GUIDE TO
DRUGS
IN CANADA

Canadian Pharmacists Association

GUIDE TO
DRUGS
IN CANADA

EDITOR-IN-CHIEF

Lalitha Raman-Wilms

BSCPHM, PHARMD, FCSHP

FOURTH EDITION

CANADIAN PHARMACISTS ASSOCIATION

President Paula MacNeil, B.Sc. (Pharm)
Executive Director Jeff Poston, PhD, MRPharmS
Senior Director, Digital Publishing Solutions
James de Gaspé Bonar
Editor-in-Chief Carol Repchinsky

Editors Lamya Arman, Jo-Anne Hutsul, Barbara Jovaisas, Geoff Lewis, Hélène Perrier, Marc Riachi, Angela Ross

DORLING KINDERSLEY LIMITED

Editor, Canada Barbara Campbell
Production Mary Slater
Editor, India Ritu Mishra
DTP Coordinator Balwant Singh
DTP Designer Shanker Prasad

Photography Gary Ombler
Illustrations Karen Cochrane, Tony Graham, Mike Johnson, Kevin Marks, Coral Mula, Lynda Payne, Richard Tibbitts

Fourth Canadian edition, 2013.

DK Publishing is represented in Canada by Tourmaline Editions Inc., 662 King Street West, Suite 304, Toronto, Ontario M5V 1M7

13 14 15 16 17 10 9 8 7 6 5 4 3 2 1
001—187362—January 2013

The *Canadian Pharmacists Association Guide to Drugs in Canada* provides information on a wide range of medications, drugs, and related subjects. The book is not a substitute for expert medical advice, however, and you are advised always to consult your physician or pharmacist for specific information on personal health matters. Never disregard expert medical advice or delay in seeking medical advice due to information obtained from this book. The naming of any product, treatment, or organization in this book does not imply endorsement by the Editor-in-Chief, the Canadian Pharmacists Association (CPhA), or the publisher, nor does the omission of any such names indicate disapproval. The Editor-in-Chief, the CPhA, and publisher do not accept any legal responsibility for any personal injury or other damage or loss arising from any use or misuse of the information and advice in this book.

Library and Archives Canada Cataloguing in Publication
    Canadian Pharmacists Association guide to drugs in Canada / editor-in-chief, Lalitha Raman-Wilms. – 4th ed.

Includes index.
ISBN 978-1-55363-185-9

    1. Drugs – Popular works. I. Raman-Wilms, Lalitha II. Canadian Pharmacists Association III. Title: Guide to Drugs in Canada.

RM301.15.C35 2013   615.1   C2012-903767-2

DK books are available at special discounts when purchased in bulk for corporate sales, sales promotions, premiums, fund-raising, or educational use. For details, please contact specialmarkets@tourmaline.ca.

Printed and bound in China by Leo Paper Products Ltd
Discover more at www.dk.com

PREFACE

New developments in drug research move at a tremendous pace, and often generate multiple options for the treatment of various conditions. With more new drugs, and with many patients taking multiple medications, it is important to be vigilant to prevent potential adverse drug events. Increasingly, this vigilance requires that patients and their caregivers be more knowledgeable about the specifics of a particular therapy – which drugs have been prescribed, how they work, what can be expected from the therapy, potential side effects, possible interactions with their other medications, and how to monitor for long-term effectiveness and safety. Moreover, an increasing number of people are using the internet for information or to purchase medications. Although some websites may be well researched and referenced, there are others where opinions of individuals who may not be qualified health professionals are posted. Whether you are searching the internet for reliable information or purchasing medications online, it is always advisable to consult with a qualified health professional and to obtain medications from pharmacies which are registered and regulated by your provincial Pharmacy College.

The fourth edition of the Canadian Pharmacists Association *Guide to Drugs in Canada* aims to address common questions related to drug therapy by providing factual information in a clear and easy-to-read format. Chapter 1 discusses what drugs are, how they work in the body, drug use in special risk groups such as children and pregnant women, and important information on how best to manage your drug therapy. The chapter on Major Drug Groups describes how drugs work on the different body systems such as the heart and lungs, and indicates common drugs used in conditions affecting these systems. The A–Z of Drugs chapter provides detailed profiles of nearly 300 specific drugs, including information on doses, how best to take the medication, special precautions, and potential side effects. Information is also provided on vitamins, minerals, and alternative medicines. A Drug Finder Index as well as a general index are provided for ease of identifying the drugs by their various names.

Our goal is that by providing you with a better understanding of drugs and how they work, and alerting you to early signs of adverse effects, this guide will help you use your medications safely and effectively. This book is not intended to replace advice provided by your physician or pharmacist but, rather, to help you to work in partnership with them. Your healthcare professionals can best explain the reasons why any drug has been prescribed for you and how it may affect you.

We hope that this book will enable you to improve your overall health through informed use of drug therapy.

Lalitha Raman-Wilms, PharmD, FCSHP
Editor-in-Chief

Jeff Poston, PhD, MRPharmS
Executive Director, Canadian Pharmacists Association

CONTENTS

4 A–Z OF DRUGS

5 GLOSSARY AND INDEX

INTRODUCTION

The *Guide to Drugs in Canada* has been planned and written to provide clear information and practical advice on drugs and medications in a way that can be readily understood by a non-medical reader. The text reflects current drug usage knowledge and standard medical practice in this country. It is intended to complement and reinforce the advice of your physician and pharmacist.

How the book is structured

The book is divided into five parts. The first part, Understanding and Using Drugs, provides a general introduction to the effects of drugs and gives general advice on practical questions, such as the administration and storage of drugs. The second part, the Drug Finder Index, provides the means of locating information on specific drugs through an index to over 2,000 generic and brand-name drugs. Part 3, Major Drug Groups, will help

you understand the uses and mechanisms of action of the principal classes of drugs. Part 4, the A–Z of Drugs, consists of 292 detailed profiles of commonly prescribed generic drugs, profiles of vitamins, minerals, supplements, drugs of abuse, and information on drugs in sport and travel. Part 5 contains a glossary of drug-related terms (italicized in the text) and a general index.

Finding your way into the book

The information you require, whether on the specific characteristics of an individual drug or on the general effects and uses of a group of drugs, can be easily obtained without prior knowledge of the medical names of drugs or drug classification through one of the two indexes: the Drug Finder or the General Index. The diagram on the facing page shows how you can obtain information throughout the book on the subject concerning you from each of these starting points.

---

1 UNDERSTANDING AND USING DRUGS

The introductory part of the book, Understanding and Using Drugs, gives a grounding in the fundamental principles underlying the medical use of drugs. Covering such topics as classifications of drugs, mechanisms of action, and the proper use of medicines, it provides valuable background information that backs up the more detailed descriptions and advice given in Parts 3 and 4. You should read this section before seeking further specific information.

2 DRUG FINDER INDEX

The Drug Finder Index helps you to find information on specific brand-name drugs and generic substances, and lists the drug names alphabetically by both generic and trade names. References are provided to the profiles for individual drugs in Part 4.

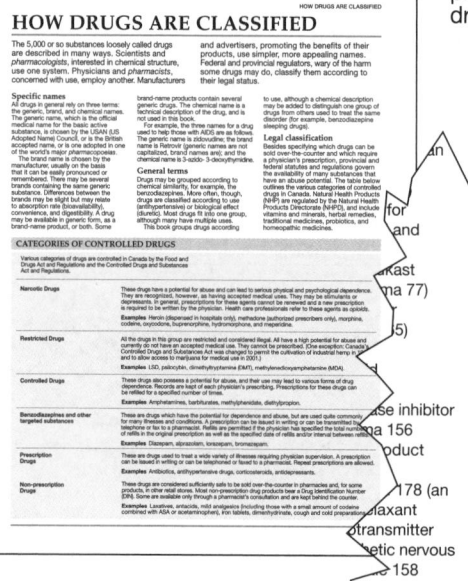

Finding your information

Whether you start by looking up an individual drug or a group of drugs, you will be led by cross-references to relevant information in all parts of the book.

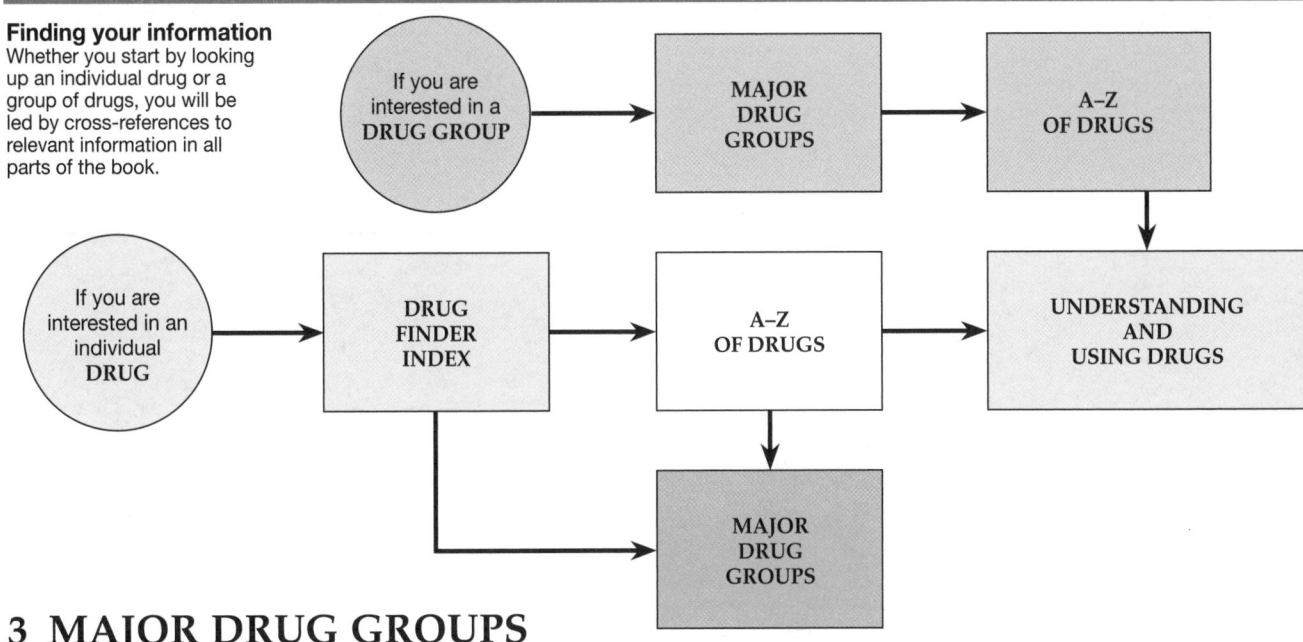

If you are interested in a DRUG GROUP → **MAJOR DRUG GROUPS** → **A–Z OF DRUGS**

If you are interested in an individual DRUG → **DRUG FINDER INDEX** → **A–Z OF DRUGS** → **UNDERSTANDING AND USING DRUGS**

MAJOR DRUG GROUPS

3 MAJOR DRUG GROUPS

Subdivided into sections dealing with each body system (for example, heart and circulation) or major disease grouping (for example, malignant and immune disease), this part of the book contains descriptions of the principal classes of drugs. Information is given on the uses, actions, effects, and risks associated with each group of drugs and is backed up by helpful illustrations and diagrams. Individual drugs in each group are listed to allow cross-reference to Part 4.

4 A–Z OF DRUGS

This contains profiles of 292 generic drugs, written to a standard format to help you find specific information quickly and easily; cross-references to the relevant major drug groups are provided. Supplementary sections profile vitamins, minerals, supplements, drugs of abuse, alternative medicine, and drugs in sport and travel.

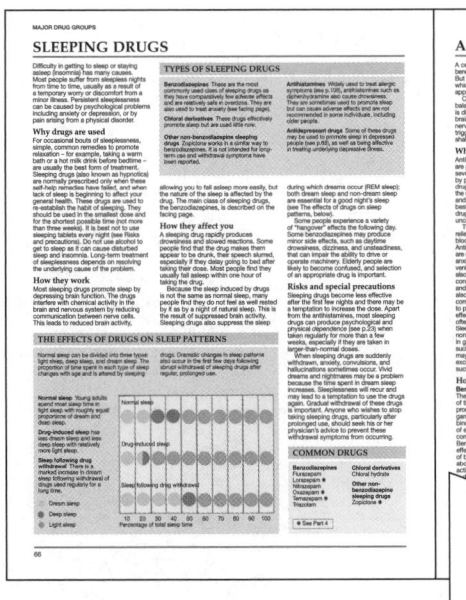

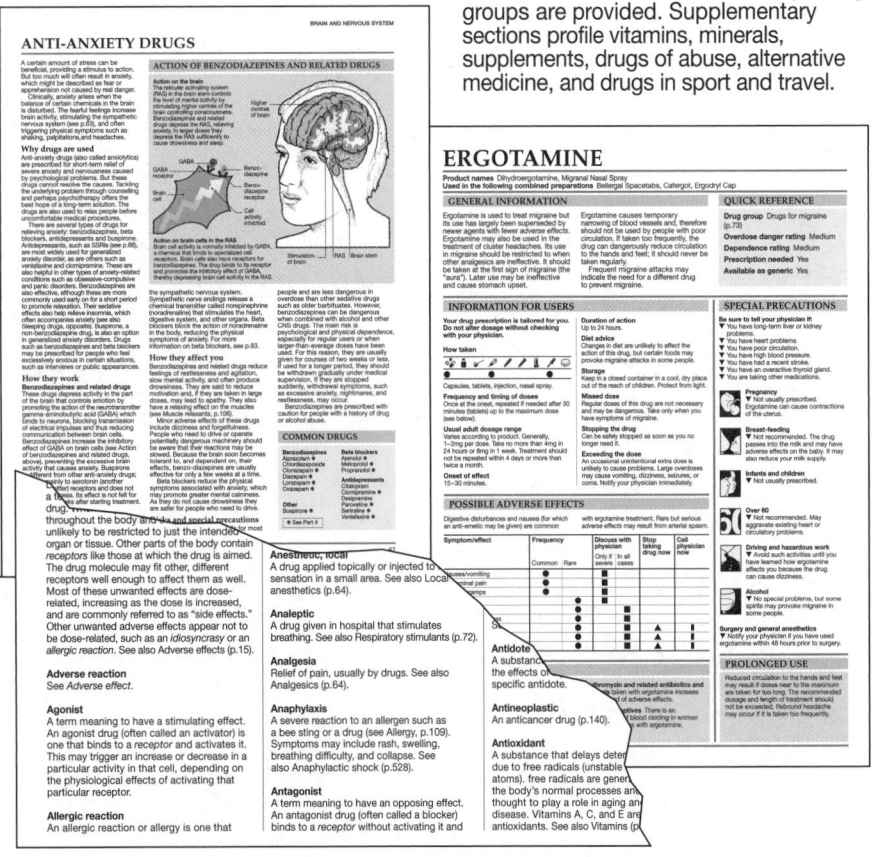

5 GLOSSARY AND INDEX

A glossary of terms explains technical words italicized in the text. The general index enables you to look up references throughout the book.

Adverse reaction
See *Adverse effect*.

Agonist
A term meaning to have a stimulating effect. An agonist drug (often called an activator) is one that binds to a *receptor* and activates it. This may trigger an increase or decrease in a particular activity in that cell, depending on the physiological effects of activating that particular receptor.

Allergic reaction
An allergic reaction or allergy is one that

Anesthetic, local
A drug applied topically or injected to reduce sensation in a small area. See also Local anesthetics (p.64).

Analeptic
A drug given in hospital that stimulates breathing. See also Respiratory stimulants (p.72).

Analgesia
Relief of pain, usually by drugs. See also Analgesics (p.64).

Anaphylaxis
A severe reaction to an allergen such as a bee sting or a drug (see Allergy, p.109). Symptoms may include rash, swelling, breathing difficulty, and collapse. See also Anaphylactic shock (p.528).

Antagonist
A term meaning to have an opposing effect. An antagonist drug (often called a blocker) binds to a *receptor* without activating it and

Anesthetic, local

Antineoplastic
An anticancer drug (p.140).

Antioxidant
A substance that delays deterioration due to free radicals (unstable atoms). Free radicals are generated by the body's normal processes and are thought to play a role in aging and disease. Vitamins A, C, and E are antioxidants. See also Vitamins (p.

UNDERSTANDING AND USING DRUGS

WHAT ARE DRUGS?

The health professions use the word "drugs" to refer to medicines – substances that can cure or arrest disease, relieve symptoms, ease pain, and provide other benefits. This definition does not include essential vitamins and minerals that may be given to correct deficiency diseases, or herbal products.

Powerful drugs often have marked *adverse effects*. Commonly used drugs with less potential to cause harm are sold over-the-counter (OTC) in *pharmacies*. Some OTC drugs can only be obtained with a pharmacist's consultation, and these are kept behind the pharmacy counter. More powerful drugs (those that cannot be used safely without medical supervision) require a doctor's prescription.

A different use of the word "drugs" refers to those substances on which a person may become dependent. These range from mild stimulants such as caffeine (found in coffee) to powerful agents that alter mood and behaviour. Some addictive drugs have no medical use and cannot be obtained legally.

Where drugs come from

At one time, the only available drugs were substances extracted from plants, or, in some cases, animals. Herbalism, the study and medicinal use of plants, was practised by the Chinese more than 5,000 years ago and is becoming popular in many parts of the world today.

Virtually all the drugs in current use have been developed in the laboratory and are manufactured through various chemical processes. About a quarter of these are derived from plants or other organisms. Most drugs are synthetic chemical copies, but some are still extracted from natural sources. For example, the *opioid* drugs, including morphine, are made from a species of poppy. Many *antibiotics* and some anticancer drugs are still of natural origin. The main difference between drugs of plant origin and "herbal medicines" is that drugs have been thoroughly tested to prove that they work and are safe.

Some drugs can now be made through genetic engineering, in which the genes (which control a cell's function) of certain microorganisms are altered, changing the products of cell activity to the desired drug. For example, the *hormone* insulin can now be manufactured by genetically engineered bacteria. This could eliminate the need to extract insulin from animal pancreas glands, the source until recently, benefiting those people who experience *adverse reactions* to material derived from animal sources.

Purely synthetic drugs are either modifications of naturally occurring ones, with the aim of increasing effectiveness or safety, or drugs developed after scientific investigation of a disease process with the intention of changing it biochemically and/or pharmacologically.

Developing and marketing new drugs

Pharmaceutical manufacturers find new products in a variety of ways. New drugs are usually developed for one purpose but quite commonly a variant will be found that will be useful for something entirely different.

When a new drug is discovered, the manufacturer often undertakes a program of molecular tinkering, or elaboration. This refers to investigations into variants of the drug to see if a version can be made that is more effective or has fewer adverse effects. In some cases that experimental process has unexpected results. The elaboration process, for example, transformed some sulfa drugs, which were originally valued for their antibacterial properties, into widely used oral antidiabetics, diuretics, and antiepileptics.

All new drugs undergo a long, careful test period before they are approved for marketing by the Therapeutic Products Directorate (TPD) (see Testing and approving new drugs). Once approval has been given, the manufacturer can then market the drug under a brand or trade name. Technically, patent protection gives the manufacturer exclusive rights for 20 years, but this protection starts from when the drug is first identified. The time remaining after TPD approval can be much less than 20 years.

When patent protection ends, other manufacturers may produce the drug, although they must use a different brand name or the generic name (see How drugs are classified, facing page).

Testing and approving new drugs

Before a drug is cleared by the TPD it undergoes a cautious, step-by-step period of testing, often lasting six to ten years. By law, a drug must be both safe and medically effective. Safety is established through various means, including tests on animals and human volunteers. Efficacy is proven through complex tests (including *double-blind* trials) on groups of healthy and ill patients. The testing is done in various research institutions under government-approved procedures.

The approval process also involves weighing a new drug's risks against its benefits. A dangerous drug whose only potential might be the relief of an ordinary headache undoubtedly would not win approval. Yet an equally *toxic* drug, effective against cancer, might. Medical judgment is an important part of the approval process.

Deadly nightshade
The drug belladonna is derived from this plant.

Opium poppy
This poppy is the basis for drugs such as morphine.

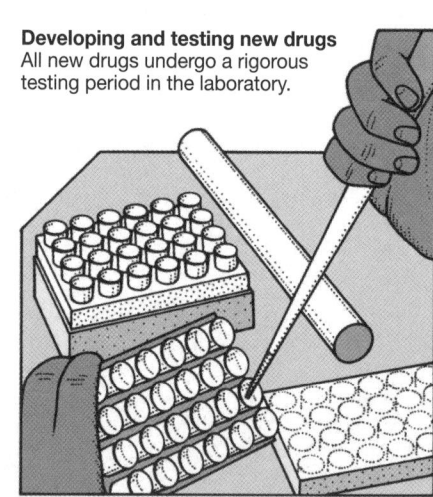

Developing and testing new drugs
All new drugs undergo a rigorous testing period in the laboratory.

HOW DRUGS ARE CLASSIFIED

The 5,000 or so substances loosely called drugs are described in many ways. Scientists and *pharmacologists*, interested in chemical structure, use one system. Physicians and *pharmacists*, concerned with use, employ another. Manufacturers and advertisers, promoting the benefits of their products, use simpler, more appealing names. Federal and provincial regulators, wary of the harm some drugs may do, classify them according to their legal status.

Specific names

All drugs in general rely on three terms: the generic, brand, and chemical names. The generic name, which is the official medical name for the basic active substance, is chosen by the USAN (US Adopted Name) Council, or is the British accepted name, or is one adopted in one of the world's major *pharmacopoeias*.

The brand name is chosen by the manufacturer, usually on the basis that it can be easily pronounced or remembered. There may be several brands containing the same generic substance. Differences between the brands may be slight but may relate to absorption rate (bioavailability), convenience, and digestibility. A drug may be available in generic form, as a brand-name product, or both. Some brand-name products contain several generic drugs. The chemical name is a technical description of the drug, and is not used in this book.

For example, the three names for a drug used to help those with AIDS are as follows. The generic name is zidovudine; the brand name is Retrovir (generic names are not capitalized, brand names are); and the chemical name is 3-azido- 3-deoxythymidine.

General terms

Drugs may be grouped according to chemical similarity, for example, the benzodiazepines. More often, though, drugs are classified according to use (antihypertensive) or biological effect (diuretic). Most drugs fit into one group, although many have multiple uses.

This book groups drugs according to use, although a chemical description may be added to distinguish one group of drugs from others used to treat the same disorder (for example, benzodiazepine sleeping drugs).

Legal classification

Besides specifying which drugs can be sold over-the-counter and which require a physician's prescription, provincial and federal statutes and regulations govern the availability of many substances that have an abuse potential. The table below outlines the various categories of controlled drugs in Canada. Natural Health Products (NHP) are regulated by the Natural Health Products Directorate (NHPD), and include vitamins and minerals, herbal remedies, traditional medicines, probiotics, and homeopathic medicines.

CATEGORIES OF CONTROLLED DRUGS

Various categories of drugs are controlled in Canada by the Food and Drugs Act and Regulations and the Controlled Drugs and Substances Act and Regulations.

Narcotic Drugs	These drugs have a potential for abuse and can lead to serious physical and psychological *dependence*. They are recognized, however, as having accepted medical uses. They may be stimulants or depressants. In general, prescriptions for these agents cannot be renewed and a new prescription is required to be written by the physician. Health care professionals refer to these agents as *opioids*. **Examples** Heroin (dispensed in hospitals only), methadone (authorized prescribers only), morphine, codeine, oxycodone, buprenorphine, hydromorphone, and meperidine.
Restricted Drugs	All the drugs in this group are restricted and considered illegal. All have a high potential for abuse and currently do not have an accepted medical use. They cannot be prescribed. (One exception: Canada's Controlled Drugs and Substances Act was changed to permit the cultivation of industrial hemp in 1998, and to allow access to marijuana for medical use in 2001.) **Examples** LSD, psilocybin, dimethyltryptamine (DMT), methylenedioxyamphetamine (MDA).
Controlled Drugs	These drugs also possess a potential for abuse, and their use may lead to various forms of drug dependence. Records are kept of each physician's prescribing. Prescriptions for these drugs can be refilled for a specified number of times. **Examples** Amphetamines, barbiturates, methylphenidate, diethylpropion.
Benzodiazepines and other targeted substances	These are drugs which have the potential for dependence and abuse, but are used quite commonly for many illnesses and conditions. A prescription can be issued in writing or can be transmitted by telephone or fax to a pharmacist. Refills are permitted if the physician has specified the total number of refills in the original prescription as well as the specified date of refills and/or interval between refills. **Examples** Diazepam, alprazolam, lorazepam, bromazepam.
Prescription Drugs	These are drugs used to treat a wide variety of illnesses requiring physician supervision. A prescription can be issued in writing or can be telephoned or faxed to a pharmacist. Repeat prescriptions are allowed. **Examples** Antibiotics, antihypertensive drugs, corticosteroids, antidepressants.
Non-prescription Drugs	These drugs are considered sufficiently safe to be sold over-the-counter in pharmacies and, for some products, in other retail stores. Most non-prescription drug products bear a Drug Identification Number (DIN). Some are available only through a pharmacist's consultation and are kept behind the counter. **Examples** Laxatives, antacids, mild analgesics (including those with a small amount of codeine combined with ASA or acetaminophen), iron tablets, dimenhydrinate, cough and cold preparations.

HOW DRUGS WORK

Before the discovery of the sulfa drugs in 1935, medical knowledge of drugs was limited to possibly only a dozen or so drugs that had a clear medical value. Most of these were the extracts of plants (such as digitalis, from foxgloves), while others, such as ASA, were chemically closely related to plant extracts (in this case, salicylic acid, from the willow tree). It was soon realized, however, that crude plant extracts had two disadvantages: they were of variable potency, and the same plant could contain a number of different substances with different actions. These might even oppose each other, or cause serious *adverse effects*. Now, thousands of effective drugs are available and scientific knowledge regarding drugs and their actions has virtually exploded.

Today's physician and *pharmacist* understands the complexity of drug actions in the body, both beneficial and adverse. As a result of extensive research and clinical experience, they can now also recognize that some drugs interact harmfully with others, or with certain foods and alcohol.

DRUG ACTIONS

While the exact workings of some drugs are not fully understood, medical science provides clear knowledge as to what most of them do once they enter or are applied to the human body. Drugs serve different purposes: sometimes they cure a disease, sometimes they only alleviate symptoms. Their impact occurs in various parts of the anatomy. Although different drugs act in different ways, their actions generally fall into one of three categories.

Replacing chemicals that are deficient

To function normally, the body requires sufficient levels of certain chemical substances. These include vitamins and minerals, which the body obtains from food. A balanced diet usually supplies what is needed. But when deficiencies occur, various deficiency diseases result. Lack of vitamin C causes scurvy, iron deficiency causes anemia, and lack of vitamin D leads to rickets in children and osteomalacia in adults.

Other deficiency diseases arise from a lack of various *hormones* which are the chemical substances produced by glands. Hormones act as internal "messengers". Diabetes mellitus, hypothyroidism, and Addison's disease all result from deficiencies of different hormones.

Deficiency diseases are treated with drugs that replace the substances that are missing or, in the case of some hormone deficiencies, with animal or synthetic replacements.

Interfering with cell function

Many drugs can change the way cells work by increasing or reducing the normal level of activity. Inflammation, for example, is due to the action of certain natural hormones and other chemicals on blood vessels and blood cells . Anti-inflammatory drugs block the action of the inflammatory components or slow their production. Drugs that act in a similar way are used in the treatment of a variety of conditions: hormone disorders, blood clotting problems, and heart and kidney diseases.

Many such drugs do their work by altering the transmission system by which messages are sent from one part of the body to another.

A message – such as to contract a muscle – originates in the brain and enters a nerve cell through its receiving end. The message, in the form of an electrical impulse, travels the nerve cell to the sending end. Here a chemical substance called a *neurotransmitter* is released, conducting the message across the tiny gap (synapse) separating it from an adjacent nerve cell. That process is repeated until the message reaches the appropriate muscle.

Many drugs can alter this process, often by their effect on receptor sites on cells (see left). Some drugs (*agonists*) intensify the response to cell receptor activation while other drugs (*antagonists*) reduce it.

Acting against invading organisms or abnormal cells

Infectious diseases are caused by viruses, bacteria, protozoa, and fungi invading the body. We now have a wide choice of drugs that destroy these microorganisms, either by halting their multiplication or by killing them directly. Other drugs treat disease by killing abnormal cells produced by the human body – cancer cells, for example.

RECEPTOR SITES

Many drugs produce their effects through their action on special sites called *receptors*, which may be on the surface of cells or inside them. Natural body chemicals such as *neurotransmitters* bind to these sites, initiating a response in the cell. A cell may have many types of receptors, each with an affinity for a different chemical. Drugs may also bind to receptors, either adding to the effect of the body's natural chemicals and enhancing cell response (agonists) or preventing such a chemical from binding to its receptor, and thereby blocking a particular cell response (antagonists).

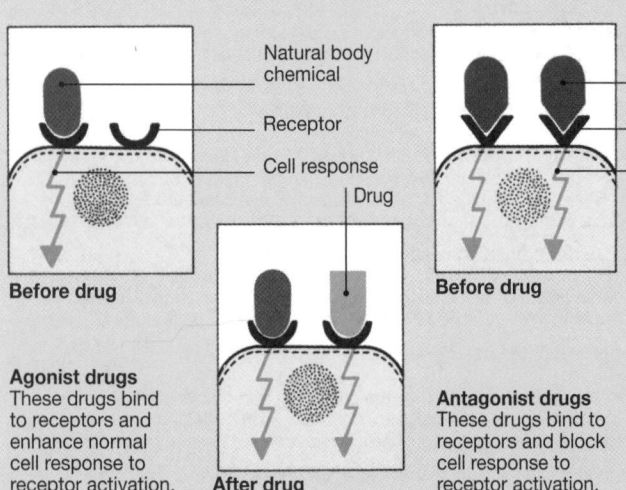

Natural body chemical
Receptor
Cell response
Drug

Before drug

Agonist drugs
These drugs bind to receptors and enhance normal cell response to receptor activation.

After drug

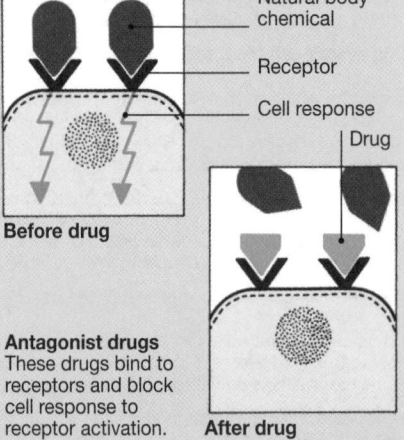

Natural body chemical
Receptor
Cell response
Drug

Before drug

Antagonist drugs
These drugs bind to receptors and block cell response to receptor activation.

After drug

THE EFFECTS OF DRUGS

Before a physician selects a drug to be used in the treatment of a sick person, he or she carefully weighs the benefits and the risks. Obviously, the physician expects a positive result from the drug – a cure for the condition or at least the relief of symptoms. At the same time, the physician has to consider the risks, since all drugs are potentially harmful, some of them considerably more so than others.

Reaction time

Some drugs can produce rapid and spectacular relief from the symptoms of disease. Nitroglycerin frequently provides almost immediate relief from the pain of angina; other drugs can quickly alleviate the symptoms of an asthmatic attack. Conversely, some drugs take much longer to produce a response. It may, for example, require several weeks of treatment with an antidepressant drug before a person experiences maximum benefit. This can add to anxiety unless the individual is informed of the possibility of a delay in the onset of beneficial effects.

Adverse effects

The *adverse effects* of a drug (also known as side effects or adverse reactions) are its undesired effects. When drugs are taken, they are distributed throughout the body and their effects are unlikely to be restricted just to the organ or tissue we want them to affect. Other parts of the body contain *receptor* sites like those the drug is targeting. In addition, the drug molecule may fit other, different receptors well enough to activate or block them too.

For example, *anticholinergic* drugs, given to relieve spasm of the intestinal wall, may also cause blurred vision, dry mouth, and retention of urine. Such effects may gradually disappear as the body becomes used to the drug. If they persist, the dose may have to be reduced, or the time between doses may need to be increased. Reducing the dose will often reduce the severity of the adverse effect for those effects that are called "dose-related".

DOSE AND RESPONSE

People respond in different ways to a drug, and often the dose has to be adjusted to allow for a person's age, weight, or general health. Children and the elderly usually require different doses than adults.

The dose of any drug should be sufficient to produce a beneficial response but not so great that it will cause excessive adverse effects. If the dose is too low, the drug may not have any effect; if it is too high, it will not produce any additional benefits and may produce adverse effects. The aim of drug treatment is to achieve a concentration of drug in the blood or tissue that lies between the lowest effective level and the maximum safe concentration. This is known as the therapeutic window (or range).

For certain drugs the therapeutic window is quite narrow, so the safety/effectiveness margin is small. Other drugs have a much wider therapeutic window.

Wide therapeutic window

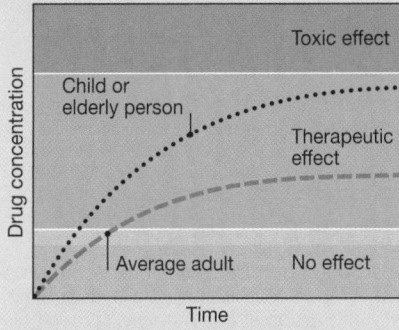

Dosage of drugs with a wide therapeutic range can vary considerably without altering the drug's effect. The effect of some drugs can be greater in children and the elderly.

Narrow therapeutic window

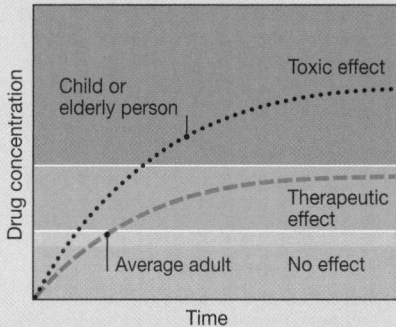

Dosage of drugs with a narrow therapeutic range must be carefully calculated to achieve the desired effect without toxicity. Children or the elderly require adjustment in doses.

Adverse effects of some drugs can be quite serious. Such drugs are given because they may be the only treatment for an otherwise fatal disease. But all drugs are chemicals, with a potential for producing serious, *toxic* reactions.

Some adverse effects seem not to be dose-related, and where the effect appears on first use and is unexpected, the phenomenon is called *idiosyncrasy*. People are genetically different and, as a result, their response to drugs differs, perhaps because they lack a particular *enzyme* or because it is less active than usual. For this reason, not everyone suffers the "common" adverse effects; but, occasionally, a new adverse effect, due to a rare and unsuspected genetic variation, will be discovered only after the drug has been taken by a large number of people.

Other adverse effects that are not dose-related are *allergic reactions*. These reactions do not usually appear on the first exposure to the drug but on a subsequent occasion. The symptoms are similar to those caused by other allergens and, in extreme cases, may cause anaphylactic shock (see p.528).

Beneficial vs. adverse effects

In evaluating the risk/benefit ratio of a prescribed drug, the doctor has to weigh the drug's therapeutic benefit against the possible adverse effects. For example, such side effects as nausea, headache, and diarrhea may result from taking an antibiotic. But the possible risks of these side effects will be considered acceptable if the problem is a life-threatening infection requiring immediate medical treatment. However, such side effects would be considered unacceptable for an over-the-counter drug for the relief of headaches.

Because some people are more at risk from adverse drug reactions than others (particularly those who have a history of drug allergy), the physician normally checks whether there is any reason why a certain drug should not be prescribed (see Drug treatment in special risk groups, p.20). The *pharmacist* should also verify that the individual has no known contraindications to the drug.

PLACEBO RESPONSE

The word placebo – Latin for "I will please" – is used to describe any chemically inert substance given as a substitute for a drug. Any benefit gained from taking a placebo occurs because the person taking it believes that it will produce good results.

New drugs are almost always tested against a placebo preparation in clinical trials as a way of assessing the efficacy of a drug before it is marketed. The placebo is made to look identical to the active preparation, and the volunteers are not told whether they have been given the active drug or the placebo. Sometimes the physician is also unaware of which preparation an individual has been given. This is known as a *double-blind* trial. In this way, the purely placebo effect can be eliminated and the effectiveness of the drug determined more realistically.

Sometimes the mere taking of a medicine has a psychological effect that produces a beneficial physical response. This type of placebo response can make an important contribution to the overall effectiveness of a chemically active drug. It is most commonly seen with analgesics, antidepressants, and anti-anxiety drugs. Some people, known as placebo responders, are more likely to experience this sort of reaction than the rest of the population.

DRUG INTERACTIONS

When different drugs are taken together, or when a drug is taken in combination with certain foods or with alcohol, effects different from those when the drug is taken alone may be produced. Often, this is beneficial and physicians sometimes make use of interactions to increase the effectiveness of a treatment. Often, more than one drug may be used to treat conditions such as cancer or high blood pressure.

Other interactions, however, are unwanted and may be harmful. They may occur not only between prescription drugs, but also between prescription and over-the-counter drugs. It is important to read warnings on drug labels and tell your physician and pharmacist if you are taking any preparations – both prescription and over-the-counter, and even herbal or homeopathic remedies.

A drug may interact with another drug or with food or alcohol for a number of reasons (see below).

Altered absorption
Alcohol and some drugs (particularly *opioids* and drugs with an *anticholinergic* effect) slow the digestive process that empties the stomach contents into the intestine. This may delay the absorption, and therefore the effect, of another drug. Other drugs (for example, metoclopramide, an anti-emetic drug) may speed the rate at which the stomach empties and may, therefore, increase the rate at which another drug is absorbed and takes effect.

Some drugs also combine with another drug or food in the intestine to form a compound that is not absorbed as readily. This occurs when tetracycline and iron tablets or antacids are taken together. Milk and dairy products also reduce the

Drug absorption in the intestine

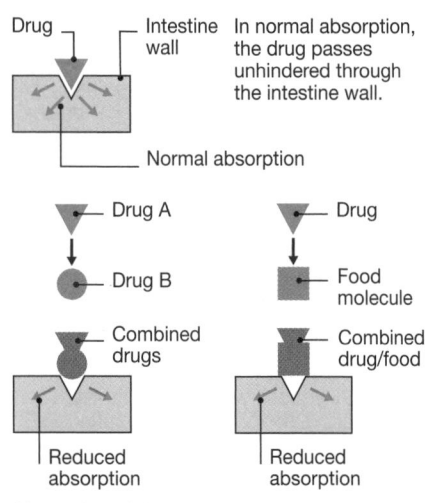

In normal absorption, the drug passes unhindered through the intestine wall.

Normal absorption

Absorption of drug (A) may be reduced if it combines with another drug (B).

Absorption of a drug may be reduced if it combines with a food molecule.

EXAMPLES OF IMPORTANT INTERACTIONS

Adverse interactions between drugs may vary from a simple blocking of a drug's beneficial effect to a serious reaction between two drugs that may be life-threatening. Some of the more serious adverse interactions occur between the following:

Drugs that depress the central nervous system (opioids, sedating antihistamines, sleeping drugs, and alcohol). The effects of two or more of these drugs together may be additive, causing dangerous oversedation.

Drugs that lower blood sugar levels and such drugs as sulfonamides and alcohol. The drug interaction increases the effect of blood-sugar-lowering drugs, thus further depressing blood sugar levels.

Oral anticoagulants and other drugs, particularly ASA and antibiotics. As these drugs may increase the tendency to bleed, it is essential to check the effects in every case.

Monoamine oxidase inhibitors (MAOIs). Many drugs and foods can produce a severe increase in blood pressure when taken with MAOIs. Such drugs include amphetamines and decongestants; foods include cheese, herring, chocolate, red wine, and beer. Some of the newer MAOIs, however, are much less likely to interact with food and drugs.

absorption of tetracycline and some other drugs, such as ciprofloxacin, by combining with the drugs in this manner.

Enzyme effects
Some drugs increase the production of *enzymes* in the liver that break down drugs, while others inhibit or reduce enzyme production. Thus, they affect the rate at which other drugs are activated or inactivated.

Excretion in the urine
A drug may reduce the kidneys' ability to excrete another drug, raising the drug level in the blood and increasing its effect.

Receptor effects
Drugs that act on the same *receptor sites* (p.14) sometimes add to each other's effect on the body, or compete with each other in occupying certain receptor sites. For example, naloxone blocks receptors used by opioid drugs, thereby helping to reverse the effects of opioid poisoning.

Similar or opposite effects
Drugs that produce similar effects (but act on different receptors) add to each others' actions. Often, lower doses are possible as a result, with fewer *adverse effects*. This is common practice in the treatment of high blood pressure and cancer. Antibiotics are given together as the infecting organisms are less likely to develop resistance to the drugs. Drugs with *antagonistic* effects reduce the useful activity of one or both drugs. For example, some antidepressants oppose the effects of anticonvulsants.

Reduced protein binding
Some drugs circulate around the body in the bloodstream with a proportion of the drug attached to the proteins of the blood

plasma. The amount of drug attached to the plasma proteins is inactive. If another drug is taken, some of the second drug may also bind to the plasma proteins and displace the first drug; more of the first drug is then active in the body.

Interaction between protein-bound drugs

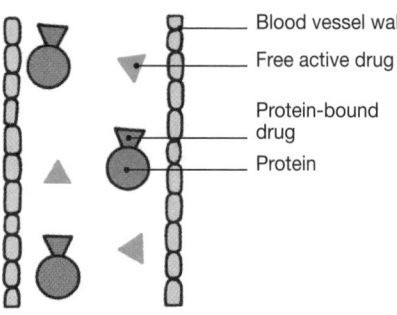

Blood vessel wall

Free active drug

Protein-bound drug

Protein

Protein-bound drug taken alone
Drug molecules that are bound to proteins in the blood are unable to pass into body tissues. Only free drug molecules are active.

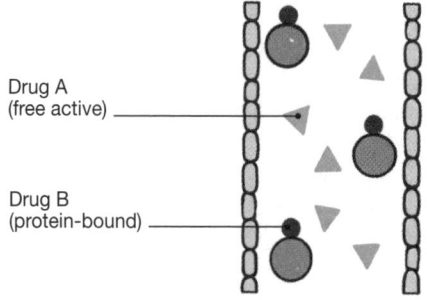

Drug A (free active)

Drug B (protein-bound)

Taken with another protein-bound drug
If a drug (B) with a greater ability to bind with proteins is also taken, drug (A) is displaced, increasing the amount of active drug.

METHODS OF ADMINISTRATION

The majority of drugs must be absorbed into the bloodstream in order for them to reach the site where their effects are needed. The method of administering a drug determines the route it takes to get into the bloodstream and the speed at which it is absorbed into the blood.

When a drug is meant to enter the bloodstream it is usually administered in one of the following ways: through the mouth or rectum, by injection, or by inhalation. Drugs that are implanted under the skin or enclosed in a skin patch also enter the bloodstream. These types are discussed under Slow-release preparations (p.18).

When it is unnecessary or undesirable for a drug to enter the bloodstream in large amounts, it may be applied *topically* so that its effect is limited mainly to the site of the disorder, such as the surface of the skin or mucous membranes (the membranes of the nose, eyes, ears, vagina, or rectum). Drugs are administered topically in a variety of preparations, including creams, sprays, drops, and suppositories. Most inhaled drugs also have a local effect on the respiratory tract.

Very often, a particular drug may be available in different forms. Many drugs are available both as tablets and injectable fluid. The choice between a tablet and an injection depends on a number of factors, including the severity of the illness, the urgency with which the drug effect is needed, the part of the body requiring treatment, and the patient's general state of health, in particular his or her ability to swallow.

The various administration routes are discussed in greater detail below. For a description of the different forms in which drugs are given, see Drug forms (p.19).

ADMINISTRATION BY MOUTH

Giving drugs by mouth is the most common method of administration. Most of the drugs that are given by mouth are absorbed into the bloodstream through the walls of the intestine. The speed at which the drug is absorbed and the amount of active drug that is available for use depend on several factors, including the form in which the drug is given (for example, as a tablet or a liquid) and whether it is taken with food or on an empty stomach. If a drug is taken when the stomach is empty (before meals, for example) it may act more quickly than a drug that is taken after a meal when the stomach is full.

Some drugs (like antacids, which neutralize stomach acidity) are taken by mouth to produce a direct effect on the stomach or digestive tract.

In-mouth administration
Products are available that are placed in the mouth but not swallowed. They are absorbed quickly into the bloodstream through the lining of the mouth, which has a rich supply of blood vessels. Sublingual tablets are placed under the tongue, wafers are placed on the tongue, and buccal tablets are placed in the pouch between the cheek and teeth.

HOW DRUGS PASS THROUGH THE BODY

Most drugs taken by mouth reach the bloodstream by absorption through the wall of the small intestine. Blood vessels supplying the intestine then carry the drug to the liver, where it may be broken down into a form that can be used by the body. The drug (or its breakdown product) then enters the general circulation, which carries it around the body. It may pass back into the intestine before being reabsorbed into the bloodstream. Some drugs are rapidly excreted via the kidneys; others may build up in fatty tissues in the body.

Certain insoluble drugs cannot be absorbed through the intestinal wall and pass through the digestive tract unchanged. These drugs are useful for treating bowel disorders, but if they are intended to have *systemic* effects elsewhere they must be given by intravenous injection.

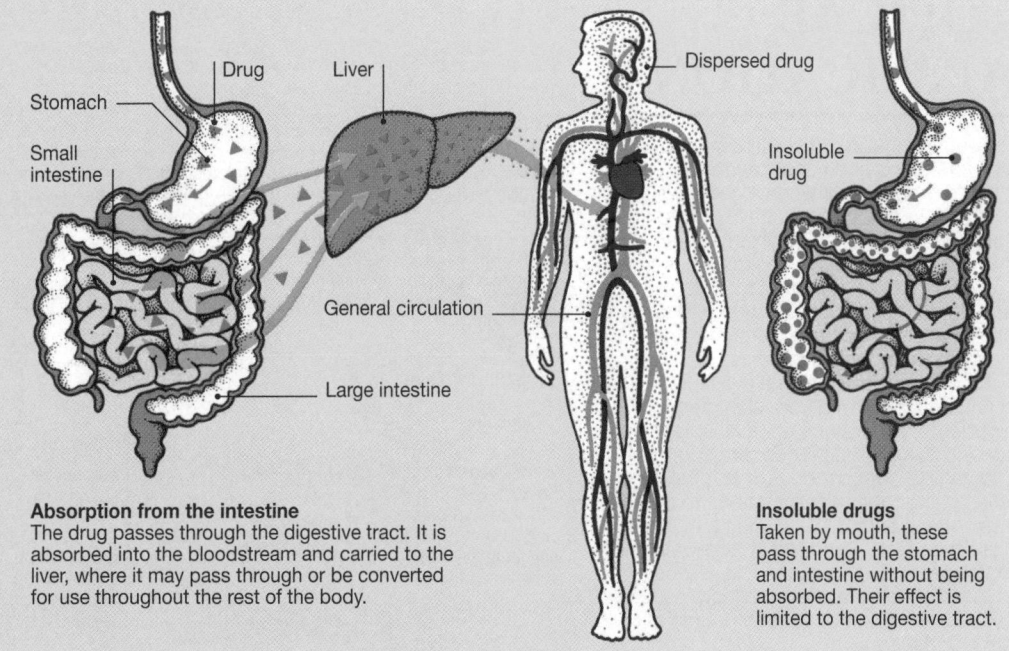

Absorption from the intestine
The drug passes through the digestive tract. It is absorbed into the bloodstream and carried to the liver, where it may pass through or be converted for use throughout the rest of the body.

Insoluble drugs
Taken by mouth, these pass through the stomach and intestine without being absorbed. Their effect is limited to the digestive tract.

RECTAL ADMINISTRATION

Drugs intended to have a *systemic* effect may be given in the form of *suppositories* inserted into the rectum, from where they are absorbed into the bloodstream. This method may be used to give drugs that might be destroyed by the stomach's digestive juices. It is also sometimes used to administer drugs to people who cannot take medication by mouth, such as those who are suffering from nausea and vomiting.

Drugs may also be given rectally for local effect, either as suppositories (to relieve hemorrhoids) or as enemas (for ulcerative colitis).

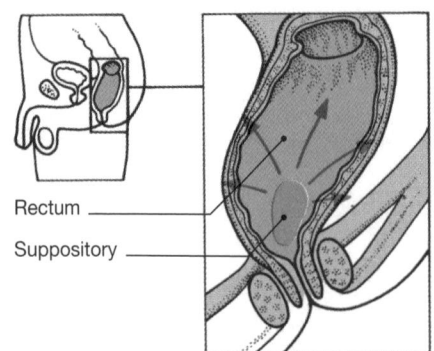

Rectum

Suppository

INHALATION

Drugs may be inhaled to produce a *systemic* effect or a direct local effect on the respiratory tract.

Gases to produce *general anesthesia* are administered by inhalation and are absorbed into the bloodstream through the lungs, producing a general effect on the body, particularly the brain.

Bronchodilators, used to treat certain types of asthma, emphysema, and bronchitis, are a common example of drugs administered by inhalation for their direct effect on the respiratory tract, although some of the active drug also reaches the bloodstream. (See also p.76).

ADMINISTRATION BY INJECTION

Drugs may be injected into the body to produce a *systemic* effect. One reason for injecting drugs is the rapid response that follows. Other circumstances that call for injection are when: a person is intolerant to the drug when taken by mouth; the drug would be destroyed by the stomach's digestive juices (insulin, for example); or the drug cannot pass through the intestinal walls into the bloodstream. Drug injections may also be given to produce a local effect, as is often done to relieve the pain of arthritis.

The three most common methods of injection – *intramuscular*, *intravenous*, and *subcutaneous* – are described in the illustration (see right). The type of injection depends both on the nature of the drug and the condition being treated.

Muscle | Vein | Skin | Fatty tissue

Intramuscular (IM) injection
The drug is injected into a muscle, usually of the thigh, the upper arm, or the buttock.

Subcutaneous (SC) injection
The drug is injected directly under the surface of the skin.

Intravenous (IV) injection
The drug is injected directly into a vein and therefore directly into the bloodstream. Drugs given by this route act more quickly than drugs given by other types of injection.

TOPICAL APPLICATION

In treating localized disorders such as skin infections and nasal congestion, it is often preferable when a choice is available to prescribe drugs in a form that has a *topical*, or localized, rather than a *systemic* effect. The reason is that it is much easier to control the effects of drugs administered locally and to ensure that they produce the maximum benefit with minimum *adverse effects*.

Topical preparations are available in a variety of forms, from skin creams, ointments, and lotions to nasal sprays, ear and eye drops, bladder irrigations, and vaginal suppositories. It is important when using topical preparations to follow instructions carefully, avoiding a higher dose than recommended or application for longer than necessary. This will help to avoid adverse systemic effects caused by the absorption of larger amounts into the bloodstream.

SLOW-RELEASE AND MODIFIED-RELEASE PREPARATIONS

Some disorders can be treated with specially formulated preparations that can release the active drug slowly. Such preparations may be beneficial when it is inconvenient for a person to visit the physician regularly, or when only small amounts of the drug need to be released into the body, and can decrease the number of doses needed in one day. Slow release of drugs can be achieved by *depot injections*, *transdermal patches*, *capsules* and tablets, and implants. Modified-release tablets and capsules are a more advanced version in which release of the active ingredient is related to time.

Slow-release capsule
Contains pellets of drug in a specially formulated coating.

Capsule — Outer coating — Drug

Transdermal patch
An adhesive, drug-impregnated pad is placed on the skin. The drug passes slowly into the skin.

Transdermal patch

Skin

Drug

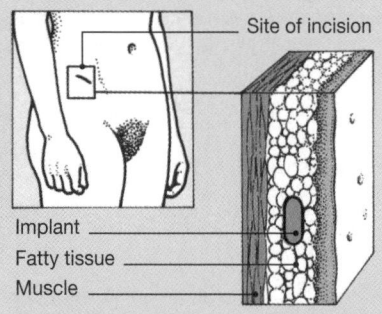

Site of incision

Implant
Fatty tissue
Muscle

Implants
A pellet containing the drug is implanted under the skin. By this rarely used method, a drug (usually a hormone) is slowly released into the bloodstream over a period of months.

DRUG FORMS

Most drugs are specially prepared in a form designed for convenience of administration. This helps to ensure that dosages are accurate and that taking the medication is as easy as possible. Inactive ingredients (those with no therapeutic effect) are often added to flavour or colour the medicine, or to improve its chemical stability, extending the period during which it is effective.

The more common drug forms are described in detail below.

Tablets

This contains the drug compressed with other ingredients (see right) into a solid plug. Some are coated with a membrane that allows the drug to be slowly released, to produce a sustained effect; others are composed of granules that are individually layered to give the slow release.

Capsules

The drug is contained in a cylindrically shaped gelatin shell that breaks open after the capsule has been swallowed, releasing the drug. Slow-release capsules contain pellets that dissolve in the gastrointestinal tract, releasing the drug slowly (facing page).

Wafers

The drug is contained in a small wafer, which is placed on the tongue and allowed to dissolve.

Liquids

Some drugs are available in liquid form, the active substance being combined in a solution, suspension, or emulsion with other ingredients – preservatives, solvents, and flavouring or colouring agents. Many liquid preparations should be shaken before use to ensure that the active drug is evenly distributed. If it is not, inaccurate dosages may result.

Mixture

A mixture is one or more drugs, either dissolved to form a solution or suspended in a liquid (often water).

Elixir

An elixir is a solution of a drug in a sweetened mixture of alcohol and water. It is often highly flavoured.

Emulsion

An emulsion is a drug dispersed in oil and water. An emulsifying agent is often included to stabilize the product.

Syrup

A syrup is a concentrated solution of sugar containing the active drug, with flavouring and stabilizing agents added.

Topical skin preparations

These are designed for application to the skin and other surface body tissues. Preservatives are usually included to

WHAT A TABLET CONTAINS

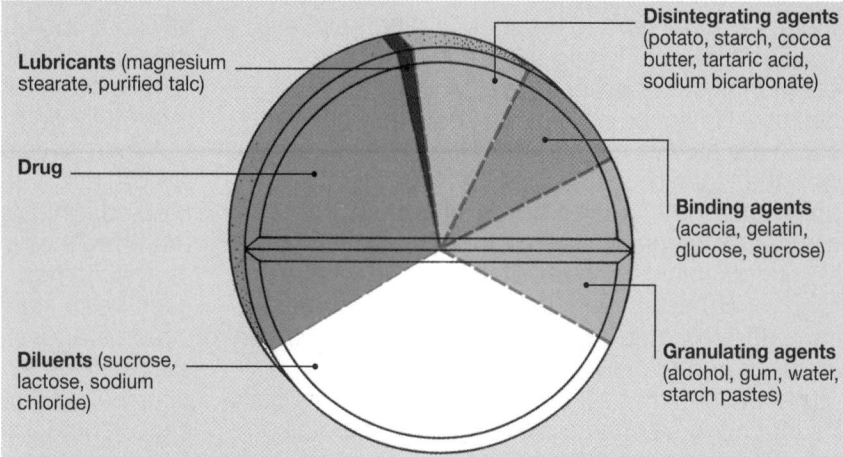

Lubricants (magnesium stearate, purified talc)

Drug

Diluents (sucrose, lactose, sodium chloride)

Disintegrating agents (potato, starch, cocoa butter, tartaric acid, sodium bicarbonate)

Binding agents (acacia, gelatin, glucose, sucrose)

Granulating agents (alcohol, gum, water, starch pastes)

Diluents add bulk. Binders and granulating agents bind the ingredients. Lubricants ensure a smooth surface by allowing the ingredients to flow during the manufacturing process.

Disintegrating agents help the tablet dissolve. A sugar coating or a transparent film protects the surface or modifies the drug's release rate. Dyes and imprints make it recognizable.

reduce the growth of bacteria. The most commonly used skin preparations are described below. (See also Bases for skin preparations, p.160.)

Creams, ointments, and gels

A cream is a non-greasy preparation that is used to apply drugs to an area of the body or to cool or moisten the skin. It is less noticeable than an ointment.

An ointment is a greasy preparation used to apply drugs to an area of the body, or as a protective or lubricant layer for the relief of dry skin conditions.

A gel is a jelly-like suspension consisting of small, insoluble particles dispersed through a liquid. Most gels are non-greasy and are most commonly used for face and scalp preparations.

Lotion

A lotion is a solution or suspension applied to unbroken skin to cool and dry the affected area. Some are more suitable for use in hairy areas because they are not as sticky as creams or ointments.

Injection solutions

Solutions used for injections are sterile (germ-free) preparations of a drug that are dissolved or suspended in a liquid. Other chemicals (e.g. anti-oxidants and buffers) are often added to preserve the stability of the drug or to regulate the acidity or alkalinity of the solution. Most injectable drugs used today are packaged in sterile, disposable syringes. For details on different types, see Administration by injection, facing page.

Suppositories

These are solid, bullet-shaped dosage forms designed for easy insertion into

the rectum (rectal suppository) or vagina (vaginal suppository). They contain a drug and an inert (pharmacologically and chemically inactive) substance often derived from cocoa butter or vegetable oil. The drug is gradually released in the rectum or vagina as the suppository dissolves at body temperature.

Eye drops

A sterile drug solution (or suspension) dropped behind the eyelid.

Ear drops

A solution (or suspension) containing a drug introduced into the ear by dropper. Ear drops are usually given to produce an effect on the outer ear canal.

Nasal drops/spray

A solution of a drug for introduction into the nose to produce a local effect.

Inhalers

Aerosol inhalers contain a solution or suspension of a drug under pressure. A valve ensures delivery of a recommended dosage when the inhaler is activated. A mouthpiece facilitates inhalation as the drug is released from the canister. The correct technique is important; the printed instructions should be followed carefully or your physician, pharmacist, or nurse will show you. Aerosol inhalers are widely used for asthma (see also p.77).

Transdermal patches

These adhesive pads are impregnated with a drug and placed on the skin. The drug is released slowly through the skin (facing page). Examples include fentanyl and nitroglycerin patches. (See also p.133).

DRUG TREATMENT IN SPECIAL RISK GROUPS

Different people tend to respond in different ways to drug treatment. Taking the same drug, one person may suffer *adverse effects* while another does not. However, physicians know that certain people are always more at risk from adverse effects when they take drugs; the reason is that in those people the body handles drugs differently, or the drug has an atypical effect. Those people at special risk include infants and children, women who are pregnant or breast-feeding, the elderly, and people with long-term medical conditions, especially those who have impaired liver or kidney function.

The reasons that such people may be more likely to suffer adverse effects are discussed in detail on the following pages. Others who may need special attention include those already taking regular medication who may risk complications when they take another drug. Drug interactions are discussed more fully on p.16.

When physicians prescribe drugs for people at special risk, they take extra care to select appropriate medication, adjust dosages, and closely monitor the effects of treatment. If you think you may be at special risk, be sure to tell your physician in case he or she is not fully aware of your particular circumstances. Similarly, if you are buying over-the-counter drugs, you should ask your physician or *pharmacist* if you think you may be at risk of experiencing any possible adverse effects or hazardous drug interactions.

INFANTS AND CHILDREN

Infants and children need a lower dosage of drugs than adults because children have a relatively low body weight. In addition, because of differences in body composition and the distribution and amount of body fat, as well as differences in the state of development and function of organs such as the liver and kidneys at different ages, children cannot simply be given a proportion of an adult dose as if they were small adults. Dosages need to be calculated in a more complex way, taking into account the child's age and weight. While newborn babies often have to be given very small doses of drugs, older children may need relatively large doses of some drugs compared to the adult dosage.

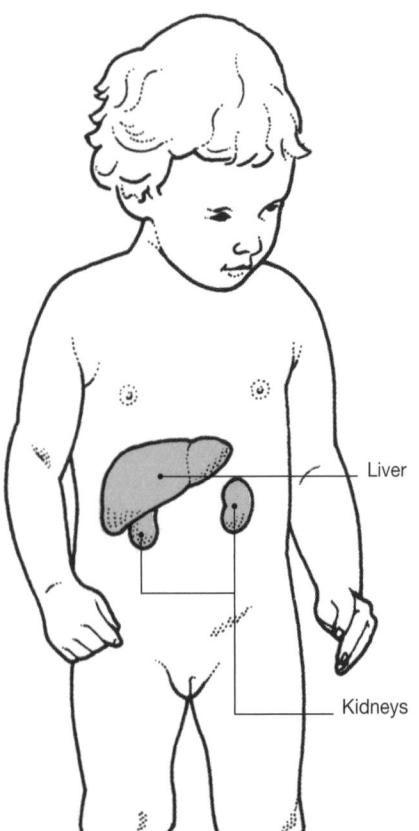

Liver

Kidneys

The liver
The liver's enzyme systems are not fully developed when a baby is born. This means that drugs are not broken down as rapidly as in an adult, and may reach dangerously high concentrations in the baby's body. For this reason, many drugs are not prescribed for babies or are given in very reduced doses. In older children, because the liver is relatively large compared to the rest of the body, some drugs may need to be given in proportionately higher doses.

The kidneys
During the first six months, a baby's kidneys are unable to excrete drugs as efficiently as an adult's kidneys. This may lead to a dangerously high concentration of a drug in the blood. The dose of certain drugs may therefore need to be reduced. Between one and two years of age, kidney function improves, and higher doses of some drugs may then be needed.

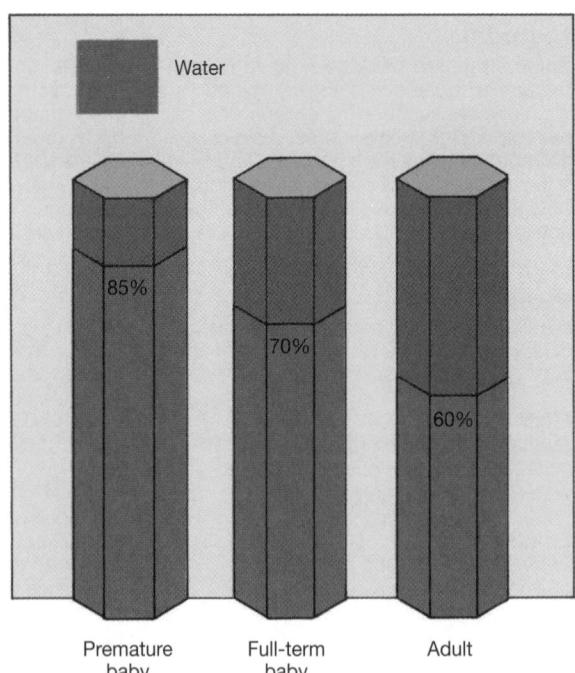

Water

85%

70%

60%

Premature baby   Full-term baby   Adult

Body composition
The proportion of water in the body of a premature baby is about 85 per cent of its body weight, that of a full-term baby is 70 per cent, and that of an adult is only 60 per cent. This means that drugs that stay in the body water will not be as concentrated in an infant's body as in an adult's, unless a higher dose relative to body weight is given.

PREGNANT WOMEN

Great care is needed during pregnancy to protect the fetus so that it develops into a healthy baby. Drugs taken by the mother can cross the placenta and enter the baby's bloodstream. With certain drugs, and at certain stages of pregnancy, there is a risk of developmental abnormalities, retarded growth, or post-delivery problems affecting the newborn baby. In addition, some drugs may affect the health of the mother during pregnancy.

Many drugs are known to have *adverse effects* during pregnancy; others are known to be safe, but in a large number of cases there is no firm evidence to decide on risk or safety. Therefore, the most important rule if you are pregnant or trying to conceive is to consult your physician before taking any prescribed or over-the-counter medication.

Drugs such as marijuana, nicotine, and alcohol should also be avoided during pregnancy. A high daily intake of caffeine should be reduced if possible. Your physician will assess the potential benefits of drug treatment against any possible risks to decide whether or not a drug should be taken. This is particularly important if you need to take medication regularly for a chronic condition such as epilepsy, high blood pressure, or diabetes.

Drugs and the stages of pregnancy

Pregnancy is divided into three three-month stages called trimesters. Depending on the trimester in which they are taken, drugs can have different effects on the mother, the fetus, or both. Some drugs may be considered safe during one trimester, but not during another. Physicians, therefore, often need to substitute one medication for another given during the course of pregnancy and/or labour.

The trimesters of pregnancy

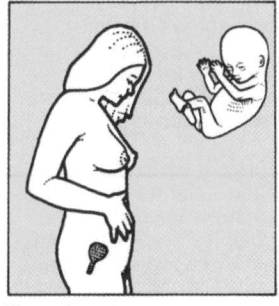 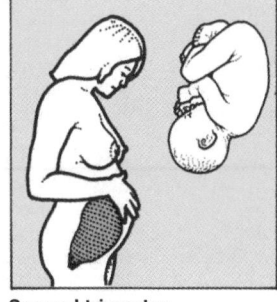 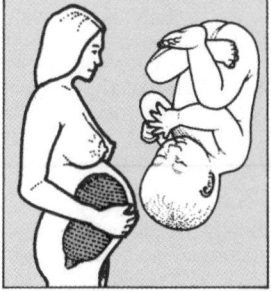

First trimester
During the first three months of pregnancy – the most critical period – drugs may affect the development of fetal organs, leading to congenital malformations. Very severe defects may result in miscarriage.

Second trimester
From the fourth to the sixth month some drugs may retard the growth of the fetus. This may also result in a low birth weight. Other drugs may affect the development of the nervous system.

Third trimester
During the last three months of pregnancy, major risks include breathing difficulties in the newborn baby. Some drugs may also affect labour, causing it to be premature, delayed, or prolonged.

How drugs cross the placenta
The placenta acts as a filter between the mother's bloodstream and that of the baby. It allows small molecules of nutrients to pass into the baby's blood, while preventing larger particles such as blood cells from doing so. Most drug molecules are comparatively small and pass easily through the placental barrier.

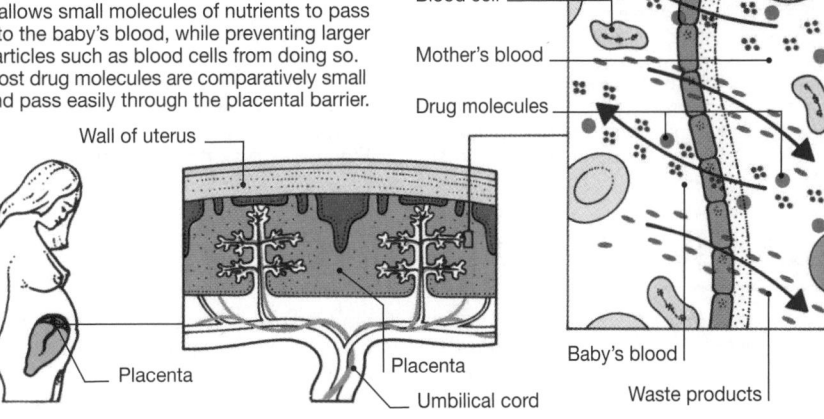

Wall of uterus — Placenta — Placenta — Umbilical cord — Nutrients — Blood cell — Mother's blood — Drug molecules — Baby's blood — Waste products

BREAST-FEEDING

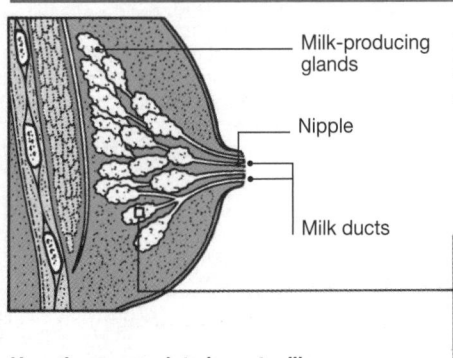

Milk-producing glands — Nipple — Milk ducts

How drugs pass into breast milk
The milk-producing glands in the breast are surrounded by a network of fine blood vessels. Small molecules of substances such as drugs pass from the blood into the milk. Drugs that dissolve easily in fat may pass across in greater concentrations than other drugs.

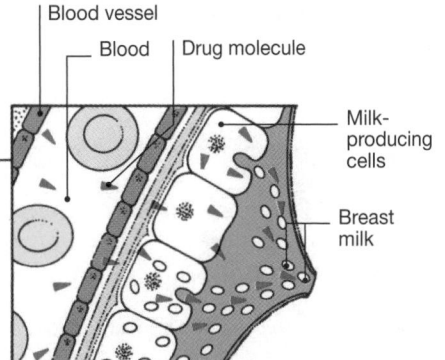

Blood vessel — Blood — Drug molecule — Milk-producing cells — Breast milk

Just as drugs may cross from the mother's bloodstream into the baby's through the placenta, they may also pass to the baby from the mother's milk. This means that a breast-fed baby will receive small doses of whatever drugs the mother is taking. In many cases this is not a problem, because the amount of drug that passes into the milk is too small to have any significant effect on the baby. However, some drugs can produce unwanted effects on the baby. Antibiotics may sensitize the infant and consequently prevent their use later in life. *Sedative* drugs may make the baby drowsy and cause feeding problems. Moreover, some drugs may reduce the amount of milk produced by the mother.

Physicians usually advise breast-feeding women to take only essential drugs. When a mother needs to take regular medication while breast-feeding, her baby may also need to be closely monitored for possible adverse effects.

THE ELDERLY

Older people are particularly at risk when taking drugs. This is partly due to the physical changes associated with aging, and partly because many elderly people need to take several different drugs at the same time. They may also be at risk because they may be unable to manage their treatment properly, or they may lack the information to do so.

Physical changes

Elderly people have a greater risk of accumulating drugs in their body tissues because the liver is less efficient at breaking drugs down and the kidneys are less efficient at excreting them. Because of this, in some cases the normal adult dose will produce *side effects*, and a smaller dose may be needed to produce a therapeutic effect without the side effects. (See also Liver and kidney disease, below.)

Older people tend to take more drugs than younger people – many take three or more drugs at the same time. Apart from increasing the number of drugs in their systems, adverse drug interactions (see p.16) are more likely.

As people grow older, some parts of the body, such as the brain and nervous system, become more sensitive to drugs, thus increasing the likelihood of *adverse reactions* from drugs acting on those sites (see right). A similar problem may occur due to changes in the percentage of body fat. Although allergic reactions (see

Allergy, p.109) do not become more common due to increasing age, they are more likely because more drugs are prescribed. Accordingly, physicians prescribe more carefully for older people, especially those with disorders that are likely to correct themselves in time.

Incorrect use of drugs

Elderly people often suffer harmful effects from their drug treatment because they may fail to take their medication regularly or correctly. This may happen because they have been misinformed about how to take it or receive vague instructions. Problems arise sometimes because the elderly person cannot remember whether he or she has taken the drug and takes a double dose (see Exceeding the dose, p.30). Problems may also occur because the person is confused; this is not necessarily due to age or illness, but can arise as a result of drug treatment, especially if an elderly person is taking a number of different drugs or a *sedative*.

Prescriptions for the elderly should be clearly and fully labelled, and information about the drug and its use should be provided either for the individual or for the person taking care of him or her. When appropriate, containers with memory aids should be used to dispense the medication in single doses.

Elderly people often find it difficult to swallow medicine in *capsule* or tablet

Effect of drugs that act on the brain

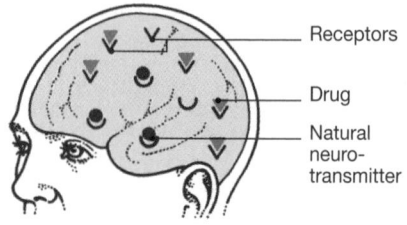

In young people
There are plenty of *receptors* to take up the drug as well as natural *neurotransmitters*.

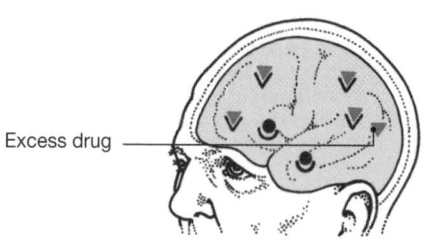

In older people
There may be fewer receptors so that even a reduced drug dose may be excessive.

form; they should always take capsules or tablets with a full glass or cup of liquid. A liquid medicine may be prescribed instead.

LIVER AND KIDNEY DISEASE

Long-term illness affects the way in which people respond to drugs. This is especially true of liver and kidney problems. The liver alters the chemical structure of many drugs that enter the body (see How drugs pass through the body, p.17) by breaking them down into simpler substances, while the kidneys excrete drugs in the urine. If the effectiveness of the liver or kidneys is reduced by illness, the action of drugs on the individual can be significantly altered. In most cases, people with liver or kidney disease will be prescribed a smaller number of drugs and lower doses. In addition, certain drugs may, in rare cases, damage the liver or kidneys. For

example, tetracycline can cause kidney failure in those with poor kidney function. A physician may be reluctant to prescribe such a drug to someone with already reduced liver or kidney function in order to avoid the risk of further damage.

Drugs and liver disease

Severe liver diseases, such as cirrhosis and hepatitis, affect the way the body breaks down drugs. This can lead to a dangerous accumulation of certain drugs in the body. People suffering from these diseases should consult their physician before taking any medication (including over-the-counter drugs) or alcohol. Many

drugs must be avoided completely, since they could cause coma in someone with liver damage.

Drugs and kidney disease

People with poor kidney function are at risk from drug side effects. There are two reasons for this. First, drugs build up in the system because smaller amounts are excreted in urine. Second, kidney disease can cause protein loss through the urine, which lowers the level of protein in the blood. Some drugs bind to blood proteins, and if there are fewer protein molecules, a greater proportion of drug becomes free and active in the body.

Drug passing through body

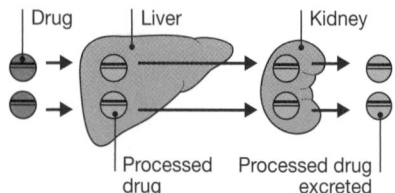

Normal liver and kidneys
Drugs are processed in the liver before being excreted by the kidneys.

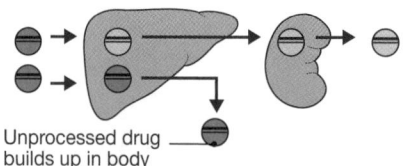

In liver damage
The liver cannot process sufficient drug and this builds up in the body tissues.

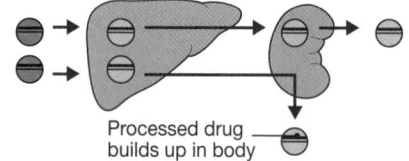

In kidney damage
The kidneys cannot excrete the processed drug in the urine and drug levels in the body rise.

DRUG TOLERANCE AND DEPENDENCE

In the course of treatment with many common drugs, the body acquires the ability to adapt to the drug's effect. This response is known as tolerance. As a result, the drug dose has to be increased to achieve the same effect as before. Tolerance is not always associated with dependence (often called addiction), which is the compulsion to continue taking a drug in order to experience a desired effect, or in order to avoid the unpleasant effects that occur when it is not taken. Dependence is almost always confined to drugs which act on the brain and nervous system, such as opiates, tobacco, and alcohol.

TOLERANCE

Drug tolerance occurs as the body adapts to a drug's actions. A person taking the drug needs larger and larger doses to achieve the original effect and as the dose increases, so too do the risks of toxic effects and dependence. Although people can develop a tolerance to many drugs, it is a dangerous characteristic of virtually all the drugs of dependence.

How tolerance develops

Drug tolerance can develop through a variety of different mechanisms, many of which are not fully understood. In some cases, the liver becomes more efficient at breaking the drug down to an inactive form. In other cases, the drug receptors adapt to the presence of the drug, In yet other cases, the drug exhausts the body's supply of chemicals necessary to produce a response.

Tolerance to one particular drug may result in the reduced effect of a drug that has similar properties or is processed in the body in the same way. This is known as cross tolerance. For example, a regular drinker, who can tolerate high levels of alcohol (a depressant), can have a dangerous tolerance to other depressants such as sleeping drugs and anti-anxiety drugs. While cross-tolerance can often cause problems, it sometimes has a beneficial effect in allowing a substance with a less addictive potential to replace the original drug. For example, the symptoms of alcohol withdrawal can be controlled by the anti-anxiety drug diazepam, which is also a depressant.

Tolerance to some drugs has its benefits. A person can develop tolerance to the side effects of a drug while still benefiting from its useful effects. For example, many people taking antidepressants find that side effects such as dry mouth slowly disappear, with the primary action of the drug continuing (see below).

Increasing drug tolerance has dangers. A person who has developed tolerance to a drug may keep raising the dose to sometimes toxic levels in order to achieve the desired effect.

Effects of tolerance

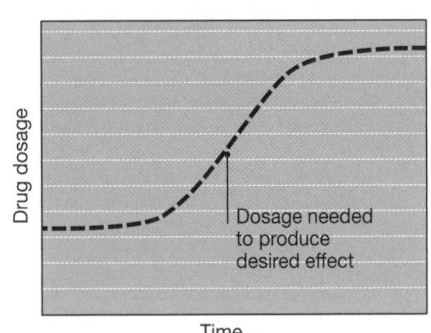

Development of tolerance
A gradually increasing dose of the drug is needed to produce the desired effect as tolerance develops over time.

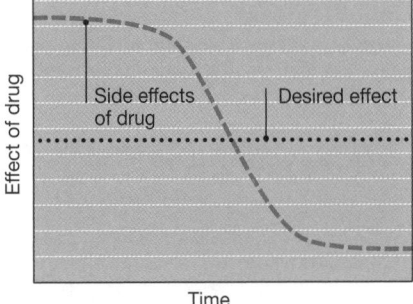

Beneficial effect of tolerance
During treatment with many drugs, the unwanted side effects decrease with time, while the desired effect of the drug is maintained.

DEPENDENCE

Drug addiction is characterized by behaviour that includes a loss of control over drug use, and/or a compulsive use and craving for a substance resulting in physical, psychological, or social harm to the user, with continued use despite the harm.

Drug dependence (a more widely used term than the word addiction) applies far more widely than most people realize. It is usually thought of in association with the use of illegal drugs, such as heroin, or with excessive intake of alcohol. But millions of people are dependent on other drugs, including stimulants – such as caffeine found in coffee and tea, and nicotine in tobacco – and certain prescription medicines, such as analgesics, sleeping drugs, amphetamines, and tranquillizers.

Psychological and physical dependence

Drug dependence, implying that a person is reliant on the continued use of a substance with potential for abuse, is of two types. Psychological dependence is an emotional state of craving for a drug whose presence has a desired effect on the mind, or whose absence has an undesired effect. Physical dependence, which may or may not accompany psychological dependence, involves physiological adaptation to a medicine that is characterized by severe physical disturbances – withdrawal symptoms – during a period of abstinence. Physical dependence alone does not incite addiction.

Drugs that cause dependence

Many people who need to take regular medication worry that they may become dependent on their drugs. In fact, only a few groups of drugs produce physical or psychological dependence, and most of them are substances that alter mood or behaviour. Such drugs include heroin and other *opioid* analgesics such as morphine and meperidine, sleeping and anti-anxiety drugs (benzodiazepines and barbiturates), depressants (alcohol), and nervous system stimulants (cocaine, caffeine, amphetamines, and nicotine).

Antidepressant drugs do not cause psychological dependence. When a depressive illness has been treated effectively, drugs can usually be stopped

DEPENDENCE continued

without any problems, although some people may experience physical withdrawal symptoms if drugs are stopped suddenly. Consult the drug profile in Part 4 of this book to discover the dependence rating of any drug you are taking.

The use of nicotine, in the form of tobacco, and of opioid analgesics, whether controlled or uncontrolled, invariably produces physical dependence if taken regularly over a period of time. However, it is also true that not all regular users of alcohol become alcoholics. There is much argument over the definition of an alcoholic. A widely used definition is: a person who has experienced physical, psychological, social, or occupational impairment as a consequence of habitual, excessive consumption of alcohol.

Recognizing the dangers of drug dependence

Factors that determine a person's risk of developing physical dependence include the characteristics of the drug itself, the strength and frequency of doses, and the duration of use. However, the presence of these factors does not always result in dependence. Psychological and physiological factors that are unique to each individual also enter into the equation, and there may be other, as yet unknown, factors involved. For example, when the use of opioid analgesics is

DRUG MISUSE

The term is defined as any use of drugs that causes physical, psychological, economic, legal, or social harm to the user, or to persons who may be affected by the user's behaviour. Drug abuse commonly refers to taking drugs obtained illegally (such as heroin), but may also be used to describe the misuse of drugs generally obtainable legally (nicotine, alcohol), and to drugs obtainable through a physician's prescription only (everything from sleeping drugs and tranquillizers to analgesics and stimulants).

The misuse of prescription drugs deserves more attention than it usually receives. The practice can include the personal use of drugs left over from a previous course of treatment, the sharing with others of drugs that have been prescribed for yourself, the deliberate deception of physicians, the forgery of prescriptions, and the theft of drugs from pharmacies. All of these practices can have dangerous consequences. Careful

attention to the advice in the section on Managing your drug treatment (p.25) will help to avoid inadvertent misuse of drugs. The dangers associated with abuse of individual drugs are discussed under Drugs of abuse (pp.483–493).

Commonly misused drugs	
Alcohol	Magic mushrooms
Amphetamines	Mephedrone
Barbiturates	Mescaline
Benzodiazepines	Naphyrone
Cannabis	Nicotine
Cocaine (including	Nitrates
crack)	Opioids
Ecstasy	(including
GHB	heroin and
Ketamine	methadone)
Khat	Phencyclidine
Lysergide (LSD)	Solvents

restricted to the short-term relief of pain in a medical setting or long-term use in patients with cancer, dependence is rare. Yet there is a high risk of physical dependence when these drugs, or other drugs of abuse, are taken for non-medical reasons. There is also a risk in some cases of low-dose use when the drug is continued over a long period (e.g. with

benzodiazepines, p.67). No one can say for sure exactly what leads a person to drug-dependent behaviour. A person's psychological and physical make-up are thought to be factors, as well as his or her social environment, occupational pressures, and outlook on life.

The indiscriminate use of certain prescription drugs can also cause drug dependence. Benzodiazepine drugs can produce dependence, and this is one reason why physicians today discourage the use of any drug to induce sleep or calm anxiety for more than a few weeks. Appetite suppressants (see p.72) require close medical supervision. Amphetamines are no longer prescribed as appetite suppressants because of the frequency with which they are abused.

Treating drug dependence

Treatment for drug dependence can only be effective if the person is sufficiently motivated. There are two parts to treatment. The first part, detoxification, can take different forms. In some cases, if it is possible to do so, abstinence may be abruptly imposed. Sometimes, the drug may be gradually withdrawn or other safer substances substituted. For example, methadone (p.352) is substituted for heroin. Physical or mental withdrawal symptoms may need close monitoring, for instance, withdrawal from depressants such as barbiturates or alcohol may result in seizures. Once the drug has been cleared from the body, the second part of treatment is directed at preventing a recurrence. This can involve psychological therapies to tackle the initial cause of the dependence, such as social problems. Psychotherapy, counselling, and support organizations, such as Alcoholics Anonymous, may all play a role in the rehabilitation of the alcoholic or addict.

SYMPTOMS OF WITHDRAWAL

These can range from the mild (sneezing, sweating) to the serious (vomiting, confusion) to the extremely serious (seizures, coma). Alcohol withdrawal may be associated with delirium tremens, very occasionally fatal. Withdrawal from benzodiazepines can sometimes involve hallucinations and seizures. Under medical guidance, withdrawal symptoms can be relieved

with doses of the original drug, or with less addictive substitutes.

Withdrawal symptoms occur because the body has adapted to the action of the drug (see Drug tolerance, p.23). When a drug is continuously present, the body may stop the release of a natural chemical necessary to normal function, like endorphins (below).

Pain and heroin withdrawal

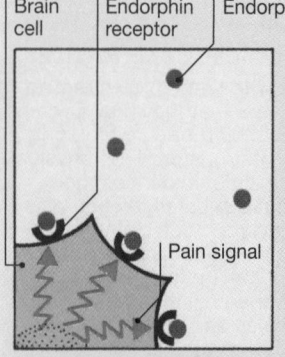

Normal brain
When no drug is present, natural substances called endorphins inhibit the transmission of pain signals.

Effect of heroin
Heroin occupies the same receptors in the brain as endorphins, suppressing production of endorphins.

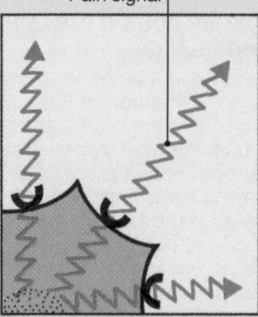

Heroin withdrawal
Abrupt withdrawal of heroin leaves the brain without a buffer to pain signals, even from minor stimuli.

MANAGING YOUR DRUG TREATMENT

A prescribed drug does not automatically produce a beneficial response. For a drug to have maximum benefit, it must be taken as directed by your physician, pharmacist, or manufacturer. It is estimated that two out of every five people for whom a drug is prescribed do not take it properly, if at all. The reasons include failure to understand or remember instructions, fear of adverse reactions, and lack of motivation, often arising from the disappearance of symptoms.

It is your responsibility to take a prescribed drug at the correct time, and in the manner recommended. To do this, you need to know where to obtain information about the drug (see Questioning your physician, p.26) and to make certain that you fully understand the instructions.

The following pages describe the practical aspects of drug treatment, from obtaining a prescription and buying over-the-counter drugs to storing drugs and disposing of old medications safely. Problems caused by mismanaging drug treatment – overdosing, underdosing, or stopping the drug altogether – and long-term drug treatment are dealt with on pp.28–31. Information regarding specific drugs is given in Part 4.

OVER-THE-COUNTER DRUGS

Over-the-counter drugs are those for which a prescription is not required. All are available from pharmacies (many only from pharmacies).

It is generally accepted that over-the-counter drugs are suitable for self-treatment and are unlikely to produce serious adverse reactions if taken as directed. But, as with all medicines, they can be harmful if they are misused. The ease with which they can be purchased is no guarantee of their absolute safety. For this reason, the same precautions should be taken when using any over-the-counter medicine as when using a drug prescribed by your physician or other health care provider.

Using over-the-counter drugs

A number of minor ailments and problems, ranging from coughs and colds to minor cuts and bruises, can be adequately dealt with by taking or using over-the-counter medicines. However, when using these treatments, you must be sure to read the directions on the label and follow them carefully, particularly those advising on dosage and under what circumstances a physician should be consulted. Most over-the-counter drugs are clearly labelled. They may warn of conditions under which the drug should not be taken, or advise you to consult a doctor if symptoms persist.

The *pharmacist* is a good source of information about over-the-counter drugs and can usually tell you what is suitable for your complaint. He or she can also determine when an over-the-counter drug may not be effective and can warn you if self-treatment or prolonged treatment is not advisable. When consulting the pharmacist regarding over-the-counter drugs, you should inform him or her if you are taking prescription drugs or other medications for any other illnesses.

BUYING MEDICINES OVER THE INTERNET

There are many websites offering over-the-counter (OTC) and prescription-only medicines (POM) for sale over the Internet. Buying medicines from non-accredited *pharmacy* sites can be potentially very dangerous. Many of them operate outside of Canada and so are not subject to Canadian law, and the drugs sold, as well as the advice given, may not be regulated in the same way as in Canada. This means the quality of the drugs they supply cannot be guaranteed. You may receive either substandard or fake drugs, with the risk that you could suffer under- or overdosing or even toxic adverse effects from taking the wrong drug or a toxic contaminant. You should be especially suspicious if the site will supply you with a POM without a prescription. The home page of an official accredited Canadian pharmacy website must identify that the website belongs (or refers) to a pharmacy and should indicate that it is accredited by the provincial pharmacy college – e.g. a pharmacy in Ontario will indicate that it is accredited by the Ontario College of Pharmacists (OCP). Also, the physical location of the pharmacy including the address, telephone number, and information on when licensed pharmacists are available for consultation should be included. For further details on internet pharmacies, please refer to the provincial pharmacy college's website.

Buying over-the-counter medications
Various drugs are available over-the-counter, ranging from cough medicines to eye drops.

Your pharmacist can help you to select the appropriate medication.

Medicated creams, lotions, and powders

Analgesics

Eye preparations

Laxatives

Cough and cold treatments

Antacids

It is important to speak to your physician before buying over-the-counter drugs for children. Some symptoms, such as diarrhea in young children, should be treated only by a physician since they may be caused by a serious condition.

PRESCRIPTION DRUGS

Drugs prescribed by a physician are not necessarily "stronger" or more likely to have *side effects* than those you can buy without prescription. Indeed, physicians often prescribe drugs that are also available over-the-counter (OTC). Drugs that are available only on prescription are drugs whose safe use is difficult to ensure without medical supervision.

When a physician prescribes a drug, he or she usually starts treatment at the normal dosage for the disorder being treated. The dosage may later be adjusted (lowered or increased) if the drug is not producing the desired effect or if you experience adverse side effects. The physician may also decide to switch to an alternative drug that may be more effective at treating the disorder.

Prescribing generic and brand-name drugs

When writing a prescription for a drug, the physician often has a choice between a generic and a brand-name product. Although the active ingredient is the same and the products are considered equivalent, two versions of the same drug may act in slightly different ways, as each manufacturer may formulate their product differently. They may also look different. Generic drugs are often cheaper than brand-name products. For this reason, certain brand-name products are not available on certain drug plans. These are factors that a physician must consider when writing a prescription.

Your *pharmacist* usually needs to consider which drug is covered on your plan and may consult with you in substituting a generic drug. Physicians may indicate "no substitution" on the prescription if they feel that the brand name product would be most suitable for treatment.

If you are prescribed a generic drug, the pharmacist is free to dispense whatever version of this drug is available. This means that your regular medication may vary in appearance when you renew your prescription. If your medication does look different, always check with your pharmacist to reassure yourself that it is the correct drug.

Hospital pharmacies often dispense only generic versions of certain drugs. Therefore, if you are in hospital, the regular medication you receive may look different from that which you are used to at home.

Your prescription

Prescriptions usually have the same information. Your name and address will be listed, and the name of the medication you are being prescribed. The prescription will also state the dose or strength of the medication to be prescribed, how much to take (the number of tablets or amount of liquid), and how frequently it should be taken. The prescription informs the pharmacist of the amount of the drug to be dispensed, and the information that should be put on the label.

In some cases, your physician will indicate that the prescription can be refilled a certain number of times without having to obtain a repeat prescription. The pharmacist will record this information. When your supply of the drug is exhausted, you can return to the pharmacist to obtain a refill without having to get a new prescription. If treatment needs to be continued after the set number of refills have been prescribed, you will have to see your physician again. He or she will decide if a repeat prescription is necessary, or if the treatment should be altered.

Your physician's signature, phone number, and address are included on the prescription, so that the pharmacist can contact him or her if there is a query about the drug to be prescribed.

In addition to medication information provided to you verbally by the pharmacist, he or she may also provide a Patient Information Leaflet, which gives details about the drug, its *adverse effects*, whether it is safe for you, when not to use it, and so on. Compare this with your physician's instructions, and ask the pharmacist about any differences. You should also consult with the pharmacist if the label on your medication differs from the information on the prescription.

It is advisable for you to obtain all of your prescription drugs from the same pharmacist or at least from the same pharmacy, so that your pharmacist can advise you about any particular problems you may have, and keep supplies of any unusual drugs you may be taking.

If you need to take drugs that are prescribed by more than one physician, or by your dentist in addition to your physician, the pharmacist is able to call attention to possible harmful interactions. Physicians do ask if you are taking other medicines before prescribing, but your regular pharmacist provides valuable additional advice.

Questioning your physician

Countless surveys unmistakably point to lack of information as the most common reason for failure of drug treatment. Responses such as "The doctor is too busy to be bothered with a lot of questions" or "The doctor will think I'm stupid if I ask that" recur over and over. Be certain you understand the instructions for a drug before leaving your physician's office, and don't leave with any questions unanswered.

It is a good idea to make a list of the questions you may want to ask before your visit, and to make notes while you are there about what you are told (see page 31). It is not uncommon to forget some of the instructions your physician gives you during a consultation. You can check your instructions from the physician with the pharmacist.

Know what you are taking

Your physician should tell you the generic or brand name of the drug he or she is prescribing, and exactly what condition or symptom it has been prescribed to treat.

As well as telling you the name of the drug prescribed, your physician should explain what dose you should take, how often to take it, and whether the prescription should be repeated. Be certain you understand the instructions about how and when to take the drug (see also Taking your medication, facing page). For example, does four times a day mean four times during the time you are awake, or four times in 24 hours? Ask your physician how long the treatment should last; some medications cause harmful effects if you stop taking them abruptly, or do not have beneficial effects unless the full course of drug treatment is completed.

To help you remember, the label on your dispensed medicine may repeat the instructions, further explaining how to take the medicine. The pharmacist can also help by answering your questions, if you have forgotten to ask the physician.

Risks and special precautions

All drugs have adverse effects (see The effects of drugs, p.15), and you should know what these are. Ask your physician what the possible adverse effects of the drug are and what you should do if they occur. Also ask if there are any foods or other drugs you should avoid during treatment, whether the drug can cause drowsiness, and if you can drink alcohol while taking the drug.

PRESCRIPTION TERMS

ac before meals	**po** by mouth
ad lib freely	**prn** as needed
AM morning	**qid** four times
bid twice a day	a day
c with	**s** without
cap capsule	**sr** slow release
cc cubic centimetre	**stat** at once
ext for external use	**tab** tablet
gtt drops	**tid** three times
mg milligrams	a day
ml millilitres	**top** apply topically
nocte at night	**ud** use as directed
pc after meals	**x** times
PM evening	

TAKING YOUR MEDICATION

Among the most important aspects of managing your drug treatment is knowing how often the drug is to be taken. Should it be taken on an empty stomach? With food? Mixed with something? Specific instructions on such points are given in the individual drug profiles in Part 4.

When to take your drugs

Certain drugs, such as analgesics and drugs for migraine, are taken only as necessary, when warning symptoms occur. Others are meant to be taken regularly at specified intervals. The prescription or label instructions can be confusing, however. For instance, does four times a day mean once every six hours out of 24 – at 8 am, 2 pm, 8 pm, and 2 am? Or does it mean take at four equal intervals during waking hours – morning, lunchtime, late afternoon, and bedtime? The latter is usually the case, but you need to ask your physician or pharmacist for precise directions.

The actual time of day that you take a drug is generally flexible, so you can normally schedule your doses to fit your daily routine. This has the additional advantage of making it easier for you to remember to take your drugs. For example, if you are to take the drug three times during the day, it may be most convenient to take the first dose at 7 am, the second at 3 pm, and the third at 11 pm, while it may be more suitable for another person on the same regimen to take the first dose at 8 am, and so on. You must, however, establish with your pharmacist or your physician whether the drug should be taken with food, in which case you would probably need to take it with your breakfast, lunch, and dinner. Try to take your dose at the recommended intervals; if you take them

Four times a day?

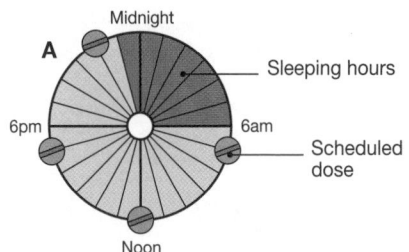

A
Midnight — Sleeping hours
6pm — 6am
— Scheduled dose
Noon

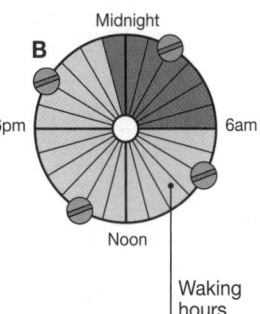

B
Midnight
6pm — 6am
Noon
Waking hours

Check with your physician whether your prescription means (A) take your drug 4 times a day during waking hours, or (B) take 4 times over a 24-hour period.

TIPS ON TAKING MEDICINES

● Whenever possible, take capsules and tablets while standing up or in an upright sitting position, and take them with water. If you take them when you are lying down, or without enough water, it is possible for the capsules or tablets to become stuck in the esophagus. This can delay the action of the drug and may damage the esophagus.

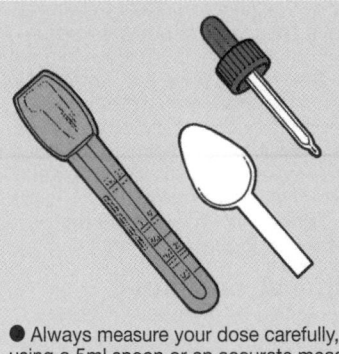

● Always measure your dose carefully, using a 5ml spoon or an accurate measure such as a dropper, children's medicine spoon, or oral syringe.

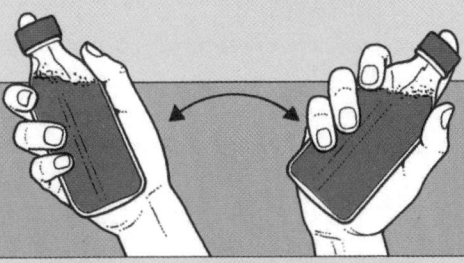

● When taking liquid medicines, shake the bottle before measuring each dose, or you may take improper dosages if the active substance has risen to the top or settled at the bottom of the bottle.

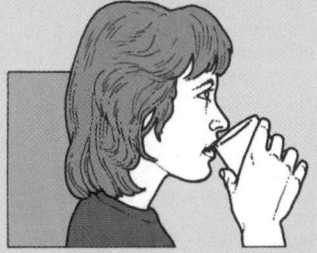

● A drink of cold water immediately after an unpleasantly flavoured medicine may hide the taste and help prevent tablets from lodging in the esophagus.

too close together, the risk of side effects occurring is increased.

If you are taking several different drugs, ask your doctor or pharmacist if they can be taken together, or if they must be taken at different times in order to avoid any adverse effects or reduced effectiveness caused by an interaction between them.

How to take your drugs

If your prescription specifies taking your drug with food – or without food – it is very important to follow this instruction if you are to get the maximum benefit from your treatment.

Certain drugs, such as ampicillin, should be taken on an empty stomach (usually one to two hours before eating) so they will be absorbed more quickly into the bloodstream; others, such as ibuprofen, should be taken with food to avoid stomach irritation. Similarly, you should comply with any instructions to avoid particular foods. Milk and dairy products may inhibit the absorption of some drugs, such as tetracycline; grapefruit juice may affect the way certain drugs are broken down in the body and significantly increase their effectiveness; alcohol is best avoided with many drugs. (See also Drug interactions, p.16.) In some cases, when taking diuretics, for example,

you may be advised to eat foods rich in potassium. But do not take potassium supplements unless you are advised to do so by your physician (see Potassium, p.476). If you use any of the salt substitutes (all of which contain potassium), remember to tell your doctor.

GIVING MEDICINES TO CHILDREN

A number of over-the-counter medicines are specifically prepared for children. Many other medicines have labels that give both adult's and children's dosages. For the purposes of drug labelling, anyone 12 years of age or under is considered a child.

When giving over-the-counter medicines to children, you should always follow the instructions on the label exactly and under no circumstances exceed the dosage recommended for a child. Never give a child even a small amount of a medicine intended for adult use without the advice of your physician.

Never leave a child's medicine within reach, and remember that adult's tablets may look like candy. Also, be aware that apparently simple adult remedies may be extremely toxic to children at an adult dose (e.g. iron tablets).

MISSED DOSES

Missing a dose of your medication can be a problem only if you are taking the drug as part of a regular course of treatment. Missing a drug dose is not uncommon and it is not a cause for concern in most cases. The missed dose may sometimes produce a recurrence of symptoms or a change in the action of the drug, so you should know what to do when you have forgotten to take your medication. Ask your pharmacist how to deal with missed doses. For advice on individual drugs, consult the drug profile in Part 4.

Additional measures

With some drugs, the timing of doses depends on how long the actions of the drugs last. When you miss a dose, the amount of drug in your body is lowered, and the effect of the drug may be diminished. You may therefore have to take other steps to avoid unwanted consequences. For example, if you are taking an oral contraceptive and you forget to take one pill at your usual time, you should take the pill as soon as you remember, and for the next week use another form of contraception.

If you miss more than one dose of any drug you are taking regularly, you should tell your physician. Missed doses are especially important with insulin and drugs for epilepsy.

If you frequently forget to take your medication, you should tell your physician. He or she may be able to simplify your treatment schedule by prescribing a preparation that contains several drugs, or a preparation that releases the drug slowly into the body over time, and only needs to be taken once or twice daily.

REMEMBERING YOUR MEDICATION

If you take several different drugs, it is useful to draw up a chart to remind yourself of when each drug should be taken. This will also help anyone who looks after you, or a physician who is unfamiliar with your treatment.

The example given here is of a dosage chart for an elderly woman suffering from osteoarthritis and a heart condition who has trouble sleeping. Her physician has prescribed the following treatment:

Hydrochlorothiazide (a diuretic to counter fluid retention), one 25mg tablet in the morning.

Amiloride (another diuretic to counter the potassium loss caused by hydrochlorothiazide), two 5mg tablets in the morning.

Acetaminophen (for osteoarthritis), three 500mg tablets daily.

Verapamil (to treat heart condition), three 80mg tablets a day.

Zopiclone (a sleeping drug), one 5mg tablet at bedtime.

Dosage Chart

8am	1pm
2 x Amiloride	1 x Acetaminophen
1 x Acetaminophen	1 x Verapamil
1 x Verapamil	
1 x Hydrochlorothiazide	

7pm	11pm
1 x Acetaminophen	1 x Verapamil
	1 x Zopiclone

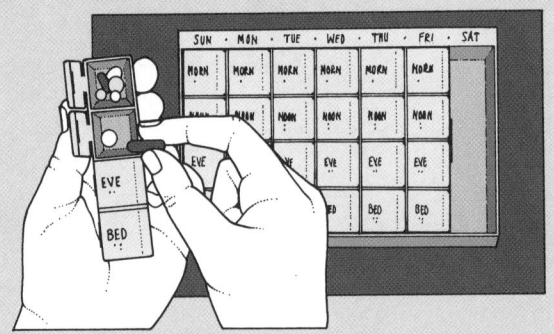

Pill box
Using a pill box is a handy way of making sure you take your tablets in the right order. They are also useful for carers of people with dementia. The boxes have a strip for each day of the week, and compartments for morning, afternoon, evening, and bedtime.

ENDING DRUG TREATMENT

As with missed doses, ending drug treatment too soon can be a problem when you are taking a regular course of drugs. With medication that you take as required, you can stop treatment as soon as you feel better.

Advice on stopping individual drugs is given in the drug profiles in Part 4. Some general guidelines for ending drug treatment are given below.

Risks of stopping too soon

Suddenly stopping drug treatment before completing your course of medication may cause the original condition to recur or lead to other complications, including withdrawal symptoms. The disappearance of the symptoms does not necessarily mean that a disorder is cured. Even if you feel better, do not stop taking the drug unless your physician advises you to do so. People taking antibiotics often stop too soon, but the full course of treatment prescribed should always be followed.

Adverse effects

Do not stop taking a medication simply because it produces unpleasant side effects. Many adverse effects disappear or become bearable after a while. But if they do not, check with your physician, who may want to reduce the dosage of the drug gradually or, alternatively, substitute another drug that does not produce the same side effects.

Gradual reduction

While many medications can be stopped abruptly, others need to be reduced gradually to prevent a reaction when treatment ends. This is the case with long-term corticosteroid therapy (see right) as well as with *dependence*-inducing drugs.

Phased reduction of corticosteroids

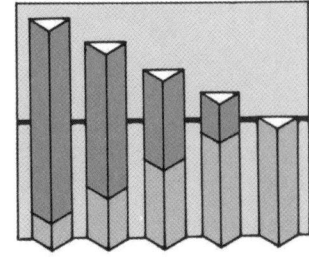

■ Corticosteroid drug

□ Natural adrenal hormone

Normal hormone level

Corticosteroid drugs suppress production in the body of natural adrenal hormones. A phased reduction of the dosage allows levels of the natural hormones to revert to normal. The last stages of withdrawal are made very slowly.

STORING DRUGS

Once you have completed a medically directed course of treatment, you should not keep any unused drugs. But most families will want to keep a supply of remedies for indigestion, headaches, colds, and so forth. Such medicines should not be used if they show any signs of deterioration, or if they have reached their expiry date (see When to dispose of drugs, right).

How to store drugs

All drugs, including cough medicines, iron tablets, and oral contraceptives, should be kept out of the reach of children. If you are in the habit of keeping your medicines where you will see them as a reminder to take them, leave a previously emptied medicine container out instead, and put the drug itself safely out of reach.

Over-the-counter and prescription drugs should normally be stored in the container in which you purchased them. If it is necessary to put them into other containers, such as special containers designed for the elderly, make sure you keep the original container with the label, as well as any separate instructions, for future reference.

Make certain that caps and lids are replaced and tightly closed after use; loose caps may leak and spill, or hasten deterioration of the drug.

Where to store drugs

The majority of drugs should be stored in a cool, dry place out of direct sunlight, even those in plastic containers or tinted glass. Room temperature, away from sources of direct heat, is suitable for most medicines. A few drugs should be stored in the refrigerator. Storage information for individual drugs is given in the drug profiles in Part 4.

Wall cabinets that can be locked are ideal for storing drugs, as long as the cabinet itself is located in a cool, dry place and not, as often happens, in the bathroom, which is frequently warm and humid.

WHEN TO DISPOSE OF DRUGS

Old drugs should be returned to the pharmacist for proper disposal. Always dispose of:

● Any drug that is past its expiry date.

● ASA tablets that smell of vinegar.

● Tablets that are chipped, cracked, or discoloured, and capsules that have softened, cracked, or stuck together.

● Liquids that have thickened or discoloured, or that taste or smell different in any way from the original product.

● Tubes that are cracked, leaky, or hard.

● Ointments and creams that have changed odour, or changed appearance by discolouring, hardening, or separating.

● Any liquid needing refrigeration that has been kept for over two weeks, unless otherwise specified on the bottle.

LONG-TERM DRUG TREATMENT

Many people require regular, prolonged treatment with one or more drugs. People who suffer from chronic or recurrent disorders often need lifelong treatment with drugs to control symptoms or prevent complications. Antihypertensive drugs for high blood pressure and insulin or oral antidiabetic drugs for diabetes mellitus are familiar examples. Many other disorders take a long time to cure; for example, people with tuberculosis usually need at least six months' treatment with antituberculous drugs. Long-term drug treatment may also be necessary to prevent a condition from occurring, and will have to be taken for as long as the individual is at risk. Antimalarial drugs are a good example.

Possible adverse effects

You may worry that taking a drug for a long period will reduce its effectiveness or that you will become dependent on it. However, *tolerance* develops only with a few drugs; most medicines continue to have the same effect indefinitely without necessitating an increase in dosage or change in drug. Similarly, taking a drug for more than a few weeks does not normally create *dependence*.

Changing drug treatment

If you are taking a drug regularly, you will need to know what to do if something else occurs to affect your health. If you wish to become pregnant, for example, you should ask your physician right away if it is preferable to continue on your regular medicine or switch to another less likely to affect your pregnancy. If you contract a new illness, for which an additional drug is prescribed, your regular treatment may be altered.

There are a number of other reasons for changing a drug. You may have had an *adverse reaction*, or an improved preparation may have become available.

Adjusting to long-term treatment

You should establish a daily routine for taking your medication in order to reduce the risk of a missed dose. Usually you should not stop taking your medication, even if there are *side effects*, without consulting your physician (see Ending drug treatment, facing page). If you fear possible side effects from the drug, discuss this with your physician.

Many people deliberately stop their drugs because they feel well or their symptoms disappear. This can be dangerous, especially with a disease like high blood pressure, which has no noticeable symptoms. Stopping treatment may lead to a recurrence or worsening of a disease. If you are uncertain about why you have to keep taking a drug, ask your physician.

Only a few drugs require an alteration in habits. Some drugs should not be taken with alcohol; with a few drugs you should avoid certain foods. If you require a drug that makes you drowsy, you should not drive a car or operate dangerous equipment.

If you are taking a drug that should not be stopped suddenly or that may interact with other drugs, it is a good idea to carry a warning card or bracelet, a MedicAlert for example. Such information might be essential for emergency medical treatment in an accident.

Monitoring treatment

If you are on long-term treatment, you need to visit your physician for periodic check-ups. He or she will check your underlying condition and monitor any *adverse effects* of treatment. Levels of the drug in the blood may be measured. With insulin, in addition to checks with the physician, you need to monitor blood glucose and/or urine levels each day.

If a drug is known to cause damage to an organ, tests may be done to check the function of the organ. For example, blood and urine tests to check kidney function, or a blood count to check the bone marrow, may be indicated.

Medical check-ups
Blood pressure is commonly checked in people on long-term drug treatment.

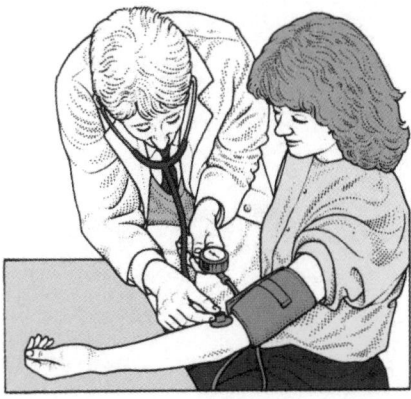

EXCEEDING THE DOSE

Most people associate drug overdoses with attempts at suicide or the fatalities and near fatalities brought on by abuse of street drugs. However, drug overdoses can also occur among people who deliberately or inadvertently exceed the stated dose of a drug that has been prescribed for them by their physician.

A single extra dose of most drugs is unlikely to be a cause for concern, although accidental overdoses can create anxiety in the individual and his or her family, and may cause overdose symptoms, which can appear in a variety of different forms.

Overdose of some drugs, however, is potentially dangerous even when the dose has been exceeded by only a small amount. Each of the drug profiles in Part 4 gives detailed information on the consequences of exceeding the dose, symptoms to look out for, and what to do. Each drug has an overdose danger rating of low, medium, or high, which are described fully on p.174.

Taking an extra dose

People sometimes exceed the stated dose in the mistaken belief that by increasing dosage they will obtain more

Effects of repeated overdose
Repeated overdose of a drug over an extended period may lead to a build-up of high levels of the drug in the body, especially if liver or kidney function is reduced.

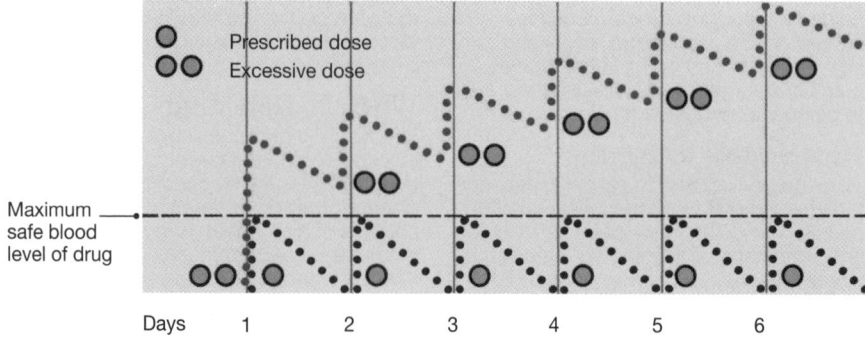

Days   1   2   3   4   5   6

immediate action or a more effective cure. This action is a particular risk with *tolerance*-inducing drugs (see Drug tolerance and dependence, p.23). Others exceed their dose accidentally, by miscalculating the amount or forgetting that the dose has already been taken.

Taking extra doses is often a problem in the elderly, who may repeat their dose

through forgetfulness or confusion. This is a special risk with medicines that cause drowsiness (see also p.22).

In some cases, especially when liver or kidney function deteriorates, the drug builds up in the blood because the body cannot break down and excrete the extra dose quickly enough, so that symptoms of poisoning may result. Symptoms of excessive intake may not be apparent for many days.

When and how to get help

If you are not sure whether or not you have taken your medicine, think back and check again. If you honestly cannot remember, assume that you have missed the dose and follow the advice given in the individual drug profiles in Part 4 of this book. If you cannot find your drug, consult your physician. Make a note to use some system in the future which will help you remember to take your medicine.

If you are looking after an elderly person on regular drug treatment who suddenly develops unusual symptoms such as confusion, drowsiness, or unsteadiness, consider the possibility of an inadvertent drug overdose and consult the physician as soon as possible.

Deliberate overdose

While many cases of drug overdose are accidental or the result of a mistaken belief that increasing the dose will enhance the benefits of drug treatment, sometimes an excessive amount of a drug is taken with the intention of causing harm or even as a suicide attempt. Whether or not you think a dangerous amount of a drug has been taken, deliberate overdoses of this kind should always be brought to the attention of your doctor. Not only is it necessary to ensure that no physical harm has occurred as a result of the overdose, but the psychological condition of anyone who takes such action may indicate the need for additional medical help.

THE EFFECT OF DRUG OVERDOSE ON THE BODY

The effect of drug overdose on the body depends on the type of drug involved. Some drugs produce an exaggeration of the desired effect, for instance overdose of tranquillizers leads to unconsciousness. With many drugs, the toxic overdose effects are unrelated to the action or side effects of the drug when it is taken in normal doses.

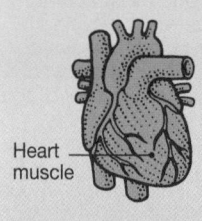

Heart and circulation
Some antidepressants cause severe, and possibly fatal, arrhythmias in overdose.

Heart muscle

Liver
Fatal liver damage can occur with as few as 20 tablets of acetaminophen. Treatment can prevent damage but must be given within 12 hours of taking the drug.

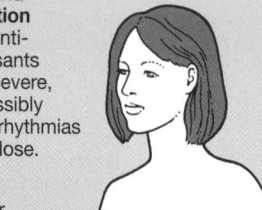

Liver

Gallbladder

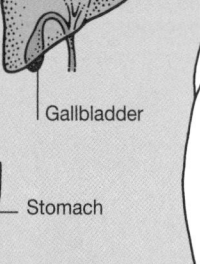

Stomach

Small intestine

Stomach and intestines
Iron overdose causes bleeding in the digestive tract. An overdose of NSAIDs causes ulceration of the stomach and intestines.

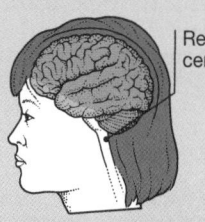

Respiratory centre

Brain
Depression of the respiratory centre in the brain is common with overdose of barbiturates and tranquillizers. ASA in overdose can result in convulsions.

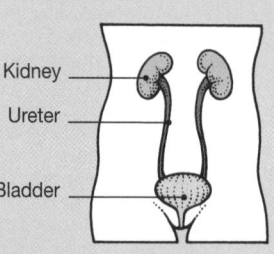

Kidney

Ureter

Bladder

Kidney
An overdose of NSAIDs, particularly in people who have impaired kidney function, can result in kidney failure.

DOs AND DON'Ts

On this page you will find a summary of the most important practical points concerning the management of your drug treatment. The advice is arranged under general headings, explaining the safest methods of storing drugs and following treatment, whether it is a prescribed medicine or an over-the-counter drug. This information is equally applicable whether you are taking medicine yourself or supervising the drug treatment of someone in your care.

At the physician's office

DO
✓ Tell the person prescribing your drugs about all drugs you are already taking: prescription, over-the-counter, street drugs, and herbal or natural products.
✓ Tell them if you are pregnant, intending to become pregnant, or breast-feeding.
✓ Tell them about any allergic reactions you have experienced to past drug treatments.
✓ Tell them if you have a current health problem or if you think you might be at risk from drug treatment.

✓ Ask them how your prescribed medication will help you and when you will know it is working.
✓ Make sure you understand the reasons why you have been prescribed a particular drug and how long you will need to take it. People who do not understand the reasons for their treatment often fail to take their prescribed drug correctly.

DON'T
✗ Leave your physician's office before you have a clear understanding of how and when to take your drug.

At the pharmacy

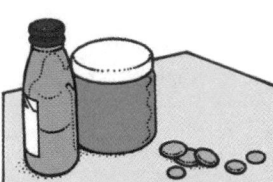

DO
✓ Ask your pharmacist's advice about over-the-counter drugs if you are not sure what you should buy, or if you think you may react adversely to a drug.
✓ Try to see the same pharmacist or use the same pharmacy to obtain your regular prescriptions.
✓ Be sure you know the name of the drug you have been prescribed. If you are getting a repeat prescription and your physician has specified that you should always use the same brand, make sure the brand is correct.

✓ Make sure you understand what is on the drug label.
✓ Ask the pharmacist to put your drug in a container with an easy-to-remove cap if you have difficulty using child-resistant containers.
✓ Ask the pharmacist if the medication will interact with any other drugs you are taking, foods, or vitamins.

DON'T
✗ Send children to the pharmacy to get your medicine for you.

Giving medicines to children

DO
✓ Check the dose on the label carefully before giving medicines to children.
✓ Make sure over-the-counter preparations you give to children under 16 years old do not contain ASA.

DON'T
✗ Pretend to children that medicines are candies or soft drinks.
✗ Give any medicines to children under the age of five, except on the advice of your physician.

Taking your drug

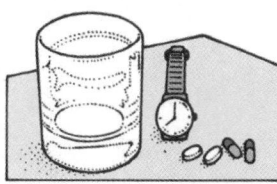

DO
✓ Make sure that your drug will not make you drowsy or otherwise affect your ability before you drive or perform difficult or dangerous tasks.
✓ Read the label carefully and do what it says. This is equally important with all types of drugs, creams, and lotions as well as drugs taken by mouth.
✓ Finish the drug treatment prescribed for you.
✓ Consult your physician for advice if you experience side effects.

DON'T
✗ Take any prescribed or over-the-counter drugs without first consulting your physician if you are pregnant or trying to conceive.
✗ Offer your medicine to other people or take medicine that has been prescribed for someone else (even if the symptoms are the same).

Food, drink, and drugs of abuse

DO
✓ Check with your physician and pharmacist whether it is safe to take alcohol with the drugs you are prescribed.
✓ Check that there are no foods you should avoid.
✓ Follow the timing of your drugs with respect to meals, when instructed to do so by your physician or pharmacist.

DON'T
✗ Take drugs (except those prescribed by your physician or other qualified prescriber) or alcohol if you are pregnant or trying to conceive. They may adversely affect the unborn baby.
✗ Take drugs of abuse under any circumstances.

Storing drugs

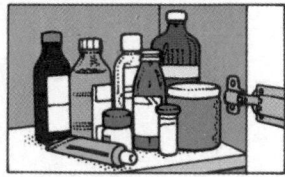

DO
✓ Take care to store drugs in a cool, dry place and protect them from light or refrigerate them, if advised to do so.
✓ Keep all drugs, including seemingly harmless ones such as cough preparations, locked away out of the reach of children.
✓ Check your medicine chest regularly in case other members of the family have left their unwanted drugs in it, and to make sure that none of the normal supplies are out of date.

✓ Keep drugs in their original containers with the original instructions to avoid confusion.

DON'T
✗ Keep drugs you no longer need at home. When you have stopped taking a prescribed drug, take it to your pharmacist to dispose of it unless it is part of your family's first aid kit.

DRUG FINDER INDEX

THE DRUG FINDER

THE DRUG FINDER

This section contains the names of approximately 2,000 individual drug products and substances. It provides a quick and easy reference for readers interested in learning about a specific drug or medication. There is no need for you to know whether the item is a brand name or a generic name, or whether it is a prescription or an over-the-counter drug; all types of drug are listed.

What it contains
The drugs are listed alphabetically and include all major generic drugs and many less widely used substances. A broad range of brand names, as well as many vitamins and minerals, are also included. This comprehensive selection reflects the wide diversity of products available in Canada for the treatment and prevention of disease. Inclusion of a drug or product does not imply endorsement by the publishers or the CPhA, nor does the exclusion of any particular drug or product indicate their disapproval.

How the references work
Entries with an upper case letter are the product names of drugs. References are to the pages in Part 4, containing the drug profiles of each principal generic drug, and to the section in Part 3 that describes the relevant drug group, as appropriate. For products that contain a combination of drugs or substances, page references are given for each drug. Some entries for generic drugs that do not have a full profile in Part 4 have a brief description here. Certain technical terms within the entries are printed in italics to indicate that they are defined in the Glossary (pp.503–508).

---

222 Tablets a combination product containing codeine 244 (an *opioid analgesic* 64) and caffeine

282/292 Tablets a combination product containing codeine 244 (an *opioid analgesic* 64) and caffeine

282 MEP C8 a combination product containing codeine 244 (an *opioid analgesic* 64) and caffeine

5-ASA 176 (a drug for inflammatory bowel disease 98)

642 Tablets a product name for propoxyphene (an *opioid analgesic* 64)

A

abacavir an antiretroviral drug for HIV/AIDS 144

abatacept a biological response modifier for rheumatoid arthritis 103

abciximab an antiplatelet drug 90

Abelcet a product name for amphotericin B 194 (an antifungal 124)

Abenol a product name for acetaminophen 178 (an non-opioid *analgesic* 64)

Abstral a product name for fentanyl 289 (an *analgesic* 64)

acarbose 177 (an oral antidiabetic 128)

Accel-Amlodipine a product name for amlodipine 192 (an anti-angina 87 and antihypertensive drug 88)

Accolate a product name for zafirlukast (a leukotriene *antagonist* for asthma 77)

Accutane Roche a product name for isotretinoin 324 (a drug for acne 165)

acebutolol a beta blocker 83

acetaminophen 178 (non-opioid *analgesic* 64)

acetazolamide a carbonic anhydrase inhibitor diuretic 85 and drug for glaucoma 156

Acetazone Forte a combination product containing codeine 244 (an *opioid analgesic* 64) with acetaminophen 178 (an *analgesic* p.64) and a muscle relaxant

acetylcholine a chemical neurotransmitter that stimulates the parasympathetic nervous system 62 and is used as a miotic 158

acetylcysteine a *mucolytic* 80

acetylsalicylic acid *see* ASA

acitretin a drug for psoriasis 166

Aclasta a product name for zoledronic acid (a drug used for treatment of bone disorders 108)

Actifed Plus a product name for a combination of pseudoephedrine 408 (a decongestant), acetaminophen 178 (an *analgesic* 64), and triprolidine (an antihistamine 110)

Activase a product name for alteplase (a thrombolytic drug 91)

Activelle a product name for a combination of norethindrone 374 and estradiol 281 (female sex *hormones* 133)

Actonel a product name for risedronate 421 (a drug for bone disorders 108)

Acular a product name for ketorolac (a non-steroidal anti-inflammatory 102)

acyclovir 179 (an antiviral 119)

Adalat XL a product name for nifedipine 372 (a calcium channel blocker 87)

adalimumab 180 (a biological response modifier 103)

adapalene a retinoid for acne 165

Adasept Skin Cleanser a product name for triclosan (a *topical* antimicrobial 163)

Adderall a product name for mixed salts amphetamine (an amphetamine 72)

Adefovir an antiviral drug 119

Adenocard a product name for adenosine (an antiarrhythmic 86)

adenosine an antiarrhythmic 86

Adriamycin PFS a product name for doxorubicin 271 (a *cytotoxic* anticancer drug 140)

Adrucil a product name for fluorouracil (an anticancer drug 140)

Advair a product name for a combination of salmeterol 430 (a *bronchodilator* 76) and fluticasone 296 (a corticosteroid 127)

Advicor a combination product containing lovastatin 343 (a lipid-lowering drug 89) and nicotinic acid (a lipid-lowering drug 89)

Advil a product name for ibuprofen 315 (a non-opioid *analgesic* 64 and non-steroidal anti-inflammatory 102)

Aerius a product name for desloratadine 334 (an antihistamine 110)

Airomir a product name for salbutamol 429 (a *bronchodilator* 76)

Akineton a product name for biperiden (an *anticholinergic* for *parkinsonism* 71)

Alcomicin a product name for gentamicin 304 (an *antibiotic* 110)

Aldactazide a product name for a combination of spironolactone 437 (a potassium-sparing diuretic 85) and hydrochlorothiazide 311 (a thiazide diuretic 85)

Aldactone a product name for spironolactone 437 (a potassium-sparing diuretic 85)

alefacept a drug for psoriasis 166

alendronate 181 (a drug for treatment of bone disorders 108)

Alertec a product name for modafinil (a drug used in narcolepsy 72)

Alesse a product name for levonorgestrel 333 (a female sex *hormone* 133 and oral contraceptive 149) and ethinyl estradiol 283 (an estrogen 133)

Aleve a product name for naproxen 370 (an NSAID 102)

alfacalcidol vitamin D 481 (a vitamin 135)

alfuzosin a drug used in urinary disorders 154

alginates/alginic acid 182 (substances extracted from brown seaweed used to protect stomach and esophagus from acid reflux (antacids 94)

aliskiren 183 an antihypertensive drug 88

Alka-Seltzer Morning Relief a combination product with ASA 198 (a non-opioid *analgesic* 64) and caffeine

ALKERAN–APO-PIROXICAM

Alkeran a product name for melphalan (an anticancer drug 140)

allantoin a uric acid derivative. Applied *topically*, is said to encourage healing of minor wounds

Allegra a product name for fexofenadine (an antihistamine 110)

allopurinol 184 (a drug for gout 105)

almotriptan a drug for migraine 73

Alomide a product name for lodoxamide (a drug for allergy 109)

Alphagan a product name for brimonidine (a drug for glaucoma 156)

alpha tocopheryl vitamin E 481 (a vitamin 135)

alprazolam 185 (a benzodiazepine anti-anxiety drug 67)

alprostadil 186 a *prostaglandin* used for male impotence 152

Alprostadil Injection USP a product name for alprostadil 186 (a drug for erectile dysfunction 152)

Altace a product name for ramipril 416 (an ACE inhibitor 100)

Altace HCT a product name for combination of hydrochlorothiazide 311 (a thiazide diuretic 85) and ramipril 416 (an ACE inhibitor 84)

alteplase a thrombolytic 91

aluminum acetate an *astringent* used for inflammation of the skin or outer ear canal 159

aluminum hydroxide 187 (an antacid 94)

Alvesco a product name for ciclesonide (an inhaled corticosteroid 127 used in asthma 78)

amantadine 188 (an antiviral 119 and drug used for *parkinsonism* 71)

Amaryl a product name for glimepiride 306 (an oral antidiabetic 128)

AmBisome a product name for amphotericin B 194 (an antifungal124)

Amcinonide a *topical* corticosteroid 162

Amerge a product name for naratriptan (a drug for migraine 73)

amethocain a local *anesthetic* 64

Ametop a product name for tetracaine (also known as amethocain, a local *anesthetic* 64)

amikacin an *antibiotic* 114

Amikin a product name for amikacin (an aminoglycoside *antibiotic* 114)

amiloride 189 (a potassium-sparing diuretic 85)

aminobenzoic acid an ingredient of sunscreens 169

aminophylline 449 (a *bronchodilator* 76)

amiodarone 190 (an anti-arrhythmic 86)

amitriptyline 191 (a tricyclic antidepressant 68)

amlodipine 192 (a calcium channel blocker 87)

ammonium chloride a drug that increases urine acidity 154

amoxicillin 193 (a penicillin *antibiotic* 114)

amoxicillin/clavulinic acid a combination of amoxicillin 193 (a penicillin *antibiotic* 114) and clavulinic acid (a substance given with it to make amoxicillin more effective)

Amphojel a product name for aluminum hydroxide 187 (an antacid 94)

amphotericin B 194 (an antifungal 124)

ampicillin a penicillin *antibiotic* 116

Anafranil a product name for clomipramine 238 (a tricyclic antidepressant 68)

Anakinra 195 an immunomodulatory drug for rheumatoid arthritis 103

Anaprox a product name for naproxen 370 (a non-steroidal anti-inflammatory 102)

anastrozole 196 (an anticancer drug 140)

Andriol a product name for testosterone 447 (a male sex *hormone* 132)

Androcur a product name for cyproterone (a synthetic sex *hormone* used for acne 165, cancer of the prostate 140, and male sexual disorders 132)

Androderm a product name for testosterone 447 (a male sex *hormone* 132)

AndroGel a product name for testosterone 447 (a male sex *hormone* 132)

anidulafungin an antifungal drug 124

Ansaid a product name for flurbiprofen (a non-steroidal anti-inflammatory 102)

Anthraforte a product name for anthralin (a drug used in psoriasis 166)

anthralin a drug used in psoriasis 166

Anthranol a product name for anthralin (a drug used in psoriasis 166)

Anthrascalp a product name for anthralin (a drug used in psoriasis 166)

antihemophilic factor a blood protein used to promote blood clotting in hemophilia 90

Anugesic-HC a combination drug with hydrocortisone 313 (a corticosteroid 127 and antipruritic 161) and other drugs

Anusol a product-name preparation for hemorrhoids 101 containing zinc sulfate

Anuzinc HC Plus a combination drug with hydrocortisone 313 (a corticosteroid 127 and antipruritic 161) and other drugs

Anzemet a product name for dolasetron (an anti-emetic 74)

apixaban an anticoagulant drug 91

Apo-Acetaminophen a generic company version of acetaminophen 178(an non-opioid *analgesic* 64)

Apo-Acyclovir a generic company version of acyclovir 179 (an antiviral 119)

Apo-Alendronate a product name for alendronate 181 (a drug for bone disorders 108)

Apo-Allopurinol a generic company version of allopurinol 184 (a drug for gout 105)

Apo-Alpraz a generic company version of alprazolam 185 (a benzodiazepine anti-anxiety drug 67)

Apo-Alpraz TS a generic company version of alprazolam 185 (a benzodiazepine anti-anxiety drug 67)

Apo-Amiloride a product name for amiloride 189 (a diuretic 85)

Apo-Amitriptyline a generic company version of amitriptyline 191 (a tricyclic antidepressant 68)

Apo-Amlodipine a product name for amlodipine 192 (an anti-angina 87 and antihypertensive drug 88)

Apo-Amoxi a generic company version of amoxicillin 193 (a penicillin *antibiotic* 114)

Apo-Amoxi-Clav a generic company version of amoxicillin/clavulinic acid (a combination of amoxicillin 193 (a penicillin *antibiotic* 114) and clavulinic acid (a substance given with it to make amoxicillin more effective)

Apo-Atenolol a generic company version of atenolol 199 (a beta blocker 83)

Apo-Atomoxetine a product name for atomoxetine 200 (a drug used for ADHD 72)

Apo-Atorvastatin a product name for atorvastatin 201 (a lipid-lowering drug 89)

Apo-Azathioprine a generic company version of azathioprine 203

Apo-Baclofen a product name for baclofen 205 (a muscle-relaxant drug 106)

Apo-Beclomethasone a product name for beclomethasone 206 (a corticosteroid 127, 162)

Apo-Benztropine a generic company version of benztropine (an *anticholinergic* for *parkinsonism* 71)

Apo-Bromocriptine a generic company version of bromocriptine (a pituitary agent 131 and drug for *parkinsonism* 71)

Apo-Buspirone a generic company version of buspirone 216 (anti-anxiety drug 67)

Apo-Capto a generic company version of captopril 217 (an ACE inhibitor 84)

Apo-Carbamazepine a generic company version of carbamazepine 218 (an antiepileptic 70)

Apo-Carvedilol a generic company version of carvedilol 219 (a beta blocker 83)

Apo-Cefaclor a generic company version of cefaclor 220 (an antibiotic 114)

Apo-Cefprozil a generic company version of cefprozil 221 (an antibiotic 114)

Apo-Cefuroxime a generic company version of cefuroxime 222 (a cephalosporin antibiotic 114)

Apo-Cephalex a generic company version of cephalexin 224 (a cephalosporin *antibiotic* 114)

Apo-Cetirizine a generic company version of cetirizine 225 (an antihistamine 110)

Apo-Chlorpropamide a generic company version of chlorpropamide (a drug for diabetes 128)

Apo-Chlorthalidone a generic company version of chlorthalidone (a thiazide diuretic 85)

Apo-Ciproflox a generic company version of ciprofloxacin 231 (an antibacterial drug 117)

Apo-Citalopram a generic version of citalopram 233 (an antidepressant 68)

Apo-Clindamycin a generic company version of clindamycin 235 (an antibiotic 114)

Apo-Clomipramine a generic company version of clomipramine 238 (an antidepressant 68)

Apo-Clonazepam a generic company version of clonazepam 239 (a benzodiazepine anti-anxiety drug 67 and antiepileptic 70)

Apo-Clonidine a generic company version of clonidine (an antihypertensive 88)

Apo-Clorazepate a generic company version of clorazepate (a benzodiazepine anti-anxiety drug 67)

Apo-Cloxi a generic company version of cloxacillin 242 (a penicillin *antibiotic* 114)

Apo-Clozapine a generic company version of clozapine 243 (an antipsychotic 69)

Apo-Cyclobenzaprine a generic company version of cyclobenzaprine 247 (a muscle relaxant 106)

Apo-Desipramine a generic company version of desipramine (a tricyclic antidepressant 68)

Apo-Diazepam a generic company version of diazepam 257 (a benzodiazepine anti-anxiety drug 67, *sedative* 67, muscle relaxant 106, and antiepileptic 70)

Apo-Diclo a generic company version of diclonefac 254 (a non-steroidal anti-inflammatory 102)

Apo-Diflunisal a generic company version of diflunisal (a non-steroidal anti-inflammatory 102)

Apo-Diltiaz a generic company version of diltiazem 261 (an antihypertensive 88 and calcium channel blocker 87)

Apo-Dipivefrin a generic company version of dipivefrin (a *sympathomimetic* for glaucoma 156)

Apo-Dipyridamole a generic company version of dipyridamole 265 (an antiplatelet drug)

Apo-Divalproex a generic company version of divalproex (an antiepileptic 70)

Apo-Domperidone a generic company version of domperidone 267 (an anti-emetic 74)

Apo-Dorzo-Timop a product name for a combination of dorzolamide 269 and timolol 451 (drugs for glaucoma 156)

Apo-Doxazosin a generic company version of doxazosin 270 (a *sympatholytic* antihypertensive 88)

Apo-Doxepin a generic company version of doxepin (a tricyclic antidepressant 68)

Apo-Doxy a generic company version of doxycycline 272 (a tetracycline *antibiotic* 114)

Apo-Enalapril Maleate/HCTZ a generic company version of a combination of enalapril 275 (an ACE inhibitor 84 and antihypertensive drug 88) and hydrochlorothiazide 311 (a diuretic 85)

Apo-Erythro-ES a generic company version of erythromycin 279 (an *antibiotic* 114)

Apo-Erythromycin a generic company version of erythromycin 279 (an *antibiotic* 114)

Apo-Famciclovir a generic company version of famciclovir 287 (an antiviral drug 119)

Apo-Fenofibrate a generic company version of fenofibrate (a lipid-lowering drug 89)

Apo-Feno-Micro a generic company version of fenofibrate (a lipid-lowering drug 89)

Apo-Fluconazole a generic company version of fluconazole 292 (an antifungal drug 124)

Apo-Flunisolide a generic company version of flunisolide (a corticosteroid 127)

Apo-Flutamide a generic company version of flutamide 295 (an anticancer drug 140)

Apo-Fluoxetine a generic company version of fluoxetine 293 (an antidepressant 68)

Apo-Fluphenazine a generic company version of fluphenazine (an phenothiazine antipsychotic 69)

Apo-Flurazepam a generic company version of flurazepam (a benzodiazepine sleeping drug 66)

Apo-Flurbiprofen a generic company version of flurbiprofen (a non-steroidal anti-inflammatory 102)

Apo-Flutamide a generic company version of flutamide 295 (an anticancer drug 140)

Apo-Fluvoxamine a generic name for fluvoxamine 297 (an antidepressant 68)

Apo-Gabapentin a generic company version of gabapentin 300 (an antiepileptic 70)

Apo-Gain a generic company version of minoxidil 362 (an antihypertensive 88)

Apo-Gemfibrozil a generic product name for gemfibrozil 303 (a lipid-lowering drug 89)

Apo-Glimepiride a generic company version of glimepiride 306 (a drug used in diabetes 128)

Apo-Haloperidol a generic company version of haloperidol 309 (an antipsychotic 69)

Apo-Hydroxyzine a generic company version of hydroxyzine (an antihistamine used as an anti-anxiety drug 67)

Apo-Ibuprofen a generic company version of ibuprofen 315 (a non-opioid *analgesic* 64 and non-steroidal anti-inflammatory 102)

Apo-Imipramine a generic company version of imipramine 316 (a tricyclic antidepressant 68)

Apo-Indapamide a generic company version of indapamide 317 (a thiazide-like diuretic 85)

Apo-Ipravent a generic company version of ipratropium bromide 320 (a *bronchodilator* 76)

Apo-Ketoconazole a generic company version of ketoconazole 325 (an antifungal drug 124)

Apo-Ketotifen a generic company version of ketotifen (a drug used in asthma 77)

Apo-lactulose a generic company version of lactulose 327 (an osmotic laxative 97)

Apo-Lamotrigine a generic company version of lamotrigine 328 (an antiepileptic drug 70)

Apo-Lansoprazole a generic company version of lansoprazole 329 (an anti-ulcer drug 95)

Apo-Latanoprost a generic company version of latanoprost 330 (a drug for glaucoma 156)

Apo-levobunolol a generic company version of levobunolol (a beta blocker 83 and drug for glaucoma 156)

Apo-Levocarb a generic company version of a combination of levodopa 331 and carbidopa (drugs for parkinsonism 71)

Apo-Loperamide a generic company version of loperamide 338 (an antidiarrheal 96)

Apo-Loratadine a generic company version of loratadine 340 (an antihistamine 110)

Apo-Lorazepam a generic company version of lorazepam 341 (a benzodiazepine anti-anxiety drug 67 and sleeping drug 66)

Apo-Lovastatin a generic company version of lovastatin 343 (a lipid-lowering drug 89)

Apo-Loxapine a generic company version of loxapine (an antipsychotic 69)

Apo-Meloxican a generic company version of meloxicam 348 (an NSAID 102)

Apo-Memantine a generic company version of memantine 349 (a drug for dementia 71)

Apo-Metformin a generic company version of metformin 351 (a drug for diabetes 128)

Apo-Metoclop a generic company version of metoclopramide 357 (a gastrointestinal motility regulator and anti-emetic 74)

Apo-Metoprolol a generic company version of metoprolol 354 (a beta blocker 83)

Apo-Methotrimeprazine a generic company version of methotrimeprazine (a phenothiazine antipsychotic 69)

Apo-Minocycline a generic company version of minocycline 361 (a tetracycline *antibiotic* 114)

Apo-Moclobemide a generic company version of moclobemide 365 (an antidepressant 68)

Apo-Montelukast a generic company version of montelukast 367 (an anti-allergy drug 109)

Apo-Nabumetone a generic company version of nabumetone (a non-steroidal anti-inflammatory 102)

Apo-Naproxen SR a generic company version of naproxen 370 (a non-steroidal anti-inflammatory 102)

Apo-Nifed a product name for nifedipine 372 (a calcium channel blocker 87)

Apo-Nifed PA a generic company version of nifedipine 372 (a calcium channel blocker 87)

Apo-Nortriptyline a generic company version of nortriptyline (a tricyclic antidepressant 68)

Apo-Ondansetron a generic company version of ondansetron 379 (anti-emetic drug 74)

Apo-Orciprenaline a generic company version of orciprenaline (a *bronchodilator* 76)

Apo-Oxazepam a generic company version of oxazepam 382 (a benzodiazepine anti-anxiety drug 67)

Apo-Oxtriphylline a generic company version of oxtriphylline (a *bronchodilator* 76)

Apo-Pen VK a generic company version of penicillin V 386 (a penicillin *antibiotic* 114)

Apo-Perphenazine a generic company version of perphenazine (a phenothiazine antipsychotic 69)

Apo-Pioglitazone a generic company version of pioglitazone 392 (a drug for diabetes 128)

Apo-Piroxicam a generic company version of piroxicam 393 (a non-steroidal anti-inflammatory 102)

APO-PRAMIPEXOLE–BOTULINUM TOXIN

Apo-Pramipexole a generic company version of pramipexole 396 (an antiparkinsonism drug 71)

Apo-Pravastatin a generic company version of Pravastatin 398 (a lipid-lowering drug 89)

Apo-Prazo a generic company version of prazosin (a *sympatholytic* antihypertensive 88)

Apo-Prednisone a generic company version of prednisone 399 (a corticosteroid 127)

Apo-Primidone a generic company version of primidone (an antiepileptic 70)

Apo-Procainamide a generic company version of procainamide (an anti-arrhythmic 86)

Apo-Prochlorperazine a generic company version of prochlorperazine 402 (a phenothiazine anti-emetic 74 and antipsychotic 69)

Apo-Propafenone a generic company version of propafenone (an anti-arrhythmic 86)

Apo-Propranolol a generic company version of propranolol 406 (a beta blocker 83)

Apo-Quinidine a generic company version of quinidine 413 (an anti-arrhythmic drug 86)

Apo-Risperidone a generic company version of risperidone 422 (an antipsychotic drug 69)

Apo-Rivastigmine a generic company version of rivastigmine 425 (a drug for dementia 71)

Apo-Salvent a generic company version of salbutamol 429 (a *bronchodilator* 76)

Apo-Salvent-HFA a generic company version of salbutamol 429 (a *bronchodilator* 76)

Apo-Selegiline a generic company version of selegiline 431 (an antiparkinonism drug 71)

Apo-Sertraline a generic company version of sertraline 432 (an antidepressant 68)

Apo-Sotalol a generic company version of sotalol, (a beta blocker 83)

Apo-Sulfinpyrazone a generic company version of sulfinpyrazone (a drug for gout 105)

Apo-Sulin a generic company version of sulindac (a non-steroidal anti-inflammatory 102)

Apo-Temazepam a generic company version of temazepam 443 (a benzodiazepine sleeping drug 66)

Apo-Tenoxicam a generic company version of tenoxicam (a non-steroidal anti-inflammatory 102)

Apo-Terazosin a generic company version of terazosin 444 (a *sympatholytic* antihypertensive 88)

Apo-Terbinafine a generic company version of terbinafine 445 (an antifungal 124)

Apo-Theo LA a generic company version of theophylline 449 (a *bronchodilator* 76)

Apo-Thioridazine a generic company version of thioridazine (an antipsychotic 69)

Apo-Tiaprofenic a generic company version of tiaprofenic acid (a non-steroidal anti-inflammatory 102)

Apo-Tramadol/ACET a generic company version of a combination of tramadol 456 (an *opioid analgesic* 65) and acetaminophen 178 (an *analgesic* 64)

Apo-Trazodone a generic company version of trazodone (an antidepressant 68)

Apo-Trazodone D a generic company version of trazodone (an antidepressant 68)

Apo-Triazo a generic company version of temazepam 443 (a benzodiazepine sleeping drug 66)

Apo-Trihex a generic company version of trihexyphenidyl (a drug for *parkinsonism* 71)

Apo-Trimip a generic company version of trimipramine (a tricyclic antidepressant 68)

Apo-Warfarin a generic company version of warfarin 463 (an anticoagulant drug 90)

Apo-Zidovudine a generic company version of zidovudine 466 (a drug for HIV and immune deficiency 144)

Apo-Zopiclone a generic company version of zopiclone 467 (a sleeping drug 66)

apraclonidine a drug for glaucoma 156

aprepitant 197 (an anti-emetic drug 74)

Apresoline a product name for hydralazine (an antihypertensive 102)

Apri a product name for an oral contraceptive 149

aprotinin an antifibrinolytic 90 used to promote blood clotting

Aptivus a product name for tipranavir (an antiretroviral drug used in the treatment of HIV and AIDS 144)

Aranesp a product name for darbepoetin 275 (a kidney *hormone* 126 used for *anemia* due to kidney failure).

Arava a product name for leflunomide (an antirheumatic drug 103)

Aricept a product name for donepezil 268 (a drug for Alzheimer's disease 71)

Aricept RDT a product name for donepezil 268 (a drug for dementia 71)

Arimidex a product name for anastrozole 196 (an anticancer drug 140)

aripiprazole an antipsychotic drug 69

Aristocort a product name for triamcinolone (a corticosteroid 127)

Aristospan a product name for triamcinolone (a corticosteroid 127)

Arixtra a product name for fondaparinux (an anticoagulant 91)

Arthrotec a product-name combination drug containing diclofenac 258 (a non-steroidal anti-inflammatory drug 102) and misoprostol 364 (an antiulcer drug 95)

ASA 198 (a non-opioid *analgesic* 64 and antiplatelet drug 90)

Asacol a product name for 5-ASA 176 (a drug for inflammatory bowel disease 98)

Asaphen a product name for ASA 198 (a non-opioid *analgesic* 64 and antiplatelet drug 90)

Asaphen EC a product name for ASA 198 (a non-opioid *analgesic* 64 and antiplatelet drug 90)

Asatab a product name for ASA 198 (an *analgesic* 64 and antiplatelet drug 90)

ascorbic acid vitamin C 480 (a vitamin 135)

Asmanex a product name for mometasone 366 (a corticosteroid 127)

Aspergum a product name for ASA 198 (an *analgesic* 64 and antiplatelet drug 90)

Aspirin a product name for ASA 198 (a non-opioid *analgesic* 64 and antiplatelet drug 90)

Aspirin Backache a combination product with ASA 198 (a non-opioid *analgesic* 64) and methocarbamol (a muscle relaxant 106)

Atacand a product name for candesartan (a *vasodilator* 84 and an antihypertensive drug 88)

Atarax a product name for hydroxyzine (an antihistamine used as an anti-anxiety drug 67)

Atasol a product name for acetaminophen 177 (an non-opioid *analgesic* 64)

Atazanavir an antiretroviral drug for HIV infection and AIDS 144

atenolol 199 a beta blocker 83

Ativan a product name for lorazepam 341 (a benzodiazepine anti-anxiety drug 67 and sleeping drug 66)

atomoxatine 196 (a drug used to treat hyperactivity 72)

atorvastatin 201 a lipid-lowering drug 89

atovaquone an antiprotozoal 122 and antimalarial 123

Atridox a product name for doxycycline 272 (an antibiotic 114)

Atripla a product combination product containing emtricitabine, tenofovir disoproxil, and efavirenz 274 (drugs used in HIV and immune deficiency 144)

atropine 202 (an *anticholinergic* for irritable bowel syndrome 98 and a *mydriatic* 158)

Atrovent a product name for ipratropium bromide 320 (a *bronchodilator* 76)

auranofin an antirheumatic 103

Auro-Cyclobenzaprine a product name for cyclobenzaprine 247 (a muscle relaxant 106)

Ava-Atenolol a product name for atenolol 199 (a beta blocker 83)

Ava-Atorvastatin a product name for atorvastatin 201 (a lipid-lowering drug 89)

Ava-Bupropion a product name for bupropion 215 (a nicotine withdrawal aid 24, 367)

Ava-Cyclobenzaprine a product name for cyclobenzaprine 247 (a muscle relaxant 106)

Ava-Glyburide a product name for glyburide 307 (an antidiabetic drug 128)

Avalide a combination drug containing irbesartan 321 (a *vasodilator* 84 and antihypertensive drug 88) and hydrochlorothiazide 311 (a diuretic 85)

Avamys a product name for fluticasone 296 (a corticosteroid 127)

Avandamet a product name for a combination of metformin 351 and rosiglitazone 427 (antidiabetic drugs 128)

Avandia a product name for rosiglitazone 427 (a drug for diabetes 128)

Ava-Pramipexole a product name for pramipexole 396 (an antiparkinsonism drug 71)

Avapro a product name for irbesartan 321 (a *vasodilator* 84 and antihypertensive drug 88)

Avastin a product name for bevacizumab (a monoclonal *antibody* 140)

Ava-Valsartan a product name for valsartan 459 (a *vasodilator* 84 and antihypertensive drug 88)

Ava-Valsartan-HCT a product name for a combination of valsartan 459 (a *vasodilator* 84 and antihypertensive drug 88) and hydrochlorothiazide 311 (a diuretic drug 85)

Avelox a product name for moxifloxacin 369 (an antibacterial 117)

Aviane a product name for a combination of levonorgestrel 333 and ethinyl estradiol 283 (female sex *hormones* 133 and oral contraceptives 149)

Avirax a product name for acyclovir 179 (an antiviral drug 119)

avobenzone an ingredient of sunscreens 169

Avodart a product name for dutasteride (a drug used in urinary disorders 154)

Avonex a product name for interferon beta-1a 314 (a drug used in multiple sclerosis)

Axert a product name for almotripton (a drug for migraine 73)

Azarga a product name for a combination of timolol 451 (a beta blocker 83 and drug for glaucoma 156) and brinzolamide (a drug for glaucoma 156)

azathioprine 203 (an antirheumatic 103 and immunosuppressant 143)

Azilect a product name for rasagiline 418 (a drug used for parkinsonism 71)

azithromycin 204 (an *antibiotic* 114)

Azopt a product name for brinzolamide (a drug for glaucoma 156)

B

Baciguent a product name for bacitracin (an *antibiotic* 114)

bacitracin an *antibiotic* 114

baclofen 205 (a muscle relaxant 106)

Bactigras a product name for chlorhexidine (a skin *antiseptic* 163)

Bactroban a product name for mupirocin (an antibacterial for skin infections 163)

Balminil Codeine Night-Time and Expectorant a combination drug with ammonium chloride (an *expectorant* 80), codeine 244 (an opioid *analgesic* 64), and diphenhydramine 263 (an antihistamine 110)

Balminil DM a product name for dextromorphan 252 (a cough suppressant 80)

Balminil DM-D-E a combination product containing guafenesin (an *expectorant* 80) and dextromorphan 252 (a cough suppressant)

Baraclude a product name for entecavir (an antiviral 119)

basiliximab an immunosuppressant 143

beclomethasone 206 (a corticosteroid 127)

Beech Nut Cough Drops Honey-Lemon a lozenge with eucalyptus and menthol

Beech Nut Cough Drops Menthol a lozenge with eucalyptus and menthol

Beech Nut Cough Drops Wild Cherry a lozenge with eucalyptus and menthol

belladonna an *antispasmodic anticholinergic* for irritable bowel syndrome 98

Bellergal Spacetabs a product name for ergotamine 278 (a drug for migraine 73) with belladonna (an *antispasmodic*), and pentobarbital (a barbiturate *sedative* 66)

Benadryl a product name for diphenhydramine 263 (an antihistamine 110, anti-emetic 74, and antipruritic 161)

Benoxyl a product name for benzoyl peroxide 207 (a drug for acne 165)

benserazide a drug used to enhance the effect of levodopa 331 (a drug for *parkinsonism* 71)

Bentylol a product name for dicyclomine 259 (a drug for irritable bowel syndrome 98)

Benuryl a product name for probenecid 401 (a drug for gout 105)

Benylin DM a product name for dextromorphan 252 (a cough suppressant 80)

Benylin DM-E Extra Strength a combination product containing guafenesin (an *expectorant* 80) and dextromorphan 252 (a cough suppressant)

Benylin First Defence Syrup a *syrup* with menthol and echinacea

Benzac AC a product name for benzoyl peroxide 207 (a drug for acne 165)

Benzac W Wash a product name for benzoyl peroxide 207 (a drug for acne 165)

Benzaclin a product name for a combination of benzoyl peroxide 207 (a drug for acne 165) and clindamycin 235 (an antibiotic 114) and tretinoin (a drug for acne 165)

Benzamycin a combination of benzoyl peroxide 207 (a drug for acne 165) and erythromycin 279 (an *antibiotic* 114)

benzocaine a local *anesthetic* 64

benzophones an ingredient of sunscreens 169

benzoyl peroxide 207 (a drug for acne 165)

benztropine an *anticholinergic* for *parkinsonism* 71

Benztropine Mesylate a product name for benztropine (an *anticholinergic* for *parkinsonism* 71)

Benztropine Omega a product name for benztropine (an *anticholinergic* for *parkinsonism* 71)

benzylpenicillin see penicillin G (a penicillin *antibiotic* 114)

Berotec a product name for fenoterol (a *sympathomimetic bronchodilator* 76)

beta-carotene vitamin A 479 (a vitamin 135 and food additive)

Betadine Topical a product name for povidone-iodine (a skin *antiseptic* 163)

Betagan a product name for levobunolol (a beta blocker 83 and drug for glaucoma 56)

betahistine 208 (an antivertigo 74)

Betaject a product name for betamethasone 209 (a corticosteroid 127)

Betaloc a product name for metoprolol 354 (a beta blocker 83)

Betaloc Durules a product name for metoprolol 354 (a beta blocker 83)

betamethasone 209 (a corticosteroid 127)

Betaseron a product name for interferon beta-1b 319. (a drug used in multiple sclerosis)

betaxolol a beta blocker 83 also used in glaucoma 156

bethanechol a para*sympathomimetic* for urinary retention 154

Betnesol a product name for betamethasone 209 (a corticosteroid 127)

Betoptic S a product-name drug for glaucoma 156 containing betaxolol

Bevacizumab a monoclonal *antibody* 140

Biaxin a product name for clarithromycin 234 (a macrolide *antibiotic* 114)

Biaxin BID a product name for clarithromycin 234 (a macrolide *antibiotic* 114)

Biaxin XL a product name for clarithromycin 234 (a macrolide *antibiotic* 114)

Biacna a product name for a combination of clindamycin 235 (an antibiotic 116) and trentinoin (a drug for acne 165)

bimatoprost a drug for glaucoma 156

Bio-Amitriptylinea product name for amitriptyline 191 (an antidepressant drug 68)

Bioderm Ointment a product name for a combination of polymixin B 395 and bacitracin (antibiotic drugs 114)

Bio-Oxazepam a product name for oxazepam 382 (an anti-anxiety drug 67)

biotin 469 (a vitamin 135)

bisacodyl 210 (a laxative 97)

Bismutal a product name combination of bismuth (a metal given in compound form for gastric and duodenal ulcers 95 that is also used for sore throats) and guaifenesin (an *expectorant* 80)

Bismutal Adults a product name for a combination of bismuth subsalicylate 211 (an antacid and adsorbent 94) and guaifenesin (an *expectorant* drug 80)

bismuth a metal given in compound form for gastric and duodenal ulcers 95 and is also used for sore throats

Bismuth + Antacid a product name for a combination of bismuth subsalicylate 211 (an antacid and adsorbent 94) and calcium carbonate 469 (a mineral)

Bismuth Chewtabs a product name for bismuth subsalicylate 211 (an antacid and adsorbent 94)

bismuth subsalicylate 211 (an antacid and adsorbent 94)

Bisocolax a product name for bisacodyl 210 (a laxative 97**)**

Blephamide a product name for a combination of prednisolone 395 (a corticosteroid 127) and sulfacetamide (a sulfonamide antibacterial 117) for use in the eye

Bonamine a product name for meclizine (an antihistamine used as an anti-emetic drug 74)

Botox a product name for botulinum toxin type A 212 (a muscle relaxant 106)

Botox Cosmetic a product name for botulinum toxin type A 212 (a muscle relaxant 106)

botulinum toxin 212 (a muscle relaxant 106)

BRETYLIUM–CONTACT HEAD

bretylium an anti-arrhythmic 86

Bretylium Tosylate a product name for bretylium (an anti-arrhythmic 86)

Brevibloc a product name for esmolol (a beta blocker 83)

Brevicon 0.5/35 a product-name oral contraceptive 149 containing ethinyl estradiol 283 and norethindrone 374

Brilinta a product name for ticagrelor 450 (an antiplatelet drug 90)

brimonidine a drug for glaucoma 156

brinzolamide a drug for glaucoma 156

brompheniramine an antihistamine 110

buclizine an antihistamine 110 used for motion sickness

budesonide 213 a corticosteroid 127

bupivacaine a long-lasting local *anesthetic* 64 used in labour 153

buprenorphine 214 (an *opioid analgesic* 64)

bupropion 215 (an antidepressant 68 used as an aid when stopping smoking in addition to counselling)

Buro-Sol a combination of aluminum (an *astringent* used for inflammation of the skin or outer ear canal 163) and benzethonium chloride

buserelin a drug for menstrual disorders 148

buspirone 216 (a non-benzodiazepine anti-anxiety drug 67)

butaconazole an antifungal 124

BuTrans a product name for buprenorphine 214 (an *opioid analgesic* 64)

Byetta a product name for exenatide 285 (an antihyperglycemic drug 128)

C

cabergoline a drug to treat infertility 152 or to stop milk production in women who do not want to breast-feed, also used for Parkinson's disease 71

Caduet a product name for combination product containing amlodipine 192 (a calcium channel blocker 87) and atorvastatin 201 (a lipid-lowering drug 89)

Caelyx a product name for doxorubicin 271 (a *cytotoxic* anticancer drug 140)

Cafergot a product name for ergotamine 278 (a drug for migraine 73) with caffeine (a stimulant 72)

Cafergot-PB a product name for ergotamine 278 (a drug for migraine 73) with belladonna (an *antispasmodic* drug), caffeine (a stimulant 72), and pentobarbital (a barbiturate *sedative* 66)

caffeine a stimulant 72 in coffee, tea, and cola, added to some *analgesics* 64

calamine a substance containing zinc carbonate (an antipruritic 161) used to soothe irritated skin

calcifediol vitamin D 481 (a vitamin 135)

Calcimar a product name for calcitonin (a drug for bone disorders 108)

Calcite 500 a product name for calcium carbonate (a calcium salt (a mineral 137) used as an antacid 94)

Calcite D-500 a combination product with calcium carbonate (a calcium salt (a mineral 137) used as an antacid 94) and vitamin D 481

calcitonin a drug for bone disorders 108

calcitriol vitamin D 481 (a vitamin 135)

calcium 469 (a mineral 152)

Calcium 500 a product name for calcium carbonate (a calcium salt (a mineral 137) used as an antacid 94)

calcium acetate calcium 469 (a mineral 152)

calcium carbonate a calcium salt (a mineral 137) used as an antacid 94

calcium chloride calcium 469 (a mineral 152)

Calcium D 500 a combination product with calcium carbonate (a calcium salt (a mineral 137) used as an antacid 94) and vitamin D 481 (a vitamin 135)

calcium gluconate calcium 469 (a mineral 152)

Calcium Oyster Shell a product name for calcium carbonate (a calcium salt (a mineral 137) used as an antacid 94)

Caltine a product name for calcitonin (a drug for bone disorders 108)

camphor a *topical* antipruritic 161

Camptosar a product name for irinotecan (an anticancer drug 140)

Cancidas a product name for caspofungin (an antifungal drug 124)

Candesartan a *vasodilator* 84 and an antihypertensive drug 88

Candistatin a product name for nystatin 376 (an antifungal 124)

Canesten a product name for clotrimazole 241 (an antifungal 124)

cannabidiol an *analgesic* (64) used in multiple sclerosis

Capex shampoo a product name for fluocinolone (a *topical* corticosteroid 162)

Capoten a product name for captopril 217 (an ACE inhibitor 84)

capreomycin an antituberculous drug 118

captopril 217 (an ACE inhibitor 84)

carbachol a drug used for its miotic effect in glaucoma 156 and as a para*sympathomimetic*

Carbachol a product name for carbachol (a drug used for its miotic effect in glaucoma 156 and as a para*sympathomimetic*)

carbamazepine 218 (an antiepileptic 70)

carbidopa a substance that enhances the therapeutic effect of levodopa 331 (a drug for *parkinsonism* 71)

carbocysteine a *mucolytic* 95

Carbolith a product name for lithium 337 (a drug for mania 69)

carboplatin an anticancer drug 140

Cardizem CD a product name for diltiazem 261 (an antihypertensive 88 and calcium channel blocker 87)

Cardura a product name for doxazosin 270 (a *sympatholytic* antihypertensive 88)

carnitine an amino acid used as a nutritional supplement 134

carvedilol 219 (a beta blocker 83)

cascara a laxative 97

caspofungin an antifungal drug 124

castor oil a stimulant laxative 97

Catapres a product name for clonidine (an antihypertensive 88)

Caverject a product name for alprostadil 186 (a *prostaglandin* used for male impotence 134, 152)

Ceclor a product name for cefaclor 220 (an antibiotic 114)

cefaclor 220 (an antibiotic 114)

cefadroxil a cephalosporin *antibiotic* 114

cefamandole a cephalosporin *antibiotic* 114

cefazolin an *antibiotic* 114

cefepime an *antibiotic* 114

cefixime a cephalosporin *antibiotic* 114

Cefizox a product name for ceftizoxime (a cephalosporin *antibiotic* 114)

Cefotan a product name for cefotetan (a cephalosporin *antibiotic* 114)

cefotaxime a cephalosporin *antibiotic* 114

cefoxitin a cephalosporin *antibiotic* 114

cefprozil 221 (an antibiotic 114)

ceftazidime a cephalosporin *antibiotic* 114

Ceftin a product name for Cefuroxime axetil 222 (a cephalosporin *antibiotic* 115)

ceftriaxone an *antibiotic* 114

Cefuroxime 222 (a cephalosporin *antibiotic* 114)

Cefzil a product name for cefprozil 221 (an antibiotic 114)

Celebrex a product name for celecoxib 223 (a non-steroidal anti-inflammatory 102)

celecoxib 223 a non-steroidal anti-inflammatory 102

Celestone a product name for betamethasone 209 (a corticosteroid 127)

Celexa a product name for citalopram 233 (a tricyclic antidepressant 68)

CellCept a product name for mycophenolate mofetil (an immunosuppressant 143)

Celontin a product name for methsuximide (an antiepileptic 70)

Celsentri a product name for Maraviroc (an antiretroviral drug used in the treatment of HIV and AIDS 144)

cephalexin 224 (a cephalosporin *antibiotic* 114)

Cerebyx a product name for fosphenytoin 390 (an antiepileptic 70)

Cesamet a product name for nabilone (an anti-emetic 74)

cetirizine 225 (an antihistamine 110)

cetrimide a skin *antiseptic* 163

Champix a product name for varenicline 460 (a drug used in smoking cessation)

Cheracol a product name for a combination product containing codeine 244 (an *opioid analgesic* 64) and cough/cold medications

chloral hydrate a sleeping drug 66

chlorambucil an anticancer drug 140 used for chronic lymphocytic leukemia and lymphatic and ovarian cancers, and as an immunosuppressant 143 for rheumatoid arthritis 103

chloramphenicol 226 (an *antibiotic* 114)

chlorhexidine a skin *antiseptic* 179

Chloromycetin a product name for chloramphenicol 226 (an *antibiotic* 114)

chloroquine 227 (an antimalarial 123 and antirheumatic 103)

chlorpheniramine 228 (an antihistamine 110)

chlorpropamide a drug for diabetes 128

chlorthalidone a thiazide diuretic 85

Choledyl a product name for oxtriphylline (a *bronchodilator* 76)

cholestyramine 229 (a lipid-lowering drug 89)

chromium 470 (a mineral 137)

Cialis a product name for tadalafil (a drug used for the treatment of sexual impotence 152)

Cicatrin a combination of bacitracin (an *antibiotic* 114), amino acids, and neomycin

ciclesonide an inhaled corticosteroid 127 used in asthma 78

Ciclopirox an antifungal drug 124

Ciloxan a product name for ciprofloxacin 231 (a quinolone antibacterial 117)

cimetidine 230 (an anti-ulcer drug 95)

Cipralex a product name for escitalopram (an antidepressant 68)

Cipro a product name for ciprofloxacin 231 (an antibacterial 117)

Ciprodex a combination product containing ciprofloxacin 231 (an antibacterial 117) and dexamethasone 255 (a corticosteroid 127) used in ear infections

ciprofloxacin 231 (an antibacterial 117)

Cipro HC a combination of ciprofloxacin 231 (an antibacterial 117) and hydrocortisone 313 (a corticosteroid 127) used in ear infections

Cipro XL a product name for ciprofloxacin 231 (an antibacterial drug 117)

cisplatin 232 (an anticancer drug 140)

citalopram 233 (a tricyclic antidepressant 68)

Citalopram-Odan a product name for citalopram 233 (an antidepressant drug 68)

Citrate 600 a product name for calcium carbonate used as an antacid 94

Citro-Mag a product name for magnesium citrate (an osmotic laxative 97)

Claforan a product name for cefotaxime (a cephalosporin *antibiotic* 114)

clarithromycin 234 (a macrolide *antibiotic* 114)

Claritin a product name for loratadine 340 an antihistamine 110

Claritin Allergy and Sinus a product name for a combination of loratadine 340 (an antihistamine 110) and pseudoephedrine 408 (a decongestant 79)

Claritin Allergic Congestion Relief a product name product containing oxymetazoline (a *topical* decongestant 79)

Claritin Eye Allergy Relief a product name product containing oxymetazoline (a *topical* decongestant 79)

Claritin Skin Itch Relief a product name for hydrocortisone 313 (a corticosteroid 127 and antipruritic 161)

Clarus a generic version of isotretinoin 324 (a drug for acne 165)

clavulinic acid a substance given with amoxicillin 193 (a penicillin *antibiotic* 114) to make it more effective

Clavulin a product name for amoxicillin/ clavulinic acid (a combination of amoxicillin

193 (a penicillin *antibiotic* 114) and clavulinic acid (a substance given with it to make amoxicillin more effective))

clemastine an antihistamine 110

clindamycin 235 a lincosamide *antibiotic* 114

Clindasol a product name for clindamycin 235 (an antibiotic 116)

Clindets a product name for *topical* clindamycin 235 (a lincosamide antibiotic 114)

Clindoxyl Gel a product name for a combination of benzoyl peroxide 207 (a drug for acne 165) and clindamycin 235 (an antibiotic 114)

clioquinol an antibacterial 117 and antifungal 124

Clioquinol a product name for clioquinol (an antibacterial 117 and antifungal drug 124)

clobazam a benzodiazepine drug used as an antiepileptic 70

clobetasol 236 (a *topical* corticosteroid drug 162)

clobetasone a *topical* corticosteroid 162

Clomid a product name for clomiphene 237 (a drug for infertility 152)

clomiphene 237 (a drug for infertility 152)

clomipramine 238 (a tricyclic antidepressant 68)

clonazepam 239 (a benzodiazepine anti-anxiety drug 67 and antiepileptic 70)

clonidine an antihypertensive drug 88

clopidogrel 240 (an antiplatelet drug 90)

Clopixol a product name for zuclopenthixol (an antipsychotic drug 69)

Clopixol-Acuphase a product name for zuclopenthixol (an antipsychotic 69)

Clopixol-Depot a product name for zuclopenthixol (an antipsychotic 69)

Clotrimaderm a product name for clotrimazole 241 (an antifungal 124

clotrimazole 241 (an antifungal 124)

cloxacillin 242 (a penicillin *antibiotic* 114)

clozapine 243 (an antipsychotic 69)

Clozaril a product name for clozapine 243 (an antipsychotic 69)

CoActifed Tablets a combination product containing codeine 244 (an *opioid analgesic* 64) and cough/cold medications.

CO Alendronate a product name for alendronate 181 (a drug for bone disorders 108)

coal tar a substance for psoriasis 166 and eczema 167

Coated Aspirin a product name for ASA 198 (a non-opioid *analgesic* 64 and antiplatelet drug 90)

CO Betahistine a product name for betahistine 208 (a drug for Ménière's disease 74)

cocaine a local *anesthetic* 64 and drug of abuse 488

CO Citalopram a product name for citalopram 233 (an antidepressant drug 68)

CO Clomipramine a product name for clomipramine 238 (an antidepressant 68)

CO Clopidogrel a product name for clopidogrel 240 (an antiplatelet drug 90)

codeine 244 (an *opioid analgesic* 64, cough suppressant 80, and antidiarrheal 96)

Codeine Contin a product name for codeine 244 (an *opioid analgesic* 64)

Codeine Phosphate a product name for codeine 244 (an *opioid analgesic* 64)

CO Diltiazem CD a product name for diltiazem 261 (a calcium channel blocker 87 and antihypertensive drug 88)

CO Enalapril a product name for enalapril 275 (an ACE inhibitor 84 and antihypertensive drug 88)

co-enzyme Q$_{10}$ a supplement 470

CO Etidrocal a product name for a combination of etidronate 284 (a drug for bone disorders 108) and calcium carbonate 469 (a mineral)

CO Etidronate a product name for etidronate 284 (a drug for bone disorders 108)

CO Fluconazole a product name for fluconazole 292 (an antifungal drug 124)

CO Fluoxetine a product name for fluoxetine 293 (a tricyclic antidepressant 68)

Cogentin a product name for benztropine (an *anticholinergic* for *parkinsonism* 71)

Co-Glimepiride a generic company version of glimepiride 306 (a drug used in diabetes 128)

CO Irbesartan a product name for irbesartan 321 (a *vasodilator* 84 and antihypertensive drug 88)

Colace a product name for docusate sodium 266 (a stool softener, laxatives 97)

CO Latanoprost a product name for latanoprost 330 (a drug for glaucoma 156)

colchicine 245 (a drug for gout 105)

colecalciferol vitamin D 481 (a vitamin 135)

colestipol a lipid-lowering drug 89

CO Levofloxacin a product name for levofloxacin 332 (an antibacterial drug 117)

colistin an *antibiotic* 114

collodion a substance that dries to form a sticky film, protecting broken skin

CO Losartan a product name for losartan 342 (a *vasodilator* 84 and antihypertensive drug 88)

Combigan a product name for a combination of brimonidine (an alpha *adrenergic* receptor agonist used in glaucoma 156) and timolol 451 (a beta blocker 83 and drug for glaucoma 156)

Combivent UDV a product name for a combination of ipratropium bromide 320 and salbutamol 429 (*bronchodilator* drugs 76)

CO Memantine a product name for memantine 349 (a drug for dementia 71)

CO Mirtazapine a product name for mirtazapine 363 (an antidepressant drug 68)

Comtan a product name for entacapone (a drug for *parkinsonism* 71)

Concerta a product name for methylphenidate 355 (a nervous system stimulant 72)

Condyline a product name for podophyllotoxin (a drug for genital warts 135)

Contact Head and Chest Congestion a combination product containing guafenesin (an *expectorant* 80) and pseudoephedrine 408 (a decongestant)

COPHYLAC DROPS–DRISTAN N.D.

Cophylac Drops a product name for a combination of methadone 352 (an *analgesic* 64) and ephedrine (a *bronchodilator* 76 and decongestant 79)

Co-Pioglitazone a generic company version of pioglitazone 392 (a drug for diabetes 128)

copper 471 (a mineral 137)

CO Ramipril a product name for ramipril 416 (an ACE inhibitor 84 and drug for hypertension 88)

Cordarone a product name for amiodarone 190 (an anti-arrhythmic 86)

CO Repaglinide a product name for repaglinide 419 (a drug for diabetes 128**)**

CO Risperidone a product name for risperidone 422 (an antipsychotic drug 69)

CO Rizatriptan ODT a product name for rizatriptan 426 (a drug for migraine 73)

Cortate a product name for hydrocortisone 313 (a corticosteroid 127 and antipruritic 161)

Cortef a product name for hydrocortisone 313 (a corticosteroid 127)

Cortenema a product name for hydrocortisone 313 (a corticosteroid 127)

corticotropin a pituitary *hormone* 131

Cortifoam a product name for hydrocortisone 308 (a corticosteroid 127)

Cortimyxin ointment a combination of polymyxin B 395 (a skin *antiseptic* 163) and bacitracin zinc (an *antibiotic* 114), hydrocortisone 313 (a corticosteroid 127 and antipruritic 161) and neomycin (an *antibiotic* 114)

cortisol an old name for hydrocortisone 313

cortisone a corticosteroid 127

Cortisone acetate a product name for cortisone (a corticosteroid 127)

Cortisporin ointment a combination of polymyxin B 395 (a skin *antiseptic* 163), bacitracin zinc (an *antibiotic* 114), hydrocortisone 313 (a corticosteroid 127 and antipruritic 161), and neomycin (an *antibiotic* 114)

Cortoderm a product name for hydrocortisone 313 (a corticosteroid 127 and antipruritic 161)

Cosopt a combination of dorzolamide 269 (a carbonic anhydrase inhibitor for glaucoma 156) and timolol 451 (a beta blocker 83)

CO Topiramate a product name for topiramate 455 (an antiepileptic drug 70)

Coumadin a product name for warfarin 463 (an anticoagulant 90)

CO Valsartan a product name for valsartan 459 (a *vasodilator* 84 and antihypertensive drug 88)

Coversyl a product name for perindopril 387 (an ACE inhibitor 84)

Coversyl Plus a combination of perindopril 387 (an ACE inhibitor 84) and indapamide 317 (a thiazide-like diuretic 85)

Coversyl Plus LD a product name for a combination of indapamide 317 (a thiazide-like diuretic 85) and perindopril 387 (an ACE inhibitor 84)

Cozaar a product name for losartan 342 (an antihypertensive 88)

Creon a product name for pancreatin (a preparation of pancreatic *enzymes* 114)

Crestor a product name for rosuvastatin 428 (a lipid-lowering drug 89)

Crinone a product name for progesterone (a female sex *hormone* 133)

Crixivan a product name for indinavir (a drug for HIV/AIDS 144)

Cromolyn a product name for sodium cromoglycate 436 (an anti-allergy drug 109)

crotamiton an antipruritic 161 and antiparasitic 164 for scabies

Crystapen a product name for benzylpenicillin (a penicillin *antibiotic* 114)

CTP 30 a product name for citalopram 233 (an antidepressant drug 68)

Cubicin a product name for daptomycin (an antibacterial 117)

Cuprimine a product name for penicillamine (an antirheumatic 103)

Cutivate a product name for fluticasone 296 (a corticosteroid 127)

cyanocobalamin vitamin B12 480 (a vitamin 135)

Cyclen a product name for an oral contraceptive 149

cyclizine an antihistamine 110 used as an anti-emetic 74

cyclobenzaprine 247 (a muscle relaxant 106)

Cyclogyl a product name for cyclopentolate (an *anticholinergic mydriatic* 158)

Cyclomen a product name for danazol 251 (a drug for menstrual disorders 148)

cyclopentolate an *anticholinergic mydriatic* 158

cyclophosphamide 248 (an anticancer drug 140)

cyclosporine 249 (an immunosuppressant 143)

Cyklokapron a product name for tranexamic acid (an antifibrinolytic used to promote blood clotting 90)

Cymbalta a product name for duloxetine 273 (an antidepressant 68)

cyproheptadine an antihistamine 111

cyproterone a synthetic sex *hormone* used for acne 165, cancer of the prostate 140, and male sexual disorders 134

cytarabine a drug for leukemia 140

Cytomel a product name for liothyronine (a thyroid *hormone* 130)

Cytovene a product name for ganciclovir (an antiviral 119)

D

dabigatran etexilate 250 (anticoagulant drug 90)

Dalacin C a product name for clindamycin 235 (a lincosamide *antibiotic* 114)

dalfopristin an *antibiotic* 114

Dalmacol a product name combination product with doxylamine (a sleeping drug 66) and a cough suppressant 80

dalteparin 305 (an anticoagulant 91)

danazol 251 (a drug for menstrual disorders 148)

Dantrium a product name for dantrolene (a muscle relaxant 106)

dantrolene tizanidine a muscle relaxant 106

dapsone an antibacterial 117

Daptomycin an antibiotic drug 114

Daraprim a product name for pyrimethamine 411 (an antimalarial 123)

darbepoetin 275 (a kidney *hormone* 126 used for *anemia* due to kidney failure)

darifenacin 252 (a drug for urinary disorders 154)

darunavir an antiretroviral drug used in the treatment of HIV and AIDS 144

Daypro a product name for oxaprozin (a non-steroidal anti-inflammatory 102)

Deca-Durabolin a product name for nandrolone (an anabolic steroid 134)

Delatestryl a product name for testosterone 447 (a male sex *hormone* 132)

Delavirdine an antiretroviral drug used in the treatment of HIV and AIDS 144

Delestrogen a product name for estradiol 281 (an estrogen 133)

Demerol a product name for meperidine (an *opioid analgesic* 64 and drug used in labour 153)

Denavir a product name for penciclovir (an antiviral 119)

Denorex a product name for coal tar (a substance for psoriasis 166 and eczema 167)

denosumab 253 (a human monoclonal *antibody* 141)

Depakene a product name for valproic acid 458 (an antiepileptic 70)

DepoCyt a product name for cytarabine (a drug for leukemia 140)

Depo-Medrol a product name for methyl-prednisolone 352 (a corticosteroid 127)

Depo-Provera a product name for medroxyprogesterone 345 (a female sex *hormone* 133)

Depo-Testosterone a product name for testosterone 447 (a male sex *hormone* 132)

Derma-Smooth/FS a product name for fluocinolone (a *topical* corticosteroid 162)

Dermovate a product name for clobetasol 236 (a *topical* corticosteroid 162)

desipramine a tricyclic antidepressant 68

desloratadine 334 (an antihistamine 110)

Deslym DM a product name for dextromethorphan 256 (a cough suppressant 80)

desmopressin 254 (a pituitary *hormone* 131 used for diabetes insipidus 128)

desogestrel a progestin 133

desonide a *topical* corticosteroid 127

Desoxi a product name for desoximetasone (a *topical* corticosteroid 162)

desoximetasone a *topical* corticosteroid 162

Desquam-X a product name for benzoyl peroxide 207 (a drug for acne 165)

Desyrel a product name for trazodone (an antidepressant 68)

Desyrel Dividose a product name for trazodone (an antidepressant 68)

DRONABINOL–GEN-BACLOFEN

dronabinol an anti-emetic 74

drospirenone a synthetic progestin 133

Dulcolax a product name for bisacodyl 210 (laxative 97)

duloxetine 273 (an antidepressant drug 68)

Duofilm a product name for salicylic acid (a keratolytic for treating acne 165, dandruff 168, psoriasis 166, and warts)

Duovent UDV a product name for fenoterol with ipratropium bromide 320 (both *bronchodilator*s 76)

Duragesic a product name for fentanyl 289 (an *opioid analgesic* 64 used in the management of pain)

Duricef a product name for cefadroxil (a cephalosporin *antibiotic* 114)

dutasteride a drug used in urinary disorders 154

E

Ebixa a product name for memantine 349 (a drug for dementia 71)

Ecostatin a product name for econazole (an antifungal 124)

edrophonium a drug for diagnosis of myasthenia gravis 107

EES a product name for erythromycin 279 (an *antibiotic* 114)

efavirenz 274 (a drug for HIV and immune deficiency 144)

Effexor XR a product name for venlafaxine 461 (an antidepressant 68)

Effient a product name for aprepitant 197 (an antiplatelet drug 90)

Efudex a product name for fluorouracil (an anticancer drug 140)

Elavil a product name for amitriptyline 191 (an antidepressant drug 68)

eletriptan a drug for migraine 73

Elocom a product name for mometasone 366 (a *topical* corticosteroid 162)

Eltor a product name for pseudoephedrine 408 (a decongestant 79)

Eltroxin a product name for levothyroxine 334 (a thyroid *hormone* 130)

Emend a product name for aprepitant 197 (an anti-emetic 74)

EMLA Cream a combination product with lidocaine and prilocaine (both local *anesthetic*s 64)

EMLA Patch a combination product with lidocaine and prilocaine (both local *anesthetic*s 64)

Emo-Cort a product name for hydrocortisone 313 (a corticosteroid 127)

emtricitabine an antiretroviral drug used in the treatment of HIV and AIDS 144

Enablex a product name for darifenacin 252 (a drug for urinary disorders 154)

enalapril 275 (a *vasodilator* 84 and antihypertensive 88)

Enbrel a product name for etanercept (a biological response modifier for rheumatoid arthritis 103)

Endocet a product name for oxycodone (an *opioid analgesic* 64)

enfuvirtide a drug for HIV/AIDS 144

Enlon a product name for edrophonium (a drug for diagnosis of myasthenia gravis 107)

enoxaparin 300 (an anticoagulant 91)

entacapone a drug for *parkinsonism* 71

entecavir an antiviral drug 119

Entocort a product name for budesonide 213 (a corticosteroid 143)

Entrophen a product name for ASA 198 (a non-opioid *analgesic* 64 and antiplatelet drug 90)

epinephrine 276 (a *bronchodilator* 76)

epirubicin a *cytotoxic* anticancer drug 140

Epival a product name for valproic acid 458 (an antiepileptic 70)

Epival ER a product name for divalproex (an antiepileptic 70)

eplerenone 277 a potassium-sparing diuretic 85

epoprostenol a *prostaglandin* used for its *vasodilator* effects 84

Eprex a product name for erythropoietin 275 (a kidney *hormone* 126 used for *anemia* due to kidney failure)

Ergamisol a product name for levamisole (an anthelmintic 125)

ergocalciferol vitamin D 481 (a vitamin 135)

Ergodryl Cap a product name for ergotamine 278 (a drug for migraine 73) with caffeine (a stimulant 72), and diphenhydramine 263 (an antihistamine 110 and anti-emetic 74)

ergometrine another name for ergonovine (a uterine stimulant 153)

ergonovine a uterine stimulant 153

Ergonovine maleate a product name for ergonovine (a uterine stimulant 153)

ergotamine 278 (a drug for migraine 73)

ertapenem an *antibiotic* 114

Erybid a product name for erythromycin 279 (an *antibiotic* 114)

Eryc a product name for erythromycin 279 (an *antibiotic* 114)

Erythro Base a product name for erythromycin 279 (an *antibiotic* 114)

erythromycin 279 (an *antibiotic* 114)

erythropoietin 275 (a kidney *hormone* 126 used for *anemia* due to kidney failure). Also known as epoetin

escitalopram an antidepressant 68

esmolol a beta blocker 83

Estalis a product name for a combination product containing estradiol 281 (an estrogen 135)

Estalis-Sequi a product-name combination oral contraceptive 149 containing estradiol 281 and norethindrone 374

Estar a product name for coal tar (a substance for psoriasis 166 and eczema 167)

Estrace a product name for estradiol 281 (an estrogen 135)

Estraderm a product name for estradiol 281 (an estrogen 133)

estradiol 281 (an estrogen 133)

Estring a product name for estradiol 281 (an estrogen 133)

Estrogel a product name for estradiol 281 (an estrogen 133)

estrone estropipate an estrogen 133

etanercept a biological response modifier for rheumatoid arthritis 103

ethambutol 282 (an antituberculous drug 118)

ethinyl estradiol 283 (a female sex *hormone* 133 and oral contraceptive 149)

ethopropazine a drug used for parkinsonism 71

ethosuximide an antiepileptic 70

ethynodiol diacetate a progestin 151

Etibi Tab a product name for ethambutol 282 (an antituberculous drug 118)

Etidrocal a product name for a combination of etidronate 284 (a drug for bone disorders 108) and calcium carbonate 469 (a mineral)

etidronate 284 (a drug for bone disorders 108)

etodolac a non-steroidal anti-inflammatory 102

etomidate a drug for induction of general anesthesia

Etonogestrel a progestin 151

etoposide a drug for cancers of the lung, lymphatic system, and testes 140

etravirine an antiretroviral drug 145

eucalyptus a cough medication 80

Euflex a product name for flutamide 295 (an anticancer drug 140)

Euglucon a product name for glyburide 307 (an oral antidiabetic drug 128)

Eumovate a product name for clobetasone (a *topical* corticosteroid 162)

Eurax a product name for crotamiton (an antipruritic 162)

Eurthyrox a product name for levothyroxine 334 (a thyroid *hormone* 130)

Evista a product name for raloxifene 415 (a selective estrogen *receptor* modulator 133 for osteoporosis 108)

Evra a product name for a transdermal contraceptive containing norelgestromin and ethinyl estradiol 283 (female sex *hormone*s 133)

Exdol-8 a combination product containing codeine 244 (an *opioid analgesic* 64) with acetaminophen 177 (an analgesic 64) and caffeine

Exdol-15 a combination product containing codeine 244 (an *opioid analgesic* 64) with acetaminophen 177 (an analgesic 64), and caffeine

Exdol-30 a combination product containing codeine 244 (an *opioid analgesic* 64) with acetaminophen 177 (an analgesic 64), and caffeine

Exelon a product name for rivastigmine 425 (a drug for Alzheimer's disease 71)

exenatide 285 (drug for diabetes 128)

ezetimibe 286 (a cholesterol-lowering drug 89)

Ezetrol a product name for ezetimibe 286 (a cholesterol lowering drug 89)

F

famciclovir 287 (an antiviral 119)

famotidine 288 (an anti-ulcer drug 95)

Famvir a product name for famciclovir 287 (an antiviral 119)

felodipine a calcium channel blocker 87 and an antihypertensive 88

Femara a product name for letrozole (an anticancer drug 140)

FemHRT a product-name oral contraceptive 149 containing ethinyl estradiol 283 and norethindrone 374

fenofibrate a lipid-lowering drug 89

fenoprofen a non-steroidal anti-inflammatory 102

fenoterol a *sympathomimetic bronchodilator* 76

fentanyl 289 (an *opioid analgesic* 64 used in the management of pain)

Ferrlecit a product name for sodium ferric gluconate complex, an intravenous iron preparation 473 (a mineral 137)

ferrous fumarate iron 473 (a mineral 137)

ferrous gluconate iron 473 (a mineral 137)

ferrous sulfate iron 473 (a mineral 137)

Feva-Galantamine a product name for galantamine 301 (a drug for dementia 71)

fexofenadine an antihistamine 110

filgrastim 290 (a blood growth stimulant)

finasteride 291 (a drug for benign prostatic hypertrophy)

Fiorinal-C a combination product containing codeine 244 (an *opioid analgesic* 64) with ASA 198, bultalbital (a barbiturate sleeping drug p.66), and caffeine.

Flagyl a product name for metronidazole 359 (an antibacterial 117 and antiprotozoal 122)

Flagystatin a combination of metronidazole 359 (an antibacterial 117 and antiprotozoal 122) and nystatin 376 (an antifungal 124)

flavoxate a urinary *antispasmodic* 154

flecainide an anti-arrhythmic 86

Flexeril a product name for cyclobenzapine (a muscle relaxant 106)

Flolan a product name for epoprostenol (a *prostaglandin* used for its *vasodilator* effects 84)

Flomax CR a product name for fluticasone 296 (an alpha-blocking drug for prostate disorders 134)

Flonase a product name for fluticasone 296 (a corticosteroid 127)

Florazole ER a product name for metronidazole 359 (an antibacterial 117 and antiprotozoal 122)

Florinef a product name for fludrocortisone (a corticosteroid 127)

Flovent Diskus a product name for fluticasone 296 (a corticosteroid 127)

Flovent HFA a product name for fluticasone 296 (a corticosteroid 127)

Fluanxol a product name for flupentixol 294 (an antipsychotic 69)

Fluanxol Depot a product name for flupentixol 294 (an antipsychotic 69)

fluconazole 292 (an antifungal 124)

fludrocortisone a corticosteroid 127

flumazenil an *antidote* for benzodiazepine overdose

flumethasone a corticosteroid 127

flunarizine a calcium channel blocker used in the prevention of migraine 73

flunisolide a corticosteroid 127

fluocinolone a *topical* corticosteroid 162

fluocinonide a *topical* corticosteroid 162

Fluoderm a product name for fluocinolone (a *topical* corticosteroid 162)

fluoride 471 (a mineral 137)

fluorometholone a corticosteroid 127 for eye disorders

fluorouracil an anticancer drug 140

Fluotic a product name for fluoride 457 (a mineral 137)

fluoxetine 293 (an antidepressant 68)

flupentixol 294 (an antipsychotic 69 used in depression 68)

fluphenazine an phenothiazine antipsychotic 69

Fluphenazine Omega a product name for fluphenazine (an phenothiazine antipsychotic 69)

flurazepam a benzodiazepine sleeping drug 66

flurbiprofen a non-steroidal anti-inflammatory 102

flutamide 295 (an anticancer drug 140)

fluticasone 296 (a corticosteroid 127)

fluvastatin a lipid-lowering drug 89

fluvoxamine 297 (an antidepressant 68)

folic acid 472 (a vitamin 135)

folinic acid a vitamin 135

follitropin alpha a drug for infertility 152

follitropin beta a drug for treatment of infertility 152

fondaparinux an anticoagulant 91

Foradil a product name for formoterol 298 (a *bronchodilator* 76)

formoterol 298 (a *bronchodilator* 76)

Fortaz a product name for ceftazidime (a cephalosporin *antibiotic* 114)

Forteo a product name for teriparatide 446 (a drug for osteoporosis 108)

Fosamax a product name for alendronate 181 (a drug for bone disorders 108)

Fosamprenavir a drug for HIV/AIDS 144

Fosavance a combination product with alendronate 181 (a drug for treatment of bone disorders 108) and vitamin D 481 (a vitamin 135)

fosfomycin tromethamine an *antibiotic* 114

fosinopril an ACE inhibitor 98

fosphenytoin 390 (an antiepileptic 70)

Fragmin a product name for LMWH (low molecular weight heparin) 310 (an anticoagulant 91)

framycetin a *topical* aminoglycoside *antibiotic* 114 used for the treatment of ear, eye, and skin infections

Fraxiparine a product name for LMWH (low molecular weight heparin) 310 (an anticoagulant 91)

Frisium a product name for clobazam (a benzodiazepine drug used as a antiepileptic 70)

Froben SR a product name for flurbiprofen (a non-steroidal anti-inflammatory drug 102)

FSH follicle-stimulating (a natural *hormone* for infertility 166)

Fucidin a product name for fusidic acid (an *antibiotic* 114)

Fucidin H a product name for a combination drug with hydrocortisone 313 (a corticosteroid 127 and antipruritic 161) and other drugs

Fucithalmic a product name for fusidic acid (an *antibiotic* 114)

Fulvicin U/F a product name for griseofulvin (an antifungal 124)

Fungizone Intravenous a product name for amphotericin B 194 (an antifungal 126)

furosemide 299 (a loop diuretic 85)

fusidic acid an *antibiotic* 114

Fuzeon a product name for enfuvirtide (a drug for HIV/AIDS 144)

G

gabapentin 300 (an antiepileptic 70)

galantamine 301 (a drug for Alzheimer's disease 71)

gamma benzene hexachloride also called lindane; used in the treatment of pediculosis and scabies 164

ganciclovir an antiviral 119

ganirelix a drug for treatment of infertility 152

Garamycin a product name for gentamicin 304 (an aminoglycoside *antibiotic* 114)

Gardasil a product name for human papilloma virus (HPV), used in prevention of cervical cancer 139

Gasulsol a product name combination product containing aluminum hydroxide 187 (an antacid 94) and magnesium trisilicate (an antacid 94)

gatifloxacin 302 (an antibacterial drug 117)

Gaviscon Heartburn Relief Formula a combination product with alginic acid 180 (used to protect stomach and esophagus from acid reflux) and magnesium carbonate (an antacid 94)

GD-Latanoprost a product name for latanoprost 330 (a drug for glaucoma 156)

gemfibrozil 303 (a lipid-lowering drug 89)

Gen-Acyclovir a generic company version of acyclovir 179 (an antiviral 119)

Gen-Alprazolam a generic company version of alprazolam 185 (a benzodiazepine anti-anxiety drug 67)

Gen-Amoxicillin a generic company version of amoxicillin 193 (a penicillin *antibiotic* 114)

Gen-Atenolol a generic company version of atenolol 199 (a beta blocker 83)

Gen-Azathioprine a generic company version of azathioprine 203 (an antirheumatic 103 and immunosuppressant 143)

Gen-Baclofen a generic company version of baclofen 205 (a muscle relaxant 106)

GEN-BUSPIRONE–LETROZOLE

Gen-Buspirone a generic company version of buspirone 216 (an anti-anxiety drug 67)

Gen-Carbamazepine a generic company version of carbamazepine 218 (an antiepileptic 70)

Gen-Clobetasol a generic company version of clobetasol 236 (a *topical* corticosteroid 162)

Gen-Clomipramine a generic company version of clomipramine 238 (a tricyclic antidepressant 68)

Gen-Clonazepam a generic company version of clonazepam 239 (a benzodiazepine anti-anxiety drug 67 and antiepileptic 70)

Gen-Clozapine a generic company version of clozapine 243 (an antipsychotic drug 69)

Gen-Cyclobenzaprine a generic company version of cyclobenzaprine 247 (a muscle relaxant 106)

Gen-Cyproterone a generic company version of cyproterone (a synthetic sex *hormone* used for acne 165, cancer of the prostate 140, and male sexual disorders 134)

Gen-Diltiazem a generic company version of diltiazem 261 (an antihypertensive 88 and calcium channel blocker 87)

Gen-Doxazosin a generic company version of doxazosin 270 (a *sympatholytic* antihypertensive 88)

Gen-Fenofibrate Micro a generic company version of fenofibrate (a lipid-lowering drug 89)

Gen-Fluoxetine a generic company version of fluoxetine 293 a tricyclic antidepressant 68)

Gen-Gemfibrozil a generic company version of gemfibrozil 303 (a lipid-lowering drug 89)

Gen-Gliclazide a generic company version of gliclazide 305 (an oral antidiabetic 128)

Gen-Ipratropium a product name for ipratropium bromide 320 (a *bronchodilator* 76)

Gen-Medroxy a generic company version of medroxyprogesterone 345 (a female sex *hormone* 133)

Gen-metformin a generic company version of metformin 351 (a drug for diabetes 128)

Gen-Metoprolol a product name for metoprolol 354 (a beta blocker 83)

Gen-Minocycline a generic company version of minocycline 361 (a tetracycline *antibiotic* 114)

Gen-Mirtazapine a generic product name for mirtazapine 363 (an antidepressant 68)

Gen-Nabumetone a generic company version of nabumetone (a non-steroidal anti-inflammatory 102)

Gen-Nortriptyline a generic company version of ortriptyline (a tricyclic antidepressant 68)

Gen-Oxybutynin a generic company version of oxybutynin 383 (an *anticholinergic* and *antispasmodic* for urinary disorders 154)

Gen-Piroxicam a product name for piroxicam 393 (a non-steroidal anti-inflammatory 102)

Gen-Salbutamol a generic company version of salbutamol 429 (a *bronchodilator* 76)

Gen-Selegiline a generic company version of selegiline 431 (a drug for *parkinsonism* 71)

Gen-Sertraline a generic company version of sertraline 432 (an antidepressant 68)

Gen-Sotalol a generic company version of sotalol (a beta blocker 83)

gentamicin 304 (an aminoglycoside *antibiotic* 114)

Gen-Temazepam a product name for temazepam 443 (a benzodiazepine sleeping drug 66)

Gen-Terbinafine a generic company version of terbinafine 445 (an antifungal 124)

Gen-Trazodone a generic company version of trazodone (an antidepressant 68)

Gen-Triazolam a generic company version of temazepam 443 (a benzodiazepine sleeping drug 66)

Gen-Valproic a generic company version of valproic acid 458 (an antiepileptic 70)

Gen-Verapamil a generic company version of verapimil 462 (an antihypertensive 88 and calcium channel blocker 87)

Gen-Zopiclone a product name for zopiclone 467 (a sleeping drug 66)

Gleevec a product name for imatinib (an anticancer drug 140)

gliclazide 305 (an oral antidiabetic 128)

glimepiride 306 (an oral antidiabetic 128)

glucagon a pancreatic *hormone* for hypoglycemia 126

Glucobay a product name for acarbose 177 (an oral antidiabetic 128)

GlucoNorm a product name for repaglinide 419 (a drug for diabetes 128)

Glucophage a product name for metformin 351 (a drug for diabetes 128)

glucosamine 472 a supplement

Glumetza a product name for metformin 351 (an antidiabetic drug 128)

glyburide 307 (an oral antidiabetic drug 128)

Glycon a product name for metformin 351 (an antidiabetic drug 128)

gold sodium thiomalate a drug for rheumatoid arthritis 103

gonadorelin a drug for infertility 152

Gonal-F a product name for follitropin alpha (a drug for infertility 152)

goserelin 308 (a female sex *hormone* 133 and anticancer drug 140, also used for menstrual disorders 148 and infertility 152)

gramicidin an aminoglycoside *antibiotic* 114 or eye, ear, and skin infections

granisetron an anti-emetic 74

Gravol Preparations a product name for dimenhydrinate 262 (an anti-emetic 74 and an anti-vertigo drug 74)

growth hormone somatropin (pituitary hormones 131)

guaifenesin an *expectorant* 80

Gynazole-I a product name for butaconzole (an antifungal 124)

H

Halcion a product name for triazolam (a benzodiazepine sleeping drug 66)

halobetasol a *topical* corticosteroid 162

Halog a product name for halcinonide (a *topical* corticosteroid 162)

haloperidol 309 (an antipsychotic 69)

Haloperidol LA a product name for haloperidol 309 (an antipsychotic 69)

Haloperidol-LA Omega a product name for haloperidol 309 (an antipsychotic 69)

halothane a gas used to induce general anesthesia

heparin 310 (an anticoagulant 91)

Heparin Leo a product name for heparin 310 (an anticoagulant 91)

Hepsera a product name for adefovir (an antiviral 119)

herceptin a product name for trastuzumab (an anticancer drug 140)

heroin diamorphine (an opioid 492)

Herplex-D a product name for idoxuridine (an antiviral 119)

hexachlorophene a skin *antiseptic* 163

Histanil a product name for promethazine 405 (an antihistamine 110 and anti-emetic 74)

homatropine a *mydriatic* 158

Hp-PAC a combination of clarithromycin 234 (a macrolide *antibiotic* 114), amoxicillin 193 (an *antibiotic* 114) and lansoprazole 329 (an antiulcer drug 95)

Humalog a product name for insulin lispro (a drug for diabetes 128)

human chorionic gonadotropin 302 (a drug for infertility 152)

Humatrope a product name for somatropin, a pituitary *hormone* 131 (a synthetic pituitary *hormone* 131)

Humira a product name for adalimumab 180 (an antirheumatic drug 103)

Humulin a product name for insulin lente (a drug for diabetes 128)

Humulin N a product name for insulin NPH (a drug for diabetes 128)

hyaluronidase helps injections penetrate tissues

Hycodan a product name for hydrocodone 312 (an opioid used in cough preparations 80)

Hycort a product name for hydrocortisone 313 (a corticosteroid 127 and anti-pruritic 161)

Hyderm a product name for hydrocortisone 313 (a corticosteroid 127 and antipruritic 161)

hydralazine an antihypertensive 88

hydrochlorothiazide 311 (a thiazide diuretic 85)

hydrocodone 312 (a cough suppressant 80)

hydrocortisone 313 (a corticosteroid 127 and antipruritic 161)

Hydromorph Contin a product name for hydromorphone 314 (an *opioid analgesic* 64 used in the management of pain)

hydromorphone 314 (an *opioid analgesic* 64 used in the management of pain)

Hydromorphone HP a product name for hydromorphone 314 (an *opioid analgesic* 64 used in the management of pain)

Hydromorphone HP Forte a product name for hydromorphone 314 (an *opioid analgesic* 64 used in the management of pain)

hydroxocobalamin vitamin B_{12} 480 (a vitamin 135)

hydroxychloroquine an antimalarial 123 and antirheumatic drug 103

hydroxyzine an antihistamine used as an anti-anxiety drug 67

Hygroton a product name for chlortalidone (a thiazide diuretic 101)

Hypurin a product name for insulin 318 (a drug for diabetes 128)

Hytrin a product name for terazosin 444 (a *sympatholytic* antihypertensive 88)

I

ibuprofen 315 (a non-*opioid analgesic* 64 and non-steroidal anti-inflammatory 102)

ibutulide an anti-arrhythmic 86

ichthammol a substance in skin preparations for eczema 167

idoxuridine an antiviral 119

imatinib an anticancer drug 140

Imdur a product name for isosorbide mononitrate 318 (a nitrate *vasodilator* 84 and anti-angina drug 87)

imipenem-cilastin an *antibiotic* 114

imipramine 316 (a tricyclic antidepressant 68)

Imitrex DF a product name for sumatriptan 440 (a drug for migraine 73)

Imodium a product name for loperamide 338 (an antidiarrheal 96)

Imovane a product name for zopiclone 467 (a sleeping drug 66)

Impril a product name for imipramine 316 (an antidepressant 68 and drug for urinary disorders 154)

Imuran a product name for azathioprine 203 (an antirheumatic 103 and immunosuppressant 143)

indacaterol a broncodilator 76

indapamide 317 (a thiazide-like diuretic 85)

Inderal-LA a product name for propranolol 406 (a beta blocker 83)

indinavir a drug for HIV/AIDS 144

Indocid P.D.A. a product name for indomethacin (a non-steroidal anti-inflammatory 102)

indomethacin a non-steroidal anti-inflammatory 102

infliximab a biological response modifier for rheumatoid arthritis 103 and Crohn's disease 98

Innohep a product name for LMWH 305 (an anticoagulant 91)

inosiplex an antiviral 119

Inspra a product name for eplerenone 277 (a diuretic 85)

insulin 318 (a drug for diabetes 128)

insulin aspart a drug for diabetes 128

insulin detemir a drug for diabetes 128

insulin glargine a drug for diabetes 128

insulin NPH a drug for diabetes 128

insulin ultralente a drug for diabetes 128

interferon 319 (an antiviral 119 and anticancer drug 140)

Interferon alfa-2b an antiviral 119 and anticancer drug 140

Interferon beta-1a a drug used in multiple sclerosis

Interferon beta-1b a drug used in multiple sclerosis

Intron-A a product name for interferon alfa-2b (an antiviral 119 and anticancer drug 140)

Invirase a product name for saquinavir (a drug for HIV/AIDS 144)

iodine 473 (a mineral 137)

iopidine a product name for apraclonidine (a drug for glaucoma 156)

ipecac a drug used to induce vomiting in drug overdose and poisoning, also used as an *expectorant* 80

ipratropium bromide 320 (a *bronchodilator* 76)

irbesartan 321 (a *vasodilator* 84 and antihypertensive drug 88)

irinotecan an anticancer drug 140

iron 473 (a mineral 137)

ISDN a product name for isosorbide dinitraten 323 (a *vasodilator* 84 and anti-angina drug 87)

Isentress a product name for raltegravir (an antiretroviral drug used in the treatment of HIV and AIDS 144)

isoflurane a volatile liquid inhaled as a general *anesthetic*

isoniazid 322 (an antituberculous drug 134)

isopropyl myristate a drug to treat skin parasites 164

isoproterenol a *sympathomimetic*

Isoproterenol Hydrochloride a product name for isoproterenol (a *sympathomimetic*)

Isoptin SR a product name for verapimil 462 (an antihypertensive 88 and calcium channel blocker 87)

Isopto Atropine a product name for atropine 202 (an *anticholinergic mydriatic* 158)

Isopto Carbachol a product name for carbachol eye drops (a miotic for glaucoma 156)

Isopto Homatropine a product name for homatropine (a *mydriatic* 158)

isopropyl myristate a drug to treat skin parasites 164

isosorbide dinitrate 323 (a nitrate *vasodilator* 84 and anti-angina drug 87)

isosorbide mononitrate 318 (a nitrate *vasodilator* 84 and anti-angina drug 87)

Isotamine a product name for isoniazid 322 (an antituberculous drug 134)

isotretinoin 324 (a drug for acne 165)

itraconazole an antifungal 124

JK

Jaa Tetra a product name for tetracycline 448 (an antibiotic 114)

Janumet a product name for a combination of sitagliptin phosphate 435 (an antihyperglycemic drug 128) and metformin 351 (an antidiabetic drug 128)

Januvia a product name for sitagliptin phosphate 435 (an antihyperglycemic drug 128)

Kadian a product name for morphine 368 (an *opioid analgesic* 64)

Kaletra a product name for lopinavir/ritonavir 339 (a drug for HIV and immune deficiency 144)

Kefzol a product name for cefazolin (a cephalosporin *antibiotic* 114)

Kenalog a product name for triamcinolone (a corticosteroid 127)

Keppra a product name for levetiracetam (an antiepileptic 70)

ketamine a drug used to induce general anesthesia, also a drug of abuse 489

Ketek a product name for telithromycin (an antibiotic 114)

ketoconazole 325 (an antifungal 124)

Ketoderm a product name for ketoconazole 325 (an antifungal 124)

ketoprofen 326 (a non-steroidal anti-inflammatory 102)

ketorolac a non-steroidal anti-inflammatory 102

ketotifen a drug used in asthma 77

Kineret a product name for anakinra 195 (an immunomodulatory drug for rheumatoid arthritis 103)

K-Lyte a product name for potassium citrate (a drug used in the treatment of low potassium)

Koffex DM a product name for dextromorphan 252 (a cough suppressant 80)

Kwellada-P a product name for permethrin 388 (a *topical* antiparasitic 164)

Kytril a product name for granisetron (an anti-emetic 74)

L

lactic acid an ingredient in preparations for warts, *emollients*, and vaginal suppositories

lactulose 327 (an osmotic laxative 113)

Lamictal a product name for lamotrigine 328 (an antiepileptic 70)

Lamisil a product name for terbinafine 445 (an antifungal 124)

lamivudine 466 (an antiretroviral drug used for HIV/AIDS 144)

lamotrigine 328 (an antiepileptic 70)

Lanoxin a product name for digoxin 260 (a digitalis drug 82)

lansoprazole 329 (an anti-ulcer drug 95)

Lariam Tab a product name for mefloquine 346 (an antimalarial 123)

Lasix a product name for furosemide 299 (a loop diuretic 85)

latanoprost 330 (a drug for glaucoma 156)

Leflunomide an antirheumatic drug 103

Lescol a product name for fluvastatin (a lipid-lowering drug 89)

letrozole an anticancer drug 140

LEUKERAN–MUCAINE

Leukeran a product name for chlorambucil (an anticancer drug 140 used for chronic lymphocytic leukemia and lymphomas)

Levaquin a product name for levofloxacin 332 (an antibacterial 117)

Levate a product name for amitriptyline 191 (an antidepressant drug 68)

Levetiracetam an antiepileptic 70

Levitra a product name for vardenafil (a drug used for the treatment of sexual impotence 152)

levobunolol a beta blocker 83 and drug for glaucoma 156

levocabastine a *topical* antihistamine 110

levodopa 331 (a drug for *parkinsonism* 71)

levodopa/benserazide a combination of levodopa 331 and benserazide for *parkinsonism* 71

levodopa/carbidopa 331 (a combination of levodopa 331 and carbidopa for *parkinsonism* 71)

levofloxacin 332 (an antibacterial 117)

levonorgestrel 333 (a female sex *hormone* 133 and oral contraceptive 149)

levothyroxine previously known as thyroxine 334 (a thyroid *hormone* 130)

Levsin a product name for hyoscine (an *antispasmodic* drug 96)

Lidemol a product name for fluocinonide (a *topical* corticosteroid 162)

Lidex a product name for fluocinonide (a *topical* corticosteroid 162)

lidocaine a local *anesthetic* 64 and anti-arrhythmic 86

Lidocaine Parenteral a product name for lidocaine (a local *anesthetic* 64 and anti-arrhythmic 86)

Lidodan Endotracheal a product name for lidocaine (a local *anesthetic* 64 and anti-arrhythmic 86)

Lidomyxin a product name for a combination of polymixin B 395 (an antibiotic 114) and lidocaine (a local anesthetic 64)

Lin-Buspirone a generic company version of buspirone 216 (an anti-anxiety drug 67)

lindane also called gamma benzene hexachloride; used in the treatment of pediculosis and scabies 164

linezolid an *antibiotic* 114

Lipidil EZ a product name for fenofibrate (a lipid-lowering drug 89)

Lipidil-Micro a product name for fenofibrate (a lipid-lowering drug 89)

Lipidil Supra a product name for fenofibrate (a lipid-lowering drug 89)

Lipitor a product name for atorvastatin 201 (a lipid-lowering drug 89)

Lioresal a product name for baclofen 205 (a muscle relaxant 106)

liothyronine a thyroid *hormone* 130

liraglutide 335 (a drug for diabetes 128)

lisdexamfetamine a drug for ADHD 72

lisinopril 336 (an ACE inhibitor 84)

Lithane a product name for lithium 337 (a drug for mania 69)

lithium 337 (a drug for mania 69)

Litmax a product name for lithium 337 (an antimanic drug 69)

Livostin a product name for levocabastine (an antihistamine 110)

LMWH 305 (an anticoagulant 91)

Locacorten Vioform a combination of clioquinol (an antibacterial 117 and antifungal 124) and flumethasone (a corticosteroid 127)

Iodoxamide an anti-allergy drug 109

Loestrin a product-name oral contraceptive 149 containing ethinyl estradiol 283 and norethindrone 374

Lomotil a product name for diphenoxylate 264 (an opioid antidiarrheal 96) and atropine 202

Loniten a product name for minoxidil 362 (an antihypertensive 88)

Loperacap a product name for loperamide 338 (an antidiarrheal drug 96)

loperamide 338 (an antidiarrheal 96)

Lopid a product name for gemfibrozil 303 (a lipid-lowering drug 89)

lopinavir/ritonavir 339 (a drug for HIV/AIDS 144)

Lopresor a product name for metoprolol 354 (a cardioselective beta blocker 83)

loratadine 340 (an antihistamine 110)

lorazepam 341 (a benzodiazepine anti-anxiety drug 67 and sleeping drug 66)

losartan 342 (an antihypertensive 88)

Losec a product name for omeprazole 378 (an antiulcer drug 95)

Losec 1-2-3A a product name for a combination of amoxicillin 193, clarithromycin 234 (antibiotic drugs 114), and omeprazole 378 (an anti-ulcer drug 95)

Lotriderm a product-name product containing betamethasone 209 (a corticosteroid 127) and clotrimazole 241 (an antifungal 124)

lovastatin 343 (a lipid-lowering drug 89)

Lovenox a product name for LMWH 305 (an anticoagulant 91)

Lovenox HP a product name for LMWH 305 (an anticoagulant 91)

Low molecular weight heparin see LMWH

Loxapac a product name for loxapine (an antipsychotic 69)

loxapine an antipsychotic 69

Lozide Tab a product name for indapamide 317 a thiazide-like diuretic 85

Lugol's solution an iodine 473 solution for overactive thyroid gland

Lumigan a product name for bimatoprost (a drug for glaucoma 156)

lutein 474 a natural supplement

Lutrepulse a product name for gonadorelin (a drug for infertility 152)

Luvox a product name for fluvoxamine 297 (an antidepressant 68)

Luxiq a product name for betamethasone 209 (a corticosteroid 127)

Lyderm a product name for fluocinonide (a *topical* corticosteroid 162)

Lyrica a product name for pregabalin 400 (an antiepileptic 70)

M

Maalox Antacid with Anti-Gas a combination product with aluminum hydroxide 187 (an antacid 94), magnesium hydroxide 338 (an antacid 94), and simethicone (antiflatulent 98)

Maalox Antacid with Anti-Gas Extra Strength a combination product with aluminum hydroxide 187 (an antacid 94), magnesium hydroxide 344 (an antacid 94), and simethicone (an antiflatulent 98)

Maalox Quick Dissolve a product name for calcium carbonate (a calcium salt and a mineral 137 used as an antacid 94)

Maalox TC a combination product with aluminum hydroxide 187 and magnesium hydroxide 344 (both antacids 94)

magnesium 474 (a mineral 137)

magnesium carbonate an antacid 94

magnesium citrate an osmotic laxative 97

magnesium hydroxide 344 (an antacid 94 and laxative 97)

magnesium oxide an antacid 94

magnesium sulfate an osmotic laxative 97

magnesium trisilicate an antacid 94

Malarone a combination of proguanil and atovaquone 404 (both antimalarials 123)

Manerix a product name for moclobemide 365 (a reversible MAOI antidepressant 68)

mannitol an osmotic diuretic 85

maprotiline antidepressant 68

Maraviroc an antiretroviral drug used in the treatment of HIV and AIDS 144

Marcaine a product name for bupivacaine local *anesthetic* 64 used in labour 153)

Marinol a product name for dronabinol (an anti-emetic 74)

Marvelon a product name for an oral contraceptive 149

Maxidex a product name for dexamethasone 255 (a corticosteroid 127)

Maxitrol a product name for a combination of polymixin B 395, neomycin (antibiotic drugs 114), and dexamethasone 255 (a corticosteroid 127)

Maxalt a product name for rizatriptan 426 (a drug for migraine 73)

Maxalt RPD a product name for rizatriptan 426 (a drug for migraine 73)

Maxitrol a product name for a combination of polymixin B 395, neomycin (antibiotic drugs 114), and dexamethasone 255 (a corticosteroid 127)

mebendazole an anthelmintic 125

meclizine an antihistamine used as an anti-emetic drug 74

Medrol a product name for methylprednisolone 356 (a corticosteroid 127)

medroxyprogesterone 345 (a female sex *hormone* 133 and anticancer drug 140)

mefloquine 346 (an antimalarial 123)

Mefoxin a product name for cefoxitin (a cephalosporin *antibiotic* 114)

Megace a product name for megestrol 347 (a female sex *hormone* 133 and anticancer drug 140)

Megace OS a product name for megestrol 347 (a female sex hor-mone 135 and anticancer drug 140)

megestrol acetate a progestin 133

meloxicam 348 (a non-steroidal anti-inflammatory 102)

melphalan an alkylating agent for multiple myeloma 140

memantine 349 a drug for dementia 71

menadiol vitamin K 482 (a vitamin 135)

menotropins a drug for infertility 152

menthol an alcohol from mint oils used as an inhalation and *topical* anti-pruritic 161

menthyl anthranilate an ingredient of sunscreens 169

mepacrine an *antiprotozoal* 122 for giardiasis

meperidine an *opioid analgesic* 64 and drug used in labour 153

mepivacaine a local anesthetic 64

Mepron a product name for atovaquone (an antimalarial 123)

mercaptopurine 350 (an anticancer drug 140)

meropenem an *antibiotic* 114

Mersyndol with Codeine a combination product with doxylamine (a drug used to aid sleep 66), acetaminophen 177 (an *analgesic* 64), and codeine 244 (an *opioid analgesic* 64)

M-Eslon a product name for morphine 368 (an *opioid analgesic* 64)

Mesasal a product name for 5-ASA 176 (a drug for inflammatory bowel disease 98)

Mesavant a product name for 5-ASA 176 (a drug for inflammatory bowel disease 98)

Mestinon a product name for pyridostigmine 410 (a drug for myasthenia gravis 107)

Mestinon-SR a product name for pyridostigmine 410 (a drug for myasthenia gravis 107)

Metadol a product name for methadone 352 (an opioid used in the maintenance treatment of opioid-dependent individuals and as an *analgesic* 64 in acute and chronic pain)

Metamucil a fiber laxative containing psyllium 409 (laxative 97)

metformin 351 (a drug for diabetes 128)

methadone 352 (an opioid used in the maintenance treatment of opioid-dependent individuals and as an *analgesic* 64 in acute and chronic pain)

methazolamide a drug used in glaucoma 156

methenamine a drug for urinary tract infections 154

methimazole an antithyroid drug 130

methocarbamol a muscle relaxant 106

methotrexate 353 (an antimetabolite anticancer drug 140)

methotrimeprazine a phenothiazine antipsychotic 69

Methoxacet-C a combination product containing codeine 244 (an *opioid analgesic* 64) with acetaminophen 177 (an analgesic p.64) and a muscle relaxant 106

Methoxisal a combination product with ASA 198 (a non-*opioid analgesic* 64) and methocarbamol (a muscle relaxant 106)

methoxsalen a drug used in the treatment of psoriasis (166) and atopic dermatitis

Methsuximide an antiepileptic 70

methylcobalamin vitamin B12 480 (a vitamin 135)

methyldopa 354 (an antihypertensive 88)

methylphenidate 355 (a drug used to treat hyperactivity in children 72)

methylprednisolone 356 (a corticosteroid 127)

methyl salicylate a topical *analgesic* 64 for muscle and joint pain

metoclopramide 357 (a gastrointestinal motility regulator and anti-emetic 74)

Metoclopramide Omega a product name for metoclopramide 357 (a gastrointestinal motility regulator and anti-emetic 74)

Metoject a product name for methotrexate 353 (an anticancer 140, antirheumatic 103, and drug for psoriasis 166)

metolazone a thiazide-like diuretic 85

metoprolol 354 (a beta blocker 83)

Metreton a combination of prednisone 399 (a corticosteroid 127), chlorpheniramine 228 (an antihistamine 110), and vitamin C 480 (a vitamin 135)

MetroCream a product name for metronidazole 359 (an antibacterial 117 and antiprotozoal 122)

MetroGel a product name for *topical* metronidazole 359 (an antibacterial 117)

metronidazole 359 (an antibacterial 117 and antiprotozoal 122)

Mevacor a product name for lovastatin 343 (a lipid-lowering drug 89)

mexiletine an anti-arrhythmic 86

mexoryl SX an ingredient of sunscreens 169

Mezavant a product name for 5-ASA 176 (a drug for inflammatory bowel disease 98)

Miacalcin NS a product name for calcitonin (a drug for bone disorders 108)

micafungin an antifungal 124

Micardis a product name for telmisartan (a *vasodilator* 84 and antihypertensive 88)

Micatin a product name for miconazole 360 (an antifungal 124)

miconazole 360 (an antifungal 124)

Micozole a product name for miconazole 360 (an antifungal 124)

Micronor a product name for norethindrone 374 (a female sex *hormone* 133)

Migranal Nasal Spray a product name for ergotamine 278 (a drug for migraine 73)

mineral oil a lubricant laxative 97

Minestrin a product-name oral contraceptive 149 containing ethinyl estradiol 283 and norethindrone 374

Minims Atropine a product name for atropine 202 (an *anticholinergic mydriatic* 158)

Minims Cyclopentolate a product name for cyclopentolate (an *anticholinergic mydriatic* 158)

Minims Phenylephrine a product name for phenylephrine (a decongestant eye drop 79)

Minims Tetracaine a product name for tetracaine (also known as amethocain, a local anesthetic 64)

Minims Tropicamide a product name for tropicamide (a *mydriatic* 158)

Minipress a product name for prazosin (a *sympatholytic* antihypertensive 88)

Minitram a product name for nitroglycerin 373 (an anti-angina drug 87)

Minocin a product name for minocycline 361 (a tetracycline *antibiotic* 114)

minocycline 361 (a tetracycline *antibiotic* 114)

Min-Ovral a product name for levonorgestrel 333 (a female sex *hormone* 133 and oral contraceptive 149) and ethinyl estradiol 283 (an estrogen 135)

minoxidil 362 (an antihypertensive drug 88 and treatment for hair loss 168)

Mintezol a product name for tiabendazole (an anthelmintic 125)

Miostat a product name for carbachol (a miotic drug used in glaucoma 156 and a para*sympathomimetic*)

Mirapex a product name for pramipexole 396 (a drug for *parkinsonism* 71)

Mirena a product name for levonorgestrel 333 (a female sex *hormone* 133 and oral contraceptive 149)

mirtazapine 363 (an antidepressant 68)

misoprostol 364 (an antiulcer drug 95)

Mobicox a product name for meloxicam 348 (a non-steroidal anti-inflammatory 102)

moclobemide 365 a reversible MAOI antidepressant 68

modafinil a drug used in treatment of narcolepsy

Modecate a product name for fluphenazine (a phenothiazine antipsychotic 69)

molybdenum a mineral 137 required in minute amounts in the diet, poisonous if ingested in large quantities

mometasone 366 (a *topical* corticosteroid 162)

Monicure a product name for fluconazole 292 (an antifungal drug 124)

Monistat a product name for miconazole 360 (an antifungal 124)

montelukast 367 (a leukotriene *antagonist* for asthma 77)

Monurol a product name for fosfomycin tromethamine (an *antibiotic* 114)

morphine 368 (an opioid analgesic 64)

Morphine Sulfate a product name for morphine 368 (an *opioid analgesic* 64)

M.O.S. a product name for morphine 368 (an *opioid analgesic* 64)

Motrin a product name for ibuprofen 315 (a non-steroidal anti-inflammatory 102)

moxifloxacin 369 (an antibacterial 117)

MS Contin a product name for morphine 368 (an *opioid analgesic* 64)

MSD Enteric Coated ASA a product name for ASA 198 (a non-*opioid analgesic* 64 and antiplatelet drug 90)

MS-IR a product name for morphine 368 (an *opioid analgesic* 64)

Mucaine a product name for a combination of aluminum hydroxide 187, magnesium hydroxide 344 (antacids 94), and oxethazaine (a local anesthetic 64)

MUPIROCIN–NOVO-TERAZOSIN

mupirocin an antibacterial for skin infections 163

MUSE a product name for alprostadil 186 (a *prostaglandin* used for male impotence 134, 152)

Mycamine a product name for micafungin (an antifungal 124)

Mycobutin a product name for rifabutin (an antituberculosis drug 118)

mycophenolate mofetil an immunosuppressant 143

Mydfrin a product name for phenylephrine (used as a *mydriatic* 158)

Mydriacil a product name for tropicamide (a *mydriatic* 158)

Mylan-Acyclovir a product name for acyclovir 179 (an antiviral drug 119)

Mylan-Amantadine a product name for amantadine 188 (a drug for parkinsonism 71 and antiviral drug 119)

Mylan-Amilazide a product name for a combination of amiloride 189 and hydrochlorothiazide 311 (diuretic drugs 85)

Mylan-Amiodarone a product name for amiodarone 190 (an anti-arrhythmic drug 86)

Mylan-Atenolol a product name for atenolol 199 (a beta blocker 83)

Mylan-Azathioprine a product name for azathioprine 203 (an antirheumatic 103 and immunosuppressant drug 143)

Mylan-Beclo AQ a product name for beclomethasone 206 (a corticosteroid 127, 162)

Mylan-Captopril a product name for captopril 217 (an ACE inhibitor 84 and antihypertensive drug 88)

Mylan-Combo Sterinebs a product name for a combination of salbutamol 429 and ipratropium 320 (*bronchodilators* 76)

Mylan-Enalapril a product name for enalapril 275 (an ACE inhibitor 84 and antihypertensive drug 88)

Mylan-Etidronate a product name for etidronate 284 (a drug for bone disorders 108)

Mylan-Galantamine a product name for galantamine 301 (a drug for dementia 71)

Mylan-Selegiline a product name for selegiline 431 (an antiparkinonism drug 71)

Mylan-Tizanidine a product name for tizanidine 453 (a muscle relaxant drug 106)

Mylan-Verapamil a product name for verapamil 462 (an anti-angina 87, anti-arrhythmic 86, and antihypertensive drug 88)

Mylanta Double Strength Plain a combination product with aluminum hydroxide 187 (an antacid 94) and magnesium hydroxide 344 (an antacid 94)

Mylanta Extra Strength a combination product with aluminum hydroxide 187 (an antacid 94), magnesium hydroxide 344 (an antacid 94), and simethicone (an antiflatulent 98)

Myocet a product name for doxorubicin 271 (a *cytotoxic* anticancer drug 140)

Myochrysine a product name for gold sodium thiomalate (an antirheumatic 117)

Myotonachol a product name for bethanechol (a parasympathomimetic for urinary retention 154)

Mysoline a product name for primidone (an antiepileptic 70)

N

nabilone an anti-emetic 74

nabumetone a non-steroidal anti-inflammatory 102

nadolol a beta blocker 97

nadroparin 305 (an anticoagulant 91)

nafarelin a drug for menstrual disorders 148

nalbuphine an *opioid analgesic* 64

Nalcrom a product name for sodium cromoglycate 436 (an anti-allergy drug 109)

Nalfon a product name for fenoprofen (a non-steroidal anti-inflammatory 102)

naloxone an *antidote* for opioid 507 poisoning

naltrexone a drug used in formally opioid dependent individuals; also used in alcohol dependence

nandrolone an anabolic steroid 134

Naprosyn a product name for naproxen 370 (a non-steroidal anti-inflammatory 102)

naproxen 370 (a non-steroidal anti-inflammatory 102)

naratriptan a drug for migraine 73

Narcan a product name for naloxone (an *antidote* for opioid 490 poisoning)

Nardil a product name for phenelzine (an MAOI antidepressant 68)

Nasacort AQ a product name for triamcinolone (a corticosteroid 127)

Nasonex a product name for mometasone 366 (a *topical* corticosteroid 162)

nateglinide a drug for diabetes 128

Navane a product name for thiothixene (an antipsychotic 69)

Nebcin a product name for tobramycin (an aminoglycoside *antibiotic* 114)

nedocromil a drug used to prevent asthma attacks 77

nelfinavir an antiretroviral drug for HIV/AIDS 144

Neocitran Cough and Cold Night a product name for a combination of dextromethorphan 256 (a cough suppressant 80), pseudoephedrine 408 (a decongestant 79), and chlorpheniramine 228 (an antihistamine 110)

Neo-Laryngobis a product name for bismuth subsalicylate 211 (an antacid and adsorbent 94)

Neo-Medrol Acne Lotion a combination product with methylprednisolone 356 (a corticosteroid 127), neomycin (an *antibiotic* 114), aluminum chlorhydroxide, and sulfur

neomycin an aminoglycoside *antibiotic* 114 used in ear drops 175

Neoral a product name for cyclosporine 249 (an immunosuppressant 143)

neostigmine a drug for myasthenia gravis 107

NeoStrata Canada Blemish Spot Gel a product name for salicylic acid (a keratolytic

for acne 165, dandruff 168, psoriasis 166, and warts)

Neo-Synephrine Parenteral a product name for phenylephrine (used as a vasoconstrictor)

Nerisalik a combination of diflucortolone (a *topical* corticosteroid 162) with alicyclic acid

Nerisone a product name for diflucortolone (a *topical* corticosteroid 162)

Neulasta a product name for filgrastim 290 (a blood stimulant)

Neuleptil a product name for pericyazine (an antipsychotic 69)

Neupogen a product name for filgrastim 290 (a blood growth stimulant)

Neurontin a product name for gabapentin 300 (an antiepileptic 70)

nevirapine an antiretroviral drug for HIV/AIDS 144

Nexium a product name for omeprazole 378 (an anti-ulcer drug 95)

Nexium 1–2–3A a product name for a combination of amoxicillin 193 (an antibiotic drug 114) and omeprazole 378 (an anti-ulcer drug 95)

niacin 475 (a vitamin 135)

niacinamide another name for niacin 475 (a vitamin 135)

Nicoderm a product name for nicotine 371 (used in smoking cessation)

Nicorette a product name for nicotine 371 (used in smoking cessation)

nicotinamide a B vitamin 475 (a vitamin 135)

nicotine 371

nicotinic acid see niacin; a lipid-lowering drug 103 and vitamin 135

nicotinyl alcohol tartrate niacin 475 (a vitamin 135)

NidaGel Vaginal a product name for metronidazole 359 (an antibacterial 117 and antiprotozoal 122)

Nidazol a product name for metronidazole 359 (an antibacterial 117 and antiprotozoal 122)

nifedipine 372 (a calcium channel blocker 87)

Nitro-Dur a product name for nitroglycerin 373 (an anti-angina drug 87)

nitrofurantoin an antibacterial 117

nitroglycerin 373 (an anti-angina drug 87)

Nitrol a product name for nitroglycerin 373 (an anti-angina drug 87)

Nitrolingual Pumpspray a product name for nitroglycerin 373 (an anti-angina drug 87)

Nitrostat a product name for nitroglycerin 373 (an anti-angina drug 87)

nitrous oxide *anesthetic* gas

Nix a product name for permethrin 388 (a *topical* antiparasitic 164)

nizatidine an antiulcer drug 95

Nizoral a product name for ketoconazole 325 (an antifungal 124)

Nolvaldex D a product name for tamoxifen 441 (an anticancer drug 140)

nonacog alfa a synthetic form of factor IX to promote blood clotting

nonoxynol '9' a spermicidal agent

noradrenaline see norepinephrine

Norelgestromin a progestin 151

norepinephrine a drug similar to epinephrine 276 used to raise the blood pressure during shock

norethindrone 374 (a female sex *hormone* 133 and oral contraceptive 149)

norfloxacin 375 (an antibacterial 117)

norgestimate a progestin (133) used as an oral contraceptive 149

Noritate a product name for metronidazole 359 (an antibacterial 117 and antiprotozoal 122)

NorLevo a product name for levonorgestrel 333 (a female sex *hormone* 133 and oral contraceptive 149)

Norlutate a product name for norethindrone 374 (a female sex *hormone* 133)

Noroxin a product name for norfloxacin 375 (a fluoroquinolone antibiotic 115)

Norpramin a product name for desipramine (a tricyclic antidepressant 68)

nortriptyline a tricyclic antidepressant 68

Norvasc a product name for amlodipine 192 (an anti-hypertensive 88 and calcium channel blocker 87)

Novahistex DH a combination product with phenylephrine (a decongestant 79) and hydrocodone 312 (a cough suppressant 80)

Novahistine DH a combination product with phenylephrine (a decongestant 79) and hydrocodone 312 (a cough suppressant 80)

Novamoxin a product name for amoxicillin 193 (an *antibiotic* 114)

Novo-AZT a generic company version of zidovudine 466 (a drug for HIV and immune deficiency 144)

Novo-Betahistine a generic company version of betahistine 208 (a drug for Ménière's disease 74)

Novo-Carbamaz a generic company version of carbamazepine 218 (an antiepileptic 70)

Novo-Cefaclor a generic company version of cefaclor 220 (a cephalosporin *antibiotic* 114)

Novo-Clobetasol a generic company version of clobetasol 236 (a *topical* corticosteroid 162)

Novo-Clobazam a product name for clobazam (a benzodiazepine drug used as a antiepileptic 70)

Novo-Clonazepam a generic company version of clonazepam 239 (a benzodiazepine antiepileptic 70)

Novo-Clonidine a generic company version of clonidine (an antihypertensive 88)

Novo-Clopamine a generic company version of clomipramine 238 (a tricyclic antidepressant 68)

Novo-Clopate a generic company version of clorazepate (a benzodiazepine anti-anxiety drug 67)

Novo-Cycloprine a generic company version of cyclobenzaprine 247 (muscle relaxant 106)

Novo-Cyproterine a product name for cyproterone (a synthetic sex *hormone* used for acne 165, cancer of the prostate 140, and male sexual disorders 132)

Novo-Desipramine a generic company version of desipramine (a tricyclic antidepressant 68)

Novo-Diflunisal a generic company version of diflunisal (a non-steroidal anti-inflammatory 102)

Novo-Diltiazem a generic company version of diltiazem 261 (an antihypertensive 88 and calcium channel blocker 87)

Novo-Divalproex a generic company version of divalproex (an antiepileptic 70)

Novo-Doxazosin a generic company version of doxazosin 270 (a *sympatholytic* antihypertensive 88)

Novo-Doxepin a generic company version of doxepin (a tricyclic antidepressant 68)

Novo-Doxylin a generic company version of doxycycline 272 (a tetracycline *antibiotic* 114)

Novo-Fluoxetine a generic company version of fluoxetine 293 (a tricyclic antidepressant 68)

Novo-Flutamide a generic company version of flutamide 295 (an anticancer drug 140)

Novo-Fluprofen a generic company version of flurbiprofen (a non-steroidal anti-inflammatory 102)

Novo-Fluvoxamine a generic company version of fluvoxamine 297 (an antidepressant 68)

Novo-Gabapentin a generic company version of gabapentin 300 (an antiepileptic 70)

Novo-Gemfibrozil a generic company version of gemfibrozil 303 (a lipid-lowering drug 89)

Novo-Gesic C8 a combination product containing codeine 244 (an *opioid analgesic* 64) with acetaminophen 177 (an analgesic 64), and caffeine.

Novo-Gliclazide a product name for gliclazide 305 (an oral antidiabetic 128)

Novo-Hydroxyzin a generic company version of hydroxyzine (an antihistamine used as an anti-anxiety drug 67)

Novo-Ipramide a generic company version of ipratropium bromide 320 (a *bronchodilator* 76)

Novo-Ketoconazole a generic company version of ketoconazole 325 (an antifungal 124)

Novo-Ketotifen a generic company version of ketotifen (a drug used in asthma 77)

Novo-Levodicarbidopa a generic company version of levodopa/carbidopa 331 (a combination of levodopa 331 and carbidopa for *parkinsonism* 71)

Novo-Levobunolol a generic company version of levobunolol (a beta blocker 83 and drug for glaucoma 156)

Novolin ge NPH a product name for insulin NPH (a drug for diabetes 128)

Novo-Loperamide a generic company version of loperamide 338 (an antidiarrheal 96)

Novo-Lorazem a generic company version of lorazepam 341 (a benzodiazepine anti-anxiety drug 67 and sleeping drug 66)

Novo-Maprotiline a generic company version of maprotiline (an antidepressant 68)

Novo-Medopa a generic company version of methyldopa 354 (an antihypertensive drug 88)

Novo-Medrone a generic company version of medroxyprogesterone 345 (a female sex *hormone* 133)

Novo-Metformin a product name or metformin 351 (drug for diabetes 128)

Novo-Methacin a generic company version of indomethacin (a non-steroidal anti-inflammatory 102)

Novo-Metoprol a generic company version of metoprolol 354 (a beta blocker 83)

Novo-Mexiletine a generic company version of mexiletine (an anti-arrhythmic 86)

Novo-Minocycline a generic company version of minocycline 361 (an *antibiotic* 114)

Novo-Misoprostol Tablets a generic company version of misoprostol 364 (an anti-ulcer drug 95)

Novo-Nifedin a product name for nifedipine 372 (a calcium channel blocker 87)

Novo-Norfloxacin a generic company version of norfloxacin 375 (a fluoroquinolone antibiotic 115)

Novo-Nortriptyline a generic company version of nortriptyline (a tricyclic antidepressant 68)

Novo-Oxybutynin a generic company version of oxybutynin 383 (an *anticholinergic* and *antispasmodic* for urinary disorders 154)

Novo-Pen VK a generic company version of penicillin V 386 (a penicillin antibiotic 114)

Novo-Peridol LA a generic company version of haloperidol 309 (an antipsychotic 69)

Novo-Pirocam a generic company version of piroxicam 393 (a non-steroidal anti-inflammatory 102)

Novo-Prazin a generic company version of prazosin (a *sympatholytic* antihypertensive 88)

Novo-Prednisone a generic company version of prednisone 399 (a corticosteroid 127)

Novo-Profen a generic company version of ibuprofen 315 (a non-*opioid analgesic* 64 and non-steroidal anti-inflammatory 102)

Novo Rapid a product name for insulin aspart (a drug for diabetes 128)

Novo-Salmol a generic company version of salbutamol 429 (a *bronchodilator* 76)

Novo-Semide Tab a generic company version of furosemide 299 (a diuretic 85 and antihypertensive drug 88)

Novo-Sertraline a generic company version of sertraline 432 (an antidepressant 68)

Novo-Sundac a generic company version of sulindac (a non-steroidal anti-inflammatory 102)

Novo-Temazepam a generic company version of temazepam 443 (a benzodiazepine sleeping drug 66)

Novo-Terazosin a generic company version of terazosin 444 (a *sympatholytic* antihypertensive 88)

THE DRUG FINDER

NOVO-TERBINAFINE–PEPCID

Novo-Terbinafine a generic company version of terbinafine 445 (an antifungal 124)

Novo-Theophyl SR a generic company version of theophylline 449 (a *bronchodilator* 76)

Novo-Tiaprofenic a generic company version of tiaprofenic acid (a non-steroidal anti-inflammatory 102)

Novo-Trazodone a generic company version of trazodone (an antidepressant 68)

Novo-Tripamine a generic company version of imipramine 316 (an antidepressant 68 and drug for urinary disorders 154)

Novo-Valproic a generic company version of valproic acid 458 (an antiepileptic 70)

Novo-Veramil a generic company version of verapimil 462 (an antihypertensive 88 and calcium channel blocker 87)

Novo-Zopiclone a generic company version of zopiclone 467 (a sleeping drug 66)

Nozinan a product name for methotrimeprazine (an antipsychotic 69)

Nu-Acyclovir a generic company version of acyclovir 178 (an antiviral 119)

Nu-Alpraz a generic company version of alprazolam 185 (a benzodiazepine anti-anxiety drug 67)

Nu-Amilazide a generic company version of a combination of amiloride 189 and hydrochlorothiazide 311 (diuretic drugs 85)

Nu-Amoxi a generic company version of amoxicillin 193 (a penicillin *antibiotic* 114)

Nu-Ampi a generic company version of ampicillin (a penicillin *antibiotic* 114)

Nu-Atenol a generic company version of atenolol 199 (a beta blocker 83)

Nu-Baclo a generic company version of baclofen 205 (a muscle relaxant 106)

Nubain a product name for nalbuphine (an *opioid analgesic* 64)

Nu-Buspirone a generic company version of buspirone 216 (an anti-anxiety drug 67)

Nu-Cefaclor a generic company version of cefaclor 220 (an *antibiotic* 114)

Nu-Cephalex a generic company version of cephalexin 224 (a cephalosporin *antibiotic* 114)

Nu-Cimet a generic company version of cimetidine 230 (an anti-ulcer drug 95)

Nu-Clonazepam a generic company version of clonazepam 239 (a benzodiazepine anti-anxiety drug 67 and antiepileptic 70)

Nu-Clonidine a product name for clonidine (an antihypertensive 88)

Nu-Cloxi a generic company version of cloxacillin 242 (a penicillin *antibiotic* 114)

Nu-Cotrimox a product name for co-trimoxazole

Nu-Cromolyn a generic company version of sodium cromoglycate 436 (an anti-allergy drug 109)

Nu-Cyclobenzaprine a generic company version of cyclobenzaprine 247 (a muscle relaxant 106)

Nu-Desipramine a generic company version of desipramine (a tricyclic antidepressant 68)

Nu-Diclo a generic company version of diclonefac 250 (a non-steroidal anti-inflammatory 102)

Nu-Diflunisal a generic company version of diflunisal (a non-steroidal anti-inflammatory 102)

Nu-Diltiaz a generic company version of diltiazem 261 (an antihypertensive 88 and calcium channel blocker 87)

Nu-Divalproex a product name for divalproex (an antiepileptic 70)

Nu-Doxycycline a product name for doxycycline 272 (a tetracycline *antibiotic* 114)

Nu-Fenofibrate a generic company version of fenofibrate (a lipid-lowering drug 89)

Nu-Fluoxetine a generic company version of fluoxetine 293 (a tricyclic antidepressant 68)

Nu-Flurbiprofen a generic company version of flurbiprofen (a non-steroidal anti-inflammatory 102)

Nu-Fluvoxamine a generic company version of fluvoxamine 297 (an antidepressant 68)

Nu-Gemfibrozil a generic company version of gemfibrozil 303 (a lipid-lowering drug 89)

Nu-Ibuprofen a generic company version of ibuprofen 315 (a non-*opioid analgesic* 64 and non-steroidal anti-inflammatory 102)

Nu-Indo a generic company version of indomethacin (a non-steroidal anti-inflammatory 102)

Nu-Ipratropium a generic company version of ipratropium bromide 320 (a *bronchodilator* 76)

Nu-Ketocon a generic company version of ketoconazole 325 (an antifungal drug 124)

Nu-Ketoprofen a generic company version of ketoprofen 326 (a non-steroidal anti-inflammatory 102)

Nu-Levocarb a generic company version of levodopa/carbidopa 331 (a combination of levodopa 331 and carbidopa used in the treatment of *parkinsonism* 71)

Nu-Loraz a generic company version of lorazepam 341 (a benzodiazepine anti-anxiety drug 67 and sleeping drug 66)

Nu-Loxapine a generic company version of loxapine (an antipsychotic 69)

Nu-Medopa a generic company version of methyldopa 354 (an antihypertensive drug 88)

Nu-Megestrol a generic company version of megestrol 347 (a female sex *hormone* 133 and anticancer drug 140)

Nu-Metoclopramide a product name for metoclopramide 357 (a gastrointestinal motility regulator and anti-emetic 74)

Nu-Metop a generic company version of metoprolol 354 (a beta blocker 83)

Nu-Moclobemide a generic company version of moclobemide 365 (an antidepressant 68)

Nu-Naprox a generic company version of naproxen 370 (an NSAID 102)

Nu-Nifed a generic company version of nifedipine 372 (a calcium channel blocker 87)

Nu-Nifedipine-PA a product name for nifedipine 372 (a calcium channel blocker 87)

Nu-Nortriptyline a generic company version of nortriptyline (a tricyclic antidepressant 68)

Nu-Oxybutyn a product name for oxybutynin 383 (an *anticholinergic* and *antispasmodic* for urinary disorders 154

Nu-Pen VK a generic company version of penicillin V 386 (a penicillin antibiotic 114)

Nu-Pirox a generic company version of piroxicam 393 (an NSAID 102)

Nu-Pravastatin a generic company version of pravastatin 398 (a lipid-lowering drug 89)

Nu-Prazo a generic company version of prazosin (a *sympatholytic* antihypertensive 88)

Nu-Prochlor a generic company version of prochlorperazine 402 (a phenothiazine anti-emetic 74 and antipsychotic 69)

Nu-Propranolol a generic company version of propranolol 406 (a beta blocker 83)

Nu-Salbutamol a generic company version of salbutamol 429 (a *bronchodilator* 76)

Nu-Selegiline a generic company version of selegiline 431 (an antiparkinonism drug 71)

Nu-Sotalol a generic company version of sotalol (a beta blocker 83)

Nu-Sulfinpyrazone a generic company version of sulfinpyrazone (a drug for gout 105)

Nu-Sulindac a generic company version of sulindac (a non-steroidal anti-inflammatory 102)

Nu-Temazepam a product name for temazepam 443 (a benzodiazepine anti-anxiety drug 67 and sleeping drug 66)

Nu-Terazosin a generic company version of terazosin 444 (a *sympatholytic* antihypertensive 88)

Nu-Terbinafine a generic company version of terbinafine 445 (an antifungal drug 124)

Nu-Tetra a generic company version of tetracycline 448 (an antibiotic 114)

Nu-Tiaprofenic a generic company version of tiaprofenic acid (a non-steroidal anti-inflammatory 102)

Nu-Trazodone a generic company version of trazodone (an antidepressant 68)

Nu-Trazodone-D a generic company version of trazodone (an antidepressant 68)

Nu-Triazide a generic company version of a combination of triamterene 457 and hydrochlorothiazide 311 (diuretic drugs 85)

Nu-Trimipramine a generic company version of trimipramine (a tricyclic antidepressant 68)

Nu-Tripamine a generic company version of imipramine 316 (an antidepressant 68 and drug for urinary disorders 154)

Nutropin a product name for somatropin, a pituitary *hormone* 131 (a synthetic pituitary hormone 131)

Nu-Valproic a generic company version of valproic acid 458 (an antiepileptic drug 70)

Nu-Verap a generic company version of verapimil 462 (an antihypertensive 88 and calcium channel blocker 87)

Nu-Zopiclone a product name for zopiclone 467 (a sleeping drug 66)
Nyaderm a product name for nystatin 376 (an antifungal 124)
nystatin 376 (an antifungal 124)
Nytol a product name for diphenhydramine 263 used as a sleep aid (an antihistamine 110, anti-emetic 74, and antipruritic 161)

O

octocrylene an ingredient of sunscreens 169
octoxynol a spermicidal agent
octreotide a synthetic pituitary *hormone* 131 used to relieve symptoms of cancer of the pancreas
Ocufen a product name for flurbiprofen (a non-steroidal anti-inflammatory 102)
Oesclim a product name for estradiol 281 (a female sex *hormone* 133)
ofloxacin an antibacterial 117
Ogen a product name for estropipate (an estrogen 135)
olanzapine 377 (an antipsychotic 69)
Olestyr a product name for cholestyramine 229 (a lipid-lowering drug 89)
olopatadine an antihistamine 111
olsalazine a drug for ulcerative colitis 98
omalizumab a monoclonal *antibody* 140
omega-3 fatty acids 475 a supplement
omeprazole 378 (an anti-ulcer drug 95)
ondansetron 379 (an anti-emetic 74)
Onsolis a product name for fentanyl 289 (an *analgesic* 64)
opium an extract of poppy seeds; basis for *opioid analgesics* 64
Opticrom a product name for sodium cromoglycate 436 (an anti-allergy drug 109)
Optimine a product name for azatadine (an antihistamine 110)
Optimyxin ointment a combination of polymyxin B and bacitracin zinc (both *antibiotics* 114)
Oracort a product name for triamcinolone (a corticosteroid 127)
Orap a product name for pimozide (an antipsychotic 69)
orciprenaline a *bronchodilator* 76
Orencia a product name for abatacept (a biological response modifier 103)
Orgalutran a product name for ganirelix (a drug for infertility 152)
orlistat 380 (a drug that blocks the action of *enzymes* that digest fats)
Ortho 0.5/35 a product-name oral contraceptive 149 containing ethinyl estradiol 283 (an estrogen 133 and oral contraceptive 149) and norethindrone 374 (a progestin 133)
Ortho 7/7/7 a product-name oral contraceptive 149 containing ethinyl estradiol 283 (an estrogen 133) and norethindrone 374 (a progestin 133)
Ortho-Cept a product-name oral contraceptive 149 containing ethinyl estradiol 283 (an estrogen 133) and desogestrel (a progestin 133)

Ortho-Novum a product-name oral contraceptive 149 containing mestranol (an estrogen 133 and oral contraceptive 149) and norethindrone 374 (a progestin 133)
Os-Cal a product name for calcium carbonate (a calcium salt (a mineral 137) used as an antacid 94)
oseltamivir 381 (an anitiviral drug 119)
Ostoforte a product name for ergocalciferol (a vitamin 135)
Otrivin a product name for xylometazoline 464 (a decongestant 79)
Ovol a product name for simethicone (an antiflatulent 98)
oxaprozin non-steroidal anti-inflammatory 102
oxazepam 382 (a benzodiazepine anti-anxiety drug 67)
oxcarbazepine an antiepileptic 70
Oxeze Turbuhaler a product name for formoterol 298 (a *bronchodilator* 76)
Oxpam a product name for oxazepam 382 (an anti-anxiety drug 67)
Oxipar Lotion a product name for coal tar (a substance for psoriasis 166 and eczema 167)
oxprenolol a beta blocker 97
Oxsoralen a product name for methoxsalen a drug used in the treatment of psoriasis (166) and atopic dermatitis
Oxsoralen-Ultra a product name for methoxsalen a drug used in the treatment of psoriasis (166) and atopic dermatitis
oxtriphylline a *bronchodilator* 76
oxybenzone a sunscreen 169
oxybuprocaine a local anesthetic 64
oxybutynin 383 (an *anticholinergic* and *antispasmodic* for urinary disorders 154)
oxycodone an *opioid analgesic* 64
OxyContin a product name for oxycodone (an *opioid analgesic* 64)
Oxyderm a product name for benzoyl peroxide 207 (a drug for acne 165)
Oxy.IR a product name for oxycodone (an *opioid analgesic* 64)
oxymetazoline a *topical* decongestant 79
oxymorphone an *opioid analgesic* 64
oxytocin an uterine stimulant 153
Oxytrol a product name for oxybutynin 383 (an *anticholinergic* and *antispasmodic* for urinary disorders 154)
Ozonol a product name for a combination of polymixin B 395, bacitracin (antibiotic drugs 114) and lidocaine (a local anesthetic 64)
Ozurdex a product name for dexamethasone 255 (a corticosteroid 127)

P

paclitaxel an anticancer drug 140
padimate-O an ingredient of sunscreens 169
paliperidone an antipsychotic drug 69
palivizumab an antiviral drug 119
pamidronate a drug for bone disorders 108
pancrealipase a preparation of pancreatic *enzymes* 100
Pancrease a product name for pancrelipase (a preparation of pancreatic *enzymes* 100)

pancreatin a preparation of pancreatic *enzymes* 100
panthenol pantothenic acid 476 (a vitamin 135)
PANTO IV a product name for pantoprazole 384 (an anti-ulcer drug 95)
Pantoloc a product name for pantoprazole 384 (an anti-ulcer drug 95)
pantoprazole 384 (an anti-ulcer drug 95)
pantothenic acid 476 (a vitamin 135)
papaverine a muscle relaxant 106
paraldehyde an antiepileptic 84 used for status epilepticus
Paraplatin-AQ a product name for carboplatin (an anticancer drug 140)
Parnate a product name for tranylcypromine (an MAOI antidepressant 68)
paroxetine 385 (an antidepressant 68)
Parsitan a product name for ethopropazine (drug for parkinsonism 71)
Parvolex a product name for acetylcysteine (a *mucolytic* 94)
Patanol a product name for olopatadine (an antihistamine 111)
Paxil a product name for paroxetine 385 (an antidepressant 68)
Pediatrix a product containing acetaminophen 177 (an *analgesic* 64)
Pegasys a product name for interferon 319 (an antiviral 119 and anticancer drug 140)
Pegasys RBV a product name for a combination of interferon 319 (an antiviral 119 and anticancer drug 140) and ribavirin (an antiviral drug 119)
Pegetron a product name for a combination of interferon 319 (an antiviral 119 and anticancer drug 140)
peginterferon alfa-2a a biological response modifier used in hepatitis B and C 119
peginterferon alfa-2b a biological response modifier used in hepatitis C 119
Peg-Intron a product name for peginterferon alfa-2b (an antiviral 119)
Penbritin a product name for ampicillin (a penicillin *antibiotic* 114)
penciclovir an antiviral 119
penicillamine an antirheumatic 103
penicillin *antibiotics* 114
penicillin G a penicillin *antibiotic* 114
penicillin V 386 (a penicillin *antibiotic* 114)
Penlac a product name for ciclopirox (an antifungal 124)
Pennsaid a product name for diclofenac 258 (an NSAID 102, *analgesic* 64, and drug for gout 105)
Pentacarinat a product name for pentamidine (an antiprotozoal 122)
pentamidine an antiprotozoal 122
Pentamycetin a product name for chloramphenicol 226 (an *antibiotic* 114)
Pentasa a product name for 5-ASA 176 (a drug for inflammatory bowel disease 98)
pentoxifylline a *vasodilator* 98 used to improve blood flow to the limbs in peripheral vascular disease
Pepcid a product name for famotidine 288 (an anti-ulcer drug 95)

PEPCID COMPLETE–QUINIDINE

Pepcid Complete a combination product name containing famotidine 288 (an anti-ulcer drug 95), calcium carbonate 137, and magnesium hydroxide 344 (an antacid 94)

Pepto-Bismol a product name for bismuth subsalicylate 211 (an antacid and adsorbent 94)

Percocet a product name for oxycodone (an *opioid analgesic* 64) and acetaminophen 177 (a non-*opioid* analgesic 64)

Pergonal a product name for menotropins (a drug for infertility 152)

pericyazine an antipsychotic 69

Peridex a product name for chlorhexidine (a skin *antiseptic* 163)

perindopril 387 (an ACE inhibitor 84)

Periostat a product name for doxycycline 272 (an antibiotic 114)

permethrin 388 (a *topical* antiparasitic 164)

perphenazine a phenothiazine antipsychotic 69

Persantine a product name for dipyridamole 265 (an antiplatelet drug 89)

Peru balsam an *antiseptic* 163 for hemorrhoids

Pharmorubicin PFS a product name for epirubicin (a *cytotoxic* anticancer drug 140)

Phazyme a product name for simethicone (an antiflatulent 98)

phenelzine an MAOI antidepressant 68

Phenobarb a product name for phenobarbital 389 (an antiepileptic drug 70)

phenobarbital 389 (a barbiturate antiepileptic 70)

phenol an *antiseptic* used in throat lozenges and sprays 163

phentolamine an antihypertensive 102

phenylephrine a decongestant 79

phenytoin 390 (an antiepileptic 70)

pHisoHex a product name for hexachlorophene (a skin *antiseptic* 163)

PHL Dialproex a generic company version of valproic acid 458 (an antiepileptic drug 70)

phosphorus a mineral 137

phytomenadione vitamin K 482 (a vitamin 135)

phytonadione vitamin K 482 (a vitamin 135)

picosulfate sodium a laxative 97

pilocarpine 391 (a miotic for glaucoma 156)

Pilopine HS a product name for pilocarpine 391 (a miotic for glaucoma 156)

pimecrolimus a drug for dermatitis 167

pimozide an antipsychotic 69

pioglitazone 392 (a drug for diabetes 128)

piperacillin a penicillin *antibiotic* 114

piperonyl butoxide used to treat pediculosis and scabies 164

Piportil L4 a product name for pipotiazine (an antipsychotic 69)

pipotiazine an antipsychotic 69

Pipracil a product name for piperacillin (a penicillin *antibiotic* 114)

piroxicam 393 (a non-steroidal anti-inflammatory 102)

pizotifen 394 (a drug for migraine 73)

Plan B a product name for levonorgestrel 333 (a female sex *hormone* 133) used as emergency contraception

Plaquenil a product name for hydroxychloroquine (an antimalarial 123 and antirheumatic 103)

Plavix a product name for clopidogrel 240 (an antiplatelet drug 90)

Plendil a product name for felodipine (an antihypertensive 88 and calcium channel blocker 87)

PMS-Atenolol a generic company version of atenolol 199 (a beta blocker 83)

PMS-Baclofen a generic company version of baclofen 205 (a muscle relaxant 106)

PMS-Bromocriptine a generic company version of bromocriptine (a pituitary agent 131 and drug for *parkinsonism* 71)

PMS-Buspirone a generic company version of buspirone 216 (an anti-anxiety drug 67)

PMS-Carvedilol a generic company version of carvedilol 219 (a beta blocker 83)

PMS-Cefaclor a generic company version of cefaclor 220 (an antibiotic 114)

PMS-Cetirizine a generic company version of cetirizine 225 (an antihistamine 110)

PMS-Chloral Hydrate a generic company version of chloral hydrate (a sleeping drug 66)

PMS-Cholestyramine a generic company version of cholestyramine 229 (a lipid-lowering drug 89)

PMS-Clonazepam a generic company version of clonazepam 239 (a benzodiazepine antiepileptic 70)

PMS-Desipramine a generic company version of desipramine (a tricyclic antidepressant 68)

PMS-Dexamethasone a generic company version of dexamethasone 255 (a corticosteroid 127)

PMS-Diclofenac a generic company version of diclonefac 258 (a non-steroidal anti-inflammatory 102)

PMS-Dipivefrin a generic company version of dipivefrin (a *sympathomimetic* for glaucoma 156)

PMS-Dopazide a generic company version of methyldopa 354 (an antihypertensive 889) and hydrochlorothiazide 311 (a thiazide diuretic 85)

PMS-Fluphenazine a generic company version of fluphenazine (an phenothiazine antipsychotic 69)

PMS-Flutamide a product name for flutamide 295 (an anticancer drug 140)

PMS-Fluvoxamine a generic company version of fluvoxamine 297 (an antidepressant 68)

PMS-Gabapentin a generic company version of gabapentin 300 (an antiepileptic 70)

PMS-Gemfibrozil a generic company version of gemfibrozil 303 (a lipid-lowering drug 89)

PMS-Hydrocodone a generic company version of hydrocodone 312 (a cough suppressant 80)

PMS Hydroxyzine a generic company version of hydroxyzine (an antihistamine used as an anti-anxiety drug 67)

PMS-Indapamide a generic company version of indapamide 317 (a thiazide-like diuretic 85)

PMS-ISMN a generic company version of mononitrate (a *vasodilator* 84 and anti-angina drug 87)

PMS-Isoniazid a generic company version of isoniazid 322 (an antituberculous drug 134)

PMS-Isosorbide a generic company version of isosorbide dinitrate 323 (a *vasodilator* 84 and anti-angina drug 87)

PMS-lactulose a generic company version of lactulose 327 (an osmotic laxative 113)

PMS Lindane Lotion a generic company version of Lindane (also called gamma benzene hexachloride) used to treat pediculosis and scabies 164

PMS-Levobunolol a generic company version of levobunolol (a beta blocker 83 and drug for glaucoma 156)

PMS-Loperamide a generic company version of loperamide 338 (an antidiarrheal 96)

PMS-Loxapine a generic company version of loxapine (an antipsychotic 69)

PMS-Mefenamic Acid a generic company version of mefenamic acid (a non-steroidal anti-inflammatory 102)

PMS-Methylphenidate a generic company version of methylphenidate 355 (a drug for hyperactivity in children 72)

PMS-Metoprolol-B a generic company version of metoprolol 354 (a beta blocker 83)

PMS-Misoprostol a generic company version of misoprostol 364 (an anti-ulcer drug 95)

PMS-Moclobemide a generic company version of moclobemide 365 (an antidepressant 68)

PMS-Nifedipine a generic company version of nifedipine 372 (an anti-angina 87 and antihypertensive drug 88)

PMS-Nortriptyline a generic company version of nortriptyline (a tricyclic antidepressant 68)

PMS-Nystatin a generic company version of nystatin 376 (an antifungal 124)

PMS-Oxybutynin a generic company version of oxybutynin 383 (an *anticholinergic* and *antispasmodic* for urinary disorders 154)

PMS-Prochlorperazine a generic company version of prochlorperazine 402 (an antipsychotic 69 and anti-emetic drug 74)

PMS-Procyclidine a generic company version of procyclidine 403 (a drug for parkinsonism 71)

PMS-Promethazine a generic company version of promethazine 405 (an antihistamine 110 and anti-emetic drug 74)

PMS-Raloxifene a generic company version of raloxifene 415 (a drug for bone disorders 108)

PMS-Risedronate a generic company version of risedronate 421 (a drug for bone disorders 108)

PMS-Rivastigmine a generic company version of rivastigmine 425 (a drug for dementia 71)

PMS-Sodium Cromoglycate a generic company version of sodium cromoglycate

436 (an anti-allergy drug 109 used to prevent asthma attacks 77)

PMS-Sotalol a generic company version of sotalol (a beta blocker 83)

PMS-Temazepam a generic company version of temazepam 443 (a benzodiazepine anti-anxiety drug 67 and sleeping drug 66)

PMS-Terazosin a generic company version of terazosin 444 (a *sympatholytic* antihypertensive 88)

PMS-Terbinafine a generic company version of terbinafine 445 (an antifungal 124)

PMS-Tiaprofenic a generic company version of tiaprofenic acid (a non-steroidal anti-inflammatory 102)

PMS-Timolol a generic company version of timolol 451 (a beta blocker 83 and drug for glaucoma 156)

PMS-Trazodone a generic company version of trazodone (an antidepressant 68)

PMS-Valproic Acid a product name for valproic acid 458 (an antiepileptic 70)

podophyllin a *topical* treatment for genital warts

Polycitra-K a product name for potassium citrate (a drug used in the treatment of low potassium)

polyethylene glycol a laxative 97

polymixin B 395 (an antibiotic 114)

Polysporin ear drops a product name combination of polymyxin B and gramiacidin (both *antibiotics* 114, 159)

Polysporin ointment a product name combination of polymyxin B and bacitracin zinc (both *antibiotics* 114)

polyvinyl alcohol an ingredient of artificial tear preparations 160

Pontocaine a product name for tetracaine (also known as amethocain, a local anesthetic 64)

Portia a product name for an oral contraceptive 149

posaconazole an antifungal drug 124

potassium 476 (a mineral 137)

potassium bicarbonate an antacid 94

potassium citrate a drug used in the treatment of low potassium

potassium iodide a drug used for overactive thyroid before surgery

potassium permanganate a skin *antiseptic* 163

povidone-iodine a skin *antiseptic* 163

Pradax a product name for dabigatran etexilate 250 (an anticoagulant drug 90)

pralidoxime mesylate *antidote* for organophosphorus poisoning

pramipexole 396 (a drug for *parkinsonism* 71)

Pramox HC a combination drug with hydrocortisone 313 (a corticosteroid 127 and antipruritic 161) and pramoxine (a local anesthetic 64)

Pramoxine a local anesthetic 161

prasugrel 397 (an antiplatelet drug 90)

Pravachol a product name for pravastatin 398 (a lipid-lowering drug 89)

pravastatin 398 (a lipid-lowering drug 89)

praziquantel an anthelmintic 125 for tapeworms

prazosin a *sympatholytic* antihypertensive 88 also used to relieve urinary obstruction 154

Pred Forte a product name for prednisolone 395 (a corticosteroid 127)

Pred Mild a product name for prednisolone 395 (a corticosteroid 127)

Prednicarbate a *topical* corticosteroid 162

prednisone 399 (a corticosteroid 127)

prednisolone the active form of prednisone 399 (a corticosteroid 127)

pregabalin 400 (an antiepileptic 70)

Prevacid a product name for lansoprazole 329 (an anti-ulcer drug 95)

Prevex HC a product name for hydrocortisone 313 (a corticosteroid 127 and antipruritic 161)

Prezista a product name for darunavir (an antiretroviral drug used in the treatment of HIV and AIDS 144)

prilocaine a local *anesthetic* 64

primaquine an antimalarial 123 and antiprotozoal 122

Primaquine sulfate a product name for primaquine (an antimalarial 123 and antiprotozoal 122)

Primaxim a product name for imipenem (an *antibiotic* 114) with cilastatin (used to make imipenem more effective)

primidone an antiepileptic 70

Prinivil a product name for lisinopril 336 (an ACE inhibitor 98)

Pristiq a product name for venlafaxine 461 (an antidepressant 68)

probenecid 401 (a uricosuric for gout 105)

Probeta a combination of levobunolol (a beta blocker 83 and drug for glaucoma 156) and dipivefrin (a *sympathomimetic* for glaucoma 156)

procainamide an anti-arrhythmic 86

Procan-SR a product name for procainamide (an anti-arrhythmic 86)

prochlorperazine 402 (a phenothiazine anti-emetic 74 and antipsychotic 69)

Proctodan HC a combination drug with hydrocortisone 313 (a corticosteroid 127 and antipruritic 161) and pramoxine (a local anesthetic 64)

Proctofoam HC a combination drug with hydrocortisone 313 (a corticosteroid 127 and antipruritic 161) and other drugs

procyclidine 403 (an *anticholinergic* for *parkinsonism* 71)

Procytox a product name for cyclophosphamide 246 (an anticancer drug 140)

Pro-Fluoxetine a product name for fluoxetine 293 (an antidepressant drug 68)

progesterone a female sex *hormone* 133

progestin a female sex *hormone* 133

Prograf a product name for tacrolimus (an immunosuppressant 143)

proguanil 400 (an antimalarial 123)

Prolia a product name for denosumab 253 (a human monoclonal *antibody* 141)

Prolopa a product name for levodopa/benserazide (a combination of levodopa 331 and benserazide for *parkinsonism* 71)

Proloprim a product name for trimethoprim 444 (an antibacterial 117)

promethazine 405 (an antihistamine 110 and anti-emetic 74)

Prometrium a product name for progesterone (a female sex *hormone* 133)

Pronestyl-SR a product name for procainamide (an anti-arrhythmic 86)

propafenone an anti-arrhythmic 86

Propecia a product name for finasteride 291 (a drug for benign prostatic hypertrophy)

Propine a product name for dipivefrin (a *sympathomimetic* for glaucoma 156)

propranolol 406 (a beta blocker 83)

propylthiouracil 407 (an antithyroid drug 130)

Propyl-Thyracil a product name for propylthiouracil 407 (an antithyroid drug 130)

Proscar a product name for finasteride 291 (a drug for benign prostatic hypertrophy)

Prostin VR a product name for alprostadil 186 (a *prostaglandin* used for male impotence 134, 152)

protirelin test of thyroid function

Protopic a product name for tacrolimus (an immunosuppressant 143)

Pro-Triazide a product name for a combination of triamterene 457 and hydrochlorothiazide 311 (diuretic drugs 85)

Protylol a product name for dicyclomine 259 (drug for irritable bowel syndrome 96)

Provera a product name for medroxyprogesterone 345 (a female sex hormone 133)

Proviodine a product name for povidone-iodine (a skin *antiseptic* 163)

Prozac a product name for fluoxetine 293 (an antidepressant 68)

pseudoephedrine 408 (a decongestant 79)

Psyllium 409 (a laxative 97)

Pulmicort a product name for budesonide 213 (a corticosteroid 127)

Pulmozyme a product name for dornase alfa (a drug for cystic fibrosis 80)

Pumicort Nebuamp a product name for budesonide 213 (a corticosteroid 127)

Puregon a product name for follitropin beta (a drug for infertility 152)

Purinethol a product name for mercaptopurine 350 (an anticancer drug 140)

pyrantel a drug used in the treatment of intestinal worms, such as pinworms (125)

pyrazinamide an antituberculous drug 118

pyridostigmine 410 (a drug for myasthenia gravis 107)

pyridoxine another name for vitamin B6 477 (a vitamin 135)

pyrimethamine 411 (an antimalarial 123)

pyrvinium pamoate a drug used in the treatment of pinworms (125)

Q

quetiapine 412 (an antipsychotic 69)

quinapril an ACE inhibitor 98

quinidine 413 (an anti-arrhythmic drug 86)

QUINIDINE SULFATE–SEPTRA

quinidine sulfate quinidine 413 (an anti-arrhythmic drug 86)

quinine 414 (an antimalarial 123 and muscle relaxant 106)

Quinine-Odan a product name for quinine 414 (an antimalarial 123 and muscle relaxant 106)

Qvar a product name for beclomethasone 206 (a corticosteroid 127)

R

radioactive iodine see iodine

Ralivia a product name for tramadol 456 (an *opioid analgesic* 64)

raloxifene 415 (a selective estrogen *receptor* modulator 133 for osteoporosis 108)

raltegravir an antiretroviral drug used in the treatment of HIV and AIDS 144

ramipril 416 (an ACE inhibitor 98)

RAN-Carvedilol a product name for carvedilol 219 (a beta blocker 83)

RAN-Cefprozil a product name for cefprozil 221 (an antibiotic 114)

R and C II Shampoo/Conditioner a product name for piperonyl butoxide (used in the treatment of pediculosis and scabies 164)

R and C II Spray a product name for piperonyl butoxide (used in the treatment of pediculosis and scabies 164)

ranitidine 417 (an anti-ulcer drug 95)

rasagiline 418 (used for parkinsonism 71)

Rasilez a product name for aliskiren 183 (an antihypertensive drug 88)

Rasilez HCT a product name for a combination of aliskiren 183 (an antihypertensive drug 88) and hydrochlorothiazide 311 (a diuretic drug 85)

ratio-Aclavulanate a product name for amoxicillin/clavulinic acid (a combination of amoxicillin 193 (a penicillin *antibiotic* 114) and clavulinic acid (a substance given with it to make amoxicillin more effective)

ratio-Amiodarone a generic company version of amiodarone 190 (an antiarrhythmic 86)

ratio-Atenolol a generic company version of atenolol 199 (a beta blocker 83)

ratio-Baclofen a generic company version of baclofen 205 (a muscle relaxant 106)

ratio-Brimonidine a product name for brimonidine (a drug for glaucoma 156)

ratio-Buspirone a generic company version of buspirone 216 (an anti-anxiety drug 67)

ratio-Calmydone a combination of doxylamine (an antihistamine 110), hydrocodone 312 (a cough suppressant 80), and etafedrine (a decongestant 79)

ratio-Carvedilol a product name for carvedilol 219 (a beta blocker 83)

ratio-Clobazam a generic company version of clobazam (a benzodiazepine drug used as a antiepileptic 70)

ratio-Clobetasol a generic company version of clobetasol 236 (a *topical* corticosteroid 162)

ratio-Clonazepam a generic company version of clonazepam 239 (a benzodiazepine antiepileptic 70)

ratio-Codeine a generic company version of codeine 244 (an *opioid analgesic* 64)

ratio-Colchicine a generic company version of colchicine 245 (a drug for gout 105)

ratio-Coristex-DH a combination product with phenylephrine (a decongestant 79) and hydrocodone 312 (a cough suppressant 80)

ratio-Cyclobenzapine a generic company version of cyclobenzapine (a muscle relaxant 106)

ratio-Desipramine a generic company version of desipramine (a tricyclic antidepressant 68)

ratio-Dexamethasone a generic company version of dexamethasone 255 (a corticosteroid 127)

ratio-Doxazosin a generic company version of doxazosin 270 (a *sympatholytic* antihypertensive 88)

ratio-Fentanyl a generic company version of fentanyl 289 (an *analgesic* drug 64)

ratio-Flunisolide a generic company version of flunisolide (a corticosteroid 127)

ratio-Fluoxetine a generic company version of fluoxetine 293 (an antidepressant 68)

ratio-Fluvoxamine a generic company version of fluvoxamine 297 (an antidepressant 68)

ratio-Gentamicin a generic company version of gentamicin 304 (an *antibiotic* 114)

ratio-Indomethacin a generic company version of indomethacin (a non-steroidal anti-inflammatory 102)

ratio-Ipratropium UDV a generic company version of ipratropium bromide 320 (a *bronchodilator* 76)

ratio-Lovastatin a generic company version of lovastatin 343 (a lipid-lowering drug 89)

ratio-Methotrexate a generic company version of methotrexate 353 (an antimetabolite anticancer drug 140)

ratio-Methylphenidate a generic company version of methylphenidate 355 (a nervous system stimulant 72)

ratio-Morphine a generic company version of morphine 368 (an *opioid analgesic* 64)

ratio-MPA a generic company version of medroxyprogesterone 345 (a female sex hormone 133)

ratio-Nortriptyline a generic company version of nortriptyline (a tricyclic antidepressant 68)

ratio-Nystatin a generic company version of nystatin 376 (an antifungal drug 124)

ratio-Oxycodone a generic company version of oxycodone (an *opioid analgesic* 64)

ratio-Prednisolone a generic company version of prednisolone 395 (a corticosteroid 127)

ratio-Risperidone a generic company version of risperidone 422 (an antipsychotic drug 69)

ratio-Salbutamol HFA a generic company version of salbutamol 429 (a *bronchodilator* 76)

ratio-Sertraline a generic company version of sertraline 432 (an antidepressant 68)

ratio-Sildenafil R a generic company version of sildenafil 433 (a drug for erectile dysfunction 152)

ratio-Terazosin a generic company version of terazosin 444 (a *sympatholytic* antihypertensive 88)

ratio-Topilene a generic company version of betamethasone 209 (a corticosteroid 127)

ratio-Trazodone a generic company version of trazodone (an antidepressant 68)

ratio-Triacomb a combination of nystatin 376 (a drug for fungal infections 124), gramicidin and neomycin sulfate (both *antibiotic*s 114), and triamcinolone acetonide (a corticosteroid 127)

ratio-Valproic a generic company version of valproic acid 458 (an antiepileptic 70)

ratio-Zopiclone a generic company version of zopiclone 467 (a sleeping drug 66)

Reactine a product name for cetirizine 225 (an antihistamine 110)

Reactine Allergy and Sinus a product name for a combination of cetirizine 225 (an antihistamine 110) and pseudoephedrine 408 (a decongestant 79)

Rebif a product name for interferon beta-1a (a drug used for the treatment of multiple sclerosis)

Rectogel HC a product name combination product with hydrocortisone 313 (a corticosteroid 127), benzocaine (an *anesthetic* 64), and zinc sulfate monohydrate

Rejuva-A a product name for tretinoin (a drug for acne 165)

Relenza a product name for zanamivir 465 (an antiviral drug 119)

Relpax a product name for eletriptan (a drug for migraine 73)

Remeron a product name for mirtazapine 363 (an antidepressant 68)

Remicade a product name for infliximab (a biological response modifier for rheumatoid arthritis 103 and Crohn's disease 98)

Renedil a product name for felodipine (an antihypertensive 88 and calcium channel blocker 87)

Renova a product name for tretinoin (a drug for acne 165)

repaglinide 419 (a drug for diabetes 128)

ReQuip a product name for ropinirole (a drug for *parkinsonism* 71)

Rescriptor a product name for delavirdine (an antiretroviral drug used in the treatment of HIV and AIDS 144)

resorcinol a keratolytic mainly for acne 165

Restasis a product name for cyclosporine 249 (an immunosuppressant drug 143)

Restoril a product name for temazepam 443 (a benzodiazepine sleeping drug 66)

Retin-A a product name for tretinoin (a drug for acne 165)

Retin-A Micro a product name for tretinoin (a drug for acne 165)

retinoic acid vitamin A 479 (a vitamin 135)

retinol vitamin A 479 (a vitamin 135)

Retrovir a product name for zidovudine 466 (an antiretroviral drug used for the treatment of HIV infection and AIDS 144)

Revatio a product name for sildenafil 433 (drug for impotence 152)

Reyataz a product name for atazanavir (an antiretroviral drug for HIV infection and AIDS 144)

Rhinaris CS Anti-allergic a product name for sodium cromoglycate 436 (an anti-allergy drug 109)

Rhinocort Aqua a product name for budesonide 213 (a corticosteroid 143)

Rhodacine a product name for indomethacin (a non-steroidal anti-inflammatory 102)

Rho-Nitro Pumpspray a product name for nitroglycerin 373 (an anti-angina drug 87)

Rhovane a product name for zopiclone 467 (a sleeping drug 66)

Rhoxal-loperamide a generic company version of loperamide 338 (an antidiarrheal drug 96)

Rhoxal-Sotalol a generic company version of sotalol (a beta blocker 83)

Rhythmol a product name for propafenone (an anti-arrhythmic 86)

ribavirin an antiviral 119

riboflavin 477 (a vitamin 135)

Ridaura a product name for auranofin (a drug used for the treatment of rheumatoid arthritis 117)

rifabutin an antituberculous drug 118

Rifadin a product name for rifampin 420 (an antituberculous drug 118**)**

rifampin 420 (an antituberculous drug 118)

Rifater a combination of isoniazid 322 (an antituberculous drug 118) and rifampin 420 (an antituberculous drug 118)

rilpivirin a drug for HIV 144

Rimso-50 a product name for dimethyl sulfoxide (a drug for urinary infection 154)

risedronate 421 (drug for bone disorders 108)

Risperdal a product name for risperidone 422 (an antipsychotic 69)

risperidone 422 (an antipsychotic 69)

Ritalin a product name for methylphenidate 355 (a drug for hyperactivity in children 72)

ritodrine a uterine muscle relaxant 167

Rituxan a product name for rituximab 423 (an anticancer drug 140)

rituximab 423 (an anticancer drug 140)

Riva-Loperamide a generic company version of loperamide 338 (an antidiarrheal drug 96)

Rivanase AQ a product name for beclomethasone 206 (a corticosteroid 143)

rivaroxaban 424 (an anticoagulant drug 90)

rivastigmine 425 (a drug for Alzheimer's disease 71)

Rivotril a product name for clonazepam 239 (a benzodiazepine anticonvulsant 84)

rizatriptan 426 (drug for migraine 73)

Robaxacet-8 a combination product containing codeine 244 (an *opioid analgesic* 64) with acetaminophen 177 (an analgesic 64) and methocarbamol (a muscle relaxant 106)

Robaxin a product name for methocarbamol (a muscle relaxant 106)

Robaxisal a combination of ASA 198 (a non-*opioid analgesic* 64) and methocarbamol (a muscle relaxant 106)

Robaxisal Extra Strength a combination product with ASA 198 (a non-opioid *analgesic* 64) and methocarbamol (a muscle relaxant 106)

Robitussin DM a product name combination product containing guafenesin (an *expectorant* 80) and dextromorphan 252 (a cough suppressant)

Robitussin Honey Cough DM a product name for dextromorphan 252 (a cough suppressant 80)

Rocaltrol a product name for calcitriol 481 (a vitamin 135)

Rofact a product name for rifampin 420 (an antituberculous drug 118)

Rogaine Topical Solution a product name for minoxidil 362 (an antihypertensive 88) used for hair regrowth

Ropinirole a drug for *parkinsonism* 71

rosiglitazone 427 (a drug for diabetes 128)

rosuvastatin 428 (a lipid-lowering drug 89)

Royvac a product name combination product with bisacodyl 210 and magnesium citrate (laxatives 97)

Rythmodan a product name for disopyramide (an anti-arrhythmic 86)

Rythmodan-LA a product name for disopyramide (an anti-arrhythmic 86)

S

Sabril a product name for vigabatrin (an antiepileptic 70)

Saizen a product name for somatropin, a pituitary hormone 131 (a synthetic pituitary hormone 131)

Salagen Tablets a product name for pilocarpine 391 (used in the treatment of dry mouth and dry eyes)

salbutamol 429 (a *bronchodilator* 76)

salicylic acid a keratolytic for acne 165, dandruff 168, psoriasis 166, and warts.

salmeterol 430 (a *bronchodilator* 76)

Salofalk a product name for 5-ASA 176 (a drug for inflammatory bowel disease 98)

Sandimmune IV a product name for cyclosporine 249 (an immunosuppressant 143)

Sandomigran a product name for pizotifen 394 (a drug for migraine 73)

Sandomigran DS a product name for pizotifen 394 (a drug for migraine 73)

Sandostatin a product name for octrotide (a synthetic pituitary *hormone* 131 used to relieve symptoms of cancer of the pancreas)

Sandostatin LAR a product name for octrotide (a synthetic pituitary *hormone* 131 used to relieve symptoms of cancer of the pancreas)

Sandoz Cefprozil a generic company version of cefprozil 221 (an antibiotic 114)

Sandoz Dorzolamide a generic company version of dorzolamide 269 (a drug for glaucoma 156)

Sandoz Dorzolamide/Timolol a generic company version of a combination of dorzolamide 269 and timolol 451 (drugs for glaucoma 156)

Sandoz Famciclovir a generic company version of famciclovir 287 (an antiviral drug 119)

Sandoz Glimepiride a generic company version of glimepiride 306 (a drug used in diabetes 128)

Sandoz Levofloxacin a generic company version of levofloxacin 332 (an antibacterial drug 117)

Sandoz Pioglitazone a generic company version of pioglitazone 392 (a drug for diabetes 128)

Sandoz Rosuvastatin a generic company version of rosuvastatin 428 (a lipid-lowering drug 89)

Sansert a product name for methysergide (a drug for migraine 73)

Saquinavir a drug for HIV/AIDS 144

Sarna HC a product name for hydrocortisone 313 (a corticosteroid 127 and antipruritic 161)

Sativex a product name combination product with cannabidiol and delta-9-tetrahydrocannabinol (cannabis sativa extract) (an *analgesic* used in multiple sclerosis 64)

Scabene Aerosol a product name for piperonyl butoxide (used in the treatment of pediculosis and scabies 164)

scopolamine a drug for prevention of nausea and vomiting 74

Seasonale a product name for an oral contraceptive 149

Seasonique a product name for an oral contraceptive 149

Sebcur a product name for salicylic acid (a keratolytic for acne 165, dandruff 168, psoriasis 166, and warts)

Sebivo a product name for telbivudine (an antiviral 119)

Select 1/35 a product-name oral contraceptive 149 containing ethinyl estradiol 283 and norethindrone 374

selegiline 431 (a drug for severe *parkinsonism* 71)

selenium 478 (a mineral 137)

selenium sulfide a substance for skin inflammation 163 and dandruff 168

Selsun a product-name dandruff shampoo 168 containing selenium sulfide

senna a stimulant laxative 97

Sensorcaine a product name for bupivacaine (a local *anesthetic* 64 used in labour 153)

Sensorcaine with Epinephrine a product name for a combination of epinephrine 276 and bupivacaine (a local *anesthetic* 64)

Septra a product name for sulfamethoxazole-trimethoprim 439 (an antibacterial drug 117)

SERC–TRANS-PLANTAR

Serc a product name for betahistine 208 (a drug for Ménière's disease 74)

Serevent a product name for salmeterol 430 (a *bronchodilator* 76)

Serophene a product name for clomiphene 237 (a drug for infertility 152)

Seroquel a product name for quetiapine 412 (an antipsychotic 69)

Serostim a product name for somatropin, a pituitary *hormone* 131 (a synthetic pituitary hormone 131)

sertraline 432 (an antidepressant 68)

Sibelium a product name for flunarizine (a calcium channel blocker used in the prevention of migraine 73)

Sildenafil 433 (a drug used for the treatment of sexual impotence 152)

silver sulfiadiazine a *topical* antibacterial 117 used to prevent infection in burns

simethicone an antiflatulent 98

Simply Sleep a product name for diphenhydramine 263 (an antihistamine 110, anti-emetic 74, and antipruritic 161)

simvastatin 434 (a lipid-lowering drug 89)

Simulect a product name for basiliximab (an immunosuppressant 143)

Sinemet a product name for levodopa/carbidopa 331 (a combination of levodopa 331 and carbidopa for *parkinsonism* 71)

Singulair a product name for montelukast 367 (a leukotriene *antagonist* for asthma 77)

Sinomet CR a product name for levodopa/carbidopa 331 (a combination of levodopa 331 and carbidopa for *parkinsonism* 71)

Sinutab N.T Extra Strength a product name for a combination of diphenhydramine 263 (an antihistamine 110), acetaminophen 178 (an *analgesic* 64), and pseudoephedrine 408 (a decongestant 79)

Sinutab Sinus and Allergy a combination product with pseudoephedrine 408 (a decongestant 79), acetaminophen 177 (an *analgesic* 64), and chlorpheniramine 228 (an antihistamine 110)

Sinutab with Codeine a combination product containing codeine 244 (an *opioid analgesic* 64) pseudoephedrine 408 (a decongestant 79), acetaminophen 177 (an analgesic 64), and chlorpheniramine 228 (an antihistamine 110)

sitagliptin a drug for diabetes 128

sitagliptin phosphate 435 (an antihyperglycemic drug 128)

Slow-Fe a product name for iron 473 (a mineral 137)

Slow-Fe Folic a product name for folic acid 472 (a vitamin 135) with iron 473 (a mineral 137)

Slow-K a product name for potassium 476 (a mineral 137)

sodium 478 (a mineral 137)

sodium cellulose phosphate an agent used to reduce levels of calcium 462 in the blood

sodium chloride common salt, a source of sodium 478 (a mineral 137)

sodium cromoglycate 436 (an anti-allergy drug 109 used to prevent asthma attacks 77)

sodium ferric gluconate an intravenous iron preparation 473 (a mineral 137)

sodium fluoride 471 (a mineral 137)

Sofracort Sterile Ear/Eye Drops a product name for a combination of dexamethasone 255 (a cortiosteroid 127), framycetin, and gramicidin (antibiotics 114)

Soframycin a product name for framycetin (an *antibiotic* 114)

sofra-Tulle a product name for framycetin (an *antibiotic* 114)

solifenacin a drug used in urinary disorders 154

Solugel a product name for benzoyl peroxide 207 (a drug for acne 165)

Solu-Medrol a product name for methyl-prednisolone 356 (a corticosteroid 127)

Soluver a product name for salicylic acid (a keratolytic for acne 165, dandruff 168, psoriasis 166, and warts)

Somatostatin a drug used in the management of esophageal variceal bleeding

somatropin a synthetic pituitary *hormone* 131

Soriatane a product name for acitretin (a drug for psoriasis 166)

Spiriva a product name for tiotropium 452 (a *bronchodilator* 76)

spironolactone 437 (a potassium-sparing diuretic 85)

Sporanox a product name for itraconazole (an antifungal 124)

Spriafil a product name for posaconazole (an antifungal 124)

Stalevo a product name for a combination of levodopa 331, carbidopa, and entacapone (drugs for parkinsonism 71)

Starlix a product name for nateglinide (a drug for diabetes 128)

stavudine an antiretroviral drug for HIV/AIDS 144

Stieva-A a product name for tretinoin (a drug for acne 165)

Stievamycin a product name for a combination of erythromycin 279 (an *antibiotic* 114) and tretinoin (a drug for acne 165)

Stilamine a product name for somatostatin (a drug used in the management of esophageal variceal bleeding)

stilboestrol see diethylstilbestrol (a female sex *hormone* 133)

Strattera a product name for atomoxatine 196 (a drug for hyperactivity 72)

streptomycin an antituberculous drug 118 and aminoglycoside *antibiotic* 114

Suboxone a product name for a combination of buprenorphine 214 (an opioid *analgesic* 64) and naloxone (an *antidote* for opioid poisoning)

sucralfate 438 (an ulcer-healing drug 95)

Sudafed Decongestant 12 Hour a product name for pseudoephedrine 408 (a decongestant 79)

Sulcrate a product name for sucralfate 438 (an ulcer-healing drug 95)

sulfacetamide a sulfonamide antibacterial 117

sulfadiazine a sulfonamide antibacterial 117

sulfamethoxazole-trimethoprim 439 (an antibacterial drug 117)

sulfinpyrazone a drug for gout 105

sulindac a non-steroidal anti-inflammatory 102

sumatriptan 440 (a drug for migraine 73)

Supeudol a product name for oxycodone (an opioid analgesic 64)

Suprax a product name for cefixime (a cephalosporin *antibiotic* 114)

Suprefact a product name for buserelin (a drug for menstrual disorders 148)

Suprefact Depo a product name for buserelin (a drug used in the treatment of menstrual disorders 148)

Surgam a product name for tiaprofenic acid (a non-steroidal anti-inflammatory 102)

Surgam SR a product name for tiaprofenic acid (a non-steroidal anti-inflammatory 102)

Surmontil a product name for trimipramine (a tricyclic antidepressant 68)

Sustiva a product name for efavirenz 274 (a drug for HIV and immune deficiency 144)

Symbicort Turbuhaler a product name for a combination of formoterol 298 (a *bronchodilator* 76) and budesonide 213 (a corticosteroid 127)

Synagis a product name for palivizumab (an antiviral drug 119)

Synalar a product name for fluocinolon (a *topical* corticosteroid 162)

Synarel a product name for nafarelin (a drug for menstrual disorders 148)

Synphasic a product-name oral contraceptive 149 containing ethinyl estradiol 283 (an estrogen 133) and norethindrone 374 (a progestin 133)

Synthroid a product name for levothyroxine 334 (a thyroid *hormone* 130)

T

tacrolimus an immunosuppressant 143

Tactuo a product name for a combination of benzoyl peroxide 207 and adapalene (drugs for acne 165)

tadalafil a drug used for the treatment of sexual impotence 152

Talwin a product name for pentazocine (an opioid analgesic 64)

Tambocor a product name for flecainide (an anti-arrhythmic 86)

Tamiflu a product name for oseltamavir 381 (an antiviral drug 119)

tamoxifen 441 (an anticancer drug 140)

tamsulosin 442 (an alpha-blocking drug for prostate disorders 134)

Tapazole a product name for methimazole (an antithyroid drug 130)

tapentadol an *opioid analgesic* 65

Tardan a combination of triclosan (a *topical* antimicrobial 161), coal tar, and salicyclic acid

Tarka a product name for verapamil 462 (an antihypertensive 88 and calcium channel blocker 87) and trandolapril (an antihypertensive and an ACE inhibitor 88)

Taro-Sone a product name for betamethasone 209 (a corticosteroid 127)

Taro-Warfarin a product name for warfarin 463 (an anticoagulant drug 90)

Taxol a product name for paclitaxel (an anticancer drug 140)

Taxotere a product name for docetaxel (an anticancer drug 140)

Tazidime a product name for ceftazidime (a cephalosporin *antibiotic* 114)

tazarotene a retinoid (see vitamin A 479) for psoriasis 166

tazobactam an *antibiotic* 114

Tazocin a product name for piperacillin (an *antibiotic* 114) with tazobactam (a substance that increases the effectiveness of piperacillin)

Tazorac a product name for tazarotene (a retinoid (see vitamin A 479) for psoriasis 166)

Tears Naturale a product-name artificial tear preparation containing hydroxypropylmethylcellulose

Tebrazid a product name for pyrazinamide (an antituberculous drug 118)

Tegretol a product name for carbamazepine 218 (an antiepileptic 70)

telbivudine an antiviral drug 119

telithromycin an *antibiotic* 114

telmisartan a *vasodilator* 84 and an antihypertensive drug 88

Telzir a product name for fosamprenavir (a drug for HIV/AIDS 144)

temazepam 443 (a benzodiazepine sleeping drug 66)

Tempra a product name for acetaminophen 177 (an *analgesic* 64)

tenofovir a drug for HIV/AIDS 144

Tenoretic a product name product with a combination of chlorthalidone (a thiazide diuretic 85) and atenolol 199 (a beta blocker 83)

Tenormin a product name for atenolol 199 (a beta blocker 83)

tenoxicam a non-steroidal anti-inflammatory 102

Tequin a product name for gatifloxacin 302 (an antibacterial drug 117)

Terazol a product name for terconazole (an antifungal 124)

terazosin 444 (a *sympatholytic* antihypertensive 88)

terbinafine 445 (an antifungal 124)

terconazole an antifungal drug 124

teriparatide 446 (a drug used in osteoporosis 108)

Tersaseptic a product name for triclosan (a *topical* antimicrobial 161)

testosterone 447 (a male sex *hormone* 132)

tetracaine also known as amethocain, a local *anesthetic* 64

tetracycline 448 (an *antibiotic* 114 and antimalarial 123)

Teva-5 ASA a product name for 5-ASA 176 (a drug for inflammatory bowel disease 98)

Teva-Alendronate a product name for alendronate 181 (a drug for bone disorders 108)

Teva-Allopurinol a product name for allopurinol 184 (a drug for gout 105)

Teva-Alprazolam a product name for alprazolam 185 (an anti-anxiety drug 67)

Teva-Amiodarone a product name for amiodarone 190 (an anti-arrhythmic drug 86)

Teva-Amoloride HCTZ a product name for a combination of amiloride 189 and hydrochlorothiazide 311 (diuretic drugs 85)

Teva-Atenolol a product name for atenolol 199 (a beta blocker 83)

Teva-Azathioprine a product name for azathioprine 203 (an antirheumatic 103 and immunosuppressant drug 143)

Teva-Baclofen a product name for baclofen 205 (a muscle-relaxant drug 106)

Teva-Buspirone a product name for buspirone 216 (an anti-anxiety drug 67)

Teva-Chloroquine a product name for chloroquine 227 (an antimalarial 123 and antirheumatic drug 103)

Teva-Cimetidine a product name for cimetidine 230 (an anti-ulcer drug 95)

Teva-Clindamycin a product name for clindamycin 235 (an antibiotic 116)

Teva-Cloxin a product name for cloxacillin 242 (an antibiotic 114)

Teva-Domperidone a product name for domperidone 267 (an anti-emetic drug 74)

Teva-Enalapril/HTCZ a product name for a combination of enalarpil 275 (an ACE inhibitor 84 and antihypertensive drug 88) and and hydrochlorothiazide 311 (a diuretic 85)

Teva-Lexin a product name for cephalexin 224 (an antibiotic 114)

Teva-Montelukast a product name for montelukast 367 (an anti-allergy drug 109)

Teva-Paroxetine a product name for paroxetine 385 (an antidepressant drug 68)

Teva-Quetiapine a product name for quetiapine 412 (an antipsychotic 69)

Teva-Quinine a product name for quinine 414 (an antimalarial drug 123)

Teva-Rosuvastatin a product name for rosuvastatin 428 (a lipid-lowering drug 89)

Teva-Selegiline a product name for selegiline 431 (an antiparkinonism drug 71)

Teva-Sertraline a product name for sertraline 432 (an antidepressant 68)

Teva-Spironolactone a product name for spironolactone 437 (a diuretic 85)

Teva-Sumatriptan a product name for sumatriptan 440 (a drug for migraine 73)

Teva-Tamoxifen a product name for tamoxifen 441 (an anticancer drug 140)

Teva-Terazosin a product name for terazosin 444 (an antihypertensive 88 and drug for urinary disorders 154)

Teva-Terbinafine a product name for terbinafine 445 (an antifungal drug 124)

Theolair a product name for theophylline 449 (a *bronchodilator* 76)

theophylline 449 (a *bronchodilator* 76)

thiamine 479 (a vitamin 135)

thiopental a fast-acting barbiturate used to induce general anesthesia

thiothixene an antipsychotic 69

Tiamol a product name for fluocinonide (a *topical* corticosteroid 162)

tiaprofenic acid a non-steroidal anti-inflammatory 102

Tiazac a product name for diltiazem 261 (an antihypertensive 88 and calcium channel blocker 87)

ticagrelor 450 (an antiplatelet drug 90)

ticarcillin an *antibiotic* 114

tigecycline an antibiotic 114

Tilade a product name for nedocromil (a drug for asthma 77)

timolol 451 (a beta blocker 83 and drug for glaucoma 156)

Timoptic a product name for timolol 451 (a beta blocker 83 and drug for glaucoma 156)

Timoptic-XE a product name for timolol 451 (a beta blocker 83 and drug for glaucoma 156)

tinidazole an antibacterial 117 and antiprotozoal 122

tinzaparin 305 (an anticoagulant 91)

tiotropium 452 (a *bronchodilator* 76)

tipranavir an antiretroviral drug used in the treatment of HIV and AIDS 144

titanium dioxide an ingredient of sunscreens 169

tizanidine 453 (an antispastic agent 106)

TOBI a product name for tobramycin (an *antibiotic* 114)

Tobradex a combination of dexamethasone 255 (a corticosteroid 127) and tobramycin (an *antibiotic* 114)

tobramycin an aminoglycoside *antibiotic* 114

tocopherol vitamin E 481 (a vitamin 135)

tocopheryl acetate vitamin E 481 (a vitamin 135)

tolnaftate an antifungal 124

Toloxin a product name for digoxin 260 (a digitalis drug 82)

tolterodine 454 (an *anticholinergic* and *antispasmodic* for urinary disorders 154)

Topamax a product name for topiramate 455 (an antiepileptic 70, a drug for migraine 73)

Topicort a product name for desoximet-asone (a *topical* corticosteroid 162)

topiramate 455 (an antiepileptic 70, a drug for migraine 73)

Topsyn a product name for fluocinonide (a *topical* corticosteroid 162)

Tramacet a combination product containing tramadol 456 (an *opioid analgesic* 64) with acetaminophen 177 (an analgesic 64)

tramadol 456 (an *opioid analgesic* 64)

tranexamic acid an antifibrinolytic used to promote blood clotting 90

Transderm-Nitro a product name for nitroglycerin 373 (an anti-angina drug 87)

Trans-Plantar a product name for salicylic acid (a keratolytic for acne 165, dandruff 168, psoriasis 166, and warts)

TRANS VER SAL–ZYVOXAM

Trans Ver Sal a product name for salicylic acid (a keratolytic for acne 165, dandruff 168, psoriasis 166, and warts)

tranylcypromine an MAOI antidepressant 68

trastuzumab an anticancer drug 140

Travatan a product name for travoprost (a drug for glaucoma 156)

travoprost a drug for glaucoma 156

trazodone an antidepressant 68

Trelstar a product name for triptorelin (a drug for menstrual disorders 148)

Trental a product name for pentoxifylline (a *vasodilator* 98)

tretinoin a drug for acne 165

triamcinolone a corticosteroid 127

Triaderm a product name for triamcinolone (a corticosteroid 127)

Triaminic Cold and Cough a product name for a combination of dextromethorphan 256 (a cough suppressant and pseudoephedrine 408 (a decongestant 79)

Triaminic Pediatric Oral Cold Drops a product name for pseudoephedrine 408 (a decongestant 79)

triamterene 457 (a potassium-sparing diuretic 85)

Triatec-8 a combination product containing codeine 244 (an *opioid analgesic* 64) with acetaminophen 177 (an analgesic 64), and caffeine.

Triatec-30 a combination product containing codeine 244 (an *opioid analgesic* 64) with acetaminophen 177 (an analgesic 64).

Tridural a product name for tramadol 456 (an *opioid analgesic* 64)

trifluridine an antiviral drug 119

Trilafon a product name for perphenazine (a phenothiazine antipsychotic 69)

Trileptal a product name for oxcarbazepine (an antiepileptic 70)

trimeprazine an antihistamine 124

trimipramine a tricyclic antidepressant 68

Trinalin a combination of azatadine (an antihistamine 110) and pseudoephedrine 408 (a decongestant 79)

triptorelin a drug for menstrual disorders 148

Triquilar a product name for a combination of levonorgestrel 333 and ethinyl estradiol 283 (female sex *hormones* 133 and oral contraceptives 149)

tropicamide a *mydriatic* 158

Trosec a product name for trospium (a drug used in urinary disorders 154)

trospium a drug used in urinary disorders 154

Trusopt a product name for dorzolamide 269 (a carbonic anhydrase inhibitor for glaucoma 156)

Truvada a product name combination of emtricitabine and tenofovir (drugs used for HIV and AIDS 144)

tryptophan an antidepressant 68

T-Stat a combination of erythromycin 279 (an *antibiotic* 114) and ethyl alcohol

Tussionex a product name for a combination of hydrocodone 312 (a cough suppressant 80) and phenyltoloxamine (an antihistamine 110)

Twinject Auto-Injector a product name for epinephrine 276 (an anti-allergy drug 109)

Twynsta a product name for a combination of amlodipine 192 (an anti-angina 87 and antihypertensive drug 88) and telmisartan (a *vasodilator* 84 and an antihypertensive drug 88)

Tygacil a product name for tigecycline (an antibiotic 114)

Tylenol a product name for acetaminophen 177 (an *analgesic* 64)

Tylenol Allergy Sinus a combination product with pseudoephedrine 408 (a decongestant 79), acetaminophen 177 (an *analgesic* 64), and chlorpheniramine 228 (an antihistamine 110)

Tylenol Cold a product name for a combination of chlorpheniramine 228 (an antihistamine 110), acetaminophen 178 (an *analgesic* 64), and pseudoephedrine 408 (a decongestant 79)

Tylenol Cold Suspension Children's a combination product containing pseudoephedrine 408 (a decongestant 79), acetaminophen 177 (an *analgesic* 64), and chlorpheniramine 228 (an antihistamine 110)

Tylenol Elixir with Codeine a combination product containing codeine 244 (an *opioid analgesic* 64) with acetaminophen 177 (an analgesic 64)

Tylenol No. 1 a combination product containing codeine 244 (an *opioid analgesic* 64) with acetaminophen 177 (an analgesic 64), and caffeine

Tylenol No.1 Forte a combination product containing codeine 244 (an *opioid analgesic* 64) with acetaminophen 177 (an analgesic 64), and caffeine

Tylenol No. 2 with Codeine a combination product containing codeine 244 (an *opioid analgesic* 64) with acetaminophen 177 (an analgesic 64), and caffeine

Tylenol No. 4 with Codeine a combination product containing codeine 244 (an *opioid analgesic* 64) with acetaminophen 177 (an analgesic 64)

U

Ultradol a product name for etodolac (a non-steroidal anti-inflammatory drug 102)

Ultram a product name for tramadol 456 (an *opioid analgesic* 65)

Ultramop capsules a product name for methoxsalen (a drug used in the treatment of psoriasis (166) and atopic dermatitis)

Ultramop lotion a product name for methoxsalen (a drug used in the treatment of psoriasis (166) and atopic dermatitis)

Uniphyl a product name for theophylline 449 (a *bronchodilator* 76)

Unisom a product name for diphenhydramine 263 (an antihistamine 110, anti-emetic 74, and antipruritic 161)

Unisom-2 a product name for doxylamine

succinate (a drug used to aid sleep 66, and an antihistamine 110)

Urispas a product name for flavoxate (a urinary *antispasmodic* 154)

urofollitropin a drug for pituitary disorders 147

Uromax a product name for oxybutynin 383 (a drug used in urinary disorders 154)

Urozide a product name for hydrochlorothiazide 311 (a diuretic drug 85)

Urso a product name for ursodiol (a drug for cholestatic liver disease 100)

ursodeoxycholic acid a substance present in bile used to treat gallstones 100

Ursodiol a drug for cholestatic liver disease 100

ustekinumab a drug for psoriasis 166

V

Vagifem a product name for estradiol 281 (an estrogen 135)

valacyclovir an antiviral 119

Valcyte a product name for valganciclovir (an antiviral 144 used for cytomegalovirus)

valganciclovir an antiviral 144 used for cytomegalovirus

Valisone a product name for betamethasone 209 (a corticosteroid 127)

Valium 5 Tab a product name for diazepam 257 (an anti-anxiety 67, muscle relaxant 106, and antiepileptic drug 70)

valproic acid 458 (an antiepileptic 70 and an antimanic drug 69)

valsartan 459 (a *vasodilator* 84 and antihypertensive drug 88)

Valtrex a product name for valacyclovir (an antiviral 119)

Vancocin a product name for vancomycin (an *antibiotic* 114)

vancomycin an *antibiotic* 114

vardenafil a drug used for the treatment of erectile dysfunction 152

varenicline 460 (a drug used in smoking cessation)

Vasotec a product name for enalapril 275 (a *vasodilator* 84 and anti-hypertensive 88)

venlafaxine 461 (an antidepressant 68)

Ventodisks a product name for salbutamol 429 (a *bronchodilator* 76)

Ventolin a product name for salbutamol 429 (a *bronchodilator* 76)

Vepesid a product name for etoposide (an anticancer drug 140)

Veramil a product name for verapamil 462 (an antihypertensive 88 and calcium channel blocker 87)

verapamil 462 (an antihypertensive 88 and calcium channel blocker 87)

Verelan a product name for verapamil 462 (an anti-angina 87, anti-arrhythmic 86, and antihypertensive drug 88)

Vermox a product name for mebendazole (an anthelmintic 125)

Vesanoid a product name for tretinoin (a drug for acne 165)

Vesicare a product name for solifenacin (a drug used for urinary disorders 154)

Vfend a product name for variconazole (an antifungal drug 124)

Viaderm-K.C. a product name combination of nystatin 376 (an antifungal 124), gramicidin and neomycin sulfate (both *antibiotic*s 114), and triamcinolone acetonide (a corticosteroid 127)

Viagra a product name for sildenafil 433 (a drug for impotence 134, 152)

Vibramycin a product name for doxycycline 272 (a tetracycline *antibiotic* 114)

Vibra-Tabs a product name for doxycycline 272 (a tetracycline *antibiotic* 114)

Victoza a product name for liraglutide 335 (an antihyperglycemic drug 128)

Victrelis Triple a product name for a combination of interferon 319 (an antiviral 119 and anticancer drug 140), boceprevir (a drug for hepatitis), and ribavirin (an antiviral drug 119)

Videx a product name for didanosine (an antiretroviral drug used in the treatment of HIV infection and AIDS 144)

vigabatrin an antiepileptic 70

Vigamox a product name for moxifloxacin 369 (an antibacterial 117)

Vimovo a product name for a combination of naproxen 370 (an NSAID 102) and omeprazole 378 (anti-ulcer drug 95)

vinblastine a drug used in cancer treatment 140

vincristine a drug used in cancer treatment 140

Vioform Hydrocortisone a product name combination of clioquinol (an antibacterial 117 and antifungal 124) and hydrocortisone 313 (a corticosteroid 127)

Virazole a product name for ribivirin (an antiviral 119)

Viread a product name for tenofovir (a drug for HIV/AIDS 144)

Viroptic a product name for trifluridine (an antiviral 119)

Visine Workplace Eye Drops a product name product containing oxymetazoline (a *topical* decongestant 79)

vitamin A 479 (a vitamin 135)

Vitamin A Acid a product name for tretinoin (a drug for acne 165)

vitamin B complex (see vitamins 135)

vitamin B1 another name for thiamine 479 (a vitamin 135)

vitamin B2 another name for riboflavin 477 (a vitamin 135)

vitamin B6 another name for pyridoxine 477 (a vitamin 135)

vitamin B12 480 (a vitamin 135)

vitamin C another name for ascorbic acid 480 (a vitamin 135)

vitamin D 481 (a vitamin 135)

vitamin E 481 (a vitamin 135)

vitamin K 482 (a vitamin 135)

Voltaren a product name for diclonefac 254 (a non-steroidal anti-inflammatory 102)

Voltaren Ophtha a product name for diclonefac 254 (a non-steroidal anti-inflammatory 102 used as eye drops)

voriconazole an antifungal drug 124

W

warfarin 463 (an anticoagulant 90)

Wellbutrin SR a product name for bupropion 215 (an antidepressant 68 used as an aid when stopping smoking in addition to counselling)

Westcort a product name for hydrocortisone 313 (a corticosteroid 127 and antipruritic 161)

X

Xalatan a product name for latanoprost 330 (a drug for glaucoma 156)

Xamiol a product name for a combination of betamethasone 209 (a corticosteroid 127) and calcipotriol (a drug for psoriasis 166)

Xanax a product name for alprazolam 185 (an anti-anxiety drug 67)

Xarelto a product name for rivaroxaban 424 (an anticoagulant drug 90)

Xatral a product name for alfuzosin (an alpha-*adrenergic* blocker for prostate disorders 148)

Xenical a product name for orlistat 380 (a drug that blocks the action of *enzymes* that digest fats)

Xgeva a product name for denosumab 253 (a human monoclonal *antibody* 141)

Xolair a product name for omalizumab (a monoclonal *antibody* 140)

Xylocaine a product name for lidocaine (a local *anesthetic* 64)

Xylocaine Jelly 2% a product name for lidocaine (a local *anesthetic* 64 and anti-arrhythmic 86)

Xylocaine Parenteral with Epinephrine a product name for a combination of epinephrine 276 and lidocaine (a local *anesthetic*)

Xylocard a product name for lidocaine (a local *anesthetic* 64 and anti-arrhythmic 86)

xylometazoline 464 (*topical* decongestant 79)

Y

Yasmin a product name for oral contraceptive 149 containing drospirenone (a progestin 151) and ethinyl estradiol 283 (an estrogen 133)

Yaz a product name for an oral contraceptive 149

Z

Zaditen a product name for ketotifen (a drug used to prevent asthma 77)

zafirlukast a leukotriene *antagonist* for asthma 77

Zanaflex a product name for tizanidine 453 (a muscle relaxant 106)

zanamivir 465 (an antiviral drug 119)

Zantac a product name for ranitidine 417 (an anti-ulcer drug 95)

Zarontin a product name for ethosuximide (an antiepileptic 70)

ZeaSorb AF a product name for tolnaftate (an antifungal 124)

Zenapax a product name for daclizumab (an immunosuppressant 142)

Zenhale a product name for a combination of formoterol 298 (a bronchodilator 76) and mometasone 366 (a corticosteroid 127)

Zestoretic a product name for lisinopril 336 (an ACE inhibitor 98) and hydrochlorothiazide 311 (a diuretic 101)

Zestril a product name for lisinopril 336 (an ACE inhibitor 98)

zidovudine (AZT) 466 (an antiretroviral for HIV infection and AIDS 144)

zinc 482 (a mineral 137)

Zincofax a product name for zinc oxide (a soothing agent 163)

zinc oxide a soothing agent 163

zinc pyrithione an antimicrobial with antibacterial 117 and antifungal properties used for dandruff

zinc sulfate zinc 482 (a mineral 137)

Zithromax a product name for azithromycin 204 (an *antibiotic* 114)

Zmax SR a product name for azithromycin 204 (an antibiotic 114)

Zocor a product name for simvastatin 434 (a lipid-lowering drug 89))

Zofran a product name for ondansetron 379 (an anti-emetic 74)

Zofran ODT a product name for ondansetron 379 (an anti-emetic 74)

Zoladex a product name for goserelin 308 (a female sex *hormone* 133 and anticancer drug 140)

Zoladex LA a product name for goserelin 308 (a female sex *hormone* 133 and anticancer drug 140)

zoledronic acid a drug for treatment of bone disorders 108

zolmitriptan a drug for migraine 73

Zoloft a product name for sertraline 432 (an antidepressant 68)

Zomig a product name for zolmiptran (a drug for migraine 73)

Zomig Rapimelt a product name for zolmiptran (a drug for migraine 73)

Zopiclone 467 (a sleeping drug 66)

Zovirax a product name for acyclovir 178 (an antiviral 119)

Zuclopenthixol an antipsychotic 69

Zyban a product name for bupropion 213 (an antidepressant 68 used as an aid when stopping smoking in addition to counselling)

Zyloprim a product name for allopurinol 184 (a drug for gout 105)

Zyprexa a product name for olanzapine 377 (an antipsychotic 69)

Zyprexa Zydis a product name for olanzapine 377 (an antipsychotic 69)

Zytram a product name for tramadol 456 (an *opioid analgesic* 64)

Zyvoxam a product name for linezolid (an *antibiotic* 114)

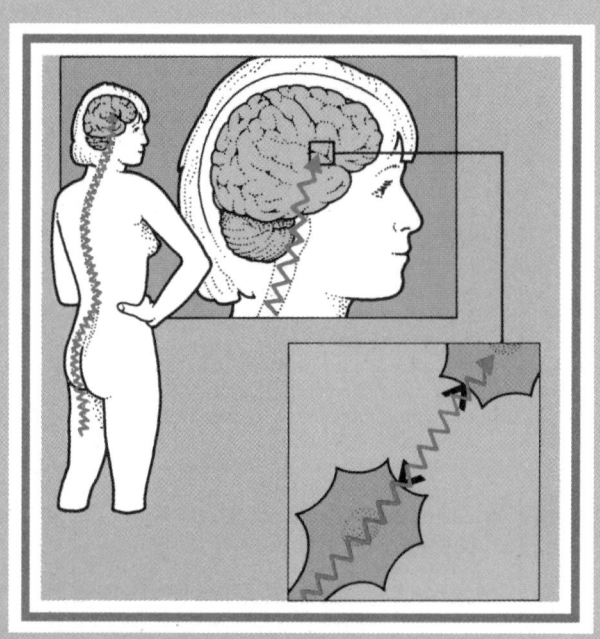

BRAIN AND NERVOUS SYSTEM

The human brain contains over 100 billion nerve cells (neurons). These nerve cells receive electro-chemical impulses from everywhere in the body. They interpret these impulses and send responsive signals back to various glands and muscles. The brain functions continuously as a switchboard for the human communications system. At the same time, it serves as the seat of emotions and mood, of memory, personality, and thought. Extending from the brain is an additional cluster of nerve cells that forms the spinal cord. Together, these two elements compose the central nervous system.

Radiating from the central nervous system is the peripheral nervous system, which has three parts. One branches off the spinal cord and extends to skin and muscles throughout the body. Another, in the head, links the brain to the eyes, ears, nose, and taste buds. The third is a semi-independent network called the autonomic, or involuntary, nervous system. This is the part of the nervous system that controls unconscious body functions such as breathing, digestion, and glandular activity (see facing page).

Signals traverse the nervous system by electrical and chemical means. Electrical impulses carry signals from one end of a neuron to the other. To cross the gap between neurons, chemical *neurotransmitters* are released from one cell to bind on to the *receptor* sites of nearby cells. *Excitatory* transmitters stimulate action; *inhibitory* transmitters reduce it.

What can go wrong

Disorders of the brain and nervous system may manifest as illnesses that show themselves as physical impairments, such as epilepsy or strokes, or as mental and emotional impairments (for example, schizophrenia or depression).

Illnesses causing physical impairments can result from different types of disorder of the brain and nervous system. Death of nerve cells resulting from poor circulation can result in paralysis, while electrical disturbances of certain nerve cells cause the seizures of epilepsy. Temporary changes in neurons and blood vessels within and around the brain are associated with migraine. Parkinson's disease is caused by a lack of dopamine, a neurotransmitter that is produced by specialized brain cells.

The causes of disorders that trigger mental and emotional impairment are not known, but these illnesses are thought to result from the defective functioning of nerve cells and neurotransmitters. The nerve cells may be underactive, overactive,

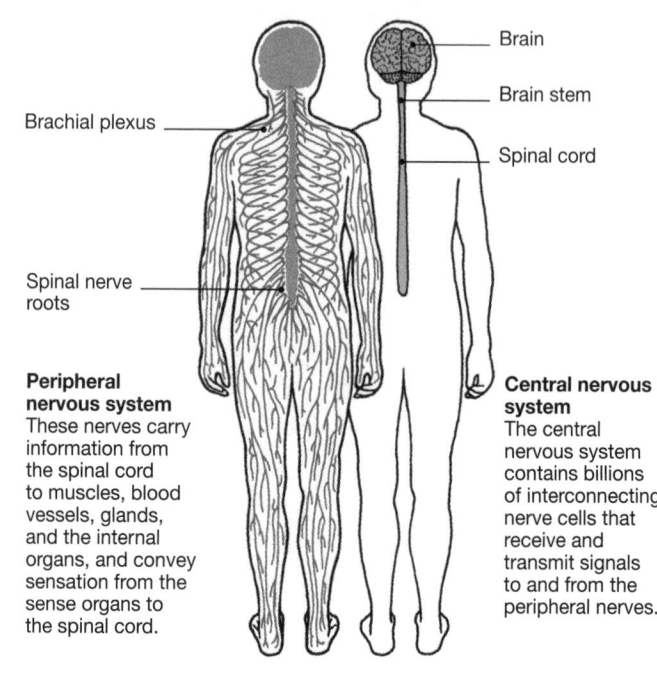

Peripheral nervous system
These nerves carry information from the spinal cord to muscles, blood vessels, glands, and the internal organs, and convey sensation from the sense organs to the spinal cord.

Central nervous system
The central nervous system contains billions of interconnecting nerve cells that receive and transmit signals to and from the peripheral nerves.

Brain
Brain stem
Spinal cord
Brachial plexus
Spinal nerve roots

How nerve signals are transmitted
A nerve signal is an electrical impulse produced by chemical reactions on the surface of the cell body of a neuron (nerve cell). The signal is transmitted by a neurotransmitter, released from the ends of a nerve fibre, that binds to a *receptor* on the neighbouring cell body. This, in turn, transmits the signal to another neuron or triggers a response in a muscle or organ.

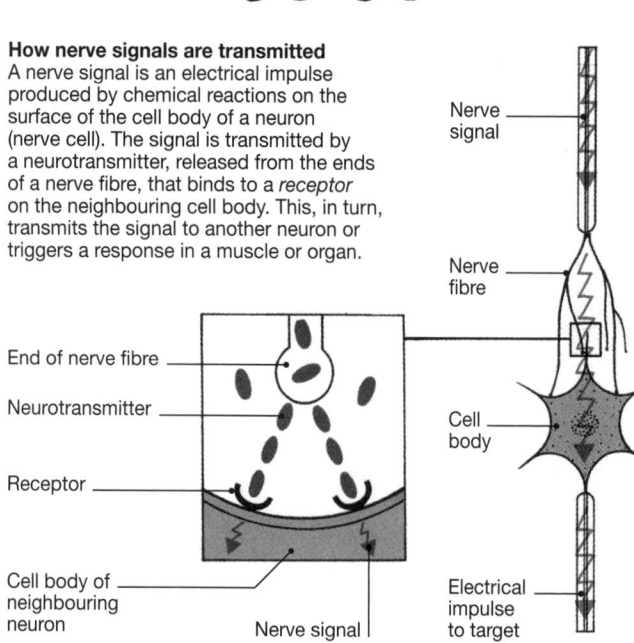

End of nerve fibre
Neurotransmitter
Receptor
Cell body of neighbouring neuron
Nerve signal
Nerve signal
Nerve fibre
Cell body
Electrical impulse to target

or poorly coordinated. Alternatively, mental and emotional impairment may be due to too much or too little neurotransmitter in one area of the brain.

Why drugs are used

By and large, the drugs described in this section do not eliminate nervous system disorders. Their function is to correct or modify the communication of the signals that traverse the nervous system. By doing so they can relieve symptoms or restore normal functioning and behaviour. In some cases,

AUTONOMIC NERVOUS SYSTEM

The autonomic, or involuntary, nervous system governs the actions of the muscles of the organs and glands. Such vital functions as heart beat, salivation, and digestion continue without conscious direction, whether we are awake or asleep.

The autonomic system is divided into two parts, the effects of one generally balancing those of the other. The *sympathetic* nervous system has an *excitatory* effect. For example, it widens the airways to the lungs, increases the heart rate, and also increases the flow of blood to the arms and legs. The *parasympathetic* system, by contrast, has an opposing effect. It slows the heart rate, narrows the large airways, and redirects blood from the limbs to the gut.

Although the functional pace of most organs results from the interplay between the two systems, the muscles surrounding the blood vessels respond only to the signals of the sympathetic system. Whether a vessel is dilated or constricted is determined by the relative stimulation of two sets of receptor sites: alpha sites and beta sites.

Neurotransmitters
The parasympathetic nervous system depends on the neurotransmitter acetylcholine to transmit signals from one cell to another. The sympathetic nervous system relies on adrenaline and noradrenaline, substances that act as both hormones and neurotransmitters.

Drugs that act on the sympathetic nervous system
The drugs that stimulate the sympathetic nervous system are called adrenergics (or sympathomimetics, see chart). They either promote the release of adrenaline and noradrenaline or mimic their effects. Drugs that interfere with the action of the sympathetic nervous system are called sympatholytics. Alpha blockers act on alpha receptors; beta blockers act on beta receptors (see also Beta blockers, p.83).

Drugs that act on the parasympathetic nervous system
Drugs that stimulate the parasympathetic nervous system are called cholinergics (or parasympathomimetics), and drugs that oppose its action are called *anticholinergics*. Many prescribed drugs have anticholinergic properties (see chart, right).

Effects of stimulation of the autonomic nervous system

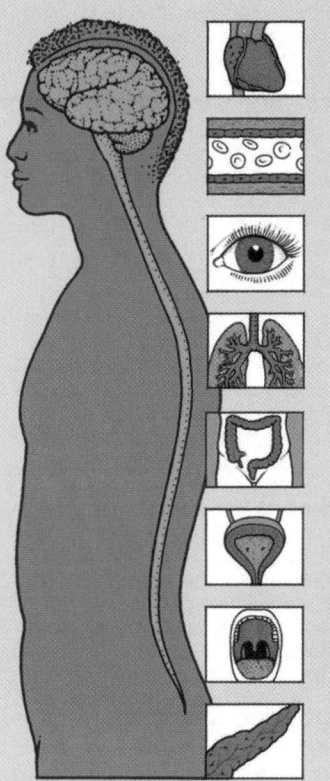

	Sympathetic	Parasympathetic
Heart	The rate and strength of the heart beat are increased.	The rate and strength of the heart beat are reduced.
Blood vessels in skin	These are constricted by stimulation of alpha receptors.	No effect.
Pupils	The pupils are dilated.	The pupils are constricted.
Airways	The bronchial muscles relax and widen the airways.	The bronchial muscles contract and narrow the airways.
Intestines	Activity of the muscles of the intestinal wall is reduced.	Activity of the muscles of the intestinal wall is increased.
Bladder	The bladder wall relaxes and the sphincter muscle contracts.	The bladder wall contracts and the sphincter muscle relaxes.
Salivary glands	Secretion of thick saliva increases.	Secretion of watery saliva increases.
Pancreas	Insulin secretion is increased (beta receptors) or reduced (alpha receptors).	Insulin secretion is increased.

Drugs that act on the autonomic nervous system

	Sympathetic	Parasympathetic
Stimulated by		
Natural neurotransmitters	Epinephrine (adrenaline) Norepinephrine (noradrenaline)	Acetylcholine
Drugs	Adrenergic drugs (including alpha agonists, beta agonists) Sympathomimetics	Cholinergic drugs Parasympathomimetics
Blocked by		
Drugs	Alpha blockers (antagonists) Beta blockers (antagonists)	Anticholinergic drugs

such as anxiety and insomnia, drugs are used to lower the level of activity in the brain. In other disorders – depression, for example – drugs are given to encourage the opposite effect, increasing the level of activity.

Drugs that act on the nervous system are also used for conditions that outwardly have nothing to do with nervous system disorders. Vomiting, for example, may be treated with drugs that directly affect the vomiting centre in the brain or block stimulatory nerve signals to the vomiting centre.

MAJOR DRUG GROUPS

Analgesics
Sleeping drugs
Anti-anxiety drugs
Antidepressant drugs
Antipsychotic drugs
Antiepileptic drugs
Drugs for parkinsonism
Drugs for dementia
Nervous system stimulants
Drugs for migraine
Anti-emetics
Anti-vertigo

ANALGESICS

Analgesics are drugs that relieve pain. Pain is not a disease but a symptom, long-term relief depends on treatment of the underlying cause. For example, toothache can be relieved by drugs but can be cured only by appropriate dental treatment. If the underlying disorder is irreversible, such as some rheumatic conditions, long-term analgesic treatment may be necessary.

Damage to body tissues as a result of disease or injury is detected by nerve endings that transmit signals to the brain. The interpretation of these sensations can be affected by the psychological state of the individual, so that pain is worsened by anxiety and fear, for example. Often a reassuring explanation of the cause of discomfort makes pain easier to bear and may even relieve it altogether. Anti-anxiety drugs (see p.67) are helpful when pain is accompanied by anxiety, and some of these drugs are also used to reduce painful muscle spasms. Antidepressant drugs (see p.68) act to block the transmission of impulses signalling pain and are particularly useful for nerve pains (neuralgia), which do not always respond to analgesics. Other medications used to treat nerve pains include anticonvulsant drugs (see p.70) like valproic acid, gabapentin, or pregabalin.

Types of analgesics

Analgesics are divided into the opioids (with similar properties to drugs derived from opium, such as morphine) and non-opioids. Non-opioids include all the other analgesics, including acetaminophen and non-steroidal anti-inflammatory drugs (NSAIDs), the most well known of which is ASA. Non-opioids are less powerful painkillers than opioids. Local anesthetics are also used to relieve pain (see below).

Opioid drugs and acetaminophen act directly on the brain and spinal cord to alter the perception of pain. Opioids act like the endorphins, hormones naturally produced in the brain that stop the cell-to-cell transmission of pain sensation. NSAIDs block the formation of pain-modulating substances (e.g. prostaglandins) at nerve endings at the site of pain.

When pain is treated under medical supervision, it is common to start with acetaminophen or an NSAID; if neither provides adequate pain relief, they may be combined. A mild opioid (for example, codeine) may also be used. If the less powerful drugs are ineffective, a strong opioid such as morphine may be given. As there is now a wide variety of oral analgesic formulations, injections are seldom necessary to control even the most severe pain.

When treating pain with an over-the-counter preparation, for example, taking ASA for a headache, you should seek medical advice if pain persists for longer than 48 hours, recurs, or is worse or different from previous pain.

Non-opioid analgesics

Acetaminophen

This analgesic is believed to act by reducing the production of chemicals called prostaglandins in the brain. It does not affect prostaglandin production in the rest of the body, so it does not reduce inflammation, although it can reduce fever. Acetaminophen can be used for everyday aches and pains, such as headaches and joint pains.

As well as being the most widely used analgesic, it is one of the safest when taken correctly. It does not usually irritate the stomach and allergic reactions are rare. However, an overdose can cause severe and possibly fatal liver or kidney damage.

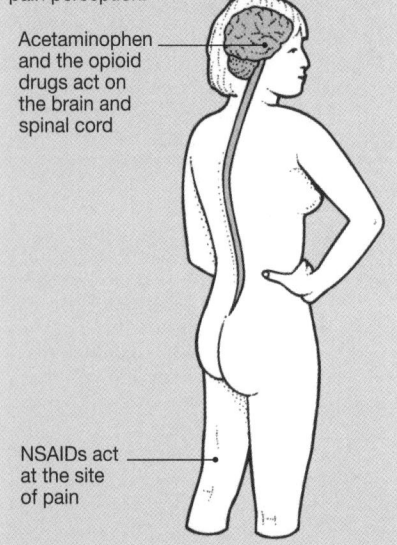
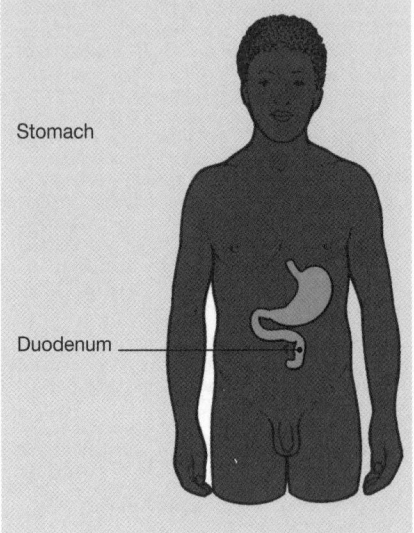
Its toxic potential may be increased in heavy drinkers or those who are malnourished.

Non-steroidal anti-inflammatory drugs (NSAIDs): ASA (acetylsalicylic acid)
Used for many years to relieve pain and reduce fever, ASA also acts to reduce inflammation by blocking the production of prostaglandins, which contribute to the swelling and pain in inflamed tissue (see Action of analgesics, facing page). ASA is useful for headaches, toothaches, mild rheumatic pain, sore throat, and discomfort caused by feverish illnesses. Given regularly, it can also relieve the pain and inflammation of chronic rheumatoid arthritis (see Antirheumatic drugs, p.103).

ASA is found in combination with other substances in a variety of medicines (see Cold cures, p.80). It is also used in the treatment of some blood disorders since ASA helps to prevent abnormal clotting of blood by preventing platelets from sticking together (see Drugs that affect blood clotting, p.90).

ASA in the form of soluble tablets, dissolved in water before being taken, is absorbed into the bloodstream more quickly, thereby relieving pain faster than tablets. Soluble ASA is not, however, less irritating to the stomach lining.

ASA is available in many forms, all of which have a similar effect, but because the amount of ASA in a tablet of each type varies, it is important to read the package for the correct dosage. It is not recommended for children aged under 16 years with flu-like symptoms because its use has been linked to Reye's syndrome, which is a very rare but potentially fatal liver and brain disorder.

Other non-steroidal anti-inflammatory drugs (NSAIDs)
These drugs can relieve both pain and inflammation. NSAIDs are related to ASA and also work by blocking the production of *prostaglandins* in the brain. They are most commonly used to treat muscle and joint pain and may also be prescribed for other types of pain including menstrual pain. For further information on these drugs, see p.102.

Combined analgesics
Mild opioids, such as codeine, are often found in combination preparations with non-opioids, such as acetaminophen or ASA. These mixtures may add the advantages of analgesics that act on the brain to the benefits of those acting at the site of pain. Another advantage of combining analgesics is that the reductions in dose of the components may reduce the side effects of the preparation. Combinations can be helpful in reducing the number of tablets taken during long-term treatment.

Opioid analgesics
These drugs are related to opium, an extract of poppy seeds. They act directly on several sites in the central nervous system to block the transmission of pain signals (see Action of analgesics, above). Because they act directly on the parts of the brain where pain is perceived, opioids are the strongest analgesics and are used to treat the pain arising from surgery, serious injury, and cancer. These drugs are particularly valuable for relieving severe pain during terminal illnesses. In addition, their ability to produce a state of relaxation and euphoria is often of help in relieving the stress that accompanies severe pain.

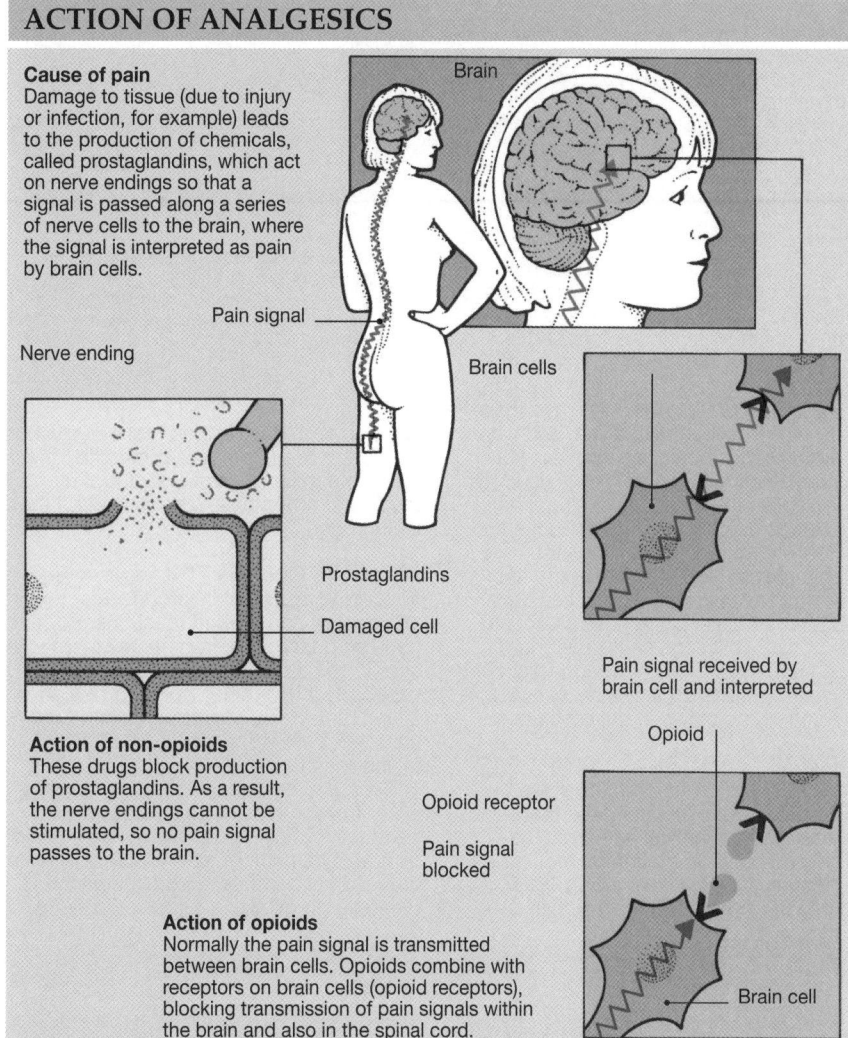

ACTION OF ANALGESICS

Cause of pain
Damage to tissue (due to injury or infection, for example) leads to the production of chemicals, called prostaglandins, which act on nerve endings so that a signal is passed along a series of nerve cells to the brain, where the signal is interpreted as pain by brain cells.

Brain

Pain signal

Nerve ending

Brain cells

Prostaglandins

Damaged cell

Pain signal received by brain cell and interpreted

Action of non-opioids
These drugs block production of prostaglandins. As a result, the nerve endings cannot be stimulated, so no pain signal passes to the brain.

Opioid

Opioid receptor

Pain signal blocked

Action of opioids
Normally the pain signal is transmitted between brain cells. Opioids combine with receptors on brain cells (opioid receptors), blocking transmission of pain signals within the brain and also in the spinal cord.

Brain cell

Morphine is the best known of the strong *opioid* analgesics. Others include oxycodone and meperidine. The use of these powerful opioids is strictly controlled because they produce feelings of euphoria, which can lead to abuse and addiction. However, when these powerful opioids are given under medical supervision to treat severe pain, the risk of addiction is minimal.

Opioid analgesics may prevent clear thought and cloud consciousness. Other possible adverse effects include nausea, vomiting, constipation, drowsiness, and depressed breathing. When they are taken in overdose, these drugs may induce a deep coma and lead to fatal breathing difficulties.

There are also some less powerful analgesics in this group that are used to relieve mild to moderate pain. They include hydrocodone, codeine, tapentadol, tramadol, and diphenoxylate. Their normally unwanted side effects of depressing respiration and causing constipation make

them useful as cough suppressants (p.80) and as antidiarrheal drugs (p.96).

COMMON DRUGS

Opioids
Buprenorphine *
Codeine *
Fentanyl *
Hydromorphone *
Methadone *
Meperidine
Morphine *
Oxycodone
Tapentadol
Tramadol *

Cox-2 Selective Inhibitor
Celecoxib *

NSAIDs (see p.102)
ASA *
Diclofenac *
Etodolac

Flurbiprofen
Ibuprofen *
Indomethacin
Ketoprofen *
Ketorolac
Mefenamic acid *
Meloxicam *
Naproxen *
Oxaprozin
Piroxicam *

Other drugs
Acetaminophen *
Cannabis Sativa
    Extract
    (Cannabidiol,
    Delta-9-tetrahydro-
    cannabinol)

    * See Part 4

SLEEPING DRUGS

Difficulty in getting to sleep or staying asleep (insomnia) has many causes. Most people suffer from sleepless nights from time to time, usually as a result of a temporary worry or discomfort from a minor illness. Persistent sleeplessness can be caused by psychological problems including anxiety or depression, or by pain arising from a physical disorder.

Why drugs are used

For occasional bouts of sleeplessness, simple, common remedies to promote relaxation – for example, taking a warm bath or a hot milk drink before bedtime – are usually the best form of treatment. Sleeping drugs (also known as hypnotics) are normally prescribed only when these self-help remedies have failed, and when lack of sleep is beginning to affect your general health. These drugs are used to re-establish the habit of sleeping. They should be used in the smallest dose and for the shortest possible time (not more than three weeks). It is best not to use sleeping tablets every night (see Risks and precautions). Do not use alcohol to get to sleep as it can cause disturbed sleep and insomnia. Long-term treatment of sleeplessness depends on resolving the underlying cause of the problem.

How they work

Most sleeping drugs promote sleep by depressing brain function. The drugs interfere with chemical activity in the brain and nervous system by reducing communication between nerve cells. This leads to reduced brain activity,

allowing you to fall asleep more easily, but the nature of the sleep is affected by the drug. The main class of sleeping drugs, the benzodiazepines, is described on the facing page.

How they affect you

A sleeping drug rapidly produces drowsiness and slowed reactions. Some people find that the drug makes them appear to be drunk, their speech slurred, especially if they delay going to bed after taking their dose. Most people find they usually fall asleep within one hour of taking the drug.

Because the sleep induced by drugs is not the same as normal sleep, many people find they do not feel as well rested by it as by a night of natural sleep. This is the result of suppressed brain activity. Sleeping drugs also suppress the sleep

during which dreams occur (REM sleep); both dream sleep and non-dream sleep are essential for a good night's sleep (see The effects of drugs on sleep patterns, below).

Some people experience a variety of "hangover" effects the following day. Some benzodiazepines may produce minor side effects, such as daytime drowsiness, dizziness, and unsteadiness, that can impair the ability to drive or operate machinery. Elderly people are likely to become confused, and selection of an appropriate drug is important.

Risks and special precautions

Sleeping drugs become less effective after the first few nights and there may be a temptation to increase the dose. Apart from the antihistamines, most sleeping drugs can produce psychological and physical *dependence* (see p.23) when taken regularly for more than a few weeks, especially if they are taken in larger-than-normal doses.

When sleeping drugs are suddenly withdrawn, anxiety, convulsions, and hallucinations sometimes occur. Vivid dreams and nightmares may be a problem because the time spent in dream sleep increases. Sleeplessness will recur and may lead to a temptation to use the drugs again. Gradual withdrawal of these drugs is important. Anyone who wishes to stop taking sleeping drugs, particularly after prolonged use, should seek his or her physician's advice to prevent these withdrawal symptoms from occurring.

(see p.109), (see facing page), (see p.68), (see p.23)

TYPES OF SLEEPING DRUGS

Benzodiazepines These are the most commonly used class of sleeping drugs as they have comparatively few *adverse effects* and are relatively safe in overdose. They are also used to treat anxiety (see facing page).

Chloral derivatives These drugs effectively promote sleep but are used little now.

Other non-benzodiazepine sleeping drugs Zopiclone works in a similar way to benzodiazepines. It is not intended for long-term use and withdrawal symptoms have been reported.

Antihistamines Widely used to treat allergic symptoms (see p.109), antihistamines such as diphenhydramine also cause drowsiness. They are sometimes used to promote sleep but can cause adverse effects and are not recommended in some individuals, including older people.

Antidepressant drugs Some of these drugs may be used to promote sleep in depressed people (see p.68), as well as being effective in treating underlying depressive illness.

THE EFFECTS OF DRUGS ON SLEEP PATTERNS

Normal sleep can be divided into three types: light sleep, deep sleep, and dream sleep. The proportion of time spent in each type of sleep changes with age and is altered by sleeping drugs. Dramatic changes in sleep patterns also occur in the first few days following abrupt withdrawal of sleeping drugs after regular, prolonged use.

Normal sleep Young adults spend most sleep time in light sleep with roughly equal proportions of dream and deep sleep.

Drug-induced sleep has less dream sleep and less deep sleep with relatively more light sleep.

Sleep following drug withdrawal There is a marked increase in dream sleep following withdrawal of drugs used regularly for a long time.

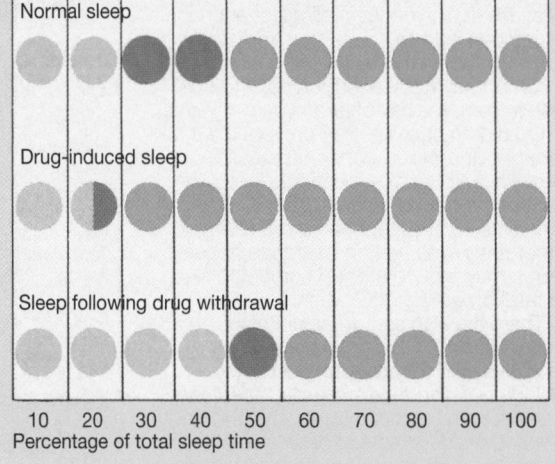

- ● Dream sleep
- ● Deep sleep
- ● Light sleep

Normal sleep

Drug-induced sleep

Sleep following drug withdrawal

10 20 30 40 50 60 70 80 90 100
Percentage of total sleep time

COMMON DRUGS

Benzodiazepines
Flurazepam
Lorazepam *
Nitrazepam
Oxazepam *
Temazepam *
Triazolam

Chloral derivatives
Chloral hydrate

Other non-benzodiazepine sleeping drugs
Zopiclone *

* See Part 4

ANTI-ANXIETY DRUGS

A certain amount of stress can be beneficial, providing a stimulus to action. But too much will often result in anxiety, which might be described as fear or apprehension not caused by real danger.

Clinically, anxiety arises when the balance of certain chemicals in the brain is disturbed. The fearful feelings increase brain activity, stimulating the sympathetic nervous system (see p.63), and often triggering physical symptoms such as shaking, palpitations,and headaches.

Why drugs are used

Anti-anxiety drugs (also called anxiolytics) are prescribed for short-term relief of severe anxiety and nervousness caused by psychological problems. But these drugs cannot resolve the causes. Tackling the underlying problem through counselling and perhaps psychotherapy offers the best hope of a long-term solution. The drugs are also used to relax people before uncomfortable medical procedures.

There are several types of drugs for relieving anxiety: benzodiazepines, beta blockers, antidepressants and buspirone. Antidepressants, such as SSRIs (see p.68), are most widely used for generalized anxiety disorder, as are others such as venlafaxine and clomipramine. These are also helpful in other types of anxiety-related conditions such as obsessive-compulsive and panic disorders. Benzodiazepines are also effective, although these are more commonly used early on for a short period to promote relaxation. Their sedative effects also help relieve insomnia, which often accompanies anxiety (see also Sleeping drugs, opposite). Buspirone, a non-benzodiazepine drug, is also an option in generalized anxiety disorders. Drugs such as benzodiazepines and beta blockers may be prescribed for people who feel excessively anxious in certain situations, such as interviews or public appearances.

How they work

Benzodiazepines and related drugs
These drugs depress activity in the part of the brain that controls emotion by promoting the action of the *neurotransmitter* gamma-aminobutyric acid (GABA) which binds to neurons, blocking transmission of electrical impulses and thus reducing communication between brain cells. Benzodiazepines increase the inhibitory effect of GABA on brain cells (see Action of benzodiazepines and related drugs, above), preventing the excessive brain activity that causes anxiety. Buspirone is different from other anti-anxiety drugs; it binds mainly to serotonin (another neurotransmitter) receptors and does not cause drowsiness. Its effect is not felt for at least two weeks after starting treatment.

Beta blockers
The physical symptoms of anxiety are produced by an increase in the activity of the sympathetic nervous system. Sympathetic nerve endings release a chemical transmitter called norepinephrine (noradrenaline) that stimulates the heart, digestive system, and other organs. Beta blockers block the action of noradrenaline in the body, reducing the physical symptoms of anxiety. For more information on beta blockers, see p.83.

How they affect you

Benzodiazepines and related drugs reduce feelings of restlessness and agitation, slow mental activity, and often produce drowsiness. They are said to reduce motivation and, if they are taken in large doses, may lead to apathy. They also have a relaxing effect on the muscles (see Muscle relaxants, p.106).

Minor *adverse effects* of these drugs include dizziness and forgetfulness. People who need to drive or operate potentially dangerous machinery should be aware that their reactions may be slowed. Because the brain soon becomes tolerant to, and dependent on, their effects, benzo-diazepines are usually effective for only a few weeks at a time.

Beta blockers reduce the physical symptoms associated with anxiety, which may promote greater mental calmness. As they do not cause drowsiness they are safer for people who need to drive.

Risks and special precautions

The benzodiazepines are safe for most people and are less dangerous in overdose than other sedative drugs such as older barbiturates. However, benzodiazepines can be dangerous when combined with alcohol and other CNS drugs. The main risk is psychological and physical *dependence*, especially for regular users or when larger-than-average doses have been used. For this reason, they are usually given for courses of two weeks or less. If used for a longer period, they should be withdrawn gradually under medical supervision. If they are stopped suddenly, withdrawal symptoms, such as excessive anxiety, nightmares, and restlessness, may occur.

Benzodiazepines are prescribed with caution for people with a history of drug or alcohol abuse.

ACTION OF BENZODIAZEPINES AND RELATED DRUGS

Action on the brain
The reticular activating system (RAS) in the brain stem controls the level of mental activity by stimulating higher centres of the brain controlling consciousness. Benzodiazepines and related drugs depress the RAS, relieving anxiety. In larger doses they depress the RAS sufficiently to cause drowsiness and sleep.

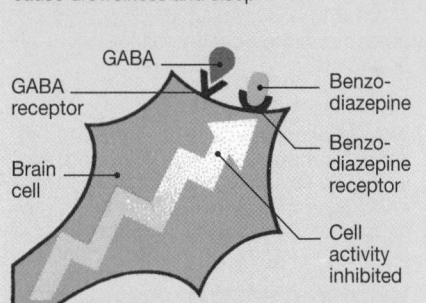

GABA

GABA receptor

Brain cell

Benzo-diazepine

Benzo-diazepine receptor

Cell activity inhibited

Higher centres of brain

Stimulation of brain   RAS   Brain stem

Action on brain cells in the RAS
Brain cell activity is normally inhibited by GABA, a chemical that binds to specialized cell *receptors*. Brain cells also have receptors for benzodiazepines. The drug binds to its receptor and promotes the inhibitory effect of GABA, thereby depressing brain cell activity in the RAS.

COMMON DRUGS

Benzodiazepines
Alprazolam ✳
Chlordiazepoxide
Clonazepam ✳
Diazepam ✳
Lorazepam ✳
Oxazepam ✳

Other
Buspirone ✳

✳ See Part 4

Beta blockers
Atenolol ✳
Metoprolol ✳
Propranolol ✳

Antidepressants
Citalopram
Clomipramine ✳
Desipramine
Paroxetine ✳
Sertraline ✳
Venlafaxine ✳

ANTIDEPRESSANT DRUGS

Occasional moods of discouragement or sadness are normal and usually pass quickly. But more severe depression, accompanied by despair, lethargy, loss of sex drive, and often poor appetite, may call for medical attention. Such depression can arise from life stresses such as the death of someone close, an illness, or sometimes from no apparent cause.

Several types of drugs are used to treat depression: tricyclic antidepressants (TCAs), selective serotonin re-uptake inhibitors (SSRIs), monoamine oxidase inhibitors (MAOIs), and others (see Types of antidepressant, below). Lithium, a metallic element, is used to treat bipolar disorder (see Antimanic drugs, facing page). It is sometimes used with an anti-depressant drug for treating resistant depression. Several other antidepressants may be prescribed, including venlafaxine, maprotiline, mirtazapine, or trazodone.

Why drugs are used

Minor depression does not usually require drug treatment. Cognitive behavioural therapy, support and help in coming to terms with the cause of the depression is often all that is needed. Moderate or severe depression usually requires drug treatment, which is effective in most cases. Antidepressant drugs may have to be taken for many months. Treatment should not be stopped too soon because symptoms are likely to reappear if it is. When treatment is stopped, the dose should be gradually reduced over several weeks because withdrawal symptoms may occur if they are stopped suddenly.

How they work

Depression is thought to be caused by a reduction in the level of certain chemicals in the brain called *neurotransmitters*, which affect mood by stimulating brain cells. Antidepressants increase the level of these *excitatory* neurotransmitters. See Action of antidepressants (right).

TYPES OF ANTIDEPRESSANT

Tricyclic antidepressants (TCAs)
Some TCAs, such as amitriptyline, cause drowsiness, which is useful for sleep problems in depression. TCAs also cause *anticholinergic* effects, including blurred vision, a dry mouth, and difficulty urinating.

Selective serotonin re-uptake inhibitors (SSRIs)
The SSRIs generally have fewer *side effects* than TCAs. The main unwanted effects of the SSRIs are nausea and vomiting. Anxiety, headache, and restlessness may also occur at the beginning of treatment.

Other antidepressants
Other drugs such as venlafaxine, moclobemide, and mirtazapine can all be effective options in those with depression.

Tricyclics (TCAs)

TCAs and venlafaxine block the re-uptake of the neurotransmitters serotonin and norepinephrine (noradrenaline), increasing neurotransmitter levels at receptors.

Selective serotonin re-uptake inhibitors (SSRIs)

SSRIs act by blocking the re-uptake of only one neurotransmitter, serotonin.

Monoamine oxidase inhibitors (MAOIs)

MAOIs act by blocking the breakdown of neurotransmitters, mainly serotonin, norepinephrine (noradrenaline), and dopamine.

How they affect you

The antidepressant effect of these drugs starts after about 14 days treatment and it may be six to eight weeks before the full effect is seen. However, side effects may happen at once. *Tolerance* to these usually occurs and treatment should be continued.

Risks and special precautions

Ongoing monitoring of individuals with depression, by their physician and other care providers, with regards to feelings of self-harm is important. Overdose can be dangerous: tricyclics can produce coma, seizures, and disturbed heart rhythm, which may be fatal; MAOIs can also cause muscle spasms and even death. Both are prescribed with caution for people with heart problems or epilepsy.

Monoamine oxidase inhibitors taken with certain drugs or foods rich in tyramine (for example, cheese, meat, yeast extracts, and red wine) can produce a dramatic rise in blood pressure, with headache or vomiting. People taking MAOIs are given a list of prohibited drugs and foods. However, moclobemide is a reversible inhibitor of MAOI-A and strict dietary precautions are usually not required at standard doses. Because of this adverse interaction, MAOIs are used much less frequently today. SSRIs are more commonly prescribed in preference.

COMMON DRUGS

Tricyclics	**MAOIs**
Amitriptyline *	Moclobemide *
Clomipramine *	Phenelzine
Desipramine	Tranylcypromine
Doxepin	
Imipramine *	**Other drugs**
Nortriptyline	Bupropion *
Trimipramine	Duloxetine *
	Maprotiline
SSRIs	Mirtazapine *
Citalopram *	Trazodone
Escitalopram	Venlafaxine *
Fluoxetine *	
Fluvoxamine *	
Paroxetine *	* See Part 4
Sertraline *	

ACTION OF ANTIDEPRESSANTS

Normally, the brain cells release sufficient quantities of excitatory chemicals (known as neurotransmitters) to stimulate neighbouring cells. The neurotransmitters are constantly reabsorbed into the brain cells where they are broken down by an enzyme called monoamine oxidase. In depression, fewer neurotransmitters are released. The levels of neurotransmitters in the brain are raised by antidepressant drugs.

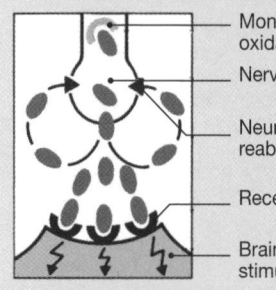

Monoamine oxidase
Nerve ending
Neurotransmitters reabsorbed
Receptor
Brain cell stimulated

Normal brain activity
In a normal brain neurotransmitters are constantly being released, reabsorbed, and broken down.

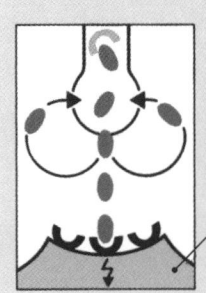

Brain activity in depression
The brain cells release fewer neurotransmitters than normal, leading to reduced stimulation.

Brain cell poorly stimulated

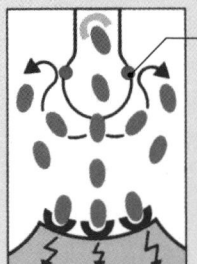

Drug blocks reabsorption of neurotransmitter

Action of TCAs and SSRIs
TCA and SSRI drugs increase the levels of neurotransmitters by blocking their reabsorption.

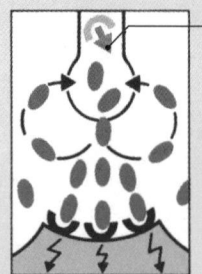

Drug blocks enzyme

Action of MAOIs
MAOIs increase the neurotransmitter levels by blocking the action of the enzyme (monoamine oxidase) that breaks them down.

ANTIPSYCHOTIC DRUGS

Psychosis is a term used to describe mental disorders that prevent the sufferer from thinking clearly, recognizing reality, and acting rationally. These disorders include schizophrenia and sometimes bipolar disorder (manic depression). The precise causes of these disorders are unknown, although a number of factors, including stress, heredity, and brain injury, may be involved. Temporary psychosis can also arise as a result of alcohol withdrawal or the abuse of mind-altering drugs (see Drugs of abuse, p.483). Various drugs are used to treat psychotic disorders (see Common drugs, below), most of which have similar actions and effects. One exception is lithium, which is particularly useful for bipolar disorder (see Antimanic drugs, right).

Why drugs are used

A person with a psychotic illness may recover spontaneously, and so a drug will not always be prescribed. Long-term treatment is started only when normal life is seriously disrupted. Antipsychotic drugs (sometimes called neuroleptics) do not cure the disorder, but they do help to control symptoms.

By controlling the symptoms of psychosis, antipsychotic drugs make it possible for most sufferers to live in the community and be admitted to hospital for acute episodes.

The drug given to a particular individual depends on the nature of his or her illness and the expected *adverse effects* of that drug. Drugs differ in the amount of sedation produced; the need for sedation also influences the choice of drug.

Antipsychotics may also be given to calm or sedate a highly agitated or agressive person, whatever the cause. Some antipsychotic drugs also have a powerful action against nausea and vomiting (see p.74), and are therefore sometimes used as premedication before a person has surgery.

How they work

It is thought that some forms of mental illness are caused by an increase in communication between brain cells due to overactivity of an *excitatory* chemical called dopamine. This may disturb normal thought processes and produce abnormal behaviour. Dopamine combines with *receptors* on the brain cells. Antipsychotic drugs reduce the transmission of nerve signals by binding to these receptors, thereby making the brain cells less sensitive to dopamine (see Action of antipsychotics, below). Some antipsychotic drugs, such as clozapine and risperidone, also bind to receptors for the chemical serotonin.

How they affect you

Because antipsychotics depress the action of dopamine, they can disturb its balance with another chemical in the brain, acetylcholine. If an imbalance occurs, extrapyramidal side effects (EPS) may appear. These include restlessness, disorders of movement, and *parkinsonism* (see Drugs for parkinsonism, p.71).

In these circumstances, a change in medication to a different type of antipsychotic may be necessary. If this is not possible, an *anticholinergic* drug (see p.71) may be prescribed.

Antipsychotics may block the action of noradrenaline, another neurotransmitter in the brain. This lowers the blood pressure, especially when you stand up, causing dizziness. This effect on noradrenaline may also prevent ejaculation.

Risks and special precautions

It is important to continue taking these drugs even if all symptoms have gone, because the symptoms are controlled only by taking the prescribed dose.

Because antipsychotic drugs can have permanent as well as temporary side effects, the minimum necessary dosage is used. This minimum dose is determined by starting with a low dose and increasing

ANTIMANIC DRUGS

Changes in mood are normal, but when a person's mood swings become grossly exaggerated, with peaks of elation or mania alternating with troughs of depression, it becomes an illness known as bipolar disorder, or manic depression. It is usually treated with a mood stabilizer such as lithium, a drug that reduces the intensity of the mania, lifts the depression, and lessens the frequency of mood swings. Because it may take weeks or even months before the lithium starts to work, an antipsychotic may be prescribed with lithium at first to give immediate relief of symptoms.

Lithium can be toxic; regular checks on the blood concentration of lithium should therefore be carried out during treatment. Symptoms of lithium poisoning include blurred vision, tremor, vomiting, and diarrhea (see p.337).

Some antiepileptic drugs are also used as mood stabilizers.

it until the symptoms are controlled. Sudden withdrawal after more than a few weeks can cause nausea, sweating, headache, and restlessness. Therefore, the dose is reduced gradually when treatment needs to be stopped.

The most serious long-term risk of antipsychotic treatment is a disorder known as *tardive dyskinesia*, which may develop after one to five years of therapy. This consists of repeated jerking movements of the mouth, tongue, and face, and sometimes of the hands and feet.

The condition is less common with the second-generation antipsychotics (atypical antipsychotics) than the older drugs (first-generation).

How they are administered

Antipsychotics may be given by mouth as tablets, *capsules*, syrup, or by injection. They can also be given in the form of an intramuscular *depot injection* which releases the drug slowly over several weeks. This is helpful for people who might forget to take their drugs or who might overdose.

ACTION OF ANTIPSYCHOTICS

Brain activity is partly governed by the action of a chemical called dopamine, which transmits signals between brain cells. In psychotic illness the brain cells release too much dopamine, resulting in excessive stimulation. The antipsychotic drugs help to reduce the adverse effects of excess dopamine.

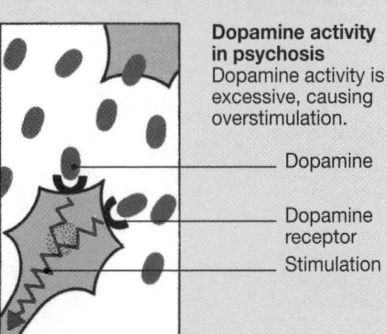

Dopamine activity in psychosis
Dopamine activity is excessive, causing overstimulation.

Dopamine

Dopamine receptor

Stimulation

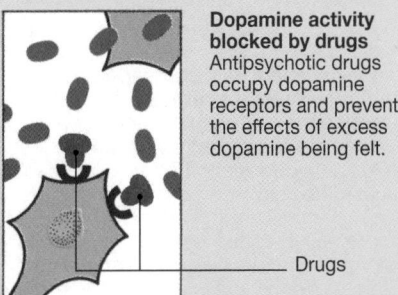

Dopamine activity blocked by drugs
Antipsychotic drugs occupy dopamine receptors and prevent the effects of excess dopamine being felt.

Drugs

COMMON DRUGS

First–generation antipsychotics
Chlorpromazine
Flupenthixol ✳
Fluphenazine
Haloperidol ✳
Loxapine
Methotrimeprazine
Perphenazine
Pimozide
Pipotiazine
Thiothixene
Trifluoperazine
Zuclopenthixol

✳ See Part 4

Second– generation (atypical) antipsychotics
Aripiprazole
Clozapine ✳
Olanzapine ✳
Paliperidone
Quetiapine ✳
Risperidone ✳
Ziprasidone

Antimanic drugs
Carbamazepine ✳
Divalproex
Lithium ✳
Valproic acid

ANTIEPILEPTIC DRUGS

Electrical signals from nerve cells in the brain are normally finely coordinated to produce smooth movements of arms and legs, but these signals can become irregular and chaotic, and trigger the disorderly muscular activity and mental changes that are characteristic of a seizure (also called a convulsion). The most common cause of seizures is the disorder known as epilepsy, which is caused by brain disease or injury. In patients with epilepsy, a seizure may be triggered by an outside stimulus such as a flashing light. Seizures can also result from the *toxic* effects of certain drugs and, in young children, by a high temperature.

Antiepileptic drugs are used both to reduce the risk of an epileptic seizure and to stop one that is in progress.

Why drugs are used

Isolated convulsions seldom require drug treatment, but antiepileptic drugs are the usual treatment for controlling seizures that are caused by epilepsy. These drugs permit most people with epilepsy to lead a normal life.

ACTION OF ANTIEPILEPTICS

Normally, the electrical activity of the brain is under good control. If an area of the brain is electrically unstable and there is an uncontrolled discharge of electrical impulses, epilepsy may occur (see Types of epilepsy, right). Antiepileptics stabilize the electrical activity of brain cells, thus reducing the likelihood of a seizure.

Normal brain activity

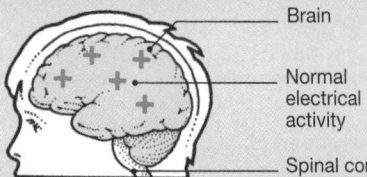

Brain

Normal electrical activity

Spinal cord

Brain activity in a fit

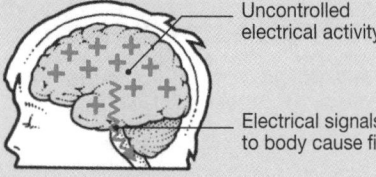

Uncontrolled electrical activity

Electrical signals to body cause fit

Drug action on brain activity

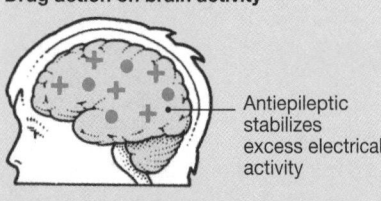

Antiepileptic stabilizes excess electrical activity

Most people with epilepsy need to take antiepileptics on a regular basis to prevent seizures. Usually a single drug is used, and treatment continues until there have been no attacks for at least two years. The particular drug prescribed depends on the type of epilepsy (see Types of epilepsy, right). If one drug is not effective, a different antiepileptic will be tried. Occasionally, it is necessary to take a combination of drugs. A person can suffer seizures even when on treatment. A prolonged seizure can be halted by injection of diazepam or a similar drug.

How they work

Brain cells bring about body movement by electrical activity that passes through the nerves to the muscles. In an epileptic seizure, uncontrolled electrical activity starts in one part of the brain and spreads to other parts, causing uncontrolled stimulation of brain cells. Most antiepileptics have an *inhibitory* effect on brain cells and damp down electrical activity, preventing the excessive build-up that causes epileptic seizures (see Action of antiepileptics, left).

How they affect you

Ideally, the only effect an antiepileptic should have is to reduce or prevent epileptic seizures. Unfortunately, no drug prevents seizures without potentially affecting normal brain function, leading to poor memory, inability to concentrate, lack of coordination, and lethargy. It is important, therefore, to find a dosage sufficient to prevent seizures without causing unacceptable *side effects*. The dose has to be carefully tailored to the individual. It is usual to start with a low dose of a selected drug and to increase it gradually until a balance is achieved between the control of seizures and the occurrence of side effects, many of which wear off after the first weeks of treatment.

Blood tests are used to monitor levels of some antiepileptics in the body as an aid to dose adjustment. Finding the correct dose may take several months.

Risks and special precautions

Each antiepileptic drug has its own specific *adverse effects* and risks. In addition, some affect the liver's ability to break down other drugs (see Drug interactions, p.16) and so may influence the action of other drugs you are taking. Physicians try to prescribe the minimum number of antiepileptics needed to control the person's seizures in order to reduce the risk of such interactions.

Some antiepileptics have risks for a fetus – if you wish to become pregnant, discuss the risks and whether to change your medication, with your physician. People taking antiepileptics need to take their medicine regularly as prescribed. If the antiepileptic levels in the body are allowed to fall suddenly, seizures are very

TYPES OF EPILEPSY

The selection of antiepileptic drug depends on the type of epilepsy, the age of the patient, and his or her particular response to individual drug treatment.

Generalized epilepsy In this form of epilepsy, there is a widespread disturbance of the electrical activity in the brain and loss of consciousness occurs at the outset. In its simplest form, a momentary loss of consciousness occurs during which the sufferer may stare into space. This is called an absence seizure, and mainly affects children. Convulsions do not occur.

Another form of generalized epilepsy causes a brief jerk of a limb (myoclonus).

The most severe type is a tonic-clonic (grand mal) seizure, which is characterized by loss of consciousness, and convulsions that may last for a few minutes. Sufferers may have one or more of these types of generalized epilepsy.

Valproic acid, lamotrigine, carbamazepine, topiramate, phenytoin, or the benzodiazepines are normally used for these types of epilepsy.

Partial (focal) epilepsy This type of epilepsy is caused by an electrical disturbance in only one part of the brain. The result is a disturbance of function, such as an abnormal sensation or movement of a limb, without loss of consciousness. Known as a simple partial seizure, this may precede a more serious attack associated with loss of consciousness (complex partial seizure), which may in turn progress to a generalized convulsive seizure.

Carbamazepine, lamotrigine, or phenytoin may be prescribed for this type of epilepsy.

Status epilepticus Repeated epileptic attacks without full recovery between them, or a single attack lasting more than 10 minutes, is called status epilepticus and it requires emergency treatment.

likely to occur. The dose should not be reduced or the treatment stopped, except on the advice of a doctor.

If, for any reason, antiepileptic drug treatment needs to be stopped, the dose should be reduced gradually. People on antiepileptic therapy are advised to carry an identification tag giving full details of their condition and treatment (see p.29).

COMMON DRUGS

Carbamazepine *	Nitrazepam *
Clobazam	Oxcarbazepine
Clonazepam *	Phenobarbital *
Diazepam *	Phenytoin *
Divalproex	Primidone
Ethosuximide	Topiramate *
Fosphenytoin	Valproic acid *
Gabapentin *	Vigabatrin
Lamotrigine *	
Levetiracetam	
Lorazepam *	
Methsuximide	* See Part 4

DRUGS FOR PARKINSONISM

Parkinsonism is a general term used to describe shaking of the head and limbs, muscular stiffness, an expressionless face, and inability to control or initiate movement. It is caused by an imbalance of chemicals in the brain; the effect of acetylcholine is increased by a reduction in the action of dopamine.

Parkinsonism has a variety of causes, but the most common is Parkinson's disease, degeneration of the dopamine-producing cells in the brain. Other causes include the *side effects* of certain drugs, notably antipsychotics (see p.69), and narrowing of the blood vessels in the brain.

Why drugs are used
Drugs can relieve the symptoms of parkinsonism but, unfortunately, the degeneration of brain cells in Parkinson's disease cannot be halted, although drugs can minimize symptoms for many years.

How they work
Drugs to treat parkinsonism restore the balance between the chemicals dopamine and acetylcholine. They fall into two main groups: those that reduce the effect of acetylcholine (*anticholinergic* drugs) and those that boost the effect of dopamine.

Anticholinergics combine with *receptors* on brain cells, preventing acetylcholine from binding to them. This action reduces acetylcholine's relative overactivity and restores the balance with dopamine.

Dopamine cannot pass from the blood to the brain, and therefore cannot be given to boost its levels in the brain. Instead, levodopa (L-dopa), the chemical from which it is naturally produced in the brain, is combined with carbidopa or benserazide to prevent it from being converted to dopamine before it reaches the brain. Amantadine (also used as an antiviral, see p.119) boosts levels of dopamine in the brain by stimulating its release. The action

of dopamine can also be boosted by other drugs, including bromocriptine, pergolide, pramipexole, or ropinirole, which mimic the action of dopamine.

Choice of drug
Anticholinergics are often effective in the early stages of Parkinson's disease and are used to treat parkinsonism due to anti-psychotic drugs, which have dopamine-blocking properties. L-dopa is usually given when the disease impairs walking. Its effectiveness usually wanes after two to five years, in which case other dopamine-boosting drugs may also be prescribed.

ACTION OF DRUGS FOR PARKINSONISM

Normal movement depends on a balance in the brain between dopamine and acetylcholine, which combine with receptors on brain cells. In parkinsonism, there is less dopamine present, with the result that acetylcholine is relatively overactive. The balance between acetylcholine and dopamine may be restored by anticholinergic drugs, which combine with the receptor for acetylcholine to block the action of acetylcholine on the brain cell, or by dopamine-boosting drugs, which increase the level of dopamine activity in the brain.

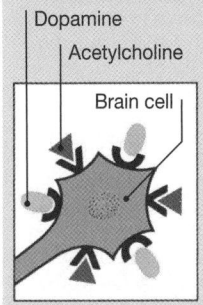 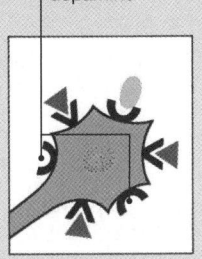 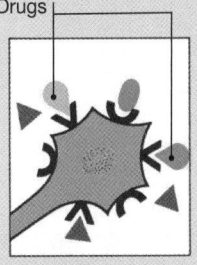 

Normal chemical balance
Normally dopamine and acetylcholine are balanced.

Chemical imbalance in parkinsonism
If dopamine activity is low, acetylcholine is overactive.

Action of anticholi-nergic drugs
Anticholinergic drugs displace acetylcholine and restore balance.

Action of dopamine-boosting drugs
These drugs increase dopamine activity and restore balance.

COMMON DRUGS

Dopamine-boosting drugs	Ropinirole
Amantadine *	Selegiline *
Bromocriptine	
Entacapone	**Anticholinergic drugs**
Ethopropazine	
Levodopa/	Benztropine
benserazide *	Procyclidine *
Levodopa/	Trihexyphenidyl
carbidopa *	
Pramipexole *	
Rasagiline *	

* See Part 4

DRUGS FOR DEMENTIA

Dementia is a decline in mental function that is severe enough to affect normal social or occupational activities. It can be sudden and irreversible, for example due to a stroke or a head injury. It can also develop gradually and may be a feature of a number of disorders, including poor circulation in the brain, multiple sclerosis, and Alzheimer's disease. Much research is in progress on the cause of Alzheimer's disease, which is the most common cause of dementia.

Why they are used
Drugs called acetylcholinesterase inhibitors (AchIs) have been found to improve the symptoms of dementia in Alzheimer's disease, although they do not prevent its long-term progression.

How they work
In healthy people, acetylcholinesterase (an enzyme in the brain) breaks down the *neurotransmitter* acetylcholine, balancing its levels and limiting its effects. In Alzheimer's disease, there is a deficiency of acetylcholine. AchIs block the action of the enzyme acetylcholinesterase, raising brain levels of acetylcholine, thus increasing the patient's alertness and slowing the rate of deterioration.

How they affect you
Drug treatment is started at a low dose following an assessment by a specialist of mental function. The dosage is increased gradually to minimize *side effects*. Any improvements should begin to appear in about 3 weeks. Assessment

is repeated after 3 months to see if the treatment is beneficial.

Risks and special precautions
It is important to continue taking these drugs because there is a gradual loss of improvement after they are stopped. Side effects include urinary difficulties, nausea, vomiting, and diarrhea. These drugs may increase the risk of seizures in some people.

COMMON DRUGS

Acetylcholinesterase inhibitors	**Other**
Donepezil *	Memantine *
Galantamine *	
Rivastigmine *	* See Part 4

NERVOUS SYSTEM STIMULANTS

A person's state of mental alertness varies throughout the day and is under the control of chemicals in the brain, some of which are depressant, causing drowsiness, and others that are stimulant, heightening awareness.

It is thought that an increase in the activity of the depressant chemicals may be responsible for a condition called narcolepsy, which is a tendency to fall asleep during the day for no obvious reason. In this case, the nervous system stimulants are administered to increase wakefulness. These drugs include the amphetamines (usually dextroamphetamine), the related drug methylphenidate, and modafinil. Amphetamines are used less often these days because of the risk of *dependence*. A common home remedy for increasing alertness is caffeine, a mild stimulant that is present in coffee, tea, and cola. Respiratory stimulants related to caffeine are used to improve breathing (see right).

Why drugs are used

In adults who suffer from narcolepsy, some of these drugs prevent excessive drowsiness during the day. Stimulants do not cure narcolepsy and, since the disorder usually lasts throughout the sufferer's lifetime, may have to be taken indefinitely. Methylphenidate, lisdexamfetamine, mixed salts amphetamine, or dextroamphetamine are sometimes given to children suffering from attention deficit hyperactivity disorder (ADHD). Stimulants were once used as part of the treatment for obesity because reduced appetite is a *side effect* of amphetamines but they are no longer appropriate for weight reduction. Diet is now the main treatment, together with orlistat if necessary.

Apart from their use in narcolepsy, nervous system stimulants are not useful in the long term because the brain soon develops *tolerance* to them.

How they work

The level of wakefulness is controlled by a part of the brain stem called the reticular activating system (RAS). Activity in this area depends on the balance between chemicals, some of which are *excitatory* (including norepinephrine (noradrenaline)) and some *inhibitory,* such as gamma aminobutyric acid (GABA). Stimulants promote release of noradrenaline, increasing activity in the RAS and other parts of the brain, so raising alertness.

How they affect you

In adults, the central nervous system stimulants taken in the prescribed dose for narcolepsy increase wakefulness, thereby allowing normal concentration and thought processes to occur. They may also reduce appetite and cause tremors. In children with ADHD, they improve

RESPIRATORY STIMULANTS

Some stimulants (for example, aminophylline and theophylline) act on the part of the brain – the respiratory centre – that controls respiration. They are sometimes used in hospitals to help people who have difficulty breathing, mainly very young babies and adults with severe chest infections.

core symptoms such as inattention, hyperactivity, and impulsivity.

Risks and special precautions

Some people, especially the elderly or those with previous psychiatric problems, are particularly sensitive to stimulants and may experience *adverse effects*, even when the drugs are given in comparatively low doses. They need to be used with caution in children because they can retard growth if taken for prolonged periods. An excess of these drugs given to a child may depress the nervous system, producing drowsiness or even loss of consciousness. Palpitations may also occur. These medications are generally not recommended in those with an overactive thyroid, high blood pressure, or abnormalities of the heart or heart disease. Modafinil is generally not recommended for use in children.

These drugs reduce the level of natural stimulants in the brain, so after regular use for a few weeks a person may become physically dependent on them for normal function. If they are abruptly withdrawn, the excess of natural *inhibitory* chemicals in the brain depresses central nervous system activity, producing *withdrawal symptoms*. These may include lethargy, depression, increased appetite, and difficulty staying awake.

Stimulants can produce overactivity in the brain if used inappropriately or in excess, resulting in extreme restlessness, sleeplessness, nervousness, or anxiety. They also stimulate the sympathetic branch of the autonomic nervous system (see p.63), causing shaking, sweating, and palpitations. More serious risks of exceeding the prescribed dose are seizures and a major disturbance in mental functioning that may result in delusions and hallucinations. Because these drugs have been abused, amphetamines and methylphenidate are classified as controlled drugs (see pp.13 and 483).

ACTION OF NERVOUS SYSTEM STIMULANTS

Wakefulness is controlled by a part of the brain stem called the reticular activating system (RAS).

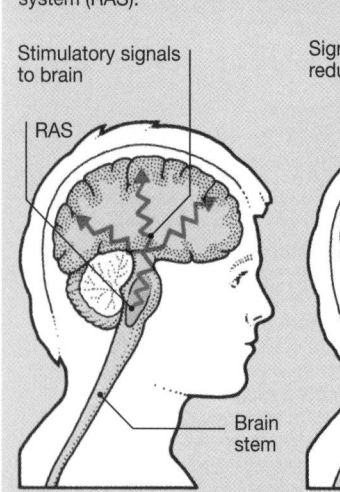

Stimulatory signals to brain

RAS

Brain stem

Normal brain activity
When the brain is functioning normally, signals from the RAS stimulate the upper parts of the brain, which control thought processes and alertness.

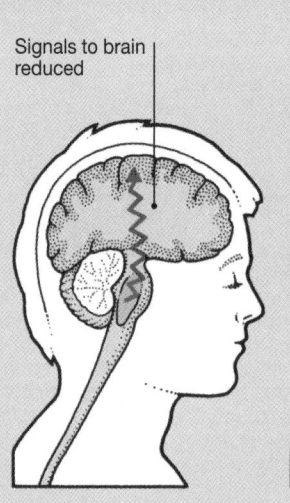

Signals to brain reduced

Brain activity in narcolepsy
In narcolepsy, the level of signals from the RAS is greatly reduced.

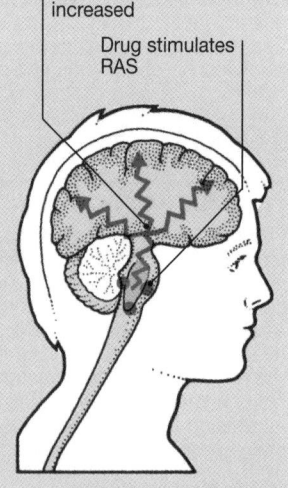

Signals to brain increased

Drug stimulates RAS

Normal brain activity restored
Central nervous system stimulants act on the RAS to increase the level of stimulatory signals to the brain.

COMMON DRUGS

Nervous system stimulants	Mixed salts amphetamine
Dextroamphetamine	Modafinil
Methylphenidate ✳	✳ See Part 4

DRUGS FOR MIGRAINE

Migraine is a term applied to recurrent severe headaches affecting only one side of the head and caused by changes in the blood vessels around the brain and scalp. They may be accompanied by nausea and vomiting and sometimes preceded by warning signs, usually an impression of flashing lights or numbness and tingling in the arm. Occasionally, speech may be impaired, or the attack may be disabling. The underlying cause of migraine is uncertain, but an attack may be triggered by a blow to the head, physical exertion, certain foods and drugs, or emotional factors such as excitement, tension, or shock. A family history of migraine also increases the chance of an individual suffering from it.

Why drugs are used

Drugs are used either to relieve symptoms or to prevent attacks. Different drugs are used in each approach, but none cures the underlying disorder. However, a susceptibility to migraine headaches can clear up spontaneously, and if you are taking drugs regularly, your physician may recommend that you stop them after a few months to see if this has happened.

In most people, migraine headaches can be relieved by a mild analgesic (painkiller), for example, acetaminophen, ibuprofen, or ASA, or a stronger one like naproxen, ergotamine, or a triptan (see Analgesics, p.64). If nausea and vomiting accompany the migraine, tablets may not be absorbed sufficiently from the gut. Absorption can be increased if drugs are taken as soluble tablets in water or with an anti-emetic.

Some drugs used to relieve attacks can be given by injection, inhaler, nasal spray, or *suppository*. Preparations that contain caffeine should be avoided since headaches may be caused by excessive use or on stopping treatment. 5HT$_1$ *agonist* drugs (triptans, such as sumatriptan) are used if analgesics are not effective. Ergotamine is used less often now.

The factors that trigger an individual's attacks should be identified and avoided. Anti-anxiety drugs such as benzodiazepines are not usually prescribed if stress is a precipitating factor because of the potential for dependence. If the attacks occur more than 3 or 4 times a month or if the abortive therapy is not effective, drugs to prevent the attacks may be prescribed. Drugs used to prevent migraine are beta blockers (such as propranolol, see p.83), calcium channel blockers (such as flunarizine and verapamil), antidepressants (such as amitriptyline, see p. 68) and pizotifen (an antihistamine and serotinin blocker). Methysergide is not commonly used because of its serious *side effects*.

How they work

The mechanism of how a migraine headache occurs is not completely understood. It is believed that a complex set of neurological events, which also

affects the blood vessels, occurs during a migraine episode. Sensory cells in certain parts of the brain are triggered; this also causes the release of several substances, resulting in changes in *neurotransmitters* levels such as that of serotonin and dopamine. Drugs such as sumatriptan (triptans) work by stimulating specific serotonin (5-HT) receptors, located on blood vessels and on nerve terminals. Pizotifen and propranolol block the effect of chemicals on blood vessels and thereby prevent attacks (see Action of drugs used for migraine, above).

ASA and acetaminophen relieve pain by blocking prostaglandins. Ergotamine relieves pain by narrowing dilated blood vessels in the scalp.

How they affect you

Each drug has its own *adverse effects*. 5HT$_1$ agonists may cause chest tightness and drowsiness. Ergotamine may cause drowsiness, tingling sensations in the skin, cramps, and weakness in the legs, and vomiting may be made worse. Pizotifen may cause drowsiness and weight gain. For effects of beta blockers such as propranolol, see p.406, and for analgesics, see p.64.

Risks and special precautions

5HT$_1$ agonists should not usually be used by those with high blood pressure, angina, or coronary heart disease. Ergotamine

can damage blood vessels by prolonged overconstriction so it should be used with caution by those with poor circulation. Excessive use can lead to dependence and many adverse effects, including headache. You should not take more than what your physician advises in any one week.

How they are administered

These drugs are usually taken by mouth as tablets or *capsules*. Sumatriptan can also be taken as an injection and dihydroergotamine, zolmitriptan, and sumatriptan are available as a nasal spray. Ergotamine can be taken orally or as an injection.

ACTION OF DRUGS USED FOR MIGRAINE

The underlying cause of migraines is uncertain, but symptoms occur when chemicals in the bloodstream affect blood vessels around the brain and in the scalp. In the first stage of a migraine attack, the blood vessels surrounding the brain constrict, causing warning signs (below left). In the second stage, the blood vessels in the scalp dilate, causing a severe headache (below right).

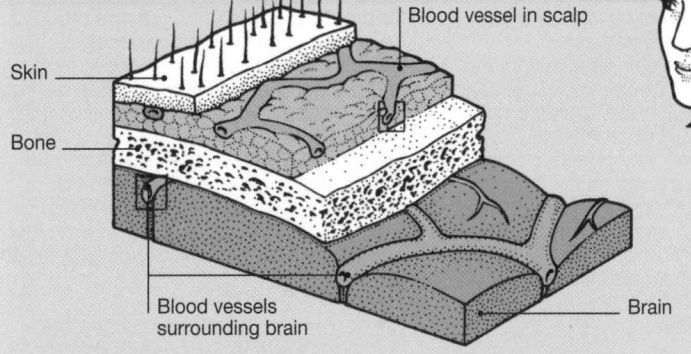

Skin

Bone

Blood vessel in scalp

Blood vessels surrounding brain

Brain

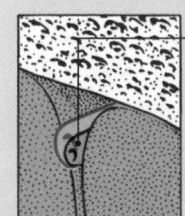

Constricted blood vessel

Preventing migraine
Migraine-preventing drugs block the action of chemicals that cause constriction of the blood vessels surrounding the brain.

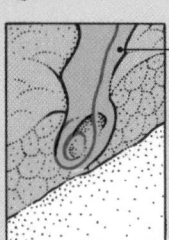

Dilated blood vessel

Stopping an attack
Ergotamine and 5HT$_1$ agonists taken during a migraine attack return the dilated blood vessels in the scalp to their normal size.

COMMON DRUGS

Drugs to prevent migraine
Amitriptyline ✱
Atenolol ✱
Flunarizine
Metoprolol ✱
Nadolol
Pizotifen ✱
Propranolol ✱
Topiramate ✱
Valproic acid ✱
Verapamil ✱

5HT$_1$ agonists
Almotriptan
Eletriptan
Frovatriptan
Naratriptan
Rizatriptan ✱
Sumatriptan ✱
Zolmitriptan

Other drugs to relieve migraine
Acetaminophen ✱
ASA ✱
Dihydroergotamine
Ergotamine ✱
Ibuprofen ✱

✱ See Part 4

ANTI-EMETICS

Drugs used to treat or prevent vomiting or nausea are known as anti-emetics. Vomiting is a reflex action for getting rid of harmful substances, but it may also be a symptom of disease. Vomiting and nausea are often caused by a digestive tract infection, travel sickness, pregnancy, or vertigo (a balance disorder involving the inner ear). They can also occur as a *side effect* of some drugs, especially those used for cancer, radiation therapy, or general anesthesia.

Commonly used anti-emetics include metoclopramide, domperidone, cyclizine, haloperidol, ondansetron, granisetron, prochlorperazine, and promethazine. The phenothiazine and butyrophenone drug groups are also used as antihistamines (see p.110) and prescribed to treat some types of mental illness (see Antipsychotic drugs, p.69). Corticosteroids like dexamethasone may also be used in the prevention of chemotherapy related nausea and vomiting.

Why drugs are used

Physicians usually diagnose the cause of vomiting before prescribing an anti-emetic because vomiting may be due to a digestive tract infection or some other condition of the abdomen that might require treatment such as surgery. Treating only the vomiting and nausea might delay diagnosis, correct treatment, and recovery. Anti-emetics may be taken to prevent travel sickness (using one of the antihistamines), vomiting resulting from anticancer (see p.140) and other drug treatments (metoclopramide, haloperidol, domperidone, ondansetron, and prochlorperazine), to help the nausea in vertigo (see right), and occasionally to relieve cases of severe vomiting during pregnancy. You should not take an anti-emetic during pregnancy except on medical advice. No anti-emetic drug should be taken for longer than a couple of days without consulting your physician.

How they work

Nausea and vomiting occur when the vomiting centre in the brain is stimulated by signals from three places in the body: the digestive tract, the part of the inner ear controlling balance, and the brain

VERTIGO AND MÉNIÈRE'S DISEASE

Vertigo is a spinning sensation in the head, which is often accompanied by nausea and vomiting. It is usually caused by a disease affecting the organ of balance in the inner ear. Anti-emetic drugs are prescribed to relieve the symptoms.

Ménière's disease is a disorder in which excess fluid builds up in the inner ear, causing vertigo, noises in the ear, and gradual deafness. It is usually treated with betahistine, prochlorperazine, or an anti-anxiety drug (see p.67). A diuretic (see p.85) may also be given in order to reduce the excess fluid in the ear.

itself via thoughts and emotions and via its chemoreceptor trigger zone, which responds to harmful substances in the blood. Anti-emetic drugs may act at one or more of these places (see Action of anti-emetics, left). Some help the stomach to empty its contents into the intestine. A combination may be used that works at different sites and has an additive effect.

How they affect you

As well as treating vomiting and nausea, many anti-emetic drugs may make you feel drowsy. However, for preventing travel sickness on long journeys, a sedating antihistamine may be an advantage.

Some anti-emetics (in particular, the phenothiazines and antihistamines) can block the parasympathetic nervous system (see p.63), causing dry mouth, blurred vision, or difficulty in passing urine. The phenothiazines may also lower blood pressure, leading to dizziness or fainting.

Risks and special precautions

As some antihistamines can make you drowsy, it may be advisable not to drive while taking them. Phenothiazines, butyrophenones, and metoclopramide can produce uncontrolled movements of the face and tongue, so they are used with caution in people with *parkinsonism*.

ACTION OF ANTI-EMETICS

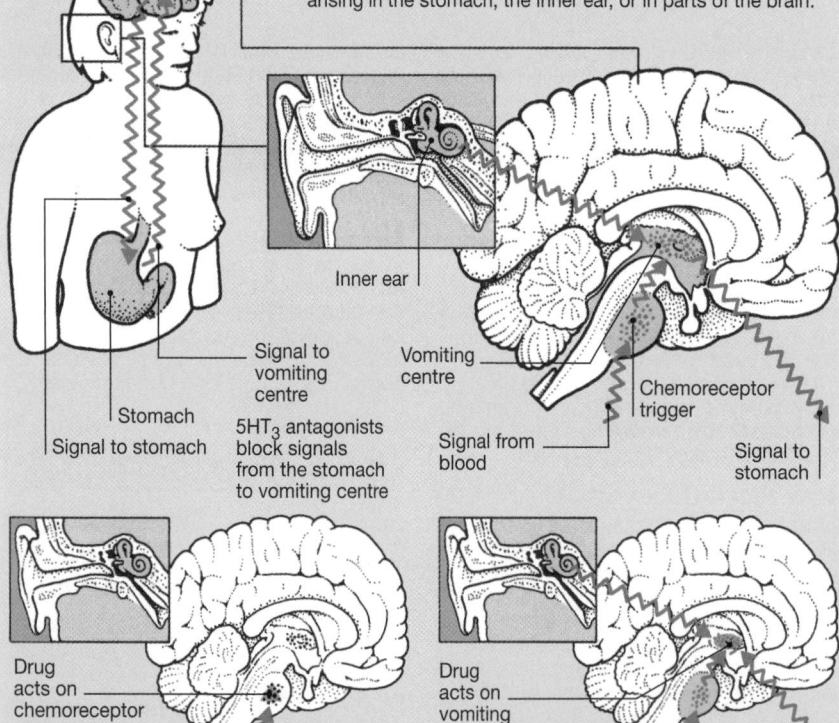

The vomiting reflex, in which the muscles of the stomach contract to expel the stomach contents, is triggered when the vomiting centre in the brain is stimulated by signals arising in the stomach, the inner ear, or in parts of the brain.

Brain

Inner ear

Signal to vomiting centre

Stomach
Signal to stomach

5HT$_3$ antagonists block signals from the stomach to vomiting centre

Vomiting centre

Signal from blood

Chemoreceptor trigger

Signal to stomach

Drug acts on chemoreceptor trigger

Drug acts on vomiting centre

Phenothiazines, butyrophenones and 5HT$_3$ antagonists prevent the chemoreceptor trigger from stimulating vomiting.

Antihistamines reduce the sensitivity of the vomiting centre.

COMMON DRUGS

Antihistamines
Dimenhydrinate *
Hydroxyzine
Meclizine
Promethazine *

Phenothiazines
Chlorpromazine
Perphenazine
Prochlorperazine *
Trifluoperazine

Anti-vertigo
Betahistine *

5HT$_3$ antagonists
Dolasetron
Granisetron
Ondansetron *

Butyrophenones
Haloperidol *

Other drugs
Aprepitant *
Dexamethasone *
Dronabinol
Metoclopramide *
Nabilone
Scopolamine

* See Part 4

RESPIRATORY SYSTEM

The respiratory system consists of the lungs and the passageways, such as the trachea and bronchi, by which air reaches them. Through the process of inhaling and exhaling air – breathing – the body is able to obtain the oxygen necessary for survival, and to expel carbon dioxide, which is the waste product of the basic human biological processes.

What can go wrong

Difficulty in breathing may be due to narrowing of the air passages, from spasm, as in asthma and bronchitis, or from swelling of the linings of the air passages, as in bronchiolitis, bronchitis, and asthma. Breathing difficulties may also be due to a bacterial or viral infection of the lung tissue, as in pneumonia and acute bronchitis, or to damage to the small air sacs (alveoli) from emphysema or from inhaled dusts or moulds, which cause pneumoconiosis and farmer's lung. Smoking and air pollution can affect the respiratory system in many ways, leading to diseases such as lung cancer and bronchitis.

Sometimes difficulty in breathing may be due to congestion of the lungs from heart disease, to an inhaled object such as a peanut, or to infection or inflammation of the throat. Symptoms of breathing difficulties often include a cough and a tight feeling in the chest.

Why drugs are used

Drugs with a variety of actions are used to clear the air passages, soothe inflammation, and reduce the production of mucus. Some can be bought without a prescription as single-ingredient or combined-ingredient preparations, often with an analgesic.

Decongestants (p.79) reduce the swelling inside the nose, thereby making it possible to breathe more freely. If the cause of the congestion is an allergic response, an antihistamine (p.110) is often recommended to relieve symptoms or to prevent attacks. Bacterial infections of the respiratory tract are usually treated with antibiotics (p.114).

Bronchodilators are drugs that widen the bronchi (p.76). They are used to prevent and relieve asthma attacks. Corticosteroids (p.127) reduce inflammation in the swollen inner layers of the airways. They are used to prevent asthma attacks. Other drugs, such as sodium cromoglycate, may be used for treating allergies and preventing asthma attacks but they are not effective once an asthma attack has begun.

A variety of drugs are used to relieve a cough, depending on the type of cough involved. Some drugs make it easier to eliminate phlegm; others suppress the cough by inhibiting the cough reflex.

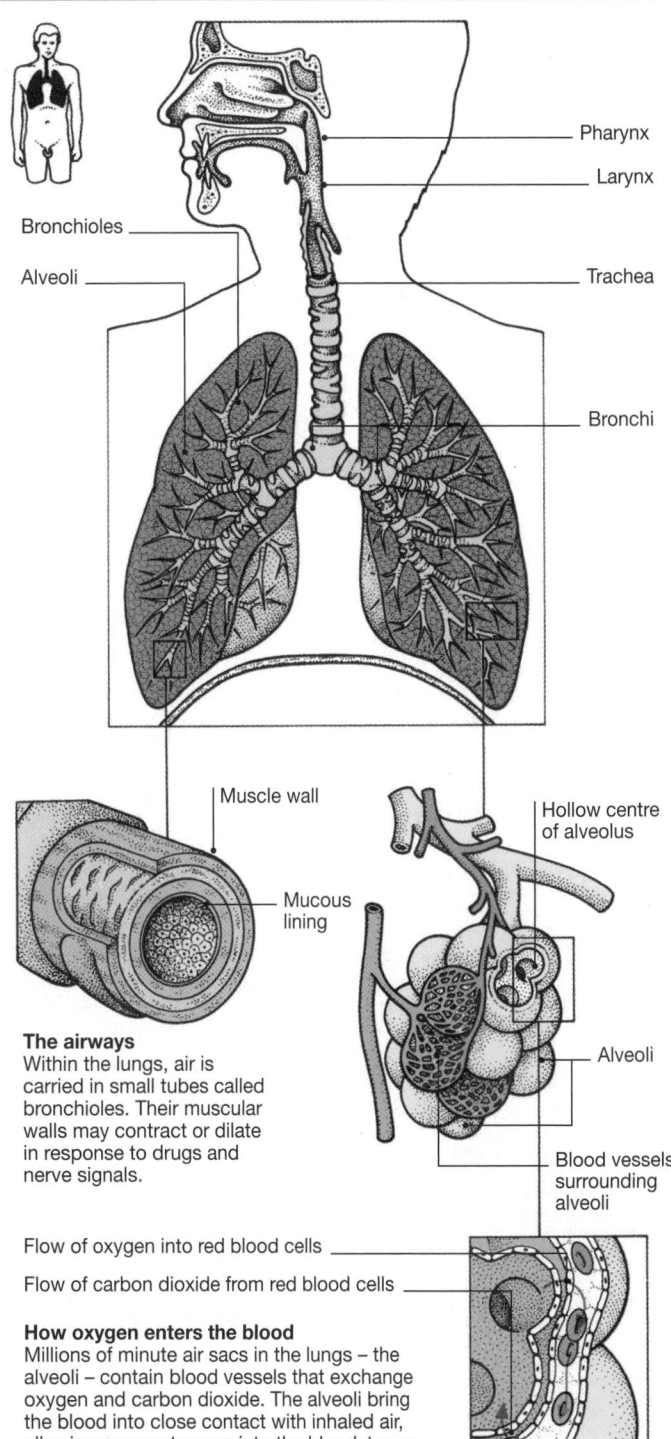

Pharynx
Larynx
Bronchioles
Alveoli
Trachea
Bronchi
Muscle wall
Hollow centre of alveolus
Mucous lining
Alveoli
Blood vessels surrounding alveoli

The airways
Within the lungs, air is carried in small tubes called bronchioles. Their muscular walls may contract or dilate in response to drugs and nerve signals.

Flow of oxygen into red blood cells
Flow of carbon dioxide from red blood cells

How oxygen enters the blood
Millions of minute air sacs in the lungs – the alveoli – contain blood vessels that exchange oxygen and carbon dioxide. The alveoli bring the blood into close contact with inhaled air, allowing oxygen to pass into the bloodstream and carbon dioxide to pass out of the body for expiration.

MAJOR DRUG GROUPS

Bronchodilators
Drugs for asthma
Decongestants
Drugs to treat coughs

See also sections on Allergy (p.109) and Infections (p.112)

BRONCHODILATORS

Chronic Obstructive Pulmonary Disease (COPD) affects airways (both large and small) and the lung tissue. Air entering the lungs passes through narrow tubes called bronchioles. In asthma and COPD the bronchioles become narrower, either as a result of contraction of the muscles in their walls, or as a result of mucus congestion. This narrowing of the bronchioles obstructs the flow of air into and out of the lungs and causes breathlessness.

Bronchodilators are prescribed to widen the bronchioles and improve breathing. There are three main groups of bronchodilators: *sympathomimetics*, *anticholinergics*, and xanthine drugs, which are related to caffeine. They are all used for relief of symptoms, and do not affect the underlying disease process. Anticholinergics are thought to be more effective in, and are used particularly for, COPD. In chronic asthma, they are less effective, and are usually prescribed as additional therapy when control with other drugs is inadequate. Sympathomimetics or beta$_2$-agonists are the mainstay of asthma treatment, and are also frequently used in COPD. Xanthines have been used for many years, both for asthma and COPD. They usually need precise adjustment of dosage to be effective while avoiding *side effects*. This makes them more difficult to use, and they are reserved for people whose condition cannot be controlled by other bronchodilators alone.

Why drugs are used

Bronchodilators help to dilate the bronchioles of people suffering from asthma and COPD. However, they are of little benefit to those suffering from severe COPD.

Bronchodilators can either be taken when they are needed in order to relieve an attack of breathlessness that is in progress, or on a regular basis to prevent such attacks from occurring. Some people find it helpful to take an extra dose of their bronchodilator immediately before undertaking any activity likely to provoke an attack of breathlessness.

A patient who requires treatment with a beta$_2$-agonist inhaler more than twice a week or at night should see his or her physician about preventative treatment with an inhaled corticosteroid.

Beta$_2$-agonist drugs are mainly used for the rapid relief of breathlessness; anticholinergic and xanthine drugs are used long term.

How they work

Bronchodilator drugs act by relaxing the muscles surrounding the bronchioles. Beta$_2$-agonist and anticholinergic drugs achieve this by interfering with nerve signals passed to the muscles through the autonomic nervous system (see p.63). Xanthine drugs are thought to relax the muscle in the bronchioles by a direct effect on the muscle fibres, but their precise action is not known.

Bronchodilator drugs usually improve breathing within a few minutes of administration. Corticosteroids act more slowly, and it may be several days before the capacity for exercise increases substantially. Eventually the corticosteroids should reduce the need for bronchodilators.

Because beta$_2$-agonist drugs stimulate a branch of the autonomic nervous system that controls heart rate, they may sometimes cause palpitations and trembling. Typical side effects of anticholinergic drugs include dry mouth, blurred vision, and difficulty in passing urine. However, when used in an inhaler, these effects are rarely reported. Xanthine drugs may cause headaches and nausea.

Risks and special precautions

Since most bronchodilators are not taken by mouth, but inhaled, they do not usually cause serious side effects. However, because of their possible effect on heart rate, xanthine and beta$_2$-agonist drugs need to be prescribed with caution to people with heart problems, high blood pressure, or an overactive thyroid gland. Smoking tobacco and drinking alcohol increase excretion of xanthines from the body, reducing their effects. Stopping smoking after being stabilized on xanthine may result in a rise in blood concentration, and an increased risk of side effects. It is advisable to stop smoking before starting treatment. The anticholinergic drugs may not be suitable for people with urinary retention or those who have a tendency to glaucoma.

ACTION OF BRONCHODILATORS

When the bronchioles are narrowed following contraction of the muscle layer and swelling of the mucous lining, the passage of air is impeded. Bronchodilators act on the nerve signals that govern muscle activity. Sympatho-mimetics or Beta$_2$-agonists enhance the action of neurotransmitters that encourage muscle relaxation. Anticholinergics block the neurotransmitters that trigger muscle contraction and reduce production of mucus. Xanthines promote muscle relaxation by a direct effect on the muscles.

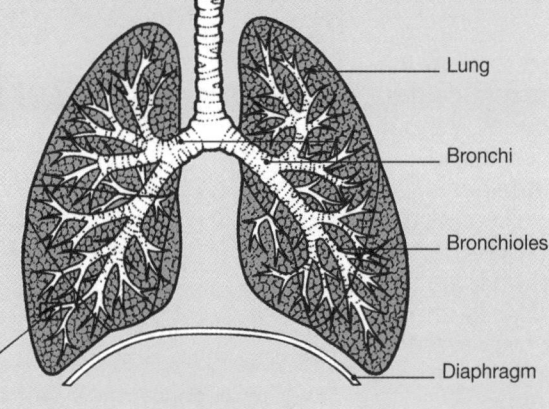

Trachea

Lung

Bronchi

Bronchioles

Diaphragm

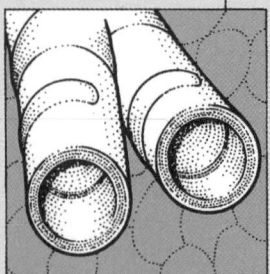

Normal bronchioles
The muscle surrounding the bronchioles is relaxed, thus leaving the airway open.

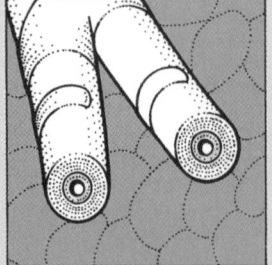

Asthma attack
The bronchiole muscle contracts and the lining swells, narrowing the airway.

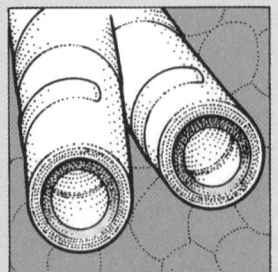

After drug treatment
The muscles relax, thereby opening the airway, but the lining remains swollen.

COMMON DRUGS

Sympathomimetics	Xanthines
Fenoterol	Aminophylline *
Formoterol *	Oxtriphylline
Indacaterol	Theophylline *
Orciprenaline	
Salbutamol *	
Salmeterol *	
Terbutaline	

Anticholinergics	
Ipratropium *	
Tiotropium *	* See Part 4

DRUGS FOR ASTHMA

Asthma is a chronic lung disease characterized by episodes in which the bronchioles constrict due to over-sensitivity. The attacks are usually, but not always, reversible; asthma is also known as reversible airways obstruction. About 5 per cent of adults and 10 per cent of children have the disease. Sometimes the inflammation causing the constriction is due to an identifiable allergen in the atmosphere, such as house dust mites, but often there is no obvious trigger. Breathlessness is the main symptom. Wheezing, coughing, and chest tightness are common. Asthma sufferers often have attacks during the night and wake up with breathing difficulty. The illness varies in severity, and it can be life threatening.

There are a number of drugs that are used in the control of asthma. Where drugs are needed only to control an occasional attack (relievers), a *sympathomimetic* bronchodilator will probably be used in inhaler form. When the patient needs continuous preventative treatment (preventers/controllers) there are a number of choices: often an inhaled corticosteroid may be used (with a sympathomimetic inhaler if attacks persist). More severe cases may require higher dose corticosteroids or the addition of a long-acting sympathomimetic bronchodilator. If this is not adequate, a high dose corticosteroid will be used with an *anticholinergic* drug, or these in combination with others already tried. There are also leukotriene antagonists, which may be used when corticosteroids cannot be used in an individual.

Theophylline may also be considered. Some people who suffer from very severe asthma may need such large doses of corticosteroids that tablets have to be taken. In those who still have asthma symptoms while on inhaled corticosteroids, omalizumab can help reduce the number of asthma attacks. Omalizumab blocks IgE, which is a naturally occurring substance in the body that plays a role in asthma. Antihistamines were prescribed for asthma in the past but this has not proved to be a successful treatment.

Why drugs are used

In asthma, the airways (bronchioles) constrict making it difficult to get air in or out of the lungs. Bronchodilators (sympathomimetics, anticholinergics, and theophylline) relax the constricted muscles around the bronchioles (p.76). Short-acting sympathomimetics act within a few minutes when inhaled and are used to provide relief of symptoms during an attack, and in more severe cases the long-acting sympathomimetics may be used to help with continuous protective cover. They are particularly useful for preventing symptoms overnight. Theophylline/aminophylline must be given by mouth or injection; the tablets are used for regular continuous dosing, and the injection is used in hospital to gain control of severe asthma. Drugs that are not bronchodilators, such as corticosteroids and leukotriene receptor antagonists (see p.78), are effective for long-term protection. Corticosteroids are also given orally for severe acute attacks. Although

they have a delayed onset of action (12–24 hours), they help prevent a recurrence of symptoms in the days after the acute attack.

In some cases, an intravenous injection of magnesium sulfate may be given to treat a severe asthma attack.

How they work

Inhaling a drug directly into the lungs is the best way of getting benefit without excessive *side effects*. A selection of devices for delivering the drug into the airways is illustrated below.

Inhalers or puffers release a small dose when they are pressed, but require some skill to use effectively. A large hollow plastic "spacer" can help you to inhale your drug more easily. Insufflation cartridges (dry powder inhalers) are easier to use because the drug is taken in as you breathe normally.

Nebulizers pump compressed air through a solution of drug to produce a fine mist that is inhaled through a face mask. They deliver large doses of the drug to the lungs, rapidly relieving breathing difficulty.

Bronchodilators act by relaxing the muscles surrounding the bronchioles (see p.76). Corticosteroids are used for their anti-inflammatory properties. By suppressing airway inflammation they reduce the swelling inside the bronchioles, complementing the relaxation of the walls by the bronchodilators in opening up the tubes. Reducing the inflammation also reduces the amount of mucus produced, and this again helps to clear the airways.

DIFFERENT TYPES OF INHALER

Inhalers are used to deliver drugs to relieve or prevent the symptoms of asthma. A wide range of different types of inhaler is available and the most commonly prescribed ones are shown here. Many people are prescribed a reliever and a preventer drug and these may come in different types of inhaler, depending on the drugs that are given. Although every inhaler works on the same broad principle to deliver the drug directly to the bronchioles through a mouthpiece, there are individual differences in the actions required. Therefore, it is important to read the instructions carefully and practise using the inhaler before you need it in an emergency. Some inhalers are activated by taking in a breath, and these may be easier for some people to use. If you have trouble operating an inhaler, you can ask your physician for a spacer device (see p.78); this requires less coordination between releasing the drug and breathing in, and is particularly suitable for children and the elderly. Always check how to use your particular device with the *pharmacist*.

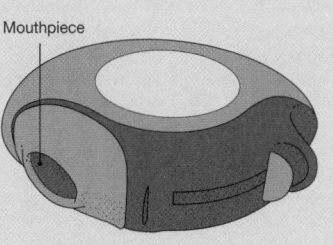

Diskus

Mouthpiece

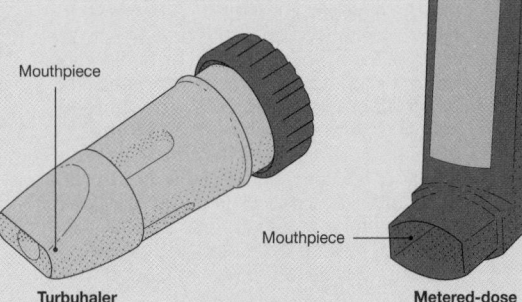

Turbuhaler

Mouthpiece

Mouthpiece

Metered-dose

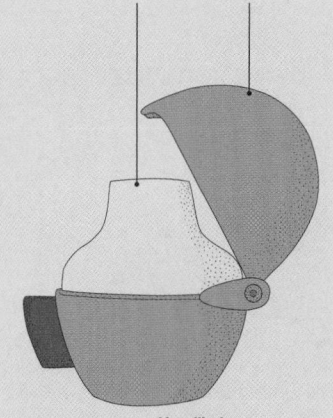

Mouthpiece   Cover

Handihaler

DRUGS FOR ASTHMA continued

HOW TO USE A SPACER

A spacer is a large, hollow plastic device that has a mouthpiece at one end and a slot for an inhaler at the other; it can be split in two for easy cleaning and transporting. A spacer is ideal for groups such as children and the elderly as it avoids special breathing techniques and allows the patient to breathe in the drug at a normal rate. For small children and the very sick, the mouthpiece can be fitted with a mask that covers the mouth and nose. The spacer should be cleaned once a week to remove deposits and reduce the build-up of static electricity because this can reduce the amount of drug that reaches the airways.

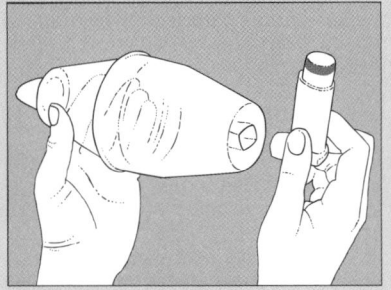

1 Click the two halves of the spacer together securely. Remove the cap from the inhaler's mouthpiece and shake the inhaler.

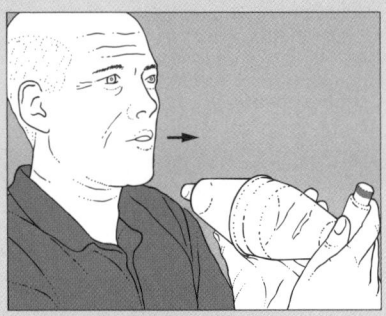

2 Push the mouthpiece of the inhaler into the slot at the blunt end of the spacer. Breathe out as deeply as possible; prepare to place the spacer in your mouth.

3 Press the canister to release a dose of the drug. Breathe in, hold breath for 10 seconds, breathe out into the spacer, and repeat. Another dose can be taken.

HOW TO USE A METERED-DOSE INHALER

The metered-dose inhaler is one of the most commonly prescribed devices for treating asthma, and is used to deliver a range of drugs. It is easy to use, and it takes only a matter of seconds for the drug to reach the airways and relieve breathing. Practise the technique before you need to use the inhaler in an emergency.

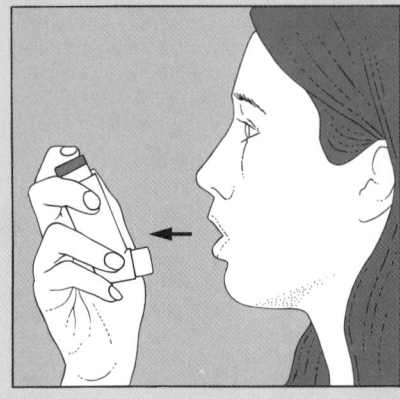

1 Remove the cap from the mouthpiece and shake the inhaler. Breathe out gently. Get ready to place the mouthpiece in the mouth.

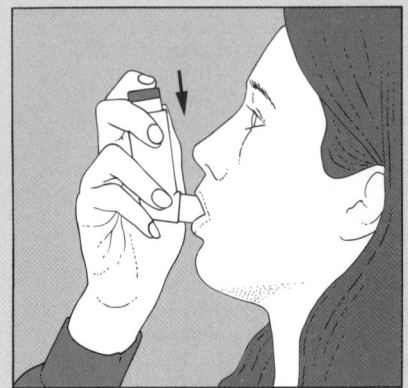

2 Tilt back the head, breathe in slowly and deeply, and at the same time press the canister. Hold breath for 10 seconds.

Corticosteroids usually start to increase the sufferer's capacity for exercise within a few days, and most people find that the frequency of their attacks is reduced.

Leukotrienes occur naturally in the body; they used to be called "slow-reacting substances". They are chemically related to the prostaglandins, but much more potent in producing an inflammatory reaction; they are also much more potent than histamine at causing broncho-constriction. Leukotrienes seem to play an important part in asthma. Drugs have been developed that block their receptors (leukotriene receptor antagonists) and therefore reduce the inflammation and bronchoconstriction of asthma. Cromoglycate acts by stabilizing mast cells in the lungs, preventing them from releasing histamine, leukotrienes, and other inflammation-causing chemicals.

Risks and special precautions

The drugs taken by inhalation act locally and are used in much lower doses than would be needed as tablets. They do not commonly cause serious side effects, but the dry powder inhalations can cause a reflex bronchospasm as the powder hits the lining of the airways; this can be avoided by using a short-acting sympathomimetic first. Inhaled corticosteroids may encourage fungal growth in the mouth and throat (thrush). This can be minimized by using a spacer and/or by rinsing the mouth with water after each use. High doses of inhaled corticosteroids may suppress adrenal gland function, reduce bone density, cause bruising, increase the risk of glaucoma, and retard growth in children.

Sympathomimetics and theophylline taken by mouth may affect heart rate, and should be prescribed with caution to people with heart problems, high blood pressure, or an overactive thyroid gland. The effects of theophylline may last longer if you have a viral infection, heart failure, or liver cirrhosis. The drugs also interact with many other drugs. The anticholinergic drugs must be used with caution in patients who have prostate problems or urinary retention. Leukotriene *receptor antagonists* may rarely produce a syndrome with several potentially serious effects including worsening lung function and heart complications.

COMMON DRUGS

Sympathomimetics
Fenoterol
Formoterol ✳
Orciprenaline
Salbutamol ✳
Salmeterol ✳
Terbutaline ✳

Anticholinergics
Ipratropium ✳
Tiotropium ✳

Leukotriene antagonists
Montelukast ✳
Zafirlukast

Xanthines
Aminophylline ✳
Oxtriphylline
Theophylline ✳

Corticosteroids
Beclomethasone ✳
Budesonide ✳
Ciclesonide
Fluticasone ✳
Mometasone
Prednisolone/
  prednisone ✳

IgE blocker
Omalizumab

Other drugs
Sodium
  cromoglycate ✳
Ketotifen

✳ See Part 4

DECONGESTANTS

The usual cause of a blocked nose is swelling of the delicate mucous membrane that lines the nasal passages and excessive production of mucus as a result of inflammation. This may be caused by an infection (for example, a common cold) or it may be caused by an allergy (for example, to pollen), a condition known as allergic rhinitis or hay fever. Congestion can also occur in the sinuses (the air spaces in the skull), resulting in sinusitis. Decongestants are drugs that reduce swelling of the mucous membrane and suppress the production of mucus, helping to clear blocked nasal passages and sinuses. Antihistamines counter the allergic response in allergy- related conditions (see p.110). If the symptoms are persistent, either *topical* corticosteroids (see p.127) or sodium cromoglycate may be preferred. For children under 6 years of age, consult a physician or *pharmacist* before using a cough or cold product.

Why drugs are used

Decongestants aren't necessary for most common colds and blocked noses. Simple home remedies, for example, steam inhalation, possibly with the addition of an aromatic oil – such as menthol or eucalyptus – are often effective. Decongestants are used when such measures are ineffective or when there is a particular risk from untreated congestion – for example, in people who suffer from recurrent middle-ear or sinus infections.

Decongestants are available in the form of drops or sprays applied directly into the nose or they can be taken by mouth. Decongestant drugs are added to many over-the-counter cold remedies (see p.80).

How they work

When the mucous membrane lining the nose is irritated by infection or allergy, the blood vessels supplying the membrane become enlarged. This leads to fluid accumulation in the surrounding tissue and encourages the production of larger-than-normal amounts of mucus.

Most decongestants belong to the *sympathomimetic* group of drugs that stimulate the sympathetic branch of the

ACTION OF DECONGESTANTS

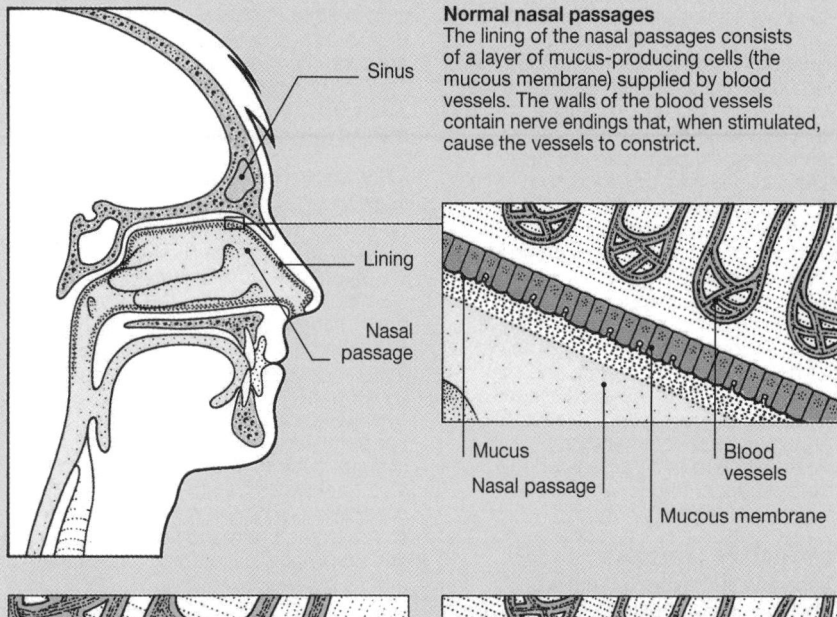

Normal nasal passages
The lining of the nasal passages consists of a layer of mucus-producing cells (the mucous membrane) supplied by blood vessels. The walls of the blood vessels contain nerve endings that, when stimulated, cause the vessels to constrict.

Sinus

Lining

Nasal passage

Mucus
Nasal passage
Blood vessels
Mucous membrane

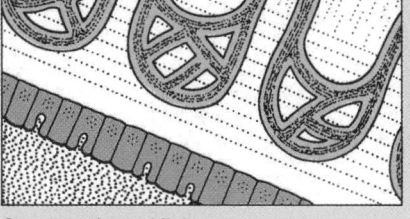

Congested nasal lining
When the blood vessels enlarge in response to infection or irritation, increased amounts of fluid pass into the mucous membrane, which swells and produces more mucus.

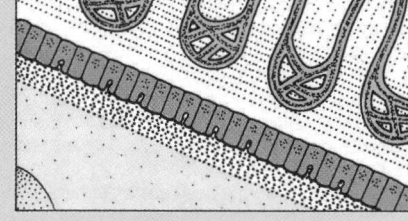

Effect of decongestants
Decongestants enhance the action of chemicals that stimulate constriction of the blood vessels. Narrowing of the blood vessels reduces swelling and mucus production.

autonomic nervous system (see p.63). One effect of this action is to constrict the blood vessels, reducing swelling of the lining of the nose and sinuses.

How they affect you

When applied topically in the form of drops or sprays, these drugs start to relieve congestion within a few minutes. Decongestants by mouth take a little longer to act, but their effect may also last

longer. Used in moderation, topical decongestants have few *adverse effects*, because they are not absorbed by the body in large amounts. Used for too long or in excess, topical decongestants can, after giving initial relief, do more harm than good, causing a "rebound congestion" (see left). This effect can be prevented by taking the minimum effective dose and by using decongestant preparations only when absolutely necessary. Decongestants taken by mouth do not cause rebound congestion but are more likely to cause other *side effects*.

REBOUND CONGESTION

This can happen when decongestant nose drops and sprays are withdrawn or overused. The result is a sudden increase in congestion due to widening of the blood vessels in the nasal lining because blood vessels are no longer constricted by the decongestant.

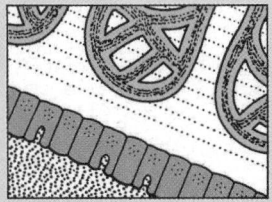

Congestion before drug treatment

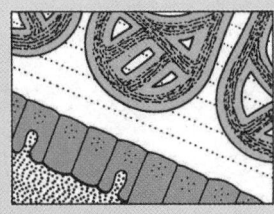

Congestion after stopping drug treatment

COMMON DRUGS

Used topically
Ephedrine
Oxymetazoline
Phenylephrine
Xylometazoline ✳

Taken by mouth
Ephedrine ✳
Phenylephrine
Pseudoephedrine ✳

✳ See Part 4

DRUGS TO TREAT COUGHS

Coughing is a natural response to irritation of the lungs and air passages, designed to expel harmful substances from the respiratory tract. Common causes of coughing include infection of the respiratory tract (for example, bronchitis or pneumonia), inflammation of the airways caused by asthma, or exposure to certain irritant substances such as smoke or chemical fumes. Depending on their cause, coughs may be productive – that is, phlegm-producing – or they may be dry.

In most cases, coughing is a helpful reaction that assists the body in ridding itself of excess phlegm and substances that irritate the respiratory system; suppressing the cough may actually delay recovery. However, repeated bouts of coughing can be distressing, and may increase irritation of the air passages. In such cases, medication to ease the cough may be recommended.

There are two main groups of cough remedies, according to whether the cough is productive or dry.

Productive coughs

Mucolytics and expectorants are sometimes recommended for productive coughs when simple home remedies such as steam inhalation have failed to "loosen" the cough and make it easier to cough up phlegm. Mucolytics alter the consistency of the phlegm, making it less sticky and easier to cough up. These are often given by inhalation. However, there is little evidence that they are effective.

Dornase alfa may be given to people who suffer from cystic fibrosis; the drug, given by inhalation via a nebulizer, is an enzyme that improves lung function by thinning the mucus. Expectorant drugs are taken by mouth to loosen a cough. There is some evidence that guaifenesin is effective. Expectorants are included in many over-the-counter cough remedies.

Dry coughs

In dry coughs there is no advantage to be gained from promoting the expulsion of phlegm. Drugs used for dry coughs are given to suppress the coughing mechanism by calming the part of the brain that governs the coughing reflex. Antihistamines are often given for mild coughs, particularly in children. Dextromethorphan (DM) is used in many over-the-counter cough products. For persistent coughs, mild opioid drugs such as codeine may be prescribed (see also Analgesics, p.64). All cough suppressants have a generally sedating effect on the brain and nervous system and commonly cause drowsiness and other *side effects*.

Selecting a cough medication

There is a bewildering variety of over-the-counter medications available for the treatment of coughs. Most consist of a syrupy base to which active ingredients and flavourings are added. Many contain a number of different active ingredients, sometimes with contradictory effects: it is

COLD CURES

Many preparations are available over-the-counter to treat different symptoms of the common cold. The main ingredient in most preparations is a mild analgesic, such as ASA or acetaminophen, accompanied by a decongestant (p.79), an antihistamine (p.110), and sometimes caffeine. Often the dose of each added ingredient is too low to provide any benefit. There is no evidence that vitamin C (see p.480) speeds recovery, but zinc supplements (see p.482) may be effective in shortening the cold's duration.

While some people find these drugs help to relieve symptoms, over-the-counter "cold cures" do not alter the course of the illness. Most doctors recommend using a product with a single analgesic, as the best way of alleviating symptoms. Other decongestants or antihistamines may be taken if needed, although antihistamines may cause sedation. These medicines are not harmless: take care to avoid overdose if using different brands.

not uncommon to find an expectorant (for a productive cough) and a decongestant included in the same preparation.

It is important to select the correct type of medication for your cough to avoid the risk that you may make your condition worse. For example, using a cough suppressant for a productive cough may prevent you getting rid of excess infected phlegm and may delay your recovery. It is best to choose a preparation with a single active ingredient that is appropriate for your type of cough. Diabetics may need to select a sugar-free product. If you are in any doubt about which product to choose, ask your physician or pharmacist for advice. Since there is a danger that use of over-the-counter cough remedies to alleviate symptoms may delay the diagnosis of a more serious underlying disorder, it is important to seek medical advice for any cough that persists for longer than a few days or if a cough is accompanied by additional symptoms such as fever or blood in the phlegm. For children under 2 years of age, a physician or pharmacist should be consulted before using a cough or cold product.

ACTION OF COUGH REMEDIES

Cough remedies are divided into two main groups: those that alter the consistency or production of phlegm (mucolytics and expectorants); and those that suppress the coughing reflex (opioid and non-opioid cough suppressants). Mucolytics are usually given by inhalation and act directly on the lungs and airways. Expectorants are taken by mouth, and are supposed to help bring up phlegm. Cough suppressants are taken by mouth and they act on the coughing centre in the brain.

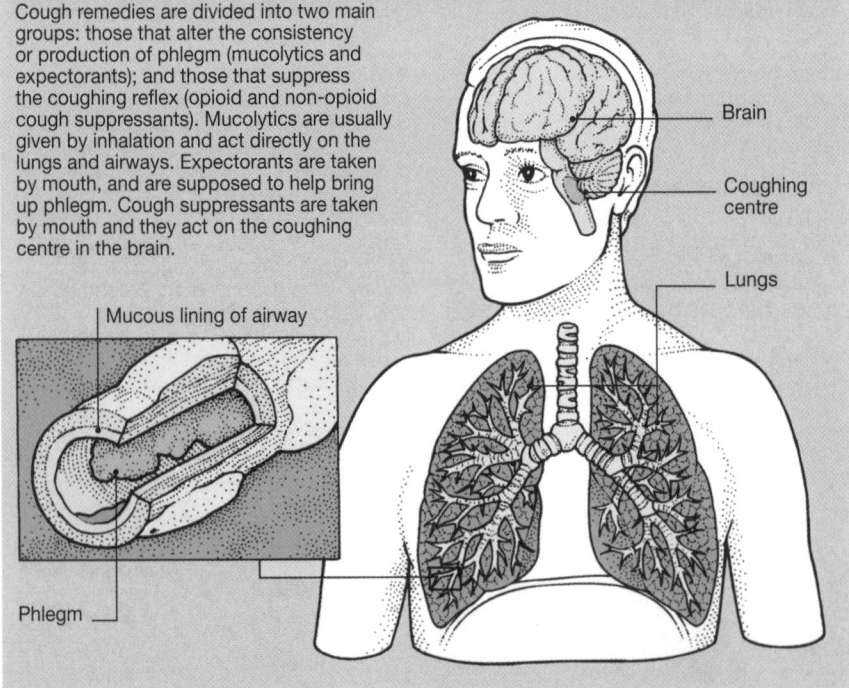

Brain

Coughing centre

Lungs

Mucous lining of airway

Phlegm

COMMON DRUGS

Expectorants
Guaifenesin

Mucolytics
Dornase alfa

Steam inhalation
Eucalyptus
Menthol

Opioid cough suppressants
Codeine ✱
Hydrocodone ✱

Non-opioid cough suppressants
Antihistamines (see p.110)
Dextromethorphan ✱

✱ See Part 4

HEART AND CIRCULATION

The blood transports oxygen, nutrients, and heat, contains chemical messages in the form of drugs and hormones, and carries away waste products for excretion by the kidneys. It is pumped by the heart to and from the lungs, and then in a separate circuit to the rest of the body, including the brain, digestive organs, muscles, kidneys, and skin.

What can go wrong

The efficiency of the circulation may be impaired by weakening of the heart's pumping action (heart failure) or irregularity of heart rate (arrhythmia). In addition, the blood vessels may be narrowed and clogged by fatty deposits (atherosclerosis). This may reduce blood supply to the brain, the extremities (peripheral vascular disease), or the heart muscle (coronary heart disease), causing angina. These last disorders can be complicated by the formation of clots that may block a blood vessel. A clot in the arteries supplying the heart muscle is known as coronary thrombosis; a clot in an artery inside the brain is the most frequent cause of stroke.

One common circulatory disorder is abnormally high blood pressure (hypertension), in which the pressure of circulating blood on the vessel walls is increased for reasons not yet fully understood. One factor may be loss of elasticity of the vessel walls (arteriosclerosis). Several other conditions, such as migraine and Raynaud's disease, are caused by temporary alterations to blood vessel size.

Why drugs are used

Because those suffering from heart disease often have more than one problem, several drugs may be prescribed at once. Many act directly on the heart to alter the rate and rhythm of the heart beat. These are known as anti-arrhythmics and include beta blockers, calcium channel blockers, and digoxin.

Other drugs affect the diameter of the blood vessels, either dilating them (vasodilators) to improve blood flow and reduce blood pressure, or constricting them (vasoconstrictors).

Drugs may also reduce blood volume and fat levels, and alter clotting ability. Diuretics (used in the treatment of hypertension and heart failure) increase the body's excretion of salt and water. Lipid-lowering drugs reduce blood cholesterol levels, thereby minimizing the risk of atherosclerosis. Drugs to reduce blood clotting are administered if there is a risk of abnormal blood clots forming in the heart, veins, or arteries. Drugs that increase clotting are given when the body's natural clotting mechanism is defective.

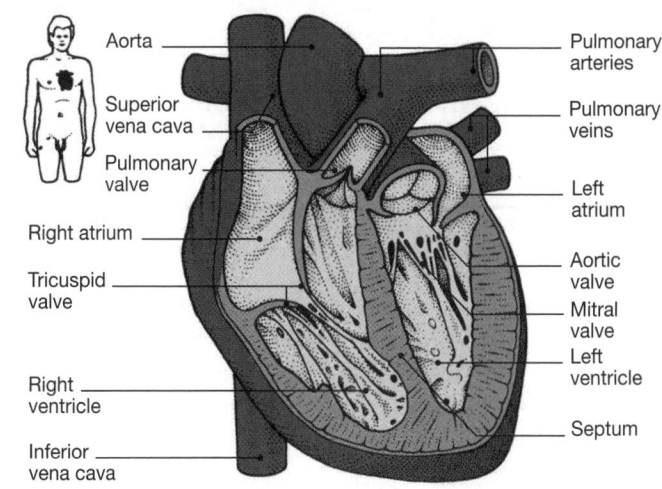

The heart
The heart is a pump with four chambers. The atrium and ventricle on the left side pump oxygenated blood to the body, while the chambers on the right pump deoxygenated blood to the lungs. Backflow of blood is stopped by valves at the chamber exits.

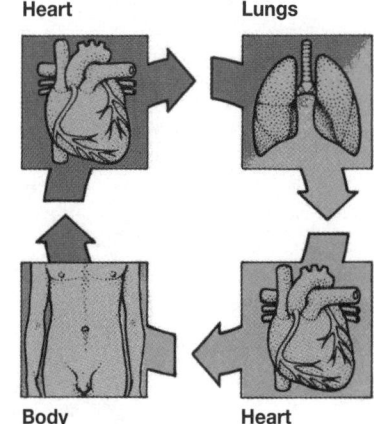

How blood circulates
Deoxygenated blood is carried to the heart from all parts of the body. It is then pumped to the lungs, where it becomes oxygenated. The oxygenated blood returns to the heart and from there is pumped throughout the body.

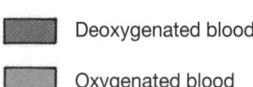

Deoxygenated blood

Oxygenated blood

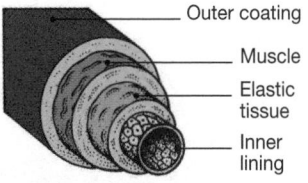

Arteries
Arteries carry blood away from the heart. Muscle walls contract and dilate in response to nerve signals.

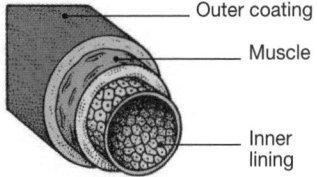

Veins
Veins carry blood back to the heart. The walls are less elastic than artery walls.

MAJOR DRUG GROUPS

Digitalis
Beta blockers
Vasodilators
Diuretics
Anti-arrhythmics

Anti-angina drugs
Antihypertensive drugs
Lipid-lowering drugs
Drugs that affect blood
  clotting

DIGITALIS

Digitalis is the collective term for the naturally occurring substances (also called cardiac glycosides) that are found in the leaves of plants of the foxglove family and used to treat certain heart disorders.

The principal drug in this group is digoxin. Digoxin dosage is usually adjusted to a therapeutic drug level in the blood (see also Risks and special precautions, below).

Why it is used

Digoxin does not cure heart disease but improves the heart's pumping action and so relieves many of the symptoms that result from poor heart function. It is useful for treating conditions in which the heart beats irregularly or too rapidly (notably in atrial fibrillation, see Anti-arrhythmic drugs, p.86), when it pumps too weakly (in congestive heart failure), or when the heart muscle is damaged and weakened following a heart attack.

Digoxin can be used for a short period when the heart is working poorly, but in many cases it has to be taken indefinitely. Its effect does not diminish with time. In cases of heart failure, this digitalis drug is often given together with a diuretic drug (see p.85).

How it works

The normal heart beat results from electrical impulses generated in nerve tissue within the heart. These impulses cause the heart muscle to contract and pump blood to the body. Digoxin reduces the flow of electrical impulses in the heart, therefore making the heart contract more slowly.

The force with which the heart muscle contracts depends on chemical changes in the heart muscle. By promoting these chemical changes, digoxin increases the force of muscle contraction each time the heart is stimulated. This compensates for the loss of power that occurs when some of the muscle is damaged following a heart attack. The stronger heart beat increases blood flow to the kidneys. This leads to increased urine production and therefore helps to remove the excess fluid that often accumulates as a result of heart failure.

How it affects you

Digoxin relieves the symptoms of heart failure – fatigue, breathlessness, and swelling of the legs – and increases your capacity for exercise. The frequency with which you need to pass urine may also be increased initially.

Risks and special precautions

Digoxin can be *toxic* and, if blood levels of digoxin rise too high, the symptoms of digitalis poisoning may be produced. These symptoms include excessive tiredness, confusion, loss of appetite, nausea, vomiting, visual disturbances, and diarrhea. If such symptoms occur during treatment with digoxin, it is important to report them to your physician promptly.

Digoxin is normally removed from the body by the kidneys; if kidney function is impaired, the drug is more likely to accumulate in the body and cause toxic side effects.

Digoxin is more toxic when blood potassium levels are low. Potassium deficiency is commonly caused by diuretic drugs, therefore people taking these drugs as well as digoxin need to have the effects of both the drugs and their blood potassium levels carefully monitored. Potassium supplements may be required.

ACTION OF DIGITALIS

The heart beat is triggered by electrical impulses that are generated by the pacemaker, a small mass of nerve tissue in the right atrium. Electrical signals are passed from the pacemaker to the atrio-ventricular node. From here a wave of impulses spreads throughout the heart muscle, causing it to contract and pump blood to the body. The pumping action of the heart can become weak if the heart muscle is damaged, as sometimes happens after a heart attack, or if the heart beat is too fast, as in atrial fibrillation. In this condition (shown right), rapid signals from the pacemaker trigger fast and inefficient contractions of both the atria and the ventricles.

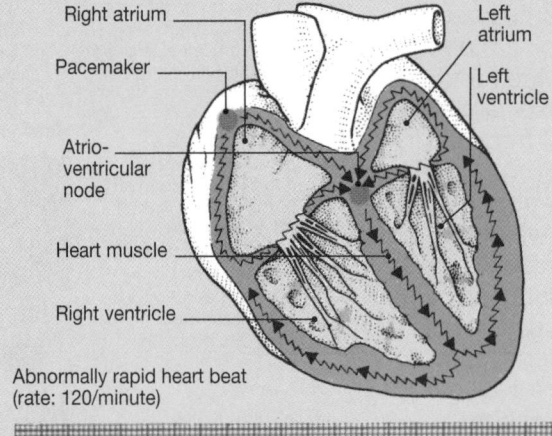

Right atrium
Pacemaker
Atrio-ventricular node
Heart muscle
Right ventricle
Left atrium
Left ventricle

Abnormally rapid heart beat (rate: 120/minute)

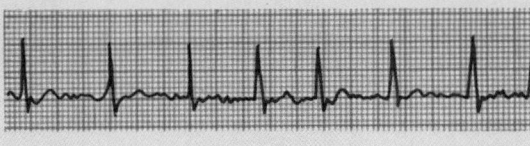

The effect of digitalis
The digitalis drug digoxin reduces the flow of electrical impulses through the atrioventricular node so that the ventricles contract less often. In addition, by promoting the chemical changes in muscle cells necessary for muscular contraction, this drug increases the force with which the heart muscle contracts and thereby improves the efficiency of each heart beat.

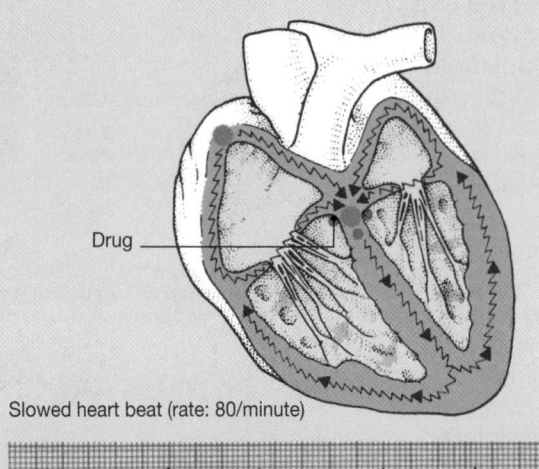

Drug

Slowed heart beat (rate: 80/minute)

COMMON DRUGS

Digoxin *

---

* See Part 4

BETA BLOCKERS

Beta blockers are drugs that interrupt the transmission of stimuli through the beta *receptors* of the body. Since the actions they block originate in the adrenal glands (and elsewhere) they are also sometimes called beta adrenergic blocking agents. Used mainly in heart disorders, these drugs are occasionally prescribed for other conditions.

Why they are used

Beta blockers are used for treating angina (see p.87), hypertension (see p.88), and irregular heart rhythms (see p.86). They are also given after a heart attack to reduce the likelihood of abnormal heart rhythms or further damage to the heart muscle. These drugs are also prescribed to improve heart function in heart muscle disorders, known as cardiomyopathies.

Beta blockers may also be given to prevent migraine headaches (see p.73), or to reduce the physical symptoms of anxiety (see p.67). The drugs may also be given to control symptoms of an overactive thyroid gland. A beta blocker is sometimes given in the form of eye drops in glaucoma to lower the fluid pressure inside the eye (see p.156).

How they work

By occupying the beta receptors, beta blockers nullify the stimulating action of norepinephrine (noradrenaline), the main "fight or flight" hormone. As a result, they reduce the force and speed of the heart

BETA RECEPTORS

Signals from the sympathetic nervous system are carried by noradrenaline, a *neurotransmitter* produced in the adrenal glands and at the ends of the sympathetic nerve fibres. Beta blockers stop the signals from the neurotransmitter.

Neurotransmitter

Beta blocker

Types of beta receptor
There are two types of beta receptor: beta 1 and beta 2. Beta 1 receptors are located mainly in the heart muscle; beta 2 receptors are found both in the airways and blood vessels. Cardioselective drugs act mainly on beta 1 receptors; non-cardioselective drugs act on both types of receptor.

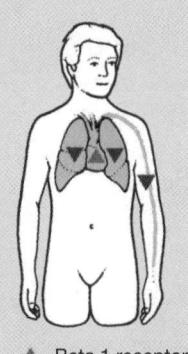

▲ Beta 1 receptors
▼ Beta 2 receptors

THE USES AND EFFECTS OF BETA BLOCKERS

Blocking the transmission of signals through beta receptors in different parts of the body produces a wide variety of benefits and side effects depending on the disease being treated. The illustration (right) shows the main areas and body systems affected by the action of beta blockers.

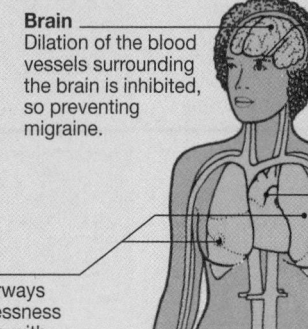

Brain
Dilation of the blood vessels surrounding the brain is inhibited, so preventing migraine.

Eye
Beta blocker eye drops reduce fluid production and so lower pressure inside the eye.

Heart
Slowing of the heart rate and reduction of the force of the heart beat reduces the workload of the heart, helping to prevent angina and abnormal heart rhythms. But this action may worsen heart failure.

Lungs
Constriction of the airways may provoke breathlessness in asthmatics or those with chronic bronchitis.

Blood vessels
Constriction of the blood vessels may cause coldness of the hands and feet.

Blood pressure
This is lowered because the rate and force at which the heart pumps blood into the circulatory system is reduced.

Muscles
Muscle tremor due to anxiety or to over activity of the thyroid gland is reduced.

beat and prevent the dilation of the blood vessels surrounding the brain and leading to the extremities. The effect of this "beta blockade" in a variety of disorders is shown in the box above.

How they affect you

Beta blockers are taken to treat angina. They reduce the frequency and severity of attacks. As part of the treatment for hypertension, beta blockers help to lower blood pressure and thus reduce the risks that are associated with this condition. Beta blockers help to prevent severe attacks of arrhythmia, in which the heart beat is wild and uncontrolled.

Because beta blockers affect many parts of the body, they often produce minor *side effects*. By reducing heart rate and air flow to the lungs, they may reduce capacity for strenuous exercise, although this is unlikely to be noticed by somebody whose physical activity was previously limited by heart problems. Many people experience cold hands and feet while taking these drugs as a result of the reduction in the blood supply to the limbs. Reduced circulation can also lead to temporary erectile dysfunction during treatment.

Risks and special precautions

The main risk of beta blockers is that of provoking breathing difficulties as a result of their blocking effect on beta receptors in the lungs. Cardioselective beta blockers, which act principally on the heart, are thought to be less likely than non-cardioselective ones to cause such problems. But all beta blockers are

prescribed with caution for people who have asthma, bronchitis, or other forms of respiratory disease.

Beta blockers are not commonly prescribed for people who have poor circulation in the limbs because they reduce the flow of blood and may aggravate such conditions. They may be given, very cautiously, to people who are subject to heart failure because they may further reduce the force of the heart beat. Diabetics who need to take beta blockers should be aware that they may notice a change in the warning signs of low blood sugar; in particular, they may find that symptoms such as palpitations and tremor are suppressed.

Beta blockers should not be stopped suddenly after prolonged use; this may provoke a sudden and severe recurrence of symptoms of the original disorder, even a heart attack. The blood pressure may also rise markedly. When treatment with beta blockers needs to be stopped, it should be withdrawn gradually under medical supervision.

COMMON DRUGS

Cardioselective	Non-cardioselective
Acebutolol	Carvedilol ✳
Atenolol ✳	Labetalol
Betaxolol	Nadolol
Bisoprolol	Oxprenolol
Esmolol	Pindolol
Metoprolol ✳	Propranolol ✳
	Sotalol
	Timolol ✳

✳ See Part 4

VASODILATORS

Vasodilators are drugs that widen blood vessels. Their most obvious use is to reverse narrowing of the blood vessels when this leads to reduced blood flow and, consequently, a lower oxygen supply to parts of the body. This problem occurs in angina, when narrowing of the coronary arteries reduces blood supply to the heart muscle. Vasodilators are also often used to treat high blood pressure (hypertension).

Why they are used

Vasodilators improve the blood flow and thus the oxygen supply to areas of the body where they are most needed. In angina, dilation of blood vessels throughout the body reduces the force with which the heart needs to pump and thereby eases its workload (see also Anti- angina drugs, p.87). Specifically, ACE (angiotensin-converting enzyme) Inhibitors are helpful in treating congestive heart failure.

Because blood pressure is dependent partly on the diameter of blood vessels, vasodilators are often helpful in treating hypertension (see p.88).

In peripheral vascular disease, narrowed blood vessels in the legs cannot supply sufficient blood to the extremities, often leading to pain in the legs during exercise. Unfortunately, because the vessels are narrowed by atherosclerosis, vasodilators have little effect.

How they work

Vasodilators widen the blood vessels by relaxing the muscles surrounding them. They achieve this either by affecting the action of the muscles directly (nitrates, hydralazine, and calcium channel blockers) or by interfering with the nerve signals that govern contraction of the blood vessels (alpha blockers). ACE inhibitors block the activity of an *enzyme* in the blood that is responsible for producing angiotensin II, a powerful

vasoconstrictor (see box below). Angiotensin II blockers prevent angiotensin II from constricting the blood vessels by blocking its receptors within the vessels.

How they affect you

As well as relieving the symptoms of the disorders for which they are taken, vasodilators can have many minor *side effects* related to their action on the circulation. Flushing and headaches are common at the start of treatment. Dizziness and fainting may also occur as a result of lowered blood pressure, which is often worse on standing.

Dilation of the blood vessels can also cause fluid build-up, leading to swelling, particularly of the ankles.

Risks and special precautions

The major risk is that blood pressure may fall too low. Therefore vasodilator drugs are prescribed with caution for people with unstable blood pressure. It is also advisable to sit or lie down after taking the first dose of a vasodilator drug.

ACTION OF VASODILATORS

The diameter of blood vessels is governed by the contraction of the surrounding muscle. The muscle contracts in response to signals from the sympathetic nervous system (p.63). Vasodilators encourage the muscles to relax, thus increasing the size of blood vessels.

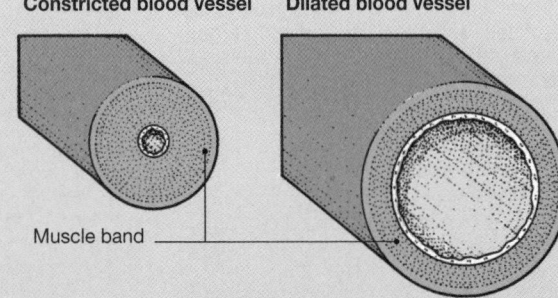

Constricted blood vessel **Dilated blood vessel**

Muscle band

Where they act
Each type of vasodilator acts on a different part of the mechanism controlling blood vessel size in order to prevent contraction of the surrounding layer of muscles.

Nerves – Alpha blockers interfere with nerve signals to the muscles.

Muscle layer – Nitrates and calcium channel blockers act directly on the muscle to inhibit contraction.

Blood – ACE inhibitors block enzyme activity in the blood (see box below).

COMMON DRUGS

ACE inhibitors	Calcium channel blockers
Benazepril	Amlodipine *
Captopril *	Diltiazem *
Cilazapril	Felodipine
Enalapril *	Nifedipine *
Fosinopril	Verapamil *
Lisinopril *	
Perindopril *	**Angiotensin II blockers**
Quinapril	Candesartan
Ramipril *	Eprosartan
Trandolapril	Irbesartan *
	Losartan *
Alpha blockers	Telmisartan
Doxazosin *	Valsartan *
Prazosin	
Terazosin *	**Other drugs**
	Hydralazine
Nitrates	Minoxidil *
Nitroglycerin *	
Isosorbide dinitrate/	
mononitrate *	

ACE INHIBITORS

The ACE (angiotensin-converting enzyme) inhibitors are powerful vasodilators. They act by blocking the action of an enzyme in the bloodstream that is responsible for converting a chemical called angiotensin I into angiotensin II. Angiotensin II encourages constriction of the blood vessels, and its absence permits them to dilate (see right).

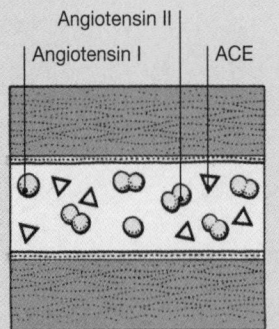

Angiotensin II
Angiotensin I | ACE

Before drug
Angiotensin I is converted by the enzyme into angiotensin II. The blood vessel constricts.

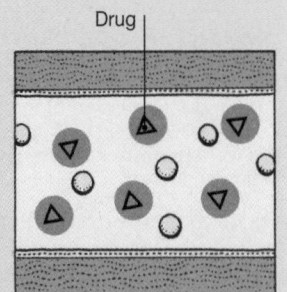

Drug

Drug action
ACE inhibitors block enzyme activity, thereby preventing the formation of angiotensin II. The blood vessel dilates.

* See Part 4

DIURETICS

Diuretic drugs help to turn excess body water into urine. As the urine is expelled, two disorders are relieved: the tissues become less water-swollen (edema) and the heart action improves because it has to pump a smaller volume of blood. There are several classes of diuretics, each of which has different uses, modes of action, and effects (see Types of diuretic, below). But all diuretics act on the kidneys, the organs that govern the water content of the body.

Why they are used

Diuretics are most commonly used in the treatment of high blood pressure (hypertension). By removing a larger amount of water than usual from the bloodstream, the kidneys reduce the total volume of blood circulating. This drop in volume causes a reduction of the pressure within the blood vessels (see Antihypertensive drugs, p.88).

Diuretics are also widely used to treat heart failure in which the heart's pumping mechanism has become weak. In the treatment of this disorder, they remove fluid that has accumulated in the tissues and lungs. The resulting drop in blood volume reduces the work of the heart.

Other conditions for which diuretics are often prescribed include nephrotic syndrome (a kidney disorder that causes edema) and cirrhosis of the liver (in which fluid may accumulate in the abdominal cavity).

Less commonly, diuretics are used to treat glaucoma (see p.156) and Ménière's disease (see p.74).

How they work

The kidneys' normal filtration process takes water, salts (mainly potassium and sodium), and waste products out of the bloodstream. Most of the salts and water are returned to the bloodstream, but some are expelled from the body together with the waste products in the urine. Diuretics interfere with this filtration process by reducing the amounts of sodium and water taken

ACTION OF DIURETICS

As blood passes through the kidney, water, sodium, and potassium salts, and waste products are filtered out of the bloodstream. Most of the water and filtered salts are then reabsorbed by the bloodstream from the tubule; the remainder is excreted as urine.

By blocking the movement of sodium back into the bloodstream, diuretics prevent the reabsorption of water, so that more is expelled from the body as urine. Different diuretic drugs act on different parts of the tubule (see right).

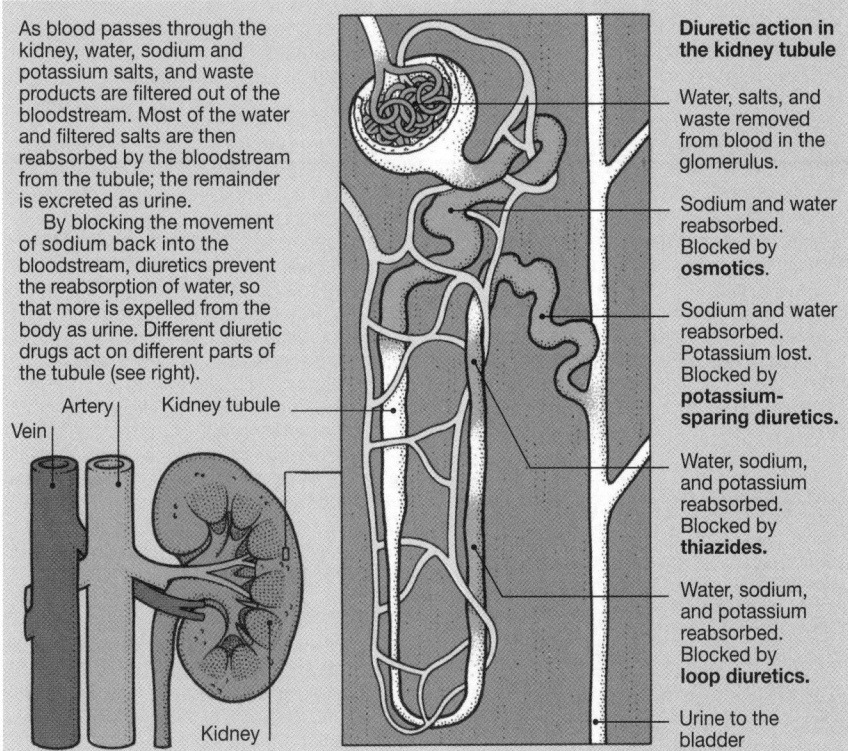

Artery | Kidney tubule
Vein
Kidney

Diuretic action in the kidney tubule

Water, salts, and waste removed from blood in the glomerulus.

Sodium and water reabsorbed. Blocked by **osmotics**.

Sodium and water reabsorbed. Potassium lost. Blocked by **potassium-sparing diuretics.**

Water, sodium, and potassium reabsorbed. Blocked by **thiazides.**

Water, sodium, and potassium reabsorbed. Blocked by **loop diuretics.**

Urine to the bladder

back into the bloodstream, thus increasing the volume of urine produced. Modifying the filtration process in this way means that the water content of the blood is reduced; less water in the blood causes excess water present in the tissues to be drawn out and eliminated in urine.

How they affect you

All diuretics increase the frequency with which you need to pass urine. This is most noticeable at the start of treatment. People who have suffered from edema may notice that swelling – particularly of the ankles – is reduced, and those with heart failure may find that breathlessness is relieved.

Risks and special precautions

Diuretics can cause blood chemical imbalances, of which a fall in potassium levels (hypokalemia) is the most common. Hypokalemia can cause confusion, weakness, and trigger abnormal heart rhythms (especially in people taking digitalis drugs). Potassium supplements or a potassium-sparing diuretic usually corrects the imbalance. A diet that is rich in potassium (containing plenty of fresh fruits and vegetables) may be helpful.

Some diuretics may raise blood levels of uric acid, increasing the risk of gout. They may also raise blood sugar levels, causing problems for diabetics.

TYPES OF DIURETIC

Thiazides The diuretics most commonly prescribed, thiazides may lead to potassium deficiency and they are, therefore, sometimes given together with a potassium supplement or in conjunction with a potassium-sparing diuretic (see right).

Loop diuretics These fast-acting, powerful drugs increase the output of urine for a few hours, and are therefore sometimes used in emergencies. They may cause excessive loss of potassium, which may need to be countered as for thiazides. Large doses may disturb hearing.

Potassium-sparing diuretics These mild diuretics are usually used in conjunction with a thiazide or a loop diuretic to prevent excessive potassium loss.

Osmotic diuretics Prescribed only rarely, these drugs are used to maintain the flow of urine through the kidneys after surgery or injury, and to reduce pressure rapidly within fluid-filled cavities.

Acetazolamide This mild diuretic drug is used principally in the treatment of glaucoma (see p.156).

COMMON DRUGS

Loop diuretics
Bumetanide
Furosemide ✳

Potassium-sparing diuretics
Amiloride ✳
Eplerenone ✳
Spironolactone ✳
Triamterene ✳

Thiazides
Chlorthalidone
Hydrochlorothiazide ✳
Indapamide ✳
Metolazone

Others
Ethacrynic acid

✳ See Part 4

ANTI-ARRHYTHMICS

The heart contains two upper and two lower chambers, which are known as the atria and ventricles (see p.81). The pumping actions of these two sets of chambers are normally coordinated by electrical impulses that originate in the pacemaker and then travel along conducting pathways so that the heart beats with a regular rhythm. If this coordination breaks down, the heart will beat abnormally, either irregularly, or faster or slower than usual. The general term for abnormal heart rhythm is arrhythmia.

Arrhythmias may occur as a result of a birth defect, coronary heart disease, or other less common heart disorders. A variety of more general conditions, including overactivity of the thyroid gland, and certain drugs – such as caffeine and *anticholinergic* drugs – can also disturb heart rhythm.

SITES OF DRUG ACTION

Anti-arrhythmic drugs either slow the flow of electrical impulses to the heart muscle, or inhibit the muscle's ability to contract. Beta blockers reduce the ability of the pacemaker to pass electrical signals to the atria. Digoxin reduces the passage of signals from the atrioventricular node. Calcium channel blockers interfere with the ability of the heart muscle to contract by impeding the flow of calcium into muscle cells. Other drugs, such as quinidine and disopyramide, reduce the sensitivity of muscle cells to electrical impulses.

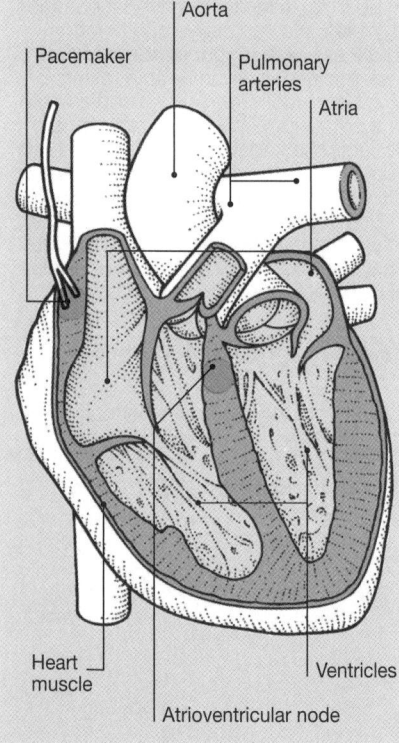

Aorta

Pacemaker

Pulmonary arteries

Atria

Heart muscle

Ventricles

Atrioventricular node

A broad selection of drugs is used to regulate heart rhythm, including beta blockers, the digitalis drug digoxin, and calcium channel blockers. Other drugs used are amiodarone, disopyramide, procainamide, and quinidine.

Why drugs are used

Minor disturbances of heart rhythm are common and do not usually require drug treatment. However, if the pumping action of the heart is seriously affected, the circulation of blood throughout the body may become inefficient, and drug treatment may be necessary.

Drugs may be taken to treat individual attacks of arrhythmia, or they may be taken on a regular basis to prevent or control abnormal heart rhythms. The particular drug prescribed depends on the type of arrhythmia to be treated, but because people differ in their response, it may be necessary to try several in order to find the most effective one. When the arrhythmia is sudden and severe, it may be necessary to inject a drug immediately to restore normal heart function.

How they work

The heart's pumping action is governed by electrical signals under the control of the sympathetic nervous system (see Autonomic nervous system, p.63). These signals pass through the heart muscle, causing the two pairs of chambers – the atria and ventricles – to contract in turn (see Sites of drug action, left).

All anti-arrhythmic drugs alter the conduction of electrical signals in the heart. However, each drug or drug group has a different effect on the sequence of events controlling the pumping action. Some block the transmission of signals to the heart (beta blockers); some affect the way in which signals are conducted within the heart (digoxin); others affect the response of the heart muscle to the signals received (calcium channel blockers, amiodarone, disopyramide, procainamide, and quinidine).

How they affect you

These drugs usually prevent symptoms of arrhythmia and may restore a regular heart rhythm. Although they do not prevent all arrhythmias, they usually reduce the frequency and severity of any symptoms.

Unfortunately, as well as suppressing arrhythmias, many of these drugs tend to depress normal heart function, and may produce dizziness on standing up, or increased breathlessness on exertion. Mild nausea and visual disturbances are also fairly frequent. Verapamil can cause constipation, especially when it is prescribed in high doses. Disopyramide may interfere with the parasympathetic nervous system (see p.63), resulting in a number of *anticholinergic* effects.

TYPES OF ARRHYTHMIA

Atrial fibrillation In this common type of arrhythmia, the atria contract irregularly at such a high rate that the ventricles cannot keep pace. It is treated with digoxin, calcium channel blockers such as verapamil, or a beta blocker.

Ventricular tachycardia In this condition, abnormal electrical activity in the ventricles causes them to contract rapidly. For those with ongoing symptoms, regular treatment with amiodarone or other anti-arrhythmics may be effective, although implanted defibrillators are replacing drug treatment for this condition.

Supraventricular tachycardia This condition occurs when extra electrical impulses arise in the pacemaker or atria. These extra impulses stimulate the ventricles to contract rapidly. Attacks may disappear on their own without treatment, but drugs such as adenosine, digoxin, verapamil, or propranolol may be given.

Heart block When impulses are not conducted from the atria to the ventricles, the ventricles start to beat at a slower rate. Some cases of heart block do not require treatment. For more severe heart block accompanied by dizziness and fainting, it is usually necessary to fit the patient with an artificial pacemaker.

Risks and special precautions

These drugs may further disrupt heart rhythm under certain circumstances and therefore they are used only when the likely benefit outweighs the risks.

Amiodarone may accumulate in the tissues over time, and may lead to light-sensitive rashes, changes in thyroid function, and lung problems.

COMMON DRUGS

Beta blockers
Propranolol ✳
Sotalol
(see also p.83)

Calcium channel blockers
Diltiazem ✳
Verapamil ✳

Digitalis
(see also p.82)
Digoxin ✳

Other drugs
Amiodarone ✳
Bretylium
Disopyramide
Flecainide
Ibutilide
Lidocaine
Mexiletine
Procainamide
Propafenone
Quinidine ✳

✳ See Part 4

ANTI-ANGINA DRUGS

Angina is chest pain, or chest discomfort, produced when the heart muscle receives insufficient oxygen. Women may not always feel pain, just chest tightness with some shortness of breath. Angina is usually caused by narrowing of the blood vessels (coronary arteries) that transport blood and oxygen to the heart muscle.

In the most common type of angina (classic angina), narrowing of the coronary arteries results from deposits of fat – called atheroma – on the walls of the arteries. Symptoms usually occur during emotional stress or physical exertion. In variant angina, the arteries are narrowed by contraction (spasm) of the muscle fibres in the artery walls, and pain may also occur at rest.

Atheroma deposits build up more rapidly in the arteries of smokers and people who eat a high-fat diet. This is why, as a basic component of angina treatment, doctors recommend giving up smoking and changing the diet. Overweight people are also advised to lose weight to reduce the demands placed on the heart. While such changes in lifestyle often produce an improvement in symptoms, drug treatment to relieve angina is also often necessary.

The drugs used to treat angina include beta blockers, nitrates, and calcium channel blockers. Other drugs that may also be used include ASA (see p.90), statins such as simvastatin (see p.89), and ACE inhibitors (see p.84).

Why drugs are used

Frequent episodes of angina can be disabling and, if left untreated, can lead to an increased risk of a heart attack. Drugs can be used both to relieve angina attacks and to reduce their frequency. People who suffer from only occasional episodes are usually prescribed a rapid-acting drug to take at the first signs of an attack, or before an activity that is known to bring on an attack. A rapid-acting nitrate – nitroglycerin – is usually prescribed for this purpose.

If attacks become more frequent or more severe, regular preventative treatment may be advised. Beta blockers, long-acting nitrates, and calcium channel blockers are used as regular medication to prevent attacks. The introduction of adhesive patches to administer nitrates through the patient's skin has extended the duration of action of nitroglycerin, making treatment easier.

Drugs can often control angina for many years, but they cannot cure the disorder. When severe angina cannot be controlled by drugs, surgery to increase the blood flow to the heart may be recommended.

How they work

Nitrates and calcium channel blockers dilate blood vessels by relaxing the muscle layer in the blood vessel walls (see also Vasodilators, p.84). Blood is more easily pumped through the dilated vessels, reducing the strain on the heart.

Beta blockers reduce heart muscle stimulation during exercise or stress by interrupting signal transmission in the heart. Decreased heart muscle stimulation means less oxygen is required, reducing the risk of angina attacks. For further information on beta blockers, see p.83.

How they affect you

Treatment with one or more of these medicines usually effectively controls angina. Drugs to prevent attacks allow sufferers to undertake more strenuous

ACTION OF ANTI-ANGINA DRUGS

Angina pain occurs when the heart muscle runs short of oxygen as it pumps blood round the circulatory system. Nitrates, calcium channel blockers, and potassium channel openers reduce the heart's work by dilating blood vessels. Beta blockers impede the stimulation of heart muscle, reducing its oxygen requirement, thus relieving angina.

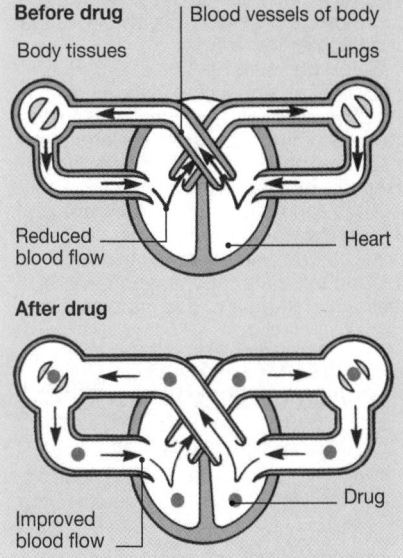

Before drug
Body tissues | Blood vessels of body
Lungs
Reduced blood flow | Heart

After drug
Improved blood flow | Drug

activities without provoking pain, and if an attack does occur, nitroglycerin usually provides immediate effective relief.

These drugs do not usually cause serious *adverse effects*, but they can produce a variety of minor symptoms. By dilating blood vessels throughout the body, the nitrates and calcium channel blockers can cause dizziness (especially when standing) and may cause fainting. Other possible side effects are headaches at the start of treatment, flushing of the skin (especially of the face), and ankle swelling. Beta blockers often cause cold hands and feet, and sometimes they may produce tiredness and a feeling of heaviness in the legs.

CALCIUM CHANNEL BLOCKERS

The passage of calcium through special channels into muscle cells is an essential part of the mechanism of muscle contraction (see right). These drugs prevent movement of calcium in the muscles of the blood vessels and so encourage them to dilate (see far right). The action helps to reduce blood pressure and relieves the strain on the heart muscle in angina by making it easier for the heart to pump blood throughout the body (see Action of anti-angina drugs, above right). Verapamil also slows the passage of nerve signals through the heart muscle. This can be helpful for correcting certain arrhythmias.

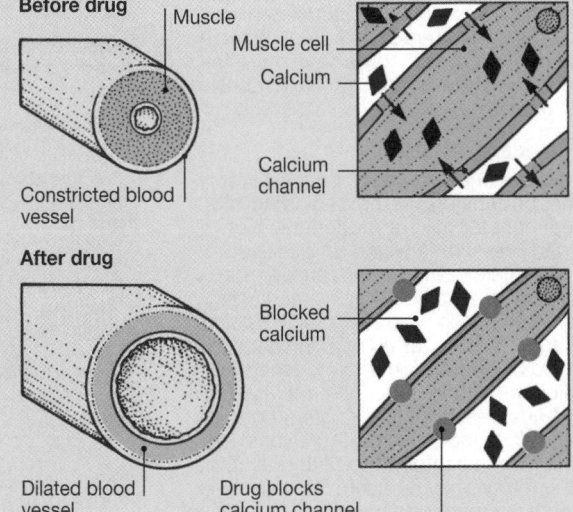

Before drug
Muscle
Muscle cell
Calcium
Calcium channel
Constricted blood vessel

After drug
Blocked calcium
Dilated blood vessel
Drug blocks calcium channel

COMMON DRUGS

Beta blockers
(see p.83)

Calcium channel blockers
Amlodipine ✳
Diltiazem ✳
Felodipine ✳
Nifedipine ✳
Verapamil ✳

Nitrates
Isosorbide dinitrate/ mononitrate ✳
Nitroglycerin ✳

Other drugs
ASA ✳
Ramipril ✳
Simvastatin ✳

✳ See Part 4

ANTIHYPERTENSIVE DRUGS

Blood pressure is the force exerted by the blood against the walls of the arteries. Two measurements are taken: one indicates force while the heart's ventricles are contracting (systolic pressure). This reading is a higher figure than the other one, which measures the blood pressure during ventricle relaxation (diastolic pressure). Blood pressure varies among individuals and normally increases with age. If a person's blood pressure is higher than normal on at least three separate occasions, a physician may diagnose the condition as hypertension.

Blood pressure may be elevated as a result of an underlying disorder, which the physician will try to identify. Usually, however, it is not possible to determine a cause. This condition is referred to as essential hypertension.

Although hypertension does not usually cause any symptoms, severely raised blood pressure may produce headaches, palpitations, and general feelings of ill-health. It is important to reduce high blood pressure because it can have serious consequences, including stroke, heart attack, heart failure, and kidney damage. Certain groups are particularly at risk from high blood pressure. These risk groups include diabetics, smokers, people with pre-existing heart damage, and those whose blood contains a high level of fat. High blood pressure is more common among black people than among whites, and in countries, such as Japan, where the diet is high in salt.

A small reduction in blood pressure may be brought about by reducing weight, exercising regularly, and avoiding an excessive amount of salt in the diet. But for more severely raised blood pressure, one or more antihypertensive drugs may be prescribed. Several classes of drugs have antihypertensive properties, including the centrally acting antihypertensives, diuretics (p.85), beta blockers (p.83), calcium channel blockers (p.87), ACE (angiotensin-converting enzyme) inhibitors (p.84), and alpha blockers. See also Vasodilators, p.84.

Why drugs are used

Antihypertensive drugs are prescribed when diet, exercise, and other lifestyle changes have not brought about an adequate reduction in blood pressure, and your physician sees a risk of serious consequences if the condition is not treated. These drugs do not cure hypertension and may have to be taken indefinitely.

How they work

Blood pressure depends not only on the force with which the heart pumps blood, but also on the diameter of blood vessels and the volume of blood in circulation: blood pressure is increased either if the vessels are narrow or if the volume of blood is high. Antihypertensive drugs lower blood pressure either by dilating the blood vessels or by reducing blood volume. Antihypertensive drugs work in different ways and some have more than one action (see Action of antihypertensive drugs, left).

Choice of drug

Drug treatment depends on the severity of hypertension. At the beginning of treatment for mild or moderately high blood pressure, a single drug is used. A thiazide diuretic is often chosen for initial treatment, but it is also increasingly common to use a beta blocker, a calcium channel blocker, or an ACE inhibitor. For those of African American descent, a calcium channel blocker is usually the first-line treatment. If a single drug does not reduce the blood pressure sufficiently, a diuretic in combination with one of the other drugs may be used. Some people who have moderate hypertension require a third drug, in which case a vasodilator, centrally acting antihypertensive, or alpha blocker, may also be prescribed.

Severe hypertension is usually controlled with a combination of several drugs, which may need to be given in high doses. Your physician may need to try a number of drugs before finding a combination that controls blood pressure without unacceptable *side effects*.

How they affect you

Treatment with antihypertensive drugs relieves symptoms such as headache and palpitations. However, since most people with hypertension have no symptoms, side effects may be more noticeable than any immediate beneficial effect. Some antihypertensive drugs may cause dizziness and fainting at the start of treatment because they can sometimes cause an excessive fall in blood pressure. It may take a while for your physician to determine a dosage that avoids such effects. For detailed information on the *adverse effects* of drugs used to treat hypertension, consult the individual drug profiles in Part 4.

Risks and special precautions

Since your physician needs to know exactly how treatment with a particular drug affects your hypertension – the benefits as well as the side effects – it is important for you to keep using the antihypertensive medication as prescribed, even though you may feel the problem is under control. Sudden withdrawal of some of these drugs may cause a potentially dangerous rebound increase in blood pressure. To stop treatment, the dose needs to be reduced gradually under medical supervision.

ACTION OF ANTI-HYPERTENSIVE DRUGS

Each type of antihypertensive drug acts on a different part of the body to lower blood pressure.

Centrally acting drugs act on the brain's mechanism that controls blood vessel size.

Beta blockers reduce the force of the heart beat.

Diuretics act on the kidneys to reduce blood volume.

ACE inhibitors act on enzymes in the blood to dilate blood vessels.

Vasodilators and calcium channel blockers act on the arterial wall muscles to prevent constriction.

Alpha blockers block nerve signals that trigger constriction of blood vessels.

COMMON DRUGS

ACE inhibitors (see p.84)

Angiotensin II blockers (see p.84)

Beta blockers (see p.83)

Calcium channel blockers (see p.87)
Amlodipine *
Diltiazem *
Felodipine
Nifedipine *
Verapamil *

Renin inhibitor
Aliskiren *

Centrally acting antihypertensives
Clonidine
Methyldopa *

Diuretics (see p.85)

Alpha blockers
Doxazosin *
Prazosin
Terazosin *

Vasodilators (see p.84)

* See Part 4

LIPID-LOWERING DRUGS

The blood contains several types of fats, or lipids. They are necessary for normal body function but can be damaging if present in excess, particularly saturated fats such as cholesterol. The main risk is atherosclerosis, in which fatty deposits called atheroma build up in the arteries, restricting and disrupting the flow of blood. This can increase the likelihood of the formation of abnormal blood clots, leading to potentially fatal disorders such as stroke and heart attack.

For most people, cutting down the amount of fat in the diet is sufficient to reduce the risk of atherosclerosis. For others, and for those with an inherited tendency to high levels of fat in the blood (hyperlipidemia or dyslipidemia), lipid-lowering drugs may also be prescribed.

Why drugs are used

Lipid-lowering drugs are generally given only when dietary measures have failed. The drugs may be given at an earlier stage to individuals at increased risk of atherosclerosis – such as diabetics and people already suffering from circulatory disorders. The drugs may remove existing atheroma in the blood vessels and prevent accumulation of new deposits.

For maximum benefit, these drugs are used in conjunction with a low-fat diet and a reduction in other risk factors such as obesity and smoking. The choice of drug depends on the type of lipid causing problems, so a full medical history, examination, and laboratory analysis of blood samples are needed before drug treatment is given.

How they work

Cholesterol and triglycerides are two of the major fats in the blood. One or both may be raised, influencing the choice of lipid-lowering drug. Ezetimibe prevents the absorption of cholesterol from the bowel. Drugs like cholestyramine act on bile salts, which contain a large amount of cholesterol and are normally released into the bowel to aid digestion before being reabsorbed into the blood. Drugs that bind to bile salts reduce cholesterol levels by blocking their reabsorption, allowing them to be lost from the body.

Other drugs act on the liver. Fibrates and niacin can reduce the level of cholesterol and triglycerides. Statins lower blood cholesterol. Fish oil preparations reduce blood triglycerides, but they may raise cholesterol levels.

Lipid-lowering drugs do not correct the underlying cause of raised levels of fat in the blood, so it is usually necessary to continue with diet and drug treatment indefinitely. Stopping treatment usually leads to a return of high blood lipid levels.

How they affect you

Because dyslipidemia and atherosclerosis are usually without symptoms, you are

ACTION OF LIPID-LOWERING DRUGS

Lipid-lowering drugs reduce the levels of fats in the blood by interfering with the absorption of bile salts in the bowel, or by altering the way in which the liver converts fatty acids in the blood into different types of lipids.

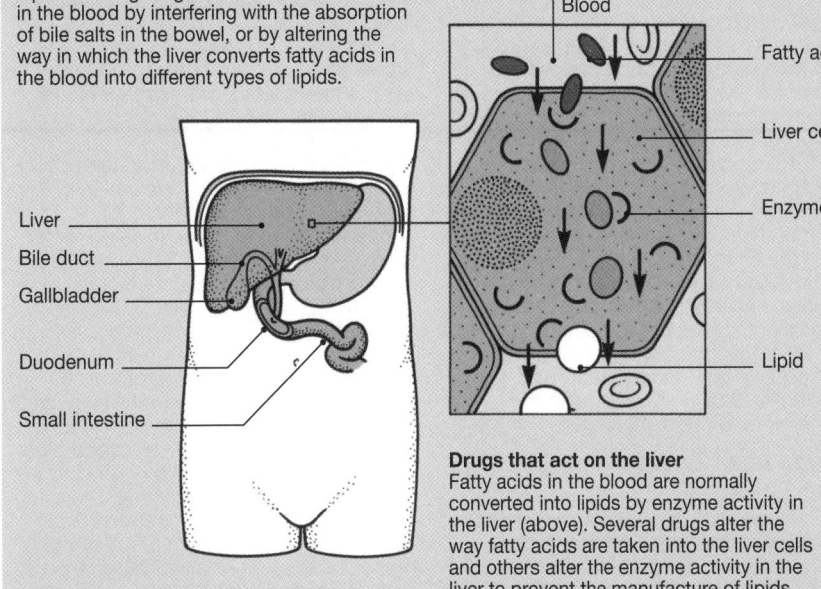

Liver
Bile duct
Gallbladder
Duodenum
Small intestine

Blood
Fatty acid
Liver cell
Enzyme
Lipid

Drugs that act on the liver
Fatty acids in the blood are normally converted into lipids by enzyme activity in the liver (above). Several drugs alter the way fatty acids are taken into the liver cells and others alter the enzyme activity in the liver to prevent the manufacture of lipids.

Drugs that bind to bile salts
Bile is produced by the liver and released into the small intestine via the bile duct to aid digestion. Salts in the bile carry large amounts of cholesterol and are normally reabsorbed from the intestine into the bloodstream during digestion (right). Some drugs bind to bile salts in the intestine and prevent their reabsorption (far right). This action reduces the levels of bile salts in the blood, and triggers the liver to convert more cholesterol into bile salts, thus reducing blood cholesterol levels.

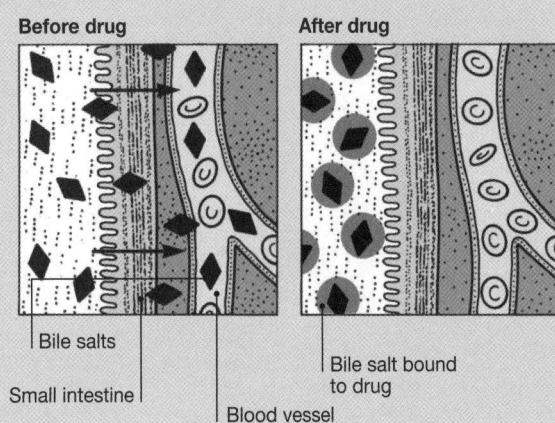

Before drug

After drug

Bile salts
Small intestine
Blood vessel

Bile salt bound to drug

unlikely to notice any short-term benefits from these drugs. Rather, the aim of treatment is to reduce long-term complications. There may be minor *side effects* from some of these drugs.

By increasing the amount of bile in the digestive tract, several drugs can cause gastrointestinal disturbances such as nausea and constipation or diarrhea, especially at the start of treatment. Statins appear to be well tolerated and are widely used to lower cholesterol levels when diet alone does not work.

Risks and special precautions

Drugs that bind to bile salts can limit absorption of some fat-soluble vitamins, so vitamin supplements may be needed. Fibrates can increase susceptibility to gallstones and occasionally upset the balance of fats in the blood. Statins are

used with caution in people with reduced kidney or liver function, and monitoring of blood samples is often advised.

COMMON DRUGS

Fibrates	**Nicotinic acid**
Bezafibrate	Niacin ✳
Fenofibrate	
Gemfibrozil ✳	**Drugs that bind**
	to bile salts
Statins	Cholestyramine ✳
Atorvastatin ✳	Colestipol
Fluvastatin	
Lovastatin ✳	**Other drugs acting**
Pravastatin ✳	**on the liver**
Rosuvastatin ✳	Omega-3 acid ethyl
Simvastatin ✳	esters
	Omega-3 marine
Cholesterol	triglycerides
absorption inhibitor	
Ezetimibe ✳	✳ See Part 4

DRUGS THAT AFFECT BLOOD CLOTTING

When bleeding occurs from injury or surgery, the body normally acts swiftly to stem the flow by sealing the breaks in the blood vessels. This occurs in two stages – first, when cells called platelets accumulate as a plug at the opening in the blood vessel wall, and then when these platelets produce chemicals that activate clotting factors in the blood to form a protein called fibrin. Vitamin K plays an important role in this process (see The clotting mechanism, below). An *enzyme* in the blood called plasmin ensures that clots are broken down when the injury has been repaired.

Some disorders interfere with this process, either preventing clot formation or creating clots uncontrollably. If the blood does not clot, there is a danger of excessive blood loss. Inappropriate development of clots may block the supply of blood to a vital organ.

Drugs used to promote blood clotting

Fibrin formation depends on the presence in the blood of several clotting-factor proteins. When Factor VIII is absent or at low levels, an inherited disease called hemophilia exists; the symptoms almost always appear only in males. Factor IX deficiency causes another bleeding condition called Christmas disease, named after the person in whom it was first identified. Lack of these clotting factors can lead to uncontrolled bleeding or excessive bruising following even minor injuries.

Regular drug treatment for hemophilia is not normally required. However, if severe bleeding or bruising occurs, a concentrated form of the missing factor, extracted from normal blood, may be injected in order to promote clotting and thereby halt bleeding. Injections may need to be repeated for several days after injury.

It is sometimes useful to promote blood clotting in non-hemophiliacs when bleeding is difficult to stop (for example, after surgery). In such cases, blood clots are sometimes stabilized by reducing the action of plasmin with an antifibrinolytic (or hemostatic) drug like tranexamic acid; this is also occasionally given to hemophiliacs before minor surgery such as tooth extraction.

A tendency to bleed may also occur as a consequence of vitamin K deficiency (see the box below).

Drugs used to prevent abnormal blood clotting

Blood clots normally form only as a response to injury. In some people, however, there is a tendency for clots to form in the blood vessels without apparent cause. Disturbed blood flow occurring as a result of the presence of fatty deposits – atheroma – inside the blood vessels increases the risk of the formation of this type of abnormal clot (or thrombus). In addition, a portion of a blood clot (known as an embolus) formed in response to injury or surgery may sometimes break off and be removed in the bloodstream. The likelihood of this happening is increased by long periods of little or no activity. When an abnormal clot forms, there is a risk that it may become lodged in a blood vessel, thereby blocking the blood supply to a vital organ such as the brain or heart.

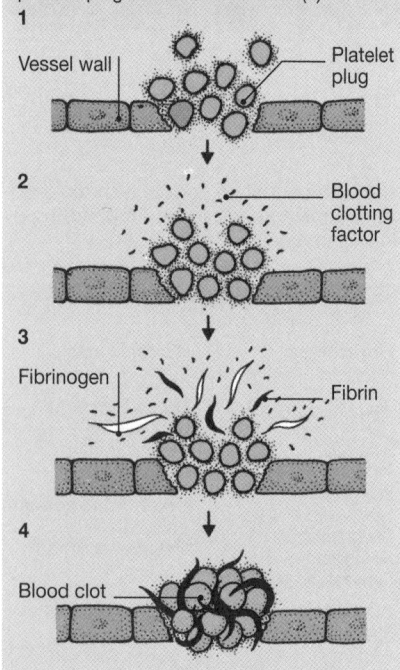
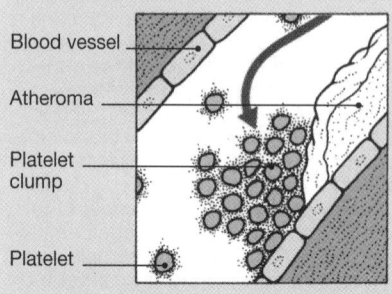
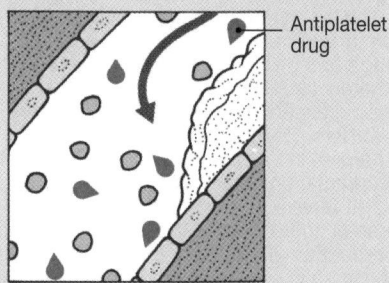
Three main types of drugs are used to prevent and disperse clots: antiplatelet drugs, anticoagulants, and thrombolytics.

Antiplatelet drugs

Taken regularly by people with a tendency to form clots in the fast-flowing blood of the heart and arteries, these drugs are also given to prevent clots from forming after heart surgery. They reduce the tendency of platelets to stick together when blood flow is disrupted (see Action of antiplatelet drugs, above).

The most widely used antiplatelet drug is ASA (see also Analgesics, p.64). This drug has an antiplatelet action even when given in much lower doses than would be necessary to reduce pain. In these low doses *adverse effects* that may occur when ASA is given in pain-relieving doses are unlikely. Other antiplatelet drugs are clopidogrel, dipyridamole, prasugrel, and ticagrelor.

Anticoagulants

Anticoagulant drugs help to maintain normal blood flow in people who are at risk from clot formation. They can either prevent the formation of blood clots in the veins or stabilize an existing clot so that it does not break away and become a circulation-stopping embolism. All of the anticoagulant drugs reduce the activity of certain blood clotting factors, although the mode of action of each drug differs (see Action of anticoagulant drugs, right). However, these medicines do not dissolve the clots that have already formed: these clots are treated with thrombolytic drugs (below).

Anticoagulants fall into two groups: those that are given by *intravenous* or *subcutaneous injection* and act immediately, and those that are given by mouth and take effect after a few days.

Injected anticoagulants

Heparin is the most widely used drug of this type and it is used mainly in hospital during or after surgery. In addition, it is also given during kidney dialysis to prevent clots from forming in the dialysis equipment. Because heparin cannot be taken by mouth, it is less suitable for long-term treatment in the home.

A number of synthetic injected anticoagulants called low molecular weight heparins (LMWH) have recently been developed. Some act for a longer time than heparin. Others are alternatives for people who react adversely to heparin.

Oral anticoagulants

Warfarin is the most widely used of the oral anticoagulants. Dabigatran and rivaroxaban are newer anticoagulants. These drugs are mainly prescribed to prevent the formation of clots in veins and in the chambers of the heart – they are less likely to prevent the formation of blood clots in arteries. Oral anticoagulants may be given after injury

or surgery (in particular, heart valve replacement) when there is a high risk of embolism. They are also given long term as a preventative treatment to people at risk from strokes. A common problem experienced with these drugs is that overdosage may lead to bleeding from the nose or gums, or in the urinary tract. For this reason, the dosage needs to be carefully calculated; for warfarin, regular blood tests are performed to ensure that the clotting mechanism is correctly adjusted.

The action of oral anticoagulant drugs may be affected by many other drugs. It may therefore be necessary to alter the dosage of anticoagulant when other drugs also need to be given. People who have been prescribed oral anticoagulants should carry a warning list of drugs that they should not be given. In particular, none of the anticoagulants should be taken with ASA except on the direction of a physician.

ACTION OF ANTICOAGULANT DRUGS

Anticoagulant drugs block the action of certain blood clotting factors that convert fibrinogen into fibrin, the protein that binds platelets into blood clots.

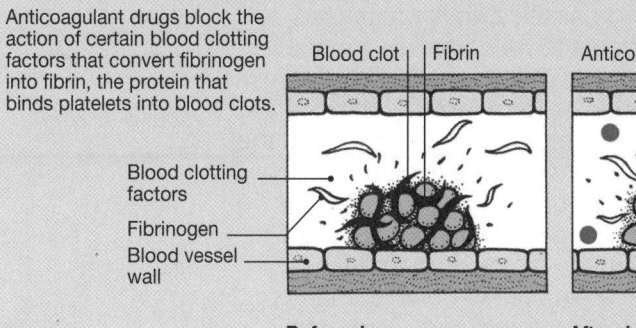

Blood clot | Fibrin

Anticoagulant drug

Blood clotting factors

Fibrinogen

Blood vessel wall

Before drug

After drug

Thrombolytics

Also known as fibrinolytics, these drugs are used to dissolve clots that have already formed. They are usually given in hospital intravenously to clear a blocked blood vessel – for example, in coronary thrombosis. The sooner they are given after the start of symptoms, the more likely they are to reduce the size and severity of a heart attack. Thrombolytic drugs may be given either intravenously or directly into the blocked blood vessel. The main thrombolytics are alteplase and tenecteplase, which act by increasing the blood level of plasmin, the enzyme that breaks down fibrin (see Action of thrombolytic drugs, below).

The most common problem with use of these drugs is increased susceptibility to bleeding and bruising.

COMMON DRUGS

Blood clotting factors
Factor VIIa
Factor VIII
Factor IX

Antifibrinolytic or haemostatic drugs
Aprotinin
Tranexamic acid

Vitamin K
Phytonadione

Antiplatelet drugs
Abciximab
ASA *
Clopidogrel *
Dipyridamole *
Eptifibatide
Prasugrel *
Ticagrelor *
Ticlopidine
Tirofiban

Injected anticoagulants
Antithrombin III
Dalteparin * (see Heparin)
Danaparoid
Enoxaparin *
Epoprostenol
Fondaparinux
Heparin *
Lepirudin
Nadroparin
Tinzaparin

Thrombolytic drugs
Alteplase
Tenecteplase

Oral anti-coagulant
Apixaban
Dabigatran etexilate *
Rivaroxaban *
Warfarin *

| * See Part 4 |

ACTION OF THROMBOLYTIC DRUGS

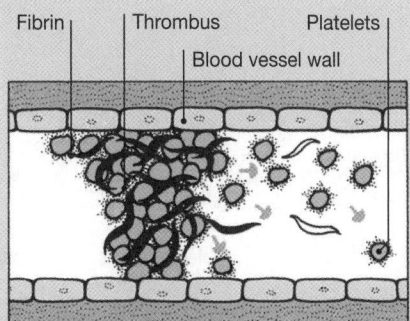

Fibrin | Thrombus | Platelets
Blood vessel wall

Before drug
When platelets accumulate in a blood vessel and are reinforced by strands of fibrin, the resultant blood clot, which is known as a thrombus, cannot be dissolved either by antiplatelet drugs or anticoagulant drugs.

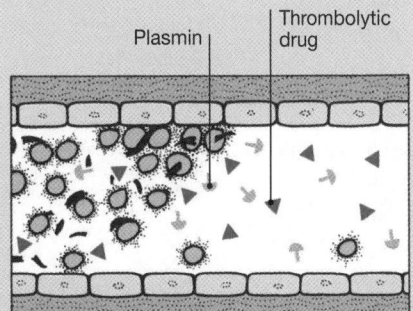

Plasmin | Thrombolytic drug

After drug
Thrombolytic drugs boost the action of plasmin, an enzyme in the blood that breaks up the strands of fibrin that bind the clot together. This allows the accumulated platelets to disperse and restores normal blood flow.

GASTROINTESTINAL TRACT

The gastrointestinal tract, also known as the digestive or alimentary tract, is the pathway through which food passes as it is processed to enable the nutrients to be absorbed for use by the body. It consists of the mouth, esophagus, stomach, small intestine (duodenum, jejunum, and ileum), large intestine, and rectum. In addition, the salivary glands in the mouth, the liver, pancreas, and gallbladder are involved in the digestion of food. These tissues, together with the gastrointestinal tract, form the digestive system.

The digestive system breaks down the large, complex chemicals – proteins, carbohydrates, and fats – present in the food we eat into simpler molecules that can be used by the body (see also Nutrition, p.134). Undigested or indigestible material, together with some of the body's waste products, pass to the large intestine, and, when a sufficient mass of such matter has accumulated, it is expelled from the body as feces.

What can go wrong
Inflammation of the lining of the stomach or intestine (gastroenteritis) is usually the result of an infection or parasitic infestation. Damage may also be done by the inappropriate production of digestive juices, leading to complaints of pain (dyspepsia) and major disorders like peptic ulcers. The lining of the intestine can be damaged by the immune system (inflammatory bowel disease). The rectum and anus can become painful and irritated by damage to the lining, tears in the skin at the opening of the anus (anal fissure), or enlarged veins (hemorrhoids).

The most commonly experienced gastrointestinal symptoms are constipation, diarrhea and irritable bowel syndrome. There can be several causes for these, one being the disruption of the normal muscle contraction that propels the contents of the food through the bowel.

Why drugs are used
Many drugs for gastrointestinal disorders are taken by mouth and act directly on the digestive tract without first entering the bloodstream. Such drugs include certain antibiotics and other drugs used to treat infestations and inflammation. Some antacids for peptic ulcers and excess stomach acidity, and the bulk-forming agents for constipation and diarrhea, also pass through the system unabsorbed.

However, for many disorders, drugs with a *systemic* effect are required, including anti-ulcer drugs, *opioid* antidiarrheal drugs, and some of the drugs for inflammatory bowel disease.

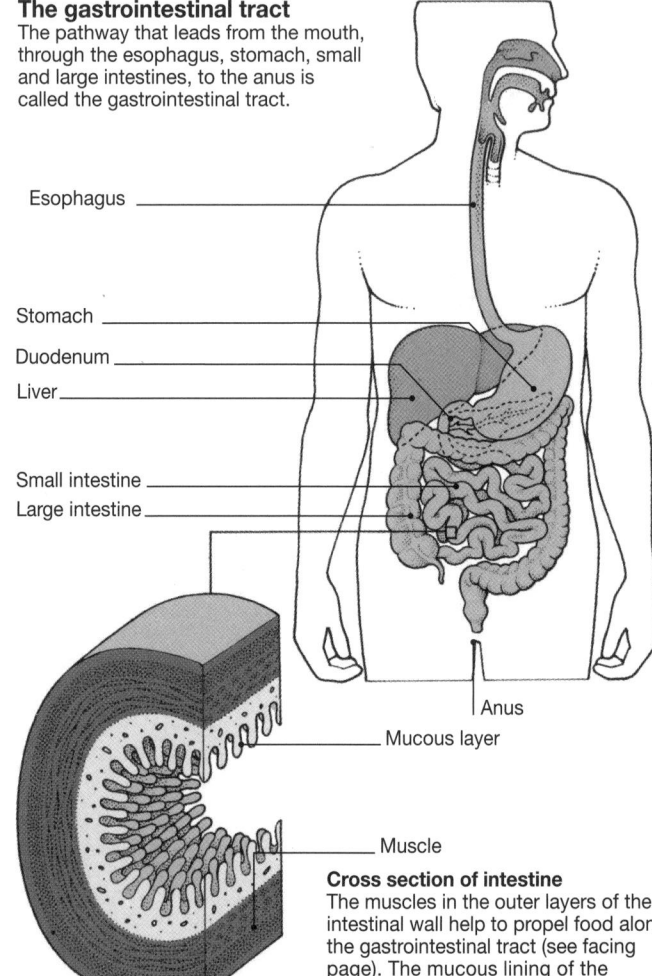

The gastrointestinal tract
The pathway that leads from the mouth, through the esophagus, stomach, small and large intestines, to the anus is called the gastrointestinal tract.

Esophagus

Stomach

Duodenum

Liver

Small intestine

Large intestine

Anus

Mucous layer

Muscle

Cross section of intestine
The muscles in the outer layers of the intestinal wall help to propel food along the gastrointestinal tract (see facing page). The mucous lining of the intestine allows nutrients to be absorbed into the bloodstream.

Pancreas
The pancreas produces *enzymes* that digest fats, carbohydrates, and proteins into simpler substances. Pancreatic juices neutralize acidity of the stomach contents.

Gallbladder
Bile produced by the liver is stored in the gallbladder and released into the small intestine. Bile assists the digestion of fats by reducing them to smaller units that are more easily acted upon by digestive enzymes.

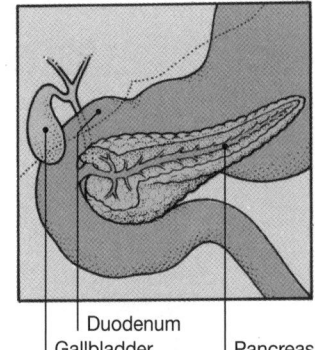

Duodenum

Gallbladder

Pancreas

MAJOR DRUG GROUPS

Antacids	Drugs for rectal and
Anti-ulcer drugs	anal disorders
Antidiarrheal drugs	Drug treatment
Laxatives	for gallstones
Drugs for inflammatory	
bowel disease	

The lining of the gastrointestinal tract

The lining of the different sections of the gastrointestinal tract varies according to the function of that part, depending, for example, on whether its principal role is to secrete digestive juices or to absorb nutrients.

Stomach
The stomach stores food and passes it to the intestine. The lining of the stomach releases gastric juice that partly digests food. The stomach wall continuously produces thick mucus that forms a protective coating.

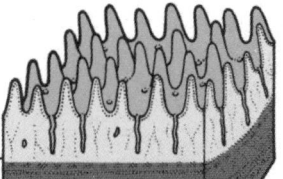

Duodenum (part of the small intestine)
This is the tube that connects the stomach to the intestine. Its lining may be damaged by excess acid produced by the stomach.

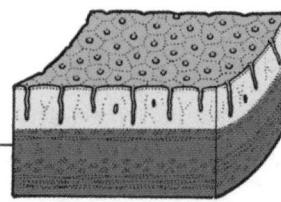

Small intestine
The small intestine is a long tube in which food is broken down by digestive juices. The mucous lining is covered with tiny projections called villi that provide a large surface area through which the products of digestion are absorbed into the bloodstream.

Large intestine
The large intestine receives both undigested food and indigestible material from the small intestine. Water and mineral salts pass through the lining into the bloodstream.

MOVEMENT OF FOOD THROUGH THE GASTROINTESTINAL TRACT

Food is propelled through the gastrointestinal tract by rhythmic waves of muscular contraction called peristalsis. The illustration shows how peristaltic contractions of the bowel wall push food through the intestine.

Muscle contraction in the tract is controlled by the autonomic nervous system (p.63) and is therefore easily disrupted by drugs that either stimulate or inhibit the activity of the autonomic nervous system. Excessive peristaltic action may cause diarrhea; slowed peristalsis may cause constipation.

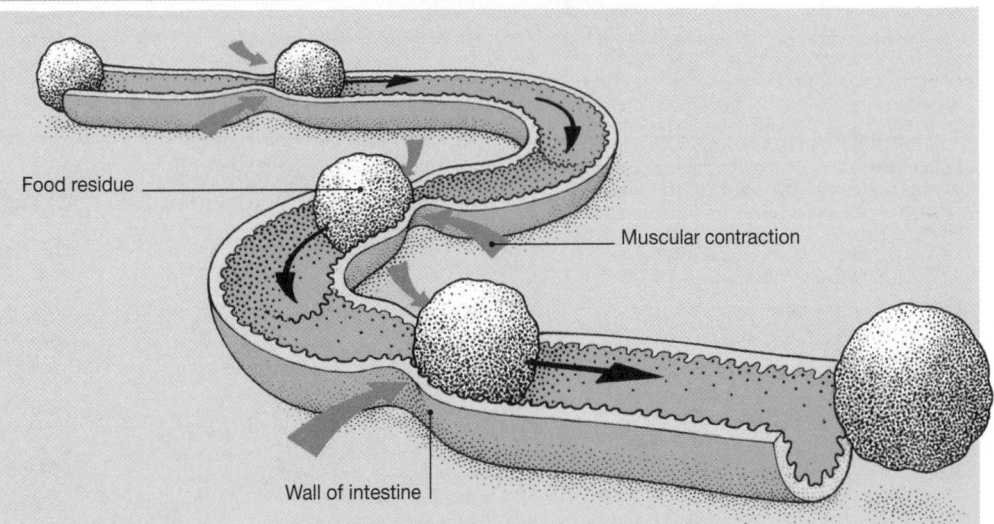

Food residue

Muscular contraction

Wall of intestine

ANTACIDS

Digestive juices in the stomach contain acid and *enzymes* that break down food before it passes into the intestine. The stomach wall is normally protected from the action of digestive acid by a layer of mucus secreted by the stomach lining. Problems arise when the stomach lining is damaged or too much acid is produced and eats away at the mucous layer.

Excess acid that leads to discomfort, commonly referred to as indigestion, may result from anxiety, overeating or eating certain foods, coffee, alcohol, or smoking. Some drugs, notably acetylsalicylic acid (ASA) and non-steroidal anti-inflammatory drugs (NSAIDs), can irritate the stomach lining and even cause ulcers to develop.

Antacids are used to neutralize acid and thus relieve pain. They are simple chemical compounds that are mildly alkaline, and some also act as chemical buffers. Their chalky taste is often disguised with flavourings.

Why drugs are used

Antacids may be needed when simple remedies (a change in diet) fail to relieve indigestion. They are especially useful one to three hours after meals to neutralize after-meal acid surge.

Physicians prescribe these drugs in order to relieve dyspepsia (pain in the chest or upper abdomen caused by or aggravated by acid) in disorders such as inflammation of the esophagus, stomach lining, and duodenum. Antacids usually relieve pain resulting from dyspepsia within a few minutes. Regular treatment with antacids reduces the acidity of the stomach, thereby encouraging the healing of ulcers that may have formed.

How they work

By neutralizing stomach acid, antacids prevent inflammation, relieve pain, and

ACTION OF ANTACIDS

Excess acid in the stomach may eat away at the layer of mucus that protects the stomach. When this occurs, or when the mucous lining is damaged, for example, by an ulcer, stomach acid comes into contact with the underlying tissues, causing pain and inflammation (right). Antacids combine with stomach acid to reduce the acidity of the digestive juices. This helps to prevent pain and inflammation, and allows the mucous lining to repair itself (far right).

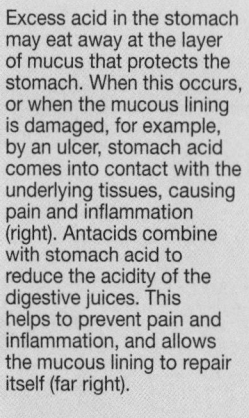
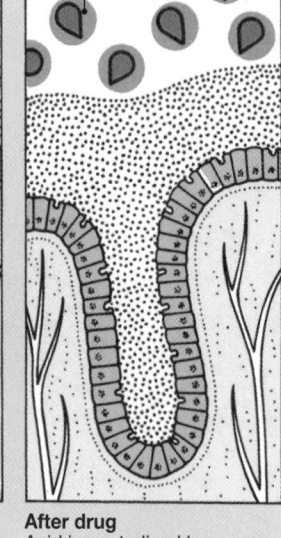

Acid   Drug

Mucus

Mucous lining

Stomach wall

Before drug
Acid damages mucous layer of stomach lining.

After drug
Acid is neutralized by antacid action.

allow the mucous layer and lining to mend. When used to treat ulcers, they prevent acid from attacking damaged stomach lining, allowing the ulcer to heal.

How they affect you

If antacids are taken according to the instructions, they are usually effective in relieving abdominal discomfort caused by acid. The speed of action, dependent on the ability to neutralize acid, varies. Their duration of action also varies; the

short-acting drugs may have to be taken quite frequently.

Although most antacids have few serious *side effects* when used only occasionally, some may cause diarrhea, and others may cause constipation (see Types of antacids, below).

Risks and special precautions

Antacids should not be taken to prevent abdominal pain on a regular basis except under medical supervision, as they may suppress the symptoms of stomach cancer. Your physician is likely to want to arrange tests such as endoscopy or barium X-rays before prescribing long-term treatment.

Antacids can interfere with the absorption of other drugs. If you are taking a prescription medicine, you should check with your physician or *pharmacist* before taking an antacid.

TYPES OF ANTACIDS

Aluminum compounds These drugs have a prolonged action and are widely used, especially for indigestion and dyspepsia. They may cause constipation, but this is often countered by combining this type of antacid with one that contains magnesium. Aluminum compounds can interfere with the absorption of phosphate from the diet, causing weakness and bone damage if taken in high doses over a long period. A high blood-level of aluminium may build up in people with kidney failure, causing a dementia-like illness.

Calcium compounds These are commonly available as calcium carbonate. They act to neutralize the stomach acid and can work rapidly, but can cause constipation. If taken in high doses, especially with vitamin D, they can increase calcium levels in the blood, potentially leading to kidney failure.

Magnesium compounds Like the aluminum compounds, these have a prolonged action. In large doses they can cause diarrhea, and

in people who have impaired kidney function, a high blood magnesium level may build up, causing weakness, lethargy, and drowsiness.

Sodium bicarbonate This antacid acts quickly, but its effect soon passes. It reacts with stomach acids to produce gas, which may cause bloating and belching. Sodium bicarbonate is not advised for people with heart or kidney disease, as it can lead to the accumulation of water (edema) in the legs and lungs, or serious changes in the acid-base balance of the blood.

Combined preparations Antacids may be combined with other substances called alginates and antifoaming agents. Alginates are intended to float over the contents of the stomach and subdue acid that can otherwise rise into the esophagus. Antifoaming agents are intended to relieve flatulence. The value of these additives is dubious.

COMMON DRUGS

Antacids
Aluminum
  hydroxide ✳
Bismuth subsalicylate ✳
Calcium carbonate
Magnesium
  hydroxide ✳
Magnesium
  trisilicate
Sodium
  bicarbonate

Antifoaming agent
Simethicone

Other drugs
Alginates/alginic
  acid ✳

✳ See Part 4

ANTI-ULCER DRUGS

Normally, the linings of the esophagus, stomach, and duodenum are protected from the irritant action of stomach acids or bile by a thin covering layer of mucus. If this is damaged, or if large amounts of stomach acid are formed, the underlying tissue may become eroded, causing a peptic ulcer. Some may experience abdominal pain, vomiting, and changes in appetite with an ulcer, while others may have no symptoms. The most common type of ulcer occurs just beyond the stomach, in the duodenum. The exact cause of peptic ulcers is not understood, but a number of risk factors have been identified, including heavy smoking, the regular use of ASA or NSAIDs, and family history. An organism found in almost all patients who have peptic ulcers, *Helicobacter pylori*, is now believed to be the main causative agent.

The symptoms caused by ulcers may be relieved by an antacid (see facing page), but healing is slow. Sucralfate may also be used to allow ulcers to heal. The usual treatment is with an anti-ulcer drug, such as a proton pump inhibitor (PPI) or an H_2 blocker, which is sometimes combined with bismuth and antibiotics to eradicate the *Helicobacter pylori* infection.

Why drugs are used

Anti-ulcer drugs are used to relieve symptoms and heal the ulcer. Untreated ulcers may erode blood vessel walls or perforate the stomach or duodenum. Eradication of *Helicobacter pylori* by an antisecretory drug (such as a proton pump inhibitor) combined with two antibiotics (triple therapy) can provide a cure in one to two weeks. Surgery is reserved for complications such as obstruction, perforation, hemorrhage, and when there is a possibility of cancer.

How they work

Drugs protect ulcers from the action of stomach acid, allowing the tissue to heal. H_2 blockers and proton pump inhibitors reduce the amount of acid released; misoprostol encourages mucous production; bismuth and sucralfate form a protective coating over the ulcer. Bismuth also has an antibacterial effect.

How they affect you

These drugs begin to reduce pain in a few hours and usually allow the ulcer to heal in four to eight weeks. They produce few side effects, although H_2 blockers such as cimetidine can cause confusion in the elderly. Bismuth and sucralfate may cause constipation; misoprostol, diarrhea; and proton pump inhibitors, either constipation or diarrhea. Triple therapy is given for one or two weeks. If *Helicobacter pylori* is eradicated, maintenance therapy should not be necessary. H_2 blockers and PPIs may mask the symptoms of cancer; sometimes tests to rule out this disorder may be done before they are prescribed. In those with a high risk for ulcers, PPIs or misoprostol may be given to prevent ulcers.

ACTION OF ANTI-ULCER DRUGS

Proton pump inhibitors

Acid secretion by the cells lining the stomach depends on an *enzyme* system (also known as the proton pump) that transports hydrogen ions across the cell walls. Omeprazole, lansoprazole, and similar drugs work by blocking the proton pump. They can stop stomach acid production until a new supply of the enzyme can be made by the body and, therefore, have a long duration of action.

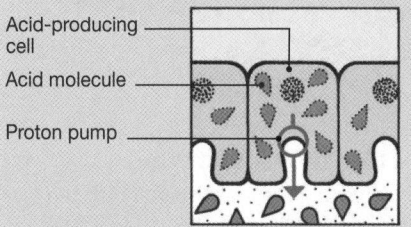

The proton pump
This enzyme system transports hydrogen ions across the cell wall into the stomach, thereby stimulating acid secretion.

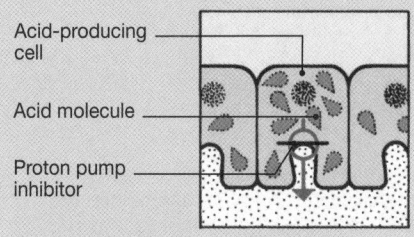

The action of proton pump inhibitors
Proton pump inhibitors block the enzyme system, stopping the transport of hydrogen ions and, thus, the secretion of acid.

H_2 blockers

Histamine is a chemical released by mast cells (see Allergies, p.109) that can produce a number of effects in different parts of the body. In the stomach, histamine stimulates H_2 *receptors*, causing acid production. To control stomach acid production, a class of antihistamine drugs was developed that acts by blocking the H_2 receptors. These drugs are known as H_2 blockers to distinguish them from antihistamines used for allergic disorders (see p.110), which are sometimes called H_1 blockers because they block H_1 receptors.

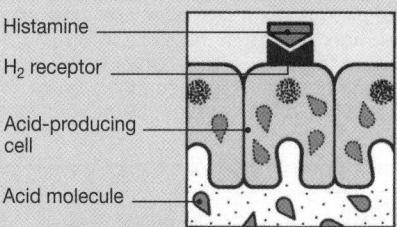

The action of histamine on the stomach
Histamine binds to specialized H_2 receptors and stimulates acid-producing cells in the stomach wall to release acid.

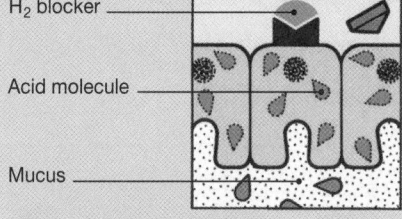

The action of H_2 blockers
H_2 blockers occupy H_2 receptors, preventing histamine from triggering the production of acid. This allows the mucous lining to heal.

Sucralfate and bismuth

Sucralfate forms a coating over the ulcer, protecting it from the action of stomach acid and allowing it to heal. Bismuth kills the bacteria that are thought to cause most peptic ulcers. Bismuth is used in triple therapy with antibiotics to cure ulcers.

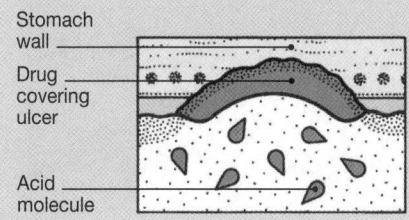

COMMON DRUGS

Proton pump inhibitors
Esomeprazole
Lansoprazole ✳
Omeprazole ✳
Pantoprazole ✳
Rabeprazole

H_2 blockers
Cimetidine ✳
Famotidine ✳
Nizatidine
Ranitidine ✳

Other drugs
Antacids (see p.94)
Antibiotics (see p.114)
Bismuth subsalicylate ✳
Misoprostol ✳
Sucralfate ✳

✳ See Part 4

ANTIDIARRHEAL DRUGS

Diarrhea is an increase in the fluidity and frequency of bowel movements. In some cases diarrhea protects the body from harmful substances in the intestine by hastening their removal. The most common causes are viral infection, food poisoning, and parasites. But it also occurs as a symptom of other illnesses. It can be a *side effect* of some drugs and may follow radiation and drug therapy for cancer. Diarrhea may also be caused by anxiety.

An attack of diarrhea usually clears up quickly without medical attention. Treatment may involve abstaining from food and drinking plenty of clear fluids. Rehydration solutions containing sugar as well as potassium and sodium salts are widely recommended for preventing dehydration and chemical imbalances, particularly in children. You should consult your physician if: the condition does not improve within 48 hours; the diarrhea contains blood; severe abdominal pain and vomiting or fever are present; you have just returned from a foreign country; or if the diarrhea occurs in a small child or an elderly person.

Severe diarrhea can impair absorption of drugs, and anyone taking a prescribed drug should seek advice from a physician or *pharmacist*. A woman taking oral contraceptives may need additional contraceptive measures (see p.149).

The main types of drugs used to relieve non-specific diarrhea are *opioids*, and bulk-forming and *adsorbent* agents. Antispasmodic drugs may also be used to relieve accompanying pain (see Drugs for irritable bowel syndrome, below).

Why drugs are used
An antidiarrheal drug may be prescribed to provide relief when simple remedies are not effective, and once it is certain the diarrhea is neither infectious nor *toxic*.

ACTION OF ANTIDIARRHEAL DRUGS

Opioid antidiarrheals
These drugs reduce the transmission of nerve signals to the intestinal muscles, thus reducing muscle contraction. This allows more time for water to be absorbed from the food residue and therefore reduces the fluidity as well as the frequency of bowel movements.

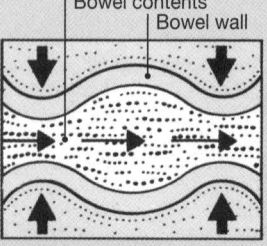
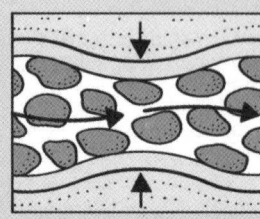

Before drug
Rapid bowel contraction prevents water from being absorbed.

After drug
Slowed bowel action allows more water to be absorbed.

Bulk-forming agents
These preparations contain particles that swell up as they absorb water from the large intestine. This makes the feces firmer and less fluid. It is thought that bulk-forming agents may absorb irritants and harmful chemicals along with excess water.

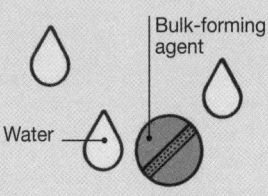

Water is attracted by bulk-forming agent.

Bulk-forming agent swells as water is absorbed.

Opioid drugs are the most effective antidiarrheals. They are used when the diarrhea is severe and debilitating. The bulking and adsorbent agents have a milder effect and are often used when it is necessary to regulate bowel action over a prolonged period – for example, in people with colostomies or ileostomies.

How they work
Opioids decrease the intestinal muscles' propulsive activity so that fecal matter passes more slowly through the bowel.

Bulk-forming agents and adsorbents absorb water and irritants present in the bowel, thereby producing larger and firmer stools at less frequent intervals.

How they affect you
Drugs that are used to treat diarrhea reduce the urge to move the bowels. Opioids and antispasmodics may relieve abdominal pain. All antidiarrheals may cause constipation if used in excess.

Risks and special precautions
Used in relatively low doses for a limited period of time, the opioid drugs are unlikely to produce *adverse effects*. However, these drugs should be used under medical supervision when diarrhea is caused by an infection, since they may slow the elimination of microorganisms from the intestine. All antidiarrheals should be taken with plenty of water. It is important not to take a bulk-forming agent together with an opioid or antispasmodic drug, because a bulky mass could form and obstruct the bowel.

DRUGS FOR IRRITABLE BOWEL SYNDROME

Irritable bowel syndrome (IBS) is a common stress-related condition in which the normal coordinated waves of muscular contraction responsible for moving the bowel contents smoothly through the intestines become strong and irregular, often causing pain, and associated with diarrhea or constipation.

Symptoms are often relieved by adjusting the amount of fibre in the diet, although medication may also be required. Bulk-forming agents may be given to regulate the consistency of the bowel contents. Tegaserod may be used for symptomatic treatment of constipation associated with IBS. If pain is severe, an antispasmodic drug may be prescribed. These *anticholinergic* drugs reduce the transmission of nerve signals to the bowel wall, thus preventing spasm.

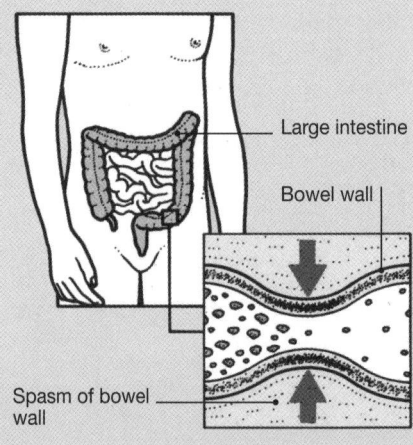

Large intestine

Bowel wall

Spasm of bowel wall

COMMON DRUGS

Antispasmodics
Atropine *
Dicyclomine *
Scopolamine

Opioids
Codeine *
Diphenoxylate *
Loperamide *

Bulk-forming agents and adsorbents
Attapulgite
Bismuth
  subsalicylate *
Ispaghula
Psyllium *

Antibacterials
Ciprofloxacin *
Sulfamethoxazole-
  trimethoprim *

* See Part 4

LAXATIVES

When your bowels do not move as frequently as usual and the feces are hard and difficult to pass, you are suffering from constipation. The most common cause is lack of sufficient fibre in your diet; fibre supplies the bulk that makes the feces soft and easy to pass. The simplest remedy is more fluid and a diet that contains plenty of foods that are high in fibre, but laxative drugs may also be used.

Ignoring the urge to defecate can also cause constipation, because the feces become dry, hard to pass, and too small to stimulate the muscles that propel them through the intestine.

Certain drugs may be constipating: for example, *opioid* analgesics, tricyclic antidepressants, and antacids containing aluminium. Some diseases, such as hypothyroidism (underactive thyroid gland) and scleroderma (a rare disorder of connective tissue characterized by the hardening of the skin), can also lead to constipation.

The onset of constipation in a middle-aged or elderly person may be an early symptom of bowel cancer. Consult your physician about any persistent change in bowel habit.

Why drugs are used

Since prolonged use is harmful, laxatives should be used for very short periods only (except for psyllium, which is fine for long-term use). They may prevent pain and straining in people suffering from either hernias or hemorrhoids (p.99). Physicians may prescribe laxatives for the same reason after childbirth or abdominal surgery. Laxatives are also used to clear the bowel before investigative procedures such as colonoscopy. They may be prescribed for patients who are elderly or bedridden because lack of exercise can often lead to constipation.

How they work

Laxatives act on the large intestine – by increasing the speed with which fecal matter passes through the bowel, or

ACTION OF LAXATIVES

Bulk-forming agents
Taken after a meal, these agents are not absorbed as they pass through the digestive tract. They contain particles that absorb many times their own volume of water. By doing so, they increase the bulk of the bowel movements and thus encourage bowel action.

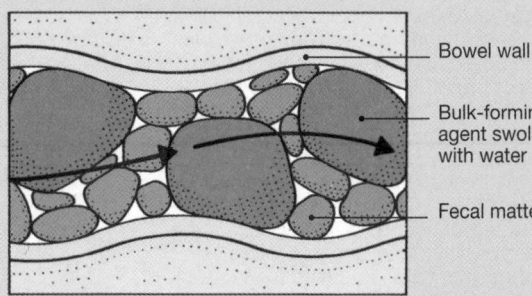

Bowel wall

Bulk-forming agent swollen with water

Fecal matter

Stimulant laxatives
These laxatives are thought to encourage bowel movements by acting on nerve endings in the wall of the intestines that trigger contraction of the intestinal muscles. This speeds the passage of fecal matter through the large intestine, allowing less time for water to be absorbed. Thus feces become more liquid and are passed more frequently.

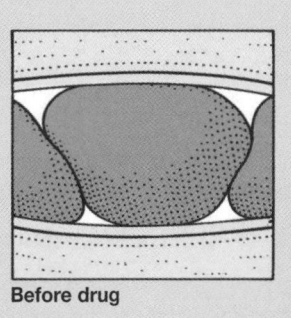

Before drug

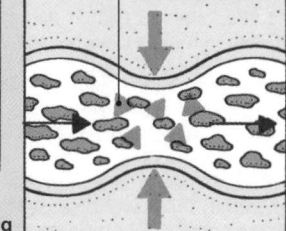

Increased contractions speed passage of fecal matter

After drug

increasing its bulk and/or water content. Stimulants cause the bowel muscles to contract, increasing the speed at which fecal matter goes through the intestine. Bulk-forming laxatives absorb water in the bowel, thereby increasing the volume of feces, making them softer and easier to pass. Lactulose also causes fluid to accumulate in the intestine. Osmotic laxatives act by keeping water in the bowel, and thereby make the bowel movements softer. This also increases the bulk of the feces and enables them to be passed more easily. Lubricant liquid paraffin preparations make bowel

movements softer and easier to pass without increasing their bulk. Prolonged use can interfere with absorption of some essential vitamins.

Risks and special precautions

Laxatives can cause diarrhea if taken in overdose, and can make constipation worse if overused. Use of a laxative should therefore be discontinued as soon as normal bowel movements have been re-established. Children should not be given laxatives except in special circumstances on the advice of a physician.

TYPES OF LAXATIVES

Bulk-forming agents These are relatively slow acting but are less likely than other laxatives to interfere with normal bowel action. Only after consultation with your physician should they be taken for constipation accompanied by abdominal pain because of the risk of intestinal obstruction.

Stimulant (contact) laxatives These are for occasional use when other treatments have failed or when rapid onset of action is needed. Stimulant laxatives should not normally be used for longer than a week as they can cause abdominal cramps and diarrhea.

Softening agents These are often used when hard bowel movements cause pain on defecation – for example, when hemorrhoids

are present, or after surgery when straining must be avoided. Docusate sodium is often recommended for this.

Osmotic laxatives Salts such as magnesium citrate may be used to evacuate the bowel before surgery or investigative procedures. They are not normally used for the long-term relief of constipation because they can cause chemical imbalances in the blood.

Lactulose is an alternative to bulk-forming laxatives for the long-term treatment of chronic constipation. It may cause stomach cramps and flatulence but is usually well tolerated.

COMMON DRUGS

Stimulant laxatives
Bisacodyl ✳
Cascara
Castor oil
Sennosides

Bulk-forming agents
Bran
Psyllium ✳

Softening agents
Docusate sodium ✳
Liquid paraffin

Osmotic laxatives
Glycerin
Lactulose ✳
Magnesium citrate
Magnesium hydroxide ✳
Magnesium sulfate
Polyethylene glycol
Picosulfate sodium

Lubricant laxative
Mineral oil

✳ See Part 4

DRUGS FOR INFLAMMATORY BOWEL DISEASE

Inflammatory bowel disease is the term used for disorders in which inflammation of the intestinal wall causes recurrent attacks of abdominal pain, general feelings of ill-health, and frequently diarrhea, with blood and mucus present in the feces. Loss of appetite and poor absorption of food may often result in weight loss.

There are two main types of inflammatory bowel disease (IBD): Crohn's disease (CD) and ulcerative colitis (UC). In Crohn's disease (also called regional enteritis), any part of the digestive tract may become inflamed, although the small intestine is the most commonly affected site. In ulcerative colitis, it is the large intestine (colon) that becomes inflamed and ulcerated, often producing bloodstained diarrhea (see right).

The exact cause of these disorders is unknown, although stress-related, dietary, infectious, and genetic factors may all be important.

Establishing a proper diet and a less stressful lifestyle may help to alleviate these conditions. Bed rest during attacks is also advisable. However, these simple measures alone do not usually relieve or prevent attacks, and drug treatment is often necessary.

Three types of drug are used to treat inflammatory bowel disease: corticosteroids (p.127), immunosuppressants (p.143), and aminosalicylate anti-inflammatory drugs such as sulfasalazine. Nutritional supplements (used especially for Crohn's disease) and antidiarrheal drugs (p.96) may also be used. Surgery to remove damaged areas of the intestine may be needed in severe cases.

SITES OF BOWEL INFLAMMATION

The two main types of bowel inflammation are ulcerative colitis and Crohn's disease. The former occurs in the large intestine. Crohn's disease can occur anywhere along the gastrointestinal tract, but it most often affects the small intestine.

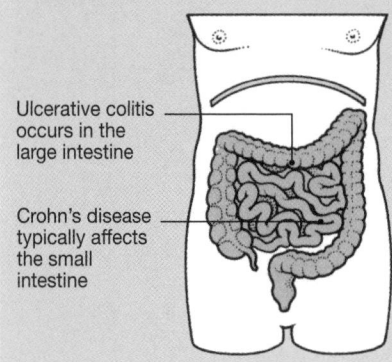

Ulcerative colitis occurs in the large intestine

Crohn's disease typically affects the small intestine

Why drugs are used

Drugs help control symptoms and prevent complications of IBD, especially perforation of the intestinal wall. Aminosalicylates are used to treat acute attacks of UC and CD, and they may be continued as maintenance therapy. With severe bowel inflammation, a course of corticosteroids may be prescribed, particularly during a sudden flare-up. Once symptoms are controlled, an immunosuppressant drug may be prescribed to prevent a relapse.

How they work

Corticosteroids and sulfasalazine damp down the inflammatory process, allowing the damaged tissue to recover. They act in different ways to prevent migration of white blood cells into the bowel wall, which may be responsible in part for the inflammation of the bowel. Newer drugs such as infliximab and adalimumab act by blocking the actions of a substance called tumor necrosis factor-alpha or TNF-alpha, which causes inflammation in the body.

How they affect you

Taken to treat attacks, these drugs relieve symptoms within a few days, and general health improves gradually over a period of a few weeks. Aminosalicylates usually provide long-term relief from the symptoms of inflammatory bowel disease.

Treatment with an immunosuppressant drug may take several months before the condition improves; regular blood tests to monitor possible *side effects* are often required.

Risks and special precautions

Immunosuppressant and corticosteroid drugs can cause serious *adverse effects* and are only prescribed when potential benefits outweigh the risks involved.

The side effects of corticosteroids can be reduced by the use of budesonide in a topical preparation that releases the drug at the site of inflammation.

It is important to continue taking these drugs as instructed because stopping them abruptly may cause a sudden flare-up of the disorder. Physicians usually supervise a gradual reduction in dosage when such drugs are stopped, even when they are given as a short course for an attack. Antidiarrheal drugs should not be taken on a routine basis because they may mask signs of deterioration or cause sudden bowel dilation or rupture.

How they are administered

Many of these drugs are usually taken in the form of tablets, although mild ulcerative colitis in the last part of the large intestine may be treated with suppositories or an enema containing a corticosteroid or aminosalicylate. Drugs such as adalimumab are given by injection.

ACTION OF DRUGS IN ULCERATIVE COLITIS

The most common form of inflammatory bowel disease is ulcerative colitis. It affects the large intestine, causing ulceration of the lining and producing pain and violent blood-stained diarrhea. It is often treated with corticosteroids and aminosalicylates.

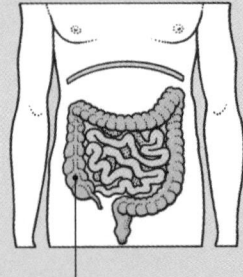

Large intestine

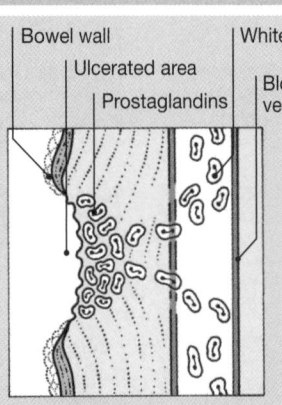

Bowel wall

Ulcerated area

Prostaglandins

Before drug
Damage to the intestinal lining provokes the formation of chemicals known as prostaglandins, which trigger the migration of white blood cells into the ulcerated area. The accumulation of white blood cells in the bowel wall causes inflammation.

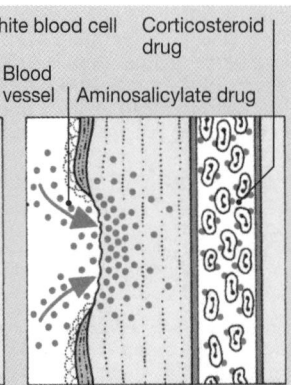

White blood cell   Corticosteroid drug

Blood vessel   Aminosalicylate drug

Drug action
Aminosalicylate drugs pass into the ulcerated area from inside the bowel. They prevent prostaglandins from forming in the damaged tissue. Corticosteroids in the bloodstream reduce the ability of white blood cells to pass into the bowel wall.

COMMON DRUGS

Corticosteroids	**Aminosalicylates**
Betamethasone ✳	5-Aminosalicylic
Budesonide ✳	Acid (5-ASA)
Hydrocortisone ✳	Olsalazine
Methylprednisolone ✳	Sulfasalazine
Prednisolone/	
prednisone ✳	**Other drugs**
	Adalimumab ✳
Immunosuppressants	Infliximab
Azathioprine ✳	Metronidazole ✳
Cyclosporine ✳	
Mercaptopurine ✳	✳ See Part 4
Methotrexate ✳	

DRUGS FOR RECTAL AND ANAL DISORDERS

The most common disorder affecting the rectum (the last part of the large intestine) and anus (the opening from the rectum) is hemorrhoids, also known as piles. They occur when hemorrhoidal veins become swollen or irritated, often as a result of prolonged local pressure such as that caused by a pregnancy or a job requiring long hours of sitting. Hemorrhoids may cause irritation and pain, especially on defecation. The condition is aggravated by constipation and straining during defecation. In some cases hemorrhoids may bleed and occasionally clots form in the swollen veins, leading to severe pain, a condition called thrombosed hemorrhoids.

Other common disorders affecting the anus include anal fissure (painful cracks in the anus) and pruritus ani (itching around the anus). Anal disorders of all kinds occur less frequently in people who have soft, bulky stools.

A number of both over-the-counter and prescription-only preparations are available for the relief of such disorders.

Why drugs are used

Preparations for relief of hemorrhoids and anal discomfort fall into two main groups: creams or suppositories that act locally to relieve inflammation and irritation, and measures that relieve constipation, which contributes to the formation of, and the discomfort from, hemorrhoids and anal fissure.

Preparations from the first group often contain a soothing agent with *antiseptic*, *astringent*, or *vasoconstrictor* properties. Ingredients of this type include zinc oxide or sulfate, bismuth, hamamelis (witch hazel), and phenylephrine or naphazoline. Some of these products include a mild local anesthetic (see p.64) such as benzocaine, dibucaine, or pramoxine. A physician may also prescribe an ointment containing a corticosteroid to relieve inflammation around the anus (see Topical corticosteroids, p.162).

People who suffer from hemorrhoids or anal fissure are generally advised to include in their diets plenty of fluids and fibre-rich foods, such as fruits, vegetables, and whole grain products, both to prevent constipation and to ease defecation. A mild bulk-forming or softening laxative may also be prescribed (see p.97).

Neither of these treatments can shrink large hemorrhoids, although they may provide relief while anal fissures heal naturally. Severe, persistently painful hemorrhoids that continue to be troublesome in spite of these measures may need to be removed surgically or, more commonly, by banding with specially applied small rubber bands (see below left).

How they affect you

The treatments described above usually relieve discomfort, especially during defecation. Most people experience no adverse effects, although preparations containing local anesthetics may cause irritation or even a rash in the anal area. It is rare for ingredients in locally acting preparations to be absorbed into the body in sufficient quantities to cause generalized *side effects*.

The main risk is that self-treatment of hemorrhoids may delay diagnosis of bowel cancer. It is therefore always wise to consult your physician if symptoms of hemorrhoids are present, especially if you have noticed bleeding from the rectum or a change in bowel habits.

DISORDERS OF THE RECTUM AND ANUS

The rectum and anus form the last part of the digestive tract. Common conditions affecting the area include swelling of the veins around the anus (hemorrhoids), cracks in the anus (anal fissure), and inflammation or irritation of the anus and surrounding area (pruritus ani).

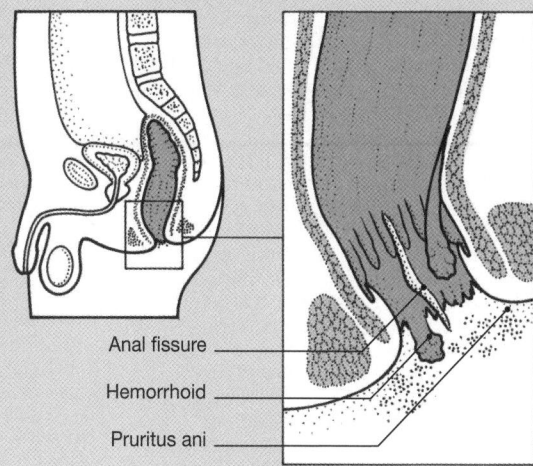

Anal fissure
Hemorrhoid
Pruritus ani

COMMON DRUGS

Soothing and astringent agents	Topical corticosteroids
Aluminium acetate	Hydrocortisone *
Bismuth	
Zinc oxide	**Local anesthetics** (see p.64)
Vasoconstrictors	
Ephedrine *	**Laxatives** (see p.97)

* See Part 4

SITES OF DRUG ACTION

The illustration below shows how and where drugs for the treatment of rectal disorders act to relieve symptoms.

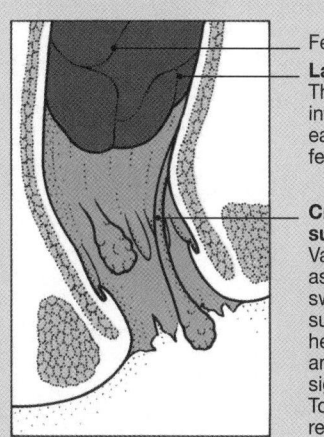

Fecal matter

Laxatives
These act in the large intestine to soften and ease the passage of feces.

Creams and suppositories
Vasoconstrictors and astringents reduce the swelling and restrict blood supply, helping to relieve hemorrhoids. Local anesthetics numb pain signals from the anus. Topical corticosteroids relieve inflammation.

Banding treatment
A small rubber band is applied tightly to a hemorrhoid, thereby blocking off its blood supply. The hemorrhoid will eventually wither away.

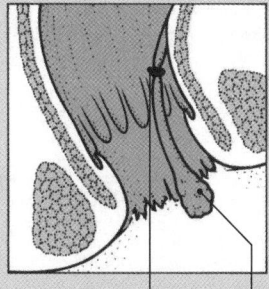

Rubber band

Hemorrhoid

DRUG TREATMENT FOR GALLSTONES

The formation of gallstones is the most common disorder of the gallbladder, which is the storage and concentrating unit for bile, a digestive juice produced by the liver. During digestion, bile passes from the gallbladder via the bile duct into the small intestine, where it assists in the digestion of fats. Bile is composed of several ingredients, including bile acids, bile salts, and bile pigments. It also has a significant amount of cholesterol, which is dissolved in bile acid. If the amount of cholesterol in the bile increases, or if the amount of bile acid is reduced, a proportion of the cholesterol cannot remain dissolved, and under certain circumstances this excess accumulates in the gallbladder as gallstones.

Gallstones may be present in the gallbladder for years without causing symptoms. However, if they become lodged in the bile duct they cause pain and block the flow of bile. If the bile accumulates in the blood, it may cause an attack of jaundice, or the gallbladder may become infected and inflamed.

Drug treatment with ursodeoxycholic acid, also known as ursodiol, is only effective against stones made principally of cholesterol (some contain other substances), and even these take many months to dissolve. Therefore, surgery and ultrasound have become widely used, especially the use of laparoscopic ("keyhole") surgery. Surgery and ultrasound treatments are always used to remove stones blocking the bile duct.

Why drugs are used

Even if you have not experienced any symptoms, once gallstones have been diagnosed your physician may advise treatment because of the risk of blockage of the bile duct. Drug treatment is usually preferred to surgery for small cholesterol stones or when there is a possibility that surgery may be risky.

How they work

Ursodeoxycholic acid is a substance that is naturally present in bile. It acts on chemical processes in the liver to regulate the amount of cholesterol in the blood by controlling the amount that passes into the bile. Once the cholesterol level in the bile is reduced, the bile acids are

DIGESTION OF FATS

The digestion of fats (or lipids) in the small intestine is assisted by the action of bile, a digestive juice produced by the liver and stored in the gallbladder. A complex sequence of chemical processes enables fats to be absorbed through the intestinal wall, broken down in the liver, and converted for use in the body. Cholesterol, a lipid present in bile, plays an important part in this chain.

2 Bile salts act on fats to enable them to pass from the small intestine into the bloodstream, either directly or via the lymphatic system.

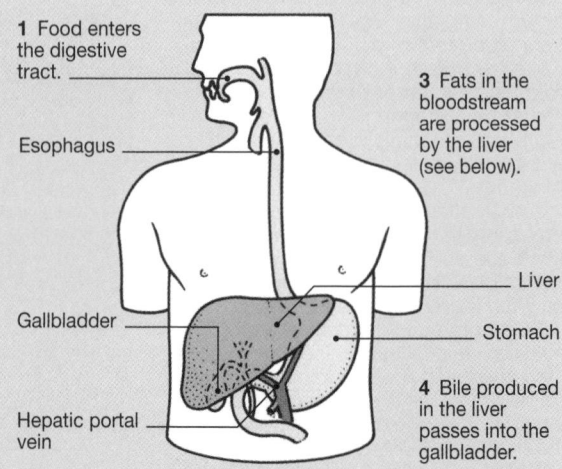

1 Food enters the digestive tract.

Esophagus

Gallbladder

Hepatic portal vein

3 Fats in the bloodstream are processed by the liver (see below).

Liver

Stomach

4 Bile produced in the liver passes into the gallbladder.

How fats are processed in the liver

Fat molecules are broken down in the liver into fatty acids and glycerol. Glycerol, as well as some of the fatty acids, pass back into the bloodstream. Other fatty acids are used to form cholesterol, some of which in turn is used to make bile salts. Unchanged cholesterol is dissolved in the bile, which then passes into the gallbladder.

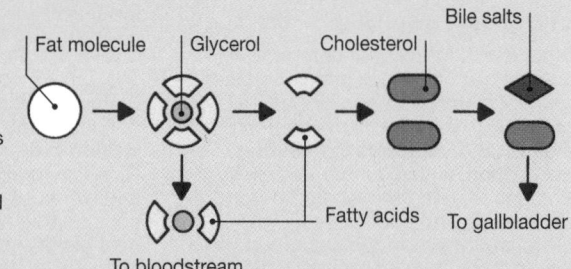

Fat molecule | Glycerol | Cholesterol | Bile salts

To bloodstream | Fatty acids | To gallbladder

able to start dissolving the stones in the gallbladder. To achieve maximum effect, ursodeoxycholic acid treatment usually needs to be accompanied by adherence to a low-cholesterol, high-fibre diet.

How they affect you

Drug treatment may often take years to dissolve gallstones completely. You will not, therefore, feel any immediate benefit from the drug, but you may have some minor *side effects*, the most usual of which is diarrhea. If this occurs, your physician may adjust the dosage. The effect of drug treatment on the gallstones is usually monitored at regular intervals by means of ultrasound or X-ray examinations.

Even after successful treatment with drugs, gallstones often recur when the drug is stopped. In some cases drug treatment and dietary restrictions may be continued even after the gallstones have dissolved, to prevent a recurrence.

Although the drug reduces cholesterol in the gallbladder, it increases the level of cholesterol in the blood because it reduces its excretion in the bile. Physicians therefore prescribe it with caution to people who have atherosclerosis (fatty deposits in the blood vessels). The drug is not usually given to people who have liver disorders because it can interfere with normal liver function. Surgical or ultrasound treatment is used for those with liver problems.

AGENTS USED IN DISORDERS OF THE PANCREAS

The pancreas releases certain *enzymes* into the small intestine that are necessary for digestion of a range of foods. If the release of pancreatic enzymes is impaired (caused by, for example, chronic pancreatitis or cystic fibrosis), enzyme replacement therapy may be necessary. Replacement of enzymes does not cure the underlying disorder, but it restores normal digestion. Pancreatic enzymes should

be taken just before or with meals, and usually take effect immediately. Your physician will probably advise you to eat a diet that is high in protein and carbohydrates and low in fat.

Pancreatin, the generic name for those preparations containing pancreatic enzymes, is extracted from pig pancreas. Treatment must be continued indefinitely as long as the pancreatic disorder persists.

COMMON DRUGS

Drug for gallstones
Ursodeoxycholic acid (Ursodiol)

Drug for cholestatic liver disease
Ursodeoxycholic acid (Ursodiol)

Pancreatic enzymes
Pancreatin

MUSCLES, BONES, AND JOINTS

The basic architecture of the human body relies on 206 bones, over 600 muscles, and a complex assortment of ligaments, tendons, and cartilage that enable the body to move with remarkable efficiency.

What can go wrong

Although tough, these structures often suffer damage. Muscles, tendons, and ligaments can be strained or torn by stretching, over use, or violent movement, causing inflammation, making the affected tissue swollen and painful. Joints, especially those that bear the body's weight – hips, knees, ankles, and vertebrae – are prone to wear and tear. The cartilage covering the bone ends may tear, causing inflammation and pain. Some may develop osteoarthritis as a result of cartilage damage. Joint damage also occurs in rheumatoid arthritis, which is an autoimmune disorder. Gout, in which uric acid crystals form in some joints may cause inflammation, a condition known as gouty arthritis.

The muscles and joints can also suffer nerve injury or degeneration, altering nerve control over muscle contraction. Myasthenia gravis, in which transmission of signals between nerves and muscles is reduced, affects muscle control. Bones may also be weakened by vitamin, mineral, or hormone deficiencies.

Why drugs are used

An analgesic or an anti-inflammatory drug provides pain relief in most of these conditions. For severe inflammation, a doctor may inject a drug with a more powerful anti-inflammatory effect, such as a corticosteroid, into the affected site. In progressive rheumatoid arthritis, antirheumatic drugs may halt the disease's progression and relieve symptoms. Glucosamine, a natural health product, has been tried in osteoarthritis, but beneficial effects are unclear.

Drugs that help to eliminate excess uric acid from the body are often prescribed to treat gout. Muscle relaxants that inhibit transmission of nerve signals to the muscles are used to treat muscle spasm. Drugs that increase nervous stimulation of the muscle are prescribed for myasthenia gravis. Bone disorders in which the mineral content of the bone is reduced are treated with supplements of minerals, vitamins, hormones, and other drugs.

MAJOR DRUG GROUPS

Non-steroidal anti-inflammatory drugs	Muscle-relaxant drugs
Antirheumatic drugs	Drugs used for myasthenia gravis
Locally acting corticosteroids	Drugs for bone disorders
Drugs for gout	

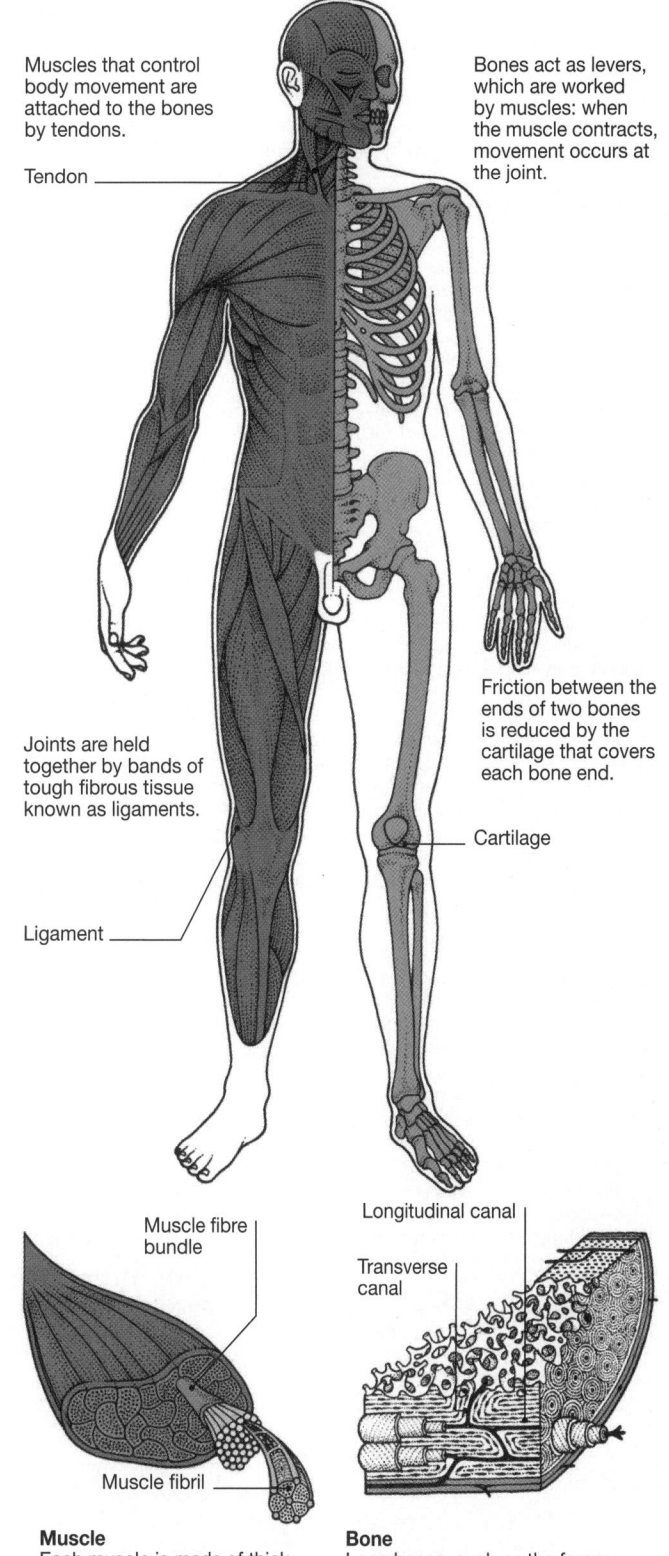

Muscles that control body movement are attached to the bones by tendons.

Tendon

Bones act as levers, which are worked by muscles: when the muscle contracts, movement occurs at the joint.

Joints are held together by bands of tough fibrous tissue known as ligaments.

Ligament

Friction between the ends of two bones is reduced by the cartilage that covers each bone end.

Cartilage

Muscle fibre bundle

Muscle fibril

Longitudinal canal

Transverse canal

Muscle
Each muscle is made of thick bundles of fibres: each bundle in turn is made of fibrils. Tiny nerves and blood vessels enable the muscle to function.

Bone
Long bones, such as the femur, contain a network of longitudinal and transverse canals to carry blood, nerves, and lymph vessels through the bone.

NON-STEROIDAL ANTI-INFLAMMATORY DRUGS

These drugs are used to relieve the pain, stiffness, and inflammation of painful conditions affecting the muscles, bones, and joints. NSAIDs are called "non-steroidal" to distinguish them from corticosteroid drugs (see p.127), which also decrease inflammation.

Why they are used

NSAIDs are widely prescribed for the treatment of osteoarthritis, rheumatoid arthritis, and other rheumatic conditions. They reduce inflammation and thus relieve pain and swelling of joints.

The response to the various drugs in this group varies between individuals. It is sometimes necessary to try several different NSAIDs before finding the one that best suits a particular individual.

NSAIDs do not change the progress of a disease. Medications called DMARDs are used in rheumatoid arthritis to decrease disease progression (see facing page).

NSAIDs are also commonly prescribed to relieve back pain, headaches, gout (p.105), menstrual pain (p.148), mild pain following surgery, and pain from soft tissue injuries, such as sprains and strains (see also Analgesics, p.64).

How they work

Prostaglandins are chemicals released by the body at the site of injury. They are responsible for producing inflammation and pain following tissue damage. NSAIDs block an enzyme, cyclo-oxygenase (COX) which is involved in the production of prostaglandins, and thus reduce pain and inflammation (see p.65).

How they affect you

NSAIDs are rapidly absorbed from the digestive system and most start to relieve pain within an hour. When used regularly they reduce pain, inflammation, and stiffness and may restore or improve the function of a damaged or painful joint.

Most NSAIDs are short acting and need to be taken a few times a day in order to provide optimal relief from pain. Some need to be taken only twice daily. Others, such as piroxicam, are very slowly eliminated from the body and are effective when taken once a day.

Risks and special precautions

Nausea, indigestion, and altered bowel action are common *side effects*. However, the main risk from NSAIDs is that, occasionally, they can cause ulcers and bleeding in the stomach or duodenum. They should therefore be avoided by people who have suffered from peptic ulcers.

Most NSAIDs may not be recommended during pregnancy or for breast-feeding mothers. Caution is also advised for those with kidney or liver abnormalities or with a history of hypersensitivity to other drugs. NSAIDs may impair blood clotting and are, therefore, prescribed with caution for

ACTION OF NSAIDs IN OSTEOARTHRITIS

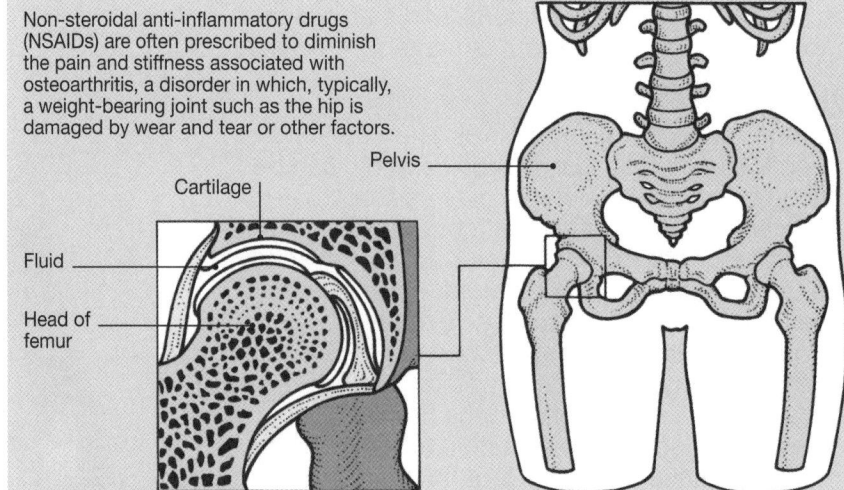

Non-steroidal anti-inflammatory drugs (NSAIDs) are often prescribed to diminish the pain and stiffness associated with osteoarthritis, a disorder in which, typically, a weight-bearing joint such as the hip is damaged by wear and tear or other factors.

Pelvis

Cartilage

Fluid

Head of femur

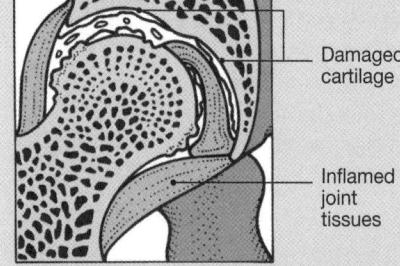

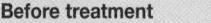

Damaged cartilage

Inflamed joint tissues

Before treatment
The protective layers of cartilage surrounding the joint are worn away and the joint becomes inflamed and painful.

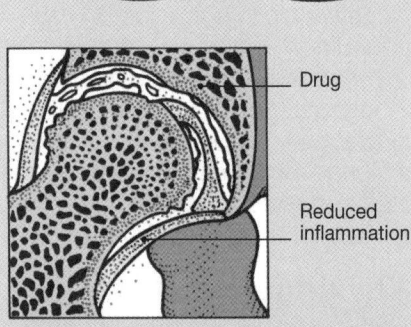

Drug

Reduced inflammation

Effect of NSAIDs
NSAIDs reduce inflammation and may thus relieve pain, but damage to the joint remains and symptoms are likely to worsen or recur if the drug is stopped.

people with bleeding disorders or who are taking drugs that reduce blood clotting. Long-term use of some NSAIDs is associated with an increased risk of cardiovascular events such as a heart attack and stroke. The risk may be greater in those with heart disease or at risk for heart disease.

Anti-ulcer drugs

An NSAID may cause bleeding when its antiprostaglandin action occurs in the digestive tract. To protect against this side effect, proton-pump inhibitors (PPIs) or misoprostol are used. Misoprostol is sometimes combined in one pill with the NSAID.

COX-2 selective inhibitors

NSAIDs block two types of COX enzymes, COX-1 and COX-2, at different sites in the body. Blocking COX-1 leads to the stomach irritation of NSAIDs, while blocking COX-2 leads to the anti-inflammatory effect. As a result, one class of NSAIDs, COX-2 selective inhibitors,

was developed to block COX-2 only. Thus, the benefits of NSAIDs can be obtained with less risk of stomach pain, peptic ulcers, or intestinal bleeding. Celecoxib is a COX-2 selective inhibitor, and is useful in people at risk of stomach problems, but should be used cautiously in those with kidney or heart disease.

COMMON DRUGS

ASA *	Mefenamic acid *
Diclofenac *	Meloxicam *
Diflunisal	Nabumetone
Etodolac	Naproxen *
Flurbiprofen	Oxaprozin
Ibuprofen *	Piroxicam *
Indomethacin	Sulindac
Ketoprofen *	Tenoxicam
Ketorolac	Tiaprofenic acid

COX-2 selective inhibitor
Celecoxib *

* See Part 4

ANTIRHEUMATIC DRUGS

These drugs are used in the treatment of various rheumatic disorders, the most crippling and deforming of which is rheumatoid arthritis (RA), an autoimmune disease in which the body's immune system causes damage of its own joint tissue. The disease causes pain, stiffness, and swelling of the joints that, over many months, can lead to deformity. Flare-ups of RA also cause a general feeling of being unwell, fatigue, and loss of appetite.

Treatments for RA include drugs, rest, changes in diet, physiotherapy, and immobilization of joints. RA cannot yet be cured, although with treatment, disability can be prevented. It sometimes subsides spontaneously for prolonged periods.

Why drugs are used

The aim of drug treatment is to relieve the symptoms of pain and stiffness, maintain mobility, and prevent deformity. There are two main forms of drug treatment for RA: one to alleviate symptoms, and the second to modify, halt, or slow the underlying disease process. Drugs in the first category include ASA (p.198) and the other non-steroidal anti-inflammatory drugs (NSAIDs, facing page). These drugs are usually prescribed for early relief of pain and inflammation.

The second category of drugs, called disease-modifying antirheumatic drugs (DMARDs) are also started early in the disease, as these drugs may prevent any further joint damage and disability. They are usually prescribed in moderate to severe disease and can have potentially severe *adverse effects*. For individuals with aggressive, debilitating arthritis, biologic agents called Biological Response Modifiers (BRM) may be considered. These target specific components of the body's immune system and can reduce inflammation. BRMs are administered by injection and may need to be given daily, weekly, or every 2–4 weeks, depending on the agent. There are important health cautions in using these, which need to be discussed with your physician. BRMs are generally expensive. Corticosteroids (p.127) are sometimes used in the

THE EFFECTS OF ANTIRHEUMATIC DRUGS

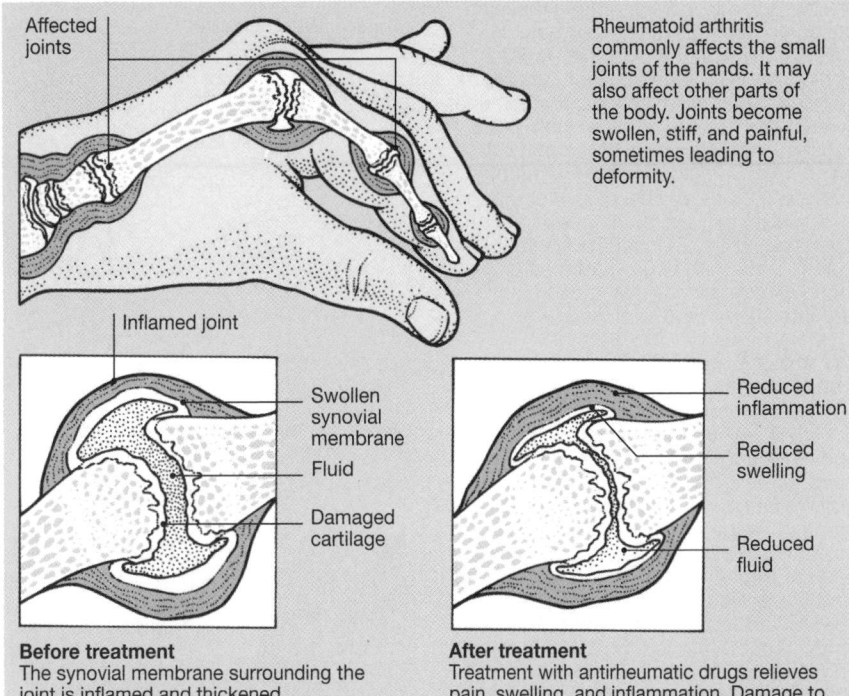

Rheumatoid arthritis commonly affects the small joints of the hands. It may also affect other parts of the body. Joints become swollen, stiff, and painful, sometimes leading to deformity.

Affected joints

Inflamed joint

Swollen synovial membrane
Fluid
Damaged cartilage

Reduced inflammation
Reduced swelling
Reduced fluid

Before treatment
The synovial membrane surrounding the joint is inflamed and thickened, producing increased fluid within the joint. The surrounding tissue is inflamed and joint cartilage is damaged.

After treatment
Treatment with antirheumatic drugs relieves pain, swelling, and inflammation. Damage to cartilage and bone may be halted so that further deformity is minimized.

treatment of RA, but only for limited periods because these drugs depress the immune system, thereby increasing susceptibility to infection.

How they work

It is not known precisely how most antirheumatic drugs slow the disease process. Some may reduce the body's immune response (see Immunosuppressant drugs, p.143). Antirheumatic drugs prevent damage to the cartilage and bone, reducing progressive deformity and disability. The effectiveness of each drug varies with the individual response.

How they affect you

These drugs are generally slow acting; it may be weeks or even months before benefit is noticed. NSAID treatment is usually continued until remission occurs. Prolonged treatment with antirheumatic drugs can cause a marked improvement in symptoms. Arthritic pain is relieved, joint mobility increased, and general symptoms of ill health fade.

Some *side effects* may be noticed before any beneficial effect is evident, so patience is required. Severe adverse effects may necessitate abandoning the treatment.

TYPES OF ANTIRHEUMATIC DRUGS (DMARDs)

Hydroxychloroquine Originally developed to treat malaria (see p.123), this drug is less effective than penicillamine or gold. Since prolonged use may cause eye damage, regular eye checks are needed.

Immunosuppressants (e.g.methotrexate) These are prescribed if other drugs do not provide relief and if RA is severe and disabling. Regular observation and blood tests must be carried out because immunosuppressants can cause severe complications.

Sulfasalazine Used mainly for ulcerative colitis (p.98), sulfasalazine was first introduced to treat RA and is effective in some cases.

Gold-based drugs These may be given orally or by injection for many years. Side effects can include a rash and digestive disturbances. Gold may sometimes damage the kidneys, which recover on stopping treatment; regular urine tests are usually carried out. It can suppress blood cell production in bone marrow, so periodic blood tests are also carried out.

Penicillamine This drug may be used when RA is worsening, or when gold cannot be given. Improvement in symptoms may take 3 to 6 months. It has similar side effects to gold, and periodic blood and urine tests are usually performed.

COMMON DRUGS

Immunosuppressants
Azathioprine ✳
Cyclosporine ✳
Cyclophosphamide ✳
Leflunomide
Methotrexate ✳

NSAIDs
(see facing page)

Gold-based drugs
Auranofin
Sodium aurothiomalate (Myochrysine)

Biological Response Modifiers
Abatacept
Adalimumab ✳
Anakinra ✳
Etanercept
Infliximab
Rituximab ✳

Other drugs
Hydroxychloroquine
Penicillamine
Prednisone ✳
Sulfasalazine

✳ See Part 4

LOCALLY ACTING CORTICOSTEROIDS

The adrenal glands, which lie on the top of the kidneys, produce a number of important *hormones*. Among these are the corticosteroids, so named because they are made in the outer part (cortex) of the glands. The corticosteroids play an important role, influencing the immune system and regulating the carbohydrate and mineral *metabolism* of the body. A number of drugs that mimic the natural corticosteroids have been developed.

These drugs have many uses and are discussed in detail under Corticosteroids (p.127). This section concentrates on those corticosteroids injected into an affected site to treat joint disorders.

Why they are used

Corticosteroids given by injection are particularly useful for treating joint disorders – notably rheumatoid arthritis and osteoarthritis – when one or only a few joints are involved, and when pain and inflammation have not been relieved by other drugs. In such cases, it is possible to relieve symptoms by injecting each of the affected joints individually. Corticosteroids may also be injected to relieve pain and inflammation caused by strained or contracted muscles, ligaments, and/or tendons – for example, in frozen shoulder or tennis elbow. They may also be given for bursitis, tendinitis, or swelling that is compressing a nerve. Corticosteroid injections are sometimes used in order to relieve pain and stiffness sufficiently to permit physiotherapy.

How they work

Corticosteroid drugs have two important actions that are believed to account for their effectiveness. They block the production of prostaglandins – chemicals responsible for triggering inflammation and pain – and depress the accumulation

and activity of the white blood cells that cause the inflammation (below). Injection concentrates the corticosteroids, and their effects, at the site of the problem, thus giving the maximum benefit where it is most needed.

How they affect you

Corticosteroids usually produce dramatic relief from symptoms when the drug is

COMMON INJECTION SITES

Corticosteroids are often injected into joints affected by osteo- and rheumatoid arthritis. Joints commonly treated in this way are knee, shoulder, and finger joints.

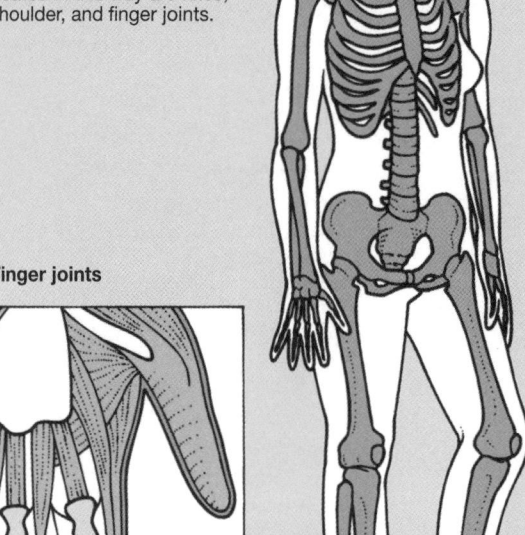

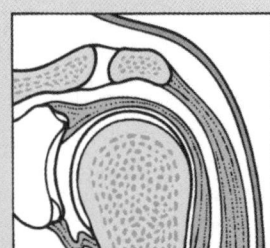

Shoulder joint

Finger joints

Knee joint

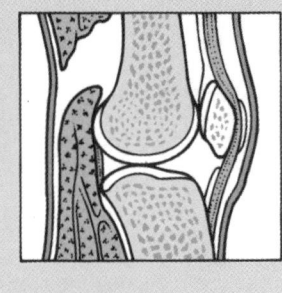

injected into a joint. Often a single injection is sufficient to relieve pain and swelling, and to improve mobility. When used to treat muscle or tendon pain, they may not always be effective because it is difficult to position the needle so that the drug reaches the right spot. In some cases, repeated injections are necessary.

Because these drugs are concentrated in the affected area, rather than being dispersed in significant amounts in the body, the generalized *adverse effects* that sometimes occur when corticosteroids are taken by mouth are unlikely. Minor *side effects*, such as loss of skin pigment at the injection site, are uncommon. Occasionally, a temporary increase in pain (steroid flare) may occur. In such cases, rest, local application of ice, and analgesic medication may relieve the condition. Sterile injection technique is critically important.

ACTION OF CORTICOSTEROIDS ON INFLAMED JOINTS

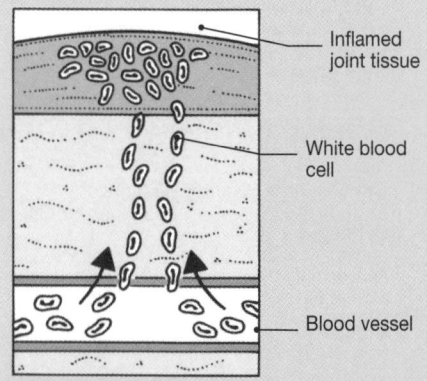

Inflamed joint tissue

White blood cell

Blood vessel

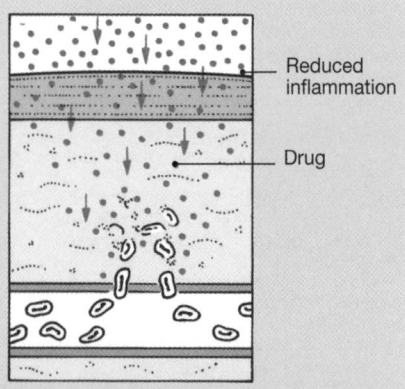

Reduced inflammation

Drug

Inflamed tissue
Inflammation occurs when disease or injury causes large numbers of white blood cells to accumulate in the affected area. In joints this leads to swelling and stiffness.

Action of corticosteroids
Corticosteroids, when injected into the area, permeate the joint lining (synovial membrane), blocking prostaglandin production and preventing white blood cells accumulating.

COMMON DRUGS

Dexamethasone *   Prednisolone
Hydrocortisone *   Triamcinolone
Methylprednisolone *

* See Part 4

DRUGS FOR GOUT

Gout is a disorder that arises when the blood contains increased levels of uric acid, which is a by-product of normal body *metabolism*. When its concentration in the blood is excessive, uric acid crystals may form in various parts of the body, especially in the joints of the foot (most often the big toe), the knee, and the hand, causing intense pain and inflammation known as gout. Crystals may form as white masses, known as tophi, in soft tissue, and in the kidneys as stones. Attacks of gout can recur, and may lead to damaged joints and deformity, known as gouty arthritis. Kidney stones can cause kidney damage.

An excess of uric acid can be caused either by increased production or by decreased elimination by the kidneys, which remove it from the body. The disorder tends to run in families and is far more common in men than women. The risk of attack is increased by high alcohol intake, the consumption of certain foods (red meat, sardines, anchovies, and offal such as liver, brains, and sweetbreads), and obesity. In susceptible individuals, an attack may be triggered by drugs such as thiazide diuretics (see p.85) or anticancer drugs (see p.140), or excessive drinking. Changes in diet and a reduction in the consumption of alcohol may be an important part of treatment.

Drugs used to treat acute attacks of gout include non-steroidal anti-inflammatory drugs (NSAIDs, see p.102), and colchicine. Sometimes, corticosteroids may be injected into a joint to decrease inflammation. Other drugs, which lower the blood level of uric acid, are used for the long-term prevention of gout. These include the uricosuric drugs (probenecid and sulfinpyrazone), as well as allopurinol and febuxostat. ASA is not prescribed for pain relief because it slows the excretion of uric acid.

Why drugs are used

Drugs may be prescribed either to treat an attack of gout or to prevent recurrent attacks that could lead to deformity of affected joints and kidney damage. The NSAIDs and colchicine are both used to treat an attack of gout and should be taken as soon as an attack begins. Colchicine is relatively specific in relieving the pain and inflammation arising from gout.

If symptoms recur, your physician may advise long-term treatment with either allopurinol or an uricosuric drug. One of these drugs must usually be taken indefinitely. Since they can trigger attacks of gout at the beginning of treatment, colchicine may sometimes be given with these drugs for a few months.

How they work

Allopurinol and febuxostat reduce the level of uric acid in the blood by interfering with the activity of xanthine oxidase, an *enzyme* involved in the production of uric acid in the body. Both sulfinpyrazone and probenecid increase the rate at which uric acid is excreted by the kidneys. The process by which colchicine reduces inflammation and relieves pain is not understood. The actions of NSAIDs are described on p.102.

How they affect you

Drugs used in the long-term treatment of gout are usually successful in preventing attacks and joint deformity. However, response may be slow.

Colchicine can disturb the digestive system, causing abdominal pain and diarrhea, which your physician can control by reducing the dose or prescribing other drugs.

Risks and special precautions

Since they increase the output of uric acid through the kidneys, uricosuric drugs can cause uric acid crystals to form in the kidneys. They are not, therefore, usually prescribed for those people who already have impaired kidney function or urate stones. In such cases, allopurinol may be preferred. It is always important to drink plenty of fluids while taking drugs for gout in order to prevent kidney crystals from forming. Monitoring of *side effects* and regular blood tests to monitor levels of uric acid in the blood may be required.

ACTION OF URICOSURIC DRUGS

Uric acid is removed from the blood by the kidneys and excreted in the urine. Excess uric acid, caused by increased production or impaired kidney function, requires treatment with uricosuric drugs, which increase the rate at which uric acid is expelled.

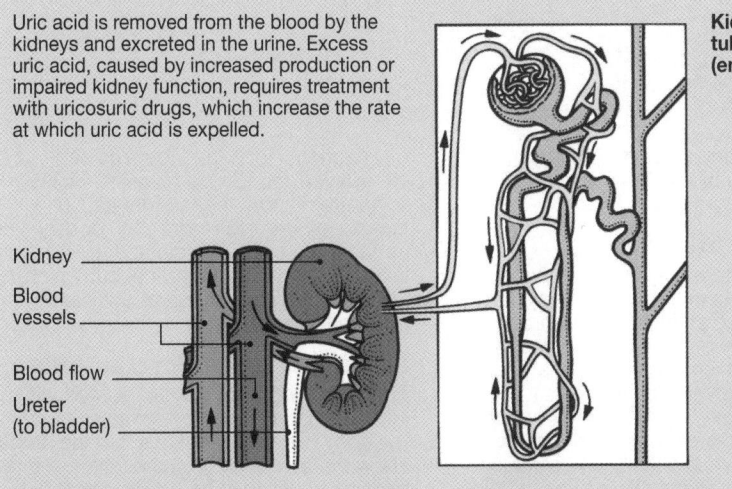

Kidney tubule (enlarged)

Kidney

Blood vessels

Blood flow

Ureter (to bladder)

Uric acid and gout
Gout occurs when uric acid crystals form in a joint, often a toe, knee, or hand, causing inflammation and pain. This is the result of excessively high levels of uric acid in the blood. In some cases this is caused by overproduction of uric acid, while in others it is the result of reduced excretion of uric acid by the kidneys.

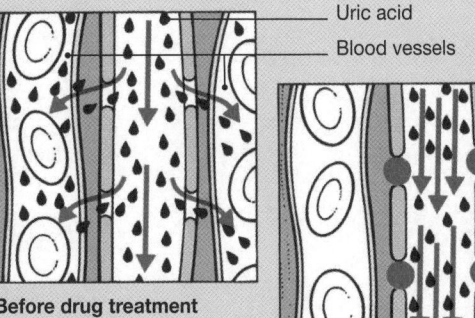

Uric acid

Blood vessels

Drug

Before drug treatment
Excess uric acid from the kidney tubule is reabsorbed into the surrounding blood vessels. This leads to the formation of uric acid crystals, which can cause gout.

After drug treatment
By blocking the reabsorption of uric acid into the blood vessels, the amount of uric acid excreted in the urine is increased.

COMMON DRUGS

Drugs to treat attacks	Drugs to prevent attacks
Colchicine *	Allopurinol *
Methylprednisolone *	Probenecid *
NSAIDs (see p.102)	Sulfinpyrazone

Drugs to treat high uric acid caused by cytotoxic drugs
Allopurinol *

* See Part 4

MUSCLE RELAXANTS

Several drugs are available to treat muscle spasm – the involuntary, painful contraction of a muscle or a group of muscles that can stiffen an arm or leg, or make it nearly impossible to straighten your back. There are various causes. It can follow an injury, or come on without warning. It may also be brought on by a disorder such as osteoarthritis, the pain in the affected joint triggering abnormal tension in a nearby muscle.

Spasticity is another form of muscle tightness seen in some neurological disorders, such as multiple sclerosis, stroke, or cerebral palsy. Spasticity can sometimes be helped by physiotherapy but in severe cases drugs may be used to relieve symptoms.

Why drugs are used

Muscle spasm resulting from direct injury is usually treated with a non-steroidal anti-inflammatory drug (see p.102) or an analgesic. However, if the spasm is severe, a muscle relaxant may also be tried for a short period.

In spasticity, the sufferer's legs may become so stiff and uncontrollable that walking unaided is impossible. In such cases, a drug may be used to relax the muscles. Relaxation of the muscles often permits physiotherapy to be given for longer-term relief from spasms.

The muscle relaxant botulinum toxin may be injected locally to relieve muscle spasm in small groups of accessible muscles, such as those around the eye or in the neck.

How they work

Muscle-relaxant drugs work in one of several ways. The centrally acting drugs damp down the passage of the nerve signals from the brain and spinal cord that cause muscles to contract, thus reducing excessive stimulation of muscles as well as unwanted muscular contraction. Dantrolene reduces the sensitivity of the muscles to nerve signals. When injected

SITES OF ACTION OF MUSCLE RELAXANTS

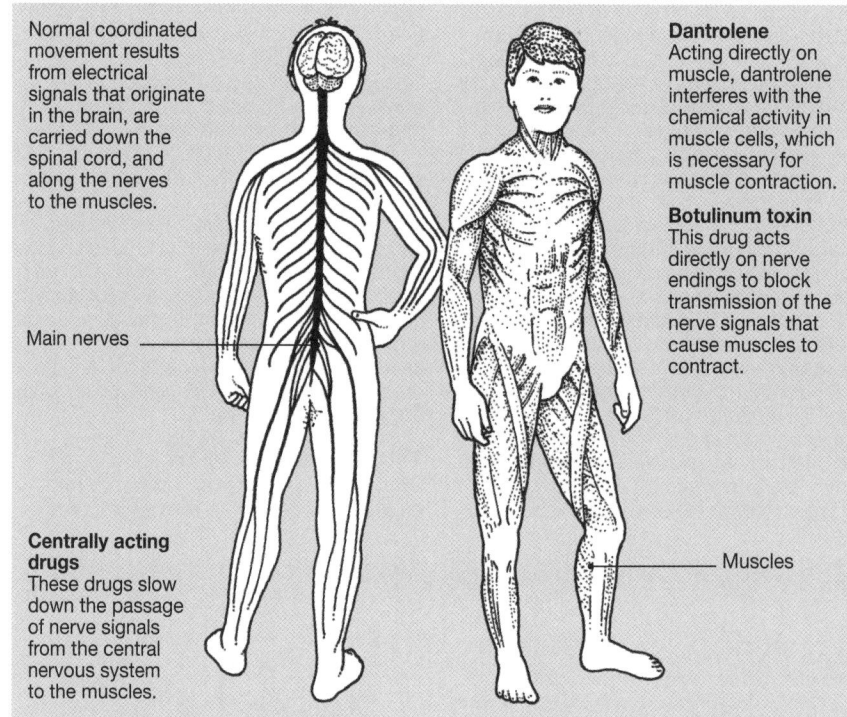

Normal coordinated movement results from electrical signals that originate in the brain, are carried down the spinal cord, and along the nerves to the muscles.

Main nerves

Centrally acting drugs
These drugs slow down the passage of nerve signals from the central nervous system to the muscles.

Dantrolene
Acting directly on muscle, dantrolene interferes with the chemical activity in muscle cells, which is necessary for muscle contraction.

Botulinum toxin
This drug acts directly on nerve endings to block transmission of the nerve signals that cause muscles to contract.

Muscles

locally, botulinum toxin prevents transmission of impulses between nerves and muscles.

How they affect you

Drugs taken regularly for a spastic disorder of the central nervous system usually reduce stiffness and improve mobility. They may restore the use of the arms and legs when this has been impaired by muscle spasm.

Unfortunately, most centrally acting drugs can have a generally depressant effect on nervous activity and produce drowsiness, particularly at the beginning

of treatment. Too high a dosage can excessively reduce the muscles' ability to contract and can therefore cause weakness. For this reason, the dosage needs to be carefully adjusted to find a level that controls symptoms but which, at the same time, maintains sufficient muscle strength.

Risks and special precautions

The main long-term risk associated with centrally acting muscle relaxants is that the body becomes dependent. If the drugs are withdrawn suddenly, the stiffness may become worse than before drug treatment.

Rarely, dantrolene can cause serious liver damage. Anyone who is taking this drug should have his or her blood tested regularly to assess liver function.

Unless used very cautiously, botulinum toxin can paralyse unaffected muscles, and might interfere with functions such as speech and swallowing.

ACTION OF CENTRALLY ACTING DRUGS

Centrally acting muscle relaxants restrict passage of nerve signals to the muscles by occupying a proportion of the *receptors* in the central nervous system that are normally used by *neurotransmitters* to transmit such impulses. Reduced nervous stimulation allows the muscles to relax; however, if the dose of the drug is too high, this action may give rise to excessive muscle weakness.

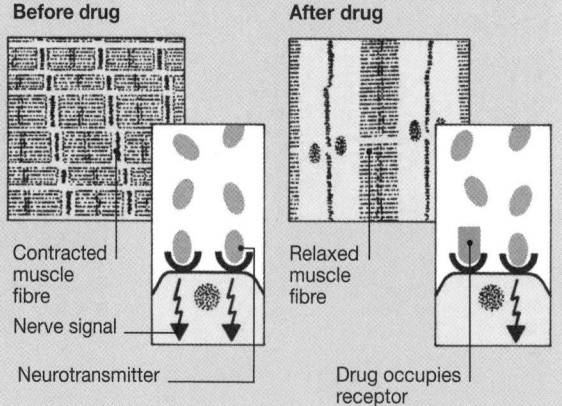

Before drug

Contracted muscle fibre

Nerve signal

Neurotransmitter

After drug

Relaxed muscle fibre

Drug occupies receptor

COMMON DRUGS

Centrally acting drugs
Baclofen ✳
Cyclobenzaprine ✳
Diazepam ✳
Tizanidine ✳

Methocarbamol
Orphenadrine

Other drugs
Botulinum toxin
   type A ✳
Dantrolene

✳ See Part 4

DRUGS USED FOR MYASTHENIA GRAVIS

Myasthenia gravis is a disorder that occurs when the immune system (see p.138) becomes defective and produces antibodies that disrupt the signals being transmitted between the nervous system and muscles that are under voluntary control. As a result, the body's muscular response is progressively weakened. The first muscles to be affected are those controlling the eyes, eyelids, face, pharynx, and larynx, with muscles in the arms and legs becoming involved as the disease progresses. The disease is often linked to a disorder of the thymus gland, which is the source of the destructive antibodies concerned.

Various methods can be used in the treatment of myasthenia gravis, including the removal of the thymus gland (called a thymectomy) or temporarily clearing the blood of antibodies using a procedure known as plasmapheresis. Drugs that improve muscle function, principally neostigmine and pyridostigmine, may be prescribed. They may be used alone or together with other drugs that depress the immune system – usually azathioprine (see Immunosuppressant drugs, p.143) or corticosteroids (see p.127).

THE EFFECTS OF MYASTHENIA GRAVIS

Myasthenia gravis initially causes weakness of the muscles in the face and throat, affecting the muscles around the eyes and the mouth. In the later stages, arms and legs may be affected.

Late stages

Early stages

The thymus gland
Located in the upper part of the chest, this gland is thought to be partly responsible for the abnormal antibody activity in this disease.

Principal muscles affected

Why drugs are used

Drugs that improve the muscle response to nerve impulses have several uses. One such drug, edrophonium, acts very quickly and, once administered intravenously, it brings about a dramatic improvement in the symptoms. This effect is used to confirm the diagnosis of myasthenia gravis. However, because of its short duration of action, edrophonium is not used for long-term treatment. Pyridostigmine and neostigmine are preferred for long-term treatment, especially when surgery to remove the thymus gland is not feasible or does not provide adequate relief.

These drugs may be given to non-myasthenic patients after surgery to reverse the effects of a drug given as part of the general anesthetic that causes muscle paralysis.

How they work

Normal muscle action occurs when a nerve impulse triggers a nerve ending to release a *neurotransmitter*, which combines with a specialized *receptor* on the muscle cells and causes the muscles to contract. In myasthenia gravis, the body's immune system destroys many of these receptors, so that the muscle is less responsive to nervous stimulation. Drugs used to treat the disorder increase the amount of neurotransmitter at the nerve ending by blocking the action of an *enzyme* that normally breaks it down. Increased levels of the neurotransmitter

permit the remaining receptors to function more efficiently (see Action of drugs used for myasthenia gravis, below).

How they affect you

These drugs usually restore the muscle function to a normal or near-normal level, particularly when the disease takes a mild form. Unfortunately, the drugs can produce unwanted muscular activity by enhancing the transmission of nerve impulses elsewhere in the body.

Common *side effects* include vomiting, nausea, diarrhea, and muscle cramps in the arms, legs, and abdomen.

Risks and special precautions

Muscle weakness can suddenly worsen even when it is being treated with drugs. Should this occur, it is important not to take larger doses of the drug in an attempt to relieve the symptoms, since excessive levels can interfere with the transmission of nerve impulses to muscles, causing further weakness. The administration of other drugs, including some antibiotics, can also markedly increase the symptoms of myasthenia gravis. If your symptoms suddenly become worse, consult your physician.

COMMON DRUGS

Azathioprine ✳
Corticosteroids (see p.127)

Edrophonium
Neostigmine
Pyridostigmine ✳

✳ See Part 4

ACTION OF DRUGS USED FOR MYASTHENIA GRAVIS

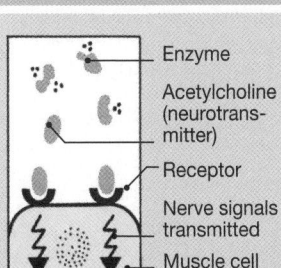

Enzyme
Acetylcholine (neurotransmitter)
Receptor
Nerve signals transmitted
Muscle cell

Normal nerve transmission
Muscles contract when a neurotransmitter (acetylcholine) binds to receptors on muscle cells. An enzyme breaks down acetylcholine.

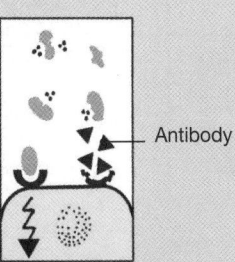

Antibody

In myasthenia gravis
Abnormal antibody activity destroys many receptors, reducing stimulation of the muscle cells and weakening the muscle action.

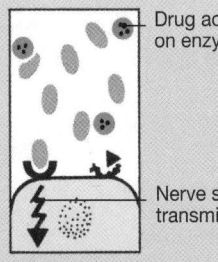

Drug acts on enzyme

Nerve signals transmitted

Drug action
Anticholinesterase drugs block enzyme action, increasing acetylcholine and prolonging the muscle cell response to nervous stimulation.

DRUGS FOR BONE DISORDERS

Bone is a living structure. Its hard, mineral quality is created by the action of the bone cells. These cells continuously deposit and remove phosphorus and calcium, stored in a honeycombed protein framework called the matrix. Because the rates of deposit and removal (the bone metabolism) are about equal in adults, the bone mass remains fairly constant.

Removal and renewal is regulated by *hormones* and influenced by a number of factors, notably the level of calcium in the blood, which depends on the intake of calcium and vitamin D from the diet, the actions of various hormones, plus everyday movement and weight-bearing stress. When normal bone metabolism is altered, various bone disorders result.

Osteoporosis

In osteoporosis, the strength and density of bone are reduced. Such wasting occurs when the rate of removal of mineralized bone exceeds the rate of deposit. In most people, bone density decreases very gradually from the age of 30. But bone loss can dramatically increase when a person is immobilized for a period, an important cause of osteoporosis in elderly people. Hormone deficiency is another important cause, commonly occurring in women with lowered estrogen levels after menopause or removal of the ovaries. It also occurs in disorders in which there is excess production of adrenal or thyroid hormones and can result from long-term treatment with corticosteroid drugs.

People with osteoporosis often have no symptoms, but, if the vertebrae become so weakened that they are unable to bear the body's weight, they may collapse spontaneously or after a minor accident. Subsequently, the individual suffers from back pain, reduced height, and a round-shouldered appearance. Osteoporosis also leads to fracture of the arm, leg, or hip.

Most doctors emphasize the need to prevent the disorder by an adequate intake of protein, calcium, and vitamin D, and by regular exercise throughout adult life. Estrogen supplements given to manage menopausal symptoms can minimize bone loss. (See Hormone replacement therapy, p.133.)

Drug treatment can help prevent further deterioration and help fractures to heal. For people whose diet is deficient in calcium or vitamin D, supplements may be prescribed. However, these are of limited value on their own. Drugs that inhibit removal of calcium from the bones are usually prescribed for osteoporosis, along with adequate calcium and vitamin D intake. Drugs such as etidronate, alendronate, and risedronate (known as bisphosphonates) bind very tightly to bone matrix, preventing its removal by bone cells. Bisphosphonates may be administered as a daily, weekly, or monthly dose. An injectable bis-phosphonate, zoledronic acid, is administered once yearly.

Osteomalacia and rickets

In osteomalacia – called rickets when it affects children – lack of vitamin D leads to loss of calcium, resulting in softening of the bones. It causes pain and tenderness and there is a risk of fracture and bone deformity. In children, growth is retarded.

Osteomalacia is most commonly caused by a lack of vitamin D. This can result from an inadequate diet, inability to absorb the vitamin, or insufficient exposure of the skin to sunlight (the action of the sun on the skin produces vitamin D inside the body). People who are at special risk include those whose absorption of vitamin D is impaired by an intestinal disorder, such as Crohn's disease or celiac disease. People with dark skins living in Northern Europe are also susceptible. Chronic kidney disease is an important cause of rickets in children and of osteomalacia in adults, since healthy kidneys play an essential role in the body's metabolism of vitamin D.

Long-term relief depends on treating the underlying disorder where possible. In rare cases, treatment may be lifelong.

Vitamin D

A number of substances that are related to vitamin D may be used in the treatment of bone disorders. These drugs include alfacalcidol, calcitriol, and ergocalciferol. The one prescribed depends on the underlying problem (see also page 481).

BONE WASTING

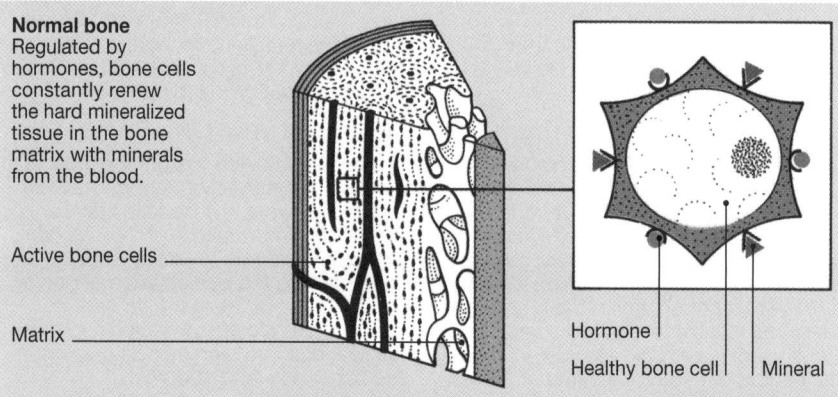

Normal bone
Regulated by hormones, bone cells constantly renew the hard mineralized tissue in the bone matrix with minerals from the blood.

Active bone cells

Matrix

Hormone

Healthy bone cell | Mineral

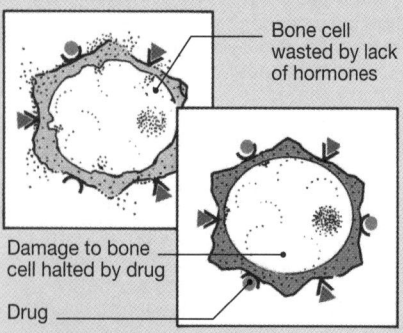

Bone cell wasted by lack of hormones

Damage to bone cell halted by drug

Drug

In osteoporosis
Hormonal disturbance leads to wasting of active bone cells. The bones become less dense and more fragile. Drug treatment with hormone and mineral supplements usually only prevents further bone loss.

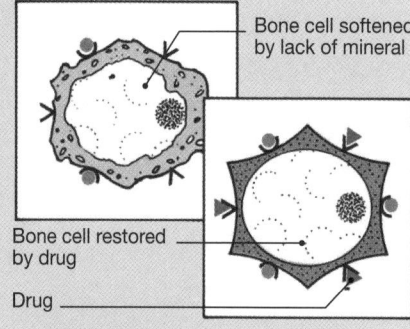

Bone cell softened by lack of mineral

Bone cell restored by drug

Drug

In osteomalacia
Deficiency of calcium or vitamin D causes softening of the bone tissue. The bones become weaker and sometimes deformed. Drug treatment with vitamin D and minerals usually restores bone strength.

COMMON DRUGS

Bisphosphonates
Alendronate ✱
Etidronate ✱
Risedronate ✱
Zoledronic acid

Supplements
Calcium carbonate ✱
Calcium citrate
Vitamin D ✱

Other drugs
Calcitonin
Calcitriol
Conjugated
 estrogens ✱
Ergocalciferol
Raloxifene ✱
Teriparatide ✱

| ✱ See Part 4 |

ALLERGY

Allergy, which is a hypersensitivity to certain substances, is an extreme reaction of the body's immune system. Through a variety of mechanisms (see Malignant and immune disease, p.138), the immune system protects the body by eliminating foreign substances that it does not recognize, such as microorganisms (bacteria or viruses).

One way in which the immune system acts is through the production of *antibodies*. When the body encounters a particular foreign substance (or allergen) for the first time, one type of white blood cell, the lymphocyte, produces antibodies that attach themselves to another type of white blood cell, the mast cell. If the same substance is encountered again, the allergen binds to the antibodies on the mast cells, causing the release of chemicals known as mediators.

The most important mediator is histamine. This can produce a rash, swelling, narrowing of the airways, and a drop in blood pressure. Although these effects are important in protecting the body against infection, they may also be triggered inappropriately in an *allergic reaction*.

What can go wrong

One of the most common allergic disorders, hay fever, is caused by an allergic reaction to inhaled grass pollen leading to allergic rhinitis – swelling and irritation of the nasal passages and watering of the nose and eyes. Other substances, such as house-dust mites, animal fur, and feathers, may cause a similar reaction in susceptible people.

Asthma, another allergic disorder, may result from the action of leukotrienes rather than histamine. Other allergic conditions include urticaria (hives) or other rashes (sometimes in response to a drug), some forms of eczema and dermatitis, and allergic alveolitis (farmer's lung). Anaphylaxis is a serious systemic allergic reaction (p.528) that occurs when an allergen reaches the bloodstream.

Why drugs are used

Antihistamines and drugs that inhibit mast cell activity are used to prevent and treat allergic reactions. Other drugs minimize allergic symptoms, such as decongestants (p.79) to clear the nose in allergic rhinitis, bronchodilators (p.76) to widen the airways of those with asthma, and corticosteroids applied to skin affected by eczema (p.167).

MAJOR DRUG GROUPS

Antihistamines	Corticosteroids (see p.127)
Leukotriene antagonists	Drugs for asthma (see pp.77-79)

Allergic response

Lymphocytes produce antibodies to allergens and these attach to mast cells. If the allergen enters the body again, it binds to the antibodies, and the mast cells release histamine.

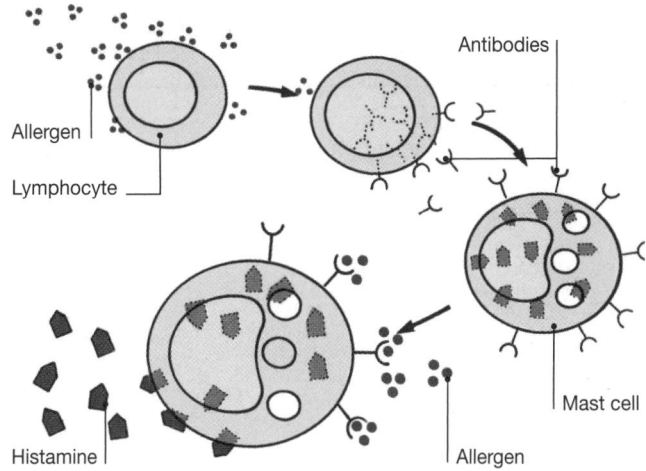

Histamine and histamine receptors

Histamine, released in response to injury or the presence of allergens, acts on H_1 *receptors* in the skin, blood vessels, nasal passages, and airways, and on H_2 receptors in the stomach lining, salivary glands, and lacrimal (tear) glands. It provokes dilation of blood vessels, inflammation and swelling of tissues, and narrowing of the airways. In some cases a reaction called anaphylactic shock may occur, caused by a dramatic fall in blood pressure, which may lead to collapse. Antihistamine drugs block the H_1 receptors, and H_2 blockers block the H_2 receptors (see also Antihistamines, p.110, and Anti-ulcer drugs, p.95).

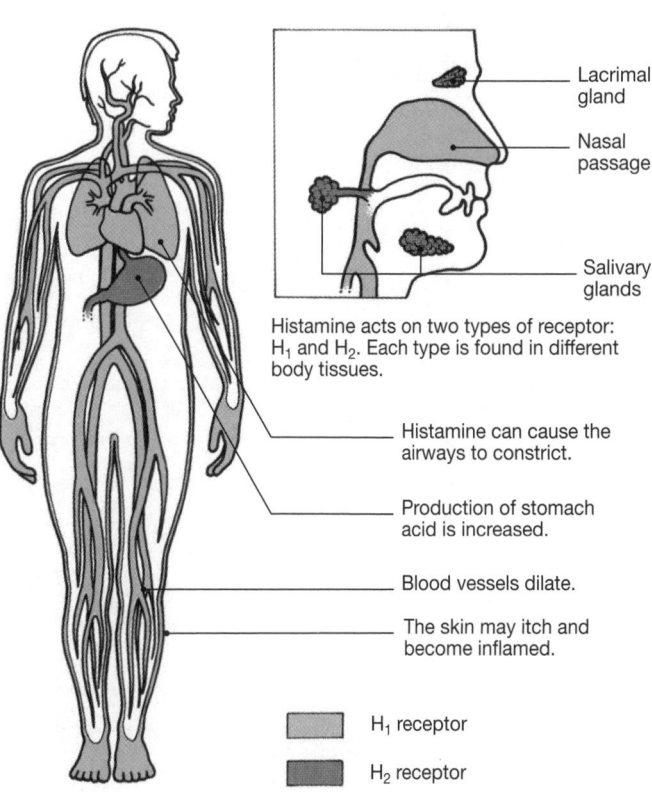

Histamine acts on two types of receptor: H_1 and H_2. Each type is found in different body tissues.

- Histamine can cause the airways to constrict.
- Production of stomach acid is increased.
- Blood vessels dilate.
- The skin may itch and become inflamed.

H_1 receptor

H_2 receptor

ANTIHISTAMINES

Antihistamines are the most widely used drugs in the treatment of allergic reactions of all kinds. They can be subdivided according to their chemical structure, each subgroup having slightly different actions and characteristics (see table on facing page). Their main action is to counter the effects of histamine, one of the chemicals released in the body when there is an allergic reaction. (For a full explanation of the allergy mechanism, see p.109).

Histamine is also involved in other body functions, including blood vessel dilation and constriction, contraction of muscles in the respiratory and gastrointestinal tracts, and the release of digestive juices in the stomach. The antihistamine drugs described here are also known as H_1 blockers because they only block the action of histamine on certain *receptors*, known as H_1 receptors. Another group of antihistamines, known as H_2 blockers, is used in the treatment of peptic ulcers (see Anti-ulcer drugs, p.97).

Some antihistamines have a significant *anticholinergic* action. This has benefits in a variety of conditions, but it also accounts for certain undesired *side effects*.

Why they are used

Antihistamines relieve allergy-related symptoms when it is not possible or practical to prevent exposure to the substance that has provoked the reaction. They are most commonly used in the prevention of allergic rhinitis (hay fever), the inflammation of the nose and upper airways that results from an allergic reaction to a substance such as pollen, house dust, or animal fur. Antihistamines are more effective when taken before the start of an attack. If they are taken only after an attack has begun, beneficial effects may be delayed.

Antihistamines are not usually effective in asthma caused by similar allergens because the symptoms of this allergic disorder are not solely caused by the action of histamine, but are likely to be the result of more complex mechanisms. Antihistamines are usually the first drugs to be tried in the treatment of allergic disorders but there are alternatives that can be prescribed (see below).

Antihistamines are also prescribed to relieve the itching, swelling, and redness that are characteristic of allergic reactions involving the skin – for example, urticaria (hives). Irritation from chickenpox may be reduced by these drugs. Allergic reactions to insect stings may also be reduced by antihistamines. Applied as drops, antihistamines can reduce inflammation and irritation of the eyes and eyelids in allergic conjunctivitis.

An antihistamine is often included as an ingredient in cough and cold preparations (see p.80), when the anticholinergic effect of drying mucus secretions and their *sedative* effect on the coughing mechanism may be helpful.

Because some antihistamines have a depressant effect on the brain, they are sometimes used to promote sleep, especially when discomfort from itching is disturbing sleep (see also Sleeping drugs, p.66). The depressant effect of antihistamines on the brain also extends to the centres that control nausea and vomiting. Antihistamines are therefore often effective for preventing and controlling these symptoms (see Anti-emetics, p.74).

Occasionally, antihistamines are used to treat fever, rash, and breathing difficulties that may occur in adverse reactions to blood transfusions and allergic reactions to drugs. Promethazine may also be used as *premedication* to provide sedation and to dry secretions during surgery, particularly in children.

How they work

Antihistamines block the action of histamine on H_1 receptors. These are found in various body tissues, particularly the small blood vessels in the skin, nose, and eyes. This helps prevent the dilation of the vessels, thus reducing the redness, watering, and swelling. The anticholinergic action of these drugs also contributes to this effect by reducing the secretions from tear glands and nasal passages.

SITES OF ACTION

Antihistamines act on a variety of sites and systems throughout the body. Their main action is on the muscles surrounding the small blood vessels that supply the skin and mucous membranes. They also act on the airways in the lungs and on the brain.

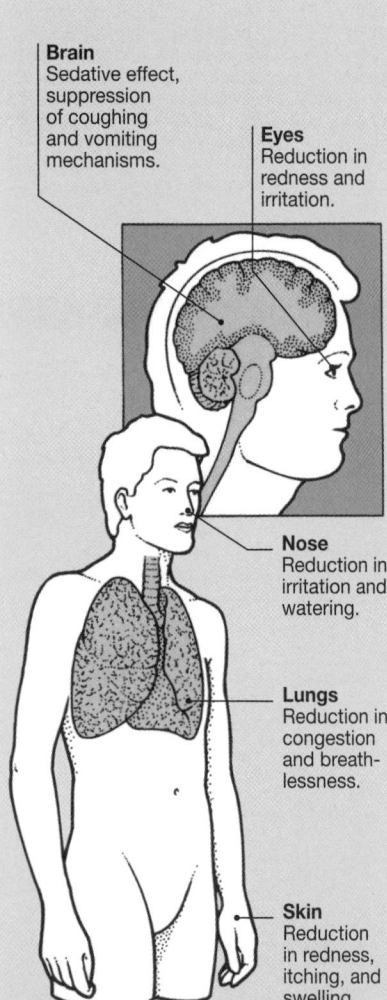

Brain
Sedative effect, suppression of coughing and vomiting mechanisms.

Eyes
Reduction in redness and irritation.

Nose
Reduction in irritation and watering.

Lungs
Reduction in congestion and breath-lessness.

Skin
Reduction in redness, itching, and swelling.

OTHER ALLERGY TREATMENTS

Sodium cromoglycate
This drug prevents the release of histamine from mast cells (see p.109) in response to exposure to an allergen, thus preventing the physical symptoms of allergies. It is given as eye drops for the prevention of allergic conjunctivitis or hay fever conjunctivitis.

Leukotriene antagonists
Like histamines, leukotrienes are substances that occur naturally in the body and seem to play an important part in asthma. Montelukast (p.367), known as a leukotriene antagonist, has been developed to prevent asthma attacks. It is not a *bronchodilator* and will not relieve an existing attack (see Drugs for asthma, p.78).

Corticosteroids
These are used to treat allergic rhinitis and asthma. They are given by inhaler, which use much lower doses than tablets.

Desensitization
This may be tried in conditions such as allergic rhinitis due to pollen sensitivity and insect venom hypersensitivity, when avoidance, antihistamines, and other treatments have not been effective and tests have shown one or two specific allergens to be responsible. Desensitization often provides incomplete relief and can be time consuming.

Treatment involves giving a series of injections containing gradually increasing doses of an extract of the allergen. The way in which this prevents *allergic reactions* is not understood. Perhaps controlled exposure triggers the immune system into producing increasing levels of *antibodies* so that the body no longer responds dramatically when the allergen is encountered naturally.

Desensitization must be carried out under medical supervision because it can provoke a severe allergic response. It is important to remain near emergency medical facilities for at least one hour after each injection.

COMPARISON OF ANTIHISTAMINES

Although antihistamines have broadly similar effects and uses, differences in their strength of anticholinergic action and the amount of drowsiness they produce, as well as in their duration of action, affect the uses for which each drug is commonly selected. The table indicates the main uses of some of the common antihistamines and gives an indication of the relative strengths of their anticholinergic and sedative effects and of their duration of action.

- ● Drug used
- ■ Strong
- ◪ Medium
- □ Minimal
- ▲ Long (over 12 hours)
- ◭ Medium (6–12 hours)
- △ Short (4–6 hours)

Drugs	Common uses						Actions and effects		
	Allergic rhinitis	Skin allergy	Sedation	Premedication	Nausea/vomiting	Cough/cold remedies	Drowsiness	Anticholinergic action	Duration of action
Brompheniramine	●	●				●	◪	◪	△
Cetirizine	●	●					□	□	▲
Chlorpheniramine	●	●	●			●	◪	■	△
Cyproheptadine	●	●					◪	◪	△
Desloratidine	●	●					□	□	▲
Diphenhydramine			●	●		●	■	■	△
Fexofenadine	●	●					□	□	▲
Hydroxyzine		●	●				■	◪	△
Loratadine	●	●					□	□	▲
Promethazine	●	●	●	●	●		■	■	◭

How they affect you
Antihistamines frequently cause a degree of drowsiness and may adversely affect coordination, leading to clumsiness. Some of the newer drugs have little or no sedative effect (see table above).

Anticholinergic side effects, including dry mouth, blurred vision, and difficulty passing urine, are common. Most side effects diminish with continued use and can often be helped by an adjustment in dosage or a change to a different drug.

Risks and special precautions
It may be advisable to avoid driving or operating machinery while taking antihistamines, particularly those that are more likely to cause drowsiness (see table above). The sedative effects of alcohol, sleeping drugs, opioid analgesics, and anti-anxiety drugs can also be increased by antihistamines.

In high doses, or in children, some antihistamines can cause excitement, agitation, and even, in extreme cases, hallucinations and convulsions. Abnormal heart rhythms have occurred after high doses with some antihistamines or when drugs that interact with them, such as antifungals and *antibiotics*, have been taken at the same time. Heart rhythm problems may also affect people with liver disease, electrolyte disturbances, or abnormal heart activity. A person who has these conditions, or who has glaucoma or prostate trouble, should seek medical advice before taking antihistamines because their various drug actions may make such conditions worse.

ANTIHISTAMINES AND ALLERGIC RHINITIS

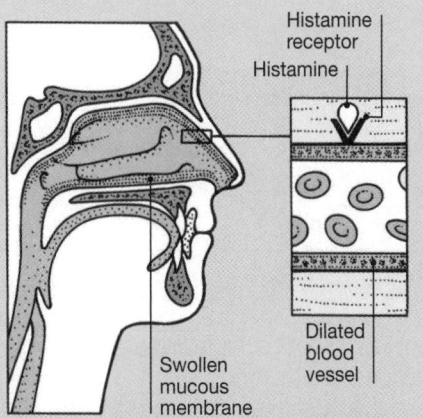

Before drug treatment
In allergic rhinitis, histamine released in response to an allergen acts on histamine receptors and produces dilation of the blood vessels supplying the lining of the nose, leading to swelling and increased mucus production. There is also irritation that causes sneezing, and often redness and watering of the eyes.

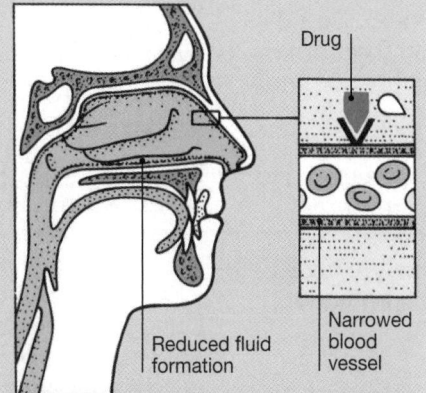

After drug treatment
Antihistamine drugs prevent histamine from attaching to histamine receptors, thereby preventing the body from responding to allergens. Over a period of time, the swelling, irritation, sneezing, and watery discharge are reduced, and further contact with the allergen responsible usually produces only minor allergic symptoms.

COMMON DRUGS

Generally non-sedating
Cetirizine ✳
Desloratadine ✳
Fexofenadine
Loratadine ✳

Sedating
Brompheniramine
Chlorpheniramine ✳
Clemastine
Cyproheptadine
Diphenhydramine ✳
Hydroxyzine
Promethazine ✳

Anti-allergic eye preparations
Emedastine
Ketotifen
Lodoxamide
Nedocromil
Olopatadine
Sodium cromoglycate

✳ See Part 4

INFECTIONS AND INFESTATIONS

The human body provides a suitable environment for the growth of many types of microorganisms, including bacteria, viruses, fungi, yeasts, and protozoa. It may also become the host for animal parasites such as insects, worms, and flukes.

Microorganisms (microbes) exist all around us and can be transmitted from person to person in many ways: direct contact, inhalation of infected air, and consumption of contaminated food or water (see Transmission of infection, facing page). Not all microorganisms cause disease; many types of bacteria exist on the skin surface or in the bowel without causing ill effects, while others cannot live either in or on the body.

Normally the immune system protects the body from infection. Invading microbes are killed before they can multiply in sufficient numbers to cause serious disease. (See also Malignant and immune disease, p.138.)

What can go wrong

Infectious diseases occur when the body is invaded by microbes. This may be caused by the body having little or no natural immunity to the invading organism, or the number of invading microbes being too great for the body's immune system to overcome. Serious infections can occur when the immune system does not function properly or when a disease weakens or destroys the immune system, as occurs in AIDS (acquired immune deficiency syndrome).

Infections (such as childhood infectious diseases or those with flu-like symptoms) can cause generalized illness or they may affect a specific part of the body (as in wound infections). Some parts are more susceptible to infection than others – respiratory tract infections are relatively common, whereas bone and muscle infections are rare.

Some symptoms are the result of damage to body tissues by the infection, or by *toxins* released by the microbes. In other cases, the symptoms result from the body's defence mechanisms.

Most bacterial and viral infections cause fever. Bacterial infections may also cause inflammation and pus formation in the affected area.

Why drugs are used

Treatment of an infection is necessary only when the type or severity of symptoms shows that the immune system has not overcome the infection.

Bacterial infection can be treated with *antibiotic* or antibacterial drugs. Some of these drugs actually kill the infecting bacteria, whereas others merely prevent them from multiplying.

Types of infecting organisms
Bacteria
A typical bacterium (right) consists of a single cell that has a protective wall. Some bacteria are aerobic – that is, they require oxygen – and therefore are more likely to infect surface areas such as the skin or respiratory tract. Others are anaerobic and multiply in oxygen-free surroundings such as the bowel or deep puncture wounds.

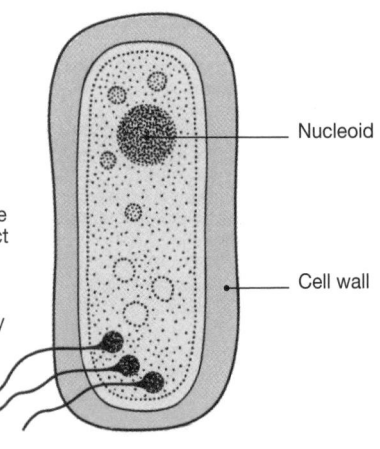

Nucleoid

Cell wall

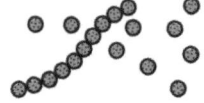

Cocci (spherical)
Streptococcus (above) can cause sore throats and pneumonia.

Bacilli (rod-shaped)
Mycobacterium tuberculosis (above) causes tuberculosis.

Spirochaete (spiral-shaped) This group includes bacteria that cause syphilis and gum infections.

Viruses
These infectious agents are smaller than bacteria and consist simply of a core of genetic material surrounded by a protein coat. A virus can multiply only in a living cell by using the host tissue's replicating material.

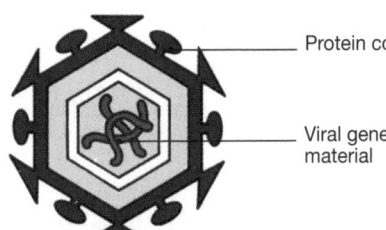

Protein coat

Viral genetic material

Protozoa
These single-celled parasites are slightly bigger than bacteria. Many protozoa live in the human intestine and are harmless. However, some types cause malaria, sleeping sickness, and dysentery.

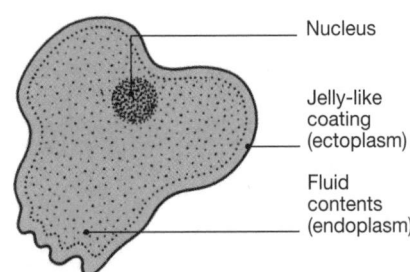

Nucleus

Jelly-like coating (ectoplasm)

Fluid contents (endoplasm)

Unnecessary use of antibiotics may result in the development of resistant bacteria.

Some antibiotics can be used to treat a broad range of infections, while others are effective against a particular type of bacterium or in a certain part of the body. Antibiotics are most commonly given by mouth, or by injection in severe infections, but they may be applied topically for a local action.

Antiviral drugs are used for severe viral infections that threaten body organs or survival. Antivirals may

How bacteria affect the body

Bacteria can cause symptoms of disease in two principal ways: first, by releasing toxins that harm body cells; second, by provoking an inflammatory response in the infected tissues.

Effects of toxins

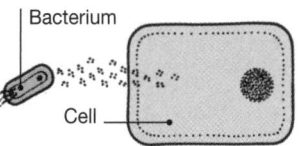
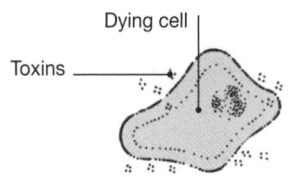

The invading bacterium gives off poisons (toxins) that attack the body cell.

The toxins emanating from the bacterium break through the cell structure and destroy the cell.

Inflammatory response

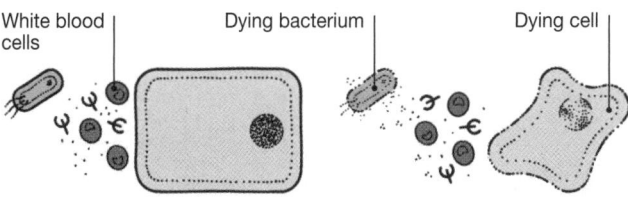

White blood cells of the immune system attack the bacterium directly by releasing inflammatory substances and, later, *antibodies*.

A *side effect* of this attack of the immune system on the bacterium is damage to, and inflammation of, the body's own cells.

Transmission of infection

Infecting organisms can enter the human body through a variety of routes, including direct contact between an infected person and someone else, and eating or inhaling infected material.

Droplet infection
Coughing and sneezing spread infected secretions.

Insects
Insect bites may transmit infection.

Physical contact
Everyday contact may spread infection.

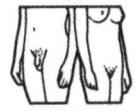

Sexual contact
Certain infections and infestations may be spread by genital contact.

Food
Many infecting organisms can be ingested in food.

Water
Infections can be spread in polluted water.

be used in *topical* preparations, given by mouth, or administered in hospital by injection.

Other drugs used in the fight against infection include antiprotozoal drugs for protozoal infections such as malaria; antifungal drugs for infection by fungi and yeasts, including *Candida* (thrush); and anthelmintics to eradicate worm and fluke infestations. Cases of infestation by skin parasites are usually treated with the topical application of insecticides (see p.164).

INFESTATIONS

Invasion by parasites that live on the body (such as lice) or in the body (such as tapeworms) is known as infestation. Since the body lacks strong natural defences against infestation, antiparasitic treatment is necessary. Infestations may be associated with tropical climates and poor standards of hygiene.

Tapeworms and roundworms live in the intestines and may cause diarrhea and *anemia*. Roundworm eggs may be passed in feces. Hookworm larvae in infected soil usually enter the body through the skin. Tapeworms may grow to 9m (30 feet) and infection occurs through undercooked meat containing larvae.

Flukes are of various types. The liver fluke (acquired from infected vegetation) lives near the bile duct in the liver and can cause jaundice. A more serious type (which lives in small blood vessels supplying the bladder or intestines) causes schistosomiasis and is acquired from contact with infected water.

Lice and scabies spread by direct contact. Head, clothing, and pubic lice need human blood to survive and die away from the body. Dried feces of lice on clothing spread typhus by infecting wounds or being inhaled. Scabies (caused by a tiny mite that does not carry disease) makes small, itchy tunnels in the skin.

Life cycle of a roundworm

Many roundworms have a complex life cycle. The life cycle of the roundworm that causes the group of diseases known as filariasis is illustrated below.

A mosquito ingests the filarial larvae and bites a human, thereby transmitting the larvae.

The mature larvae enter the lymph glands and vessels and reproduce there, often causing no ill effects.

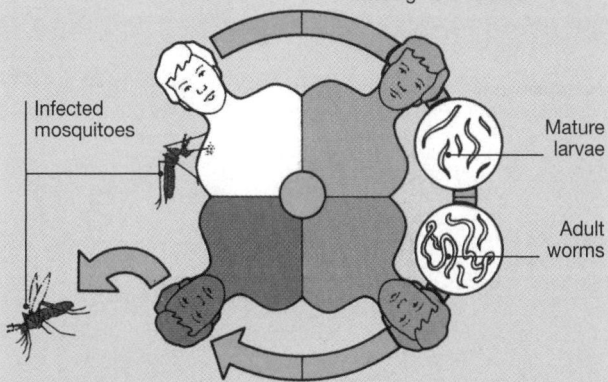

The infestation is spread by mosquitoes biting infected people and restarting the cycle.

The larvae grow into adult worms, which release larvae into the bloodstream.

MAJOR DRUG GROUPS

Antibiotics
Antibacterial drugs
Antituberculosis drugs
Antiviral drugs
Vaccines and immunizations

Antiprotozoal drugs
Antimalarial drugs
Antifungal drugs
Anthelmintic drugs

ANTIBIOTICS

Antibiotics are one of the most commonly prescribed drugs. These drugs are usually safe and effective in the treatment of bacterial disorders ranging from minor infections, like conjunctivitis, to life-threatening diseases like pneumonia, meningitis, and septicemia. They are similar in function to the antibacterial drugs (see p.117), but the early antibiotics all had a natural origin in moulds and fungi, although most antibiotics are now synthesized.

Since the 1940s, when penicillin was introduced, many different classes of antibiotics have been developed. Each one has a different chemical composition and is effective against a particular range of bacteria. None is effective against viral infections (see Antiviral drugs, p.119).

Some of the antibiotics have a broad spectrum of activity against a wide variety of bacteria. Others are used in the treatment of infection by only a few specific organisms. For a description of each common class of antibiotic, see Classes of antibiotics p.116.

Why they are used

We are surrounded by bacteria – in the air we breathe, on the mucous membranes of our mouth and nose, on our skin, and in our intestines – but we are protected, most of the time, by our immunological defences. When these break down, or when bacteria already present migrate to a vulnerable new site, or when harmful

ANTIBIOTIC RESISTANCE

The increasing use of antibiotics in the treatment of infection has led to resistance in certain types of bacteria to the effects of particular antibiotics. This resistance to the drug usually occurs when bacteria develop mechanisms of growth and reproduction that are not disrupted by the effects of the antibiotics. In other cases, bacteria produce *enzymes* that neutralize the antibiotics.

Antibiotic resistance may develop in a person during prolonged treatment when a drug has failed to eliminate the infection quickly. The resistant strain of bacteria is able to multiply, thereby prolonging the illness.

It may also infect other people, and result in the spread of resistant infection. One particularly important example is methicillin-resistant staphylococcus aureus, which resists most antibiotics but can be treated with other drugs such as vancomycin.

Physicians try to prevent the development of antibiotic resistance by selecting the drug most likely to eliminate the bacteria present in each individual case as quickly and as thoroughly as possible. Failure to complete a course of antibiotics that has been prescribed by your physician increases the likelihood that the infection will recur in a resistant form.

bacteria not usually present invade the body, infectious disease sets in.

The bacteria multiply uncontrollably, destroying tissue, releasing *toxins*, and, in some cases, threatening to spread via the bloodstream to such vital organs as the heart, brain, lungs, and kidneys. The symptoms of infectious disease vary widely, depending on the site of the infection and the type of bacteria.

Confronted with a sick person and suspecting a bacterial infection, the physician should identify the organism causing the disease before prescribing any drug. However, tests to analyse blood, sputum, urine, stool, or pus usually take 24 hours or more. In the meantime, especially if the person is in discomfort or pain, the

physician usually makes a preliminary drug choice, something of an educated guess as to the causative organism. In determining this empirical treatment, as it is called, the physician is guided by the site of the infection, the nature and severity of the symptoms, the likely source of infection, and the prevalence of any similar illnesses in the community at that time.

In such circumstances, pending laboratory identification of the trouble-making bacteria, the physician may initially prescribe a broad-spectrum antibiotic, which is effective against a wide variety of bacteria. As soon as tests provide more exact information, he or she may switch the person to the recommended antibiotic treatment for the identified bacteria. In some cases, more than one antibiotic is prescribed, to be sure of eliminating all strains of bacteria.

In most cases, antibiotics can be given by mouth. However, in serious infections when high blood levels of the drug are needed rapidly, or when a type of antibiotic is needed that cannot be given by mouth, the drug may be given by injection. Antibiotics are also included in *topical* preparations for localized skin, eye, and ear infections (see also Anti-infective skin preparations, p.163, and Drugs for ear disorders, p.159).

How they work

Depending on the type of drug and the dosage, antibiotics are either bactericidal, killing organisms directly, or bacteriostatic, halting the multiplication of bacteria and enabling the body's natural defences to overcome the remaining infection.

Penicillins and cephalosporins are bactericidal, destroying bacteria by preventing them from making normal cell walls; most other antibiotics act inside the bacteria by interfering with the chemical activities essential to their life cycle.

How they affect you

Antibiotics stop most common types of infection within days. Because they do not relieve symptoms directly, you may be advised to take other *medication*, such as

ACTION OF ANTIBIOTICS

Penicillins and cephalosporins
Drugs from these groups are bactericidal – that is, they kill bacteria. They interfere with the chemicals needed by bacteria to form normal cell walls (right). The cell's outer lining disintegrates and the bacterium dies (far right).

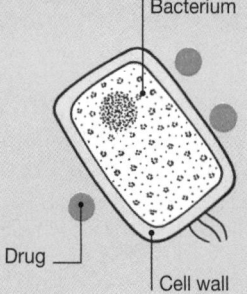
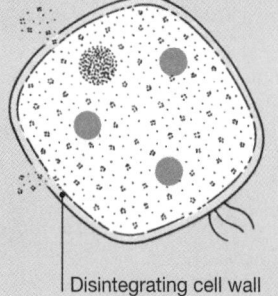

Bacterium

Drug

Cell wall

Disintegrating cell wall

Other antibiotics
These drugs alter chemical activity inside the bacteria, thereby preventing the production of proteins that the bacteria need to multiply and survive (right). This may have a bactericidal effect in itself, or it may prevent reproduction (bacteriostatic action) (far right).

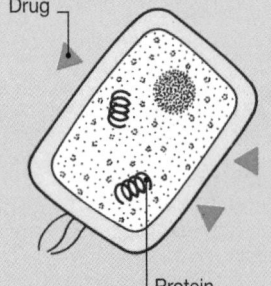
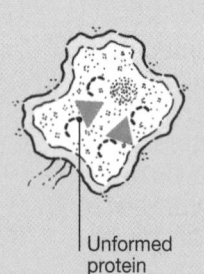

Drug

Protein

Unformed protein

USES OF ANTIBIOTICS

The table below shows which common drugs in each class of antibiotic are used for the treatment of infections in different parts of the body. For the purposes of comparison, this table also includes (in the Other drugs category) some antibacterial drugs that are discussed on page 117. This table is not intended to be used as a guide to prescribing but indicates the possible applications of each drug. Some drugs have a wide range of possible uses; this table concentrates on the most common ones.

Antibiotic / Site of infection	Ear, nose, throat, and mouth	Respiratory tract	Skin and soft tissue	Gastrointestinal tract	Eye	Kidney and urinary tract	Brain and nervous system	Heart and blood	Bones and joints	Genital tract
Penicillins										
Amoxicillin	●	●	●			●		●	●	●
Amoxicillin/clavulinic acid	●	●	●			●			●	
Ampicillin	●	●	●			●	●		●	●
Cloxacillin	●		●					●	●	
Penicillin G	●	●	●				●	●	●	●
Penicillin V	●	●	●							
Cephalosporins										
Cefaclor	●	●				●				
Cefazolin		●	●			●			●	
Cefotaxime		●			●		●	●		
Cefoxitin		●	●			●				●
Cefprozil	●	●	●							
Cefuroxime	●	●	●							●
Cephalexin		●	●			●				
Macrolides										
Azithromycin	●	●	●							●
Clarithromycin	●	●	●	●						
Erythromycin	●	●	●	●	●				●	●
Tetracyclines										
Doxycycline	●	●				●				●
Tetracycline	●	●			●	●				●
Aminoglycosides										
Amikacin		●	●	●		●	●		●	
Gentamicin		●	●	●	●	●		●	●	
Tobramycin		●	●	●		●			●	
Sulfonamide combination										
Sulfamethoxazole-trimethoprim		●				●				
Other drugs										
Clindamycin		●	●	●					●	
Fusidic acid			●					●	●	
Metronidazole	●		●	●			●	●	●	●
Nitrofurantoin						●				
Trimethoprim		●		●		●				
Vancomycin				●				●		
Quinolones										
Ciprofloxacin		●	●			●				●
Levofloxacin		●								
Moxifloxacin		●								
Norfloxacin			●			●				

ANTIBIOTICS continued

analgesics (see p.64), to relieve pain and fever until the antibiotics take effect.

It is important to complete the course of medication as it has been prescribed by your physician, even if all your symptoms have disappeared. Failure to do this can lead to a resurgence of the infection in an antibiotic-resistant form (see Antibiotic resistance, p.114).

Most antibiotics used in the home do not usually cause *adverse effects* if taken in the recommended dosage. In people who do experience adverse effects, nausea and diarrhea are among the more common ones. Some people may be sensitive to certain types of antibiotics, which can result in a variety of serious adverse effects.

DRUG TREATMENT FOR MENINGITIS

Meningitis is inflammation of the meninges (the membranes surrounding the brain and spinal cord) and is caused by both bacteria and viruses. Bacterial meningitis can kill previously well individuals within hours.

If bacterial meningitis is suspected, intravenous antibiotics are needed immediately and admission to hospital is arranged.

In cases of bacterial meningitis caused by *Haemophilus influenzae* or *Neisseria meningitidis*, close contacts of these patients are advised to have a preventative course of antibiotics, usually rifampin.

Risks and special precautions

Most antibiotics used for short periods outside a hospital setting are safe for most people. The most common risk, particularly with cephalosporins and penicillins, is an *allergic reaction* that causes a rash. Very rarely, the reaction may be severe, causing swelling of the throat and face, breathing difficulty, and circulatory collapse – a potentially fatal condition called anaphylactic shock. If you have an allergic reaction, the drug should be stopped and immediate medical advice sought. If you have had a previous allergic reaction to an antibiotic, all other drugs in that class and related classes should be avoided. It is important to inform your physician and your *pharmacist* if you have suffered an *adverse reaction* to treatment with an antibiotic (with the exception of minor bowel disturbances).

Another risk of antibiotic treatment, especially if it is prolonged, is that the balance among microorganisms normally inhabiting the body may be disturbed. Antibiotics may destroy the bacteria that normally limit the growth of *Candida*, a yeast that is often present in the body in small amounts. This can lead to overgrowth of *Candida* (thrush) in the mouth, vagina, or bowel, and an antifungal drug (p.124) may be needed. A rarer, but more serious, result of disruption of normal bacterial activity in the body is a disorder known as pseudomembranous colitis, in which bacteria (called *Clostridium difficile*) resistant to the

antibiotic multiply in the bowel, causing violent, bloody diarrhea. This potentially fatal disorder can occur with any antibiotic, but is more commonly reported with cephalosporins and clindamycin.

COMMON DRUGS

Aminoglycosides
Amikacin
Gentamicin ✳
Neomycin
Streptomycin
Tobramycin

Cephalosporins
Cefaclor ✳
Cefadroxil
Cefazolin
Cefotaxime
Cefoxitin
Cefprozil ✳
Ceftriaxone
Cefuroxime ✳
Ceftazidime
Cephalexin ✳

Lincosamides
Clindamycin ✳

Macrolides
Azithromycin ✳
Clarithromycin ✳
Erythromycin ✳

Penicillins
Amoxicillin ✳
Ampicillin
Cloxacillin ✳

Penicillin G
Penicillin V ✳
Piperacillin
Ticarcillin/
   clavulinic acid

Tetracyclines
Doxycycline ✳
Tetracycline ✳
Tigecycline

Other drugs
Chloramphenicol ✳
Daptomycin
Fosfomycin
   Tromethamine
Fusidic acid
Imipenem-cilastin
Linezolid
Meropenem
Metronidazole ✳
Polymixin B ✳
Rifampin ✳
Sulfamethoxazole/
   trimethoprim ✳
Telithromycin
Trimethoprim ✳
Vancomycin ✳

✳ See Part 4

CLASSES OF ANTIBIOTICS

Penicillins
First introduced in the 1940s, penicillins are still widely used to treat many common infections. Some penicillins are not effective when they are taken by mouth and therefore have to be given by injection in hospital. Unfortunately, certain strains of bacteria are resistant to penicillin treatment, and other drugs may have to be substituted. Penicillins often cause allergic reactions.

Cephalosporins
These are broad-spectrum antibiotics similar to the penicillins. They are often used when penicillin treatment has proved ineffective. Some cephalosporins can be given by mouth, but others are only given by injection. About 1 per cent of people who are allergic to penicillins may be allergic to phalosporins. Some cephalosporins can occasionally damage the kidneys, particularly if used with aminoglycosides. Another serious, although rare, adverse effect of a few cephalosporins is that they occasionally interfere with normal blood clotting, leading to abnormally heavy bleeding, especially in the elderly.

Macrolides
Erythromycin is the most common drug in this group. It is a broad-spectrum antibiotic that is often prescribed as an alternative to penicillins or cephalosporins. Erythromycin is also effective against certain diseases, such as Legionnaires' disease (a rare type of

pneumonia), that cannot be treated with other antibiotics. The main risk with erythromycin is that it can occasionally impair liver function.

Tetracyclines
These have a broader spectrum of activity than other classes of antibiotic. However, increasing bacterial resistance (see Antibiotic resistance, p.114) has limited their use, although they are still widely prescribed. As well as being used for the treatment of infections, tetracyclines are also used in the long-term treatment of acne, although this application is probably not related to their antibacterial action. A major drawback to the use of tetracycline antibiotics in young children and in pregnant women is that they are deposited in developing bones and teeth.

With the exception of doxycycline, drugs from this group are poorly absorbed through the intestines, and when given by mouth they have to be administered in high doses in order to reach effective levels in the blood. Such high doses increase the likelihood of diarrhea as a side effect. The absorption of tetracyclines can be further reduced by interaction with calcium and other minerals. Drugs from this group should not therefore be taken with iron tablets or milk products. Tetracyclines deteriorate and may become poisonous with time, so leftover tablets or capsules should always be discarded.

Aminoglycosides
These potent drugs are effective against a broad range of bacteria. However, they are not

as widely used as some other antibiotics since they have to be given by injection and they have potentially serious side effects especially on the kidneys and the middle ear. They are usually used in a hospital setting for treatment of serious infections. They are often given with other antibiotics.

Lincosamides
The lincosamide clindamycin is not commonly used as it is more likely to cause serious disruption of bacterial activity in the bowel than other antibiotics. It is mainly reserved for the treatment of bone, joint, abdominal, and pelvic infections that do not respond well to other antibiotics. Clindamycin is also used for dental infections and topically for acne and vaginal infections.

Quinolones (see p.117)
This group of drugs consists of nalidixic acid and substances chemically related to it, including the fluoroquinolones. Fluoroquinolones have a broad spectrum of activity. They are used to treat urinary and respiratory infections, and acute diarrheal diseases, including that caused by salmonella, as well as in the treatment of enteric fever.

The absorption of fluoroquinolones is reduced by antacids containing magnesium and aluminium. They should be avoided by epileptics, as they may rarely cause convulsions, and by children, as studies have shown that they may damage joints.

ANTIBACTERIAL DRUGS

This broad classification of drugs comprises agents that are similar to the *antibiotics* (p.114) in function but dissimilar in origin. The original antibiotics were derived from living organisms, for example, moulds and fungi. Antibacterials were developed from chemicals. The sulfonamides were the first drugs to be given for the treatment of bacterial infections and provided the mainstay of the treatment of infection before penicillin (the first antibiotic) became generally available. Increasing bacterial resistance and the development of antibiotics that are more effective and less toxic have reduced the use of sulfonamides.

Why they are used

Sulfonamides are especially useful for treating urinary tract infections because high concentrations of the drug reach the urine. They are also used for middle ear infections, although their use is limited due to resistance.

Trimethoprim is used for chest and urinary tract infections. The drug is also combined with sulfamethoxazole as co-trimoxazole.

Antibacterials used for tuberculosis are discussed on p.118. Others, sometimes classified as antimicrobials, include metronidazole, prescribed for a variety of genital infections and for some serious infections of the abdomen, pelvic region, heart, and central nervous system. Other antibacterials are used to treat urinary infections. These include nitrofurantoin and drugs in the quinolone group (see facing page) used to cure or prevent recurrent urinary tract infections. The quinolones are effective against a broad spectrum of bacteria. More potent relatives of nalidixic acid include norfloxacin, used to treat urinary tract infections, and ciprofloxacin,

ACTION OF SULFONAMIDES

Before drug treatment
Folic acid, a chemical that is necessary for the growth of bacteria, is produced within bacterial cells by an *enzyme* that acts on a chemical called para-aminobenzoic acid.

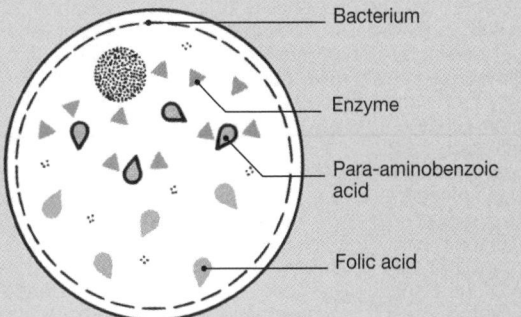

- Bacterium
- Enzyme
- Para-aminobenzoic acid
- Folic acid

After drug treatment
Sulfonamides interfere with the release of the enzyme. This prevents folic acid from being formed. The bacterium is therefore unable to function properly and dies.

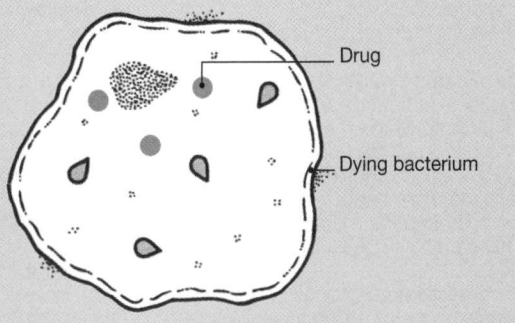

- Drug
- Dying bacterium

levofloxacin, and ofloxacin. These drugs are all used to treat many serious bacterial infections.

How they work

Most antibacterials function by preventing growth and multiplication of bacteria (see also Action of antibiotics, p.114, and Action of sulfonamides, above).

How they affect you

Antibacterials usually take several days to eliminate bacteria. During this time your physician may recommend additional medication to alleviate pain and fever. Possible *side effects* of sulfonamides include loss of appetite, nausea, a rash, and drowsiness.

Risks and special precautions

Like antibiotics, most antibacterials can cause *allergic reactions* in susceptible people. Possible symptoms that should always be brought to your physician's attention include rashes and fever. If such symptoms occur, a change to another drug is likely to be necessary.

Treatment with sulfonamides carries a number of serious, but uncommon risks. Some drugs in this group can cause crystals to form in the kidneys, a risk that can be reduced by drinking adequate amounts of fluid during prolonged treatment. Because sulfonamides may also occasionally

damage the liver, they are not usually prescribed for people with impaired liver function. There is also a slight risk of damage to bone marrow, lowering the production of white blood cells and thereby increasing the chances of a serious infection. Sulfonamides are therefore not prescribed for prolonged periods. Liver function and blood composition are often monitored during unavoidable long-term treatment.

DRUG TREATMENT FOR HANSEN'S DISEASE

Hansen's disease, also known as leprosy, is a bacterial infection caused by *Mycobacterium leprae*. It is rare in Canada, but relatively common in parts of Africa, Asia, and Latin America.

The disease progresses slowly, first affecting the peripheral nerves and causing loss of sensation in the hands and feet. This leads to frequent unnoticed injuries or burns and consequent scarring. Later, the nerves of the face may also be affected.

Treatment uses three drugs together to prevent the development of resistance. Usually, dapsone, rifampin, and clofazimine will be given for at least 2 years. If one of these cannot be used, then a second line drug (ofloxacin, minocycline, or clarithromycin) might be substituted. Complications during treatment sometimes require the use of prednisone, ASA, chloroquine, or even thalidomide.

COMMON DRUGS

Quinolones
Ciprofloxacin ✳
Gemifloxacin
Levofloxacin ✳
Moxifloxacin ✳
Norfloxacin ✳
Ofloxacin

Sulfonamides
Sulfamethoxazole (available in combination with trimethoprim) ✳

Urinary antiseptic
Nitrofurantoin ✳

Other drugs
Clindamycin ✳
Metronidazole ✳
Trimethoprim

✳ See Part 4

ANTITUBERCULOUS DRUGS

Tuberculosis is an infectious bacterial disease acquired, often in childhood, by inhaling the tuberculosis bacilli present in the spray caused by a sneeze or cough from someone who is actively infected. It may also be acquired from infected unpasteurized cow's milk. The disease usually starts in a lung and takes one of two forms: either primary infection or reactivated infection.

In 90 to 95 per cent of those with a primary infection, the body's immune system suppresses the infection but does not kill the bacilli. They remain alive but dormant and may cause the reactivated form of the disease. After they are reactivated, the tuberculosis bacilli may spread via the lymphatic system and bloodstream throughout the body (see Sites of infection, below).

The first symptoms of the primary infection may include a cough, fever, tiredness, night sweats, and weight loss. Tuberculosis is confirmed through clinical investigations, which may include a chest X-ray, isolation of the bacilli from the person's sputum, and a positive reaction – localized inflammation – to a skin test (in which tuberculin, a protein extracted from tuberculosis bacilli, is injected into the skin).

The gradual emergence in adults of the destructive and progressive form of tuberculosis is caused by the reactivated infection. It occurs in 5 to 10 per cent of those who have had a previous primary infection. Another form, reinfection

tuberculosis, occurs when someone with the dormant, primary form is reinfected. This type of tuberculosis is clinically identical to the reactivated form. Reactivation is more likely in those people whose immune system is suppressed, such as the elderly, those on corticosteroids or other immunosuppressant drugs, and those who have HIV/AIDS. Reactivation tuberculosis may be difficult to identify because the symptoms may start in any part of the body seeded with the bacilli. It is most often first seen in the upper lobes of the lung, and is frequently diagnosed after a chest X-ray. The early symptoms may be identical to those of primary infection: a cough, night sweats, tiredness, fever, and weight loss.

If left untreated, tuberculosis continues to destroy tissue, spreading throughout the body and eventually causing death. It was one of the most common causes of death in developed countries until the 1940s but the disease is now on the increase again worldwide. Vulnerable groups are people with suppressed immune systems and the homeless.

Why drugs are used

A person who has been diagnosed as having tuberculosis is likely to be treated with three or four antituberculous drugs. This helps to overcome the risk of drug-resistant strains of the bacilli emerging (see Antibiotic resistance, p.114).

The standard drug combination for the treatment of tuberculosis consists of rifampin, isoniazid, and pyrazinamide. In areas where there is a high prevalence of drug-resistant tuberculosis ethambutol may be added. However, other drugs may be substituted if the initial treatment fails or if drug sensitivity tests indicate that the bacilli are resistant to these drugs.

The standard duration of treatment for a newly diagnosed tuberculosis infection is a six-month regimen as follows: isoniazid, rifampin, pyrazinamide with or without ethambutol depending on susceptibility of bacteria, daily for two months, followed by isoniazid and rifampin for four months. The duration of treatment can be extended from nine months to up to two years in people at particular risk, such as those with a suppressed immune system.

Corticosteroids may be added to the treatment in specific situations, if the patient does not have a suppressed immune system, to reduce the amount of tissue damage.

Both the number of drugs required and the long duration of treatment may make treatment difficult, particularly for those who are homeless. To help with this problem, supervised administration of treatment is available when required, both in the community and in hospital.

Tuberculosis infection in patients with HIV infection or AIDS is treated with the standard antituberculous drug regimen.

SITES OF INFECTION

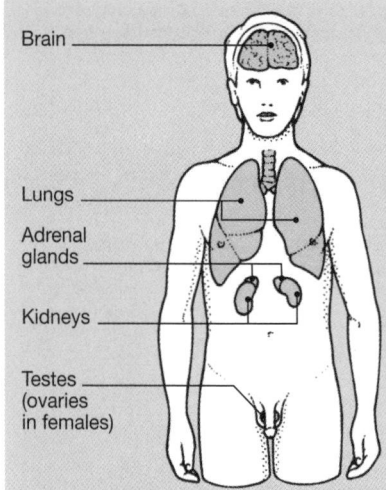

Brain

Lungs

Adrenal glands

Kidneys

Testes (ovaries in females)

Tuberculosis usually affects only part of one lung at first. However, later outbreaks usually spread to both lungs and may also affect the kidneys, leading to pyelonephritis; the adrenal glands, causing Addison's disease; and the membranes surrounding the brain, which may lead to meningitis. The testes (in men) and the ovaries (in women) may also be affected.

TUBERCULOSIS PREVENTION

A vaccine prepared from an artificially weakened strain of cattle tuberculosis bacteria can provide immunity from tuberculosis by provoking the development of natural resistance to the disease (see Vaccines and immunization, p.120). The BCG (Bacille Calmette-Guérin) vaccine is a form of tuberculosis bacillus that provokes the body's immune response but does not cause the illness because it is not infectious. The vaccine is given to some children between the ages of 10 and 14 years who are shown to have no natural immunity when given a skin test. BCG vaccination may be given to newborn babies if, for example, someone in the family has tuberculosis.

How it is done
The vaccine is usually injected into the upper arm. A small pustule usually appears 6–12 weeks later, by which time the person can be considered immune.

How they work

Antituberculous drugs act in the same way as antibiotics, either by killing bacilli or preventing them from multiplying (see Action of antibiotics, p.114).

How they affect you

Although the drugs start to combat the disease within days, benefits of drug treatment are not usually noticeable for a few weeks. As the infection is eradicated, the body repairs the damage caused by the disease. Symptoms such as fever and coughing gradually subside, and appetite and general health improve.

Risks and special precautions

Antituberculous drugs may cause *adverse effects* (nausea, vomiting, and abdominal pain), and they occasionally lead to serious *allergic reactions*. When this happens, another drug is substituted.

Rifampin and isoniazid may affect liver enzymes; isoniazid may adversely affect the nerves as well. Ethambutol can cause changes in colour vision. Dosage is carefully monitored, especially in children, the elderly, and those with reduced kidney function.

COMMON DRUGS

Ethambutol ✻	Rifabutin
Isoniazid ✻	Rifampin ✻
Pyrazinamide	Streptomycin

✻ See Part 4

ANTIVIRAL DRUGS

Viruses are simpler and smaller organisms than bacteria and are less able to sustain themselves. These organisms can survive and multiply only by penetrating body cells (see Action of antiviral drugs, right). Because viruses perform few functions independently, medicines that disrupt or halt their life cycle without harming human cells have been difficult to develop.

There are many different types of virus, and viral infections cause illnesses with various symptoms and degrees of severity. Common viral illnesses include the cold, influenza and flu-like illnesses, cold sores, and the usual childhood diseases such as chickenpox and mumps. Throat infections, pneumonia, acute bronchitis, gastroenteritis, and meningitis are often, but not always, caused by a virus.

Fortunately, the natural defences of the body are usually strong enough to overcome infections such as these, with drugs given to ease pain and lower fever. However, the more serious viral diseases, such as pneumonia and meningitis, need close medical supervision.

Another difficulty with viral infections is the speed with which the virus multiplies. By the time symptoms appear, the viruses are so numerous that antiviral drugs have little effect. Antiviral agents must be given early in the course of a viral infection or they may be used *prophylactically* (as a preventative). Some viral infections can be prevented by vaccination (see p.120).

Why drugs are used

Antiviral drugs are helpful in the treatment of various conditions caused by the herpes virus: cold sores, encephalitis, genital herpes, chickenpox, and shingles.

Acyclovir is applied topically to treat outbreaks of cold sores, herpes eye infections, and genital herpes. They can reduce the severity and duration of an outbreak, but they do not eliminate the infection permanently. The drugs acyclovir, famciclovir, and valacyclovir are given by mouth or, under exceptional circumstances by injection, to prevent chickenpox or severe, recurrent attacks of the herpes virus infections in those people who are already weakened by other conditions.

Influenza may sometimes be prevented or treated using oseltamivir or zanamivir. They are indicated for treatment in those older than a year, if symptoms have been present for no more than two days. They can also be used in the prevention of influenza, following close contact with an infected individual.

The interferons are proteins produced by the body and involved in the immune response and cell function. Interferon alpha and beta are effective in reducing the activity of hepatitis B and hepatitis C. Lamivudine is also used to treat hepatitis B, and ribavirin for hepatitis C.

Ganciclovir is sometimes used for cyto-megalovirus (CMV). Respiratory syncytial

ACTION OF ANTIVIRAL DRUGS

In order to reproduce, a virus requires a living cell. The invaded cell eventually dies and the new viruses are released, spreading and infecting other cells. Most antiviral drugs act to prevent the virus from using the host cell's genetic material, DNA, to multiply. Unable to divide, the virus dies and the spread of infection is halted.

Before drug

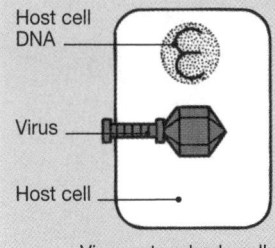
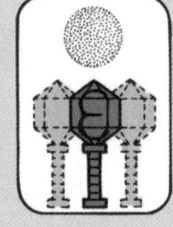

Host cell DNA

Virus

Host cell

Virus enters body cell.

Virus uses host cell's DNA to reproduce.

Host cell dies and new viruses are released.

After drug

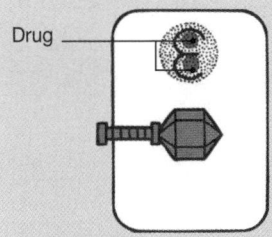
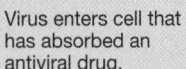
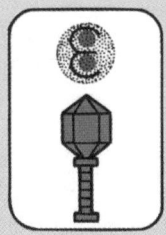
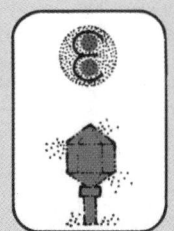

Drug

Virus enters cell that has absorbed an antiviral drug.

Cell DNA is altered by drug action and virus cannot use it.

Virus dies and spread of infection is thereby halted.

virus (RSV) has been treated with ribavirin, and prevented by palivizumab. Drug treatment for AIDS is discussed on p.144.

How they work

Some antiviral drugs, such as idoxuridine, act by altering the cell's genetic material (DNA) so that the virus cannot use it to multiply. Other drugs stop multiplication of viruses by blocking enzyme activity within the host cell. Halting multiplication prevents the virus from spreading to uninfected cells and improves symptoms rapidly. However, in herpes infections, it does not eradicate the virus from the body. Infection may therefore flare up on another occasion.

Amantadine has a different action: it prevents the virus from entering the cells. It is therefore most effective when it is given as a *prophylactic*, before the infection has spread widely.

How they affect you

Topical antiviral drugs usually start to act immediately. Providing that the treatment is applied early enough, an outbreak of herpes can be cut short. Symptoms usually clear up within two to four days.

Antiviral ointments may cause irritation and redness. Antiviral drugs given by mouth or injection can occasionally cause nausea and dizziness.

Risks and special precautions

Because some of these drugs may affect the kidneys adversely, they are prescribed with caution for people with reduced kidney function. Some antiviral drugs can adversely affect the activity of normal body cells, particularly those in the bone marrow. Idoxuridine is, for this reason, available only for topical application.

COMMON DRUGS

Acyclovir ✳	Peginterferon
Adefovir	alfa-2a
Amantadine ✳	Peginterferon
Entecavir	alfa-2b
Famciclovir ✳	Penciclovir
Ganciclovir	Ribavirin
Idoxuridine	Telbivudine
Interferon alfa-2b ✳	Trifluridine
Lamivudine ✳	Valacyclovir
Oseltamivir ✳	Valganciclovir
Palivizumab	Zanamivir ✳

✳ See Part 4	See also Drugs for HIV, p.144

VACCINES AND IMMUNIZATION

Many infectious diseases, including most of the common viral infections, occur only once during a person's lifetime. The reason is that the antibodies produced in response to the disease remain afterwards, prepared to repel any future invasion by the infectious organisms. The duration of such immunity varies, but it can last a lifetime.

Protection against many infections can now be provided artificially by using vaccines derived from altered forms of the infecting organism. These vaccines stimulate the immune system in the same way as a genuine infection, and provide lasting, active immunity. Because each type of microbe stimulates the production of a specific antibody, a different vaccine must be given for each disease.

Another type of *immunization*, called passive immunization, relies on giving antibodies (see Immune globulins, below).

Why they are used

Some infectious diseases cannot be treated effectively or are so serious that prevention is the best course. Routine immunization not only protects the individual but may gradually eradicate the disease completely, as with smallpox.

Newborn babies receive *antibodies* for many diseases from their mothers, but this protection lasts only for about three months. Most children are vaccinated against common childhood infectious diseases. In addition, travellers are advised to be vaccinated against the diseases common in the areas they are visiting.

Effective lifelong immunization can sometimes be achieved by a single dose of the vaccine. However, in many cases reinforcing doses (booster shots) are needed later to maintain reliable immunity.

Vaccines do not provide immediate protection, and it may be up to four weeks before full immunity develops. When immediate protection is needed, it may be necessary to establish passive immunity with immune globulins (see below).

ACTIVE AND PASSIVE IMMUNIZATION

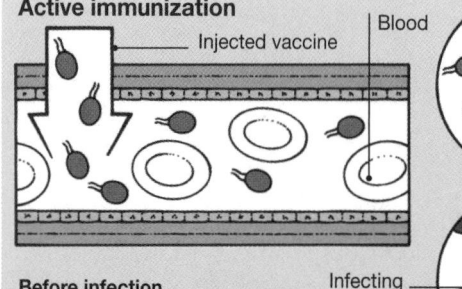

Active immunization

Injected vaccine

Blood

Antibody formation
The vaccine causes antibodies to form against the infection.

Antibodies

Before infection
A vaccine containing altered forms of the infection is injected.

Infecting organism attacked by antibodies

Immunity
Invasion of the body by a similar organism causes antibodies to form as a result of the vaccine and eliminate the infection.

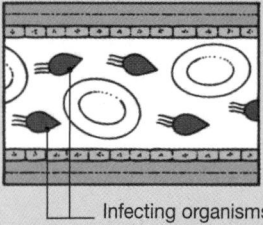

Passive immunization

Injected antibodies

Infecting organisms

Infecting organism attacked by antibodies

After infection
Passive immunization is needed when the infection has entered the blood.

Immune globulin injection
A serum containing antibodies (immune globulin) extracted from donated blood is injected. This helps the body to fight the infection.

How they work

Vaccines provoke the immune system into creating antibodies that help the body to resist specific infectious diseases. Some vaccines (live vaccines) are made from artificially weakened forms of the disease-causing organism. Others rely either on inactive (or killed) disease-causing organisms or inactive derivatives of them. Whatever their type, all vaccines stimulate antibody production and establish active immunity.

How they affect you

The degree of protection varies among different vaccines. Some provide reliable lifelong immunity; others may not give full protection against a disease, or the effects may last for as little as six months. Influenza vaccines usually protect only against the variety of virus causing the latest outbreak of flu.

Any vaccine may cause *side effects* but they are usually mild and soon disappear. The most common reactions are a red, slightly raised, tender area at the site of injection, and a slight fever or a flu-like illness lasting for one or two days.

Risks and special precautions

Serious reactions are rare and, for most children, the risk is far outweighed by the protection given. A family or personal history of seizures is not necessarily a contraindication to immunization, but immunization may be delayed, if the condition is unstable. Children who have any infection more severe than a common cold will not be given any routine vaccination until they have recovered.

Live vaccines should not be given during pregnancy because they can affect the developing baby, nor should they be given to people whose immune systems are weakened by disease or drug treatment. It is also advisable for

IMMUNE GLOBULINS

Antibodies, which can result from exposure to snake and insect venom as well as infectious disease, permeate the serum of the blood (the part remaining after the red cells and clotting agents are removed). The concentrated serum of people who have survived diseases or poisonous bites is called immune globulin, and, given by injection, it creates passive immunity. Immune globulin from blood donated by a wide cross-section of donors is likely to contain antibodies to most common diseases. Specific immune globulins against rare diseases or toxins are derived from the blood of selected donors likely to have high levels of antibodies to that disease. These are called hyperimmune globulins. Some

immune globulins are extracted from horse blood following repeated doses of the toxin.

Because immune globulins do not stimulate the body to produce its own antibodies, their effect is not long-lasting and diminishes progressively over three or four weeks. Continued protection requires repeated injections of immune globulins.

Adverse effects from immune globulins are uncommon. Some people are sensitive to horse globulins, and about a week after the injection they may experience a reaction known as serum sickness, with fever, a rash, joint swelling, and pain. This usually ends in a few days but should be reported to your physician before any further immunization.

those taking high doses of corticosteroids (p.127) to delay their vaccinations until the end of drug treatment.

The risk of high fever following the DTaP–IPV (combined diphtheria, tetanus, acellular pertussis, and polio) vaccine can be reduced by giving acetaminophen at the time of vaccination. The pertussis vaccine may rarely cause a mild seizure, which is brief, usually associated with fever, and stops without treatment. Children who have experienced such seizures recover completely without neurological or developmental problems.

COMMON VACCINATIONS

Disease	Age at which vaccination is given	How given	General information
Diphtheria	2 months, 4 months, 6 months, 18 months, 4–6 years.	Injection	Infants: given with tetanus, pertussis, and polio vaccines. In later life immunity may diminish. Adults: booster every 10 years.
Tetanus	2 months, 4 months, 6 months, 18 months, 4–6 years.	Injection	Infants: given with diphtheria, pertussis, and polio. Protection lasts 5–10 years. Booster shots given for injuries that would likely result in tetanus infection. Adults: booster every 10 years.
Acellular pertussis	2 months, 4 months, 6 months, 18 months, 4–6 years.	Injection	Preferable to use products in which diptheria toxin is combined with acellular pertussis. Preschool booster. Adults: give one dose as Tdap if not previously received.
Polio	2 months, 4 months, 6 months, 18 months, 4–6 years.	Injection	Many physicians may recommend a booster every 10 years, especially if primary series during childhood is not complete, and especially for people who are travelling to countries where polio is still prevalent. Single booster dose recommended for those at high risk of exposure.
Haemophilus influenzae type b (Hib)	2 months, 4 months, 6 months, 18 months.	Injection	Routinely given in infancy to prevent serious disease up to the age of 4 years.
Rubella (German measles)	12 months and at 18 months or 4–6 years.	Injection	Given in infancy with measles and mumps vaccines (MMR). Rubella is important because it can damage the fetus if it affects a woman in early pregnancy.
Measles	12 months and at 18 months or 4–6 years.	Injection	Given with mumps and rubella vaccines (MMR) in infancy.
Mumps	12 months and at 18 months or 4–6 years.	Injection	Given with measles and rubella vaccines (MMR) in infancy.
Varicella (chickenpox)	1–2 doses for people over 12 months who have not had chickenpox	Injection	Although most children recover from chickenpox with no problems, the infection can pose serious health risks to newborns and some adults.
Influenza	Recommended for all children 6–23 months. Also children and adults of any age who are at risk of serious illness or death if they develop influenza and their household carers, health care workers, as well as those wishing to be protected against influenza, and all adults 65 years of age and over.	Injection	Long-term immunity against all forms of influenza is impossible. Annual vaccinations are needed to protect against the latest strains. Also given to individuals capable of transmitting influenza to those at high risk (e.g. health care workers). Safe in pregnant and breast-feeding women.
Hepatitis A	Single dose for people any age who are at risk. Booster 6–12 months after initial shot.	Injection	Given to people travelling to areas of poor hygiene or where hepatitis infection is likely and to those exposed at school or work.
Hepatitis B	3 inoculations any age, with the second and third shots 1 and 6 months after the first.	Injection	Efficacy is checked by a blood test. Recommended for "at risk" groups, such as health-care providers, intravenous drug users, and long-stay travellers. Adolescents (11–15 years) may be given a 2-dose regimen of adult formulation.
Pneumococcal pneumonia	2 months, 4 months, 6 months, and at 12–15 months of age (pneumococcal conjugate vaccine). Single dose for people any age who are at risk and adults 65 years of age and over (pneumococcal polysaccharide).	Injection	Persons at risk of contracting pneumococcal pneumonia include those who have had their spleen removed, immunodeficient persons, or those with chronic liver or lung disease or diabetes mellitus. Single booster dose after 5 years recommended in those at high risk.
Meningococcal meningitis A/C/Y/W–135	Recommended for all children in early adolescence. Single dose for people any age who are at risk. Schedule depends on age of individual.	Injection	Given to persons at risk of contracting meningitis; for example to travellers to the "Meningitis belt" of tropical and subtropical countries where there is a high risk of meningitis infection, also contacts of cases in Canada.
Meningococcal meningitis C	2 months, 4 months, 6 months (less than 2 years old).	Injection	Given in infancy to protect against one of the most common types of childhood meningitis.
Typhoid	Single dose for people of any age who are at risk.	Injection	Travellers to areas with poor sanitation.

ANTIPROTOZOAL DRUGS

Protozoa are single-celled organisms that are present in soil and water. They may be transmitted to or between humans through contaminated food or water, sexual contact, or insect bites. There are many types of protozoal infection, each of which causes a different disease depending on the organism involved. Trichomoniasis, toxoplasmosis, cryptosporidium, giardiasis, and pneumocystis pneumonia are probably the most common protozoal infections. The rarer infections are usually contracted as a result of exposure to infection in another part of the world.

Many types of protozoa infect the bowel, causing diarrhea and generalized symptoms of ill-health. Others may infect the genital tract or skin. Some protozoa may penetrate vital organs such as the lungs, brain, and liver. Prompt diagnosis and treatment are important in order to limit the spread of the infection within the body and, in some cases, prevent it from spreading to other people. Increased attention to hygiene is an important factor in controlling the spread of the disease.

A variety of medicines is used in the treatment of these diseases. Some, such as metronidazole and tetracycline, are also commonly used for their antibacterial action. Others, such as pentamidine, are rarely used except in treating specific protozoal infections.

How they affect you

Protozoa are often difficult to eradicate from the body. Drug treatment may therefore need to be continued for several months in order to eliminate the infecting organisms completely and thus prevent recurrence of the disease. In addition, unpleasant *side effects* such as nausea, diarrhea, and abdominal cramps are often unavoidable because of the limited choice of drugs and the need to maintain dosage levels that will effectively cure the disease. For detailed information on the risks and *adverse effects* of individual antiprotozoal drugs, consult the appropriate drug profile in Part 4.

The table below describes the principal protozoal diseases, the organisms that cause them, and some of the drugs used in their treatment. Malaria, which is probably the most common protozoal disease in the world today, is discussed on the facing page.

SUMMARY OF PROTOZOAL DISEASES

Disease	Protozoan	Description	Drugs
Amoebiasis (amoebic dysentery)	*Entamoeba histolytica*	Infection of the bowel and sometimes of the liver and other organs. Usually transmitted in contaminated food or water. Major symptom is violent, sometimes bloody, diarrhea.	Metronidazole
Balantidiasis	*Balantidium coli*	Infection of the bowel, specifically the colon. Usually transmitted through contact with infected pigs. Possible symptoms include diarrhea and abdominal pain.	Tetracycline Metronidazole Iodoquinol
Cryptosporidiosis	*Cryptosporidium*	Infection of the bowel, also occasionally of the respiratory tract and bile ducts. Symptoms include diarrhea and abdominal pain.	No specific drugs but paromomycin and azithromycin may be effective.
Giardiasis (lambliasis)	*Giardia lamblia*	Infection of the bowel. Usually transmitted in contaminated food or water but may also be spread by some types of sexual contact. Major symptoms are general ill health, diarrhea, flatulence, and abdominal pain.	Metronidazole
Leishmaniasis	*Leishmania*	A mainly tropical and subtropical disease caused by organisms spread through sandfly bites. It affects the mucous membranes of the mouth, nose, and throat, and may in its severe form invade organs such as the liver.	Paromomycin Pentamidine Amphotericin
Pneumocystis pneumonia	*Pneumocystis carinii*	Potentially fatal lung infection that usually affects only those with reduced resistance to infection, such as AIDS sufferers. The symptoms include cough, breathlessness, fever, and chest pain.	Atovaquone Sulfamethoxazole–trimethoprim Pentamidine
Toxoplasmosis	*Toxoplasma gondii*	Infection is usually spread via cat feces or by eating undercooked meat. Although usually symptomless, infection may cause generalized ill-health, mild fever, and eye inflammation. Treatment is necessary only if the eyes are involved or if the patient is immunosuppressed (such as in AIDS). It may also pass from mother to baby during pregnancy, leading to severe disease in the fetus.	Pyrimethamine with sulfadiazine or with azithromycin, clarithromycin, or clindamycin Spiramycin (during pregnancy)
Trichomoniasis	*Trichomonas vaginalis*	Infection most often affects the vagina, causing irritation and an offensive discharge. In men, infection may occur in the urethra. The disease is usually sexually transmitted.	Metronidazole
Trypanosomiasis	*Trypanosoma*	African trypanosomiasis (sleeping sickness) is spread by the tsetse fly and causes fever, swollen glands, and drowsiness. South American trypanosomiasis (Chagas' disease) is spread by assassin bugs and causes inflammation, enlargement of internal organs, and infection of the brain.	Pentamidine (sleeping sickness) Primaquine (Chagas' disease)

ANTIMALARIAL DRUGS

Malaria is one of the main killing diseases in the tropics (see map below). It is most likely to affect people who live in or travel to such places.

The disease is caused by protozoa (see also facing page) whose life cycle is far from simple. The malaria parasite, which is called *Plasmodium*, lives in and depends on the female *Anopheles* mosquito during one part of its life cycle. It lives in and depends on human beings during other parts of its life cycle.

Transferred to humans in the saliva of the female mosquito as she penetrates ("bites") the skin, the malaria parasite enters the bloodstream and settles in the liver, where it multiplies.

Following its stay in the liver, the parasite (or plasmodium) enters another phase of its life cycle, circulating in the bloodstream, penetrating and destroying red blood cells, and reproducing again. If the plasmodia then transfer back to a female *Anopheles* mosquito via another "bite", they breed, and are again ready to start a human infection.

Following the emergence of plasmodia from the liver, the symptoms of malaria occur: episodes of high fever and profuse sweating alternate with equally agonizing episodes of shivering and chills. One of the four strains of malaria, *Plasmodium falciparum*, can produce a single severe attack that can be fatal unless treated.

The others cause recurrent attacks, sometimes extending over many years.

A number of drugs are available for preventing malaria, the choice depending on the region in which the disease can be contracted and the resistance to the commonly used drugs. In most areas, *Plasmodium falciparum* is resistant to chloroquine (see Choice of drugs, below). In all regions, five drugs are commonly used for treating malaria: quinine, mefloquine, Malarone, doxycicline, and primaquine.

Why drugs are used
The medical response to malaria takes three forms: prevention, treatment of attacks, and the complete eradication of the plasmodia (radical cure).

For someone planning a trip to an area where malaria is prevalent, drugs are given that destroy the parasites in the liver. Dosing begins one week (2–3 weeks for mefloquine) before the traveller arrives in the malarial area and should continue for four to six weeks after return from the area.

Drugs such as mefloquine can produce a radical cure but chloroquine does not. After chloroquine treatment of non-falciparum malaria, a 14- to 21-day course of primaquine is administered. Although highly effective in destroying plasmodia in the liver, the drug is weak against the plasmodia in the blood.

Primaquine is recommended only after a person leaves the malarial area because of the high risk of reinfection.

How they work
Taken to prevent the disease, some drugs kill the plasmodia in the liver, preventing them from multiplying. Once plasmodia have multiplied, the other drugs may be used in higher doses to kill plasmodia that re-enter the bloodstream. If these drugs are not effective, primaquine may be used to destroy any plasmodia that are still present in the liver.

How they affect you
The low doses of antimalarial drugs taken for prevention rarely produce noticeable effects. Drugs taken for an attack usually begin to relieve symptoms within a few hours. Most of them can cause nausea, vomiting, and diarrhea. Quinine can cause disturbances in vision and hearing. Mefloquine can cause sleep disturbance, dizziness, and difficulties in coordination.

Risks and special precautions
When drugs are given to prevent or cure malaria, the full course of treatment must be taken. No drugs give long-term protection; a new course of treatment is needed for each journey.

Most of these drugs do not produce severe *adverse effects*, but primaquine can cause the blood disorder hemolytic *anemia*, particularly in people with glucose-6-phosphate dehydrogenase (G6PD) deficiency. Blood tests are taken before treatment to identify susceptible individuals. Mefloquine is not prescribed for those who have had psychological disorders or seizures.

Other protective measures
Because *Plasmodium* strains continually develop resistance to the available drugs, prevention using drugs is not absolutely reliable. Protection from mosquito bites is of the highest priority. Such protection includes the use of insect repellents and mosquito nets impregnated with permethrin insecticide, as well as covering any exposed skin after dark.

CHOICE OF DRUGS

The parts of the world in which malaria is prevalent (illustrated on the map, right), and travel to which may make antimalarial drug treatment advisable, can be divided into six zones. The table below indicates the drug(s) currently used for the prevention of malaria in each zone. As prevalent strains of malaria change very rapidly, you must always seek specific medical advice before travelling to these areas.

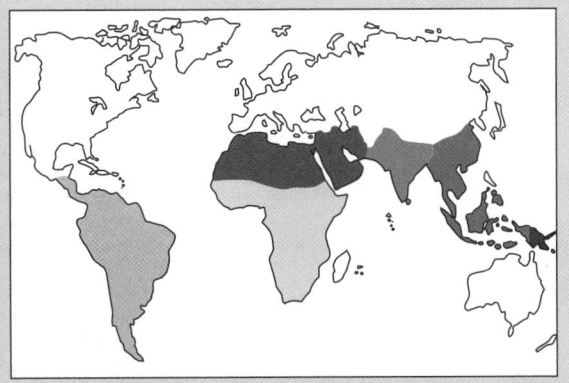

Zone	Countries	Recommended antimalarial drugs for prevention
1	North Africa and the Middle East	Chloroquine, plus proguanil in areas of chloroquine resistance
2	Sub-Saharan Africa	Mefloquine, or chloroquine with proguanil, or doxycycline, or Malarone
3	South Asia	Mefloquine, or chloroquine with proguanil, or doxycycline, or Malarone
4	Southeast Asia	Mefloquine in high-risk areas, or chloroquine with proguanil; doxycycline or Malarone in mefloquine-resistant areas
5	Oceania	Mefloquine, or doxycycline, or Malarone
6	Latin America	Central America except Panama: chloroquine or proguanil. Panama and South America: mefloquine, or doxycycline, or Malarone in high-risk areas, or chloroquine with proguanil

COMMON DRUGS

Drugs for prevention	Drugs for treatment
Chloroquine ✳	Chloroquine ✳
Doxycycline ✳	Mefloquine ✳
Hydroxychloroquine	Primaquine
Mefloquine ✳	Proguanil with atovaquone ✳
Primaquine	Pyrimethamine ✳
Proguanil ✳	Quinine ✳
Proguanil with atovaquone ✳	

✳ See Part 4

ANTIFUNGAL DRUGS

We are continually exposed to fungi – in the air we breathe, the food we eat, and the water we drink. Fortunately, most of them cannot live in the body, and few are harmful. But some can grow in the mouth, skin, hair, or nails, causing irritating or unsightly changes, and a few can cause serious and possibly fatal disease. The most common fungal infections are caused by the tinea group. These include tinea pedis (athlete's foot), tinea cruris (jock itch), tinea corporis (ringworm), and tinea capitis (scalp ringworm). Caused by a variety of organisms, they are spread by direct or indirect contact with infected humans or animals. Infection is encouraged by warm, moist conditions.

Problems may also result from the proliferation of a fungus normally present in the body; the most common example is excessive growth of *Candida*, a yeast that causes thrush infection of the mouth, vagina, and bowel. It can also infect other organs if it spreads through the body via the bloodstream. Overgrowth of *Candida* may occur in people taking *antibiotics* (p.114) or oral contraceptives (p.149), in pregnant women, or in those with diabetes or immune system disorders such as AIDS.

Superficial fungal infections – those that attack only the outer layer of the skin and mucous membranes – are relatively common and, although irritating, do not usually present a threat to general health. Internal fungal infections – for example, of the lungs, heart, or other organs – are rare, but may be serious and prolonged.

As antibiotics and other antibacterial drugs have no effect on fungi and yeasts, a different type of drug is needed. Drugs for fungal infections are either applied *topically* to treat minor infections of the skin, nails, and mucous membranes, or they are given by mouth or injection to eliminate serious fungal infections of the internal organs and nails.

Why drugs are used

Drug treatment is necessary for most fungal infections since they rarely improve alone. Measures such as careful washing and drying of affected areas may help but are not a substitute for antifungal drugs. The use of over-the-counter preparations to increase the acidity of the vagina is not usually effective.

Fungal infections of the skin and scalp are usually treated with a cream or shampoo. Drugs for vaginal thrush are most commonly applied in the form of vaginal suppositories or cream applied with a special applicator. For very severe or persistent vaginal infections, fluconazole or itraconazole may be given as a short course by mouth. Mouth infections are usually eliminated by lozenges dissolved in the mouth or an antifungal solution or gel applied to the affected areas. When *Candida* infects the bowel, an antifungal drug that is not absorbed into the bloodstream, such as nystatin, is given in tablet form. For severe or persistent infections of the nails, terbinafine or itraconazole are given by mouth until the infected nails have grown out.

In the rare cases of fungal infections affecting internal organs, such as the blood, the heart, or the brain, potent drugs such as fluconazole and itraconazole are given by mouth, or amphotericin and flucytosine are given by injection. These drugs pass into the bloodstream to fight the fungi.

ACTIONS OF ANTIFUNGAL DRUGS

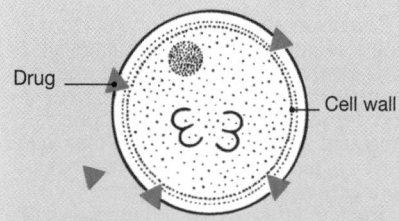

Drug — Cell wall

Stage one
The drug acts on the wall of the fungal cell.

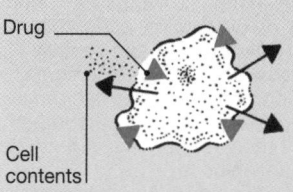

Drug — Cell contents

Stage two
The drug damages the cell wall and the cell contents leak out. The cell dies.

How they work

Most antifungals alter the permeability of the fungal cell's walls. Chemicals needed for cell life leak out and the fungal cell dies.

How they affect you

The speed with which antifungal drugs provide benefit varies with the type of infection. Most fungal or yeast infections of the skin, mouth, and vagina improve within a week. The condition of nails affected by fungal infections improves only when new nail growth occurs, which takes months. *Systemic* infections of the internal organs can take weeks to cure.

Antifungal drugs applied topically rarely cause side effects, although they may irritate the skin. However, treatment by mouth or injection for systemic and nail infections may produce more serious side effects. Amphotericin, injected in cases of life-threatening, systemic infections, can cause potentially dangerous effects, including kidney damage.

CHOICE OF ANTIFUNGAL DRUG

The table below shows the range of uses for some antifungal drugs. The particular drug chosen in each case depends on the precise nature and site of the infection. The usual route of administration for each drug is also indicated.

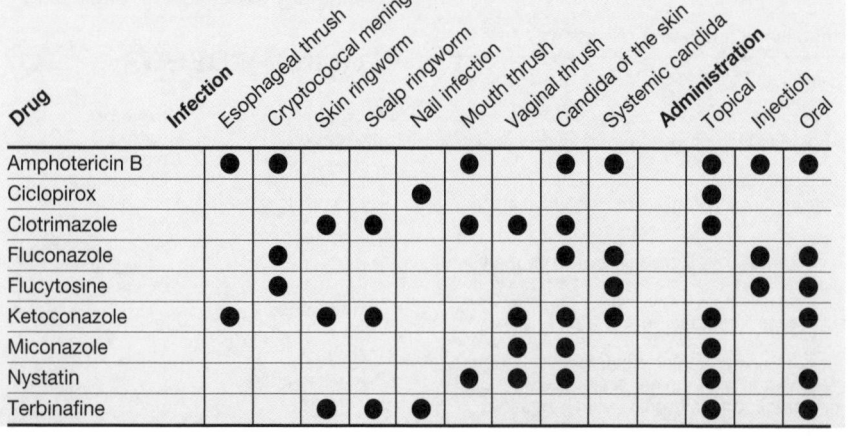

Drug	Infection									Administration		
	Esophageal thrush	Cryptococcal meningitis	Skin ringworm	Scalp ringworm	Nail infection	Mouth thrush	Vaginal thrush	Candida of the skin	Systemic candida	Topical	Injection	Oral
Amphotericin B	●	●				●		●	●	●	●	●
Ciclopirox					●					●		
Clotrimazole			●	●		●	●	●		●		
Fluconazole		●					●		●		●	●
Flucytosine		●							●		●	●
Ketoconazole	●		●	●			●	●		●		●
Miconazole							●	●		●		
Nystatin						●	●	●		●		●
Terbinafine			●	●	●					●		●

COMMON DRUGS

Amphotericin B ✳
Anidulafungin
Caspofungin
Ciclopirox
Clotrimazole ✳
Fluconazole ✳
Itraconazole
Ketoconazole ✳
Micafungin
Miconazole ✳
Nystatin ✳

Posaconazole
Terbinafine ✳
Terconazole
Tolnaftate
Voriconazole

✳ See Part 4

ANTHELMINTIC DRUGS

Anthelmintics are drugs that are used to eliminate the many types of worm (helminths) that can enter the body and live there as parasites, producing a general weakness in some cases and serious harm in others. The body may be host to many different worms (see Types of Worm infestations, below). Most species spend part of their life cycle in another animal, and the infestation is often passed on to humans in food contaminated with the eggs or larvae. In some cases, such as hookworm, larvae enter the body through the skin. Larvae or adults may attach themselves to the intestinal wall and feed on the bowel contents; others feed off the intestinal blood supply, causing *anemia*. Worms can also infest the bloodstream or lodge in the muscles or internal organs.

Many people have worms at some time during their life, especially during childhood; most can be effectively eliminated with anthelmintic drugs.

Why drugs are used

Most common worms cause only mild symptoms and usually do not pose a serious threat to general health. Anthelmintic drugs are usually necessary, however, because the body's natural defences against infection are not effective against most worm infestations. Certain types of infestation must always be treated since they can cause serious complications. In some cases, such as threadworm infestation, physicians may recommend anthelmintic treatment for the whole family to prevent reinfection. If worms have invaded tissues and formed cysts, they may have to be removed surgically. Other drugs may be prescribed to ease symptoms or to compensate for any blood loss or nutritional deficiency.

How they work

The anthelmintic drugs act in several ways. Many of them kill or paralyse the worms, which pass out of the body in the faeces. Others, which act *systemically*, are used to treat infection in the tissues.

Many anthelmintics are specific for particular worms, and the physician must identify the nature of the infection before selecting the most appropriate treatment (see Choice of drug, below). Most of the common intestinal infestations are easily treated, often with only one or two doses of the drug. However, tissue infections may require more prolonged treatment.

How they affect you

Once the drug has eliminated the worms, symptoms caused by infestation rapidly disappear. Taken as a single dose or a short course, anthelmintics do not usually produce side effects. However, treatment can disturb the digestive system, causing abdominal pain, nausea, and vomiting.

COMMON DRUGS

Mebendazole
Praziquantel
Pyrantel

TYPES OF WORM INFESTATIONS

Threadworm or pinworm (enterobiasis)
A common worm infection, particularly among young children. The worm lives in the intestine, but it travels to the anus at night to lay eggs. This causes itching; scratching leaves eggs on the fingers, usually under the fingernails. These eggs are transferred to the mouth, often by sucking the fingers or eating food with unwashed hands. Keeping nails short and good hygiene, including washing the hands after using the toilet and before each meal, and an early morning bath to remove the eggs, are all important elements in the eradication of infection.
Drugs Mebendazole, pyrantel. All members of the family should be treated simultaneously.

Common roundworm (ascariasis)
The most common worm infection worldwide. Transmitted to humans in contaminated raw food or in soil. Infects the intestine. The worms are large and dense clusters of them can block the intestine.
Drugs Mebendazole

Tropical threadworm (strongyloidiasis)
Occurs in the tropics and southern Europe. Larvae from contaminated soil penetrate skin, pass into the lungs, and are swallowed into the gut.
Drugs Albendazole, ivermectin*

Whipworm (trichuriasis)
Mainly occurs in tropical areas as a result of eating contaminated raw vegetables. Worms infest the intestines.
Drug Mebendazole

Hookworm (uncinariasis)
Mainly found in tropical areas. Worm larvae penetrate skin and pass via the lymphatic system and bloodstream to the lungs. They then travel up the airways, are swallowed, and attach themselves to the intestinal wall, where they feed off the intestinal blood supply.
Drug Mebendazole

Pork roundworm (trichinosis)
Transmitted in infected undercooked pork. Initially worms lodge in the intestines, but larvae may invade muscle to form cysts that are often resistant to drug treatment and may require surgery.
Drug Mebendazole

Toxocariasis (visceral larva migrans)
Usually occurs as a result of eating soil or eating with fingers contaminated with dog or cat feces. Eggs hatch in the intestine and may travel to the lungs, liver, kidney, brain, and eyes. Treatment is not always effective.
Drug Mebendazole

Creeping eruption (cutaneous larva migrans)
Mainly occurs in tropical areas and coastal areas of southeastern United States as a result of skin contact with larvae from cat and dog feces. Infestation is usually confined to the skin.
Drug Ivermectin*

Filariasis (including onchocerciasis and loiasis)
Tropical areas only. Infection by this group of worms is spread by bites of insects that are carriers of worm larvae or eggs. May affect the lymphatic system, blood, eyes, and skin.
Drug Ivermectin*

Flukes
Sheep liver fluke (fascioliasis) is indigenous to the United Kingdom. Infestation usually results from eating watercress grown in contaminated water. Mainly affects the liver and biliary tract. Flukes found in other countries may infect the lungs, intestines, or blood.
Drug Praziquantel

Tapeworms (including beef, pork, fish, and dwarf tapeworms)
Depending on the type may be carried by cattle, pigs, or fish and transmitted to humans in undercooked meat. Most types affect the intestines. Larvae of the pork tapeworm may form cysts in muscle and other tissues.
Drug Praziquantel

Hydatid disease (echinococciasis)
Eggs are transmitted in dog faeces. Larvae may form cysts over many years, commonly in the liver. Surgery is the usual treatment for cysts.
Drug Albendazole*

Bilharzia (schistosomiasis)
Occurs in polluted water in tropical areas. Larvae may be swallowed or penetrate the skin; they migrate to the liver: adult worms live in the bladder.
Drug Praziquantel

✳ Some drugs are obtained through special access only; check with your physician.

HORMONES AND ENDOCRINE SYSTEM

The endocrine system is a collection of glands located throughout the body that produce *hormones* and release them into the bloodstream. Each endocrine gland produces one or more hormones, each of which governs a particular body function, including growth and repair of tissues, sexual development and reproductive function, and the body's response to stress.

Most hormones are released continuously from birth, but the amount produced fluctuates with the body's needs. Others are produced mainly at certain times – for example, growth hormone is released mainly during childhood and adolescence. Sex hormones are produced by the testes and ovaries from puberty onwards (see p.146).

Many endocrine glands release their hormones in response to triggering hormones produced by the pituitary gland. The pituitary gland releases a variety of pituitary hormones, each of which, in turn, stimulates the appropriate endocrine gland to produce its hormone.

A "feedback" system usually regulates blood hormone levels: if the blood level rises too high, the pituitary gland responds by reducing the amount of stimulating hormone produced, thereby allowing the blood hormone level to return to normal.

What can go wrong

Endocrine disorders, usually resulting in too much or too little of a particular hormone, have a variety of causes. Some are congenital in origin; others may be caused by autoimmune disease (including some forms of diabetes mellitus), malignant or benign tumours, injury, or certain drugs.

Why drugs are used

Natural hormone preparations or their synthetic versions are often prescribed to treat deficiency. Sometimes drugs are given to stimulate increased hormone production in the endocrine gland, such as oral antidiabetic drugs, which act on the insulin-producing cells of the pancreas. When too much hormone is produced, drug treatment may reduce the activity of the gland.

Hormones or related drugs are also used to treat certain other conditions. Corticosteroids related to adrenal hormones are prescribed to relieve inflammation and to suppress immune system activity (see p.143). Several types of cancer are treated with sex hormones (see p.140). Female sex hormones are used as contraceptives (see p.149) and to treat menstrual disorders (see p.148).

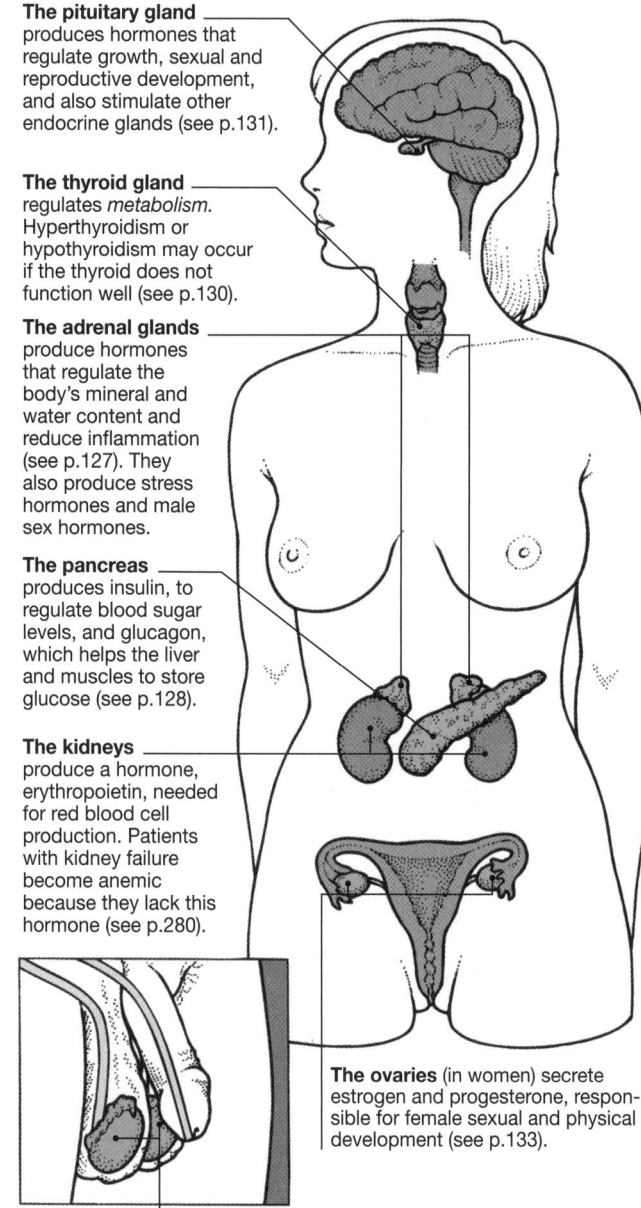

The pituitary gland produces hormones that regulate growth, sexual and reproductive development, and also stimulate other endocrine glands (see p.131).

The thyroid gland regulates *metabolism.* Hyperthyroidism or hypothyroidism may occur if the thyroid does not function well (see p.130).

The adrenal glands produce hormones that regulate the body's mineral and water content and reduce inflammation (see p.127). They also produce stress hormones and male sex hormones.

The pancreas produces insulin, to regulate blood sugar levels, and glucagon, which helps the liver and muscles to store glucose (see p.128).

The kidneys produce a hormone, erythropoietin, needed for red blood cell production. Patients with kidney failure become anemic because they lack this hormone (see p.280).

The ovaries (in women) secrete estrogen and progesterone, responsible for female sexual and physical development (see p.133).

The testes (in men) produce testosterone, which controls the development of male sexual and physical characteristics (see p.132).

MAJOR DRUG GROUPS

Corticosteroids
Drugs used in diabetes
Drugs for thyroid disorders
Drugs for pituitary disorders
Male sex hormones
Female sex hormones

CORTICOSTEROIDS

Corticosteroid drugs – often referred to simply as steroids – are derived from, or are synthetic variants of, the natural corticosteroid *hormones* formed in the outer part (cortex) of the adrenal glands, situated on top of each kidney. Release of these hormones is governed by the pituitary gland (see p.131).

Corticosteroids may have either mainly glucocorticoid or mainly mineralocorticoid effects. Glucocorticoid effects include the maintenance of normal levels of sugar in the blood and the promotion of recovery from injury and stress. Main mineralocorticoid effects are the regulation of the balance of mineral salts and the water content of the body. When present in large amounts, they reduce inflammation and suppress allergic reactions and immune system activity. They are distinct from another group of steroid hormones, the anabolic steroids (see p.132). Although corticosteroids have broadly similar actions to each other, they vary in their relative strength and duration of action. The mineralocorticoid effects of these drugs also vary in strength.

ADVERSE EFFECTS OF CORTICOSTEROIDS

Corticosteroids are effective and useful drugs that often provide benefit in cases where other drugs are ineffective. However, long-term use of high doses can lead to a variety of unwanted effects on the body, as shown below.

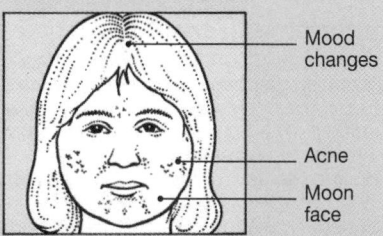

Mood changes

Acne

Moon face

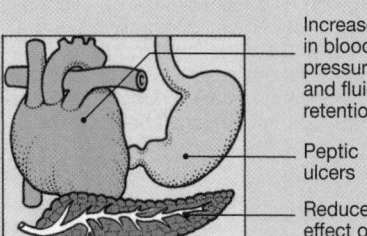

Increase in blood pressure and fluid retention

Peptic ulcers

Reduced effect of insulin

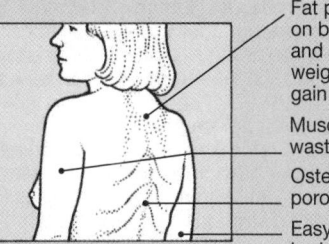

Fat pad on back and weight gain

Muscle wasting

Osteo-porosis

Easy bruising

Why they are used

Corticosteroid drugs are used primarily for their effect in controlling inflammation, whatever its cause. Topical preparations containing corticosteroids are often used for the treatment of many inflammatory skin disorders (see p.162). These drugs may also be injected directly into a joint or around a tendon to relieve inflammation caused by injury or disease (see p.104). However, when local administration of the drug is either not possible or not effective, corticosteroids may be given systemically, either by mouth or by intravenous injection.

Corticosteroids are commonly part of the treatment of many disorders in which inflammation is thought to be caused by excessive or inappropriate activity of the immune system. These disorders include inflammatory bowel disease (p.98), rheumatoid arthritis (p.103), glomerulonephritis (a kidney disease), and some rare connective tissue disorders, such as systemic lupus erythematosus. In these conditions corticosteroids relieve symptoms and may also temporarily halt the disease.

Corticosteroids may be given regularly by mouth or inhaler to treat asthma, although they are not effective for the immediate relief of asthma attacks in progress (see Bronchodilators, p.76 and Drugs for asthma, p.78).

An important use of oral corticosteroids is to replace the natural hormones that are deficient when adrenal gland function is reduced, as in Addison's disease. In these cases, the drugs most closely resembling the actions of the natural hormones are selected and a combination of these may be used.

Some cancers of the lymphatic system (lymphomas) and the blood (leukemias) may also respond to corticosteroid treatment. These drugs are also widely used to prevent or treat rejection of organ transplants, usually in conjunction with other drugs, such as azathioprine (see Immunosuppressants, p.143).

How they work

Given in high doses, corticosteroid drugs reduce inflammation by blocking the action of chemicals such as prostaglandins that are responsible for triggering the inflammatory response. These drugs also temporarily suppress the immune system by reducing the activity of certain types of white blood cells.

How they affect you

Corticosteroid drugs often produce a dramatic improvement in symptoms. Given systemically, corticosteroids may also act on the brain to produce a heightened sense of well-being and, in some people, a sense of euphoria. Troublesome day-to-day side effects are rare. Long-term corticosteroid treatment, however, carries a number of serious risks for the patient.

Risks and special precautions

In the treatment of Addison's disease, corticosteroids can be considered as "hormone replacement therapy", with drugs replacing the natural hormone hydrocortisone. Because replacement doses are given, the adverse effects of high-dose corticosteroids do not occur.

Drugs with strong mineralocorticoid effects, such as fludrocortisone, may cause water retention, swelling (especially of the ankles), and an increase in blood pressure. Because corticosteroids reduce the effect of insulin, they may create problems in diabetics, and may even give rise to diabetes in susceptible individuals. They also increase the risk of peptic ulcers, especially when given concurrently with non-steroidal anti-inflammatory drugs (NSAIDs).

Because corticosteroids suppress the immune system, they increase susceptibility to infection. They also suppress symptoms of infectious disease. People who are taking corticosteroids should avoid exposure to chickenpox or shingles, but if they catch either disease, acyclovir or valacyclovir tablets may be prescribed. With long-term use, corticosteroids may cause a variety of adverse effects (see left). Physicians try to avoid long-term use of corticosteroids to children because prolonged use may retard growth.

Long-term use of corticosteroids suppresses the production of the body's own corticosteroid hormones. For this reason, treatment that lasts for more than a few weeks should be withdrawn gradually to give the body time to adjust. If the drug is stopped abruptly, the lack of corticosteroid hormones may lead to sudden collapse.

People taking corticosteroids by mouth for longer than one month are advised to carry a warning card. If someone who is taking steroids long-term has an accident or serious illness, his or her defences against shock may need to be quickly strengthened with extra hydrocortisone, administered intravenously.

COMMON DRUGS

Beclomethasone *
Betamethasone *
Budesonide *
Clobetasol *
Clobetasone
Cortisone
Desonide
Desoximetasone
Dexamethasone *
Diflucortolone
Fludrocortisone
Flumethasone

Flunisolide
Fluocinolone
Fluocinonide
Fluticasone *
Halcinonide
Halobetasol
Hydrocortisone *
Methyl-
    prednisolone *
Mometasone *
Prednisolone/
    prednisone *
Triamcinolone

* See Part 4

DRUGS USED IN DIABETES

The body obtains most of its energy from glucose, a simple form of sugar made in the intestine from the breakdown of starch and other sugars. Insulin, one of the hormones produced in the pancreas, enables body tissues to take up glucose from the blood, either to use it for energy or to store it. In diabetes mellitus, there is either a complete lack of insulin or too little is produced. This results in reduced uptake of glucose by the tissues and thus the glucose level in the blood rises abnormally. A high blood glucose level is medically known as hyperglycemia.

There are two main types of diabetes mellitus. Type 1 diabetes usually appears in young people, 50 per cent of cases occurring around the time of puberty. The insulin-secreting cells in the pancreas are gradually destroyed. An autoimmune condition (where the body recognizes its pancreas as "foreign" and tries to eliminate it) or a childhood viral infection is the most likely cause. Although the decline in insulin production is slow, the condition often appears suddenly, brought on by periods of stress (for example, infection or puberty) when the body's insulin requirements are high. Symptoms of Type 1 diabetes include extreme thirst, increased urination, lethargy, and weight loss. This type of diabetes is fatal if it is left untreated.

In Type 1 diabetes, insulin treatment is the only treatment option. It has to be continued for life. Several types of insulin are available, which are broadly classified by their duration of action (short-, medium-, and long-acting).

Type 2 or maturity-onset diabetes tends to appear at an older age (usually over 40, although it has become increasingly common in younger age groups) and tends to come on much more gradually – there may be a delay in its diagnosis for several years because of the gradual onset of symptoms. In this type of diabetes, the levels of insulin in the blood are usually high initially. However, the cells of the body are resistant to the effects of insulin and have a reduced glucose uptake despite the high insulin levels. This

ADMINISTRATION OF INSULIN

The non-diabetic body produces a background level of insulin, with additional insulin being produced as required during meals. The insulin delivery systems that are currently available cannot mimic this precisely. In people with Type 1 diabetes, short-acting insulin is usually given before meals, and a medium-acting insulin is given either before the evening meal or at bedtime. Insulin pen injectors are particularly useful for administration during the day because

they are discreet and easy to carry and use. In patients with Type 2 diabetes who require insulin, a mixture of short- and medium-acting insulin may be given twice a day. Special pumps that deliver continuous subcutaneous insulin appear to have no advantage over multiple subcutaneous injections. Some new types of insulins called insulin analogues (e.g. Insulin lispro) may be better at mimicking the insulin-producing behaviour of the normal pancreas.

Duration of action of types of insulin

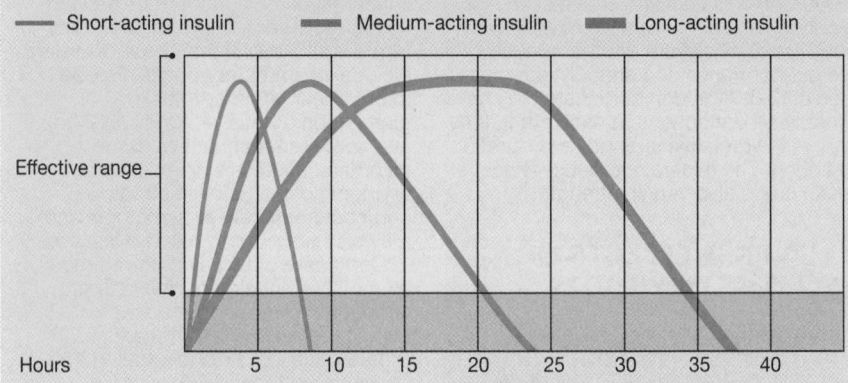

— Short-acting insulin ■ Medium-acting insulin ■ Long-acting insulin

Effective range

Hours · 5 · 10 · 15 · 20 · 25 · 30 · 35 · 40

results in hyperglycemia. Obesity is the most common cause of Type 2 diabetes.

In both types of diabetes, an alteration in diet is vital. A healthy diet consisting of a low-fat, high-fibre, low simple sugar (cakes, sweets), and high complex sugar (pasta, rice, potatoes) intake is advised. In Type 2 diabetes, a reduction in weight alone may be sufficient to lower the body's energy requirements and restore blood glucose to normal levels. If an alteration in diet fails, oral antidiabetic drugs, such as metformin, acarbose, or sulfonylureas, are prescribed. Insulin may need to be given to people with Type 2 diabetes if the above treatments fail, or in pregnancy, during severe illness,

and before the patient undergoes any surgery requiring a general anesthetic.

Importance of treating diabetes

If diabetes is left untreated, the continuous high blood glucose levels damage various parts of the body. The major problems are caused by the build-up of atherosclerosis in arteries, which narrows the vessels, reducing the flow of blood. This can result in heart attacks, blindness, kidney failure, reduced circulation in the legs, and even gangrene. The risk of these conditions is greatly reduced with treatment. Careful control of diabetes in young people, during puberty and afterwards, is of great importance in reducing possible long-term complications. Good diabetic control before conception reduces the chance of miscarriage or abnormalities in the baby.

How antidiabetic drugs work

Insulin treatment directly replaces the natural hormone that is deficient in diabetes mellitus. Human and pork insulins are the most widely available. When transferring between animal and human insulin, alteration of the dose may be required.

Insulin cannot be given by mouth because it is broken down in the digestive tract before it reaches the bloodstream. Regular injections are therefore necessary (see Administration of insulin, above). Sulfonylurea oral antidiabetic drugs encourage the pancreas to produce insulin.

ACTION OF SULFONYLUREA DRUGS

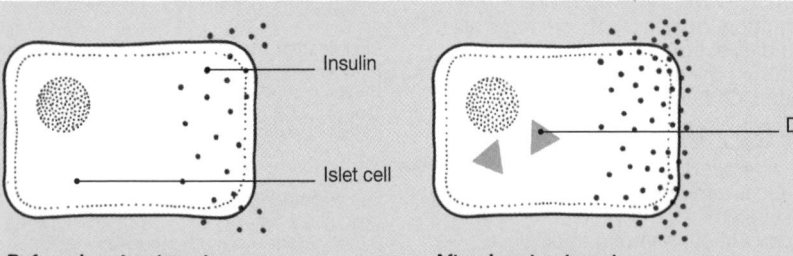

Before drug treatment
In Type 2 diabetes, the islet cells of the pancreas secrete insufficient insulin to meet the body's needs.

After drug treatment
The drug stimulates the islet cells to release increased amounts of insulin.

They are effective only when some insulin-secreting cells remain active, and this is why they are ineffective in the treatment of Type 1 diabetes. Metformin alters the way in which the body *metabolizes* sugar. Acarbose slows digestion of starch and sugar. Both slow the increase in blood sugar that occurs after a meal. Nateglinide and repaglinide stimulate insulin release. Pioglitazone reduces the body's resistance to insulin. Exenatide and sitagliptin stimulate insulin release and block the release of glucagon (a substance that raises blood glucose), thereby helping to prevent the rise in blood sugar after a meal.

Insulin treatment and you

The insulin requirements in diabetes vary greatly between individuals and also depend on physical activity and calorie intake. Hence, insulin regimens are tailored to particular needs, and the diabetic is encouraged to take an active role in his or her own management.

A regular record of home blood glucose monitoring should be kept. This is the basis on which insulin doses are adjusted, preferably by diabetics themselves.

A person with diabetes should learn to recognize the warning signs of hypoglycemia or low blood sugar. A hypoglycemic event may be induced by giving insulin under medical supervision. The symptoms of sweating, faintness, or palpitations are produced but disappear with the administration of glucose, so a diabetic should always carry glucose tablets or sweets. Recurrent "hypos" at specific times of the day or night may require a reduction of insulin dose. Rarely, undetected low glucose levels may lead

to coma. The injection of glucagon rapidly reverses this. A relative may be instructed how to perform this procedure.

Repeated injection at the same site may disturb the fat layer beneath the skin, producing either swelling or dimpling. This alters the rate of insulin absorption and can be avoided by regularly rotating injection sites.

Insulin requirements are increased during illness and pregnancy. During an illness, the urine should be checked for ketones, which are produced when there is insufficient insulin to permit the normal uptake of glucose by the tissues. If high ketone levels occur in a diabetic's urine during an illness, urgent medical advice should be sought. The combination of high blood sugars, high urinary ketones, and vomiting is a diabetic emergency and the person should be taken to an Emergency department without delay.

Exercise increases the body's need for glucose, and therefore extra calories may be needed before and during exertion. The effects of vigorous exercise on blood sugar levels may last up to 18 hours, and the subsequent (post-exercise) doses of insulin may need to be reduced by 10–25 per cent to avoid hypoglycemia.

It is advisable for diabetics to carry a card or bracelet detailing their condition and treatment. This may be useful in a medical emergency.

Antidiabetic drugs and you

The sulfonylureas may lower the blood glucose too much, causing a condition called hypoglycemia. This condition can be avoided by starting treatment with low doses of these drugs and ensuring that

SITES OF INJECTION

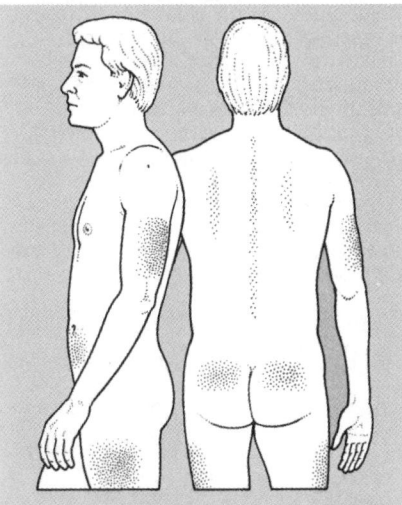

The shaded areas indicate suitable sites for the injection of insulin.

food intake is regular. Rarely, these drugs cause a decrease in the blood cell count, a rash, or intestinal or liver disturbances. Interactions may occur with other drugs, so your physician should be informed of your treatment before prescribing any medicines for you.

Unlike the sulfonylureas, metformin does not cause hypoglycemia. Its most common side effects are nausea, weight loss, abdominal distension, and diarrhea. Metformin should not be used in people with liver, kidney, or heart problems. Acarbose does not cause hypoglycemia if used on its own. However, the tablets must be taken with the first mouthful of food at mealtimes. Sitagliptin is taken orally once a day, either with or without food. Exenatide, used mainly in obese patients, is given by injection twice a day before meals.

MONITORING BLOOD GLUCOSE

Diabetics need to check either their blood or urine glucose level at home. Blood tests give the most accurate results and are usually recommended.

There are a variety of devices that can measure blood glucose to help monitor diabetes. These meters, called glucometers, measure the blood sugar level in a drop of blood obtained from a finger prick.

Glucometers can be purchased at most pharmacies. If you have diabetes, ask your diabetes educator, physician, or pharmacist which meter would be best for you. You should also ask for training on how to use the chosen meter properly. Your physician may be able to recommend a Diabetes Education Centre, which can provide support and training.

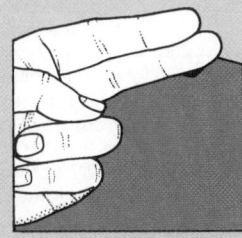

1 Prick your finger to give a large drop of blood.

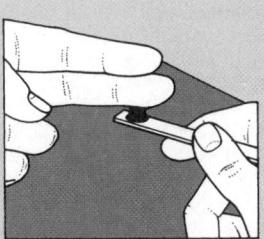

2 Touch the blood on to the test pads of the testing strip.

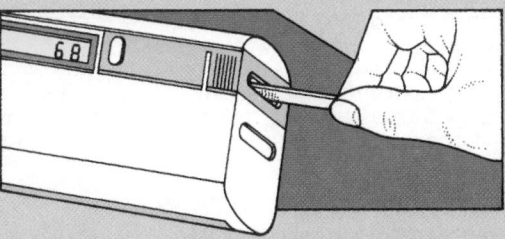

3 Insert the strip into the meter. Your reading (e.g. 6.8) will appear as a digital readout.

COMMON DRUGS

Sulfonylurea drugs	Insulins cont.
Chlorpropamide	Lente (pork)
Gliclazide ✻	Lispro
Glimepiride ✻	NPH (human
Glyburide ✻	biosynthetic,
Tolbutamide	pork)
	Regular (human
Antiobesity agent	biosynthetic)
Orlistat ✻	Liraglutide ✻
	Metformin ✻
Other drugs	Nateglinide
Acarbose ✻	Pioglitazone ✻
Exenatide ✻	Repaglinide ✻
Glucagon	Rosiglitazone ✻
Insulins ✻	Sitagliptin
Aspart	phosphate ✻
Detemir	
Glargine	

✻ See Part 4

DRUGS FOR THYROID DISORDERS

The thyroid gland produces the *hormone* thyroxine, which regulates the body's *metabolism*. During childhood, thyroxine is essential for normal physical and mental development. Calcitonin, also produced by the thyroid, regulates calcium metabolism and is used as a drug for certain bone disorders (p.108).

Hyperthyroidism

In this condition (often called thyrotoxicosis), the thyroid is overactive and produces too much thyroxine. Women are more commonly affected than men.

ACTION OF DRUGS FOR THYROID DISORDERS

Thyroid hormone production
Iodine combines with other chemicals (precursors) in the thyroid gland to make thyroid hormones.

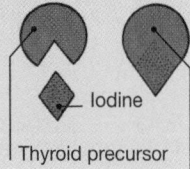

Iodine

Thyroid precursor

Thyroid hormone

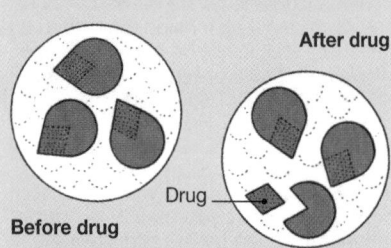

Thyroid hormone

Normal output of thyroid hormones
Thyroid output is normally regulated according to the body's needs.

After drug

Drug

Before drug

Action of antithyroid drugs
In hyperthyroidism, antithyroid drugs partly reduce the production of thyroid hormones by preventing iodine from combining with thyroid precursors in the thyroid gland.

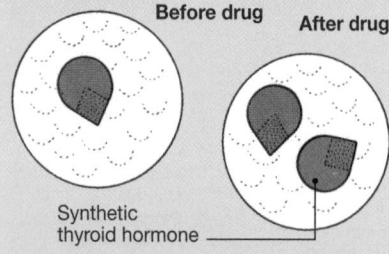

Before drug

After drug

Synthetic thyroid hormone

Action of thyroid hormones
In hypothyroidism, when the thyroid gland is underactive, supplements of synthetic or (rarely) natural thyroid hormones restore hormone levels to normal.

Symptoms include anxiety, palpitations, weight loss, increased appetite, heat intolerance, diarrhea, and menstrual disturbances. Graves' disease is the most common form of hyperthyroidism. It is an autoimmune disease in which the body produces antibodies that stimulate the thyroid to produce excess thyroxine. Patients with Graves' disease may develop abnormally protuberant eyes (exophthalmos) or a swelling involving the skin over the shins (pretibial myxedema). Hyperthyroidism can be caused by a benign single tumour of the thyroid (an adenoma) or a pre-existing multinodular goitre. Rarely, an overactive thyroid may follow a viral infection, a condition called thyroiditis. Inflammation of the gland leads to the release of stored thyroxine.

Management of hyperthyroidism

There are three possible treatments for hyperthyroidism: antithyroid drugs, radioactive iodine, and surgery. The most commonly used antithyroid drug is methimazole. This drug inhibits the formation of thyroid hormones and reduces their levels to normal over a period of about 4–8 weeks. In the early stage of treatment, a beta blocker (p.83) may be prescribed to control symptoms. This should be stopped once thyroid function returns to normal. Long-term methimazole is usually given for 12–18 months to prevent relapse. A "block and replace" regimen may also be used. In this treatment, the thyroid gland is blocked by high doses of methimazole and thyroxine is added when the level of thyroid hormone in the blood falls below normal.

Methimazole may produce minor side effects such as nausea, vomiting, skin rashes, or headaches. Rarely, the drug may reduce the white blood cell count. Propylthiouracil may be used as an alternative antithyroid drug.

Radioactive iodine is frequently chosen as a first-line therapy, especially in the elderly, and is the second choice if hyperthyroidism recurs following use of methimazole. It acts by destroying thyroid tissue. Hypothyroidism occurs in up to 80 per cent of people within 20 years after treatment. Long-term studies show radioactive iodine to be safe, but its use should be avoided during pregnancy and breast-feeding, and in patients with thyroid eye disease.

Surgery is a third-line therapy. Its use may be favoured for patients with a large goitre, particularly if it causes difficulty in swallowing or breathing. Exophthalmos may require corticosteroids (p.127) as it does not respond to other treatments.

Hypothyroidism

This is a condition resulting from too little thyroxine. Sometimes it may be caused by an autoimmune disorder, in which the body's immune system attacks the

TREATMENT FOR GOITRE

A goitre is a swelling of the thyroid gland. It may occur only temporarily, during puberty or pregnancy, or it may be due to an abnormal growth of thyroid tissue that requires surgical removal. It may rarely be brought about by iodine deficiency. This last cause is treated with iodine supplements (see also p.473).

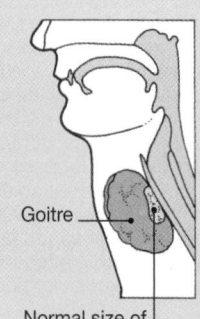

Goitre

Normal size of thyroid gland

thyroid gland. Other cases may follow treatment for hyperthyroidism. In newborn babies, hypothyroidism may be the result of an inborn *enzyme* disorder. In the past, it also arose from a deficiency of iodine in the diet.

The symptoms of adult hypothyroidism develop slowly and include weight gain, mental slowness, dry skin, hair loss, increased sensitivity to cold, and heavy menstrual periods. In babies, low levels of thyroxine cause permanent mental and physical retardation and, for this reason, babies are tested for hypothyroidism within a week of birth.

Management of hypothyroidism

Lifelong oral treatment with synthetic thyroid hormones (thyroxine (levothyroxine), or liothyronine) is the only option. Blood tests are performed regularly to monitor the treatment and permit dosage adjustments. In the elderly, as well as people with heart disease, gradual introduction of thyroxine is used to prevent heart strain.

In severely ill patients, thyroid hormone may be given by injection. This method of administration may also be used to treat newborn infants with low levels of thyroxine.

Symptoms of thyrotoxicosis may appear if excess thyroxine replacement is given. Otherwise, no adverse events occur since treatment is adjusted to replace the natural hormone that the body should produce itself.

COMMON DRUGS

Drugs for hypothyroidism
Liothyronine
Levothyroxine
  (thyroxine) ✳

Drugs for hyperthyroidism
Iodine ✳
Methimazole
Metopolol ✳
Propranolol ✳
Propylthiouracil
Radioactive iodine

✳ See Part 4

DRUGS FOR PITUITARY DISORDERS

The pituitary gland, which lies at the base of the brain, produces a number of *hormones* that regulate physical growth, *metabolism*, sexual development, and reproductive function. Many of these hormones act indirectly by stimulating other glands, such as the thyroid, adrenal glands, ovaries, and testes, to release their own hormones. A summary of the actions and effects of each pituitary hormone is given below.

An excess or a lack of one of the pituitary hormones may produce serious effects, the nature of which depends on the hormone involved. Abnormal levels of a particular hormone may be caused by a pituitary tumour, which may be treated surgically, with radiotherapy, or with drugs. In other cases, drugs may be used to correct the hormonal imbalance.

The more common pituitary disorders that can be treated with drugs are those involving growth hormone, antidiuretic hormone, prolactin, adrenal hormones, and the gonadotrophins. The first three are discussed below. For information on the use of drugs to treat infertility arising from inadequate levels of gonadotrophins, see p.152. Lack of corticotrophin, leading to inadequate production of adrenal hormones, is usually treated with corticosteroids (see p.127).

Drugs for growth hormone disorders
Growth hormone (somatotropin) is the principal hormone required for normal growth in childhood and adolescence.

Lack of growth hormone impairs normal physical growth. Physicians administer hormone treatment only after tests have proven that a lack of this hormone is the cause of the disorder. If treatment is started at an early age, regular injections of somatropin, a synthetic form of natural growth hormone, administered until the end of adolescence usually allow normal growth and development to take place.

Growth hormone deficiency in adults is rare but may cause loss of strength and stamina, reduced bone mass, weight gain, and psychological symptoms such as poor memory and depression. In some cases it may be treated with somatropin.

Less often, the pituitary produces an excess of growth hormone. In children this can result in pituitary gigantism; in adults, it can produce a disorder known as acromegaly. This disorder, which is usually the result of a pituitary tumour, is characterized by thickening of the skull, face, hands, and feet, and enlargement of some internal organs.

The pituitary tumour may either be surgically removed or destroyed by radiotherapy. In the frail or elderly, drugs such as bromocriptine and octreotide are used to reduce growth hormone levels. Octreotide is also used as an adjunctive treatment before surgery and in those with increased growth hormone levels occurring after surgery. People who have undergone surgery and/or radiotherapy may require long-term replacement with other hormones (such as sex hormones, thyroid hormone, or corticosteroids).

Drugs for diabetes insipidus
Antidiuretic hormone (also known as ADH or vasopressin) acts on the kidneys, controlling the amount of water retained in the body and returned to the blood. A lack of ADH is usually caused by damage to the pituitary, and this in turn causes diabetes insipidus. In this rare condition, the kidneys cannot retain water and large quantities pass into the urine. The chief symptoms of diabetes insipidus are constant thirst and the production of large volumes of urine.

Diabetes insipidus is treated with ADH or a related synthetic drug, desmopressin. These replace naturally produced ADH. Alternatively, a thiazide diuretic (such as chlorthalidone) may be prescribed for mild cases (see Diuretics, p.85). The usual effect of such drugs is to increase urine production, but in diabetes insipidus they have the opposite effect, reducing water loss from the body.

Drugs used to reduce prolactin levels
Prolactin, also called lactogenic hormone, is produced in both men and women. In women, prolactin controls the secretion of breast milk following childbirth. The function of this hormone in men is not understood, although it appears to be necessary for normal sperm production.

The disorders associated with prolactin are all concerned with overproduction. High levels of prolactin in women can cause lactation that is unassociated with pregnancy and birth (galactorrhea), lack of menstruation (amenorrhea), and infertility. If excessive amounts are produced in men, the result may be galactorrhea, erectile dysfunction, or infertility.

Some drugs, notably methyldopa, estrogen, and the phenothiazine antipsychotics, can raise the prolactin level in the blood. More often, however, the increased prolactin results from a pituitary tumour and is usually treated with bromocriptine or cabergoline. These drugs inhibit prolactin production.

THE EFFECTS OF PITUITARY HORMONES

The pituitary gland produces a large number of hormones, many of which control the activities of other glands. The illustration shows the principal sites of action of the major pituitary hormones.

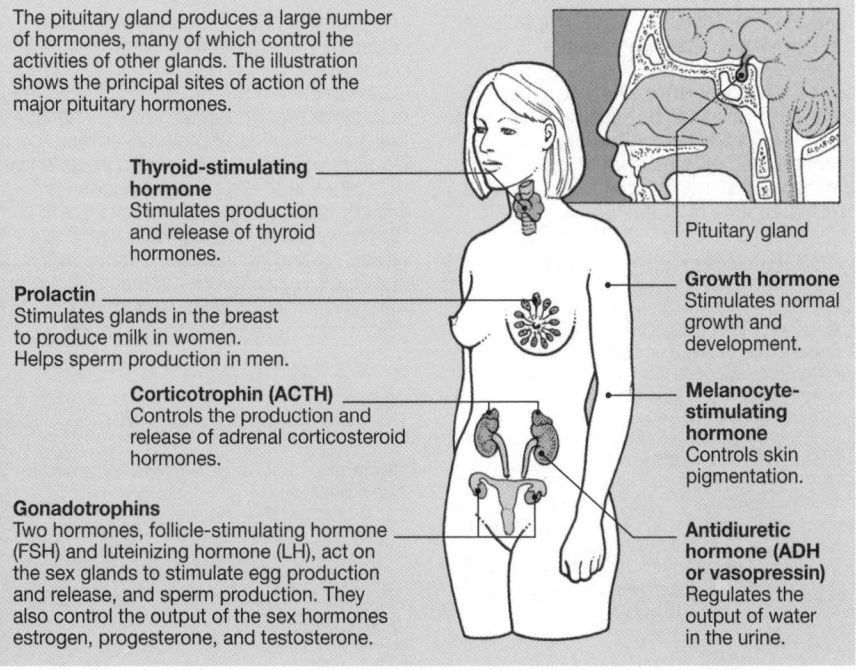

Thyroid-stimulating hormone Stimulates production and release of thyroid hormones.

Prolactin Stimulates glands in the breast to produce milk in women. Helps sperm production in men.

Corticotrophin (ACTH) Controls the production and release of adrenal corticosteroid hormones.

Gonadotrophins Two hormones, follicle-stimulating hormone (FSH) and luteinizing hormone (LH), act on the sex glands to stimulate egg production and release, and sperm production. They also control the output of the sex hormones estrogen, progesterone, and testosterone.

Pituitary gland

Growth hormone Stimulates normal growth and development.

Melanocyte-stimulating hormone Controls skin pigmentation.

Antidiuretic hormone (ADH or vasopressin) Regulates the output of water in the urine.

COMMON DRUGS

Drugs for growth hormone disorders
Bromocriptine
Octreotide
Somatostatin
Somatropin

Drugs for diabetes insipidus
Carbamazepine ✳
Chlorpropamide
Chlorthalidone
Desmopressin ✳
Vasopressin (ADH)

Drugs to reduce prolactin levels
Bromocriptine ✳
Cabergoline

✳ See Part 4

MALE SEX HORMONES

Male sex *hormones* – androgens – are responsible for the development of male sexual characteristics. The principal androgen is testosterone, which in men is produced by the testes from puberty onwards. Women produce testosterone in small amounts in the adrenal glands, but its exact function in the female body is not known.

Testosterone has two major effects: an androgenic effect and an anabolic effect. Its androgenic effect is to stimulate the appearance of the secondary sexual characteristics at puberty, such as the growth of body hair, deepening of the voice, and an increase in genital size. Its anabolic effects are to increase muscle bulk and accelerate growth rate.

There are a number of synthetically produced derivatives of testosterone that produce varying degrees of the androgenic and anabolic effects mentioned above. Derivatives that have a mainly anabolic effect are known as anabolic steroids (see box below).

Testosterone and its derivatives have been used under medical supervision in both men and women to treat a number of conditions.

Why they are used
Male sex hormones are mainly given to men to promote the development of male sexual characteristics when hormone production is deficient. This may be the result of an abnormality of the testes or of inadequate production of the pituitary hormones that stimulate the testes to release testosterone.

A course of treatment with male sex hormones is sometimes prescribed for adolescent boys in whom the onset of puberty is delayed by pituitary problems. The treatment may also help to stimulate development of secondary male sexual characteristics and to increase sex drive (libido) in adult men who are producing inadequate testosterone levels. However, this type of hormone treatment has been found to reduce the production of sperm. (For information on the drug treatment of male infertility, see p.152.)

EFFECTS OF MALE SEX HORMONES

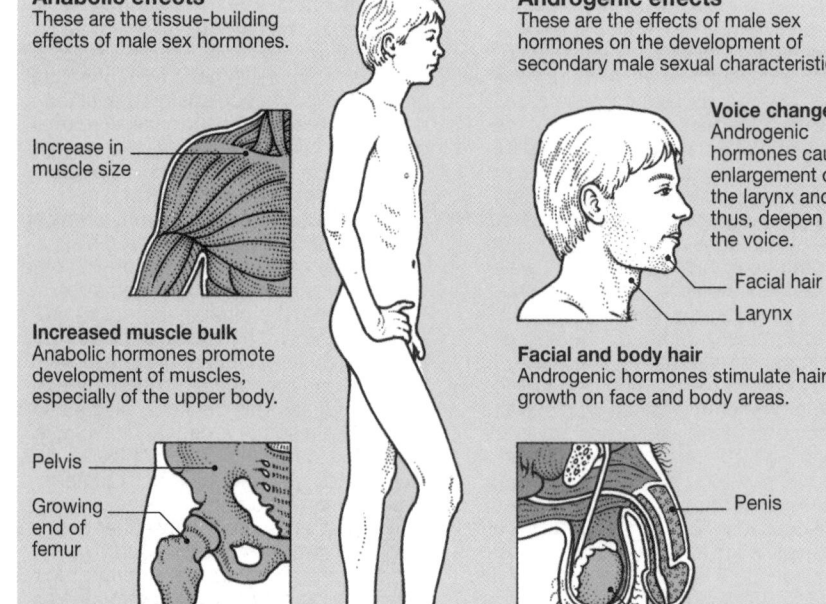

Anabolic effects
These are the tissue-building effects of male sex hormones.

Increase in muscle size

Increased muscle bulk
Anabolic hormones promote development of muscles, especially of the upper body.

Pelvis

Growing end of femur

Bone growth
Anabolic hormones increase bone density. They also halt growth of the bone ends.

Androgenic effects
These are the effects of male sex hormones on the development of secondary male sexual characteristics.

Voice changes
Androgenic hormones cause enlargement of the larynx and, thus, deepen the voice.

Facial hair

Larynx

Facial and body hair
Androgenic hormones stimulate hair growth on face and body areas.

Penis

Testis

Genital development
Androgenic hormones stimulate enlargement of the testes and penis.

Androgens may also be prescribed for women to treat certain types of cancer of the breast and uterus (see Anticancer drugs, p.140). Testosterone can be given by injection, *gel*, or patches.

How they work
Taken in low doses as part of replacement therapy when natural production is low, male sex hormones act in the same way as the natural hormones. In adolescents suffering from delayed puberty, hormone treatment produces both androgenic and anabolic effects (above), initiating the development of secondary sexual characteristics over a few months; full

sexual development usually takes place over three to four years. When sex hormones are given to adult men, the effects on physical appearance and libido may begin to be felt within a few weeks.

Risks and special precautions
The main risks with these drugs occur when they are given to boys with delayed puberty and to women with breast cancer. Given to initiate the onset of puberty, they may stunt growth by prematurely sealing the growing ends of the long bones. Doctors normally try to avoid prescribing hormones in these circumstances until growth is complete. High doses given to women have various masculinizing effects, including increased facial and body hair, and a deeper voice. The drugs may also produce enlargement of the clitoris, changes in libido, and acne.

ANABOLIC STEROIDS

Anabolic steroids are synthetically produced variants that mimic the anabolic effects of the natural hormones. They increase muscle bulk and body growth.

Doctors occasionally prescribe anabolic steroids and a high-protein diet to promote recovery after serious illness or major surgery. The steroids may also help to increase the production of blood cells in some forms of anemia and to reduce itching in chronic obstructive jaundice.

Anabolic steroids have been widely abused by athletes because these drugs speed up

the recovery of muscles after a session of intense exercise. This enables the athlete to go through a more demanding daily exercise programme, which results in a significant improvement in muscle power. The use of anabolic steroids by athletes to improve their performance is condemned by doctors and athletic organizations because of the risks to health, particularly for women. The side effects range from acne and baldness to fluid retention, reduced fertility in men and women, hardening of the arteries, a long-term risk of liver disease, and certain forms of cancer.

COMMON DRUGS

Primarily androgenic
Testosterone ✳

Primarily anabolic
Nandrolone

Anti-androgens
Cyproterone
Finasteride ✳

| ✳ See Part 4 |

FEMALE SEX HORMONES

There are two types of female sex hormones: estrogen and progesterone. In women, these hormones are secreted by the ovaries from puberty until the menopause. Each month, the levels of estrogen and progesterone fluctuate, producing the menstrual cycle (see p.148). During pregnancy, estrogen and progesterone are produced by the placenta. Production of estrogen and progesterone is regulated by the two gonadotrophin hormones (FSH and LH) produced by the pituitary gland (see p.131).

Estrogen is responsible for the development of female sexual characteristics, including breast development and widening of the pelvis. Progesterone prepares the lining of the uterus for implantation of a fertilized egg. This hormone is also important for the maintenance of pregnancy.

Synthetic forms of these hormones are used medically to treat a number of conditions and are known as estrogens and progestins.

Why they are used

The best-known use of estrogens and progestins is in oral contraceptives. These drugs are discussed on p.149. Other uses include the treatment of menstrual disorders (p.148) and certain hormone-sensitive cancers (p.140). This page discusses the drug treatments that are used for natural hormone deficiency.

Hormone deficiency

Deficiency of female sex hormones may occur as a result of deficiency of gonadotrophins caused by a pituitary disorder or by abnormal development of the ovaries (ovarian failure). This may lead to the absence of menstruation and lack of sexual development. If tests show a deficiency of gonadotrophins, preparations of these hormones may be prescribed (see p.152). These trigger the release of estrogen and progesterone from the ovaries. If pituitary function is normal and ovarian failure is diagnosed as the cause of hormone deficiency, estrogens and progestins may be given as supplements. In this situation, these supplements ensure development of normal female sexual characteristics but cannot stimulate ovulation.

Menopause

A decline in levels of estrogen and progesterone occurs naturally after the menopause, when the menstrual cycle ceases. The sudden reduction in levels of estrogen often causes distressing symptoms. Various options are available for the management of these, including hormone replacement therapy (HRT). Nonhormonal therapies such as venlafaxine, gabapentin, and clonidine may alleviate hot flashes associated with menopause. HRT can also delay some of the long-term consequences of reduced estrogen levels, such as osteoporosis (p.108). A balance between the benefits and risk for individual women must be considered, however, because there can be a slight increase in risk of breast cancer and thrombosis. It should be used with caution, especially in women with heart disease. It is used together with a progestin unless the woman has had a hysterectomy, in which case the estrogen alone is used. Some women with very severe symptoms respond poorly to oral drugs and may be helped by estrogen implants. When dryness of the vagina is a particular problem, a cream containing an estrogen drug may be prescribed. Hormone replacement therapy may also be prescribed for women who have undergone early or premature menopause, for example, as a result of surgical removal of the ovaries or radiotherapy for ovarian cancer.

How they affect you

Hormones given to treat ovarian failure or delayed puberty take three to six months to produce a noticeable effect on sexual development. Taken for menopausal symptoms, they can dramatically reduce the number of hot flushes within a week.

Both estrogens and progestins can cause fluid retention, and estrogens may also cause nausea, vomiting, breast tenderness, headache, dizziness, and depression. Progestins may cause breakthrough bleeding between menstrual periods. In the comparatively low doses used to treat these disorders, side effects are unlikely.

Risks and special precautions

The use of estrogens and progestins as replacement in ovarian failure carries few risks for otherwise healthy young women. Because estrogens increase the risk of hypertension (raised blood pressure), thrombosis (abnormal blood clotting), and breast cancer, there are risks associated with long-term HRT in older women. Treatment is prescribed with caution for women who have heart or circulatory disorders, and in those who are overweight or smoke. Your physician may order regular breast cancer checks. Estrogens may also trigger the onset of diabetes mellitus or aggravate blood sugar control in diabetic women.

EFFECTS OF HORMONE REPLACEMENT THERAPY (HRT)

Besides alleviating the symptoms of the menopause, such as hot flashes and vaginal dryness, HRT has a beneficial effect in preventing osteoporosis (p.108). Benefits must, however, be weighed against a slightly increased risk of breast cancer.

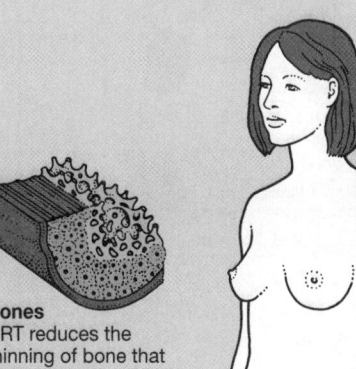

Bones
HRT reduces the thinning of bone that occurs in osteoporosis and thus protects against fractures.

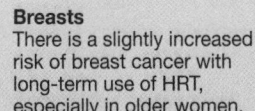

Breasts
There is a slightly increased risk of breast cancer with long-term use of HRT, especially in older women.

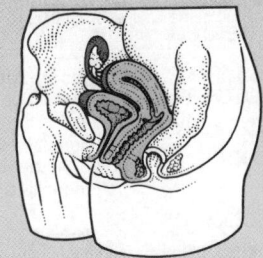

Reproductive organs
Thinning of the vaginal tissues leading to painful intercourse can be prevented by HRT.

COMMON DRUGS

Estrogens	Progestins
Conjugated estrogens *	Desogestrel
Ethinyl estradiol *	Drospirenone
Estrone	Levonorgestrel *
Estropipate	Medroxyprogesterone acetate *
	Megestrol acetate
	Norethindrone *
	Norgestimate
	Progesterone

| * See Part 4 |

NUTRITION

Food provides energy (as calories) and materials called nutrients needed for growth and renewal of tissues. Protein, carbohydrate, and fat are the three major nutrient components of food. Vitamins and minerals are found only in small amounts in food, but are just as important for normal function of the body. Fibre, found only in foods from plants, is needed for a healthy digestive system.

During digestion, large molecules of food are broken down into smaller molecules, releasing nutrients that are absorbed into the bloodstream. Carbohydrate and fat are then *metabolized* by body cells to produce energy. They may also be incorporated with protein into the cell structure. Each metabolic process is promoted by a specific *enzyme* and often requires the presence of a particular vitamin or mineral.

Why drugs are used

Dietary deficiency of essential nutrients can lead to illness. In poorer countries where there is a shortage of food, marasmus (resulting from lack of food energy) and kwashiorkor (from lack of protein) are common. In the developed world, however, excessive food intake leading to obesity is more common. Nutritional deficiencies in developed countries result from poor food choices and usually stem from a lack of a specific vitamin or mineral, such as in iron-deficiency anemia.

Some nutritional deficiencies may be caused by an inability of the body to absorb nutrients from food (malabsorption) or to utilize them once they have been absorbed. Malabsorption may be caused by lack of an enzyme or an abnormality of the digestive tract. Errors of metabolism are often inborn and are not yet fully understood. They may be caused by failure of the body to produce the chemicals required to process nutrients for use.

Why supplements are used

Deficiencies such as kwashiorkor or marasmus are usually treated by dietary improvement and, in some cases, food supplements, rather than drugs. Vitamin and mineral deficiencies are usually treated with appropriate supplements. Malabsorption disorders may require changes in diet or long-term use of supplements. Metabolic errors are not easily treated with supplements or drugs, and a special diet may be the main treatment.

The preferred treatment of obesity is reduction of food intake, altered eating patterns, and increased exercise. When these methods are not effective, and the *body mass index (BMI)* is 30 or more, an anti-obesity drug may be used.

Major food components

Proteins
Vital for tissue growth and repair. In meat and dairy products, cereals, and pulses. Moderate amounts required.

Carbohydrates
A major energy source, stored as fat when taken in excess. In cereals, sugar, and vegetables. Starchy foods preferable to sugar.

Fats
A concentrated energy form that is needed only in small quantities. In animal products such as butter and in plant oils.

Fibre (non-starch polysaccharides)
The indigestible part of any plant product that, although it contains no nutrients, adds bulk to feces.

Absorption of nutrients

Food passes through the mouth, esophagus, and stomach to the small intestine. The lining of the small intestine secretes many enzymes and is covered by tiny projections (villi) that enable nutrients to pass into the blood.

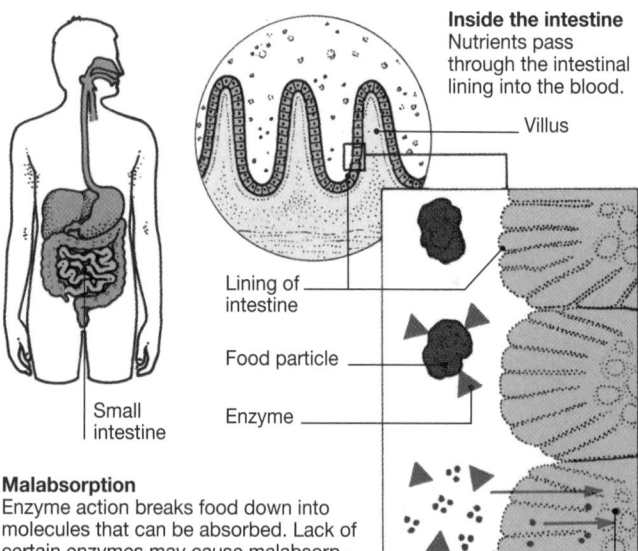

Inside the intestine
Nutrients pass through the intestinal lining into the blood.

Villus

Lining of intestine

Food particle

Enzyme

Small intestine

Food molecule absorbed

Malabsorption
Enzyme action breaks food down into molecules that can be absorbed. Lack of certain enzymes may cause malabsorption of nutrients. Other causes include flattened villi and scars on the intestine.

MAJOR DRUG GROUPS

Vitamins
Minerals

VITAMINS

Vitamins are complex chemicals that are essential for a variety of body functions. With the exception of vitamin D, the body cannot manufacture these substances itself and therefore we need to include them in our diet. There are 13 major vitamins: A, C, D, E, K, and the B complex vitamins – thiamine (B_1), riboflavin (B_2), niacin (B_3), pantothenic acid (B_5), pyridoxine (B_6), and cobalamin (B_{12}), folic acid, and biotin. Most vitamins are required in very small amounts and each vitamin is present in one or more foods (see Main food sources of vitamins, p.136). Vitamin D is also produced in the body when the skin is exposed to sunlight. Vitamins fall into two groups, depending on whether they dissolve in fat or water (see Fat-soluble and water-soluble vitamins, p.137).

A number of vitamins (such as vitamins A, C, and E) have now been recognized as having strong antioxidant properties. Antioxidants neutralize the effect of free radicals, substances produced during the body's normal processes that may be potentially harmful if they are not neutralized. Free radicals are believed to play a role in cardiovascular disease, aging, and cancer.

A balanced diet that includes a variety of different types of food is likely to contain adequate amounts of all the vitamins. Inadequate intake of any vitamin over an extended period can lead to symptoms of deficiency. The nature of these symptoms depends on the vitamin concerned.

A doctor may recommend taking supplements of one or more vitamins in a variety of circumstances: to prevent vitamin deficiency occurring in people who are considered at special risk, to treat symptoms of deficiency, and in the treatment of certain medical conditions.

Why they are used
Preventing deficiency
Most people in Canada obtain sufficient quantities of vitamins in their diet, and it is therefore not usually necessary to take additional vitamins in the form of supplements. People who are unsure if their present diet is adequate are advised to look at the table on p.136 to check that foods that are rich in vitamins are eaten regularly. Vitamin intake can often be boosted simply by increasing the quantities of fresh foods and raw fruit and vegetables in the diet. Certain groups in the population are, however, at increased risk of vitamin

deficiency. These include people who have an increased need for certain vitamins that may not be met from dietary sources – in particular, women who are pregnant or breast-feeding, and infants and young children. The elderly, who may not be eating a varied diet, may also be at risk. Strict vegetarians, vegans, and others on restricted diets may not receive adequate amounts of all vitamins.

In addition, people who suffer from disorders in which absorption of nutrients from the bowel is impaired, or who need to take drugs that reduce the absorption of vitamins (for example, some types of lipid-lowering drugs), are usually given additional vitamins.

In these cases, the physician is likely to advise supplements of one or more vitamins. Although most preparations are available without a prescription, it is important to seek specialist advice before starting a course of vitamin supplements, so that a proper assessment is made of your individual requirements.

Vitamin supplements should not be used as a general tonic to improve well-being – they are not effective for this purpose – nor should they ever be used as a substitute for a balanced diet.

PRIMARY FUNCTIONS OF VITAMINS

The role of vitamins in the body is not yet fully understood; much of our knowledge is based on the evidence that is provided by symptoms occurring as a result of deficiency of a particular vitamin. Most vitamins have been found to have a number of important actions on one or more body systems or functions. Many are involved in the activity of *enzymes* (substances that promote or enable biochemical reactions in the body). The illustration below indicates the organs and body systems on which each vitamin has its principal effect.

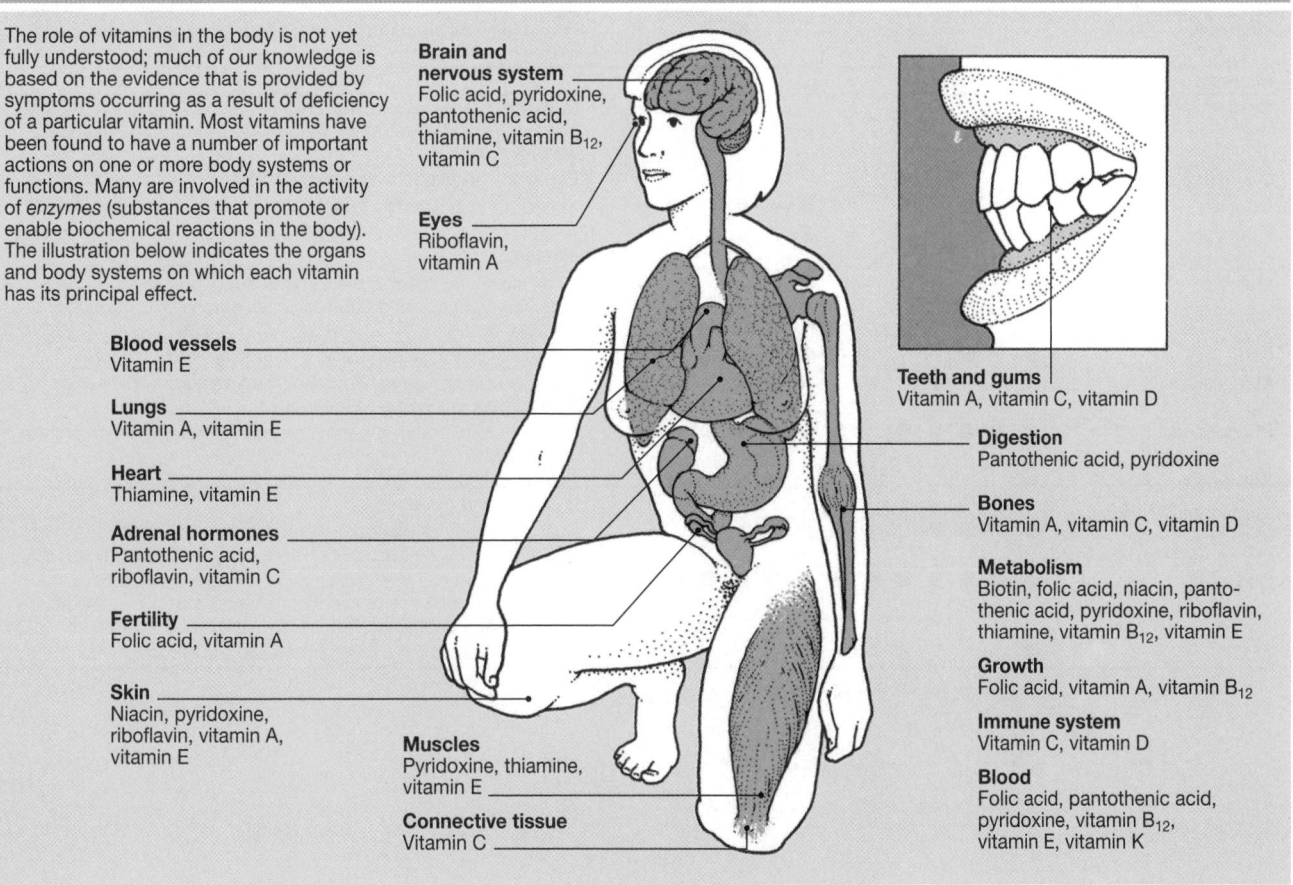

Brain and nervous system
Folic acid, pyridoxine, pantothenic acid, thiamine, vitamin B_{12}, vitamin C

Eyes
Riboflavin, vitamin A

Blood vessels
Vitamin E

Lungs
Vitamin A, vitamin E

Heart
Thiamine, vitamin E

Adrenal hormones
Pantothenic acid, riboflavin, vitamin C

Fertility
Folic acid, vitamin A

Skin
Niacin, pyridoxine, riboflavin, vitamin A, vitamin E

Muscles
Pyridoxine, thiamine, vitamin E

Connective tissue
Vitamin C

Teeth and gums
Vitamin A, vitamin C, vitamin D

Digestion
Pantothenic acid, pyridoxine

Bones
Vitamin A, vitamin C, vitamin D

Metabolism
Biotin, folic acid, niacin, pantothenic acid, pyridoxine, riboflavin, thiamine, vitamin B_{12}, vitamin E

Growth
Folic acid, vitamin A, vitamin B_{12}

Immune system
Vitamin C, vitamin D

Blood
Folic acid, pantothenic acid, pyridoxine, vitamin B_{12}, vitamin E, vitamin K

VITAMINS continued

MAIN FOOD SOURCES OF VITAMINS AND MINERALS

The table below indicates which foods are especially good sources of particular vitamins and minerals. Ensuring that you regularly select foods from a variety of categories helps to maintain adequate intake for most people, without a need for supplements. It is important to remember that processed and overcooked foods are likely to contain fewer vitamins than fresh, raw, or lightly cooked foods.

Vitamins	Red meat	Poultry	Liver	Milk	Cheese	Butter/margarine	Eggs	Fish	Cereals and bread	Green vegetables	Root vegetables	Pulses/legumes	Nuts	Fruit	Other	
Biotin			●				●					●	●			Especially peanuts. Cauliflower and mushrooms are good sources.
Folic acid			●				●			●					●	Wheat germ and mushrooms are rich sources.
Niacin as nicotinic acid	●	●	●					●	●			●	●			Protein-rich foods such as milk and eggs contain tryptophan, which can be converted to niacin in the body.
Pantothenic acid			●					●	●							Each food group contributes some pantothenic acid.
Pyridoxine	●	●	●				●	●	●							Especially white meat (poultry), fish, and wholegrain cereals.
Riboflavin		●	●	●	●		●		●			●	●	●		Found in most foods.
Thiamine	●		●				●					●	●			Brewer's yeast, wheat germ, and bran are also good sources.
Vitamin A		●	●	●	●	●	●			●	●				●	Fish liver oil, dark green leafy vegetables such as spinach, and orange or yellow-orange vegetables and fruits such as carrots, apricots, and peaches, are especially good sources of vitamin A.
Vitamin B_{12}	●		●	●	●		●	●								Obtained only from animal products, especially liver and red meat.
Vitamin C										●	●				●	Especially citrus fruits, tomatoes, potatoes, broccoli, strawberries, and melon.
Vitamin D				●		●	●	●								Fish liver oils, margarine, and milk are the best sources, but the vitamin is also produced when the skin is exposed to sunlight.
Vitamin E					●	●			●	●		●	●			Vegetable oils, wholegrain cereals, and wheat germ are the best sources.
Vitamin K									●	●						Found In small amounts in fruits, seeds, root vegetables, dairy and meat products.

Minerals	Red meat	Poultry	Liver	Milk	Cheese	Butter/margarine	Eggs	Fish	Cereals and bread	Green vegetables	Root vegetables	Pulses/legumes	Nuts	Fruit	Other	
Calcium				●	●				●		●	●				Dark green leafy vegetables, soya bean products, and nuts are good non-dairy alternatives. Also present in hard, or alkaline, water supplies.
Chromium	●			●					●	●						Especially unrefined wholegrain cereals.
Copper	●	●	●					●	●	●						Especially shellfish, wholegrain cereals, and mushrooms.
Fluoride								●								Primarily obtained from fluoridated water supplies. Also in seafood and tea.
Iodine				●	●			●	●							Provided by "iodized" table salt, but adequate amounts can be obtained without using table salt from dairy products, saltwater fish, and bread.
Iron	●	●	●				●	●	●	●						Especially liver, red meat, and enriched or whole grains.
Magnesium				●				●	●	●		●	●			Dark green leafy vegetables such as spinach are rich sources. Also present in alkaline water supplies.
Phosphorus	●	●	●	●	●		●	●	●	●	●	●	●	●		Common food additive. Large amounts found in some carbonated beverages.
Potassium									●	●		●			●	Best sources are fruits and vegetables, especially oranges, bananas, and potatoes.
Selenium	●		●	●				●	●							Seafood is the richest source. Amounts in most foods are variable, depending on soil where plants were grown and animals grazed.
Sodium	●	●	●	●	●	●	●	●	●	●	●	●	●		●	Sodium is present in all foods, especially table salt, processed foods, potato chips, crackers, and pickled, cured, or smoked meats, seafood, and vegetables. Also present in "softened" water.
Zinc	●			●				●	●			●				Highest amounts in wholegrain breads and cereals.

Vitamin deficiency

It is rare for a diet to be completely lacking in a particular vitamin. But if intake of a particular vitamin is regularly lower than the body's requirements, over a period of time the body's stores of vitamins may become depleted and symptoms of deficiency may begin to appear. In Canada, vitamin deficiency disorders are most common among malnourished individuals and alcoholics. Deficiencies of water-soluble vitamins are more likely since most of these are not stored in large quantities in the body. For descriptions of individual deficiency disorders, see the appropriate vitamin profile in Part 4.

Dosages of vitamins prescribed to treat vitamin deficiency are likely to be larger than those used to prevent deficiency. Medical supervision is required when correcting vitamin deficiency.

Other medical uses of vitamins

Various claims have been made for the value of vitamins in the treatment of medical disorders other than vitamin deficiency. High doses of vitamin C have been said to be effective in the prevention and treatment of the common cold, but such claims are not yet proved; zinc, however, may be helpful for this purpose. Vitamin and mineral supplements do not improve IQ in well-nourished children.

Certain vitamins have recognized medical uses apart from their nutritional role. Vitamin D has long been used to treat bone-wasting disorders (p.108). Niacin is sometimes used as a lipid-lowering drug (p.89). Derivatives of vitamin A (retinoids) are an established part of the treatment for severe acne (p.165). Many women who suffer from pre-menstrual syndrome take pyridoxine

MINERALS

Minerals are elements – the simplest form of substances – many of which are essential in trace amounts for normal metabolic processes. A balanced diet usually contains all of the minerals that the body requires; mineral deficiency diseases, except iron-deficiency *anemia*, are uncommon.

Dietary supplements are necessary only when a physician has diagnosed a specific deficiency or as part of the prevention or treatment of a medical disorder. Physicians often prescribe minerals for people with intestinal diseases that reduce the absorption of minerals from the diet. Iron supplements are often advised for pregnant or breast-feeding women, and iron-rich foods are recommended for infants over six months.

Much of the general advice given for vitamins also applies to minerals: taking supplements unless under medical direction is not advisable, exceeding the body's daily requirements is not beneficial, and large doses may be harmful.

CALCULATING DAILY VITAMIN REQUIREMENTS

Everyone needs a minimum amount of each vitamin for maintenance of health. The amount may vary with age, sex, and whether a woman is pregnant or breast-feeding. Guidelines for assessing the nutritional value of diets are called Recommended Daily Allowances (RDA), and are based on the amount of a nutrient that is enough, or more than enough, for 97 per cent of people. Those consuming much less than the RDA on a daily basis may not be consuming less than their needs but the risk of doing so is increased.

The current RDA (see table below) were set by Health Canada.

Daily reference nutrient intakes of vitamins for adults (aged 19–50)

Vitamin (unit)	Recommended Daily Allowance		
	Men	Women	Pregnancy and breast-feeding
Biotin (mcg)	30	30	30–35
Folic acid as folate (mcg)	400	400	500–600
Niacin (mg)	16	14	17–18
Pantothenic acid (mg)	5	5	6–7
Pyridoxine (mg)	1.3	1.3	1.9–2.0
Riboflavin (mg)	1.3	1.1	1.4–1.6
Thiamine (mg)	1.2	1.1	1.4
Vitamin A (mcg)	900	700	770–1300
Vitamin B_{12} (mcg)	2.4	2.4	2.6–2.8
Vitamin C (mg)	90	75	85–120
Vitamin D (mcg) *1	15	15	15
Vitamin E (mg)	15*	15*	15–19*

*as alpha-tocophenol   1 adequate intake

(vitamin B_6) supplements to relieve their symptoms. See also Drugs for menstrual disorders, p.148.

Risks and special precautions

Vitamins are essential for health, and supplements can be taken without risk by most people. It is important, however, not to exceed the recommended dosage, particularly in the case of fat-soluble vitamins, which may accumulate in the body. Dosage needs to be carefully calculated, taking into account the degree of deficiency, the dietary intake, and the duration of treatment. Overdosage has at best no therapeutic value and at worst it may incur the risk of serious harmful effects. Multivitamin preparations containing a large number of different vitamins are widely available. Fortunately, the amounts of each vitamin contained in each tablet are not usually large and are not likely to be harmful unless the dose is greatly exceeded. Single vitamin supplements can be harmful because an excess of one vitamin may increase requirements for others; hence, they should be used only on medical advice. For specific information on each vitamin, see Part 4, pp.468–482.

FAT-SOLUBLE AND WATER-SOLUBLE VITAMINS

Fat-soluble vitamins

Vitamins A, D, E, and K are absorbed from the intestine into the bloodstream together with fat (see also How drugs pass through the body, p.17). Deficiency of these vitamins may occur as a result of any disorder that affects the absorption of fat (for example, celiac disease). These vitamins are stored in the liver and reserves of some of them may last for several years. Taking an excess of a fat-soluble vitamin for a long period may cause it to build up to a harmful level in the body. Ensuring that foods rich in these vitamins are regularly included in the diet usually provides a sufficient supply without the risk of overdosage.

Water-soluble vitamins

Vitamin C and the B vitamins dissolve in water. Most are stored in the body for only a short period and are rapidly excreted by the kidneys if taken in higher amounts than the body requires. Vitamin B_{12} is the exception; it is stored in the liver, which may hold up to six years' supply. For these reasons, foods containing water-soluble vitamins need to be eaten daily. They are easily lost in cooking, so uncooked foods containing these vitamins should be regularly eaten. An overdose of water-soluble vitamins does not usually cause toxic effects, but *adverse reactions* to large dosages of vitamin C and pyridoxine (vitamin B_6) have been reported.

MALIGNANT AND IMMUNE DISEASE

New cells are continuously needed by the body to replace those that wear out and die naturally and to repair injured tissue. Normally the rate at which cells are created is carefully regulated. However, abnormal cells that multiply uncontrollably are sometimes formed. They may form lumps of abnormal tissue. These tumours are usually confined to one place and cause few problems; these are benign growths, such as warts. In other types of tumour the cells may invade or destroy the structures around it, and abnormal cells may spread to the rest of the body, forming metastatic tumours. These are malignant growths, also called cancers.

Opposing tumour growth is the body's immune system. This recognizes invading bacteria and viruses, and also transplanted tissue and cells that have become cancerous as foreign. The immune system relies on different types of white blood cells produced in the lymph glands and the bone marrow. They respond to foreign cells in a variety of ways, which are described on the facing page.

What can go wrong

A single cause for cancer has not been identified, and an individual's risk of developing cancer may depend upon both genetic predisposition and exposure to external risk factors, known as carcinogens. These include tobacco smoke, which increases the risk of lung cancer, and ultraviolet light from the sun. Long-term suppression of the immune system by disease (as in AIDS) or by drugs – for example, those given to prevent rejection of transplanted organs – also increases the risk of developing infections and certain cancers. This demonstrates the importance of the immune system in removing abnormal cells with the potential to cause a tumour.

Overactivity of the immune system may also cause problems. It may respond excessively to an innocuous stimulus, as in hay fever (see Allergy, p.109), or may mount a reaction against normal tissues, leading to autoimmune diseases. These include rheumatoid arthritis, systemic lupus erythematosus, pernicious anemia, and some forms of hypothyroidism. Immune system activity can also be troublesome following a transplant, when it may lead to rejection of the foreign tissue. Medication is then needed to damp down the immune system and enable the body to accept the foreign tissue.

Why drugs are used

In cancer treatment, conventional chemotherapy involves using cytotoxic (cell-killing) drugs to

Types of cancer

Uncontrolled multiplication of cells leads to the formation of tumours that may be benign or malignant. Benign tumours do not spread to other tissues; however, malignant (cancerous) tumours do. Some of the main types of cancer are defined below.

Type of cancer	Tissues affected
Carcinoma	Skin and glandular tissue lining cells of internal organs
Sarcoma	Muscles, bones, and fibrous tissues and lining cells of blood vessels
Leukemia	White blood cells
Lymphoma	Lymph glands

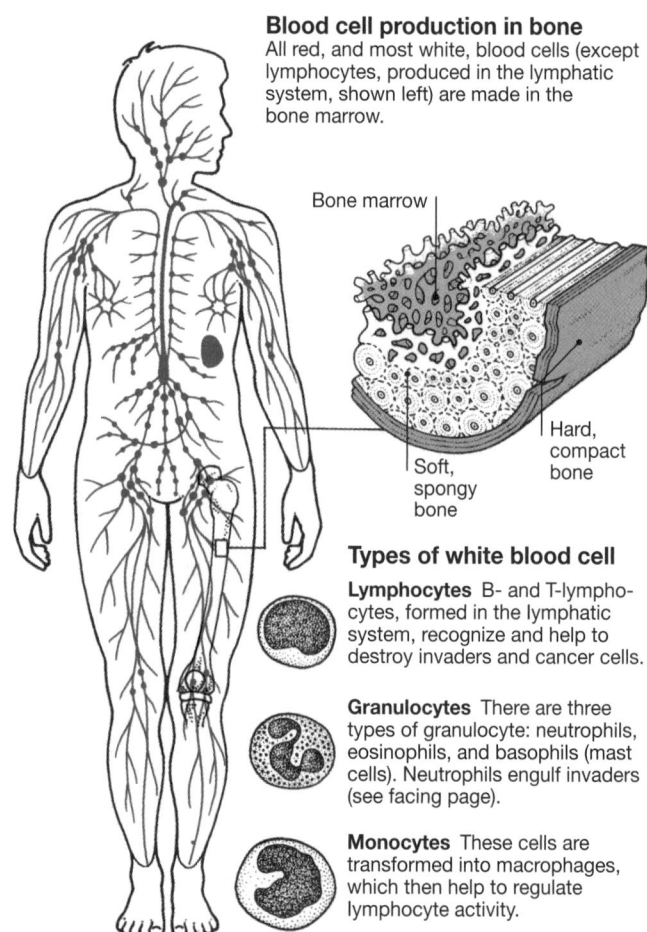

Blood cell production in bone

All red, and most white, blood cells (except lymphocytes, produced in the lymphatic system, shown left) are made in the bone marrow.

Bone marrow

Hard, compact bone

Soft, spongy bone

Types of white blood cell

Lymphocytes B- and T-lymphocytes, formed in the lymphatic system, recognize and help to destroy invaders and cancer cells.

Granulocytes There are three types of granulocyte: neutrophils, eosinophils, and basophils (mast cells). Neutrophils engulf invaders (see facing page).

Monocytes These cells are transformed into macrophages, which then help to regulate lymphocyte activity.

eliminate abnormally dividing cells. These slow the growth rate of tumours and sometimes lead to their complete disappearance. Because these drugs act against all rapidly dividing cells, they also reduce the number of normal cells, including blood cells, being produced from bone marrow. This can produce serious adverse effects, like *anemia* and neutropenia in cancer patients, but it can be useful in limiting white cell activity in autoimmune disorders. Some newer anticancer drugs are more selective in the cells they target.

Types of immune response

A specific response occurs when the immune system recognizes an invader. Two types of specific response, humoral and cellular, are described below. Phagocytosis, a non-specific response that does not depend on recognition of the invader, is also described.

Humoral response

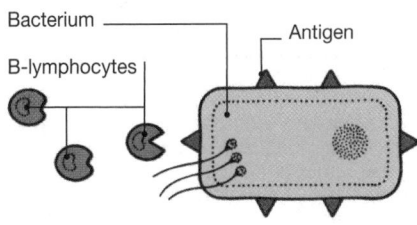

B-lymphocytes are activated by unfamiliar proteins (antigens) on the surface of the invading bacterium.

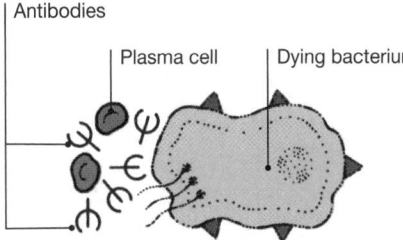

The activated B-lymphocytes form plasma cells, which release antibodies that bind to the invader and kill it.

Cellular response

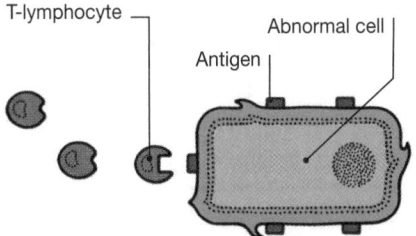

T-lymphocytes recognize the antigens on abnormal or invading cells.

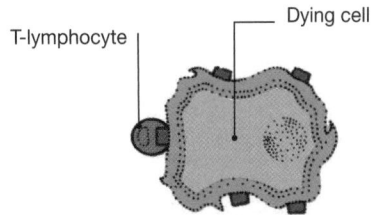

The T-lymphocytes bind to the abnormal cell and destroy it by altering chemical activity within the cell.

Engulfing invaders (phagocytosis)

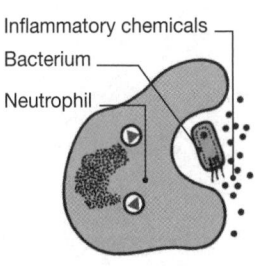

Certain cells, such as neutrophils, are attracted by inflammatory chemicals to an area of bacterial infection.

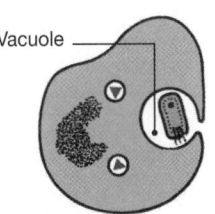

The neutrophil flows around the bacterium, enclosing it within a fluid-filled space called a vacuole.

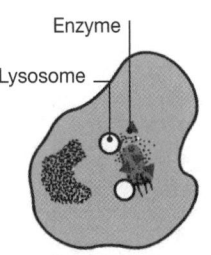

When the vacuole is formed, enzymes from areas called lysosomes in the neutrophil destroy the bacterium.

Interferons are natural proteins that limit viral infection by inhibiting viral replication within body cells. These substances also assist in the destruction of some types of cancer cells.

Effect on viral infection

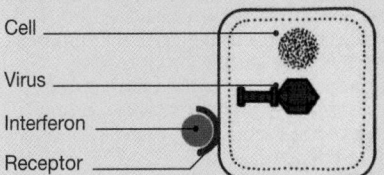

Interferon binds to receptors on a virus-infected cell.

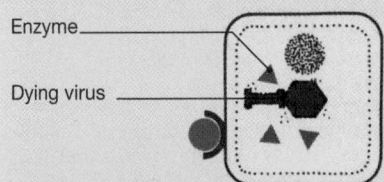

The presence of interferon triggers the release of enzymes that block viral replication. The virus is thus destroyed.

Effect on cancer cells

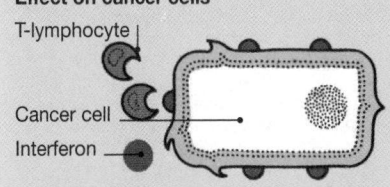

Interferon produced in response to a cancer cell activates T-lymphocytes.

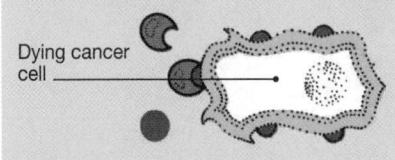

T-lymphocytes attack and destroy the cancer cell.

Other drugs that have immunosuppressant effects include corticosteroids, azathioprine, and cyclosporine, which are used after transplant surgery. No drugs are yet available that directly stimulate the entire immune system. However, growth factors may be used to increase the number and activity of some white blood cells, and antibody infusions may help those with deficient production or be used against specific targets in organ transplantation and cancer. For cervical cancer, there is a new preventive strategy.

As a majority of cervical cancers are caused by a human papilloma virus (HPV) infection, vaccination against HPV in young women can reduce the risk of cervical cancer. HPV vaccine is recommended for females between the age of 9 and 26.

MAJOR DRUG GROUPS

Anticancer drugs
Immunosuppressant drugs
Drugs for immunodeficiency and AIDS

ANTICANCER DRUGS

Cancer is a general term that covers a wide range of disorders, ranging from the leukemias (blood cancers) to solid tumours of the lung, breast, and other organs. In all cancers, a group of cells escape from the normal controls on cell growth and multiplication. As a result, the malignant (cancerous) cells begin to crowd out the normal cells and a tumour develops. Cancerous cells are frequently unable to perform their usual functions, and this may lead to progressively impaired function of the organ or area concerned. Cancers may develop from cells of the blood, skin, muscle, or any other tissue.

Malignant tumours spread into nearby structures, blocking blood vessels and compressing nerves and other structures. Fragments of the tumour may become detached and carried in the bloodstream to other parts of the body, where they form secondary growths (metastases).

Many different factors, or a combination of them, can provoke cancerous changes in cells. These include an individual's genetic background, immune system failure, and exposure to cancer-causing

agents (carcinogens). Known carcinogens include strong sunlight, tobacco smoke, radiation, certain chemicals, viruses, and dietary factors.

Treating cancer is a complicated process that depends on the type of cancer, its stage of development, and the patient's condition and wishes. Any of the following treatments may be used alone or in combination with the others: surgery, radiation treatment, and drug therapy.

Until recently, drug treatment of cancer relied heavily on hormonal drugs and cytotoxic agents (usually referred to as chemotherapy). Hormone treatments are suitable for only a few types of cancer, and cytotoxic drugs, although valuable, can have severe side effects because of the damage that they do to normal tissues. In recent years, as understanding of cancer biology has increased, new drugs have been developed. These include cytokines, such as interferon and interleukin-2, that stimulate the immune system to attack certain cancers, and monoclonal antibodies and growth factor inhibitors that attack the cancer cells much more selectively.

Why drugs are used

Cytotoxic drugs can cure rapidly growing cancers and are the treatment of choice for leukemias, lymphomas, and certain cancers of the testis. They are less effective against slow-growing solid tumours, such as those of the breast and bowel, but they can relieve symptoms and prolong life when given as palliative chemotherapy (treatment that relieves symptoms but does not cure the disease). *Adjuvant* chemotherapy is increasingly being used after surgery, especially for breast and bowel tumours, to prevent regrowth of the cancer from cells left behind after surgery. Neoadjuvant, or primary, chemotherapy is sometimes used before surgery to reduce the size of the tumour. Hormone treatment is offered in cases of hormone-sensitive cancer, such as breast, uterine, and prostatic cancers, where they can be used to relieve disease symptoms or provide palliative treatment in advanced disease. Cytokines, monoclonal antibodies, and growth factor inhibitors are increasingly used alongside or instead of conventional chemotherapy. Sometimes these can be curative, but often they produce or prolong disease remission.

SUCCESSFUL CHEMOTHERAPY

Not all cancers respond to treatment with anticancer drugs. Some cancers can be cured by drug treatment. In others, drug treatment can slow or temporarily halt the progress of the disease. The table (right) summarizes the main cancers that fall into each of these two groups. In certain individual cases, drug treatment has no beneficial effect, but in some of these,

other treatments, such as surgery, often produce significant benefits.

Successful drug treatment of cancer usually requires repeated courses of anticancer drugs because the treatment needs to be halted periodically to allow the blood-producing cells in the bone marrow to recover. The diagram below shows the number of cancer cells and normal blood

cells before and after each course of treatment with cytotoxic anticancer drugs during successful chemotherapy. Both cancer cells and blood cells are reduced, but the blood cells recover quickly between courses of drug treatment. When treatment is effective, the number of cancer cells is reduced, so they no longer cause symptoms.

Response to chemotherapy

Cancers that can be cured by drugs
Some cancers of the lymphatic system (including Hodgkin's disease)
Acute leukemias (forms of blood cancer)
Choriocarcinoma (cancer of the placenta)
Germ cell tumours (cancers affecting sperm and egg cells)
Wilms' tumour (a rare form of kidney cancer that affects children)
Cancer of the testis

Cancers in which drugs produce worthwhile benefits
Breast cancer
Ovarian cancer
Some leukemias
Multiple myeloma (a bone marrow cancer)
Many types of lung cancer
Head and neck cancers
Cancer of the stomach
Cancer of the prostate
Some cancers of the lymphatic system
Bladder cancer
Endometrial cancer (cancer affecting the lining of the uterus)
Cancer of the large intestine
Cancer of the esophagus
Cancer of the pancreas
Cancer of the cervix

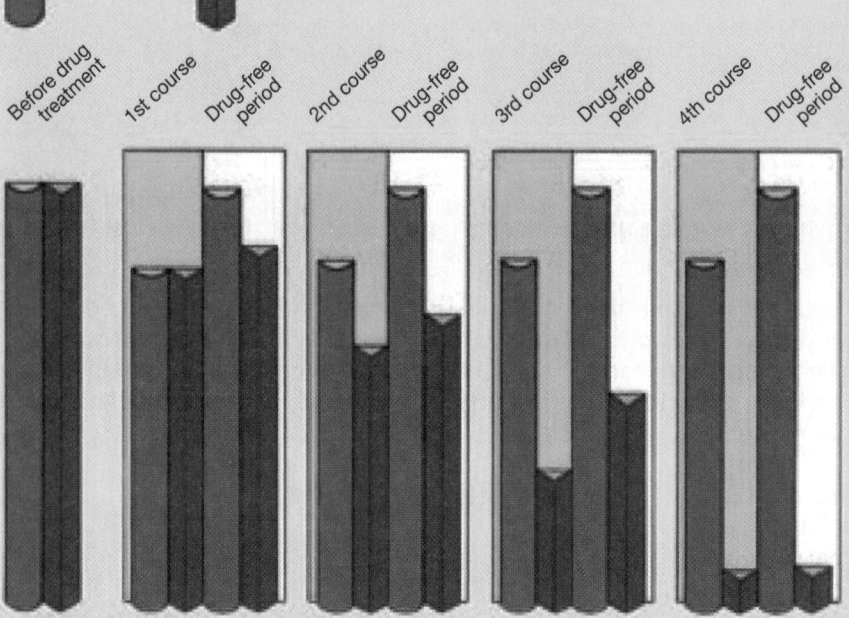

Blood cells   Cancer cells

Before drug treatment | 1st course | Drug-free period | 2nd course | Drug-free period | 3rd course | Drug-free period | 4th course | Drug-free period

ACTION OF CYTOTOXIC ANTICANCER DRUGS

Each type of cytotoxic drug affects a separate stage of the cancer cell's development, and each type of drug kills the cell by a different mechanism of action. The action of some of the principal classes of cytotoxic drugs is described below.

Alkylating agents and cytotoxic antibiotics
These act within the cell's nucleus to damage the cell's genetic material, DNA. This prevents the cell from growing and dividing.

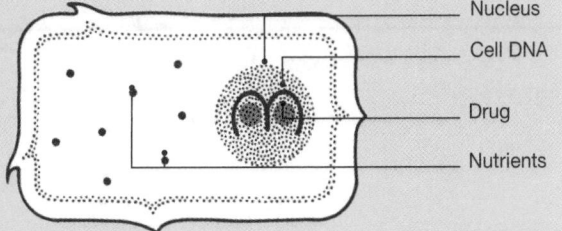

- Nucleus
- Cell DNA
- Drug
- Nutrients

Antimetabolites
These drugs prevent the cell from *metabolizing* (processing) nutrients and other substances that are necessary for normal activity in the cell.

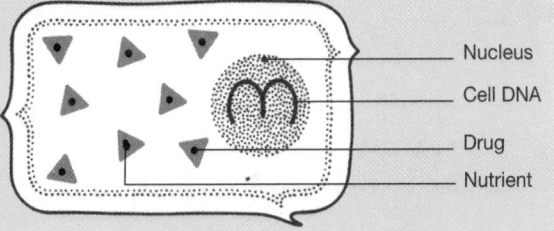

- Nucleus
- Cell DNA
- Drug
- Nutrient

Most anticancer drugs, especially cytotoxic drugs, have side effects that are sometimes severe, and so treatment decisions have to balance possible benefits against the side effects. Often a combination of several drugs is used. Special regimes of different drugs used together and in succession have been devised to maximize their activity and minimize side effects.

Certain anticancer drugs are also used for their effect in suppressing immune system activity (see p.143).

How they work
Anticancer drugs work in many different ways. The main groups of drugs and how they work are described in this section.

Cytotoxic drugs
There are several classes of cytotoxic drugs, including the alkylating agents, antimetabolites, taxanes, and cytotoxic antibiotics. Each class has a different mechanism of action, but all act by interfering with basic processes of cell replication and division. They are particularly potent against rapidly dividing cells. These include cancer cells but also certain normal cells, especially those in the hair follicles, gut lining, and bone marrow. This explains their side effects and why treatment needs careful scheduling (see panel, p.140).

Hormone therapies
Hormone treatments act by counter-acting the effects of the hormone that is encouraging growth of the cancer.

For example, some breast cancers are stimulated by the female sex hormone estrogen; the action of estrogen is opposed by the drug tamoxifen. Other cancers are damaged by very high doses of a particular sex hormone. An example is medroxyprogesterone, a progesterone, that is often used to halt the spread of endometrial cancer.

Cytokines
The cytokines, interferon alfa and interleukin-2, stimulate the immune system to attack certain cancers. The mechanisms responsible for this action are not entirely understood.

Monoclonal antibodies
Antibodies are a fundamental building block of the immune system. They recognize and bind very specifically to foreign proteins on the surface of bacteria, viruses, and parasites, marking them out for destruction by other parts of the immune system. Monoclonal antibodies are produced in tissue culture using cells genetically engineered to make antibodies against a particular target protein. If the target is carefully selected, the antibodies can be used to identify cancer cells for destruction. If the target is found only on cancer cells, or on the cancer cells and the normal tissue from which it arose, the damage to healthy tissues during treatment is limited. Monoclonal antibodies are being used increasingly in cancer treatment. Examples include trastuzumab (Herceptin), which binds to a protein produced by certain types of breast cancer cells, and

alemtuzumab and rituximab, which recognize different types of proteins on white blood cells and are used to treat leukemias and lymphomas. These antibodies are very specific for certain types of cancer, and they cause little of the toxicity of conventional chemotherapy. They can, however, cause allergy-type reactions, especially at the beginning of treatment.

Growth-factor inhibitors
The growth of cells is controlled by a complex network of growth factors that bind very specifically to receptor sites on the cell surface. This triggers a complex series of chemical reactions that transmit the "grow" message to the nucleus, triggering cell growth and replication. In many cancers, this system is faulty and there are either too many receptors on the cell surface or other abnormalities that result in inappropriate "grow" messages. The extra or abnormal cell surface receptors can be used as targets for monoclonal antibodies (see above).

Other defects in this system are being used as the basis for other new drugs. For example, imatinib very selectively interferes with an abnormal version of an enzyme that is found in certain leukemic cells. This abnormal enzyme results in the cell nucleus receiving a "grow" signal continuously, resulting in the uncontrolled growth of cancer. By stopping the enzyme working, it is possible to selectively "turn off" the growth of the abnormal cells. Imatinib is proving very successful in treating certain types of leukemia, with few serious side effects.

Another new area of cancer treatment is the use of drugs that inhibit the growth of new blood vessels to tumours (anti-angiogenesis agents), thereby depriving the tumours of the nutrients and oxygen they need to grow. One example is bevacizumab, a monoclonal antibody that blocks vascular endothelial growth factor (VEGF), a protein produced by certain tumours that promotes blood vessel growth. Bevacizumab is used to treat advanced cancer of the bowel, breast, lung, or kidney. Other new drugs are being developed that work in similar ways.

How they affect you
Cytotoxic drugs are generally associated with more side effects than other anti-cancer drugs. At the start of treatment, adverse effects of the drugs may be more noticeable than benefits. The most common side effect is nausea and vomiting, for which an anti-emetic drug (see p.74) will usually be prescribed. Effects on the blood are also common. Many cytotoxic drugs cause hair loss because of the effect of their activity on the hair follicle cells, but the hair usually starts to grow back after chemotherapy has been completed. Individual drugs may produce other side effects.

ACTION OF MONOCLONAL ANTIBODIES

Antibodies are a vital part of the body's immune system. They identify rogue cells, which are then destroyed in different ways by the action of the immune system; killer leukocytes are one type of immune response. Monoclonal antibodies are manufactured antibodies in the form of drugs that are designed to bind to proteins on the surface of specific cancer cells. The immune system is triggered into action and destroys the "tagged" cancer cells causing little or no harm to nearby normal cells.

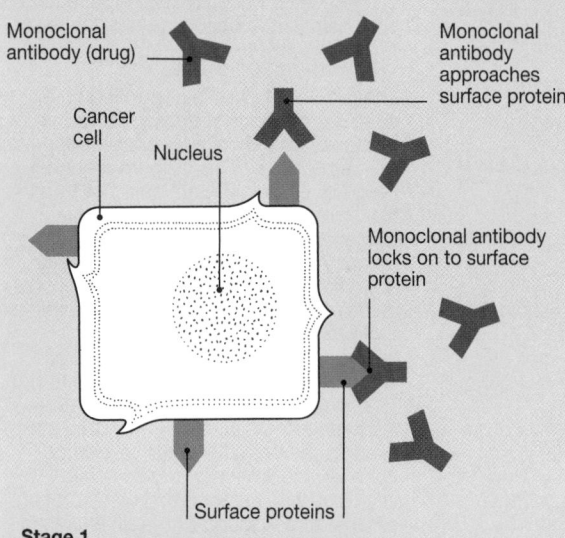

Monoclonal antibody (drug)

Cancer cell

Nucleus

Monoclonal antibody approaches surface protein

Monoclonal antibody locks on to surface protein

Surface proteins

Killer leukocyte is attracted to attached monoclonal antibody

Antibody-recognition sites

Nucleus

Cancer cell begins to disintegrate

Killer leukocyte is attached to cancer cell via monoclonal antibody

Stage 1
Monoclonal antibodies are introduced into the body. They are attracted to the surface proteins on a cancer cell and lock on to them. When sufficient antibodies have attached, the cell is recognized as rogue.

Stage 2
The "tagged" cancer cell becomes a target for destruction by killer leukocytes. Their antibody-recognition sites lock on to the monoclonal antibodies. This initiates destruction of the cell.

Cytotoxic drugs are, in most cases, administered in the highest doses that can be tolerated by the patient in order to kill as many cancer cells as quickly as possible.

The unpleasant side effects of intensive chemotherapy, combined with a delay of several weeks before any beneficial effects are seen, and the seriousness of the underlying disease often lead to depression in patients receiving anticancer drugs. Specialist counselling, support from family and friends, and, in some cases, treatment with antidepressant drugs, may help.

Risks and special precautions

All cytotoxic anticancer drugs interfere with the activity of noncancerous cells and, for this reason, they often produce serious adverse effects during long-term treatment. In particular, these drugs often adversely affect rapidly dividing cells such as the blood-producing cells in the bone marrow. The numbers of red and white cells and the number of platelets (particles in the blood responsible for clotting) may all be reduced. In some cases, symptoms of *anemia* (weakness and fatigue) and an increased risk of abnormal or excessive bleeding may develop as a result of treatment with anticancer drugs. Reduction in the number of white blood cells may result in an increased susceptibility to infection.

A simple infection such as a sore throat may be a sign of depressed white cell production in a patient taking anticancer drugs, and it must be reported to the physician without delay. In addition, wounds may take longer to heal, and susceptible people can develop gout as a result of increased uric acid production due to cells being broken down.

Several short courses of drug treatment are usually given, thus allowing the bone marrow time to recover in the period between courses (see Successful chemotherapy, p.140). Blood tests are performed regularly. When necessary, blood transfusions, antibiotics, or other forms of treatment are used to overcome the adverse effects. When relevant, contraceptive advice is given early in treatment because most anticancer drugs can damage a developing baby. In some cases, egg or sperm may be harvested before chemotherapy for later in vitro fertilization after the chemotherapy is completed.

Individual drugs may also have adverse effects on particular organs. These are described under individual drug profiles in Part 4.

By contrast, other anticancer drugs, such as hormonal drugs, antibodies, and growth-factor inhibitors, are much more selective in their actions and generally have less serious side effects.

COMMON DRUGS

Alkylating agents
Chlorambucil
Cyclophosphamide ✳
Melphalan

Antimetabolites
Cytarabine
Fluorouracil
Mercaptopurine ✳
Methotrexate ✳

Cytotoxic antibiotics
Doxorubicin ✳
Epirubicin

Hormone treatments
Anastrozole ✳
Cyproterone acetate
Flutamide ✳
Goserelin ✳
Letrozole
Leuprolide
Medroxy-
    progesterone
    acetate ✳
Megestrol ✳
Tamoxifen ✳

Cytokines
Interferon alfa-2a ✳
Interferon alfa-2b ✳

Taxanes
Docetaxel
Paclitaxel

Monoclonal antibodies
Basiliximab
Bevacizumab
Daclizumab
Denosumab ✳
Trastuzumab
Rituximab

Growth-factor inhibitors
Gefitinib
Imatinib

Vinca alkaloids and Analogs
Vinblastine
Vincristine
Vinorelbine

Other drugs
Carboplatin
Cisplatin ✳
Etoposide
Irinotecan

✳ See Part 4

IMMUNOSUPPRESSANT DRUGS

The body is protected against attack from bacteria, fungi, and viruses by the specialized cells and proteins in the blood and tissues that make up the immune system (see p.138). White blood cells known as lymphocytes either kill invading organisms directly or produce special proteins (*antibodies*) to destroy them. These mechanisms are also responsible for eliminating abnormal or unhealthy cells that could otherwise multiply and develop into a cancer.

In certain conditions it is medically necessary to damp down the activity of the immune system. These include a number of autoimmune disorders in which the immune system attacks normal body tissue. Autoimmune disorders may affect a single organ – for example, the kidneys in Goodpasture's syndrome or the thyroid gland in Hashimoto's disease – or they may result in widespread damage, for example, in rheumatoid arthritis or systemic lupus erythematosus.

Immune system activity may also need to be reduced following an organ transplant, when the body's defences would otherwise attack and reject the transplanted tissue.

Several types of drugs are used as immunosuppressants: anticancer drugs (p.140), corticosteroids (p.127), cyclosporine (p.249); and monoclonal antibodies.

Why drugs are used

Immunosuppressant drugs are given to treat autoimmune disorders, such as rheumatoid arthritis, when symptoms are severe and other treatments have not provided adequate relief. Corticosteroids are usually prescribed initially. The pronounced anti-inflammatory effect of these drugs, as well as their immuno-suppressant action, helps to promote healing of tissue damaged by abnormal immune system activity. Anticancer drugs such as methotrexate may be used in addition to corticosteroids if these do not produce sufficient improvement or if their effect wanes (see also Antirheumatic drugs, p.103).

Immunosuppressant drugs are given before and after organ and other tissue transplants. Treatment may have to be continued indefinitely to prevent rejection. A number of drugs and drug combinations are used, depending on which organ is being transplanted and the underlying condition of the patient. However, cyclosporine, along with the related drug tacrolimus, is now the most widely used drug for preventing organ rejection. It is also increasingly used to treat autoimmune disorders. It is often used in combination with a corticosteroid or the more specific drug, mycophenolate mofetil.

Monoclonal antibodies, which destroy specific cells of the immune system, are also used to aid transplantation and are increasingly being used to treat autoimmune disorders. For example, adalimumab is used to treat certain types of arthritis while rituximab is also used for vasculitis.

How they work

Immunosuppressant drugs reduce the effectiveness of the immune system, either by depressing the production of lymphocytes or by altering their activity.

How they affect you

When immunosuppressants are given to treat an autoimmune disorder, they reduce the severity of the symptoms and may temporarily halt the progress of the disease. However, they cannot restore major tissue damage.

Immunosuppressant drugs can produce a variety of unwanted side effects. The side effects caused by corticosteroids are described in more detail on p.127. Anticancer drugs, when prescribed as immunosuppressants, are given in low doses that produce only mild side effects. They may cause nausea and vomiting, for which an anti-emetic drug (p.74) may be prescribed. Hair loss is rare and regrowth usually occurs when the drug treatment is discontinued. Cyclosporine may cause increased growth of facial hair, swelling of the gums, and tingling in the hands.

Risks and special precautions

All of these drugs may produce potentially serious adverse effects. By reducing the activity of the patient's immune system, immunosuppressant drugs can affect the body's ability to fight invading micro-organisms, thereby increasing the risk of serious infections. Because lymphocyte activity is also important for preventing the multiplication of abnormal cells, there is an increased risk of certain types of cancer. A major drawback of anticancer drugs is that, in addition to their effect on the production of lymphocytes, they interfere with the growth and division of other blood cells in the bone marrow. Reduced production of red blood cells can cause *anemia*; when the production of blood platelets is suppressed, blood clotting may be less efficient.

Although cyclosporine is more specific in its action than either corticosteroids or anticancer drugs, it can cause kidney damage and, in too high a dose, may affect the brain, causing hallucinations or seizures. Cyclosporine also tends to raise blood pressure, and another drug may be required to counteract this effect (see Antihypertensive drugs, p.88).

ACTION OF IMMUNOSUPPRESSANTS

Before treatment
Many types of blood cell, each with a distinct role, form in the bone marrow. Lymphocytes respond to infection and foreign tissue. B-lymphocytes produce antibodies to attack invading organisms, whereas T-lymphocytes directly attack invading cells. Other blood cells help the action of the B- and T-cells.

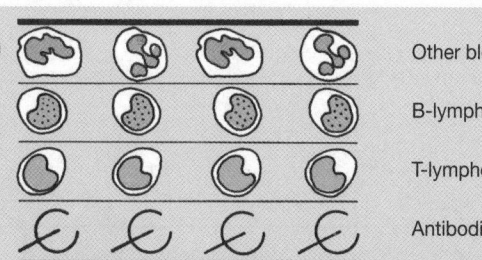

Other blood cells

B-lymphocytes

T-lymphocytes

Antibodies

  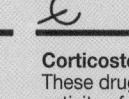 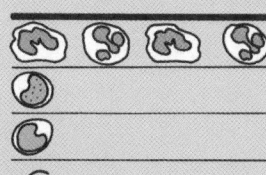 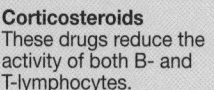 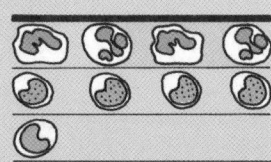

Anticancer drugs
These drugs slow the production of all cells in the bone marrow.

Corticosteroids
These drugs reduce the activity of both B- and T-lymphocytes.

Cyclosporine
This inhibits the activity of T-lymphocytes only, and not the activity of B-lymphocytes.

COMMON DRUGS

Anticancer drugs
Azathioprine ✻
Chlorambucil
Cyclophosphamide ✻
Methotrexate ✻
Mycophenolate
 mofetil

Corticosteroids
(see p.127)

Antibodies
Lymphocyte immune globulin/
 anti-thymocyte globulin
Adalimumab ✻

Basiliximab
Bevacizumab
Rituximab ✻

Other drugs
Cyclosporine ✻
Tacrolimus

✻ See Part 4

DRUGS FOR HIV AND AIDS

AIDS (acquired immune deficiency syndrome) is caused by infection with the human immunodeficiency virus (HIV). This virus invades certain cells of the immune system, particularly the white blood cells called T-helper lymphocytes (or CD$_4$ cells), which normally activate other immune cells to fight infection. Since HIV kills T-helper lymphocytes, the body cannot fight the virus or subsequent infections. In recent years, the number of drugs available to treat HIV has increased considerably, as has the knowledge about how best to use the drugs in combination.

Why drugs are used

Drug treatments for HIV infection can be divided into the treatment of the initial infection and treatment of diseases and complications associated with AIDS.

Drugs that act directly against HIV are known as antiretrovirals. The two most common groups work by interfering with enzymes vital for virus replication. The first inhibits the reverse transcriptase enzyme. They are divided according to their chemical structure into nucleoside inhibitors (also called nucleoside analogues), nucleotide inhibitors (nucleotide analogues), and non-nucleoside inhibitors. The second group interferes with an enzyme called protease. Entry, or fusion, inhibitors are a new group that interferes with the entry of the virus into the cell. Other groups include integrase inhibitors to prevent the virus from injecting its DNA into the cell nucleus; and others to target the receptor sites for entry into cells.

Antiretrovirals are much more effective in combination. Treatment usually starts with two nucleoside transcriptase inhibitors and a non-nucleoside drug or a protease inhibitor. If combination antiretroviral therapy (cART) is started before damage

to the immune system is too great, it can reduce the level of HIV virus in the body and improve the outlook for HIV-infected individuals, but it is not a cure and such people remain infectious. The mainstay of drug treatment for AIDS-related diseases are antimicrobial drugs for the bacterial, viral, fungal, and protozoal infections to which people with AIDS are particularly susceptible. These drugs include the antituberculous drugs (p.118), sulfamethoxazole-trimethoprim for pneumocystis pneumonia, and ganciclovir to treat CMV (cytomegalovirus) infection.

COMMON DRUGS

Nucleoside reverse transcriptase inhibitors	Non-nucleoside reverse transcriptase inhibitors
Abacavir	Delavirdine
Didanosine (ddI) ✳	Efavirenz ✳
Emtricitabine	Etravirine
Lamivudine (3TC)✳	Nevirapine
Stavudine (d4T)	Rilpivirine
Zidovudine (AZT or ZDV) ✳	**Protease inhibitors**
Nucleotide reverse transcriptase inhibitor	Amprenavir
Tenofovir	Atazanavir
	Darunavir
Fusion inhibitor	Fosamprenavir
Enfuvirtide	Indinavir
Maraviroc	Lopinavir/ritonavir ✳
	Nelfinavir
Integrase inhibitor	Saquinavir
Raltegravir	Tipranavir

| ✳ See Part 4 |

HIV INFECTION AND POSSIBLE TREATMENTS

The illustrations below show how the human immunodeficiency virus (HIV) enters CD$_4$ cells and, once inside, replicates itself to produce new viruses. The action of already existing drugs, along with the possible actions of future drugs are also described.

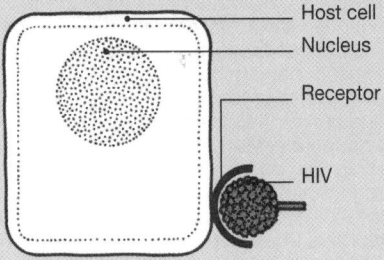

Host cell
Nucleus
Receptor
HIV

Stage 1
The virus binds to a specialized site (receptor) on a body cell.

Possible drug intervention
Drugs such as enfuvirtide and maraviroc have been developed to block the entry of HIV into CD$_4$ cells.

Stage 2
The virus enters the cell.

Reverse transcriptase

Viral RNA

Stage 3
The virus loses its protective coat and releases RNA, its genetic material, and an enzyme known as reverse transcriptase.

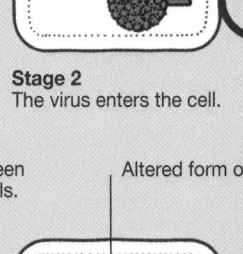

Altered form of RNA

Drug intervention
The reverse transcriptase inhibitor drugs, such as zidovudine, efavirenz, and tenofovir, act here. Integrase inhibitors work by blocking the process here.

Stage 4
The enzyme reverse transcriptase converts viral RNA into a form that can enter the host cell's nucleus (DNA) and may become integrated with the cell's genetic material. This viral DNA is integrated into the DNA of the host cell by the enzyme integrase.

Protein

Viral RNA

Stage 5
The host cell starts to produce new viral RNA and protein from the viral material that has been incorporated into its nucleus.

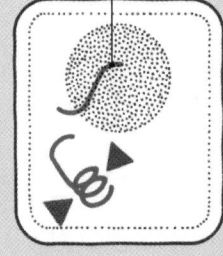

New HIV viruses

Dying host cell

Stage 6
The new viral RNA and proteins assemble to produce new viruses. These leave the host cell (which then dies) and are free to attack other cells in the body.

Drug intervention
The protease inhibitors prevent formation of viral proteins and viral assembly.

ANTIRETROVIRAL DRUGS

Your dosage will be tailored to your specific situation. Do not change your dose without consulting your physician.

Drug name	Cautions	Drug name	Cautions
Abacavir *Ziagen* (NRTI)	Can cause a severe allergic-type reaction.	**Atazanavir (ATZ)** *Reyataz* (PI)	Should be taken with food.
Lamivudine (3TC), zidovudine (AZT) *Combivir* (NRTI)		**Darunavir (TMC-114)** *Prezista* (PI)	Used only with ritonavir.
Didanosine (ddI) *Videx EC* (NRTI)		**Tipranavir (TPV)** *Aptivus* (PI)	Used only with ritonavir.
Emtricitabine (FTC) *Truvada*: emtricitabine and tenovir (NtRTI). *Atripla*: emtricitabine, tenovir (NtRTI), and efavirenz (NNRTI).	May be taken with, or without food.	**Fosamprenavir (f-APV)** *Telzir* (PI)	Used only with ritonavir. Take solution on empty stomach.
Lamivudine (3TC)	Can also be used to treat hepatitis B.	**Indinavir (IDV)** *Crixivan* (PI)	Adequate fluid intake recommended.
Stavudine (d4T) *Zerit* (NRTI)		**Nelfinavir (NFV)** *Viracept* (PI)	Doses must be taken with a meal. Discuss risks with physician before initiating therapy.
Lamivudine, zidovudine (AZT or ZDV), abacavir *Trizivir* (NRTI)	The abacavir contained within trizivir can cause a severe allergic-type reaction.	**Ritonavir (RTV)** *Norvir* (PI)	Doses should be taken with food.
Zidovudine (AZT) *Retrovir* (NRTI)	Can cause *anemia*.	**Lopinavir/ritonavir (LPV/RTV)** *Kaletra* (PI)	Doses of solution should be taken with food.
Tenofovir *Viread* (NtRTI). Also see emtricitabine for combination products.		**Saquinavir (SQV)** *Invirase* (PI)	Doses should be taken within 2 hours of a full meal.
Nevirapine *Viramune* (NNRTI)	Can cause a severe allergic-type reaction.	**Enfuvirtide** *Fuzeon* (FI)	Injected subcutaneously. Reconstituted solution to be stored in refrigerator for no longer than 24 hours.
Efavirenz (EFV) *Sustiva* (NNRTI). Also see emtricitabine for combination products.	Can cause a severe allergic-type rash. Can cause psychiatric symptoms.	**Maraviroc** *Celsentri* (FI)	Swallow tablets and do not chew them.
Delavirdine (DLV) *Rescriptor* (NNRTI)	May be dispersed in water for easier swallowing.	**Raltegravir** *Isentress* (II)	Dose may be increased when given with rifampin.
Etravirine (TMC-125) *Intelence* (NNRTI)	Rare reports of a severe skin reaction.		
Rilpivirine (RPV) *Edurant* (NNRTI)	Caution in patients with a history of depression. Must be taken with food.	**Several combination products are also available.**	

KEY: NRTI = nucleoside reverse transcriptase inhibitor; NtRTI = nucleotide reverse transcriptase inhibitor; NNRTI = non-nucleoside reverse transcriptase inhibitor; PI = protease inhibitor; FI = fusion inhibitor; II = Integrase inhibitor.

REPRODUCTIVE & URINARY TRACTS

The reproductive systems of men and women consist of those organs that produce and release sperm (male), or store and release eggs, and then nurture a fertilized egg until it develops into a baby (female).

The urinary system filters wastes and water from the blood, producing urine, which is then expelled from the body. The reproductive and urinary systems of men are partially linked, but those of women form two physically close but functionally separate systems.

The female reproductive organs comprise the ovaries, fallopian tubes, and uterus (womb). The uterus opens via the cervix (neck of the uterus) into the vagina. The principal male reproductive organs are the two sperm-producing glands, the testes (testicles), which lie within the scrotum, and the penis. Other structures of the male reproductive tract include the prostate gland and several tubular structures – the tightly coiled epididymides, the vas deferens, the seminal vesicles, and the urethra (see right).

The urinary organs in both sexes comprise the kidneys, which filter the blood and excrete urine (see also p.85), the ureters down which urine passes, and the bladder, where urine is stored until it is released from the body via the urethra.

What can go wrong
The reproductive and urinary tracts are both subject to infection. Such infections (apart from those transmitted by sexual activity) are relatively uncommon in men because the long male urethra prevents bacteria and other organisms passing easily to the bladder and upper urinary tract, and to the male sex organs. The shorter female urethra allows urinary tract infections, especially of the bladder (cystitis) and of the urethra (urethritis), to occur commonly. The female reproductive tract is also vulnerable to infection, which, in some cases, is sexually transmitted.

Reproductive function may also be disrupted by hormonal disturbances that lead to reduced fertility. Women may be troubled by symptoms arising from normal activity of the reproductive organs, including menstrual disorders as well as problems associated with childbirth.

The most common urinary problems apart from infection are those related to bladder function. Urine may be released involuntarily (incontinence) or it may be retained in the bladder. Such disorders may be caused by factors such as abnormal nerve signals to the bladder or sphincter muscle or hormonal changes in aging women. The filtering action of the kidneys

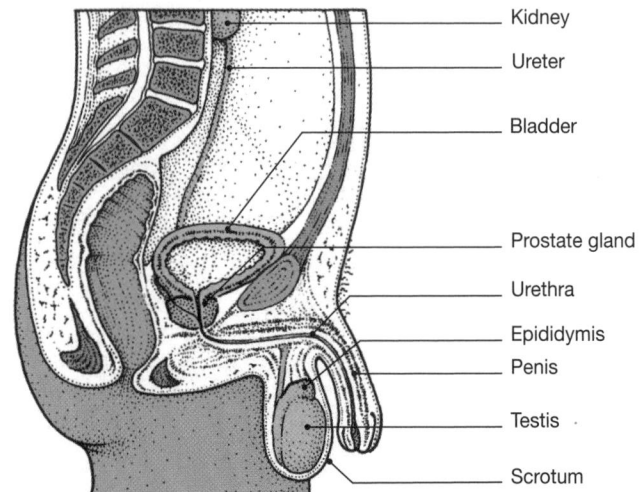

Male reproductive system
Sperm produced in each testis pass into the epididymis, a tightly coiled tube in which the sperm mature before passing along the vas deferens to the seminal vesicle. Sperm are stored in the seminal vesicle until they are ejaculated from the penis via the urethra, together with seminal fluid and secretions from the prostate gland.

Kidney
Ureter
Bladder
Prostate gland
Urethra
Epididymis
Penis
Testis
Scrotum

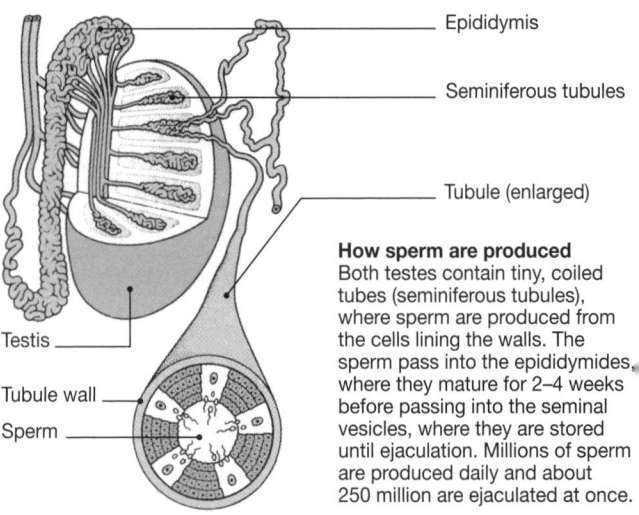

Epididymis
Seminiferous tubules
Tubule (enlarged)

Testis
Tubule wall
Sperm

How sperm are produced
Both testes contain tiny, coiled tubes (seminiferous tubules), where sperm are produced from the cells lining the walls. The sperm pass into the epididymides, where they mature for 2–4 weeks before passing into the seminal vesicles, where they are stored until ejaculation. Millions of sperm are produced daily and about 250 million are ejaculated at once.

may be affected by alteration of the composition of the blood or the *hormones* that regulate urine production, or by damage (from infection or inflammation) to the filtering units themselves.

Why drugs are used
Antibiotic drugs (p.114) are used to eliminate both urinary and reproductive tract infections (including sexually transmitted infections). Certain infections of the vagina are caused by fungi or yeasts and require antifungal drugs (p.124).

Hormone drugs are used both to reduce fertility deliberately (oral contraceptives) and to increase fertility in certain conditions in which it has not been

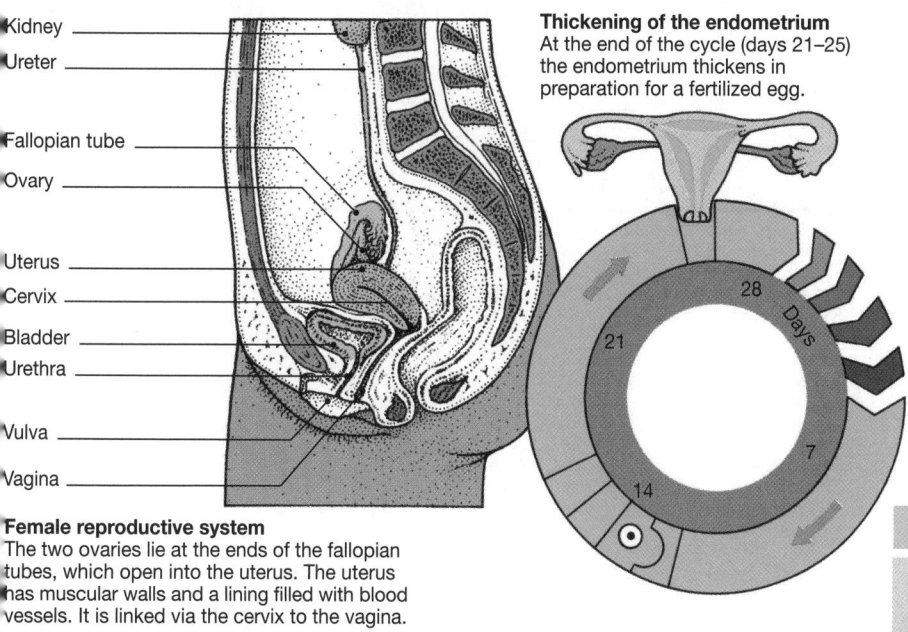

Thickening of the endometrium
At the end of the cycle (days 21–25) the endometrium thickens in preparation for a fertilized egg.

28 Days 21 14 7

Female reproductive system
The two ovaries lie at the ends of the fallopian tubes, which open into the uterus. The uterus has muscular walls and a lining filled with blood vessels. It is linked via the cervix to the vagina.

Kidney
Ureter
Fallopian tube
Ovary
Uterus
Cervix
Bladder
Urethra
Vulva
Vagina

Menstrual cycle

A monthly cycle of hormone interactions allows an egg to be released and, if it is fertilized, creates the correct environment for it to implant in the uterus. Major body changes occur, the most obvious being monthly vaginal bleeding (menstruation). The cycle usually starts between the ages of 11 and 14 years and continues until the menopause, which occurs at around 50. After the menopause, childbearing is no longer possible. The cycle is usually 28 days, but this varies with individuals.

Menstruation
If no egg is fertilized, the endometrium is shed (days 1–5).

Fertile period
Conception may take place in the 24 hours after ovulation (days 14–16).

URINARY SYSTEM

The kidneys extract waste and excess water from the blood. The waste liquid (urine) passes into the bladder, from which it is expelled via the urethra.

Endometrium

The fertilized egg divides continually on the way down the fallopian tube.

One sperm fuses with the egg in the fallopian tube.

Fallopian tube

Ovarian follicle

A fluid-filled cell cluster (follicle) nourishes the maturing egg. When the egg is ripe, it is released from the follicle.

Ovary

The fertilized egg implants in the uterine wall and develops into an embryo.

Journey of the egg
Every month, hormone activity causes an egg within an ovarian follicle in one of the ovaries to ripen. It is then released (ovulation) and travels down the fallopian tube to the uterus.

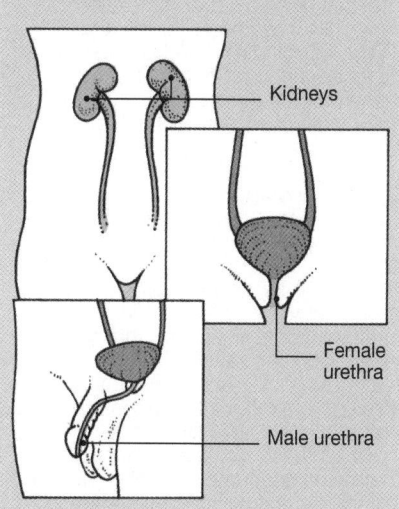

Kidneys

Female urethra

Male urethra

possible for a couple to conceive. Hormones may also be used to regulate menstruation when it is irregular or excessively painful or heavy. NSAIDs (p.102) are used to treat menstrual period pain, and analgesics (p.64) are used for pain relief in labour. Other drugs used in labour include those that increase contraction of the muscles of the uterus and those that limit blood loss after the birth. Drugs may also be employed to halt premature labour.

Drugs that alter the transmission of nerve signals to the bladder muscles have an important role in the treatment of urinary incontinence and retention. Drugs that increase the kidneys' filtering action are commonly used to reduce blood pressure and fluid retention (see Diuretics, p.85). Other drugs may alter the composition of the urine – for example, the uricosuric drugs that are used in the treatment of gout (p.105) increase the amount of uric acid.

MAJOR DRUG GROUPS

Drugs used to treat menstrual disorders
Oral contraceptives
Drugs for infertility
Drugs used in labour
Drugs used for urinary disorders
Antibiotics

DRUGS USED TO TREAT MENSTRUAL DISORDERS

The menstrual cycle results from the actions of female sex *hormones* that cause ovulation (the release of an egg) and thickening of the endometrium (the lining of the uterus) each month in preparation for pregnancy. Unless the egg is fertilized, the endometrium will be shed about two weeks later during menstruation (see also p.147).

The main problems associated with menstruation that may require medical treatment are excessive blood loss (menorrhagia), pain during menstruation (dysmenorrhea), and distressing physical and psychological symptoms occurring prior to menstruation (premenstrual syndrome). The absence of periods (amenorrhea) is discussed under female sex hormones (p.133).

The drugs most commonly used to treat the menstrual disorders described above include estrogens, progestins, and analgesics.

Why drugs are used

Drug treatment for menstrual disorders is undertaken only when the physician has ruled out the possibility of an underlying gynecological disorder, such as a pelvic infection or fibroids. In some cases, especially in women over the age of 35, a D and C (dilatation and curettage) may be recommended. When no underlying reason for the problem is found, drug treatment aimed primarily at the relief of symptoms is usually prescribed.

Dysmenorrhea

Painful menstrual periods are usually treated with an analgesic such as a non-steroidal anti-inflammatory drug (NSAID; see p.102). These are most effective because they counter the effects of prostaglandins, chemicals that are partly responsible for transmission of pain to the brain. Diclofenac and mefenamic acid are also used to reduce the excessive blood loss of menorrhagia (see below).

When these drugs are not sufficient to provide adequate pain relief, hormonal drug treatment may be recommended. If contraception is also required, treatment may involve an oral contraceptive pill containing both an estrogen and a progestin, or a progestin alone. The treatment of dysmenorrhea caused by endometriosis is described in the box above right. Non-hormonal progestin preparations may also be prescribed.

Menorrhagia

Excessive blood loss during menstruation can sometimes be reduced by some NSAIDs. Tranexamic acid, an antifibrinolytic drug, is an effective treatment for menorrhagia. Alternatively, danazol, a drug that reduces production of the female sex hormone estrogen, may be prescribed to reduce blood loss.

ENDOMETRIOSIS

Endometriosis is a condition in which fragments of endometrial tissue (uterine lining) occur outside the uterus in the pelvic cavity. This disorder causes severe pain during menstruation, often causes pain during intercourse, and may sometimes lead to infertility.

Drugs used for this disorder are similar to those prescribed for heavy periods (menorrhagia). However, in this case the intention is to suppress endometrial development for an extended period so that the abnormal tissue eventually withers away. Progesterone supplements that suppress endometrial thickening may be prescribed throughout the menstrual cycle. Alternatively, danazol, which suppresses endometrial development by reducing estrogen production, may be prescribed. Any drug treatment usually needs to be continued for a minimum of six months.

When drug treatment is unsuccessful, surgical removal of the abnormal tissue is usually necessary.

Premenstrual syndrome

This is a collection of psychological and physical symptoms that affect many women to some degree in the days before menstruation. Psychological symptoms include mood changes such as increased irritability, depression, and anxiety. Principal physical symptoms are bloating, headache, and breast tenderness. Oral contraceptives or progestin-only preparations may be considered. Other drugs sometimes used include pyridoxine (vitamin B_6) and diuretics (p.85) if bloating due to fluid retention is a problem. Anti-anxiety drugs (p.67) may be prescribed in rare cases where severe premenstrual psychological disturbance is experienced.

How they work

Drugs used in menstrual disorders act in a variety of ways. Hormonal treatments are aimed at suppressing the pattern of hormonal changes that is causing troublesome symptoms. Contraceptive preparations override the woman's normal menstrual cycle. Ovulation does not occur, and the endometrium does not thicken normally. Bleeding that occurs at the end of a cycle is less likely to be abnormally heavy, to be accompanied by severe discomfort, or to be preceded by distressing symptoms. For further information on oral contraceptives, see facing page.

Non-contraceptive progestin such as medroxyprogesterone taken in the days before menstruation do not suppress ovulation. Increased progesterone during this time reduces premenstrual symptoms and prevents excessive thickening of the endometrium.

Danazol, a potent drug, prevents the thickening of the endometrium, thereby correcting excessively heavy periods. Blood loss is reduced, and in some cases menstruation ceases altogether during treatment.

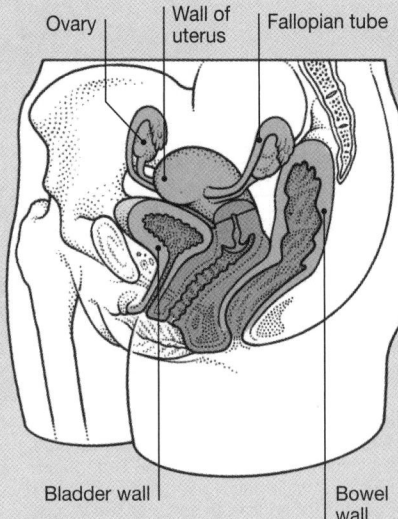

Sites of endometriosis

Ovary | Wall of uterus | Fallopian tube

Bladder wall | Bowel wall

▢ Endometrial tissue

COMMON DRUGS

Estrogens and progestins
(see p.133)

NSAID analgesics
ASA ✳
Celecoxib ✳
Diclofenac ✳
Diflunisal
Flurbiprofen
Ibuprofen ✳
Ketoprofen ✳
Mefenamic acid
Naproxen ✳

Diuretics
(see p.85)

Other drugs
Bromocriptine ✳
Buserelin
Danazol ✳
Goserelin ✳
Leuprolide
Nafarelin
Pyridoxine
Tranexamic acid
Triptorelin pamoate

✳ See Part 4

ORAL CONTRACEPTIVES

There are many different methods of ensuring that pregnancy does not follow sexual intercourse, but for most women the oral contraceptive is the most effective method. It has the advantage of being convenient and unobtrusive during lovemaking. Oral contraceptives are the method of choice for most young couples, especially teens, when combined with condoms, which are used for protection from sexually transmitted diseases.

Hormonal contraceptive formulations include oral tablets, vaginal ring, a patch applied on the skin, an injection, and an intrauterine system (IUS). Each vaginal ring and patch is left in/on for a period of 3 weeks; then a new package is used after a one-week hormone-free interval (i.e. a new one used every 4 weeks). The ring and the patch contain a combination of an estrogen and a progestin hormone. The injection is administered every 3 months and contains only a progestin hormone. The IUS contains a progestin that is released continuously over 5 years. Oral contraceptives are available as a combined pill of estrogen and progestin or a progestin-only pill.

Why they are used
The combined pill
The combined pill is widely prescribed and has the lowest failure rate in terms of unwanted pregnancies. It is referred to as the "pill" and is the type thought most suitable for young women who want to use a hormonal form of contraception. The combined pill is particularly suitable for those women who regularly experience exceptionally painful, heavy, or prolonged periods (see Drugs used to treat menstrual disorders, facing page).

COMPARISON OF RELIABILITY OF DIFFERENT METHODS OF CONTRACEPTION

The table indicates the number of pregnancies that occur with each method of contraception among 100 women using that method in a year. The wide variation that occurs with some methods takes into account pregnancies that occur as a result of incorrect use of the method.

Method	Pregnancies*
Combined and phased pills	2–3
Progestin-only pill	2.5–10
IUD (Intrauterine device)	up to 5
Condom	10–14
Diaphragm	10–14
Rhythm	25–30
Contraceptive sponge	10–14
Vaginal spermicide alone	2–30
Medroxyprogesterone depot	Less than 1
No contraception	80–85
"Morning after" pill	11–25

* Per 100 users per year.

There are many different products available containing a fixed dose of an estrogen and a progestin drug. They are usually divided into three groups according to their estrogen content (see Hormone content of common oral contraceptives, below). Low-dose products are chosen when possible to minimize the risk of adverse effects.

The combined pill is also available as "phased pills," where each pack is divided into two or three groups or phases. Each phase contains a different proportion of an estrogen and a progestin. The aim is to provide a hormonal balance that closely resembles the fluctuations of a normal menstrual cycle. Phased pills provide effective protection for many women who suffer side effects from other available forms of oral contraceptive.

Progestin-only pill
The progestin-only pill is often prescribed for women who react adversely to the estrogen in the combined pill or for whom the combined pill is considered unsuitable due to their age or medical history (see Risks and special precautions, p.150). It is also prescribed for women who are breast-feeding since it does not reduce milk production. The progestin pill has a higher failure rate than the combined pill and must be taken at precisely the same time each day for maximum contraceptive effect.

How they work
In a normal menstrual cycle, the ripening and release of an egg and the preparation of the uterus for implantation of the fertilized egg are the result of a complex interplay between the natural female sex hormones, estrogen and progesterone, and the pituitary hormones, follicle-stimulating hormone (FSH) and luteinizing hormone (LH) (see also p.133). The estrogen and progestin contained in oral contraceptives disrupt the normal menstrual cycle in such a way that conception is less likely.

With combined and phased pills, the increased levels of estrogen and progesterone produce similar effects to the hormonal changes of pregnancy. The actions of the hormones inhibit the production of FSH and LH, thereby preventing the egg from ripening in the ovary and from being released.

The progestin-only pill has a slightly different effect. It does not always prevent release of an egg; its main contraceptive action may be on the mucus that lines the cervix, which thickens so sperm cannot cross it. This effect occurs to some extent with combined pills and phased pills.

How they affect you
Most courses of combined and phased pills last for 21 days, followed by a pill-free

HORMONE CONTENT OF COMMON ORAL CONTRACEPTIVES

The estrogen-containing forms are classified according to estrogen content as follows:
Low: 20 micrograms; standard: 30–35 micrograms; phased pills: 30–40 micrograms.

Type of contraception (estrogen content)	Brand names
Combined (20mcg)	Alesse, Apri, Aviane, Cyclen, Marvelon, Minestrin 1/20, Portia Seasonale, Seasonique, Yaz
(30–35mcg)	Brevicon 0.5/35, Brevicon 1/35, Cyclen Marvelon, Demulen 30, Diane-35, Loestrin 1.5/30, Min-Ovral, Ortho 0.5/35, Ortho 1/35, Ortho-Cept, Select 1/35, Yasmin
Phased (30–40mcg)	Linessa, Ortho7/7/7, Synphasic, Tri-cyclen, Tri-cyclen Lo, Triquilar
Progestin-only (no estrogen)	Micronor
Postcoital (morning after) (no estrogen)	Plan B

ORAL CONTRACEPTIVES continued

BALANCING THE RISKS AND BENEFITS OF ORAL CONTRACEPTIVES

Oral contraceptives are safe for the vast majority of young women. However, every woman considering oral contraception should discuss with her physician and pharmacist the risks and possible adverse effects of the drugs before deciding that a hormonal method is the most suitable in her case. A variety of factors must be taken into account, including the woman's age, her own medical history and that of her close relatives, and factors such as whether she is a smoker. The importance of such factors varies depending on the type of contraceptive. The table below gives the main advantages and disadvantages of estrogen-containing and progestin-only pills.

Type of oral contraceptive	Estrogen-containing combined and phased	Progestin-only
Advantages	● Very reliable ● Convenient/unobtrusive ● Regularizes menstruation ● Reduced menstrual pain and blood loss ● Reduced risk of: ▼ benign breast disease ▼ endometriosis ▼ ectopic pregnancy ▼ ovarian cysts ▼ pelvic infection ▼ ovarian and endometrial cancer	● Reasonably reliable ● Convenient/unobtrusive ● Suitable during breast-feeding ● Avoids estrogen-related side effects and risks ● Allows rapid return to fertility
Side effects	● Weight gain ● Depression ● Breast swelling ● Reduced sex drive ● Headaches ● Increased vaginal discharge ● Nausea	● Irregular menstruation ● Breast tenderness
Risks	● Thrombosis/embolism ● Heart disease ● High blood pressure ● Jaundice ● Cancer of the liver (rare) ● Gallstones	● Ectopic pregnancy ● Ovarian cysts
Factors that may prohibit use	● Previous thrombosis* ● Heart disease or high levels of lipid in blood ● Breast cancer ● Liver disease ● Blood disorders ● High blood pressure ● Unexplained vaginal bleeding ● Migraine with aura ● Otosclerosis ● Presence of several risk factors (below)	● Previous ectopic pregnancy ● Heart or circulatory disease ● Unexplained vaginal bleeding ● Breast cancer
Factors that increase risks	● Smoking* ● Obesity* ● Increasing age ● Diabetes mellitus ● Family history of heart or circulatory disease* ● Current treatment with other drugs	● As for estrogen-containing pills, but to a lesser degree

*Products containing desogestrel have a higher excess risk with these factors than other progestins.

How to minimize your health risks while taking the pill

▼ Give up smoking.
▼ Maintain a healthy weight and diet.
▼ Have regular blood pressure and blood lipid checks.
▼ Have regular cervical smear tests.

▼ Remind your physician that you are taking oral contraceptives before taking other prescription drugs.
▼ Stop taking estrogen-containing oral contraceptives four weeks before planned major surgery (use alternative contraception).

seven days during which time menstruation occurs. Some brands contain seven additional inactive pills (28-day pack). With these, the new course directly follows the last so the habit of taking the pill is not broken. Progestin-only pills are taken for 28 days each month. Menstruation usually occurs during the last few days of the menstrual cycle.

Women taking oral contraceptives, especially drugs that contain estrogen, usually find that their menstrual periods are lighter and relatively pain-free. Some women cease to menstruate altogether. This is not a cause for concern in itself, provided no pills have been missed, but it may make it difficult to determine if pregnancy has occurred. An apparently missed period probably indicates a light one, rather than pregnancy. However, if you have missed two consecutive periods and you feel that you may be pregnant, it is advisable to have a pregnancy test.

All forms of oral contraceptive may cause spotting of blood in mid-cycle ("breakthrough bleeding"), especially at first, but this can be a particular problem of the progestin-only pill.

Oral contraceptives that contain estrogen may produce any of a large number of mild side effects depending on the dose. Symptoms similar to those experienced early in pregnancy may occur, particularly in the first few months of pill use: some women complain of nausea and vomiting, weight gain, depression, altered libido, increased appetite, and cramps in the legs and abdomen. The pill may also affect the circulation, producing minor headaches and dizziness. All these effects usually disappear within a few months, but if they persist, it may be advisable to change to a brand containing a lower dose of estrogen or to some other contraceptive method.

Risks and special precautions

All oral contraceptives need to be taken regularly for maximum protection against pregnancy. Contraceptive protection can be reduced by missing a pill (see What to do if you miss a pill, below). It may also be reduced by vomiting or diarrhea. If you suffer from either of these symptoms, it is advisable to act as if you had missed your last pill. Many drugs may also affect the action of oral contraceptives and it is essential to tell your physician and pharmacist that you are taking oral contraceptives before taking additional prescribed medications.

Oral contraceptives, particularly those containing an estrogen, have been found to carry a number of risks. These are summarized in the box on the facing page. One of the most serious potential adverse effects of estrogen-containing pills is development of a thrombus (blood clot) in a vein or artery. The thrombus may travel to the lungs or cause a stroke or heart attack. The risk of thrombus formation increases with age and other factors, notably obesity, high blood pressure, and smoking. Physicians assess these risk factors for each person when prescribing oral contraceptives. A woman who is over 35 may be advised against taking a

POSTCOITAL CONTRACEPTION

Pregnancy following intercourse without contraception may be avoided by taking a short course of postcoital ("morning after") pills. The preparation used for this purpose contains a progestin; usually two tablets are taken together within 72 hours following intercourse. This regime may also be taken in two doses, as one tablet 12 hours apart. These drugs postpone ovulation and act on the lining of the uterus to prevent implantation of the egg. However, the high doses required make them unsuitable for regular use. This method has a higher failure rate than the usual oral contraceptives.

combined pill, especially if she smokes or has an underlying medical condition such as diabetes mellitus. Concerns have been expressed about contraceptive pills containing the progestins desogestrel and drospirenone because several studies have found that preparations with this progestin carry a higher risk of thrombus formation than those containing other progestins. The drugs that contain desogestrel include Marvelon and Ortho-Cept. These preparations should be used only by those women who are intolerant of other contraceptive pills and are aware of the higher risk.

High blood pressure is a possible complication of oral contraceptives for some women. All women taking oral contraceptives should have their blood pressure measured before the pill is prescribed and monitored at six-month intervals thereafter.

Some very rare liver cancers have occurred in contraceptive pill-users, and breast cancer may be slightly more common. However, cancers of the ovaries and uterus are less common in women who take the contraceptive pill.

Although there is no evidence that oral contraceptives reduce a woman's fertility or that they damage the babies conceived after they are discontinued, physicians recommend that you wait for at least one normal menstrual period after stopping the pill before you attempt to become pregnant.

WHAT TO DO IF YOU MISS A PILL

Contraceptive protection may be reduced if blood levels of the *hormones* in the body fall as a result of missing a pill. It is particularly important to ensure that the progestogen-only pills are taken punctually. If you miss a pill, the action you should take depends on the degree of lateness and the type of pill being used (see below).

	Combined and phased pills	Progestin-only pills
3–12 hours late	Take the missed pill now. No additional precautions necessary.	Take the missed pill now. Take additional precautions for the next 7 days.
Over 12 hours late	Take the missed pill now and take the next pill on time (even if on the same day). If more than one pill has been missed, take the latest missed pill now and the next on time. Take additional precautions for the next 7 days. If the 7 days extends into the pill-free (or inactive pill) period, start the next pack without a break (or without taking inactive pills).	Take the missed pill now, and take the next on time. Take additional precautions for the next 7 days.

COMMON DRUGS

Progestins	Estrogens
Desogestrel	Ethinyl estradiol *
Drospirenone	
Ethynodiol diacetate	
Etonogestrel	
Levonorgestrel *	
Norelgestromin	
Norethindrone *	* See Part 4
Norgestimate	

DRUGS FOR INFERTILITY

Conception and the establishment of pregnancy require a healthy reproductive system in both partners. The man must be able to produce sufficient numbers of healthy sperm; the woman must be able to produce a healthy egg that is able to pass freely down the fallopian tube to the uterus. The lining of the uterus must be in a condition that allows the implantation of the fertilized egg.

The cause of infertility may sometimes remain undiscovered, but in the majority of cases it is due to one of the following factors: intercourse taking place at the wrong time during the menstrual cycle; the man producing too few or unhealthy sperm; the woman either failing to ovulate (release an egg) or having blocked fallopian tubes perhaps as a result of previous pelvic infection. Alternatively, production of gonadotrophin *hormones* – follicle-stimulating hormone (FSH) and luteinizing hormone (LH) – needed for ovulation and implantation of the egg may be affected by illness or psychological stress.

If no simple explanation can be found, the man's semen will be analyzed. If these tests show that abnormally low numbers of sperm are being produced, or if a large proportion of the sperm produced are unhealthy, drug treatment may be tried.

If no abnormality of sperm production is discovered, the woman will be given a thorough medical examination. Ovulation is monitored and blood tests may be performed to assess hormone levels. If ovulation does not occur, the woman may be offered drug treatment.

Why drugs are used

In men, low sperm production may be treated with gonadotrophins (FSH or hCG) or a pituitary-stimulating drug (for example, clomiphene).

In women, drugs are useful in helping to achieve pregnancy only when a hormone defect inhibiting ovulation has been diagnosed. Treatment may continue for months and does not always produce a pregnancy. Women in whom the pituitary gland produces some FSH and LH may be given courses

ACTION OF FERTILITY DRUGS

Ovulation (release of an egg) and implantation are governed by hormones that are produced by the pituitary gland. FSH stimulates ripening of the egg follicle. LH triggers ovulation and ensures that progesterone is produced to prepare the uterus for the implantation of the egg. Drugs for female infertility boost the actions of these hormones.

FSH and hCG FSH adds to the action of the natural FSH early in the menstrual cycle. hCG mimics the action of natural LH at mid-cycle.

Clomiphene Normally, estrogen suppresses the output of FSH and LH by the pituitary gland. Clomiphene opposes the action of estrogen so that FSH and LH continue to be produced.

Comparison of normal hormone fluctuation and timing of drug treatment

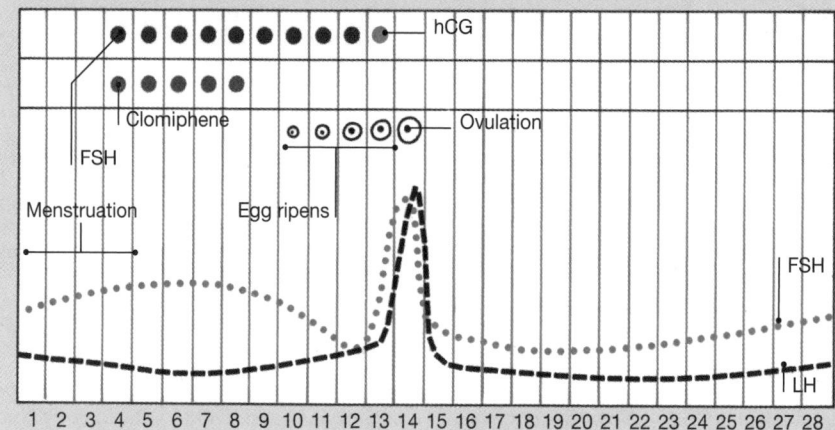

of clomiphene for several days during each month. Usually, up to three courses may be tried. An effective dose produces ovulation five to ten days after the last tablet is taken.

Clomiphene may thicken the cervical mucus, impeding the passage of sperm but the advantage of achieving ovulation outweighs the risk of this side effect. If treatment with clomiphene fails to produce ovulation, or if a disorder of the pituitary gland prevents the production of FSH and LH, treatment with FSH and human chorionic gonadotropin may be given. FSH is given during the second week of the menstrual cycle, followed by an injection of human chorionic gonadotropin.

How they work

Fertility drugs raise the chance of ovulation by boosting levels of LH and FSH. Clomiphene stimulates the pituitary gland to increase its output of these hormones. Artificially produced FSH and hCG mimic the action of naturally produced FSH and LH respectively. Both treatments, when successful, stimulate ovulation and implantation of the fertilized egg.

How they affect you

Clomiphene may produce hot flushes, nausea, headaches, and, rarely, ovarian cysts and visual disturbance, while hCG can cause tiredness, headaches, and mood changes. FSH can cause the ovaries to enlarge, producing abdominal discomfort. These drugs increase the likelihood of multiple births, usually twins.

DRUGS FOR ERECTILE DYSFUNCTION

Erectile dysfunction, or impotence, is a common male disorder and is defined as the inability to achieve or maintain an erection. The penis contains three cylinders of erectile tissue, the corpora cavernosa and the corpus spongiosum. Normally, when a man is sexually aroused, the arteries in the penis relax and widen, allowing more blood than usual to flow into the organ, filling the corpora cavernosa and the corpus spongiosum. As these tissues expand and harden, the veins that carry blood out of the penis become compressed, reducing outflow and resulting

in an erection. In some forms of erectile dysfunction, this does not happen. Drugs can then be used to increase the blood flow into the penis to produce an erection.

Drugs like sildenafil (p.433) not only increase the blood flow into the penis but also prevent the muscle wall from relaxing, so the blood does not drain out of the blood vessels and the penis remains erect.

Alprostadil (p.183) is a prostaglandin drug that helps men achieve an erection by widening the blood vessels, but it must be injected directly into the penis, or applied into the urethra using a special syringe.

COMMON DRUGS

Buserelin
Clomiphene
Follitropin alpha
Follitopin beta
Ganirelix
Gonadorelin
Goserelin ✳
Human chorionic gonadotropin
Menotropins
Nafarelin

Drugs for erectile dysfunction
Alprostadil ✳
Sildenafil ✳
Tadalafil
Vardenafil

✳ See Part 4

DRUGS USED IN LABOUR

Normal labour has three stages. In the first stage, the uterus begins to contract, initially irregularly and then gradually more regularly and powerfully, while the cervix dilates until it is fully stretched. During the second stage, powerful contractions of the uterus push the baby down the mother's birth canal and out of her body. The third stage involves the delivery of the placenta.

Drugs may be required during one or more stages of labour for any of the following reasons: to induce or augment labour; to delay premature labour (see Uterine muscle relaxants, below right); and to relieve pain. The administration of some drugs may be viewed as part of normal obstetric care; for example, the uterine stimulant ergometrine may be injected routinely before the third stage of labour. Other drugs are administered only when the condition of the mother or baby requires intervention. The possible adverse effects of the drug on both mother and baby are always carefully balanced against the benefits.

Drugs to induce or augment labour

Induction of labour may be advised when a physician considers it risky for the health of the mother or baby for the pregnancy to continue – for example, if natural labour does not occur within two weeks of the due date or when a woman has pre-eclampsia. Other common reasons for inducing labour include premature rupture of the membrane surrounding the baby (breaking of the waters), slow growth of the baby due to poor nourishment by the placenta, or death of the fetus in the uterus.

When labour needs to be induced, oxytocin, a uterine stimulant, may be administered intravenously. Alternatively, a prostaglandin vaginal suppository may be given to soften and dilate the cervix. If these methods are ineffective or cannot be used because of potential adverse effects (see Risks and special precautions, above right), a cesarean delivery may have to be performed.

DRUGS USED TO TERMINATE PREGNANCY

Drugs may be used in a hospital or in a clinic to terminate a pregnancy up to the end of the 23rd week, or to empty the uterus after the death of the baby. A prostaglandin may be given first to dilate the cervix. Before 14 weeks of pregnancy, the fetus is then removed under anesthetic. After 14 weeks of pregnancy, labour is induced with a prostaglandin. These methods may be supplemented by oxytocin given by intravenous drip (see Drugs to induce or augment labour, above).

Oxytocin may also be used to strengthen the force of contractions in labour that has started spontaneously but has not continued normally.

A combination of oxytocin and another uterine stimulant, ergometrine, is given to most women as the baby is being born or immediately following birth to prevent excessive bleeding after the delivery of the placenta. This combination encourages the uterus to contract after delivery, which restricts the flow of blood.

Risks and special precautions
When oxytocin is used to induce labour, the dosage is carefully monitored throughout to prevent the possibility of excessively violent contractions. It is administered to women who have had surgery of the uterus only with careful monitoring. The drug is not known to affect the baby adversely. Ergometrine is not given to women who have suffered from high blood pressure during the course of pregnancy.

Drugs used for pain relief
Opioid analgesics
Meperidine, morphine, or other opioids may be given once active labour has been established (see Analgesics, p.64). Possible side effects for the mother include drowsiness, nausea, and vomiting. Opioid drugs may cause breathing difficulties for the new baby, but these problems may be reversed by the antidote naloxone.

Epidural anesthesia
This provides pain relief during labour and birth by numbing the nerves leading to the uterus and pelvic area. It is often used during a planned cesarean delivery, thus enabling the mother to be fully conscious for the birth.

An epidural involves the injection of a local anesthetic drug (see p.64) into the epidural space between the spinal cord and the vertebrae. An epidural may block the mother's urge to push during the second stage, and a forceps delivery may be necessary. Headaches may occasionally occur following epidural anesthesia.

Oxygen and nitrous oxide
These gases are combined to produce a mixture that reduces the pain caused by contractions. During the first and second stages of labour, gas is self-administered by inhalation through a mouthpiece or mask. If it is used over too long a period, it may produce nausea, confusion, and dehydration in the mother.

Local anesthetics
These drugs are injected inside the vagina or near the vaginal opening and are used to numb sensation during forceps delivery, before an episiotomy (an incision

WHEN DRUGS ARE USED IN LABOUR

The drugs used in each stage of labour are described below.

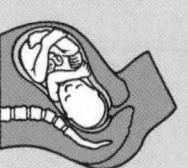

Before labour
Oxytocin
Prostaglandins

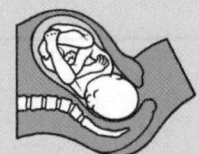

First stage
Epidural anesthetics
Morphine
Oxytocin
Meperidine

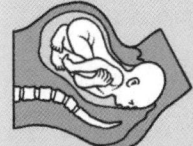

Second stage
Local anesthetics
Nitrous oxide
Oxytocin

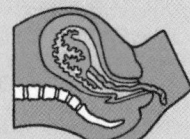

Third stage
Ergometrine
Oxytocin

made to enlarge the vaginal opening), and when stitches are necessary. Side effects are rare.

Uterine muscle relaxants
When contractions of the uterus start before the 34th week of pregnancy, doctors usually advise bed rest and may also administer a drug that relaxes the muscles of the uterus and thus halts labour. Initially, the drug is given in hospital by injection, but it may be continued orally at home. These drugs work by stimulating the sympathetic nervous system (see Autonomic nervous system, p.63) and may cause palpitations and anxiety in the mother. They have not been shown to have adverse effects on the baby.

COMMON DRUGS

Prostaglandins
Dinoprostone

Pain relief
Fentanyl ✳
Morphine ✳
Meperidine

Uterine stimulants
Ergonovine
Oxytocin

Local anesthetics
Bupivacaine
Lidocaine

✳ See Part 4

DRUGS USED FOR URINARY DISORDERS

Urine is produced by the kidneys and stored in the bladder. As the urine accumulates, the bladder walls stretch and pressure within the bladder increases. Eventually, the stretching stimulates nerve endings that produce the urge to urinate. The ring of muscle (sphincter) around the bladder neck normally keeps the bladder closed until it is consciously relaxed, allowing urine to pass via the urethra out of the body.

A number of disorders can affect the urinary tract. The most common of these disorders are infection in the bladder (cystitis) or the urethra (urethritis), and loss of reliable control over urination (urinary incontinence). A less common problem is inability to expel urine (urinary retention). Drugs used to treat these problems include *antibiotics* and antibacterial drugs, analgesics, drugs to increase the acidity of the urine, and drugs that act on nerve control over the muscles of the bladder and sphincter.

Drugs for urinary infection

Nearly all infections of the bladder are caused by bacteria. Symptoms include a continual urge to urinate, although often nothing is passed; pain on urinating; and lower abdominal pain.

Many antibiotic and antibacterial drugs are used to treat urinary tract infections. Among the most widely used – because of their effectiveness – are cephalexin and norfloxacin (see Antibiotics, p.114, and Antibacterial drugs, p.117).

Measures are also sometimes taken to increase the acidity of the urine, thereby making it hostile to bacteria. Ascorbic acid (vitamin C) and acid fruit juices have this effect. Cranberry juice has also been tried in preventing urinary infections. Once appropriate antibiotic treatment is started, symptoms are commonly relieved within a few hours.

For maximum effect, all drug treatments prescribed for urinary tract infections need to be accompanied by increased fluid intake.

Drugs for urinary incontinence

Urinary incontinence can occur for several reasons. A weak sphincter muscle allows the involuntary passage of urine when abdominal pressure is raised by coughing or physical exertion. This is known as stress incontinence and commonly affects women who have had children and post-menopausal women. Urgency – the sudden need to urinate – stems from oversensitivity of the bladder muscle; small quantities of urine stimulate the urge to urinate frequently.

Incontinence can also occur due to loss of nerve control in neurological disorders such as multiple sclerosis. In children, inability to control urination at night (nocturnal enuresis) is also a form of urinary incontinence.

Drug treatment is not necessary or appropriate for all forms of incontinence. In stress incontinence, exercises to strengthen the pelvic floor muscles or surgery to support the urethra (e.g. midurethral sling or TVT procedure) may be effective. Vaginal estrogen may be tried in postmenopausal women. In urgency, regular emptying of the bladder can often avoid the need for medical intervention. Incontinence caused by loss of nerve control is unlikely to be helped by drug treatment. Frequency of urination in urgency may be reduced by *anticholinergic* and *antispasmodic* drugs. These reduce nerve signals from the muscles in the bladder, allowing greater volumes of urine to accumulate without stimulating the urge to pass urine. Tricyclic antidepressants, such as imipramine, have a strong anticholinergic action, and have been prescribed for nocturnal enuresis in children, but many doctors believe the risk of overdosage is unacceptable. Desmopressin, a synthetic derivative of antidiuretic hormone (see p.131), is preferred for nocturnal enuresis.

Drugs for urinary retention

Urinary retention is the inability to empty the bladder. This usually results from the failure of the bladder muscle to contract sufficiently to expel accumulated urine. Possible causes include an enlarged prostate gland or tumour, or a long-standing neurological disorder. Some drugs can cause urinary retention.

Most cases of urinary retention need to be relieved by inserting a tube catheter into the urethra. Surgery may be needed to prevent a recurrence of the problem. Drugs that relax the sphincter or stimulate bladder contraction are now rarely used in the treatment of urinary retention, but two types of drug are used in the long-term management of prostatic enlargement. Finasteride prevents production of the male hormones that stimulate prostatic growth and alpha blockers, such as prazosin and terazosin, relax smooth muscle in the prostate gland and in the urethra, thereby improving urine outflow. Long-term drug treatment can relieve symptoms and delay the need for surgery.

ACTION OF DRUGS ON URINATION

Normal bladder action
Urination occurs when the sphincter keeping the exit from the bladder into the urethra closed is consciously relaxed in response to signals from the bladder indicating that it is full. As the sphincter opens, the bladder wall contracts and urine is expelled.

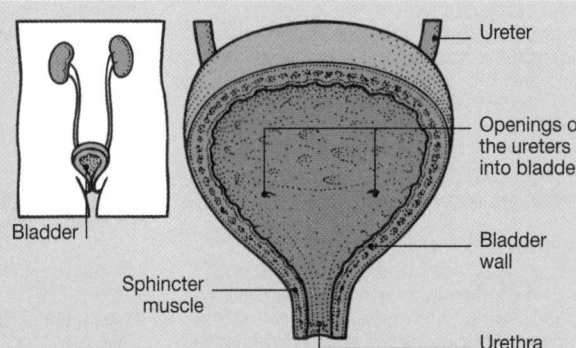

Bladder

Sphincter muscle

Ureter

Openings of the ureters into bladder

Bladder wall

Urethra

How drugs act to improve bladder control

Anticholinergic drugs relax the bladder muscle by interfering with the passage of nerve impulses to the muscle.

Sympathomimetics act directly on the sphincter muscle, causing it to contract.

How drugs act to relieve urinary retention

Parasympathomimetics (cholinergics) stimulate contraction of the bladder wall.

Alpha blockers relax the muscle of the sphincter and urethra.

COMMON DRUGS

Antibiotics and antibacterials
(see pp.114–117)

Anticholinergic/ antispasmodic
Darifenacin ✳
Desipramine
Flavoxate
Imipramine ✳
Nortriptyline
Oxybutynin ✳
Solifenacin
Tolterodine ✳
Trospium

Alpha blockers
Alfuzosin
Doxazosin ✳
Tamsulosin ✳
Terazosin

Other drugs
Desmopressin ✳
Dutasteride
Finasteride ✳
Vitamin C ✳

✳ See Part 4

EYES AND EARS

The eyes and ears are the two sense organs that provide us with the most information about the world around us. The eye is the organ of vision that converts light images into nerve signals, which are transmitted to the brain for interpretation into images. The ear not only provides the means by which sound is detected and communicated to the brain, but it also contains the organ of balance that tells the brain about the position and movement of the body. It is divided into three parts – outer, middle, and inner ear.

What can go wrong

The most common eye and ear disorders are infection and inflammation (sometimes caused by allergy). Many parts of the eye may be affected, notably the conjunctiva (the membrane that covers the front of the eye and lines the eyelids) and the iris. The middle and outer ear are more commonly affected by infection than the inner ear.

The eye may also be damaged by glaucoma, a disorder in which pressure of fluid within the eye builds up and may eventually threaten vision. Eye problems such as retinopathy (disease of the retina) or cataracts (clouding of the lens) may occur as a result of diabetes or for other reasons, but both are now treatable. Disorders for which no drug treatment is appropriate are beyond the scope of this book.

Other disorders affecting the ear include build-up of wax (cerumen) in the outer ear canal and disturbances to the balance mechanism (see Vertigo and Ménière's disease, p.74).

Why drugs are used

Doctors usually prescribe *antibiotics* (see p.114) to clear ear and eye infections. These may be given by mouth or *topically*. Topical eye and ear preparations may contain a corticosteroid (p.127) to reduce inflammation. When inflammation has been caused by allergy, antihistamines (p.110) may also be taken. Decongestant drugs (p.79) are often prescribed to help clear the eustachian tube in middle ear infections.

Various drugs are used to reduce fluid pressure in glaucoma. These include certain diuretics (p.85), beta blockers (p.83), and *miotics* to narrow the pupil. In other cases, the pupil may need to be widened by *mydriatic* drugs.

MAJOR DRUG GROUPS

Drugs for glaucoma	Drugs for ear disorders
Drugs affecting the pupil	

How the eye works
Light enters the eye through the cornea. The muscles of the iris control pupil size and thus the amount of light passing into the eye. In the eye, light hits the retina, which converts it to nerve signals that are carried by the optic nerve to the brain.

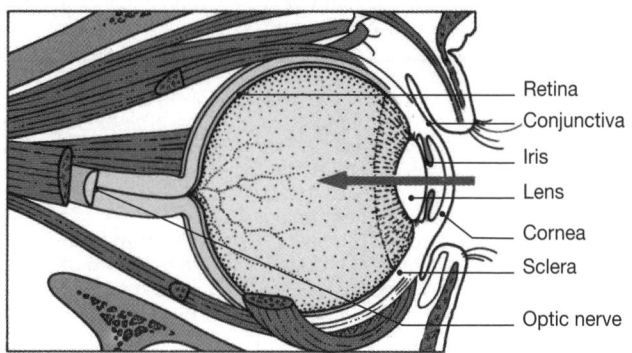

Retina
Conjunctiva
Iris
Lens
Cornea
Sclera
Optic nerve

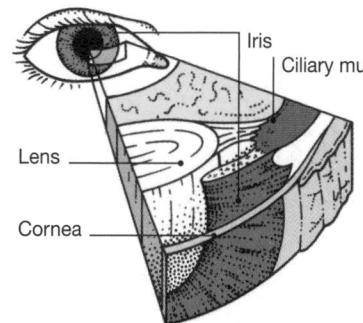

Iris
Ciliary muscle
Lens
Cornea

The eye muscles
Both focusing and pupil size are governed by muscles controlled by the autonomic nervous system (p.63), which may be affected by many drugs. Disturbed vision is often a *side effect* of such drugs.

The ear
The outer ear canal is separated from the middle ear by the eardrum. Three bones in the middle ear connect it to the inner ear. This contains the cochlea (organ of hearing) and the labyrinth (organ of balance).

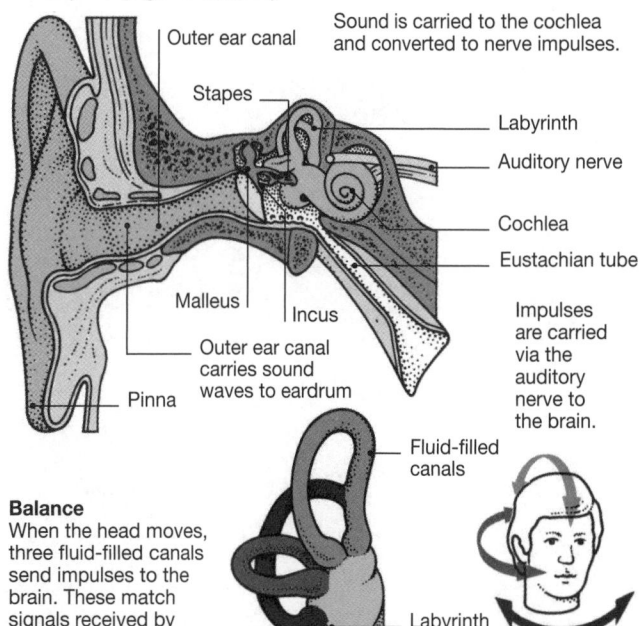

Outer ear canal
Stapes
Malleus
Incus
Pinna
Outer ear canal carries sound waves to eardrum

Sound is carried to the cochlea and converted to nerve impulses.

Labyrinth
Auditory nerve
Cochlea
Eustachian tube

Impulses are carried via the auditory nerve to the brain.

Fluid-filled canals
Labyrinth

Balance
When the head moves, three fluid-filled canals send impulses to the brain. These match signals received by eyes and limb muscles.

DRUGS FOR GLAUCOMA

Glaucoma is the name given to a group of conditions in which the optic nerve is damaged, and pressure in the eye may be at an abnormally high level. This compresses the blood vessels that supply the nerve connecting the eye to the brain (optic nerve) and may result in irreversible nerve damage and permanent loss of vision.

In the most common type of glaucoma, called chronic (or open-angle) glaucoma, reduced drainage of fluid from the eye causes pressure inside the eye to build up slowly. Progressive reduction in the peripheral field of vision may take months or years to be noticed. Acute (or angle closure) glaucoma occurs when drainage of fluid is suddenly blocked by the iris. Fluid pressure usually builds up quite suddenly, blurring vision in the affected eye (see below). The eye becomes red and painful, accompanied by a headache and sometimes vomiting. The main attack is often preceded by milder warning attacks, such as seeing haloes around

lights in the previous weeks or months. Elderly, far-sighted people are particularly at risk of developing acute glaucoma. The angle may also narrow suddenly following injury or after taking certain drugs, for example, *anticholinergic* drugs. Closed-angle glaucoma may develop more slowly (chronic closed-angle glaucoma).

Drugs are used in the treatment of both types of glaucoma. These include miotics (see Drugs affecting the pupil, p.158) and beta blockers (p.83), as well as certain diuretics (carbonic anhydrase inhibitors and osmotics, p.85).

Why drugs are used
Chronic glaucoma
In this form of glaucoma, drugs are used to reduce pressure inside the eye. These drugs will prevent further deterioration of vision but cannot restore damage that has already been sustained, and therefore these drugs may be required lifelong. In most patients, treatment is begun with

eyedrops containing a beta blocker or prostaglandin to reduce the production of fluid inside the eye. Cholinergic *agonist* eye drops to contract the ciliary muscle and improve fluid drainage may be given. Prostaglandins are also used to increase fluid outflow. If none of these drugs are effective, brimonidine may be tried to reduce secretion and help outflow. Sometimes a carbonic anhydrase inhibitor such as acetazolamide may be given by mouth to reduce fluid production. Laser treatment and surgery may also be used to improve fluid drainage from the eye.

Acute glaucoma
In acute glaucoma immediate medical treatment is required in order to prevent total loss of vision. Drugs are used initially to bring down the pressure within the eye. Laser treatment or surgery is then carried out to prevent a recurrence of the problem so that long-term drug treatment is seldom required.

WHAT HAPPENS IN GLAUCOMA

Normal eye
The ciliary body, situated at the root of the iris, continuously produces aqueous humour – a watery fluid that helps to maintain the normal shape of the eyeball. Aqueous humour drains via the angle between the cornea and iris through a mesh of fibres (the trabecular meshwork) into a channel in the sclera (white of the eye).

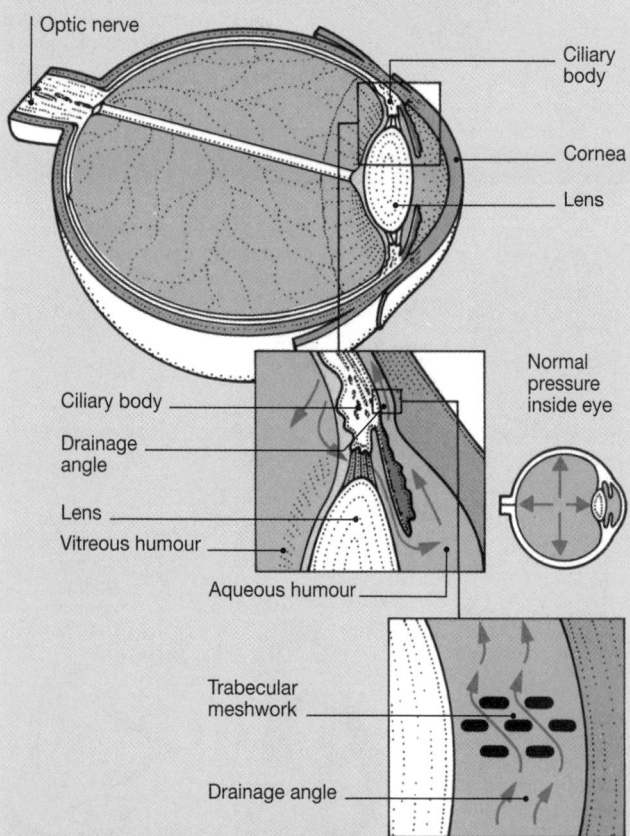

Optic nerve
Ciliary body
Cornea
Lens
Ciliary body
Drainage angle
Lens
Vitreous humour
Aqueous humour
Trabecular meshwork
Drainage angle

Normal pressure inside eye

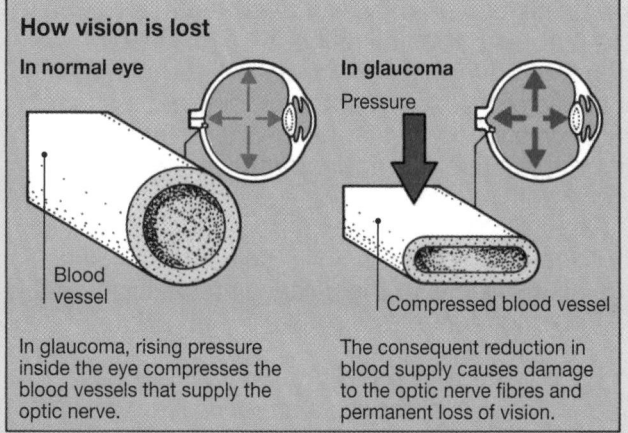

How vision is lost
In normal eye

Blood vessel

In glaucoma, rising pressure inside the eye compresses the blood vessels that supply the optic nerve.

In glaucoma
Pressure

Compressed blood vessel

The consequent reduction in blood supply causes damage to the optic nerve fibres and permanent loss of vision.

Acute glaucoma
In acute glaucoma, the drainage angle between the cornea and the iris becomes completely closed, so the pressure inside the eye rises rapidly. This may cause permanent damage to the nerve fibres.

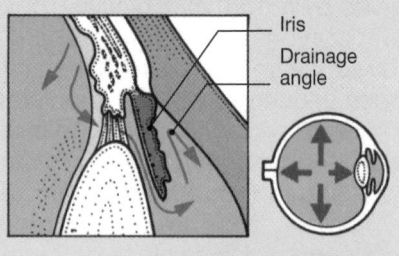

Iris
Drainage angle

Chronic glaucoma
In chronic glaucoma, the trabecular mesh-work through which the aqueous humour normally drains slowly closes off, so that fluid pressure builds up gradually and damages the optic nerve.

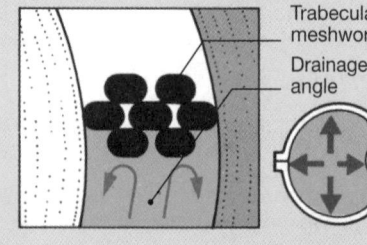

Trabecular meshwork
Drainage angle

Acetazolamide is often the first drug administered when the condition is diagnosed. This drug may be injected for rapid effect and thereafter administered by mouth. Frequent applications of eye drops containing pilocarpine or carbachol are given. An osmotic diuretic such as mannitol may be administered. This draws fluid out of all body tissues, including the eye, and reduces pressure within the eye.

How they work

Drugs for glaucoma act in various ways to reduce fluid pressure in the eye. Cholinergic agonists improve the drainage of the fluid out of the eye. In chronic glaucoma, this is achieved by increasing the outflow of aqueous humour through the drainage channel called the trabecular meshwork. In acute glaucoma, the pupil constricting effect of cholinergic agonists pulls the iris away from the drainage channel, allowing the aqueous humour to flow out in the normal way. Prostaglandin analogues act by increasing fluid flow from the eye. Beta blockers and carbonic anhydrase inhibitors act on the fluid-producing cells inside the eye to reduce the output of aqueous humour. Sympathomimetic drugs such as epinephrine, brimonidine, and apraclonidine are also thought to act partly in this way and partly by improving fluid drainage.

How they affect you

Drugs for acute glaucoma relieve pain and other symptoms within a few hours of their being used. The benefits of treatment in chronic glaucoma, however, may not be immediately apparent since treatment is only able to halt a further deterioration of vision.

People receiving cholinergic agonist eye drops are likely to notice darkening of vision and difficulty seeing in the dark. Increased shortsightedness may be noticeable. Some cholinergic agonists also cause irritation and redness of the eyes.

Beta blocker eye drops have few day-to-day side effects but carry risks for a few people (see right). Oral acetazolamide usually causes an increase in frequency of urination and thirst. Nausea and general malaise are also common.

ACTION OF DRUGS FOR GLAUCOMA

Cholinergic agonists

These act on the circular muscle in the iris to reduce the size of the pupil. In acute glaucoma, this relieves any obstruction to the flow of aqueous humour by pulling the iris away from the cornea (right). In chronic glaucoma, these drugs act directly to increase the outflow of aqueous humour.

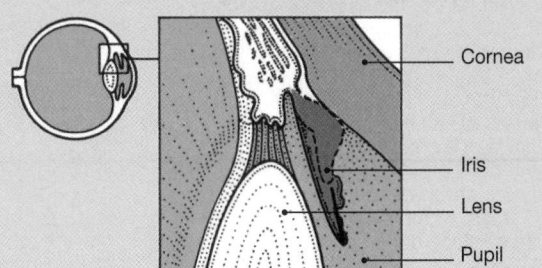

- Cornea
- Iris
- Lens
- Pupil

Beta blockers

The fluid-producing cells in the ciliary body are stimulated by signals passed through beta receptors. Beta blocking drugs prevent the transmission of signals through these receptors, thereby reducing the stimulus to produce fluid.

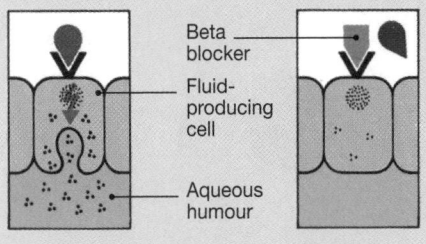

- Beta blocker
- Fluid-producing cell
- Aqueous humour

Before drug   **After drug**

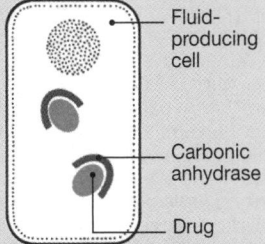

- Fluid-producing cell
- Carbonic anhydrase
- Drug

Carbonic anhydrase inhibitors

These block carbonic anhydrase, an *enzyme* involved in the production of aqueous humour in the ciliary body.

Risks and special precautions

Cholinergic agonists can cause alteration in vision. Beta blockers are absorbed into the body and can affect the lungs, heart, and circulation. As a result, a cardio-selective beta blocker, such as betaxolol, may be prescribed with caution to people with asthma or certain circulatory disorders and, in some cases, such drugs are withheld altogether. The amount of the drug absorbed into the body can be reduced by applying the eye drops carefully, as described (left). Acetazolamide may cause troublesome adverse effects, including painful tingling of the hands and feet, the formation of kidney stones, and rarely, kidney damage. People with existing kidney problems are not usually given this drug.

APPLYING EYE DROPS IN GLAUCOMA

To reduce the amount of drug absorbed into the blood via the lacrimal (tear) duct, apply eye drops as described. This also improves the effectiveness of the drug.

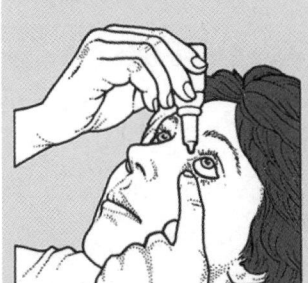

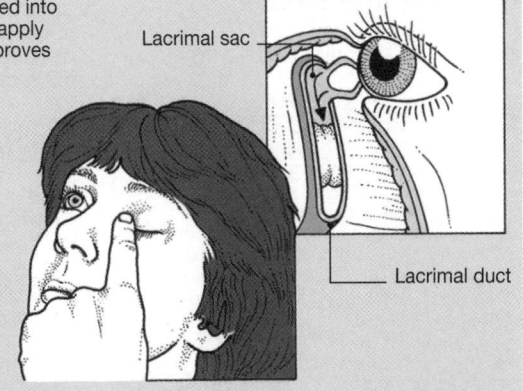

- Lacrimal sac
- Lacrimal duct

1 Press firmly on the lacrimal sac in the corner of the eye and apply the number of drops prescribed by your doctor.

2 Maintain pressure on the lacrimal sac for a few moments after applying the drops.

COMMON DRUGS

Cholinergic agonists
Carbachol
Pilocarpine *

Carbonic anhydrase inhibitors
Acetazolamide
Brinzolamide
Dorzolamide *
Methazolamide

Prostaglandin analogues
Bimatoprost

Latanoprost *
Travoprost

Beta blockers
Betaxolol
Levobunolol
Timolol *

Sympathomimetics
Apraclonidine
Brimonidine

* See Part 4

DRUGS AFFECTING THE PUPIL

The pupil of the eye is the circular opening in the centre of the iris (the coloured part of the eye) through which light enters. It continually changes in size to adjust to variations in the intensity of light; in bright light it becomes quite small (constricts), but in dim light the pupil enlarges (dilates).

Eye drops containing drugs that act on the pupil are widely used by specialists. They are grouped into two categories: *mydriatics*, which dilate the pupil, and *miotics*, which constrict it.

Why drugs are used

Mydriatics are most often used to allow the physician to view the inside of the eye – particularly the retina, the optic nerve head, and the blood vessels that supply the retina. Many of these drugs cause a temporary paralysis of the eye's focusing mechanism, a state called cycloplegia. Cycloplegia is sometimes induced to help determine the presence of any focusing errors, especially in babies and young children. By producing cycloplegia, it is possible to determine the precise optical prescription required for a small child, especially in the case of a squint.

Dilation of the pupil is part of the treatment for uveitis, an inflammatory disease of the iris and focusing muscle. In uveitis, the inflamed iris may stick to the lens, and thus cause severe damage to the eye. This complication can be prevented by early dilation of the pupil so that the iris is no longer in contact with the lens.

Constriction of the pupil with miotic drugs is often required in the treatment of glaucoma (see p.157). Miotics can also be used to restore the pupil to a normal size after dilation is induced by mydriatics.

How they work

The size of the pupil is controlled by two separate sets of muscles in the iris, the circular muscle and the radial muscle. The two sets of muscles are governed by separate branches of the autonomic nervous system (see p.63): the radial muscle is controlled by the sympathetic

ACTION OF DRUGS AFFECTING THE PUPIL

The muscles of the iris
Pupil size is controlled by the coordinated action of the circular and radial muscles in the iris. The circular muscle forms a ring around the pupil; when this muscle contracts, the pupil becomes smaller. The radial muscle is composed of fibres that run from the pupil to the base of the iris like the spokes of a wheel. Contraction of these fibres causes the pupil to become larger.

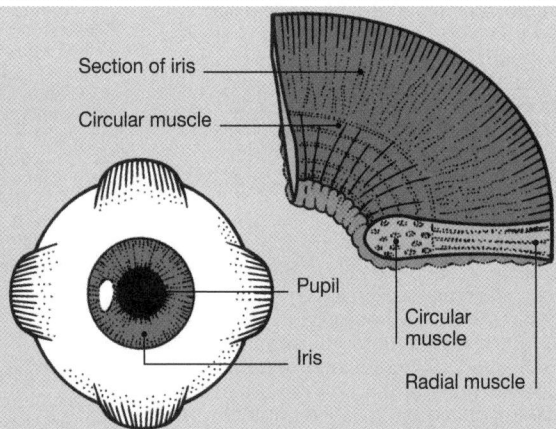

Section of iris
Circular muscle
Pupil
Iris
Circular muscle
Radial muscle

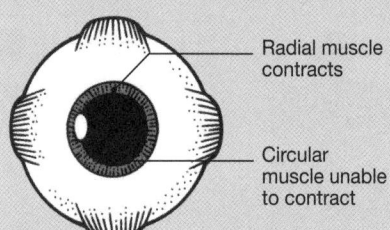

Radial muscle contracts
Circular muscle unable to contract

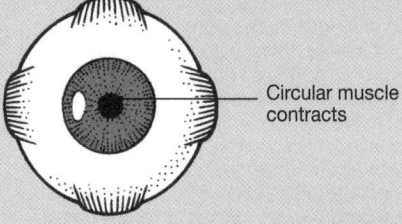

Circular muscle contracts

Mydriatics
Mydriatics enlarge the pupil in one of two ways. The *sympathomimetics* stimulate the radial muscle to contract. The *anticholinergics* prevent the circular muscle from contracting.

Miotics
Most miotics reduce the size of the pupil by stimulating the activity of the parasympathetic nervous system, which causes the circular muscle to contract.

nervous system, and the circular muscle is controlled by the parasympathetic nervous system.

Individual mydriatic and miotic drugs affect different branches of the autonomic nervous system, and cause the pupil to dilate or to contract, depending on the type of drug used (see above).

How they affect you

Mydriatic drugs – especially the long-acting types – impair the ability to focus

the eye(s) for several hours or even days after use. This interferes particularly with close activities such as reading. Bright light may cause discomfort. Miotics often interfere with night vision and may cause temporary short sight.

Normally, these eye drops produce few serious *adverse effects*. *Sympathomimetic* mydriatics may raise blood pressure and are used with caution in people with hypertension or heart disease. Miotics may irritate the eyes, but rarely cause generalized effects.

ARTIFICIAL TEAR PREPARATIONS

Tears are continually produced to keep the front of the eye covered with a thin moist film. This is essential for clear vision and for keeping the front of the eye free from dirt and other irritants. In some conditions, known collectively as dry eye syndromes (for example, Sjögren's syndrome), inadequate tear production may make the eyes feel dry and sore. Sore eyes can also occur in disorders where the eyelids do not close properly, causing the eye to become dry.

Why they are used
Since prolonged deficiency of natural tears can damage the cornea, regular application

of artificial tears in the form of eye drops is recommended for all of the conditions described above. Artificial tears may also be used to provide temporary relief from any feeling of discomfort and dryness in the eye caused by irritants, exposure to wind or sun, or following the initial wearing of contact lenses.

Although artificial tears are non-irritating, they often contain a preservative (for example, thimerosal or benzalkonium chloride) that may cause irritation. This risk of irritation is increased for wearers of soft contact lenses, who should ask their optician for advice before using any type of eye drops.

COMMON DRUGS

Sympathomimetic mydriatics
Phenylephrine

Miotics
Carbachol
Pilocarpine *

Anticholinergic mydriatics
Atropine *
Cyclopentolate
Homatropine
Tropicamide

* See Part 4

DRUGS FOR EAR DISORDERS

Inflammation and infection of the outer and middle ear are the most common ear disorders that are treated with drugs. Drug treatment for Ménière's disease, a condition that affects the inner ear, is described under Vertigo and Ménière's disease, p.74.

The type of drug treatment given for ear inflammation depends on the cause of the trouble and the site affected.

Inflammation of the outer ear

Inflammation of the external ear canal (otitis externa) can be caused by eczema or by a bacterial or fungal infection. The risk of inflammation is increased by swimming in dirty water, accumulation of wax in the ear, or scratching or poking too frequently at the ear.

Symptoms vary, but in many cases there is itching, pain (which may be severe if there is a boil in the ear canal), tenderness, and possibly some loss of hearing. If the ear is infected there will probably be a discharge.

Drug treatment

A corticosteroid (see p.127) in the form of ear drops may be used to treat inflammation of the outer ear when there is no infection. Aluminum acetate solution, as drops or applied on a piece of gauze, may also be used. Relief is usually obtained within a day or two. Prolonged use of corticosteroids is not advisable because they may reduce the ear's resistance to infection.

If there is both inflammation and infection, your physician may prescribe ear drops containing an *antibiotic* (see p.114) combined with a corticosteroid to relieve the inflammation. Usually, a combination of antibiotics is prescribed to make the treatment effective against a wide range of bacteria. Commonly used antibiotics include framycetin, neomycin, and polymyxin B. These antibiotics are not used if the eardrum is perforated.

EAR WAX REMOVAL

Ear wax (cerumen) is a natural secretion from the outer ear canal that keeps it free from dust and skin debris. Occasionally, wax may build up in the outer ear canal and become hard, leading to irritation and/or hearing loss.

A number of over-the-counter remedies are available to soften ear wax and hasten its expulsion. Such products may contain irritating substances that can cause inflammation. Some physicians advise application of olive or almond oil instead. A cotton plug should be inserted to retain the oil in the outer ear. When ear wax is not dislodged by such home treatment, a physician may syringe the ear with warm water. Do not use a stick or cotton swab.

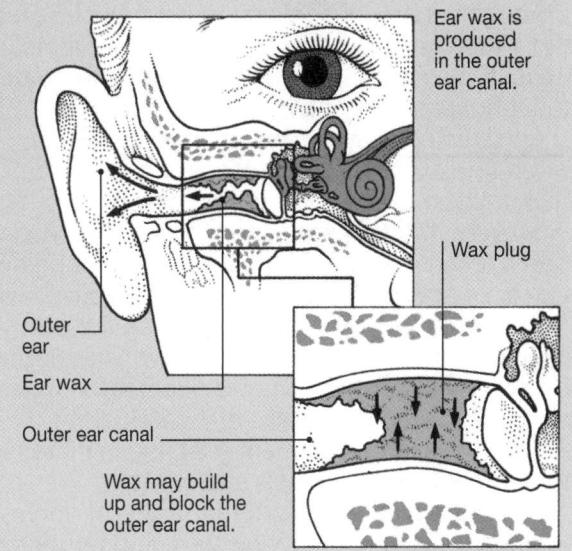

Ear wax is produced in the outer ear canal.

Wax plug

Outer ear

Ear wax

Outer ear canal

Wax may build up and block the outer ear canal.

They are not usually applied for long periods because prolonged application can irritate the skin lining the ear canal.

Sometimes an antibiotic given in the form of drops is not effective, and another type of antibiotic may also have to be taken by mouth.

Infection of the middle ear

Infection of the middle ear (otitis media) often causes severe pain and hearing loss. It is particularly common in young children in whom infecting organisms are able to spread easily into the middle ear from the nose or throat via the eustachian tube.

Viral infections of the middle ear usually cure themselves and are less serious than those caused by bacteria, which are sometimes treated with antibiotics given by mouth or injection. Bacterial infections often cause the eustachian tube to swell and become blocked. When a blockage occurs, pus builds up in the middle ear and puts pressure on the eardrum, which may perforate as a result.

Drug treatment

Sometimes, an antibiotic is given by mouth to clear the infection.

Although antibiotics are not effective against viral infections, it is often difficult to distinguish between a viral and a bacterial infection of the middle ear, so your physician may prescribe an antibiotic as a precautionary measure. Acetaminophen or ibuprofen, an analgesic (see p.64), may be given to relieve pain.

HOW TO USE EAR DROPS

Ear drops for outer ear disorders are more easily and efficiently administered if you have someone to help you. Lie on your side while the other person drops the medication into the ear cavity, ensuring that the dropper does not touch the ear. If possible, it is advisable to remain lying in that position for a few minutes in order to allow the drops to bathe the ear canal. Ear drops should be discarded when the course of treatment has been completed.

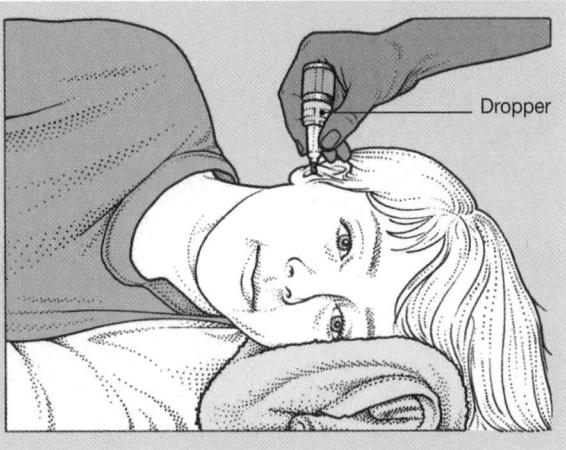

Dropper

COMMON DRUGS

Antibiotic and antibacterial ear drops
Chloramphenicol *
Ciprofloxacin *
Clioquinol
Framycetin
Gentamicin *
Neomycin
Polymyxin B *

Oral antibiotics
Amoxicillin
Amoxicillin/clavulanate
Cefprozil
Cefuroxime axetil

Corticosteroids
Betamethasone *
Dexamethasone *
Flumethasone

Other drugs
Aluminum acetate

* See Part 4

SKIN

The skin waterproofs, cushions, and protects the rest of the body and is, in fact, its largest organ. It provides a barrier against innumerable infections and infestations, it helps the body to retain its vital fluids; it plays a major role in temperature control, and it houses the sensory nerves of touch.

The skin consists of two main layers: a thin, tough top layer, the epidermis, and below it a thicker layer, the dermis. The epidermis also has two layers: the skin surface, or stratum corneum (horny layer) consisting of dead cells, and below, a layer of active cells. The cells in the active layer divide and eventually die, maintaining the horny layer. Living cells produce keratin, which toughens the epidermis and is the basic substance of hair and nails. Some living cells in the epidermis produce melanin, a pigment released in increased amounts following exposure to sunlight.

The dermis contains different types of nerve ending for sensing pain, pressure, and temperature; sweat glands to cool the body; sebaceous glands that release an oil (sebum) that lubricates and waterproofs the skin; and white blood cells that help to keep the skin clear of infection.

What can go wrong

Most skin complaints are not serious, but they may be distressing if visible. They include infection, inflammation and irritation, infestation by skin parasites, and changes in skin structure and texture (for example, psoriasis, eczema, and acne).

Why drugs are used

Skin problems often resolve themselves without drug treatment. Over-the-counter preparations containing medicinal ingredients are available, but physicians generally advise against their use without medical supervision because they could aggravate some skin conditions if used inappropriately. Drugs prescribed by physicians, however, are often highly effective, including antibiotics (p.114) for bacterial infections, antifungal drugs (p.124) for fungal infections, antiparasitic agents for skin parasites (p.164), and topical corticosteroids (p.162) for inflammatory conditions. Specialized drugs are available for conditions such as psoriasis and acne.

Although many drugs are *topical* medications, they must be used carefully because, like drugs taken orally, they can also cause adverse effects.

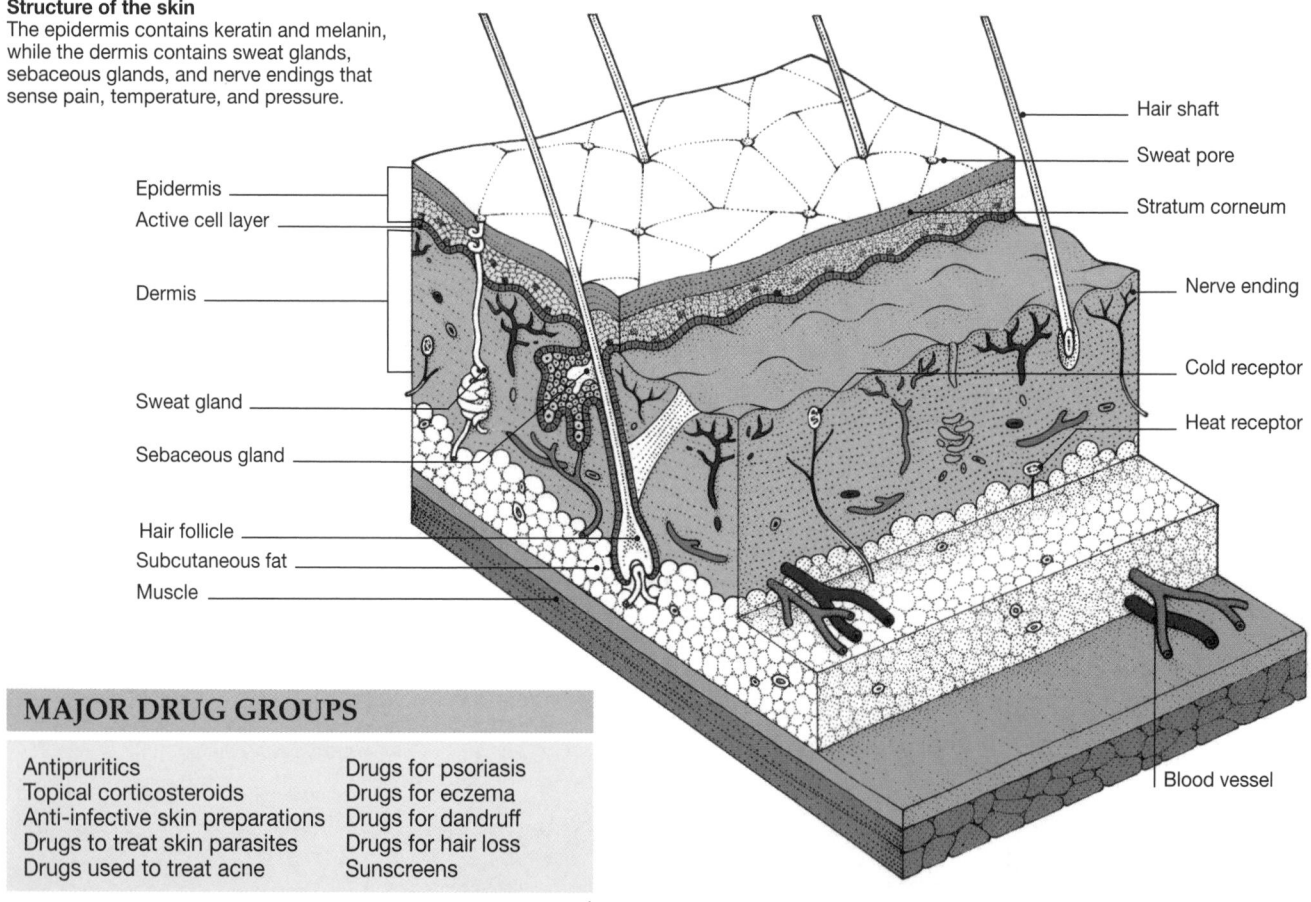

Structure of the skin
The epidermis contains keratin and melanin, while the dermis contains sweat glands, sebaceous glands, and nerve endings that sense pain, temperature, and pressure.

Epidermis
Active cell layer
Dermis
Sweat gland
Sebaceous gland
Hair follicle
Subcutaneous fat
Muscle

Hair shaft
Sweat pore
Stratum corneum
Nerve ending
Cold receptor
Heat receptor
Blood vessel

MAJOR DRUG GROUPS

Antipruritics	Drugs for psoriasis
Topical corticosteroids	Drugs for eczema
Anti-infective skin preparations	Drugs for dandruff
Drugs to treat skin parasites	Drugs for hair loss
Drugs used to treat acne	Sunscreens

ANTIPRURITICS

Itching (irritation of the skin that creates the urge to scratch), also known as pruritus, most often occurs as a result of minor physical irritation or chemical changes in the skin caused by disease, allergy, inflammation, or exposure to irritant substances. People differ in their tolerance to itching, and an individual's threshold can be altered by stress and other psychological factors.

Itching is a common symptom of many skin disorders, including eczema and psoriasis and allergic conditions such as urticaria (hives). It is also sometimes caused by a localized fungal infection or parasitic infestation. Diseases such as chickenpox may also cause itching. Less commonly, itching may also occur as a symptom of diabetes mellitus, jaundice, or kidney failure.

In many cases, generalized itching is caused by dry skin. Itching in particular parts of the body is often caused by a specific problem. For example, itching around the anus (pruritus ani) may result from hemorrhoids or worm infestation, while genital itching in women (pruritus

vulvae) may be caused either by vaginal infection or, in older women, may be the result of a hormone deficiency.

Although scratching frequently provides temporary relief, it can often increase skin inflammation and make the condition worse. Continued scratching of an area of irritated skin may occasionally lead to a vicious circle of scratching and itching that continues long after the original cause of the trouble has been removed.

There are a number of different types of medicines used to relieve skin irritation. These products include soothing *topical* preparations applied to the affected skin and drugs that are taken by mouth. The main drugs used in antipruritic products include corticosteroids (see Topical corticosteroids, p.162), antihistamines (p.110), and local anesthetics (p.64). Simple *emollient* or cooling creams or ointments, which do not contain active ingredients, are often recommended.

Why drugs are used

For mild itching arising from sunburn, urticaria, or insect bites, a cooling lotion

such as calamine, perhaps containing menthol, phenol, or camphor, may be the most appropriate treatment. Local anesthetic creams are sometimes helpful for small areas of irritation, such as insect bites, but are unsuitable for widespread itching. The itching caused by dry skin is often soothed by a simple emollient. Avoiding excessive bathing and using moisturizing bath oils may also help.

Severe itching from eczema or other inflammatory skin conditions may be treated with a topical corticosteroid preparation. When the irritation prevents sleep, a physician may prescribe an antihistamine drug to be taken at night to promote sleep as well as to relieve itching (see also sleeping drugs, p.66). Antihistamines are also often included in topical preparations for the relief of skin irritation, but their effectiveness when administered in this way is doubtful. For the treatment of pruritus ani, see drugs for rectal and anal disorders (p.99). Post-menopausal pruritus vulvae may be helped by vaginal creams containing estrogen; for further information, see female sex hormones (p.133). Itching that is caused by an underlying illness cannot be helped by skin creams and requires treatment for the principal disorder.

Risks and special precautions

The main risk from any antipruritic, with the exception of simple emollient and soothing preparations, is skin irritation, and therefore aggravated itching, that is caused by prolonged or heavy use. Antihistamine and local anesthetic creams are especially likely to cause a reaction, and must be stopped if they do so. Some antihistamines taken by mouth to relieve itching are likely to cause drowsiness. The special risks of topical corticosteroids are discussed on p.162.

Because itching can be a symptom of many underlying conditions, self-treatment should be continued for no longer than a week before seeking medical advice.

ACTION OF ANTIPRURITICS

Irritation of the skin such as during an allergic reaction causes the release of substances, such as histamine, that cause blood vessels to dilate and fluid to accumulate under the skin, which results in itching and inflammation. Antipruritic drugs act either by reducing inflammation, and therefore irritation, or by numbing the nerve impulses that transmit sensation to the brain.

Corticosteroids applied to the skin surface reduce itching caused by allergy within a few days, although the soothing effect of the cream may produce an immediate improvement. They pass into the underlying tissues and blood vessels and cause a decreased activity of histamine, prostaglandins, kinins and other substances which promote inflammation, leading to a

decrease in inflammation. They also reverse the dilation of blood vessels in the area, causing a decrease in redness, swelling and itching.

Antihistamines act within a few hours to reduce allergy-related skin inflammation. Applied to the skin or taken orally, they pass into the underlying tissue and block the effects of histamine on the blood vessels beneath the skin.

Local anesthetics absorbed through the skin may numb the transmission of signals from the nerves in the skin to the brain.

Soothing and emollient creams Calamine lotion and similar preparations applied to the skin surface reduce inflammation and itching by cooling the skin. Emollient creams lubricate the skin surface and prevent dryness.

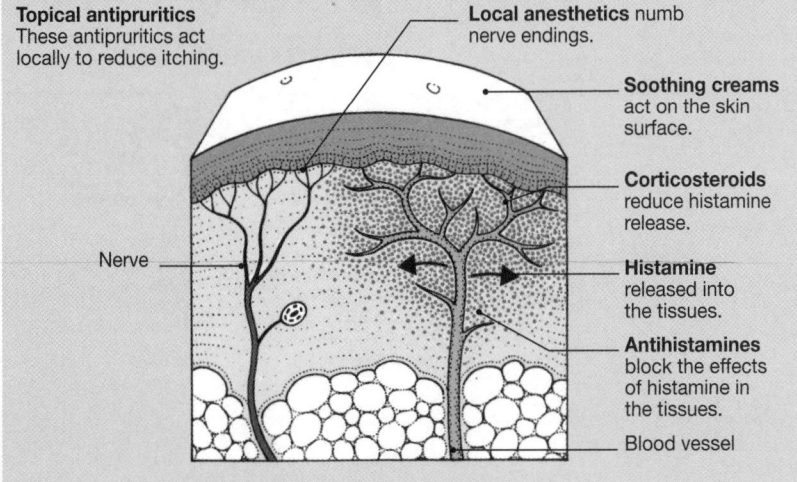

Topical antipruritics
These antipruritics act locally to reduce itching.

Local anesthetics numb nerve endings.

Soothing creams act on the skin surface.

Corticosteroids reduce histamine release.

Histamine released into the tissues.

Antihistamines block the effects of histamine in the tissues.

Nerve

Blood vessel

COMMON DRUGS

Antihistamines
(see also p.110)
Diphenhydramine *
Hydroxyzine

Corticosteroids
(see also p.127)
Hydrocortisone *

Local anesthetics
Benzocaine
Lidocaine
Tetracaine
Pramoxine

Emollient and cooling preparations
Aqueous cream
Calamine lotion
Cold cream
Emulsifying ointment

Other drugs
Crotamiton

* See Part 4

TOPICAL CORTICOSTEROIDS

Corticosteroid drugs (often simply called steroids) are related to the hormones produced by the adrenal glands. For a full description of these drugs, see p.127. *Topical* preparations containing a corticosteroid drug are often used to treat skin conditions in which inflammation is a prominent symptom.

Why they are used

Corticosteroid creams and ointments are most commonly given to relieve itching and inflammation associated with skin diseases such as eczema and dermatitis. These preparations may also be prescribed for psoriasis (see p.166). Corticosteroids do not affect the underlying cause of skin irritation, and the condition is therefore likely to recur unless the substance (allergen or irritant) that has provoked the irritation is removed, or the underlying condition is treated.

A physician might not prescribe a corticosteroid as the initial treatment, preferring to try a topical medicine that has fewer *adverse effects* (see Antipruritics, p.161). In most cases, treatment is started with a preparation containing a low concentration of a mild corticosteroid drug. A stronger preparation may be prescribed subsequently if the first product is ineffective.

How they affect you

Corticosteroids prevent the release of chemicals that trigger inflammation (see Action of corticosteroids on the skin, above right). Conditions treated with these drugs often improve within a few days of starting the drug. Applied topically, corticosteroids rarely cause side effects, but the stronger drugs used in high concentrations have certain risks.

Risks and special precautions

Prolonged use of potent corticosteroids in high concentrations may lead to changes

ACTION OF CORTICOSTEROIDS ON THE SKIN

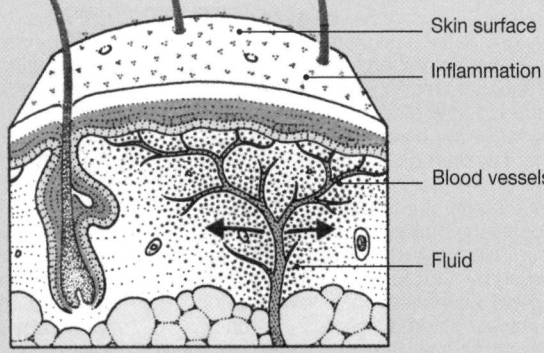

Skin inflammation
Irritation of the skin, caused by allergens or irritant factors, provokes white blood cells to release substances that dilate the blood vessels. This makes the skin hot, red, and swollen.

Skin surface
Inflammation
Blood vessels
Fluid

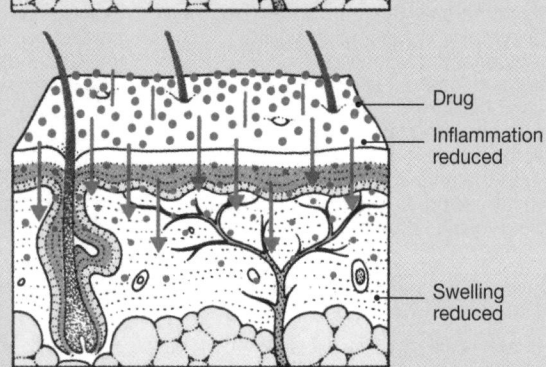

Drug action
Applied to the skin surface, corticosteroids are absorbed into the underlying tissue. There they inhibit the action of the substances that cause inflammation, allowing the blood vessels to return to normal and reducing the swelling.

Drug
Inflammation reduced
Swelling reduced

(either permanent or reversible) in the skin. The most common effect is thinning of the skin, sometimes resulting in permanent stretch marks. Fine blood vessels under the skin surface may become prominent (this condition is known as telangiectasia). Because the skin on the face is especially vulnerable to such damage, only weak corticosteroids should be prescribed for use on the face. Dark-skinned people sometimes suffer a temporary reduction in pigmentation at the site of application.

When corticosteroids have been used on the skin for a prolonged period, abrupt discontinuation can cause a reddening of the skin called rebound erythroderma. This effect may be avoided by a gradual reduction in dosage. Corticosteroids suppress the body's immune system (see p.143), thereby increasing the risk of infection. For this reason, they are never used alone to treat skin inflammation caused by bacterial or fungal infection. However, they are sometimes included in a topical preparation that also contains an *antibiotic* or antifungal agent (see Anti-infective skin preparations, facing page).

LONG-TERM EFFECTS OF TOPICAL CORTICOSTEROIDS

Prolonged use of topical corticosteroids causes drying and thinning of the epidermis, so that tiny blood vessels close to the skin surface become visible. In addition, long-term use of these drugs weakens the underlying connective tissue of the dermis, leading to an increased susceptibility to stretch marks.

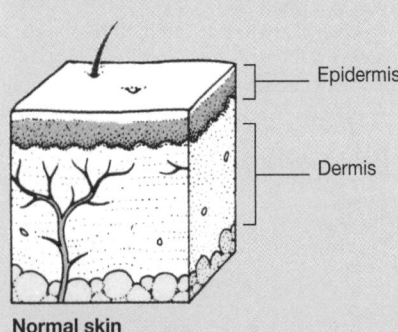

Epidermis
Dermis

Normal skin

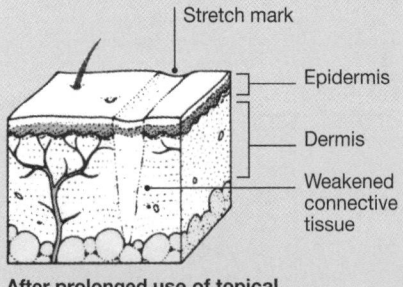

Stretch mark
Epidermis
Dermis
Weakened connective tissue

After prolonged use of topical corticosteroids

COMMON DRUGS

Very potent
Betamethasone dipropionate *
Clobetasol *
Halobetasol

Potent
Amcinonide
Betamethasone valerate *
Desoximetasone
Diflucortolone
Fluocinolone
Fluocinonide *
Mometasone *

Moderate
Clobetasone
Flumethasone
Hydrocortisone valerate *
Prednicarbate
Triamcinolone

Mild
Desonide
Hydrocortisone *

* See Part 4

ANTI-INFECTIVE SKIN PREPARATIONS

The skin is the body's first line of defence against infection. Yet the skin can also become infected itself, especially if the outer layer (epidermis) is damaged by a burn, cut, scrape, insect bite, or an inflammatory skin condition – for example, dermatitis.

Several different types of organism may infect the skin, including bacteria, viruses, fungi, and yeasts. This page concentrates on drugs applied topically to treat bacterial skin infections. These drugs include antiseptics, *antibiotics*, and other antibacterial agents. Infection by other organisms is covered elsewhere (see Antiviral drugs, p.119, Antifungal drugs, p.124, and Drugs used to treat skin parasites, p.164).

Why drugs are used

Bacterial infection of a skin wound can usually be prevented by thorough cleansing of the damaged area and the application of antiseptic creams or lotions as described in the box (right). If infection does occur, the wound usually becomes inflamed and swollen, and pus may form. If you develop these signs, you should see your physician. The usual treatment for a wound infection is an antibiotic taken orally, although often an antibiotic cream will be prescribed.

An antibiotic or antibacterial skin cream may also be used to prevent infection when your physician considers this to be a particular risk – for example, in the case of severe burns.

Other skin disorders in which *topical* antibiotic treatment may be prescribed include impetigo and infected eczema, skin ulcers, bedsores, and diaper rash.

Rarely, a preparation containing two or more antibiotics is used in order to ensure that all bacteria are eradicated.

ANTISEPTICS

Antiseptics (sometimes called germicides or skin disinfectants) are chemicals that kill or prevent the growth of microorganisms. They are weaker than household disinfectants, which are irritating to the skin.

Antiseptic lotions, creams, *gels*, and solutions may be effective for preventing infection following wounds to the surface of the skin. Solutions can be added to water to clean wounds (if they are used undiluted,

Soaps, shampoos, throat lozenges and mouthwashes, skin lotions, creams, and ointments may contain antiseptic ingredients.

they may cause inflammation and increase the risk of infection). Creams may be applied to wounds after cleansing.

Antiseptics are also included in some soaps and shampoos for the prevention of acne and dandruff, but their benefit in these disorders is doubtful. They are also included in some throat lozenges, but their effectiveness in curing throat infections is unproven.

The antibiotics selected for inclusion in topical preparations are usually drugs that are poorly absorbed through the skin (for example, the aminoglycosides). Thus the drug remains concentrated on the surface and in the skin's upper layers where it is intended to have its effect. However, if the infection is deep under the skin, or is causing fever and malaise, antibiotics may need to be given by mouth or injection.

Risks and special precautions

Any topical antibiotic product can irritate the skin or cause an allergic reaction. Irritation is sometimes provoked by another ingredient of the preparation rather than the active drug, for example, a preservative contained in the product. An allergic reaction causing swelling and reddening of the skin is more likely to be caused by the antibiotic drug itself. Any adverse reaction of this kind should be reported to your physician, who may substitute another drug, or prescribe a different preparation.

Always follow your doctor's instructions on how long the treatment with antibiotics should be continued. Stopping too soon may cause the infection to flare up again.

Never use a skin preparation that has been prescribed for someone else since it may aggravate your condition. Always throw away any unused medication.

BASES FOR SKIN PREPARATIONS

Drugs that are applied to the skin are usually in a preparation known as a base (or vehicle), such as a cream, lotion, ointment, or paste. Many bases are beneficial on their own.

Creams These have an *emollient* effect. They are usually composed of an oil-in-water emulsion and are used in the treatment of dry skin disorders, such as psoriasis and dry eczema. They may contain other ingredients, such as camphor or menthol.

Barrier preparations These may be creams or ointments. They protect the skin against water and irritating substances. They may be used in the treatment of diaper rash and to protect the skin around an open sore. They may contain powders and water-repellent substances, such as silicones.

Lotions These thin, semi-liquid preparations are often used to cool and soothe inflamed skin. They are most suitable for use on large, hairy areas. Preparations known as shake lotions contain fine powder that remains on

the surface of the skin when the liquid has evaporated. They are used to encourage scabs to form.

Ointments These are usually greasy and are suitable for treating some types of eczema.

Gels These are jelly-like in consistency and are often water based. They are used increasingly for a wide variety of topical skin treatments because they are easy to apply, usually non-greasy, and more rapidly absorbed than ointments.

Pastes These are ointments containing large amounts of finely powdered solids such as starch or zinc oxide. Pastes protect the skin and absorb unwanted moisture.

Collodions These are preparations that, when applied to damaged areas of the skin such as ulcers and minor wounds, dry to form a protective film. They are sometimes used to keep a dissolved drug in contact with the skin.

COMMON DRUGS

Antibiotics	Antiseptics and other antibacterials
Bacitracin	Chlorhexidine
Clindamycin ✳	Hexachlorophene
Framycetin	Metronidazole ✳
Fusidic acid	Povidone iodine
Gentamicin ✳	Silver sulfadiazine
Mupirocin	Triclosan
Neomycin	
Polymyxin B ✳	

✳ See Part 4

DRUGS TO TREAT SKIN PARASITES

Mites and lice are the most common parasites that live on the skin. One common mite causes the skin disease scabies. The mite burrows into the skin and lays eggs, causing intense itching. Scratching the affected area results in bleeding and scab formation, as well as increasing the risk of infection.

There are three types of lice, each of which infests a different part of the human body: the head louse, the body (or clothes) louse, and the crab louse, which often infests the pubic areas but is also sometimes found on other hairy areas such as the eyebrows. All of these lice cause itching and lay eggs (nits) that look like white grains attached to hairs.

Both mites and lice are passed on by direct contact with an infected person (pubic lice are passed on during sexual intercourse) or, particularly in the case of body lice, by contact with infected bedding or clothing.

The drugs most often used to eliminate skin parasites are insecticides that kill both the adult insects and their eggs. The most effective drug for scabies is permethrin; lindane and precipitated sulfur in petrolatum are occasionally used. Very severe scabies may require oral ivermectin as well. For lice infestations, permethrin, pyrethrins with piperonyl butoxide, or lindane are used.

Why drugs are used

Skin parasites do not represent a serious threat to health, but they can cause severe irritation and spread rapidly if untreated. Prompt treatment of any parasite is essential. Drugs are used to eradicate the parasites from the body, but bedding and clothing may need to be disinfected to avoid the possibility of reinfestation.

How they are used

Lotions for the treatment of scabies (*topical* scabicides) should be applied to the entire body from the neck down. It

SITES AFFECTED BY SKIN PARASITES

Scabies
The female scabies mite burrows into the skin and lays its eggs under the skin surface. After hatching, larvae travel to the skin surface, where they mature for 10–17 days before starting the cycle again.

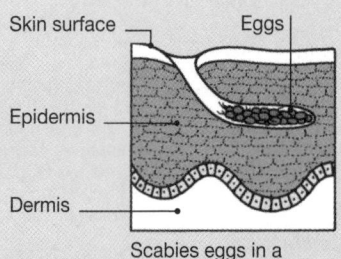

Skin surface / Eggs / Epidermis / Dermis

Scabies eggs in a burrow under the skin

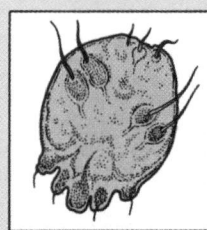

Scabies mite

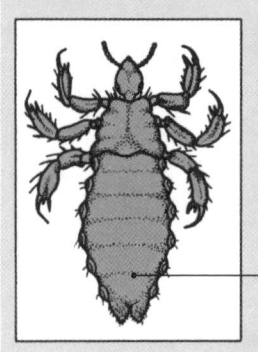

Head louse

Head lice
These tiny brown insects are transmitted from person to person (commonly among children). Their bites often cause itching.

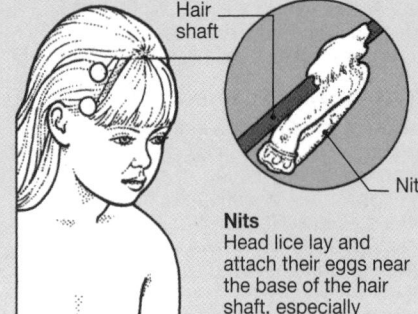

Hair shaft

Nit

Nits
Head lice lay and attach their eggs near the base of the hair shaft, especially around the ears, the crown, and the nape.

may be best to apply the lotion after showering and drying the skin thoroughly. After application of the scabicide, clothes can be worn. The lotion should be left on for 12 hours, then must be washed off.

One or two treatments are normally sufficient to remove the scabies mites. However, the itch associated with scabies may persist after the mite has been removed, so it may be necessary to use a soothing cream or medication containing an antipruritic drug (see p.161) to ease this. People who have direct skin-to-skin contact with a sufferer from scabies, such as family members and sexual partners, should also be treated with antiparasitic preparations at the same time. Head and

pubic lice infestations are usually treated by applying a preparation of one of the products and washing it off with water when and as instructed by the leaflet given with the preparation. If the skin has become infected as a result of scratching at the affected area, a topical *antibiotic* (see Anti-infective skin preparations, p.163) may also be prescribed.

Risks and special precautions

Lotions prescribed to control parasites can cause irritation and stinging that may be intense if the medication is allowed to come into contact with the eyes, mouth, or other moist membranes. Therefore, lotions and shampoos should be applied carefully, following the instructions of your physician or the manufacturer.

Because they are applied topically, antiparasitic drugs do not usually have generalized effects. Nevertheless, it is important not to apply these preparations more often than directed.

ELIMINATING PARASITES FROM BEDDING AND CLOTHING

Most skin parasites may also infest bedding and clothing that has been next to an infected person's skin. Therefore, to avoid reinfestation following removal of the parasites from the body, any insects and eggs lodged in the bedding or clothing must be eradicated.

Washing
Since all skin parasites are killed by heat, washing affected items of clothing and bedding in hot water and drying them in a hot dryer is an effective and convenient method of dealing with the problem.

Non-washable items
Items that cannot be washed should be isolated in plastic bags. The insects and their eggs cannot survive long without their human

hosts and die within days. The length of time they can survive, and therefore the period of isolation, varies depending on the type of parasite (see the table below).

Parasite	Maximum survival time away from host Insects	Eggs	Isolation period
Scabies	2 days	0 days	2 days
Head lice	2 days	10 days	10 days
Crab lice	1 day	10 days	10 days
Body lice	10 days	30 days	30 days

COMMON DRUGS

Crotamiton
Dimeticone
Isopropyl myristate
Lindane
Permethrin ✽

Pyrethrins/Pipernoyl butoxide
Sulfur

✽ See Part 4

DRUGS USED TO TREAT ACNE

Acne, known medically as acne vulgaris, is a common condition caused by excess production of the skin's natural oil (sebum), leading to blockage of hair follicles (see What happens in acne, right). It chiefly affects adolescents but it may occur at any age, due to taking certain drugs, exposure to industrial chemicals, oily cosmetics, or hot, humid conditions.

Acne primarily affects the face, neck, back, and chest. The primary symptoms are blackheads, papules (inflamed spots), and pustules (raised pus-filled spots with a white centre). Mild acne may produce only blackheads and an occasional papule or pustule. Moderate cases are characterized by larger numbers of pustules and papules. In severe cases of acne, painful, inflamed cysts also develop. These can cause permanent pitting and scarring.

Medication for acne can be divided into two groups: *topical* preparations applied directly to the skin and *systemic* treatments taken by mouth.

Why drugs are used

Mild acne usually does not need medical treatment. A topical preparation containing benzoyl peroxide or salicylic acid, available over-the-counter, can be used. Over-the-counter antibacterial soaps and lotions are limited in use and may cause irritation.

When a physician or dermatologist thinks acne is severe enough to need

CLEARING BLOCKED HAIR FOLLICLES

The most common treatment for acne is the application of keratolytic skin ointments. These encourage the layer of dead and hardened skin cells that form the skin surface to peel off. At the same time, this clears blackheads that block hair follicles and give rise to the formation of acne spots.

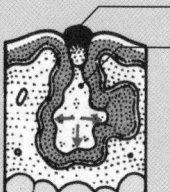

Blackhead
Trapped sebum

Blocked hair follicle
A hair follicle blocked by a plug of skin debris and sebum is ideal for acne spot formation.

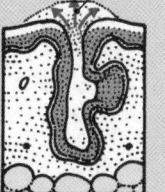

Freed sebum

Cleared hair follicle
Once the follicle is unblocked, sebum can escape and air can enter, thereby limiting bacterial activity.

WHAT HAPPENS IN ACNE

In normal, healthy skin, sebum produced by a sebaceous gland attached to a hair follicle is able to flow out of the follicle along the hair. An acne spot forms when the flow of the sebum from the sebaceous gland is blocked by a plug of skin debris and hardened sebum, leading to an accumulation of sebum.

Acne papules and pustules
Bacterial activity leads to the formation of pustules and papules. Irritant substances may leak into the surrounding skin, causing inflammation.

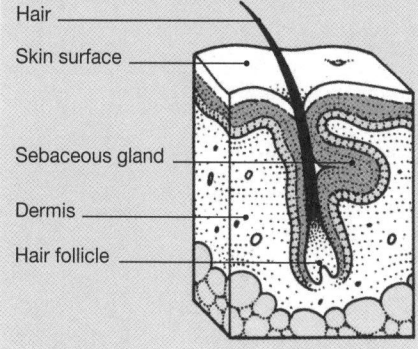

Hair
Skin surface
Sebaceous gland
Dermis
Hair follicle

Sebum
Blackhead
Cyst

Cystic acne
When acne is severe, cysts may form in the inflamed dermis. These are pockets of pus enclosed within scar tissue.

medical treatment, an ointment containing a retinoid (drugs related to vitamin A) or an *antibiotic* may be prescribed.

If acne is severe or does not respond to topical treatments, a doctor may prescribe a course of antibiotics by mouth (usually tetracycline or minocycline). If these measures are unsuccessful, the more powerful vitamin A-like drug isotretinoin, taken by mouth, may be prescribed.

Estrogen drugs may have a beneficial effect on acne. A woman suffering from acne who also needs contraception may be given an estrogen-containing oral contraceptive (p.149). Alternatively, a preparation containing an estrogen and cyproterone or drospirenone (drugs that oppose male sex *hormones*) may be prescribed.

How they work

Drugs used to treat acne act in different ways. Some have a keratolytic effect – that is, they loosen the dead cells on the skin surface (see Clearing blocked hair follicles, left). Other drugs work by countering bacterial activity in the skin or reducing sebum production.

Topical preparations, such as benzoyl peroxide, salicylic acid, and tretinoin, have a keratolytic effect. Benzoyl peroxide also has an antibacterial effect. Topical or systemic antibiotics reduce bacteria but may also have a direct anti-inflammatory effect on the skin. Isotretinoin reduces sebum production, soothes inflammation, and helps to unblock hair follicles.

How they affect you

Keratolytic preparations often cause soreness of the skin, especially at the start of treatment. If this persists, a change to a milder preparation may be

recommended. Day-to-day *side effects* are rare with antibiotics.

Treatment with isotretinoin often causes dry and scaly skin, particularly on the lips. The skin may become itchy and rarely, some hair loss may occur.

Risks and special precautions

Antibiotics in skin ointments may, in rare cases, provoke an allergic reaction requiring discontinuation of treatment. The tetracyclines, which are some of the most commonly used antibiotics for acne, are not suitable for use by mouth in pregnancy since they can affect the bones and teeth of the developing baby.

Isotretinoin sometimes increases levels of lipids in the blood. More seriously, the drug is known to damage the developing baby if taken during pregnancy. Women taking this drug need to make sure that they avoid conception during treatment.

COMMON DRUGS

Topical treatments	Other oral drugs
Adapalene	Cyproterone/
Benzoyl peroxide ✳	ethinyl estradiol
Dapsone	(women) ✳
Salicylic acid	Drospirenone/ethinyl
Tazarotene	estradiol
Tretinoin	Isotretinoin ✳
	Levonorgestrel/
Oral and/or topical	ethinyl estradiol
antibiotics	(women) ✳
Clindamycin ✳	
Doxycycline ✳	
Erythromycin ✳	
Minocycline ✳	
Tetracycline ✳	

✳ See Part 4

DRUGS FOR PSORIASIS

The skin is constantly being renewed; as fast as dead cells in the outermost layer (epidermis) are shed, they are replaced by cells from the base of the epidermis. Psoriasis occurs when the production of new cells increases while the shedding of old cells remains normal. As a result of increased cell production, the live skin cells accumulate and produce patches of inflamed, thickened skin covered by silvery scales. In some cases, the area of skin affected is extensive and causes severe embarrassment and physical discomfort. There are different types of psoriasis; the most common form is plaque psoriasis. Psoriasis can also affect the scalp and nails. Psoriasis may occasionally be accompanied by arthritis, called psoriatric arthritis, in which the joints become swollen and painful.

The underlying cause of psoriasis is not known. The disorder usually first occurs between the ages of 10 and 30, and it recurs throughout life. Outbreaks may be triggered by emotional stress, skin damage, drugs, and physical illness. Psoriasis can also worsen as a consequence of the withdrawal of corticosteroid drugs.

There is no complete cure for psoriasis. An *emollient* cream (see Antipruritics, p.161) often soothes the irritation. Careful sunbathing or using an ultraviolet lamp under medical supervision may help to clear mild psoriasis. When such measures fail to provide adequate relief, additional drug therapy is needed.

Why drugs are used

Drugs are used to decrease the size of affected skin areas and to reduce inflammation and scaling. Mild and moderate psoriasis are usually treated with a *topical* preparation. Coal tar preparations, available in creams, pastes, or bath additives, are often helpful, although some people dislike the smell. Applied to the affected areas, the preparation is left for a few minutes or overnight (depending on which product is used), after which it is washed off. Coal tar can stain clothes and bed linen.

Salicylic acid may be applied to help remove thick scale and crusts, especially from the scalp.

Topical corticosteroids (see p.162) are often used when treatment with emollients is ineffective. They may also be given to counter irritation caused by dithranol, a drug that is also used to treat psoriasis.

Ultraviolet light therapy in the form of regulated exposure to natural sunlight or to ultraviolet lamps (UVB) may also be advised. If psoriasis is very severe and other treatments have not been effective, specialist treatment may include the use of more powerful drugs. These drugs include vitamin A derivatives (oral retinoids), biologic response modifiers (e.g. adalimumab, alefacept, infliximab,

ustekinumab), and methotrexate. Another form of specialist treatment, PUVA, is described in the box above.

How they work

Salicylic acid and coal tar remove the layers of dead skin cells. Corticosteroids reduce inflammation of underlying skin. Methotrexate slows down the rapid rate of cell division that causes thickening of the skin. Acitretin also reduces the production of keratin, the hard protein that forms in the outer layer of skin.

How they affect you

Appropriate treatment of psoriasis usually improves the appearance of the skin. However, since drugs cannot cure the underlying cause of the disorder, psoriasis tends to recur, even following successful treatment of an outbreak.

Individual drugs may cause *side effects*. Topical preparations can cause stinging and inflammation, especially if applied to normal skin. Coal tar increases the skin's sensitivity to sunlight; excessive

sunbathing or overexposure to artificial ultraviolet light may damage skin and worsen the condition.

Acitretin and methotrexate can have several serious side effects, including gastrointestinal upsets. Acitretin can cause liver damage and methotrexate can cause bone marrow damage. Both are contraindicated in pregnancy, and women are advised not to become pregnant for three years after completing treatment with acitretin. Topical corticosteroids may cause rebound worsening of psoriasis when these drugs are stopped.

PUVA

PUVA is the combined use of a psoralen drug (methoxsalen) and ultraviolet A light (UVA). The drug is applied *topically* or taken by mouth some hours before exposure to UVA, which enhances the effect of the drug on skin cells.

This therapy is given two to three times a week and produces an improvement in skin condition within about four to six weeks.

Possible *adverse effects* include nausea, itching, and painful reddening of the normal areas of skin. More seriously, there is a risk of the skin aging prematurely and a long-term risk of skin cancer, particularly in fair-skinned people. For these reasons, PUVA therapy is generally recommended only for severe psoriasis, when other treatments have failed.

In psoriasis
Skin cells form at the base of the epidermis faster than they can be shed from the skin surface. This causes the formation of patches of thickened, inflamed skin covered by a layer of flaking dead skin.

Normal skin

Skin in psoriasis

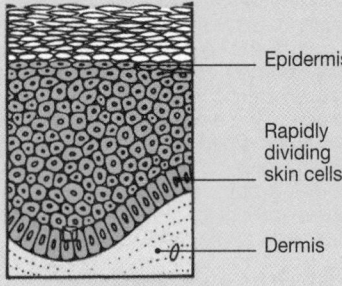

- Epidermis
- Rapidly dividing skin cells
- Dermis

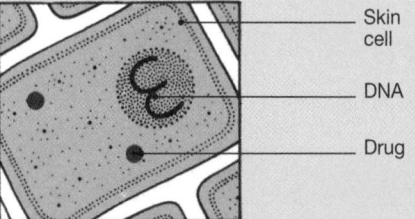

- Skin cell
- DNA
- Drug

Psoralen drugs
In PUVA, psoralen drugs administered by mouth or as ointment penetrate the skin cells.

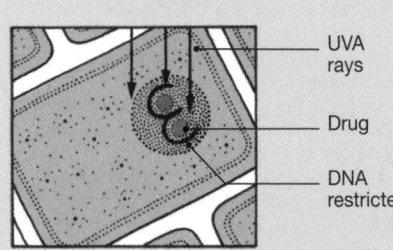

- UVA rays
- Drug
- DNA restricted

Ultraviolet light
The drug is activated by exposure of the skin to ultraviolet light. It acts on the cell's genetic material (DNA) to regulate its rate of division.

COMMON DRUGS

Acitretin	Infliximab
Adalimumab ✳	Methotrexate ✳
Alefacept	Methoxsalen
Anthralin	Salicylic acid
Calcipotriol	Tazarotene
Calcitriol	Topical cortico-
Cyclosporine ✳	steroids (see p.162)
Coal tar	Ustekinumab
Dithranol	
Etanercept	✳ See Part 4

DRUGS FOR DERMATITIS

Dermatitis is a skin condition causing a dry, itchy rash that may be inflamed and blistered. There are several types. Dermatitis can be triggered by allergy but often occurs for no known reason. In the long term, it can thicken the skin as a result of persistent scratching.

The most common type, atopic dermatitis (eczema), may appear in infancy, but many children grow out of it. There is often a family history of eczema, asthma, or allergic rhinitis. Atopic dermatitis commonly appears on the hands, due to their exposure to detergents, and the feet, due to the warm, moist conditions of enclosed footwear.

Contact dermatitis, another common form, is caused by chemicals, detergents, or soap. It may only appear after repeated exposure to the substance, but strong acids or alkalis can cause a reaction within minutes. It can also result from irritation of the skin by traces of detergent on clothes and bedding.

Allergic contact dermatitis can appear days after initial contact has been made (or after years of problem-free contact) with triggers such as nickel, rubber, elastic, or drugs (such as *antibiotics*, antihistamines, antiseptics, or local anesthetics). Sunlight can also trigger contact dermatitis following use of aftershave, perfume or *medication*.

Nummular eczema causes circular dry, scaly, itchy, patches to develop anywhere on the body, and bacteria are often found in these areas. The cause of nummular eczema is unknown.

Seborrhoeic dermatitis mainly affects the scalp and face (see Dandruff and hair loss, p.168).

Why drugs are used

Emollients are used to soften and moisten the skin. Oral antihistamines (p.110) may be prescribed for a particularly itchy rash (*topical* antihistamines make the skin more sensitive and should not be used). Coal tar

COMMON SUBSTANCES THAT CAUSE DERMATITIS

Some substances produce an allergic reaction and some irritate the skin, causing dermatitis. The most common are listed below.

Allergens	Irritants
● Nickel, chromium	● Detergents
● Perfumes	● Soaps
● Plants	● Disinfectants
● Drugs	● Household cleaning products
● Rubber, elastic	
● Adhesive bandages (especially zinc oxide ones)	● Paints
	● Glues and resins
● Cats and dogs	● Vegetable and fruit juices
● Tanning agents and dyes in leather and clothing	● Extremes of weather

PATCH TESTING

Low concentrations of the suspected substances are applied as spots to the skin of the back and held in place with non-absorbent adhesive tape. This method allows a number of potential allergens (substances that can cause an allergic reaction) to be tested at the same time.

Patches being applied

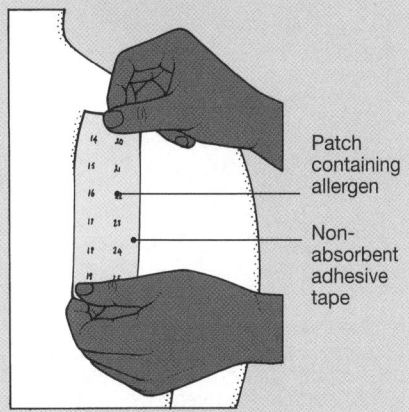

Patch containing allergen

Non-absorbent adhesive tape

After 48 hours, the adhesive tape is removed and the skin inspected for any redness, swelling, or blistering that has developed, which would indicate a positive reaction. The skin will be checked after a further 24 and 48 hours, in case the reaction has taken longer to develop.

Results of patch test

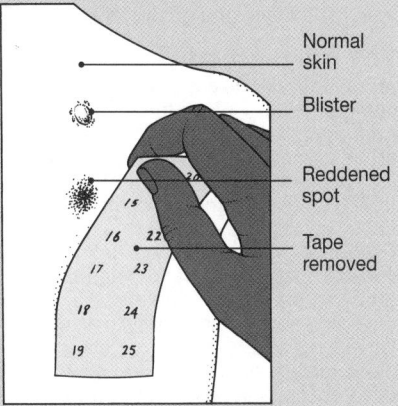

Normal skin

Blister

Reddened spot

Tape removed

may be used for chronic atopic dermatitis, but topical corticosteroids (p.162) may be needed to help control a flare up. Tacrolimus ointment and pimecrolimus cream, both classified as calcineurin inhibitors, may also be used in moderate to severe atopic dermatitis. Rarely, severe cases that are resistant to other treatments may need to be treated with the immuno-suppressant drug cyclosporine (p.249). Oral corticosteroids may be used to treat contact dermatitis. Nummular eczema usually requires corticosteroid treatment. If it is resistant, antibiotics (p.114) may be prescribed because infection is likely.

How they work

Emollients make the skin less dry and itchy. They are available as ointments, creams, lotions, soap substitutes, or bath oils. The effect is not long-lasting, so they need to be applied frequently. Emollients do not usually contain an active drug.

Antihistamines block the action of histamine (a chemical present in all cells). Histamine dilates the blood vessels in the skin, causing redness and swelling of the surrounding tissue due to fluid leaking from the circulation. Antihistamines also prevent histamine from irritating the nerve fibres, which causes itching.

Topical corticosteroids are absorbed into the tissues to relieve itching and inflammation. The least potent one that is effective is given. Hydrocortisone one per cent is often used in 1–2-week courses.

Oral or topical antibiotics destroy the bacteria sometimes present in broken, oozing, or blistered skin. The exact mechanism of calcineurin inhibitors is not known, but it controls inflammation,

itchiness, and redness related to atopic dermatitis. Cyclosporine blocks the action of white blood cells, which are involved in the immune response. The drug is given in short courses when the immune system responds inappropriately to an allergen.

Risks and special precautions

All types of dermatitis can become infected, and antibiotics may be needed. Herpes virus may infect atopic dermatitis, so direct contact with people who have a herpes infection, such as a cold sore, should be avoided. Emollients are generally well tolerated as are short-term topical mild corticosteroids. Cyclosporine, however, may produce some *adverse effects*.

Preventing dermatis

Trigger substances can be identified using patch testing (see above) and avoided. PVC gloves should be worn to protect the hands from detergents. Cotton clothing should be worn next to the skin. Cosmetic moisturizers should be avoided because they usually contain perfumes and other sensitizers.

COMMON DRUGS

Emollient and cooling preparations	Corticosteroids (see also p.162)
Aqueous cream	Hydrocortisone ✳
Cold cream	
Emulsifying ointment	**Other drugs**
Calamine lotion	Cyclosporine ✳
	Coal tar
Antihistamines	Pimecrolimus
(see also p.110)	Tacrolimus
Chlorpheniramine ✳	
Diphenhydramine ✳	
Hydroxyzine	✳ See Part 4

DRUGS FOR DANDRUFF

Dandruff is an irritating, but harmless, condition that involves an acceleration in the normal shedding of skin cells from the scalp (see right). Extensive dandruff is considered to be a mild form of a type of dermatitis known as seborrhoeic dermatitis, which may be caused by an overgrowth of a yeast organism that lives in the scalp. In severe cases of seborrhoeic dermatitis, a rash and reddish yellow, scaly pimples appear along the hairline and on the face.

Why drugs are used

Frequent washing with a detergent shampoo usually keeps the scalp free of dandruff, but more persistent dandruff can be treated with shampoos medicated with zinc pyrithione or selenium sulfide (p.478), or with shampoos containing coal tar or salicylic acid. Severe cases of seborrhoeic dermatitis are best treated with shampoo containing the antifungal, ketoconazole (p.325). Ointments containing coal tar and salicylic acid are also available. Corticosteroid gels and lotions may be needed to treat an itchy rash, especially in cases of severe seborrhoeic dermatitis.

How they work

Coal tar and salicylic acid preparations

WHAT HAPPENS IN DANDRUFF

All skin cells are replaced regularly as new cells grow from the epidermis. They gradually flatten as they die, and are shed on reaching the surface. Increased rate of production and

sticking together of the cells produces dandruff. In children, dandruff may produce thick scaly flakes that can be 1–2cm across. In adults, smaller flakes are produced.

Normal shedding

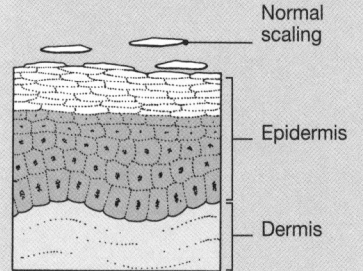

Normal scaling

Epidermis

Dermis

Dandruff

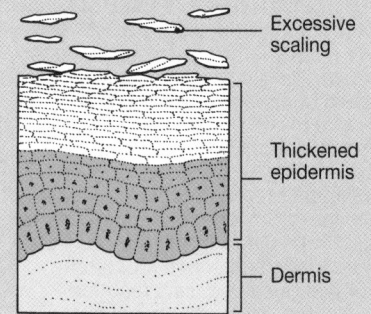

Excessive scaling

Thickened epidermis

Dermis

reduce the overproduction of new skin cells and break down scales which are then washed off while shampooing. Antifungals (p.124) reduce the overgrowth of yeast on the scalp by altering the permeability of the fungal cell walls. Corticosteroids (p.127) help to relieve an itchy rash by reducing inflammation of the underlying skin.

COMMON DRUGS

Antifungals	**Other drugs**
Ketoconazole ✳	Coal tar
Selenium sulfide ✳	Corticosteroids
Zinc pyrithione	Salicylic acid

✳ See Part 4

DRUGS FOR HAIR LOSS

Hair loss (alopecia) is the result of greater than normal shedding of hairs, or reduced hair production. Hair loss can be caused by a skin condition, such as scalp ringworm or scalp psoriasis, or by a hormonal imbalance.

Other forms of hair loss are due to a disorder of the follicles themselves and may be a response to illness, malnutrition,

or a reaction to some drugs, such as anticancer drugs or anticoagulants. The hair loss may be diffuse or in a pattern, as in male-pattern baldness which is caused by oversensitivity to testosterone.

Why drugs are used

If the hair loss is caused by a skin disorder such as scalp ringworm, an antifungal will

be used to kill the fungal growth. If male-pattern baldness is a response to the male hormone, testosterone, finasteride could be used to reduce the effect of the hormone. The antihypertensive drug minoxidil can be applied to the scalp to promote hair growth.

How they work

Hair loss can be reversed when the underlying illness is treated, or the drug treatment is stopped. Finasteride, taken by mouth, inhibits conversion of testosterone to its more active form and reduces sensitivity to androgens. The role of minoxidil (p.362) in hair growth is not fully understood, although it is thought to stimulate the hair follicles (see left).

Risks and special precautions

Finasteride can lead to loss of libido or impotence. Anyone with a history of heart disease or hypertension should consult their physician before using minoxidil, as the drug can be absorbed through skin.

HAIR REGROWTH IN MALE-PATTERN BALDNESS

Follicles on the scalp have periods of activity and rest. During the rest phase, the bottom of the hair detaches from the follicle and the hair

falls out. Regular applications of minoxidil, the antihypertensive drug, stimulate follicles to produce new hair growth.

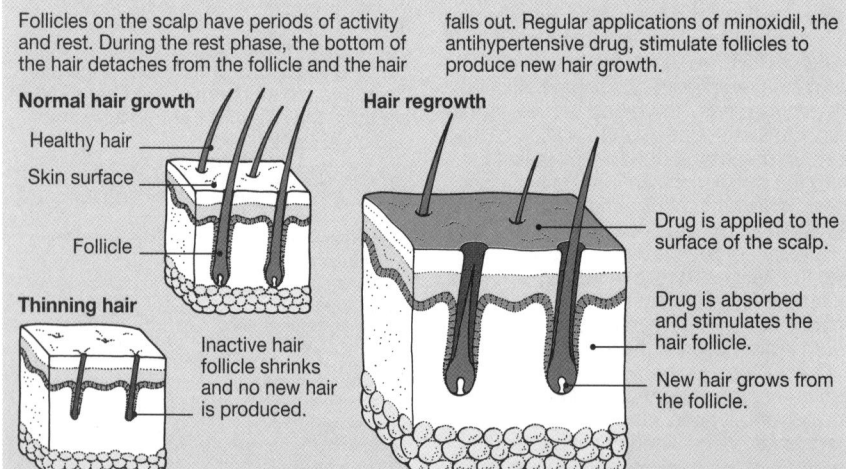

Normal hair growth

Healthy hair

Skin surface

Follicle

Thinning hair

Inactive hair follicle shrinks and no new hair is produced.

Hair regrowth

Drug is applied to the surface of the scalp.

Drug is absorbed and stimulates the hair follicle.

New hair grows from the follicle.

COMMON DRUGS

Antifungals	**Other drugs**
Ketoconazole ✳	Minoxidil ✳
Terbinafine ✳	Finasteride ✳

✳ See Part 4

SUNSCREENS

Sunscreens and sunblocks are chemicals, usually formulated as creams or oils, that protect the skin from the damaging effects of ultraviolet radiation from the sun.

People vary in their sensitivity to sunlight. Fair-skinned people generally have the least tolerance and tend to burn easily when exposed to the sun, while those with darker skin, especially brown or black skin, can withstand exposure to the sun for longer periods.

In a few cases, the skin's sensitivity to sunlight is increased by a disease such as pellagra (see p.475) or herpes simplex infection. Some drugs, such as thiazide diuretics, phenothiazine antipsychotics, psoralens, sulfonamide antibacterials, tetracycline *antibiotics*, and nalidixic acid, can also increase the skin's sensitivity.

Apart from sunburn and premature ageing of the skin, the most serious effect from sunlight is skin cancer. Reducing the skin's exposure to sunlight can help to prevent skin cancers.

How they work

Sunlight consists of different wavelengths of radiation. Of these, ultraviolet (UV) radiation is particularly harmful to the skin. UV radiation ages the skin and causes burning. Excessive exposure to UV radiation also increases the risk of developing skin cancer. UV radiation is mainly composed of UVA and UVB rays, both of which age the skin. Especially vulnerable are fair-skinned people and those being treated with immuno-suppressant drugs. Sunscreens absorb

ACTION OF SUNSCREENS

Fair skin unprotected by a sunscreen suffers damage as ultraviolet rays pass through to the layers beneath, causing pain and inflammation. Sunscreens act by blocking out some of these ultraviolet rays, while allowing a proportion of them to pass through the skin surface to the epidermis to stimulate the production of melanin, the pigment that gives the skin a tan and helps to protect it during further exposure to the sun.

Skin unprotected

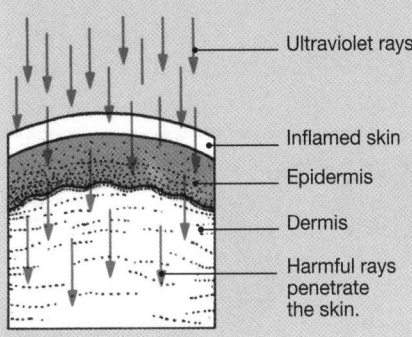

- Ultraviolet rays
- Inflamed skin
- Epidermis
- Dermis
- Harmful rays penetrate the skin.

Skin protected by sunscreen

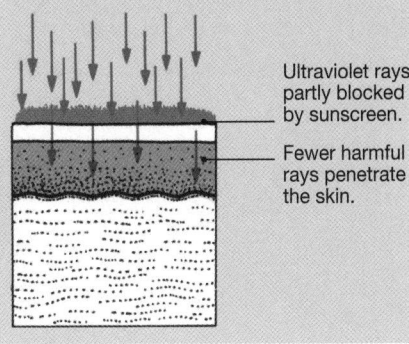

- Ultraviolet rays partly blocked by sunscreen.
- Fewer harmful rays penetrate the skin.

some of the UVA and UVB radiation, ensuring that less of it reaches the skin. Sunscreens are graded using the Sun Protection Factor (SPF) (see below). Some preparations contain chemicals such as zinc oxide and titanium dioxide, which reflect both UVB and UVA rays.

Sunscreens must be applied before exposure to the sun and are particularly advisable for visitors to tropical, subtropical, and mountainous areas. People with fair skin should use a sunscreen with a higher SPF than people with darker skin.

Risks and special precautions

Sunscreens either partially absorb or form a physical barrier to the passage of UV radiation. They do not alter the skin to make it more resistant to sunlight. Sunscreen lotions must be applied frequently during exposure to the sun to maintain protection. People who are very fair skinned or are known to be very sensitive to sunlight should never expose their skin to direct sunlight, even if they are using a sunscreen, since not even sunscreens with high SPF values give complete protection.

Sunscreens can irritate the skin and some preparations may cause an allergic rash. People who are sensitive to some drugs, such as procaine and benzocaine and some hair dyes, might develop a rash after applying a sunscreen containing aminobenzoic acid or a benzophenone derivative such as oxybenzone.

SUN PROTECTION FACTORS

Sun protection factor (SPF) refers to the degree of protection given by a sunscreen against sunburn. It is a measure of the amount of UVB radiation a sunscreen absorbs. The higher the number, the greater the protection. The table below shows the major skin types and the minimum SPF recommended for each skin type.

This number only describes the protection against UVB radiation. Some sunscreens protect against UVA radiation as well.

Skin type	Type 1	Type 2	Type 3	Type 4	Type 5/6
Skin/hair tone	White or light skin, blue eyes, freckles	White or fair skin, fair hair	Medium white skin, brown hair	Olive skin, dark hair and eyes	Brown/black skin, dark hair and eyes
Sun sensitivity	Always burns, never tans	Burns easily, tans eventually	Tans slowly, burns sometimes	Tans easily burns occasionally	Very rarely burns
Minimum SPF	SPF 30 +	SPF 25 +	SPF 25	SPF 15 + SPF 25 for vulnerable areas	May not need; SPF 15 if at risk of burning

COMMON DRUGS

Ingredients in sunscreens and sunblocks
Aminobenzoic acid
Avobenzone
Benzophenones
Methyl anthranilate
Mexoryl Sx
Octocrylene

Octyl methoxy-cinnamate
Oxybenzone
Padimate-O
Titanium dioxide
Zinc oxide

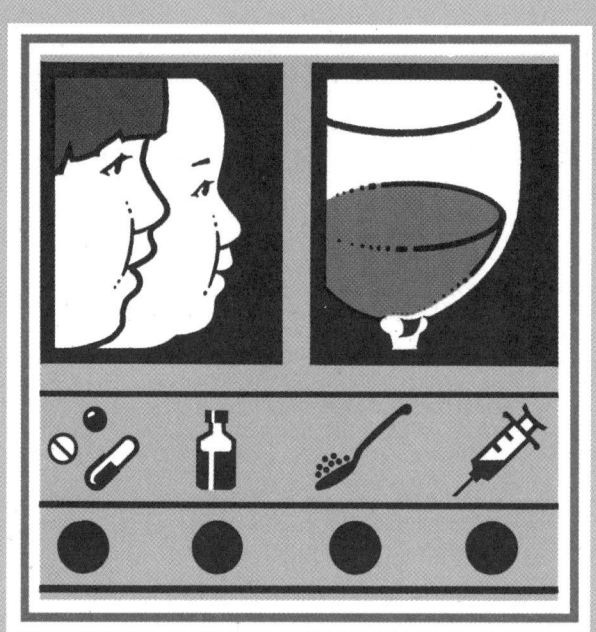

PART

4

A–Z
OF DRUGS

A–Z OF MEDICAL DRUGS
A–Z OF VITAMINS, MINERALS,
AND SUPPLEMENTS
DRUGS OF ABUSE
ALTERNATIVE MEDICINE
DRUGS IN SPORT
MEDICINES AND TRAVEL

A–Z OF MEDICAL DRUGS

The drug profiles in this section provide information and practical advice on 292 individual drugs. It is intended that the profiles should provide reference and guidance for non-medical readers taking drug treatment. However, it is impossible for this kind of book to take into account every variation in individual circumstances; readers should always follow their physician's or pharmacist's instructions in instances where these differ from the advice in this section.

The drugs have been selected in order to provide representative coverage of the principal classes of drugs in medical use today. For disorders for which a number of drugs are available, the most commonly used drugs have been selected.

Emphasis has also been placed on the drugs likely to be used in the home, although in a few cases drugs administered only in hospital have been included when the drug has been judged to be of sufficient general interest. At the end of this section, there are supplementary profiles on vitamins, minerals, and supplements (pp.468–482), drugs of abuse (pp.483–493), alternative medicine (pp.494–495), drugs in sport (p.496), and medicine and travel (pp.497–499).

Each drug profile is organized in the same way, using standard headings (see sample page, below). To help you make the most of the information provided, the terms used and the instructions given under each heading are discussed and explained on the following pages.

HOW TO UNDERSTAND THE PROFILES

For ease of reference, the information on each drug is arranged in a consistent format under standard headings.

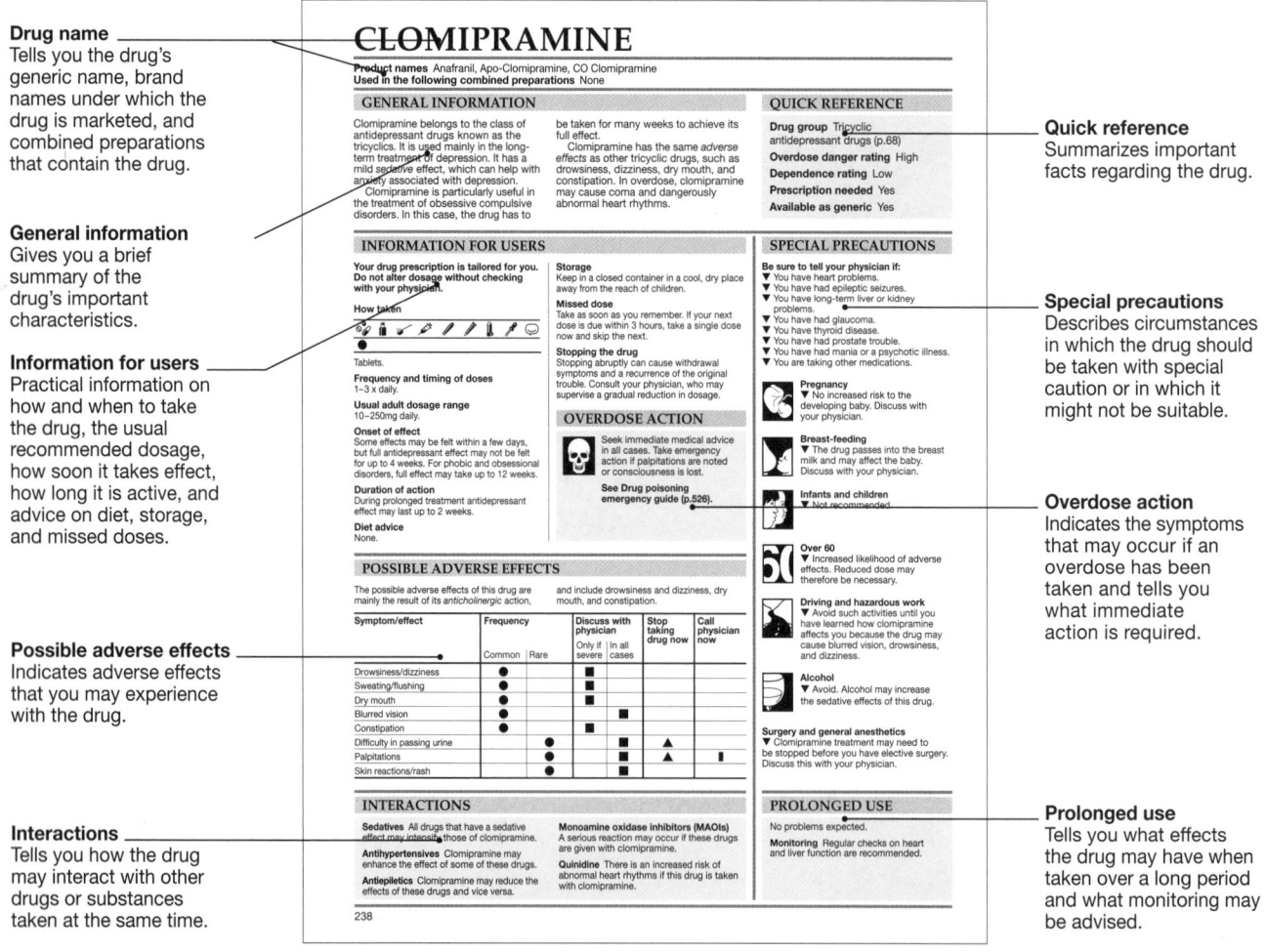

Drug name
Tells you the drug's generic name, brand names under which the drug is marketed, and combined preparations that contain the drug.

General information
Gives you a brief summary of the drug's important characteristics.

Information–for users
Practical information on how and when to take the drug, the usual recommended dosage, how soon it takes effect, how long it is active, and advice on diet, storage, and missed doses.

Possible adverse effects
Indicates adverse effects that you may experience with the drug.

Interactions
Tells you how the drug may interact with other drugs or substances taken at the same time.

Quick reference
Summarizes important facts regarding the drug.

Special precautions
Describes circumstances in which the drug should be taken with special caution or in which it might not be suitable.

Overdose action
Indicates the symptoms that may occur if an overdose has been taken and tells you what immediate action is required.

Prolonged use
Tells you what effects the drug may have when taken over a long period and what monitoring may be advised.

Generic name

The main heading on the page is the drug's shortest generic name, unless the short name causes confusion with another drug, in which case the full generic name is given. For example, the antimalarial drug proguanil hydrochloride is listed as proguanil because there is no other generic drug of this name. However, magnesium hydroxide, an antacid, is listed under its full name to avoid confusing it with the mineral magnesium or other compounds, such as magnesium sulfate. If the drug has recently been renamed, the old name appears in brackets after the new one.

Brand names

Under the generic name are the brand names of products in which the drug is the major single active ingredient. If there are many different brand names of the drug, only commonly used ones are given because of limitations of space. The names of the principal preparations, if any, in which the drug is combined with other drugs, are also listed. For more information about brand names and generic names, see p.13.

AMILORIDE

Product name Apo-Amiloride
Used in the following combined preparati

GENERAL INFORMATION

GENERAL INFORMATION

The information here gives an overall picture of the drug. It may include notes on the drug's history (for example, when it was first introduced) and the principal disorders for which it is prescribed. This section also discusses the drug's major advantages and disadvantages.

Used in the following combined preparati

GENERAL INFORMATION

Cyclosporine is one of the immuno-suppressants, a group of drugs that suppress the body's natural defences against infection and foreign cells. This action is of particular use following organ transplants when the recipient's

QUICK REFERENCE

The text in this box summarizes the important facts regarding your drug, and is organized under five headings, which are explained in detail below.

Drug group

This tells you which of the major groups the drug belongs to, and the page on which you can find out more about the drugs in the group and the various disorders or conditions they are used to treat. Where a drug belongs to more than one group, each group mentioned in the book is listed. For example, interferon is listed as an antiviral drug (p.119) and an anticancer drug (p.140).

Overdose danger rating

Gives an indication of the seriousness of the drug's effects if the dosage prescribed by your physician, or that recommended on the label of an over-the-counter drug, is exceeded. The

QUICK REFERENCE

Drug group Immunosuppressant drug (p.143)

Overdose danger rating Medium

Dependence rating Low

Prescription needed Yes

ratings – low, medium, and high – are explained more fully on p.174.

● **Low** Symptoms unlikely. Death unknown.

● **Medium** Medical advice needed. Death rare.

● **High** Medical attention needed urgently. Potentially fatal.

If you do exceed the dose, advice is given under Exceeding the dose, or in an "Overdose action" panel.

Dependence rating

Drugs are rated low, medium, or high on the basis of the risk of dependence.

● **Low** Dependence unknown.

● **Medium** Rare possibility of dependence.

● **High** Dependence is likely in long-term use.

Prescription needed

This tells you whether or not you need a prescription to obtain the drug. Some drugs are available over-the-counter (also known as nonprescription drugs) in lower strength preparations or restricted amounts but require a prescription for higher doses or larger amounts. Certain prescription drugs are subject to government regulations (see How drugs are classified, p.13).

Available as generic

Tells you if the drug is available as a generic product.

INFORMATION FOR USERS

This section contains information on the following: administration, i.e., the forms in which the drug is available, dosage frequency and amount, effects and actions, and advice on diet, storage, missed doses, stopping drug treatment, and overdose. All the information is generalized and should not be taken as a recommendation for an individual dosing schedule. Always follow your physician's instructions carefully when taking prescription drugs, and those of your pharmacist or the manufacturer when you buy over-the-counter medications.

How taken

The symbols in the box show how drugs can be administered. The dot below the symbol indicates the form in which a drug is available. This is a visual backup to the written information below the box.

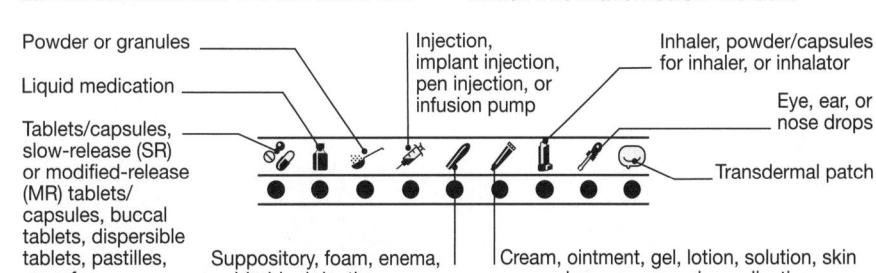

Powder or granules

Liquid medication

Tablets/capsules, slow-release (SR) or modified-release (MR) tablets/ capsules, buccal tablets, dispersible tablets, pastilles, or wafers

Suppository, foam, enema, or bladder irrigation

Injection, implant injection, pen injection, or infusion pump

Cream, ointment, gel, lotion, solution, skin spray, shampoo, or scalp application

Inhaler, powder/capsules for inhaler, or inhalator

Eye, ear, or nose drops

Transdermal patch

INFORMATION FOR USERS continued

Frequency and timing of doses

This refers to the standard number of times each day that the drug should be taken and, where relevant, whether it should be taken with liquid, with meals, or on an empty stomach.

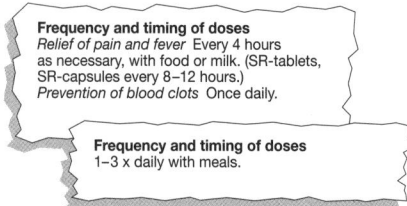

Frequency and timing of doses
Relief of pain and fever Every 4 hours as necessary, with food or milk. (SR-tablets, SR-capsules every 8–12 hours.)
Prevention of blood clots Once daily.

Frequency and timing of doses
1–3 x daily with meals.

Usual dosage range

This is generally given as the normal dosage range for an adult. In cases where the dosages for specific age groups vary significantly from the normal adult dosage, these will also be given. Where dosage varies according to use, the dosage for each is included.

The vast majority of drug dosages are expressed in metric units, usually milligrams (mg) or micrograms (mcg). In a few, dosage is given in units (u) or international units (IU). See also weights and measures, facing page.

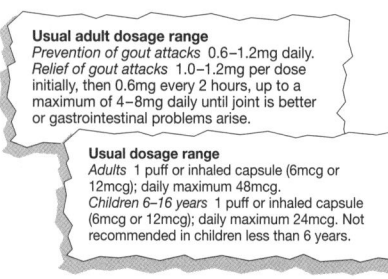

Usual adult dosage range
Prevention of gout attacks 0.6–1.2mg daily.
Relief of gout attacks 1.0–1.2mg per dose initially, then 0.6mg every 2 hours, up to a maximum of 4–8mg daily until joint is better or gastrointestinal problems arise.

Usual dosage range
Adults 1 puff or inhaled capsule (6mcg or 12mcg); daily maximum 48mcg.
Children 6–16 years 1 puff or inhaled capsule (6mcg or 12mcg); daily maximum 24mcg. Not recommended in children less than 6 years.

Onset of effect

The onset of effect is the time it takes for the drug to become active in the body; sometimes the time it takes to see improvement in symptoms may be listed. There may sometimes be an interval between the time when a drug is pharmacologically active and when you start to notice improvement in your symptoms or your underlying condition.

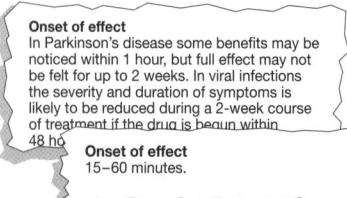

Onset of effect
In Parkinson's disease some benefits may be noticed within 1 hour, but full effect may not be felt for up to 2 weeks. In viral infections the severity and duration of symptoms is likely to be reduced during a 2-week course of treatment if the drug is begun within 48 h...

Onset of effect
15–60 minutes.

Duration of action

The information given here refers to the length of time that one dose of the drug remains active in the body.

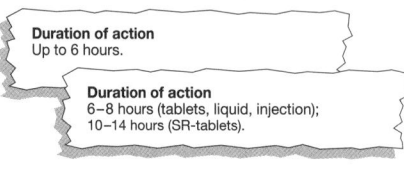

Duration of action
Up to 6 hours.

Duration of action
6–8 hours (tablets, liquid, injection); 10–14 hours (SR-tablets).

Diet advice

With some drugs, it is important to avoid certain foods, either because they reduce the effect of the drug or because they interact adversely. This section of the profile tells you what, if any, dietary changes are necessary.

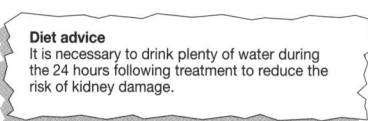

Diet advice
It is necessary to drink plenty of water during the 24 hours following treatment to reduce the risk of kidney damage.

Storage

Drugs will deteriorate and may become inactive if they are not stored under suitable conditions. The advice usually given is to store in a cool, dry place out of the reach of children. Some drugs must also be protected from light. Others, especially liquid medications, need to be kept in a refrigerator, but should not be frozen. For further advice on storing drugs, see p.29.

Storage
Keep in a closed container in a cool, dry place out of the reach of children. Protect from light.

Missed dose

This section gives advice on what to do if you forget a dose of your drug, so that the effectiveness and safety of your treatment is maintained as far as possible. If you forget to take several doses in succession, consult your physician. You can read more about missed doses on p.28.

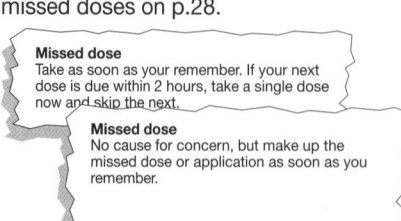

Missed dose
Take as soon as your remember. If your next dose is due within 2 hours, take a single dose now and skip the next.

Missed dose
No cause for concern, but make up the missed dose or application as soon as you remember.

Stopping the drug

If you are taking a drug regularly you should know how and when you can safely stop taking it. Some drugs can be safely stopped as soon as you feel better, or as soon as your symptoms have disappeared. Others must not be stopped until the full course of treatment has been completed, or they must be gradually withdrawn under the supervision of a doctor. Failure to comply with instructions for stopping a drug may lead to adverse effects. It may also cause your condition to worsen or your symptoms to reappear. See also Ending drug treatment, p.28.

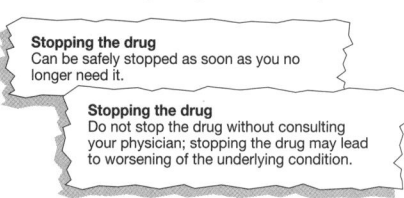

Stopping the drug
Can be safely stopped as soon as you no longer need it.

Stopping the drug
Do not stop the drug without consulting your physician; stopping the drug may lead to worsening of the underlying condition.

Exceeding the dose

The information in this section expands on that in the quick reference box on the drug's overdose danger rating. It explains possible consequences of exceeding the dose and what to do if an overdose is taken. Examples of wording used for low, medium, and high overdose ratings are:

Low
An occasional extra dose is unlikely to be a cause for concern. But if you notice any unusual symptoms, or if a large overdose has been taken, notify your physician.

Medium
An occasional extra dose is unlikely to cause problems. Large overdoses may cause (symptoms listed). Notify your physician.

High
Seek immediate medical advice in all cases. Take emergency action if (relevant symptoms listed) occur.

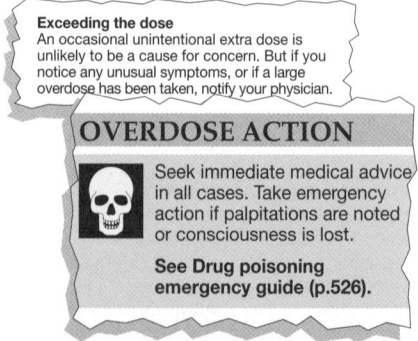

Exceeding the dose
An occasional unintentional extra dose is unlikely to be a cause for concern. But if you notice any unusual symptoms, or if a large overdose has been taken, notify your physician.

OVERDOSE ACTION

Seek immediate medical advice in all cases. Take emergency action if palpitations are noted or consciousness is lost.

See Drug poisoning emergency guide (p.526).

SPECIAL PRECAUTIONS

Many drugs need to be taken with care by people with a history of particular conditions. The profile lists conditions you should tell your physician about when you are prescribed a drug, or about which you should consult your physician or pharmacist before taking an over-the-counter drug. Certain groups of people (pregnant women, breast-feeding mothers, children, and the over 60s) may also be at special risk from drug treatment. Advice for each of these groups is given in every profile. Information is also included about driving, undertaking hazardous work, and drinking alcohol.

SPECIAL PRECAUTIONS

Cyclosporine is prescribed only under close medical supervision, taking account of your present condition and medical history.

Pregnancy
▼ Safety in pregnancy not established. Discuss with your physician.

Breast-feeding
▼ The drug passes into the breast milk and may affect the baby. Discuss with your physician.

Infants and children
▼ Not recommended.

Over 60
▼ No special problems.

Driving and hazardous work
▼ No special problems.

Alcohol
▼ Excessive intake of alcohol may irritate the stomach and increase the risk of bleeding.

WEIGHTS AND MEASURES

Metric equivalents of measurements used in this book:

1,000mcg (microgram) = 1mg (milligram)
1,000mg = 1g (gram)
1,000ml (millilitre) = 1l (litre)

Units or international units
Units (u) and international units (IU) are also used to express drug dosages. They represent the biological activity of a drug (its effect on the body). This ability cannot be measured in terms of weight or volume, but must be calculated in a laboratory.

POSSIBLE ADVERSE EFFECTS

The adverse effects discussed in the drug profile are symptoms or reactions that may arise when you take the drug. The emphasis is on symptoms that you, the patient, are likely to notice, rather than on the findings of laboratory tests that your physician may order – it is not an all-inclusive list. The bulk of the section is in the form of a table that lists the adverse effects and indicates how commonly they occur, when to tell your physician about them, and when to stop the drug. The headings in the table are explained below.

Frequency
Tells you whether the adverse effect is common or rare. Common effects are listed first.

Discuss with physician
The marker in this section indicates under what circumstances you need to inform your physician about an adverse effect you are experiencing.

Only if severe A marker in this column means that the symptom is unlikely to be serious, but that you should seek your physician's advice if it troubles you. *In all cases* Adverse effects marked in this column require prompt, but not necessarily emergency, medical attention. (See also Call physician now, below.)

Stop taking drug now
In cases where certain unpleasant or dangerous adverse effects of a drug may override its beneficial effects, you are advised to stop taking the drug immediately, if necessary before seeing your physician.

Call physician now
Effects marked in this column require immediate medical help. They indicate a potentially dangerous response to the drug treatment, for which you should seek emergency medical attention.

Symptom/effect	Frequency		Discuss with physician		Stop taking drug now	Call physician now
	Common	Rare	Only if severe	In all cases		
Indigestion	●			■		
Weight gain		●		■		
Acne		●		■		
Muscle weakness		●		■		
Mood changes		●		■		
Bloody/black feces		●		■	▲	▮

INTERACTIONS

The interactions that are discussed here are those that may occur between the drug under discussion and other drugs, and sometimes food. Information includes the name of the interacting drug or group of drugs and the effect of the interaction.

INTERACTIONS

General note Cyclosporine may interact with a large number of drugs. Check with your physician or pharmacist before taking

PROLONGED USE

The information given here concerns the adverse, and sometimes beneficial, effects of the drug that may occur during long-term use. These may differ from those listed under Possible adverse effects. This section of the profile also includes information on monitoring the effects of the drug during long-term treatment, explaining the tests you may be given if your physician thinks they are necessary.

PROLONGED USE

No problems expected from use of calcipotriol in low doses. If the effects of the skin preparation decline after several weeks, they may be regained by suspending use for a few weeks and then recommencing treatment.

Monitoring Regular checks on calcium levels in the blood or urine are required

5-AMINOSALICYLIC ACID (5-ASA)

Product names Asacol, Mesasal, Pentasa, Salofalk, Mezavant, Teva-5 ASA
Used in the following combined preparations None

GENERAL INFORMATION

5-Aminosalicylic Acid (5-ASA), also known as mesalamine, is prescribed for patients with ulcerative colitis and is sometimes used for Crohn's disease. The drug is given to relieve symptoms in an acute attack and is also taken as a preventative measure. When 5-ASA is used to treat severe cases, it is often taken with other drugs such as corticosteroids. When taken in tablet form, the active component of the drug is released in the intestine, where its local effect relieves the inflamed mucosa. It is important to stick to the same brand of tablet. Enemas and suppositories are also available and are particularly useful when the disease affects the rectum and lower colon.

This drug produces fewer *side effects* than some older treatments, such as sulfasalazine. Patients who are unable to tolerate sulfasalazine may be able to take 5-ASA without any problems. However, those who are hypersensitive to salicylates, for example ASA, and those with kidney impairement should not take 5-ASA.

QUICK REFERENCE

Drug group Drug for inflammatory bowel disease (p.98)

Overdose danger rating Low

Dependence rating Low

Prescription needed Yes

Available as a generic Yes

INFORMATION FOR USERS

Your drug prescription is tailored for you. Do not alter dosage without checking with your physician.

How taken

Tablets, SR-tablets, rectal suppositories, enema (foam or liquid).

Frequency and timing of doses
3 x daily, swallowed whole and not chewed (tablets); 3 x daily (suppositories); once daily at bedtime (enema).

Usual adult dosage range
800mg–2.4g daily (acute attack); 750mg–2.4g daily (maintenance dose).

Onset of effect
Adverse effects may be noticed within a few days, but full beneficial effects may not be felt for a couple of weeks.

Duration of action
Up to 12 hours.

Diet advice
Your physician may advise you, taking account of the condition affecting you.

Storage
Keep in a closed container in a cool, dry place out of the reach of children. Protect from light. Keep aerosol container out of direct sunlight.

Missed dose
Take as soon as you remember. If your next dose is due within 2 hours, take a single dose now and skip the next.

Stopping the drug
Do not stop taking the drug without consulting your physician; symptoms may recur.

Exceeding the dose
An occasional unintentional extra dose is unlikely to be a cause for concern. But if you notice any unusual symptoms, or if a large overdose has been taken, notify your physician.

SPECIAL PRECAUTIONS

Be sure to tell your physician if:
▼ You have long-term liver or kidney problems.
▼ You are allergic to ASA or mesalamine.
▼ You are taking other medications.

Pregnancy
▼ Negligible amounts of the drug cross the placenta. However, safety in pregnancy is not established. Discuss with your physician.

Breast-feeding
▼ Negligible amounts of the drug pass into the breast milk. However, safety is not established. Discuss with your physician.

Infants and children
▼ Not recommended under 15 years.

Over 60
▼ Dosage reduction not normally necessary unless there is kidney impairment.

Driving and hazardous work
▼ No special problems.

Alcohol
▼ No special problems.

POSSIBLE ADVERSE EFFECTS

The common side effects of 5-ASA are related to the gastrointestinal tract. Other problems rarely occur. However, unexplained bleeding, bruising, sore throat, fever, or malaise should be reported to your physician, who will carry out a blood test to eliminate blood disorders.

Symptom/effect	Frequency		Discuss with physician		Stop taking drug now	Call physician now
	Common	Rare	Only if severe	In all cases		
Nausea	●		■			
Abdominal pain	●		■			
Diarrhea	●		■			
Fever/wheezing		●		■	▲	■
Colitis worsening		●		■	▲	
Rash		●		■	▲	
Bleeding/bruising		●		■	▲	■
Sore throat/malaise		●		■	▲	■

PROLONGED USE

Monitoring Kidney function will be evaluated periodically.

INTERACTIONS

Lactulose The release of 5-ASA/mesalamine at its site of action may be reduced by lactulose.

Warfarin 5-ASA/mesalamine may reduce the effect of warfarin.

ACARBOSE

Product name Glucobay
Used in the following combined preparations None

GENERAL INFORMATION

Acarbose is used in Type 2 Diabetes mellitus, usually in combination with other antidiabetic drugs. It inhibits an enzyme, alpha glucosidase, in the intestinal wall, which causes a delay in the breakdown of ingested carbohydrates and thereby reduces blood glucose levels after eating. As it works differently than other antidiabetic agents, it can be used with other antidiabetic drugs. Acarbose should be taken with the first bite of a meal. To increase tolerability, it should be started once daily, then gradually increased up to three times daily. Common side effects with acarbose are flatulence, diarrhea, and abdominal discomfort. These effects can be minimized by starting with a small dose.

QUICK REFERENCE

Drug group Oral antidiabetic drugs (p.128)

Overdose danger rating Medium

Dependence rating Low

Prescription needed Yes

Available as generic No

INFORMATION FOR USERS

Your drug prescription is tailored for you. Do not alter dosage without checking with your physician.

How taken

Tablets.

Frequency and timing of doses
1–3 x daily at mealtimes.

Usual adult dosage range
Starting dose: 25–50mg once daily.
Daily dose: 25–100mg.
Maximum dose: 300mg.

Onset of effect
Peak effect in 1 hour.

Duration of action
2–4 hours.

Diet advice
A diabetic diet will be recommended by your physician. Follow his or her advice.

Storage
Keep in a closed container in a cool, dry place out of the reach of children. Protect from light.

Missed dose
Skip the dose, and take the next dose with a meal. Acarbose should not be taken between meals. Do not take more doses each day than prescribed by your physician.

Stopping the drug
Do not stop the drug without consulting your physician; symptoms may recur.

Exceeding the dose
An occasional unintentional extra dose is unlikely to cause problems. Large overdoses may cause abdominal distension, flatulence, and diarrhea. Drinks and food containing carbohydrates should be avoided for 4–6 hours. If patient was also taking another drug, such as insulin for diabetes, overdose of this may cause low blood sugar. Should symptoms of low blood sugar occur, seek immediate medical advice.

SPECIAL PRECAUTIONS

Be sure to tell your physician if:
- ▼ You have had an allergic reaction to acarbose.
- ▼ You have irritable bowel syndrome, inflammation or ulceration of the bowel (Crohn's disease or ulcerative colitis).
- ▼ You have or have had a bowel obstruction.
- ▼ You have a kidney disorder.
- ▼ You have a large hernia.
- ▼ You are taking any digestive enzymes.
- ▼ You are taking other medications.

Pregnancy
▼ Safety not established. Discuss with your physician.

Breast-feeding
▼ Safety not established. Discuss with your physician.

Infants and children
▼ Not recommended.

Over 60
▼ Close monitoring may be required.

Driving and hazardous work
▼ Avoid such activities until you have learned how acarbose affects you.

Alcohol
▼ Avoid. Alcoholic drinks may upset diabetic control and increase the risk of hypoglycemia.

POSSIBLE ADVERSE EFFECTS

Adverse effects associated with acarbose tend to be mild and transient in nature. The adverse effects predominantly affect the skin and gastrointestinal tract.

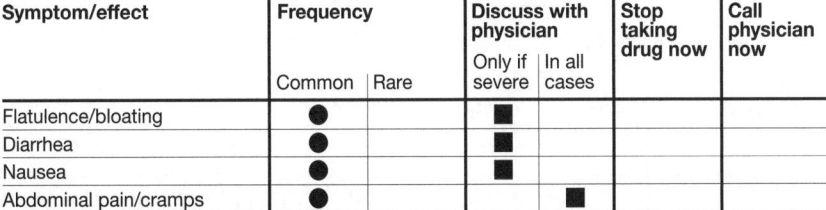

Symptom/effect	Frequency		Discuss with physician		Stop taking drug now	Call physician now
	Common	Rare	Only if severe	In all cases		
Flatulence/bloating	●		■			
Diarrhea	●		■			
Nausea	●		■			
Abdominal pain/cramps	●			■		

INTERACTIONS

Diuretics, corticosteroids, estrogens, oral contraceptives, phenytoin, and sympathomimetics These drugs can increase blood glucose level and effect diabetic control.

Digestive enzymes These can decrease the effect of acarbose and should be avoided.

Chloestyramine This may enhance the effect of acarbose; monitor closely.

Digoxin Acarbose can effect digoxin absorption; dose adjustment of digoxin may be required.

PROLONGED USE

No problems expected.

Monitoring Regular testing of after-meal blood sugar levels is required.

ACETAMINOPHEN

Product names Abenol, Apo-Acetaminophen, Atasol, Tempra, Tylenol, and many others
Used in the following combined preparations Atasol-8, Dimetapp Nighttime Cold, Dristan, Exdol-15, Tylenol Cold, and others

GENERAL INFORMATION

Although acetaminophen has been known since the early 1900s, it was not widely used as an analgesic until the 1950s. One of a group of drugs known as the non-*opioid* analgesics, it is used to relieve occasional bouts of mild pain and to reduce fever. It is also used in the management of chronic painful conditions such as osteoarthritis. It is suitable for children as well as adults.

One of its primary advantages is that it does not cause stomach upset or bleeding problems. This makes it a useful alternative for people who suffer from peptic ulcers or those who cannot tolerate ASA. The drug is also safe for occasional use by those who are being treated with anticoagulants.

Although safe when used as directed, acetaminophen is dangerous when it is taken in overdose, and it is capable of causing serious damage to the liver and kidneys. Large doses of acetaminophen may also be *toxic* if you regularly drink even moderate amounts of alcohol or are malnourished.

QUICK REFERENCE

Drug group Non-opioid analgesics (p.64)

Overdose danger rating High

Dependence rating Low

Prescription needed No

Available as generic Yes

INFORMATION FOR USERS

Follow instructions on the label. Call your physician if symptoms worsen.

How taken

Tablets, capsules, liquid, suppositories.

Frequency and timing of doses
Every 4–6 hours as necessary, but not more than 4 doses per 24 hours in children.

Usual dosage range
Adults 325mg–1g per dose up to 4g daily.
Children 60mg (aged 2–3 months); 60–120mg per dose (aged 3 months–1 year); 120–250mg per dose (aged 1–5 years); 250–500mg per dose (aged 6–12 years).

Onset of effect
Within 15–60 minutes.

Duration of action
Up to 6 hours.

Diet advice
None.

Storage
Keep in a closed container in a cool, dry place out of the reach of children.

Missed dose
Take as soon as you remember if required to relieve pain. Otherwise do not take the missed dose, and take a further dose only when you are in pain.

Stopping the drug
Can be safely stopped as soon as you no longer need it.

OVERDOSE ACTION

 Seek immediate medical advice in all cases. Take emergency action if nausea, vomiting, or stomach pain occur.

See Drug poisoning emergency guide (p.526).

SPECIAL PRECAUTIONS

Be sure to consult your physician or pharmacist before using this drug if:
▼ You have long-term liver or kidney problems.
▼ You are taking other medications.

 Pregnancy
▼ No evidence of risk with occasional use.

 Breast-feeding
▼ The drug passes into the breast milk but only in amounts too small to be harmful.

 Infants and children
▼ Infants aged 2–3 months on doctor's advice for post-immunization fever. Reduced dose necessary up to 12 years.

 Over 60
▼ No special problems.

 Driving and hazardous work
▼ No special problems.

 Alcohol
▼ Heavy intake of alcohol in combination with excess acetaminophen may substantially increase the risk of injury to the liver.

POSSIBLE ADVERSE EFFECTS

Acetaminophen has rarely been found to produce any side effects when taken as recommended. The drug should be stopped and your physician notified if a rash occurs.

Symptom/effect	Frequency		Discuss with physician		Stop taking drug now	Call physician now
	Common	Rare	Only if severe	In all cases		
Nausea		●	■			
Rash		●		■	▲	

PROLONGED USE

You should not normally take this drug for longer than 48 hours except on the advice of your physician. However, there is no evidence of harm from long-term use.

INTERACTIONS

Anticoagulants such as warfarin may need dosage adjustment if acetaminophen is taken regularly in high doses.

Carbamazepine, isoniazid, phenytoin, and rifampin may accelerate the rate at which acetaminophen is metabolized in the body.

Cholestyramine reduces the absorption of acetaminophen and may reduce its effectiveness.

Probenacid may increase the level of acetaminophen.

ACYCLOVIR

Product names Avirax, Mylan-Acyclovir, Zovirax, and others
Used in the following combined preparations None

GENERAL INFORMATION

Acyclovir is an antiviral drug used in the treatment of herpes infections, which can cause cold sores and genital herpes. It is available as a cream, ointment, tablets, and injection. The cream is commonly used to treat cold sores. It can speed up the healing of the lesions, provided application is started as soon as symptoms occur and as the lesions appear. Acyclovir tablets and injection are used to treat severe herpes infections, shingles, chickenpox, and genital herpes. The tablets can also be used to prevent the development of herpes infection in people who have reduced immunity.

QUICK REFERENCE

Drug group Antiviral drugs (p.119)
Overdose danger rating Low
Dependence rating Low
Prescription needed Yes
Available as generic Yes

INFORMATION FOR USERS

Your drug prescription is tailored for you. Do not alter dosage without checking with your physician.

How taken

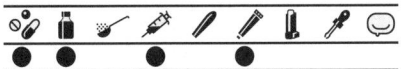

Tablets, liquid, injection, cream, ointment.

Frequency and timing of doses
2–5 x daily. Start as soon as possible.

Usual adult dosage range
Tablets, liquid 1–4g daily (treatment);
600mg–1g daily (prevention).
Cream, ointment 5 x daily.

Onset of effect
Within 24 hours.

Duration of action
Up to 8 hours.

Diet advice
It is necessary to drink plenty of water when taking high doses by mouth or injection.

Storage
Keep in a closed container in a cool, dry place out of the reach of children. Protect from light.

Missed dose
Tablets/liquid Take as soon as you remember.
Cream, ointment Do not apply the missed dose. Apply your next dose as usual.

Stopping the drug
Complete the full course as directed.

Exceeding the dose
An occasional unintentional extra dose is unlikely to be a cause for concern. But if you notice any unusual symptoms, or if a large overdose has been taken, notify your physician.

SPECIAL PRECAUTIONS

Be sure to tell your physician if:
▼ You have a long-term kidney problem.
▼ You have reduced immunity.
▼ You are taking other medications.

Pregnancy
▼ Topical preparations carry no known risk. Oral and injectable forms may be prescribed if the benefits outweigh the risks. Discuss with your physician.

Breast-feeding
▼ No evidence of risk with topical forms. The drug passes into the breast milk following injection or oral administration. Discuss with your physician.

Infants and children
▼ Reduced dose necessary in young children.

Over 60
▼ Reduced dose may be necessary.

Driving and hazardous work
▼ No known problems.

Alcohol
▼ No known problems.

POSSIBLE ADVERSE EFFECTS

Serious *adverse effects* are rare. The cream commonly causes discomfort at the site of application. Confusion and hallucinations occur rarely with oral and injections.

Symptom/effect	Frequency		Discuss with physician		Stop taking drug now	Call physician now
	Common	Rare	Only if severe	In all cases		
Topical applications						
Burning/stinging/itching	●		■			
Rash		●		■	▲	
By mouth						
Nausea/vomiting		●	■			
Headache/dizziness/fatigue		●		■		
Confusion/hallucinations		●		■		
Rash		●		■	▲	
Injection						
Inflammation at injection site		●		■		
Confusion/hallucinations		●		■		

PROLONGED USE

Acyclovir is usually given as a single course of treatment and is not given long term, except for people with reduced immunity.

INTERACTIONS (by mouth or injection only)

General note Any drug that affects the kidneys increases the risk of *side effects* with acyclovir.

Mycophenolate mofetil Acyclovir may increase the levels of this drug in the blood and vice versa.

ADALIMUMAB

Product name Humira
Used in the following combined preparations None

GENERAL INFORMATION

Adalimumab is a recombinant human immunoglobulin (IgG) monoclonal antibody. It is used in the management of rheumatoid arthritis (RA), psoriasis, psoriatric arthritis, ankylosing spondylitis, and Crohn's disease (CD). Adalimumab binds to a protein called TNF-α, decreasing inflammation. This medication can help improve the daily functioning of the individual.

Adalimumab is administered by subcutaneous injection. Prior to starting therapy, patients should be evaluated for risk of tuberculosis (TB), hepatitis B and C, and varicella as this drug should not be started in those with an active infection. Also, patients should not receive live vaccinations during treatment with adalimumab. This drug is usually ordered by specialist physicians who are familiar with its use and monitoring. The medication is available as a Pen or as a pre-filled syringe. The needle cover contains a natural rubber (latex) and should not be handled by those who are sensitive to latex.

QUICK REFERENCE

Drug group Biological Response Modifier (Tumor Necrosis Factor [TNF] alpha inhibitor) (p.103)

Overdose danger rating Medium

Dependence rating Low

Prescription needed Yes

Available as generic No

INFORMATION FOR USERS

Your drug prescription is tailored for you. Do not alter dosage without checking with your physician.

How taken

Injection given subcutaneously.

Frequency and timing of doses
Injection every other week.

Usual adult dosage range
RA: 40mg every other week.
CD: Initial loading dose of 160mg; 80mg the following week; 40mg maintenance dose every other week, starting week 4.

Onset of effect
Effect achieved within 12 weeks of treatment.

Duration of action
Up to several weeks.

Diet advice
None.

Storage
The medication should be refrigerated between 2 and 8°C. Do not freeze. Protect from light.

Missed dose
Administer as soon as you remember, then continue with the next scheduled dose.

Stopping the drug
Do not stop the drug without consulting your physician; symptoms may recur.

Exceeding the dose
Monitor closely. But if you notice any unusual symptoms, or if a large overdose has been taken, notify your physician.

SPECIAL PRECAUTIONS

Be sure to tell your physician if:
▼ You have had infections such as tuberculosis and other infections.
▼ You are planning on receiving vaccinations in the near future.
▼ You have heart failure.
▼ You or the person administering the drug has sensitivity to latex.
▼ You are taking other medications.

 Pregnancy
▼ No adequate, well-controlled studies available. Discuss with your physician.

 Breast-feeding
▼ No adequate, well-controlled studies available. Discuss with your physician.

 Infants and children
▼ Safety and efficacy not fully established.

 Over 60
▼ No special problems.

 Driving and hazardous work
▼ No special problems.

 Alcohol
▼ No special problems.

POSSIBLE ADVERSE EFFECTS

Common *side effects* of adalimumab include mild injection site reactions. There is an increased risk of lymphoma, leukemia, and other malignancies; close monitoring is required.

Symptom/effect	Frequency		Discuss with physician		Stop taking drug now	Call physician now
	Common	Rare	Only if severe	In all cases		
Nausea	●		■			
Injection site reactions (redness, itching, pain, swelling)	●		■			
Infections (such as upper respiratory infections)	●		■	■		
Headache/dizziness	●		■			
Neurologic effects (optic neuritis)		●		■		

PROLONGED USE

Usually used for specified duration.

INTERACTIONS

Anakinra, abatacept, and other immunosuppressants may have their adverse effects enhanced by adalimumab; avoid using together.

Tacrolimus (topical) may enhance the adverse effects of adalimumab.

Echinacea may decrease the effect of adalimumab.

Denosumab may enhance the adverse effects of adalimumab.

Vaccines Adalimumab may diminish the effectiveness of vaccines and may enhance the toxic effects of live vaccines; avoid using together.

ALENDRONATE

Product names Apo-Alendronate, CO Alendronate, Fosamax, Teva-Alendronate, and others
Used in the following combined preparation Fosavance

GENERAL INFORMATION

Alendronate is used to treat osteoporosis in men and post-menopausal women. It is also used in the treatment of Paget's disease. Alendronate tablets should be taken on getting up in the morning, and swallowed whole with a full glass of tap water (mineral water or other drinks should not be used due to a possible negative effect on absorption of the drug). Following this, the individual should remain upright for at least 30 minutes to prevent the drug from staying in the esophagus, where it could cause irritation or, rarely, ulcers. Alendronate should be taken on an empty stomach. Calcium or vitamin D supplements, or other medications and food may be consumed 30 minutes (preferably longer) after taking alendronate.

QUICK REFERENCE

Drug group Drugs for bone disorders (p.108)

Overdose danger rating Medium

Dependence rating Low

Prescription needed Yes

Available as generic Yes

INFORMATION FOR USERS

Your drug prescription is tailored for you. Do not alter dosage without checking with your physician.

How taken

Tablets, oral solution.

Frequency and timing of doses
Once daily or once weekly, first thing in the morning.

Usual adult dosage range
Treatment: men and postmenopausal women, 10mg daily or 70mg weekly.

Prevention: 5mg (postmenopausal women).
Prevention and treatment of corticosteroid-induced osteoporosis: 5mg daily for men and women; postmenopausal women not taking HRT, 10mg.
Paget's disease: 40mg daily for 6 months.

Onset of effect
It may take months to notice an improvement.

Duration of action
Some effects may persist for months or years.

Diet advice
Absorption of alendronate is reduced by foods, especially those containing calcium (e.g. dairy products); take on an empty stomach. The diet must contain adequate calcium and vitamin D; supplements may be given.

Storage
Keep in a closed container in a cool, dry place out of the reach of children.

Missed dose
Take the next dose at the usual time next morning.

Stopping the drug
Do not stop without consulting your physician; the underlying condition may worsen.

Exceeding the dose
An occasional unintentional extra dose is unlikely to cause problems. Large overdoses may cause stomach problems including heartburn, irritation, and ulcers. Notify your physician at once, and try to remain upright.

SPECIAL PRECAUTIONS

Be sure to tell your physician if:
▼ You have difficulty swallowing or have an abnormality of the esophagus.
▼ You have any unusual bone pain.
▼ You have stomach problems or a history of ulcers.
▼ You are unable to stand or sit upright for at least 30 minutes.
▼ You have hypocalcemia (low calcium).
▼ You have kidney impairment.
▼ You are on any other medications.

Pregnancy
▼ Not recommended.

Breast-feeding
▼ Not recommended.

Infants and children
▼ Not recommended.

Over 60
▼ No special problems.

Driving and hazardous work
▼ No special problems.

Alcohol
▼ May cause further stomach irritation.

PROLONGED USE

Alendronate is usually prescribed for several years for osteoporosis without causing any problems.

Monitoring Blood and urine tests may be carried out at intervals.

POSSIBLE ADVERSE EFFECTS

The most frequent *adverse effect* caused by alendronate is abdominal pain as a result of irritation to the esophagus, stomach, or the small intestine.

Symptom/effect	Frequency		Discuss with physician		Stop taking drug now	Call physician now
	Common	Rare	Only if severe	In all cases		
Abdominal pain/distension	●		■			
Diarrhea/constipation	●		■			
Muscle/bone pain	●			■		
Headache	●		■			
Pain on/difficulty swallowing	●			■	▲	
New or worsening heartburn	●			■	▲	
Nausea/vomiting		●	■			
Rash/photosensitivity		●	●			
Eye inflammation/discomfort		●				
Dull, aching pain in thigh, hip, or groin		●		■		▮
Jaw pain		●		■	▲	▮

INTERACTIONS

Antacids and calcium and iron salts reduce the absorption of alendronate and should be taken at a different time of day.

ALGINATES/SODIUM ALGINATE

Product name Gaviscon
Used in the following combined preparations Gaviscon Heartburn Relief, Maalox HRF

GENERAL INFORMATION

"Alginates" is a group term that refers to a mixture of acidic compounds extracted from brown algae (seaweeds). When the powder extract is mixed with water, alginates become a thick viscous fluid or gel depending on the chemicals used. Alginates combined with antacids form a "raft" that floats on the surface of the stomach contents, which reduces reflux and protects the lining of the esophagus. Alginates are used to treat mild symptoms of gastro-esophageal reflux disease. A number of indigestion remedies on sale to the public also contain alginates. These are often used in combination with antacids.

The properties of alginates are also used in wound dressings where, in the form of a woven pad, they absorb fluids from the surface of the wound, keeping it moist and allowing it to heal.

QUICK REFERENCE

Drug group Antacids (p.94)
Overdose danger rating Low
Dependence rating Low
Prescription needed No
Available as generic Yes

INFORMATION FOR USERS

Follow instructions on the label. Call your physician if symptoms worsen.

How taken

Tablets, liquid, powder.

Frequency and timing of doses
4 x daily after meals and at bedtime.

Usual adult dosage range
800–2000mg daily (tablets and liquid).

Onset of effect
10–20 minutes.

Duration of action
3–4 hours.

Diet advice
None.

Storage
Keep in a closed container in a cool, dry place out of the reach of children.

Missed dose
Take as soon as you remember, if you need it.

Stopping the drug
Alginates can be safely stopped as soon as you no longer need them.

Exceeding the dose
Overdose of alginates is likely to produce abdominal distension, without any other symptoms. Notify your physician if symptoms are severe.

POSSIBLE ADVERSE EFFECTS

The antacid salts used in combined oral preparations of alginates may cause abdominal discomfort and distension.

Symptom/effect	Frequency		Discuss with physician		Stop taking drug now	Call physician now
	Common	Rare	Only if severe	In all cases		
Stomach distension	●		■			
Nausea		●	■			

INTERACTIONS

Alginates combined with antacids could affect the absorption of some drugs. Please discuss with your pharmacist.

SPECIAL PRECAUTIONS

Be sure to consult your physician or pharmacist before taking this drug if:
▼ You are on a salt-restricted diet.
▼ You are taking any other medications.

Pregnancy
▼ No evidence of risk to developing baby. Some products can be used for heartburn in pregnancy.

Breast-feeding
▼ No evidence of risk.

Infants and children
▼ Reduced dose necessary.

Over 60
▼ No special problems.

Driving and hazardous work
▼ No known problems.

Alcohol
▼ No known problems.

PROLONGED USE

No problems expected. If symptoms of indigestion last more than 2 weeks, or worsen, consult with your physician.

ALISKIREN

Product name Rasilez
Used in the following combined preparation Rasilez HCT

GENERAL INFORMATION

Aliskiren, a renin inhibitor, is indicated for the treatment of high blood pressure (hypertension). This drug works differently than other antihypertensives and blocks an *enzyme*, thereby causing blood vessels to relax and lower blood pressure. It can be used alone or in combination with another antihypertensive drug, commonly with hydrochlorothiazide (Rasilez HCT). When used in patients with Type 2 diabetes, there is a concern about increased risk of stroke, kidney problems, and other complications. ACE inhibitors or angiotensin receptor blockers (ARBs) should not be used with aliskiren in these patients.

QUICK REFERENCE

Drug group Antihypertensive drugs; renin inhibitor (p.88)

Overdose danger rating Medium

Dependence rating Low

Prescription needed Yes

Available as generic No

INFORMATION FOR USERS

Your drug prescription is tailored for you. Do not alter dosage without checking with your physician.

How taken

Tablets. Do not chew or crush.

Frequency and timing of doses
Once daily.

Usual adult dosage range
150–300mg.

Onset of effect
May take up to 4 weeks to see its full effect.

Duration of action
Up to 24 hours.

Diet advice
None.

Storage
Keep in a closed container in a cool, dry place out of the reach of children.

Missed dose
If you miss a dose, take it as soon as you remember. However, if it is almost time for your next dose, skip the missed dose and go back to the regular schedule. Do not double up on a dose.

Stopping the drug
Do not stop the drug without consulting your physician; symptoms may recur.

Exceeding the dose
An occasional unintentional extra dose is unlikely to be a cause for concern. But if you notice any unusual symptoms, or if an overdose has occurred, seek medical attention immediately.

SPECIAL PRECAUTIONS

Be sure to tell your physician if:
▼ You have kidney problems.
▼ You have gastrointestinal problems.
▼ You have Type 2 diabetes.
▼ You have had a serious allergic reaction called angioedema to a medication.
▼ You are taking cyclosporine or itraconazole.
▼ You are taking other medications.

Pregnancy
▼ Not recommended.

Breast-feeding
▼ Not recommended.

Infants and children
▼ Not recommended for use in those under 18 years of age.

Over 60
▼ Dosage reduction is not normally necessary unless there is significant kidney impairment.

Driving and hazardous work
▼ No special problems.

Alcohol
▼ No special problems.

POSSIBLE ADVERSE EFFECTS

Diarrhea may occur. The incidence of dry cough is much less than with ACE inhibitors. Use with other blood pressure medications may cause a low blood pressure (hypotension). When used with ACE inhibitors or ARBs, the risk for high potassium is greater and should be monitored.

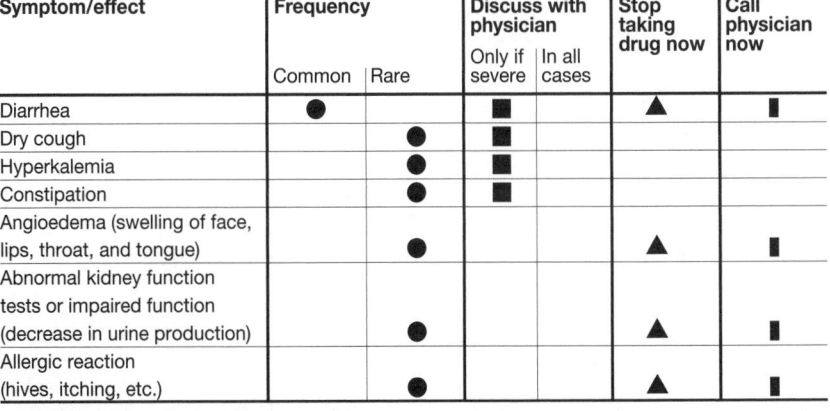

Symptom/effect	Frequency		Discuss with physician		Stop taking drug now	Call physician now
	Common	Rare	Only if severe	In all cases		
Diarrhea	●		■		▲	▮
Dry cough		●	■			
Hyperkalemia		●	■			
Constipation		●	■			
Angioedema (swelling of face, lips, throat, and tongue)		●			▲	▮
Abnormal kidney function tests or impaired function (decrease in urine production)		●			▲	▮
Allergic reaction (hives, itching, etc.)		●			▲	▮

PROLONGED USE

Appropriate assessment of renal function is recommended.

Monitoring Ongoing monitoring of potassium.

INTERACTIONS

Itraconazole or cyclosporine should not be taken with aliskiren.

Potassium-sparing diuretics or potassium supplements, when used with aliskiren, may result in increased levels of potassium.

Irbesartan may decrease the levels of aliskiren.

Furosemide Aliskiren may decrease the effects of furosemide.

ALLOPURINOL

Product names Teva-Allopurinol, Zyloprim
Used in the following combined preparations None

GENERAL INFORMATION

Allopurinol is used to prevent gout, which is caused by deposits of uric acid crystals in joints. Allopurinol blocks an enzyme called xanthine oxidase that is involved in forming uric acid. It is also used to lower high uric acid levels (hyperuricemia) caused by other drugs, such as anticancer drugs. Allopurinol should never be started until an acute attack is over because it may cause a further episode. Treatment with the drug should be continued indefinitely to prevent further attacks.

At the start of treatment, an acute attack may occur and colchicine or an anti-inflammatory drug may also be given, until uric acid levels are reduced. If an acute attack occurs while on allopurinol, treatment should continue along with an anti-inflammatory drug.

QUICK REFERENCE

Drug group Drugs for gout (p.105)
Overdose danger rating Medium
Dependence rating Low
Prescription needed Yes
Available as generic Yes

INFORMATION FOR USERS

Your drug prescription is tailored for you. Do not alter dosage without checking with your physician.

How taken

Tablets.

Frequency and timing of doses
1–3 x daily after food.

Usual adult dosage range
100–300mg daily.

Onset of effect
Within 24–48 hours. Full effect may not be felt for several weeks.

Duration of action
Up to 30 hours. Some effect may last for 1–2 weeks after the drug has been stopped.

Diet advice
A high fluid intake (2 litres of fluid daily) is recommended.

Storage
Keep in a closed container in a cool, dry place out of the reach of children.

Missed dose
If your next dose is not due for another 12 hours or more, take a dose as soon as you remember and take the next one as usual. Otherwise skip the missed dose and take your next dose on schedule.

Stopping the drug
Do not stop the drug without consulting your physician; symptoms may recur.

Exceeding the dose
An occasional unintentional extra dose is unlikely to cause problems. Large overdoses may cause nausea, vomiting, abdominal pain, diarrhea, and dizziness. Notify your physician.

SPECIAL PRECAUTIONS

Be sure to tell your physician if:
▼ You have long-term liver or kidney problems.
▼ You have had a previous sensitivity reaction to allopurinol.
▼ You have a current attack of gout.
▼ You are taking other medications.

Pregnancy
▼ Risks versus benefits need to be assessed. Discuss with your physician.

Breast-feeding
▼ The drug passes into the breast milk but is not known to be harmful to the baby. Discuss with your physician.

Infants and children
▼ May be used in malignancy-related increase in uric acid levels. Reduced dose necessary.

Over 60
▼ Reduced dose may be necessary.

Driving and hazardous work
▼ Avoid such activities until you have learned how allopurinol affects you because the drug can cause drowsiness.

Alcohol
▼ Avoid. Alcohol may worsen gout.

POSSIBLE ADVERSE EFFECTS

Adverse effects of allopurinol are not very common. The most serious is an allergic rash that may require the drug to be stopped and an alternative treatment substituted. Nausea can be avoided by taking allopurinol after food.

Symptom/effect	Frequency		Discuss with physician		Stop taking drug now	Call physician now
	Common	Rare	Only if severe	In all cases		
Nausea	●		■			
Rash/itching	●			■	▲	
Drowsiness/dizziness		●	■			
Headache		●		■		
Sore throat		●		■	▲	
Metallic taste		●		■		
Fever and chills		●		■	▲	
Visual disturbances		●		■		

PROLONGED USE

Apart from an increased risk of gout in the first weeks or months, no problems are expected.

Monitoring Periodic checks on uric acid levels in the blood and liver function tests are usually performed, and the dose of allopurinol adjusted if necessary.

INTERACTIONS

ACE inhibitors Allopurinol may increase the risk of hypersensitivity reactions.

Oral anticoagulant drugs Allopurinol may increase the effects of these drugs.

Theophylline Allopurinol may increase levels of this drug.

Mercaptopurine and azathioprine Allopurinol blocks the breakdown of these drugs, requiring a reduction in their dosage.

Cyclosporine Allopurinol may increase the effects of this drug.

Amoxicillin and ampicillin Concurrent use may increase the incidence of skin rash.

Antacids may decrease the absorption of allopurinol. Separate by 3 hours.

ALPRAZOLAM

Product names Apo-Alpraz, Nu-Alpraz, Teva-Alprazolam, Xanax, Xanax TS
Used in the following combined preparations None

GENERAL INFORMATION

Alprazolam belongs to a group of drugs called the benzodiazepines. The actions and adverse effects of this group of drugs are described more fully under Anti-anxiety drugs (p.69).

Alprazolam is indicated for the short-term symptomatic relief of excessive anxiety. It is also used in the treatment of panic disorders and agoraphobia (fear of open spaces), other phobias, and anxiety disorders of a general nature.

Panic disorders are characterized by recurrent panic attacks, which may present as periods of intense fear or discomfort.

Like other benzodiazepines, alprazolam can be habit-forming if taken regularly over a long period. Its effects may also grow weaker over time. For these reasons, treatment with alprazolam is reviewed by the physician at regular intervals.

QUICK REFERENCE

Drug group Benzodiazepine anti-anxiety drug (p.67)

Overdose danger rating Medium

Dependence rating High

Prescription needed Yes

Available as generic Yes

INFORMATION FOR USERS

Your drug prescription is tailored for you. Do not alter dosage without checking with your physician.

How taken

Tablets.

Frequency and timing of doses
2–3 x daily.

Usual dosage range
0.75–1.5mg daily. Occasionally, larger doses may be prescribed.

Onset of effect
1–2 hours.

Duration of action
Up to 24 hours.

Diet advice
None.

Storage
Keep in a tightly closed container in a cool, dry place away from reach of children. Protect from light.

Missed dose
No cause for concern, but take when you remember. If your next dose is due within 2 hours, take a single dose now and skip the next one.

Stopping the drug
If you have been taking the drug continuously for less than 2 weeks, it can be safely stopped as soon as you feel you no longer need it. However, if you have been taking it for longer, consult your physician, who may advise a gradual reduction in dosage. Stopping abruptly may lead to withdrawal symptoms.

Exceeding the dose
An occasional unintentional extra dose is unlikely to cause problems. Larger overdoses may cause unusual drowsiness, unsteadiness, or coma. Notify your physician.

SPECIAL PRECAUTIONS

Be sure to consult your physician or pharmacist before taking this drug if:
▼ You have impaired liver or kidney function.
▼ You have myasthenia gravis.
▼ You have glaucoma.
▼ You have had problems with alcohol or drug abuse.
▼ You are taking other medications.

Pregnancy
▼ Generally avoided. Discuss with your physician.

Breast-feeding
▼ The drug passes into the breast milk. Its effects on the baby are not clearly known. Discuss with your physician.

Infants and children
▼ Not recommended in patients under 18 years.

Over 60
▼ Increased likelihood of adverse effects. Reduced dose may therefore be necessary.

Driving and hazardous work
▼ Avoid such activities until you have learned how the drug affects you: it can cause reduced alertness, blurred vision, and slowed reactions.

Alcohol
▼ Avoid. Alcohol may increase the sedative effects of this drug.

POSSIBLE ADVERSE EFFECTS

The principal adverse effects of this drug are related to its sedative and tranquilizing properties. These effects normally diminish after the first few days of treatment. If adverse effects persist, they can often be reduced by adjustment of dosage.

Symptom/effect	Frequency		Discuss with physician		Stop taking drug now	Call physician now
	Common	Rare	Only if severe	In all cases		
Drowsiness	●		■			
Dizziness/unsteadiness	●			■		
Blurred vision		●		■		
Forgetfulness/confusion		●		■		
Headache		●	■			
Rash		●		■		
Jaundice		●		■		

INTERACTIONS

Sedatives All drugs that have a *sedative* effect on the central nervous system are likely to increase the sedative properties of alprazolam. Such drugs include alcohol, sleeping drugs, antihistamines, antidepressants, *narcotic* analgesics, and antipsychotics.

Clarithromycin, erythromycin, azithromycin, indinavir, lopinavir, ritonavir, droperidol, ketoconazole, itraconozole, and grapefruit juice can all increase the effect of alprazolam. Avoid using together.

PROLONGED USE

Regular use of this drug over several weeks can lead to a reduction in its effect as the body adapts. It may also be habit-forming when taken for extended periods, especially if larger-than-average doses are taken.

ALPROSTADIL

Product names Alprostadil Injection USP, Caverject, MUSE, Prostin VR
Used in the following combined preparations None

GENERAL INFORMATION

Alprostadil is a member of the prostaglandin group of drugs and is used to help men with erectile dysfunction to achieve an erection. It is either injected directly into the penis or applied as a micro-*suppository* into the urethra. The most common *side effect* of alprostadil is pain in the penis.

The first dose must be given by medically trained personnel, and self-administration may only be undertaken after proper training.

The drug Prostin VR is also used to treat patent ductus arteriosus, a congenital heart disorder in newborn babies. It works by keeping the ductus blood vessel (normally shut off at birth) open until it can be closed permanently by surgery. It is usually only administered to babies in hospital. *Side effects* such as heart and respiratory problems are common, and there is a risk of unusual bone growth, particularly after long use.

INFORMATION FOR USERS

Your drug prescription is tailored for you. Do not alter dosage without checking with your physician.

How taken

Injection, suppository.

Frequency and timing of doses
Caverject up to 3 x per week. Not more than one dose in any 24 hour period.
MUSE no more than 2 doses in 24 hours.

Usual dosage range
Starts at 2.5mcg, individually adjusted by your physician to produce an erection lasting not more than 1 hour.

Onset of effect
Within a few minutes.

Duration of action
Erection should not last more than 1 hour.

Diet advice
None.

Storage
Store in a refrigerator, out of the reach of children. Do not freeze.

Missed dose
Take the next dose when needed. Use no more than one dose in any 24-hour period and no more than 3 doses per week.

Stopping the drug
Can be safely stopped as soon as you no longer need it.

Exceeding the dose
If an unintentional extra dose has been used close to the regular dose, notify your physician. If you notice any unusual symptoms or if a large overdose has been taken, notify your physician.

SPECIAL PRECAUTIONS

Be sure to tell your physician if:
▼ You are taking other medications for erectile dysfunction.
▼ You have sickle cell anemia, multiple myeloma, or leukemia.
▼ You have a penile implant.

Pregnancy
▼ Not prescribed.

Breast-feeding
▼ Not prescribed.

Infants and children
▼ Other than Prostin VR for newborn babies, not prescribed.

Over 60
▼ Doses are adjusted individually.

Driving and hazardous work
▼ No special problems.

Alcohol
▼ Excessive use of alcohol with alprostadil can contribute to erectile problems.

POSSIBLE ADVERSE EFFECTS

Breathing difficulties are a side effect of the drug in newborn babies. Less often, it may cause convulsions. In men, there is a risk of prolonged erection. You should report any erection lasting for more than 3 hours to your physician and stop taking the drug immediately.

Symptom/effect	Frequency		Discuss with physician		Stop taking drug now	Call physician now
	Common	Rare	Only if severe	In all cases		
Newborn babies						
Breathing difficulties		●		■		▮
Convulsions		●		■		▮
Men						
Penile pain	●		■			
Bruising/swelling	●			■		
Bleeding	●			■		
Prolonged erection	●			■	▲	▮
Testicular pain/swelling		●		■		
Dizziness/fainting		●		■		
Chest pain/palpitations		●		■		

PROLONGED USE

Prolonged use in newborn babies may cause abnormal bone development and weakening of some blood vessel walls.

Prolonged use for erectile dysfunction may lead to development of fibrosis of the penis.

Monitoring Regular examinations for penile fibrosis are required.

INTERACTIONS

Antihypertensive and vasodilator drugs The effects of these drugs may be increased by alprostadil.

ALUMINUM HYDROXIDE

Product name Amphojel
Used in the following combined preparations Diovol, Gelusil, Gaviscon Heartburn Relief Formula, and others

GENERAL INFORMATION

Aluminum hydroxide is a common ingredient of many over-the-counter remedies for indigestion and heartburn. Because the drug is constipating (it is sometimes used to treat diarrhea), it is usually combined with a magnesium-containing antacid with a balancing laxative effect.

The prolonged action of the drug makes it useful in preventing the pain of stomach and duodenal ulcers or heartburn. Aluminum hydroxide can also promote the healing of ulcers. The drug may be more effective as an antacid in liquid form rather than

as tablets. Some antacid preparations include large amounts of sodium and these should be used with caution by those on low-sodium diets.

In the intestine, aluminum hydroxide binds with, and thereby reduces the absorption of, phosphate. This makes it helpful in treating high blood phosphate (hyperphosphatemia), which occurs in some people with impaired kidney function. However, prolonged heavy use can lead to phosphate deficiency and a consequent weakening of the bones.

INFORMATION FOR USERS

Follow instructions on the label. Call your physician if symptoms worsen.

How taken

Tablets, capsules, liquid (gel suspension). The tablets should be well chewed.

Frequency and timing of doses
As antacid 4–6 x daily as needed, or 1 hour before and after meals.
Peptic ulcer 6–7 x daily.
Hyperphosphatemia 3–4 x daily with meals.
Diarrhea 2–6 x daily.

Usual dosage range
Adults Up to 70ml daily (liquid), 2–10g daily (tablets or capsules).
Children over 6 years Reduced dose according to age and weight.

Onset of effect
Within 15 minutes.

Duration of action
2–4 hours.

Diet advice
For hyperphosphatemia, a low-phosphate diet may be advised in addition to aluminum hydroxide treatment.

Storage
Keep in a closed container in a cool, dry place out of the reach of children.

Missed dose
Do not take the missed dose. Take your next dose as usual.

Stopping the drug
Can be safely stopped as soon as you no longer need it (indigestion). When taken as ulcer treatment or for hyperphosphatemia resulting from kidney failure, do not stop without consulting your physician.

Exceeding the dose
An occasional unintentional extra dose is unlikely to be a cause for concern. But if you notice any unusual symptoms, or if a large overdose has been taken, notify your physician.

SPECIAL PRECAUTIONS

Be sure to consult your physician or pharmacist before taking this drug if:
▼ You have a long-term kidney problem.
▼ You have heart problems.
▼ You have high blood pressure.
▼ You suffer from constipation.
▼ You have a bone disease.
▼ You have porphyria.
▼ You are taking other medications.

Pregnancy
▼ Safety in pregnancy not established. Discuss with your physician.

Breast-feeding
▼ No evidence of risk.

Infants and children
▼ Not recommended under 6 years except on the advice of a physician.

Over 60
▼ Increased likelihood of adverse effects. Reduced dose may therefore be necessary.

Driving and hazardous work
▼ No known problems.

Alcohol
▼ No known problems.

POSSIBLE ADVERSE EFFECTS

Constipation is common with aluminum hydroxide; nausea and vomiting may occur due to the granular, powdery nature of the drug. Bone pain occurs only when large doses have been taken regularly for months or years.

Symptom/effect	Frequency		Discuss with physician		Stop taking drug now	Call physician now
	Common	Rare	Only if severe	In all cases		
Constipation distension	●		■			
Nausea		●	■			
Vomiting		●			■	

INTERACTIONS

General note Aluminum hydroxide may interfere with the absorption or excretion of many drugs, including oral anticoagulants, digoxin, many antibiotics, penicillamine, corticosteroids, antipsychotics, and phenytoin. It should only be taken at least 2 hours before or after other drugs.

Enteric-coated tablets Aluminum hydroxide may lead to the break-up of the enteric coating of tablets (e.g., bisacodyl, or enteric-coated ASA) before they leave the stomach, leading to stomach irritation.

PROLONGED USE

Aluminum hydroxide should not be used for longer than 4 weeks without consulting your physician. Prolonged use of high doses in people with normal kidney function may deplete blood phosphate and calcium levels, leading to weakening of the bones and fractures.

AMANTADINE

Product name Mylan-Amantadine
Used in the following combined preparations None

GENERAL INFORMATION

Amantadine was first used in the 1960s as an antiviral drug, originally for the prevention and treatment of influenza A. However, flu viruses have recently shown resistance to amantadine, so the drug is no longer used as a first choice for this purpose. It can also reduce pain following herpes zoster (shingles). In 1969, amantadine was found to be helpful in *parkinsonism*, except when the condition is caused by drugs. Amantadine usually produces improvement of symptoms during the first few weeks, but its effectiveness wears off over six to eight weeks, requiring replacement by another drug. It is sometimes given with levodopa (see p.331), another drug for parkinsonism.

(see p.331)

QUICK REFERENCE

Drug group Drugs for parkinsonism (p.71) and antiviral drugs (p.119)

Overdose danger rating Low

Dependence rating Low

Prescription needed Yes

Available as generic Yes

INFORMATION FOR USERS

Your drug prescription is tailored for you. Do not alter dosage without checking with your physician.

How taken

Capsules, liquid.

Frequency and timing of doses
1–2 x daily.

Usual dosage range
100–200mg daily.

Onset of effect
In parkinsonism the full effect may not be felt for up to 2 weeks. In viral infections the severity and duration of symptoms is likely to be reduced if the drug is begun within 48 hours of the onset of symptoms.

Duration of action
Up to 24 hours.

Diet advice
None.

Storage
Keep in a closed container in a cool, dry place out of the reach of children.

Missed dose
Take as soon as you remember. If your next dose is due within 2 hours, take a single dose now and skip the next dose.

Stopping the drug
Do not stop taking the drug without consulting your physician; symptoms may recur.

Exceeding the dose
An occasional unintentional extra dose is unlikely to cause problems. But if you notice any unusual symptoms, or if a large overdose has been taken, notify your physician.

SPECIAL PRECAUTIONS

Be sure to tell your physician if:
▼ You have long-term liver or kidney problems.
▼ You have a peptic ulcer.
▼ You have had epileptic seizures.
▼ You have heart disease.
▼ You suffer from eczema.
▼ You are taking other medications.

Pregnancy
▼ Safety not established. Discuss with your physician.

Breast-feeding
▼ The drug passes into the breast milk and may affect the baby. Discuss with your physician.

Infants and children
▼ Not usually prescribed. Reduced dose necessary.

Over 60
▼ Increased likelihood of adverse effects. Reduced dose necessary.

Driving and hazardous work
▼ Avoid such activities until you have learned how amantadine affects you because the drug may cause blurred vision, dizziness, inability to concentrate, hallucinations, agaitation, and confusion.

Alcohol
▼ No known problems.

POSSIBLE ADVERSE EFFECTS

Adverse effects are uncommon and often wear off during continued treatment. They are rarely serious enough to require treatment to be stopped.

Symptom/effect	Frequency		Discuss with physician		Stop taking drug now	Call physician now
	Common	Rare	Only if severe	In all cases		
Nervousness/agitation	●		■			
Nausea	●		■			
Confusion/hallucinations	●			■		
Insomnia	●		■			
Dizziness	●			■		
Blurred vision		●		■		
Loss of appetite		●		■		
Ankle swelling		●		■		
Rash		●	■		▲	

INTERACTIONS

Anticholinergic drugs Amantadine may add to the effects of *anticholinergic* drugs. In that event your physician will probably reduce the dosage of the anticholinergic drugs.

Antipsychotics, such as haloperidol, olanzapine, and quetiapine, may reduce the effectiveness of amantadine when used for parkinsonism.

PROLONGED USE

The beneficial effects of this drug usually diminish during continuous treatment for parkinsonism. When this occurs, another drug may be substituted for or given together with amantadine. Sometimes the effectiveness of amantadine can be restored if it is withdrawn by your physician for a few weeks and later reintroduced.

AMILORIDE

Product name Apo-Amiloride
Used in the following combined preparations Apo-Amilzide, Mylan-Amilazide, Nu-Amilzide, Teva-Amiloride HCTZ

GENERAL INFORMATION

Amiloride is a diuretic. It acts on the kidneys to increase the amount of urine that is passed, although the diurectic effect of amiloride is very mild. It is used in the treatment of edema (fluid retention), which can result from heart failure or liver disease and for hypertension (high blood pressure).

Amiloride's effect on urine flow may last for several hours, so it should be taken in the morning.

Amiloride causes the kidneys to conserve potassium (potassium-sparing diuretic) and should not be used when there is a high blood level of potassium. The drug is prescribed with caution in people taking potassium supplements or those with kidney disease. The drug is often combined with other diuretics.

INFORMATION FOR USERS

Your drug prescription is tailored for you. Do not alter dosage without checking with your physician.

How taken

Tablets.

Frequency and timing of doses
Once or twice daily, usually in the morning.

Usual adult dosage range
5–20mg daily.

Onset of effect
Within 2–4 hours.

Duration of action
12 hours.

Diet advice
Avoid foods that are high in potassium – for example, dried fruit, bananas, tomatoes, and "low salt" salt substitutes.

Storage
Keep in a closed container in a cool, dry place out of the reach of children.

Missed dose
Take as soon as you remember. However, if it is late in the day, do not take the missed dose, or you may need to get up at night to pass urine. Take the next scheduled dose as usual.

Stopping the drug
Do not stop the drug without consulting your physician; symptoms may recur.

Exceeding the dose
An occasional unintentional extra dose is unlikely to be a cause for concern. But if you notice any unusual symptoms, or if a large overdose has been taken, notify your physician.

SPECIAL PRECAUTIONS

Be sure to tell your physician if:
▼ You have long-term liver or kidney problems.
▼ You are taking other medications.

Pregnancy
▼ Not usually prescribed. May cause a reduction in the blood supply to the developing baby. Discuss with your physician.

Breast-feeding
▼ Not usually prescribed during breast-feeding. Discuss with your physician.

Infants and children
▼ Not recommended.

Over 60
▼ Increased likelihood of adverse effects. Reduced dose may be necessary.

Driving and hazardous work
▼ No known problems.

Alcohol
▼ No special problems.

POSSIBLE ADVERSE EFFECTS

Amiloride has few adverse effects; the main problem is the possibility that potassium may be retained by the body, causing muscle weakness and numbness.

Symptom/effect	Frequency		Discuss with physician		Stop taking drug now	Call physician now
	Common	Rare	Only if severe	In all cases		
Digestive disturbance		●	■			
Confusion		●		■		
Muscle weakness/cramps		●		■		
Rash		●		■	▲	
Dry mouth/thirst		●		■		
Dizziness		●		■		

PROLONGED USE

Monitoring Blood tests may be carried out to monitor levels of body salts.

INTERACTIONS

Lithium Amiloride may increase the blood levels of lithium, leading to an increased risk of lithium poisoning.

ACE inhibitors, angiotensin II blockers, renin inhibitors, cyclosporine, and NSAIDs These drugs may increase the risk of potassium retention if taken with amiloride.

AMIODARONE

Product names Apo-Amiodarone, Cordarone, Mylan-Amiodarone, Teva-Amiodarone, and others
Used in the following combined preparations None

GENERAL INFORMATION

Amiodarone is used to treat a variety of abnormal heart rhythms (arrhythmias). It works by slowing nerve impulses in the heart muscle.

Amiodarone is given to prevent recurrent atrial and ventricular fibrillation and to treat ventricular and supraventricular tachycardias and Wolff-Parkinson-White Syndrome. Often the last choice when other treatments have failed, especially for long-term use, it has serious *adverse effects* including liver damage, thyroid problems, and eye and lung damage.

Treatment should be started only under specialist supervision or in hospital and the dosage carefully controlled in order to achieve the desired effect using the lowest possible dose.

QUICK REFERENCE

Drug group Anti-arrhythmic drugs (p.86)

Overdose danger rating Medium

Dependence rating Low

Prescription needed Yes

Available as generic Yes

INFORMATION FOR USERS

Your drug prescription is tailored for you. Do not alter dosage without checking with your physician.

How taken

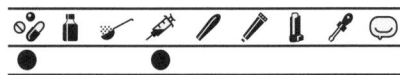

Tablets, injection.

Frequency and timing of doses
3 x daily or by injection initially, then 2 x daily, then 1 x every 1 or 2 days (maintenance dose).

Usual adult dosage range
600–800mg daily, reduced gradually. Maintenance dose: 200–400mg.

Onset of effect
By mouth, some effects may occur in 72 hours; full benefits may take some weeks to show. By injection, effects may occur within 30 minutes.

Duration of action
3–12 months.

Diet advice
None.

Storage
Keep in a closed container in a cool, dry place out of the reach of children. Protect from light.

Missed dose
Take as soon as you remember. If your next dose is due within 12 hours, do not take the missed dose. Take your next dose as usual.

Stopping the drug
Do not stop the drug without consulting your physician; symptoms may recur.

OVERDOSE ACTION

 Seek immediate medical advice in all cases. Take emergency action if palpitations are noted or consciousness is lost.

See Drug poisoning emergency guide (p.526).

SPECIAL PRECAUTIONS

Be sure to tell your physician if:
▼ You have long-term liver problems.
▼ You have heart problems.
▼ You have eye disease.
▼ You have a lung disorder such as asthma or bronchitis.
▼ You have a thyroid disorder.
▼ You are sensitive to iodine.
▼ You are taking other medications.

 Pregnancy
▼ Not prescribed. Discuss with your physician.

 Breast-feeding
▼ The drug passes into the breast milk and may affect the baby. Discuss with your physician.

 Infants and children
▼ Not recommended.

 Over 60
▼ Increased likelihood of adverse effects. Reduced dose necessary.

 Driving and hazardous work
▼ Avoid these activities until you have learned how amiodarone affects you because the drug can cause the eyes to be dazzled by bright light.

 Alcohol
▼ No known problems.

POSSIBLE ADVERSE EFFECTS

Amiodarone has a number of unusual adverse effects, including metallic taste in the mouth, greyish skin, and increased sensitivity of the skin to sunlight (photosensitivity). Patients are advised to use sun block, wear a hat, and cover exposed skin.

Symptom/effect	Frequency		Discuss with physician		Stop taking drug now	Call physician now
	Common	Rare	Only if severe	In all cases		
Nausea/vomiting	●		■			
Liver damage	●			■		
Photosensitivity	●			■		
Visual disturbances	●			■		
Thyroid problems		●		■		
Heart rate disturbances		●		■		
Numb, tingling extremities		●		■		
Shortness of breath/cough		●		■		
Headache/weakness/fatigue		●		■		
Grey skin colour		●		■		

PROLONGED USE

Prolonged use of this drug may cause a number of adverse effects on the eyes, lungs, thyroid gland, and liver.

Monitoring A chest X-ray may be taken before treatment starts. Blood tests are done before treatment starts and then every 6 months to check thyroid and liver function. Regular eye examinations are required.

INTERACTIONS

General note Amiodarone can interact with many drugs. Consult your physician or *pharmacist* before taking other medications. Grapefruit juice can increase levels of oral amiodarone and should be avoided.

Diuretics These cause potassium loss that may increase amiodarone's *toxic* effects.

Other anti-arrhythmic drugs Amiodarone may increase the effects of drugs such as beta blockers, digoxin, diltiazem, or verapamil.

Warfarin Amiodarone may increase the anticoagulant effect of warfarin.

AMITRIPTYLINE

Product names Bio-Amitriptyline, Dom-Amitriptyline, Elavil, Levate, and others
Used in the following combined preparations None

GENERAL INFORMATION

Amitriptyline belongs to the tricyclic group of antidepressant drugs. They are effective for long-term depression but are less well tolerated and dangerous in overdose so they are second-line choices after SSRI antidepressants. The *sedative* effect of amitriptyline is useful when depression is accompanied by anxiety or insomnia. Taken at night, the drug encourages sleep and reduces the need for additional sleeping drugs. Amitriptyline may also be used to treat neuropathic pain such as postherpetic neuralgia after shingles and to prevent migraine. For many of these other conditions, it is used in smaller doses than when used as an antidepressant. In overdose, amitriptyline may cause abnormal heart rhythms, seizures, and *coma*.

QUICK REFERENCE

Drug group Tricyclic antidepressant drugs (p.68)
Overdose danger rating High
Dependence rating Low
Prescription needed Yes
Available as generic Yes

INFORMATION FOR USERS

Your drug prescription is tailored for you. Do not alter dosage without checking with your physician.

How taken

Tablets.

Frequency and timing of doses
1–4 x daily, usually as a single dose at night.

Usual adult dosage range
Depression: 50–200mg daily.
Neuropathic pain: 10–150mg daily.

Onset of effect
Sedation can appear within hours but full antidepressant effect may take 4 weeks.

Duration of action
Antidepressant effect may last for 6 weeks; common adverse effects, only a few days.

Diet advice
None.

Storage
Keep in a closed container in a cool, dry place out of the reach of children. Protect from light.

Missed dose
Take as soon as you remember. If your next dose is due within 3 hours, take a single dose now and skip the next.

Stopping the drug
An abrupt stop can cause withdrawal symptoms and a recurrence of the original trouble. Consult your physician, who may supervise a gradual reduction in dosage.

OVERDOSE ACTION

Seek immediate medical advice in all cases. Take emergency action if palpitations are noted or consciousness is lost.

See Drug poisoning emergency guide (p.526).

SPECIAL PRECAUTIONS

Be sure to tell your physician if:
▼ You have heart problems.
▼ You have had epileptic seizures.
▼ You have long-term liver or kidney problems.
▼ You have glaucoma.
▼ You have prostate trouble.
▼ You have thyroid disease.
▼ You have had mania or a psychotic illness.
▼ You are taking other medications.

Pregnancy
▼ Safety in pregnancy not established. Discuss risks versus benefits with your physician.

Breast-feeding
▼ The drug passes into the breast milk and may affect the baby. Discuss with your physician.

Infants and children
▼ Not recommended under 16 years for depression, or under 6 years for enuresis.

Over 60
▼ Reduced dose may be necessary.

Driving and hazardous work
▼ Avoid such activities until you have learned how amitriptyline affects you because the drug may cause blurred vision and reduced alertness.

Alcohol
▼ Avoid. Alcohol may increase the sedative effects of this drug.

Surgery and general anesthetics
▼ Amitriptyline treatment may need to be reassessed before you have surgery. Discuss this with your physician.

POSSIBLE ADVERSE EFFECTS

The possible adverse effects of this drug are mainly the result of its *anticholinergic* action and its blocking action on the transmission of signals through the heart.

Symptom/effect	Frequency		Discuss with physician		Stop taking drug now	Call physician now
	Common	Rare	Only if severe	In all cases		
Drowsiness	●		■			
Sweating	●		■			
Dry mouth/constipation	●		■			
Blurred vision	●			■		
Dizziness/fainting	●			■		
Difficulty passing urine		●		■	▲	
Sore throat		●		■	▲	
Palpitations		●		■	▲	■

INTERACTIONS

Monoamine oxidase inhibitors (MAOIs)
In the rare cases where these drugs are given with amitriptyline, close monitoring is required due to the possibility of serious interactions.

Antiepileptics The effects of these drugs are reduced by amitriptyline as it lowers the threshold for seizures.

Sedatives All drugs that have *sedative* effects intensify those of amitriptyline.

Antiarrhythmic drugs There is an increased risk of abnormal heart rhythms when these drugs are taken with amitriptyline. Cimetidine, SSRIs, and beta blockers may increase amitriptyline levels.

PROLONGED USE

No problems expected.

AMLODIPINE

Product name Accel-Amlodipine, Apo-Amlodipine, Norvasc, and others
Used in the following combined preparations Caduet, Twynsta

GENERAL INFORMATION

Amlodipine belongs to a group of drugs known as calcium channel blockers, which interfere with the conduction of signals in the muscles of the heart and blood vessels.

Amlodipine is used in the treatment of angina to help prevent attacks of chest pain. Unlike some other anti-angina drugs (such as beta blockers), it can be used safely by asthmatics and noninsulin-dependent diabetics.

Amlodipine is also used to reduce high blood pressure (hypertension).

In common with other drugs of its class, amlodipine may cause blood pressure to fall too low at the start of treatment. In rare cases, angina may become worse at the start of amlodipine treatment. The drug may sometimes cause mild to moderate leg and ankle swelling.

INFORMATION FOR USERS

Your drug prescription is tailored for you. Do not alter dosage without checking with your physician.

How taken

Tablets.

Frequency and timing of doses
Once daily.

Usual adult dosage range
5–10mg daily.

Onset of effect
6–12 hours.

Duration of action
24 hours.

Diet advice
None.

Storage
Keep in a closed container in a cool, dry place out of the reach of children.

Missed dose
If you remember a missed dose within 12 hours, take it as soon as you remember. Otherwise do not take the missed dose and do not double up the next one. Instead, go back to your regular schedule.

Stopping the drug
Do not stop without consulting your physician; the underlying condition may worsen.

Exceeding the dose
An occasional unintentional extra dose is unlikely to cause problems. Large overdoses may cause a marked lowering of blood pressure. Notify your physician immediately.

SPECIAL PRECAUTIONS

Be sure to tell your physician if:
▼ You have long-term liver or kidney problems.
▼ You have heart failure or aortic stenosis.
▼ You have diabetes.
▼ You are taking other medications.

Pregnancy
▼ Safety in pregnancy not established. Discuss with your physician.

Breast-feeding
▼ It is not known if the drug passes into the breast milk. Discuss with your physician.

Infants and children
▼ Not recommended.

Over 60
▼ No special problems.

Driving and hazardous work
▼ Avoid such activities until you have learned how amlodipine affects you because the drug can cause dizziness owing to lowered blood pressure.

Alcohol
▼ Avoid. Alcohol may further reduce blood pressure, causing dizziness or other symptoms.

POSSIBLE ADVERSE EFFECTS

Amlodipine can cause a variety of minor *adverse effects*, including leg and ankle swelling, headache, dizziness, fatigue, and nausea. Dizziness, especially on rising, may be the result of an excessive reduction in blood pressure.

Symptom/effect	Frequency		Discuss with physician		Stop taking drug now	Call physician now
	Common	Rare	Only if severe	In all cases		
Leg and ankle swelling	●		■			
Headache	●		■			
Dizziness/fatigue	●		■			
Flushing	●		■			
Nausea/abdominal pain		●		■		
Palpitations		●		■		
Worsening of angina		●		■	▲	■
Skin rash		●		■	▲	
Breathing difficulties		●		■	▲	

INTERACTIONS

Alpha blockers, beta blockers, ACE inhibitors, and diuretics Amlodipine may increase the effect of these drugs and vice versa.

Ketoconazole, itraconazole, and ritonavir These drugs may increase blood levels and adverse effects of amlodipine.

St John's wort This reduces the blood level of amlodipine.

Simvastatin Amlodipine may increase levels of simvastatin.

Carbamazepine may decrease the effect of amlodipine.

PROLONGED USE

No problems expected.

AMOXICILLIN

Product names Apo-Amoxi, Gen-Amoxicillin, and others
Used in the following combined preparations Clavulin, Hp-PAC, Losec 1-2-3 A, Nexium 1-2-3 A

GENERAL INFORMATION

Amoxicillin is a penicillin *antibiotic*. It is prescribed to treat a variety of infections, but is particularly useful for treating ear, nose, and throat infections, respiratory tract infections, and cystitis. It is also used to treat urethral or rectal Chlamydia infections. The drug is absorbed well by the body when taken orally.

Amoxicillin can cause minor stomach upsets and a skin rash. It can also provoke a severe *allergic reaction* with fever, swelling of the mouth and tongue, itching, and breathing difficulties. This suggests that the patient is allergic to penicillin antibiotics.

QUICK REFERENCE

Drug group Penicillin antibiotics (p.116)

Overdose danger rating Low

Dependence rating Low

Prescription needed Yes

Available as generic Yes

INFORMATION FOR USERS

Your drug prescription is tailored for you. Do not alter dosage without checking with your physician.

How taken

Tablets, capsules, powder (dissolved in water)

Frequency and timing of doses
Normally 3 x daily.

Usual dosage range
Adults 750mg–1.5g daily. A single dose of 2g may be given as a preventative for infective endocarditis.
Children Reduced dose according to age and weight.

Onset of effect
1–2 hours.

Duration of action
Up to 8 hours.

Diet advice
None.

Storage
Keep in a closed container in a cool, dry place out of the reach of children.

Missed dose
Take as soon as you remember. Take your next dose at the scheduled time.

Stopping the drug
Take the full course. Even if you feel better, the original infection may still be present and symptoms may recur if treatment is stopped too soon.

Exceeding the dose
An occasional unintentional extra dose is unlikely to be a cause for concern. But if you notice any unusual symptoms, or if a large overdose has been taken, notify your physician.

SPECIAL PRECAUTIONS

Be sure to tell your physician if:
▼ You have a long-term kidney problem.
▼ You have an allergy (for example, asthma, hay fever, or eczema).
▼ You have had a previous allergic reaction to a penicillin or cephalosporin antibiotic.
▼ You have ulcerative colitis.
▼ You have glandular fever.
▼ You have chronic leukemia.
▼ You are taking other medications.

Pregnancy
▼ No evidence of risk.

Breast-feeding
▼ The drug passes into the breast milk, but at normal doses adverse effects on the baby are unlikely. Discuss with your physician.

Infants and children
▼ Reduced dose necessary.

Over 60
▼ No known problems.

Driving and hazardous work
▼ No known problems.

Alcohol
▼ No known problems.

POSSIBLE ADVERSE EFFECTS

The most common *adverse effects* are gastrointestinal. If you develop a rash, itching, wheezing or breathing difficulties, or joint swelling (signs of an allergic reaction), or *jaundice* which may occur weeks or even months after finishing treatment, call your physician.

Symptom/effect	Frequency		Discuss with physician		Stop taking drug now	Call physician now
	Common	Rare	Only if severe	In all cases		
Diarrhea/nausea	●		■			
Rash	●		■			
Abdominal pain		●		■		
Bruising		●		■		
Sore throat/fever		●		■		
Itching		●		■		
Breathing difficulties/wheezing		●		■	▲	▌
Jaundice		●		■	▲	▌

PROLONGED USE

Amoxicillin is usually given only for short courses of treatment.

INTERACTIONS

Oral contraceptives Amoxicillin may reduce the effectiveness of the oral contraceptive pill and also increase the risk of breakthrough bleeding.

Anticoagulant drugs Amoxicillin may alter the anticoagulant effect of these drugs.

Allopurinol Amoxicillin may increase the likelihood of allergic skin reactions.

Oral typhoid vaccine Amoxicillin inactivates this vaccine. Avoid taking drug for 3 days before and after having the vaccine; discuss with your physician.

Methotrexate Amoxicillin can increase levels of this drug.

AMPHOTERICIN

Product names Abelcet, AmBisome, Fungizone
Used in the following combined preparations None

GENERAL INFORMATION

Amphotericin is a highly effective and powerful antifungal drug. When given by injection, it is used to treat serious *systemic* fungal infections. It may also be administered by aerosol to treat lung infection. Treatment administered by injection is carefully supervised, usually in hospital, because of potentially serious *adverse effects*. A test dose for allergy may be given before a full injection. The new, recently introduced formulations of this drug appear to be less toxic than the original injection.

QUICK REFERENCE

Drug group Antifungal drugs (p.124)

Overdose danger rating Medium

Dependence rating Low

Prescription needed Yes

Available as generic No

INFORMATION FOR USERS

Your drug prescription is tailored for you. Do not alter dosage without checking with your physician.

How taken

Injection.

Frequency and timing of doses
Daily, usually over a 6-hour period (injection).

Usual dosage range
The dosage for injection is determined individually and depends on the formulation.

Onset of effect
Improvement may be noticed after 2–4 days.

Duration of action
Up to several days.

Diet advice
When given by injection, this drug may reduce the levels of potassium and magnesium in the blood. To correct this, mineral supplements may be recommended by your physician.

Storage
Keep in a closed container in a cool, dry place out of the reach of children. Some brands of injection should be stored in the fridge.

Missed dose
Unlikely to happen since the drug is given under close medical supervision.

Stopping the drug
Take the full course as prescribed, Even if symptoms improve, the original infection may still be present and symptoms may recur if treatment is stopped too soon.

Exceeding the dose
Unlikely to happen since the drug is given under close medical supervision. But if dosage is exceeded, seek medical assistance immediately.

SPECIAL PRECAUTIONS

Be sure to tell your physician if:
▼ You have a long-term kidney problem.
▼ You have previously had an allergic reaction to amphotericin.
▼ You are taking other medications.

Pregnancy
▼ Injections are given only when the infection is very serious.

Breast-feeding
▼ It is not known whether the drug passes into the breast milk. Discuss with your physician.

Infants and children
▼ Reduced dose may be necessary.

Over 60
▼ No special problems.

Driving and hazardous work
▼ No known problems.

Alcohol
▼ No known problems.

POSSIBLE ADVERSE EFFECTS

Amphotericin is given by injection only under close medical supervision. Adverse effects are thus carefully monitored and promptly treated.

Symptom/effect	Frequency		Discuss with physician		Stop taking drug now	Call physician now
	Common	Rare	Only if severe	In all cases		
Injection						
Pain at injection site	●			■		
Nausea/vomiting	●			■		
Headache/fever	●			■		
Low blood pressure	●			■		
Unusual bleeding		●		■		
Muscle and joint pain		●		■		
Indigestion/abdominal pain		●		■		

PROLONGED USE

Given by injection, the drug may cause a reduction in blood levels of potassium and magnesium. It may also damage the kidneys and cause blood disorders.

Monitoring Regular blood tests to monitor liver and kidney function, blood cell counts, and potassium and magnesium levels are advised during treatment by injection.

INTERACTIONS

Digoxin Amphotericin may increase the *toxicity* of digoxin.

Diuretics Amphotericin increases the risk of low potassium levels with diuretics.

Aminoglycoside antibiotics Taken with amphotericin, these drugs increase the likelihood of kidney damage.

Corticosteroids may increase loss of potassium from the body caused by amphotericin.

Cyclosporine increases the likelihood of kidney damage.

ANAKINRA

Product name Kineret
Used in the following combined preparations None

GENERAL INFORMATION

Anakinra may be used alone, or with other *medications*, to decrease the pain and swelling associated with moderate to severe rheumatoid arthritis (RA). This class of medications, called biologic response modifiers, works by blocking receptors for interleukins, which are mediators released in the body and can cause inflammation.

Anakinra is administered by *subcutaneous* injection, usually in the outer thigh, back of arms, stomach, or buttocks. It can be self-administered. The syringes should not be shaken prior to use and should not be used if there is any discoloration. While on anakinra, patients should consult their physician before receiving any vaccinations such as the flu shot.

QUICK REFERENCE

Drug group Immunosuppressant drugs (p.143)

Overdose danger rating Medium

Dependence rating Low

Prescription needed Yes

Available as generic No

INFORMATION FOR USERS

Your drug prescription is tailored for you. Do not alter dosage without checking with your physician.

How taken

Parenteral (subcutaneous injection).

Frequency and timing of doses
Once daily.

Usual adult dosage range
100mg daily.

Onset of effect
Several weeks to see full benefit.

Duration of action
Up to 24 hours.

Diet advice
None.

Storage
Store in refrigerator, but do not freeze. Keep away from light. Keep in a closed container and out of the reach of children.

Missed dose
If you miss a dose, take it as soon as you remember. If it is near the time of the next dose, skip the missed dose and resume your usual dosing schedule. Do not double up to catch up on a missed dose.

Stopping the drug
Do not stop the drug without consulting your physician. Stopping the drug may lead to worsening of the underlying condition.

Exceeding the dose
Overdosage is unlikely since treatment is monitored closely. If an extra dose is administered, notify your physician immediately.

SPECIAL PRECAUTIONS

Be sure to tell your physician if:
▼ You have infections, asthma, HIV, or kidney disease.
▼ You are considering getting vaccinations, such as the flu shot.
▼ You have allergy to proteins from bacterial cells (*E. coli*) or latex.
▼ You are taking other medications.

Pregnancy
▼ Not usually prescribed.
Discuss with your physician.

Breast-feeding
▼ Safety not established.
Discuss with your physician.

Infants and children
▼ Safety not established.

Over 60
▼ A reduced dose may be needed depending on kidney function.

Driving and hazardous work
▼ No special problems.

Alcohol
▼ No special problems.

POSSIBLE ADVERSE EFFECTS

Common *side effects* relate to redness and pain at the site of injection. If you develop a fever or sore throat while on this medication, contact your physician right away.

Symptom/effect	Frequency		Discuss with physician		Stop taking drug now	Call physician now
	Common	Rare	Only if severe	In all cases		
Redness, swelling, pain at injection site	●		■			
Headache	●		■			
Upset stomach	●		■			
Diarrhea	●		■			
Runny nose	●		■			
Infection		●		■	▲	■
Stomach pain		●	■			
Flu-like symptoms		●		■		■
Rash		●		■		■
Fever, sore throat, chills		●		■		■
Coughing, wheezing, chest pain		●		■		■

PROLONGED USE

This medication should be reassessed periodically.

INTERACTIONS

Etanercept, adalimumab, infliximab
Anakinra should not be used with these types of agents, due to a greater risk of infection.

Vaccinations Vaccinations may not be effective if patient is on anakinra. Discuss with physician prior to receiving any vaccinations.

ANASTROZOLE

Product name Arimidex
Used in the following combined preparations None

GENERAL INFORMATION

Anastrozole is a potent non-steroidal inhibitor of the enzyme that manufactures estradiol (natural estrogen) in the body. It can reduce production of estradiol by more than 80 per cent. It works by blocking estradiol production in the peripheral tissues of the body, rather than the ovary itself, so it is not suitable for use in premenopausal women where the ovaries are still producing estrogen. The drug is used in post-menopausal women to treat types of breast cancer in which the tumour cells have estrogen receptors (known as estrogen-receptor-positive breast cancer).

Anastrozole is generally well tolerated; *adverse effects* are mainly gastrointestinal or gynecological, and are generally similar to menopausal symptoms. If there is any doubt about whether the woman to be treated is post-menopausal, a biochemical test will be performed.

INFORMATION FOR USERS

Your drug prescription is tailored for you. Do not alter dosage without checking with your physician.

How taken

Tablets.

Frequency and timing of doses
Once daily.

Usual adult dosage range
1mg.

Onset of effect
30 minutes.

Duration of action
24 hours.

Diet advice
None.

Storage
Keep in a closed container in a cool, dry place out of the reach of children.

Missed dose
Take as soon as you remember. If your next dose is due within 2 hours, take a single dose now and skip the next.

Stopping the drug
Do not stop the drug without consulting your physician. Stopping the drug may lead to worsening of the underlying condition.

Exceeding the dose
An occasional unintentional extra dose is unlikely to be a cause for concern. But if you notice any unusual symptoms, or a large overdose has been taken, notify your physician.

SPECIAL PRECAUTIONS

Be sure to tell your physician if:
▼ You are premenopausal.
▼ You have kidney or liver problems.
▼ You are allergic to anastrozole.
▼ You are taking other medications.

Pregnancy
▼ Not prescribed in pregnancy.

Breast-feeding
▼ Not prescribed when breast-feeding.

Infants and children
▼ Not recommended.

Over 60
▼ No special problems.

Driving and hazardous work
▼ Do not drive until you know how the drug affects you. It can cause drowsiness.

Alcohol
▼ No known problems.

POSSIBLE ADVERSE EFFECTS

Anastrozole is usually well tolerated, and any *side effects* are relatively minor, except for the increased risk of osteoporosis and bone fracture.

Symptom/effect	Frequency		Discuss with physician		Stop taking drug now	Call physician now
	Common	Rare	Only if severe	In all cases		
Hot flushes	●		■			
Headache/fatigue/dizziness	●		■			
Joint pain/stiffness	●		■			
Vaginal dryness	●		■			
Hair thinning	●		■			
Nausea/diarrhea	●		■			
Rash		●		■	▲	▐

INTERACTIONS

Tamoxifen and estrogens may oppose the effects of anastrozole.

PROLONGED USE

No known problems.

Monitoring Women with osteoporosis or at risk of osteoporosis will have their bone mineral density assessed at the start of treatment and at regular intervals.

APREPITANT

Product name Emend
Used in the following combined preparations None

GENERAL INFORMATION

Aprepitant is used in the prevention of acute and delayed nausea and vomiting associated with highly emetogenic cancer chemotherapy in adults. This medication will not treat nausea and vomiting that has already developed. It is used in combination with another type of anti-emetic called a 5-HT$_3$ receptor antagonist, and with dexamethasone. Aprepitant works by blocking a substance in the brain called neurokinin. Usually three doses of the drug are taken for a total of three days. Common side effects include stomach pain, tiredness or fatigue, loss of appetite, constipation or diarrhea, and hiccoughs.

INFORMATION FOR USERS

Your drug prescription is tailored for you. Do not alter dosage without checking with your physician.

How taken

Capsules.

Frequency and timing of doses
1 hour before chemotherapy and for 2 days after chemotherapy.

Usual adult dosage range
Day 1: 125mg 1 hour before chemotherapy.
Days 2 & 3: 80mg each morning.

Onset of effect
Within hours.

Duration of action
Up to 24 hours.

Diet advice
None.

Storage
Keep in a closed container in a cool, dry place out of the reach of children.

Missed dose
If you miss a dose, contact your physician or pharmacist to seek advice.

Stopping the drug
Do not stop the drug without consulting your physician; symptoms may recur.

Exceeding the dose
If you have taken an extra dose, contact your physician immediately.

SPECIAL PRECAUTIONS

Be sure to tell your physician if:
▼ You have liver problems.
▼ You drive a car or operate machinery.
▼ You are taking other medications.

Pregnancy
▼ Not recommended. Discuss with your physician.

Breast-feeding
▼ Not prescribed. Safety not established.

Infants and children
▼ Not recommended for those under 18 years of age.

Over 60
▼ No special problems.

Driving and hazardous work
▼ Avoid such activities until you know how aprepitant affects you because the drug may cause tiredness or fatigue.

Alcohol
▼ No special problems.

POSSIBLE ADVERSE EFFECTS

The common side effects of aprepitant are heartburn or dyspepsia, tiredness or fatigue, diarrhea, dizziness, constipation, and hiccoughs.

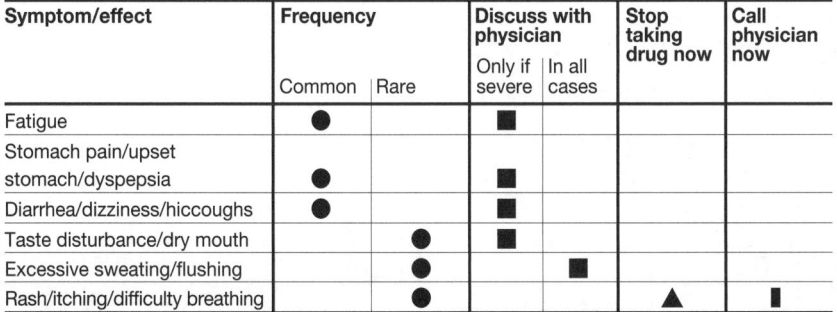

Symptom/effect	Frequency Common	Frequency Rare	Discuss with physician Only if severe	Discuss with physician In all cases	Stop taking drug now	Call physician now
Fatigue	●		■			
Stomach pain/upset stomach/dyspepsia	●		■			
Diarrhea/dizziness/hiccoughs	●		■			
Taste disturbance/dry mouth		●	■			
Excessive sweating/flushing		●		■		
Rash/itching/difficulty breathing		●			▲	■

INTERACTIONS

Pimozide and aripiprazole Aprepitant may increase the levels of these drugs; do not use with aprepitant.

Dexamethasone and midazolam Aprepitant may increase levels of these drugs.

Phenytoin and tolbutamide Aprepitant may decrease levels of these drugs.

Erythromycin, clarithromycin, itraconazole, ketoconazole, and diltiazem may increase levels of aprepitant.

Carbamazepine, phenytoin, and rifampin may decrease levels of aprepitant.

Oral contraceptives The effectiveness of these drugs may be decreased during and for 28 days after use of aprepitant.

Warfarin Aprepitant can decrease the effectiveness of warfarin; close monitoring needed.

PROLONGED USE

Usually only used for a few doses.

ASA (ACETYLSALICYLIC ACID)

Product names Asatab, Aspergum, Aspirin, Coated Aspirin, Entrophen
Used in the following combined preparations Fiorinal, 222 Tablets, Robaxisal, and others

GENERAL INFORMATION

In use for over 80 years, ASA relieves pain, reduces fever, and alleviates the symptoms of arthritis. In low doses, it helps to prevent blood clots, particularly in atherosclerosis or angina due to coronary artery disease, and it reduces the risk of heart attacks and strokes.

It is present in many medicines for colds, flu, headaches, menstrual period pains, and joint or muscular aches.

ASA may irritate the stomach and cause stomach ulcers or bleeding. Coated ASA can minimize stomach upsets.

ASA can also provoke asthma attacks, and, in children, can cause Reye's syndrome, a rare but serious brain and liver disorder. For this reason, ASA should not be given to children under the age of 16 years, except on the advice of a physician.

INFORMATION FOR USERS

Follow instructions on the label. Call your physician if symptoms worsen.

How taken

Tablets, suppositories.

Frequency and timing of doses
Relief of pain or fever Every 4–6 hours, as necessary, with or after food or milk.
Prevention of blood clots Once daily.

Usual adult dosage range
Relief of pain or fever 300–900mg per dose.
Prevention of blood clots 75–300mg daily.

Onset of effect
30–60 minutes (regular aspirin); 1½–8 hours (coated tablets or SR-capsules).

Duration of action
Up to 12 hours. Effect persists for 7–10 days when used to prevent blood clotting.

Diet advice
Take with or immediately after food.

Storage
Keep in a closed container in a cool, dry place out of the reach of children.

Missed dose
Take as soon as you remember. If your next dose is due within 2 hours, take a single dose now and skip the next.

Stopping the drug
If you have been prescribed ASA by your physician for a long-term condition, you should seek medical advice before stopping the drug. Otherwise it can be safely stopped.

OVERDOSE ACTION

 Seek immediate medical advice in all cases. Take emergency action if there is restlessness, sweating, stomach pain, ringing noises in the ears, blurred vision, or vomiting.

See Drug poisoning emergency guide (p.526).

SPECIAL PRECAUTIONS

Be sure to consult your physician or pharmacist before taking this drug if:
▼ You have long-term liver or kidney problems.
▼ You have asthma.
▼ You are allergic to ASA.
▼ You have a blood clotting disorder.
▼ You have had a stomach ulcer.
▼ You are taking other medications.

 Pregnancy
▼ Not usually recommended. Discuss with your physician.

 Breast-feeding
▼ Avoid. The drug passes into the breast milk, posing the potential threat of Reye's syndrome in your baby.

 Infants and children
▼ Do not give to children under 16 years, except on a physician's advice.

 Over 60
▼ Adverse effects more likely.

 Driving and hazardous work
▼ No special problems.

 Alcohol
▼ Avoid. Alcohol increases the likelihood of stomach irritation with this drug.

Surgery and general anesthetics
▼ Regular treatment with ASA may need to be stopped about one week before surgery. Discuss with your physician or dentist before any operation.

POSSIBLE ADVERSE EFFECTS

Adverse effects are more likely to occur with high doses of ASA, but may be reduced by taking the drug with food or in buffered or *enteric coated* forms.

Symptom/effect	Frequency		Discuss with physician		Stop taking drug now	Call physician now
	Common	Rare	Only if severe	In all cases		
Indigestion	●		■			
Nausea/vomiting		●		■		
Rash		●		■	▲	
Breathlessness/wheezing		●		■	▲	
Blood in vomit/black feces		●		■	▲	▮
Ringing in the ears/dizziness		●	■		▲	▮

INTERACTIONS

Anticoagulants ASA may add to the anticoagulant effect of such drugs, leading to an increased risk of abnormal bleeding.

Drugs for gout ASA may reduce the effect of these drugs.

Corticosteroids and some SSRI antidepressants These drugs may increase the risk of stomach bleeding with ASA.

NSAIDs These drugs may increase the likelihood of stomach irritation with ASA.

Methotrexate ASA may increase the toxicity of this drug.

Sulphonylurea antidiabetic drugs ASA may increase the effect of these drugs.

PROLONGED USE

ASA should not be taken in high doses for prolonged periods. All doses of the drug taken long term increase the risk of peptic ulcers and gastrointestinal bleeding.

ATENOLOL

Product names Apo-Atenol, Ava-Atenolol, Mylan-Atenolol, Ratio-Atenolol, Tenormin, Teva-Atenolol, and others
Used in the following combined preparation Tenoretic

GENERAL INFORMATION

Atenolol is a cardioselective beta blocker. It prevents the heart from beating too quickly and is used to treat irregular heart rhythms (arrhythmias), chest pain (angina), and high blood pressure. It may also be given following a heart attack to protect the heart from further damage. It is less likely than non-cardioselective beta blockers to provoke breathing problems but, nevertheless, it is not usually given to patients with asthma. It may also slow the body's response to low blood sugar if you are a diabetic on insulin.

QUICK REFERENCE

Drug group Beta blockers (p.83)
Overdose danger rating Medium
Dependence rating Low
Prescription needed Yes
Available as generic Yes

INFORMATION FOR USERS

Your drug prescription is tailored for you. Do not alter dosage without checking with your physician.

How taken

Tablets.

Frequency and timing of doses
Once daily.

Usual adult dosage range
25–100mg daily.

Onset of effect
2–4 hours.

Duration of action
20–30 hours.

Diet advice
None.

Storage
Keep in a tightly closed container in a cool, dry place out of the reach of children. Protect from light.

Missed dose
Take as soon as you remember. If your next dose is due within 6 hours, omit the missed dose but take the next scheduled dose as usual.

Stopping the drug
Do not stop taking the drug without consulting your physician; sudden withdrawal may lead to dangerous worsening of the underlying condition. It should be withdrawn gradually.

OVERDOSE ACTION

 Seek immediate medical advice. Take emergency action if breathing difficulties, collapse, or loss of consciousness occur.

See Drug poisoning emergency guide (p.526).

POSSIBLE ADVERSE EFFECTS

Atenolol has adverse effects that are common to most beta blockers and tend to diminish with long-term use. Fainting may be a sign that the drug has slowed the heart beat excessively.

Symptom/effect	Frequency		Discuss with physician		Stop taking drug now	Call physician now
	Common	Rare	Only if severe	In all cases		
Lethargy/fatigue	●			■		
Cold hands and feet	●			■		
Nausea/vomiting		●		■		
Nightmares/vivid dreams		●		■	▲	
Rash/dry eyes		●		■	▲	
Visual disturbances		●		■	▲	
Fainting/palpitations		●		■	▲	▮
Breathlessness/wheezing		●		■	▲	▮

INTERACTIONS

Antihypertensive drugs Atenolol may enhance the blood-pressure-lowering effect.

Calcium channel blockers may cause low blood pressure, a slow heart beat, and heart failure if used with atenolol.

Cardiac glycosides (e.g. digoxin) may increase the heart-slowing effect of atenolol.

Antidiabetic drugs used with atenolol may increase the risk of low blood sugar or mask its symptoms.

Decongestants used with atenolol may increase blood pressure and heart rate.

Anti-steroidal anti-inflammatory drugs (NSAIDS) may reduce the antihypertensive effect of atenolol.

SPECIAL PRECAUTIONS

Be sure to tell your physician if:
▼ You have heart problems.
▼ You have a long-term kidney problem.
▼ You have diabetes.
▼ You have a lung disorder such as asthma or bronchitis.
▼ You have psoriasis.
▼ You are taking other medications.

 Pregnancy
▼ Safety in pregnancy not established. Discuss with your physician.

 Breast-feeding
▼ The drug passes into the breast milk. Discuss with your physician.

 Infants and children
▼ Not recommended.

 Over 60
▼ No special problems. Reduced dose may be necessary if there is impaired kidney function.

 Driving and hazardous work
▼ Avoid such activities until you have learned how atenolol affects you because the drug can cause dizziness.

 Alcohol
▼ Avoid excessive intake. Alcohol may increase the blood-pressure-lowering effects of atenolol.

Surgery and general anesthetics
▼ Occasionally, atenolol may need to be stopped before you have a general anesthetic. Discuss this with your physician or dentist before any surgery.

PROLONGED USE

No special problems expected.

ATOMOXETINE

Product names Apo-Atomoxetine, Strattera, and others
Used in the following combined preparations None

GENERAL INFORMATION

Atomoxetine is a drug prescribed for adolescents and adults with attention-deficit hyperactivity disorder (ADHD). It can also be used in children 6 years of age or older. Studies indicate that after 6–12 weeks of treatment this drug can decrease some of the symptoms of ADHD in about 70% of cases. It is not a stimulant and may be an option in those who have not responded to, or are not able to tolerate, the stimulant class of drugs. Dosing in children is based on the individual's weight. The starting dose may be gradually increased as appropriate. It may take 3–4 weeks of regular use to start to see a benefit. It should be used cautiously in those with heart problems, high blood pressure, or uncontrolled overactive thyroid. It may also affect a child's growth and weight. Benefits and risks should be discussed with a physician prior to starting therapy.

INFORMATION FOR USERS

Your drug prescription is tailored for you. Do not alter dosage without checking with your physician.

How taken

Capsules.

Frequency and timing of doses
Usually once or twice daily.

Usual adult dosage range
Initial dose: 40mg daily to start; may increase gradually as appropriate; maximum 100mg/day.

Onset of effect
3–4 weeks; full beneficial effects take 6–12 weeks.

Duration of action
Up to 24 hours.

Diet advice
None.

Storage
Keep in a closed container in a cool, dry place out of the reach of children.

Missed dose
If you miss a dose, take it as soon as you remember. If it is near the time of the next dose, skip the missed dose and resume your usual dosing schedule. Do not take more than the total daily dose.

Stopping the drug
Do not stop the drug without consulting your physician. Stopping the drug may lead to worsening of the underlying condition.

OVERDOSE ACTION

Seek immediate medical advice in all cases. Take emergency action if loss of consciousness occurs.

See Drug poisoning emergency guide (p.526).

SPECIAL PRECAUTIONS

Be sure to tell your physician if:
▼ You have liver problems.
▼ You have tics.
▼ You or anyone else in your family has depression or bipolar disorder.
▼ You have had seizures.
▼ You have a history of glaucoma.
▼ You have any heart conditions or heart rhythm problems.
▼ You have thyroid disease.
▼ You have high blood pressure.
▼ You are involved in strenuous activities.
▼ You have a family history of sudden death related to a heart condition.
▼ You are taking other medications.

Pregnancy
▼ Safety in pregnancy not established. Discuss with your physician.

Breast-feeding
▼ Safety not established. Discuss with your physician.

Infants and children
▼ Not recommended in those less than 6 years of age. Discuss with your physician.

Over 60
▼ Safety and efficacy not established in older individuals.

Driving and hazardous work
▼ May cause drowsiness or dizziness. Do not drive a car or operate machinery until you feel you are mentally alert.

Alcohol
▼ Avoid. Alcohol may increase the risk of drowsiness caused by this drug.

POSSIBLE ADVERSE EFFECTS

The most common are upset stomach, nausea, headaches, sedation, decrease in appetite, small changes in heart rate or blood pressure. Rarely, this drug may cause liver problems.

Symptom/effect	Frequency		Discuss with physician		Stop taking drug now	Call physician now
	Common	Rare	Only if severe	In all cases		
Headache	●		■			
Dizziness/fatigue	●		■			
Abdominal discomfort/pain	●		■			
Nausea/vomiting		●	■			
Appetite changes	●		■		▲	
Jaundice		●		■		∎
Irregular heartbeat		●		■		∎
Skin rash/hives		●		■		∎
Emotional changes		●			▲	∎
Flu-like symptoms		●		■		∎

INTERACTIONS

Fluoxetine, Paroxetine, Quinidine These medications may decrease the breakdown of atomoxetine and increase its effects.

Salbutamol If used at the same time, may increase heart rate.

Phenelzine, tranylcypromine, selegiline Atomoxetine should not be taken with, or within 14 days of stopping, these drugs.

PROLONGED USE

Prolonged treatment can adversely affect liver function.

Monitoring Regular blood tests to check liver function are recommended. Tests of muscle function may be carried out if problems are suspected.

ATORVASTATIN

Product names Apo-Atorvastatin, Ava-Atorvastatin, Lipitor
Used in the following combined preparation Caduet

GENERAL INFORMATION

Atorvastatin is a member of the statin group of lipid-lowering drugs. It is used to treat hypercholesterolemia (high blood cholesterol levels) in patients who have not responded to other treatments, such as a special diet, and are at risk of developing heart disease.

Atorvastatin blocks the action, in the liver, of an enzyme that is needed for the manufacture of cholesterol. As a result, blood levels of cholesterol are lowered, which can help to prevent coronary heart disease.

Rarely, atorvastatin can cause muscle pain, inflammation, and muscle damage. The risk is increased if the drug is given with a fibrate (another kind of lipid-lowering drug).

INFORMATION FOR USERS

Your drug prescription is tailored for you. Do not alter dosage without checking with your physician.

How taken

Tablets.

Frequency and timing of doses
Once daily.

Usual adult dosage range
10–40mg; up to 80mg (inherited hypercholesterolemia).

Onset of effect
Within 2 weeks. Full beneficial effects may not be seen for 4–6 weeks.

Duration of action
20–30 hours.

Diet advice
A low-fat diet is usually recommended.

Storage
Keep in a closed container in a cool, dry place out of the reach of children.

Missed dose
Take as soon as you remember. If your next dose is due within 8 hours, do not take the missed dose, but take the next one on schedule.

Stopping the drug
Do not stop taking the drug without consulting your physician. Stopping the drug may lead to a recurrence of the original condition.

Exceeding the dose
An occasional unintentional extra dose is unlikely to cause problems. Large overdoses may cause liver problems. Notify your physician.

SPECIAL PRECAUTIONS

Be sure to tell your physician if:
▼ You have had liver problems.
▼ You are a heavy drinker.
▼ You are taking other medications.
▼ You are allergic to statins or atorvastatin.
▼ You have had kidney problems.
▼ You have thyroid problems.
▼ You have a family history of muscular disorders.
▼ You are diabetic.

Pregnancy
▼ Not recommended. May affect fetal development. Discuss with your physician if you are pregnant or intend to become pregnant.

Breast-feeding
▼ Safety not established. Discuss with your physician.

Infants and children
▼ Not recommended.

Over 60
▼ No special problems.

Driving and hazardous work
▼ No special problems.

Alcohol
▼ Avoid excessive amounts. Alcohol may increase the risk of developing liver problems with atorvastatin.

POSSIBLE ADVERSE EFFECTS

Adverse effects of atorvastatin are usually mild and transient. Muscle damage is a rare side effect and muscle aching or weakness should be reported to your physician at once.

Symptom/effect	Frequency		Discuss with physician		Stop taking drug now	Call physician now
	Common	Rare	Only if severe	In all cases		
Nausea	●		■			
Headache	●		■			
Skin rash		●		■	▲	
Muscle pain/weakness		●		■	▲	▮
Jaundice		●		■	▲	▮
Sleep disturbances		●	■			
Urine discoloration		●		■	▲	▮

INTERACTIONS

Anticoagulant drugs Atorvastatin may increase the effect of anticoagulants.

Macrolide antibiotics (e.g. erythromycin, clarithromycin), fusidic acid, and antifungals Taken with atorvastatin, these drugs may increase the risk of muscle damage.

Oral contraceptives Atorvastatin increases blood levels of ethinyl estradiol and norethisterone. The dose of these drugs may need adjustment.

Digoxin Atorvastatin increases blood levels of digoxin.

Other lipid-lowering drugs Taken with atorvastatin, these drugs may increase the risk of muscle damage.

Cyclosporine and other immuno-suppressant drugs Atorvastatin is not usually prescribed with these drugs because of the increased risk of muscle damage.

PROLONGED USE

Long-term use of atorvastatin can affect liver function.

Monitoring Regular blood tests to check liver function are needed. Tests of muscle function may be carried out if problems are suspected.

ATROPINE

Product names Isopto Atropine, Minims Atropine, and others
Used in the following combined preparation Lomotil

GENERAL INFORMATION

Atropine is an *anticholinergic* drug. Because of its *antispasmodic* action, which relaxes the muscle wall of the intestine, the drug has been used to relieve abdominal cramps in irritable bowel syndrome. Atropine may also be prescribed in combination with diphenoxylate, an antidiarrheal drug. However, this combination can be dangerous in overdosage, particularly in young children.

Atropine eye drops, used to enlarge the pupil during eye examinations, are part of the treatment for uveitis.

Atropine may be used as part of the *premedication* before a general anesthetic. It is occasionally injected to restore normal heart beat in heart block (p.86).

Atropine must be used with caution in children and the elderly due to their sensitivity to the drug's effects.

QUICK REFERENCE

Drug group Anticholinergic drugs (p.98) and mydriatic drugs (p.158)

Overdose danger rating High

Dependence rating Low

Prescription needed Yes (except powder)

Available as generic Yes

INFORMATION FOR USERS

Your drug prescription is tailored for you. Do not alter dosage without checking with your physician.

How taken

Tablets (in combination only), injection, eye ointment, eye drops.

Frequency and timing of doses
Once only, or up to 4 times daily according to condition (eye drops); as directed (other forms).

Usual adult dosage range
1–2 drops as directed (eye drops); as directed (other forms).

Onset of effect
Varies according to method of administration. 30 minutes (eye drops).

Duration of action
7 days or longer (eye drops); several hours (other forms).

Diet advice
None.

Storage
Keep in a closed container in a cool, dry place out of the reach of children. Protect from light.

Missed dose
Take as soon as you remember. If your next dose is due within 2 hours, take a single dose now and skip the next.

Stopping the drug
Do not stop the drug without consulting your physician.

OVERDOSE ACTION

Seek immediate medical advice in all cases. Take emergency action if palpitations, tremor, delirium, seizures, or loss of consciousness occur.

See Drug poisoning emergency guide (p.526).

SPECIAL PRECAUTIONS

Be sure to tell your physician if:
▼ You have long-term liver or kidney problems.
▼ You have prostate problems.
▼ You have pyloric stenosis.
▼ You have gastro-esophageal reflux.
▼ You have glaucoma.
▼ You have urinary difficulties.
▼ You have myasthenia gravis.
▼ You have ulcerative colitis.
▼ You wear contact lenses (eye drops).
▼ You have heart problems.
▼ You are taking other medications.

Pregnancy
▼ Safety in pregnancy not established. Discuss with your physician.

Breast-feeding
▼ The drug passes into the breast milk and may affect the baby. Discuss with your physician.

Infants and children
▼ Combination with diphenoxylate not recommended under 4 years; reduced dose necessary in older children.

Over 60
▼ Increased likelihood of adverse effects.

Driving and hazardous work
▼ Avoid such activities until you have learned how atropine affects you because the drug can cause blurred vision and may impair concentration.

Alcohol
▼ Avoid. Alcohol increases the likelihood of confusion when taken with atropine.

POSSIBLE ADVERSE EFFECTS

The use of this drug is limited by the frequency of anticholinergic effects.

In addition to these effects, atropine eye drops may cause stinging.

Symptom/effect	Frequency		Discuss with physician		Stop taking drug now	Call physician now
	Common	Rare	Only if severe	In all cases		
Blurred vision/dry mouth/thirst	●		■			
Constipation	●		■			
Flushing/dry skin	●		■			
Difficulty in passing urine		●		■		
Eye pain and irritation		●		■	▲	▮
Palpitations/confusion		●		■	▲	▮
Contact rash		●		■	▲	
Nausea/vomiting		●	■			
Dizziness		●	■			

INTERACTIONS

General note Atropine delays stomach emptying and may therefore alter the absorption of other drugs.

Anticholinergic drugs Atropine increases the risk of *side effects* from drugs that also have anticholinergic effects.

Ketoconazole Atropine reduces the absorption of this drug from the digestive tract. Increased dose may be necessary.

PROLONGED USE

Usually used for short duration of therapy.

AZATHIOPRINE

Product names Apo-Azathioprine, Imuran, Mylan-Azathioprine, Teva-Azathioprine
Used in the following combined preparations None

GENERAL INFORMATION

Azathioprine is an immunosuppressant drug used to prevent immune system rejection of transplanted organs. The drug is also given for severe rheumatoid arthritis that has failed to respond to conventional drug therapy.

Autoimmune and collagen diseases (including polymyositis, systemic lupus erythematosus, myasthenia gravis, and dermatomyositis) may be treated with azathioprine, usually in combination with corticosteroids.

Azathioprine is administered only under close supervision because of the risk of serious *adverse effects*. These include suppression of the production of white blood cells, thereby increasing the risk of infection as well as the risk of excessive or prolonged bleeding.

INFORMATION FOR USERS

Your drug prescription is tailored for you. Do not alter dosage without checking with your physician.

How taken

Tablets, injection.

Frequency and timing of doses
Usually once daily with or after food.

Usual dosage range
Initially according to body weight and the condition being treated and then adjusted according to response.

Onset of effect
2–4 weeks. Antirheumatic effect may not be felt for 8 weeks or more.

Duration of action
Immunosuppressant effects may last for several weeks after the drug is stopped.

Diet advice
None.

Storage
Keep in a closed container in a cool, dry place out of the reach of children. Protect from light.

Missed dose
Take as soon as you remember, then return to your normal schedule. If more than 2 doses are missed, consult your physician.

Stopping the drug
Do not stop the drug without consulting your physician. If taken to prevent graft transplant rejection, stopping treatment could provoke the rejection of the transplant.

Exceeding the dose
An occasional unintentional extra dose is unlikely to cause problems. Large overdoses may cause nausea, vomiting, abdominal pains, and diarrhea. Notify your physician.

SPECIAL PRECAUTIONS

Be sure to tell your physician if:
▼ You have long-term liver or kidney problems.
▼ You have had a previous allergic reaction to azathioprine or 6-mercaptopurine.
▼ You have recently had shingles or chickenpox.
▼ You have an infection.
▼ You have a blood disorder.
▼ You are taking other medications.

Pregnancy
▼ Azathioprine has been taken in pregnancy without problems. Discuss with your physician.

Breast-feeding
▼ A small amount of the drug passes into the breast milk. Discuss with your physician.

Infants and children
▼ No special problems.

Over 60
▼ Increased likelihood of adverse effects. Reduced dose necessary.

Driving and hazardous work
▼ Avoid such activities until you have learned how azathioprine affects you because the drug can cause dizziness.

Alcohol
▼ No known problems.

POSSIBLE ADVERSE EFFECTS

Digestive disturbances and adverse effects on the blood which could lead to sore throat, fever, and weakness are common with azathioprine. Unusual bleeding or bruising while taking this drug may be a sign of reduced levels of platelets in the blood.

Symptom/effect	Frequency		Discuss with physician		Stop taking drug now	Call physician now
	Common	Rare	Only if severe	In all cases		
Nausea/vomiting	●		■			
Hair loss	●		■			
Loss of appetite	●			■		
Weakness/fatigue		●		■		
Unusual bleeding/bruising		●		■		▌
Jaundice		●		■		▌
Rash		●		■		▌
Fever/chills		●		■		▌

INTERACTIONS

ACE inhibitors could increase risk of blood cell changes if taken with azathioprine.

Allopurinol increases effects and *toxicity* of azathioprine; dosage of azathioprine will need to be reduced.

Warfarin Azathioprine may reduce its effect.

Co-trimoxazole and trimethoprim may increase the risk of blood problems if taken with azathioprine.

Corticosteroids may increase infection risk.

PROLONGED USE

Prolonged use of this drug may reduce bone marrow activity, leading to a reduction of all types of blood cells. Some people have a genetic susceptibility to this effect. There is also a small increase in the risk of cancers affecting the immune system. Avoiding exposure to sunlight may help to prevent adverse skin effects.

Monitoring Regular checks on blood chemistry and blood cell counts are carried out.

AZITHROMYCIN

Product names Apo-Azithromycin, CO Azithromycin, Novo-Azithromycin, PMS-Azithromycin, Zithromax, Zmax SR
Used in the following combined preparations None

GENERAL INFORMATION

Azithromycin is a marcolide *antibiotic* similar to erythromycin (p.270) from which it is derived. It has similar actions and uses to erythromycin. It is used for upper respiratory tract infections, such as middle ear infections, pharyngitis and tonsilitis, and lower respiratory tract infections, such as bacterial exacerbation of chronic obstructive lung disease, bronchitis, and pneumonia, as well as for skin and soft tissue infections, and some cases of gonorrhoea.

Prolonged use with azithromycin is usually not necessary.

INFORMATION FOR USERS

Your drug prescription is tailored for you. Do not alter dosage without checking with your physician.

How taken

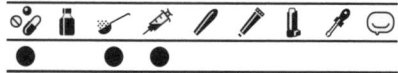

Tablets, liquid (reconstituted from powder), injection.

Frequency and timing of doses
Once daily.

Usual adult dosage range
250mg–2g daily.

Onset of effect
1–3 hours.

Duration of action
Up to 24 hours.

Diet advice
None.

Storage
Keep in a closed container in a cool, dry place out of the reach of children. Store the reconstituted solution between 5 and 30°C and discard any unused portion after 10 days.

Missed dose
If you miss a dose, take it as soon as you remember. If it is near the time of the next dose, skip the missed dose and resume your usual dosing schedule. Do not double up to catch up on a missed dose.

Stopping the drug
Take the full course. Even if you feel better, the infection may still be present and symptoms may recur if treatment is stopped too soon.

Exceeding the dose
An occasional unintentional extra dose is unlikely to be a cause for concern. But if you notice any unusual symptoms, or if a large overdose has been taken, notify your physician.

POSSIBLE ADVERSE EFFECTS

Azithromycin is usually well tolerated. Nausea and diarrhea may occur.

Symptom/effect	Frequency		Discuss with physician		Stop taking drug now	Call physician now
	Common	Rare	Only if severe	In all cases		
Abdominal pain	●		■			
Nausea	●		■			
Diarrhea	●		■			
Headache		●	■			
Rash		●		■	▲	▐
Edema of skin		●		■	▲	▐
Dizziness		●	■			
Jaundice		●		■	▲	▐

INTERACTIONS

Antacids Aluminum- and magnesium-containing antacids can affect azithromycin's peak effect. Do not take at the same time as azithromycin.

Cyclosporine, digoxin, amiodarone, quinine, pimozide, citalopram, quetiapine, and disopyramide Azithromycin may increase the effect of these drugs.

SPECIAL PRECAUTIONS

Be sure to tell your physician if:
▼ You have liver or kidney problems.
▼ You have had an allergic reaction to erythromycin, clarithromycin, or azithromycin.
▼ You have a heart problem.
▼ You have porphyria.
▼ You are taking other medications.

 Pregnancy
▼ Safety has not been established. Discuss with your physician.

 Breast-feeding
▼ Safety in breast-feeding not established. Discuss with your physician.

 Infants and children
▼ Reduced dose necessary.

 Over 60
▼ No special problems.

 Driving and hazardous work
▼ No special problems.

  Alcohol
▼ No known problems.

PROLONGED USE

Usually not used for prolonged periods. During prolonged therapy, periodic liver function tests may be done.

Monitoring Regular blood tests to check liver function are recommended.

BACLOFEN

Product names Apo-Baclofen, Ava-Baclofen, Lioresal, and others
Used in the following combined preparations None

GENERAL INFORMATION

Baclofen is a muscle-relaxant drug that acts on the central nervous system, including the spinal cord. The drug relieves the spasms, cramping, and rigidity of muscles caused by a variety of disorders, including multiple sclerosis and spinal cord injury. Baclofen is also used to treat the spasticity that results from brain injury, cerebral palsy, or stroke. Although this drug does not cure any of these disorders, it increases mobility, allowing other treatment, such as physiotherapy, to be carried out. It is available as tablets or as intrathecal injection (via a pump implanted in the abdomen).

Baclofen is less likely to cause muscle weakness than similar drugs, and its *side effects*, such as dizziness or drowsiness, are usually temporary.

QUICK REFERENCE

Drug group Muscle-relaxant drugs (p.106)

Overdose danger rating Medium

Dependence rating Low

Prescription needed Yes

Available as generic Yes

INFORMATION FOR USERS

Your drug prescription is tailored for you. Do not alter dosage without checking with your physician.

How taken

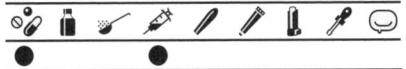

Tablets, injection (specialist use).

Frequency and timing of doses
3 x daily with food or milk.

Usual adult dosage range
15mg daily (starting dose). Daily dose may be increased by 15mg every 3 days as necessary. Maximum recommended daily dose: 80mg.

Onset of effect
Some benefits may appear after 1–3 hours, but full beneficial effects may not be felt for several weeks. A dose 1 hour before a specific task will improve mobility.

Duration of action
Up to 8 hours.

Diet advice
None.

Storage
Keep in a closed container in a cool, dry place out of the reach of children. Protect liquid from light.

Missed dose
Take as soon as you remember. If your next dose is due within 2 hours, take a single dose now and skip the next.

Stopping the drug
Do not stop taking the drug without consulting your physician who will supervise a gradual reduction in dosage. Abrupt cessation may cause hallucinations, seizures, and worsening spasticity.

Exceeding the dose
An occasional unintentional extra dose is unlikely to cause problems. Large overdoses may cause weakness, vomiting, and severe drowsiness. Notify your physician.

SPECIAL PRECAUTIONS

Be sure to tell your physician if:
▼ You have long-term liver or kidney problems.
▼ You have difficulty in passing urine.
▼ You have had a peptic ulcer.
▼ You have had epileptic seizures.
▼ You have diabetes.
▼ You are being treated for high blood pressure.
▼ You have porphyria.
▼ You suffer with breathing problems.
▼ You are taking other medications.

Pregnancy
▼ Safety in pregnancy not established. Discuss with your physician.

Breast-feeding
▼ The drug passes into the breast milk. Discuss with your physician.

Infants and children
▼ Reduced dose necessary.

Over 60
▼ Increased likelihood of adverse effects. Reduced dose may therefore be necessary.

Driving and hazardous work
▼ Avoid such activities until you have learned how baclofen affects you because the drug can cause drowsiness.

Alcohol
▼ Avoid. Alcohol may increase the sedative effects of this drug.

Surgery and general anesthetics
▼ Be sure to inform your physician or dentist that you are taking baclofen before you have a general anesthetic.

POSSIBLE ADVERSE EFFECTS

The common *adverse effects* are related to the *sedative* effects of the drug. Such effects are minimized by starting with a low dose that is gradually increased.

Symptom/effect	Frequency		Discuss with physician		Stop taking drug now	Call physician now
	Common	Rare	Only if severe	In all cases		
Dizziness	●		■			
Drowsiness	●		■			
Nausea	●		■			
Muscle fatigue/weakness	●		■			
Difficulty in passing urine	●		■			
Constipation/diarrhea		●	■			
Headache		●	■			
Confusion		●		■		

INTERACTIONS

Antihypertensive and diuretic drugs The effect of such drugs may be increased.

Drugs for *parkinsonism* Some of these drugs may cause confusion or hallucinations if taken with baclofen.

Antidiabetic drugs or insulin Dosage may need adjusting, as baclofen may increase blood glucose levels.

Sedatives These drugs may increase the sedative properties of baclofen.

Tricyclic antidepressants may increase baclofen's effects, causing muscle weakness.

PROLONGED USE

No problems expected.

BECLOMETHASONE

Product names Apo-Beclamethasone, Mylan-Beclo AQ, Qvar, Rivanase AQ
Used in the following combined preparation None

GENERAL INFORMATION

Beclomethasone is a corticosteroid drug prescribed to relieve the symptoms of allergic rhinitis (as a nasal spray) and to control asthma (as an inhalant). It controls nasal symptoms by reducing inflammation and mucus production in the nose. It also helps to reduce chest symptoms, such as wheezing and coughing. Asthma sufferers may take it regularly to reduce the severity and frequency of attacks. However, once an attack has started, the drug does not relieve symptoms.

There are few serious *adverse effects* associated with beclomethasone as it is given *topically* by nasal spray or inhaler. Fungal infections causing irritation of the mouth and throat are a possible *side effect* of inhaling beclomethasone. These can be avoided to some degree by rinsing the mouth and gargling with water after each inhalation.

INFORMATION FOR USERS

Your drug prescription is tailored for you. Do not alter dosage without checking with your physician.

How taken

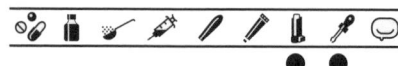

Metered-dose inhaler, nasal spray.

Frequency and timing of doses
2–4 x daily.

Usual dosage range
Adults 1–2 puffs 2 x daily according to preparation used (asthma); 1–2 sprays in each nostril 2 x daily (allergic rhinitis); *Children* Reduced dose according to age and weight.

Onset of effect
Within 1 week (asthma); 1–3 days (allergic rhinitis). Full benefit may not be felt for up to 4 weeks.

Duration of action
Several days after stopping the drug.

Diet advice
None.

Storage
Keep in a closed container in a cool, dry place out of the reach of children. Protect from light.

Missed dose
Take as soon as you remember. If your next dose is due within 2 hours, take a single dose now and skip the next.

Stopping the drug
Do not stop the drug without consulting your physician; symptoms may recur. Sometimes a gradual reduction in dosage is recommended.

Exceeding the dose
An occasional unintentional extra dose is unlikely to cause problems. But if you notice any unusual symptoms, or if a large overdose has been taken, notify your physician. Adverse effects may occur if the recommended dose is regularly exceeded over a prolonged period.

SPECIAL PRECAUTIONS

Be sure to tell your physician if:
▼ You have had tuberculosis or another nasal or respiratory infection.
▼ You have had recent nasal ulcers or nasal surgery.
▼ You have varicose ulcers (cream/ointment).

 Pregnancy
▼ No evidence of risk with inhaler.

 Breast-feeding
▼ No evidence of risk with inhaler.

 Infants and children
▼ Reduced dose necessary.

 Over 60
▼ No known problems.

 Driving and hazardous work
▼ No known problems.

 Alcohol
▼ No known problems.

POSSIBLE ADVERSE EFFECTS

The main side effects of the nasal spray and inhaler are irritation of the nasal passages and fungal infection of the throat and mouth.

Symptom/effect	Frequency		Discuss with physician		Stop taking drug now	Call physician now
	Common	Rare	Only if severe	In all cases		
Inhaler/nasal spray						
Nasal discomfort/irritation	●		■			
Cough	●		■			
Sore throat/hoarseness	●			■		
Nosebleed	●			■		

INTERACTIONS

None.

PROLONGED USE

No problem expected when used for asthma or rhinitis, but high doses of nasal spray can give systemic effects.

Monitoring Periodic checks to ensure that the adrenal glands are functioning healthily may be required if large doses are being used.

BENZOYL PEROXIDE

Product names Benoxyl, Benzac, Benzagel, Oxyderm, Panoxyl, Solugel, and many others
Used in the following combined preparations Benzaclin, Benzamycin, Clindoxyl Gel, Tactuo

GENERAL INFORMATION

Benzoyl peroxide is used in a variety of *topical* preparations for the treatment of acne. Available over the counter, it comes in concentrations of varying strengths for mild to moderate acne.

Benzoyl peroxide works by removing the top layer of skin and unblocking the sebaceous glands. It can also reduce inflammation of blocked hair follicles by killing the bacteria that infect them.

Benzoyl peroxide may cause irritation due to its drying effect on the skin, but this generally diminishes with time. The drug should be applied to the affected areas as directed on the label. Washing the area prior to application greatly enhances the drug's beneficial effects. Side effects are less likely if treatment is started with a preparation containing a low concentration of benzoyl peroxide, and changed to a stronger preparation only if necessary. Marked dryness and peeling of the skin, which may occur, can usually be controlled by reducing the frequency of application. Care should be taken to avoid contact of the drug with the eyes, mouth, and mucous membranes. It is also advisble to avoid excessive exposure to sunlight. Preparations of benzoyl peroxide may bleach clothing and hair.

QUICK REFERENCE

Drug group Drugs for acne (p.165)
Overdose danger rating Low
Dependence rating Low
Prescription needed No (most preparations)
Available as generic Yes

INFORMATION FOR USERS

Follow instructions on the label. Call your physician if symptoms worsen.

How taken

Lotion, gel, bar, facial cleanser.

Frequency and timing of doses
1–2 x daily.

Usual dosage range
Start with the lowest strength preparation (2.5 per cent) and, if necessary, increase gradually to highest strength (5 per cent).

Onset of effect
Reduces oiliness of skin immediately. Acne usually improves within 4–6 weeks.

Duration of action
24–48 hours.

Diet advice
None.

Storage
Keep in a closed container in a cool, dry place out of the reach of children.

Missed dose
Apply as soon as you remember.

Stopping the drug
Can be safely stopped as soon as you no longer need it.

Exceeding the dose
A single extra application is unlikely to cause problems. Regular overuse may result in extensive irritation, peeling, redness, and swelling of the skin.

SPECIAL PRECAUTIONS

Be sure to consult your physician or pharmacist before taking this drug if:
▼ You have eczema.
▼ You have sunburn.
▼ You have had a previous allergic reaction to benzoyl peroxide.
▼ You are taking other medications.

Pregnancy
▼ No evidence of risk.

Breast-feeding
▼ No evidence of risk.

Infants and children
▼ Not usually recommended under 12 years except under medical supervision.

Over 60
▼ Not usually required.

Driving and hazardous work
▼ No known problems.

Alcohol
▼ No known problems.

POSSIBLE ADVERSE EFFECTS

Application of benzoyl peroxide may cause temporary burning or stinging of the skin. Redness, peeling, and swelling may result from excessive drying of the skin and usually clears up if the treatment is stopped or used less frequently. If severe burning, blistering, or crusting occur, stop using benzoyl peroxide and consult your physician.

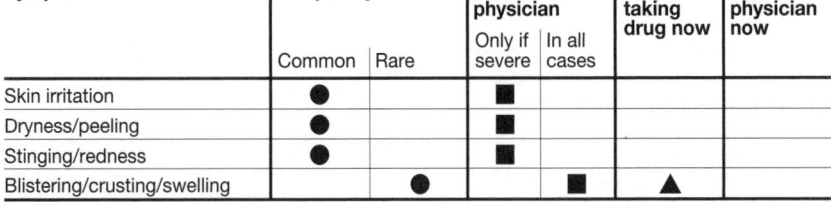

Symptom/effect	Frequency		Discuss with physician		Stop taking drug now	Call physician now
	Common	Rare	Only if severe	In all cases		
Skin irritation	●		■			
Dryness/peeling	●		■			
Stinging/redness	●		■			
Blistering/crusting/swelling		●		■	▲	

INTERACTIONS

Skin-drying preparations Medicated cosmetics, soaps, toiletries, and other anti-acne preparations increase the likelihood of dryness and irritation of the skin with benzoyl peroxide.

PROLONGED USE

Benzoyl peroxide usually takes 4–6 weeks to produce an effect. Discuss long-term use with your physician.

BETAHISTINE

Product names CO Betahistine, Novo-Betahistine, Serc
Used in the following combined preparations None

GENERAL INFORMATION

Betahistine, a drug that resembles the naturally occurring substance histamine in some of its effects, was introduced in the 1970s as a treatment for Ménière's disease, which is caused by the pressure of excess fluid in the inner ear.

Taken regularly, betahistine may reduce both the frequency and the severity of the nausea and vertigo attacks that characterize this condition. Betahistine is thought to work by reducing pressure in the inner ear, possibly by improving blood flow in the small blood vessels. Drug treatment is not successful in all cases, however, and surgery may be needed.

QUICK REFERENCE

Drug group Drugs for Ménière's disease (p.74)

Overdose danger rating High

Dependence rating Low

Prescription needed Yes

Available as generic Yes

INFORMATION FOR USERS

Your drug prescription is tailored for you. Do not alter dosage without checking with your physician.

How taken

Tablets.

Frequency and timing of doses
2–3 x daily after food.

Usual adult dosage range
24–48mg daily.

Onset of effect
Within 1 hour.

Duration of action
6–12 hours.

Diet advice
None.

Storage
Keep in a closed container in a cool, dry place out of the reach of children.

Missed dose
Take as soon as you remember. If your next dose is due within 2 hours, take a single dose now and skip the next.

Stopping the drug
Do not stop the drug without consulting your physician; symptoms may recur.

OVERDOSE ACTION

 Seek immediate medical advice in all cases. Large overdoses may cause collapse and seizures requiring emergency action.

See Drug poisoning emergency guide (p.526)

POSSIBLE ADVERSE EFFECTS

Adverse effects from betahistine are minor and rarely cause problems.

Symptom/effect	Frequency		Discuss with physician		Stop taking drug now	Call physician now
	Common	Rare	Only if severe	In all cases		
Nausea	●		■			
Indigestion	●		■			
Headache		●	■			
Rash		●		■		

INTERACTIONS

Antihistamines Although unproven, there is a possibility that betahistine may reduce the effects of these drugs.

SPECIAL PRECAUTIONS

Be sure to tell your physician if:
▼ You have asthma.
▼ You have a history of peptic ulcers.
▼ You have pheochromocytoma.
▼ You are taking other medications.

 Pregnancy
▼ Safety in pregnancy not established. Discuss with your physician.

 Breast-feeding
▼ Safety not established. Discuss with your physician.

 Infants and children
▼ Not recommended.

 Over 60
No special problems.

 Driving and hazardous work
▼ Avoid such activities until you have learned how the drug affects you because rarely it may cause drowsiness.

 Alcohol
▼ No special problems.

PROLONGED USE

No special problems.

BETAMETHASONE

Product names Betaderm, Betaject, Betnesol, Celestone, Diprosone, Luxiq, Prevex B, Taro-Sone, Valisone
Used in the following combined preparations Dovobet, Lotriderm, Diprosalic, Garasone, Valisone-G, Xamiol

GENERAL INFORMATION

Betamethasone is a corticosteroid drug used to treat a variety of conditions. It is available as different formulations such as dipropionate and valerate, with variable potency. When injected directly into the joints it relieves joint inflammation and the pain and stiffness of rheumatoid arthritis and other inflammatory conditions, such as bursitis. It is also used *topically* to treat skin complaints, such as eczema and psoriasis. It is also used as an enema to help treat inflammatory bowel disease. When taken for short periods, low or moderate doses of this drug rarely cause serious *side effects*. High dosages or prolonged use can lead to many symptoms (see below).

INFORMATION FOR USERS

Your drug prescription is tailored for you. Do not alter dosage without checking with your physician.

How taken

Injection, rectal enema, cream, ointment, scalp solution, scalp aerosolized foam, eye ointment, eye/ear drops.

Frequency and timing of doses
Usually once daily in the morning (*injection*). Otherwise varies according to disorder being treated.

Usual dosage range
Varies; follow your physician's instructions.

Onset of effect
Within 30–60 minutes (injection); within 24–48 hours (other forms).

Duration of action
Up to 24 hours.

Diet advice
None

Storage
Keep in a closed container in a cool, dry place out of the reach of children. Protect from light.

Missed dose
Take as soon as you remember. If your next dose is due within 2 hours, take a single dose now and skip the next.

Stopping the drug
Can be safely stopped as soon as you no longer need it. Dose may need to be tapered off gradually.

Exceeding the dose
An occasional unintentional extra dose is unlikely to cause problems. But if you notice any unusual symptoms, notify your physician.

POSSIBLE ADVERSE EFFECTS

Serious adverse effects occur only when high doses are taken by mouth for long periods.

Topical preparations are unlikely to cause adverse effects unless overused.

Symptom/effect	Frequency		Discuss with physician		Stop taking drug now	Call physician now
	Common	Rare	Only if severe	In all cases		
Indigestion	●			■		
Weight gain		●		■		
Acne		●		■		
Muscle weakness		●		■		
Mood changes		●		■		
Bloody/black feces		●		■	▲	▮

INTERACTIONS

Interactions with topical use or when injected into the joints are uncommon. Discuss with your physician or *pharmacist*.

SPECIAL PRECAUTIONS

Be sure to tell your physician if:
▼ You suffer from a psychiatric disorder.
▼ You have a heart condition.
▼ You have glaucoma.
▼ You have high blood pressure.
▼ You have a history of epilepsy.
▼ You have had a peptic ulcer.
▼ You have had tuberculosis.
▼ You have any infection.
▼ You have diabetes.
▼ You have liver or kidney problems.
▼ You are taking other medications.

Avoid exposure to chickenpox, measles, or shingles if you are on betamethasone injection.

Pregnancy
▼ No evidence of risk with low dose, short-term use of topical preparations. Discuss with your physician.

Breast-feeding
▼ No risk with topical preparations. Discuss with your physician.

Infants and children
▼ Reduced dose necessary.

Over 60
▼ Reduced dose may be necessary

Driving and hazardous work
▼ No known problems.

Alcohol
▼ Keep consumption low. Betamethasone tablets increase the risk of peptic ulcers.

PROLONGED USE

Prolonged use of topical treatment may lead to skin thinning. This drug can also retard growth in children.

BISACODYL

Product names Apo-Bisacodyl, Bisacolax, Correctol, Dulcolax, and others
Used in the following combined preparations None

GENERAL INFORMATION

Bisacodyl is recommended for the treatment of occasional constipation. It may also be given in preparation for diagnostic procedures. Bisacodyl is a stimulant laxative that is thought to work by acting on the nerve endings on the wall of the bowel, which triggers contraction of the intestinal muscles and speeds up the process of fecal matter moving through the bowel. Usually, long-term use of bisacodyl is not recommended.

Bisacodyl, as with other laxatives, should not be used in someone who is experiencing abdominal pain, nausea, vomiting, or fever. Bisacodyl tablets should be swallowed whole and not taken with milk or antacids.

INFORMATION FOR USERS

Follow instructions on the label. Call your physician if symptoms worsen.

How taken

Tablets, suppositories, enema.

Frequency and timing of doses
Once daily on an occasional basis.

Usual adult dosage range
Oral tablets 5–15mg.
Suppository 10mg.
Micro-enema Contents of one enema.

Onset of effect
Tablets within 6–8 hours.
Suppository and micro-enema: within 30 minutes.

Duration of action
Up to 24 hours.

Diet advice
Maintaining adequate fluid and fiber intake is important in preventing constipation.

Storage
Keep in a closed container in a cool, dry place out of the reach of children.

Missed dose
If you miss a dose, take it as soon as you remember. Resume normal dose thereafter. Do not double up on a dose.

Stopping the drug
Can be safely stopped as soon as you no longer need it.

Exceeding the dose
An occasional unintentional extra dose is unlikely to be a cause for concern. Large doses can cause watery stools, abdominal cramps, and loss of electrolytes. Notify your physician.

SPECIAL PRECAUTIONS

Be sure to consult your physician or pharmacist before taking this drug if:
▼ You have severe constipation, and/or nausea, vomiting, or abdominal pain.
▼ You have unexplained rectal bleeding.
▼ You have difficulty swallowing.
▼ You have a known narrowing of the bowel.
▼ You have any obstruction of the bowel.
▼ You have an acute appendicitis or inflammatory bowel disease.
▼ You are sensitive or allergic to triarylmethane products.
▼ You are taking other medications.

Pregnancy
▼ Safety not established. Discuss with your physician.

Breast-feeding
▼ No evidence of risk. Discuss with your physician.

Infants and children
▼ Not recommended in children under 6 years of age without medical advice.

Over 60
▼ No special problems expected.

Driving and hazardous work
▼ No known problems.

Alcohol
▼ No known problems.

POSSIBLE ADVERSE EFFECTS

Generally well tolerated.

Symptom/effect	Frequency		Discuss with physician		Stop taking drug now	Call physician now
	Common	Rare	Only if severe	In all cases		
Abdominal pain/discomfort		●		■		
Dizziness		●		■		
Diarrhea		●		■		
Muscle weakness		●		■		
Suppositories and enema:						
Local irritation	●		■			
Painful sensation		●		■		

INTERACTIONS

Diuretics Prolonged use of bisacodyl can affect electrolyte balance, which can be potentiated further with diuretic use.

Digoxin Changes in electrolytes with bisacodyl could increase the effect of digoxin.

PROLONGED USE

Prolonged use of the oral preparation can make the bowel dependent on laxatives. For regular use, consult your physician or pharmacist.

BISMUTH SUBSALICYLATE

Product names Bismuth Chewtabs, Bismuth Subsalicylate, Devrom Chewtabs, Neo-Laryngobis, Pepto-Bismol, and others
Used in the following combined preparations Bismutal Adults, Bismuth + Antacid (Chewable Tablets)

GENERAL INFORMATION

Bismuth is used for a number of different conditions and is available in a variety of forms. It has weak antacid properties as well as antidiarrheal properties. Bismuth subsalicylate (BS) is thought to have a bactericidal effect. Bismuth salts are used for indigestion, heartburn, diarrhea (non-specific and Traveller's), upset stomach and nausea in adults and in children. Bismuth subsalicylate is also indicated in the treatment of *Helicobacter pylori* gastrointestinal tract infection in adults. For this condition, it is used in conjunction with antibiotics (amoxicillin and/or metronidazole) and a proton-pump inhibitor and used up to 14 days.

QUICK REFERENCE

Drug group Antacids and adsorbents (p.94)

Overdose danger rating Low

Dependence rating Low

Prescription needed No

Available as generic Yes

INFORMATION FOR USERS

Check with your pharmacist or physician for the recommended dosage.

How taken

Caplets, chewable tablets, liquid, rectal suppository (Bismutal).

Frequency and timing of doses
Every ½ to 1 hour as needed up to 8 doses in 24 hours and not to exceed maximum allowable dose based on patient's age.

Usual adult dosage range
Usual adult dosage for diarrhea and heartburn
524mg orally every 30 min to 1 hour, to a maximum of 8 doses/day (4,192mg/day).

Usual adult dosage for H. pylori infection
525mg orally four times daily, in combination with other antibiotics, for 10 to 14 days.

Onset of effect
Diarrhea 30 minutes to an hour.
H. pylori infection May be several days to see full effect.

Duration of action
For diarrhea, may last several hours.

Diet advice
None.

Storage
Keep in the original container in a cool, dry place out of the reach of children.

Missed dose
Take as soon as you remember but if it is time for your next dose, take this as per your schedule.

Stopping the drug
For H. pylori, complete the course of the drug as prescribed, or symptoms may recur. For diarrhea, the drug may be stopped as soon as you no longer need it.

Exceeding the dose
If a significantly larger than recommended dose of bismuth subsalicylate is taken, consult with your doctor or *pharmacist* as the salicylate component is absorbed and can lead to toxicity. In general, with a large dose of any bismuth product, if you notice any unusual symptoms, seek immediate medical help.

POSSIBLE ADVERSE EFFECTS

A common *side effect* is harmless darkening or blackening of the stools. Darkening of the tongue had occurred with older formulations; this is not commonly reported now.

Symptom/effect	Frequency		Discuss with physician		Stop taking drug now	Call physician now
	Common	Rare	Only if severe	In all cases		
Darkening of the feces	●					
Nausea/diarrhea/constipation		●	■			
Rash		●		■		
Headache/dizziness		●	■			
Tinnitus/ringing in the ears (with subsalicylate salt)		●		■		

INTERACTIONS

Doxycycline, minocycline, and tetracycline In general these drugs may have decreased effectiveness when taken with BS.

Methotrexate Salicylate could increase *adverse effects* of methotrexate.

Warfarin BS in large doses may increase the risk of bleeding from warfarin.

Calcium Bismuth can increase levels of calcium.

NSAIDs BS can increase risk of peptic ulcer disease caused by NSAID and salicylate.

SPECIAL PRECAUTIONS

Be sure to tell your physician if:
▼ You are allergic to salicylates or to bismuth subsalicylate.
▼ You are taking other medications.

Pregnancy
▼ Not recommended. Discuss with your physician.

Breast-feeding
▼ Insufficient information available. Discuss with your physician.

Infants and children
▼ Reduced dose necessary depending on age; discuss with your physician. Drug should not be given to children or teenagers who have signs of a viral infection or chicken pox (varicella).

Over 60
▼ No special problems.

Driving and hazardous work
▼ No special problems.

Alcohol
▼ Alcohol can irritate the stomach, which may worsen some symptoms.

PROLONGED USE

Usually used for a short treatment period only. Prolonged use of bismuth subsalicylate can increase the risk of salicylate toxicity.

BOTULINUM TOXIN

Product names Botox, Botox Cosmetic
Used in the following combined preparations None

GENERAL INFORMATION

Botulinum toxin is a neurotoxin (nerve poison) produced naturally by the bacterium *Clostridium botulinum*. The toxin causes botulism, a rare but serious form of food poisoning,

Research has found that there are several slightly different components in the toxin. Two are used medically: botulinum A toxin and botulinum B toxin. They are used therapeutically to treat conditions in which there are painful muscle spasms, for example spastic foot deformity, blepharospasm (spasm of the eyelids, causing them

almost to close), hemifacial spasm, and spasmodic torticollis (spasms of the neck muscles, causing the head to jerk). Toxin A is also used to treat very resistant and distressing cases of hyperhidrosis (excessive sweating). The effects produced by the toxins may last for 2–3 months, until new nerve endings have formed.

Botulinum toxin is used cosmetically to remove facial wrinkles by paralysing the muscles under the skin.

QUICK REFERENCE

Drug group Muscle relaxants (p.106)

Overdose danger rating High

Dependence rating Low

Prescription needed Yes

Available as generic No

INFORMATION FOR USERS

This drug is given only under medical supervision and is not for self-administration.

How taken

Injection.

Frequency and timing of doses
Every 2–3 months, depending on response.

Usual adult dosage range
Dose depends on the particular condition being treated. Individual injections may range from 1.25 units to 50 units. The number of injection sites depends on the size and number of the muscles to be paralysed. Specialist judgement is necessary.

Onset of effect
Within 3 days to 2 weeks. The maximum benefit of the drug will be seen around 6 weeks after treatment.

Duration of action
2–3 months.

Diet advice
None.

Storage
Not applicable as the drug is not normally kept in the home.

Missed dose
Attend for treatment at the next possible time.

Stopping the drug
If having botulinum toxin for medical reasons, discuss with your physician whether you should stop receiving the drug. Cosmetic use of the drug can be stopped safely at any time.

Exceeding the dose
When used for medical reasons, overdose is unlikely since treatment is carefully monitored. If the drug was injected into your face for cosmetic reasons, the effects of an overdose will develop gradually over several days; you should be especially alert for any weakness in your neck or swallowing difficulty and, if they occur, you should contact your physician immediately.

SPECIAL PRECAUTIONS

Be sure to tell your physician if:
▼ You have any disorder of muscle activity such as myasthenia gravis.
▼ You are taking an anticoagulant drug or have a bleeding disorder.
▼ You are allergic to botulinum toxin.

Pregnancy
▼ Not prescribed.

Breast-feeding
▼ Not prescribed.

Infants and children
▼ Reduced dose necessary.

Over 60
▼ No special problems.

Driving and hazardous work
▼ Do not drive until you know how botulinum toxin affects you; the drug may impair ability.

Alcohol
▼ No known problems.

POSSIBLE ADVERSE EFFECTS

Some of the adverse effects depend on the site of injection. Misplaced injections may paralyse unintended muscle groups. All paralyses are likely to be long lasting.

Symptom/effect	Frequency		Discuss with physician		Stop taking drug now	Call physician now
	Common	Rare	Only if severe	In all cases		
Reduced blinking/dry eye	●			■		
Painful swallowing	●			■		∎
Pain at site	●			■		
Glaucoma/painful eye		●		■		
Neck weakness/head tremor		●		■		∎
Weakness (local or general)	●			■		
Hypersensitivity reactions		●		■		

INTERACTIONS

None.

PROLONGED USE

To maintain the desired effects, the drug may have to be administered at regular intervals.

BUDESONIDE

Product names Entocort, Pulmicort, Rhinocort Aqua, Pulmicort Nebuamp
Used in the following combined preparation Symbicort

GENERAL INFORMATION

Budesonide is a corticosteroid drug used in the form of slow-release capsules to relieve the symptoms of Crohn's disease and as an enema to treat ulcerative colitis. It is also used as an inhaler to prevent attacks of asthma but will not stop an existing attack. It is also used as a nasal spray to relieve the symptoms of allergic rhinitis and for nasal polyps.

Budesonide controls symptoms by reducing inflammation, whether it is in the nose, lungs, or intestine.
There are fewer, usually less serious, *side effects* when budesonide is taken by inhaler or nasal spray because the drug is absorbed by the body in much smaller quantities than when it is taken by mouth.

QUICK REFERENCE

Drug group Corticosteroids (p.127)
Overdose danger rating Low
Dependence rating Low
Prescription needed Yes
Available as generic Yes

INFORMATION FOR USERS

Your drug prescription is tailored for you. Do not alter dosage without checking with your physician.

How taken

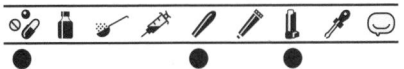

SR-capsules, enema, nebulizer, powder for inhalation, nasal spray.

Frequency and timing of doses
Once daily in morning before meal (capsules); once daily at bedtime (enema); twice daily (inhaler); once or twice daily (nasal spray).

Usual dosage range
3–9mg (capsules); 2mg (enema); 100–400mcg (nasal spray); dose individualized for nebulizer.

Onset of effect
Asthma Within 1 week.
Other conditions 1–3 days.

Duration of action
12–24 hours.

Diet advice
None.

Storage
Keep in a closed container in a cool, dry place out of the reach of children.

Missed dose
Take as soon as you remember. If your next dose is due within 2 hours, take a single dose now and skip the next.

Stopping the drug
Do not stop taking the drug without consulting your physician; symptoms may recur. The SR-capsules used in Crohn's disease should be withdrawn gradually.

Exceeding the dose
An occasional extra dose is unlikely to be a cause for concern. But if you notice any unusual symptoms, or if a large overdose has been taken, notify your physician.

POSSIBLE ADVERSE EFFECTS

The main side effects of inhalers and nasal spray are confined to the nasal passages and mouth. Capsules and enemas can cause gastrointestinal disturbances and rashes.

High doses of budesonide by any route can cause long-term side effects associated with corticosteroids.

Symptom/effect	Frequency		Discuss with physician		Stop taking drug now	Call physician now
	Common	Rare	Only if severe	In all cases		
Inhalers and nasal spray						
Nasal irritation	●		■			
Cough	●		■			
Sore throat/hoarseness	●			■		
Nosebleed		●		■		
Capsules and enema						
Diarrhea/constipation	●		■			
Rash/itching		●		■		
Mood disorders		●		■		
Weight gain		●		■		

INTERACTIONS

Ketoconazole/other azole antifungals
can increase the blood level of oral budesonide.

SPECIAL PRECAUTIONS

Be sure to tell your physician if:
▼ You have had tuberculosis or another respiratory infection.
▼ You are taking other medications.

 Pregnancy
▼ Discuss with physician, especially if used for Crohn's disease.

 Breast-feeding
▼ Discuss with physician, especially if used for Crohn's disease.

 Infants and children
▼ Reduced dose necessary.

 Over 60
▼ No special problems.

 Driving and hazardous work
▼ No special problems.

 Alcohol
▼ No special problems.

PROLONGED USE

Capsules and enema are not generally used long term. Asthma prevention is the condition for which prolonged use may be required. There may be a small risk of glaucoma, cataracts, and effects on bone with high doses inhaled for a prolonged period. Patients taking budesonide long term are advised to wear a Medic-alert bracelet.

Monitoring If budesonide is being taken in large doses, periodic checks may be needed to make sure that the adrenal glands are working properly. Children using inhalers may have their growth (height) monitored regularly.

BUPRENORPHINE

Product name BuTrans
Used in the following combined preparation Suboxone

GENERAL INFORMATION

Buprenorphine is a synthetic *opioid* available as BuTrans and Suboxone. BuTrans, a transdermal *patch* that slowly releases the medication over 7 days, is used in the management of moderate persistent pain that requires continuous opioid analgesic. Suboxone, a combination of buprenorphine and naloxone, is used for substitution therapy in adults who have opioid drug *dependence*. Both can cause drug dependence; to minimize this risk, follow your physician's instructions carefully.

Important: Follow your physician's or pharmacist's instructions on proper use and disposal of BuTrans or Suboxone.

QUICK REFERENCE

Drug group Opioid analgesics (p.64)
Overdose danger rating High
Dependence rating Medium
Prescription needed Yes
Available as generic No

INFORMATION FOR USERS

Your drug prescription is tailored for you. Do not alter dosage without checking with your physician.

How taken

Sublingual tablet, transdermal patch.

Frequency and timing of doses
BuTrans Every 7 days.
Suboxone Usually once daily.

Usual adult dosage range
BuTrans Dose individualized. Usual starting dose of 5ug/h.
Suboxone Starting dose 4mg on day 1; maximum daily dose 24mg.

Onset of effect
BuTrans Within 24 hours.
Suboxone 3–4 hours.

Duration of action
BuTrans Up to 7 days.
Suboxone More than 24 hours.

Diet advice
None.

Storage
Keep in the original container in a cool, dry place out of the reach of children.

Missed dose
BuTrans If the patch is left on for longer than 7 days, remove it and apply a new one.

Suboxone Speak to your physician or the *pharmacist* who will recommend a plan for any missed doses.

Stopping the drug
Do not stop taking the drug suddenly without consulting your physician; unwanted *side effects* may occur.

OVERDOSE ACTION

 Seek immediate medical advice in all cases. Take emergency action if loss of consciousness occurs.

See Drug poisoning emergency guide (p.526).

POSSIBLE ADVERSE EFFECTS

Withdrawal effects are common when stopping the medication. These include diarrhea, muscle aches, abdominal pain, anxiety, and sweating.

Symptom/effect	Frequency		Discuss with physician		Stop taking drug now	Call physician now
	Common	Rare	Only if severe	In all cases		
Lightheadedness/dizziness	●		■			
Headache	●		■			
Withdrawal symptoms	●			■		
Constipation	●		■			
Nausea/vomiting/dysepsia	●		■			
Breathing difficulties/ swelling of the face		●		■		■

INTERACTIONS

General note Never share this medication with someone else – it could be fatal.

Clarithromycin, itraconazole, ketoconazole, lopinavir, mifepristone and ritonavir can increase the adverse effects of buprenorphine.

Sedatives, hypnotics, and droperidol, can increase the central nervous system effects of buprenorphine.

Atazanavir may increase the level of buprenorphine; also, buprenorphine may decrease the level of atazanavir.

Other opioid medications should not be used with buprenorphine.

Alvimopan and monoamine oxidase inhibitors Buprenorphine may enhance the adverse effects of these drugs.

SPECIAL PRECAUTIONS

Be sure to tell your physician if:
▼ You have respiratory problems.
▼ You have liver problems.
▼ You are pregnant or breast-feeding.
▼ You use alcohol regularly or have experienced alcohol withdrawal symptoms.
▼ You are taking other medications.

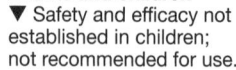

Pregnancy
▼ No adequate studies. Discuss with your physician.

Breast-feeding
▼ Not recommended.

Infants and children
▼ Safety and efficacy not established in children; not recommended for use.

Over 60
▼ Safety and efficacy not established in older individuals.

Driving and hazardous work
▼ The drug can cause drowsiness. Do not drive a car or operate machinery until you feel you are mentally alert.

Alcohol
▼ Do not take with alcohol. It increases the *sedative* effect of buprenorphine.

PROLONGED USE

Monitoring Careful monitoring by your physician and other team members is required.

BUPROPION

Product names Ava-Bupropion, Wellbutrin SR, Zyban, and others
Used in the following combined preparations None

GENERAL INFORMATION

Bupropion is an antidepressant; chemically it is unrelated to other antidepressant drugs. It is used to treat depression, and it is also generally used as an aid for people who are trying to give up tobacco smoking. The person being treated must commit in advance to a stop date. Treatment is started while the patient is still smoking and the "target stop date" decided on within the first two weeks of treatment. Bupropion will be stopped after 7 weeks if the smoker has not made significant progress in giving up smoking by then. Although the drug can be an effective aid, nicotine replacement therapy is more popular.

Bupropion should not be prescribed for people with a history of seizures or eating disorders, or who are withdrawing from benzodiazepine or alcohol. Neither should the drug be used by people with bipolar disorder (manic depression) or psychosis because there is a risk of mania developing.

QUICK REFERENCE

Drug group Nicotine withdrawal aids (pp.24, 367)

Overdose danger rating High

Dependence rating Low

Prescription needed Yes

Available as generic Yes

INFORMATION FOR USERS

Your drug prescription is tailored for you. Do not alter dosage without checking with your physician.

How taken

SR-tablets.

Frequency and timing of doses
1–2 x daily.

Usual adult dosage range
150–300mg (maximum dose).

Onset of effect
Up to 4 weeks for full effect.

Duration of action
12 hours.

Diet advice
None.

Storage
Keep in original closed container in a cool, dry place out of the reach of children.

Missed dose
Take as soon as you remember. If your next dose is due within 2 hours, take a single dose now and skip the next dose.

Stopping the drug
Do not stop the drug without consulting your physician. The physician may want to taper the dose.

OVERDOSE ACTION

 Seek immediate medical advice in all cases. Take emergency action if consciousness is lost.

See Drug poisoning emergency guide (p.526)

POSSIBLE ADVERSE EFFECTS

Some effects, for example agitation, tremor, sweating, and insomnia, may be due to the withdrawal of nicotine rather than to the effects of bupropion itself.

Symptom/effect	Frequency		Discuss with physician		Stop taking drug now	Call physician now
	Common	Rare	Only if severe	In all cases		
Insomnia/poor concentration	●		■			
Headache/dizziness/tremor	●		■			
Nausea/vomiting	●		■			
Rash/fever	●			■		
Dry mouth	●		■			
Depression	●			■		
Palpitations/fainting		●		■		
Confusion/anxiety		●		■		
Seizures		●		■	▲	■

INTERACTIONS

General note A wide range of drugs increases the likelihood of seizures when taken with bupropion. Check with your physician if you are on other medications.

Ritonavir, amantadine, and levodopa may all increase the risk of side effects with bupropion.

Antiepileptics Phenytoin and carbamazepine may reduce the blood levels and effects of bupropion. Valproate may increase its blood levels and effects.

SPECIAL PRECAUTIONS

Be sure to tell your physician if:
▼ You have a head injury or history of seizures.
▼ You have an eating disorder.
▼ You have cancer of the nervous system.
▼ You have diabetes.
▼ You have bipolar disorder (manic depression) or a psychosis.
▼ You have kidney or liver problems.
▼ You are withdrawing from alcohol or benzodiazepine dependence.
▼ You are taking other medications.

 Pregnancy
▼ Safety in pregnancy is not established. Discuss other options for quitting smoking or depression management with your physician.

 Breast-feeding
▼ Safety not established. The drug passes into the breast milk and may affect the baby.

 Infants and children
▼ Not recommended.

 Over 60
▼ Increased sensitivity to drug's effects. Reduced dose may therefore be necessary.

 Driving and hazardous work
▼ Avoid until you have learned how bupropion affects you. The drug may cause impaired concentration and dizziness.

 Alcohol
▼ Avoid. Alcohol will increase any sedative effects.

PROLONGED USE

Bupropion is used for up to 9 weeks for cessation of smoking.

Monitoring Progress will be reviewed after about 3–4 weeks, and the drug continued only if it is having some effect.

BUSPIRONE

Product names Apo-Buspirone, Teva-Buspirone, and others
Used in the following combined preparations None

GENERAL INFORMATION

Buspirone is an anti-anxiety drug that is used for the treatment of anxiety disorders marked by persistent, unrealistic, and excessive worry and anxiety. It is used in conjunction with counselling. It is thought to act by increasing 5-HT (serotonin) and dopamine levels in the brain.

Buspirone is better tolerated than benzodiazepine drugs (see p.67) when used for anxiety, but is less sedating. It may take one to two weeks to see an effect, and up to four weeks for the maximum benefit of the drug to be achieved.

see p.67

QUICK REFERENCE

Drug group Anti-anxiety (p.67)
Overdose danger rating Medium
Dependence rating Low
Prescription needed Yes
Available as generic Yes

(p.67)

INFORMATION FOR USERS

Your drug prescription is tailored for you. Do not alter dosage without checking with your physician.

How taken

Tablets.

Frequency and timing of doses
2–3 x daily.

Usual dosage range
5–30 mg daily.

Onset of effect
40–90 minutes.

Duration of action
Variable; up to 11 hours.

Diet advice
None.

Storage
Keep in a closed container in a cool, dry place away from the reach of children.

Missed dose
No cause for concern, but take when you next feel you need the drug. If your next dose is due within 2 hours, take a single dose now and skip the next dose.

Stopping the drug
If you have been taking the drug continuously for less than 2 weeks, it can be safely stopped if you no longer need it. However, if you have been taking it for a longer period of time, consult your physician. Stopping abruptly may lead to *withdrawal symptoms*.

Exceeding the dose
An occasional, unintentional extra dose is unlikely to cause problems. Larger overdoses may cause unusual drowsiness. Notify your physician.

SPECIAL PRECAUTIONS

Be sure to tell your physician if:
▼ You have impaired kidney or liver function.
▼ You have any form of epilepsy or any other convulsive disorder.
▼ You have a problem with alcohol or drug abuse.
▼ You are taking other medications.

Pregnancy
▼ Safety in pregnancy not established. Discuss with your physician.

Breast-feeding
▼ Safety in breast-feeding not established. Discuss with your physician.

Infants and children
▼ Not recommended for patients under 18 years of age.

Over 60
▼ Increased chance of adverse effects. Reduced dosage, therefore, may be necessary.

Driving and hazardous work
▼ Avoid such activities until you have learned how the drug affects you; it can cause reduced alertness and slowed reactions.

Alcohol
▼ Avoid. Alcohol may increase the sedative effects of this drug.

POSSIBLE ADVERSE EFFECTS

The most common *adverse reactions* encountered with buspirone are dizziness, headache, drowsiness, and nausea. They normally diminish after the first few days and if troublesome, they can usually be reduced by adjustment of dosage.

Symptom/effect	Frequency		Discuss with physician		Stop taking drug now	Call physician now
	Common	Rare	Only if severe	In all cases		
Dizziness/lightheadedness	●		■			
Headache	●			■		
Daytime drowsiness	●			■		
Nausea	●		■			
Skin rash		●		■	▲	▌
Sore throat		●		■	▲	▌

INTERACTIONS

Sedatives All drugs, including alcohol, that have a sedating effect on the central nervous system are likely to increase the sedative effects of buspirone.

Cyclosporine and haloperidol Buspirone may increase blood levels of these drugs.

Verapamil, diltiazem, itraconazole, and erythromycin may increase blood levels of buspirone.

Monamine oxidase inhibitors (MAOIs) Phenelzine, tranylcypromine, and moclobemide taken with buspirone may cause increased blood pressure; therefore, they should not be used together.

Grapefruit juice Regular intake of grapefruit juice can increase buspirone levels; avoid.

PROLONGED USE

If buspirone is taken for longer than 3–4 weeks, the need for continued therapy should be reassessed regularly.

CAPTOPRIL

Product names Apo-Capto, Capoten, Mylan-Captopril, and others
Used in the following combined preparations None

GENERAL INFORMATION

Captopril belongs to the class of drugs called ACE inhibitors, used to treat high blood pressure and heart failure. The drug works by relaxing the muscles around blood vessels, allowing them to dilate and thereby easing blood flow.

Captopril lowers blood pressure rapidly but may require several weeks to achieve full effect. People with heart failure may be given captopril in addition to diuretics. It can achieve dramatic results, relaxing muscle in blood vessel walls and reducing the heart's workload.

The first dose is usually very small and taken while lying down as there is a risk of a sudden fall in blood pressure. Diuretics are often given at the same time.

A variety of minor *side effects* may occur. Some people experience loss of taste, while others get a persistent dry cough. A reduction in dose may help minimize these effects.

QUICK REFERENCE

Drug group ACE inhibitors (p.84) and antihypertensive drugs (p.88)

Overdose danger rating Medium

Dependence rating Low

Prescription needed Yes

Available as generic Yes

INFORMATION FOR USERS

Your drug prescription is tailored for you. Do not alter dosage without checking with your physician.

How taken

Tablets.

Frequency and timing of doses
2–3 x daily.

Usual adult dosage range
12.5–25mg daily initially, gradually increased to 50–150mg daily. Starting doses of 6.25mg may be used.

Onset of effect
30–60 minutes. Full beneficial effect may take several weeks.

Duration of action
6–8 hours.

Diet advice
A low–salt diet may be advised to help control blood pressure.

Storage
Keep in a closed container in a cool, dry place out of the reach of children.

Missed dose
Take as soon as you remember. If your next dose is due within 2 hours, take a single dose now and skip the next.

Stopping the drug
Do not stop the drug without consulting your physician; the underlying condition may worsen.

Exceeding the dose
An occasional unintentional extra dose is unlikely to cause problems. Large overdoses may cause dizziness or fainting. Notify your physician.

SPECIAL PRECAUTIONS

Be sure to tell your physician if:
▼ You have long-term kidney or liver problems.
▼ You have heart problems.
▼ You have had an angiodema or a previous allergic reaction to ACE inhibitors.
▼ You are pregnant or intend to become pregnant.
▼ You are taking other medications.

Pregnancy
▼ Not prescribed. There is evidence of harm to the developing fetus.

Breast-feeding
▼ Safety not established. Discuss with your physician.

Infants and children
▼ Not recommended.

Over 60
▼ Reduced dose may be necessary.

Driving and hazardous work
▼ Avoid such activities until you have learned how captopril affects you because the drug can cause dizziness and fainting.

Alcohol
▼ Avoid. Alcohol may increase the blood-pressure-lowering and adverse effects of the drug.

Surgery and general anesthetics
▼ Captopril may need to be stopped before you have a general anesthetic. Discuss with your physician or dentist before any operation.

POSSIBLE ADVERSE EFFECTS

Captopril causes a variety of minor *adverse effects*, primarily rashes and gastrointestinal symptoms. These usually disappear soon after treatment has started.

Symptom/effect	Frequency		Discuss with physician		Stop taking drug now	Call physician now
	Common	Rare	Only if severe	In all cases		
Loss of taste	●		■			
Rash	●			■		
Persistent dry cough	●			■		
Mouth ulcers/sore mouth		●		■		
Dizziness/fainting		●		■		
Sore throat/fever		●		■		
Swelling of mouth/lips		●		■	▲	▮
Breathing difficulty		●		■	▲	▮

INTERACTIONS

Non-steroidal anti-inflammatory drugs (NSAIDs) may reduce the effectiveness of captopril. There is also a risk of kidney damage when they are taken with captopril.

Vasodilators, diuretics, and other antihypertensives These drugs may reduce blood pressure even further.

Cyclosporine This drug increases the risk of high potassium levels in the blood when taken with captopril.

Potassium supplements and potassium-sparing diuretics increase the risk of high potassium levels when taken with captopril.

Lithium Blood levels of lithium may be raised by captopril.

PROLONGED USE

Rarely, prolonged use can lead to changes in the blood count or kidney function.

Monitoring Periodic checks on potassium levels, white blood cell count, kidney function, and urine are usually performed.

CARBAMAZEPINE

Product names Apo-Carbamazepine, Novo-Carbamaz, Tegretol, and others
Used in the following combined preparations None

GENERAL INFORMATION

Carbamazepine is used to treat some forms of epilepsy as it reduces the likelihood of seizures caused by abnormal nerve signals in the brain.

Carbamazepine is also prescribed to relieve the intermittent severe pain caused by damage to the cranial nerves in trigeminal neuralgia. It is also prescribed to stabilize mood in bipolar disorder (manic depression) and in the treatment of acute mania.

In order to avoid *side effects*, carbamazepine therapy is usually commenced at a low dose and is gradually increased. It is recommended that patients stick to the brand of carbamazepine prescribed.

INFORMATION FOR USERS

Your drug prescription is tailored for you. Do not alter dosage without checking with your physician.

How taken

CR (controlled release) tablets, tablets chewable tablets, liquid, suppositories.

Frequency and timing of doses
1–2 x daily.

Usual adult dosage range
Epilepsy 100–2,000mg daily (low starting dose that is slowly increased every 2 weeks).
Pain relief 100–1,600mg daily.
Psychiatric disorders 400–1,600mg daily.

Onset of effect
Within 4 hours.

Duration of action
12–24 hours.

Diet advice
None.

Storage
Keep in a closed container in a cool, dry place out of the reach of children.

Missed dose
Take as soon as you remember. If your next dose is due within 2 hours, take a single dose now and skip the next.

Stopping the drug
Do not stop the drug without consulting your physician; symptoms may recur.

Exceeding the dose
An occasional unintentional extra dose is unlikely to cause problems. Large overdoses may cause tremor, convulsions, and *coma*. Notify your physician.

SPECIAL PRECAUTIONS

Be sure to tell your physician if:
▼ You have long-term liver or kidney problems.
▼ You have heart problems.
▼ You have had blood problems with other drugs or porphyria.
▼ You have been tested for specific HLA-A*3101 and HLA-B*1502 genotype.
▼ You are taking other medications.

 Pregnancy
▼ May be associated with abnormalities in the unborn baby. Folic acid supplements should be taken before and during pregnancy. Discuss with your physician.

 Breast-feeding
▼ The drug passes into the breast milk, but at normal doses *adverse effects* on the baby are unlikely. Discuss with your physician.

 Infants and children
▼ Reduced dose necessary.

 Over 60
▼ May cause confused or agitated behaviour in the elderly. Reduced dose may be necessary.

 Driving and hazardous work
▼ Discuss with your physician. Your underlying condition, as well as the possibility of reduced alertness while taking carbamazepine, may make such activities inadvisable.

 Alcohol
▼ Avoid. Alcohol may increase the *sedative* effects of this drug.

POSSIBLE ADVERSE EFFECTS

Most people experience very few *adverse effects* with this drug, but when blood levels get too high, adverse effects are common and the dose may need to be reduced. Although rare, serious blood disorders and liver problems can occur. Regular monitoring of blood tests is important. Individuals with certain genotypes may be at a higher risk for a serious skin reaction.

Symptom/effect	Frequency		Discuss with physician		Stop taking drug now	Call physician now
	Common	Rare	Only if severe	In all cases		
Dizziness/unsteadiness	●		■			
Drowsiness	●		■			
Nausea/loss of appetite	●		■			
Blurred vision	●			■		
Jaundice		●		■		
Ankle swelling		●		■		
Rash		●		■	▲	▮
Sore throat/hoarseness		●		■	▲	

PROLONGED USE

There is a slight risk of changes in liver function or of skin or blood abnormalities occurring during prolonged use.

Monitoring Periodic blood tests are usually performed to monitor levels of the drug, blood cell counts, and liver and kidney function.

INTERACTIONS

General note Many drugs may increase or reduce the effects of carbamazepine. Discuss with your physician or *pharmacist* before taking other medications.

Other antiepileptic drugs Complex and variable interactions can occur between these drugs and carbamazepine. Discuss with your physician or pharmacist.

Grapefruit juice May increase carbamazepine blood levels; avoid.

Oral contraceptives Carbamazepine may affect the blood level of oral contraceptives. Discuss contraceptive options with your physician or pharmacist.

CARVEDILOL

Product names Apo-Carvedilol, PMS-Carvedilol, RAN-Carvedilol, ratio-Carvedilol
Used in the following combined preparations None

GENERAL INFORMATION

Carvedilol is used in the treatment of heart failure and has shown to improve survival. It works differently from traditional beta blockers as it also blocks alpha receptors. The dose of this drug is usually increased gradually over 2 to 4 weeks, with close monitoring of heart rate and blood pressure, particularly when patients are on other medications that can affect the heart rate and blood pressure. Discontinuation of carvedilol usually requires a gradual withdrawal over two or more weeks. Drugs with beta-blocker activity may mask symptoms of low blood sugar in a patient with diabetes.

QUICK REFERENCE

Drug group Beta blockers (p.83)

Overdose danger rating Medium

Dependence rating Low

Prescription needed Yes

Available as generic Yes

INFORMATION FOR USERS

Your drug prescription is tailored for you. Do not alter dosage without checking with your physician.

How taken

Tablets; swallow whole, do not chew or break.

Frequency and timing of doses
Twice daily, at the same time each day.

Usual adult dosage range
6.25–50mg.

Onset of effect
May take a few weeks to see full benefit.

Duration of action
7–10 hours.

Diet advice
Take with food.

Storage
Keep in a closed container in a cool, dry place away from the reach of children.

Missed dose
Take as soon as you remember but do not take two doses within 6 hours of each other.

Stopping the drug
Do not stop the drug without consulting your physician; symptoms may worsen.

Exceeding the dose
If the dose has been exceeded or in case of overdose, seek immediate medical attention and notify your physician.

SPECIAL PRECAUTIONS

Be sure to tell your physician if:
▼ You have a lung disorder such as asthma or bronchitis.
▼ You have diabetes, thyroid problems, or Raynaud's phenomenon (coldness or spasm in hands/feet).
▼ You have low blood pressure or heart rate.
▼ You have long-term liver problems.
▼ You have other heart conditions.
▼ You are taking other medications.

Pregnancy
▼ Avoid use in pregnancy. Discuss with your physician.

Breast-feeding
▼ The drug does enter breast milk. Breast-feeding is not recommended while on carvedilol. Discuss with your physician.

Infants and children
▼ Safety and efficacy not established in children.

Over 60
▼ Dosage reduction may be required.

Driving and hazardous work
▼ The drug may cause dizziness or tiredness, especially when starting the drug or when the dose is increased. Use caution with driving and hazardous work.

Alcohol
▼ Do not take with alcohol.

POSSIBLE ADVERSE EFFECTS

The common *side effects*, especially when starting the drug or when doses are adjusted, include fatigue, dizziness or lightheadedness. Stand up slowly while supporting yourself.

Symptom/effect	Frequency		Discuss with physician		Stop taking drug now	Call physician now
	Common	Rare	Only if severe	In all cases		
Nausea/constipation	●		■			
Fatigue/tiredness	●		■			
Dizziness/lightheadedness (orthostatic hypotension)	●		■			
Low heart rate	●			■		
Worsening heart failure/fluid retention		●		■		▮
Breathing difficulties		●		■		▮
Allergic reaction/rashes		●		■		▮

INTERACTIONS

Dabigatran and colchicine Carvedilol may increase the level of this drug.

Digoxin, amiodarone, diltiazem, verapamil and beta-blockers can all decrease heart rate; close monitoring required when taken with carvedilol.

Terazoin, prazosin, and similar drugs can significantly decrease blood pressure when given with carvedilol.

Clonidine and tizanidine may cause significant increase in blood pressure when being withdrawn in the presence of carvedilol.

Epinephrine, when given with carvedilol, can increase blood pressure and decrease heart rate.

Salbutamol, formeterol, and salmetrol Carvedilol can interfere with the effectiveness of these drugs.

CYP 2D6 inhibitor drugs, such as fluoxetine and bupropion, can increase the level of carvedilol.

Rituximab Carvedilol may further decrease the low blood pressure caused during infusion of this drug.

PROLONGED USE

Monitoring Monitor for heart rate and blood pressure, particularly when carvedilol is used in combination with other medications.

CEFACLOR

Product names Apo-Cefaclor, Ceclor, Novo-Cefaclor, Nu-Cefaclor, PMS-Cefaclor
Used in the following combined preparations None

GENERAL INFORMATION

Cefaclor is a broad spectrum cephalosporin *antibiotic* used to treat a variety of bacterial infections, including infections of the upper respiratory tract, such as pharyngitis and tonsillitis, and ear infections. It is also used to treat lower respiratory tract infections such as pneumonia and bronchitis, skin and soft-tissue infections, and urinary tract infections. Cefaclor can be used to treat lower respiratory complications from cystic fibrosis. Cefaclor is prescribed for a specific time period, usually between 7 and 10 days. It is well absorbed when taken orally. Patients who are allergic to penicillins have a higher chance of being allergic to a cephalosporin antibiotic; cefaclor should be used cautiously in these individuals.

QUICK REFERENCE

Drug group Antibiotics (p.114)
Overdose danger rating Low
Dependence rating Low
Prescription needed Yes
Available as generic Yes

INFORMATION FOR USERS

Your drug prescription is tailored for you. Do not alter dosage without checking with your physician.

How taken

Capsules, suspension.

Frequency and timing of doses
2–3 x daily as instructed, at the same time daily.

Usual dosage range
Adults 750mg–1500mg; maximum 2g daily.
Children 20–40mg/kg/day in divided doses; maximum 1g daily.

Onset of effect
Within 24–72 hours.

Duration of action
8–12 hours.

Diet advice
None.

Storage
Capsules: Keep in a closed container in a cool, dry place out of the reach of children. *Suspension/liquid:* Once reconstituted, can be kept in the refrigerator for 14 days. Discard after this time.

Missed dose
Take as soon as you remember, then continue with your regular dosing regimen.

Stopping the drug
Take the full course. Even if you feel better, the original infection may still be present and may recur if treatment is stopped too soon.

Exceeding the dose
An occasional unintentional extra dose is unlikely to cause problems. But if you notice any unusual symptoms, or if a large overdose has been taken, notify your physician.

SPECIAL PRECAUTIONS

Be sure to tell your physician if:
▼ You have had a previous *allergic reaction* to a penicillin or a cephalosporin antibiotic.
▼ You have a history of blood disorders.
▼ You are taking other medications.

Pregnancy
▼ No specific studies; however, cephalosporins in general are considered safe in pregnancy. Discuss with your physician.

Breast-feeding
▼ The drug does enter breast milk. Cefaclor should be used with caution while breast-feeding. Discuss with your physician.

Infants and children
▼ Reduced dose necessary.

Over 60
▼ No special problems.

Driving and hazardous work
▼ No known problems.

Alcohol
▼ No known problems.

POSSIBLE ADVERSE EFFECTS

Most people do not suffer serious *adverse effects* while taking cefaclor. Diarrhea is common but it tends not to be severe. The rare adverse reactions are usually due to an allergic reaction and may require stopping the drug.

Symptom/effect	Frequency		Discuss with physician		Stop taking drug now	Call physician now
	Common	Rare	Only if severe	In all cases		
Diarrhea	●		■			
Nausea/vomiting		●	■			
Rash		●		■	▲	▮
Itching/swelling/wheezing		●		■	▲	▮

INTERACTIONS

Aminoglycoside antibiotics such as tobramycin or gentamicin taken with cefaclor may increase the risk of kidney toxicity.

Probenecid This drug increases the level of cefaclor in the blood. Dose of cefaclor may need to be adjusted.

Oral typhoid vaccine Antibiotics may decrease the effect of this vaccine.

PROLONGED USE

Cefaclor is usually given only for short courses of treatment.

CEFPROZIL

Product names Apo-Cefprozil, Cefzil, RAN-Cefprozil, Sandoz Cefprozil
Used in the following combined preparations None

GENERAL INFORMATION

Cefprozil is a broad spectrum cephalosporin *antibiotic* used to treat a variety of bacterial infections. It is used for upper respiratory tract infections such as pharyngitis and tonsillitis, ear infections, and sinus infections. It is also used to treat skin infections and urinary tract infections. Cefprozil is prescribed for a specific number of days, usually between 7 and 10 days. Patients who are allergic to penicillins have a higher chance of being allergic to a cephalosporin antibiotic; cefprozil should be used cautiously in these individuals.

QUICK REFERENCE

Drug group Antibiotics (p.114)
Overdose danger rating Low
Dependence rating Low
Prescription needed Yes
Available as generic Yes

INFORMATION FOR USERS

Your drug prescription is tailored for you. Do not alter dosage without checking with your physician.

How taken

Tablets, oral suspension.

Frequency and timing of doses
Once or twice daily.

Usual dosage range
Adults 500mg–1,000mg daily.
Children 6 months–12 years 15mg/kg/day–30mg/kg/day; maximum 1,000 mg daily.

Onset of effect
24–72 hours.

Duration of action
12–24 hours.

Diet advice
None.

Storage
The reconstituted suspension must be stored in the refrigerator (2–8°C) and can be kept up to14 days. Discard unused portion after 14 days.

Missed dose
Take as soon as you remember, then continue with your regular dosing regimen.

Stopping the drug
Take the full course. Even if you feel better, the original infection may still be present and may recur if treatment is stopped too soon.

Exceeding the dose
An occasional unintentional extra dose is unlikely to cause problems. But if you notice any unusual symptoms, or if a large overdose has been taken, notify your physician.

SPECIAL PRECAUTIONS

Be sure to tell your physician if:
▼ You have a long-term kidney problem.
▼ You have a history of blood disorders.
▼ You have had a previous allergic reaction to a penicillin or a cephalosporin.
▼ You are taking other medications.

 Pregnancy
▼ No specific studies; however, cephalosporins in general are considered safe in pregnancy. Discuss with your physician.

 Breast-feeding
▼ The drug does enter breast milk. Cefprozil should be used with caution while breast-feeding. Discuss with your physician.

 Infants and children
▼ May be used in children over 3 months.

 Over 60
▼ Dosage reduction may be required based on kidney function.

 Driving and hazardous work
▼ No known problems.

 Alcohol
▼ No known problems.

POSSIBLE ADVERSE EFFECTS

Most people do not suffer serious *adverse effects* while taking cefprozil. Diarrhea is common but it tends not to be severe. The rare adverse reactions are usually due to an allergic reaction and may require stopping the drug. The drug may rarely increase liver *enzymes*.

Symptom/effect	Frequency		Discuss with physician		Stop taking drug now	Call physician now
	Common	Rare	Only if severe	In all cases		
Diarrhea	●		■			
Nausea/vomiting	●		■			
Dizziness		●		■		
Rash		●		■	▲	▮
Itching/swelling/wheezing		●		■	▲	▮

INTERACTIONS

Aminoglycoside antibiotics such as tobramycin or gentamicin, when taken with cefprozil, may further increase the risk of kidney toxicity.

Probenecid This drug increases the level of cefprozil in the blood. Dose of cefprozil may need to be adjusted.

Oral typhoid vaccine Antibiotics may decrease the effect of this vaccine.

PROLONGED USE

Cefprozil is usually only given for short courses of treatment.

CEFUROXIME

Product names Apo-Cefuroxime, Ceftin, Ratio-Cefuroxime
Used in the following combined preparations None

GENERAL INFORMATION

Cefuroxime is a cephalosporin *antibiotic* that is prescribed for a variety of mild to moderately severe infections. It is used for upper respiratory tract infections such as pharyngitis, tonsillitis, ear infections, and sinus infections. It is also used in lower respiratory tract infections such as pneumonia and bronchitis. Cefuroxime may be used in some skin and soft tissue infections, and urinary tract infections.

Cefuroxime axetil is an orally active drug of cefuroxime. Absorption of the oral formulation is better when administered with food. The liquid suspension should be shaken well before use.

Patients who are allergic to penicillins have a slightly higher chance of being allergic to a cephalosporin antibiotic and cefuroxime should be used cautiously in these individuals.

INFORMATION FOR USERS

Your drug prescription is tailored for you. Do not alter dosage without checking with your physician.

How taken

Tablets, liquid, injection.

Frequency and timing of doses
Twice daily. Take oral dose with food.

Usual dosage range
Adults 500mg–1g daily.
Children 3 months to < 12 years Dose based on body weight.

Onset of effect
Within 1 hour.

Duration of action
6–12 hours.

Diet advice
None.

Storage
Keep tablets in a closed container in a cool, dry place out of the reach of children. The solution should be stored between 2 and 25°C, preferably in the refrigerator. Any leftover solution should be discarded after 10 days.

Missed dose
Take as soon as you remember, then continue with your regular dosing regiment.

Stopping the drug
Take the full course. Even if you feel better, the original infection may still be present and may recur if treatment is stopped too soon.

Exceeding the dose
An occasional unintentional extra dose is unlikely to cause problems. But if you notice any unusual symptoms, or if a large overdose has been taken, notify your physician.

SPECIAL PRECAUTIONS

Be sure to tell your physician if:
▼ You have a long-term kidney problem.
▼ You have had a previous allergic reaction to a penicillin or a cephalosporin.
▼ You have a history of blood disorders.
▼ You have a gastrointestinal disease such as colitis.
▼ You are taking other medications.

Pregnancy
▼ No known problems. Discuss with your physician.

Breast-feeding
▼ No known problems. Discuss with your physician.

Infants and children
▼ May be used in children older than 3 months.

Over 60
▼ May require a reduced dose.

Driving and hazardous work
▼ No known problems.

Alcohol
▼ No known problems.

POSSIBLE ADVERSE EFFECTS

Diarrhea can occur but is usually mild. A physician should be consulted for ongoing or worsening diarrhea or diarrhea occurring after finishing the antibiotic course.

Symptom/effect	Frequency		Discuss with physician		Stop taking drug now	Call physician now
	Common	Rare	Only if severe	In all cases		
Diarrhea	●		■			
Headache/dizziness	●		■			
Nausea/vomiting	●		■			
Rash		●		■	▲	▮
Itching/swelling/wheezing		●		■	▲	▮
Jaundice/tiredness		●		■		▮

INTERACTIONS

Aminoglycosides When administered with cefuroxime, increases risk of kidney problems. Monitor closely.

Probenecid May increase the level of cefuroxime. Monitor closely.

PROLONGED USE

Cefuroxime is usually given only for short courses of treatment. Use of large doses or prolonged therapy requires close monitoring.

CELECOXIB

Product name Celebrex
Used in the following combined preparations None

GENERAL INFORMATION

Celecoxib is a type of NSAID called a cyclo-oxygenase-2 (COX-2) selective inhibitor; these drugs are considered to have a slightly lower risk of causing ulcers of the upper gastrointestinal tract than other NSAIDs. Celecoxib reduces pain, stiffness, and inflammation and is used to relieve the symptoms of both rheumatoid arthritis and osteoarthritis. Elderly patients and those with kidney problems may be more sensitive to the drug's effects; they are usually prescribed a low dose to begin with.

Celecoxib is not prescribed to anyone who has had a heart attack or stroke because it slightly increases the risk of recurrence, nor is it prescribed to people with peripheral artery disease (poor circulation). It is prescribed with caution to anyone at risk of any of these conditions.

INFORMATION FOR USERS

Your drug prescription is tailored for you. Do not alter dosage without checking with your physician.

How taken

Capsules.

Frequency and timing of doses
1–2 x daily.

Usual adult dosage range
200–400mg daily with food.

Onset of effect
1 hour.

Duration of action
8–12 hours.

Diet advice
None.

Storage
Keep in a cool, dry place out of the reach of children.

Missed dose
Take as soon as you remember. If your next dose is due within 4 hours, take a single dose now and skip the next.

Stopping the drug
If being used short term, the drug can safely be stopped as soon as you no longer need it. If prescribed for long-term use, you should not stop taking the drug without consulting your physician.

Exceeding the dose
An occasional unintentional extra dose is unlikely to cause problems. Large overdoses can cause stomach and intestinal pain and damage. Notify your physician.

SPECIAL PRECAUTIONS

Be sure to tell your physician if:
▼ You have asthma.
▼ You are allergic to ASA or celecoxib.
▼ You are allergic to sulfonamides.
▼ You have a history of peptic ulcers.
▼ You have inflammatory bowel disease.
▼ You have heart problems.
▼ You have had a heart attack or stroke.
▼ You have liver or kidney problems.
▼ You have epilepsy.
▼ You have high blood pressure.
▼ You have ankle swelling.
▼ You are taking other medicines.

Pregnancy
▼ Not prescribed.

Breast-feeding
▼ Not prescribed.

Infants and children
▼ Not recommended.

Over 60
▼ Elderly people may be more sensitive to the drug's effects. Lower doses may be necessary.

Driving and hazardous work
▼ Avoid until you know how the drug affects you. It can cause dizziness, vertigo, and sleepiness.

Alcohol
▼ Alcohol may increase drowsiness and the risk of stomach irritation.

POSSIBLE ADVERSE EFFECTS

Gastrointestinal, nervous, and respiratory symptoms are the most likely *adverse effects*.

Symptom/effect	Frequency		Discuss with physician		Stop taking drug now	Call physician now
	Common	Rare	Only if severe	In all cases		
Indigestion/abdominal pain	●		■			
Diarrhea/flatulence	●		■			
Dizziness/insomnia	●		■			
Rash	●			■		
Swollen ankles	●			■		
Palpitations/difficulty breathing		●		■		▮
Black/bloody vomit/feces		●		■	▲	▮

INTERACTIONS

Anticoagulants The effects of warfarin are increased by celecoxib.

ACE inhibitors increase the risk of renal failure.

Antihypertensives and diuretics Blood pressure-lowering effects may be reduced by celecoxib.

Lithium levels and effects are increased when taken with celecoxib.

Cyclosporine and tacrolimus may increase the risk of renal toxicity if taken with celecoxib.

Methotrexate Excretion of this drug is slowed by NSAIDs causing increased toxicity. This effect may be minimal with celecoxib.

Carbamazepine, fluconazole, rifampin, and barbiturates reduce the effects of celecoxib.

PROLONGED USE

Long-term use increases the risk of stroke or heart attack, so the lowest effective dose is given for the shortest duration.

Monitoring Periodic tests of kidney function may be performed.

CEPHALEXIN

Product names Apo-Cephalex, Teva-Lexin, and others
Used in the following combined preparations None

GENERAL INFORMATION

Cephalexin is a cephalosporin *antibiotic* that is prescribed for a variety of mild to moderate infections. Cephalexin does not have such a wide range of uses as some other antibiotics, but it is helpful in treating cystitis, and certain skin and soft tissue infections. In some cases it is prescribed as follow-up treatment for severe infections after a more powerful cephalosporin has been given by injection.

Diarrhea is the most common *side effect* of cephalexin, although it tends to be less severe than with other cephalosporin antibiotics. In addition, patients who are allergic to penicillins have a slightly higher chance of being allergic to a cephalosporin antibiotic and cephalexin should be used cautiously in these individuals.

INFORMATION FOR USERS

Your drug prescription is tailored for you. Do not alter dosage without checking with your physician.

How taken

Tablets, capsules, liquid.

Frequency and timing of doses
Usually 4 x daily. May take with food.

Usual dosage range
Adults 1–2g daily, up to a maximum of 4g.
Children Reduced dose according to age and weight.

Onset of effect
Within 1 hour.

Duration of action
6–12 hours.

Diet advice
None.

Storage
Keep tablets and capsules in a closed container in a cool, dry place out of the reach of children. Refrigerate liquid, but do not freeze, and keep for no longer than 10 days. Protect from light.

Missed dose
Take as soon as you remember. If your next dose is due at this time, take both doses now.

Stopping the drug
Take the full course. Even if you feel better, the original infection may still be present and may recur if treatment is stopped too soon.

Exceeding the dose
An occasional unintentional extra dose is unlikely to be a cause for concern. But if you notice any unusual symptoms, or if a large overdose has been taken, notify your physician.

POSSIBLE ADVERSE EFFECTS

Most people do not suffer serious *adverse effects* while taking cephalexin. Diarrhea is common but it tends not to be severe. The rarer adverse effects are usually due to an allergic reaction and may necessitate stopping the drug.

Symptom/effect	Frequency		Discuss with physician		Stop taking drug now	Call physician now
	Common	Rare	Only if severe	In all cases		
Diarrhea	●		■			
Nausea/vomiting	●		■			
Abdominal pain		●		■		
Rash		●		■	▲	▮
Itching/swelling/wheezing		●		■	▲	▮

INTERACTIONS

Probenecid This drug increases the level of cephalexin in the blood. The dosage of cephalexin may need to be adjusted accordingly.

SPECIAL PRECAUTIONS

Be sure to tell your physician if:
▼ You have a long-term kidney problem.
▼ You have had a previous allergic reaction to a penicillin or cephalosporin antibiotic.
▼ You have a history of blood disorders.
▼ You are taking other medications.

Pregnancy
▼ No evidence of risk to the developing baby.

Breast-feeding
▼ The drug passes into the breast milk but at normal doses **adverse effects** on the baby are unlikely. Discuss with your physician.

Infants and children
▼ Reduced dose necessary.

Over 60
▼ Reduced dose may be necessary depending on kidney function.

Driving and hazardous work
▼ No known problems.

Alcohol
▼ No known problems.

PROLONGED USE

Cephalexin is usually given only for short courses of treatment. Use of large doses or prolonged therapy requires close monitoring.

CETIRIZINE

Product names Apo-Cetrizine, PMS-Cetirizine, Reactine, and others
Used in the following combined preparations Reactine Allergy and Sinus

GENERAL INFORMATION

Cetirizine is a long-acting antihistamine. Its main use is in the treatment of allergic rhinitis, particularly hay fever. It is also used to treat allergic skin conditions, such as urticaria (hives).

The principal difference between cetirizine and traditional antihistamines such as chlorpheniramine is that this has a less *sedative* effect on the central nervous system and may therefore be suitable for people when they need to avoid sleepiness – for example, when driving or at work. However, because these drugs can cause drowsiness in some people, you should learn how cetirizine affects you before you undertake any activities that require concentration.

QUICK REFERENCE

Drug group Antihistamines (p.110)
Overdose danger rating Medium
Dependence rating Low
Prescription needed No
Available as generic Yes

INFORMATION FOR USERS

Your drug prescription is tailored for you. Do not alter dosage without checking with your physician.

How taken

Tablets, liquid.

Frequency and timing of doses
1–2 x daily.

Usual adult dosage range
5–10mg daily. Maximum dose: 20mg.

Onset of effect
1–3 hours. Some effects may not be felt for 1–2 days.

Duration of action
Up to 24 hours.

Diet advice
None.

Storage
Keep in a closed container in a cool, dry place out of the reach of children.

Missed dose
No cause for concern, but take as soon as you remember. If your next dose is due within 8 hours, take a single dose now and skip the next.

Stopping the drug
Can be safely stopped as soon as you no longer need it.

Exceeding the dose
An occasional unintentional extra dose is unlikely to cause problems. Large overdoses may cause nausea or drowsiness and have adverse effects on the heart.
Notify your physician.

POSSIBLE ADVERSE EFFECTS

The most common adverse effects are drowsiness, dry mouth, and fatigue.

Side effects may be reduced if the dose of cetirizine is taken as 5mg twice a day.

Symptom/effect	Frequency		Discuss with physician		Stop taking drug now	Call physician now
	Common	Rare	Only if severe	In all cases		
Drowsiness/fatigue		●	■			
Dry mouth		●	■			
Headache		●	■			
Diarrhea		●	■			

INTERACTIONS

Anticholinergic drugs The *anticholinergic* effects of cetirizine may be increased by all drugs that have anticholinergic effects, including anti-psychotics and tricyclic antidepressants, and some drugs for parkisonism.

Sedatives Cetirizine may increase the *sedative* effects of anti-anxiety drugs, sleeping drugs, antidepressants, and antipsychotic drugs.

Allergy tests Antihistamines should be discontinued approximately 2–4 days before allergy skin testing.

SPECIAL PRECAUTIONS

Be sure to consult your physician if:
▼ You have long-term liver or kidney problems.
▼ You have glaucoma.
▼ You are allergic to hydroxyzine.
▼ You are taking other medications.

Pregnancy
▼ Safety in pregnancy not established. Discuss with your physician.

Breast-feeding
▼ The drug passes into the breast milk. Discuss with your physician.

Infants and children
▼ Not recommended under 2 years, but may be prescribed for special use under 6 years.

Over 60
▼ No problems expected.

Driving and hazardous work
▼ Avoid such activities until you have learned how cetirizine affects you because the drug can cause drowsiness in some people.

Alcohol
▼ Keep consumption low.

PROLONGED USE

No problems expected.

CHLORAMPHENICOL

Product names Chloromycetin, Pentamycetin
Used in the following combined preparation Pentamycetin/HC

GENERAL INFORMATION

Chloramphenicol is an *antibiotic* used *topically* to treat eye and ear infections. Given by mouth or injection, it is used in the treatment of meningitis and brain abscesses. It is also effective in acute infections such as typhoid, pneumonia, epiglottitis, or meningitis caused by bacteria resistant to other antibiotics.

Although most people experience few *adverse effects*, chloramphenicol occasionally causes serious or even fatal blood disorders. For this reason, chloramphenicol by mouth or injection is normally only given to treat life-threatening infections that do not respond to safer drugs.

QUICK REFERENCE

Drug group Antibiotics (p.114)
Overdose danger rating Low
Dependence rating Low
Prescription needed Yes
Available as generic Yes

INFORMATION FOR USERS

Your drug prescription is tailored for you. Do not alter dosage without checking with your physician.

How taken

Capsules, injection, cream, eye and ear drops, eye and ear ointment.

Frequency and timing of doses
Every 6 hours (by mouth or injection); every 3–6 hours (eye preparations); 3–4 x daily (ear drops).

Usual adult dosage range
Varies according to preparation and condition. Follow your doctor's instructions.

Onset of effect
1–3 days, depending on the condition and preparation.

Duration of action
6–8 hours.

Diet advice
None.

Storage
Keep in a closed container in a cool, dry place out of the reach of children. Protect from light.

Missed dose
For skin, eye, and ear preparations, apply as soon as you remember. Other preparations are usually given in hospital.

Stopping the drug
Take the full course. Even if you feel better the infection may still be present and may recur if treatment is stopped too soon.

Exceeding the dose
An occasional unintentional extra dose is unlikely to be a cause for concern. But if you notice any unusual symptoms, or if a large overdose has been taken, notify your physician.

SPECIAL PRECAUTIONS

Be sure to tell your physician if:
▼ You have long-term liver or kidney problems.
▼ You have a blood disorder.
▼ You are taking other medications.

Pregnancy
▼ No evidence of risk with eye or ear preparations. Safety in pregnancy, of other methods of administration, not established. Discuss with your physician.

Breast-feeding
▼ No evidence of risk with eye or ear preparations. Taken by mouth, the drug passes into the breast milk and may increase the risk of blood disorders in the baby. Discuss with your physician.

Infants and children
▼ Rarely used in infants and children, and then only under medical supervision.

Over 60
▼ No problems expected.

Driving and hazardous work
▼ No known problems.

Alcohol
▼ No known problems.

POSSIBLE ADVERSE EFFECTS

Transient irritation may occur with eye or ear drops. Sore throat, fever, and unusual tiredness with any form of chloramphenicol may be signs of blood abnormalities and should be reported to your physician without delay, even if treatment has been stopped.

Symptom/effect	Frequency		Discuss with physician		Stop taking drug now	Call physician now
	Common	Rare	Only if severe	In all cases		
Burning/stinging (drops)		●	■			
Nausea/vomiting/diarrhea		●	■			
Numb/tingling hands/feet		●		■		
Rash/itching		●		■		
Impaired vision		●		■	▲	▌
Sore throat		●		■	▲	▌
Fever/weakness		●		■	▲	▌
Painful mouth/tongue		●		■	▲	▌

PROLONGED USE

Rarely, prolonged or repeated use may increase the risk of serious blood disorders. Prolonged or repeated use of eye drops may make the drug less effective at treating eye infections.

Monitoring Patients given the drug by mouth or injection may have periodic blood cell counts and eye tests. In the rare cases when chloramphenicol is given to infants by mouth or injection, blood levels of the drug are usually monitored.

INTERACTIONS

General note Chloramphenicol may increase the effect of certain other drugs, including phenytoin, oral anticoagulants, and oral antidiabetics. Phenobarbital or rifampin may reduce the effect of chloramphenicol.

Antidiabetic drugs Chloramphenicol may increase the effect of antidiabetic drugs.

Cyclosporine, tacrolimus, and sirolimus
The blood levels of these drugs may rise if given at the same time as chloramphenicol capsules or injection.

CHLOROQUINE

Product name Teva-Chloroquine
Used in the following combined preparations None

GENERAL INFORMATION

Chloroquine is used for the prevention and treatment of malaria. It usually clears an attack in three days. Injections may be given for a severe attack. To prevent malaria, a low dose is given once weekly, starting one week before visiting a high-risk area and continuing through four weeks after leaving. Chloroquine is not suitable for use in all parts of the world as resistance to the drug has developed in some areas. Other uses are in the treatment of amebiasis (a parasitic disease) and autoimmune diseases, such as rheumatoid arthritis.

Common *side effects* include nausea, headache, diarrhea, and abdominal cramps. Occasionally a rash develops. Chloroquine can damage the retina during prolonged treatment, causing blurred vision that may progress to blindness. Regular eye examinations are performed to detect early changes.

QUICK REFERENCE

Drug group Antimalarial drugs (p.123) and antirheumatic drugs (p.103)

Overdose danger rating High

Dependence rating Low

Prescription needed Yes

Available as generic Yes

INFORMATION FOR USERS

Your drug prescription is tailored for you. Do not alter dosage without checking with your physician.

How taken

Tablets.

Frequency and timing of doses
By mouth 1 x weekly (prevention of malaria); 1–4 x daily (treatment of malaria).

Usual adult dosage range
Prevention of malaria 300mg (2 tablets) as a single dose on the same day each week. Start 1–2 weeks before entering endemic area, and continue for 4 weeks after leaving.
Treatment of malaria Initial dose 600mg (4 tablets) and following doses 300mg.
Rheumatoid arthritis 250mg (1 tablet) per day.

Onset of effect
2–3 days. In rheumatoid arthritis, full effect may not be felt for up to 6 months.

Duration of action
Up to 1 week.

Diet advice
None.

Storage
Keep in a closed container in a cool, dry, place out of the reach of children. Protect from light.

Missed dose
Take as soon as you remember but if your next dose is due within 24 hours (1 x weekly schedule), or 6 hours (1–2 x daily schedule), take a single dose now and skip the next.

Stopping the drug
Do not stop the drug without consulting your physician.

OVERDOSE ACTION

Seek immediate medical advice in all cases. Take emergency action if breathing difficulties, seizures, or loss of consciousness occur.

See Drug poisoning emergency guide (p.526).

POSSIBLE ADVERSE EFFECTS

Side effects such as nausea, diarrhea, and abdominal pain might be avoided by taking the drug with food. Changes in vision should be reported promptly.

Symptom/effect	Frequency		Discuss with physician		Stop taking drug now	Call physician now
	Common	Rare	Only if severe	In all cases		
Nausea	●		■			
Diarrhea/abdominal pain	●		■			
Headache/dizziness		●		■		
Hearing disorders		●		■		
Hair loss/depigmentation		●		■		
Rash/swollen lips or tongue		●		■	▲	▌
Blurred vision		●		■	▲	▌

INTERACTIONS

Antiepileptic drugs Chloroquine may reduce the effect of these drugs.

Amiodarone Chloroquine may increase the risk of abnormal heart rhythms if taken with this drug.

Digoxin The level of digoxin in the blood may be increased by chloroquine.

Cyclosporine Chloroquine increases the blood level of cyclosporine.

SPECIAL PRECAUTIONS

Be sure to tell your physician if:
▼ You have liver or kidney problems.
▼ You have glucose-6-phosphate dehydrogenase (G6PD) deficiency.
▼ You have eye or vision problems.
▼ You have psoriasis.
▼ You have a history of epilepsy.
▼ You suffer from porphyria.
▼ You are taking other medications.

Pregnancy
▼ No evidence of risk with low doses. High doses may affect the baby. Discuss with your physician.

Breast-feeding
▼ The drug may pass into breast milk in small amounts. At normal doses effects on the baby are unlikely. Discuss with your physician.

Infants and children
▼ Reduced dose necessary.

Over 60
▼ No special problems, except that it may be difficult to tell between changes in eyesight due to aging, and those that are drug-induced.

Driving and hazardous work
▼ Avoid such activities until you have learned how chloroquine affects you because the drug may cause dizziness.

Alcohol
▼ Keep consumption low.

PROLONGED USE

Prolonged use may cause eye damage and blood disorders.

Monitoring Periodic eye tests and blood counts must be carried out.

CHLORPHENIRAMINE

Product name Chlor-Tripolon
Used in the following combined preparations Dristan, Sinutab with Codeine, Tylenol Cold, and others

GENERAL INFORMATION

Chlorpheniramine has been used for over 30 years to treat allergies such as hay fever, allergic conjunctivitis, urticaria (hives), insect bites and stings, and angioedema (allergic swellings). It is included in several over-the-counter cold remedies (see p.80).

Like other antihistamines, it relieves allergic skin symptoms such as itching, swelling, and redness. It also reduces sneezing and the runny nose and itching eyes of hay fever. Chlorpheniramine also has a mild *anticholinergic* action, which suppresses mucus secretion.

Chlorpheniramine may also be used to prevent or treat *allergic reactions* to blood transfusions or X-ray contrast material.

QUICK REFERENCE

Drug group Antihistamines (p.110)
Overdose danger rating Medium
Dependence rating Low
Prescription needed No
Available as generic Yes

INFORMATION FOR USERS

Follow instructions on the label. Call your physician if symptoms worsen.

How taken

Tablets, liquid.

Frequency and timing of doses
4–6 x daily (tablets, liquid); 2 x daily (extended release tablets).

Usual dosage range
Adults 12–24mg daily.
Children Reduced dose according to age and weight.

Onset of effect
Within 60 minutes.

Duration of action
4–6 hours (tablets, liquid).

Diet advice
None.

Storage
Keep in a closed container in a cool, dry place out of the reach of children.

Missed dose
Take as soon as you remember. If your next dose is due within 2 hours, take a single dose now and skip the next.

Stopping the drug
Can be safely stopped as soon as you no longer need it.

Exceeding the dose
An occasional unintentional extra dose is unlikely to cause problems. Large overdoses may cause drowsiness, agitation, seizures, or heart problems. Notify your physician.

SPECIAL PRECAUTIONS

Be sure to consult your physician or pharmacist before taking this drug if:
▼ You have a long-term liver problem.
▼ You have had epileptic fits.
▼ You have glaucoma.
▼ You have urinary difficulties.
▼ You are taking other medications.

Pregnancy
▼ Safety in pregnancy not established. Discuss with your physician.

Breast-feeding
▼ The drug passes into the breast milk, but at normal doses adverse effects on the baby are unlikely. Discuss with your physician.

Infants and children
▼ Reduced dose necessary.

Over 60
▼ Reduced dose may be necessary. Increased likelihood of adverse effects.

Driving and hazardous work
▼ Avoid such activities until you have learned how chlorpheniramine affects you because the drug can cause drowsiness, dizziness, and blurred vision.

Alcohol
▼ Avoid. Alcohol may increase the *sedative* effects of this drug.

POSSIBLE ADVERSE EFFECTS

Drowsiness is the most common *adverse effect* of chlorpheniramine; other *side effects* are rare. Some of these, such as dryness of the mouth, blurred vision, and difficulty passing urine, are due to its *anticholinergic* effects. Gastrointestinal irritation may be reduced by taking the tablets or liquid with food or drink.

Symptom/effect	Frequency		Discuss with physician		Stop taking drug now	Call physician now
	Common	Rare	Only if severe	In all cases		
Drowsiness/dizziness	●		■			
Digestive disturbances		●	■			
Difficulty in passing urine		●	■			
Dry mouth		●	■			
Blurred vision		●		■		
Excitation (children)		●		■	▲	
Rash		●		■	▲	

PROLONGED USE

No problems expected.

INTERACTIONS

Anticholinergic drugs All drugs, including some drugs for *parkinsonism*, that have an anticholinergic effect are likely to increase the anticholinergic effect of chlorpheniramine.

Monoamine oxidase inhibitors (MAOIs) and tricyclic antidepressants These drugs may increase the side effects of chlorpheniramine.

Allergy tests Antihistamines should be discontinued approximately 2–4 days before allergy skin testing.

Sedatives All drugs with a *sedative* effect are likely to increase the sedative properties of chlorpheniramine.

Phenytoin The effects of phenytoin may be enhanced by chlorpheniramine.

CHOLESTYRAMINE

Product names Olestyr, PMS-Cholestyramine
Used in the following combined preparations None

GENERAL INFORMATION

Cholestyramine is a resin that binds bile acids in the intestine, preventing their reabsorption. Cholesterol in the body is normally converted to bile acids. Therefore, cholestyramine reduces cholesterol levels in the blood. This action on bile acids makes bowel movements bulkier, creating an antidiarrheal effect. Cholestyramine is used to treat hyperlipidemia (high levels of cholesterol in the blood) in people who have not responded to dietary changes. In liver disorders, such as primary biliary

cirrhosis, bile salts sometimes accumulate in the bloodstream, and cholestyramine may be prescribed to alleviate any accompanying itching.

Taken in large doses, cholestyramine often causes bloating, mild nausea, and constipation. It may also interfere with the body's ability to absorb fat and certain fat-soluble vitamins, causing pale, bulky, foul-smelling feces.

QUICK REFERENCE

Drug group Lipid-lowering drugs (p.89)

Overdose danger rating Low

Dependence rating Low

Prescription needed Yes

Available as generic Yes

INFORMATION FOR USERS

Your drug prescription is tailored for you. Do not alter dosage without checking with your physician.

How taken

Powder mixed with water, juice, or apple sauce.

Frequency and timing of doses
1–4 x daily before meals and at bedtime.

Usual dosage range
4–24g daily.

Onset of effect
May take several weeks to achieve full beneficial effects.

Duration of action
12–24 hours.

Diet advice
A low-fat, low-calorie diet may be advised for patients who are overweight. Use of this drug may deplete levels of certain vitamins. Supplements may be advised.

Storage
Keep in a closed container in a cool, dry place out of the reach of children.

Missed dose
Take as soon as you remember.

Stopping the drug
Do not stop taking the drug without consulting your physician.

Exceeding the dose
An occasional unintentional extra dose is unlikely to cause problems. But if you notice any unusual symptoms, or if a large overdose has been taken, notify your physician.

POSSIBLE ADVERSE EFFECTS

Adverse effects are more likely if large doses are taken by people over 60. Minor side effects such as indigestion and abdominal discomfort are rarely a cause for concern. More serious adverse effects are usually the result of vitamin deficiency.

Symptom/effect	Frequency		Discuss with physician		Stop taking drug now	Call physician now
	Common	Rare	Only if severe	In all cases		
Indigestion	●		■			
Abdominal discomfort	●		■			
Nausea/vomiting	●		■			
Constipation	●		■			
Bruising/increased bleeding		●		■		
Diarrhea (high doses)		●	■			

INTERACTIONS

General note Cholestyramine reduces the body's ability to absorb other drugs. If you are taking other medicines, you should tell either your physician or pharmacist so that they can discuss with you the best way to

take all your drugs. To avoid any problems, take other drugs at least 1 hour before, or 4–6 hours after, cholestyramine. The dosage of other drugs you take may need to be adjusted.

SPECIAL PRECAUTIONS

Be sure to tell your physician if:
▼ You have jaundice.
▼ You have a peptic ulcer.
▼ You suffer from hemorrhoids.
▼ You are taking other medications.

Pregnancy
▼ Safety in pregnancy not established. Discuss with your physician.

Breast feeding
▼ Safety not established. The drug binds fat-soluble vitamins long-term and may cause vitamin deficiency in the baby. Discuss with your physician.

Infants and children
▼ Not recommended under 6 years. Reduced dose necessary in older children.

Over 60
▼ Increased likelihood of adverse effects.

Driving and hazardous work
▼ No special problems.

Alcohol
▼ Although this drug does not interact with alcohol, your underlying condition may make it inadvisable to take alcohol.

PROLONGED USE

As this drug reduces vitamin absorption, supplements of vitamins A, D, and K and folic acid may be advised.

Monitoring Periodic blood checks are usually required to monitor the level of cholesterol in the blood.

CIMETIDINE

Product names Nu-Cimet, Teva-Cimetidine
Used in the following combined preparations None

GENERAL INFORMATION

Cimetidine reduces the secretion of gastric acid and of pepsin (an *enzyme* that helps in the digestion of protein) and thereby promotes healing of ulcers in the stomach and duodenum (see p.95). It is also used for reflux esophagitis, in which acid stomach contents may flow up the esophagus. Treatment is usually given in four- to eight-week courses, with further short courses if symptoms recur. Cimetidine also affects the actions of certain enzymes in the liver, where many drugs are broken down. It is

therefore prescribed with caution to people who are receiving other drugs, particularly drugs whose levels need to be carefully controlled. Since cimetidine promotes healing of the stomach lining, it may mask the symptoms of stomach cancer and delay diagnosis. It is therefore prescribed with caution to patients whose symptoms change or persist, and in middle-aged and older people.

INFORMATION FOR USERS

Follow instructions on the label. Call your physician if symptoms worsen.

How taken

Tablets, liquid.

Frequency and timing of doses
1–4 x daily (after meals and at bedtime).

Usual adult dosage range
800–1,600mg daily.

Onset of effect
Within 90 minutes.

Duration of action
2–6 hours.

Diet advice
None.

Storage
Keep in a closed container in a cool, dry place away from the reach of children. Protect from light.

Missed dose
Do not take the missed dose. Take your next dose as usual.

Stopping the drug
If prescribed by your physician, do not stop taking the drug without consulting him or her because symptoms may recur.

Exceeding the dose
An occasional unintentional extra dose is unlikely to be a cause for concern. But if you notice any unusual symptoms, or if a large overdose has been taken, notify your physician.

SPECIAL PRECAUTIONS

Be sure to consult your physician or pharmacist before taking this drug if:
▼ You have long-term liver or kidney problems.
▼ You are taking other medications.

 Pregnancy
▼ Safety in pregnancy not established. Discuss with your physician.

 Breast-feeding
▼ The drug passes into the breast milk, but at normal doses adverse effects on the baby are unlikely. Discuss with your physician.

 Infants and children
▼ Reduced dose necessary.

 Over 60
▼ Risk of stomach cancer is higher in the elderly and it must be excluded before cimetidine is prescribed. The drug is also more likely to cause confusion and depression in the elderly.

 Driving and hazardous work
▼ Avoid such activities until you have learned how cimetidine affects you because the drug may cause dizziness and confusion.

 Alcohol
▼ Avoid. Alcohol may aggravate the underlying condition and counter the beneficial effects of cimetidine.

POSSIBLE ADVERSE EFFECTS

Adverse effects of cimetidine are uncommon. They are usually related to dosage level and almost always disappear when the drug is stopped.

Symptom/effect	Frequency		Discuss with physician		Stop taking drug now	Call physician now
	Common	Rare	Only if severe	In all cases		
Diarrhea	●		■			
Dizziness/confusion/tiredness	●			■		
Muscle/joint pain		●		■		
Breast enlargement (men)		●		■		
Erectile dysfunction		●		■		
Confusion/hallucinations		●		■	▲	

INTERACTIONS

Benzodiazepines Cimetidine may increase the blood levels of some of these drugs, increasing the risk of adverse effects.

Theophylline/aminophylline Cimetidine may increase the blood levels of these drugs. Their dose may need to be reduced.

Sildenafil and oral contraceptives Cimetidine may increase the blood level of these drugs.

Beta blockers, antiarrhythmic drugs, anticonvulsants, cyclosporine, and tacrolimus Cimetidine may increase the blood levels of these drugs.

Anticoagulant drugs Cimetidine may increase their effect.

Ketoconazole Cimetidine may affect its absorption.

PROLONGED USE

Courses of longer than 8 weeks are not usually necessary.

CIPROFLOXACIN

Product names Apo-Ciproflox, Cipro, Cipro XL, Ciloxan, and others
Used in the following combined preparations Cipro HC

GENERAL INFORMATION

Ciprofloxacin, a quinolone antibacterial, is used to treat several types of bacteria. It is especially useful for some types of chest, skin, intestinal, and urinary tract infections.

When taken by mouth, ciprofloxacin is well absorbed by the body and works quickly and effectively. In more severe systemic bacterial infections the drug may need to be administered by injection.

The most common *side effect* is gastrointestinal disturbance. Occasionally it may cause tendon inflammation and damage (see advice for levofloxacin, p.332).

QUICK REFERENCE

Drug group Antibacterials (p.117)
Overdose danger rating Medium
Dependence rating Low
Prescription needed Yes
Available as generic Yes

INFORMATION FOR USERS

Your drug prescription is tailored for you. Do not alter dosage without checking with your physician.

How taken

Tablets, liquid, injection, eye ointment and drops, ear drops.

Frequency and timing of doses
2 x daily with plenty of fluids.

Usual adult dosage range
500mg–1.5g daily (tablets); 400mg–1.2g daily (injection).

Onset of effect
The drug begins to work within a few hours, although full beneficial effect may not be felt for several days.

Duration of action
About 12 hours.

Diet advice
Do not get dehydrated; ensure that you drink fluids regularly.

Storage
Keep in a closed container in a cool, dry place out of the reach of children. The injection must be protected from light.

Missed dose
Take as soon as you remember, and take your next dose as usual.

Stopping the drug
Take the full course. Even if you feel better the original infection may still be present, and symptoms may recur if treatment is stopped too soon.

Exceeding the dose
An occasional unintentional extra dose is unlikely to cause problems. Large overdoses may cause mental disturbance and fits. Notify your physician.

SPECIAL PRECAUTIONS

Be sure to tell your physician if:
▼ You have long-term liver or kidney problems.
▼ You have had epileptic seizures.
▼ You have glucose-6-phosphate dehydrogenase (G6PD) deficiency.
▼ You have a history of myasthenia gravis or muscle weakness.
▼ You are taking other medications.

Pregnancy
▼ Safety in pregnancy not established. Discuss with your physician.

Breast-feeding
▼ The drug passes into the breast milk and may affect the baby adversely. Discuss with your physician.

Infants and children
▼ Not usually recommended.

Over 60
▼ Reduced dose necessary. Tendon damage is more likely over the age of 60.

Driving and hazardous work
▼ Avoid such activities until you have learned how ciprofloxacin affects you because the drug can cause dizziness.

Alcohol
▼ Avoid. Alcohol may increase the sedative effects of this drug.

Sunlight
▼ Avoid excessive exposure.

POSSIBLE ADVERSE EFFECTS

Ciprofloxacin commonly causes nausea and vomiting; other side effects are less common, except when very high doses are given. Painful and inflamed tendons should be reported to your physician at once, treatment should be discontinued, and the affected limbs rested.

Symptom/effect	Frequency		Discuss with physician		Stop taking drug now	Call physician now
	Common	Rare	Only if severe	In all cases		
Nausea/vomiting	●		■			
Abdominal pain/diarrhea	●		■			
Rash/itching	●			■		
Dizziness/headache		●	■			
Joint pain		●	■			
Sleep disturbance		●	■			
Photosensitivity		●		■		
Jaundice		●		■		
Confusion/convulsions		●		■	▲	ǀ
Painful, inflamed tendons		●		■	▲	ǀ

PROLONGED USE

Ciprofloxacin is not usually prescribed for long-term use.

INTERACTIONS

Oral iron preparations and antacids containing magnesium or aluminum hydroxide interfere with absorption of ciprofloxacin. Do not take antacids within 2 hours of taking ciprofloxacin tablets.

Anticoagulants and oral antidiabetics Blood levels of these drugs may be increased; their dosage may need adjusting.

Theophylline Ciprofloxacin may increase blood levels of this drug; its dose may need adjusting and its blood levels monitored.

Phenytoin Ciprofloxacin may increase the blood levels of this drug.

Non-steroidal anti-inflammatory drugs increase the risk of epileptic seizures.

CISPLATIN

Product name None
Used in the following combined preparations None

GENERAL INFORMATION

Cisplatin is one of the most effective drugs available to treat a wide variety of cancers including those of the ovaries, testes, head, neck, bladder, cervix, and lung. It is also used in treating certain children's cancers and some cancers of the blood. It is usually given along with other anticancer drugs.

The most common and serious *adverse effect* of cisplatin is impaired kidney function. To reduce the risk of permanent kidney damage, the drug is usually given only once every three weeks, and plenty of fluid must be taken to minimize the effect of the drug in the kidneys. Nausea and vomiting may occur after administration of cisplatin. These symptoms usually start within an hour and last for up to 24 hours, in some cases persisting for up to a week. Because they may be quite severe, anti-emetic drugs are given.

Damage to hearing is common and may be more severe in children, and it may appear only after treatment has stopped. Use of cisplatin may also increase the risk of anemia, blood clotting disorders, and infection during treatment.

QUICK REFERENCE

Drug group Anticancer drugs (p.140)
Overdose danger rating High
Dependence rating Low
Prescription needed Yes
Available as generic Yes

INFORMATION FOR USERS

This drug is given only under medical supervision and is not for self-administration.

How taken

Injection.

Frequency and timing of doses
Every 3 weeks for up to 5 days; it may be given alone or in combination with other anticancer drugs.

Usual adult dosage range
Dosage is determined individually according to body height, weight, and response.

Onset of effect
Some adverse effects, such as nausea and vomiting, may appear within 1 hour of starting treatment.

Duration of action
Some adverse effects may last for up to 1 week after treatment has stopped.

Diet advice
Prior to treatment it is important that the body is well hydrated. Therefore, 1–2 litres of fluid are usually given by infusion over 8–12 hours.

Storage
Not applicable. The drug is not normally kept in the home.

Missed dose
Not applicable. The drug is given only in hospital under medical supervision.

Stopping the drug
Not applicable. The drug will be stopped under medical supervision.

Exceeding the dose
Overdosage is unlikely since treatment is carefully monitored, and the drug is given intravenously only under close supervision.

POSSIBLE ADVERSE EFFECTS

Most adverse effects appear within a few hours of injection and are carefully monitored in hospital after each dose. Some effects wear off within 24 hours. Nausea and loss of appetite may last for up to a week.

Symptom/effect	Frequency		Discuss with physician		Stop taking drug now	Call physician now
	Common	Rare	Only if severe	In all cases		
Loss of appetite/taste	●		■			
Nausea/vomiting	●			■		
Ringing in the ears/hearing loss	●			■		
Breathing difficulties		●		■		▮
Abnormal sensations		●		■		▮
Swollen face/rash		●		■		▮
Reduced urine output		●		■	▲	▮

INTERACTIONS

General note A number of drugs (e.g., antibacterials such as gentamicin) increase the adverse effects of cisplatin. Because cisplatin is given only under close medical supervision, these interactions are carefully monitored and the dosage is adjusted accordingly.

SPECIAL PRECAUTIONS

Cisplatin is prescribed only under close medical supervision, taking account of your present condition and your medical history. However, be sure to tell your physician if:
▼ You have impaired kidney function.

Pregnancy
▼ Not usually prescribed. Cisplatin may cause birth defects or premature birth. Discuss with your physician.

Breast-feeding
▼ Not advised. The drug passes into the breast milk and may affect the baby adversely. Discuss with your physician.

Infants and children
▼ The risk of hearing loss is increased. Reduced dose used.

Over 60
▼ Reduced dose may be necessary. Increased likelihood of adverse effects.

Driving and hazardous work
▼ No known problems.

Alcohol
▼ No known problems.

PROLONGED USE

There is an increased risk of long–term damage to the kidneys, nerves, and bone marrow, and to hearing. The drug may also reduce fertility and increase the risk of further cancers later in life.

Monitoring Hearing tests and blood checks to monitor kidney function and bone marrow activity are carried out regularly.

CITALOPRAM

Products names Apo-Citalopram, Celexa, Citaopram–Odan, CO Citalopram, CTP 30
Used in the following combined preparations None

GENERAL INFORMATION

Citalopram is a member of the selective serotonin re-uptake inhibitor (SSRI) group of antidepressant drugs. It is used for depressive illness and panic disorder. Citalopram gradually improves the patient's mood, increases energy levels, and restores interest in everyday pursuits.

Citalopram is generally well tolerated, and any gastrointestinal *adverse effects*, such as nausea, vomiting, or diarrhea,

are dose related and usually diminish with continued use of the drug.

Like other SSRIs, citalopram causes fewer *anticholinergic side effects* and is less sedating than the tricyclic antidepressants. It is also less likely to be harmful if taken in overdose. It can, however, cause drowsiness and impair performance of tasks such as driving.

QUICK REFERENCE

Drug group Antidepressant drugs (p.68)

Overdose danger rating Medium

Dependence rating Low

Prescription needed Yes

Available as generic Yes

INFORMATION FOR USERS

Your drug prescription is tailored for you. Do not alter dosage without checking with your physician.

How taken

Tablets.

Frequency and timing of doses
Once daily in the morning or evening.

Usual adult dosage range
Depressive illness 20–40mg.
Panic attacks 10mg (starting dose); 20–30mg (usual range).

Onset of effect
Full benefits may not be felt for 2–4 weeks.

Duration of action
Antidepressant effect may persist for some

weeks following prolonged treatment.

Diet advice
None.

Storage
Keep in a closed container in a cool, dry place out of the reach of children.

Missed dose
Take as soon as you remember. If your next dose is due within 8 hours, take a single dose now and skip the next.

Stopping the drug
Do not stop taking the drug without consulting your physician. Stopping abruptly can cause withdrawal symptoms.

Exceeding the dose
An occasional unintentional extra dose is unlikely to be a cause for concern. If you notice any unusual symptoms, or if a large overdose has been taken, notify your physician.

SPECIAL PRECAUTIONS

Be sure to tell your physician if:
▼ You have epilepsy.
▼ You have liver or kidney problems.
▼ You have had a manic-depressive illness.
▼ You have had heart problems, specifically any rhythm problems.
▼ You have a history of low potassium or magnesium.
▼ You have been taking monoamine oxidase inhibitors (MAOIs) or other antidepressants.
▼ You are taking other medications.

 Pregnancy
▼ Safety in pregnancy not established. Discuss with your physician.

 Breast-feeding
▼ The drug may pass into breast milk and may affect the baby. Discuss with your physician.

 Infants and children
▼ Not generally recommended under 18 years.

 Over 60
▼ Reduced dose necessary. 20mg maximum dose if 65 years or older.

 Driving and hazardous work
▼ Avoid such activities until you have learned how citalopram affects you because the drug can cause drowsiness.

 Alcohol
▼ Avoid. Alcohol may enhance some of citalopram's side effects.

POSSIBLE ADVERSE EFFECTS

Common adverse effects such as nausea, indigestion, and diarrhea usually diminish with

reduction in dosage. If convulsions or a rash occur, consult your physician immediately.

Symptom/effect	Frequency		Discuss with physician		Stop taking drug now	Call physician now
	Common	Rare	Only if severe	In all cases		
Nausea/indigestion	●		■			
Dry mouth/sweating	●		■			
Diarrhea/constipation	●		■			
Anxiety/insomnia	●		■			
Headache/tremor	●		■			
Dizziness/drowsiness	●		■			
Sexual dysfunction	●		■			
Abnormal dreaming/sleep disorder		●		■		
Suicidal thoughts/attempts		●		■	▲	■

INTERACTIONS

General note Any drug that affects the breakdown of others in the liver may alter blood levels of citalopram, and vice versa.

Cimetidine, ketoconazole, lansoprazole, and others may decrease the breakdown of citalopram.

Sumatriptan and other 5HT1 agonists, lithium, and tramadol There is an

increased risk of adverse effects when citalopram is taken with these drugs.

Monoamine oxidase inhibitors (MAOIs) These drugs may cause a severe reaction if they are taken with citalopram. Avoid taking citalopram if MAOIs have been taken in the last 14 days.

Anticoagulants The effect of these drugs may be increased by citalopram.

PROLONGED USE

No problems expected in adults. However, mild *withdrawal symptoms* may occur if the drug is not stopped gradually. There is also a small risk of suicidal thoughts and self-harm in children and adolescents.

Monitoring Monitor for effectiveness. Any person experiencing drowsiness, confusion, muscle cramps, or seizures should be monitored for low sodium levels in the blood.

CLARITHROMYCIN

Product names Biaxin, Biaxin BID, Biaxin XL, and others
Used in the following combined preparations Hp-PAC, Losec 1-2-3 A, and others

GENERAL INFORMATION

Clarithromycin is a macrolide *antibiotic* similar to erythromycin (p.279) from which it is derived. It has similar actions and uses to erythromycin, but is slightly more active in certain situations. It is used for upper respiratory tract infections, such as middle ear infections, sinusitis, and pharyngitis, and lower respiratory tract infections, including whooping cough, bronchitis, and pneumonia, as well as for skin and soft tissue infections. Given with anti-ulcer drugs (p.95) and other antibiotics, clarithromycin is used to eradicate *Helicobacter pylori*, the bacterium that causes many peptic ulcers.

Prolonged use of clarithromycin is not usually necessary.

QUICK REFERENCE

Drug group Antibiotics (p.114)
Overdose danger rating Low
Dependence rating Low
Prescription needed Yes
Available as generic Yes

INFORMATION FOR USERS

Your drug prescription is tailored for you. Do not alter dosage without checking with your physician.

How taken

Tablets, liquid, extended release tablets.

Frequency and timing of doses
1–2x daily, up to 14 days.

Usual adult dosage range
500mg–1g daily.

Onset of effect
1–4 hours.

Duration of action
1–12 hours.

Diet advice
None.

Storage
Keep in a closed container in a cool, dry place out of the reach of children. Protect from light.

Missed dose
Take as soon as you remember. If your next dose is due within 2 hours, take a single dose now and skip the next.

Stopping the drug
Take the full course. Even if you feel better, the infection may still be present and symptoms may recur if treatment is stopped too soon.

Exceeding the dose
An occasional unintentional extra dose is unlikely to be a cause for concern. But if you notice any unusual symptoms, or if a large overdose has been taken, notify your physician.

SPECIAL PRECAUTIONS

Be sure to tell your physician if:
▼ You have liver or kidney problems.
▼ You have had an allergic reaction to erythromycin or clarithromycin.
▼ You have a heart problem.
▼ You have myasthenia gravis.
▼ You have porphyria.
▼ You are taking other medications.

Pregnancy
▼ Safety has not been established. Discuss with your physician.

Breast-feeding
▼ Clarithromycin passes into the breast milk and may affect the baby. Discuss with your physician.

Infants and children
▼ Reduced dose necessary.

Over 60
▼ No special problems.

Driving and hazardous work
▼ No known problems.

Alcohol
▼ No known problems.

POSSIBLE ADVERSE EFFECTS

Clarithromycin is generally well tolerated. Gastrointestinal disturbances are the most common problems encountered. Hearing loss is a rare possibility, but it is usually reversible on stopping the drug.

Symptom/effect	Frequency		Discuss with physician		Stop taking drug now	Call physician now
	Common	Rare	Only if severe	In all cases		
Nausea/vomiting/diarrhea	●		■			
Indigestion	●		■			
Headache	●		■			
Joint/muscle pain		●	■			
Rash	●			■		
Altered sense of taste/smell	●			■		
Anxiety/insomnia		●		■		
Confusion/hallucinations		●		■	▲	▮
Jaundice		●		■	▲	

PROLONGED USE

In courses of over 14 days, there is a risk of developing antibiotic-resistant infections.

INTERACTIONS

General note Clarithromycin interacts with many drugs, of which only some are listed here.

Digoxin, warfarin, triazolam, midazolam, disopyramide, rifabutin, phenytoin, cyclosporine, tacrolimus, carbamazepine, and theophylline Blood levels and effects of these drugs are increased by clarithromycin.

Zidovudine Blood levels are reduced if this drug is taken at the same time as clarithromycin.

Ergot derivatives There is an increased risk of ergot toxicity if these drugs are taken with clarithromycin.

Pimozide may cause cardiac arrhythmias if taken with clarithromycin.

Lipid-lowering drugs whose names end in 'statin' If these drugs are taken with clarithromycin, there is a risk of rhabdomyolysis (muscle damage).

CLINDAMYCIN

Product names Apo-Clindamycin, Clindasol, Clinda-T, Clindets, Dalacin C, Teva-Clindamycin
Used in the following combined preparations Benzaclin topical gel, Biacna, Clindoxyl gel

GENERAL INFORMATION

Clindamycin is an *antibiotic* that is prescribed for a variety of infections. It is used to treat infections of the skin, the respiratory tract, vagina, and abdomen. It may also be used prior to certain surgical procedures. It is also available as a *topical* product, which is prescribed for acne. When taken by mouth, clindamycin is usually given every 6–8 hours. It should be taken with a full glass of water. Diarrhea can sometimes occur. If significant diarrhea occurs, the physician should be called. More serious *C. difficile*-associated diarrhea may occur even several weeks after antibiotic use; this requires immediate follow-up with your physician.

A vaginal cream is also available to treat bacterial infection; this is usually used intravaginally for 7 nights.

QUICK REFERENCE

Drug group Antibiotics (p.116)
Overdose danger rating Low
Dependence rating Low
Prescription needed Yes
Available as generic Yes

INFORMATION FOR USERS

Your drug prescription is tailored for you. Do not alter dosage without checking with your physician.

How taken

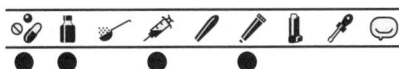

Capsules, oral solution, parenteral injection (IM, IV), topical gel, topical cream, topical pad, topical solution, vaginal cream.

Frequency and timing of doses
Orally: every 6–8 hours; topically: usually twice daily.

Usual adult dosage range
Oral dose: 600–1800mg daily; maximum 1800mg daily.

Onset of effect
Within 48 hours; for acne, may take several weeks to see effect.

Duration of action
6–8 hours for oral/IV doses.

Diet advice
None

Storage
Keep in a closed container in a cool, dry place out of the reach of children. Reconstituted oral solution should not be refrigerated and is kept at room temperature for 14 days. Discard any unused medication; talk to your *pharmacist* about proper disposal.

Missed dose
If you miss a dose, take it as soon as you remember. If it is near the time of the next dose, skip the missed dose and resume your usual dosing schedule. Do not double up to catch up on a missed dose.

Stopping the drug
Do not stop the drug without consulting your physician. Stopping the drug may lead to worsening of the underlying condition.

Exceeding the dose
An occasional unintentional extra dose is unlikely to cause problems. With large overdoses, seek help right away and notify your physician.

SPECIAL PRECAUTIONS

Be sure to tell your physician if:
▼ You are allergic to any antibiotics or tartrazine (a yellow dye used in foods).
▼ You have kidney disease.
▼ You have gastrointestinal disease.
▼ You have liver problems.
▼ You are taking other medications.

Pregnancy
▼ Safety in pregnancy not established. Discuss with your physician.

Breast-feeding
▼ Safety not established. Discuss with your physician.

Infants and children
▼ Not recommended.

Over 60
▼ When diarrhea occurs, requires more close monitoring and follow-up.

Driving and hazardous work
▼ No special problems.

Alcohol
▼ No known problems.

PROLONGED USE

Clindamycin, when used by injection, orally, or vaginally, is usually given only for short courses of treatment. When used topically, continued use should be regularly reassessed.

POSSIBLE ADVERSE EFFECTS

Clindamycin is usually well tolerated. Some may experience an upset stomach.

Symptom/effect	Frequency		Discuss with physician		Stop taking drug now	Call physician now
	Common	Rare	Only if severe	In all cases		
When used orally/ by injection						
Diarrhea	●			■		
Vomiting	●		■			
Upset stomach	●		■			
Skin rash		●		■	▲	■
Jaundice		●		■	▲	
When used topically or vaginally						
Redness/irritation	●		■			
Burning	●		■			

INTERACTIONS

Kaolin (e.g. in Kaopectate) may decrease absorption of clindamycin.

CLOBETASOL

Product names Clobex Lotion, Clobex Shampoo, Dermovate, and others
Used in the following combined preparations None

GENERAL INFORMATION

Clobetasol is a corticosteroid drug (p.127) used for short-term treatment of severe skin conditions such as discoid lupus erythematosus, lichen planus and lichen simplex, eczema, and plaque-type psoriasis. It is one of the strongest *topical* corticosteroids and is generally used only when the disorder has not responded to treatment with another topical corticosteroid.

It is important to apply clobetasol thinly and sparingly to affected areas because it can be absorbed and cause *adverse effects* such as suppression of the pituitary and adrenal glands and Cushing's syndrome. Other *side effects* include irreversible changes to the structure of the skin in the areas that have been treated. Also, clobetasol, like all steroids, can exacerbate eczema infected with a virus such as herpes simplex.

Treatment with clobetasol must only be carried out with close medical supervision.

QUICK REFERENCE

Drug group Topical corticosteroids (p.162)

Overdose danger rating Low

Dependence rating Low

Prescription needed Yes

Available as generic Yes

INFORMATION FOR USERS

Your drug prescription is tailored for you. Do not alter dosage without checking with your physician.

How taken

Cream, ointment, solution, scalp application.

Frequency and timing of doses
1 x 2 times daily.

Usual dosage range
No more than 50g weekly.

Onset of effect
12 hours. Full beneficial effect after 48 hours.

Duration of action
Up to 24 hours.

Diet advice
None.

Storage
Keep in a closed container, in a cool, dry place out of the reach of children.

Missed dose
Use as soon as you remember. If your next application is due within 8 hours, apply the usual amount now and skip the next application.

Stopping the drug
Do not stop using the drug without consulting your physician; symptoms may recur.

Exceeding the dose
An occasional unintentional extra application is unlikely to cause problems. But if you notice any unusual symptoms, notify your physician.

SPECIAL PRECAUTIONS

Be sure to tell your physician if:
▼ You have a cold sore or chickenpox.
▼ You have any other infection.
▼ You have psoriasis.
▼ You have acne or rosacea.
▼ You are taking other medications.

Pregnancy
▼ Safety in pregnancy not established. Discuss with your physician.

Breast-feeding
▼ May be used if benefits outweigh the risks. Discuss with your physician.

Infants and children
▼Safety and effectiveness not established. Not recommended for infants under 1 year. Used only with great caution for short periods in older children because overuse can cause serious side effects.

Over 60
▼ Those over 60 may be more sensitive to adverse effects.

Driving and hazardous work
▼ No special problems.

Alcohol
▼ No special problems.

POSSIBLE ADVERSE EFFECTS

Most people who use clobetasol as directed do not have problems. Adverse effects mainly affect the skin. Some of these effects cannot be reversed.

Symptom/effect	Frequency		Discuss with physician		Stop taking drug now	Call physician now
	Common	Rare	Only if severe	In all cases		
Thinning of the skin	●			■		
Stretch marks	●			■		
Increased capillary size in skin	●			■		
Acne/dermatitis around mouth	●			■		
Loss of skin pigment	●		■			
Mood changes		●		■		
Weight gain		●		■		

INTERACTIONS

None.

PROLONGED USE

Clobetasol is usually used for 2 weeks only and in some cases up to 4 weeks. If the condition has not improved in 2 to 4 weeks, you should notify your physician.

CLOMIPHENE

Product names Clomid, Serophene
Used in the following combined preparations None

GENERAL INFORMATION

Clomiphene is used to treat female infertility due to failure of ovulation. It stimulates ovulation by increasing production of *hormones* by the hypothalamus and pituitary gland.

Tablets are taken within about five days of the onset of each menstrual cycle. If clomiphene does not stimulate ovulation after several months, other drugs may be prescribed.

Multiple pregnancies (usually twins) occur more commonly in women treated with clomiphene. *Adverse effects* include an increased risk of ovarian cysts and ectopic pregnancy. Ovarian hyperstimulation syndrome (overstimulation of the ovaries) has also been reported; symptoms include pain and swelling of the abdomen, swelling of the hands and legs, shortness of breath, weight gain, nausea, and vomiting. You should consult your physician if any of these symptoms develop.

INFORMATION FOR USERS

Your drug prescription is tailored for you. Do not alter dosage without checking with your physician.

How taken

Tablets.

Frequency and timing of doses
Once daily for 5 days during each menstrual cycle, preferably starting on day 2 of the cycle.

Dosage range
50mg daily initially; dose may be increased up to 100mg daily.

Onset of effect
Ovulation occurs 4–10 days after the last dose in any cycle. However, ovulation may not occur for several months.

Duration of action
5 days.

Diet advice
None.

Storage
Keep in a closed container in a cool, dry place away from the reach of children. Protect from light.

Missed dose
Take as soon as you remember. If your next dose is due at this time, take the missed dose and the next scheduled dose together.

Stopping the drug
Take as directed by your physician. Stopping the drug will reduce the chances of conception.

Exceeding the dose
An occasional unintentional extra dose is unlikely to be a cause for concern. But if you notice any unusual symptoms, or if a large overdose has been taken, notify your physician.

SPECIAL PRECAUTIONS

Be sure to tell your physician if:
▼ You have a long-term liver problem.
▼ You are pregnant.
▼ You have uterine fibroids or abnormal vaginal bleeding.
▼ You are taking other medications.

Pregnancy
▼ Not prescribed. The drug is stopped as soon as pregnancy occurs.

Breast-feeding
▼ Not prescribed.

Infants and children
▼ Not prescribed.

Over 60
▼ Not prescribed.

Driving and hazardous work
▼ Avoid such activities until you have learned how clomiphene affects you because the drug can cause blurred vision.

Alcohol
▼ Keep consumption low.

POSSIBLE ADVERSE EFFECTS

Most *side effects* are related to the dose taken. Ovarian enlargement and cyst formation can occur. If this happens the problem usually resolves within a few weeks of stopping the drug.

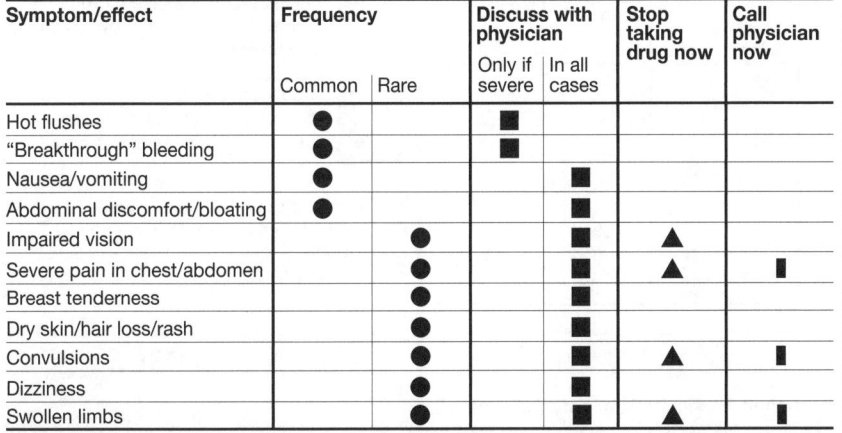

Symptom/effect	Frequency		Discuss with physician		Stop taking drug now	Call physician now
	Common	Rare	Only if severe	In all cases		
Hot flushes	●		■			
"Breakthrough" bleeding	●		■			
Nausea/vomiting	●			■		
Abdominal discomfort/bloating	●			■		
Impaired vision		●		■	▲	
Severe pain in chest/abdomen		●		■	▲	■
Breast tenderness		●		■		
Dry skin/hair loss/rash		●		■		
Convulsions		●		■	▲	■
Dizziness		●		■		
Swollen limbs		●		■	▲	■

INTERACTIONS

None.

PROLONGED USE

Prolonged use of clomiphene may cause visual impairment. Also, no more than 6 courses of treatment are recommended since this may lead to an increased risk of ovarian cancer.

Monitoring Eye tests may be recommended if symptoms of visual impairment are noticed. Monitoring of body temperature and blood or urine hormone levels or ultrasound scans of the ovaries are performed to detect signs of ovulation and pregnancy.

CLOMIPRAMINE

Product names Anafranil, Apo-Clomipramine, CO Clomipramine
Used in the following combined preparations None

GENERAL INFORMATION

Clomipramine belongs to the class of antidepressant drugs known as the tricyclics. It is used mainly in the long-term treatment of depression. It has a mild *sedative* effect, which can help with anxiety associated with depression.

Clomipramine is particularly useful in the treatment of obsessive compulsive disorders. In this case, the drug has to be taken for many weeks to achieve its full effect.

Clomipramine has the same *adverse effects* as other tricyclic drugs, such as drowsiness, dizziness, dry mouth, and constipation. In overdose, clomipramine may cause coma and dangerously abnormal heart rhythms.

INFORMATION FOR USERS

Your drug prescription is tailored for you. Do not alter dosage without checking with your physician.

How taken

Tablets.

Frequency and timing of doses
1–3 x daily.

Usual adult dosage range
10–250mg daily.

Onset of effect
Some effects may be felt within a few days, but full antidepressant effect may not be felt for up to 4 weeks. For phobic and obsessional disorders, full effect may take up to 12 weeks.

Duration of action
During prolonged treatment antidepressant effect may last up to 2 weeks.

Diet advice
None.

Storage
Keep in a closed container in a cool, dry place away from the reach of children.

Missed dose
Take as soon as you remember. If your next dose is due within 3 hours, take a single dose now and skip the next.

Stopping the drug
Stopping abruptly can cause withdrawal symptoms and a recurrence of the original trouble. Consult your physician, who may supervise a gradual reduction in dosage.

OVERDOSE ACTION

 Seek immediate medical advice in all cases. Take emergency action if palpitations are noted or consciousness is lost.

See Drug poisoning emergency guide (p.526).

SPECIAL PRECAUTIONS

Be sure to tell your physician if:
▼ You have heart problems.
▼ You have had epileptic seizures.
▼ You have long-term liver or kidney problems.
▼ You have had glaucoma.
▼ You have thyroid disease.
▼ You have had prostate trouble.
▼ You have had mania or a psychotic illness.
▼ You are taking other medications.

 Pregnancy
▼ No increased risk to the developing baby. Discuss with your physician.

 Breast-feeding
▼ The drug passes into the breast milk and may affect the baby. Discuss with your physician.

 Infants and children
▼ Not recommended.

 Over 60
▼ Increased likelihood of adverse effects. Reduced dose may therefore be necessary.

 Driving and hazardous work
▼ Avoid such activities until you have learned how clomipramine affects you because the drug may cause blurred vision, drowsiness, and dizziness.

 Alcohol
▼ Avoid. Alcohol may increase the sedative effects of this drug.

Surgery and general anesthetics
▼ Clomipramine treatment may need to be stopped before you have elective surgery. Discuss this with your physician.

POSSIBLE ADVERSE EFFECTS

The possible adverse effects of this drug are mainly the result of its *anticholinergic* action, and include drowsiness and dizziness, dry mouth, and constipation.

Symptom/effect	Frequency		Discuss with physician		Stop taking drug now	Call physician now
	Common	Rare	Only if severe	In all cases		
Drowsiness/dizziness	●		■			
Sweating/flushing	●		■			
Dry mouth	●		■			
Blurred vision	●			■		
Constipation	●		■			
Difficulty in passing urine		●		■	▲	
Palpitations		●		■	▲	▮
Skin reactions/rash		●		■		

INTERACTIONS

Sedatives All drugs that have a sedative effect may intensify those of clomipramine.

Antihypertensives Clomipramine may enhance the effect of some of these drugs.

Antiepiletics Clomipramine may reduce the effects of these drugs and vice versa.

Monoamine oxidase inhibitors (MAOIs) A serious reaction may occur if these drugs are given with clomipramine.

Quinidine There is an increased risk of abnormal heart rhythms if this drug is taken with clomipramine.

PROLONGED USE

No problems expected.

Monitoring Regular checks on heart and liver function are recommended.

CLONAZEPAM

Product names Apo-Clonazepam, Novo-Clonazepam, Rivotril, and others
Used in the following combined preparations None

GENERAL INFORMATION

Clonazepam belongs to a group of drugs known as the benzodiazepines, which are mainly used in the treatment of anxiety and insomnia (see p.67). However, clonazepam is used almost exclusively as an antiepileptic to prevent and treat epileptic seizures. It is particularly useful for the prevention of brief muscle spasms (myoclonus) and absence of seizures (petit mal) in children but other forms of epilepsy, such as sudden flaccidity or seizures induced by flashing lights, also respond to clonazepam treatment. Being a benzodiazepine, the drug also has tranquillizing and *sedative* effects.

Clonazepam is used either alone or together with other antiepileptic drugs. Its antiepileptic effect may begin to wear off after some months.

QUICK REFERENCE

Drug group Benzodiazepine antiepileptic drugs (p.70)

Overdose danger rating Medium

Dependence rating Medium

Prescription needed Yes

Available as generic Yes

INFORMATION FOR USERS

Your drug prescription is tailored for you. Do not alter dosage without checking with your physician.

How taken

Tablets, injection.

Frequency and timing of doses
1–3 x daily.

Usual dosage range
Adults 0.5mg daily at night (starting dose), increased gradually to 4–8mg daily (maintenance dose).
Children Reduced dose according to age and weight.

Onset of effect
1–4 hours.

Duration of action
24–48 hours.

Diet advice
None.

Storage
Keep in a closed container in a cool, dry place away from the reach of children.

Missed dose
No cause for concern, but take as soon as you remember. Take your next dose when it is due.

Stopping the drug
Do not stop the drug without consulting your physician because symptoms may recur.

Exceeding the dose
An occasional unintentional extra dose is unlikely to cause problems. Larger overdoses may cause excessive drowsiness and confusion. Notify your physician.

POSSIBLE ADVERSE EFFECTS

The principal *adverse effects* of this drug are related to its sedative and tranquillizing properties. These effects normally diminish after the first few days of treatment and can often be reduced by medically supervised adjustment of dosage.

Symptom/effect	Frequency		Discuss with physician		Stop taking drug now	Call physician now
	Common	Rare	Only if severe	In all cases		
Daytime drowsiness	●		■			
Dizziness/unsteadiness	●		■			
Increased salivation	●		■			
Altered behaviour	●			■		
Forgetfulness/confusion		●		■		
Muscle weakness		●		■		

SPECIAL PRECAUTIONS

Be sure to tell your physician if:
▼ You have severe respiratory disease.
▼ You have long-term liver or kidney problems.
▼ You have porphyria.
▼ You have myasthenia gravis.
▼ You have had problems with drug or alcohol abuse.
▼ You are taking other medications.

Pregnancy
▼ Safety in pregnancy not established. Discuss with your physician.

Breast-feeding
▼ The drug passes into the breast milk and may affect the baby adversely. Discuss with your physician.

Infants and children
▼ Reduced dose necessary.

Over 60
▼ Reduced dose may be necessary.

Driving and hazardous work
▼ Your underlying condition, as well as the possibility of drowsiness while taking clonazepam, may make such activities inadvisable. Discuss with your physician.

Alcohol
▼ Avoid. Alcohol may increase the sedative effects of this drug.

INTERACTIONS

Sedatives All drugs that have a sedative effect on the central nervous system are likely to increase the sedative properties of clonazepam. Such drugs include anti-anxiety and sleeping drugs, antihistamines, opioid analgesics, antidepressants, and antipsychotics.

Other anticonvulsants Clonazepam may alter the effects of other antiepileptic you are taking, or they may alter its effect. Adjustment of dosage or change of drug may be necessary.

PROLONGED USE

Both beneficial and adverse effects of clonazepam may become less marked during prolonged treatment as the body adapts.

CLOPIDOGREL

Product names CO Clopidogrel, Plavix
Used in the following combined preparations None

GENERAL INFORMATION

Clopidogrel is an antiplatelet drug that is used to prevent blood clots from forming. It is prescribed to patients who have a tendency to form clots in the fast-flowing blood of the arteries and heart, or those who have had a stroke or a heart attack.

It is also widely used to prevent clots forming in metal stents inserted into coronary arteries. It may be used alone or in combination with ASA. Clopidogrel reduces the sticking together of platelets, which can lead to abnormal bleeding. You should therefore report any unusual bleeding to your physician at once, and, if you require dental treatment, you should tell your dentist that you are taking the drug.

Adverse effects are common with clopidogrel and are usually associated with bleeding.

QUICK REFERENCE

Drug group Antiplatelet drugs (p.90)

Overdose danger rating Medium

Dependence rating Low

Prescription needed Yes

Available as generic Yes

INFORMATION FOR USERS

Your drug prescription is tailored for you. Do not alter dosage without checking with your physician.

How taken

Tablets.

Frequency and timing of doses
Once daily.

Usual dosage range
75mg.

Onset of effect
1 hour.

Duration of action
Antiplatelet effect may last up to 1 week.

Diet advice
None.

Storage
Keep in a closed container in a cool, dry place out of the reach of children.

Missed dose
Take as soon as you remember. If your next dose is due within 4 hours, take a single dose now and skip the next.

Stopping the drug
Do not stop taking the drug without consulting your physician. Stopping the drug may lead to a recurrence of the original condition.

Exceeding the dose
An occasional unintentional extra dose is unlikely to be a cause for concern. But if you notice any unusual symptoms, or if a large overdose has been taken, notify your physician.

SPECIAL PRECAUTIONS

Be sure to tell your physician if:
▼ You have liver or kidney problems.
▼ You have a peptic ulcer.
▼ You have a bleeding disorder.
▼ You are taking other medications.

Pregnancy
▼ Safety in pregnancy not established. Discuss with your physician.

Breast-feeding
▼ The drug passes into the breast milk and may affect the baby. Discuss with your physician.

Infants and children
▼ Not recommended.

Over 60
▼ No special problems.

Driving and hazardous work
▼ No special problems.

Alcohol
▼ Avoid. Alcohol can irritate the stomach and increase the risk of bleeding.

Surgery and general anesthetics
▼ Clopidogrel may need to be stopped a week before surgery. Discuss this with your physician or dentist.

PROLONGED USE

No special problems.

POSSIBLE ADVERSE EFFECTS

The most frequent adverse effects of clopidogrel are bleeding and bruising. Nausea and diarrhea are less common.

Symptom/effect	Frequency		Discuss with physician		Stop taking drug now	Call physician now
	Common	Rare	Only if severe	In all cases		
Bruising/nosebleeds	●			■		
Diarrhea/abdominal pain	●		■			
Gastrointestinal bleeding/ulcers		●		■		
Blood in urine/feces		●		■		
Nausea/vomiting		●	■			
Headache/dizziness		●	■			
Rash/itching		●		■		
Sore throat		●		■		■

INTERACTIONS

ASA and other non-steroidal anti-inflammatory drugs (NSAIDs) Clopidogrel increases the effect of ASA on platelets. The risk of gastrointestinal bleeding is increased when clopidogrel is used with these drugs.

Anticoagulant drugs (e.g. warfarin)
The anticoagulant effect of these drugs is increased if they are taken with clopidogrel.

Proton pump inhibitors (e.g. omeprazol)
These may decrease the antiplatelet effect of clopidogrel and should be used cautiously with clopidogrel.

CLOTRIMAZOLE

Product names Canesten, Clotrimaderm
Used in the following combined preparations Lotriderm

GENERAL INFORMATION

Clotrimazole is an antifungal drug that is commonly used to treat fungal and yeast infections. It is used for treating tinea (ringworm) infections of the skin, and candida (thrush) infections of the vagina or penis. The drug is applied in the form of a cream to the affected area, and inserted as vaginal *suppositories* or applied as cream for vaginal conditions such as candida.

Adverse effects from clotrimazole are very rare, although some people may experience burning and irritation on the skin surface in the area where the drug has been applied.

QUICK REFERENCE

Drug group Antifungal drugs (p.124)
Overdose danger rating Low
Dependence rating Low
Prescription needed Yes (for combined preparations)
Available as generic Yes

INFORMATION FOR USERS

Your drug prescription is tailored for you. Do not alter dosage without checking with your physician. Consult with your physician or pharmacist for non-prescription products.

How taken

Suppositories, vaginal cream, topical cream.

Frequency and timing of doses
2–3 x daily (skin cream);
once daily at bedtime (vaginal suppositories);
1–2 x daily (external vaginal cream).

Usual dosage range
Vaginal infections One applicatorful (5g) per dose (vaginal cream); 100–500mg per dose (vaginal suppositories).
Skin infections (skin cream) as directed.

Onset of effect
Within 2–3 days.

Duration of action
Up to 12 hours.

Diet advice
None.

Storage
Keep in a closed container in a cool, dry place away from the reach of children.

Missed dose
No cause for concern, but make up the missed dose or application as soon as you remember.

Stopping the drug
Apply the full course. Even if symptoms disappear, the original infection may still be present and symptoms may recur if treatment is stopped too soon.

Exceeding the dose
An occasional unintentional extra dose is unlikely to cause problems. But if you notice unusual symptoms or if a large amount has been swallowed, notify your physician.

POSSIBLE ADVERSE EFFECTS

Clotrimazole rarely causes adverse effects. Skin preparations and vaginal applications may occasionally cause localized burning and irritation.

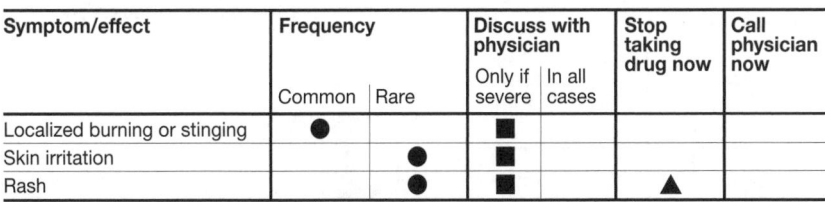

Symptom/effect	Frequency		Discuss with physician		Stop taking drug now	Call physician now
	Common	Rare	Only if severe	In all cases		
Localized burning or stinging	●		■			
Skin irritation		●	■			
Rash		●	■		▲	

INTERACTIONS

Latex contraceptives Damage may occur to these; additional precautions are needed during use of clotrimazole and for at least 5 days after.

SPECIAL PRECAUTIONS

Be sure to tell your physician if:
▼ You are taking other medications.

 Pregnancy
▼ No evidence of risk to developing baby, but only use with the advice of your physician.

 Breast-feeding
▼ No evidence of risk.

 Infants and children
▼ No special problems, but use of vaginal suppositories not advised.

 Over 60
▼ No special problems.

 Driving and hazardous work
▼ No known problems.

 Alcohol
▼ No known problems.

PROLONGED USE

No problems expected.

CLOXACILLIN

Product names Apo-Cloxi, Nu-Cloxi, Teva-Cloxin, and others
Used in the following combined preparations None

GENERAL INFORMATION

Cloxacillin, a penicillin *antibiotic* first available in 1963, is prescribed to treat staphylococcal infections. These are usually resistant to treatment with other forms of penicillin because the bacteria produce an enzyme that breaks down the antibiotic. Cloxacillin, however, is not affected by the enzyme. Common sites where staphylococcal infection may occur include the skin and the soft tissues.

For maximum effect, cloxacillin needs to be taken on an empty stomach, because food interferes with absorption of the drug from the digestive tract.

Diarrhea is the most common *side effect*. As with other penicillin antibiotics, there is a risk of an allergic reaction – rash and possibly fever, itching, swelling of the mouth and tongue, and breathing difficulty.

QUICK REFERENCE

Drug group Penicillin antibiotics (p.114)

Overdose danger rating Low

Dependence rating Low

Prescription needed Yes

Available as generic Yes

INFORMATION FOR USERS

Your drug prescription is tailored for you. Do not alter dosage without checking with your physician.

How taken

Capsules, oral liquid, injection.

Frequency and timing of doses
4 x daily at least 1 hour before, or 2 hours after eating.

Dosage range
Adults 1–2g daily (by mouth).
Children Reduced dose according to age and weight.

Onset of effect
Symptoms usually improve within 1–3 days, depending on the condition.

Duration of action
Up to 6 hours.

Diet advice
None.

Storage
Keep in a closed container in a cool, dry place away from the reach of children. Refrigerate liquid, but do not freeze, and do not keep for longer than 14 days.

Missed dose
Take as soon as you remember. If your next dose is due at this time, take both doses now.

Stopping the drug
Take the full course. Even if you feel better, the original infection may still be present and symptoms may recur if treatment is stopped too soon.

Exceeding the dose
An occasional unintentional extra dose is unlikely to cause problems. But if you notice unusual symptoms, or if a large overdose has been taken, notify your physician.

SPECIAL PRECAUTIONS

Be sure to tell your physician if:
▼ You have ulcerative colitis.
▼ You have had a rash after taking a penicillin or cephalosporin antibiotic.
▼ You are taking other medications.

Pregnancy
▼ Is prescribed during pregnancy, but risks to baby have not been fully established. Discuss with your physician.

Breast-feeding
▼ The drug passes into the breast milk but adverse effects unlikely. Discuss with your physician.

Infants and children
▼ Safety in premature and newborn infants not established. Reduced dose necessary for children.

Over 60
▼ Reduced dose necessary.

Driving and hazardous work
▼ No known problems.

Alcohol
▼ No known problems.

POSSIBLE ADVERSE EFFECTS

If you develop a rash, wheezing, itching, fever, or joint swelling, this may indicate an allergy to cloxacillin, making it necessary to take a different antibiotic.

Symptom/effect	Frequency		Discuss with physician		Stop taking drug now	Call physician now
	Common	Rare	Only if severe	In all cases		
Rash	●			■		
Nausea/vomiting		●	■			
Unusual thirst		●	■			
Tiredness/weakness		●	■			
Diarrhea		●		■		
Wheezing/breathlessness		●		■	▲	▮
Itching		●		■	▲	▮
Swollen mouth/tongue		●		■	▲	▮

INTERACTIONS

Probenecid This drug can increase blood levels of cloxacillin.

Warfarin Cloxacillin may increase the effects of this drug.

Methotrexate Cloxacillin may increase the levels of this drug.

PROLONGED USE

Cloxacillin is usually given only for short courses of treatment.

CLOZAPINE

Product names Apo-Clozapine, Clozaril, Gen Clozapine
Used in the following combined preparations None

GENERAL INFORMATION

Clozapine is an atypical antipsychotic drug for schizophrenia. It is given to patients who have not responded to other treatments or who have experienced intolerable *side effects* with other drugs. Clozapine helps control severe resistant schizophrenia. The improvement is gradual, and relief of severe symptoms can take more than three weeks. All treatment is supervised by a hospital and all patients must be registered with the Clozaril Support and Assistance Network (CSAN). The drug can cause a very serious side effect: agranulocytosis (a large decrease in white blood cells). Blood tests are done before and during treatment; the drug is supplied only if results are normal. Clozapine may also cause heart muscle problems, which requires monitoring.

INFORMATION FOR USERS

This drug is given only under strict medical supervision and continual monitoring.

How taken

Tablets.

Frequency and timing of doses
1–3 x daily; a larger dose may be given at night.

Usual adult dosage range
Initial dose of 12.5mg; usual daily range of 300–600mg; maximum 900mg daily.

Onset of effect
Gradual. Some effect may appear within 3–5 days, but the full beneficial effect may not be felt for over 3 weeks.

Duration of action
Up to 16 hours.

Diet advice
None.

Storage
Keep in a closed container in a cool, dry place away from the reach of children.

Missed dose
Take as soon as you remember. If your next dose is due within 2 hours, take a single dose now and skip the next. If you miss more than 2 days of tablets, notify your physician because you may need to restart at a lower dose.

Stopping the drug
Do not stop the drug without consulting your physician because symptoms may recur.

Exceeding the dose
An occasional unintentional extra dose is unlikely to cause problems. Large overdoses may cause unusual drowsiness, seizures, and agitation. Notify your physician.

SPECIAL PRECAUTIONS

Be sure to tell your physician if:
▼ You have long-term liver or kidney problems.
▼ You have a history of blood disorders.
▼ You have had epileptic seizures.
▼ You have heart problems.
▼ You have colon problems or have had bowel surgery.
▼ You have diabetes.
▼ You have glaucoma.
▼ You have prostate problems.
▼ You are taking other medications.

 Pregnancy
▼ Not usually prescribed. Safety not established. Discuss with your physician.

 Breast-feeding
▼ The drug passes into the breast milk and may affect the baby. Discuss with your physician.

 Infants and children
▼ Not prescribed.

 Over 60
▼ *Adverse effects* are more likely. Initial dose is low and is slowly increased.

 Driving and hazardous work
▼ Avoid such activities until you know how clozapine affects you because the drug can cause blurred vision, drowsiness, and dizziness.

 Alcohol
▼ Avoid. Alcohol may increase the sedative effects of this drug.

POSSIBLE ADVERSE EFFECTS

Unlike other antipsychotic drugs, clozapine is less likely to cause parkinsonian side effects (tremor and stiffness). The most serious side effect is agranulocytosis; strict monitoring is necessary.

Symptom/effect	Frequency		Discuss with physician		Stop taking drug now	Call physician now
	Common	Rare	Only if severe	In all cases		
Drowsiness/tiredness	●		■			
Excess saliva	●		■			
Dry mouth	●		■			
Weight gain	●		■			
Fast heartbeat	●			■		
Dizziness/fainting	●			■		
Constipation	●			■		
Blurred vision		●		■		
Fever/sore throat		●		■		▮
Seizures		●		■		▮

INTERACTIONS

General note A number of drugs increase the risk of adverse effects on the blood. Do not take other medication without checking with your physician or *pharmacist*.

Sedatives Drugs with a *sedative* effect on the central nervous system are likely to increase the sedative properties of clozapine.

Anticholinergic drugs There is a risk of severe constipation or even bowel obstruction when these drugs are used with clozapine.

PROLONGED USE

Agranulocytosis and heart muscle problems may occur, and occasionally liver function may be affected. Significant weight gain may also occur.

Monitoring Blood tests are carried out weekly for 18 weeks, fortnightly until the end of the first year, and, if blood counts are stable, every 4 weeks thereafter. Liver function tests, weighing, and tests for diabetes are performed every 3–6 months. Heart monitoring is also carried out.

CODEINE

Product Name Codeine Contin
Used in the following combined preparations 222, Atasol-8, Exdol-15, Fiorinal-C1/4, and many others

GENERAL INFORMATION

Codeine is a mild *opioid* analgesic that is similar to, but weaker than, morphine. It has been in common medical use since the beginning of the last century.

Codeine is prescribed primarily to relieve mild to moderate pain, and is often combined with a non-opioid analgesic such as acetaminophen. It is also an effective cough suppressant and, for this reason, is included as an ingredient in many non-prescription cough syrups and cold relief preparations.

Like the other opioid drugs, codeine is constipating, a characteristic that sometimes makes it useful in the short-term control of diarrhea. Other rare *adverse effects* include breathing difficulties, which should be reported to your physician without delay.

Although codeine is habit-forming, addiction seldom occurs if the drug is used for a limited period of time and the recommended dosage is followed. Codeine Contin should be swallowed whole and not chewed or crushed.

QUICK REFERENCE

Drug group Opioid analgesics (p.64), antidiarrheal drugs (p.96), and cough suppressants (p.80)

Overdose danger rating High

Dependence rating Medium

Prescription needed Yes (some preparations)

Available as generic Yes

INFORMATION FOR USERS

Your drug prescription is tailored for you. Do not alter dosage without checking with your physician.

How taken

Tablets, liquid, injection.

Frequency and timing of doses
4–6 x daily (pain); 3–4 x daily when necessary (cough); every 4–6 hours when necessary (diarrhea).

Usual adult dosage range
120–240mg daily (pain); 45–120mg daily (cough); 30–180mg daily (diarrhea).

Onset of effect
30–60 minutes.

Duration of action
4–6 hours.

Diet advice
None.

Storage
Keep in a closed container in a cool, dry place out of the reach of children. Protect from light.

Missed dose
Take as soon as you remember if needed for relief of symptoms. If not needed, do not take the missed dose, and return to your normal dose schedule when necessary.

Stopping the drug
Can be safely stopped as soon as you no longer need it.

OVERDOSE ACTION

Seek immediate medical advice in all cases. Take emergency action if there are symptoms such as slow or irregular breathing, severe drowsiness, or loss of consciousness.

See Drug poisoning emergency guide (p.526).

SPECIAL PRECAUTIONS

Be sure to tell your physician if:
▼ You have long-term liver or kidney problems.
▼ You have a lung disorder such as asthma or bronchitis.
▼ You are taking other medications.

Pregnancy
▼ No evidence of risk of malformations, but may adversely affect the baby's breathing if taken during labour. Discuss with your physician.

Breast-feeding
▼ The drug passes into the breast milk, and may affect the baby. Discuss with your physician.

Infants and children
▼ Reduced dose necessary.

Over 60
▼ Reduced dose may be necessary.

Driving and hazardous work
▼ Avoid such activities until you have learned how codeine affects you because the drug may cause dizziness and drowsiness.

Alcohol
▼ Avoid. Alcohol may increase the *sedative* effects of this drug.

POSSIBLE ADVERSE EFFECTS

Serious adverse effects are rare with codeine. Constipation occurs especially with prolonged use, but other side effects, such as nausea, vomiting, and drowsiness, are not usually troublesome at recommended doses, and usually disappear if the dose is reduced.

Symptom/effect	Frequency		Discuss with physician		Stop taking drug now	Call physician now
	Common	Rare	Only if severe	In all cases		
Constipation	●		■			
Nausea/vomiting		●		■		
Drowsiness		●		■		
Dizziness		●		■		
Agitation/restlessness		●		■	▲	
Rash/hives		●		■	▲	■
Wheezing/breathlessness		●		■	▲	■

PROLONGED USE

Codeine is normally used only for short-term relief of symptoms. It can be habit-forming if taken for extended periods, especially if higher-than-average doses are taken.

INTERACTIONS

Sedatives All drugs, including alcohol, that have a *sedative* effect on the central nervous system are likely to increase sedation with codeine. Such drugs include sleeping drugs, antidepressant drugs, and antihistamines.

COLCHICINE

Product name None
Used in the following combined preparations None

GENERAL INFORMATION

Colchicine, a drug originally extracted from the autumn crocus flower and later synthesized, has been used since the 18th century for gout. Although it has now, to some extent, been superseded by newer drugs, it is still often used to relieve joint pain and inflammation in flare-ups of gout. Colchicine is most effective when taken at the first sign of symptoms, and almost always produces an improvement. The drug may also be given during the first few months of treatment with allopurinol or probenecid (other drugs used for treating gout), because these may at first increase the frequency of gout attacks.

Colchicine is occasionally prescribed for the prevention of acute attacks of familial Mediterranean fever (FMF), a rare congenital condition.

QUICK REFERENCE

Drug group Drugs for gout (p.105)
Overdose danger rating High
Dependence rating Low
Prescription needed Yes
Available as generic Yes

INFORMATION FOR USERS

Your drug prescription is tailored for you. Do not alter dosage without checking with your physician.

How taken

Tablets.

Frequency and timing of doses
Prevention of gout attacks Twice daily.
Relief of gout attacks 2 doses one hour apart.

Usual adult dosage range
Prevention of gout attacks 0.5mg 1–4 x weekly to 1.8mg daily.
Relief of gout attacks 1.2mg initially, followed by 0.6mg 1 hour later. This course must not be repeated within 3 days.
Prevention of FMF 1–2mg daily for adults.

Onset of effect
Relief of symptoms in an attack may be felt in 6–24 hours. Full effect in gout prevention may not be felt for several days.

Duration of action
Up to 2 hours. Some effect may last longer.

Diet advice
Certain foods are known to make gout worse. Discuss with your physician.

Storage
Keep in a closed container in a cool, dry place out of the reach of children. Protect from light.

Missed dose
Take as soon as you remember. If your next dose is due within 30 minutes, take a single dose now and skip the next.

Stopping the drug
Do not stop without consulting your physician.

OVERDOSE ACTION

Seek immediate medical advice in all cases; some reactions can be fatal. Take emergency action if severe nausea, vomiting, bloody diarrhea, severe abdominal pain, or loss of consciousness occur.

See Drug poisoning emergency guide (p.526).

SPECIAL PRECAUTIONS

Be sure to tell your physician if:
▼ You have long-term liver or kidney problems.
▼ You have heart problems.
▼ You have a blood disorder.
▼ You have stomach ulcers.
▼ You have chronic inflammation of the bowel.
▼ You are taking other medications.

 Pregnancy
▼ Not usually prescribed. May cause defects in the unborn baby. Discuss with your physician.

 Breast-feeding
▼ The drug passes into the breast milk and may affect the baby. Discuss with your physician.

 Infants and children
▼ Used in the prevention of FMF in children.

 Over 60
▼ Increased likelihood of adverse effects.

 Driving and hazardous work
▼ No special problems.

 Alcohol
▼ Avoid. Alcohol may cause an increase in gout attacks, and may increase stomach irritation caused by colchicine.

POSSIBLE ADVERSE EFFECTS

The appearance of any symptom that may be an *adverse effect* of the drug is a sign that you should stop the drug until you have received further medical advice.

Symptom/effect	Frequency		Discuss with physician		Stop taking drug now	Call physician now
	Common	Rare	Only if severe	In all cases		
Nausea/vomiting	●			■	▲	
Diarrhea/abdominal pain	●			■	▲	
Numbness and tingling		●		■	▲	
Unusual bleeding/bruising		●		■	▲	
Rash		●		■	▲	

INTERACTIONS

Cyclosporine Taking cyclosporine with colchicine may lead to adverse effects on the kidneys.

Erythromycin and clarithromycin may increase the adverse effects of colchicine.

Statins and fibrates Taking these with colchicine may increase the risk of adverse effects on the muscles.

Indinavir, ritonavir, diltiazem, and verapamil can increase the levels of colchicine.

PROLONGED USE

Prolonged use of this drug may lead to hair loss, rashes, tingling in the hands and feet, muscle pain and weakness, and blood disorders.

Monitoring Periodic blood checks are usually required.

CONJUGATED ESTROGENS

Product names C.E.S., Congest, Premarin
Used in the following combined preparation Premplus

GENERAL INFORMATION

Preparations of conjugated estrogens consist of naturally occurring estrogens similar to those found in the urine of pregnant mares. Given by mouth, they are used to relieve symptoms of menopause such as hot flushes. They can also help prevent post-menopausal osteoporosis (bone loss), although they are not used to treat only osteoporosis. They are used in the lowest effective dose for the shortest period necessary to manage menopausal symptoms.

As replacement therapy, conjugated estrogens may be taken on a cyclic or daily dosing schedule, often in conjunction with a progestin. Conjugated estrogens are also available as a vaginal cream to relieve pain and dryness of the vagina or vulva after the menopause.

Conjugated estrogens do not provide contraception. A woman can still get pregnant for 2 years after her last period (if she is under 50 years) or for 1 year after the end of menstruation (if she is over 50 years). Conjugated estrogens without a progestin are not recommended for women who have a uterus.

QUICK REFERENCE

Drug group Female sex hormones (p.133) and drugs for bone disorders (p.108)

Overdose danger rating Low

Dependence rating Low

Prescription needed Yes

Available as generic Yes

INFORMATION FOR USERS

Your drug prescription is tailored for you. Do not alter dosage without checking with your physician.

How taken

Tablets, cream.

Frequency and timing of doses
Once daily.

Usual adult dosage range
0.3–1.25mg daily (tablets); 1–2g daily (cream).

Onset of effect
5–20 days.

Duration of action
1–2 days.

Diet advice
None.

Storage
Keep in a closed container in a cool, dry place out of the reach of children.

Missed dose
Take as soon as you remember.

Stopping the drug
Do not stop the drug without consulting your physician because symptoms may recur.

Exceeding the dose
An occasional unintentional extra dose is unlikely to be a cause for concern. But if you notice any unusual symptoms, or if a large overdose has been taken, notify your physician.

SPECIAL PRECAUTIONS

Be sure to tell your physician or pharmacist if:
▼ You have heart failure or hypertension.
▼ You have had blood clots or a stroke.
▼ You have a history of breast disease.
▼ You have had fibroids in the uterus or abnormal vaginal bleeding.
▼ You suffer from migraine or epilepsy.
▼ You are taking other medications.
▼ You have long-term liver or kidney problems.

Pregnancy
▼ Not prescribed. May affect the baby adversely. Discuss with your physician.

Breast-feeding
▼ Not prescribed. The drug passes into the breast milk and may inhibit its flow. Discuss with your physician.

Infants and children
▼ Not prescribed.

Over 60
▼ No special problems.

Driving and hazardous work
▼ No known problems.

Alcohol
▼ No known problems.

Surgery and general anesthetics
▼ Drug may need to be stopped before surgery. Discuss with your physician.

POSSIBLE ADVERSE EFFECTS

The most common *adverse effects* of conjugated estrogens are similar to symptoms that occur in the early stages of pregnancy, and generally diminish or disappear after 2–3 months of treatment. Women on a cyclic schedule will have a menstrual bleed towards the end of each cycle. Sudden, sharp pain in the chest, groin, or legs may indicate an abnormal blood clot that requires urgent medical attention.

Symptom/effect	Frequency		Discuss with physician		Stop taking drug now	Call physician now
	Common	Rare	Only if severe	In all cases		
Nausea/vomiting	●		■			
Breast swelling/tenderness	●		■			
Increase or decrease in weight	●		■			
Bloating/abdominal pain	●		■			
Reduced sex drive		●	■			
Headache/migraine		●		■		
Depression		●		■		
Vaginal bleeding		●		■		
Pain in chest/groin/legs		●		■		▮
Jaundice		●		■	▲	▮

INTERACTIONS

Tobacco smoking Smoking increases the risk of serious adverse effects on the heart and circulation with conjugated estrogens.

Oral anticoagulant drugs Conjugated estrogens reduce the *anticoagulant* effect of these drugs.

PROLONGED USE

There is a higher risk of breast cancer, cancer of the uterus, gallbladder disease, and abnormal blood clots in some people.

Monitoring Regular physical examinations (e.g., mammograms) and blood pressure checks are advised.

CYCLOBENZAPRINE

Product names Apo-Cyclobenzaprine, Auro-Cyclobenzaprine, Ava-Cyclobenzaprine, DOM-Cyclobenzaprine, and others
Used in the following combined preparations None

GENERAL INFORMATION

Cyclobenzaprine is used for short-term treatment of muscle spasm. It is usually used for a few days and no longer than 3 weeks. This medication is not recommended for muscle spasm related to cerebral or spinal cord disease. Although not approved by Health Canada, it has been used in fibromyalgia; when used for this condition, it is administered once daily at bedtime. A common *side effect* of cyclobenzaprine is dry mouth. Chewing sugar-free gum or sucking on sugar-free candy can help alleviate this. Older individuals may be more sensitive to some of its *adverse effects* related to its anticholinergic effect, as well as its effect on the central nervous system.

QUICK REFERENCE

Drug group Skeletal muscle relaxants (p.106)

Overdose danger rating High

Dependence rating Low

Prescription needed Yes

Available as generic Yes

INFORMATION FOR USERS

Your drug prescription is tailored for you. Do not alter dosage without checking with your physician.

How taken

Tablets.

Frequency and timing of doses
1–3 x daily.

Usual adult dosage range
10–30mg daily.

Onset of effect
Full beneficial effect may not be felt for a few days.

Duration of action
8–12 hours.

Diet advice
None.

Storage
Keep in original container in a cool, dry place out of the reach of children.

Missed dose
Take as soon as you remember but do not take two doses within 4 to 6 hours of each other.

Stopping the drug
If only taken for a few days, can be safely stopped as soon as you no longer need it.

OVERDOSE ACTION

 Seek immediate medical advice in all cases. Take emergency action if seizures, slow or irregular pulse, or loss of consciousness occur.

See Drug poisoning emergency guide (p.526).

SPECIAL PRECAUTIONS

Be sure to tell your physician if:
▼ You are recovering from a heart attack.
▼ You have a history of heart rhythm disturbances or other heart problems including heart failure.
▼ You have an overactive thyroid.
▼ You have glaucoma.
▼ You have trouble urinating.
▼ You are, or have recently taken, monoamine oxidase inhibitors such as phenelzine or moclobemide.
▼ You are taking other medications.

 Pregnancy
▼ Insufficient evidence available in pregnant women. Discuss with your physician.

 Breast-feeding
▼ Insufficient evidence available in women who are breast-feeding. Discuss with your physician.

 Infants and children
▼ Safety and efficacy not established in children less than 15 years of age.

 Over 60
▼ Use with caution. Older individuals can be more sensitive to the anticholinergic and central depressant effect of this drug.

 Driving and hazardous work
▼ May cause drowsiness or dizziness. Do not drive a car or operate machinery until you feel you are mentally alert.

 Alcohol
▼ Avoid.

POSSIBLE ADVERSE EFFECTS

Common side effects are related to cyclobenzaprine's effect on the central nervous system, as well as *anticholinergic* side effects such as dry mouth.

Symptom/effect	Frequency		Discuss with physician		Stop taking drug now	Call physician now
	Common	Rare	Only if severe	In all cases		
Drowsiness/dizziness/fatigue	●		■			
Nausea/dry mouth	●		■			
Heart rhythm problems		●		■		
High or low blood pressure		●		■		
Change in mood/feeling anxious/disorientation		●		■		▮
Yellowing skin, eyes		●	■	▲		▮

INTERACTIONS

General note Avoid using cyclobenzaprine with other drugs that have anticholinergic effects; other drugs that cause central nervous system side effects, or alcohol, can significantly increase these effects.

Fluoxetine may increase the levels of cyclobenzaprine.

Droperidol Avoid use of cyclobenzaprine with this drug as there is an increased risk for heart rhythm problems.

Drugs which enhance serotonin activity Use cautiously with cyclobenzapine due to potential for serious side effects.

Tramadol Cyclobenzaprine may increase the risk of seizures when taken with this drug.

MAO inhibitors Do not use cyclobenzaprine with, or for 14 days after discontinuing these drugs.

PROLONGED USE

Only recommended for short-term use.

CYCLOPHOSPHAMIDE

Product names Procytox
Used in the following combined preparations None

GENERAL INFORMATION

Cyclophosphamide belongs to a group of anticancer drugs known as alkylating agents. It is used for a wide range of cancers, including lymphomas (lymph gland cancers), leukemias, and solid tumours. It is commonly given together with radiotherapy or other drugs. Cyclophosphamide has also been used for autoimmune diseases.

Cyclophosphamide causes nausea, vomiting, and hair loss, and can affect the heart, lungs, and liver. It can also cause bladder damage in susceptible people because it produces a toxic substance called acrolein. To reduce toxicity, people considered to be at risk may be given a drug called mesna before and after each dose of cyclophosphamide. Also, because the drug often reduces production of blood cells, it may lead to abnormal bleeding, increased risk of infection, and reduced fertility in men and women.

QUICK REFERENCE

Drug group Anticancer drugs (p.140)

Overdose danger rating Medium

Dependence rating Low

Prescription needed Yes

Available as generic Yes

INFORMATION FOR USERS

Your drug prescription is tailored for you. Do not alter dosage without checking with your physician.

How taken

Tablets, injection.

Frequency and timing of doses
Varies from once daily to every 3 weeks, depending on the condition being treated.

Usual dosage range
Dosage is determined individually according to the nature of the condition, body weight, and response.

Onset of effect
Some effects may appear within hours of starting treatment. Full beneficial effects may not be felt for many weeks.

Duration of action
Several weeks.

Diet advice
High fluid intake with frequent bladder emptying is recommended. This will usually prevent the drug causing bladder irritation.

Storage
Keep in a closed container in a cool, dry place out of the reach of children. Protect from light.

Missed dose
Injections are given only in hospital. If you are taking tablets, take the missed dose as soon as you remember. If your next dose is due within 6 hours, take a single dose now and skip the next. Tell your physician that you missed a dose.

Stopping the drug
The drug will be stopped under medical supervision (injection). Do not stop taking the drug without consulting your physician (tablets); stopping the drug may lead to worsening of the underlying condition.

Exceeding the dose
An occasional unintentional extra dose is unlikely to cause problems. Large overdoses may cause nausea, vomiting, and bladder damage. Notify your physician.

SPECIAL PRECAUTIONS

Cyclophosphamide is prescribed only under close medical supervision, taking account of your present condition and medical history. However, be sure to tell your physician if:
▼ You have liver or kidney problems.
▼ You have porphyria.

Pregnancy
▼ Not usually prescribed. May cause birth defects. Discuss with your physician.

Breast-feeding
▼ Not advised. The drug passes into the breast milk and may affect the baby adversely. Discuss with your physician.

Infants and children
▼ Reduced dose necessary.

Over 60
▼ No special problems.

Driving and hazardous work
▼ No known problems.

Alcohol
▼ No problems expected, but avoid excessive amounts.

Surgery and general anesthetics
Infom your anesthesiologist that you are taking the drug prior to surgery.

POSSIBLE ADVERSE EFFECTS

Cyclophosphamide often causes nausea and vomiting, which usually diminish as your body adjusts. Also, women often experience irregular periods. Blood in the urine may be a sign of bladder damage and requires prompt medical attention. Those thought to be at risk of bladder damage may be given mesna before and after doses of cyclophosphamide.

Symptom/effect	Frequency		Discuss with physician		Stop taking drug now	Call physician now
	Common	Rare	Only if severe	In all cases		
Nausea/vomiting	●		■			
Hair loss	●		■			
Irregular menstruation	●			■		
Mouth ulcers		●		■		
Breathlessness		●		■		
Bloodstained urine		●		■		■

INTERACTIONS

Phenytoin Can increase the breakdown of cyclophosphamide.

Allopurinol and phenothiazines Can inhibit breakdown of cyclophosphamide.

PROLONGED USE

Prolonged use of this drug may reduce the production of blood cells in the bone marrow. It may also cause pigmentation of the nails, palms, and soles of the feet.

Monitoring Periodic checks on blood composition and blood chemistry are usually required.

CYCLOSPORINE

Product names Neoral, Restasis, Sandimmune
Used in the following combined preparations None

GENERAL INFORMATION

Cyclosporine is one of the immuno-suppressants, a group of drugs that suppress the body's natural defences against infection and foreign cells. This action is of particular use following organ transplants, when the recipient's immune system may reject the transplanted organ unless the immune system is controlled.

Cyclosporine is widely used after many types of transplant, such as heart, bone marrow, kidney, liver, and pancreas; its use has considerably reduced the risk of rejection. It is sometimes used to treat rheumatoid arthritis, severe psoriasis, and in nephrotic syndrome, when other treatments have failed.

Because cyclosporine reduces the effectiveness of the immune system, people being treated with this drug are more susceptible than usual to infections. Cyclosporine can also cause kidney damage.

Different brands of cyclosporine may reach different levels in your blood. It is important to know which brand you are taking. Do not try to make dose changes on your own. Ask your *pharmacist* for a patient information leaflet on the product you are taking.

INFORMATION FOR USERS

Your drug prescription is tailored for you. Do not alter dosage without checking with your physician.

How taken

Capsules, liquid, injection.

Frequency and timing of doses
1–2 x daily. The liquid can be mixed with water, apple juice, or orange juice just before taking. Do not mix with grapefruit juice.

Usual dosage range
Dosage is calculated on an individual basis according to age and weight.

Onset of effect
Within 12 hours.

Duration of action
Up to 3 days.

Diet advice
Avoid high-potassium foods, such as bananas and tomatoes, and potassium supplements. Avoid grapefruit juice.

Storage
Capsules should be left in the blister pack until required. Keep in a closed container in a cool, dry place out of the reach of children. Do not refrigerate liquid.

Missed dose
Take as soon as you remember. If your dose is more than 36 hours late, consult your physician.

Stopping the drug
Do not stop taking the drug without consulting your physician; stopping the drug may lead to transplant rejection.

Exceeding the dose
An occasional unintentional extra dose is unlikely to cause problems. Large overdoses may cause vomiting and diarrhea and may affect kidney function. Notify your physician.

POSSIBLE ADVERSE EFFECTS

The most common *adverse effects* are gum swelling, excessive hair growth, nausea and vomiting, and tremor. Headache and muscle cramps may also occur. Less common effects are diarrhea, facial swelling, flushing, "pins and needles" sensations, rash, and itching.

Symptom/effect	Frequency		Discuss with physician		Stop taking drug now	Call physician now
	Common	Rare	Only if severe	In all cases		
Increased body hair	●		■			
Nausea/vomiting	●			■		
Tremor	●			■		
Headache	●			■		
Sore throat/chills		●		■		
Swelling of gums	●			■		
High blood pressure	●			■		■

INTERACTIONS

General note Cyclosporine may interact with a large number of drugs. Check with your physician or pharmacist before taking any new prescription or over-the-counter medications.

Grapefruit juice can increase blood levels of cyclosporine. Avoid grapefruit juice.

SPECIAL PRECAUTIONS

Cyclosporine is prescribed only under close medical supervision, taking account of your present condition and medical history.

Pregnancy
▼ Not usually prescribed. Safety in pregnancy not established. Discuss with your physician.

Breast-feeding
▼ Not recommended. The drug passes into the breast milk and safety has not been established. Discuss with your physician.

Infants and children
▼ Safety not established; used only with great caution.

Over 60
▼ Reduced dose may be necessary.

Driving and hazardous work
▼ No known problems.

Alcohol
▼ No known problems.

Sunlight
▼ Avoid prolonged, unprotected exposure.

PROLONGED USE

Long-term use, especially in high doses, can affect kidney and/or liver function. It may reduce numbers of white blood cells, thus increasing susceptibility to infection.

Monitoring Regular blood tests should be carried out as well as tests for liver and kidney function. Cyclosporine blood levels and blood pressure should also be checked regularly.

DABIGATRAN ETEXILATE

Product name Pradax
Used in the following combined preparations None

GENERAL INFORMATION

Dabigatran is an anticoagulant used to prevent blood clots in certain conditions. It works by blocking the activity of a protein called thrombin. The drug is used to reduce the risk of clot formation after elective orthopedic surgery of the hip and knee (replacements) and to prevent the risk of stroke in individuals with atrial fibrillation. Unlike oral anticoagulants such as warfarin, this drug starts to work sooner. Treatment is usually started within 1 to 4 hours following surgery and is continued for 10 days following knee surgery, and for 28 to 35 days following hip surgery. For stroke prevention, the drug is administered for as long as needed.

QUICK REFERENCE

Drug group Anticoagulant drugs (p.90)

Overdose danger rating High

Dependence rating Low

Prescription needed Yes

Available as generic No

INFORMATION FOR USERS

Your drug prescription is tailored for you. Do not alter dosage without checking with your physician.

How taken

Capsules; swallow whole and do not chew, break, or open capsules.

Frequency and timing of doses
Once daily, at the same time each day.
Atrial fibrillation Twice daily, 12 hours apart.

Usual adult dosage range
Post orthopedic surgery 110–220mg daily.
Atrial fibrillation 220–300mg daily.

Onset of effect
Within 30 minutes–2 hours.

Duration of action
24 hours or longer.

Diet advice
None.

Storage
Keep in original container in a cool, dry place out of the reach of children. Protect from light.

Missed dose
Take a missed dose as soon as you remember. Take the following dose on your original schedule. Do not double up on your doses. Discuss with your physician.

Stopping the drug
Short-term therapy: Complete your course of drugs. Long-term therapy: Do not stop taking the drug without consulting your physician; the underlying condition may worsen.

OVERDOSE ACTION

 Seek immediate medical advice in all cases. Take emergency action if severe bleeding or loss of consciousness occur.

See Drug poisoning emergency guide (p.526).

SPECIAL PRECAUTIONS

Be sure to tell your physician if:
▼ You have liver disease or kidney problems.
▼ You have had a previous stroke.
▼ You have had any problems with bleeding or peptic ulcers.
▼ You are considering any surgery, including dental surgery.
▼ You are taking ketoconazole or other medications or natural health products.

 Pregnancy
▼ Safety and efficacy not established in pregnant women; not recommended. Discuss with your physician.

 Breast-feeding
▼ Safety and efficacy not established in women who are breast-feeding; not recommended. Discuss with your physician.

 Infants and children
▼ Safety and efficacy not established in patients less than 18 years of age.

 Over 60
▼ Dose reduction may be needed for those over 75 years of age.

 Driving and hazardous work
▼ Use caution with driving and hazardous work; even minor bumps can cause bad bruises and excessive bleeding cause drowsiness and visual disturbances.

 Alcohol
▼ No known problems.

▼ **Surgery and general anesthetics**
Consult with your physician or dentist before any surgery.

POSSIBLE ADVERSE EFFECTS

Bleeding is the most common and serious *side effect* with dabigatran. If you experience any signs of bruising or bleeding, such as a nose bleed, discuss with your doctor and *pharmacist*.

Symptom/effect	Frequency		Discuss with physician		Stop taking drug now	Call physician now
	Common	Rare	Only if severe	In all cases		
Nausea/diarrhea	●		■			
Nose bleed or minor bleeding		●	■			
Bleeding from the rectum, vagina, urinary tract, or coughing blood		●		■	▲	▌
Bruising/rash		●		■		

INTERACTIONS

Amiodarone, atorvastatin, clarithromycin, itraconazole, verapamil, amiodarone, quinidine, clarithromycin and grapefruit juice can all increase the level of dabigatran.

Ketoconazole should not be used with dabigatran.

Quinidine can increase the level of dabigatrin; not recommended to be used together.

Rifampin and St. John's wort may decrease the effectivness of dabigatrin.

Other drugs that act as anticoagulants should not be used with dabigatran as the risk of bleeding is increased.

ASA and NSAIDs should be used cautiously with dabigatran.

PROLONGED USE

Monitoring Ongoing monitoring for bleeding.

DANAZOL

Product name Cyclomen
Used in the following combined preparations None

GENERAL INFORMATION

Danazol is a synthetic steroid *hormone* that inhibits hormones called pituitary gonadotrophins.

It is used in a range of conditions, including endometriosis (fragments of endometrial tissue growing outside the uterus), menorrhagia, and, in men, to reduce gynecomastia (breast swelling). Danazol has also been used, long term, to treat hereditary angioedema (a rare allergic disorder that causes facial swelling).

Danazol is also used to relieve pain, tenderness, and lumpiness in the breasts caused by fibrocystic disease. Treatment commonly disrupts normal menstrual periods and in some cases periods may stop altogether. Women taking high doses may notice unusual hair growth and deepening of the voice.

INFORMATION FOR USERS

Your drug prescription is tailored for you. Do not alter dosage without checking with your physician.

How taken

Capsules.

Frequency and timing of doses
2–4 x daily.

Usual adult dosage range
200–800mg daily, depending on the condition being treated, its severity, and the response to the drug.

Onset of effect
Some effects occur after a few days. Full beneficial effects may take some months.

Duration of action
1–2 days.

Diet advice
None.

Storage
Keep in a closed container in a cool, dry place out of the reach of children.

Missed dose
Take as soon as you remember. If your next dose is due within 2 hours, take a single dose now and skip the next.

Stopping the drug
Do not stop the drug without consulting your physician; symptoms may recur.

Exceeding the dose
An occasional unintentional extra dose is unlikely to cause problems. But if you notice any unusual symptoms, or if a large overdose has been taken, notify your physician.

SPECIAL PRECAUTIONS

Be sure to tell your physician if:
▼ You have long-term liver or kidney problems.
▼ You have heart disease.
▼ You have had epileptic seizures.
▼ You suffer from migraine.
▼ You suffer from unexplained vaginal bleeding.
▼ You have diabetes mellitus.
▼ You are taking other medications.

Pregnancy
▼ Not prescribed. May cause masculine characteristics in a female baby. Non-hormonal methods of contraception should be used for women of childbearing age; and pregnancy should be avoided for 3 months after the end of treatment.

Breast-feeding
▼ The drug passes into the breast milk and may affect the baby. Discuss with your physician.

Infants and children
▼ Not recommended.

Over 60
▼ Unlikely to be required.

Driving and hazardous work
▼ No known problems.

Alcohol
▼ No known problems.

POSSIBLE ADVERSE EFFECTS

Danazol rarely causes *adverse effects* in low doses. Adverse effects from higher doses, including acne, weight gain, and nausea, are the result of hormonal changes. Voice changes and unusual hair growth in women are largely reversed after treatment.

Symptom/effect	Frequency		Discuss with physician		Stop taking drug now	Call physician now
	Common	Rare	Only if severe	In all cases		
Swollen feet/ankles	●		■			
Weight gain	●		■			
Nausea/dizziness	●		■			
Acne/oily skin	●		■			
Backache/cramps	●		■			
Women only						
Unusual hair growth and loss	●			■		
Menstrual disturbances	●			■		
Reduced breast size		●	■			
Voice changes		●		■		

PROLONGED USE

The drug is normally taken for 3–9 months depending on the condition being treated. There is a slight risk of liver damage. See also Possible adverse effects, left.

Monitoring Periodic liver function tests may be carried out.

INTERACTIONS

Oral anticoagulant drugs Danazol may increase the effects of these drugs.

Anticonvulsant drugs Danazol may increase the effects of carbamazepine, and possibly other antiepileptic drugs.

Immunosuppressants Danazol may increase the effects of cyclosporine and tacrolimus.

Oral antidiabetic drugs Danazol may reduce the effects of these drugs.

DARIFENACIN

Product name Enablex
Used in the following combined preparations None

GENERAL INFORMATION

Darifenacin is used to treat an overactive bladder, and can help minimize symptoms of frequent urination and the urgency to urinate. It works by relaxing the bladder muscle. Darifenacin is available as an extended-release tablet and is taken once daily. The tablets should be swallowed whole and should not be chewed, split, or crushed. It is best to take it at the same time every day. As darifenacin can decrease sweating, precautions should be taken in hot environments to prevent heat prostration.

QUICK REFERENCE

Drug group Drugs for urinary disorders (p.154)

Overdose danger rating Medium

Dependence rating Low

Prescription needed Yes

Available as generic No

INFORMATION FOR USERS

Your drug prescription is tailored for you. Do not alter dosage without checking with your physician.

How taken

Extended-release tablets.

Frequency and timing of doses
Usually once daily.

Usual adult dosage range
7.5–15mg daily.

Onset of effect
May take 1–2 weeks to see full benefit.

Duration of action
Up to 24 hours.

Diet advice
None.

Storage
Keep in a closed container in a cool, dry place out of the reach of children.

Missed dose
If you miss a dose, skip the missed dose and continue your usual dosing schedule. Do not double up to catch up on a missed dose.

Stopping the drug
Do not stop the drug without consulting your physician. Stopping the drug may lead to worsening of the underlying condition.

Exceeding the dose
An occasional unintentional extra dose is unlikely to cause problems. With large overdoses, seek help right away and notify your physician.

SPECIAL PRECAUTIONS

Be sure to tell your physician if:
▼ You are allergic to darifenacin or other medications.
▼ You have had difficulty passing urine.
▼ You have or have had prostate enlargement.
▼ You have had severe constipation.
▼ You have or have had liver disease.
▼ You have or have had glaucoma.
▼ You have or have had any disorders of the nervous system.
▼ You are taking other medications.

 Pregnancy
▼ Not usually prescribed. Safety in pregnancy not established. Discuss with your physician.

 Breast-feeding
▼ Safety not established. Discuss with your physician.

 Infants and children
▼ Not recommended.

 Over 60
▼ No special problems.

 Driving and hazardous work
▼ May cause blurred vision or dizziness. Do not drive a car or operate machinery until you know how this medication affects you.

 Alcohol
▼ No special problems

POSSIBLE ADVERSE EFFECTS

Common *side effects* include dry mouth, constipation, and an upset stomach. Additional side effects are associated with higher doses.

Symptom/effect	Frequency		Discuss with physician		Stop taking drug now	Call physician now
	Common	Rare	Only if severe	In all cases		
Dry mouth	●		■			
Constipation	●		■			
Upset stomach	●		■			
Dry eyes	●		■			
Diarrhea		●	■			
Difficulty urinating		●				▮
Burning pain during urination		●				▮
Rash		●				▮
Itching		●				▮

INTERACTIONS

Flavoxate, oxybutynin, tolterodine, solifenacin These drugs also affect the bladder muscle. These are not usually used at the same time as darifenacin.

Flecainide Darifenacin can increase levels of flecainide, leading to possible adverse effects.

Ketoconazole, telithromycin, clarithromycin, erythromycin Some antifungals and antibiotics increase the level of darifenacin. May require dose adjustment.

Anticholinergics Drugs with anticholinergic properties can affect urination and should generally not be used with darifenacin. Examples include diphenhydramine, amitriptyline, clozapine, benztropine, and scopolamine.

Donepezil, galantamine, rivastigmine, tacrine Taking darifenacin with these medications can make both drugs less effective. Patients on both should be closely monitored.

PROLONGED USE

No problems expected.

DENOSUMAB

Product names Prolia, Xgeva
Used in the following combined preparations None

GENERAL INFORMATION

Denosumab is a biologic agent, used for the treatment of severe osteoporosis in postmenopausal women who are at high risk of fracture (Prolia®). This drug is also available in a higher dose for reducing the risk of developing bone-related complications from cancer, such as broken bones and/or bone pain (Xgeva®). It may also be used in women who have not responded to, or can't tolerate, other osteoporosis therapies. Denosumab increases bone mineral density and decreases the risk of fractures. For osteoporosis, it is administered by injection every six months. Single-use, prefilled syringes are administered subcutaneously in the upper arm, thigh, or abdomen. Maintain good oral hygiene and inform your dentist that you are on this medication.

INFORMATION FOR USERS

Your drug prescription is tailored for you. Do not alter dosage without checking with your physician.

How taken

Subcutaneous injection.

Frequency and timing of doses
Osteoporosis Once every 6 months.
Bone-related complications with cancer Once every 4 weeks.

Usual adult dosage range
Osteoporosis 60mg every 6 months.
Bone-related complications from cancer 120mg every 4 weeks.

Onset of effect
May take several months to see full benefits.

Duration of action
Up to 6 months.

Diet advice
Adequate intake of calcium and vitamin D is recommended.

Storage
Store in the refrigerator (between 2 and 8°C). Do not freeze. Avoid shaking vigorously. May be kept at room temperature (up to 25°C) in the original package if used within 30 days.

Missed dose
Take as soon as you remember. Inform your physician. The next dose should be scheduled 6 months from the date of your last injection.

Stopping the drug
Do not stop taking the drug without consulting your physician.

Exceeding the dose
In rare cases of excess dose, notify your physician right away. In cases of overdose, seek immediate assistance.

SPECIAL PRECAUTIONS

Be sure to tell your physician if:
▼ You have low calcium levels.
▼ You are hypersensitive/allergic to the drug or to any ingredient in the injection.
▼ You are premenopausal.
▼ You are unable to take adequate calcium and vitamin D daily.
▼ You or the person administering the drug has sensitivity to latex.
▼ You have had thyroid or parathyroid surgery.
▼ You plan to have dental surgery or have your teeth removed.
▼ You have a history of cancer.
▼ You are taking other medications.

 Pregnancy
▼ Not recommended.

 Breast-feeding
▼ Not recommended.

 Infants and children
▼ Not recommended.

 Over 60
▼ No special problems.

 Driving and hazardous work
▼ No special problems.

 Alcohol
▼ No special problems.

POSSIBLE ADVERSE EFFECTS

In general, the drug is well tolerated. There may be an increased risk of skin infection, especially in the leg. If you develop symptoms such as red, swollen, painful skin, see a physician right away.

Symptom/effect	Frequency		Discuss with physician		Stop taking drug now	Call physician now
	Common	Rare	Only if severe	In all cases		
Fatigue/asthenia	●			■		
Itching, redness, dryness (eczema)	●		■			
Fever or chills		●		■		
Low calcium level in blood		●		■		
Skin infection/swollen, red area on skin (cellulitis)		●		■		■
Paresthesias		●		■		
Muscle spasms, twitches, cramps, numbness or tingling of fingers or toes		●		■		
Sore mouth, gums or jaw (may indicate osteonecrosis of jaw)		●		■		■
Any fracture		●		■		■

PROLONGED USE

For osteoporosis, the drug has been used up to 3 years in clinical trials. Discuss longer use with physician.

Monitoring Calcium levels should be monitored.

INTERACTIONS

Interactions with other drugs have not been studied.

Immunosuppressants Denosumab may enhance the *adverse effects* of these drugs.

DESMOPRESSIN

Product names DDAVP, Minirin, Octostim, and others
Used in the following combined preparations None

GENERAL INFORMATION

Desmopressin is a synthetic form of the *hormone* vasopressin. Low levels of vasopressin in the body can lead to diabetes insipidus, which causes frequent urination and continual thirst.

Desmopressin can be used to correct the deficiency of vasopressin. It is also used to test for diabetes insipidus, to check kidney function, and to treat nocturnal enuresis (bedwetting) in both children and adults. When given by injection, it helps to boost clotting factors in hemophilia.

Side effects of the drug include low blood sodium and fluid retention (which sometimes requires monitoring of body weight and blood pressure to check the body's water balance).

Desmopressin should not be taken during an episode of vomiting and diarrhea because the body's fluid balance may be upset.

QUICK REFERENCE

Drug group Drugs for diabetes insipidus (p.128)

Overdose danger rating Medium

Dependence rating Low

Prescription needed Yes

Available as generic Yes

INFORMATION FOR USERS

Your drug prescription is tailored for you. Do not alter dosage without checking with your physician.

How taken

Tablets, injection, nasal solution, nasal spray.

Frequency and timing of doses
Diabetes insipidus 3 x daily (tablets); 1–2 x daily (nasal spray/solution). *Nocturnal enuresis* At bedtime (tablets, nasal spray/solution). Avoid fluids from 1 hour before bedtime to 8 hours afterwards.

Usual dosage range
Diabetes insipidus: *Adults* 300–600mcg daily (tablets); 1–4 puffs (nasal spray); 10–40mcg daily (nasal solution). *Children* 300–600mcg daily (tablets); up to 2 puffs (nasal spray); 20mcg (nasal solution). Nocturnal enuresis: 200–400mcg for children over 5 years only (tablets); 20–40mcg (nasal solution); 2–4 puffs (nasal spray).

Onset of effect
Begins within a few minutes with full effects in a few hours (injection, nasal solution, and nasal spray); 30–90 minutes (tablets).

Duration of action
Tablets 8 hours; injection and nasal solutions 8–12 hours; nasal spray 10–12 hours.

Diet advice
Your physician may advise you to monitor your fluid intake.

Storage
Keep in a cool, dry place (tablets) or in a refrigerator, without freezing (nasal solution and nasal spray), out of the reach of children. Protect from light.

Missed dose
Take as soon as you remember. If your next dose is due within 2 hours, take a single dose now and skip the next.

Stopping the drug
Do not stop the drug without consulting your physician; symptoms of diabetes insipidus may recur.

Exceeding the dose
An occasional unintentional extra dose is unlikely to cause problems. Large overdoses may prevent the kidneys from eliminating fluid, with ensuing problems including convulsions. Notify your physician immediately.

SPECIAL PRECAUTIONS

Be sure to tell your physician if:
▼ You have heart problems.
▼ You have high blood pressure.
▼ You have kidney problems.
▼ You have cystic fibrosis.
▼ You have asthma or allergic rhinitis.
▼ You have epilepsy.
▼ You are taking other medications.

Pregnancy
▼ Used with caution in pregnancy.

Breast-feeding
▼ The drug passes into breast milk, in small amounts, but adverse effects on the baby are unlikely.

Infants and children
▼ No special problems in children; infants may need monitoring to ensure that fluid balance is correct.

Over 60
▼ May need monitoring to ensure that fluid balance is correct.

Driving and hazardous work
▼ No known problems.

Alcohol
▼ Your physician may advise on fluid intake.

PROLONGED USE

Diabetes insipidus: no problems expected.

Nocturnal enuresis: the drug will be withdrawn for at least a week after 3 months for assessment of the need to continue treatment.

Monitoring The levels of electrolytes (such as sodium) in the blood should be monitored periodically.

POSSIBLE ADVERSE EFFECTS

Desmopressin can cause fluid retention and low blood sodium (in serious cases with convulsions). Headache, nausea, vomiting, and epistaxis (nosebleeds) may also occur.

Symptom/effect	Frequency		Discuss with physician		Stop taking drug now	Call physician now
	Common	Rare	Only if severe	In all cases		
Headache		●	■			
Nausea/vomiting		●	■			
Nasal congestion		●	■			
Nosebleeds		●	■			
Increased body weight		●		■		
Stomach pain		●		■		
Convulsions		●		■	▲	■

INTERACTIONS

Antidepressants, chlorpropamide, and carbamazepine These drugs may increase the effects of desmopressin.

Indomethacin This anti-inflammatory drug may increase the body's response to desmopressin.

DEXAMETHASONE

Product names Maxidex, Ozurdex, and others
Used in the following combined preparations Maxitrol, Sofracort Sterile Ear/Eye Drops, Tobradex OPM, and others

GENERAL INFORMATION

Dexamethasone is a long-acting and potent corticosteroid drug that is prescribed to suppress inflammatory and allergic disorders, such as rheumatoid arthritis, shock, macular edema, and brain swelling (due to injury or tumour).

It is also used in conjunction with other drugs to alleviate the nausea and vomiting associated with chemotherapy.

Dexamethasone is available in different forms, including tablets, oral solution, injection, and eye and ear drops.

Low doses of dexamethasone taken for short periods rarely cause serious *side effects*. However, as with other corticosteroids, long-term treatment with high doses can cause unpleasant or dangerous side effects.

INFORMATION FOR USERS

Your drug prescription is tailored for you. Do not alter dosage without checking with your physician.

How taken

Tablets, liquid, injection, intravitreal implant, eye ointment, eye/ear drops.

Frequency and timing of doses
1–4 x daily (with food when taken by mouth); 1–6 hourly (eye drops); 1–4 x daily (ear drops); 1–2 x daily (eye ointment).

Usual dosage range
0.5–10mg daily (by mouth). Higher doses may sometimes be used.

Onset of effect
1–4 days.

Duration of action
Some effects may last several days.

Diet advice
None.

Storage
Keep in a closed container in a cool, dry place out of the reach of children. Protect from light.

Missed dose
Take as soon as you remember. If your next dose is due within 2 hours, take a single dose now and skip the next.

Stopping the drug
Do not stop taking the drug without consulting your physician. It may be necessary to withdraw the drug gradually.

Exceeding the dose
An occasional unintentional extra dose is unlikely to be a cause for concern. But if you notice any unusual symptoms, or if a large overdose has been taken, notify your physician.

POSSIBLE ADVERSE EFFECTS

The more serious adverse effects only occur when dexamethasone is taken systemically in high doses for long periods of time. These are carefully monitored during prolonged treatment. Side effects primarily related to systemic use are listed here.

Symptom/effect	Frequency		Discuss with physician		Stop taking drug now	Call physician now
	Common	Rare	Only if severe	In all cases		
Indigestion	●		■			
Fluid retention	●			■		
Weight gain		●	■			
Acne and other skin effects		●	■			
Muscle weakness		●		■		
Mood changes		●		■		

INTERACTIONS

Antidiabetic drugs Dexamethasone reduces the action of these drugs. Dosage may need to be adjusted accordingly to prevent abnormally high blood sugar.

Barbiturates, phenytoin, rifampin, and carbamazepine These drugs may reduce the effectiveness of dexamethasone. The dosage may need to be adjusted accordingly.

Oral anticoagulant drugs Dexamethasone may increase the effects of these drugs.

Non-steroidal anti-inflammatory drugs These drugs may increase the likelihood of indigestion from dexamethasone.

Antacids These drugs may reduce the effectiveness of, and should be taken at least 2 hours apart from, dexamethasone.

Vaccines Dexamethasone can interact with some vaccines. Discuss with your physician before having any vaccinations.

SPECIAL PRECAUTIONS

Be sure to tell your physician if:
▼ You have had a peptic ulcer.
▼ You have glaucoma.
▼ You have had tuberculosis.
▼ You have suffered from depression or mental illness.
▼ You have a herpes infection.
▼ You are taking an NSAID regularly.
▼ You are taking other medications.

Avoid exposure to chickenpox or shingles if you are on *systemic* treatment.

Pregnancy
▼ Safety in pregnancy not established. Discuss with your physician.

Breast-feeding
▼ The drug passes into the breast milk, but at normal doses adverse effects on the baby are unlikely. Discuss with your physician.

Infants and children
▼ Reduced dose necessary.

Over 60
▼ No known problems.

Driving and hazardous work
▼ No known problems.

Alcohol
▼ Avoid. Alcohol may increase the risk of peptic ulcer with this drug.

Surgery and general anesthetics
▼ Tell your physician that you are taking the drug; close monitoring is required.

PROLONGED USE

Prolonged use of this drug can lead to weight gain, peptic ulcers, glaucoma, cataracts, diabetes, mental disturbances, muscle wasting, fragile bones, and thin skin, and can retard growth in children. People receiving long-term treatment with this drug are advised to carry a 'steroid treatment' card.

DEXTROMETHORPHAN

Product names Balminil DM, Benylin DM, Deslym DM, Koffex DM, and many others
Used in the following combined preparations Neocitran Cold and Cough Night, Triaminic Cold and Cough, and many others

GENERAL INFORMATION

Dextromethorphan is a cough suppressant available over-the-counter in a large number of cough and cold remedies. It is useful for suppressing persistent, dry coughing, especially if the cough is causing disturbed sleep.

Dextromethorphan has little general *sedative* effect. Additionally, unlike the stronger *opioid* cough suppressants, its use is unlikely to lead to *dependence* when it is taken as recommended.

Like other cough suppressants, dextromethorphan should not be used to treat phlegm-producing coughs. This is because its use may prolong a chest infection by preventing the normal elimination of sputum through coughing.

Although dextromethorphan is less sedating than many similar cough suppressants, its principal *adverse effect* is drowsiness. However, *side effects* from this drug are rare when it is taken in recommended doses.

INFORMATION FOR USERS

Follow instructions on the label. Call your physician if symptoms worsen.

How taken

Tablets, SR-tablets, capsules, liquid, powder for solution.

Frequency and timing of doses
Up to 4 x daily as required. SR products 1–2 x daily.

Usual adult dosage range
Adults 12 years and older, 15–30mg per dose, up to a maximum of 120mg/24 hours.
Children 6–11 years, 15mg per dose up to a maximum of 60mg/24 hours.

Onset of effect
Within 30 minutes.

Duration of action
4–8 hours.

Diet advice
None.

Storage
Keep in a closed container in a cool, dry place out of the reach of children.

Missed dose
Take as soon as you remember if needed to relieve coughing. If you are using a sustained release product, and if your next dose is less than 4 hours away, take a dose now and skip the next dose.

Stopping the drug
Can be safely stopped as soon as you no longer need it.

Exceeding the dose
An occasional unintentional extra dose is unlikely to cause problems. Larger overdoses may cause nausea, vomiting, stomach pain, dizziness, drowsiness, and breathing problems. Notify your physician.

SPECIAL PRECAUTIONS

Be sure to consult your physician or pharmacist before taking this drug if:
▼ You have a liver disorder.
▼ You suffer from asthma or another serious respiratory problem.
▼ You are taking other medications.

Pregnancy
▼ No evidence of risk to the developing baby when normal doses are used for short periods Discuss with your physician.

Breast-feeding
▼ The drug passes into the breast milk, but at normal doses adverse effects on the baby are unlikely. Discuss with your physician.

Infants and children
▼ Not recommended for children under 6 years of age. Consult with your physician or pharmacist before using this medication in children.

Over 60
▼ Reduced dose necessary.

Driving and hazardous work
▼ Avoid such activities until you have learned how the drug affects you; it may reduce alertness.

Alcohol
▼ Avoid. Alcohol may increase the sedative effects of this drug.

POSSIBLE ADVERSE EFFECTS

The principal adverse effects of this drug are related to its sedative properties. The effects normally diminish after a few days and can often be reduced by adjustment of dosage.

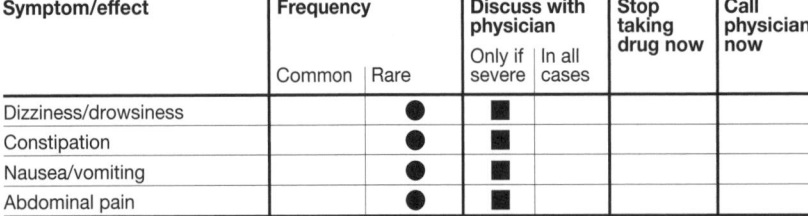

Symptom/effect	Frequency		Discuss with physician		Stop taking drug now	Call physician now
	Common	Rare	Only if severe	In all cases		
Dizziness/drowsiness		●	■			
Constipation		●	■			
Nausea/vomiting		●	■			
Abdominal pain		●	■			

INTERACTIONS

Sedatives All drugs, including alcohol, that have a *sedative* effect on the central nervous system can increase the sedative properties of dextromethorphan. Such drugs include anti-anxiety and sleeping drugs, antihistamines, opioid analgesics, antidepressants, and antipsychotics.

Monoamine oxidase inhibitors (MAOIs)
These drugs may interact dangerously with dextromethorphan to cause excitation and fever.

Fluoxetine, quinidine, paroxetine, rizatriptan and similar drugs can increase dextromethorphan levels.

PROLONGED USE

Dextromethorphan should not be taken for longer than 1 week except on the advice of a physician.

DIAZEPAM

Product names Apo-Diazepam, Diastat, Diazemuls, Valium 5 Tab
Used in the following combined preparations None

GENERAL INFORMATION

Introduced in the early 1960s, diazepam is the best known and most widely used of the benzodiazepine group of drugs. The benzodiazepines help relieve tension and nervousness, relax muscles, and encourage sleep. Their actions and *adverse effects* are described more fully on page 67.

Diazepam has a wide range of uses. Besides being commonly used in the treatment of anxiety and anxiety-related insomnia, it is prescribed as a muscle relaxant, in the treatment of alcohol withdrawal, and for the relief of epileptic seizures. Given intravenously, it is used to sedate people undergoing certain uncomfortable medical procedures.

Diazepam can be habit-forming if taken regularly over a long period. Its effects may also diminish with time. For these reasons, courses of treatment with diazepam are limited to two weeks whenever possible.

QUICK REFERENCE

Drug group Benzodiazepine anti-anxiety drugs (p.67), muscle relaxant (p.106), and antiepileptic drugs (p.70)

Overdose danger rating Medium

Dependence rating High

Prescription needed Yes

Available as generic Yes

INFORMATION FOR USERS

Your drug prescription is tailored for you. Do not alter dosage without checking with your physician.

How taken

Tablets, injection, rectal solution.

Frequency and timing of doses
1–4 x daily.

Usual adult dosage range
Anxiety 6–30mg daily.
Muscle spasm 2–60mg daily.

Onset of effect
Immediate effect (injection); 30 minutes–2 hours (other methods of administration).

Duration of action
Up to 24 hours. Some effect may last up to 4 days.

Diet advice
None.

Storage
Keep in a closed container in a cool, dry place out of the reach of children.

Missed dose
Take as soon as you remember. If your next dose is due within 2 hours, take a single dose now and skip the next.

Stopping the drug
If you have been taking the drug continuously for less than 2 weeks, it can be safely stopped as soon as you no longer need it. However, if you have been taking it for longer, consult your physician, who will supervise a gradual reduction in dosage. Stopping abruptly may lead to withdrawal symptoms (see p.63).

Exceeding the dose
An occasional unintentional extra dose is unlikely to cause problems. Larger overdoses may cause excessive drowsiness. Notify your physician.

SPECIAL PRECAUTIONS

Be sure to tell your physician if:
▼ You have severe respiratory disease.
▼ You have long-term liver or kidney problems.
▼ You have had problems with alcohol or drug abuse.
▼ You are taking other medications.

Pregnancy
▼ Not usually recommended; may cause adverse effects on newborn baby at time of delivery. Discuss with your physician.

Breast-feeding
▼ The drug passes into the breast milk and may affect the baby. Discuss with your physician.

Infants and children
▼ Reduced dose necessary.

Over 60
▼ Increased likelihood of adverse effects. Not commonly used in this age group. Reduced dose necessary.

Driving and hazardous work
▼ Recommended to avoid such activities. Diazepam can cause reduced alertness, slowed reactions, and increased aggression.

Alcohol
▼ Avoid. Alcohol may increase the sedative effects of this drug.

POSSIBLE ADVERSE EFFECTS

The principal adverse effects of this drug are related to its *sedative* properties. The effects normally diminish after a few days and can often be reduced by adjustment of dosage.

Symptom/effect	Frequency		Discuss with physician		Stop taking drug now	Call physician now
	Common	Rare	Only if severe	In all cases		
Daytime drowsiness	●		■			
Dizziness/unsteadiness	●			■		
Forgetfulness/confusion	●			■		
Headache		●	■			
Blurred vision		●		■		

INTERACTIONS

Sedatives All drugs that have a sedative effect on the central nervous system can increase the sedative properties of diazepam.

Grapefruit juice may increase diazepam level.

Cimetidine, fluconazole, fluoxetine, erythromycin, clarithromycin, ciprofloxacin, isoniazid, ritonavir, and indinavir These drugs may inhibit the breakdown of diazepam leading to increased levels in the blood and risk of adverse effects.

PROLONGED USE

Regular use of this drug over several weeks can lead to a reduction in its effect as the body adapts. It may also be habit-forming when taken for extended periods, and severe withdrawal reactions can occur.

DICLOFENAC

Product names Apo-Diclo, Nu-Diclo, Pennsaid, Voltaren, Voltaren Rapide, and others
Used in the following combined preparation Arthrotec

GENERAL INFORMATION

Taken as a single dose, diclofenac has analgesic properties similar to those of acetaminophen. It is taken to relieve mild to moderate headache, menstrual pain, and pain following minor surgery. When diclofenac is given regularly over a long period, it exerts an anti-inflammatory effect and is used to relieve the pain and stiffness associated with rheumatoid arthritis and advanced osteoarthritis. Diclofenac may also be prescribed to treat acute attacks of gout and to treat eye inflammation when an infection is not present.

The combined preparation, Arthrotec, contains diclofenac and misoprostol (see p.374). Misoprostol helps prevent gastroduodenal ulceration, which is sometimes caused by diclofenac, and may be particularly useful in patients at risk of developing this problem.

INFORMATION FOR USERS

Your drug prescription is tailored for you. Do not alter dosage without checking with your physician.

How taken

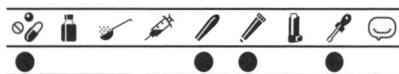

Tablets, extended-release tablets, rectal suppository, topical solution, ophthalmic solution.

Frequency and timing of doses
1–3 x daily with food.

Usual adult dosage range
75–150mg daily.

Onset of effect
Around 1 hour (pain relief); full anti-inflammatory effect may take 2 weeks.

Duration of action
Up to 12 hours; up to 24 hours (SR-preparations).

Diet advice
None.

Storage
Keep in a closed container in a cool, dry place out of the reach of children.

Missed dose
Take as soon as you remember. If your next dose is due within 2 hours, take a single dose now and skip the next.

Stopping the drug
When taken for short-term pain relief, diclofenac can be safely stopped as soon as you no longer need it. If prescribed for long-term treatment (e.g., for arthritis), speak to your physician before stopping the drug.

Exceeding the dose
An occasional unintentional extra dose is unlikely to be a cause for concern. But if you notice any unusual symptoms or if a large overdose has been taken, notify your physician.

SPECIAL PRECAUTIONS

Be sure to tell your physician if:
▼ You have long-term liver or kidney problems.
▼ You have a bleeding disorder.
▼ You have had a peptic ulcer or suffer from indigestion.
▼ You have porphyria.
▼ You are allergic to ASA or other NSAIDs.
▼ You suffer from asthma, heart problems, or high blood pressure.
▼ You have congestive heart failure.
▼ You are taking other medications.

Pregnancy
▼ The drug may increase the risk of adverse effects on the baby's heart and may prolong labour if taken in the third trimester. Discuss with your physician.

Breast-feeding
▼ Small amounts of the drug pass into the breast milk, but adverse effects on the baby are unlikely. Discuss with your physician.

Infants and children
▼ Reduced dose necessary.

Over 60
▼ Increased risk of adverse effects. Reduced dose may be necessary.

Driving and hazardous work
▼ Avoid such activities until you have learned how the drug affects you because it can cause dizziness.

Alcohol
▼ Avoid. Alcohol may increase the risk of stomach irritation.

Surgery and general anesthetics
▼ Discuss with your physician or dentist before any surgery.

POSSIBLE ADVERSE EFFECTS

The most common *adverse effects* are gastrointestinal disturbances. Black or blood-stained vomit or feces should be reported to your physician without delay.

Symptom/effect	Frequency		Discuss with physician		Stop taking drug now	Call physician now
	Common	Rare	Only if severe	In all cases		
Heartburn/indigestion	●		■			
Nausea/vomiting	●		■			
Headache		●	■			
Drowsiness/dizziness		●	■			
Swollen feet/ankles		●		■		
Rash/itching		●		■	▲	
Wheezing/breathlessness		●		■	▲	▮
Black/bloodstained feces/vomit		●		■	▲	▮

INTERACTIONS

General note Interacts with other NSAIDs, oral anticoagulants, and corticosteroids to increase the risk of bleeding and/or ulcers.

Antihypertensive drugs and diuretics The beneficial effects of these drugs may be reduced with diclofenac.

Cyclosporine Diclofenac may increase the risk of kidney problems.

Lithium, digoxin, and methotrexate Diclofenac may increase the blood levels of these drugs to an undesirable extent.

PROLONGED USE

There is an increased risk of bleeding from peptic ulcers and in the bowel with prolonged use of diclofenac. There is also a small risk of a heart attack or stroke, especially in those with cardiovascular conditions.

DICYCLOMINE

Product names Bentylol, Dicyclomine hydrochloride, Protylol
Used in the following combined preparations None

GENERAL INFORMATION

Dicyclomine is a mild *anticholinergic antispasmodic* drug that relieves painful abdominal cramps caused by spasms of the smooth muscle in the wall of the gastrointestinal tract. It can be used to treat irritable bowel syndrome, indigestion and colicky conditions in babies (only over 6 months). Dicyclomine relieves symptoms but does not cure the underlying condition. Additional treatment with other drugs and self-help measures,

such as dietary changes, may be recommended by your physician.

Side effects with dicyclomine are rare, but they include headaches, constipation, urinary difficulties, and palpitations.

INFORMATION FOR USERS

Your drug prescription is tailored for you. Do not alter dosage without checking with your physician.

How taken

Tablets, liquid.

Frequency and timing of doses
3–4 x daily before or after meals.

Usual dosage range
Adults 30–80mg daily.
Children Reduced dose according to age and weight.

Onset of effect
Within 1–2 hours.

Duration of action
4–6 hours.

Diet advice
None.

Storage
Keep in a closed container in a cool, dry place out of the reach of children. Protect from light.

Missed dose
Take as soon as you remember. If your next dose is due within 2 hours, take a single dose now and skip the next.

Stopping the drug
The drug can be stopped without causing problems when it is no longer needed.

Exceeding the dose
An occasional unintentional extra dose is unlikely to cause problems. Large overdoses may cause drowsiness, dizziness, and difficulty in swallowing. Notify your physician.

SPECIAL PRECAUTIONS

Be sure to tell your physician if:
▼ You have glaucoma.
▼ You have urinary problems and/or an enlarged prostate gland.
▼ You have hiatus hernia or suffer from heartburn or acid reflux.
▼ You have a heart condition.
▼ You have myasthenia gravis.
▼ You are taking other medications.

Pregnancy
▼ No evidence of risk.

Breast-feeding
▼ The drug passes into the breast milk, but at normal doses adverse effects on the baby are unlikely. Discuss with your physician.

Infants and children
▼ Reduced dose necessary. Not recommended in infants under 6 months.

Over 60
▼ Reduced dose necessary. The elderly are more susceptible to anticholinergic side effects.

Driving and hazardous work
▼ Avoid such activities until you have learned how dicyclomine affects you because the drug can cause drowsiness and blurred vision.

Alcohol
▼ Avoid. Alcohol may increase the sedative effects of this drug.

POSSIBLE ADVERSE EFFECTS

Most people do not notice any *adverse effects* when taking dicyclomine. Those that do occur are related to its anticholinergic properties and include drowsiness and dry mouth. Such symptoms may be overcome by adjusting the dosage, or they may disappear after a few days of usage as your body adjusts to the drug.

Symptom/effect	Frequency		Discuss with physician		Stop taking drug now	Call physician now
	Common	Rare	Only if severe	In all cases		
Dry mouth		●	■			
Headache		●	■			
Blurred vision		●	■			
Constipation		●	■			
Drowsiness/dizziness		●	■			
Difficulty in passing urine		●		■		
Palpitations		●		■		

INTERACTIONS

Sedatives All drugs that have a *sedative* effect on the central nervous system may increase the sedative properties of dicyclomine.

Anticholinergic drugs These drugs may increase the adverse effects of dicyclomine.

PROLONGED USE

No problems expected.

DIGOXIN

Product names Lanoxin, Toloxin
Used in the following combined preparations None

GENERAL INFORMATION

Digoxin is the most widely used extract of digitalis, a compound obtained from the leaves of the foxglove plant. It is sometimes given in the treatment of congestive heart failure and certain alterations of heart rhythm.

Digoxin increases the force of the heartbeat making it more effective in pumping blood around the body. This in turn helps to control breathlessness, fluid retention, and tiredness in people with heart failure.

The effective dose of digoxin can be close to the toxic dose and, therefore, treatment needs careful monitoring to prevent toxic doses being reached. A number of *adverse effects* (see below) may indicate that the toxic level is close and should be reported to your physician.

INFORMATION FOR USERS

Your drug prescription is tailored for you. Do not alter dosage without checking with your physician.

How taken

Tablets, liquid, injection.

Frequency and timing of doses
Usually once daily. Starting dose may be given up to 3 x daily.

Usual adult dosage range
0.0625–0.25mg daily (by mouth).

Onset of effect
Within a few minutes (injection); within 1–2 hours (by mouth).

Duration of action
Up to 4 days.

Diet advice
This drug may be more toxic if potassium levels are depleted, so you should include potassium-rich fruit and vegetables, such as bananas and tomatoes, in your diet.

Storage
Keep in a closed container in a cool, dry place out of the reach of children. Protect from light.

Missed dose
Take as soon as you remember. If your next dose is due within 8 hours, take a dose now and skip the next.

Stopping the drug
Do not stop the drug without consulting your physician; stopping the drug may lead to worsening of the underlying condition.

OVERDOSE ACTION

 Seek immediate medical advice in all cases. Take emergency action if palpitations, severe weakness, chest pain, or loss of consciousness occur.

See Drug poisoning emergency guide (p.526).

SPECIAL PRECAUTIONS

Be sure to tell your physician if:
▼ You have a long-term liver problem.
▼ You have thyroid trouble.
▼ You are taking other medications.

Pregnancy
▼ No evidence of risk, but adjustment in dose may be necessary.

Breast-feeding
▼ The drug passes into breast milk, but at normal doses adverse effects on the baby are unlikely. Discuss with your physician.

Infants and children
▼ Reduced dose necessary.

Over 60
▼ Increased likelihood of adverse effects. Reduced dose may therefore be necessary.

Driving and hazardous work
▼ Special problems are unlikely, but do not undertake these activities until you know how digoxin affects you.

Alcohol
▼ No special problems.

POSSIBLE ADVERSE EFFECTS

The possible adverse effects of digoxin are usually due to increased levels of the drug in the blood. Any symptoms should be reported to your physician without delay.

Symptom/effect	Frequency		Discuss with physician		Stop taking drug now	Call physician now
	Common	Rare	Only if severe	In all cases		
Tiredness	●		■			
Nausea/loss of appetite	●			■		
Confusion		●		■		
Visual disturbance		●		■	▲	▮
Palpitations		●		■	▲	▮

INTERACTIONS

General note Many drugs interact with digoxin. Do not take any medication without the advice of your physician or pharmacist.

Diuretics may increase the risk of adverse effects from digoxin.

Antacids may reduce the effects of digoxin. The effect of digoxin may increase when such drugs are stopped.

Anti-arrhythmic drugs may increase blood levels of digoxin.

PROLONGED USE

No problems expected.

Monitoring Periodic checks on blood levels of digoxin and body salts may be advised.

DILTIAZEM

Product names Cardizem CD, CO Diltiazem CD, CO Diltiazem T, Tiazac
Used in the following combined preparations None

GENERAL INFORMATION

Diltiazem belongs to the group of drugs known as calcium channel blockers (p.87). These drugs interfere with the conduction of signals in the muscles of the heart and blood vessels.

Diltiazem is used in the treatment of angina and longer acting formulations are used to treat high blood pressure. When this drug is taken regularly, it reduces the frequency of angina attacks but does not work quickly enough to reduce the pain of an angina attack that is already in progress.

Diltiazem does not adversely affect breathing and is valuable for people who suffer from asthma, for whom other anti-angina drugs may not be suitable.

Different brands of diltiazem may not be equivalent so you should always take the same brand.

QUICK REFERENCE

Drug group Calcium channel blockers (p.87) and antihypertensive drugs (p.88)

Overdose danger rating Medium

Dependence rating Low

Prescription needed Yes

Available as generic Yes

INFORMATION FOR USERS

Your drug prescription is tailored for you. Do not alter dosage without checking with your physician.

How taken

Tablets, SR-capsules, CD-capsules.

Frequency and timing of doses
3 x daily (tablets); 2 x daily (SR-capsules), 1 x daily (CD capsules).

Usual adult dosage range
180–360mg daily.

Onset of effect
2–3 hours.

Duration of action
6–8 hours.

Diet advice
None.

Storage
Keep in a closed container in a cool, dry place out of the reach of children.

Missed dose
Take as soon as you remember. If your next dose is due within 2 hours, take a single dose now and skip the next.

Stopping the drug
Do not stop taking the drug without consulting your physician; symptoms may recur. Stopping suddenly may worsen angina.

Exceeding the dose
An occasional unintentional extra dose is unlikely to cause problems. Large overdoses may cause dizziness or collapse. Notify your physician urgently.

SPECIAL PRECAUTIONS

Be sure to tell your physician if:
▼ You have long-term liver or kidney problems.
▼ You have heart failure.
▼ You are taking other medications.

Pregnancy
▼ Not usually prescribed. Discuss with your physician.

Breast-feeding
▼ The drug passes into the breast milk and may affect the baby. Discuss with your physician.

Infants and children
▼ Not recommended.

Over 60
▼ Increased likelihood of adverse effects. Reduced dose may therefore be necessary.

Driving and hazardous work
▼ Avoid such activities until you have learned how diltiazem affects you because the drug can cause dizziness due to lowered blood pressure.

Alcohol
▼ Avoid. Alcohol may lower blood pressure, causing dizziness.

POSSIBLE ADVERSE EFFECTS

Diltiazem can cause various minor symptoms that are common to other calcium channel blockers as well. These include headache and nausea. The most serious effect is the possibility of a slowed heart beat, which may cause tiredness or dizziness. These effects can sometimes be controlled by an adjustment in dosage.

Symptom/effect	Frequency		Discuss with physician		Stop taking drug now	Call physician now
	Common	Rare	Only if severe	In all cases		
Headache	●		■			
Nausea/vomiting	●		■			
Dry mouth	●		■			
Leg and ankle swelling	●		■			
Breast/gum enlargement		●		■		
Dizziness/tiredness		●		■		
Rash		●		■		

PROLONGED USE

No problems expected.

INTERACTIONS

Antihypertensive drugs Diltiazem increases the effects of these drugs, leading to a further reduction in blood pressure.

Anticonvulsant drugs Levels of these drugs may be altered by diltiazem.

Anti-arrhythmic drugs There is a risk of side effects on the heart if these are taken with diltiazem.

Digoxin Blood levels and adverse effects of this drug may be increased if it is taken with diltiazem. The dosage of digoxin may need to be reduced.

Theophylline/aminophylline Diltiazem may increase the levels of this drug.

Beta blockers increase the risk of the heart slowing.

DIMENHYDRINATE

Product names Apo-Dimenhydrinate, Gravol, Novo-Dimenate, PMS Dimenhydrinate, Travel Tabs
Used in the following combined preparations None

GENERAL INFORMATION

Dimenhydrinate is an antihistamine that is mainly used as an anti-emetic drug. It is especially effective for treating the nausea and vomiting that occur with vertigo. It is also prescribed to relieve the symptoms of inner ear disorders such as Ménière's disease and to prevent and treat motion sickness. Dimenhydrinate may be effective in treating other forms of nausea and vomiting, including those caused by drugs and radiation treatments for cancer.

Like other antihistamines, dimenhydrinate has a *sedative* effect that can cause problems if you need to drive or operate machinery.

QUICK REFERENCE

Drug group Antihistamines (p.110) and anti-emetic drugs (p.74)

Overdose danger rating Medium

Dependence rating Low

Prescription needed No

Available as generic Yes

INFORMATION FOR USERS

Follow instructions on the label. Call your physician if symptoms worsen.

How taken

Tablets, chewable tablets, slow-release (SR) capsules, oral liquid, injection, rectal suppositories.

Frequency and timing of doses
Adults Every 4 hours
Children Every 6–8 hours. To prevent motion sickness the first dose should be taken 30 minutes before travel.

Usual oral dosage range
Adults 50–100mg per dose (maximum 400mg/24 hours)
Children 2–6 years, 15–25mg per dose (maximum 75mg/24 hours); 6–12 years, 25–50mg per dose (maximum 150mg/24 hours); 12 years and over, 50mg per dose (maximum 300mg/24 hours).

Onset of effect
Within 30 minutes.

Duration of action
6–8 hours

Diet advice
None.

Storage
Keep in a closed container in a cool, dry place away from reach of children.

Missed dose
Take when you remember. Adjust the timing of your next dose accordingly.

Stopping the drug
Can be safely stopped as soon as you no longer need it.

Exceeding the dose
An occasional unintentional extra dose is unlikely to cause problems. Larger overdoses may cause unusual drowsiness. Notify your physician.

SPECIAL PRECAUTIONS

Be sure to consult your physician or pharmacist before taking this drug if:
▼ You have impaired liver or kidney function.
▼ You have chronic lung disease.
▼ You have had glaucoma.
▼ You have prostate trouble.
▼ You have had seizures.
▼ You are taking other medications.

Pregnancy
▼ While there is no evidence of risk to the developing baby, absolute safety in pregnancy has not been established. Discuss with your physician.

Breast-feeding
▼ The drug passes into the breast milk. Its effects on the baby are not clearly known. Discuss with your physician.

Infants and children
▼ Only as prescribed by your physician in children under 2 years. Reduced dose necessary in older children.

Over 60
▼ No special problems.

Driving and hazardous work
▼ Because of the possibility of drowsiness, avoid such activities until you have learned how the drug affects you .

Alcohol
▼ Avoid. Alcohol may increase the sedative effects of this drug.

POSSIBLE ADVERSE EFFECTS

The principal *adverse effects* of this drug are related to its *anticholinergic* properties and, if troublesome, can sometimes be reduced by adjustment of dosage.

Symptom/effect	Frequency		Discuss with physician		Stop taking drug now	Call physician now
	Common	Rare	Only if severe	In all cases		
Drowsiness	●		■			
Dry mouth	●		■			
Blurred vision	●			■		
Confusion/nervousness		●		■		

INTERACTIONS

Alcohol and other sedatives All drugs that have a sedative effect on the central nervous system are likely to increase the sedative properties of dimenhydrinate. Such drugs include alcohol, anti-anxiety and sleeping drugs, antidepressants, opioid analgesics, and antipsychotics.

PROLONGED USE

No special problems, but this drug should not be used for more than a few days except on medical advice.

Anti-emetics may mask the presence of underlying organic abnormalities or the toxic effects of other drugs.

Antihistamines should be discontinued approximately 48 hours prior to allergy skin testing.

DIPHENHYDRAMINE

Product names Benadryl, Nytol, Simply Sleep, Unisom, and others
Used in the following combined preparations Balminil Night-Time, Sinutab N.T. Extra Strength, and others

GENERAL INFORMATION

Diphenhydramine, one of the oldest antihistamines, is used for treating allergies such as allergic rhinitis and urticaria (hives). Injected diphenhydramine is also used in the treatment of anaphylaxis and hypersensitivity reactions to food, drugs, or insect stings.

Because it has *anticholinergic* properties, it is useful in the treatment of *parkinsonism* and movement disorders caused by antipsychotic drugs (p.69). It is also an effective anti-emetic, used to prevent and treat vertigo and motion sickness.

Diphenhydramine has a marked *sedative* action and often causes drowsiness. It is included in several over-the-counter sleeping preparations.

QUICK REFERENCE

Drug group Antihistamines (p.110), anti-emetic drugs (p.74), and sleeping drugs (p.66)

Overdose danger rating Medium

Dependence rating Low

Prescription needed No

Available as generic No

INFORMATION FOR USERS

Follow instructions on the label. Call your physician if symptoms worsen.

How taken

Tablets, chewable tablets, capsules, oral liquid, injection, cream.

Frequency and timing of doses
By mouth 3–4 x daily (allergic conditions); 30 minutes before travelling and before meals (motion sickness); 30 minutes before bedtime (insomnia).
Injection Every 2–3 hours (adults).
Cream As directed.

Usual dosage range
Adults 25–200mg daily (by mouth); up to 400mg daily (by injection).
Children Reduced dose necessary according to age and weight.

Onset of effect
Within 1 hour (by mouth); within 20 minutes (injection).

Duration of action
4–6 hours.

Diet advice
None.

Storage
Keep in a closed container in a cool, dry place away from reach of children. Do not freeze.

Missed dose
Take as soon as you remember. If your next dose is due within 2 hours, take a single dose now and skip the next.

Stopping the drug
Can be safely stopped as soon as you no longer need it.

Exceeding the dose
An occasional, unintentional extra dose is unlikely to cause problems. Large overdoses may cause drowsiness or agitation. Notify your physician.

SPECIAL PRECAUTIONS

Be sure to consult your physician or pharmacist before taking this drug if
▼ You have impaired liver function.
▼ You have chronic lung disease.
▼ You have had epileptic seizures.
▼ You have glaucoma.
▼ You have urinary difficulties.
▼ You are taking other medications.

Pregnancy
▼ No evidence of risk to the developing baby when normal doses are used for short periods. Discuss with your physician.

Breast-feeding
▼ The drug passes into the breast milk and may make the baby drowsy or irritable. Discuss with your physician.

Infants and children
▼ Not recommended for newborn or premature infants. Reduced dose necessary for older children.

Over 60
▼ Reduced dose may be necessary. Discuss with your physician.

Driving and hazardous work
▼ Avoid such activities until you have learned how the drug affects you; it can cause drowsiness.

Alcohol
▼ Avoid. Alcohol may increase the sedative effects of this drug.

POSSIBLE ADVERSE EFFECTS

Drowsiness is the most common *adverse effect* of diphenhydramine. Other *side effects*, such as dry mouth and blurred vision, are due to its anticholinergic action.

Symptom/effect	Frequency		Discuss with physician		Stop taking drug now	Call physician now
	Common	Rare	Only if severe	In all cases		
Drowsiness	●		■			
Dry mouth		●	■			
Nausea/abdominal pain		●	■			
Blurred vision		●		■		
Urinary difficulties		●		■		
Disorientation/excitation		●		■		

INTERACTIONS

Sedatives All sedatives, including alcohol, are likely to enhance the sedative effect of this drug.

Anticholinergic drugs are likely to increase the anticholinergic effects of diphenhydramine.

PROLONGED USE

The effect of this drug may become weaker with prolonged use over a period of weeks or months as the body adapts. Transfer to a different antihistamine may be recommended.

Antihistamines should be discontinued approximately 48 hours prior to allergy skin testing.

DIPHENOXYLATE

Product name None
Used in the following combined preparation Lomotil

GENERAL INFORMATION

Diphenoxylate is an antidiarrheal drug that is chemically related to the *opioid* analgesics. It reduces bowel contractions and, therefore, the fluidity and frequency of bowel movements. Available in tablet form, it is prescribed for the relief of sudden or recurrent bouts of diarrhea.

The drug is not suitable for diarrhea that is caused by infection, poisons, or antibiotics as it may delay recovery by slowing expulsion of harmful substances from the bowel. Diphenoxylate can cause toxic megacolon, a dangerous dilation of the bowel that shuts off blood supply to the wall of the bowel and increases the risk of perforation.

At recommended doses, serious *adverse effects* are rare. To guard against abuse, atropine is added to diphenoxylate tablets. If these are taken in excessive amounts, the atropine will cause highly unpleasant *anticholinergic* effects. Diphenoxylate is especially dangerous for young children; be sure to store the drug out of their reach.

QUICK REFERENCE

Drug group Opioid antidiarrheal drugs (p.96)

Overdose danger rating Medium

Dependence rating Medium

Prescription needed Yes

Available as generic No

INFORMATION FOR USERS

Your drug prescription is tailored for you. Do not alter dosage without checking with your physician.

How taken

Tablets.

Frequency and timing of doses
3–4 x daily.

Usual dosage range
Adults 5mg initially, followed by doses of 2.5–5mg. Maximum dose: 20mg in 24 hours. *Children* Reduced dose necessary according to age and weight.

Onset of effect
Within 1 hour. Control of diarrhea may take some hours.

Duration of action
Up to 24 hours.

Diet advice
Ensure adequate fluid intake during an attack of diarrhea.

Storage
Keep in a closed container in a cool, dry place out of the reach of children. Protect from light.

Missed dose
Take as soon as you remember. If your next dose is due within 3 hours, take a single dose now and skip the next.

Stopping the drug
Can be safely stopped as soon as you no longer need it.

Exceeding the dose
An occasional, unintentional extra dose is unlikely to cause problems. Large overdoses may cause unusual drowsiness, dryness of the mouth and skin, restlessness, and in extreme cases, loss of consciousness. Symptoms of overdose may be delayed. Notify your physician.

SPECIAL PRECAUTIONS

Be sure to tell your physician if
▼ You have a long-term liver problem.
▼ You have severe abdominal pain.
▼ You have bloodstained diarrhea.
▼ You have ulcerative colitis.
▼ You have recently taken antibiotics.
▼ You have recently travelled abroad.
▼ You are taking other medications.

Pregnancy
▼ Safety in pregnancy not established. Discuss with your physician.

Breast-feeding
▼ The drug passes into the breast milk and may cause drowsiness in the baby. Discuss with your physician.

Infants and children
▼ Not recommended under 4 years. Reduced dose necessary for older children.

Over 60
▼ Reduced dose may be necessary.

Driving and hazardous work
▼ Avoid such activities until you have learned how diphenoxylate affects you because the drug may cause drowsiness and dizziness.

Alcohol
▼ Avoid. Alcohol may increase the *sedative* effects of this drug.

POSSIBLE ADVERSE EFFECTS

Side effects occur infrequently with diphenoxylate. If abdominal pain or distension, nausea or vomiting occur, notify your physician.

Symptom/effect	Frequency		Discuss with physician		Stop taking drug now	Call physician now
	Common	Rare	Only if severe	In all cases		
Drowsiness	●		■			
Restlessness		●	■			
Headache		●	■			
Skin rash/itching		●		■		
Dizziness		●		■		
Nausea/vomiting		●		■	▲	!
Abdominal discomfort		●		■	▲	!

PROLONGED USE

Not usually recommended.

INTERACTIONS

Sedatives All drugs that have a sedative effect on the central nervous system may increase the sedative effect of diphenoxylate.

Monoamine oxidase inhibitors (MAOIs) There is a risk of a dangerous rise in blood pressure if MAOIs are taken together with diphenoxylate.

DIPYRIDAMOLE

Product names Apo-Dipyridamole, Dipyridamole for injection, Persantine injection
Used in the following combined preparation Aggrenox

GENERAL INFORMATION

Dipyridamole was introduced in the late 1970s as an anti-angina drug; its purpose was to improve the capability of people with angina to exercise. More effective drugs are now available to help with this problem, but dipyridamole is still prescribed as an antiplatelet drug. It acts by reducing the ability of platelets to stick to each other and to blood vessel walls, which reduces the likelihood of clots forming. This is especially important in people who have had a stroke or have undergone heart valve replacement surgery. Dipyridamole is usually given together with other drugs such as warfarin or ASA. The drug can also be given by injection during certain types of diagnostic test on the heart.

Side effects may occur, especially during the early days of treatment. If they persist, your physician may advise a reduction in dosage.

QUICK REFERENCE

Drug group Antiplatelet drugs (p.90)

Overdose danger rating Medium

Dependence rating Low

Prescription needed Yes

Available as generic Yes

INFORMATION FOR USERS

Your drug prescription is tailored for you. Do not alter dosage without checking with your physician.

How taken

Tablets, capsules, injection (for diagnostic tests only).

Frequency and timing of doses
4 x daily (tablets);
2 x daily (Aggrenox capsules).

Usual adult dosage range
300–400mg daily.

Onset of effect
Within 1 hour. Full therapeutic effect may not be reached for 2–3 weeks.

Duration of action
Up to 8 hours.

Diet advice
None.

Storage
Keep in a closed container in a cool, dry place out of the reach of children. Protect from light.

Missed dose
Take as soon as you remember. If your next dose is due within 2 hours, take a single dose now and skip the next.

Stopping the drug
Do not stop taking the drug without consulting your physician; withdrawal of the drug could lead to abnormal blood clotting.

Exceeding the dose
An occasional unintentional extra dose is unlikely to be a cause for concern. Large overdoses may cause dizziness or vomiting. Notify your physician.

SPECIAL PRECAUTIONS

Be sure to tell your physician if:
▼ You have low blood pressure.
▼ You have a blood clotting disorder.
▼ You suffer from migraine.
▼ You have angina or heart valve problems.
▼ You have had a recent heart attack.
▼ You have myasthenia gravis.
▼ You are taking other medications.

Pregnancy
▼ Safety in pregnancy not established. Discuss with your physician.

Breast-feeding
▼ The drug passes into the breast milk but at normal doses adverse effects on the baby are unlikely. Discuss with your physician.

Infants and children
▼ Reduced dose necessary.

Over 60
▼ No special problems.

Driving and hazardous work
▼ Avoid such activities until you have learned how dipyridamole affects you because the drug may cause dizziness and faintness.

Alcohol
▼ No known problems.

POSSIBLE ADVERSE EFFECTS

Adverse effects are rare. Possible symptoms include dizziness, headache, fainting, stomach upsets including nausea, and rash. In rare cases, the drug may aggravate angina.

Symptom/effect	Frequency		Discuss with physician		Stop taking drug now	Call physician now
	Common	Rare	Only if severe	In all cases		
Stomach upset/nausea	●		■			
Headache	●			■		
Flushing	●		■			
Breathing difficulties/ swollen lips		●	■	▲	■	
Diarrhea		●	■			
Dizziness/fainting		●		■		
Rash		●		■	▲	

PROLONGED USE

No known problems.

INTERACTIONS

Adenosine should not be given to somebody who is taking dipyridamole as the combination can cause a serious drop in blood pressure.

Antacids may reduce the effectiveness of dipyridamole.

Anticoagulant drugs The effect of these drugs may be increased by dipyridamole, thereby increasing the risk of uncontrolled bleeding. The dosage of the anticoagulant should be reduced accordingly.

Antihypertensives Dipyridamole may increase the effect of these drugs.

Cholinesterase inhibitors Used to treat myasthenia gravis, the effect of these drugs may be reduced by dipyridamole.

DOCUSATE SODIUM

Product names Colace, Correctol Stool Softener, Novo-Docusate, Selax, Soflax
Used in the following combined preparations Senokot-S

GENERAL INFORMATION

Docusate is a stool softener and is used in the management of constipation due to hard stools. Taking it regularly makes the stools softer and easier to pass. Docusate may be recommended to be used by those with heart conditions to ease the passage of stools and to avoid straining on defecation.

Laxatives, including docusate, should not be used in those experiencing vomiting, abdominal pain, or fever.

INFORMATION FOR USERS

Follow instructions on the label. Call your physician if symptoms worsen.

How taken

Capsules, liquid, drops.

Frequency and timing of doses
Once to twice daily.

Usual adult dosage range
100–200mg.

Onset of effect
Within 1–2 days.

Duration of action
Up to 24 hours.

Diet advice
None.

Storage
Keep in a closed container in a cool, dry place out of the reach of children.

Missed dose
If you miss a dose, take it as soon as you remember. Resume normal dose thereafter.

Stopping the drug
Can be safely stopped as soon as you no longer need it.

Exceeding the dose
An occasional unintentional extra dose is unlikely to be a cause for concern. But if you notice unusual symptoms, or if a large overdose has been taken, notify your physician. Large overdoses may cause constipation and cramping. Notify your physician.

POSSIBLE ADVERSE EFFECTS

Generally well tolerated.

Symptom/effect	Frequency		Discuss with physician		Stop taking drug now	Call physician now
	Common	Rare	Only if severe	In all cases		
Abdominal pain		●		■		
Cramping		●		■		
Rash		●		■		

INTERACTIONS

Mineral oil Docusate should not be administered with mineral oil as this may increase the absorption of the oil.

All medications Generally recommended that docusate not be administered within 2 hours of other medications.

SPECIAL PRECAUTIONS

Be sure to consult your physician or pharmacist before taking this drug if:
▼ You have severe constipation, and/or nausea, vomiting, or abdominal pain.
▼ You have unexplained rectal bleeding.
▼ You have difficulty swallowing.
▼ You have a known narrowing of the bowel.
▼ You are taking other medications.

Pregnancy
▼ Safety in pregnancy not established. Discuss with your physician.

Breast-feeding
▼ Safety in breast-feeding not established. Discuss with your physician.

Infants and children
▼ Reduced dose recommended in children.

Over 60
▼ No special problems expected.

Driving and hazardous work
▼ No known problems.

Alcohol
▼ No known problems.

PROLONGED USE

No problems expected.

DOMPERIDONE

Product names Apo-Domperidone, Teva-Domperidone, and others
Used in the following combined preparations None

GENERAL INFORMATION

Domperidone, which increases gastric motility, is particularly effective for treating nausea and vomiting caused by gastroenteritis, chemotherapy or radiotherapy. It is not effective for treating motion sickness or nausea caused by inner ear disorders such as Ménière's disease.

The main advantage of domperidone over other anti-emetic drugs is that it does not usually cause drowsiness or other *adverse effects* such as abnormal movement. Domperidone is not suitable, however, for the long-term treatment of gastrointestinal disorders, for which an alternative drug treatment is often prescribed.

Domperidone may also be used to relieve dyspepsia (indigestion and heartburn); and, in combination with acetaminophen, it is sometimes used to treat acute attacks of migraine.

INFORMATION FOR USERS

Your drug prescription is tailored for you. Do not alter dosage without checking with your physician.

How taken

Tablets, liquid, suppositories.

Frequency and timing of doses
Nausea/vomiting Every 4–8 hours as required.
Dyspepsia 3 x daily with water before meals and at night (tablets only).

Usual adult dosage range
Nausea/vomiting 10–20mg (by mouth); 30–60mg (rectally).

Onset of effect
Within 1 hour. The effects of the drug may be delayed if taken after the onset of nausea.

Duration of action
Approximately 6 hours.

Diet advice
None.

Storage
Keep in a closed container in a cool, dry place out of the reach of children. Protect from light.

Missed dose
Take as soon as you remember for dyspepsia. If your next dose is due within 4 hours, take a single dose now and skip the next. Then return to your normal dose schedule.

Stopping the drug
Can be stopped when you no longer need it.

Exceeding the dose
An occasional unintentional extra dose is unlikely to cause problems. Large overdoses may cause dizziness. Notify your physician.

SPECIAL PRECAUTIONS

Be sure to tell your physician if:
▼ You have a long-term kidney problems or liver disease.
▼ You have thyroid disease.
▼ You have a pituitary tumour.
▼ You are taking other medications.

Pregnancy
▼ Safety in pregnancy not established. Discuss with your physician.

Breast-feeding
▼ The drug may pass into the breast milk, but at normal doses adverse effects on the baby are unlikely. Discuss with your physician.

Infants and children
▼ Prescribed only to treat nausea and vomiting caused by anticancer drugs or radiation therapy. Reduced dose necessary.

Over 60
▼ No special problems.

Driving and hazardous work
▼ No special problems.

Alcohol
▼ No special problems, but alcohol is best avoided in cases of nausea and vomiting.

POSSIBLE ADVERSE EFFECTS

Adverse effects from this drug are rare.

Symptom/effect	Frequency		Discuss with physician		Stop taking drug now	Call physician now
	Common	Rare	Only if severe	In all cases		
Breast enlargement		●		■		
Milk secretion from breast		●		■		
Muscle spasms/tremors		●		■		
Reduced libido		●		■		
Rash		●		■		
Abnormal heart rhythm		●		■	▲	∎

INTERACTIONS

Anticholinergic drugs These may reduce the beneficial effects of domperidone.

Opioid analgesics These may reduce the beneficial effects of domperidone.

Bromocriptine and cabergoline Domperidone may reduce the effects of these drugs in some people.

Ketoconazole, erythromycin, azithromycin, SSRIs These drugs can increase the level of domperidone, resulting in adverse effects.

Grapefruit juice Can potentially increase the effect of domperidone.

PROLONGED USE

Not prescribed for longer than 12 weeks.

DONEPEZIL

Product names Aricept, Aricept RDT
Used in the following combined preparations None

GENERAL INFORMATION

Donepezil is an inhibitor of the *enzyme* acetylcholinesterase. This enzyme breaks down the natural *neurotransmitter* acetylcholine to limit its effects. Blocking the enzyme raises the levels of acetylcholine which, in the brain, increases alertness. Donepezil has been found to improve the symptoms of dementia in Alzheimer's disease and is used to diminish deterioration in that disease. It is not currently recommended for dementia due to other causes. It is usual to assess anyone being treated with donepezil after about three months to decide whether the drug is helping and whether it is worth continuing treatment.

Side effects may include bladder outflow obstruction and psychiatric problems, such as agitation and aggression, which might be thought due to the disease.

INFORMATION FOR USERS

Your drug prescription is tailored for you. Do not alter dosage without checking with your physician.

How taken

Tablets.

Frequency and timing of doses
Once daily in the evening.

Usual adult dosage range
5mg/day to start; may be increased up to 10mg/day if needed.

Onset of effect
1 hour. Full effects might take up to 3 months.

Duration of action
1–2 days.

Diet advice
None.

Storage
Keep in a closed container in a cool, dry place out of the reach of children.

Missed dose
Take as soon as you remember. A carer should ensure that the maximum dose taken in 24 hours does not exceed 10mg.

Stopping the drug
Do not stop taking the drug without consulting your physician; symptoms may recur.

Exceeding the dose
An occasional unintentional extra dose is unlikely to be a cause for concern. But if you notice any unusual symptoms, or if a large overdose has been taken, notify your physician.

SPECIAL PRECAUTIONS

Be sure to tell your physician if:
▼ You have a heart problem.
▼ You have asthma or respiratory problems.
▼ You have had a gastric or duodenal ulcer.
▼ You are taking an NSAID regularly.
▼ You are taking other medications.

Pregnancy
▼ Safety in pregnancy not established.

Breast-feeding
▼ Not recommended.

Infants and children
▼ Not recommended.

Over 60
▼ No special problems.

Driving and hazardous work
▼ Your underlying condition may make such activities inadvisable. Discuss with your physician.

Alcohol
▼ Avoid. Alcohol may reduce the effect of donepezil.

Surgery and general anesthetics
▼ Treatment with donepezil may need to be stopped before you have a general anesthetic. Discuss this with your physician or dentist before any operation.

POSSIBLE ADVERSE EFFECTS

Adverse effects include such problems as accidents, which are common in this group of people even when not treated.

Symptom/effect	Frequency		Discuss with physician		Stop taking drug now	Call physician now
	Common	Rare	Only if severe	In all cases		
Nausea/vomiting	●		■			
Diarrhea	●		■			
Fatigue/insomnia	●		■			
Muscle cramps	●		■			
Headache		●	■			
Fainting/dizziness		●		■		
Palpitations		●		■		
Difficulty in passing urine		●		■		

INTERACTIONS

General note If changes to the effect of donepezil are noticed when other drugs are started or stopped, discuss with your physician.

Paroxetine, erythromycin, and grapefruit juice could increase donepezil levels in the blood and possibly its side effects.

Muscle relaxants used in surgery Donepezil may increase the effect of some muscle relaxants, but it may also block some others.

Carbamazepine, phenytoin, and rifampin These drugs can all decrease the effectiveness of donepezil.

PROLONGED USE

May be continued for as long as there is benefit. Stopping the drug leads to a gradual loss of the improvements.

Monitoring Periodic checks should be carried out at 6-month intervals to test whether the drug is still providing some benefit.

DORZOLAMIDE

Product names Sandoz Dorzolamide, Trusopt
Used in the following combined preparations Apo-Dorzo-Timop, Cosopt, Sandoz Dorzolamide/Timolol

GENERAL INFORMATION

Dorzolamide is a carbonic anhydrase inhibitor (a kind of diuretic) that is used, in the form of eye drops only, to treat glaucoma by lowering intraocular pressure (fluid pressure inside the eye). The drug relieves the pressure by reducing production of aqueous humour, the fluid in the front chamber of the eye.

Dorzolamide may be used alone or combined with a beta blocker by people resistant to the effects of beta blockers or for whom beta blockers are not suitable.

Most *side effects* of dorzolamide are local to the eye, but *systemic* effects may occur if enough of the drug is absorbed by the body.

QUICK REFERENCE

Drug group Drugs for glaucoma (p.156)

Overdose danger rating Low

Dependence rating Low

Prescription needed Yes

Available as generic Yes

INFORMATION FOR USERS

Your drug prescription is tailored for you. Do not alter dosage without checking with your physician.

How taken

Eye drops.

Frequency and timing of doses
3 x daily (on its own); 2 x daily (combined preparation).

Usual adult dosage range
1 drop in the affected eye(s) or as directed.

Onset of effect
15–30 minutes.

Duration of action
4–8 hours.

Diet advice
None.

Storage
Keep in a closed container in a cool, dry place out of the reach of children. Protect from light. Discard eye drops 4 weeks after opening.

Missed dose
Use as soon as you remember. If your next dose is due, skip the missed dose and then go back to your normal dosing schedule.

Stopping the drug
Do not stop the drug without consulting your physician; symptoms may recur.

Exceeding the dose
An occasional unintentional extra application is unlikely to cause problems. Excessive use may provoke side effects as described below.

SPECIAL PRECAUTIONS

Be sure to tell your physician if:
▼ You have liver or kidney problems.
▼ You are allergic to sulfonamide drugs.
▼ You are allergic to benzalkonium chloride.
▼ You are taking other medications.

Pregnancy
▼ Not prescribed. Discuss with your physician.

Breast-feeding
▼ Not recommended. Discuss with your physician.

Infants and children
▼ Not recommended.

Over 60
▼ No special problems.

Driving and hazardous work
▼ Avoid such activities until you have learned how dorzolamide affects you because the drug can affect your vision.

Alcohol
▼ No special problems.

POSSIBLE ADVERSE EFFECTS

Local side effects of dorzolamide include conjunctivitis and keratitis (inflammation of the cornea, the transparent part of the eye). *Systemic* side effects may also occur but are rare. If you develop an itchy rash, swelling of the lips or tongue, or breathing difficulties, you should consult your physician urgently.

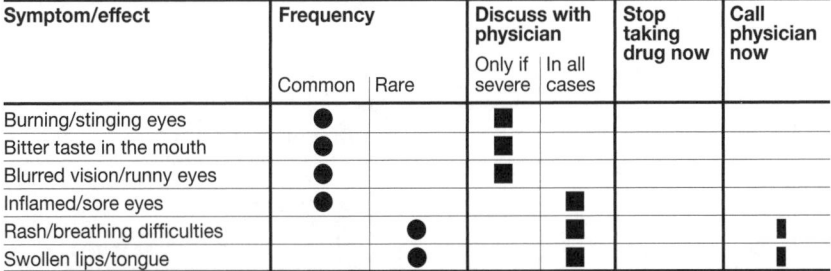

Symptom/effect	Frequency		Discuss with physician		Stop taking drug now	Call physician now
	Common	Rare	Only if severe	In all cases		
Burning/stinging eyes	●		■			
Bitter taste in the mouth	●		■			
Blurred vision/runny eyes	●		■			
Inflamed/sore eyes	●			■		
Rash/breathing difficulties		●		■		▮
Swollen lips/tongue		●		■		▮

INTERACTIONS

General note Dorzolamide, although used topically in the eye, can be absorbed systemically and has the potential for drug interactions. Consult your physician.

PROLONGED USE

Rarely, prolonged use of this drug may lead to development of kidney stones.

DOXAZOSIN

Product names Cardura-1, Cardura-2, Cardura-4, Doxazosin-1, Doxazosin-2, Doxazosin-4, and others
Used in the following combined preparations None

GENERAL INFORMATION

Doxazosin is an antihypertensive vasodilator drug that relieves hypertension (high blood pressure) by relaxing the muscles in the blood vessel walls. It may be administered together with other antihypertensive drugs, including beta blockers, since its effects on blood pressure are increased when it is combined with most other antihypertensives. Doxazosin can also be given to patients with an enlarged prostate gland. It relaxes the muscles around the bladder exit and prostate gland, making bladder emptying easier. However, this effect may cause incontinence when the drug is used in some women.

Dizziness and fainting may occur with doxazosin. Typically, this occurs on standing and may improve with continued use, but it may limit the drug's use, especially in elderly people.

QUICK REFERENCE

Drug group A vasodilator (p.84), antihypertensive drug (p.88), and drugs for urinary disorders (p.154)

Overdose danger rating Medium

Dependence rating Low

Prescription needed Yes

Available as generic Yes

INFORMATION FOR USERS

Your drug prescription is tailored for you. Do not alter dosage without checking with your physician.

How taken

Tablets.

Frequency and timing of doses
Once daily, at the same time each day.

Usual adult dosage range
Hypertension 1mg (starting dose), increased gradually as necessary up to 16mg.
Enlarged prostate 1mg (starting dose), increased gradually at 1–2-week intervals up to 8mg.

Onset of effect
Within 2 hours.

Duration of action
24 hours.

Diet advice
None.

Storage
Keep in a closed container in a cool, dry place out of the reach of children.

Missed dose
If you forget to take a tablet, skip that dose completely but carry on as normal the following day.

Stopping the drug
Do not stop taking the drug without consulting your physician; stopping the drug may lead to a rise in blood pressure.

Exceeding the dose
An occasional unintentional extra dose is unlikely to be a cause for concern. Larger overdoses may cause dizziness or fainting. Notify your physician.

SPECIAL PRECAUTIONS

Be sure to tell your physician if:
▼ You have long-term liver or kidney problems.
▼ You have heart problems.
▼ You have had an allergic reaction to doxazosin in the past.
▼ You are due to have an operation.
▼ You are taking other medications.

Pregnancy
▼ Safety in pregnancy not established. Discuss with your physician.

Breast-feeding
▼ Safety not established. The drug passes into the breast milk. Discuss with your physician.

Infants and children
▼ Not recommended.

Over 60
▼ Reduced dose may be necessary. Take extra care when standing up until you have learned how the drug affects you.

Driving and hazardous work
▼ Avoid such activities until you have learned how doxazosin affects you because the drug can cause drowsiness, dizziness, and fainting.

Alcohol
▼ Avoid excessive amounts. Alcohol may increase some of the *adverse effects* of this drug, such as dizziness, drowsiness, and fainting.

Surgery and general anesthetics
▼ A general anesthetic may increase the low blood pressure effect of doxazosin.

POSSIBLE ADVERSE EFFECTS

Nausea and weakness are common with doxazosin, but the main problem is that it may cause dizziness or fainting when you stand up.

Symptom/effect	Frequency		Discuss with physician		Stop taking drug now	Call physician now
	Common	Rare	Only if severe	In all cases		
Nausea	●		■			
Weakness/drowsiness	●		■			
Dizziness/fainting		●	■			
Stuffy/runny nose		●	■			
Incontinence (in women)		●		■		
Palpitations/chest pain		●		■		▮
Rash		●		■		

INTERACTIONS

Hypotensive drugs Any drugs that can reduce blood pressure are likely to increase the blood-pressure-lowering effect of doxazosin. These include diuretics, beta blockers, ACE inhibitors, nitrates, calcium channel blockers, some antipsychotics and antidepressants, and drugs for erectile dysfunction.

PROLONGED USE

No known problems.

DOXORUBICIN

Product names Adriamycin PFS, Caelyx, Myocet, and others
Used in the following combined preparations None

GENERAL INFORMATION

Doxorubicin is one of the most effective anticancer drugs. It is prescribed to treat a wide variety of cancers, usually in conjunction with other anticancer drugs. It is used in cancer of the lymph nodes (Hodgkin's disease), lung, breast, bladder, stomach, thyroid, and reproductive organs. It is also used to treat Kaposi's sarcoma in AIDS patients.

Nausea and vomiting after injection are the most common *side effects*. Although these symptoms are unpleasant, they tend to be less severe as the body adjusts to treatment. The drug may stain the urine bright red, but this is not harmful. More seriously, because

doxorubicin interferes with the production of blood cells, blood clotting disorders, *anemia*, and infections may occur. Hair loss is also a common side effect. Heart rhythm disturbance and heart failure are possible, although less common, dose-dependent side effects. The heart failure is usually irreversible and is worsened by trastuzumab (Herceptin).

The brand-name drugs Caelyx and Myocet are special formulations in which the doxorubicin is enclosed in fatty spheres. This makes the drug more suitable for treating certain types of cancers, for example AIDS-related Kaposi's sarcoma.

INFORMATION FOR USERS

This drug is given only under medical supervision and is not for self-administration.

How taken

Injection, bladder instillation.

Frequency and timing of doses
Every 1–4 weeks.

Usual adult dosage range
Dosage is determined individually according to body height, weight, and response.

Onset of effect
Some adverse effects may appear within one hour of starting treatment, but full beneficial effects may not be felt for up to 4 weeks.

Duration of action
Adverse effects can persist for up to 2 weeks or longer after stopping treatment.

Diet advice
None.

Storage
Not applicable. The drug is not normally kept in the home.

Missed dose
The drug is administered in hospital under close medical supervision. If for some reason you skip your dose, contact your physician as soon as you can.

Stopping the drug
Discuss with your physician. Stopping the drug prematurely may lead to a worsening of the underlying condition.

Exceeding the dose
Overdosage is unlikely since treatment is carefully monitored and supervised.

POSSIBLE ADVERSE EFFECTS

Patients are given an antiemetic drug to treat the effects of nausea and vomiting. Palpitations and shortness of breath may indicate an *adverse effect* of the drug on the heart. Since treatment is closely supervised in hospital, all adverse effects are monitored.

Symptom/effect	Frequency		Discuss with physician		Stop taking drug now	Call physician now
	Common	Rare	Only if severe	In all cases		
Nausea/vomiting	●			■		
Loss of appetite	●			■		
Hair loss	●			■		
Diarrhea		●		■		
Mouth ulcers		●		■		
Skin irritation/ulcers		●		■		
Palpitations		●		■	■	
Breathlessness		●		■		■

INTERACTIONS

Cyclosporine can increase adverse effects of doxorubicin

Phenytoin levels may be increased by doxorubicin.

SPECIAL PRECAUTIONS

Doxorubicin is prescribed only under close medical supervision, taking account of your present condition and medical history.

Pregnancy
▼ Not usually prescribed. Doxorubicin may cause birth defects or premature birth. Discuss with your physician.

Breast-feeding
▼ Not advised. The drug passes into the breast milk and may affect the baby adversely. Discuss with your physician.

Infants and children
▼ Reduced dose necessary.

Over 60
▼ Increased risk of adverse effects. Reduced dose may be necessary.

Driving and hazardous work
▼ No known problems.

Alcohol
▼ No known problems.

PROLONGED USE

Prolonged use of doxorubicin may suppress the activity of the bone marrow, leading to reduced production of all types of blood cells. It may also affect the pumping capacity of the heart.

Monitoring Periodic checks on blood composition are usually required. Regular heart examinations are also carried out.

DOXYCYCLINE

Product names Atridox, Periostat, Vibramycin, Vibra-Tabs, and others
Used in the following combined preparations None

GENERAL INFORMATION

Doxycycline is a tetracycline *antibiotic*. It is used to treat infections of the urinary, respiratory, and gastrointestinal tracts. It is also prescribed for treatment of some oral and dental infections, sexually transmitted diseases, skin, eye, and prostate infections, acne, and malaria prevention (in some parts of the world, see p.123).

Doxycycline is less likely to cause diarrhea than other tetracyclines, and its absorption is not significantly impaired by milk and food. It can therefore be taken with meals to reduce *side effects* such as nausea or indigestion. It is also safer than most other tetracyclines for people with impaired kidney function. Like other tetracyclines, it can stain developing teeth and may affect development of bone; it is therefore usually avoided in children under 12 years old and pregnant women.

QUICK REFERENCE

Drug group Tetracycline antibiotics (p.114)

Overdose danger rating Low

Dependence rating Low

Prescription needed Yes

Available as generic Yes

INFORMATION FOR USERS

Your drug prescription is tailored for you. Do not alter dosage without checking with your physician.

How taken

Tablets, capsules.

Frequency and timing of doses
1–2 x daily with water, or with or after food, in a sitting or standing position, and well before going to bed to avoid risk of throat irritation.

Usual dosage range
100–200mg daily.

Onset of effect
1–12 hours; several weeks (acne).

Duration of action
Up to 24 hours; several weeks (acne).

Diet advice
None.

Storage
Keep in closed container in a cool, dry place out of the reach of children.

Missed dose
Take as soon as you remember. If your next dose is due within 6 hours, take a single dose now and skip the next.

Stopping the drug
Take the full course. Even if you feel better, the original infection may still be present and symptoms may recur if treatment is stopped too soon.

Exceeding the dose
An occasional unintentional extra dose is unlikely to be a cause for concern. But if you notice any unusual symptoms, or if a large overdose has been taken, notify your physician.

POSSIBLE ADVERSE EFFECTS

Adverse effects from doxycycline are rare, although nausea, vomiting, or diarrhea may occur. Rash, itching, and photosensitivity of the skin are other possible adverse effects.

Symptom/effect	Frequency		Discuss with physician		Stop taking drug now	Call physician now
	Common	Rare	Only if severe	In all cases		
Nausea/vomiting	●		■			
Diarrhea		●	■			
Rash/itching		●		■	▲	
Photosensitivity		●		■	▲	
Headache/visual disturbances		●		■	▲	■

INTERACTIONS

Penicillin antibiotics Doxycycline interferes with the antibacterial action of these drugs.

Barbiturates, carbamazepine, and phenytoin All these drugs reduce the effectiveness of doxycycline. Doxycycline dosage may need to be increased.

Oral contraceptives There is a slight risk of doxycycline reducing the effectiveness of oral contraceptives. Discuss with your physician.

Oral anticoagulant drugs Doxycycline may increase the anticoagulant action of these drugs.

Antacids and preparations containing iron, calcium, or magnesium may impair absorption of this drug. Do not take within 2–3 hours of doxycycline.

SPECIAL PRECAUTIONS

Be sure to tell your physician if:
▼ You have a long-term liver problem.
▼ You have previously suffered an allergic reaction to a tetracycline antibiotic.
▼ You have porphyria.
▼ You have systemic lupus erythematosus.
▼ You have myasthenia gravis.
▼ You are taking other medications.

Pregnancy
▼ Not used in pregnancy. May discolour the teeth of the developing baby.

Breast-feeding
▼ The drug passes into the breast milk and may lead to discoloration of the baby's teeth and may also have other adverse effects. Discuss with your physician.

Infants and children
▼ Not recommended under 12 years. Reduced dose necessary for older children.

Over 60
▼ No special problems. Ensure that medication is taken in upright position to minimize esophageal irritation or ulceration.

Driving and hazardous work
▼ No known problems.

Alcohol
▼ Excessive amounts may decrease the effectiveness of doxycycline.

Surgery and general anesthetics
▼ Notify your physician or dentist that you are taking doxycycline.

PROLONGED USE

Not usually prescribed long term, except for acne.

DULOXETINE

Product name Cymbalta
Used in the following combined preparations None

GENERAL INFORMATION

Duloxetine is an antidepressant medication that is used for depression and excessive anxiety. It relieves symptoms such as depressed mood, lack of energy, and lack of interest in usual activities. Duloxetine is also used to treat pain associated with diabetic peripheral neuropathy and fibromyalgia, and for persistent long-term lower back pain. Initially, the drug may cause some nausea; this can be minimized when taken with food. You may be started on a small initial dose, which may then be gradually increased. Dosage adjustment may be required with kidney impairment.

INFORMATION FOR USERS

Your drug prescription is tailored for you. Do not alter dosage without checking with your physician.

How taken

Delayed-release capsules. Swallow whole and do not chew, crush, or open.

Frequency and timing of doses
Once daily, at the same time each day.

Usual adult dosage range
60mg.

Onset of effect
Full antidepressant effect may not be felt for 2–4 weeks or more.

Duration of action
Up to 24 hours.

Diet advice
None.

Storage
Store in its original package in a cool, dry place out of the reach of children.

Missed dose
If you missed your dose by a few hours, take your dose as soon as you remember. Otherwise, wait until your next scheduled dose. Do not double up on doses.

Stopping the drug
Do not stop taking the drug without consulting your physician. Stopping abruptly can cause withdrawal symptoms.

OVERDOSE ACTION

Seek immediate medical advice in all cases. Take emergency action if seizures, slow or irregular pulse, or loss of consciousness occur.

See Drug poisoning emergency guide (p.526).

POSSIBLE ADVERSE EFFECTS

Common *side effects* may wear off or become less bothersome. At the start of treatment or during dosage adjustments, a drop in blood pressure may occur when standing.

Symptom/effect	Frequency		Discuss with physician		Stop taking drug now	Call physician now
	Common	Rare	Only if severe	In all cases		
Nausea/drowsiness/dizziness	●		■			
Decreased appetite	●		■			
Increased sweating	●			■		
Decrease in sexual desire		●		■		
Change in behavior/ Suicidal thoughts		●		■		▮
Nausea/vomiting/yellowing of of the skin, eyes/itching		●		■		▮
Bruising/unusual bleeding		●		■		▮
Allergic reaction		●		■	▲	▮

INTERACTIONS

Monoamine oxidase inhibitors should not be used with duloxetine and should be stopped at least 14 days before starting.

Epinephrine and pseudophedrine Avoid using with duloxetine.

Tamoxifen Duloxetine may decrease the effect of this drug.

Abiraterone, ciprofloxacin, fluvoxamine, ketoconazole, methoxsalen, norfloxacin, paroxetine, ritonavir, tipranavir, and terbinafine can increase the effects of duloxetine.

Drugs which enhance serotonin activity can increase adverse effects when used with duloxetine.

SPECIAL PRECAUTIONS

Be sure to tell your physician if:
▼ You have liver or kidney problems.
▼ You have high blood pressure.
▼ You have low sodium levels.
▼ You have glaucoma.
▼ You drink substantial amounts of alcohol.
▼ You are, or have recently taken, monoamine oxidase inhibitors such as phenelzine or moclobemide.
▼ You are taking other medications.

Pregnancy
▼ Safety not established. Discuss with your physician.

Breast-feeding
▼ The drug does enter breast milk. Safety not established. Discuss with your physician.

Infants and children
▼ Safety and efficacy not established.

Over 60
▼ No special problems.

Driving and hazardous work
▼ May cause dizziness or drowsiness. Do not drive a car or operate machinery until you feel you are mentally alert.

Alcohol
▼ Avoid. Alcohol may increase the *sedative* effects of the drug.

PROLONGED USE

Monitoring Blood pressure may be monitored.

EFAVIRENZ

Product name Sustiva
Used in the following combined preparations Atripla

GENERAL INFORMATION

Efavirenz is a non-nucleoside reverse transcriptase inhibitor, which is a type of antiretroviral drug that is used to treat HIV infection. It is active against HIV type 1 but not against type 2 (which is rare in Canada). It is never used alone but is combined with other antiretrovirals, for example, two nucleoside analogues, as combination therapy to reduce viral replication. The aim of this treatment is to minimize damage to the immune system by the virus and to make the emergence of drug resistance less likely. Combination antiretroviral therapy (known as highly active antiretroviral therapy or HAART) is not a cure for HIV. If the drugs are taken regularly on a long-term basis, they can reduce the viral load and improve the outlook for the patient. However, the patient will remain infectious, and will suffer a relapse if treatment is stopped.

INFORMATION FOR USERS

Your drug prescription is tailored for you. Do not alter dosage without checking with your physician.

How taken

Capsules.

Frequency and timing of doses
Once daily, usually at night to minimize adverse effects.

Usual adult dosage range
Up to 600mg according to body weight.

Onset of effect
1 hour.

Duration of action
24 hours.

Diet advice
None.

Storage
Keep in the original container in a cool, dry place out of the reach of children.

Missed dose
Take as soon as you remember. If your next dose is due within 2 hours, take a single dose now and skip the next. It is very important not to miss doses on a regular basis as this can lead to the development of drug-resistant HIV.

Stopping the drug
Do not stop taking the drug without consulting your physician. It may be necessary to withdraw all your drugs gradually, starting with efavirenz.

Exceeding the dose
An occasional unintentional extra dose is unlikely to cause problems. But if you notice any unusual symptoms, or if a large overdose has been taken, notify your physician.

SPECIAL PRECAUTIONS

Be sure to tell your physician if:
▼ You have liver or kidney problems.
▼ You have an infection such as hepatitis B or C.
▼ You are pregnant or planning pregnancy.
▼ You are taking other medications.

Pregnancy
▼ Should not be used during first trimester of pregnancy. Pregnancy should be avoided when taking efavirenz by using barrier methods of contraception in addition to other methods. Discuss with your physician.

Breast-feeding
▼ Safety in breast-feeding not established. Breast-feeding is not recommended for HIV-positive mothers as the virus may be passed to the baby.

Infants and children
▼ Not prescribed to children under 3 years. Reduced dose necessary in older children.

Over 60
▼ Reduced dose may be necessary to minimize adverse effects.

Driving and hazardous work
▼ Avoid such activities until you have learned how efavirenz affects you because the drug can cause dizziness.

Alcohol
▼ No known problems, although some people may find the effects of alcohol are more pronounced while taking efavirenz.

POSSIBLE ADVERSE EFFECTS

Gastrointestinal upset and rash are the most common *adverse effects*. Efavirenz can cause vivid dreams and changes in sleep patterns, but these tend to wear off with time.

Symptom/effect	Frequency		Discuss with physician		Stop taking drug now	Call physician now
	Common	Rare	Only if severe	In all cases		
Nausea/vomiting	●		■			
Diarrhea	●		■			
Vivid dreams	●		■			
Rash	●			■		▮
Mood changes	●			■		▮

INTERACTIONS

General note A wide range of drugs may interact with efavirenz, causing either an increase in adverse effects or a reduction in the effect of the antiretroviral drugs. Check with your physician or *pharmacist* before taking any new drugs, including those from the dentist and supermarket, and herbal medicines.

PROLONGED USE

No known problems.

Monitoring Your physician will take regular blood samples to check the drug's effects on the viral load. Blood will also be checked for changes in lipid, cholesterol, and sugar levels.

ENALAPRIL

Product names CO Enalapril, Mylan-Enalapril, Vasotec, and others
Used in the following combined preparations Apo-Enalapril Maleate/HCTZ, Teva-Enalapril/HCTZ, Vaseretic

GENERAL INFORMATION

Enalapril belongs to the ACE inhibitor group of *vasodilator* drugs, which are used to treat hypertension (high blood pressure) and heart failure (inability of the heart to cope with its workload). It is also given to patients after a heart attack.

The first dose of enalapril may cause a sudden drop in blood pressure. For this reason, you should be resting at the time and be able to lie down for 2 to 3 hours afterwards.

The more common *adverse effects* of enalapril usually diminish with long-term treatment. Rashes can also occur but usually disappear when the drug is stopped. In some cases, they clear up on their own despite continued treatment with enalapril.

QUICK REFERENCE

Drug group ACE inhibitors (p.84) and antihypertensive drugs (p.88)

Overdose danger rating Medium

Dependence rating Low

Prescription needed Yes

Available as generic Yes

INFORMATION FOR USERS

Your drug prescription is tailored for you. Do not alter dosage without checking with your physician.

How taken

Tablets, injection.

Frequency and timing of doses
1–2 x daily.

Usual adult dosage range
2.5–5mg daily (starting dose), increased to 10–40mg daily (maintenance dose).

Onset of effect
30–60 minutes; full beneficial effect may take several weeks.

Duration of action
24 hours.

Diet advice
A low-salt diet may be recommended.

Storage
Keep in a closed container in a dry place below 25°C out of the reach of children. Protect from light.

Missed dose
Take as soon as you remember. If your next dose is due within 8 hours, take a single dose now and skip the next.

Stopping the drug
Do not stop without consulting your physician; the underlying condition may worsen.

Exceeding the dose
An occasional unintentional extra dose is unlikely to be a cause for concern. Large overdoses may cause dizziness or fainting. Notify your physician.

POSSIBLE ADVERSE EFFECTS

Common adverse effects usually diminish with long-term treatment. Less common problems may also diminish with time but dose adjustment may be necessary. If a diuretic was recently started, excessive decrease in blood pressure may occur.

Symptom/effect	Frequency		Discuss with physician		Stop taking drug now	Call physician now
	Common	Rare	Only if severe	In all cases		
Rash	●			■		
Persistent dry cough	●			■		
Mouth ulcers/sore mouth		●		■		
Dizziness		●		■		
Sore throat/fever		●		■		
Swelling of mouth/lips		●		■	▲	▮
Breathing difficulty		●		■	▲	▮

INTERACTIONS

Vasodilators, diuretics, and antihypertensives may increase the blood-pressure-lowering effect of enalapril.

Lithium Enalapril increases the levels of lithium in the blood, and serious adverse effects from lithium excess may occur.

Potassium supplements and potassium-sparing diuretics Enalapril may enhance the effect of these drugs, leading to raised levels of potassium in the blood.

Non-steroidal anti-inflammatory drugs (NSAIDs) Some of these drugs may reduce the effectiveness of enalapril. There is also risk of kidney damage when they are taken with enalapril.

Losartan and similar drugs can increase adverse effects of enalapril; dose monitoring required.

SPECIAL PRECAUTIONS

Be sure to tell your physician if:
▼ You have long-term kidney or liver problems.
▼ You have a heart problem.
▼ You have had angioedema or a previous allergic reaction to an ACE inhibitor drug.
▼ You have porphyria.
▼ You are pregnant or intend to become pregnant.
▼ You are taking other medications.

Pregnancy
▼ Not normally prescribed. May cause abnormalities in the fetus. Discuss with your physician.

Breast-feeding
▼ Safety not established. Discuss with your physician.

Infants and children
▼ Not recommended.

Over 60
▼ Reduced dose may be necessary.

Driving and hazardous work
▼ Avoid such activities until you have learned how enalapril affects you because the drug can cause dizziness and fainting.

Alcohol
▼ Avoid. Alcohol may increase the blood-pressure-lowering and adverse effects of the drug.

Surgery and general anesthetics
▼ Enalapril may have to be stopped before you have a general anesthetic. Discuss with your physician or dentist before any operation.

PROLONGED USE

No problems expected.

Monitoring Periodic tests on potassium levels, white blood cell count, kidney function, and urine are usually performed.

EPINEPHRINE (ADRENALINE)

Product names Anapen, EpiPen/EpiPen Jr, Twinject Auto-Injector, and others
Used in the following combined preparations Sensorcaine with epinephrine, Xylocaine with epinephrine, and others

GENERAL INFORMATION

Epinephrine is a *neurotransmitter* that is produced in the centre (medulla) of the adrenal glands. Synthetic epinephrine has been made since 1900. The drug is given in an emergency to stimulate heart activity and raise low blood pressure. It also narrows blood vessels in the skin and intestine, and opens airways in the lungs.

Epinephrine is injected to counteract cardiac arrest, or to relieve severe *allergic reactions* (anaphylaxis) to drugs, food, or insect stings. For patients who are at risk of anaphylaxis, it is provided as a pre-filled syringe for immediate self-injection at the start of an attack.

Because it constricts blood vessels, epinephrine is used to control bleeding and to slow the dispersal, and thereby prolong the effect, of local *anesthetics*.

QUICK REFERENCE

Drug group Drugs for cardiac resuscitation and anaphylaxis

Overdose danger rating High

Dependence rating Low

Prescription needed Yes

Available as generic Yes

INFORMATION FOR USERS

Your drug prescription is tailored for you. Do not alter dosage without checking with your physician.

How taken

Injection, intranasal solution.

Frequency and timing of doses
As directed; by itself, the drug is for use in emergencies.

Usual dosage range
As directed according to method of administration and underlying disorder.

Onset of effect
Within 5 minutes (injection).

Duration of action
Up to 4 hours (injection).

Diet advice
None.

Storage
Keep in a closed container in a cool, dry place out of the reach of children. Protect from light.

Missed dose
Not applicable. By itself, the drug is used for one-off emergencies.

Stopping the drug
Not applicable. By itself, the drug is used for one-off emergencies.

OVERDOSE ACTION

 Seek immediate medical advice in all cases. Take emergency action if palpitations, breathing difficulties, or loss of consciousness occur.

See Drug poisoning emergency guide (p.526).

SPECIAL PRECAUTIONS

Be sure to tell your physician if:
▼ You have a heart problem.
▼ You have an overactive thyroid gland.
▼ You have high blood pressure.
▼ You are taking other medications, especially a beta blocker.

 Pregnancy
▼ Discuss with your physician. Although the drug may cause defects in the fetus and prolong labour, epinephrine by itself is used only for medical emergencies and its use may be life-saving.

 Breast-feeding
▼ Adverse effects on the baby are unlikely. Discuss with your physician.

 Infants and children
▼ Reduced dose necessary.

 Over 60
▼ Increased likelihood of adverse effects. Reduced dose may therefore be necessary.

 Driving and hazardous work
▼ Not applicable. By itself, the drug is used for one-off emergencies.

 **Alcohol**
▼ No known problems.

POSSIBLE ADVERSE EFFECTS

The principal *adverse effects* of this drug are related to its stimulant action on the heart and central nervous system.

Symptom/effect	Frequency		Discuss with physician		Stop taking drug now	Call physician now
	Common	Rare	Only if severe	In all cases		
Dry mouth	●		■			
Nervousness/restlessness	●		■			
Nausea/vomiting	●		■			
Cold extremities	●		■			
Palpitations	●			■		
Headache/blurred vision	●			■		

PROLONGED USE

Not used long term.

INTERACTIONS

General note A variety of drugs interact with epinephrine to increase the risk of palpitations and/or high blood pressure. Such drugs include monoamine oxidase inhibitors (MAOIs) and tricyclic antidepressants, such as amitriptyline.

Beta blockers These drugs may cause reduced effectiveness of epinephrine for treatment of anaphylaxis.

EPLERENONE

Product name Inspra
Used in the following combined preparations None

GENERAL INFORMATION

Eplerenone is a potassium-sparing diuretic that works by blocking the action of aldosterone, a substance produced in the body. It is used in conjunction with other medications to help prevent heart failure following a heart attack.

Eplerenone is usually started within 3 to 14 days after a heart attack. The potassium level in the blood and kidney function is usually checked before starting therapy and periodically thereafter, especially with any dose changes.

QUICK REFERENCE

Drug group Diuretics; aldosterone antagonists (p.85)

Overdose danger rating Medium

Dependence rating Low

Prescription needed Yes

Available as generic No

INFORMATION FOR USERS

Your drug prescription is tailored for you. Do not alter dosage without checking with your physician.

How taken

Tablets.

Frequency and timing of doses
Once daily.

Usual adult dosage range
25mg–50mg.

Onset of effect
Full beneficial effect seen within a couple of days.

Duration of action
Up to 14 hours.

Diet advice
None.

Storage
Keep in a closed container in a cool, dry place out of the reach of children.

Missed dose
Take as soon as you remember. If it is almost time for your next dose, do not take the missed dose and go back to your normal schedule.

Stopping the drug
Do not stop taking the drug suddenly without consulting your physician; symptoms may worsen.

Exceeding the dose
An occasional unintentional extra dose is unlikely to be a cause for concern. But if you notice any unusual symptoms, or if a large overdose has been taken, notify your physician.

SPECIAL PRECAUTIONS

Be sure to tell your physician if:
▼ You have high levels of potassium (hyperkalemia).
▼ You have kidney problems.
▼ You have liver problems.
▼ You have diabetes.
▼ You are taking potassium supplements or salt substitutes.
▼ You are on lithium.
▼ You are taking other medications.

Pregnancy
▼ Limited clinical information available. Discuss with your physician.

Breast-feeding
▼ Limited clinical information available. Discuss with your physician.

Infants and children
▼ Safety and efficacy not established.

Over 60
▼ Dosage reduction may be required based on kidney function.

Driving and hazardous work
▼ The drug may cause dizziness. Caution required.

Alcohol
▼ No special problems.

POSSIBLE ADVERSE EFFECTS

Withdrawal effects are common when stopping the *medication*. This includes diarrhea, muscle aches, abdominal pain, anxiety, and sweating.

Symptom/effect	Frequency		Discuss with physician		Stop taking drug now	Call physician now
	Common	Rare	Only if severe	In all cases		
Dizziness/lightheadedness	●		■			
Diarrhea	●		■			
Nausea	●			■		
Confusion/numbness or tingling in hands, feet, or lips/heaviness in the legs		●		■		
Swelling of the feet, hands, lips, throat		●			▲	▮
Yellowing of the skin or eyes		●		■		▮

PROLONGED USE

Monitoring Potassium levels and kidney function will be monitored periodically.

INTERACTIONS

General note Other diuretics, such as amiloride, ACE-inhibitors, NSAIDs, angiotensin receptor blockers, and potassium supplements, can increase the risk for high blood potassium levels.

Ketoconazole, itraconazole, fluconazole, voriconazole, ritonavir, nelfinavir, clarithromycin, telithromycin, and nefazodone can all increase the effect of eplerenone; do not use together.

Erythromycin, saquinavir, amiodarone, diltiazem, and verapamil can increase the effect of eplerenone.

Carbamazepine, phenytoin, phenobarbital, St John's wort, and rifampin can decrease the effect of eplerenone.

Tacrolimus, cyclosporine, and herbal preparations containing potassium can cause hyperkalemia when administered with eplerenone.

ERGOTAMINE

Product names Dihydroergotamine, Migranal Nasal Spray
Used in the following combined preparations Bellergal Spacetabs, Cafergot, Ergodryl Cap

GENERAL INFORMATION

Ergotamine is used to treat migraine but its use has largely been superseded by newer agents with fewer *adverse effects*. Ergotamine may also be used in the treatment of cluster headaches. Its use in migraine should be restricted to when other analgesics are ineffective. It should be taken at the first sign of migraine (the "aura"). Later use may be ineffective and cause stomach upset.

Ergotamine causes temporary narrowing of blood vessels and, therefore should not be used by people with poor circulation. If taken too frequently, the drug can dangerously reduce circulation to the hands and feet; it should never be taken regularly.

Frequent migraine attacks may indicate the need for a different drug to prevent migraine.

INFORMATION FOR USERS

Your drug prescription is tailored for you. Do not alter dosage without checking with your physician.

How taken

Capsules, tablets, injection, nasal spray.

Frequency and timing of doses
Once at the onset, repeated if needed after 30 minutes (tablets) up to the maximum dose (see below).

Usual adult dosage range
Varies according to product. Generally, 1–2mg per dose. Take no more than 4mg in 24 hours or 8mg in 1 week. Treatment should not be repeated within 4 days or more than twice a month.

Onset of effect
15–30 minutes.

Duration of action
Up to 24 hours.

Diet advice
Changes in diet are unlikely to affect the action of this drug, but certain foods may provoke migraine attacks in some people.

Storage
Keep in a closed container in a cool, dry place out of the reach of children. Protect from light.

Missed dose
Regular doses of this drug are not necessary and may be dangerous. Take only when you have symptoms of migraine.

Stopping the drug
Can be safely stopped as soon as you no longer need it.

Exceeding the dose
An occasional unintentional extra dose is unlikely to cause problems. Large overdoses may cause vomiting, dizziness, seizures, or coma. Notify your physician immediately.

SPECIAL PRECAUTIONS

Be sure to tell your physician if:
▼ You have long-term liver or kidney problems.
▼ You have heart problems.
▼ You have poor circulation.
▼ You have high blood pressure.
▼ You have had a recent stroke.
▼ You have an overactive thyroid gland.
▼ You are taking other medications.

Pregnancy
▼ Not usually prescribed. Ergotamine can cause contractions of the uterus.

Breast-feeding
▼ Not recommended. The drug passes into the milk and may have adverse effects on the baby. It may also reduce your milk supply.

Infants and children
▼ Not usually prescribed.

Over 60
▼ Not recommended. May aggravate existing heart or circulatory problems.

Driving and hazardous work
▼ Avoid such activities until you have learned how ergotamine affects you because the drug can cause dizziness.

Alcohol
▼ No special problems, but some spirits may provoke migraine in some people.

Surgery and general anesthetics
▼ Notify your physician if you have used ergotamine within 48 hours prior to surgery.

POSSIBLE ADVERSE EFFECTS

Digestive disturbances and nausea (for which an anti-emetic may be given) are common with ergotamine treatment. Rare but serious *adverse effects* may result from arterial spasm.

Symptom/effect	Frequency		Discuss with physician		Stop taking drug now	Call physician now
	Common	Rare	Only if severe	In all cases		
Nausea/vomiting	●		■			
Abdominal pain	●		■			
Muscle cramps	●		■			
Diarrhea		●	■			
Dizziness		●		■		
Muscle pain/stiffness		●		■		
Chest pain		●		■	▲	▮
Leg/groin pain		●		■	▲	▮
Cold/numb fingers/toes		●		■	▲	▮

INTERACTIONS

Beta blockers These drugs may increase circulatory problems with ergotamine.

Sumatriptan and related drugs There is an increased risk of adverse effects on the blood circulation if ergotamine is used with these drugs.

Erythromycin and related antibiotics and antivirals taken with ergotamine increase the likelihood of adverse effects.

Oral contraceptives There is an increased risk of blood clotting in women taking these drugs with ergotamine.

PROLONGED USE

Reduced circulation to the hands and feet may result if doses near to the maximum are taken for too long. The recommended dosage and length of treatment should not be exceeded. Rebound headache may occur if it is taken too frequently.

ERYTHROMYCIN

Product names EES 200, EES 400, EryC Delayed Release Capsules, and others
Used in the following combined preparations Benzamycin, Erysol, Stievamycin

GENERAL INFORMATION

One of the safest and most widely used *antibiotics*, erythromycin is effective against many bacteria. It is commonly used as an alternative in people allergic to penicillin and related antibiotics.

Erythromycin is used to treat throat and chest infections (including some rare types of pneumonia such as Legionnaires' disease). It is also used for sexually transmitted diseases such as chlamydial infections, and in some forms of gastroenteritis.

Erythromycin may also be included as part of the treatment for diphtheria and is sometimes given to treat, and reduce the likelihood of infecting others with, pertussis (whooping cough).

When taken by mouth, erythromycin may sometimes cause nausea and vomiting. Other possible *adverse effects* include rash as well as a rare risk of liver disorders. Oral administration or *topical* application of the drug is sometimes helpful in treating acne.

QUICK REFERENCE

Drug group Antibiotic (p.114)
Overdose danger rating Low
Dependence rating Low
Prescription needed Yes
Available as generic Yes

INFORMATION FOR USERS

Your drug prescription is tailored for you. Do not alter dosage without consulting your physician.

How taken

Tablets, capsules, liquid, injection, topical solution, eye ointment.

Frequency and timing of doses
Every 6–12 hours before or with meals.

Usual dosage range
1–4g daily.

Onset of effect
1–4 hours.

Duration of action
6–12 hours.

Diet advice
None.

Storage
Keep in a closed container in a cool, dry place out of the reach of children.

Missed dose
Take as soon as you remember. If your next dose is due within 2 hours, take a single dose now and skip the next.

Stopping the drug
Take the full course. Even if you feel better, the original infection may still be present and symptoms may recur if treatment is stopped too soon.

Exceeding the dose
An occasional unintentional extra dose is unlikely to be a cause for concern. But if you notice any unusual symptoms, or if a large overdose has been taken, notify your physician.

SPECIAL PRECAUTIONS

Be sure to tell your physician if:
▼ You have a long-term liver problem.
▼ You have had a previous *allergic reaction* to erythromycin.
▼ You have porphyria.
▼ You are taking other medications.

 Pregnancy
▼ No evidence of risk to the developing fetus, although some formulations may increase the risk of liver damage in the mother. Discuss with your physician.

 Breast-feeding
▼ The drug passes into the breast milk, but at normal doses adverse effects on the baby are unlikely. Discuss with your physician.

 Infants and children
▼ Reduced dose necessary.

 Over 60
▼ No special problems.

 Driving and hazardous work
▼ No known problems.

 Alcohol
▼ Avoid.

POSSIBLE ADVERSE EFFECTS

Nausea and vomiting are common and most likely with large doses taken by mouth. Fever, rash, and *jaundice* may be signs of a liver disorder; inform your physician.

Symptom/effect	Frequency		Discuss with physician		Stop taking drug now	Call physician now
	Common	Rare	Only if severe	In all cases		
Nausea/vomiting	●		■			
Diarrhea	●		■			
Rash/itching	●			■	▲	
Hearing loss (reversible)		●		■		❚
Jaundice		●		■	▲	❚
Unexplained fever		●		■	▲	❚
Skin blisters/ulcers		●		■	▲	❚

PROLONGED USE

Courses of longer than 14 days may increase the risk of liver damage.

INTERACTIONS

General note Erythromycin interacts with a number of other drugs, particularly:

Warfarin Erythromycin increases the risk of bleeding with warfarin.

Ergotamine Erythromycin increases the risk of side effects with this drug.

Carbamazepine, digoxin, and some immunosuppressants Erythromycin may increase blood levels of these drugs.

Theophylline/aminophylline Erythromycin increases the risk of adverse effects with these drugs.

Lipid-lowering drugs ending in -statin Erythromycin may increase the risk of muscular aches and pains with statins.

ERYTHROPOIESIS STIMULATORS

Product names Aranesp, Eprex
Used in the following combined preparations None

GENERAL INFORMATION

Epoetin alfa (erythropoietin) and darbepoetin are both erythropoiesis-stimulating agents (ESA). Erythropoietin is a *hormone* naturally produced by the kidneys; it stimulates the body to produce red blood cells. Epoetin and darbepoetin are manufactured forms of erythropoetin that are used to treat anemia associated with chronic kidney disease.

ESA are also used to treat anemia caused by certain cancer treatments. They are also used to boost the level of red blood cells before surgery. Patients donate blood before surgery and this is then used during or after the surgery. Epoetin may also be used as an alternative to blood transfusions in major orthopedic (bone) surgery.

Darbepoetin is a derivative of epoetin and it has a longer duration of action. It can, therefore, be given less frequently.

The doses of these drugs are titrated gradually, with close monitoring of the hemoglobin level.

INFORMATION FOR USERS

Your drug prescription is tailored for you. Do not alter dosage without checking with your physician.

How taken

Injection.

Frequency and timing of doses
1–3 x weekly, depending on the product and condition being treated.

Usual dosage range
Dosage is calculated on an individual basis according to body weight. The dosage also varies depending on the product and condition being treated.

Onset of effect
Active inside the body within 4 hours, but effects may not be noted for 2–3 months.

Duration of action
Some effects may persist for several days.

Diet advice
None. However, if you have kidney failure, you may have to follow a special diet.

Storage
Store at 2–8°C, out of the reach of children. Do not freeze or shake. Protect from light.

Missed dose
Do not make up any missed doses.

Stopping the drug
Discuss with your physician.

Exceeding the dose
A single excessive dose is unlikely to be a cause for concern. Too high a dose over a long period can increase the likelihood of adverse effects.

SPECIAL PRECAUTIONS

Be sure to tell your physician if:
▼ You have high blood pressure.
▼ You have a long-term liver problem.
▼ You have previously suffered allergic reactions to any drugs.
▼ You have peripheral vascular disease.
▼ You have had epileptic fits.
▼ You are taking other medications.

 Pregnancy
▼ Not usually prescribed. Safety in pregnancy not established. Discuss with your physician.

 Breast-feeding
▼ Safety not established. Discuss with your physician.

 Infants and children
▼ Reduced dose necessary.

 Over 60
▼ No known problems.

 Driving and hazardous work
▼ Not applicable.

 Alcohol
▼ Follow your physician's advice regarding alcohol.

POSSIBLE ADVERSE EFFECTS

The most common effects are increased blood pressure and problems at the site of the injection; all unusual symptoms should be discussed with your physician immediately.

Symptom/effect	Frequency		Discuss with physician		Stop taking drug now	Call physician now
	Common	Rare	Only if severe	In all cases		
Increased blood pressure	●			■		
Problems at injection site	●			■		
Flu symptoms/bone pain		●		■		
Epileptic fits		●		■		▎
Skin reactions		●		■		
Headache (stabbing pain)		●		■		▎
Chest pain, difficulty breathing		●				▎
Blurred vision, changes in speech		●			▎	

INTERACTIONS

ACE inhibitor drugs These drugs may increase the level of potassium in the blood and epoetin may enhance their blood-pressure-lowering effect.

Iron supplements These may increase the effect of epoetin if you have a low level of iron in your blood.

Cyclosporine Erythropoietin may affect the blood level of cyclosporine.

PROLONGED USE

If the level of anemia is overcorrected, there is an increased risk of thrombosis, which is potentially fatal, hence the need for careful monitoring. Prolonged use of erythropoietin may also reduce survival in some patients with cancer.

Monitoring Regular blood tests to monitor blood composition and blood pressure monitoring are required.

ESTRADIOL

Product names Climara, Estrace, Estraderm, Estring, Estrogel, Oesclim, and others
Used in the following combined preparations Estalis and others

GENERAL INFORMATION

Estradiol is a naturally occurring estrogen (a female sex *hormone*). It is mainly used as hormone replacement therapy (HRT) to treat menopausal and post-menopausal symptoms such as hot flushes, night sweats, and vaginal atrophy. It is also used in contraceptive products with a progestin (another female sex hormone p.133). HRT also helps prevent the loss of bone tissue that occurs in osteoporosis. Estradiol is often given with a progestin, either as separate drugs or as a combined product. Estradiol is not recommended on its own for women with a "working" uterus.

Use of estradiol may increase the risk of developing a blood clot (thrombosis) particularly in the veins of the legs. Women with a history of these conditions should discuss this with their physician.

Estradiol is available in a variety of forms, including *topical gels* and skin patches. Skin patches of the drug may cause local rash and itching.

INFORMATION FOR USERS

Your drug prescription is tailored for you. Do not alter dosage without checking with your physician.

How taken

Tablets, vaginal tablets, vaginal rings, skin gel, patches.

Frequency and timing of doses
Once daily (tablets, gel); every 1–7 days (skin patches); daily to twice weekly (vaginal tablets); every 3 months (vaginal ring).

Usual adult dosage range
1–2mg daily (tablets); 2–4 measures daily (skin gel); 25–100mcg daily (skin patches); 10–25mcg per dose (vaginal tablets); 7.5mcg daily (vaginal ring).

Onset of effect
10–20 days.

Duration of action
Up to 24 hours; some effects may be longer lasting.

Diet advice
None.

Storage
Keep in a closed container in a cool, dry place out of the reach of children.

Missed dose
Take as soon as you remember. If your next daily treatment is due within 4 hours, take a single dose now and skip the next.

Stopping the drug
Do not stop the drug without consulting your physician; symptoms may recur.

Exceeding the dose
An occasional unintentional extra dose is unlikely to be a cause for concern. But if you notice any unusual symptoms, or if a large overdose has been taken, notify your physician.

SPECIAL PRECAUTIONS

Be sure to tell your physician if:
▼ You have long-term liver problems or gallstones.
▼ You have heart or circulation problems.
▼ You have porphyria.
▼ You have had blood clots or a stroke.
▼ You have diabetes.
▼ You are a smoker.
▼ You suffer from migraine or epilepsy.
▼ You are taking other medications.

Pregnancy
▼ Not prescribed.

Breast-feeding
▼ Not prescribed. The drug passes into breast milk and may inhibit its flow. Discuss with your physician.

Infants and children
▼ Not usually prescribed.

Over 60
▼ No special problems.

Driving and hazardous work
▼ No problems expected.

Alcohol
▼ No known problems.

Surgery and general anesthetics
▼ You may need to stop taking estradiol several weeks before having major surgery.

POSSIBLE ADVERSE EFFECTS

The most common *adverse effects* are similar to symptoms of early pregnancy, and generally diminish with time. Sudden sharp pain in the chest, groin, or legs may indicate a blood clot.

Symptom/effect	Frequency		Discuss with physician		Stop taking drug now	Call physician now
	Common	Rare	Only if severe	In all cases		
Nausea/vomiting	●		■			
Breast swelling/tenderness	●			■		
Weight gain	●		■			
Headache		●	■			
Depression		●		■		
Pain in chest/groin/legs		●		■	▲	▮

INTERACTIONS

Anticoagulant drugs The effects of these drugs are reduced by estradiol.

St John's wort May reduce the effect of estradiol.

Rifampin This drug may reduce the effects of estradiol.

Tobacco smoking This increases the risk of serious adverse effects on the heart and circulation with estradiol.

Antiepileptics The effects of estradiol are reduced by carbamazepine, phenytoin, and phenobarbital.

PROLONGED USE

As part of HRT, not usually prescribed long term. Prolonged use increases the risk of invasive breast cancer, venous thrombosis, heart attack, and stroke.

Monitoring Blood pressure checks and physical examinations, including regular mammograms, may be performed.

ETHAMBUTOL

Product name Etibi Tab
Used in the following combined preparations None

GENERAL INFORMATION

Ethambutol is an antibiotic used in the treatment of tuberculosis. It is combined with other antituberculous drugs to enhance its effect and reduce the risk of the infection becoming drug resistant. Ethambutol is not used in all cases of tuberculosis. It is more likely to be used in people with a history of tuberculosis; those with a low immune status; and in those in whom the infection may be caused by a resistant organism.

Although the drug has few common *adverse effects*, it may occasionally cause optic neuritis, a type of eye damage leading to blurring and fading of vision. As a result, ethambutol is not usually prescribed for children under six years of age or for other patients who are unable to communicate their symptoms adequately. Before starting treatment, a full ophthalmic examination is recommended.

INFORMATION FOR USERS

Your drug prescription is tailored for you. Do not alter dosage without checking with your physician.

How taken

Tablets.

Frequency and timing of doses
Once daily.

Usual adult dosage range
According to body weight.

Onset of effect
It may take several days for symptoms to improve.

Duration of action
Up to 24 hours.

Diet advice
None.

Storage
Keep in a closed container in a cool, dry, place out of the reach of children.

Missed dose
Take as soon as you remember. If your next dose is due within 6 hours, take a single dose now and skip the next.

Stopping the drug
Take the full course. Even if you feel better the original infection may still be present and may recur if treatment is stopped too soon.

Exceeding the dose
An occasional unintentional extra dose is unlikely to cause problems. Large overdoses may cause headache and abdominal pain. Notify your physician.

POSSIBLE ADVERSE EFFECTS

Side effects are uncommon with this drug but are more likely after prolonged treatment at high doses. Blurred vision or eye pain require prompt medical attention.

Symptom/effect	Frequency		Discuss with physician		Stop taking drug now	Call physician now
	Common	Rare	Only if severe	In all cases		
Nausea/vomiting		●	■			
Dizziness		●	■			
Numb/tingling hands/feet		●		■		
Blurred vision		●		■	▲	▮
Eye pain		●		■	▲	▮
Loss of colour vision		●		■	▲	▮
Rash/itching		●		■	▲	

INTERACTIONS

General note Medications that have the potential for causing optic or peripheral neuropathy may increase the adverse effects of ethambutol.

Antacids Those containing aluminium salts may decrease levels of ethambutol, and should be taken at least 2 hours before or after ethambutol.

SPECIAL PRECAUTIONS

Be sure to tell your physician if:
▼ You have a kidney problem.
▼ You have cataracts or other eye problems.
▼ You have gout.
▼ You have had a previous allergic reaction to this drug.
▼ You are taking other medications.

Pregnancy
▼ Ethambutol crosses the placenta. Discuss with your physician.

Breast-feeding
▼ The drug passes into the breast milk, but at normal doses adverse effects on the baby are unlikely. Discuss with your physician.

Infants and children
▼ Not generally prescribed under 6 years, unless the child can reliably report any vision changes.

Over 60
▼ Reduced dose may be necessary based on kidney function.

Driving and hazardous work
▼ Avoid such activities until you have learned how ethambutol affects you because the drug may cause dizziness.

Alcohol
▼ No known problems.

PROLONGED USE

Prolonged use may increase the risk of eye damage.

Monitoring Periodic eye tests are usually necessary.

ETHINYL ESTRADIOL

Used in the following combined preparations Combined oral contraceptives (e.g. Diane-35, Marvelon, Ortho-Cept, Demulen 30, Alesse, Min-Ovral, and others)

GENERAL INFORMATION

Ethinyl estradiol is a synthetic estrogen similar to estradiol, a natural female sex *hormone*. It is widely used in oral contraceptives, in combination with a synthetic progestin. It can also treat an irregular menstrual cycle and conditions in women due to high levels of male sex hormones, such as polycystic ovary syndrome and hirsutism; it may also be used as hormone therapy for the short-term relief of menopausal symptoms and preventing osteoporosis. Ethinyl estradiol may also be used to treat hypogonadism (late or absent sexual development) and acne in women, and more rarely, prostate cancer.

There is an increased risk of venous thrombosis when taking contraceptives containing ethinyl estradiol, particularly in those who are overweight and smokers.

INFORMATION FOR USERS

Your drug prescription is tailored for you. Do not alter dosage without checking with your physician.

How taken

Tablets, transdermal patch.

Frequency and timing of doses
Once daily. Often at certain times of the menstrual cycle.

Usual adult dosage range
Hormone deficiency 2.5–5mcg daily.
Combined contraceptive pills 20–35mcg daily depending on preparation.
Acne Usually 35mcg daily.

Onset of effect
10–20 days. Contraceptive protection is effective after 7 days in most cases.

Duration of action
1–2 days.

Diet advice
None.

Storage
Keep in a closed container in a cool, dry place out of the reach of children.

Missed dose
Take as soon as you remember. If your next dose is due within 4 hours, take a single dose now and skip the next. If you are taking the drug for contraceptive purposes, see What to do if you miss a pill (p.151).

Stopping the drug
Do not stop the drug without consulting your physician. Contraceptive protection is lost unless an alternative is used.

Exceeding the dose
An occasional unintentional extra dose is unlikely to be a cause for concern. If you notice any unusual symptoms, or if a large overdose has been taken, notify your physician.

SPECIAL PRECAUTIONS

Be sure to tell your physician or pharmacist before taking this drug if:
▼ You have heart failure or high blood pressure.
▼ You have had venous thrombosis or a stroke.
▼ You have a long-term liver or kidney problem.
▼ You have had breast or endometrial cancer.
▼ You have sickle cell anemia, porphyria, or diabetes.
▼ You are a smoker.
▼ You suffer from migraine or epilepsy.
▼ You are taking other medications.

Pregnancy
▼ Not prescribed. High doses may adversely affect the baby. Discuss with your physician.

Breast-feeding
▼ The drug passes into the breast milk; it may also inhibit milk flow. Discuss with your physician.

Infants and children
▼ Not usually prescribed.

Over 60
▼ No special problems.

Driving and hazardous work
▼ No known problems.

Alcohol
▼ No known problems.

Surgery and general anesthetics
▼ Ethinyl estradiol may need to be stopped several weeks before you have major surgery. Discuss this with your physician.

POSSIBLE ADVERSE EFFECTS

The most common *adverse effects* with ethinyl estradiol are similar to symptoms in the early stages of pregnancy and generally diminish with time. Sudden, sharp pain in the chest, groin, or legs may indicate an abnormal blood clot and requires urgent attention.

Symptom/effect	Frequency		Discuss with physician		Stop taking drug now	Call physician now
	Common	Rare	Only if severe	In all cases		
Nausea/vomiting	●		■			
Breast swelling/tenderness	●		■			
Weight gain/fluid retention	●		■			
Bleeding between periods	●		■			
Headache		●	■			
Depression		●		■		
Pain in chest/groin/legs		●		■	▲	▮
Sudden breathlessness		●		■	▲	▮
Itching/jaundice		●	■	■	▲	▮

INTERACTIONS

Tobacco smoking This increases the risk of serious adverse effects on the heart and circulation with ethinyl estradiol.

Rifampin and anticonvulsant drugs These drugs significantly reduce the effectiveness of oral contraceptives containing ethinyl estradiol.

Antihypertensive drugs, anticoagulants, and diuretics Ethinyl estradiol may reduce the effectiveness of these drugs.

Antibiotics and St John's wort May reduce the effectiveness of oral contraceptives containing ethinyl estradiol. Discuss with your physician or pharmacist.

PROLONGED USE

As part of HRT, not usually prescribed long term. Prolonged use increases the risk of breast cancer, venous thrombosis, heart attack, and stroke.

Monitoring Physical examinations and blood pressure checks may be performed.

ETIDRONATE

Product names CO Etidronate, Mylan-Etidronate
Used in the following combined preparations CO Etidrocal, Didrocal, Etidrocal, and others

GENERAL INFORMATION

Etidronate is given for the treatment of bone disorders such as Paget's disease. It acts only on the bones, reducing bone cell activity and thereby stopping the progress of the disease. This action also stops calcium from being released from the bones into the bloodstream, so it reduces the amount of calcium in the blood. Etidronate is also used together with calcium tablets to treat osteoporosis in post-menopausal women and to prevent steroid-induced osteoporosis. The drug's *side effects* are usually mild. If taken at high doses (20mg/kg body weight daily), the drug can lead to thinning of the bones and fractures. The effect is reversed on stopping the drug. When used for osteoporosis, the drug is taken for 14 days, followed by a gap of 76 days before the next 14 day cycle. In Didrocal, calcium carbonate tablets are included, to be taken for the 76 days.

INFORMATION FOR USERS

Your drug prescription is tailored for you. Do not alter dosage without checking with your physician.

How taken

Tablets.

Frequency and timing of doses
Once daily on an empty stomach, 2 hours before or after food.

Usual dosage range
Paget's disease 5–20mg/kg body weight daily for a maximum of 3–6 months. Courses may be repeated after a break of at least 3 months.
Osteoporosis 400mg daily for 2 weeks, repeated every 3 months.

Onset of effect
Within 1 month.

Duration of action
Some effects may persist for several weeks or months.

Diet advice
Absorption of etidronate is reduced by foods, especially those containing calcium (e.g., dairy products), so the drug should be taken on an empty stomach. Iron and antacids also reduce absorption. The diet must contain adequate calcium and vitamin D; supplements may be given.

Storage
Keep in a closed container in a dry place below 30°C out of the reach of children. Protect from light.

Missed dose
Take as soon as you remember. If your next dose is due within 6 hours, take a single dose now and skip the next.

Stopping the drug
Do not stop without consulting your physician; the underlying condition may worsen.

Exceeding the dose
An occasional unintentional extra dose is unlikely to cause problems. Large overdoses may cause numbness and muscle spasm. Notify your physician.

SPECIAL PRECAUTIONS

Be sure to tell your physician if:
▼ You have kidney problems.
▼ You are/may be pregnant or are planning pregnancy.
▼ You have had pain or difficulty in swallowing or problems with your esophagus.
▼ You have low levels of calcium in your blood.
▼ You have colitis.
▼ You are taking other medications.

 Pregnancy
▼ Not recommended.

 Breast-feeding
▼ Not recommended.

 Infants and children
▼ Not recommended.

 Over 60
▼ No special problems.

 Driving and hazardous work
▼ No special problems.

 Alcohol
▼ No special problems.

POSSIBLE ADVERSE EFFECTS

Diarrhea is more likely if the dose is increased above 5mg/kg daily. In Paget's disease, bone pain may be increased initially, but this symptom usually disappears with further treatment.

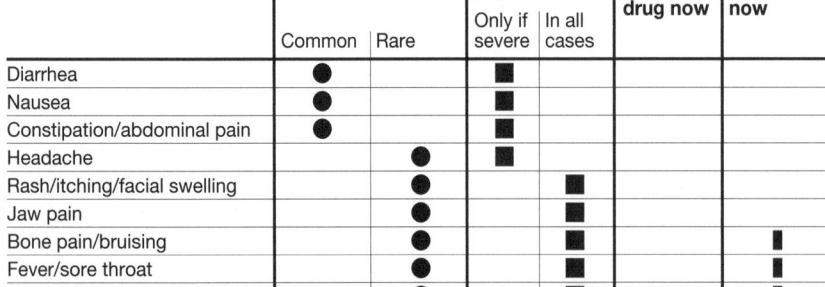

Symptom/effect	Frequency		Discuss with physician		Stop taking drug now	Call physician now
	Common	Rare	Only if severe	In all cases		
Diarrhea	●		■			
Nausea	●		■			
Constipation/abdominal pain	●		■			
Headache		●	■			
Rash/itching/facial swelling		●		■		
Jaw pain		●		■		
Bone pain/bruising		●		■		■
Fever/sore throat		●		■		■
Dull pain in thigh, hip, or groin		●		■		■

INTERACTIONS

Antacids and products containing calcium, magnesium, or iron These products should be given at least 2 hours before or after etidronate to minimize the risk of reduced absorption of etidronate.

Warfarin Close monitoring may be required with etidronate.

PROLONGED USE

When used in bone disorders such as Paget's disease, courses of treatment longer than 3 to 6 months are not usually prescribed, but repeat courses may be required. This drug can be used long term for osteoporosis.

Monitoring Your physician may monitor your bone mineral density. Blood and urine tests may be carried out.

EXENATIDE

Product name Byetta
Used in the following combined preparations None

GENERAL INFORMATION

Exenatide is an injectable drug used in the management of Type 2 diabetes. This drug is a glucagon-like peptide-1 (GLP-1) *receptor agonist* and works by mimicking certain natural substances, causing more release of insulin from the pancreas when the blood sugar is high. It is used in combination with oral medications such as metformin or a sulfonylurea, when these medications alone don't provide adequate control of blood sugar. Exenatide can increase satiety, which may result in some weight loss. It helps decrease glucose levels following a meal. It is not recommended in those with severe renal impairment.

INFORMATION FOR USERS

Your drug prescription is tailored for you. Do not alter dosage without checking with your physician.

How taken

Subcutaneous injection in the thigh, abdomen, or upper arm.

Frequency and timing of doses
Twice daily, any time up to 60 minutes prior to the morning and evening meals; each dose should be at least 6 hours apart.

Usual adult dosage range
10–20mcg daily.

Onset of effect
Within 15–60 minutes.

Duration of action
Up to 6 hours.

Diet advice
Follow your recommended diabetic diet.

Storage
Store injections in the original package in the refrigerator at 2–8°C. Do not freeze. Store your new, unused Pen in the original carton in a refrigerator, protected from light. After first use, store the pen between 2 and 25°C (do not store with needle attached). The remaining doses may be used up to 30 days. Discard any remaining medication.

Missed dose
Skip the missed dose and take your next dose at the regularly scheduled time. Do not take an extra dose.

Stopping the drug
Do not stop the drug without consulting your physician; symptoms may recur.

Exceeding the dose
Seek immediate medical help with an overdose.

POSSIBLE ADVERSE EFFECTS

When used with other medications for blood glucose control, low blood sugar may occur. The drug may cause or worsen poor kidney function.

Symptom/effect	Frequency		Discuss with physician		Stop taking drug now	Call physician now
	Common	Rare	Only if severe	In all cases		
Nausea/vomiting when starting therapy	●		■			
Diarrhea	●		■			
Rash/itching/bruising at injection site		●		■		
Low blood sugar (headache, weakness, sweating)		●		■		▮
Severe nausea/vomiting/ abdominal pain (pancreatitis)		●		■		▮
Dizziness/palpitations or pounding heart		●		■		▮

INTERACTIONS

Corticosteroids and hydrochlorothiazide may decrease the hypoglycemic effects of exenatide.

Warfarin Exenatide may enhance the effect of warfarin.

Somatropin and goserelin, leuprolide, and similar drugs may decrease the effect of exenatide.

Oral contraceptives and some antibiotics should be taken at least one hour before taking exenatide.

Acetaminophen and some antibiotics may have their absorption rate affected by exenatide.

SPECIAL PRECAUTIONS

Be sure to tell your physician if:
▼ You have type 1 diabetes mellitus or require insulin therapy.
▼ You have any kidney problems.
▼ You have experienced diabetic ketoacidosis or diabetic coma.
▼ You have severe stomach problems.
▼ You have pancreatitis, gallstones, or high triglyceride blood levels.
▼ You have a fast pulse or heart rhythm problems.
▼ You have electrolyte disturbances or have nausea or vomiting.
▼ You are allergic to exenatide or any ingredients in the injection.
▼ You have low body weight (BMI ≤ 25 kg/m²).
▼ You have had pituitary or adrenal failure.
▼ You exercise intensely.
▼ You drink alcohol heavily.
▼ You or a relation has had medullary thyroid cancer or multiple endocrine neoplasia syndrome type 2.
▼ You are taking other medications.

Pregnancy
▼ Not recommended.

Breast-feeding
▼ Not recommended.

Infants and children
▼ Not recommended.

Over 60
▼ Dosage reduction not normally necessary. Not to be used with severe kidney impairment.

Driving and hazardous work
▼ Avoid driving and hazardous work if you have warning signs of low blood sugar.

Alcohol
▼ Avoid alcohol as it increases the risk of low blood sugar.

PROLONGED USE

Monitoring Close monitoring of blood sugar is required.

EZETIMIBE

Product name Ezetrol
Used in the following combined preparations None

GENERAL INFORMATION

Ezetimibe is a lipid-lowering drug that is used in the treatment of high cholesterol in people at risk of developing heart disease. It lowers blood cholesterol by blocking the absorption of cholesterol, including dietary cholesterol, from the intestines. It is prescribed in conjunction with a low-fat diet and usually in combination with another lipid-lowering medication, a statin (p.89). It is also prescribed alone to people in whom a statin is considered inappropriate or is not tolerated.

When ezetimibe is combined with statins, it can, rarely, cause marked muscle pain, weakness, or tenderness, which should be reported to your physician immediately. This is less likely to occur when ezetimibe is used alone.

Ezetimibe can be taken at any time, once daily, and preferably taken at the same time.

QUICK REFERENCE

Drug group Lipid-lowering drugs (p.89)

Overdose danger rating Low

Dependence rating Low

Prescription needed Yes

Available as generic No

INFORMATION FOR USERS

Your drug prescription is tailored for you. Do not alter dosage without checking with your physician.

How taken

Tablets.

Frequency and timing of doses
Once daily.

Usual adult dosage range
10mg daily.

Onset of effect
1–4 hours.

Duration of action
Up to 24 hours.

Diet advice
Patients should be on a cholesterol-lowering diet.

Storage
Keep in a closed container in a cool, dry place out of the reach of children.

Missed dose
If you miss a dose, take it as soon as you remember. If it is near the time of the next dose, skip the missed dose and resume your using dosing schedule.

Stopping the drug
Do not stop the drug without consulting your physician. Stopping the drug may lead to worsening of the underlying condition.

Exceeding the dose
An occasional unintentional extra dose is unlikely to cause problems. However, if you notice any unusual symptoms, or if a large overdose has been taken, notify your physician.

SPECIAL PRECAUTIONS

Be sure to tell your physician if:
▼ You have ever had an allergic reaction to ezetimibe.
▼ You have liver problems or liver disease.
▼ You have kidney problems or kidney disease.
▼ You are taking a statin.
▼ You have lactose intolerance or glucose-galactose malabsorption.
▼ You are on any other medications.

Pregnancy
▼ Safety in pregnancy not established. Discuss with your physician.

Breast-feeding
▼ Safety in breast-feeding not established. Discuss use with your physician.

Infants and children
▼ Not recommended in children less than 10 years of age.

Over 60
▼ No special problems.

Driving and hazardous work
▼ No known problems.

Alcohol
▼ No known problems.

POSSIBLE ADVERSE EFFECTS

Ezetimibe is usually well tolerated and serious *side effects* are rare. Any unusual symptoms should be discussed with your physician.

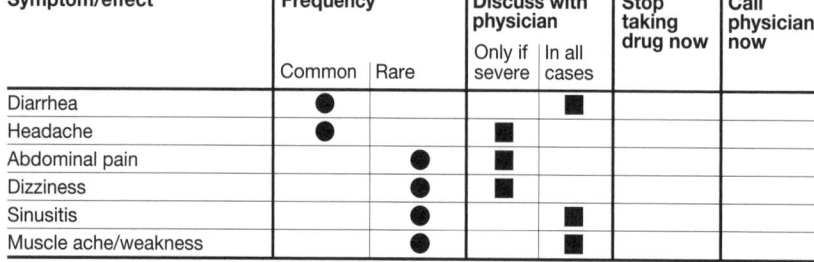

Symptom/effect	Frequency		Discuss with physician		Stop taking drug now	Call physician now
	Common	Rare	Only if severe	In all cases		
Diarrhea	●			■		
Headache	●			■		
Abdominal pain		●	■			
Dizziness		●	■			
Sinusitis		●		■		
Muscle ache/weakness		●		■		

INTERACTIONS

Antacids May decrease the rate of absorption of ezetimibe, although these do not significantly affect the total amount of ezetimibe absorbed.

Cholestyramine May decrease absorption of ezetimibe, when taken at the same time.

Fibrates Ezetimibe is not recommended to be used with fibrates (p.89) which also decrease cholesterol.

Cyclosporine May increase levels of ezetimibe; close monitoring recommended.

PROLONGED USE

No known problems.

Monitoring If administered with a statin, certain blood tests will be done periodically.

FAMCICLOVIR

Product names Apo-Famciclovir, Famvir Tablets, Sandoz Famciclovir, and others
Used in the following combined preparations None

GENERAL INFORMATION

Famciclovir is an antiviral drug used in the treatment of shingles (herpes zoster), genital herpes, and cold sores.

Early treatment in shingles can decrease symptoms. For optimal benefit, treatment should be initiated within 48 hours of the appearance of rash. Famciclovir is also beneficial in those with shingles who are over 50 years of age or those who are experiencing severe pain.

In genital herpes, it may be used to treat an acute episode or to suppress recurrent episodes in those who have had 6 or more episodes in a year. Famciclovir should be started in the prodrome stage or as soon as lesions appear.

QUICK REFERENCE

Drug group Antiviral drugs (p.119)
Overdose danger rating Low
Dependence rating Low
Prescription needed Yes
Available as generic Yes

INFORMATION FOR USERS

Your drug prescription is tailored for you. Do not alter dosage without checking with your physician.

How taken

Tablets.

Frequency and timing of doses
Herpes zoster: 3 times daily.
Suppression of recurrent genital herpes: twice daily.
Cold sores: Twice daily.

Usual adult dosage range
250–1500mg daily.

Onset of effect
Within 24 hours.

Duration of action
Up to 8–12 hours.

Diet advice
None.

Storage
Keep in a closed container in a cool, dry place out of the reach of children.

Missed dose
If you miss a dose, take it as soon as you remember. If it is near the time of the next dose, skip the missed dose and resume your usual dosing schedule. Do not double up to catch up on a missed dose.

Stopping the drug
Complete the full course as directed.

Exceeding the drug
An occasional unintentional extra dose is unlikely to cause problems. However, if you notice any unusual symptoms, or if a large overdose has been taken, notify your physician.

SPECIAL PRECAUTIONS

Be sure to tell your physician if:
▼ You have ever had an allergic reaction to famciclovir or another antiviral drug.
▼ You have impaired liver or kidney function or disease.
▼ You have reduced immunity.
▼ You are on any other medications.

 Pregnancy
▼ Safety in pregnancy not established. Discuss with your physician.

 Breast-feeding
▼ Safety in breast-feeding not established. Discuss use with your physician.

 Infants and children
▼ Not recommended.

 Over 60
▼ No special problems.

 Driving and hazardous work
▼ No known problems.

 Alcohol
▼ No known problems.

POSSIBLE ADVERSE EFFECTS

Common *side effects* include headache, nausea, and diarrhea. These effects are generally not bothersome after the first few days.

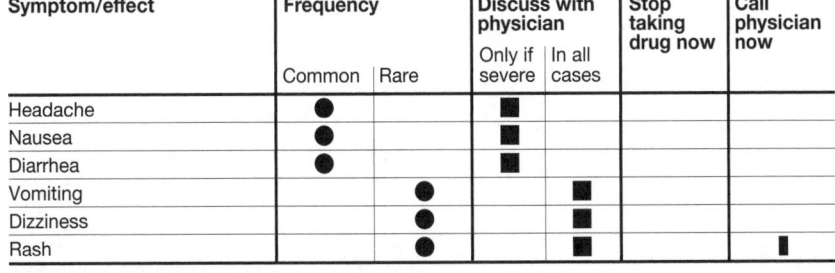

Symptom/effect	Frequency		Discuss with physician		Stop taking drug now	Call physician now
	Common	Rare	Only if severe	In all cases		
Headache	●		■			
Nausea	●		■			
Diarrhea	●		■			
Vomiting		●			■	
Dizziness		●			■	
Rash		●			■	■

INTERACTIONS

Probenecid Drugs such as probenecid, which are eliminated by the kidneys, may decrease the elimination of famciclovir, resulting in its effects being increased.

PROLONGED USE

Famciclovir is usually given for 5 or 7 days. It may be used up to a year in prevention of genital herpes.

Monitoring When used for longer than a few days, periodic monitoring of liver and kidney function may be done.

FAMOTIDINE

Product names Apo-Famotidine, Famotidine Omega, Novo-Famotidine Tab, Nu-Famotidine Tab, Pepcid AC, Pepcid Tablets
Used in the following combined preparation Pepcid Complete

GENERAL INFORMATION

Famotidine is prescribed in the treatment of stomach and duodenal ulcers. It is also used to protect against duodenal ulcers in people taking NSAIDs (p.102), who may be prone to ulcers. This drug reduces the discomfort and ulceration of reflux esophagitis, and may prevent stress ulceration and gastric bleeding in severely ill patients. Famotidine reduces the amount of stomach acid produced, allowing ulcers to heal. It is usually given in courses lasting four to eight weeks, with further courses if symptoms recur. Unlike the similar drug cimetidine, famotidine does not increase blood levels of other drugs such as anticoagulants and anticonvulsants, which might reduce the effectiveness of treatment. It is available in smaller doses over-the-counter for self-management of the discomfort of acid indigestion.

Most people experience no serious effects during famotidine treatment. As it promotes healing of the stomach lining, there is a risk that famotidine may mask stomach cancer, delaying diagnosis. It is therefore usually prescribed only when the possibility of stomach cancer has been ruled out.

QUICK REFERENCE

Drug group Anti-ulcer drugs (p.95)

Overdose danger rating Low

Dependence rating Low

Prescription needed Yes, for most doses

Available as generic Yes

INFORMATION FOR USERS

Your drug prescription is tailored for you. Do not alter dosage without checking with your physician.

How taken

Tablets, chewable tablets, injection.

Frequency and timing of doses
Once to twice daily. For prevention of acid-related symptoms associated with food intake, take 15 minutes before eating.

Usual dosage range
10–40mg daily.

Onset of effect
1 hour.

Duration of action
Up to 12 hours.

Diet advice
None.

Storage
Keep in a closed container in a cool, dry place out of the reach of children. Protect from light.

Missed dose
If you miss a dose, take it as soon as you remember. If your next dose is within 3 hours, take a single dose now and skip the next.

Stopping the drug
Do not stop the drug without consulting your physician; symptoms may recur.

Exceeding the dose
An occasional unintentional extra dose is unlikely to be a cause for concern. But if you notice any unusual symptoms, or if a large overdose has been taken, notify your physician.

SPECIAL PRECAUTIONS

Be sure to tell your physician if:
▼ You have liver or kidney problems.
▼ You have porphyria.
▼ You have had an allergic reaction to famotidine or another H_2 blocker.
▼ You are taking other medications.

Pregnancy
▼ Safety in pregnancy not established. Discuss with your physician.

Breast-feeding
▼ The drug passes into the breast milk and may affect the baby. Discuss with your physician.

Infants and children
▼ Not recommended.

Over 60
▼ No special problems.

Driving and hazardous work
▼ No known problems. Dizziness may occur in a very small proportion of patients.

Alcohol
▼ Avoid. Alcohol may aggravate your underlying condition and reduce the beneficial effects of this drug.

POSSIBLE ADVERSE EFFECTS

Adverse effects such as headache is usually related to dosage level and almost always disappear when treatment finishes.

Symptom/effect	Frequency		Discuss with physician		Stop taking drug now	Call physician now
	Common	Rare	Only if severe	In all cases		
Headache	●		■			
Diarrhea		●	■			
Dizziness		●	■			
Drowsiness		●	■			
Constipation		●	■			
Jaundice		●		■		
Mental problems		●		■		

PROLONGED USE

No problems expected.

INTERACTIONS

Ketoconazole Famotidine may reduce the absorption of ketoconazole.

FENTANYL

Product names Abstral, Duragesic, Duragesic Mat, Fentanyl citrate injection, Onsolis, ratio-Fentanyl, and others
Used in the following combined preparations None

GENERAL INFORMATION

Fentanyl is an *opioid* analgesic indicated in the management of persistent, moderate to severe, chronic pain in individuals already requiring continous opioid *medication*. It is available as buccal or sublingual tablets, a patch or an injection. The patch provides a more constant management of pain.

It is recommended that the patches not be cut or divided as this may lead to uncontrolled release of the drug. The patch should be applied to non-irritated skin on a flat surface such as the chest, back, flank, or upper arm. When applying a new patch, ensure that the old patch is removed and disposed of safely by folding it so that the adhesive side sticks to itself and flushing it down the toilet. Fentanyl injection may be used to help with anesthesia.

Individuals at risk of serious side effects include those with a fever, those whose patch area is exposed to sources of heat such as heating pads and hot water bottles, and those using drugs that may interact with this medication. The elderly are more susceptible to *adverse effects*.

INFORMATION FOR USERS

Your drug prescription is tailored for you. Do not alter dosage without checking with your physician.

How taken

Buccal tablets, sublingual tablets, injection, patch.

Frequency and timing of doses
One patch every 72 hours (3 days.)

Usual adult dosage range
Dose indiviualized. Patch available in 4 different strengths.

Onset of effect
Patch: around 12 hours.
Tablets: within 30 minutes.

Duration of action
Up to 72 hours; 2–4 hours for tablets.

Diet advice
To relieve constipation, increase intake of fluids and high fiber foods.

Storage
Keep in a closed container in a cool, dry place out of the reach of children before and after use.

Missed dose
If you miss a dose, apply the patch when you remember; the next patch should be used at the appropriate interval of 72 hours. Do not double up a dose.

Stopping the drug
Always discuss with your physician. When stopping opioid medications, a gradual downward titration is recommended.

OVERDOSE ACTION

 Seek immediate medical advice. Take emergency action in cases of slow, shallow, or irregular breathing, severe drowsiness, inability to think, or slow pulse.

See Drug poisoning emergency guide (p.526).

SPECIAL PRECAUTIONS

Be sure to tell your physician if:
▼ You have impaired liver or kidney function.
▼ You have heart or circulatory problems.
▼ You have a lung disorder such as asthma, bronchitis, or emphysema.
▼ You have sleep apnea.
▼ You have thyroid disease.
▼ You are taking other medications.

 Pregnancy
▼ Safety in pregnancy not established. Taken near the time of delivery, the drug may cause breathing difficulties in the newborn baby. Discuss with your physician.

 Breast-feeding
▼ Low levels of the drug have been detected in human milk. Safety in breast-feeding not established. Discuss with your physician.

 Infants and children
▼ Not recommended.

 Over 60
▼ Increased likelihood of adverse effects. Reduced dose necessary.

 Driving and hazardous work
▼ Patients receiving fentanyl are unlikely to be well enough to undertake such activities.

 Alcohol
▼ Avoid. Alcohol increases the sedative effects of fentanyl.

POSSIBLE ADVERSE EFFECTS

As with other opioids, fentanyl may produce nausea, vomiting, dizziness, loss of appetite, and constipation. Dosage adjustments may lessen some effects.

Symptom/effect	Frequency		Discuss with physician		Stop taking drug now	Call physician now
	Common	Rare	Only if severe	In all cases		
Sedation	●		■			
Constipation	●		■			
Nausea/vomiting	●			■		
Dizziness/light headedness	●			■		
Wheezing/difficulty breathing		●		■	▲	▮
Confusion/vivid dreams		●		■		

INTERACTIONS

CNS depressants Fentanyl increases the sedative properties of all drugs that have a sedative effect.

Ritonavir, ketoconazole, itraconazole, troleandomycin, clarithromycin, nelfinavir These drugs increase the effect of fentanyl, leading to serious effects on breathing. If any of these drugs is used with fentanyl, very close monitoring is required.

Monoamine oxidase inhibitors These may produce a severe rise in blood pressure when taken with fentanyl.

PROLONGED USE

The effects of fentanyl usually become weaker during prolonged use as the body adapts. This is known as tolerance. Other effects of long-term use include physical dependence and risk of psychological dependence.

FILGRASTIM

Product names Neulasta, Neupogen
Used in the following combined preparations None

GENERAL INFORMATION

Filgrastim is a synthetic form of G-CSF (granulocyte-colony stimulating factor), a naturally occurring protein responsible for the manufacture of white blood cells, which fight infection. Deficiency of G-CSF, therefore, increases the risk of infection. The drug works by stimulating bone marrow to produce white blood cells. It also causes bone marrow cells to move into the bloodstream, where they can be collected for use in the treatment of bone marrow disease, or to replace bone marrow lost during intensive cancer treatment.

Filgrastim is used to treat patients with congenital neutropenia (deficiency of G-CSF from birth), some AIDS patients, and those who have recently received high doses of chemo- or radiotherapy during bone-marrow transplantation or cancer treatment. Such patients are prone to frequent and severe infections.

Bone pain is a common *adverse effect* but it can be controlled using painkillers. There is an increased risk of leukemia (cancer of white blood cells) if filgrastim is given to patients with certain rare blood disorders.

QUICK REFERENCE

Drug group Blood stimulants
Overdose danger rating Medium
Dependence rating High
Prescription needed Yes
Available as generic No

INFORMATION FOR USERS

Your drug prescription is tailored for you. Do not alter dosage without checking with your physician.

How taken

Injection.

Frequency and timing of doses
Once daily.

Usual adult dosage range
0.5mcg/kg body weight–12mcg/kg body weight per day, depending upon condition being treated and response to treatment.

Onset of effect
24 hours (increase in numbers of white blood cells); several weeks (recovery of normal numbers of white blood cells).

Duration of action
1–7 days.

Diet advice
None.

Storage
Store in a refrigerator out of the reach of children.

Missed dose
Take as soon as you remember. If your next dose is due within 6 hours, do not take the missed dose. Take the next scheduled dose as usual.

Stopping the drug
Do not stop taking the drug without consulting your physician; stopping the drug may lead to worsening of the underlying condition.

Exceeding the dose
An occasional unintentional extra dose is unlikely to cause problems. But if you notice any unusual symptoms or if a large overdose has been taken, notify your physician.

SPECIAL PRECAUTIONS

Be sure to tell your physician if:
▼ You suffer from any blood disorders.
▼ You have osteoporosis.
▼ You are taking other medications.

Pregnancy
▼ Safety in pregnancy not established. Discuss with your physician.

Breast-feeding
▼ Safety in breast-feeding not established. Discuss with your physician.

Infants and children
▼ No special problems.

Over 60
▼ No special problems.

Driving and hazardous work
▼ No known problems.

Alcohol
▼ No known problems.

POSSIBLE ADVERSE EFFECTS

Adverse effects resulting from short courses of filgrastim are unusual. Most common is bone pain, which is probably linked to the stimulant effect of the drug on bone marrow.

Symptom/effect	Frequency		Discuss with physician		Stop taking drug now	Call physician now
	Common	Rare	Only if severe	In all cases		
Bone/muscle pain	●		■			
Skin rash		●		■		
Cough/breathlessness		●		■		

INTERACTIONS

***Cytotoxic* chemotherapy or radiotherapy** should not be administered within 24 hours of taking filgrastim because of the risk of increasing the damage these treatments inflict on the bone marrow.

PROLONGED USE

Prolonged use may lead to a slightly increased risk of certain leukemias. Cutaneous vasculitis (inflammation of blood vessels of the skin), osteoporosis (weakening of the bones), hair thinning, enlargement of the spleen and liver, and bleeding due to reduction in platelet numbers may also occur.

Monitoring Blood checks and regular physical examinations are performed, as well as bone scans to check for bone thinning.

FINASTERIDE

Product names Finasteride, Propecia, Proscar, and others
Used in the following combined preparations None

GENERAL INFORMATION

Finasteride is an an anti-androgen drug (see Male sex hormones, p.132) used to treat benign prostatic hyperplasia (BPH), in which the prostate gland, which surrounds the urethra, increases in size, making urination difficult. It is used in those with BPH to decrease the risk of urinary retention. The drug works by gradually shrinking the prostate gland, which improves urine flow and other obstructive symptoms such as difficulty in starting urination.

Because finasteride is excreted in semen and can feminize a male fetus, you should use a condom if your sexual partner may be, or is likely to become, pregnant. Also, women of childbearing age should not handle broken or crushed tablets because small quantities of the drug are absorbed through the skin.

The symptoms of BPH are similar to those of prostate cancer and so the drug is used only when the possibility of cancer has been ruled out.

Finasteride is also used in men, at a lower dose, to reverse male-pattern baldness by preventing the hair follicles from becoming inactive. Noticeable improvements may take about three months but will disappear within a year of treatment being stopped.

INFORMATION FOR USERS

Your drug prescription is tailored for you. Do not alter dosage without checking with your physician.

How taken

Tablets.

Frequency and timing of doses
Once daily.

Usual adult dosage range
Prostate disease 5mg.
Male-pattern baldness 1mg.

Onset of effect
Within several months.

Duration of action
24 hours.

Diet advice
None.

Storage
Keep in a closed container, in a cool, dry place out of the reach of children. Protect from light.

Missed dose
Do not take the missed dose, but take your next scheduled dose as usual.

Stopping the drug
Do not stop taking the drug without consulting your physician; stopping the drug may lead to worsening of the underlying condition.

Exceeding the dose
An occasional unintentional extra dose is unlikely to cause problems. But if you notice any unusual symptoms, or if a large overdose has been taken, notify your physician.

POSSIBLE ADVERSE EFFECTS

Most people experience very few adverse effects when taking finasteride.

Symptom/effect	Frequency		Discuss with physician		Stop taking drug now	Call physician now
	Common	Rare	Only if severe	In all cases		
Erectile dysfunction/ decreased libido	●		■			
Reduced ejaculate volume	●		■			
Breast swelling or tenderness	●			■		
Testicular pain		●		■		
Rash/lip swelling/wheezing		●		■	▲	▮

INTERACTIONS

None.

SPECIAL PRECAUTIONS

Be sure to tell your physician if:
▼ You are taking other medications.

 Pregnancy
▼ Not prescribed.

 Breast-feeding
▼ Not prescribed.

 Infants and children
▼ Not prescribed.

 Over 60
▼ No special problems.

 Driving and hazardous work
▼ No special problems.

Alcohol
▼ No special problems.

PROLONGED USE

Treatment with finasteride for benign prostatic hyperplasia and male-pattern baldness is reviewed after about six months to see if it has been effective. Long-term use of the drug carries a small increase in the risk of men developing breast cancer.

FLUCONAZOLE

Product names CO Fluconazole, Diflucan, Diflucan One, Monicure, and others
Used in the following combined preparations None

GENERAL INFORMATION

Fluconazole is an antifungal drug that is used to treat local candida infections ("thrush") affecting the vagina, mouth, and skin as well as *systemic* or more widespread candida infections. The drug is also used to treat some more unusual fungal infections, including cryptococcal meningitis. It may also be used to prevent fungal infections in patients with defective immunity. The dosage and length of course will depend on the condition being treated.

The drug is generally well tolerated, although *side effects* such as nausea and vomiting, diarrhea, and abdominal discomfort are common.

QUICK REFERENCE

Drug group Antifungal drugs (p.124)
Overdose danger rating Medium
Dependence rating Low
Prescription needed Yes
Available as generic Yes

INFORMATION FOR USERS

Your drug prescription is tailored for you. Do not alter dosage without checking with your physician.

How taken

Tablets, liquid, injection.

Frequency and timing of doses
Once daily; single 150mg dose for vaginal candidiasis.

Usual adult dosage range
50–400mg daily.

Onset of effect
Within a few hours, but full beneficial effects may take several days.

Duration of action
Up to 24 hours.

Diet advice
Avoid grapefruit juice.

Storage
Keep in a closed container in a cool, dry place out of the reach of children. Store liquid in a refrigerator (do not freeze) for no longer than 14 days.

Missed dose
Take as soon as you remember. If your next dose is due within 6 hours, take a single dose now and skip the next.

Stopping the drug
Take the full course. Even if you feel better, the original infection may still be present and may recur if treatment is stopped too soon.

Exceeding the dose
An occasional unintentional extra dose is unlikely to be a cause for concern. But if you notice any unusual symptoms, or a large overdose has been taken, notify your physician.

SPECIAL PRECAUTIONS

Be sure to tell your physician if:
▼ You have long-term liver or kidney problems.
▼ You have previously had an allergic reaction to antifungal drugs.
▼ You have acute porphyria.
▼ You are taking other medications.

Pregnancy
▼ Avoid. May adversely affect the fetus if taken during pregnancy.

Breast-feeding
▼ The drug passes into the breast milk, although probably in amounts too small to be harmful. Discuss with your physician.

Infants and children
▼ Reduced dose necessary.

Over 60
▼ Normal dose used as long as kidney function is not impaired.

Driving and hazardous work
▼ No known problems.

Alcohol
▼ No known problems.

POSSIBLE ADVERSE EFFECTS

Fluconazole is generally well tolerated. Most side effects affect the gastrointestinal tract.

Rarely, a rash may occur and should be reported to your physician.

Symptom/effect	Frequency		Discuss with physician		Stop taking drug now	Call physician now
	Common	Rare	Only if severe	In all cases		
Nausea/vomiting	●		■			
Abdominal discomfort	●		■			
Diarrhea	●		■			
Flatulence	●		■			
Rash		●		■	▲	

INTERACTIONS

Statins, colchicine, diazepam, and quinidine Fluconazole may increase the level of these drugs.

Erythromycin, azithromycin and clarithromycin can increase the level of fluconazole.

Rifampin The effect of fluconazole may be reduced by rifampin. Avoid using both drugs together.

Bosentan, ergotamine, methysergide, and eletriptan These drugs should not be used with fluconazole because of potentially dangerous interactions.

Oral antidiabetic drugs Fluconazole may increase the risk of hypoglycemia with sulfonylureas and other drugs such as nateglinide and repaglinide.

Phenytoin, theophylline/aminophylline, cyclosporine, tacrolimus, and zidovudine Fluconazole may increase the blood levels of these drugs.

Anticoagulant drugs Fluconazole may increase the effect of oral anticoagulants such as warfarin.

Anti-epileptics Fluconazole may increase blood levels of phenytoin and carbamazepime.

Estrogens Contraceptive failure has occasionally been reported during treatment of fluconazole.

PROLONGED USE

Fluconazole is usually given for short courses of treatment. However, for prevention of relapse of cryptococcal meningitis in patients with defective immunity, it may be administered indefinitely.

FLUOXETINE

Product names Pro-Fluoxetine, Prozac, and others
Used in the following combined preparations None

GENERAL INFORMATION

Fluoxetine belongs to the group of antidepressants called selective serotonin re-uptake inhibitors (SSRIs). These drugs tend to cause less sedation, have different *side effects*, and are safer if taken in overdose than older antidepressants. Fluoxetine is used to treat depression, to reduce binge eating and purging activity (bulimia nervosa), and to treat obsessive-compulsive disorder. When used to treat depression, it elevates mood, increases energy, and restores interest in everyday pursuits. Fluoxetine is broken down slowly and remains in the body for several weeks after treatment is stopped.

INFORMATION FOR USERS

Your drug prescription is tailored for you. Do not alter dosage without checking with your physician.

How taken

Capsules, liquid.

Frequency and timing of doses
Once daily in the morning.

Usual adult dosage range
20–60mg daily.

Onset of effect
Full benefits may not be felt for 4 weeks or more.

Duration of action
Beneficial effects may last for up to 6 weeks following prolonged treatment.

Diet advice
None.

Storage
Keep in a closed container in a cool, dry place out of the reach of children.

Missed dose
Take as soon as you remember. If your next dose is due within 8 hours, take a single dose now and skip the next.

Stopping the drug
Do not stop without consulting your physician; gradual dosage reduction required.

Exceeding the dose
An occasional unintentional extra dose is unlikely to cause problems. Large overdoses may cause adverse effects. Notify your physician.

SPECIAL PRECAUTIONS

Be sure to tell your physician if:
▼ You have long-term liver or kidney problems.
▼ You have heart problems.
▼ You have diabetes.
▼ You have had epileptic seizures.
▼ You have previously had an allergic reaction to fluoxetine or other SSRIs.
▼ You are taking other medications.

Pregnancy
▼ Safety in pregnancy not established. Discuss with your physician.

Breast-feeding
▼ The drug passes into the breast milk. Discuss with your physician.

Infants and children
▼ Safety and effectiveness not established. Discuss with your physician.

Over 60
▼ Reduced dose may be necessary.

Driving and hazardous work
▼ Avoid such activities until you have learned how fluoxetine affects you because the drug can cause drowsiness and can affect your judgment and coordination.

Alcohol
▼ No special problems.

POSSIBLE ADVERSE EFFECTS

The most common adverse effects of this drug are restlessness, insomnia, and intestinal irregularities. Fluoxetine produces fewer *anticholinergic* side effects than the tricyclics.

Symptom/effect	Frequency		Discuss with physician		Stop taking drug now	Call physician now
	Common	Rare	Only if severe	In all cases		
Headache/nervousness	●		■			
Insomnia/anxiety	●			■		
Nausea/diarrhea	●			■		
Weight loss	●			■		
Drowsiness		●	■			
Sexual dysfunction		●	■			
Rash		●		■	▲	∎

INTERACTIONS

General note: Any drug that affects the breakdown of other drugs in the liver may alter blood levels of fluoxetine.

Sedatives All drugs having a *sedative* effect may increase the sedative effects of fluoxetine.

Monoamine oxidase inhibitors (MAOIs) Fluoxetine should not be started less than 14 days after stopping an MAOI (except moclobemide) as serious adverse effects can occur. An MAOI should not be started less than 5 weeks after stopping fluoxetine.

ASA and other NSAIDs may have an increased risk of internal bleeding when taken with fluoxetine.

Tricyclic antidepressants Fluoxetine reduces the breakdown of tricyclics and may increase the toxicity of these drugs.

Lithium Fluoxetine increases blood levels and *toxicity* of lithium.

Carbamezepine Fluoxetine may decrease the breakdown of carbamezepine.

Tryptophan Taken together, tryptophan and fluoxetine may produce agitation, restlessness, and gastric distress.

Anticoagulants Fluoxetine can increase the effect of warfarin so dose may need adjustment.

PROLONGED USE

No problems expected in adults. Side effects tend to decrease with time. If a decision is made to stop the drug, a gradual withdrawal over several weeks should be discussed with your physician, although compared to other similar drugs, the potential for withdrawal effects are less with fluoxetine.

Monitoring Any person experiencing drowsiness, confusion, muscle cramps, or seizures should be monitored for low sodium levels in the blood.

FLUPENTIXOL

Product name Fluanxol
Used in the following combined preparations None

GENERAL INFORMATION

Flupentixol is an antipsychotic drug that is prescribed to treat schizophrenia and similar illnesses. Flupentixol's *side effects* are similar to those of phenothiazines, but it is less sedating. The drug may not be suitable for patients who suffer from mania because it may worsen the symptoms.

The drug has fewer *anticholinergic* effects than the phenothiazines but because it has antidopamingeric effects, it can cause side effects such as *parkinsonism*. Control of severe symptoms can take six months; a lower maintenance dose is then prescribed.

INFORMATION FOR USERS

Your drug prescription is tailored for you. Do not alter dosage without checking with your physician.

How taken

Tablets, injection.

Frequency and timing of doses
1–3 x daily no later than 4 pm (tablets); every 2–4 weeks (injection).

Usual adult dosage range
Schizophrenia and other psychoses 3–12mg daily (tablets); from 20–40mg every 4 weeks (injection).

Onset of effect
10 days (side effects may appear much sooner).

Duration of action
Up to 12 hours (by mouth); 2–4 weeks (by injection).

Diet advice
None.

Storage
Store at room temperature out of the reach of children. Protect injections from light.

Missed dose
Take as soon as you remember. If your next dose is due within 2 hours, do not take the missed dose, but take your next scheduled dose as usual.

Stopping the drug
Do not stop without consulting your physician, who will supervise a gradual reduction in dosage. Abrupt cessation may cause withdrawal symptoms and a recurrence of the original problem.

Exceeding the dose
An occasional unintentional extra dose is unlikely to cause problems. Larger overdoses may cause severe drowsiness, seizures, low blood pressure, high or low body temperature, or shock. Notify your physician.

SPECIAL PRECAUTIONS

Be sure to tell your physician if:
▼ You have long-term liver or kidney problems.
▼ You have heart problems.
▼ You have porphyria.
▼ You have had epileptic seizures.
▼ You have thyroid disease.
▼ You have Parkinson's disease.
▼ You have glaucoma.
▼ You are taking other medications.

Pregnancy
▼ Not usually prescribed. May cause lethargy in the baby during labour. Discuss with your physician.

Breast-feeding
▼ The drug passes into the breast milk and may affect the baby. Discuss with your physician.

Infants and children
▼ Not recommended.

Over 60
▼ Reduced dose necessary. Increased risk of late-appearing movement disorders or confusion.

Driving and hazardous work
▼ Avoid such activities until you have learned how flupentixol affects you because the drug can cause drowsiness and slowed reactions.

Alcohol
▼ Avoid. Flupentixol enhances the *sedative* effect of alcohol.

Surgery and general anesthetics
▼ Treatment may need to be stopped before you have any surgery. Discuss this with your physician or dentist.

POSSIBLE ADVERSE EFFECTS

The possible adverse effects of this drug are mainly the result of its anticholinergic and antidopamingeric actions and its blocking action on the transmission of signals through the heart.

Symptom/effect	Frequency		Discuss with physician		Stop taking drug now	Call physician now
	Common	Rare	Only if severe	In all cases		
Blurred vision	●			■		
Weight gain	●		■			
Nausea	●		■			
Drowsiness	●		■			
Rapid heartbeat/palpitations	●			■		▮
Dizziness/fainting/confusion	●			■		▮
Parkinsonism/tremor	●			■		
Epileptic seizures		●		■	▲	▮
Rash		●		■	▲	
Persistent infection/sore throat		●		■		
Jaundice		●		■	▲	

INTERACTIONS

Anti-arrhythmic drugs Taken with these drugs, flupentixol may increase the risk of arrhythmias.

Anticholinergic drugs Flupentixol may increase the effects of these drugs.

Antiepileptic drugs Flupentixol may reduce the effects of these drugs.

Sedatives Flupentixol enhances the effect of all sedative drugs.

Antihypertensive drugs Flupentixol may increase the effects of some antihypertensives.

Antiparkinson drugs Flupentixol may reduce the effects of these drugs.

PROLONGED USE

The risk of late-appearing movement disorders increases as treatment with flupentixol continues. Blood disorders, as well as *jaundice* and other liver disorders, are occasionally seen.

Monitoring Blood tests may be performed, particularly if there is persistent infection.

FLUTAMIDE

Product names Apo-Flutamide, Euflex, and others
Used in the following combined preparations None

GENERAL INFORMATION

Flutamide is an anti-androgen drug used in the treatment of advanced prostate cancer, often in combination with drugs such as goserelin that control the production of the male sex hormones (androgens). Both drugs are effective because the cancer is dependent on androgens for its continued development. Treatment with goserelin-type drugs causes an initial increase in release of the hormone testosterone, leading to a growth spurt of the cancer ("tumour flare"), which flutamide is prescribed to stop. Flutamide treatment is begun in combination with the goserelin-type drug. Flutamide is also used to treat prostate cancer when goserelin-type drugs are not prescribed.

Flutamide may discolour the urine amber or yellow-green, but this is harmless. However, you should always notify your physician straight away if your urine becomes dark coloured, because this may be an indication of liver damage.

QUICK REFERENCE

Drug group Anticancer drugs (p.140)

Overdose danger rating Medium

Dependence rating Low

Prescription needed Yes

Available as generic Yes

INFORMATION FOR USERS

Your drug prescription is tailored for you. Do not alter dosage without checking with your physician.

How taken

Tablets.

Frequency and timing of doses
3 x daily, starting 3 days before the goserelin-type drug and continuing for 3 weeks.

Usual adult dosage range
250mg.

Onset of effect
1 hour.

Duration of action
8 hours.

Diet advice
None.

Storage
Keep in a closed container in a cool, dry place out of the reach of children.

Missed dose
Take as soon as you remember. If your next dose is due within 2 hours, take a single dose now and skip the next.

Stopping the drug
Do not stop taking the drug without consulting your physician because the condition may worsen rapidly.

Exceeding the dose
An occasional unintentional extra dose is unlikely to be a cause for concern. But if you notice any unusual symptoms, or if a large overdose has been taken, notify your physician.

POSSIBLE ADVERSE EFFECTS

Nausea and tiredness are common. Breast swelling and tenderness also occur when the drug is given in an effective dose; this is usually reversible when treatment stops or dosage is reduced.

Symptom/effect	Frequency		Discuss with physician		Stop taking drug now	Call physician now
	Common	Rare	Only if severe	In all cases		
Breast swelling/tenderness	●		■			
Nausea/vomiting/diarrhea	●		■			
Insomnia/tiredness/headache	●		■			
Dizziness/blurred vision		●	■			
Skin reactions		●		■		
Jaundice/dark urine		●		■	▲	▮

INTERACTIONS

Warfarin Flutamide increases the effect of this drug.

Theophylline Flutamide may increase the level of theophylline.

SPECIAL PRECAUTIONS

Be sure to tell your physician if:
▼ You have heart problems.
▼ You have liver problems.
▼ You are taking other medications.

Pregnancy
▼ Not prescribed.

Breast-feeding
▼ Not prescribed.

Infants and children
▼ Not prescribed.

Over 60
▼ No special problems.

Driving and hazardous work
▼ Do not undertake such activities until you have learned how flutamide affects you because the drug can cause blurred vision and dizziness.

Alcohol
▼ No special problems, but excessive consumption should be avoided.

PROLONGED USE

Prolonged use of flutamide may cause liver damage. Because it is an anti-androgen, the drug also reduces sperm count.

Monitoring Periodic liver-function tests are usually performed.

FLUTICASONE

Product names Avamys, Cutivate, Flonase, Flovent
Used in the following combined preparation Advair

GENERAL INFORMATION

Fluticasone is a corticosteroid drug used to control inflammation in asthma and allergic rhinitis. It does not produce relief immediately, so it is important to take the drug regularly. For allergic rhinitis, treatment with the nasal spray needs to begin two to three weeks before the hay fever season commences. Fluticasone should be taken regularly by inhaler in order to prevent asthma attacks. Proper instruction is essential to ensure that the inhaler is used correctly. Fluticasone is also prescribed in the form of cream to treat dermatitis and eczema (see Topical corticosteroids p.162).

Fluticasone has few serious *adverse effects* because it is administered directly into the lungs (by the inhaler) or nasal mucosa (by the nasal spray). Fungal infection of the mouth and throat is a possible *side effect* of the inhaled form but can be minimized by thoroughly rinsing the mouth and gargling with water after each inhalation.

QUICK REFERENCE

Drug group Corticosteroids (p.127)
Overdose danger rating Low
Dependence rating Low
Prescription needed Yes
Available as generic Yes

INFORMATION FOR USERS

Your drug prescription is tailored for you. Do not alter dosage without checking with your physician.

How taken

Cream, inhaler, nasal spray.

Frequency and timing of doses
Allergic rhinitis 1–2 x daily; *asthma* 2 x daily.

Usual adult dosage range
Allergic rhinitis 2 sprays into each nostril; *asthma* 200–1000mcg per day.

Onset of effect
4–7 days (asthma); 3–4 days (allergic rhinitis).

Duration of action
The effects can last for several days after stopping the drug.

Diet advice
None.

Storage
Keep in a cool, dry place out of the reach of children.

Missed dose
Take as soon as you remember.

Stopping the drug
Do not stop the drug without consulting your physician; symptoms may recur.

Exceeding the dose
An occasional unintentional extra dose is unlikely to be a cause for concern. Adverse effects may occur if the recommended dose is regularly exceeded over a prolonged period.

SPECIAL PRECAUTIONS

Be sure to tell your physician if:
▼ You have chronic sinusitis.
▼ You have had nasal ulcers or surgery.
▼ You have had tuberculosis or another respiratory infection.
▼ You are taking other medications.

Pregnancy
▼ Safety in pregnancy not established. Discuss with your physician.

Breast-feeding
▼ Safety in breast-feeding not established. Discuss with your physician.

Infants and children
▼ Not recommended under 4 years. Reduced dose necessary in older children. For use in children 12 years and older, discuss with their physician.

Over 60
▼ No known problems.

Driving and hazardous work
▼ No known problems.

Alcohol
▼ No known problems.

POSSIBLE ADVERSE EFFECTS

Adverse effects are unlikely to occur. The main side effect is fungal infection of the throat and mouth (inhaler). This can be minimized by thoroughly rinsing the mouth, brushing the teeth, or gargling with water.

Symptom/effect	Frequency		Discuss with physician		Stop taking drug now	Call physician now
	Common	Rare	Only if severe	In all cases		
Inhaler/nasal spray						
Nasal irritation	●		■			
Cough	●		■			
Sore throat/mouth/hoarseness	●			■		
Nose bleeds	●			■		
Cream						
Skin changes (long-term use)	●		■			

INTERACTIONS

None.

PROLONGED USE

Although not common when used as an inhaler or topically, long-term use can cause muscle weakness, osteoporosis, growth retardation in children, and rarely, adrenal gland suppression. Rarely, nasal spray may cause glaucoma. Prolonged use of topical treatment may also lead to skin thinning.

Monitoring Periodic checks on adrenal gland function may be required if large doses are being taken. Children should have their height monitored.

FLUVOXAMINE

Product names Apo-Fluvoxamine, Apo-Fluvoxamine Tablets, Dom-Fluvoxamine, Luvox, and others
Used in the following combined preparation None

GENERAL INFORMATION

Fluvoxamine belongs to the group of antidepressants called selective serotonin re-uptake inhibitors (SSRIs). These drugs tend to cause less sedation than older antidepressants such as amitriptyline (tricyclic antidepressants).

Fluvoxamine is indicated in the management of depression and obsessive-compulsive disorder. Like other SSRIs, it elevates mood, increases energy, and restores interest in the individual's usual activities.

QUICK REFERENCE

Drug group Antidepressant (p.68)

Overdose danger rating Medium

Dependence rating Low

Prescription needed Yes

Available as generic Yes

INFORMATION FOR USERS

Your drug prescription is tailored for you. Do not alter dosage without checking with your physician.

How taken

Tablets.

Frequency and timing of doses
Once daily.

Usual adult dosage range
Initial dose: 50mg at bedtime; may increase gradually as appropriate; maximum 300mg/day.

Onset of effect
Full benefits may not be felt for 4 weeks or more.

Duration of action
Up to 24 hours.

Diet advice
None.

Storage
Keep in a closed container in a cool, dry place out of the reach of children.

Missed dose
If you miss a dose, take it as soon as you remember. If it is near the time of the next dose, skip the missed dose and resume your usual dosing schedule. Do not take more than the total daily prescribed dose in a day.

Stopping the drug
Do not stop without consulting your physician; gradual dosage reduction required.

Exceeding the dose
An occasional unintentional extra dose is unlikely to cause problems. For overdoses seek immediate medical advice and contact your physician right away. Take emergency action if seizures or loss of consciousness occurs. **See Drug poisoning emergency guide (p.526).**

SPECIAL PRECAUTIONS

Be sure to tell your physician if:
▼ You have diabetes.
▼ You have seizure disorders or epilepsy.
▼ You or anyone else in your family has depression or obsessive compulsive disorder.
▼ You have a history of mania or hypomania.
▼ You have had seizures.
▼ You have liver or kidney disease.
▼ You have high blood pressure.
▼ You are taking medications that can affect bleeding.
▼ You are taking other medications.

Pregnancy
▼ Safety in pregnancy not established. Discuss with your physician.

Breast-feeding
▼ Safety not established. Discuss with your physician.

Infants and children
▼ Safety not established. Discuss risks and benefits with your physician.

Over 60
▼ A reduced dose may be necessary.

Driving and hazardous work
▼ Avoid such activities until you have learned how fluvoxamine affects you because the drug can cause drowsiness and can affect your judgment and coordination.

Alcohol
▼ No special problems.

POSSIBLE ADVERSE EFFECTS

The most common are nausea, headaches, upset stomach, sedation, small changes in heart rate or blood pressure, decrease in appetite. Rarely, may cause liver problems.

Symptom/effect	Frequency		Discuss with physician		Stop taking drug now	Call physician now
	Common	Rare	Only if severe	In all cases		
Tiredness/drowsiness	●		■			
Nausea	●		■			
Diarrhea		●		■		
Insomnia		●	■			
Tremor/agitation		●		■		
Constipation/headache	●		■			
Changes in sexual performance		●		■		
Mental/mood changes		●		■		■

INTERACTIONS

Grapefruit juice can increase the level of fluvoxamine.

Tizanidine and Monoamine Oxidase Inhibitors (MAOIs) Fluvoxamine should not be used with these drugs. Fluvoxamine and MAOIs should not be used within 2 weeks of each other.

Cimetidine may decrease the breakdown of fluvoxamine.

ASA and other NSAIDs may have an increased risk of internal bleeding when taken with fluvoxamine.

St John's wort, lithium, tryptophan Use with caution with fluvoxamine as there is a potential for interaction.

Anticoagulants Fluvoxamine can increase the effect of warfarin; may require dose adjustment.

Carbamazepine and clozapine Fluvoxamine may decrease the breakdown of these drugs.

PROLONGED USE

If a decision is made to stop the drug, a gradual withdrawal over several weeks should be discussed with your physician to minimize withdrawal effects which include: dizziness, electric-shock sensations, abnormal dreams, agitation, anxiety, tremor, and sweating.

FORMOTEROL

Product names Foradil, Oxeze Turbuhaler
Used in the following combined preparations Symbicort Turbuhaler, Zenhale

GENERAL INFORMATION

Formoterol is a long-acting sympathomimetic bronchodilator that relaxes the muscle surrounding the bronchioles (airways in the lungs).

This drug is used in the maintenance therapy (as a "preventer") of asthma, chronic bronchitis, and emphysema. A shorter-acting bronchodilator may be used for relief of acute symptoms. In those over 6 years of age, Oxeze can be used for exercise-induced asthma, and Symbicort can be used in those over 12 years of age as a reliever. Formoterol is used by inhalation and is very effective because the drug is delivered directly to the bronchioles, allowing for smaller doses and causing fewer side effects. The most common side effect is fine tremor of the hands. Anxiety, tension, and restlessness may also occur.

INFORMATION FOR USERS

Your drug prescription is tailored for you. Do not alter dosage without checking with your physician.

How taken

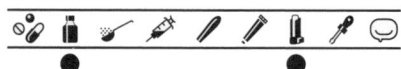

Powder in capsule for inhalation, metered dose inhaler, dry powder inhaler.

Frequency and timing of doses
2 x daily.

Usual dosage range
Adults 1 puff or inhaled capsule (6mcg or 12mcg); daily maximum 48mcg.
Children 6–16 years 1 puff or inhaled capsule (6mcg or 12mcg); daily maximum 24mcg. Not recommended in children less than 6 years.

Onset of effect
1–3 minutes; peak at about 15 minutes.

Duration of action
12 hours.

Diet advice
None.

Storage
Keep in a cool, dry place out of the reach of children. Protect from light. Do not puncture or burn inhalers.

Missed dose
If you remember within 6 hours of the missed dose, take your usual dose as soon as possible, then go back to your regular schedule. If it is longer than 6 hours, just take your next dose on time.

Stopping the drug
Do not stop the drug without consulting your physician; symptoms may recur.

Exceeding the dose
An occasional unintentional extra dose is unlikely to be a cause for concern. But if you notice any unusual symptoms, or if a large overdose has been taken, notify your physician immediately.

SPECIAL PRECAUTIONS

Be sure to tell your physician if:
▼ You have heart problems.
▼ You have high blood pressure.
▼ You have had an overactive thyroid gland.
▼ You have diabetes.
▼ You are taking other medications.

Pregnancy
▼ Safety in pregnancy not established. Discuss with your physician.

Breast-feeding
▼ Safety in breast-feeding not established. Discuss with your physician.

Infants and children
▼ Not recommended under 6 years.

Over 60
▼ Increased likelihood of adverse effects. Reduced dose may therefore be necessary.

Driving and hazardous work
▼ Avoid such activities until you have learned how formoterol affects you because the drug can cause some dizziness and tremors.

Alcohol
▼ No known problems.

POSSIBLE ADVERSE EFFECTS

Muscle tremor, which particularly affects the hands, anxiety, and restlessness are the most common adverse effects. Palpitations and headaches are rare; should these occur, see your physician.

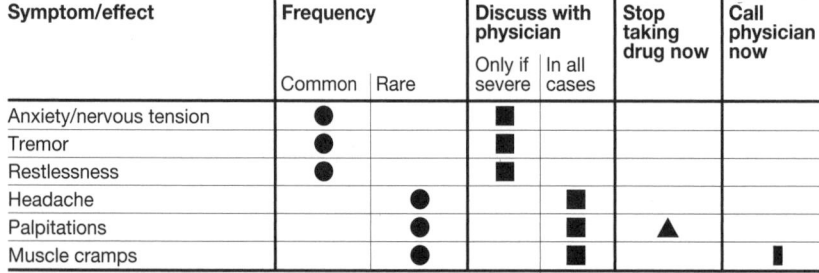

Symptom/effect	Frequency		Discuss with physician		Stop taking drug now	Call physician now
	Common	Rare	Only if severe	In all cases		
Anxiety/nervous tension	●		■			
Tremor	●		■			
Restlessness	●		■			
Headache		●		■		
Palpitations		●		■	▲	
Muscle cramps		●		■		■

INTERACTIONS

Theophylline When taken with formoterol, there is a risk of low blood potassium level.

Other sympathomimetic drugs Increase the effects of formoterol, thereby also increasing the risk of adverse effects.

Beta blockers Drugs in this group may reduce the action of formoterol.

Monoamine Oxidase Inhibitors (MAOIs) Tranylcypromine, moclobemide, and phenelzine can interact with formoterol to cause a dangerous rise in blood pressure.

PROLONGED USE

No problems expected. However, you should contact your physician if you need to use higher doses than prescribed, or require 48mcg for 3 or more days, or if you feel that your short-acting bronchodilator is not as effective.

Monitoring Periodic blood tests for potassium may be needed in people on high-dose treatment with formoterol combined with other asthma drugs.

FUROSEMIDE

Product names Lasix, Novo-Semide Tab, and others
Used in the following combined preparations None

GENERAL INFORMATION

Furosemide is a powerful, short-acting loop diuretic that has been in use for over 20 years. Like other diuretics, it is used to treat edema (accumulation of fluid in tissue spaces) caused by heart failure, and certain lung, liver, and kidney disorders.

Because it is fast acting, furosemide is often used in emergencies to relieve pulmonary edema (fluid in the lungs).

Furosemide is particularly useful for people who have impaired kidney function because they do not respond well to thiazide diuretics (see p.85).

Furosemide increases potassium loss, which can produce a wide variety of symptoms. For this reason, potassium supplements or a potassium-sparing diuretic are often given with the drug.

QUICK REFERENCE

Drug group Loop diuretics (p.85) and antihypertensive drugs (p.88)

Overdose danger rating Low

Dependence rating Low

Prescription needed Yes

Available as generic Yes

INFORMATION FOR USERS

Your drug prescription is tailored for you. Do not alter dosage without checking with your physician.

How taken

Tablets, liquid, injection.

Frequency and timing of doses
Once daily, usually in the morning; 4–6 x hourly (high dose therapy).

Usual adult dosage range
20–80mg daily. Dose may be increased to a maximum of 2g daily if kidney function is impaired.

Onset of effect
Within 1 hour (by mouth); within 5 minutes (by injection).

Duration of action
Up to 6 hours.

Diet advice
Use of this drug may reduce potassium the body. Eat plenty of potassium-rich fresh fruits and vegetables, such as bananas and tomatoes.

Storage
Keep in a closed container in a cool, dry place out of the reach of children. Protect from light.

Missed dose
No cause for concern, but take as soon as you remember. However, if it is late in the day do not take the missed dose, or you may need to get up during the night to pass urine. Take the next scheduled dose as usual.

Stopping the drug
Do not stop the drug without consulting your physician; symptoms may recur.

Exceeding the dose
An occasional unintentional extra dose is unlikely to be a cause for concern. But if you notice any unusual symptoms, or if a large overdose has been taken, notify your physician.

SPECIAL PRECAUTIONS

Be sure to tell your physician if:
▼ You have long-term liver or kidney problems.
▼ You have gout.
▼ You have previously had an allergic reaction to furosemide or sulfonamides.
▼ You have prostate trouble.
▼ You are taking other medications.

Pregnancy
▼ Safety in pregnancy not established. Discuss with your physician.

Breast-feeding
▼ The drug may reduce milk supply, but the amount in the milk is unlikely to affect the baby. Discuss with your physician.

Infants and children
▼ Reduced dose necessary.

Over 60
▼ Reduced dose may be necessary.

Driving and hazardous work
▼ Avoid such activities until you have learned how furosemide affects you because the drug may reduce mental alertness and cause dizziness.

Alcohol
▼ Keep consumption low. Furosemide increases the likelihood of dehydration and hangovers after the consumption of alcohol.

POSSIBLE ADVERSE EFFECTS

Adverse effects are caused mainly by the rapid fluid loss produced by furosemide. These tend to diminish as the body adjusts to taking the drug. The disturbance in body salts and water balance can result in muscle cramps, headaches, and dizziness.

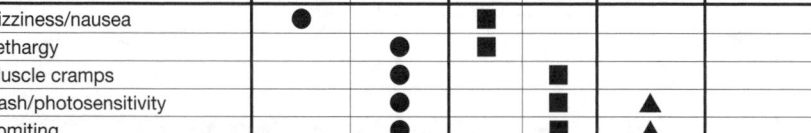

Symptom/effect	Frequency		Discuss with physician		Stop taking drug now	Call physician now
	Common	Rare	Only if severe	In all cases		
Dizziness/nausea	●		■			
Lethargy		●	■			
Muscle cramps		●		■		
Rash/photosensitivity		●		■	▲	
Vomiting		●		■	▲	

INTERACTIONS

Non-steroidal anti-inflammatory drugs (NSAIDs) Some of these drugs may reduce the diuretic effect of furosemide.

Lithium Furosemide may increase blood levels of lithium, leading to an increased risk of lithium poisoning.

Digoxin Loss of potassium may lead to digoxin toxicity when furosemide is taken with this drug.

Aminoglycoside antibiotics The risk of hearing and kidney problems may be increased when these drugs are taken with furosemide.

Thiazides Extremely large amounts of urine may be produced when these drugs are taken with furosemide.

PROLONGED USE

Serious problems are unlikely, but levels of salts, such as potassium, sodium, and calcium, may become depleted. Low blood pressure, palpitations, headaches, problems passing urine, or muscle cramps may develop, particularly in the elderly.

Monitoring Periodic tests may be performed to check kidney function and levels of body salts.

GABAPENTIN

Product name Neurontin
Used in the following combined preparations None

GENERAL INFORMATION

Gabapentin is an antiepileptic drug (see Antiepileptic drugs, p.70) used to treat partial seizures, and is often prescribed in combination with other drugs when a patient's epilepsy is not being satisfactorily controlled with the other drugs alone. Unlike some of the other antiepileptics, gabapentin does not require blood level monitoring. In addition, it does not have any interactions with the other anticonvulsant drugs.

Gabapentin has also been studied in relieving neuropathic pain, such as the pain suffered after shingles or by some people with diabetes.

Patients with impaired kidney function should be given smaller doses, and diabetic patients taking gabapentin may notice fluctuations in their blood sugar levels.

QUICK REFERENCE

Drug group Antiepileptic drugs (p.70)

Overdose danger rating Medium

Dependence rating Low

Prescription needed Yes

Available as generic Yes

INFORMATION FOR USERS

Your drug prescription is tailored for you. Do not alter dosage without checking with your physician.

How taken

Tablets, capsules.

Frequency and timing of doses
Twice daily initially, increasing to three times daily as maintenance treatment. No more than 12 hours should elapse between doses.

Usual adult dosage range
Epilepsy 900–1800mg daily; maintenance dose reached gradually over a few days.
Neuropathic pain Maximum of 1800mg daily, reached gradually over a few days.

Onset of effect
The full antiepileptic effect may not be seen for 48 hours.

Duration of action
6–8 hours.

Diet advice
None.

Storage
Keep in a cool, dry place out of the reach of children.

Missed dose
Take as soon as you remember. If your next dose is due within 4 hours, take a dose now and skip the next.

Stopping the drug
Gabapentin should not be stopped abruptly. Gradual withdrawal over at least 7 days, in consultation with a physician, is advised to reduce the risk of seizures in epileptics.

Exceeding the dose
An occasional unintentional extra dose is unlikely to be a cause for concern. Large overdoses may cause dizziness, double vision, and slurred speech. Notify your physician.

SPECIAL PRECAUTIONS

Be sure to tell your physician if:
▼ You have a kidney problem.
▼ You have diabetes.
▼ You have a history of psychiatric illness.
▼ You are taking any other medications.

 Pregnancy
▼ The drug is likely to reach the fetus and its effects are unknown. Discuss with your physician.

 Breast-feeding
▼ The drug passes into the breast milk, and the effects on the baby are unknown. Discuss with your physician.

 Infants and children
▼ Not recommended in children uner 6 years. Reduced doses based on body weight are required in children under 12 years.

 Over 60
▼ Doses may have to be adjusted to allow for decreased kidney function.

 Driving and hazardous work
▼ Avoid driving or hazardous work until you have learned how the drug affects you. Gabapentin may produce drowsiness or dizziness.

 Alcohol
▼ Alcohol may increase the sedative effects of gabapentin.

POSSIBLE ADVERSE EFFECTS

The most common *adverse effects* of gabapentin are sleepiness and dizziness. Vision difficulties are less common, as are indigestion and weight gain. The most unusual adverse effect are mood changes and rash.

Symptom/effect	Frequency		Discuss with physician		Stop taking drug now	Call physician now
	Common	Rare	Only if severe	In all cases		
Drowsiness/dizziness/fatigue	●		■			
Muscle tremor	●			■		
Vision disturbances		●		■		
Indigestion		●		■		
Weight gain		●		■		
Mood changes/hallucinations		●		■		▮
Rash		●		■		▮

PROLONGED USE

No problems expected.

INTERACTIONS

Antacids containing aluminum or magnesium These may reduce the effect of gabapentin. The drug should not be taken within 2 hours of antacid preparations.

Urinary protein tests for diabetics False-positive readings have been recorded with some tests. Special procedures are required for diabetics taking gabapentin.

GALANTAMINE

Product names Feva-Galantamine, Mylan Galantamine, Reminyl ER, and others
Used in the following combined preparations None

GENERAL INFORMATION

Galantamine is an inhibitor of the *enzyme* cholinesterase, which breaks down the naturally occurring neurotransmitter acetylcholine to limit its effect. Blocking this raises the level of acetylcholine which, in the brain, increases alertness. Galantamine can improve the symptoms of mild to moderate dementia in Alzheimer's disease, and may slow the rate of deterioration. It is not currently recommended for dementia due to other causes. It is usual to assess those on the drug after three months to decide whether it is helping and if it should be continued. As the disease progresses, the benefit obtained may diminish.

Common *side effects* include change in appetite, drowsiness, agitation, and confusion, which can appear to be similar to Alzheimer's disease.

The starting dose in usually 8mg; this can then be gradually increased up to 24mg daily. Caregiver should be overseeing the taking of tablet(s).

QUICK REFERENCE

Drug group Drugs for dementia (p.71)

Overdose danger rating Medium

Dependence rating Low

Prescription needed Yes

Available as generic Yes

INFORMATION FOR USERS

Your drug prescription is tailored for you. Do not alter dosage without checking with your physician.

How taken

Tablets, capsules.

Frequency and timing of doses
Twice daily (regular release tablets — RR); once daily (extended release capsules — ER).

Usual adult dosage range
Maintenance dose 16–24mg.

Onset of effect
1–3 hours (regular).

Duration of action
8–12 hours (RR tablets).
Up to 24 hours (ER capsules).

Diet advice
None.

Storage
Keep in a closed container in a cool, dry place out of the reach of children.

Missed dose
Take as soon as you remember. If your next regular tablet dose is within 4 hours, take a dose now and skip the next.

Stopping the drug
Do not stop taking the drug without consulting your physician; symptoms may recur.

Exceeding the dose
An occasional unintentional extra dose is unlikely to be a problem. Large overdoses may cause vomiting, diarrhea, and a low heart rate. Notify your physician.

SPECIAL PRECAUTIONS

Be sure to tell your physician if:
▼ You have a heart problem.
▼ You have liver or kidney problems.
▼ You have asthma or respiratory problems.
▼ You have had a gastric or duodenal ulcer.
▼ You have urinary incontinence or bladder problem.
▼ You are taking other medications.

Pregnancy
▼ Safety in pregnancy not established.

Breast-feeding
▼ Not recommended.

Infants and children
▼ Not recommended.

Over 60
▼ No special problems expected.

Driving and hazardous work
▼ Your underlying condition may make such activities inadvisable. Discuss with your physician.

Alcohol
▼ Avoid. Alcohol increases the sedative effects of galantamine.

POSSIBLE ADVERSE EFFECTS

Adverse effects include mental changes and intestinal problems. Although these are common, they are usually mild. However, women may be more susceptible to nausea, vomiting, and weight loss.

Symptom/effect	Frequency		Discuss with physician		Stop taking drug now	Call physician now
	Common	Rare	Only if severe	In all cases		
Nausea/vomiting	●			■		
Reduced appetite/ weight loss	●			■		
Tiredness	●		■			
Diarrhea		●		■		
Dizziness/drowsiness	●			■		
Headache	●		■			
Agitation/confusion/depression	●			■		
Low heart rate		●		■		
Convulsions		●		■		

PROLONGED USE

May be continued for as long as there is benefit. Stopping the drug leads to a gradual loss of the improvements.

Monitoring Periodic checks may be performed to test whether the drug is still providing some benefit.

INTERACTIONS

Anticholinergic medications
Cholinesterase inhibitors such as galantamine or rivastigmine may interfere with the activity of these anticholinergic agents, such as benztropine.

Ketoconazole, erythromycin, paroxetine, grapefruit juice These may increase the effect of galantamine and the dose of galantamine may need to be adjusted.

Muscle relaxants used in surgery
Galantamine may increase the effects of some muscle relaxants, but it may also block the effects of some others.

GATIFLOXACIN

Product name Zymar
Used in the following combined preparations None

GENERAL INFORMATION

Gatifloxacin, a quinolone *antibiotic*, is available as eye drops and is used in the treatment of bacterial conjunctivitis. To use the drops, wash your hands first, then tilt the head back and pull down the lower eyelid to form a pouch. Place a drop of the *medication* in the pouch. Close your eyes gently for about 30 seconds, without blinking. Do not touch the applicator tip to the eyelid as this can contaminate it.

Use the antibiotic for the full treatment period recommended by your physician, even if your eye starts to feel better. Do not wear contact lenses when you have a bacterial eye infection, until it is resolved.

INFORMATION FOR USERS

Your drug prescription is tailored for you. Do not alter dosage without checking with your physician.

How taken

Eye drops.

Frequency and timing of doses
4–8 times daily.

Usual adult dosage range
Usually for days 1 and 2, one drop every 2 hours while awake, up to 8 times daily. On days 3 to 7, one drop four times daily, spaced evenly apart.

Onset of effect
Within 48 hours.

Duration of action
2–4 hours.

Diet advice
None.

Storage
Store between 15°C and 25°C. Do not freeze. Discard container 28 days after opening.

Missed dose
If you miss a dose, apply it as soon as you remember. If it is near the time of the next dose, skip the missed dose and resume your usual dosing schedule.

Stopping the drug
Take the full course. Even if you feel better, the original infection may still be present, and symptoms may recur if treatment is stopped too soon.

Exceeding the dose
An occasional unintentional extra dose is unlikely to be a cause for concern. If too many drops are used accidentally, the eye can be flushed with warm water. If you notice any unusual symptoms, notify your physician.

SPECIAL PRECAUTIONS

Be sure to tell your physician if:
▼ You have allergy to quinolone antibiotics or any other medications.
▼ You wear contact lenses.
▼ You are using any other eye drops.
▼ You are taking other medications.

Pregnancy
▼ Safety in pregnancy not established. Discuss with your physician.

Breast-feeding
▼ Safety not established. Discuss with your physician.

Infants and children
▼ Not recommended in children less than one year of age. Limited experience in children.

Over 60
▼ No specific problems.

Driving and hazardous work
▼ Avoid such activities until you have learned how the eye drops affect your vision.

Alcohol
▼ No special problems.

POSSIBLE ADVERSE EFFECTS

The most frequently reported symptoms include eye irritation and dry eyes.

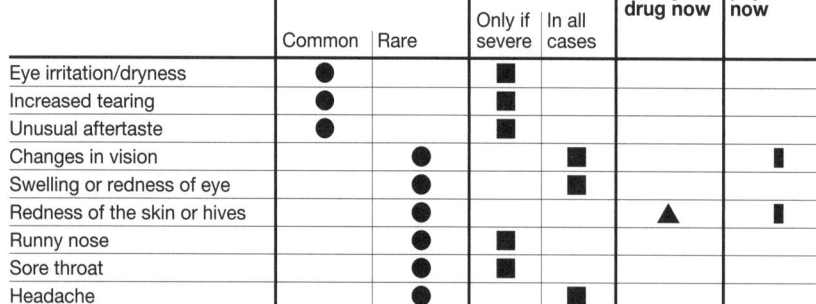

Symptom/effect	Frequency		Discuss with physician		Stop taking drug now	Call physician now
	Common	Rare	Only if severe	In all cases		
Eye irritation/dryness	●		■			
Increased tearing	●		■			
Unusual aftertaste	●		■			
Changes in vision		●		■		▮
Swelling or redness of eye		●		■		
Redness of the skin or hives		●			▲	▮
Runny nose		●	■			
Sore throat		●	■			
Headache		●		■		
Eye pain		●		■		

PROLONGED USE

This medication is usually applied for a short duration of therapy.

INTERACTIONS

Specific interactions with gatifloxacin eye drops have not been studied.

GEMFIBROZIL

Product names Apo-Gemfibrozil, Lopid, Novo-Gemfibrozil, Nu-Gemfibrozil, and others
Used in the following combined preparations None

GENERAL INFORMATION

Gemfibrozil belongs to a group of drugs, usually called fibrates, that lower lipid levels in the blood. Fibrates are particularly effective in decreasing triglyceride levels in the blood. They also reduce blood levels of cholesterol. Raised levels of lipids (fats) in the blood are associated with atherosclerosis (deposition of fat in blood vessel walls).

This can lead to coronary heart disease (for example, angina and heart attacks) and cerebrovascular disease (for example, stroke). When gemfibrozil is taken with a diet low in saturated fats, there is some evidence that the risk of coronary heart disease is reduced.

INFORMATION FOR USERS

Your drug prescription is tailored for you. Do not alter dosage without checking with your physician.

How taken

Tablets, capsules.

Frequency and timing of doses
Twice daily, 30 minutes before morning and evening meals.

Usual adult dosage range
1200mg.

Onset of effect
See onset of effect in 2–5 days; may take up to 4 weeks to see maximum benefit.

Duration of action
3–6 hours.

Diet advice
A low-fat diet is usually recommended.

Storage
Keep in a closed container in a cool, dry place out of the reach of children.

Missed dose
If you miss a dose, take it as soon as you remember. If it is near the time of the next dose, skip the missed dose and resume your usual dosing schedule. Do not double up to catch up on a missed dose.

Stopping the drug
Do not stop the drug without consulting your physician. Stopping the drug may lead to worsening of the underlying condition.

Exceeding the dose
An occasional unintentional extra dose is unlikely to cause problems. Large overdoses may cause liver problems. Notify your physician and seek medical assistance right away.

SPECIAL PRECAUTIONS

Be sure to tell your physician if:
▼ You have liver or kidney problems.
▼ You have muscle weakness.
▼ You have angina or other heart disease.
▼ You have high blood pressure.
▼ You are taking other medications.

 Pregnancy
▼ Safety not established. Discuss with your physician.

 Breast-feeding
▼ Safety not established. Discuss with your physician.

 Infants and children
▼ Not usually prescribed.

 Over 60
▼ No special problems expected.

 Driving and hazardous work
▼ No known problems.

 Alcohol
▼ No known problems.

POSSIBLE ADVERSE EFFECTS

The common *adverse effects* are those on the gastrointestinal tract, such as loss of appetite and nausea. These effects normally diminish as treatment continues.

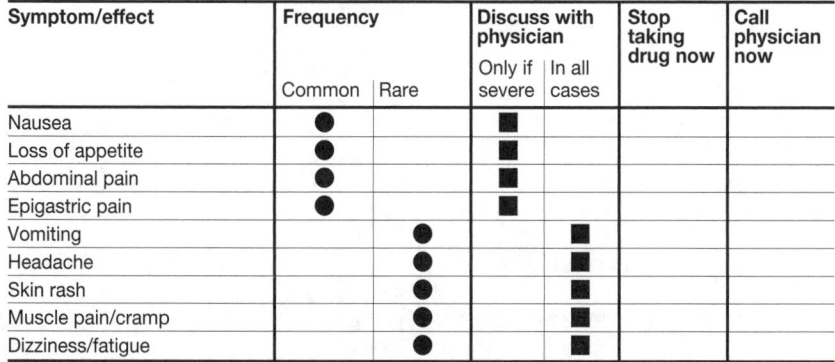

Symptom/effect	Frequency		Discuss with physician		Stop taking drug now	Call physician now
	Common	Rare	Only if severe	In all cases		
Nausea	●		■			
Loss of appetite	●		■			
Abdominal pain	●		■			
Epigastric pain	●		■			
Vomiting		●		■		
Headache		●		■		
Skin rash		●		■		
Muscle pain/cramp		●		■		
Dizziness/fatigue		●		■		

PROLONGED USE

No problems expected, but patients with kidney disease will need special care as there is a high risk of developing muscle problems.

Monitoring Blood tests will be performed occasionally to monitor the effect of the drug on lipids in the blood, and to periodically measure kidney and liver function.

INTERACTIONS

Anticoagulants Gemfibrozil may increase the effect of anticoagulants such as warfarin. Dosage adjustment may be needed.

Pravastatin, atorvastatin, simvastatin, and other lipid-lowering drugs belonging to 'statins' There is an increased risk of muscle damage if gemfibrozil is taken with these drugs.

Cholestyramine, colestipol may decrease absorption of gemfibrozil. Take two hours apart.

Repaglinide Gemfibrozil can increase the effect of repaglinide.

Amlodipine, verapamil, carvedilol, losartan, phenytoin, diazepam, tolbutamide Gemfibrozil may increase the effect of these drugs.

GENTAMICIN

Product names Diogent, Garamycin, and others
Used in the following combined preparations Garasone, Valisone-G, and others

GENERAL INFORMATION

Gentamicin is one of the aminoglycoside *antibiotics*. The injectable form is usually reserved for hospital treatment of serious infections. These include lung, urinary tract, bone, joint, and wound infections, as well as peritonitis, septicemia, and meningitis. This form is also used together with a penicillin for prevention and treatment of heart valve infections (endocarditis).

In the form of drops, gentamicin is used to treat eye and ear infections.

Gentamicin given by injection can have serious *adverse effects* on the ears and the kidneys. Damage to the ears may lead to deafness and problems with the balance mechanism in the inner ear. Courses of treatment are, therefore, limited to seven days when this is possible. Treatment is monitored by measuring blood levels of gentamicin, especially when high doses are needed or kidney function is poor.

QUICK REFERENCE

Drug group Aminoglycoside antibiotics (p.114)

Overdose danger rating Low (except for injectable form)

Dependence rating Low

Prescription needed Yes

Available as generic Yes

INFORMATION FOR USERS

Your drug prescription is tailored for you. Do not alter dosage without checking with your physician.

How taken

Injection, eye and ear drops.

Frequency and timing of doses
1–3 x daily (injection); 3–4 x daily or as directed (ear drops); every 2 hours or as directed (eye drops).

Usual adult dosage range
According to condition and response (injection); according to your physician's instructions (eye and ear drops).

Onset of effect
Within 1–2 hours.

Duration of action
8–12 hours.

Diet advice
None.

Storage
Keep in closed container in a cool, dry place out of the reach of children.

Missed dose
Apply eye and ear preparations as soon as you remember.

Stopping the drug
Complete the course. Even if you feel better, the original infection may still be present and may recur if treatment is stopped too soon.

Exceeding the dose
Although overdose by injection is dangerous, it is unlikely because treatment is carefully monitored. For other preparations of the drug, an occasional unintentional extra dose is unlikely to cause concern. But if you notice any unusual symptoms, notify your physician.

SPECIAL PRECAUTIONS

Be sure to tell your physician if:
▼ You have a long-term kidney problem.
▼ You have a hearing disorder, especially a perforated eardrum.
▼ You have myasthenia gravis.
▼ You have Parkinson's disease.
▼ You have previously had an allergic reaction to aminoglycosides.
▼ You are taking other medications.

 Pregnancy
▼ No evidence of risk with eye or ear drops. Injections can be used for serious infections in pregnancy. Discuss with your physician.

 Breast-feeding
▼ No evidence of risk with eye or ear preparations. Given by injection, the drug may pass into the breast milk. Discuss with your physician.

 Infants and children
▼ Reduced dose necessary for injections.

 Over 60
▼ Increased likelihood of adverse effects. Reduced dose may therefore be necessary.

 Driving and hazardous work
▼ No known problems from preparations for the eye or ear.

 Alcohol
▼ No known problems.

POSSIBLE ADVERSE EFFECTS

Adverse effects are rare but those that occur with the injectable form of gentamicin may be serious. Dizziness, loss of balance (vertigo), impaired hearing, and changes in the urine should be reported promptly. If ear drops are used when the eardrum is perforated, damage to the inner ear may occur. Allergic reactions, including rash and itching, may occur with all preparations that contain gentamicin. Blurred vision or eye irritation may occur with the eye preparations and should be reported to your physician.

Symptom/effect	Frequency		Discuss with physician		Stop taking drug now	Call physician now
	Common	Rare	Only if severe	In all cases		
Nausea/vomiting		●	■			
Dizziness/vertigo		●		■	▲	❚
Rash/itching		●		■	▲	❚
Ringing in the ears		●		■	▲	❚
Loss of hearing		●		■	▲	❚
Bloody/cloudy urine		●		■	▲	❚

INTERACTIONS

General note A range of drugs, including furosemide, vancomycin, amphotericin B, and cephalosporins, increase the risk of hearing loss and/or kidney failure with gentamicin given by injection.

PROLONGED USE

Not usually given for longer than seven days. When given by injection, there is a risk of adverse effects on hearing and balance.

Monitoring Blood levels of the drug are usually checked if it is given by injection. Tests on kidney function are also usually carried out.

GLICLAZIDE

Product names Apo-Gliclazide, Diamicron Tab, Diamicron MR, Novo-Gliclazide, and others
Used in the following combined preparations None

GENERAL INFORMATION

Gliclazide is an oral antidiabetic drug belonging to the sulfonylurea group. It stimulates the production and secretion of insulin from the islet cells in the pancreas. This promotes the uptake of sugar into body cells thereby lowering the level of sugar in the blood.

The drug is used to treat adult (maturity-onset or Type 2) diabetes mellitus, in conjunction with diet and exercise.

In conditions of severe illness, injury, stress, or surgery, the drug may lose its effectiveness necessitating the use of insulin injections. *Adverse effects* of gliclazide are generally mild. However, symptoms of poor diabetic control will occur if the dosage is not appropriate.

INFORMATION FOR USERS

Your drug prescription is tailored for you. Do not alter dosage without checking with your physician.

How taken

Tablets, MR-tablets.

Frequency and timing of doses
1–2 x daily (in the morning and evening with a meal).

Usual dosage range
40–320mg daily (doses above 160mg are divided into two doses).

Onset of effect
Within 1 hour.

Duration of action
12–24 hours.

Diet advice
An individualized diabetic diet must be maintained for the drug to be fully effective. Follow the advice of your physician.

Storage
Keep in a closed container in a cool, dry place out of the reach of children.

Missed dose
Take with next meal; do not double the dose to account for missed dose.

Stopping the drug
Do not stop the drug without consulting your physician; stopping the drug may lead to worsening of the underlying condition.

OVERDOSE ACTION

 Seek immediate medical advice in all cases. If early warning symptoms of excessively low blood sugar such as fainting, sweating, trembling, confusion, or headache occur, eat or drink something sugary at once. Take emergency action if seizures or loss of consciousness occur.

See Drug poisoning emergency guide (p.526).

POSSIBLE ADVERSE EFFECTS

Serious adverse effects are rare. Dizziness, confusion, tremors, sweating, and weakness may be signs of low blood sugar due to lack of food or too high a dose of gliclazide.

Symptom/effect	Frequency		Discuss with physician		Stop taking drug now	Call physician now
	Common	Rare	Only if severe	In all cases		
Weight changes	●			■		
Weakness/tremor	●			■		
Sweating	●			■		
Constipation/diarrhea	●		■			
Nausea/vomiting		●		■		
Rash/itching		●		■		
Jaundice		●		■		■
Faintness/confusion		●		■		

INTERACTIONS

General note A variety of drugs may reduce the effect of gliclazide and so may raise blood sugar levels. These include corticosteroids, estrogens, diuretics, and rifampin. Other drugs increase the risk of low blood sugar. These include warfarin, sulfonamides and other antibacterials, ASA, beta blockers, ACE inhibitors, and antifungals, particularly miconazole.

SPECIAL PRECAUTIONS

Be sure to tell your physician if:
▼ You have long-term liver or kidney problems.
▼ You are allergic to sulfonylurea drugs.
▼ You have thyroid problems.
▼ You have porphyria.
▼ You have ever had problems with your adrenal glands.
▼ You are taking other medications.

 Pregnancy
▼ Not recommended. May cause abnormally low blood sugar in the newborn baby. Insulin is generally substituted in pregnancy because it gives better diabetic control.

 Breast-feeding
▼ The drug passes into the breast milk. Discuss with your physician.

 Infants and children
▼ Not prescribed.

 Over 60
▼ Signs of low blood sugar may be more difficult to recognize. Reduced dose may be necessary.

 Driving and hazardous work
▼ Avoid such activities until you have learned how gliclazide affects you because it can cause dizziness, drowsiness, and confusion.

 Alcohol
▼ Avoid. Alcoholic drinks may upset diabetic control increasing the risk of hypoglycemia.

Surgery and general anesthetics
▼ Notify your physician or dentist that you are diabetic before undergoing any type of surgery.

PROLONGED USE

No problems expected.

Monitoring Regular testing of blood sugar control is required. Periodic assessment of the eyes, heart, and kidneys may also be advised.

GLIMEPIRIDE

Product names Amaryl, Apo-Glimepiride, Co-Glimepiride, Novo-Glimepiride, Ratio-Glimepiride, Sandoz Glimepiride, and others
Used in the following combined preparations None

GENERAL INFORMATION

Glimepiride is an oral antidiabetic drug belonging to the sulfonylurea class. Like other drugs in this class, glimepiride stimulates insulin secretion from the islets cells in the pancreas. This allows for the uptake of glucose (sugar) into the cells of the body, thereby lowering blood glucose. This drug is used in Type 2 (maturity-onset) diabetes mellitus, in conjunction with a diabetic diet low in carbohydrates and fats. Glimepiride is a long-acting drug, which can be administered once daily.

QUICK REFERENCE

Drug group Oral antidiabetics (p.128)

Overdose danger rating High

Dependence rating Low

Prescription needed Yes

Available as generic Yes

INFORMATION FOR USERS

Your drug prescription is tailored for you. Do not alter dosage without checking with your physician.

How taken

Tablets.

Frequency and timing of doses
Once daily.

Usual adult dosage range
1–8mg daily.

Onset of effect
1–3 hours.

Duration of action
24 hours.

Diet advice
A low carbohydrate, low fat diet. Follow the advice of your physician.

Storage
Keep in a closed container in a cool, dry place out of the reach of children.

Missed dose
If you miss a dose, take it as soon as you remember it. If it is time for a snack, take the medication with the snack. If it is near the time for the next dose, skip the missed dose and resume your usual dosing schedule. Do not double up to catch up on a missed dose.

Stopping the drug
Do not stop the drug without consulting your physician. Stopping the drug may lead to worsening of the underlying condition.

OVERDOSE ACTION

Seek immediate medical advice in all cases. If any early warning symptoms of excessively low blood sugar occur, eat or drink something containing sugar, e.g., 1tbsp of sugar dissolved in water or ¾ cup of juice or regular (not diet) soft drink. Take emergency action and dial 911 if seizures or loss of consciousness occur.

See Drug poisoning emergency guide (p.526).

SPECIAL PRECAUTIONS

Be sure to tell your physician if:
▼ You have liver disease.
▼ You had or have had kidney disease.
▼ You had or have had ketoacidosis.
▼ You have had problems with alcohol abuse.
▼ You are taking other medications.

Pregnancy
▼ Safety in pregnancy not established. Discuss with your physician.

Breast-feeding
▼ Not recommended. Discuss with your physician.

Infants and children
▼ Not prescribed.

Over 60
▼ No special problems.

Driving and hazardous work
▼ Usually no problems. Avoid these activities if you have warning signs of low blood sugar.

Alcohol
▼ Avoid. Alcoholic drinks may upset diabetic control, increasing the risk of hypoglycemia.

PROLONGED USE

No problems expected.

Monitoring Regular monitoring of blood glucose in blood and urine is needed. Periodic assessment of the eyes, heart, and kidneys is also advised.

POSSIBLE ADVERSE EFFECTS

This drug is generally well tolerated. The most common adverse effects include weight gain and the risk of hypoglycemia. The risk for these is lower than with other drugs in this class.

Symptom/effect	Frequency		Discuss with physician		Stop taking drug now	Call physician now
	Common	Rare	Only if severe	In all cases		
Weight gain	●		■			
Headache/dizziness	●		■			
Constipation or diarrhea	●		■			
Nausea	●		■			
Light headedness/confusion		●		■		■
Weakness/tremor		●		■		■
Sweating		●		■		■
Rash/itching		●		■		
Jaundice		●		■		■

INTERACTIONS

General note A variety of drugs may reduce the effect of glimepiride and may raise blood glucose levels. These include corticosteroids, estrogens, diuretics, and rifampin. Other drugs, including sulfonamides and other antibacterials, antifungals, ASA, warfarin, ACE inhibitors, and beta-blockers, increase the risk of low blood glucose.

GLYBURIDE

Product names Ava-Glyburide, Diabeta, Euglucon, Penta-Glyburide, Riva-Glyburide, and others
Used in the following combined preparations None

GENERAL INFORMATION

Glyburide is an oral antidiabetic drug belonging to the sulfonylurea class. Like other drugs of this type, glyburide stimulates the production and secretion of insulin from the islet cells in the pancreas. This promotes the uptake of sugar into body cells, thereby lowering the level of sugar in the blood.

This drug is used in the treatment of Type 2 (maturity-onset) diabetes mellitus, in conjunction with a diabetic diet low in carbohydrates and fats.

In conditions of severe illness, injury, or stress, glyburide may lose its effectiveness, making insulin injections necessary. *Adverse effects* are generally mild. Symptoms of poor diabetic control will occur if the dosage of glyburide is not appropriate.

QUICK REFERENCE

Drug group Oral antidiabetic drugs (p.128)

Overdose danger rating High

Dependence rating Low

Prescription needed Yes

Available as generic Yes

INFORMATION FOR USERS

Your drug prescription is tailored for you. Do not alter dosage without checking with your physician.

How taken

Tablets.

Frequency and timing of doses
Once daily in the morning with breakfast.

Usual adult dosage range
5–15mg daily.

Onset of effect
Within 3 hours.

Duration of action
10–15 hours.

Diet advice
A low-carbohydrate, low-fat diet must be maintained in order for the drug to be fully effective. Follow the advice of your physician.

Storage
Keep in a closed container in a cool, dry place out of the reach of children. Protect from light.

Missed dose
Take with next meal; do not double the dose to account for missed dose.

Stopping the drug
Do not stop the drug without consulting your physician; stopping the drug may lead to worsening of your diabetes.

OVERDOSE ACTION

 Seek immediate medical advice in all cases. If any early warning symptoms of excessively low blood sugar occur, eat or drink something containing sugar, e.g., 1tbsp of sugar dissolved in water or ¾ cup of juice or regular (not diet) soft drink. Take emergency action and dial 911 if seizures or loss of consciousness occur.

See Drug poisoning emergency guide (p.526).

SPECIAL PRECAUTIONS

Be sure to tell your physician if:
▼ You have long-term liver or kidney problems.
▼ You are allergic to sulfonylurea drugs.
▼ You have thyroid problems.
▼ You have porphyria.
▼ You have ever had problems with your adrenal glands.
▼ You are taking other medications.

 Pregnancy
▼ Not usually prescribed. Insulin is generally substituted in pregnancy because it gives better diabetic control.

 Breast-feeding
▼ The drug passes into the breast milk. Discuss with your physician.

 Infants and children
▼ Not prescribed.

 Over 60
▼ Reduced dose may be necessary. Greater likelihood of low blood sugar exists when glyburide is used.

 Driving and hazardous work
▼ Usually no problems. Avoid these activities if you have warning signs of low blood sugar.

 Alcohol
▼ Avoid. Alcoholic drinks may upset diabetic control increasing the risk of hypoglycemia.

Surgery and general anesthetics
▼ Notify your physician or dentist that you are diabetic before undergoing any type of surgery.

POSSIBLE ADVERSE EFFECTS

Serious adverse effects are rare. More common symptoms, often accompanied by hunger, may be signs of low blood sugar due to lack of food or too high a dose of the drug.

Symptom/effect	Frequency		Discuss with physician		Stop taking drug now	Call physician now
	Common	Rare	Only if severe	In all cases		
Weakness/tremor	●			■		
Sweating	●			■		
Constipation/diarrhea	●		■			
Weight changes	●			■		
Faintness/confusion		●		■		▮
Nausea/vomiting		●		■		
Rash/itching		●		■		
Jaundice		●		■		▮

INTERACTIONS

General note A variety of drugs may reduce the effect of glyburide and so may raise blood sugar levels. These include corticosteroids, estrogens, diuretics, and rifampin. Other drugs increase the risk of low blood sugar. These include warfarin, sulfonamides and other antibacterials, antifungals, ASA, beta blockers, and ACE inhibitors.

PROLONGED USE

No problems expected.

Monitoring Regular monitoring of levels of sugar in the blood and urine is needed. Periodic assessment of the eyes, heart, and kidneys may also be advised.

GOSERELIN

Product names Zoladex, Zoladex LA
Used in the following combined preparations None

GENERAL INFORMATION

Goserelin is a synthetic drug chemically related to the *hormone* gonadorelin. Like gonadorelin, it stimulates the release of other hormones from the pituitary gland, which in turn control production of the sex hormones.

Goserelin is used to suppress the production of sex hormones in breast and prostate cancer. At the start of treatment for prostate cancer, it is often given with an anti-androgen drug (see p.132) to control an initial growth spurt of the tumour – known as 'tumour flare'.

The drug is also used in the management of fibroids, infertility, and endometriosis. The first dose is normally given during menstruation to avoid the possibility that the patient may be pregnant. It is advisable for women of childbearing age to use barrier methods of contraception during treatment.

Loss of bone density is an important *side effect* in women.Therefore, repeat courses of the drug are given only for cancerous conditions.

INFORMATION FOR USERS

Your drug prescription is tailored for you. Do not alter dosage without checking with your physician.

How taken

Implant injection, long-acting implant injection.

Frequency and timing of doses

Endometriosis Every 28 days, maximum of a single 6-month treatment course only (implant).
Fibroids Implant every 28 days, maximum 3 months' treatment.
Breast and prostate cancer Every 28 days.
Prostate cancer Every 12 weeks (LA implant).

Usual adult dosage range

3.6mg every 28 days (endometriosis/ fibroids/breast cancer); 10.8mg every 3 months (prostate).

Onset of effect

Within 24 hours (endometriosis/fibroids/ breast cancer);
1–2 weeks after tumour flare (prostate).

Duration of action

28 days (implant); 12 weeks (long-acting implant).

Diet advice

None.

Storage

Not applicable. The drug is not kept in the home.

Missed dose

No cause for concern. Treatment can be resumed when possible.

Stopping the drug

Do not stop treatment without consulting your physician.

Exceeding the dose

Overdosage is unlikely since treatment is not self-administered.

SPECIAL PRECAUTIONS

Be sure to tell your physician if:
▼ You have osteoporosis.
▼ You have previously been treated with goserelin (or another gonadorelin analogue) for endometriosis or fibroids.
▼ You have polycystic ovarian disease.
▼ You are allergic to gonadorelin analogues.
▼ You are taking other medications.

Pregnancy
▼ Not prescribed.

Breast-feeding
▼ Not recommended. Discuss with your physician.

Infants and children
▼ Not recommended.

Over 60
▼ No special problems.

Driving and hazardous work
▼ No special problems.

Alcohol
▼ No special problems.

POSSIBLE ADVERSE EFFECTS

Symptoms similar to those of the menopause, such as hot flushes and changes in breast size are common. Rare adverse effects should be reported to your physician straight away.

Symptom/effect	Frequency		Discuss with physician		Stop taking drug now	Call physician now
	Common	Rare	Only if severe	In all cases		
Hot flushes/sweating	●		■			
Decreased libido/impotence	●		■			
Bone pain	●		■			
Breast enlargement/tenderness	●		■			
Rash/wheezing		●		■		■
Reaction at injection site		●		■		
Ovarian cysts		●		■		
Dizziness/fainting		●		■		

INTERACTIONS

Antidiabetic drugs Goserelin may reduce the blood-sugar-lowering effect of these drugs.

PROLONGED USE

Goserelin is only used in the long term for treatment of prostate or breast cancer. Bone density may be lost, and medication to counter this may be given.

Monitoring Women are usually monitored for changes in bone density.

HALOPERIDOL

Product names Apo-Haloperidol, Novo-Peridol, and others
Used in the following combined preparations None

GENERAL INFORMATION

First introduced in the 1960s, haloperidol is used to manage the psychotic manifestations of mental illnesses such as schizophrenia, mania, dementia, and other disorders in which delusions and/or hallucinations are experienced. It does not cure the underlying mental disorder but is used to relieve the distressing symptoms.

Haloperidol is also used in the control of Tourette's syndrome and may be of benefit in children who have severe behavioural problems for which other drugs are ineffective.

The main drawback of haloperidol is that it produces the disturbing *side effect* of abnormal, involuntary movements and stiffness of the face and limbs. As a result, it is no longer recommended for first-line maintenance treatment of schizophrenia but is still widely used for acute psychotic episodes and agitation.

INFORMATION FOR USERS

Your drug prescription is tailored for you. Do not alter dosage without checking with your physician.

How taken

Tablets, liquid, injection, *depot* injection.

Frequency and timing of doses
1–3 x daily.

Usual adult dosage range
Schizophrenia 1.5–3mg daily initially, up to a maximum of 20mg daily.

Onset of effect
2–3 hours (by mouth); 20–30 minutes (by injection).

Duration of action
6–24 hours (by mouth); 2–4 hours (injection); up to 4 weeks (depot injection).

Diet advice
None.

Storage
Keep in a closed container in a cool, dry place out of the reach of children.

Missed dose
Take as soon as you remember. If your next dose is due within 3 hours, take a single dose now and skip the next.

Stopping the drug
Do not stop the drug without consulting your physician; symptoms may recur.

Exceeding the dose
An occasional unintentional extra dose is unlikely to cause problems. Larger overdoses may cause unusual drowsiness, muscle weakness or rigidity, and/or faintness. Notify your physician.

POSSIBLE ADVERSE EFFECTS

Haloperidol can cause a variety of minor *anticholinergic* symptoms that often become less marked with time. The most significant adverse effect, abnormal movements of the face and limb stiffness (parkinsonism), may be reduced by dosage adjustment.

Symptom/effect	Frequency		Discuss with physician		Stop taking drug now	Call physician now
	Common	Rare	Only if severe	In all cases		
Drowsiness/lethargy	●		■			
Loss of appetite	●		■			
Parkinsonism	●			■		
Dizziness/fainting		●		■		
Rash		●		■	▲	
High fever/confusion		●		■	▲	■

INTERACTIONS

Sedatives *Sedatives* are likely to increase the sedative properties of haloperidol.

Rifampin and anticonvulsant drugs These drugs may reduce the effects of haloperidol, the dosage of which may need to be increased.

Lithium This drug may increase the risk of parkinsonism and effects on the nerves.

Methyldopa This drug may increase the risk of parkinsonism and low blood pressure.

Anticholinergic drugs Haloperidol may increase the side effects of these drugs.

SPECIAL PRECAUTIONS

Be sure to tell your physician if:
▼ You have long-term liver or kidney problems.
▼ You have heart or circulation problems.
▼ You have had epileptic seizures.
▼ You have an overactive thyroid gland.
▼ You have Parkinson's disease.
▼ You have had glaucoma.
▼ You have asthma, bronchitis, or another lung disorder.
▼ You have ever had an adrenal gland tumour.
▼ You are taking other medications.

Pregnancy
▼ Short-term nervous system problems may occur in babies when haloperidol is taken during the third trimester. The drug is occasionally used under psychiatric supervision. Discuss with your physician.

Breast-feeding
▼ The drug passes into the breast milk and may affect the baby. Discuss with your physician.

Infants and children
▼ Rarely required. Reduced dose necessary.

Over 60
▼ Reduced dose may be necessary.

Driving and hazardous work
▼ Avoid such activities until you have learned how haloperidol affects you because the drug may cause drowsiness and slowed reactions.

Alcohol
▼ Avoid. Alcohol may increase the sedative effect of this drug.

PROLONGED USE

Use of this drug for more than a few months may lead to *tardive dyskinesia* (abnormal, involuntary movements of the eyes, face, and tongue). Occasionally, *jaundice* may occur.

HEPARIN/LMWH

Product names Heparin-Leo; [LMWH] Fragmin, Fraxiparine, Innohep, Lovenox
Used in the following combined preparations None

GENERAL INFORMATION

Heparin is an anticoagulant drug used to prevent the formation of, and aid in the dispersion of, blood clots. As the drug acts quickly, it is useful in emergencies, for instance, to prevent further clotting when a clot has already reached the lungs or the brain. People undergoing open heart surgery or kidney dialysis are also given heparin to prevent clotting. A low dose is sometimes given after surgery to prevent the development of deep vein thromboses (clots forming in the leg veins). Heparin is often given with other slower-acting anticoagulants, such as warfarin. It is also used to treat unstable angina. Low molecular weight heparins are fragments of heparin and include dalteparin, enoxaparin, nadroparin, and tinzaparin. Their advantage is that they act longer and do not require close blood monitoring as heparin does.

The most serious *adverse effect* of heparin is the risk of excessive bleeding, so the ability of the blood to clot is monitored carefully. LMWH is used cautiously in those with kidney problems.

INFORMATION FOR USERS

Your drug prescription is tailored for you. Do not alter dosage without checking with your physician.

How taken

Injection.

Frequency and timing of doses
Every 8–12 hours or continuous intravenous infusion; once daily (LMWH).

Usual dosage range
Dosage is determined by the nature of the condition being treated or prevented.

Onset of effect
Within 15 minutes.

Duration of action
4–12 hours after treatment is stopped; 24 hours after end of treatment (LMWH).

Diet advice
None.

Storage
Keep in a cool, dry place out of the reach of children.

Missed dose
Notify your physician.

Stopping the drug
Do not stop taking the drug without consulting your physician. Stopping the drug may lead to clotting of blood.

OVERDOSE ACTION

 Seek immediate medical advice in all cases. Take emergency action if bleeding, severe headache, or loss of consciousness occur.

See Drug poisoning emergency guide (p.526).

POSSIBLE ADVERSE EFFECTS

As with all anticoagulants, bleeding is the most common adverse effect of heparin, and the risk of bleeding is increased in people with impaired kidney function. The less common effects may occur during long-term treatment.

Symptom/effect	Frequency		Discuss with physician		Stop taking drug now	Call physician now
	Common	Rare	Only if severe	In all cases		
Bleeding/bruising	●			■		▮
Alopecia		●		■		
Aching bones		●		■		
Rash		●		■	▲	▮
Breathing difficulties		●		■		▮
Jaundice/vomiting blood		●		■		▮

INTERACTIONS

Clopidogrel, ticlopidine, and dipyridamole The anticoagulant effect of heparin may be increased when it is taken with these drugs. The dosage of heparin may need to be adjusted accordingly.

ASA Do not take ASA, which may increase the anticoagulant effect of this drug and the risk of bleeding in the intestines or joints. Discuss with your physician.

ACE inhibitors and potassium supplements taken with heparins may increase the risk of high blood potassium.

SPECIAL PRECAUTIONS

Be sure to tell your physician if:
▼ You have long-term liver or kidney problems.
▼ You have high blood pressure.
▼ You bleed easily.
▼ You have any allergies.
▼ You have peptic ulcers.
▼ You are taking other medications.

 Pregnancy
▼ Careful monitoring is necessary as it may cause the mother to bleed excessively if taken near delivery. Discuss with your physician.

 Breast-feeding
▼ No evidence of risk.

 Infants and children
▼ Reduced dose necessary according to age and weight.

 Over 60
▼ Drugs like tinzaparin are not recommended in those over 70 years of age with kidney impairment.

 Driving and hazardous work
▼ Avoid risk of injury, since excessive bruising and bleeding may occur.

 Alcohol
▼ No special problems.

Surgery and general anesthetics
▼ Heparin may need to be stopped. Discuss this with your physician or dentist before having any surgery.

PROLONGED USE

Osteoporosis and hair loss may occur very rarely; tolerance to heparin may develop.

Monitoring Periodic blood and liver function tests will be required.

HYDROCHLOROTHIAZIDE

Product names Apo-Hydro Tab, Urozide, and others
Used in the following combined preparations Atacand Plus, Avalide, Hyzaar, Inhibace Plus Tab, Vaseretic, and others

GENERAL INFORMATION

Hydrochlorothiazide belongs to the thiazide group of diuretic drugs, which remove excess water from the body and reduce edema (fluid retention) in people with congestive heart failure, kidney disorders, and cirrhosis of the liver. This drug is used to treat high blood pressure (see Antihypertensive drugs, p.88).

Hydrochlorothiazide increases the loss of potassium in the urine, which can cause a variety of symptoms (see p.83), and increases the likelihood of irregular heart rhythms, particularly in patients who are taking drugs such as digoxin. For this reason, potassium supplements are often given with hydrochlorothiazide.

QUICK REFERENCE

Drug group Thiazide diuretics (p.85)

Overdose danger rating Low

Dependence rating Low

Prescription needed Yes

Available as generic Yes

INFORMATION FOR USERS

Your drug prescription is tailored for you. Do not alter dosage without checking with your physician.

How taken

Tablets.

Frequency and timing of doses
Once daily, or every 2 days, early in the day.

Usual adult dosage range
12.5–50mg daily.

Onset of effect
Within 2 hours.

Duration of action
6–12 hours.

Diet advice
Use of this drug may reduce potassium in the body. Eat plenty of fresh fruit and vegetables. Discuss with your physician the advisability of reducing your salt intake.

Storage
Keep in a closed container in a cool, dry place out of the reach of children. Protect from light.

Missed dose
No cause for concern, but take as soon as you remember. However, if it is late in the day do not take the missed dose, or you may have to get up during the night to pass urine. Take the next scheduled dose as usual.

Stopping the drug
Do not stop the drug without consulting your physician; symptoms may recur.

Exceeding the dose
An occasional unintentional extra dose is unlikely to be a cause for concern. But if you notice any unusual symptoms, or if a large overdose has been taken, notify your physician.

SPECIAL PRECAUTIONS

Be sure to tell your physician if:
▼ You have long-term liver or kidney problems.
▼ You have had gout.
▼ You have diabetes.
▼ You are taking other medications.

Pregnancy
▼ Safety not established. Discuss with your physician.

Breast-feeding
▼ The drug passes into the breast milk, but at normal doses *adverse effects* on the baby are unlikely. Discuss with your physician.

Infants and children
▼ Not usually prescribed. Reduced dose necessary.

Over 60
▼ Increased likelihood of adverse effects.

Driving and hazardous work
▼ Avoid such activities until you have learned how hydrochlorothiazide affects you because the drug may reduce mental alertness and cause dizziness.

Alcohol
▼ Keep consumption low. Hydrochlorothiazide increases the likelihood of dehydration and hangovers after consumption of alcohol.

POSSIBLE ADVERSE EFFECTS

Most effects are caused by excessive loss of potassium. This can usually be put right by taking a potassium supplement. In rare cases, gout may occur in susceptible people, and certain forms of diabetes may become more difficult to control.

Symptom/effect	Frequency		Discuss with physician		Stop taking drug now	Call physician now
	Common	Rare	Only if severe	In all cases		
Muscle cramps		●			■	
Lethargy		●	■			
Dizziness		●			■	
Constipation		●			■	
Rash		●		■		▲

INTERACTIONS

Non-steroidal anti-inflammatory drugs (NSAIDs) Some NSAIDs may reduce the diuretic effect of hydrochlorothiazide, whose dosage may need to be adjusted.

Digoxin Adverse effects may be increased if excessive potassium is lost.

Corticosteroids These drugs further increase loss of potassium from the body when taken with hydrochlorothiazide.

Lithium Hydrochlorothiazide may increase lithium levels in the blood, leading to a risk of serious *adverse effects*.

PROLONGED USE

Excessive loss of potassium and imbalances of other salts may result, especially in the elderly.

Monitoring Blood tests may be performed periodically to check kidney function and levels of potassium and other salts.

HYDROCODONE

Product names Hycodan Syrup and Tablets, PMS Hydrocodone
Used in the following combined preparations Dimetane Expectorant-DC, Tussionex, and others

GENERAL INFORMATION

Hydrocodone is a *opioid* antitussive (cough suppressant) drug with a pronounced *sedative* effect. It is used on its own or in a combined preparation with other drugs (for example, decongestants and antihistamines) to suppress troublesome dry coughs when non-opioid cough suppressants have not been effective.

Like other opioid drugs, hydrocodone can be constipating.

It may also depress breathing, and is therefore unsuitable for people with asthma or emphysema.

Hydrocodone may produce euphoria and has the potential to cause psychological and physical dependence if used in larger-than-recommended amounts over an extended period of time. It is therefore recommended to be used only for short-term treatment.

QUICK REFERENCE

Drug group Opioid cough suppressants (p.80)

Overdose danger rating High

Dependence rating Medium

Prescription needed Yes

Available as generic Yes

INFORMATION FOR USERS

Your drug prescription is tailored for you. Do not alter dosage without checking with your physician.

How taken

Tablets, oral liquid.

Frequency and timing of doses
3–4 x daily with food or milk.

Usual adult dosage range
5–15mg, not to exceed 30mg daily. Maximum single dose: 15mg.

Onset of effect
15–30 minutes.

Duration of action
4 hours.

Diet advice
None.

Storage
Keep in a closed container in a cool, dry place away from reach of children. Protect from light.

Missed dose
Take as soon as you remember. Adjust the timing of subsequent doses accordingly

Stopping the drug
Can be safely stopped following short-term treatment.

OVERDOSE ACTION

Seek immediate medical advice in all cases. Take emergency action if there are symptoms such as slow or irregular breathing, severe drowsiness, or loss of consciousness.

See Drug poisoning emergency guide (p.526).

POSSIBLE ADVERSE EFFECTS

All opioid drugs can produce a variety of adverse effects; these are more frequent in children and older persons.

Symptom/effect	Frequency		Discuss with physician		Stop taking drug now	Call physician now
	Common	Rare	Only if severe	In all cases		
Constipation	●		■			
Drowsiness/dizziness	●		■			
Nausea/vomiting		●		■		
Slow respiration		●		■	▲	▮
Slow heartbeat		●		■	▲	▮
Confusion		●		■	▲	

INTERACTIONS

Sedatives All drugs, including alcohol, that have a sedative effect on the central nervous system are likely to increase sedation with hydrocodone. Such drugs include antidepressants, antipsychotics, sleeping drugs, and antihistamines.

Monoamine oxidase inhibitors (MAOIs) Hydrocodone may interact with these drugs to cause a dangerous drop in blood pressure.

SPECIAL PRECAUTIONS

Be sure to tell your physician if:
▼ You have impaired liver or kidney function.
▼ You have a heart or circulatory disorder.
▼ You have a lung disorder such as asthma, bronchitis, or emphysema.
▼ You have thyroid disease.
▼ You are taking other medications.

Pregnancy
▼ Safety in pregnancy not established. Discuss with your physician.

Breast-feeding
▼ The drug passes into the breast milk and may affect the baby. Discuss with your physician.

Infants and children
▼ Reduced dose necessary.

Over 60
▼ Increase likelihood of adverse effects. Reduced dose necessary.

Driving and hazardous work
▼ Avoid such activities until you have learned how the drug affects you; it can cause dizziness, drowsiness, or blurred vision.

Alcohol
▼ Avoid. Alcohol may increase the sedative effects of hydrocodone.

PROLONGED USE

If hydrocodone has been taken in large doses and/or over a long period of time, withdrawal symptoms are likely to occur upon stopping the drug abruptly.

HYDROCORTISONE

Product names Cortate, Cortef Tablets, Cortenema, Cortifoam, Cortoderm, Emo-Cort, Westcort
Used in the following combined preparations Cortisporin, Fucidin H, Pentamycetin HC, Proctofoam-HC, Rectogel HC, and others

GENERAL INFORMATION

Hydrocortisone is chemically identical to the *hormone* cortisol, which is produced by the adrenal glands. For this reason, the drug is prescribed to replace natural hormones in adrenal insufficiency (Addison's disease), among other uses.

The main use of hydrocortisone is in the treatment of a variety of allergic and inflammatory conditions. Used in *topical* preparations, it provides relief from inflammation of the skin, eye, and outer ear. Oral hydrocortisone is used to treat many conditions, such as rheumatoid disorders and inflammatory bowel disease. Injected directly into the joints, the drug relieves pain and stiffness (see p.104). The drug can also be given intravenously to treat adrenal gland deficiency before an operation or in cases of serious trauma or illness.

(see p.104)

QUICK REFERENCE

Drug group Corticosteroids (p.127)

Overdose danger rating Low

Dependence rating Low

Prescription needed Yes (except for some topical preparations)

Available as generic Yes

Corticosteroids (p.127)

INFORMATION FOR USERS

Your drug prescription is tailored for you. Do not alter dosage without checking with your physician.

How taken

Oral tablets, injection, rectal suppositories, rectal enema, topical (cream, ointment, lotion), eye ointment, ear solution.

Frequency and timing of doses
Varies according to condition.

Usual dosage range
Varies according to condition.

Onset of effect
Within hours. Full effect may not be felt for several days.

Duration of action
Depends on formulation and condition.

Diet advice
Salt intake may need to be restricted when the drug is taken by mouth. Your physician may advise potassium supplements.

Storage
Keep in a closed container in a cool, dry place out of the reach of children.

Missed dose
Take as soon as you remember. If your next dose is due within 2 hours, take a single dose now and skip the next.

Stopping the drug
Do not stop taking the drug without consulting your physician. A gradual reduction in dosage is required following prolonged treatment with oral hydrocortisone.

Exceeding the dose
An occasional unintentional extra dose is unlikely to be a cause for concern. But if you notice any unusual symptoms, or if a large overdose has been taken, notify your physician.

SPECIAL PRECAUTIONS

Be sure to tell your physician if:
▼ You have liver or kidney problems.
▼ You have had a peptic ulcer.
▼ You have had a mental illness or epilepsy.
▼ You have glaucoma.
▼ You have had tuberculosis.
▼ You have diabetes or heart problems.
▼ You are taking other medications.

Avoid exposure to chickenpox, shingles, or measles if you are taking the drug by mouth or injection.

Pregnancy
▼Oral doses and high-dose *topical* preparations may adversely affect the developing baby. Discuss with your physician.

Breast-feeding
▼ The drug passes into the breast milk and may affect the baby, although topical use is generally considered safe. Discuss with your physician.

Infants and children
▼ Reduced dose necessary.

Over 60
▼ Reduced dose may be necessary.

Driving and hazardous work
▼ No special problems.

Alcohol
▼ Avoid. Alcohol may increase the risk of peptic ulcers when this drug is taken by mouth.

POSSIBLE ADVERSE EFFECTS

The most serious *adverse effects* only occur when hydrocortisone is taken by mouth in high doses for long periods of time. The *side effects* listed here are for oral and injectable forms only.

Symptom/effect	Frequency		Discuss with physician		Stop taking drug now	Call physician now
	Common	Rare	Only if severe	In all cases		
Indigestion	●		■			
Weight gain	●		■			
Acne	●		■			
Fluid retention	●			■		
Muscle weakness		●		■		
Mood changes		●		■		
Menstrual irregularities		●		■		

INTERACTIONS (by mouth only)

Barbiturates, anticonvulsants, and rifampin These drugs reduce the effectiveness of hydrocortisone.

Antidiabetic drugs Hydrocortisone reduces the action of these drugs.

ASA and other NSAIDs Increased risk of peptic ulcer and bleeding from the stomach if taken with oral or injectable hydrocortisone.

Antihypertensive drugs Hydrocortisone reduces the effects of these drugs.

Vaccines Severe reactions can occur if certain vaccines are given while taking hydrocortisone.

PROLONGED USE

Depending on method of administration, prolonged high dosage may cause diabetes, glaucoma, fragile bones, and thin skin, and may retard growth in children. People on long-term treatment are advised to carry a treatment card.

Monitoring Periodic blood tests and checks on blood pressure are usually required with oral treatment.

HYDROMORPHONE

Product names Dilaudid, Hydromorph Contin, Hydromorphone HP
Used in the following combined preparations None

GENERAL INFORMATION

Hydromorphone is chemically related to morphine. Small doses produce effective relief of acute and chronic pain. The onset of relief is faster after injection than after oral doses. Hydromorphone is used to relieve severe pain and anxiety following surgery, heart attacks, severe injuries, and in painful diseases such as cancer. The drug causes some drowsiness, although this is usually not pronounced. It is habit forming: physical and psychological dependence can occur with repeated use. However, this is usually less likely to occur when used to control chronic pain, such as that associated with cancer. When used for short periods of time for acute pain, most patients can stop taking the drug without difficulty.

INFORMATION FOR USERS

Your drug prescription is tailored for you. Do not alter dosage without checking with your physician.

How taken

Tablets, SR tablets, liquid, injection, rectal suppositories.

Frequency and timing of doses
Every 4–6 hours (tablets, SR tablets, injection). Doses by rectal suppository are required less frequently.

Usual adult dosage range
2–4mg per dose (tablets); 3 mg per dose (rectal suppository). Dosage by injection varies considerably between individuals.

Onset of effect
Within 30 minutes (tablets); within 15 minutes (injection).

Duration of action
4–6 hours.

Diet advice
To relieve constipation, increase intake of fluids and high fiber foods.

Storage
Keep in a closed container in a cool, dry place that is well secured and away from reach of children.

Missed dose
Take as soon as you remember. Return to your normal dosing schedule as soon as possible.

Stopping the drug
If the reason for taking the drug no longer exists, you may stop taking the drug after discussing it with your physician.

OVERDOSE ACTION

 Seek immediate medical advice in all cases. Take emergency action if there are symptoms such as slow or irregular breathing, severe drowsiness, loss of consciousness, or slow or irregular pulse.

See Drug poisoning emergency guide (p.526).

SPECIAL PRECAUTIONS

Be sure to tell your physician if:
▼ You have impaired liver or kidney function.
▼ You have heart or circulatory problems .
▼ You have a lung disorder such as asthma, bronchitis, or emphysema.
▼ You have thyroid disease.
▼ You are taking other medications.

 Pregnancy
▼ Not recommended. Taken near the time of delivery, the drug may cause breathing difficulties in the newborn baby. Discuss with your physician.

 Breast-feeding
▼ Low levels of opioid analgesics have been detected in human milk, and may affect the baby adversely. Discuss with your physician.

 Infants and children
▼ Not recommended.

 Over 60
▼ Increased likelihood of adverse effects. Reduced dose may therefore be necessary.

 Driving and hazardous work
▼ Persons receiving hydromorphone are unlikely to be well enough to undertake such acitivities.

 Alcohol
▼ Avoid. Alcohol increases the sedative effect of hydromorphone.

POSSIBLE ADVERSE EFFECTS

As with other opioids, hydromorphone may produce nausea, vomiting, dizziness, loss of appetite, and constipation. Dosage adjustments may lessen some effects.

Symptom/effect	Frequency		Discuss with physician		Stop taking drug now	Call physician now
	Common	Rare	Only if severe	In all cases		
Sedation	●		■			
Constipation	●		■			
Nausea/vomiting	●			■		
Dizziness/lightheadedness	●			■		
Wheezing/difficult breathing		●		■	▲	▮
Confusion/vivid dreams		●		■		

INTERACTIONS

Sedatives Hydromorphone increases the sedative properties of all drugs that have a sedative effect. Such drugs include alcohol, antidepressants, antipsychotics, sleeping drugs, and antihistamines.

Monoamine oxidase inhibitors (MAOIs) may enhance the *adverse effects* of hydromorphone.

PROLONGED USE

The effects of hydromorphone usually become weaker during prolonged use as the body adapts. This is known as *tolerance*. Other effects of long-term use include physical and psychological dependence, sexual impotence, and loss of sexual desire.

IBUPROFEN

Product names Advil, Apo-ibuprofen, Motrin, Novo-Profen, Nu-Ibuprofen
Used in the following combined preparations Advil Cold and Sinus, Sudafed Sinus Advance, and others

GENERAL INFORMATION

Ibuprofen is a non-steroidal anti-inflammatory drug (NSAID) which, like other drugs in this group, reduces pain, stiffness, and inflammation. It is an effective treatment for the symptoms of osteoarthritis, headache, and gout. In the treatment of rheumatoid arthritis, ibuprofen may be prescribed with slower-acting drugs. Other uses of the drug include the relief of mild to moderate headache, menstrual and dental pain, pain resulting from soft tissue injuries, or the pain that may follow an operation.

Ibuprofen has fewer *side effects* (especially in low doses) than many of the other NSAIDs. Unlike ASA, it has a lower risk of gastrointestinal bleeding and ulceration.

Ibuprofen in is mostly available over-the-counter.

INFORMATION FOR USERS

Follow instructions on the label. Call your physician if symptoms worsen.

How taken

Tablets, chewable tablets, gel caps, liquid.

Frequency and timing of doses
4–6 x daily (general pain relief); 3–4 x daily with food (arthritis).

Usual adult dosage range
General pain relief 600mg–1.8g daily.
Arthritis 1.2–2.4g daily.

Onset of effect
Pain relief begins in 1–2 hours. The full anti-inflammatory effect in arthritic conditions may not be felt for up to 2 weeks.

Duration of action
5–10 hours.

Diet advice
None.

Storage
Keep in a closed container in a cool, dry place out of the reach of children.

Missed dose
Take as soon as you remember. If your next dose is due within 2 hours, take a single dose now and skip the next.

Stopping the drug
When taken for short-term pain relief, the drug can be safely stopped as soon as you no longer need it. If prescribed for the long-term treatment of arthritis, however, you should seek medical advice before stopping the drug.

Exceeding the dose
An occasional unintentional extra dose is unlikely to be a cause for concern. But if you notice any unusual symptoms, or if a large overdose has been taken, notify your physician.

POSSIBLE ADVERSE EFFECTS

The most common *adverse effects* are the result of gastrointestinal disturbances. Black or bloodstained feces should be reported to your physician without delay.

Symptom/effect	Frequency		Discuss with physician		Stop taking drug now	Call physician now
	Common	Rare	Only if severe	In all cases		
Heartburn/indigestion	●		■			
Nausea/vomiting		●	■			
Headache		●	■			
Dizziness/drowsiness		●	■			
Rash/itching		●		■	▲	▮
Wheezing/breathlessness		●		■	▲	▮
Black/bloodstained feces		●		■	▲	▮
Swollen feet or legs		●		■		

INTERACTIONS

General note Ibuprofen interacts with a wide range of drugs to increase the risk of bleeding and/or peptic ulcers. Such drugs include other non-steroidal anti-inflammatory drugs (NSAIDs), ASA, oral anticoagulants, and corticosteroids.

Ciprofloxacin The risk of seizures with this drug and related antibiotics may be increased by ibuprofen.

Antihypertensive drugs and diuretics The beneficial effects of these drugs may be reduced by ibuprofen.

Lithium, digoxin, and methotrexate Ibuprofen may increase the blood levels of these drugs to an undesirable extent.

SPECIAL PRECAUTIONS

Be sure to consult your physician or pharmacist before taking this drug if:
▼ You have a long-term kidney problem.
▼ You have a long-term liver problem.
▼ You have high blood pressure.
▼ You have had a peptic ulcer, esophagitis, or acid indigestion.
▼ You are allergic to ASA.
▼ You have asthma.
▼ You are taking other medications.

Pregnancy
▼ Not usually prescribed. May affect the unborn baby and may prolong labour. Discuss with your physician.

Breast-feeding
▼ The drug passes into the breast milk, but at normal doses adverse effects on the baby are unlikely. Discuss with your physician.

Infants and children
▼ Reduced dose necessary.

Over 60
▼ Reduced dose may be necessary.

Driving and hazardous work
▼ No problems expected.

Alcohol
▼ Avoid. Alcohol may increase the risk of stomach disorders with ibuprofen.

Surgery and general anesthetics
▼ Ibuprofen may prolong bleeding. Discuss the possibility of stopping treatment temporarily with your physician or dentist.

PROLONGED USE

There is an increased risk of bleeding from peptic ulcers and in the bowel with prolonged use of ibuprofen. There is also a small risk of a heart attack or stroke.

IMIPRAMINE

Product names Impril, Novo Tripamine Tab, Nu-Tripamine Tab, and others
Used in the following combined preparations None

GENERAL INFORMATION

Imipramine belongs to the tricyclic class of antidepressant drugs. The drug is used mainly in the long-term treatment of depression to elevate mood, improve appetite, increase energy, and restore interest in everyday life. Because imipramine is less sedating than other tricyclic antidepressants, it is particularly useful when a depressed person is withdrawn or apathetic, although it can aggravate insomnia if it is taken in the evening.

Imipramine may also be prescribed to treat night-time enuresis (bedwetting) in children, although it is no longer recommended due to safer alternatives. Imipramine can cause a variety of *side effects*. In overdose, the drug may cause *coma* and dangerous heart rhythms.

INFORMATION FOR USERS

Your drug prescription is tailored for you. Do not alter dosage without checking with your physician.

How taken

Tablets.

Frequency and timing of doses
1–3 x daily.

Usual dosage range
Adults Usually 75–200mg daily (up to a maximum of 300mg in hospital patients).
Children Reduced dose according to age and weight.

Onset of effect
Some benefits and effects may appear within hours, but full antidepressant effect may not be felt for 4 weeks.

Duration of action
For a first depressive episode, once resolved, maintenance treatment is usually given for one year to prevent recurrence of symptoms.

Diet advice
None.

Storage
Keep in a closed container in a cool, dry place out of the reach of children.

Missed dose
Take as soon as you remember. If your next dose is due within 3 hours, take a single dose now and skip the next.

Stopping the drug
Do not stop taking the drug without consulting your physician, who will supervise a gradual reduction in dosage. Stopping abruptly may cause withdrawal symptoms.

OVERDOSE ACTION

 Seek immediate medical advice in all cases. Take emergency action if consciousness is lost.

See Drug poisoning emergency guide (p.526).

POSSIBLE ADVERSE EFFECTS

The possible adverse effects of this drug are mainly the result of its *anticholinergic* action and its effect on the normal rhythm of the heart.

Symptom/effect	Frequency		Discuss with physician		Stop taking drug now	Call physician now
	Common	Rare	Only if severe	In all cases		
Sweating/flushing	●		■			
Dry mouth/constipation	●		■			
Weight gain	●		■			
Blurred vision	●			■		
Dizziness/drowsiness		●		■		
Rash		●		■	▲	
Palpitations		●		■	▲	■

INTERACTIONS

Monoamine oxidase inhibitors (MAOIs)
There is a possibility of a serious interaction. Such drugs are prescribed with imipramine only under strict supervision.

Amiodarone, and sotalol These drugs may increase the risk of abnormal heart rhythms.

Sedatives Imipramine may increase the effects of sedative drugs.

Antihypertensive drugs Imipramine may reduce the effectiveness of these drugs.

Phenytoin Imipramine may increase levels of phenytoin.

SPECIAL PRECAUTIONS

Be sure to tell your physician if:
▼ You have had heart problems.
▼ You have long-term liver or kidney problems.
▼ You have had epileptic seizures.
▼ You have porphyria.
▼ You have had glaucoma.
▼ You have prostate trouble.
▼ You have had mania or a psychotic illness.
▼ You are taking other medications.

 Pregnancy
▼ Sometimes used when benefits outweigh risks. Discuss with your physician.

 Breast-feeding
▼ The drug passes into the breast milk, but at normal doses adverse effects on the baby are unlikely. Discuss with your physician.

 Infants and children
▼ Not recommended under 7 years. Reduced dose necessary in older children.

 Over 60
▼ Increased likelihood of adverse effects. Reduced dose may therefore be necessary.

 Driving and hazardous work
▼ Avoid such activities until you have learned how imipramine affects you because the drug can cause reduced alertness and blurred vision.

Alcohol
▼ Avoid. Alcohol may increase the sedative effect of imipramine.

PROLONGED USE

No problems expected. Imipramine is not usually prescribed for children as a treatment for bedwetting for longer than three months.

INDAPAMIDE

Product names Apo-Indapamide, Dom-Indapamide, Lozide Tab, PMS-Indapamide
Used in the following combined preparation Coversyl Plus

GENERAL INFORMATION

Indapamide is a drug related in its effects and uses to the thiazide diuretics, and is used to treat hypertension (high blood pressure).

The drug increases secretion of salt by the kidneys in the same way as thiazide diuretics. This causes more water to be lost from the body, which reduces the total blood volume and lowers blood pressure.

Indapamide is sometimes combined with other antihypertensive drugs but not with other diuretics. Indapamide's diuretic effects are slight at low doses, but susceptible people need to have their blood levels of potassium and uric acid monitored. These include the elderly, those taking digoxin, or those with gout or hyperaldosteronism (overproduction of the hormone aldosterone). Unlike the thiazides, indapamide does not affect control of diabetes at low doses.

INFORMATION FOR USERS

Your drug prescription is tailored for you. Do not alter dosage without checking with your physician.

How taken

Tablets.

Frequency and timing of doses
Once daily in the morning.

Usual adult dosage range
1.5–2.5mg.

Onset of effect
1–2 hours, but the full effect may not be felt for several months.

Duration of action
12–24 hours.

Diet advice
None.

Storage
Keep in a closed container in a cool, dry place out of the reach of children.

Missed dose
Take as soon as you remember. If your next dose is due within 4 hours, take a single dose now and skip the next.

Stopping the drug
Do not stop taking the drug without consulting your physician; high blood pressure may return.

Exceeding the dose
An occasional unintentional extra dose is unlikely to cause problems. But if you notice any unusual symptoms, or if a large overdose has been taken, notify your physician.

POSSIBLE ADVERSE EFFECTS

Headaches and muscle cramps are common, but other symptoms rarely cause problems.

Symptom/effect	Frequency		Discuss with physician		Stop taking drug now	Call physician now
	Common	Rare	Only if severe	In all cases		
Headache/dizziness	●		■			
Fatigue/muscle cramps	●		■			
Rash	●			■		
Diarrhea/constipation		●	■			
Palpitations/fainting		●		■		
Tingling/"pins and needles"		●		■		
Erectile dysfunction		●		■		

INTERACTIONS

Loop diuretics There is a risk of imbalance of salts in the blood if these drugs are taken with indapamide.

Lithium Blood levels of lithium are increased when it is taken with indapamide.

Antiarrhythmic drugs Loss of potassium may make these drugs less effective if they are taken with indapamide.

SPECIAL PRECAUTIONS

Be sure to tell your physician if:
▼ You have liver or kidney problems.
▼ You have gout.
▼ You have hyperaldosteronism or hyperparathyroidism.
▼ You are allergic to sulfonamide drugs.
▼ You are taking digoxin.
▼ You are taking other medications.

Pregnancy
▼ Safety not established. Discuss with your physician.

Breast-feeding
▼ Safety not established. Discuss with your physician.

Infants and children
▼ Not prescribed.

Over 60
▼ No special problems.

Driving and hazardous work
▼ No special problems.

Alcohol
▼ No special problems.

PROLONGED USE

Long-term use of indapamide may lead to potassium loss.

Monitoring Blood potassium and uric acid levels may be checked periodically.

INSULIN

Product names Humalog, Humulin, Hypurin, Innovo, Novolin
Used in the following combined preparations None

GENERAL INFORMATION

Insulin is a hormone made by the pancreas and vital to the body's ability to use sugar. It is given by injection to supplement or replace natural insulin in the treatment of diabetes mellitus. It is the only effective treatment in Type 1 diabetes and may also be prescribed in Type 2 diabetes. Insulin should be used with a carefully controlled diet. Illness, vomiting, or alterations in diet or in exercise levels may require dosage adjustment.

Insulin is available in a wide variety of preparations – short-, medium-, or long-acting. Combinations of types are often given. People receiving insulin should carry a warning card or tag. They should watch for signs of hypoglycemia and should eat something sugary if they do develop.

INFORMATION FOR USERS

Your drug prescription is tailored for you. Do not alter dosage without checking with your physician.

How taken

Injection, infusion pump, pen injection.

Frequency and timing of doses
1–5 x daily. Short-acting insulin is usually given 15–30 minutes before meals. Some newer forms can be given directly before or after eating. However, the exact timing of injections and longer-acting preparations will be tailored to your individual needs; follow the instructions you are given.

Usual dosage range
The dose (and type) of insulin is determined according to the needs of the individual.

Onset of effect
15–60 minutes (short-acting); 1–2 hours (medium- and long-acting).

Duration of action
6–8 hours (short-acting); 18–26 hours (medium-acting); 28–36 hours (long-acting).

Diet advice
A special diabetic diet is necessary. Follow your physician's advice.

Storage
Refrigerate but once opened may be stored at room temperature for 1 month. Do not freeze. Follow the instructions on the container.

Missed dose
Discuss with your physician. Appropriate action depends on dose and type of insulin.

Stopping the drug
Do not stop taking the drug without consulting your physician; confusion and coma may occur.

OVERDOSE ACTION

Seek immediate medical advice. You may notice symptoms of low blood sugar, such as faintness, hunger, sweating, trembling. Eat or drink something sugary. Take emergency action if seizures or loss of consciousness occur.

See Drug poisoning emergency guide (p.526).

SPECIAL PRECAUTIONS

Be sure to tell your physician if:
▼ You have had a previous *allergic reaction* to insulin.
▼ You are taking other medications, or your other drug treatment is changed.

Pregnancy
▼ No evidence of risk to the developing baby from insulin, but poor control of diabetes increases the risk of birth defects. Careful monitoring is required.

Breast-feeding
▼ No evidence of risk. Adjustment in dose may be necessary while breast-feeding.

Infants and children
▼ Reduced dose necessary.

Over 60
▼ No special problems.

Driving and hazardous work
▼ You may need to inform your motor vehicle licensing authority that you are taking insulin. Avoid driving or dangerous activities if you have warning signs of low blood sugar.

Alcohol
▼ Avoid. Alcoholic drinks upset diabetic control.

Surgery and general anesthetics
▼ Insulin requirements may increase during surgery, and blood glucose levels will need to be monitored during and after an operation. Notify your physician or dentist that you are diabetic before any surgery.

POSSIBLE ADVERSE EFFECTS

Symptoms such as dizziness, sweating, weakness, and confusion indicate low blood sugar. Serious allergic reactions (rash, swelling, and shortness of breath) are rare.

Symptom/effect	Frequency		Discuss with physician		Stop taking drug now	Call physician now
	Common	Rare	Only if severe	In all cases		
Injection-site irritation	●			■		
Weakness/sweating	●			■		
Dimpling at injection site		●		■		
Eyesight problems		●		■		
Rash/facial swelling		●		■		▮
Shortness of breath		●		■		▮

INTERACTIONS

General note 1 Many drugs, including some antibiotics, monoamine oxidase inhibitors (MAOIs), and oral antidiabetic drugs, increase the risk of low blood sugar.

Corticosteroids and diuretics may oppose the effect of insulin.

General note 2 Check with your physician or pharmacist before taking any medicines; some contain sugar and may upset control of diabetes.

Beta blockers may affect insulin needs and mask signs of low blood sugar.

PROLONGED USE

No problems expected.

Monitoring Regular monitoring of levels of sugar in the blood and/or urine is required.

INTERFERON

Product names Avonex, Betaseron, Intron A, Pegasys, Rebif
Used in the following combined preparations Pegasys RBV, Pegetron, Victrelis Triple, and others

GENERAL INFORMATION

Interferons are a group of substances normally produced in human and animal cells that have been infected with viruses or stimulated by other substances. They are thought to promote resistance to several types of viral infection (see p.113). Three main types of interferon (alpha, beta, and gamma) are used to treat a range of diseases. Interferon alpha is used for leukemias, other cancers, and chronic hepatitis B and C. Peginterferon alfa-2a and 2b are indicated in the management of hepatitis C; 2a is also indicated in hepatitis B. Interferon beta reduces the frequency and severity of relapses in multiple sclerosis. Interferon gamma is prescribed in conjunction with antibiotics for patients suffering from chronic granulomatous disease or from severe malignant osteopetrosis.

Interferons can cause severe *adverse effects* (see below).

INFORMATION FOR USERS

This drug is given only under medical supervision and is not for self-administration.

How taken

Injection.

Frequency and timing of doses
Once daily or once weekly depending on product and condition being treated.

Usual adult dosage range
The dosage is calculated taking account of the body surface area of the patient and the condition being treated.

Onset of effect
Active inside the body within 1 hour, but effects may not be noted for 1–2 months.

Duration of action
Immediate effects last for about 12 hours.

Diet advice
None.

Storage
Store in a refrigerator at 2–8°C (36–46°F). Do not let it freeze, and protect from light. Keep out of the reach of children.

Missed dose
Not applicable. This drug is usually given only in hospital under close medical supervision.

Stopping the drug
Discuss with your physician.

Exceeding the dose
Overdosage is unlikely since treatment is carefully monitored.

SPECIAL PRECAUTIONS

Interferon is prescribed only under close medical supervision, taking account of your present condition and medical history. However, be sure to tell your physician if:
▼ You have long-term liver or kidney problems.
▼ You have heart disease.
▼ You have very abnormal blood lipid levels.
▼ You have had epileptic seizures.
▼ You have previously suffered *allergic reactions* to any drugs.
▼ You have had asthma or eczema.
▼ You suffer from depression.
▼ You are taking other medications.

Pregnancy
▼ Not usually prescribed. Safety in pregnancy not established. Discuss with your physician.

Breast-feeding
▼ It is not known whether the drug passes into the breast milk. Discuss with your physician.

Infants and children
▼ Not usually used.

Over 60
▼ Increased likelihood of adverse effects. Reduced dose may be necessary.

Driving and hazardous work
▼ Not applicable.

Alcohol
▼ Avoid. Alcohol may increase the sedative effects of this drug.

POSSIBLE ADVERSE EFFECTS

The symptoms listed below are the most common problems. All unusual symptoms should be brought to your physician's attention without delay. Some of these symptoms are dose-related, and a reduction in dosage may be necessary to eliminate them.

Symptom/effect	Frequency		Discuss with physician		Stop taking drug now	Call physician now
	Common	Rare	Only if severe	In all cases		
Headache	●		■			
Lethargy/depression	●			■		
Dizziness/drowsiness	●			■		
Digestive disturbances	●			■		
Chills, fever, muscle-ache	●			■		
Poor appetite and weight loss	●			■		
Hair loss		●		■		
Mood changes		●		■		■

INTERACTIONS

General note A number of drugs increase the risk of adverse effects on the blood, heart, or nervous system. This is taken into account when prescribing an interferon with other drugs.

Sedatives All drugs that have a sedative effect on the central nervous system are likely to increase the sedative properties of interferon. Such drugs include *opioid* analgesics, anti-anxiety and sleeping drugs, antihistamines, antidepressants, and antipsychotics.

Vaccines Interferon may reduce the effectiveness of vaccines.

Theophylline/aminophylline The effects of this drug may be increased by interferon.

PROLONGED USE

There may be an increased risk of liver damage. Blood cell production in the bone marrow may be reduced. Repeated large doses are associated with lethargy, fatigue, collapse, and *coma*.

Monitoring Frequent blood tests are required to monitor blood composition and liver function.

IPRATROPIUM BROMIDE

Product names Atrovent and others
Used in the following combined preparations Combivent, Combivent UDV, Duovent UDV, and others

GENERAL INFORMATION

Ipratropium bromide is an *anticholinergic* bronchodilator that relaxes the muscles surrounding the bronchioles (airways in the lung). It is used primarily in the maintenance treatment of reversible airway disorders, particularly chronic obstructive pulmonary disease (COPD). It is given only by inhaler or via a *nebulizer* for these conditions. The drug is also used in treating acute attacks of asthma alone, especially severe ones in the hospital. In these cases, ipratropium bromide is usually used together with *sympathomimetic* bronchodilators, such as salbutamol. Ipratropium bromide is also prescribed as a nasal spray for the treatment of a continually runny nose due to allergy.

Unlike other anticholinergic drugs, *side effects* are rare. It is not likely to affect the heart, eyes, bowel, or bladder. Ipratropium bromide must be used with caution by people with glaucoma, but problems are unlikely at normal doses and if inhalers or nebulizers are used correctly.

QUICK REFERENCE

Drug group Bronchodilator (p.76)

Overdose danger rating Low

Dependence rating Low

Prescription needed Yes

Available as generic Yes

INFORMATION FOR USERS

Your drug prescription is tailored for you. Do not alter dosage without checking with your physician.

How taken

Inhaler, nasal spray, liquid for nebulizer.

Frequency and timing of doses
3–4 x daily.

Usual adult dosage range
80–320mcg daily (inhaler); 125–500mcg per dose (nebulizer); 2 sprays to the affected nostril 2–3 x daily (nasal spray).

Onset of effect
5–15 minutes.

Duration of action
Up to 8 hours.

Diet advice
None.

Storage
Keep in a cool, dry place out of the reach of children. Do not puncture or burn containers.

Missed dose
Take as soon as you remember. If your next dose is due within 2 hours, take a single dose now and skip the next.

Stopping the drug
Do not stop taking the drug without consulting your physician; symptoms may recur.

Exceeding the dose
An occasional unintentional extra dose is unlikely to be a cause for concern. But if you notice any unusual symptoms, or if a large overdose has been taken, notify your physician.

SPECIAL PRECAUTIONS

Be sure to tell your physician if:
▼ You have glaucoma.
▼ You have prostate problems.
▼ You have difficulty in passing urine.
▼ You are taking other medications.

Pregnancy
▼ No evidence of risk, but discuss with your physician before using in the first 3 months of pregnancy.

Breast-feeding
▼ No evidence of risk, but discuss with your physician.

Infants and children
▼ Reduced dose necessary.

Over 60
▼ No special problems.

Driving and hazardous work
▼ No special problems.

Alcohol
▼ No known problems.

POSSIBLE ADVERSE EFFECTS

Side effects are rare. The most common is dry mouth or throat. Rarely, wheezing or breathlessness may worsen immediately after inhaler use (paradoxical bronchospasm); if this happens, stop using the drug and contact your physician immediately.

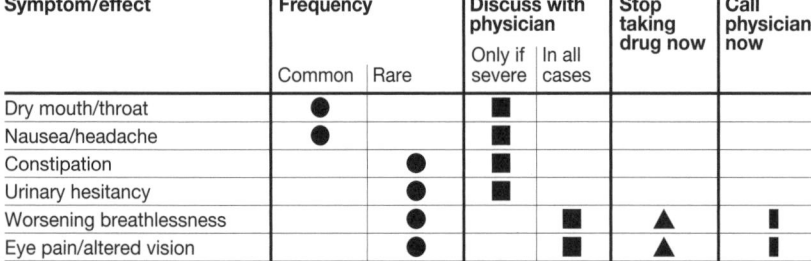

Symptom/effect	Frequency		Discuss with physician		Stop taking drug now	Call physician now
	Common	Rare	Only if severe	In all cases		
Dry mouth/throat	●			■		
Nausea/headache	●			■		
Constipation		●		■		
Urinary hesitancy		●		■		
Worsening breathlessness		●		■	▲	▮
Eye pain/altered vision		●		■	▲	▮

INTERACTIONS

Anticholinergic drugs Although absorption is minimal from the inhaler/spray, additive anticholinergic effects could occur.

PROLONGED USE

No special problems.

IRBESARTAN

Product names Avapro, CO Irbesartan, and others
Used in the following combined preparations Avalide and others

GENERAL INFORMATION

Irbesartan is a member of the group of *vasodilator* drugs called angiotensin-II blockers. Used to treat hypertension, the drug works by blocking the action of angiotensin-II (a naturally occurring substance that constricts blood vessels). This action causes the blood vessel walls to relax, thereby lowering blood pressure.

Unlike ACE inhibitors, irbesartan does not cause a persistent dry cough.

Along with other angiotensin-II blockers, it is being evaluated for the treatment of some of the other conditions, such as heart failure, for which ACE inhibitors are used. Irbesartan is also available in combination with a diuretic.

INFORMATION FOR USERS

Your drug prescription is tailored for you. Do not alter dosage without checking with your physician.

How taken

Tablets.

Frequency and timing of doses
Once daily.

Usual adult dosage range
150–300mg, but 75mg may be used in people over 75 years or with liver problems.

Onset of effect
Within 1 hour. Blood pressure is lowered within 1–2 weeks, and maximum beneficial effect is felt 4–6 weeks from start of treatment.

Duration of action
24 hours.

Diet advice
None.

Storage
Keep in a closed container in a cool, dry place out of the reach of children.

Missed dose
Take as soon as you remember. If your next dose is due within 8 hours, take a single dose now and skip the next.

Stopping the drug
Do not stop the drug without consulting your physician. Stopping the drug may lead to worsening of the underlying condition.

Exceeding the dose
An occasional unintentional extra dose is unlikely to be a cause for concern. Large overdoses may cause dizziness and fainting. Notify your physician.

SPECIAL PRECAUTIONS

Be sure to tell your physician if:
▼ You have heart problems, including heart failure.
▼ You have kidney problems or stenosis of the kidney's arteries.
▼ You have lactose/galactose intolerance or glucose/galactose malabsorption.
▼ You are taking other medications.

Pregnancy
▼ Not prescribed.

Breast-feeding
▼ Safety not established. Discuss with your physician.

Infants and children
▼ Not prescribed.

Over 60
▼ Increased risk of adverse effects. Reduced dose may be necessary.

Driving and hazardous work
▼ Avoid such activities until you have learned how irbesartan affects you because the drug can cause dizziness and fatigue.

Alcohol
▼ Avoid. Regular intake of excessive alcohol may raise the blood pressure and reduce the effectiveness of irbesartan.

POSSIBLE ADVERSE EFFECTS

Adverse effects are usually mild.

Symptom/effect	Frequency		Discuss with physician		Stop taking drug now	Call physician now
	Common	Rare	Only if severe	In all cases		
Dizziness/fatigue	●				■	
Flushing	●			■		
Headache		●		■		
Muscle or joint pains		●		■		
Rash		●			■	
Swollen face or lips		●		■	▲	■

INTERACTIONS

Diuretics There is a risk of a sudden fall in blood pressure if these drugs are being taken when irbesartan treatment is started. They may also affect the sodium and potassium levels in the blood.

Potassium supplements, potassium-sparing diuretics, and cyclosporine Irbesartan enhances the effect of these drugs, leading to raised levels of potassium in the blood.

Lithium Irbesartan increases the blood levels and *toxicity* of lithium.

NSAIDs Certain of these drugs may reduce the blood-pressure-lowering effects of irbesartan.

ACE inhibitors (e.g. enalapril, captopril, lisinopril, or ramipril) may increase potassium levels when taken with irbesartan.

Potassium salts may increase the risk of high potassium levels with irbesartan.

PROLONGED USE

No special problems.

Monitoring
Periodic checks on blood potassium levels may be performed.

ISONIAZID

Product names Dom-Isoniazid, Isotamine, and others
Used in the following combined preparations Rifater

GENERAL INFORMATION

Isoniazid (also known as INH) has been in use for over 30 years and remains an effective drug for tuberculosis. It is given alone to prevent tuberculosis and in combination with other drugs for the treatment of the disease. Treatment usually lasts for six months. However, courses lasting nine months or a year may sometimes be prescribed. Although isoniazid usually causes few

adverse effects, one of its *side effects* is the increased loss of pyridoxine (vitamin B_6) from the body. This effect, which is more likely with high doses, is rare in children but common among people with poor nutrition. Since pyridoxine deficiency can lead to irreversible nerve damage, supplements are usually given.

INFORMATION FOR USERS

Your drug prescription is tailored for you. Do not alter dosage without checking with your physician.

How taken

Tablets, liquid, injection.

Frequency and timing of doses
Normally once daily.

Usual dosage range
Adults 300mg daily. Can be given 2 or 3 x weekly in some cases.
Children According to age and weight.

Onset of effect
Over 2–3 days.

Duration of action
Up to 24 hours.

Diet advice
Isoniazid may deplete pyridoxine (vitamin B_6) levels, so supplements are usually prescribed.

Storage
Keep in a closed container in a cool, dry place out of the reach of children. Protect from light.

Missed dose
Take as soon as you remember. If your next dose is scheduled within 8 hours, take a single dose now and skip the next.

Stopping the drug
Take the full course. Even if you feel better, the infection may still be present and may recur if treatment is stopped too soon.

OVERDOSE ACTION

 Seek immediate medical advice in all cases. Take emergency action if breathing difficulties, seizures, or loss of consciousness occur.

See Drug poisoning emergency guide (p.526).

SPECIAL PRECAUTIONS

Be sure to tell your physician if:
▼ You have long-term liver or kidney problems.
▼ You have had liver damage following isoniazid treatment in the past.
▼ If you have problems with drugs or alcohol abuse.
▼ You have diabetes.
▼ You have porphyria.
▼ You have HIV infection.
▼ You have had epileptic seizures.
▼ You are taking other medications.

 Pregnancy
▼ No evidence of risk. Discuss with your physician.

 Breast-feeding
▼ The drug passes into the breast milk and may affect the baby. The infant should be monitored for signs of toxic effects. Discuss with your physician.

 Infants and children
▼ Reduced dose necessary.

 Over 60
▼ Increased likelihood of adverse effects.

 Driving and hazardous work
▼ No special problems.

 Alcohol
▼ Avoid excessive amounts.

POSSIBLE ADVERSE EFFECTS

Although serious problems are uncommon, all adverse effects of this drug should receive prompt medical attention because of the possibility of nerve or liver damage.

Symptom/effect	Frequency		Discuss with physician		Stop taking drug now	Call physician now
	Common	Rare	Only if severe	In all cases		
Nausea/vomiting	●		■			
Fatigue/weakness	●			■		
Numbness/tingling	●			■		
Rash	●			■		
Mood changes	●			■		
Blurred vision	●			■	▲	
Jaundice	●			■	▲	▮
Twitching/muscle weakness	●			■	▲	▮

INTERACTIONS

Alcohol and rifampin Large quantities of alcohol may reduce the effectiveness of isoniazid. If alcohol and isoniazid are taken together, the likelihood of liver damage is increased; if, in addition, rifampin is being taken, the risk of liver damage is increased even further.

Antiepileptics The effects of these drugs may be increased with isoniazid.

Antacids These drugs may reduce the absorption of isoniazid.

Ketoconazole Isoniazid reduces the blood concentration of ketoconazole.

PROLONGED USE

Pyridoxine (vitamin B_6) deficiency may occur with prolonged use and lead to nerve damage. Supplements are usually prescribed. There is also a risk of serious liver damage.

Monitoring Periodic blood tests are usually performed to monitor liver function.

ISOSORBIDE DINITRATE/MONONITRATE

Product names [Dinitrate] ISDN, Isosorbide Tab, PMS-Isosorbide [Mononitrate] Imdur, PMS-ISMN
Used in the following combined preparations None

GENERAL INFORMATION

Isosorbide dinitrate and mononitrate are *vasodilator* drugs similar to nitroglycerin. They are usually used to treat patients suffering from angina, and are also used in some cases of heart problems.

Unlike nitroglycerin, however, both isosorbide dintrate and isosorbide mononitrate are stable and can be stored for long periods without losing their effectiveness.

Headaches, flushing, and dizziness are common *side effects* during the early stages of treatment; gradual increase in dose can minimize these symptoms. As tolerance can develop with round-the-clock use, formulations are often designed to give a drug-free period when taken once daily. This should be discussed with your physician or *pharmacist*.

QUICK REFERENCE

Drug group Nitrate vasodilators (p.84) and anti-angina drugs (p.87)

Overdose danger rating Medium

Dependence rating Low

Prescription needed No

Available as generic Yes

INFORMATION FOR USERS

Your drug prescription is tailored for you. Do not alter dosage without checking with your physician.

How taken

Dinitrate Sublingual tablets (held under the tongue), tablets.
Mononitrate SR-tablets.

Frequency and timing of doses
Relief of angina attacks Tablets (dinitrate) sublingual under the tongue as needed.
Prevention of angina 2–4 x daily;
1 x daily (SR-tablets).

Usual adult dosage range
Relief of angina attacks 5–10mg per dose.
Prevention of angina 30–120mg daily (mononitrate).

Onset of effect
2–3 minutes when chewed or held under the tongue (certain preparations only); 30 minutes when swallowed.

Duration of action
Up to 2 hours (chewed); up to 5 hours (swallowed); up to 10 hours (SR-tablets).

Diet advice
None.

Storage
Keep in a closed container in a cool, dry place out of the reach of children. Protect from light.

Missed dose
Take as soon as you remember. If your next dose is due within 2 hours, take a single dose now and skip the next.

Stopping the drug
Do not stop taking the drug without consulting your physician; stopping the drug may lead to worsening of the underlying condition.

Exceeding the dose
An occasional unintentional extra dose is unlikely to cause problems. Large overdoses may cause dizziness and headache. Notify your physician.

SPECIAL PRECAUTIONS

Be sure to tell your physician if:
▼ You have long-term liver or kidney problems.
▼ You have any blood disorders or anemia.
▼ You have had glaucoma.
▼ You have low blood pressure.
▼ You have ever had a heart attack.
▼ You have an underactive thyroid.
▼ You are taking other medications.

Pregnancy
▼ Safety in pregnancy not established. Discuss with your physician.

Breast-feeding
▼ Safety not established. Discuss with your physician.

Infants and children
▼ Not usually prescribed.

Over 60
▼ No special problems.

Driving and hazardous work
▼ Avoid such activities until you have learned how isosorbide dinitrate or mononitrate affect you because these drugs can cause dizziness.

Alcohol
▼ Avoid. Alcohol may further lower blood pressure, depressing the heart and causing dizziness and fainting.

POSSIBLE ADVERSE EFFECTS

The most serious *adverse effect* is excessively lowered blood pressure, and this may need to be monitored on a regular basis. Other adverse effects of both forms of the drug usually improve after regular use; dose adjustment may help.

Symptom/effect	Frequency		Discuss with physician		Stop taking drug now	Call physician now
	Common	Rare	Only if severe	In all cases		
Headache	●		■			
Flushing	●		■			
Dizziness	●			■		
Fainting/weakness		●		■		

INTERACTIONS

Sildenafil The blood-pressure-lowering effect of nitrate drugs is significantly enhanced by sildenafil and the two drugs should not be used together.

Antihypertensives A further lowering of blood pressure occurs when such drugs are taken with isosorbide dinitrate.

PROLONGED USE

The initial adverse effects may disappear with continued use. To prevent tolerance, an appropriate dosing schedule will include a drug-free period during each day. Discuss this with your physician or pharmacist.

ISOTRETINOIN

Product names Accutane Roche, Clarus
Used in the following combined preparations None

GENERAL INFORMATION

Isotretinoin, a drug that is chemically related to vitamin A, is prescribed for the treatment of severe acne that has failed to respond to other treatments.

The drug reduces production of the skin's natural oils (sebum), which may reduce bacterial activity related to acne.

A 12–16-week course of treatment often clears the acne. The skin may be very dry, flaky, and itchy at first, but this usually improves as treatment continues. Very rare but serious *adverse effects* include liver damage and bowel inflammation.

INFORMATION FOR USERS

Your drug prescription is tailored for you. Do not alter dosage without checking with your physician.

How taken

Capsules.

Frequency and timing of doses
1–2 x daily (take capsules with food or milk).

Usual adult dosage range
Dosage is determined individually.

Onset of effect
2–4 weeks. Acne may worsen before it gets better during the first few weeks of treatment in some people.

Duration of action
Effects can be permanent, and should persist for at least several weeks after the drug has been stopped. Acne is usually completely cleared.

Diet advice
None.

Storage
Keep in a closed container in a cool, dry place out of the reach of children. Protect from light.

Missed dose
Take as soon as you remember. If your next dose is due within 4 hours, take a single dose now and skip the next.

Stopping the drug
Can be safely stopped as soon as you no longer need it, but best results are achieved when the course of treatment is completed as prescribed.

Exceeding the dose
An occasional unintentional extra dose is unlikely to cause problems. Large overdoses may cause headaches, vomiting, abdominal pain, facial flushing, incoordination, and dizziness. Notify your physician.

SPECIAL PRECAUTIONS

Do not donate blood during, or for at least a month after, taking oral isotretinoin. Be sure to tell your physician or pharmacist before taking this drug if:
▼ You have long-term liver or kidney problems.
▼ You suffer from arthritis.
▼ You have diabetes.
▼ You have high blood fat levels.
▼ You wear contact lenses.
▼ You suffer from gout.
▼ You are taking other medications.

Pregnancy
▼ Must not be prescribed. The drug causes abnormalities in the developing baby. All women of child-bearing age must use effective contraception during treatment and for at least a month before and after.

Breast-feeding
▼ The drug passes into the breast milk and may affect the baby. Discuss with your physician.

Infants and children
▼ Not prescribed.

Over 60
▼ Not usually prescribed.

Driving and hazardous work
▼ Avoid such activities until you have learned how the drug affects you because it can cause vision problems in dim light or darkness.

Alcohol
▼ Regular heavy drinking may raise blood fat levels with isotretinoin.

Sunlight and sunbeds
▼ Avoid exposure to the sun and sunlamps.

POSSIBLE ADVERSE EFFECTS

Dryness of the nose, mouth, and eyes, inflammation of the lips, and flaking of the skin occur in most cases. Temporary loss or increase of hair may also occur. If headache, nausea and vomiting, abdominal pain with diarrhea, blood in the feces, or visual impairment occur, consult your physician promptly.

Symptom/effect	Frequency		Discuss with physician		Stop taking drug now	Call physician now
	Common	Rare	Only if severe	In all cases		
Dry skin/nosebleeds	●		■			
Muscle/joint pain	●		■			
Lip/eye dryness/inflammation	●			■		
Headache		●		■		
Impaired vision		●		■		
Nausea/vomiting		●		■		
Abdominal pain/diarrhea		●		■	▲	■
Mood changes		●		■		

INTERACTIONS

Tetracycline antibiotics These may increase the risk of high pressure in the skull, leading to headaches, nausea, and vomiting.

Skin-drying preparations Medicated cosmetics, soaps, toiletries, and anti-acne preparations increase the likelihood of dryness and irritation of the skin with isotretinoin.

Vitamin A Supplements of this vitamin increase the risk of adverse effects from isotretinoin.

PROLONGED USE

Treatment rarely exceeds 16 weeks. Prolonged use may raise blood fat levels, and increase the risk of heart and blood vessel disease. Bone changes may occur.

Monitoring Liver function tests and checks on blood fat levels are performed.

KETOCONAZOLE

Product names Apo-Ketoconazole, Ketoderm, Nizoral, Nu-Ketocon, and others
Used in the following combined preparations None

GENERAL INFORMATION

Ketoconazole is an antifungal drug that is used to treat infections of the skin and mucous membranes, as well as severe *systemic* fungal infections. The topical preparation is used to treat athlete's foot, jock itch, and ringworm of the skin and the scalp. It can be applied as a shampoo for scalp infections and seborrhoeic dermatitis.

Given orally, it is prescribed for severe internal systemic fungal infections, such as candida infection of the body and of the mucous membranes and in people with rare fungal diseases (e.g. histoplasmosis).

The *side effect* of nausea can be reduced by taking the drug at bedtime or with meals.

QUICK REFERENCE

Drug group Antifungal drugs (p.124)
Overdose danger rating Medium
Dependence rating Low
Prescription needed Yes (except for some shampoos)
Available as generic Yes (oral)

INFORMATION FOR USERS

Your drug prescription is tailored for you. Do not alter dosage without checking with your physician.

How taken

Tablets, cream, shampoo.

Frequency and timing of doses
Once daily with food (by mouth); 1–2 x daily (cream); 1–2 times weekly (shampoo used for seborrhoeic dermatitis).

Usual dosage range
Adults 200–400mg daily (by mouth).
Children Reduced dose according to age and weight.

Onset of effect
Full beneficial effect may take several days.

Duration of action
Up to 24 hours.

Diet advice
None.

Storage
Keep in a closed container in a cool, dry place out of the reach of children.

Missed dose (oral)
Take as soon as you remember. If your next dose is due within 6 hours, take a single dose now and skip the next.

Stopping the drug
Take the full course. Symptoms may recur if treatment is stopped too soon.

Exceeding the dose
An occasional unintentional extra dose is unlikely to be a cause for concern. Large overdoses may cause gastric problems. Notify your physician.

SPECIAL PRECAUTIONS

Be sure to tell your physician if:
▼ You have liver or kidney problems.
▼ You have porphyria.
▼ You have previously had an allergic reaction to antifungal drugs.
▼ You are taking other medications.

Pregnancy
▼ When taken orally, may cause defects in the developing baby. Discuss with your physician.

Breast-feeding
▼ When taken orally, the drug passes into the breast milk and may affect the baby. Discuss with your physician.

Infants and children
▼ Reduced dose necessary.

Over 60
▼ No special problems.

Driving and hazardous work
▼ No special problems.

Alcohol
▼ Avoid. Alcohol may interact with this drug to cause flushing and nausea.

POSSIBLE ADVERSE EFFECTS

Nausea is the most common side effect of oral ketoconazole; liver damage is a rare but serious *adverse effect* causing *jaundice* that may necessitate stopping the drug.

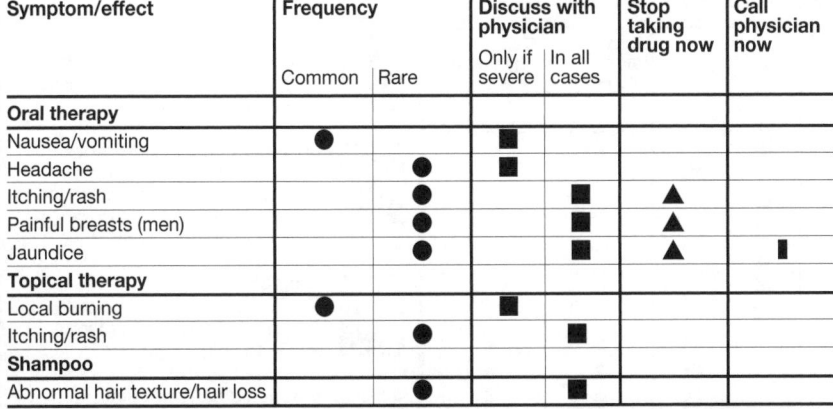

Symptom/effect	Frequency		Discuss with physician		Stop taking drug now	Call physician now
	Common	Rare	Only if severe	In all cases		
Oral therapy						
Nausea/vomiting	●		■			
Headache		●	■			
Itching/rash		●		■	▲	
Painful breasts (men)		●		■	▲	
Jaundice		●		■	▲	▮
Topical therapy						
Local burning	●		■			
Itching/rash		●		■		
Shampoo						
Abnormal hair texture/hair loss		●		■		

PROLONGED USE

The risk of liver damage increases with use for more than 14 days of the oral drug.

Monitoring Periodic blood tests are usually performed to check the effect of the drug on the liver.

INTERACTIONS (administration by mouth only)

Antacids, cimetidine, and ranitidine may reduce the effectiveness of ketoconazole if they are taken within 2 hours before or after.

Rifampin and phenytoin may reduce the effect of ketoconazole, and ketoconazole may increase the level of these drugs.

Sedatives, warfarin, cyclosporine, tacrolimus, sirolimus, theophylline, and sildenafil Ketoconazole increases

the effects of these drugs.

Eletriptan Use of this drug with ketoconazole is not recommended.

Telaprevir may need dose adjustments if used with ketoconazole.

Simvastatin and other statins Ketoconazole may increase the risk of muscle damage if these drugs are taken with it.

KETOPROFEN

Product names Ketoprofen SR, Ketoprofen-E, and others
Used in the following combined preparations None

GENERAL INFORMATION

Ketoprofen is a non-steroidal anti-inflammatory drug (NSAID) which, like other NSAIDs, relieves pain and reduces inflammation and stiffness in rheumatoid arthritis, osteoarthritis, and ankylosing spondylitis. The drug does not cure the underlying disease, however.

Ketoprofen is also given to relieve mild to moderate pain of menstruation and soft tissue injuries, and the pain that occurs following operations.

The most common *adverse reactions* to ketoprofen, as with all NSAIDs, are gastrointestinal disturbances such as nausea and indigestion. Switching to another NSAID may be recommended by your physician if unwanted effects are persistent or troublesome.

QUICK REFERENCE

Drug group Non-steroidal anti-inflammatory drugs (p.102)

Overdose danger rating Medium

Dependence rating Low

Prescription needed Yes

Available as generic Yes

INFORMATION FOR USERS

Your drug prescription is tailored for you. Do not alter dosage without checking with your physician.

How taken

Tablets, SR-tablets, capsules, SR-capsules, *suppositories.*

Frequency and timing of doses
Once daily (SR-tablets/capsules) or 2 x daily (tablets/capsules) with food; 2 x daily (suppositories).

Usual adult dosage range
100–200mg daily.

Onset of effect
Pain relief may be felt in 30 minutes to 2 hours. Full anti-inflammatory effect may not be felt for up to 2 weeks.

Duration of action
Up to 8–12 hours.

Diet advice
None.

Storage
Keep in a closed container in a cool, dry place out of the reach of children.

Missed dose
Take as soon as you remember. If your next dose is due within 4 hours, take a single dose now and skip the next.

Stopping the drug
Seek medical advice before stopping the drug.

Exceeding the dose
An occasional unintentional extra dose is unlikely to be a cause for concern. Large overdoses may cause vomiting, confusion, or irritability. Notify your physician.

SPECIAL PRECAUTIONS

Be sure to tell your physician if:
▼ You have long-term liver or kidney problems.
▼ You have heart problems.
▼ You have high blood pressure.
▼ You have asthma.
▼ You have had a peptic ulcer, esophagitis, or acid indigestion.
▼ You have bleeding problems.
▼ You are allergic to ASA or other NSAIDs.
▼ You are taking other medications.

Pregnancy
▼ The drug may increase the risk of adverse effects on the baby's heart and may prolong labour if taken in the third trimester. Discuss with your physician.

Breast-feeding
▼ The drug passes into the breast milk and may affect the baby. Discuss with your physician.

Infants and children
▼ Not recommended for children under 12 years.

Over 60
▼ Increased likelihood of adverse effects. Reduced dose may therefore be necessary.

Driving and hazardous work
▼ Avoid such activities until you have learned how ketoprofen affects you because the drug can cause dizziness and drowsiness.

Alcohol
▼ Avoid. Alcohol may increase the risk of stomach disorders with ketoprofen.

Surgery and general anesthetics
▼ Ketoprofen may prolong bleeding. Discuss with your physician or dentist before surgery.

POSSIBLE ADVERSE EFFECTS

Gastrointestinal disturbances, such as nausea, abdominal pain, and indigestion, commonly occur with ketoprofen when taken by mouth.

Suppositories may cause rectal irritation. Black or bloodstained feces should be reported promptly.

Symptom/effect	Frequency		Discuss with physician		Stop taking drug now	Call physician now
	Common	Rare	Only if severe	In all cases		
Nausea/vomiting	●		■			
Abdominal pain	●			■		
Heartburn	●		■			
Headache		●	■			
Dizziness/drowsiness		●	■			
Swollen feet or legs		●	■			
Weight gain		●	■			
Rash/itching		●		■	▲	❚
Wheezing/breathlessness		●		■	▲	❚
Black/bloodstained feces		●		■	▲	❚

INTERACTIONS

General note Ketoprofen interacts with a wide range of drugs, such as other NSAIDs including ASA, oral anticoagulants, and corticosteroids, to increase the risk of bleeding and/or stomach ulcers.

Lithium, digoxin, and methotrexate Ketoprofen may raise blood levels of these drugs to an undesirable extent.

Phenytoin Ketoprofen may enhance the effects of phenytoin.

Quinolone antibiotics Ketoprofen may increase the risk of seizures if taken with these drugs.

Antihypertensive drugs Ketoprofen may reduce the beneficial effects of these drugs.

PROLONGED USE

There is an increased risk of bleeding from peptic ulcers and in the bowel with prolonged use of ketoprofen. There is also a small risk of a heart attack or stroke. To minimize these risks, the lowest effective dose is given for the shortest duration.

LACTULOSE

Product names Apo-lactulose, PMS-lactulose, and others
Used in the following combined preparations None

GENERAL INFORMATION

Lactulose is an effective laxative that softens feces by increasing the amount of water in the large intestine. It is used for the relief of constipation and fecal impaction, especially in the elderly.

Lactulose is also used for preventing and treating brain disturbance associated with liver failure, known as hepatic encephalopathy.

Because lactulose acts locally in the large intestine and is not absorbed into the body, it is safer than many other laxatives. However, the drug can cause stomach cramps and flatulence especially at the start of treatment.

INFORMATION FOR USERS

Follow instructions on the label. Call your physician if symptoms worsen.

How taken

Liquid.

Frequency and timing of doses
2 x daily (chronic constipation);
3–4 x daily (liver failure).

Usual adult dosage range
15–30ml daily (chronic constipation);
30–120ml daily (liver failure). May dilute drug with water or juice.

Onset of effect
24–48 hours.

Duration of action
6–18 hours.

Diet advice
Maintaining adequate fluid intake is important.

Storage
Keep in a closed container in a cool, dry place out of the reach of children. Do not store after diluting.

Missed dose
Take as soon as you remember. If your next dose is due within 3 hours, take a single dose now and skip the next.

Stopping the drug
In the treatment of constipation, the drug can be safely stopped as soon as you no longer need it.

Exceeding the dose
An occasional unintentional extra dose is unlikely to be a cause for concern. But if you notice any unusual symptoms, or if a large overdose has been taken, notify your physician.

SPECIAL PRECAUTIONS

Be sure to consult your physician or pharmacist before taking this drug if:
▼ You have severe abdominal pain.
▼ You suffer from lactose intolerance or galactosemia.
▼ You are taking other medications.

Pregnancy
▼ No evidence of risk. Discuss with your physician.

Breast-feeding
▼ No evidence of risk.

Infants and children
▼ Reduced dose necessary.

Over 60
▼ No special problems.

Driving and hazardous work
▼ No known problems.

Alcohol
▼ No known problems.

POSSIBLE ADVERSE EFFECTS

Adverse effects are rarely serious and often disappear when your body adjusts to the medicine. Diarrhea may indicate that the dosage of lactulose is too high.

Symptom/effect	Frequency		Discuss with physician		Stop taking drug now	Call physician now
	Common	Rare	Only if severe	In all cases		
Flatulence/belching	●		■			
Stomach cramps	●		■			
Nausea		●	■			
Abdominal distension		●		■		
Diarrhea		●		■		

PROLONGED USE

In children, prolonged use may contribute to the development of dental caries.

INTERACTIONS

Mesalazine Lactulose may reduce the release of mesalazine at the site of action.

Anticoagulants Lactulose may increase the anticoagulant effect of warfarin.

LAMOTRIGINE

Product name Apo-Lamotrigine, Lamictal
Used in the following combined preparations None

GENERAL INFORMATION

Lamotrigine is an antiepileptic drug that is prescribed, either alone or in combination with other antiepileptic, for the treatment of epilepsy. The drug acts by restoring the balance between excitatory and inhibitory *neurotransmitters* in the brain. Lamotrigine may be less sedating than older antiepileptic, and there is no need for blood tests to determine the level of the drug in the blood.

Lamotrigine may cause a number of minor *adverse effects* (see below), most of which will respond to an adjustment in dosage. Unlike many of the older antiepileptic drugs, lamotrigine does not interfere with the action of the oral contraceptive pill.

INFORMATION FOR USERS

Your drug prescription is tailored for you. Do not alter dosage without checking with your physician.

How taken

Tablets, dispersible/chewable tablets.

Frequency and timing of doses
1–2 x daily.

Usual adult dosage range
100–500mg daily, depending on which other antiepileptic drugs are being taken (100– 200mg with valproic acid). Smaller doses are used at start of treatment.

Onset of effect
Approximately 5 days at a constant dose.

Duration of action
Up to 24 hours.

Diet advice
None.

Storage
Keep in a closed container in a cool, dry place out of the reach of children.

Missed dose
Take as soon as you remember. If your next dose is due within 2 hours, take a single dose now and skip the next.

Stopping the drug
Do not stop taking the drug without consulting your physician, who will supervise a gradual reduction in dosage over a period of about two weeks. Abrupt cessation increases the risk of rebound seizures.

Exceeding the dose
An occasional unintentional extra dose is unlikely to be a cause for concern. Large overdoses may cause sedation, double vision, loss of muscular coordination, nausea, and vomiting. Contact your physician immediately.

SPECIAL PRECAUTIONS

Be sure to tell your physician if:
▼ You have long-term liver or kidney problems.
▼ You are or intend to become pregnant.
▼ You suffer from thalassemia.
▼ You have a heart condition.
▼ You are taking other medications.

Pregnancy
▼ Safety in pregnancy not established. Some abnormalities reported when used in the first trimester. Discuss with your physician.

Breast-feeding
▼ The drug passes into the breast milk and may affect the baby. Discuss with your physician.

Infants and children
▼ Not recommended under 2 years. Not recommended as a single therapy under 12 years. Doses may be relatively higher than adult doses due to increased metabolism.

Over 60s
▼ No special problems.

Driving and hazardous work
▼ Your underlying condition, in addition to the possibility of sedation, dizziness, and vision disturbances while taking lamotrigine, may make such activities inadvisable. Discuss with your physician.

Alcohol
▼ Alcohol may increase the adverse effects of this drug.

POSSIBLE ADVERSE EFFECTS

The most common *side effects* are skin rash, nausea, headache, tiredness, insomnia, blurred or double vision, dizziness, agitation, confusion, and poor muscle coordination. Although common, a rash may indicate a serious hypersenstivity reaction, especially when accompanied by mouth ulcers; call your physician immediately. If sore throat, flu-like symptoms, or persistent or unusual bruising or bleeding occur, call your physician immediately.

Symptom/effect	Frequency		Discuss with physician		Stop taking drug now	Call physician now
	Common	Rare	Only if severe	In all cases		
Headache	●		■			
Rash	●			■		▮
Blurred vision/double vision	●			■		
Tremor/incoordination	●			■		
Nausea		●	■			
Flu-like symptoms		●		■		▮
Sore throat/bruising		●		■		▮
Swelling around the face		●		■		▮

INTERACTIONS

Valproic acid increases and prolongs the effectiveness of lamotrigine. A reduced dose of lamotrigine will be used.

Antidepressants, antipsychotics, mefloquine, and chloroquine may counteract the antiepileptic effect of lamotrigine.

Carbamazepine may reduce lamotrigine blood levels, but lamotrigine may increase the side effects of carbamazepine.

Phenytoin and phenobarbital may decrease blood levels of lamotrigine so a higher dose of lamotrigine may be needed.

PROLONGED USE

No special problems.

LANSOPRAZOLE

Product name Apo-Lansoprazole, Prevacid, and others
Used in the following combined preparation Hp-PAC

GENERAL INFORMATION

Lansoprazole is an anti-ulcer drug belonging to the group called proton pump inhibitors (p.95). It is used to treat peptic ulcers, gastro-esophageal reflux (in which the stomach acid rises into and irritates the esophagus), and Zollinger-Ellison syndrome (in which large quantities of stomach acid are produced, leading to ulceration).

Lansoprazole may be used alone or, for peptic ulcers, with two antibiotics, as part of a seven-day regimen to eradicate *Helicobacter pylori* bacteria, the main cause of such ulcers.

Because lansoprazole may mask the symptoms of stomach cancer, it is prescribed only when the possibility of this disease has been ruled out.

INFORMATION FOR USERS

Your drug prescription is tailored for you. Do not alter dosage without checking with your physician.

How taken

Capsules, oral suspension.

Frequency and timing of doses
1–2 x daily a half hour before eating.

Usual adult dosage range
Benign gastric ulcer 15–30mg daily in the morning.
NSAID-associated gastric ulcer 15–30mg daily in the morning.
Duodenal ulcer 15mg daily in the morning.
H. pylori-associated ulcer 30mg daily with appropriate antibiotics.

Onset of effect
1–2 hours.

Duration of action
24 hours.

Diet advice
None, although spicy foods and alcohol may exacerbate the condition being treated.

Storage
Keep in a closed container in a cool, dry place out of the reach of children.

Missed dose
Take as soon as you remember. If your next dose is due within 8 hours, take a single dose now and skip the next.

Stopping the drug
Do not stop taking the drug without consulting your physician; symptoms may recur.

Exceeding the dose
An occasional unintentional extra dose is unlikely to be a cause for concern. But if you notice any unusual symptoms, or if a large overdose has been taken, notify your physician.

POSSIBLE ADVERSE EFFECTS

Common *side effects* include headache, indigestion, and diarrhea. A sore throat, mouth, or tongue are very rare but should be reported to your physician at once.

Symptom/effect	Frequency		Discuss with physician		Stop taking drug now	Call physician now
	Common	Rare	Only if severe	In all cases		
Headache/dizziness	●		■			
Diarrhea/constipation	●		■			
Flatulence/abdominal pain	●		■			
Fatigue/malaise		●	■			
Bruising/swollen extremities		●		■		
Rash/itching		●		■	▲	
Sore throat/mouth/tongue		●		■	▲	▪

INTERACTIONS

Oral contraceptives, phenytoin, carbamazepine, warfarin, and theophylline Lansoprazole may reduce the effect of these drugs.

Antacids and sucralfate These drugs may reduce the absorption of, and should not be taken within an hour of, lansoprazole.

Tacrolimus Lansoprazole may increase the blood levels of tacrolimus.

Atazanavir Lansoprazole may decrease the effect of atazanavir; the two drugs should not be taken together.

SPECIAL PRECAUTIONS

Be sure to tell your physician if:
▼ You have liver problems.
▼ You are taking other medications.

Pregnancy
▼ Safety not established. Discuss with your physician.

Breast-feeding
▼ Safety not established. Discuss with your physician.

Infants and children
▼ Not recommended.

Over 60
▼ No special problems.

Driving and hazardous work
▼ No special problems.

Alcohol
▼ Avoid. Alcohol may aggravate your condition and reduce the beneficial effects of lansoprazole.

PROLONGED USE

Long-term use of lansoprazole may increase the risk of certain intestinal infections (such as *Salmonella* and *Clostridium difficile* infections) because of the loss of natural protection against such infections provided by stomach acid. Any diarrhea should be reported to your physician. Prolonged use may also increase the risk of hip fractures in women.

LATANOPROST

Product names Apo-Latanoprost, CO Latanoprost, GD-Latanoprost, Xalatan
Used in the following combined preparation Xalacom

GENERAL INFORMATION

Latanoprost is a synthetic derivative of the prostaglandin dinoprost, which constricts the smooth muscle in the blood vessels and airways. Latanoprost is used as eye drops to reduce pressure inside the eye in open angle (chronic) glaucoma (p.156) by increasing the outflow of fluid from the eye. The drug is a first-line option, and works slightly better than non-selective beta blockers (for example timolol, p.451). Sometimes, combined eye drops of latanoprost and timolol may be prescribed when

timolol alone is not adequately controlling the pressure.

Latanoprost eye drops can gradually increase the amount of brown pigment in the eye, darkening the iris. This will be particularly noticeable if only one eye needs treatment. Irises of mixed coloration are especially susceptible; pure blue eyes do not seem to be affected. Latanoprost has also been reported to cause darkening, thickening, and lengthening of eyelashes.

QUICK REFERENCE

Drug group Drugs for glaucoma (p.156)

Overdose danger rating Medium

Dependence rating Low

Prescription needed Yes

Available as generic Yes

INFORMATION FOR USERS

Your drug prescription is tailored for you. Do not alter dosage without checking with your physician.

How taken

Eye drops.

Frequency and timing of doses
1x daily, in the evening.

Usual adult dosage range
1 drop per eye, daily.

Onset of effect
15–30 minutes.

Duration of action
24 hours.

Diet advice
None.

Storage
Keep the eyedrops in the outer cardboard package to protect from light. Store in a refrigerator between 2°C and 8°C, out of the reach of children.

Missed dose
Use the next dose as normal.

Stopping the drug
Do not stop the drug without consulting your physician. Symptoms may recur.

Exceeding the dose
An occasional unintentional extra application is unlikely to cause problems. Excessive use may irritate the eye and produce *adverse effects* in other parts of the body. Notify your physician.

POSSIBLE ADVERSE EFFECTS

Darkening of the iris is very common. Changes to the eyelashes occur almost as often.

Irritation of the eye is also a very common adverse effect.

Symptom/effect	Frequency		Discuss with physician		Stop taking drug now	Call physician now
	Common	Rare	Only if severe	In all cases		
Darkening of iris	●		■			
Eye irritation	●		■			
Eyelash changes	●		■			
Eye pain	●			■		
Bloodshot eye	●			■		
Inflamed eyelids	●			■		
Eye/facial swelling		●		■		
Chest pains		●		■	▲	
Wheezing/breathing difficulty		●		■	▲	

INTERACTIONS

Thiomersal-containing eye drops should not be used within 5 minutes of using latanoprost (thiomersal is a preservative used in some eye drops).

SPECIAL PRECAUTIONS

Be sure to consult your physician or pharmacist before taking this drug if:
▼ You wear contact lenses.
▼ You are allergic to benzalkonium chloride or latanoprost.
▼ You have heart problems.
▼ You have asthma.
▼ You are taking other medications.

 Pregnancy
▼ Safety not established. Prostaglandins may affect the fetus.

 Breast-feeding
▼ The drug may pass into the breast milk and may affect the baby. Discuss with your physician.

 Infants and children
▼ Not recommended.

 Over 60
▼ No special problems.

 Driving and hazardous work
▼ The eye drops may cause temporary blurring of vision. Avoid driving and hazardous work until vision has returned to normal.

 Alcohol
▼ No known problems.

PROLONGED USE

No known problems apart from changes to iris pigment and eyelash colour.

Monitoring Although there should be no problems with long-term use, your physician will continue to monitor eye pigmentation as well as control of the glaucoma. The effect of increased pigmentation beyond 5 years is unknown.

LEVODOPA

Product name None
Used in the following combined preparations Apo-Levocarb, Prolopa, Sinemet, Sinemet CR, Stalevo, and others

GENERAL INFORMATION

The treatment of Parkinson's disease underwent dramatic change in the 1960s with the introduction of levodopa. Since the body can transform levodopa into dopamine, a chemical messenger in the brain the absence or shortage of which causes Parkinson's disease (see p.71), rapid improvements in control were obtained. These improvements were not a cure of the disease but a marked relief of symptoms.

However, it was found that, while levodopa was effective, it produced severe *side effects*, such as nausea, dizziness, and palpitations. Even when treatment was initiated gradually, it was difficult to balance the benefits against the adverse reactions.

Today the drug is combined with carbidopa or benserazide, both of which enhance the effects of levodopa in the brain and also help to reduce the side effects of levodopa.

INFORMATION FOR USERS

Your drug prescription is tailored for you. Do not alter dosage without checking with your physician.

How taken

Tablets, controlled-release tablets, capsules.

Frequency and timing of doses
3–6 x daily with food or milk.

Usual adult dosage range
125–500mg initially, increased until benefits and side effects are balanced.

Onset of effect
Within 1 hour.

Duration of action
2–12 hours.

Diet advice
None.

Storage
Keep in a closed container in a cool, dry place out of the reach of children. Protect from light.

Missed dose
Take as soon as you remember. If your next dose is due within 2 hours, take a single dose now and skip the next.

Stopping the drug
Do not stop taking the drug without consulting your physician; stopping the drug may lead to severe worsening of the underlying condition.

Exceeding the dose
An occasional unintentional extra dose is unlikely to cause problems. Larger overdoses may cause vomiting or drowsiness. Notify your physician.

SPECIAL PRECAUTIONS

Be sure to tell your physician if:
▼ You have heart problems.
▼ You have long-term liver or kidney problems.
▼ You have epilepsy.
▼ You have had glaucoma.
▼ You have a peptic ulcer.
▼ You have diabetes or any other endocrine disorder.
▼ You have any serious mental illness.
▼ You are taking other medications.

Pregnancy
▼ Unlikely to be required. Safety not established. Discuss with your physician.

Breast-feeding
▼ Unlikely to be required. May suppress milk production. Discuss with your physician.

Infants and children
▼ Not normally used in children (and rarely given to patients under 25 years).

Over 60
▼ No special problems.

Driving and hazardous work
▼ Your underlying condition, as well as the possibility of levodopa causing fainting and dizziness, may make such activities inadvisable. Discuss with your physician.

Alcohol
▼ No known problems.

POSSIBLE ADVERSE EFFECTS

Adverse effects of levodopa are related to dosage levels. At the start of treatment, on a low dosage, unwanted effects are likely to be mild. Such effects may increase in severity as dosage is increased. All adverse effects should be discussed with your physician.

Symptom/effect	Frequency		Discuss with physician		Stop taking drug now	Call physician now
	Common	Rare	Only if severe	In all cases		
Digestive disturbance	●			■		
Abnormal movement	●			■		
Nervousness/agitation	●			■		
Dark urine	●		■			
Dizziness/fainting		●		■		
Confusion/vivid dreams		●		■		
Palpitations		●		■	▲	■

INTERACTIONS

Antidepressant drugs Levodopa may interact with monoamine oxidase inhibitors (MAOIs) to cause a dangerous rise in blood pressure. It may also interact with tricyclic antidepressants.

Pyridoxine (vitamin B₆) Excessive intake of this vitamin may reduce the effect of levodopa if levodopa is used on its own.

Iron Absorption of levodopa may be reduced by iron.

Antipsychotic drugs Some of these drugs may reduce the effect of levodopa.

Bupropion The side effects of levodopa will be increased if used with this drug.

PROLONGED USE

Effectiveness usually declines in time, necessitating increased dosage and/or addition of other medications. The adverse effects may become so severe that ultimately the drug must be stopped.

LEVOFLOXACIN

Product names CO Levofloxacin, Levaquin, Sandoz Levofloxacin, and others
Used in the following combined preparations None

GENERAL INFORMATION

Levofloxacin is a quinolone antibacterial drug used for soft-tissue and respiratory and urinary tract infections that have not responded to other *antibiotics*.

The drug is usually prescribed in the form of tablets, but it is administered by intravenous *infusion* to people with serious *systemic* infections or to those who cannot take drugs by mouth. Like other quinolones, levofloxacin may occasionally cause tendon inflammation and damage, especially in the elderly, in those taking corticosteroids, and in patients undergoing certain transplants. You should, therefore, report tendon pain or inflammation to your physician straight away and stop taking the drug. The affected limb or limbs should be rested until the symptoms have subsided.

INFORMATION FOR USERS

Your drug prescription is tailored for you. Do not alter dosage without checking with your physician.

How taken

Tablets, injection.

Frequency and timing of doses
Once daily for 7–14 days depending on infection (tablets).

Usual adult dosage range
250–750mg daily.

Onset of effect
1 hour.

Duration of action
12–24 hours.

Diet advice
Drink plenty of fluids.

Storage
Keep in a closed container in a cool, dry place out of the reach of children.

Missed dose
Take as soon as you remember, then take your next dose when it is due.

Stopping the drug
Take the full course. Even if you feel better, the original infection may still be present, and symptoms may recur if treatment is stopped too soon.

Exceeding the dose
An occasional unintentional extra dose is unlikely to cause problems. Larger overdoses may cause mental disturbances and seizures. Notify your physician.

SPECIAL PRECAUTIONS

Be sure to tell your physician if:
▼ You have kidney problems.
▼ You suffer from epilepsy.
▼ You have a personal or family history of heart disease.
▼ You have myasthenia gravis.
▼ You have porphyria.
▼ You have diabetes.
▼ You are taking ASA or another NSAID.
▼ You have had a previous allergic reaction to a quinolone antibacterial.
▼ You have had a previous tendon problem with a quinolone.
▼ You are taking other medications.

Pregnancy
▼ Safety not established. Discuss with your physician.

Breast-feeding
▼ Safety not established. Discuss with your physician.

Infants and children
▼ Not recommended.

Over 60
▼ Reduced dose may be necessary. Tendon damage is more likely over the age of 60.

Driving and hazardous work
▼ Avoid such activities until you have learned how levofloxacin affects you because the drug can cause dizziness, drowsiness, and visual disturbances.

Alcohol
▼ Avoid. Alcohol may increase the sedative effects of levofloxacin.

Sunlight
▼ Avoid exposure to strong sunlight or artificial ultraviolet rays because photosensitization may occur.

POSSIBLE ADVERSE EFFECTS

Given by injection, levofloxacin may cause palpitations and a fall in blood pressure.

Nausea and vomiting are the most common *side effects* of the drug taken by mouth.

Symptom/effect	Frequency		Discuss with physician		Stop taking drug now	Call physician now
	Common	Rare	Only if severe	In all cases		
Nausea/vomiting	●		■			
Diarrhea/abdominal pain	●		■			
Headache/dizziness		●	■			
Skin rash/itching		●	■			
Drowsiness/restlessness		●	■			
Jaundice		●		■	▲	
Confusion/hallucinations		●		■	▲	
Fever/allergic reaction		●		■	▲	
Painful or inflamed tendons		●	■	▲		■

INTERACTIONS

Non-steroidal anti-inflammatory drugs (NSAIDs) and theophylline There is an increased risk of convulsions when these drugs are taken with levofloxacin.

Anticoagulants The effect of these drugs may be increased by levofloxacin.

Antacids, adsorbents, sucralfate, iron, and zinc These drugs may reduce the absorption of levofloxacin. Do not take antacids within 2 hours of taking levofloxacin tablets.

PROLONGED USE

Levofloxacin is not usually prescribed for long-term use.

LEVONORGESTREL

Product names Plan B, Mirena, NorLevo
Used in the following combined preparations Alesse, Aviane, Min-Ovral, Triquilar, and others

GENERAL INFORMATION

Levonorgestrel is a synthetic *hormone* similar to progesterone, a natural female sex hormone. The drug's primary use is in oral contraceptives; it thickens the mucus at the neck of the uterus (cervix), thereby making it difficult for sperm to enter the uterus.

Levonorgestrel is available in combined oral contraceptives (COCs) with an estrogen drug. It is also used as an emergency contraceptive (Plan B) and as part of a contraceptive intrauterine system (Mirena).

Serious *adverse effects* are rare. When it is used without an estrogen, menstrual irregularities or "breakthrough" bleeding are common.

INFORMATION FOR USERS

Your drug prescription is tailored for you. Do not alter dosage without checking with your physician.

How taken

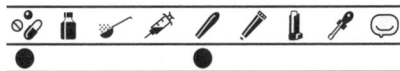

Tablets, intrauterine device (IUD).

Frequency and timing of doses
COC: Once daily, at the same time each day.

Usual adult dosage range
Oral contraceptive 0.5–1mg with estrogen.
Post-coital contraceptive 1.5mg.

Onset of effect
Levonorgestrel starts to act within 4 hours, but contraceptive protection may not be fully effective for 14 days, depending on which day of the cycle the tablets are started.

Duration of action
24 hours. Some effects, not including contraception, may persist for up to 3 months after levonorgestrel is stopped.

Diet advice
None.

Storage
Keep in a closed container in a cool, dry place out of the reach of children.

Missed dose
If a tablet is delayed by 3 hours or more, regard it as a missed dose. See What to do if you miss a pill (p.151).

Stopping the drug
The drug can be safely stopped as soon as contraceptive protection is no longer required. For treatment of menopausal symptoms, consult your physician before stopping the drug.

Exceeding the dose
An occasional unintentional extra dose is unlikely to be a cause for concern. But if you notice any unusual symptoms, or if a large overdose has been taken, notify your physician.

SPECIAL PRECAUTIONS

Be sure to consult your physician or pharmacist before taking this drug if:
▼ You have a history of breast cancer.
▼ You have liver or kidney problems, heart failure, hypertension, diabetes, asthma, epilepsy, porphyria, or sickle cell anemia.
▼ You have abnormal vaginal bleeding.
▼ You have ever had migraines, severe headaches, blood clots, or a stroke.
▼ You are taking other medications.

Pregnancy
▼ No conclusive evidence of harm. Discuss with your physician.

Breast-feeding
▼ The drug passes into the breast milk, but problems are unlikely. Discuss with your physician.

Infants and children
▼ Not prescribed.

Over 60
▼ Not prescribed.

Driving and hazardous work
▼ No known problems.

Alcohol
▼ No known problems.

Surgery or general anesthetics
▼ The drug should be stopped before surgery.

POSSIBLE ADVERSE EFFECTS

Menstrual irregularities (blood spotting between menstrual periods or absence of menstruation) are the most common side effects of levonorgestrel alone. Lower abdominal pain is a rare effect but may indicate pregnancy; consult your physician promptly.

Symptom/effect	Frequency		Discuss with physician		Stop taking drug now	Call physician now
	Common	Rare	Only if severe	In all cases		
Swollen feet/ankles	●		■			
Weight gain	●		■			
Irregular vaginal bleeding	●			■		
Nausea/vomiting		●	■			
Breast tenderness		●	■			
Depression/headache		●		■	■	
Lower abdominal pain		●		■	■	■

INTERACTIONS

General note The beneficial effects of many drugs may be affected by levonorgestrel. Many others may reduce contraceptive protection. Inform your physician before taking any other medication.

PROLONGED USE

In a COC, the drug increases the thrombosis and breast cancer risk but reduces the endometrial and ovarian cancer risk. In a POP, it carries a small increased risk of breast cancer. As part of HRT, it increases the risk of thrombosis and breast cancer. HRT is advised only for short-term use around menopause.

Monitoring Blood pressure checks and mammograms may be performed.

LEVOTHYROXINE

Product names Eltroxin, Euthyrox, Synthroid, and others
Used in the following combined preparations None

GENERAL INFORMATION

Levothyroxine is the main *hormone* produced by the thyroid gland. A deficiency of the natural hormone causes hypothyroidism, which is associated with symptoms of weight gain and slowing of body functions. A synthetic preparation is used to replace the natural hormone when it is deficient.

Levothyroxine is given (in high doses) to people who have had thyroid cancer.

Doses of levothyroxine are usually increased gradually to help prevent *adverse effects*. Particular care is required in patients with heart problems such as angina.

QUICK REFERENCE

Drug group Thyroid hormones (p.130)

Overdose danger rating Medium

Dependence rating Low

Prescription needed Yes

Available as generic Yes

INFORMATION FOR USERS

Your drug prescription is tailored for you. Do not alter dosage without checking with your physician.

How taken

Tablets, liquid.

Frequency and timing of doses
Once daily.

Usual dosage range
Adults Doses of 25–100mcg daily, increased at 3–4-week intervals as required. The usual maximum dose is 200mcg daily.

Onset of effect
Within 48 hours. Full beneficial effects may not be felt for several weeks.

Duration of action
1–3 weeks.

Diet advice
None.

Storage
Keep in a closed container in a cool, dry place out of the reach of children. Protect from light.

Missed dose
Take as soon as you remember. If your next dose is due within 8 hours, take a single dose now and skip the next.

Stopping the drug
Do not stop the drug without consulting your physician; symptoms may recur.

Exceeding the dose
An occasional unintentional extra dose is unlikely to cause problems. Large overdoses may cause palpitations during the next few days. Notify your physician.

SPECIAL PRECAUTIONS

Be sure to tell your physician if:
▼ You have high blood pressure.
▼ You have heart problems.
▼ You have diabetes.
▼ You are taking other medications.

Pregnancy
▼ No evidence of risk, but dosage adjustment may be necessary.

Breast-feeding
▼ The drug passes into the breast milk, but at normal doses adverse effects on the baby are unlikely. Discuss with your physician.

Infants and children
▼ Dosage depends on age and weight.

Over 60
▼ Reduced dose usually necessary.

Driving and hazardous work
▼ No known problems.

Alcohol
▼ No known problems.

POSSIBLE ADVERSE EFFECTS

Adverse effects are rare with levothyroxine and are usually the result of overdosage causing thyroid overactivity. These effects diminish as the dose is lowered. Too low a dose of levothyroxine may cause signs of thyroid underactivity.

Symptom/effect	Frequency		Discuss with physician		Stop taking drug now	Call physician now
	Common	Rare	Only if severe	In all cases		
Anxiety/nervousness		●		■		
Diarrhea		●		■		
Weight loss		●		■		
Sweating/flushing		●		■		
Muscle cramps/tremor		●		■		
Insomnia		●		■		
Palpitations/chest pain		●		■		■

PROLONGED USE

No special problems.

Monitoring Periodic tests of thyroid function are usually required.

INTERACTIONS

Oral anticoagulants Levothyroxine may increase the effect of these drugs.

Antidiabetic agents The doses of these drugs may need increasing once levothyroxine treatment is started.

Cholestyramine and sucralfate may both reduce absorption of levothyroxine.

Amiodarone may affect thyroid activity and levothyroxine dosage may need adjustment.

Antiepileptic drugs These drugs may reduce the effect of levothyroxine.

Oral contraceptives may increase levothyroxine requirements.

Antacids and calcium, taken at the same time, may decrease the absorption of levothyroxine.

LIRAGLUTIDE

Product name Victoza
Used in the following combined preparations None

GENERAL INFORMATION

Liraglutide is used in the management of Type 2 diabetes. This drug is a glucagon-like peptide-1 (GLP-1) *receptor agonist* and works by mimicking certain natural substances, causing the release of more insulin from the pancreas when the blood sugar is high. It is used in combination with oral medications such as metformin or a sulfonylurea, when these medications alone don't provide adequate control of blood sugar. Avoid dehydration while on this medication.

Used needles should be discarded in a puncture-resistant container as recommended by your health care provider.

QUICK REFERENCE

Drug group Antihyperglycemic drugs for diabetes (p.128)

Overdose danger rating Medium

Dependence rating Low

Prescription needed No

Available as generic No

INFORMATION FOR USERS

Your drug prescription is tailored for you. Do not alter dosage without checking with your physician.

How taken

Subcutaneous injection in thigh, abdomen, or upper arm.

Frequency and timing of doses
Once daily.

Usual adult dosage range
0.6mg daily for the first week; may be increased up to 1.8mg daily.

Onset of effect
8 hours.

Duration of action
Up to 24 hours.

Diet advice
Follow your recommended diabetic diet.

Storage
Refrigerate between 2 and 8°C. Do not freeze. Protect from light. After first use, it can be stored up to 30 days at room temperature (not above 30°C) or in the refrigerator.

Missed dose
If you miss a dose, take your usual dose on the next day. Do not take an extra dose or double up on a dose.

Stopping the drug
Do not stop taking the drug without consulting your physician; symptoms may worsen.

Exceeding the dose
Notify your physician even if you don't have symptoms. If you notice any unusual symptoms, or if a large overdose has been taken, seek immediate help.

SPECIAL PRECAUTIONS

Be sure to tell your physician if:
▼ You have a lung disorder such as asthma or bronchitis.
▼ You have diabetes, thyroid problems, or Raynaud's phenomenon (coldness or spasm in hands/feet).
▼ You have low blood pressure or heart rate.
▼ You have long-term liver problems.
▼ You have other heart conditions.
▼ You have Type-1 diabetes.
▼ You have had diabetic ketoacidosis.
▼ You are on insulin or a sulfonylurea for diabetes.
▼ You have a personal or a family history of medullary thyroid carcinoma or multiple endocrine neoplasia syndrome Type 2.
▼ You are taking other medications.

Pregnancy
▼ Avoid use in pregnancy.

Breast-feeding
▼ Avoid use while breast-feeding.

Infants and children
▼ Safety and efficacy not established in patients under 18 years of age.

Over 60
▼ No problems.

Driving and hazardous work
▼ The drug can cause drowsiness. Do not drive a car or operate machinery until you feel you are mentally alert.

Alcohol
▼ Do not take with alcohol.

POSSIBLE ADVERSE EFFECTS

If you experience sudden or severe stomach pain, nausea, lightheadedness, fever, sore throat, or symptoms of low blood sugar, call your physician right away.

Symptom/effect	Frequency		Discuss with physician		Stop taking drug now	Call physician now
	Common	Rare	Only if severe	In all cases		
Nausea/vomiting when starting therapy	●			■		
Dyspepsia/constipation	●			■		
Diarrhea	●			■		
Injection site irritation		●		■		
Low blood sugar symptoms		●		■		▮
Severe nausea/vomiting/ abdominal pain		●		■		▮
Chest pain or heart rhythm disturbances/dizziness		●			▲	▮
Lump in the neck/hoarsenes/ difficulty swallowing		●		■		▮

INTERACTIONS

General note Liraglutide may reduce the rate of absorption of some oral medications.

Sulfonylurea drugs such as glyburide, glipizide, and gliclazide may increase the risk of low blood sugar when administered with liraglutide. Dose adjustment may be required.

Somatropin may decrease the effectiveness of liraglutide.

PROLONGED USE

Monitoring Careful monitoring of the individual by his/her physician and other team members is required.

LISINOPRIL

Product names Prinivil, Zestril
Used in the following combined preparations Zestoretic Tab, Prinzide

GENERAL INFORMATION

Lisinopril is an ACE inhibitor drug used in the treatment of high blood pressure (including that caused by diabetic kidney problems), heart failure, and following a heart attack. It works by relaxing the muscles in blood vessel walls, allowing them to dilate (widen), thereby easing blood flow.

Lisinopril can initially cause a rapid fall in blood pressure, especially when taken with a diuretic drug. Therefore, treatment for heart failure is usually started under close medical supervision, in hospital in severe cases. The first dose is usually very small, and should be taken while lying down, preferably at bedtime.

INFORMATION FOR USERS

Your drug prescription is tailored for you. Do not alter dosage without checking with your physician.

How taken

Tablets.

Frequency and timing of doses
Once daily.

Usual adult dosage range
Hypertension 2.5mg (starting dose) up to 40mg.
Heart failure/diabetic nephropathy 2.5mg (starting dose) up to 20mg.
Prevention of further heart attacks 2.5–5mg (starting dose) up to 10mg.

Onset of effect
1–2 hours; full beneficial effect may take several weeks.

Duration of action
12–24 hours.

Diet advice
A reduced salt diet may be recommended to help control blood pressure.

Storage
Keep in a closed container in a cool, dry place out of the reach of children.

Missed dose
Take as soon as you remember. If your next dose is due within 8 hours, take a single dose now and skip the next.

Stopping the drug
Do not stop taking the drug without consulting your physician. Stopping the drug may lead to worsening of the underlying condition.

Exceeding the dose
An occasional unintentional extra dose is unlikely to be a cause for concern. Larger overdoses may cause dizziness or fainting. Notify your physician.

POSSIBLE ADVERSE EFFECTS

Most common *side effects* of lisinopril are persistent dry cough and a rash. A reduction of dosage may minimize these effects.

Symptom/effect	Frequency		Discuss with physician		Stop taking drug now	Call physician now
	Common	Rare	Only if severe	In all cases		
Rash	●			■		
Persistent dry cough	●			■		
Dizziness		●		■		
Sore throat/fever		●		■		
Swelling of mouth/lips		●		■	▲	❙
Breathing difficulty		●		■	▲	❙

INTERACTIONS

Potassium supplements, potassium-sparing diuretics, and cyclosporine Taken with lisinopril, these drugs increase the risk of high blood potassium levels.

Non-steroidal anti-inflammatory drugs (NSAIDs) Some of these drugs may reduce the effect of lisinopril, and the risk of kidney damage is increased.

Vasodilators, diuretics, and other drugs for hypertension These drugs may increase the blood-pressure-lowering effect of lisinopril.

Lithium Blood levels of lithium may be increased by lisinopril.

Insulin and antidiabetic drugs Lisinopril may increase the effect of these drugs.

SPECIAL PRECAUTIONS

Be sure to tell your physician if:
▼ You have had angioedema or a previous allergic reaction to ACE inhibitors.
▼ You have long-term kidney or liver problems.
▼ You have heart problems.
▼ You are pregnant or intend to become pregnant.
▼ You are taking other medications.

Pregnancy
▼ Not prescribed. May harm the developing baby.

Breast-feeding
▼ Safety not established. Discuss with your physician.

Infants and children
▼ Not recommended.

Over 60
▼ Reduced dose may be necessary.

Driving and hazardous work
▼ Avoid such activities until you have learned how lisinopril affects you because the drug can cause dizziness and fainting.

Alcohol
▼ Avoid. Alcohol may increase the blood-pressure-lowering and adverse effects of this drug.

PROLONGED USE

No problems expected.

Monitoring Periodic checks on potassium levels, white blood cell count, kidney function and urine are usually performed.

LITHIUM

Product names Carbolith, Lithane, Litmax, and others
Used in the following combined preparations None

GENERAL INFORMATION

Lithium, the lightest known metal, is used to treat acute manic episodes and to help stabilize mood in patients with bipolar disorder. Lithium decreases the intensity and frequency of the swings from extreme excitement to deep depression that characterize the disorder.

It is sometimes used along with an antidepressant drug for depression that has not responded to an antidepressant alone. Treatment with lithium may be started in hospital for the seriously ill. Careful monitoring with blood tests is required because high levels of lithium can cause serious *adverse effects*. It may take two to three weeks for any apparent benefit. Lithium is often used in conjunction with other mood-stabilizing drugs such as antipsychotics and antiepileptics.

QUICK REFERENCE

Drug group Antimanic drugs (p.69)
Overdose danger rating High
Dependence rating Low
Prescription needed Yes
Available as generic Yes

INFORMATION FOR USERS

Your drug prescription is tailored for you. Do not alter dosage without checking with your physician.

How taken

Capsules, tablets, SR-tablets, liquid.

Frequency and timing of doses
1–3 x daily with meals. Always take the same brand of lithium to ensure a consistent effect; change of brand must be closely supervised.

Usual adult dosage range
0.6–1.8g daily. Dosage may vary according to individual response and blood levels.

Onset of effect
Effects may be noticed in 3–5 days. Typical treatment trials are usually 2 weeks at therapeutic doses.

Duration of action
18–36 hours. Some effect may last for several days.

Diet advice
Lithium levels in the blood are affected by the amount of salt in the body, so do not suddenly alter the amount of salt in your diet. Be sure to drink plenty of fluids, especially in hot weather.

Storage
Keep in a closed container in a cool, dry place out of the reach of children.

Missed dose
Take as soon as you remember. If your next dose is due within 4 hours, take a single dose now and skip the next.

Stopping the drug
Do not stop the drug without consulting your physician; symptoms may recur.

OVERDOSE ACTION

 Seek immediate medical advice in all cases. Take emergency action if convulsions or loss of consciousness occur.

See Drug poisoning emergency guide (p.526).

SPECIAL PRECAUTIONS

Be sure to tell your physician if:
▼ You have long-term liver or kidney problems.
▼ You have heart or circulation problems.
▼ You have an overactive thyroid gland.
▼ You have myasthenia gravis.
▼ You have Addison's disease.
▼ You are taking other medications.

 Pregnancy
▼ Not usually prescribed. May cause defects in the unborn baby. Discuss with your physician.

 Breast-feeding
▼ The drug passes into the breast milk and may affect the baby. Discuss with your physician.

 Infants and children
▼ Not recommended.

 Over 60
▼ Increased likelihood of adverse effects. Reduced dose may therefore be necessary.

 Driving and hazardous work
▼ Avoid such activities until you have learned how lithium affects you because the drug can cause reduced alertness.

 **Alcohol**
▼ Avoid. Alcohol may increase the sedative effects of this drug.

POSSIBLE ADVERSE EFFECTS

Many of the symptoms below are signs of a high lithium level in the blood. Stop taking the drug and seek medical advice promptly if you notice any of these symptoms.

Symptom/effect	Frequency		Discuss with physician		Stop taking drug now	Call physician now
	Common	Rare	Only if severe	In all cases		
Nausea/vomiting/diarrhea	●			■	▲	
Tremor	●			■		
Weight gain		●	■			
Drowsiness/lethargy		●		■	▲	
Blurred vision		●		■	▲	
Rash		●		■	▲	
Muscle weakness/slurred speech		●		■	▲	
Increase in urine/thirst		●		■		

INTERACTIONS

General note Many drugs interact with lithium. Do not take any over-the-counter or prescription drugs without consulting your physician or pharmacist. Acetaminophen should be used in preference to other analgesics for everyday pain relief.

PROLONGED USE

Prolonged use may lead to kidney and thyroid problems. Treatment for periods of longer than 5 years is not normally advised unless the benefits are significant and tests show no sign of reduced kidney function. When the decision is made to stop lithium, it should be reduced gradually.

Monitoring Once stabilized, lithium levels should be checked every 3 months. Thyroid function should be checked every 6–12 months. Kidney function should also be monitored regularly.

LOPERAMIDE

Product names Imodium, Loperacap, and others
Used in the following combined preparation Imodium Advanced

GENERAL INFORMATION

Loperamide is an antidiarrheal drug available in tablet, capsule, or liquid form. It reduces the loss of water and salts from the bowel and slows bowel activity, resulting in the passage of firmer bowel movements at less frequent intervals.

A fast-acting drug, loperamide is widely prescribed for both sudden and recurrent bouts of diarrhea. However, it is not generally recommended for diarrhea caused by infection because it may delay the expulsion of harmful substances from the bowel. Loperamide is often prescribed for people who have had a colostomy or an ileostomy, to reduce fluid loss from the stoma (outlet).

Adverse effects from this drug are rare. It can be purchased over-the-counter in a pharmacy.

QUICK REFERENCE

Drug group Antidiarrheal drugs (p.96)

Overdose danger rating Medium

Dependence rating Low

Prescription needed No

Available as generic Yes

INFORMATION FOR USERS

Follow instructions on the label. Call your physician if symptoms worsen.

How taken

Tablets, caplets, quick dissolve tablets, chewable tablets, liquid.

Frequency and timing of doses
Acute diarrhea Take a double dose at start of treatment, then a single dose after each loose feces, up to the maximum daily dose.
Chronic diarrhea 2 x daily.

Usual dosage range
Acute diarrhea 4mg (starting dose), then 2mg after each loose bowel movement (up to 16mg daily); usual dose 6–8mg daily. Use for up to 5 days only (3 days only for children 4–8 years), then consult your physician.
Chronic diarrhea 4–8mg daily (up to 16mg daily).

Onset of effect
Within 1–2 hours.

Duration of action
6–18 hours.

Diet advice
Ensure adequate fluid, sugar, and salt intake during a diarrheal illness.

Storage
Keep in a closed container in a cool, dry place out of the reach of children.

Missed dose
Do not take the missed dose. Take your next dose if needed.

Stopping the drug
Can be safely stopped as soon as you no longer need it.

Exceeding the dose
An occasional unintentional extra dose is unlikely to be a cause for concern. Large overdoses may cause constipation, vomiting, or drowsiness, and affect breathing. Notify your physician.

SPECIAL PRECAUTIONS

Be sure to consult your physician or pharmacist before taking this drug if:
▼ You have long-term liver or kidney problems.
▼ You have had recent abdominal surgery.
▼ You have an infection or blockage in the intestine, pseudomembranous colitis, or ulcerative colitis.
▼ You are taking other medications.

Pregnancy
▼ Safety in pregnancy not established. Discuss with your physician.

Breast-feeding
▼ The drug passes into the breast milk and may affect the baby. Discuss with your physician.

Infants and children
▼ Not to be given to children under 4 years. Reduced dose necessary in older children. Children can be very sensitive to the effects of this drug so care should be taken.

Over 60
▼ No special problems.

Driving and hazardous work
▼ No known problems.

Alcohol
▼ No known problems.

POSSIBLE ADVERSE EFFECTS

Adverse effects are rare with loperamide and often difficult to distinguish from the effects of the diarrhea it is used to treat. If symptoms such as bloating, abdominal pain, or fever persist or worsen during treatment with loperamide, consult your physician.

Symptom/effect	Frequency		Discuss with physician		Stop taking drug now	Call physician now
	Common	Rare	Only if severe	In all cases		
Constipation		●	■		▲	
Bloating		●	■			
Abdominal pain		●	■			
Dry mouth		●	■			
Drowsiness or dizziness		●	■		▲	
Itching skin		●		■		
Rash		●		■	▲	

INTERACTIONS

Opioid analgesics may cause severe constipation; avoid using them with loperamide.

PROLONGED USE

Although this drug is not usually taken for prolonged periods (except by persons with a medically diagnosed long-term gastrointestinal condition), special problems are not expected during long-term use.

LOPINAVIR/RITONAVIR

Product name Kaletra
Used in the following combined preparations None

GENERAL INFORMATION

Lopinavir and ritonavir are both antiretroviral drugs from the same class of drugs, known as protease inhibitors. Combined together as a single drug, they are used in the treatment of HIV infection. The drugs work by interfering with an enzyme used by the virus to process proteins required by the virus.

The combination drug is prescribed with other antiretroviral drugs, usually two nucleoside analogues, which together slow down the production of HIV. The aim of this combination therapy is to reduce the damage done to the immune system by the virus.

Combination antiretroviral therapy is not a cure for HIV. Taken regularly on a long-term basis, it can reduce the level of the virus in the body and improve the outlook for the HIV patient. However, the patient will remain infectious, and will suffer a relapse if the treatment is stopped.

QUICK REFERENCE

Drug group Drugs for HIV and immune deficiency (p.144)

Overdose danger rating Medium

Dependence rating Low

Prescription needed Yes

Available as generic No

INFORMATION FOR USERS

Your drug prescription is tailored for you. Do not alter dosage without checking with your physician.

How taken

Capsules, liquid.

Frequency and timing of doses
1–2 x daily. Take liquid with food.

Usual adult dosage range
Dose will vary.

Onset of effect
Within 1 hour.

Duration of action
12 hours.

Diet advice
None.

Storage
Keep in the fridge at 2–5°C in the original container out of the reach of children.

Missed dose
Take as soon as you remember. If your next dose is due within 2 hours, take a single dose now and skip the next. It is very important not to miss doses on a regular basis as this can lead to the development of drug-resistant HIV.

Stopping the drug
Do not stop taking the drug without consulting your physician.

Exceeding the dose
An occasional unintentional extra dose is unlikely to cause problems. But if you notice any unusual symptoms, or if a large overdose has been taken, notify your physician.

SPECIAL PRECAUTIONS

Be sure to tell your physician if:
▼ You have long-term liver or kidney problems.
▼ You have heart problems.
▼ You take recreational drugs.
▼ You are taking other medications.

Pregnancy
▼ Safety in pregnancy not established. Discuss with your physician.

Breast-feeding
▼ Safety in breast-feeding not established. Breast-feeding is not recommended for HIV-positive mothers as the virus may be passed to the baby.

Infants and children
▼ Not recommended in children under 6 months. Reduced dose recommended in children over 6 months.

Over 60
▼ Reduced dose may be necessary to minimize adverse effects.

Driving and hazardous work
▼ No known problems.

Alcohol
▼ The liquid form of the drug contains a small amount of alcohol, so care should be taken if alcoholic drinks are consumed as well.

POSSIBLE ADVERSE EFFECTS

Gastrointestinal upset is the most common *adverse effect*. Other problems, which are more likely to occur with prolonged use, include changes in body shape, and should be discussed with your physician.

Symptom/effect	Frequency		Discuss with physician		Stop taking drug now	Call physician now
	Common	Rare	Only if severe	In all cases		
Nausea/vomiting/diarrhea	●		■			
Loss of appetite	●		■			
Fatigue	●		■			
Body shape changes		●	■			
Increased cholesterol levels	●			■		
Severe abdominal pain		●		■		▮

PROLONGED USE

Changes in body shape may occur, including redistribution of body fat from the arms and/or legs to the abdomen and back of the neck.

Monitoring Your physician will take regular blood samples to check the effect of the drugs on the virus. Blood will also be checked for changes in lipids, cholesterol, and sugar levels.

INTERACTIONS

General note A wide range of drugs may interact with lopinavir and ritonavir, causing either an increase in adverse effects or a reduction in the effect of the antiretroviral drugs. Check with your physician or *pharmacist* before taking any new drugs, including those from the dentist and supermarket, and herbal medicines. Ritonavir is known to interact with some recreational drugs, including ecstasy, and it is essential that you discuss the use of such drugs with your physician or pharmacist.

LORATADINE/DESLORATADINE

Product names Aerius, Claritin, Claritin Kids, and others
Used in the following combined preparations Claritin Allergy and Sinus, and others

GENERAL INFORMATION

Loratadine, a long-acting antihistamine drug, is used for the relief of symptoms associated with allergic rhinitis, such as sneezing, nasal discharge, and itching and burning of the eyes. Symptoms are normally relieved within an hour of oral administration. Loratadine is also used to treat allergic skin conditions such as chronic urticaria (itching). An advantage of loratadine over older antihistamines, such as chlorpheniramine, is that it has fewer

sedative and *anticholinergic* effects, so this drug is less likely to cause drowsiness.

Desloratadine is the active breakdown product of loratadine. It is available as a separate product (Aerius), but offers no advantages over loratadine itself.

Loratadine and desloratadine should be discontinued about four days prior to skin testing for allergy as they may decrease or prevent the detection of positive results.

INFORMATION FOR USERS

Follow instructions on the label. Call your physician if symptoms worsen.

How taken

Tablets, rapid-dissolve tablets (loratadine) liquid.

Frequency and timing of doses
Once daily.

Usual adult dosage range
10mg daily (loratadine); 5mg daily (desloratadine).

Onset of effect
Usually within 1 hour.

Duration of action
Up to 24 hours.

Diet advice
None.

Storage
Keep in a closed container in a cool, dry place out of the reach of children.

Missed dose
Take as soon as you remember. If your next dose is due within 6 hours, take a single dose now and skip the next.

Stopping the drug
Can be safely stopped as soon as you no longer need it.

Exceeding the dose
An occasional unintentional extra dose is unlikely to be a cause for concern. But if you notice any unusual symptoms, or if a large overdose has been taken, notify your physician.

SPECIAL PRECAUTIONS

Be sure to consult your physician or pharmacist before taking this drug if:
▼ You have liver disease.
▼ You are taking other medications.

Pregnancy
▼ Safety in pregnancy not established. Discuss with your physician.

Breast-feeding
▼ Safety not established. The drug passes into the breast milk. Discuss with your physician.

Infants and children
▼ Not recommended for children under 2 years. Reduced dose necessary for older children.

Over 60
▼ No problems expected.

Driving and hazardous work
▼ Problems are unlikely, but be aware of how the drug affects you before driving or carrying out hazardous work.

Alcohol
▼ Alcohol will increase the sedative effect of loratadine/desloratadine.

POSSIBLE ADVERSE EFFECTS

The incidence of *adverse effects* with loratadine/desloratadine is low.

Symptom/effect	Frequency		Discuss with physician		Stop taking drug now	Call physician now
	Common	Rare	Only if severe	In all cases		
Drowsiness		●	■			
Fatigue		●	■			
Nausea		●	■			
Headache		●	■			
Dry mouth		●	■			
Palpitations		●		■		

PROLONGED USE

No problems expected.

INTERACTIONS

Cimetidine, clarithromycin, erythromycin, ketoconazole, fluoxetine, fluconazole, quinidine, and others These drugs may increase the blood levels and effects of loratadine, but this has not been found to cause problems.

LORAZEPAM

Product names Apo-Lorazepam, Ativan, Novo-Lorazem, Nu-Loraz Tab, and others
Used in the following combined preparation None

GENERAL INFORMATION

Lorazepam belongs to a group of drugs known as the benzodiazepines, which help to relieve anxiety and encourage sleep. The actions and *adverse effects* of this group of drugs are described more fully on page 67.

Lorazepam is used for the short-term treatment of excessive anxiety. In those with anxiety and insomnia, taking a dose at bedtime can help with sleep. The injectable form of the drug may be used as an anticonvulsant for the control of status epilepticus (see p.70). Lorazepam is less likely than some of the other benzodiazepines to accumulate in the body.

In common with other benzodiazepines, lorazepam can be habit-forming if taken regularly over a long period of time. Its effects may also diminish with time. For those reasons, treatment should be reviewed regularly.

QUICK REFERENCE

Drug group Benzodiazepine anti-anxiety drugs (p.67)

Overdose danger rating Medium

Dependence rating High

Prescription needed Yes

Available as generic Yes

INFORMATION FOR USERS

Your drug prescription is tailored for you. Do not alter dosage without checking with your physician.

How taken

Tablets, sublingual tablets, injection.

Frequency and timing of doses
1–4 x daily.

Usual adult dosage range
1–6mg daily (by mouth); varies with condition under treatment (injection) and age.

Onset of effect
30–60 minutes (oral tablets); 5–10 minutes (intravenous injection); less than 30 minutes (intramuscular injection, sublingual tablets).

Duration of action
Up to 12 hours.

Diet advice
None.

Storage
Keep in a closed container in a cool, dry place out of the reach of children. Protect from light.

Missed dose
If you are taking the drug once daily for insomnia, a missed dose is no cause for concern. Return to your normal dose schedule the following night, if necessary. On a daytime schedule, take the missed dose when you remember. If your next dose is due within 2 hours, take a single dose now and skip the next.

Stopping the drug
If you have been taking the drug continuously for less than 2 weeks, it can be safely stopped as soon as you feel you no longer need it. However, if you have been taking the drug for longer, consult your physician, who will supervise a gradual reduction in dosage. Stopping abruptly may lead to withdrawal symptoms (see p.66)

Exceeding the dose
An occasional unintentional extra dose is unlikely to cause problems. Larger overdoses may cause unusual drowsiness. Notify your physician.

SPECIAL PRECAUTIONS

Be sure to tell your physician if:
▼ You have severe respiratory disease.
▼ You have impaired liver or kidney function.
▼ You have myasthenia gravis.
▼ You have glaucoma.
▼ You have or have had any problems with alcohol or drug abuse.
▼ You are taking other medications.

 Pregnancy
▼ Safety in pregnancy not established. Discuss with your physician.

 Breast-feeding
▼ The drug passes into the breast milk. Its effects on the baby are not clearly known. Discuss with your physician.

 Infants and children
▼ Not recommended for those under 18 years.

 Over 60
▼ Increased likelihood of adverse effects. Reduced dose may be therefore be necessary.

 Driving and hazardous work
▼ Do not undertake such activities until you have learned how the drug affects you; it can cause reduced alertness and slowed reactions.

 Alcohol
▼ Avoid. Alcohol increases the sedative effects of this drug.

POSSIBLE ADVERSE EFFECTS

The principal adverse effects of this drug are related to its *sedative* and tranquilizing properties and normally diminish after the first few days of treatment.

Symptom/effect	Frequency		Discuss with physician		Stop taking drug now	Call physician now
	Common	Rare	Only if severe	In all cases		
Daytime drowsiness	●		■			
Dizziness/unsteadiness		●		■		
Headache		●		■		
Nausea/vomiting		●		■		
Amnesia		●		■	▲	
Confusion/disorientation		●		■		❙
Rash		●		■	▲	❙

PROLONGED USE

Regular use of this drug over several weeks can lead to a reduction in its effect as the body adapts. It may also be habit-forming when taken for extended periods, especially if large doses are taken.

INTERACTIONS

Sedative All drugs, including alcohol, that have a sedative effect on the central nervous system are likely to increase the sedative properties of lorazepam. Such drugs include other anti-anxiety and sleeping drugs, antihistamines, antidepressants, *opioid* analgesics, scopolamine, and antipsychotics.

LOSARTAN

Product name CO Losartan, Cozaar, and others
Used in the following combined preparations Hyzaar, Hyzaar DS, and others

GENERAL INFORMATION

Losartan is a member of the group of vasodilator drugs called angiotensin-II blockers. Used to treat hypertension, the drug works by blocking the action of angiotensin-II (a naturally occurring substance that constricts blood vessels). This action causes the blood vessel walls to relax, thereby easing blood pressure.

Unlike ACE inhibitors, losartan does not cause a persistent dry cough, and its use is now being evaluated in conditions such as heart failure, for which ACE inhibitors are currently being used.

Adverse effects, which include diarrhea, dizziness, and fatigue, are rare.

INFORMATION FOR USERS

Your drug prescription is tailored for you. Do not alter dosage without checking with your physician.

How taken

Tablets, liquid.

Frequency and timing of doses
Once daily.

Usual adult dosage range
25–100mg. People over 75 years, and other groups that are especially sensitive to the drug's effects, and those with liver dysfunction, may start on 25mg.

Onset of effect
Blood pressure 1–2 weeks, with maximum effect in 3–6 weeks from start of treatment. *Other conditions* Within 1 hour.

Duration of action
12–24 hours.

Diet advice
None.

Storage
Keep in a closed container in a cool, dry place out of the reach of children.

Missed dose
Take as soon as you remember. If your next dose is due within 8 hours, take a single dose now and skip the next.

Stopping the drug
Do not stop the drug without consulting your physician. Stopping the drug may lead to worsening of the underlying condition.

Exceeding the dose
An occasional unintentional extra dose is unlikely to cause problems. Large overdoses may cause dizziness and fainting. Notify your physician.

POSSIBLE ADVERSE EFFECTS

Side effects, of which dizziness, headache, and diarrhea are the most common, are usually mild. If wheezing or swelling of the lips and tongue occur, stop taking the drug and contact your physician immediately.

Symptom/effect	Frequency		Discuss with physician		Stop taking drug now	Call physician now
	Common	Rare	Only if severe	In all cases		
Dizziness	●		■			
Headache		●	■			
Diarrhea		●	■			
Muscle, joint, or back pain		●		■		
Cough		●		■		
Wheezing/swollen lips or tongue		●		■	▲	▮

INTERACTIONS

Vasodilators, diuretics, and other antihypertensives These drugs may increase the blood-pressure-lowering effect of losartan.

Potassium supplements, potassium-sparing diuretics, and cyclosporine Losartan increases the effect of these drugs, leading to raised levels of potassium in the blood.

Lithium Losartan may increase the levels and *toxicity* of lithium.

Non-steroidal anti-inflammatory drugs (NSAIDs) Certain NSAIDs may reduce the blood-pressure-lowering effect of losartan.

SPECIAL PRECAUTIONS

Be sure to tell your physician if:
▼ You have stenosis of the kidney arteries.
▼ You have liver or kidney problems.
▼ You have experienced angioedema.
▼ You are taking other medications.

Pregnancy
▼ Not prescribed. May cause harm to the developing fetus.

Breast-feeding
▼ Not prescribed. Safety not established.

Infants and children
▼ Not prescribed. Safety not established.

Over 60
▼ Reduced dose may be necessary over 75 years.

Driving and hazardous work
▼ Do not undertake such activities until you have learned how losartan affects you because the drug can cause dizziness.

Alcohol
▼ Avoid. Alcohol may increase the blood-pressure-lowering and adverse effects of losartan.

PROLONGED USE

No special problems.

Monitoring Periodic checks on blood potassium levels may be performed.

LOVASTATIN

Product names Apo-Lovastatin, Mevacor, Novo-Lovastatin Tablets, Nu-Lovastatin, PMS-Lovastatin, and others
Used in the following combined preparation Advicor

GENERAL INFORMATION

Lovastatin is a lipid-lowering drug belonging to the class of statins. It blocks the action of an enzyme needed for cholesterol to be manufactured in the liver, and as a result the blood levels of cholesterol are lowered. The drug is prescribed for people with high levels of cholesterol in the blood who have not responded to a special diet, and who are at risk of developing or have existing coronary heart disease.

Lovastatin is usally taken once daily. With higher doses, the daily dosage can be split and taken with the morning and evening meals. *Side effects* are usually mild. Lovastatin may raise the levels of various liver enzymes. This effect does not usually indicate serious liver damage.

INFORMATION FOR USERS

Your drug prescription is tailored for you. Do not alter dosage without checking with your physician.

How taken

Tablets.

Frequency and timing of doses
Usually once daily with the evening meal; higher doses may be split to 2 doses.

Usual adult dosage range
20–80mg daily.

Onset of effect
Within 2 weeks; full beneficial effects may not be felt for 4–6 weeks.

Duration of action
Up to 24 hours.

Diet advice
A low-fat diet is usually recommended.

Storage
Keep in a closed container in a cool, dry place out of the reach of children.

Missed dose
If you miss a dose, take it as soon as you remember. If it is near the time of the next dose, skip the missed dose and resume your using dosing schedule. Do not double up to catch up on a missed dose.

Stopping the drug
Do not stop the drug without consulting your physician. Stopping the drug may lead to worsening of the underlying condition.

Exceeding the dose
An occasional unintentional extra dose is unlikely to cause problems. Large overdoses may cause liver problems. Notify your physician.

SPECIAL PRECAUTIONS

Be sure to tell your physician if:
▼ You have liver or kidney problems.
▼ You have eye or vision problems.
▼ You have muscle weakness.
▼ You have a thyroid disorder.
▼ You have had problems with alcohol abuse.
▼ You have porphyria.
▼ You have angina.
▼ You have high blood pressure.
▼ You are taking other medications.

Pregnancy
▼ Not usually prescribed. Safety in pregnancy not established. Discuss with your physician.

Breast-feeding
▼ Safety not established. Discuss with your physician.

Infants and children
▼ Not recommended.

Over 60
▼ No special problems.

Driving and hazardous work
▼ No special problems.

Alcohol
▼ Avoid excessive amounts. Alcohol may increase the risk of developing liver problems with this drug.

POSSIBLE ADVERSE EFFECTS

Adverse effects are usually mild and do not last long. The most common are those affecting the gastrointestinal system.

Lovastatin may very rarely cause muscle problems, and any muscle pain or weakness should be reported to your physician at once.

Symptom/effect	Frequency		Discuss with physician		Stop taking drug now	Call physician now
	Common	Rare	Only if severe	In all cases		
Abdominal pain		●	■			
Nausea/flatulence		●	■			
Constipation/diarrhea		●	■			
Headache		●	■			
Rash		●		■	▲	
Jaundice		●		■		
Muscle pain/weakness		●		■	▲	▮
Change in cognition		●				▮

INTERACTIONS

Anticoagulants Lovastatin may increase the effect of anticoagulants. Close monitoring and dose adjustment may be required.

Itraconazole, ketoconazole, clarithromycin, erythromycin, and protease inhibitors Simultaneous administration of these drugs with lovastatin may increase the risk of muscle toxicity.

Other lipid-lowering drugs The use of these with lovastatin may increase the risk of muscle toxicity.

Grapefruit juice May increase blood levels of lovastatin.

Cyclosporine and other immuno-suppressant drugs, and antiviral drugs Lovastatin and these drugs are not usually prescribed together because of the risk of muscle toxicity.

PROLONGED USE

Prolonged treatment can adversely affect liver function.

Monitoring Regular blood tests to check liver function are recommended. Tests of muscle function may be carried out if problems are suspected.

MAGNESIUM HYDROXIDE

Product name None
Used in the following combined preparations Diovol Plus, Maalox Antacid with Anti-Gas, Mucaine, and others

GENERAL INFORMATION

Magnesium hydroxide is a fast-acting antacid given to neutralize stomach acid. The drug is available in a number of over-the-counter preparations for the treatment of indigestion and heartburn. It also acts as a laxative by drawing salt and water from the wall of the bowel to soften the feces.

Magnesium hydroxide is not often used alone as an antacid because of its laxative effect. However, this effect is countered when the drug is used in combination with aluminum hydroxide, which can cause constipation.

QUICK REFERENCE

Drug group Antacids (p.94) and laxatives (p.97)

Overdose danger rating Low

Dependence rating Low

Prescription needed No

Available as generic Yes

INFORMATION FOR USERS

Follow instructions on the label. Call your physician if symptoms worsen.

How taken

Tablets, liquid, powder.

Frequency and timing of doses
1–4 x daily as needed with water, preferably an hour after food and at bedtime.

Usual adult dosage range
Antacid 2–4 tablets as needed (up to 4 x daily); 5–15ml per dose (liquid).
Laxative 5–20ml per dose (liquid).

Onset of effect
Antacid within 15 minutes.
Laxative 2–8 hours.

Duration of action
2–4 hours.

Diet advice
None.

Storage
Keep in a closed container in a cool (but not cold), dry place out of the reach of children.

Missed dose
Take as soon as you remember.

Stopping the drug
When used as an antacid, can be safely stopped as soon as you no longer need it. When given as ulcer treatment, follow your physician's advice.

Exceeding the dose
An occasional unintentional extra dose is unlikely to be a cause for concern. But if you notice any unusual symptoms, or if a large overdose has been taken, notify your physician.

SPECIAL PRECAUTIONS

Be sure to consult your physician or pharmacist before taking this drug if:
▼ You have a long-term kidney problem.
▼ You have a bowel disorder.
▼ You are taking other medications.

Pregnancy
▼ No evidence of risk, but discuss the most appropriate treatment with your physician.

Breast-feeding
▼ No evidence of risk, but discuss the most appropriate treatment with your physician.

Infants and children
▼ Not recommended under 3 years except on the advice of a physician. Reduced dose necessary for older children.

Over 60
▼ No special problems.

Driving and hazardous work
▼ No known problems.

Alcohol
▼ Avoid excessive alcohol as it irritates the stomach and may reduce the benefits of the drug.

POSSIBLE ADVERSE EFFECTS

Diarrhea is the only common *adverse effect* of this drug. Dizziness and muscle weakness due to absorption of excess magnesium in the body may occur in people with poor kidney function.

Symptom/effect	Frequency		Discuss with physician		Stop taking drug now	Call physician now
	Common	Rare	Only if severe	In all cases		
Diarrhea	●		■			

INTERACTIONS

General note Magnesium hydroxide interferes with the absorption of a wide range of drugs taken by mouth, including tetracycline antibiotics, iron supplements, diflunisal, phenytoin, and penicillamine. You should therefore allow 1–2 hours between magnesium hydroxide and other medications.

Enteric-coated tablets As with other antacids, magnesium hydroxide may allow break-up of the *enteric* coating of tablets, sometimes leading to stomach irritation.

PROLONGED USE

Magnesium hydroxide should not be used for prolonged periods without consulting your physician. If you are over 40 years of age and are experiencing long-term indigestion or heartburn, your physician will probably refer you to a specialist. Prolonged use in people with kidney damage may cause drowsiness, dizziness, and weakness, resulting from accumulation of magnesium in the body.

MEDROXYPROGESTERONE

Product names Depo-Provera, Provera, Provera-Pak, and others
Used in the following combined preparations Premplus

GENERAL INFORMATION

Medroxyprogesterone is a progestin, a synthetic female sex *hormone* similar to the natural hormone progesterone. It is used for hormonal replacement therapy to oppose effects of estrogen in women with a uterus. It is also used to treat menstrual disorders such as mid-cycle bleeding and amenorrhea (absence of periods).

Medroxyprogesterone is also often used to treat endometriosis, a condition in which there is abnormal growth of the uterine-lining tissue in the pelvic cavity. *Depot* injections of the drug are used as a contraceptive. However, since they may cause serious *side effects*, such as persistent bleeding from the uterus, amenorrhea, and prolonged infertility, their use remains controversial, and they are recommended for use only under special circumstances.

Medroxyprogesterone may be used to treat some types of cancer, such as cancer of the breast, uterus, or prostate.

INFORMATION FOR USERS

Your drug prescription is tailored for you. Do not alter dosage without checking with your physician.

How taken

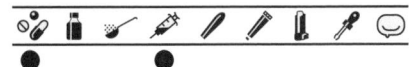

Tablets, injection.

Frequency and timing of doses
Usually once daily with plenty of water (by mouth); tablets may need to be taken at certain times during your cycle; follow the instructions you have been given; higher doses are given as individual doses. Every 3 months (depot and intramuscular injection).

Usual adult dosage range
Menstrual disorders 2.5–10mg daily.
Endometriosis 30mg daily or 150mg depot every 6–12 weeks.
Cancer 100–400mg daily.
Contraception 150mg every 12 weeks.

Onset of effect
1–2 months (cancer); 1–2 weeks (other conditions).

Duration of action
1–2 days (by mouth); up to some months (depot injection).

Diet advice
None.

Storage
Keep in a closed container in a cool, dry place out of the reach of children.

Missed dose
Take as soon as you remember. If your next dose is due within 3 hours, take a single dose now and skip the next.

Stopping the drug
Do not stop the drug without consulting your physician; symptoms may recur.

Exceeding the dose
An occasional unintentional extra dose is unlikely to be a cause for concern. But if you notice any unusual symptoms, or if a large overdose has been taken, notify your physician.

POSSIBLE ADVERSE EFFECTS

Medroxyprogesterone rarely causes serious adverse effects. Fluid retention may lead to weight gain, swollen feet or ankles, and breast tenderness.

Symptom/effect	Frequency		Discuss with physician		Stop taking drug now	Call physician now
	Common	Rare	Only if severe	In all cases		
Weight gain	●		■			
Swollen ankles	●		■			
Breast tenderness		●	■			
Nausea		●	■			
Fatigue/depression		●		■		
Irregular menstruation		●		■		
Rash/itching/acne		●		■	▲	
Jaundice		●		■	▲	

INTERACTIONS

Cyclosporine The effects of this drug may be increased by medroxyprogesterone.

SPECIAL PRECAUTIONS

Be sure to tell your physician if:
▼ You have high blood pressure.
▼ You have had venous thrombosis, a heart attack, or a stroke.
▼ You have long-term liver or kidney problems.
▼ You are taking other medications.

Pregnancy
▼ Not prescribed. May cause abnormalities in the unborn baby. Discuss with your physician.

Breast-feeding
▼ The drug passes into the breast milk, but at normal doses adverse effects on the baby are unlikely. Discuss with your physician.

Infants and children
▼ Not usually prescribed.

Over 60
▼ No special problems.

Driving and hazardous work
▼ No known problems.

Alcohol
▼ No known problems.

PROLONGED USE

Long-term use of this drug may slightly increase the risk of venous thrombosis in the leg veins. Irregular menstrual bleeding or spotting between periods may also occur during long-term use. The drug also increases the risk of osteoporosis and bone fractures. Bone loss is greatest in the first 2–3 years of treatment, then stabilizes.

Monitoring Periodic checks on blood pressure, yearly cervical smear tests, and breast examinations are usually required.

MEFLOQUINE

Product name Lariam Tab
Used in the following combined preparations None

GENERAL INFORMATION

Mefloquine is used for the prevention and treatment of malaria. It is principally recommended for use in areas where malaria is resistant to other drugs.

However, the use of mefloquine is limited by the fact that it can cause, in some patients, serious *side effects* that include depression, anxiety, nightmares, panic, confusion, hallucinations, paranoid delusions, and convulsions.

As with all antimalarials, the use of mosquito repellants and a mosquito net at night are as important in preventing malaria as taking the drug itself.

INFORMATION FOR USERS

Your drug prescription is tailored for you. Do not alter dosage without checking with your physician.

How taken

Tablets.

Frequency and timing of doses
Prevention Once weekly, starting 2–3 weeks before entering endemic area, and continuing until 4 weeks after leaving.
Treatment Up to 3 x daily, every 6–8 hours.

Usual adult dosage range
Prevention 1 tablet once weekly.
Treatment 20–25mg/kg body weight up to a maximum dose of 1.5g.

Onset of effect
2–3 days.

Duration of action
Over 1 week. Low levels of the drug may persist for several months.

Diet advice
None.

Storage
Keep in a cool, dry place out of the reach of children.

Missed dose
Take as soon as you remember. If your next dose is due within 48 hours (if taken once weekly for prevention), take a single dose now and skip the next.

Stopping the drug
If you feel it necessary to stop taking the drug, consult your physician about alternative treatment before the next dose is due.

OVERDOSE ACTION

 Seek immediate medical advice in all cases. Take emergency action if dizziness, palpitations, collapse, or loss of consciousness occur.

See Drug poisoning emergency guide (p.526).

POSSIBLE ADVERSE EFFECTS

Mefloquine commonly causes dizziness, vertigo, nausea, vomiting, and headache. In rare cases, serious *adverse effects* on the nervous system can occur, including anxiety or panic attacks, depression, hallucinations, and paranoid delusions.

Symptom/effect	Frequency		Discuss with physician		Stop taking drug now	Call physician now
	Common	Rare	Only if severe	In all cases		
Dizziness/vertigo	●		■			
Nausea/vomiting	●		■			
Headache	●		■			
Abdominal pain	●			■		
Depression		●		■	▲	
Anxiety/panic attacks		●		■	▲	
Hallucinations/delusions		●		■	▲	
Hearing disorders		●		■	▲	
Palpitations		●		■	▲	

INTERACTIONS

Antiepileptic drugs Mefloquine may decrease the effect of these drugs.

Other antimalarial drugs Mefloquine may increase the risk of adverse effects when taken with these drugs.

General note Mefloquine may increase the effects on the heart of drugs such as beta blockers, calcium channel blockers, and digoxin.

SPECIAL PRECAUTIONS

Be sure to tell your physician if:
▼ You have long-term liver or kidney problems.
▼ You have had epileptic seizures.
▼ You have had depression, anxiety, or other psychiatric illness.
▼ You have had a previous allergic reaction to mefloquine or quinine.
▼ You have heart problems.
▼ You are taking other medications.

 Pregnancy
▼ Not usually prescribed. If unavoidable, the drug is given only after the first trimester. Pregnancy must be avoided during and for 3 months after mefloquine use.

 Breast-feeding
▼ Not prescribed. The drug passes into the breast milk.

 Infants and children
▼ Not used in infants under 3 months old. Reduced dose necessary in older children.

Over 60
▼ Careful monitoring is necessary if liver or kidney problems or heart disease are present.

 Driving and hazardous work
▼ Avoid such activities when taking mefloquine for prevention until you know how the drug affects you. Also avoid during treatment and for 3 weeks afterwards as the drug can cause dizziness or disturb balance.

Alcohol
▼ Keep consumption low.

PROLONGED USE

May be taken for prevention of malaria for up to one year.

MEGESTROL

Product name Megace OS, Nu-Megestrol
Used in the following combined preparations None

GENERAL INFORMATION

Megestrol is a progestin, which is a synthetic female sex *hormone* similar to the natural hormone progesterone. The drug is used in the treatment of certain types of advanced cancer affecting the breast and uterus that are sensitive to hormone treatment. Megestrol is often prescribed when the tumour cannot be removed by surgery, when the disease has recurred after surgery, or when treatment with other anticancer drugs or radiotherapy have failed.

Successful treatment with megestrol reduces the size of the tumour; the drug may also cause secondary growths to disappear. Improvement usually occurs within two months of starting treatment. Because megestrol does not completely eradicate the cancer, the drug may need to be continued indefinitely.

Megestrol may also be used to treat anorexia, cachexia, or unexplained weight loss in those with HIV.

QUICK REFERENCE

Drug group Female sex hormones (p.133) and anticancer drugs (p.140), and anticachetic drugs.

Overdose danger rating Low

Dependence rating Low

Prescription needed Yes

Available as generic Yes

INFORMATION FOR USERS

Your drug prescription is tailored for you. Do not alter dosage without checking with your physician.

How taken

Tablets, liquid.

Frequency and timing of doses
1–4 x daily.

Usual adult dosage range
Breast cancer 160mg daily in single or divided doses.
Cancer of the uterus 40–320mg daily in single or divided doses.
Weight loss prevention 400–800mg daily as single dose.

Onset of effect
Within 2 months.

Duration of action
1–2 days.

Diet advice
None.

Storage
Keep in a closed container in a cool, dry place out of the reach of children.

Missed dose
Take as soon as you remember.

Stopping the drug
Do not stop the drug without consulting your physician. Stopping the drug may lead to worsening of your underlying condition.

Exceeding the dose
An occasional unintentional extra dose is unlikely to be a cause for concern. But if you notice any unusual symptoms, or if a large overdose has been taken, notify your physician.

SPECIAL PRECAUTIONS

Be sure to tell your physician if:
▼ You have long-term liver or kidney problems.
▼ You have had thrombosis or blood clots.
▼ You have high blood pressure.
▼ You have heart problems.
▼ You are taking other medications.

Pregnancy
▼ Not usually prescribed.

Breast-feeding
▼ Breast-feeding is usually discontinued. Discuss with your physician.

Infants and children
▼ Not usually required.

Over 60
▼ No special problems.

Driving and hazardous work
▼ No known problems.

Alcohol
▼ No known problems.

POSSIBLE ADVERSE EFFECTS

Adverse effects are rare with megestrol. It may cause weight gain owing to increased appetite and food intake. Stop taking the drug and consult your physician if a rash occurs.

Symptom/effect	Frequency		Discuss with physician		Stop taking drug now	Call physician now
	Common	Rare	Only if severe	In all cases		
Weight gain	●		■			
Swollen feet/ankles		●	■			
Nausea		●	■			
Headache		●		■		
Itching		●		■		
Hair loss		●		■		
Rash		●		■	▲	

INTERACTIONS

Cyclosporine The effects of this drug may be increased by megestrol.

PROLONGED USE

Long-term use of this drug may increase the risk of blood clots in the leg veins.

Monitoring Periodic checks on blood pressure may be performed.

MELOXICAM

Product names Apo-Meloxicam, Mobicox, and others
Used in the following combined preparations None

GENERAL INFORMATION

Meloxicam is a member of the non-steroidal anti-inflammatory (NSAID) group of drugs. It reduces pain, stiffness, and inflammation and is used to relieve the symptoms of rheumatoid arthritis, ankylosing spondylitis, and acute episodes of osteoarthritis. Meloxicam does not cure the underlying condition, however.

Meloxicam was initially thought to be safer than some other NSAIDs, with a lower risk of causing gastrointestinal bleeding, ulceration, and perforation. However, this has not been confirmed, and its main advantage is its long duration of action, so that it can be given only once a day.

QUICK REFERENCE

Drug group Nonsteroidal anti-inflammatory drugs (p.102)

Overdose danger rating Medium

Dependence rating Low

Prescription needed Yes

Available as generic Yes

INFORMATION FOR USERS

Your drug prescription is tailored for you. Do not alter dosage without checking with your physician.

How taken

Tablets.

Frequency and timing of doses
Once daily.

Usual adult dosage range
7.5–15mg.

Onset of effect
1 hour.

Duration of action
24 hours.

Diet advice
None.

Storage
Keep in a closed container in a cool, dry place out of the reach of children.

Missed dose
Take as soon as you remember. If your next dose is due within 8 hours, take a single dose now and skip the next.

Stopping the drug
The drug can be safely stopped as soon as you no longer need it (short term). Do not stop taking the drug without consulting your physician (long term).

Exceeding the dose
An occasional unintentional extra dose is unlikely to cause problems. Large overdoses can cause drowsiness, and stomach and intestinal pain and damage. Notify your physician.

SPECIAL PRECAUTIONS

Be sure to tell your physician if:
▼ You have asthma.
▼ You have cardiovascular disease.
▼ You are allergic to ASA or other NSAIDs.
▼ You have had a peptic ulcer, esophagitis, or acid indigestion.
▼ You have liver or kidney problems.
▼ You have a bleeding disorder, proctitis, or hemorrhoids.
▼ You are taking other medications.

Pregnancy
▼ Safety not established. May affect the developing fetus. Discuss with your physician.

Breast-feeding
▼ Safety not established. Discuss with your physician.

Infants and children
▼ Not recommended.

Over 60
▼ Increased likelihood of adverse effects. Reduced doses necessary.

Driving and hazardous work
▼ Avoid such activities until you have learned how meloxicam affects you because the drug can cause vertigo and drowsiness.

Alcohol
▼ Avoid. Alcohol may increase the risk of stomach irritation with meloxicam.

Surgery and general anesthetics
▼ Meloxicam may prolong bleeding. Discuss the possibility of stopping treatment temporarily with your physician or dentist.

POSSIBLE ADVERSE EFFECTS

Gastrointestinal disturbance, skin rash, and headache are common *adverse effects*. Black or bloodstained feces and wheezing should be reported to your physician without delay.

Symptom/effect	Frequency		Discuss with physician		Stop taking drug now	Call physician now
	Common	Rare	Only if severe	In all cases		
Abdominal pain/indigestion	●			■		
Headache	●		■			
Diarrhea or constipation	●		■			
Skin rash/itching	●		■			
Lightheadedness/drowsiness	●		■			
Palpitations		●	■			
Vertigo/ringing in the ears		●	■			
Wheezing/breathing difficulties		●	■		▲	▮
Black/bloodstained feces		●	■		▲	▮

INTERACTIONS

General note Meloxicam interacts with a wide range of drugs to increase the risk of bleeding and/or peptic ulcers. Such drugs include other NSAIDs, ASA, and also oral anticoagulants, and corticosteroids.

Cyclosporine There is an increased risk of kidney damage when meloxicam is taken with cyclosporine.

Lithium, digoxin, and methotrexate Meloxicam may increase the blood levels of these drugs to an undersirable extent.

Antibacterials Meloxicam may increase the risk of convulsions with ciprofloxacin and similar drugs.

ACE inhibitors and angiotensin II blockers There is an increased risk of kidney damage when meloxicam is used with these drugs.

PROLONGED USE

There is an increased risk of bleeding from peptic ulcers and in the bowel with prolonged use. The risk for cardiovascular events (such as heart attack) may also be increased.

Monitoring Periodic tests on kidney function may be performed.

MEMANTINE

Product names Apo-Memantine, CO Memantine, Ebixa, and others
Used in the following combined preparations None

GENERAL INFORMATION

Memantine is used to treat symptoms of moderate to severe Alzheimer's disease. It may be used alone or in combination with other drugs used in this condition called cholinesterase inhibitors. It works by blocking certain *receptors* in the brain, thereby decreasing abnormal excitement. It can help patients in performing daily activities more easily, but does not decrease the progression of Alzheimer's disease. The dose may be gradually increased. Doses greater than 5mg per day should be administered twice daily.

QUICK REFERENCE

Drug group Drugs for dementia (p.71)

Overdose danger rating Medium

Dependence rating Low

Prescription needed Yes

Available as generic Yes

INFORMATION FOR USERS

Your drug prescription is tailored for you. Do not alter dosage without checking with your physician.

How taken

Tablets.

Frequency and timing of doses
Usually once or twice daily.

Usual adult dosage range
5–20mg daily.

Onset of effect
Within 8 hours.

Duration of action
Up to 24 hours.

Diet advice
None

Storage
Keep in a closed container in a cool, dry place out of the reach of children.

Missed dose
If you miss a dose, take it as soon as you remember. If it is near the time of the next dose, skip the missed dose and resume your usual dosing schedule. Do not double up to catch up on a missed dose.

Stopping the drug
Do not stop the drug without consulting your physician. Stopping the drug may lead to worsening of the underlying condition.

Exceeding the dose
An occasional unintentional extra dose is unlikely to cause problems, but if you notice any unusual symptoms, or if a large overdose has been taken, notify your physician.

SPECIAL PRECAUTIONS

Be sure to tell your physician if:
- ▼ You have asthma.
- ▼ You have seizures.
- ▼ You have kidney disease.
- ▼ You have repeated urinary tract infections.
- ▼ You smoke cigarettes.
- ▼ You are taking other medications.

Pregnancy
▼ Not generally used in pregnancy. Discuss with your physician.

Breast-feeding
▼ Not generally used while breast-feeding. Discuss with your physician.

Infants and children
▼ Safety and effectiveness not established.

Over 60
▼ No special problems.

Driving and hazardous work
▼ May cause drowsiness. Do not drive a car or operate machinery until the effect of the drug wears off and you feel you are mentally alert.

Alcohol
▼ Avoid alcohol use as it may increase the effect of drowsiness caused by this drug.

POSSIBLE ADVERSE EFFECTS

Side effects include dizziness, tiredness, feeling sleepy, headache, and sometimes an increase in blood pressure.

Symptom/effect	Frequency		Discuss with physician		Stop taking drug now	Call physician now
	Common	Rare	Only if severe	In all cases		
Headache	●		■			
Dizziness	●		■			
Constipation or diarrhea	●		■			
Tiredness/sleepiness		●	■			
Loss of appetite		●	■			
Blurred vision		●		■		
Change in walk and balance		●		■		
Anxiety		●		■		
Change in behaviour		●		■		
High blood pressure		●		■		▮
Edema		●		■		▮

PROLONGED USE

May be continued for as long as there is benefit. Stopping the drug can lead to a gradual loss of the improvements.

Monitoring Periodic checks may be performed to test whether the drug is still providing some benefit.

INTERACTIONS

Hydrochlorothiazide Memantine can decrease the amount of hydrochlorothiazide in the blood.

Amantadine, Dextromethorphan (DM), ketamine There is a potential for interaction, as these drugs inhibit the same receptors as memantine.

Cimetidine, nicotine, quinidine These drugs are excreted in a similar manner to memantine in the kidneys and they can affect the levels of memantine; memantine can also affect the levels of these drugs.

Sodium bicarbonate, acetazolamide These drugs can lead to an accumulation of memantine in the body.

MERCAPTOPURINE

Product name Purinethol
Used in the following combined preparations None

GENERAL INFORMATION

Mercaptopurine is an anticancer drug that is widely used in the treatment of certain forms of leukemia. It is usually given in combination with other anticancer drugs.

Nausea and vomiting, mouth ulcers, and loss of appetite are the most common *side effects* of mercaptopurine. Such symptoms tend to be milder than those caused by other cytotoxic drugs, and often disappear as the body adjusts to the drug.

More seriously, mercaptopurine can interfere with blood cell production, resulting in blood clotting disorders and anemia, and can also cause liver damage. The likelihood of infections is also increased.

INFORMATION FOR USERS

Your drug prescription is tailored for you. Do not alter dosage without checking with your physician.

How taken

Tablets.

Frequency and timing of doses
Once daily.

Usual dosage range
Dosage is determined individually according to body weight and response.

Onset of effect
1–2 weeks.

Duration of action
Side effects may persist for several weeks after stopping treatment.

Diet advice
None.

Storage
Keep in a closed container in a cool, dry place out of the reach of children. Protect from light.

Missed dose
If your next dose is due within 6 hours, take a single dose now and skip the next. Tell your physician that you missed a dose.

Stopping the drug
Do not stop taking the drug without consulting your physician; stopping the drug may lead to worsening of your underlying condition.

Exceeding the dose
An occasional unintentional extra dose is unlikely to cause problems. Large overdoses may cause nausea and vomiting. Notify your physician.

SPECIAL PRECAUTIONS

Be sure to tell your physician if:
▼ You have long-term liver or kidney problems.
▼ You suffer from gout.
▼ You have recently had any infection.
▼ You are taking other medications.

Pregnancy
▼ Not usually prescribed. Discuss with your physician.

Breast-feeding
▼ Not advised. The drug passes into the breast milk and may affect the baby adversely. Discuss with your physician.

Infants and children
▼ No special problems.

Over 60
▼ Reduced dose may be necessary. Increased risk of adverse effects.

Driving and hazardous work
▼ No known problems.

Alcohol
▼ Avoid. Alcohol may increase the adverse effects of this drug.

POSSIBLE ADVERSE EFFECTS

The most common *adverse effects* are nausea and vomiting, and loss of appetite. *Jaundice* may also occur, but is reversible on stopping the drug. Because mercaptopurine interferes with the production of blood cells, it may cause anemia and blood clotting disorders; and infections are more likely.

Symptom/effect	Frequency		Discuss with physician		Stop taking drug now	Call physician now
	Common	Rare	Only if severe	In all cases		
Nausea/vomiting	●		■			
Loss of appetite	●		■			
Mouth ulcers	●			■		▌
Spontaneous bleeding		●		■	▲	▌
Easy bruising		●		■	▲	▌
Sore throat/fever		●		■	▲	

INTERACTIONS

Allopurinol This drug increases blood levels of mercaptopurine.

Warfarin The effects of warfarin may be decreased by mercaptopurine.

Co-trimoxazole and trimethoprim These drugs increase the risk of blood problems with mercaptopurine.

PROLONGED USE

Prolonged use of this drug may reduce bone marrow activity, leading to a reduction of all types of blood cells. Some people have a genetic susceptibility to this effect. There is also a small increase in the risk of cancers affecting the immune system.

Monitoring Regular blood checks and tests on liver function are required.

METFORMIN

Product names Glucophage, Glumetza, Glycon, and others
Used in the following combined preparations Avandamet, Janumet

GENERAL INFORMATION

Metformin is an antidiabetic drug used to treat type 2 diabetes in which some insulin is still produced by the pancreas.

The drug reduces blood sugar levels by delaying absorption of glucose, reducing glucose production in the liver, and helping your body respond better to its own insulin so that cells take up glucose more effectively from the blood.

Metformin is used in conjunction with a good diet and exercise. It can be given with insulin or other antidiabetic drugs but is often used on its own to treat people with type 2 diabetes who are obese. Metformin is also used in the treatment of polycystic ovarian syndrome.

INFORMATION FOR USERS

Your drug prescription is tailored for you. Do not alter dosage without checking with your physician.

How taken

Tablets.

Frequency and timing of doses
2–4 x daily with food.

Usual adult dosage range
1.5–2.5g daily, with a low dose at the start of treatment.

Onset of effect
Within 2 hours. It may take 2 weeks to achieve control of diabetes.

Duration of action
8–12 hours.

Diet advice
An individualized low-fat, low-sugar diet must be maintained in order for the drug to be fully effective. Follow your physician's advice.

Storage
Keep in a closed container in a cool, dry place out of the reach of children.

Missed dose
Take as soon as you remember. If your next dose is due within 2 hours, take a single dose now and skip the next.

Stopping the drug
Do not stop taking the drug without consulting your physician; stopping the drug may lead to worsening of the underlying condition.

OVERDOSE ACTION

 Seek immediate medical advice in all cases. Take emergency action if seizures or loss of consciousness occur.

See Drug poisoning emergency guide (p.526).

SPECIAL PRECAUTIONS

Be sure to tell your physician if:
▼ You have long-term liver or kidney problems.
▼ You have heart failure.
▼ You are a heavy drinker.
▼ You are taking other medications.

 Pregnancy
▼ Not usually prescribed. Insulin is usually substituted because it provides better diabetic control during pregnancy. Discuss with your physician.

 Breast-feeding
▼ Safety not established. Discuss with your physician.

 Infants and children
▼ Not recommended.

 Over 60
▼ Increased likelihood of adverse effects. Reduced dose may therefore be necessary.

 Driving and hazardous work
▼ Usually no problems. Avoid such activities if you have warning signs of low blood sugar.

 Alcohol
▼ Avoid. Alcohol increases the risk of low blood sugar, and can cause coma by increasing the acidity of the blood.

Surgery and general anesthetics
▼ Surgery may reduce the response to this drug. Notify your physician that you are diabetic before any surgery; insulin treatment may need to be substituted. Tell your physician if you are to have a contrast X-ray; metformin should be stopped before the procedure.

POSSIBLE ADVERSE EFFECTS

Minor gastrointestinal symptoms such as nausea are often helped by taking the drug with food. Diarrhea usually settles after a few days of treatment. The most serious side effect is a potentially fatal build-up of lactic acid in the blood. This is very rare and usually occurs in diabetics with impaired kidney function.

Symptom/effect	Frequency		Discuss with physician		Stop taking drug now	Call physician now
	Common	Rare	Only if severe	In all cases		
Loss of appetite/metallic taste	●		■			
Nausea/vomiting	●		■			
Diarrhea		●	■			
Dizziness/confusion		●		■		
Weakness/sweating		●		■		
Rash		●		■		

INTERACTIONS

General note A number of drugs reduce the effects of metformin. These include corticosteroids, estrogens, and diuretics. Other drugs, notably monoamine oxidase inhibitors (MAOIs) and beta blockers, increase its effects.

Warfarin Metformin may increase the effect of this anticoagulant drug. The dosage of warfarin may need to be adjusted accordingly.

PROLONGED USE

Prolonged treatment with metformin can deplete reserves of vitamin B_{12}, and this may rarely cause anemia.

Monitoring Regular checks on kidney function and on blood sugar control are usually required. Vitamin B_{12} levels may also be checked annually.

METHADONE

Product name Metadol
Used in the following combined preparations Cophylac Drops

GENERAL INFORMATION

Methadone is a synthetic drug belonging to the *opioid analgesic* group. It is used in the control of severe pain, and usually used to replace morphine or other opioids in the treatment of *dependence*. For this, methadone can be given once daily to prevent *withdrawal symptoms*. In some cases, dosage can be reduced until the drug is no longer needed.

Tolerance to methadone is marked. Although the initial dose for a person not used to opioids is very low, the dose needed by someone who is dependent could be fatal for a non-user.

QUICK REFERENCE

Drug group Opioid analgesics (p.64)
Overdose danger rating High
Dependence rating High
Prescription needed Yes
Available as generic No

INFORMATION FOR USERS

Your drug prescription is tailored for you. Do not alter dosage without checking with your physician.

How taken

Tablets, liquid.

Frequency and timing of doses
Pain 3–4 x daily; 2 x daily (prolonged use).
Opioid dependence Once daily.

Usual adult dosage range
Pain 5–10mg per dose initially, adjusted according to response.
Opioid dependence 15–30mg (starting dose); 40–60mg daily (maintenance dose).

Onset of effect
15–60 minutes.

Duration of action
36–48 hours.

Diet advice
None.

Storage
Keep in a closed container in a cool, dry place out of the reach of children. Protect liquids from light.

Missed dose
Take as soon as you remember and return to your normal dosing schedule as soon as possible. If you missed the dose because it caused you to vomit, or if you cannot swallow, consult your physician. If you miss 3 or more doses, do not resume taking; consult your physician.

Stopping the drug
Dosage should be tapered off gradually, not stopped abruptly. Discuss with your physician.

OVERDOSE ACTION

 Seek immediate medical advice in all cases. Take emergency action if symptoms such as slow or irregular breathing, severe drowsiness, or loss of consciousness occur.

See Drug poisoning emergency guide (p.526).

SPECIAL PRECAUTIONS

Be sure to tell your physician if:
▼ You have heart or circulatory problems.
▼ You have liver or kidney problems.
▼ You have lung problems such as asthma or bronchitis.
▼ You have thyroid disease.
▼ You have a history of epileptic seizures.
▼ You have a phaeochromocytoma (a type of adrenal gland tumour).
▼ You have problems with alcohol abuse.
▼ You are taking other medications.

 Pregnancy
▼ Not prescribed in late pregnancy if possible. May cause breathing difficulties in the newborn baby. Discuss with your physician.

 Breast-feeding
▼ The drug passes into breast milk and may affect the baby adversely. Discuss with your physician.

 Infants and children
▼ Not recommended.

 Over 60
▼ Not recommended.

 Driving and hazardous work
▼ Your underlying condition may make such activities inadvisable. Discuss with your physician.

 Alcohol
▼ Avoid. Alcohol increases the sedative effects of the drug and may depress breathing.

PROLONGED USE

Treatment with methadone is always closely monitored. If the drug is being taken long-term, the dose must be carefully reduced before the drug is stopped.

POSSIBLE ADVERSE EFFECTS

Drowsiness and nausea are the most common *side effects* of methadone, but these diminish as the body adapts. Constipation is also common and may be longer lasting.

Symptom/effect	Frequency		Discuss with physician		Stop taking drug now	Call physician now
	Common	Rare	Only if severe	In all cases		
Nausea/vomiting	●		■			
Drowsiness	●		■			
Constipation	●		■			
Dizziness/confusion	●			■		
Loss of consciousness		●		■	▲	▌
Slow, difficult breathing		●		■	▲	▌

INTERACTIONS

Phenytoin, carbamazepine, rifampin, and ritonavir These drugs may reduce the effects of methadone.

Monoamine oxidase inhibitors (MAOIs) and selegiline Taken with methadone, these drugs may produce a dangerous rise or fall in blood pressure.

Sedatives The effects of all drugs that have a sedative effect on the central nervous system are likely to be increased by methadone.

METHOTREXATE

Product names Metoject, ratio-Methotrexate Sodium, and others
Used in the following combined preparations None

GENERAL INFORMATION

Methotrexate is an anticancer drug used, together with other anticancer drugs, in the treatment of leukemia, lymphoma, and solid cancers such as those of the breast, bladder, head, and neck. It is also used to treat inflammatory conditions such as severe uncontrolled psoriasis, rheumatoid arthritis, and Crohn's disease.

As with most anticancer drugs, methotrexate affects both healthy and cancerous cells, so that its usefulness is limited by its *adverse effects* and toxicity. Folic acid may reduce its toxicity, and when it is given in high doses, methotrexate is usually given with folinic acid to prevent it from destroying bone marrow cells. Because of its toxicity and adverse effects, it is very important that you do not take methotrexate more often than prescribed by your doctor.

INFORMATION FOR USERS

Your drug prescription is tailored for you. Do not alter dosage without checking with your physician.

How taken

Tablets, injection.

Frequency and timing of doses
Cancer Single dose once weekly or every 3 weeks.
Other conditions Single dose once weekly.

Usual adult dosage range
Cancer Dosage is determined individually according to the nature of the condition, body weight, and response.
Rheumatoid arthritis 7.5–20mg weekly.
Psoriasis 10–25mg weekly.

Onset of effect
30–60 minutes.

Duration of action
Short-term effects last up to 24 hours.

Diet advice
None.

Storage
Keep in a closed container in a cool, dry place out of the reach of children. Wash your hands after handling the tablets.

Missed dose
Take as soon as you remember and consult your physician.

Stopping the drug
Do not stop taking the drug without consulting your physician. Stopping the drug may lead to worsening of the underlying condition.

OVERDOSE ACTION

 Seek immediate medical advice in all cases. Take emergency action if breathing problems or loss of consciousness occur.

See Drug poisoning emergency guide (p.526).

SPECIAL PRECAUTIONS

Be sure to tell your physician if:
▼ You have liver or kidney problems.
▼ You have porphyria.
▼ You have a problem with alcohol abuse.
▼ You have a peptic or other digestive-tract ulcer.
▼ You are taking other medications, especially NSAIDs or antibiotics.

 Pregnancy
▼ Not prescribed. Methotrexate may cause birth defects in the unborn baby.

 Breast-feeding
▼ Not advised. The drug passes into the breast milk and may affect the baby adversely.

 Infants and children
▼ For cancer treatment only. Reduced dose necessary.

 Over 60
▼ Increased likelihood of adverse effects. Reduced doses necessary.

 Driving and hazardous work
▼ No special problems.

 **Alcohol**
▼ Avoid. Alcohol may increase the adverse effects of methotrexate.

POSSIBLE ADVERSE EFFECTS

Nausea and vomiting may occur within a few hours of taking methotrexate. Diarrhea and mouth ulcers are also common side effects occurring a few days after starting treatment.

Symptom/effect	Frequency		Discuss with physician		Stop taking drug now	Call physician now
	Common	Rare	Only if severe	In all cases		
Nausea/vomiting	●			■		
Diarrhea	●			■		
Dry cough/chest pain	●		■			
Mouth/gum ulcers/inflammation	●			■	▲	▌
Jaundice		●		■	▲	▌
Mood changes/confusion		●		■		
Sore throat/fever		●		■	▲	▌
Rash		●		■	▲	▌
Easy bruising/bleeding		●		■	▲	▌
Breathlessness		●		■	▲	▌

INTERACTIONS

General note Many drugs, including NSAIDs, diuretics, cyclosporine, phenytoin, and probenecid, may increase blood levels and toxicity of methotrexate.

Co-trimoxazole, trimethoprim, and certain antimalarial drugs These drugs may enhance the effects of methotrexate.

PROLONGED USE

Long-term treatment with methotrexate may be needed for rheumatoid arthritis. Once the condition is controlled, the drug is reduced as much as possible to the lowest effective dose. Long-term methotrexate treatment may occasionally lead to breathing problems due to scarring of the lungs or, rarely, unusual respiratory infections, such as pneumocystis pneumonia.

Monitoring Full blood counts and kidney and liver function tests will be performed before treatment starts and at intervals during treatment.

METHYLDOPA

Product names Novo-Medopa, Nu-Medopa
Used in the following combined preparations PMS-Dopazide, and others

GENERAL INFORMATION

Introduced in the 1960s, methyldopa was, for many years, one of the most widely prescribed antihypertensive drugs for the treatment of high blood pressure. In recent years, its use has declined as newer drugs with fewer *side effects* have been introduced. However, it is effective in treating people for whom other, newer drugs are ineffective, and for treating those patients who have taken the drug for many years without experiencing any of the side effects.

Unlike some other antihypertensives, methyldopa does not reduce blood flow to the kidneys and is therefore used for patients with kidney disorders.

Methyldopa does not affect the fetus, so it is often prescribed to pregnant women who have high blood pressure.

QUICK REFERENCE

Drug group Antihypertensive drugs (p.88)

Overdose danger rating Medium

Dependence rating Low

Prescription needed Yes

Available as generic Yes

INFORMATION FOR USERS

Your drug prescription is tailored for you. Do not alter dosage without checking with your physician.

How taken

Tablets.

Frequency and timing of doses
2–3 x daily.

Usual dosage range
Adults 500mg–3g daily.
Children Reduced dose necessary.

Onset of effect
3–6 hours. Full effect begins in 2–3 days.

Duration of action
6–12 hours. Some effect may last for 1–2 days after stopping the drug.

Diet advice
None.

Storage
Keep in a closed container in a cool, dry place out of the reach of children. Protect from light.

Missed dose
Take as soon as you remember. If your next dose is due within 2 hours, take a single dose now and skip the next.

Stopping the drug
Do not stop the drug without consulting your physician, who will gradually reduce your dose. Suddenly stopping methyldopa may lead to an increase in blood pressure.

Exceeding the dose
An occasional unintentional extra dose is unlikely to cause problems. Large overdoses may cause excessive drowsiness and slow heart beat. Notify your physician.

SPECIAL PRECAUTIONS

Be sure to tell your physician if:
▼ You have long-term liver or kidney problems.
▼ You have anemia.
▼ You have porphyria.
▼ You have angina.
▼ You suffer from depression.
▼ You are taking other medications.

Pregnancy
▼ No evidence of risk.

Breast-feeding
▼ The drug passes into the breast milk, but at normal doses *adverse effects* on the baby are unlikely. Discuss with your physician.

Infants and children
▼ Reduced dose necessary.

Over 60
▼ Reduced dose necessary.

Driving and hazardous work
▼ Avoid such activities until you have learned how methyldopa affects you because the drug can cause drowsiness.

Alcohol
▼ Avoid. Alcohol may increase the hypotensive and sedative effects of this drug.

Surgery and general anesthetics
▼ Discuss the possibility of stopping methyldopa with your physician or dentist before any surgery.

POSSIBLE ADVERSE EFFECTS

Most adverse effects are uncommon and diminish in time. The fluid retention that occurs during treatment with methyldopa is counteracted by taking a diuretic.

Symptom/effect	Frequency		Discuss with physician		Stop taking drug now	Call physician now
	Common	Rare	Only if severe	In all cases		
Drowsiness	●		■			
Depression/headaches	●			■		
Nightmares	●			■		
Erectile dysfunction/ decreased libido	●		■			
Fever		●		■		
Stuffy nose		●		■		
Dizziness/fainting		●		■		
Nausea/vomiting		●		■		
Rash		●		■	▲	
Jaundice		●		■	▲	■

PROLONGED USE

Liver and blood problems may occur rarely.

Monitoring Periodic checks on blood and urine are usually required.

INTERACTIONS

Antidepressants Tricyclic antidepressants may increase the effects of methyldopa. Monoamine oxidase inhibitors (MAOIs) should not be taken at the same time as methyldopa as they may cause a dangerous drop in blood pressure.

Lithium Concurrent use of methyldopa and lithium may increase the risk of lithium *toxicity*.

Levodopa The effects of methyldopa may be enhanced by levodopa.

METHYLPHENIDATE

Product names Concerta, ratio-Methylphenidate, Ritalin, and others
Used in the following combined preparations None

GENERAL INFORMATION

Methylphenidate is a mild central nervous system stimulant used in the treatment of attention-deficit hyper-activity disorder (ADHD). People with this disorder have difficulty concentrating and are easily distracted. Medication is only one part of an ongoing treatment program, along with psychological, social, and educational interventions.

Methylphenidate tablets are usually given 2 or 3 times daily. Once its effect has worn off there are no residual effects. Slow-release (SR) tablets, and extended-release (ER) and controlled-release (CR) capsules are also available. These must be swallowed whole. SR starts to work slowly and may have a longer action than the regular tablets. ER and CR capsules are taken once daily.

Insomnia and reduced appetite are the main side effects in children; these can improve with time. Growth may be slowed in children while taking this drug and should be monitored. However, if affected, growth often returns to normal once the drug is stopped.

INFORMATION FOR USERS

Your drug prescription is tailored for you. Do not alter dosage without checking with your physician.

How taken

Tablets, slow release (SR) tablets, extended and controlled release (ER and CR) capsules.

Frequency and timing of doses
2–3 x daily (tablets), once daily (SR/ER/CR).

Usual dosage range
10–30mg daily, adjusted according to weight and response (regular); 18–54 mg daily (ER).

Onset of effect
30–60 minutes (tablets).

Duration of action
3–5 hours (tablets), 8 hrs (SR), 24 hrs (ER/CR).

Diet advice
None.

Storage
Keep in a closed container in a cool, dry place out of the reach of children.

Missed dose
Take as needed. Allow at least 4 hours between doses of regular tablets.

Stopping the drug
Can safely be stopped. Consult your physician re: overall management of your ADHD.

OVERDOSE ACTION

 Seek immediate medical advice in all cases. Take emergency action if confusion, palpitations, seizures, or loss of consciousness occur.

See Drug poisoning emergency guide (p.526).

POSSIBLE ADVERSE EFFECTS

The main adverse effects in children are insomnia and decreased appetite; these may improve with time. Abdominal pain, headache, and irritability may occur at start of treatment.

Symptom/effect	Frequency		Discuss with physician		Stop taking drug now	Call physician now
	Common	Rare	Only if severe	In all cases		
Decreased appetite	●		■			
Insomnia/nervousness	●		■			
Nausea/abdominal pain	●			■		
Headache/fatigue	●			■		
Irritability/anxiety		●		■		
Sadness/social withdrawal		●		■		
Palpitations/chest pain	●			■		■

INTERACTIONS

General note Methylphenidate may interact with many drugs to increase their effects. These include anticoagulants, anticonvulsants, and tricyclic antidepressants.

Antihypertensive drugs Methylphenidate may reverse the effect of these drugs.

Sympathomimetics and MAOIs May cause severe hypertension when used with methylphenidate (and up to 2 weeks after MAOI discontinuation).

SPECIAL PRECAUTIONS

Be sure to tell your physician if:
▼ You have high blood pressure or heart disease.
▼ You have thyroid disease or glaucoma.
▼ You have a history of seizures/epilepsy.
▼ You have a family history of Tourette's syndrome or motor tics.
▼ You are taking other medications.
▼ You are involved in strenuous exercise or activities.
▼ You have a family history of sudden death related to a heart condition.

 Pregnancy
▼ Safety in pregnancy not established. Discuss with your physician.

 Breast-feeding
▼ It is not known if the drug passes into the breast milk. Discuss with your physician.

 Infants and children
▼ Not recommended for children under 6 years.

 Over 60
▼ Increased likelihood of adverse effects. Reduced dose may therefore be necessary.

 Driving and hazardous work
▼ Avoid such activities until you have learned how the drug affects you; it can cause dizziness.

Alcohol
▼ Avoid. Effects of drug may be enhanced by alcohol.

PROLONGED USE

Continuous, long-term use may impair growth. "Drug holidays" may be recommended by your physician.

Monitoring Your physician will assess growth and blood pressure at regular intervals. In addition, periodic checks of blood count may be advised.

METHYLPREDNISOLONE

Product names Depo-Medrol, Medrol, Methylprednisolone Sodium Succinate for Injection, Solu-Medrol, and others
Used in the following combined preparations Depo-Medrol with Lidocaine, Medrol Acne Lotion, Neo-Medrol Acne Lotion

GENERAL INFORMATION

Methylprednisolone, introduced in 1957, is a synthetic corticosteroid drug derived from prednisolone. It is prescribed as a topical lotion to relieve skin conditions such as dermatitis, eczema, psoriasis, and to control acne. Methylprednisolone can be injected into joints to relieve rheumatoid arthritis and other types of joint inflammation (see p.104). It is also prescribed by mouth to replace *hormones* in pituitary or adrenal gland disorders that reduce the body's natural corticosteroid production. Occasionally, methylprednisolone tablets are given for the long-term control of severe asthma.

Side effects are rare when the drug is administered short-term. However, long-term treatment by mouth can cause *adverse effects* such as fluid retention, indigestion, fragile bones, and muscle weakness. It may also induce diabetes.

INFORMATION FOR USERS

Your drug prescription is tailored for you. Do not alter dosage without checking with your physician.

How taken

Tablets, injection, topical lotion.

Frequency and timing of doses
Varies according to preparation and condition. Follow your physician's instructions.

Usual dosage range
Considerable variation. Follow your physician's instructions.

Onset of effect
2–4 days.

Duration of action
12–36 hours.

Diet advice
A low-sodium, high-potassium diet may be recommended when the oral or injectable form of the drug is prescribed for extended periods. Follow the advice of your physician.

Storage
Keep in a closed container in a cool, dry place out of the reach of children.

Missed dose
Take as soon as you remember. If your next dose is due within 6 hours, take a single dose now and skip the next.

Stopping the drug
Do not stop tablets without consulting your physician, who may supervise a gradual reduction in dosage. Abrupt cessation may cause adrenal collapse.

Exceeding the dose
An occasional unintentional extra dose is unlikely to be a cause for concern. But if you notice unusual symptoms, or if a large overdose has been taken, notify your physician.

SPECIAL PRECAUTIONS

Be sure to tell your physician if:
▼ You have had glaucoma.
▼ You have high blood pressure.
▼ You have diabetes.
▼ You have had a peptic ulcer.
▼ You have a history of depression.
▼ You have a herpes infection.
▼ You are taking other medications.

Pregnancy
▼ No evidence of risk with topical preparations or joint injections. Prescribed in tablet form in low doses, harm to the baby is unlikely. Discuss with your physician.

Breast-feeding
▼ No evidence of risk with topical solutions or joint injections. Taken regularly by mouth, the drug may adversely affect the baby's growth. Discuss with your physician.

Infants and children
▼ Reduced dose necessary.

Over 60
▼ Reduced dose may be necessary.

Driving and hazardous work
▼ No known problems.

Alcohol
▼ Alcohol may increase the risk of peptic ulcers with methylprednisolone tablets. No special problems with other dosage forms.

POSSIBLE ADVERSE EFFECTS

The rare, but more serious, adverse effects occur only when methylprednisolone is taken by mouth in high doses for long periods of time.

Symptom/effect	Frequency		Discuss with physician		Stop taking drug now	Call physician now
	Common	Rare	Only if severe	In all cases		
Indigestion/weight gain	●		■			
Muscle weakness		●		■		
Mood changes		●		■		
Seizures		●		■	▲	❚
Black/bloody feces		●		■	▲	❚

INTERACTIONS

Oral anticoagulants Methylprednisolone may decrease the effect of anticoagulants.

Vaccines Serious reactions can occur when vaccinations are given with methylprednisolone. Discuss with your physician.

Barbiturates, phenytoin, and rifampin These drugs may reduce the effect of methylprednisolone.

Antidiabetic drugs Methylprednisolone reduces the actions of these drugs.

Antihypertensive drugs Methylprednisolone may reduce the effect of these drugs.

Diuretics Methylprednisolone may increase potassium loss.

PROLONGED USE

Prolonged use of methylprednisolone in high doses by mouth can lead to serious adverse effects, such as diabetes, glaucoma, muscle weakness, cataracts, and fragile bones. The drug may retard growth in children.

METOCLOPRAMIDE

Product names Apo-Metoclop, Metoclopramide Omega, and others
Used in the following combined preparations None

GENERAL INFORMATION

Metoclopramide has a direct action on the gastrointestinal tract. It is used for conditions in which there is a need to encourage normal propulsion of food through the stomach and intestine.

The drug has powerful anti-emetic properties and its most common use is in the prevention and treatment of nausea and vomiting. It is particularly effective for the relief of the nausea that sometimes accompanies migraine headaches. It is also prescribed to alleviate symptoms of hiatus hernia caused by acid reflux into the esophagus.

One *side effect* of metoclopramide, muscle spasm of the head and neck, is more likely to occur in children and young adults under 20 years. Other side effects are not usually troublesome.

QUICK REFERENCE

Drug group Gastrointestinal motility regulator and anti-emetic drugs (p.74)

Overdose danger rating Medium

Dependence rating Low

Prescription needed Yes

Available as generic Yes

INFORMATION FOR USERS

Your drug prescription is tailored for you. Do not alter dosage without checking with your physician.

How taken

Tablets, liquid, injection.

Frequency and timing of doses
Usually 3 x daily.

Usual adult dosage range
Usually 15–30mg daily; may be higher for nausea caused by anticancer drugs.

Onset of effect
Within 1 hour.

Duration of action
6–8 hours.

Diet advice
Fatty and spicy foods and alcohol are best avoided if nausea is a problem.

Storage
Keep in a closed container in a cool, dry place out of the reach of children.

Missed dose
Take as soon as you remember. If your next dose is due within 3 hours, take a single dose now and skip the next.

Stopping the drug
Can be safely stopped as soon as you no longer need it.

Exceeding the dose
An occasional unintentional extra dose is unlikely to be a cause for concern. Large overdoses may cause drowsiness and muscle spasms. Notify your physician.

POSSIBLE ADVERSE EFFECTS

The main *adverse effects* of metoclopramide are drowsiness and, even less commonly, uncontrolled muscle spasm. Other symptoms rarely occur.

Symptom/effect	Frequency		Discuss with physician		Stop taking drug now	Call physician now
	Common	Rare	Only if severe	In all cases		
Drowsiness		●	■			
Restlessness		●		■		
Diarrhea		●		■		
Muscle tremor/rigidity		●		■		▮
Muscle spasm of head/neck		●		■	▲	▮

INTERACTIONS

Sedatives The *sedative* properties of metoclopramide are increased by all drugs that have a sedative effect on the central nervous system. Such drugs include benzodiazepines, antihistamines, antidepressants, *opioid* analgesics, and antipsychotics.

Cyclosporine Metoclopramide may increase the blood levels of this drug.

Antipsychotics and tricyclic antidepressants Metoclopramide increases the risk of adverse effects from these drugs.

Phenothiazine antipsychotics The likelihood of adverse effects from these drugs is increased by metoclopramide.

Lithium Metoclopramide increases the risk of central nervous system side effects.

SPECIAL PRECAUTIONS

Be sure to tell your physician if:
▼ You have long-term liver or kidney problems.
▼ You have epilepsy.
▼ You have Parkinson's disease.
▼ You have porphyria.
▼ You have a history of depression.
▼ You are taking other medications.

Pregnancy
▼ Safety in pregnancy not established. Discuss with your physician.

Breast-feeding
▼ The drug passes into the breast milk but at normal doses adverse effects on the baby are unlikely. Discuss with your physician.

Infants and children
▼ Reduced dose necessary. Restricted use in patients younger than 20 years.

Over 60
▼ Reduced dose may be necessary.

Driving and hazardous work
▼ Avoid such activities until you have learned how metoclopramide affects you because the drug can cause drowsiness.

Alcohol
▼ Avoid. Alcohol may oppose the beneficial effects and increase the sedative effects of this drug. Metoclopramide may also increase the rate of absorption of alcohol.

PROLONGED USE

Not normally used long-term, except under specialist supervision for certain gastrointestinal disorders.

METOPROLOL

Product names Betaloc, Lopresor, and others
Used in the following combined preparations None

GENERAL INFORMATION

Metoprolol is a cardioselective beta blocker. It is used to prevent the heart from beating too quickly in conditions such as angina, arrhythmias, and hyperthyroidism. It is also used to treat hypertension (high blood pressure), prevent migraine attacks, and to protect the heart from further damage following a heart attack.

It is less likely to provoke breathing difficulties than other, non-cardioselective, beta blockers. However, it should be avoided in people with asthma. It may also slow the body's response to low blood sugar in diabetics on insulin.

QUICK REFERENCE

Drug group Beta-blocker (p.83)
Overdose danger rating High
Dependence rating Low
Prescription needed Yes
Available as generic Yes

INFORMATION FOR USERS

Your drug prescription is tailored for you. Do not alter dosage without checking with your physician.

How taken

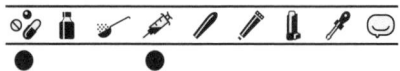

Tablets, SR-tablets, injection.

Frequency and timing of doses
1–2 x daily (hypertension); 2–3 x daily (angina/arrhythmias); 4 x daily for 2 days, then 2 x daily (heart attack prevention); 2 x daily (migraine prevention); 4 x daily (hyperthyroidism).

Usual adult dosage range
100–300mg daily.

Onset of effect
1–2 hours.

Duration of action
3–7 hours.

Diet advice
None.

Storage
Keep in a closed container in a cool, dry place out of the reach of children.

Missed dose
Take as soon as you remember. If your next dose is due within 2 hours, take a single dose now and skip the next.

Stopping the drug
Do not stop taking the drug without consulting your physician. Stopping suddenly may lead to worsening of the underlying condition.

OVERDOSE ACTION

 Seek immediate medical advice in all cases. Take emergency action if breathing difficulties, collapse, or loss of consciousness occur.

See Drug poisoning emergency guide (p.526).

POSSIBLE ADVERSE EFFECTS

Metoprolol's *adverse effects* are common to most beta blockers and tend to diminish with long-term use. Fainting may be a sign that the drug has slowed the heart beat excessively.

Symptom/effect	Frequency		Discuss with physician		Stop taking drug now	Call physician now
	Common	Rare	Only if severe	In all cases		
Cold hands and feet	●		■			
Fatigue/lethargy	●		■			
Nausea/vomiting		●	■			
Rash/dry eyes		●		■	▲	
Visual disturbances		●		■	▲	
Breathing difficulties/wheezing		●		■	▲	∎
Fainting/palpitations		●		■	▲	∎

INTERACTIONS

Antihypertensive drugs Metoprolol may enhance the blood-pressure-lowering effect.

Calcium channel blockers may cause low blood pressure, a slow heart beat, and heart failure if used with metoprolol.

Cardiac glucosides (e.g. digoxin) may increase the heart-slowing effect of metoprolol.

Antidiabetic drugs Taken with metoprolol, these drugs may increase the risk or mask the symptoms of low blood sugar.

Non-steroidal anti-inflammatory drugs (NSAIDs) may reduce the antihypertensive effects of metoprolol.

SPECIAL PRECAUTIONS

Be sure to tell your physician if:
▼ You have liver or kidney problems.
▼ You have asthma, bronchitis, or emphysema.
▼ You have heart problems.
▼ You have diabetes.
▼ You have psoriasis.
▼ You are taking other medications.

 Pregnancy
▼ Not usually prescribed. May affect the baby. Discuss with your physician.

 Breast-feeding
▼ The drug passes into the breast milk, but at normal doses adverse effects on the baby are unlikely. Discuss with your physician.

 Infants and children
▼ Not recommended.

 Over 60
▼ Reduced dose necessary. There may be an increased risk of adverse effects.

 Driving and hazardous work
▼ Avoid such activities until you have learned how metoprolol affects you because the drug can cause fatigue, dizziness, and drowsiness.

 Alcohol
▼ Avoid excessive intake. Alcohol may increase the blood-pressure-lowering effects of metoprolol.

PROLONGED USE

No special problems.

METRONIDAZOLE

Product names Flagyl, Florazole ER, MetroGel, MetroCream, Noritate, NidaGel Vaginal, and others
Used in the following combined preparations Flagystatin, and others

GENERAL INFORMATION

Metronidazole is prescribed to fight both protozoal infections and a variety of bacterial infections.

It is widely used in the treatment of trichomonas infection. Because the organism responsible for this disorder is sexually transmitted and may not cause any symptoms, a simultaneous course of treatment is usually advised for the sexual partner.

Certain infections of the abdomen, pelvis, and gums also respond well to metronidazole. The drug is used to treat septicemia, infected leg ulcers and pressure sores. It is also used to treat *Clostridium difficile* infections associated with antibiotic use. Metronidazole may be given to prevent or treat infections after surgery. Because the drug in high doses can penetrate the brain, it is prescribed to treat abscesses occurring there.

Metronidazole is also prescribed for amoebic dysentery and giardiasis, a rare protozoal infection.

QUICK REFERENCE

Drug group Antibacterial (p.117) and antiprotozoal drugs (p.122)

Overdose danger rating Low

Dependence rating Low

Prescription needed Yes

Available as generic Yes

INFORMATION FOR USERS

Your drug prescription is tailored for you. Do not alter dosage without checking with your physician.

How taken

Capsules, tablets, liquid, injection, suppositories, gel, cream, vaginal cream and gel.

Frequency and timing of doses
3 x daily for 5–10 days, depending on the condition being treated. Sometimes a single large dose is prescribed. Tablets should be taken after meals and swallowed whole with plenty of water.

Usual adult dosage range
600–1,500mg daily (by mouth); 3g daily (suppositories); 1.5g daily (injection).

Onset of effect
The drug starts to work within an hour or so, but beneficial effects may not be felt for 1–2 days.

Duration of action
6–12 hours.

Diet advice
None.

Storage
Keep in a closed container in a cool, dry place out of the reach of children. Protect from light.

Missed dose
Take as soon as you remember. If your next dose is due within 2 hours, take a single dose now and skip the next.

Stopping the drug
Take the full course. Even if you feel better, the infection may still be present and symptoms may recur if treatment is stopped too soon.

Exceeding the dose
An occasional unintentional extra dose is unlikely to be a cause for concern. But if you notice unusual symptoms, especially numbness or tingling, or if a large overdose has been taken, notify your physician.

SPECIAL PRECAUTIONS

Be sure to tell your physician if:
▼ You have long-term liver or kidney problems.
▼ You have porphyria.
▼ You have a blood disorder.
▼ You have a disorder of the central nervous system, such as epilepsy.
▼ You are taking other medications.

Pregnancy
▼ Safety in pregnancy not established. Discuss with your physician.

Breast-feeding
▼ The drug passes into the breast milk, but at normal doses adverse effects on the baby are unlikely. However, metronidazole may give the milk a bitter taste. Discuss with your physician.

Infants and children
▼ Reduced dose necessary.

Over 60
▼ No special problems.

Driving and hazardous work
▼ Avoid such activities until you have learned how metronidazole affects you because the drug can cause dizziness and drowsiness.

Alcohol
▼ Avoid. Taken with metronidazole, alcohol may cause flushing, nausea, vomiting, abdominal pain, and headache. Avoid alcohol during treatment and for 24 hours after the last dose.

POSSIBLE ADVERSE EFFECTS

Various minor gastrointestinal disturbances are common but tend to diminish with time. The drug may cause a darkening of the urine, which is of no concern. More serious *adverse effects* on the nervous system, causing numbness or tingling, are extremely rare.

Symptom/effect	Frequency		Discuss with physician		Stop taking drug now	Call physician now
	Common	Rare	Only if severe	In all cases		
Nausea/loss of appetite	●		■			
Dark urine	●		■			
Dry mouth/metallic taste		●	■			
Headache/dizziness		●	■			
Numbness/tingling		●		■		

INTERACTIONS

Oral anticoagulants, phenytoin, and fluorouracil Metronidazole may increase the effects of these drugs.

Lithium Metronidazole increases the risk of adverse effects on the kidneys.

Cimetidine This drug may increase the levels of metronidazole in the body.

Phenobarbital This drug may reduce the effects of metronidazole.

PROLONGED USE

Not usually prescribed for longer than 10 days. Prolonged treatment may cause loss of sensation in the hands and feet (usually temporary), and may also reduce production of white blood cells.

MICONAZOLE

Product names Micatin, Monistat, Micozole
Used in the following combined preparations None

GENERAL INFORMATION

Miconazole is an antifungal drug used to treat candida (yeast) infections of the vagina, and a range of other fungal infections affecting the skin.

The drug is available as a treatment for skin infections, and a variety of vaginal preparations is available.

Side effects are rare because miconazole is absorbed in only very small quantities following *topical* or vaginal application.

The vaginal *suppositories*, vaginal ovules, and vaginal cream damage latex condoms and diaphragms.

INFORMATION FOR USERS

Follow instructions on the label. Call your physician if symptoms worsen.

How taken

Vaginal suppositories, vaginal cream, vaginal ovules, cream, spray, ointment.

Frequency and timing of doses
1–2 x daily (vaginal/skin preparations).

Usual adult dosage range
Vaginal infections 1 x 5g applicatorful (cream); 1 x 100mg suppository; 1 x 400mg or 1.2g vaginal ovule.
Skin infections As directed.

Onset of effect
2–3 days.

Duration of action
Up to 12 hours.

Diet advice
None.

Storage
Keep in a closed container in a cool, dry place out of the reach of children.

Missed dose
No cause for concern, but apply missed dose or application as soon as you remember.

Stopping the drug
Apply the full course. Even if you feel better, the original infection may still be present and may recur if treatment is stopped too soon.

Exceeding the dose
An occasional unintentional extra dose is unlikely to cause problems. But if you notice any unusual symptoms or if a large amount has been swallowed, notify your physician.

POSSIBLE ADVERSE EFFECTS

Adverse effects are rare with miconazole.

Symptom/effect	Frequency		Discuss with physician		Stop taking drug now	Call physician now
	Common	Rare	Only if severe	In all cases		
Skin irritation/rash		●	■			
Nausea/vomiting		●	■			
Vaginal irritation		●		■		

INTERACTIONS

Warfarin Miconazole may increase the effects of warfarin.

SPECIAL PRECAUTIONS

Be sure to consult your physician or pharmacist before taking this drug if:
▼ You have porphyria.
▼ You have liver problems.
▼ You are taking other medications.

Pregnancy
▼ No evidence of risk with topical preparations. Safety not established for other preparations. Discuss with your physician.

Breast-feeding
▼ Safety not established. Discuss with your physician.

Infants and children
▼ Discuss with your physician.

Over 60
▼ No special problems.

Driving and hazardous work
▼ No special problems.

Alcohol
▼ No special problems.

PROLONGED USE

No problems expected. Most types of miconazole are not usually prescribed long term.

MINOCYCLINE

Product names Minocin, and others
Used in the following combined preparations None

GENERAL INFORMATION

Minocycline is tetracycline antibiotic but has a longer duration of action than tetracycline itself. The drug is most commonly used to treat acne. It may be given to treat pneumonia or to prevent infection in people with chronic bronchitis, and to treat sexually transmitted infections such as gonorrhea and non-gonococcal urethritis. The drug's most frequent *side effects* are nausea, vomiting, and diarrhea. It also interferes with the balance mechanism in the inner ear, with resultant nausea, dizziness, and unsteadiness, but these symptoms generally disappear after the drug is stopped. Minocycline is safer to use than other tetracyclines in people with poor kidney function.

QUICK REFERENCE

Drug group Tetracycline antibiotic (p.114)

Overdose danger rating Low

Dependence rating Low

Prescription needed Yes

Available as generic Yes

INFORMATION FOR USERS

Your drug prescription is tailored for you. Do not alter dosage without checking with your physician.

How taken

Capsules.

Frequency and timing of doses
1–2 x daily.

Usual dosage range
Adults 100–200mg daily.
Children Reduced dose according to age and weight.

Onset of effect
4–12 hours.

Duration of action
Up to 24 hours.

Diet advice
Milk products may impair absorption; avoid from 1 hour before to 2 hours after dosage.

Storage
Keep in a closed container in a cool, dry, well-secured place out of the reach of children.

Missed dose
Take as soon as you remember. If your next dose is due within 4 hours, take a single dose now and skip the next.

Stopping the drug
Use the full course. Even if you feel better, the original infection may still be present and symptoms may recur if treatment is stopped too soon.

Exceeding the dose
An occasional unintentional extra dose is unlikely to be a cause for concern. But if you notice any unusual symptoms, or if a large overdose has been taken, notify your physician.

POSSIBLE ADVERSE EFFECTS

Minocycline may occasionally cause nausea, vomiting, or diarrhea. Other less common *adverse effects* are rashes, an increased sensitivity of the skin to sunlight, and, in some cases, dizziness and loss of balance (vertigo).

Symptom/effect	Frequency		Discuss with physician		Stop taking drug now	Call physician now
	Common	Rare	Only if severe	In all cases		
Nausea/vomiting/diarrhea	●		■			
Dizziness/vertigo	●			■	▲	
Rash/itching		●		■	▲	
Light-sensitive rash		●		■	▲	
Headache/blurred vision		●		■	▲	

INTERACTIONS

Oral anticoagulants Minocycline may increase the anticoagulant action of these drugs.

Retinoids Taken with minocycline these drugs may increase the risk of benign intracranial hypertension (high pressure in the skull) leading to headaches, nausea, and vomiting.

Oral contraceptives Minocycline can reduce the effectiveness of these drugs.

Penicillin antibiotics Minocycline interferes with the antibacterial action of these drugs.

Antacids, bismuth, calcium, iron and milk interfere with the absorption of oral minocycline and may reduce its effectiveness. Doses should be separated by 2 hours.

SPECIAL PRECAUTIONS

Be sure to tell your physician if:
▼ You have liver or kidney problems.
▼ You have previously suffered an allergic reaction to a tetracycline antibiotic.
▼ You have porphyria or systemic lupus erythematosus.
▼ You are taking other medications.

Pregnancy
▼ Not recommended.
Discuss with your physician.

Breast-feeding
▼ Generally no problems with short-term use. Discuss with your physician.

Infants and children
▼ Not recommended under 12 years. Reduced dose necessary in older children. May discolour developing teeth.

Over 60
▼ No special problems.

Driving and hazardous work
▼ Avoid until you have learned how minocycline affects you because the drug can cause dizziness.

Alcohol
▼ No known problems.

How to take your tablets
▼ Take a small amount of water before, and a full glass of water after, each dose of minocycline. Take dose while sitting or standing and do not lie down immediately afterwards.

PROLONGED USE

Prolonged use of minocycline may occasionally cause skin darkening and discoloration of the teeth. Rarely, it may cause systemic lupus erythematosus.

Monitoring Regular blood tests should be carried out to assess liver function.

MINOXIDIL

Product names Apo-Gain, Loniten, Rogaine, and others
Used in the following combined preparations None

GENERAL INFORMATION

Minoxidil is a vasodilator drug (see p.98) that works by relaxing the muscles of artery walls and dilating blood vessels. It is effective in controlling dangerously high blood pressure. Because minoxidil is stronger acting than many other antihypertensive drugs, it is usually recommended for people whose blood pressure is not controlled by other treatment.

If minoxidil is taken for more than two months, it increases hair growth. This *side effect* is useful in treating baldness in men and women, and for this purpose, minoxidil is applied locally as a solution. Treatment of baldness is currently the most common use for this drug.

INFORMATION FOR USERS

Your drug prescription is tailored for you. Do not alter dosage without checking with your physician.

How taken

Tablets, topical solution.

Frequency and timing of doses
Once or twice daily.

Usual adult dosage range
Oral: 5mg daily initially, increasing gradually. Doses up to 40mg daily may be used.
Topical: 1ml twice daily of 2 per cent solution.

Onset of effect
Blood pressure Within 1 hour (tablets).
Hair growth 4 months–1 year (solution).

Duration of action
Oral: Up to 24 hours. Some effect may last for 2–5 days after stopping the drug.
Topical: Effect stops when drug is stopped.

Diet advice
None.

Storage
Keep in a closed container in a cool, dry place out of the reach of children.

Missed dose
Take as soon as you remember (tablets). If your next dose is due within 5 hours, take a single dose now and skip the next.

Stopping the drug
Do not stop the oral drug without consulting your physician; stopping the drug may lead to worsening of the underlying condition. If used topically for baldness, any regained hair will be lost when the drug is stopped.

Exceeding the dose
An occasional unintentional extra dose is unlikely to cause problems. Large overdoses may cause nausea, vomiting, palpitations, or dizziness. Notify your physician.

SPECIAL PRECAUTIONS

Be sure to tell your physician if:
▼ You have a long-term kidney problem.
▼ You have heart problems.
▼ You are taking other medications.

Pregnancy
▼ Safety in pregnancy not established. Discuss with your physician.

Breast-feeding
▼ The drug passes into the breast milk. Discuss with your physician.

Infants and children
▼ Reduced dose necessary.

Over 60
▼ Reduced dose may be necessary.

Driving and hazardous work
▼ Avoid such activities until you have learned how minoxidil affects you because the drug can cause dizziness and lightheadedness.

Alcohol
▼ Avoid. Alcohol may further reduce blood pressure.

Surgery and general anesthetics
▼ Minoxidil treatment may need to be stopped before you have a general anesthetic. Discuss this with your physician or dentist before any surgery.

POSSIBLE ADVERSE EFFECTS

Fluid retention is a common *adverse effect* of oral minoxidil, which may lead to an increase in weight. Diuretics are often prescribed to control this adverse effect. Allergic and irritant dermatitis may occur with minoxidil lotion.

Symptom/effect	Frequency		Discuss with physician		Stop taking drug now	Call physician now
	Common	Rare	Only if severe	In all cases		
Topical						
Increased hair growth	●		■			
Rash		●		■		
Oral						
Fluid retention/ankle swelling	●		■			
Nausea		●	■			
Breast tenderness		●		■		
Dizziness/lightheadedness		●		■		
Palpitations		●		■	▲	▮

PROLONGED USE

Prolonged use of this drug may lead to swelling of the ankles and increased hair growth.

INTERACTIONS

Antidepressant drugs The blood-pressure-lowering effects of minoxidil may be enhanced by antidepressant drugs that also lower blood pressure.

Other antihypertensives These drugs may increase the effects of minoxidil.

MIRTAZAPINE

Product names CO Mirtazapine, Gen-Mirtazapine, Remeron, Remeron RD, and others
Used in the following combined preparations None

GENERAL INFORMATION

Mirtazapine is an antidepressant chemically different than the SSRIs and tricyclic antidepressants. It is used in the treatment of mild to moderate depression. Mirtazapine is as effective as other antidepressants, and because it has little *anticholinergic* action, it is better tolerated than tricyclic antidepressants. It can cause drowsiness and weight gain. It may also cause a decrease in blood pressure on quickly sitting or standing up. Caution should be used; stand up slowly, while supporting oneself.

The RD formulation is an Orally Dispersible Tablet and rapidly disintegrates on the tongue; no water is needed to take these tablets. The regular tablets should be swallowed with water. It is best to take mirtazapine in the evening prior to sleep.

INFORMATION FOR USERS

Your drug prescription is tailored for you. Do not alter dosage without checking with your physician.

How taken

Tablets, oral disintegrating tablets.

Frequency and timing of doses
Once daily

Usual adult dosage range
15–45mg.

Onset of effect
The onset of therapeutic response usually occurs within 2 weeks of starting treatment, but full antidepressant effect may not be felt for 4–6 weeks.

Duration of action
Up to 24 hours

Diet advice
None.

Storage
Keep in a closed container in a cool, dry place out of the reach of children.

Missed dose
If you miss a dose, take it as soon as you remember. Do not double up on a dose.

Stopping the drug
Do not stop the drug without consulting your physician. Stopping abruptly can cause withdrawal symptoms. If discontinuation is prescribed by the physician, a gradual reduction in the dose over several weeks is recommended.

Exceeding the dose
An occasional unintentional extra dose is unlikely to be a cause for concern. Large doses may cause drowsiness, disorientation, impaired memory. Notify your physician and seek medical assistance right away.

SPECIAL PRECAUTIONS

Be sure to tell your physician if:
▼ You have long-term liver or kidney problems.
▼ You have a heart problem.
▼ You have had a TIA or stroke.
▼ You have a history of seizures.
▼ You are taking other medications.

Pregnancy
▼ Safety not established. Discuss with your physician.

Breast-feeding
▼ Safety not established. Discuss with your physician.

Infants and children
▼ Not recommended.

Over 60
▼ Increased likelihood of *adverse effects*. Reduced dose may be necessary.

Driving and hazardous work
▼ Avoid such activities until you have learned how mirtazapine affects you because the drug can cause drowsiness.

Alcohol
▼ Avoid. Alcohol may increase the sedative effects of this drug.

POSSIBLE ADVERSE EFFECTS

Generally well tolerated.

Symptom/effect	Frequency		Discuss with physician		Stop taking drug now	Call physician now
	Common	Rare	Only if severe	In all cases		
Drowsiness	●		■			
Dizziness	●		■			
Increased appetite/weight gain	●			■		
Muscle weakness		●		■		
Dry mouth	●		■			
Constipation		●	■			
Tiredness/fatigue		●		■		

PROLONGED USE

No problems expected.

INTERACTIONS

Diazepam and other CNS depressants
These agents will have an additive effect to the *sedative* effects of mirtazapine.

Monoamine oxidase inhibitors (MAOI)
Mirtazapine should not be used with MOAIs or within 14 days of stopping an MAOI.

Clonidine Mirtazapine may decrease the antihypertensive effects of this drug.

Ciprofloxacin, ketoconazole, captopril, carvedilol, and clarithromycin These drugs may increase the effects of mirtazapine.

MISOPROSTOL

Product names Novo-Misoprostol Tablets, PMS-Misoprostol
Used in the following combined preparation Arthrotec

GENERAL INFORMATION

Misoprostol reduces acid secretion in the stomach and promotes healing of gastric and duodenal ulcers. These types of ulcers may be caused by ASA and nonsteroidal anti-inflammatory drugs (NSAIDs, p.102), which block the synthesis of naturally occurring chemicals called prostaglandins. Misoprostol is a synthetic protaglandin that acts as a substitute for some of the natural prostaglandins and prevents ulcers from forming as well as promoting ulcer healing. Treatment with misoprostol usually causes the healing of ulcers in a few weeks. In some cases, misoprostol is given during treatment with ASA and NSAIDs as a preventative measure and combined preparations are available that reduce the likelihood of ulcers occurring. The most common *adverse effects* are diarrhea and indigestion; if they are severe it may be necessary to stop taking the drug. Diarrhea can be made worse by antacids containing magnesium; these should therefore be avoided. Misoprostol also causes the uterus to contract. This may cause premature labour and so the drug must not be used during pregnancy.

INFORMATION FOR USERS

Your drug prescription is tailored for you. Do not alter dosage without checking with your physician.

How taken

Tablets.

Frequency and timing of doses
2–4 x daily, with milk or food.

Usual adult dosage range
400–800mcg daily.

Onset of effect
Within 24 hours.

Duration of action
Up to 24 hours; some effects may be longer lasting.

Diet advice
None.

Storage
Keep in a closed container in a cool, dry place out of the reach of children.

Missed dose
Take as soon as you remember. If your next dose is due within 3 hours, take a single dose now and skip the next.

Stopping the drug
Do not stop the drug without consulting your physician; symptoms may recur.

Exceeding the dose
An occasional unintentional extra dose is unlikely to be a cause for concern. But if you notice any unusual symptoms, or if a large overdose has been taken, notify your physician.

SPECIAL PRECAUTIONS

Be sure to tell your physician if:
▼ You are pregnant, or intending to become pregnant.
▼ You have had a stroke.
▼ You have heart or circulation problems.
▼ You have high blood pressure.
▼ You have bowel problems.
▼ You are taking other medications.

Pregnancy
▼ Misoprostol should not be taken by women of childbearing years. In exceptional cases, it may be prescribed on the condition that effective contraception is used. If taken during pregnancy, the drug can cause the uterus to contract before the baby is due.

Breast-feeding
▼ Safety not established. Discuss with your physician.

Infants and children
▼ Not recommended.

Over 60
▼ No special problems.

Driving and hazardous work
▼ No problems expected.

Alcohol
▼ No problems expected, but excessive amounts may undermine the desired effect of the drug.

POSSIBLE ADVERSE EFFECTS

Adverse effects on the gastrointestinal tract can occur. These effects may be reduced by spreading the doses out during the day. Taking the drug with food may be recommended.

Symptom/effect	Frequency		Discuss with physician		Stop taking drug now	Call physician now
	Common	Rare	Only if severe	In all cases		
Diarrhea	●		■			
Indigestion	●		■			
Nausea/vomiting		●	■			
Vaginal/intermenstrual bleeding		●		■		
Abdominal pain		●		■		
Skin rashes		●		■	▲	

INTERACTIONS

Magnesium-containing antacids These may increase the severity of any diarrhea caused by misoprostol.

PROLONGED USE

No problems expected.

MOCLOBEMIDE

Product names Apo-moclobemide, Manerix, Nu-moclobemide, and others
Used in the following combined preparations None

GENERAL INFORMATION

Moclobemide is used in the treatment of depression and it belongs to the class of drugs call MAO inhibitors. This drug works by inhibiting an enzyme in the brain called monoamine oxidase type A (MAO-A), thereby increasing levels of certain neurotransmitters in the brain.

Although restrictions in foods containing tyramine is not strictly required as is for other MAO inhibitors, patients are still advised to minimize excessive use of tyramine-rich foods, such as pickled herring, aged cheeses, salami, tap beer, red wine and, soybean products.

This drug should be discontinued at least 2 days prior to receiving an anesthetic and when receiving epinephrine.

QUICK REFERENCE

Drug group Drugs for depression (p.68)

Overdose danger rating High

Dependence rating Low

Prescription needed Yes

Available as generic Yes

INFORMATION FOR USERS

Your drug prescription is tailored for you. Do not alter dosage without checking with your physician.

How taken

Tablets.

Frequency and timing of doses
Usually twice daily, taken immediately after meals.

Usual adult dosage range
200–600mg daily.

Onset of effect
May take up to 4 weeks to see full benefit from medication.

Duration of action
Up to 12 hours.

Diet advice
Minimize excessive use of tyramine-rich foods.

Storage
Keep in a closed container in a cool, dry place out of the reach of children.

Missed dose
If you miss a dose, take it as soon as you remember. If it is near the time of the next dose, skip the missed dose and resume your using dosing schedule. Do not double up to catch up on a missed dose.

Stopping the drug
Do not stop the drug without consulting your physician. Stopping the drug may lead to worsening of the underlying condition.

Exceeding the dose
An occasional unintentional extra dose is unlikely to cause problems. Large overdoses may cause serious adverse effects. Get help right away and notify your physician.

SPECIAL PRECAUTIONS

Be sure to tell your physician if:
▼ You have kidney problems.
▼ You have liver problems.
▼ You have thyroid disorder.
▼ You are taking other medications.

 Pregnancy
▼ Safety in pregnancy not established. Discuss with your physician.

 Breast-feeding
▼ Excreted in breast milk. Discuss with your physician.

 Infants and children
▼ Not recommended.

 Over 60
▼ No special problems.

 Driving and hazardous work
▼ May cause drowsiness. Do not drive a car or operate machinery until the effect of the drug wears off and you feel you are mentally alert.

 Alcohol
▼ Avoid alcohol use as it may increase the effect of drowsiness caused by this drug.

PROLONGED USE

No problems expected.

POSSIBLE ADVERSE EFFECTS

More common *adverse effects* include dizziness, headache, dry mouth, nausea, and insomnia.

Symptom/effect	Frequency		Discuss with physician		Stop taking drug now	Call physician now
	Common	Rare	Only if severe	In all cases		
Nausea	●		■			
Insomnia	●		■			
Dizziness	●		■			
Mild headache	●		■			
Dry mouth	●		■			
Sweating		●	■			
Loss of appetite		●	■			
Blurred vision		●		■		
Irregular or rapid heartbeat		●		■		▎
Chest pain		●		■		▎
Sudden and severe headache		●		■		▎

INTERACTIONS

General note Because of the wide range of possible drug interactions with moclobemide, do not take any medication, whether prescription or nonprescription, without first consulting your physician or *pharmacist*.

Meperidine, hydromorphone, carbamazepine, selegiline, sympathomimetics (in cough and cold preparations), SSRIs, TCAs, MAOIs, antipsychotics, St. John's wort Taking these with moclobemide can lead to a serious increase in blood pressure and should be avoided.

MOMETASONE

Product names Asmanex, Elocom, Nasonex, and others
Used in the following combined preparation Zenhale

GENERAL INFORMATION

Mometasone is a corticosteroid drug used in the form of a nasal spray to relieve the symptoms of allergic rhinitis. The drug is also used topically for the treatment of severe inflammatory skin disorders and in conditions such as eczema that have not responded to other corticosteroids (see Topical corticosteroids, p.162). It is also available as an inhaler for asthma.

Serious *adverse effects* are rare if the drug is used for short periods or in small amounts. However, prolonged or excessive topical use may cause local *side effects* such as thin skin with enlarged capillaries. *Systemic* side effects, such as osteoporosis and muscle weakness, may also occur with high doses of the inhaled drug. Because corticosteroids can affect growth, children using the nasal spray for prolonged periods may need to have their growth (height) monitored.

(see Topical corticosteroids, p.162)

QUICK REFERENCE

Drug group Corticosteroids (p.127)

Overdose danger rating Low

Dependence rating Low

Prescription needed Yes

Available as generic Yes (some preparations)

Corticosteroids (p.127)

INFORMATION FOR USERS

Your drug prescription is tailored for you. Do not alter dosage without checking with your physician.

How taken

Cream, ointment, lotion, inhaler, nasal spray.

Frequency and timing of doses
Once daily.

Usual dosage range
Nasal spray 100mcg (2 puffs) into each nostril.
Topical preparations As directed, applied thinly.
Inhaler 200–400mcg daily.

Onset of effect
12 hours. Full beneficial effect after 48 hours.

Duration of action
24 hours.

Diet advice
None.

Storage
Keep in a cool, dry place out of the reach of children.

Missed dose
Take as soon as you remember. If your next dose/application is due within 8 hours, take a single dose or apply the usual amount now and skip the next.

Stopping the drug
Do not stop the drug without consulting your physician; symptoms may recur.

Exceeding the dose
An occasional unintentional extra dose/application may not be a cause for concern, but if you notice unusual symptoms, notify your physician.

SPECIAL PRECAUTIONS

Be sure to tell your physician if:
▼ You have tuberculosis or another respiratory infection.
▼ You have any other nasal or skin infection.
▼ You have had recent nasal ulcers or nasal surgery.

Avoid exposure to chickenpox, measles, or shingles while using mometasone.

 Pregnancy
▼ Safety not established. Discuss with your physician.

 Breast-feeding
▼ No evidence of risk. Discuss with your physician.

 Infants and children
▼ Reduced dose necessary.

 Over 60
▼ No special problems.

 Driving and hazardous work
▼ No special problems.

 Alcohol
▼ No special problems.

POSSIBLE ADVERSE EFFECTS

Serious adverse effects are unlikely when the drug is used at low doses and/or for short periods. The most common side effects are irritation of, and sometimes bleeding from, the nose. More serious side effects, such as permanent skin changes, may occur with the cream or ointment, which should not normally be used on the face.

Symptom/effect	Frequency		Discuss with physician		Stop taking drug now	Call physician now
	Common	Rare	Only if severe	In all cases		
Inhaler/nasal spray						
Nasal discomfort/irritation	●		■			
Cough	●		■			
Sore throat/hoarseness	●			■		
Nosebleed	●			■		
Bruising		●	■			
Cream/ointment						
Skin changes (long-term use)	●			■		

INTERACTIONS

None.

PROLONGED USE

Long-term use of inhaler can rarely lead to glaucoma, muscle weakness, and osteoporosis. Also, growth retardation in children, and rarely, adrenal gland suppression may occur. Prolonged use of topical treatment may also lead to skin thinning. Patients on long-term treatment should wear a MedicAlert bracelet.

Monitoring Periodic checks on adrenal gland function may be required if large doses are being taken. Children should have their height monitored.

MONTELUKAST

Product names Apo-Montelukast, Singulair, Teva-Montelukast, and others
Used in the following combined preparations None

GENERAL INFORMATION

Montelukast belongs to the leukotriene receptor antagonist (blocker) group of anti-allergy drugs and is used in the prevention of asthma. It is thought that stimulation of leukotriene receptors by naturally occurring leukotrienes from the mast cells plays a part in causing asthma. Montelukast works by blocking these receptors.

The drug is given as an additional medication for asthma when combined treatment with corticosteroids and *bronchodilators* does not give adequate control. It is usually given by mouth as tablets, and a chewable form is available for children.

Montelukast is not a bronchodilator, and cannot be used to treat an acute attack of asthma.

INFORMATION FOR USERS

Your drug prescription is tailored for you. Do not alter dosage without checking with your physician.

How taken

Tablets, chewable tablets, granules.

Frequency and timing of doses
Once daily at bedtime, on an empty stomach.

Usual adult dosage range
10mg.

Onset of effect
2 hours.

Duration of action
24 hours.

Diet advice
None.

Storage
Keep in a closed container in a cool, dry place out of the reach of children. Protect from light.

Missed dose
Take as soon as you remember. If your next dose is due within 8 hours, take a single dose now and skip the next.

Stopping the drug
Do not stop the drug without consulting your physician, symptoms may recur.

Exceeding the dose
An occasional unintentional extra dose is unlikely to be a cause for concern. But if you notice any unusual symptoms, or if a large overdose has been taken, notify your physician.

SPECIAL PRECAUTIONS

Be sure to tell your physician if:
▼ You have phenylketonuria.
▼ You have lactose or galactose intolerance.
▼ You are taking other medications.

Pregnancy
▼ Safety not established. Discuss with your physician.

Breast-feeding
▼ Safety not established. Discuss with your physician.

Infants and children
▼ Reduced dose necessary.

Over 60
▼ No special problems.

Driving and hazardous work
▼ Avoid such activities until you have learned how montelukast affects you because the drug can cause dizziness.

Alcohol
▼ No special problems.

PROLONGED USE

No special problems.

POSSIBLE ADVERSE EFFECTS

Severe *adverse effects* are rare with montelukast. The most common adverse effects are abdominal pain and headache.

Symptom/effect	Frequency		Discuss with physician		Stop taking drug now	Call physician now
	Common	Rare	Only if severe	In all cases		
Abdominal pain	●		■			
Headache	●		■			
Nausea/diarrhea/vomiting		●	■			
Dizziness/agitation		●	■			
Weakness		●	■			
Fever		●		■		
Productive cough		●		■		
Rash		●		■		
Worsening chest symptoms		●		■		
Numbness/tingling		●		■		

INTERACTIONS

Fluconazole, ketoconazole, and fluorouracil can increase the levels of montelukast.

MORPHINE

Product names Kadian, M.O.S. Sulfate, MS Contin, MS IR, Statex, and others
Used in the following combined preparations None

GENERAL INFORMATION

Morphine is an *opioid* analgesic (see p.64) and is used to relieve severe pain that can be caused by heart attack, injury, surgery, or chronic diseases such as cancer. It is also sometimes given as *premedication* before surgery. The drug's painkilling effect wears off quickly, and it may be given in a special slow-release (long-acting) form to relieve continuous severe pain.

This drug is habit-forming, and *dependence* and addiction can occur. However, most patients who are prescribed morphine for pain relief do not become dependent and are able to stop taking it without difficulty.

QUICK REFERENCE

Drug group Opioid analgesics (p.64)
Overdose danger rating High
Dependence rating High
Prescription needed Yes
Available as generic Yes

INFORMATION FOR USERS

Your drug prescription is tailored for you. Do not alter your dosage without checking with your physician.

How taken

Tablets, SR-tablets, capsules, SR-capsules, liquid, SR-granules, injection, suppositories, SR-suppositories.

Frequency and timing of doses
Every 4 hours; every 12–24 hours (SR-preparations).

Usual adult dosage range
5–25mg per dose; however, some patients may need 75mg or more per dose. Doses vary considerably for each individual.

Onset of effect
Within 1 hour; within 4 hours (SR-preparations).

Duration of action
4 hours; up to 24 hours (SR-preparations).

Diet advice
None.

Storage
Keep in a closed container in a cool, dry place out of the reach of children.

Missed dose
Take as soon as you remember. Return to your normal dosing schedule as soon as possible.

Stopping the drug
If the reason for taking the drug no longer exists, you may stop the drug in consultation with your physician.

OVERDOSE ACTION

 Seek immediate medical advice in all cases. Take emergency action if symptoms such as slow or irregular breathing, severe drowsiness, or loss of consciousness occur.

See Drug poisoning emergency guide (p.526).

SPECIAL PRECAUTIONS

Be sure to tell your physician if:
▼ You have long-term liver or kidney problems.
▼ You have myasthenia gravis.
▼ You have heart or circulatory problems.
▼ You have a lung disorder such as asthma or bronchitis.
▼ You have thyroid disease.
▼ You have a history of epileptic seizures.
▼ You are taking other medications.

 Pregnancy
▼ Not usually prescribed. May cause breathing difficulties in the newborn baby. Discuss with your physician.

 Breast-feeding
▼ The drug passes into the breast milk, but at low doses adverse effects on the baby are unlikely. Discuss with your physician.

 Infants and children
▼ Reduced dose necessary.

 Over 60
▼ Increased likelihood of *adverse effects*. Reduced dose may therefore be necessary.

 Driving and hazardous work
▼ People on morphine treatment are unlikely to be well enough to undertake such activities.

 Alcohol
▼ Avoid. Alcohol may increase the *sedative* effects of this drug.

POSSIBLE ADVERSE EFFECTS

Nausea, vomiting, and constipation are common, especially with high doses.

Anti-nausea drugs or laxatives may be needed to counteract these symptoms.

Symptom/effect	Frequency		Discuss with physician		Stop taking drug now	Call physician now
	Common	Rare	Only if severe	In all cases		
Drowsiness	●		■			
Nausea/vomiting	●		■			
Constipation	●		■			
Dizziness	●			■		
Confusion		●		■		
Breathing difficulties		●		■	▲	▮
Impaired consciousness		●		■	▲	▮

INTERACTIONS

Esmolol The effects of esmolol may be increased by morphine.

Sedatives Morphine increases the *sedative* effects of other sedating drugs including antidepressants, antipsychotics, sleeping drugs, and antihistamines.

PROLONGED USE

The effects of this drug usually become weaker during prolonged use as the body adapts. Dependence may occur if it is taken for extended periods although this is unusual in patients taking the correct dose for pain relief.

MOXIFLOXACIN

Product names Avelox, Vigamox
Used in the following combined preparations None

GENERAL INFORMATION

Moxifloxacin is a quinolone antibacterial drug used in the treatment of respiratory infections including sinusitis, bronchitis, and pneumonia. The drug is usually prescribed as oral tablets or given as an intravenous injection for more severe infections. It is also available as a solution for eye infections. The tablets are usually taken once a day for 5 or 10 days. It may be taken with or without food. The tablets should be swallowed whole and should not be split or crushed.

Moxifloxacin may make you more sensitive to sunlight. Protect yourself with sunscreen and appropriate clothing. Occasionally, the drug may cause tendon inflammation and damage (see advice for levofloxacin, p.332).

QUICK REFERENCE

Drug group Antibacterial drugs (p.117)

Overdose danger rating High

Dependence rating Low

Prescription needed Yes

Available as generic No

INFORMATION FOR USERS

Your drug prescription is tailored for you. Do not alter dosage without checking with your physician.

How taken

Tablets, parenteral (intravenous), ophthalmic solution.

Frequency and timing of doses
Usually once daily.

Usual adult dosage range
Oral: 400mg daily.
Ophthalmic solution: 3 x daily or as directed.

Onset of effect
Within one day.

Duration of action
Up to 24 hours.

Diet advice
Drink plenty of fluids.

Storage
Keep in a closed container in a cool, dry place out of the reach of children.

Missed dose
If you miss a dose, take it as soon as you remember. If it is near the time of the next dose, skip the missed dose and resume your using dosing schedule. Do not double up to catch up on a missed dose.

Stopping the drug
Do not stop the drug without consulting your physician. Stopping the drug may lead to worsening of the underlying condition.

OVERDOSE ACTION

 Seek immediate medical advice. May experience significant gastrointestinal and CNS effects. Get help right away and notify your physician.

POSSIBLE ADVERSE EFFECTS

The most common *side effects* are nausea and abdominal discomfort.

Symptom/effect	Frequency		Discuss with physician		Stop taking drug now	Call physician now
	Common	Rare	Only if severe	In all cases		
Dizziness	●		■			
Headache	●		■			
Nausea/abdominal pain	●		■			
Diarrhea	●		■			
Skin rash, itching		●		■	▲	▮
Yellowing of skin and eyes/ dark urine/pale coloured stools		●		■	▲	▮
Mood changes		●		■		▮
Fast/irregular heartbeat		●		■		▮
Seizures/visual changes		●		■		▮
Painful, inflamed tendons		●		■	▲	▮

INTERACTIONS

Antacids, multivitamins containing iron or zinc Do not take less than 4 hours before or 8 hours after moxifloxacin.

NSAIDs Increased risk of seizures when these drugs are taken with moxifloxacin.

Antidiabetic drugs Moxifloxacin can affect blood glucose levels and affect the action of antidiabetic drugs.

Warfarin Close monitoring of INR may be required in individuals on both drugs.

SPECIAL PRECAUTIONS

Be sure to tell your physician if:
▼ You have a seizure disorder.
▼ You have liver problems.
▼ You are diabetic.
▼ You are allergic to any antibiotics.
▼ You or your family has a history of heart disease, such as irregular rhythms or heart attack.
▼ You have myasthenia gravis.
▼ You are taking other medications.

 Pregnancy
▼ Not usually prescribed. Safety in pregnancy not established. Discuss with your physician.

 Breast-feeding
▼ Safety not established. Discuss with your physician.

 Infants and children
▼ Not recommended.

 Over 60
▼ Tendon damage is more likely over the age of 60.

 Driving and hazardous work
▼ Avoid such activities until you have learned how moxifloxacin affects you because the drug can cause drowsiness and visual disturbances.

  Alcohol
▼ Avoid. Alcohol may increase the *sedative* effects of moxifloxacin.

PROLONGED USE

Usually given for a short course of treatment.

NAPROXEN

Product names Aleve, Anaprox, Apo-Naproxen, Naprosyn, Nu-Naprox Tab, and others
Used in the following combined preparations Vimovo

GENERAL INFORMATION

Naproxen, one of the non-steroidal anti-inflammatory drugs (NSAIDs), is used to reduce pain, stiffness, and inflammation.

The drug relieves the symptoms of adult and juvenile rheumatoid arthritis, ankylosing spondylitis, and osteo-arthritis, although it does not cure the underlying disease.

Naproxen is also used to treat acute attacks of gout, and may sometimes be prescribed for the relief of migraine and pain following orthopedic surgery, dental treatment, strains, and sprains. It is also effective for treating painful menstrual cramps.

Gastrointestinal *side effects* are fairly common, and there is an increased risk of bleeding. Hence, for long-term use, naproxen is often prescribed with a gastro-protective drug.

QUICK REFERENCE

Drug group Non-steroidal anti-inflammatory drugs (p.102) and drugs for gout (p.105)

Overdose danger rating Medium

Dependence rating Low

Prescription needed Yes

Available as generic Yes

INFORMATION FOR USERS

Your drug prescription is tailored for you. Do not alter dosage without checking with your physician.

How taken

Tablets, SR-tablets, liquid, suppositories.

Frequency and timing of doses
Every 6–8 hours as required (general pain relief); 1–2 x daily (muscular pain and arthritis); every 8 hours (gout).
All doses should be taken with food.

Usual adult dosage range
Mild to moderate pain, menstrual cramps 500mg (starting dose), then 250mg every 6–8 hours as required. *Muscular pain and arthritis* 500–1,250mg daily.

Onset of effect
Pain relief begins within 1 hour. Full anti-inflammatory effect may take 2 weeks.

Duration of action
Up to 12 hours.

Diet advice
None.

Storage
Keep in a closed container in a cool, dry place out of the reach of children. Protect from light.

Missed dose
Take as soon as you remember. If your next dose is due within 4 hours, take a single dose now and skip the next.

Stopping the drug
When taken for short-term pain relief, naproxen can be safely stopped as soon as you no longer need it. If prescribed for long-term treatment, however, you should seek medical advice before stopping the drug.

Exceeding the dose
An occasional unintentional extra dose is unlikely to be a cause for concern. But if you notice any unusual symptoms, or if a large overdose has been taken, notify your physician.

SPECIAL PRECAUTIONS

Be sure to tell your physician if:
▼ You have long-term liver or kidney problems.
▼ You have heart problems.
▼ You have a bleeding disorder.
▼ You have high blood pressure.
▼ You have had a peptic ulcer, esophagitis, or acid indigestion.
▼ You are allergic to ASA.
▼ You suffer from asthma.
▼ You are taking other medications.

Pregnancy
▼ The drug may increase the risk of adverse effects on the baby's heart and may prolong labour if taken in the third trimester. Discuss with your physician.

Breast-feeding
▼ The drug passes into the breast milk, but at normal doses adverse effects on the baby are unlikely. Discuss with your physician.

Infants and children
▼ Prescribed only to treat juvenile arthritis. Reduced dose necessary.

Over 60
▼ Increased likelihood of adverse effects. Reduced dose may therefore be necessary.

Driving and hazardous work
▼ Avoid such activities until you have learned how naproxen affects you because the drug may reduce your ability to concentrate.

Alcohol
▼ Avoid. Alcohol may increase the risk of stomach irritation with naproxen.

Surgery and general anesthetics
▼ Naproxen may prolong bleeding. Discuss with your physician or dentist before surgery.

POSSIBLE ADVERSE EFFECTS

Most *adverse effects* are not serious and may diminish with time. Black or bloodstained bowel movements should be reported to your physician without delay.

Symptom/effect	Frequency		Discuss with physician		Stop taking drug now	Call physician now
	Common	Rare	Only if severe	In all cases		
Heartburn/indigestion	●		■			
Nausea/vomiting		●	■			
Headache		●	■			
Dizziness/drowsiness		●	■			
Swollen feet/legs		●		■		
Weight gain		●	■			
Rash/itching		●		■	▲	
Wheezing/breathlessness		●		■	▲	▮
Black/bloodstained feces		●		■	▲	▮

INTERACTIONS

General note Naproxen interacts with a wide range of drugs to increase the risk of bleeding and/or peptic ulcers. It may also increase the blood levels of lithium, methotrexate, and digoxin.

Antihypertensive drugs and diuretics The beneficial effects of these drugs may be reduced by naproxen.

Cyclosporine Naproxen increases the risk of kidney impairment with this drug.

PROLONGED USE

There is an increased risk of bleeding from peptic ulcers and in the bowel when naproxen is used long term. There is also a small risk of a heart attack or stroke. To minimize these risks, the lowest effective dose is given for the shortest duration.

NICOTINE

Product names Nicoderm, Nicorette
Used in the following combined preparations None

GENERAL INFORMATION

Smoking is a difficult habit to stop due to the addiction to nicotine and the psychological attachment to cigarettes or a pipe. Taking nicotine in a different form can help the smoker deal with the two aspects of the habit separately.

Nicotine comes in the form of chewing gum, skin patches, or an inhaler, and is used for the relief of *withdrawal symptoms*. The patches should be applied every 24 hours to unbroken, dry, and non-hairy skin on the trunk or the upper arm.

Replacement patches should be placed on a different area, and the same area of application avoided for several days. The strength of the patch is gradually reduced, and abstinence may be achieved within three months. The chewing gum is used whenever the urge to smoke occurs. Gum is chewed slowly for up to 30 minutes, by which time all available nicotine has been released. Inhaler dose is individualized; the initial dose is usually 6–12 cartridges per day.

QUICK REFERENCE

Drug group Nicotine replacement used in smoking withdrawal.

Overdose danger rating Medium

Dependence rating Low

Prescription needed No

Available as generic No

INFORMATION FOR USERS

Follow instructions on the label. Call your physician if symptoms worsen.

How taken

Chewing gum, lozenge, inhaler, skin patch.

Frequency and timing of doses
Every 24 hours, removing the patch after 16 hours (patches); when the urge to smoke is felt (gum, lozenge); 6–12 cartridges per day (inhaler).

Usual adult dosage range
Will depend on your previous smoking habits. 7–22mg per day (patches); 1 x 2mg piece to 15 x 4mg pieces per day (gum, lozenge); dose individualized (inhaler).

Onset of effect
A few hours (patches); within minutes (gum).

Duration of action
Up to 24 hours (patches); 30 minutes (gum).

Diet advice
None.

Storage
Keep in a cool, dry place out of the reach of children.

Missed dose
Change your patch as soon as you remember, and keep the new patch on for the required amount of time before removing it.

Stopping the drug
The dose of nicotine is normally reduced gradually.

Exceeding the dose
Application of several nicotine patches at the same time could result in serious overdosage. Remove the patches and seek immediate medical help. Overdosage with the gum can occur only if many pieces of gum are chewed simultaneously. Seek immediate medical help.

SPECIAL PRECAUTIONS

Be sure to consult your physician or pharmacist before taking this drug if:
▼ You have long-term liver or kidney problems.
▼ You have diabetes mellitus.
▼ You have thyroid disease.
▼ You have heart problems.
▼ You have a history of peptic ulcers.
▼ You have pheochromocytoma.
▼ You are taking other medications.

Pregnancy
▼ Nicotine replacement during pregnancy should be disussed with your physician.

Breast-feeding
▼ Nicotine passes into the breast milk. Discuss with your physician.

Infants and children
▼ Nicotine products should not be administered to children.

Over 60
▼ No special problems.

Driving and hazardous work
▼ Usually no problems.

Alcohol
▼ No special problems.

POSSIBLE ADVERSE EFFECTS

Any skin reaction to patches will usually disappear in a couple of days. The chewing gum may cause local irritation of the throat or nose, affect your taste, and cause a dry mouth.

Symptom/effect	Frequency		Discuss with physician		Stop taking drug now	Call physician now
	Common	Rare	Only if severe	In all cases		
Local irritation	●		■			
Headache	●		■			
Dizziness	●		■			
Nausea/indigestion	●		■			
Cold/flu-like symptoms	●		■			
Insomnia	●		■			
Chest pain/palpitations		●		■		

INTERACTIONS

General note Nicotine patches and chewing gum should not be used with other nicotine-containing products, including cigarettes.

Stopping smoking may increase the blood levels of some drugs (such as warfarin and theophylline/aminophylline). Discuss with your physician or *pharmacist*.

PROLONGED USE

Nicotine replacement therapy should not normally be used for more than three months.

NIFEDIPINE

Product names Adalat XL, PMS-Nifedipine, and others
Used in the following combined preparations None

GENERAL INFORMATION

Nifedipine belongs to a group of drugs known as calcium channel blockers (p.87), which interfere with conduction of signals in the muscles of the heart and blood vessels.

Nifedipine is given as a regular medication to help prevent angina attacks. The drug can be used safely by asthmatics, unlike some other anti-angina drugs (such as beta blockers).

Nifedipine is also widely used to reduce high blood pressure and is often helpful in improving circulation to the limbs in disorders such as Raynaud's disease.

Like other drugs of its class, it may cause blood pressure to fall too low, and occasionally causes disturbances of heart rhythm. In rare cases, angina worsens as a result of taking nifedipine, and another drug must be substituted.

QUICK REFERENCE

Drug group Anti-angina drugs (p.87) and antihypertensive drugs (p.88)

Overdose danger rating Medium

Dependence rating Low

Prescription needed Yes

Available as generic Yes

INFORMATION FOR USERS

Your drug prescription is tailored for you. Do not alter dosage without checking with your physician.

How taken

Capsules, XL-tablets.

Frequency and timing of doses
3 x daily; 1–2 x daily (XL-preparations).

Usual adult dosage range
15–90mg daily.

Onset of effect
30–60 minutes.

Duration of action
6–24 hours.

Diet advice
Nifedipine should not be taken with grapefruit juice.

Storage
Keep in a closed container in a cool, dry place out of the reach of children. Protect from light.

Missed dose
Take as soon as you remember, or when needed. If your next dose is due within 3 hours, take a single dose now and skip the next.

Stopping the drug
Do not stop the drug without consulting your physician; sudden withdrawal may make angina worse.

Exceeding the dose
An occasional unintentional extra dose is unlikely to cause problems. Large overdoses may cause dizziness. Notify your physician.

SPECIAL PRECAUTIONS

Be sure to tell your physician if:
▼ You have liver or kidney problems.
▼ You have heart failure.
▼ You have had a recent heart attack.
▼ You have aortic stenosis.
▼ You have diabetes.
▼ You are taking other medications.

Pregnancy
▼ May inhibit labour, but the small risk to the baby must be weighed against the risk to the mother of uncontrolled hypertension. Discuss with your physician.

Breast-feeding
▼ The drug passes into the breast milk but only in amounts that are probably too small to harm your baby. Discuss with your physician.

Infants and children
▼ Not recommended.

Over 60
▼ Increased likelihood of adverse effects. Reduced dose may therefore be necessary.

Driving and hazardous work
▼ Avoid such activities until you have learned how nifedipine affects you because the drug can cause dizziness as a result of lowered blood pressure.

Alcohol
▼ Avoid. Alcohol may increase the blood-pressure-lowering effects of nifedipine.

Surgery and general anesthetics
▼ Nifedipine may interact with some general anesthetics causing a fall in blood pressure. Discuss this with your physician or dentist before any surgery.

POSSIBLE ADVERSE EFFECTS

Nifedipine can cause a variety of minor *adverse effects*. Dizziness, especially on rising, may be caused by reduced blood pressure. Patients with angina may notice increased severity or frequency of attacks after starting nifedipine. This should always be reported to your physician. An adjustment in dosage or a change of drug may be necessary.

Symptom/effect	Frequency		Discuss with physician		Stop taking drug now	Call physician now
	Common	Rare	Only if severe	In all cases		
Headache	●		■			
Dizziness/fatigue	●			■		
Flushing	●		■			
Ankle swelling	●		■			
Frequency in passing urine		●	■			
Rash		●		■		
Palpitations		●		■		
Increased angina		●		■	▲	■

INTERACTIONS

Antihypertensive drugs Nifedipine may increase the effects of these drugs.

Phenytoin Nifedipine may increase the effects of phenytoin.

Digoxin Nifedipine may increase the effects and *toxicity* of digoxin.

Rifampin This drug may decrease the effects of nifedipine.

Grapefruit juice This may block the breakdown of nifedipine, increasing its effects.

PROLONGED USE

No problems expected.

NITROGLYCERIN

Product names Nitro-Dur, Nitrol, Nitrolingual, Nitrolingual Pump Spray, Transiderm-Nitro, and others
Used in the following combined preparations None

GENERAL INFORMATION

Introduced in the late 1800s, nitroglycerin is one of the oldest drugs that is still in continual use. It belongs to a group of vasodilator drugs called nitrates that are used to relieve the pain of angina attacks. It is available in short-acting forms (sublingual tablets and spray) and in long-acting forms (slow-release tablets and skin patches). The short-acting forms act very quickly to relieve angina. Nitroglycerin is also given by injection in hospital for severe angina and for controlling blood pressure.

Nitroglycerin may cause a variety of minor symptoms, such as flushing and headache, most of which can be controlled by adjusting the dosage. The drug is best taken for the first time while sitting, as fainting may follow the drop in blood pressure caused by the drug.

An ointment preparation may be used for the specialist treatment of anal fissures.

QUICK REFERENCE

Drug group Anti-angina drugs (p.87)

Overdose danger rating Medium

Dependence rating Low

Prescription needed No (most preparations); yes (injection)

Available as generic Yes

INFORMATION FOR USERS

Your drug prescription is tailored for you. Do not alter dosage without checking with your physician.

How taken

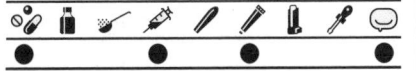

SR-tablets, sublingual tablets, injection, ointment, skin patches, spray.

Frequency and timing of doses
Prevention 3 x daily (SR-tablets); once daily (patches); every 3–4 hours (ointment).
Relief Use sublingual tablets or spray at the onset of an attack. Dose may be repeated twice in 5 minutes intervals if further relief is required. If symptoms persist after 3 doses used over 15 minutes, seek immediate medical help. The relief medication (tablets or spray) can be used immediately prior to exercise.

Usual adult dosage range
Prevention 2.6–15mg daily (SR-tablets); 5–15mg daily (patches); as directed (ointment).
Relief 0.3–1mg per dose (sublingual tablets); 1–2 sprays per dose (spray).

Onset of effect
Within minutes (sublingual tablets and spray); 1–3 hours (SR-tablets, patches, and ointment).

Duration of action
20–30 minutes (sublingual tablets and spray); 3–5 hours (ointment); 8–12 hours (SR-tablets); up to 24 hours (patches).

Diet advice
None.

Storage
Keep sublingual tablets in a tightly closed glass container fitted with a foil-lined, screw-on cap in a cool, dry place out of the reach of children. Protect from light. Do not expose to heat. Discard tablets within 3 months of opening. Check label of other preparations for storage conditions.

Missed dose
Take as soon as you remember, or when needed. If your next dose is due within 2 hours, take a single dose now and skip the next.

Stopping the drug
Do not stop taking the drug without consulting your physician.

Exceeding the dose
An occasional unintentional extra dose is unlikely to cause problems. Large overdoses may cause dizziness, vomiting, severe headache, fits, or loss of consciousness. Notify your physician.

POSSIBLE ADVERSE EFFECTS

The most serious *adverse effect* is lowered blood pressure, and this may need to be monitored periodically. Other adverse effects usually decrease in severity after regular use and they can also be controlled by an adjustment in dosage.

Symptom/effect	Frequency		Discuss with physician		Stop taking drug now	Call physician now
	Common	Rare	Only if severe	In all cases		
Headache	●		■			
Flushing	●		■			
Dizziness	●			■		

INTERACTIONS

Antihypertensive drugs These drugs increase the possibility of lowered blood pressure or fainting when taken with nitroglycerin.

Sildenafil The hypotensive effect of nitroglycerin is increased significantly by sildenafil. The two drugs should not be used together.

SPECIAL PRECAUTIONS

Be sure to tell your physician if:
▼ You have any other heart condition.
▼ You have a lung condition.
▼ You have long-term liver or kidney problems.
▼ You have any blood disorders.
▼ You have glaucoma.
▼ You have thyroid disease.
▼ You are taking other medications.

Pregnancy
▼ Safety in pregnancy not established. Discuss with your physician.

Breast-feeding
▼ It is not known whether the drug passes into the breast milk. Discuss with your physician.

Infants and children
▼ Not usually prescribed.

Over 60
▼ No special problems.

Driving and hazardous work
▼ Avoid such activities until you have learned how nitroglycerin affects you because the drug can cause dizziness.

Alcohol
▼ Avoid excessive intake. Alcohol may increase dizziness due to lowered blood pressure.

PROLONGED USE

The effects of the drug usually become slightly weaker during prolonged use as the body adapts. Timing of the doses may be changed to prevent this effect. To ensure continued effectiveness, the 3 daily doses are recommended to be taken 6 hours apart.

Monitoring Periodic checks on blood pressure are usually required.

NORETHINDRONE

Product names Micronor Tablets, Norlutate
Used in the following combined preparations Activelle, Estalis, FemHRT, Loestrin, Minestrin, Brevicon, and others

GENERAL INFORMATION

Norethindrone is a progestin, a synthetic *hormone* similar to the natural female sex hormone, progesterone. It has a wide variety of uses including the postponement of menstruation and the treatment of menstrual disorders such as endometriosis (p.148). When used for these disorders, it is taken only on certain days during the menstrual cycle. In combination with estrogen, it is also prescribed as hormone replacement therapy (HRT) and is available as tablets or patches. One of the major uses for norethindrone is as an oral contraceptive. It may be used either on its own or in conjunction with an estrogen.

Adverse effects from norethindrone are rare, but contraceptive preparations containing it may cause breakthrough bleeding (see p.151).

INFORMATION FOR USERS

Your drug prescription is tailored for you. Do not alter dosage without checking with your physician.

How taken

Tablets, skin patch.

Frequency and timing of doses
Once daily (tablets); 2 x weekly (skin patch).

Usual adult dosage range
350mcg daily (progestin-only contraceptives); 140–1000mcg daily (HRT); 500–1000mcg (in combination oral contraceptives).

Onset of effect
The drug starts to act within a few hours.

Duration of action
24 hours.

Diet advice
None.

Storage
Keep in a closed container in a cool, dry place out of the reach of children. Protect from light.

Missed dose
Take as soon as you remember. If you are taking the drug for contraception, see What to do if you miss a pill (p.147).

Stopping the drug
The drug can be safely stopped as soon as contraceptive protection is no longer required. If prescribed for an underlying disorder, do not stop taking the drug without consulting your physician.

Exceeding the dose
An occasional unintentional extra dose is unlikely to be a cause for concern. But if you notice any unusual symptoms, or if a large overdose has been taken, notify your physician.

SPECIAL PRECAUTIONS

Be sure to tell your physician if:
▼ You have liver or kidney problems.
▼ You have diabetes.
▼ You have had epileptic seizures.
▼ You suffer from migraine.
▼ You have acute porphyria.
▼ You have heart or circulatory problems, especially a history of venous thrombosis.
▼ You are taking other medications.

Pregnancy
▼ Not usually prescribed. May cause defects in the baby. Discuss with your physician.

Breast-feeding
▼ The drug passes into the breast milk, but at normal doses adverse effects on the baby are unlikely. Discuss with your physician.

Infants and children
▼ Not prescribed.

Over 60
▼ Not usually prescribed.

Driving and hazardous work
▼ No special problems.

Alcohol
▼ No special problems.

POSSIBLE ADVERSE EFFECTS

Adverse effects of norethindrone are rarely troublesome and are generally typical of drugs of this type. Prolonged treatment may cause *jaundice* due to liver damage.

Symptom/effect	Frequency		Discuss with physician		Stop taking drug now	Call physician now
	Common	Rare	Only if severe	In all cases		
Breakthrough bleeding	●			■		
Swollen feet/ankles		●	■			
Weight gain		●	■			
Acne/skin discoloration		●	■			
Depression/headache		●		■		
Jaundice		●		■	▲	

INTERACTIONS

General note Norethindrone may interfere with the beneficial effects of many drugs, including oral anticoagulants, anticonvulsants, antihypertensives, and antidiabetic drugs. Many other drugs may reduce the contraceptive effect of norethindrone-containing pills. These include anticonvulsants, antituberculous drugs, antibiotics, and St John's wort. Be sure to inform your physician that you are taking norethindrone before taking additional prescribed medication.

Cyclosporine Levels of cyclosporine may be raised by norethindrone.

PROLONGED USE

As part of HRT, norethindrone is usually only advised for short-term use after menopause. It is not normally recommended for long-term use or for treating osteoporosis. HRT increases the risk of venous thrombosis and breast cancer. The breast cancer risk reduces after stopping the drug.

Monitoring Blood-pressure checks and physical examination, including regular mammograms, may be performed.

NORFLOXACIN

Product names Apo-Norflox, Co-Norfloxacin, Noroxin, Novo-Norfloxacin, and others
Used in the following combined preparations None

GENERAL INFORMATION

Norfloxacin, a fluoroquinolone *antibiotic*, is effective against several types of bacteria that tend to be resistant to older, more commonly used antibiotics. It is particularly effective against bacteria responsible for urinary tract infections, and it is for this purpose that norfloxacin is usually prescribed. Norfloxacin is generally well tolerated, but occasional side effects occur, the most common of which involves gastrointestinal upset. Allergic reactions may also occur, and those with a history of allergies to fluoroquinolone antibiotics are not usually given this drug. Headache, dizziness, and drowsiness sometimes occur. Seizures are a rare possibility. Occasionally, the drug may cause tendon inflammation and damage (see advice for levofloxacin, p.332).

(see advice for levofloxacin, p.332).

QUICK REFERENCE

Drug group Fluoroquinolone antibiotics (p.115)

Overdose danger rating Medium

Dependence rating Low

Prescription needed Yes

Available as generic Yes

INFORMATION FOR USERS

Your drug prescription is tailored for you. Do not alter dosage without checking with your physician.

How taken

Tablets.

Frequency and timing of doses
2 x daily at least 1 hour before or 2 hours after meals.

Usual adult dosage range
800mg daily for 7–10 days (acute infections); doses of 400mg daily are used for longer courses of treatment if kidney function is impaired.

Onset of effect
1–2 days.

Duration of action
12–24 hours.

Diet advice
Do not get dehydrated. Ensure that you drink fluids regularly. Do not take calcium supplements.

Storage
Keep in a closed container in a cool, dry place out of the reach of children.

Missed dose
Take as soon as you remember. If your next dose is due within 4 hours, take a single dose now and skip the next.

Stopping the drug
Take the full course. Even if you feel better, the infection may still be present and symptoms may recur if treatment is stopped too soon.

Exceeding the dose
An occasional unintentional extra dose is unlikely to cause problems. But if you notice any unusual symptoms, or if a large overdose has been taken, notify your physician.

SPECIAL PRECAUTIONS

Be sure to tell your physician if:
▼ You have impaired kidney function.
▼ You have had epileptic seizures.
▼ You are allergic to fluoroquinolone antibiotics.
▼ You have myasthenia gravis.
▼ You are taking other medications.

 Pregnancy
▼ Safety in pregnancy not established. Discuss with your physician.

 Breast-feeding
▼ The drug passes into the breast milk and may affect the baby. Discuss with your physician.

 Infants and children
▼ Not recommended.

 Over 60
▼ Reduced dose may be necessary. Tendon damage is more likely over the age of 60.

 Driving and hazardous work
▼ Avoid such activities until you have learned how the drug affects you; it can cause dizziness, drowsiness, and blurred vision.

 Alcohol
▼ Avoid. Alcohol may increase the sedative effects of this drug.

POSSIBLE ADVERSE EFFECTS

The most common *side effects* with norfloxacin are nausea, headache, dizziness, and lightheadedness. It can also cause fatigue, rash, and drowsiness.

Symptom/effect	Frequency		Discuss with physician		Stop taking drug now	Call physician now
	Common	Rare	Only if severe	In all cases		
Nausea/vomiting	●		■			
Dizziness/lightheadedness	●		■			
Headache		●	■			
Drowsiness/fatigue		●	■			
Rash/itching		●		■		
Light-sensitive rash		●		■		
Painful, inflamed tendons		●		■	▲	∎

PROLONGED USE

No problems expected.

INTERACTIONS

Oral anticoagulants Norfloxacin may increase the anticoagulant action of these drugs.

Theophylline Norfloxacin may increase the adverse effects with theophylline.

Cyclosporine Norfloxacin may increase the blood levels of cyclosporine.

Caffeine Norfloxacin may increase the effects of caffeine: avoid excessive intake.

Antacids, iron, sucralfate These drugs decrease the absorption of norfloxacin. Avoid taking these within 2 hours of each other.

Probenecid This drug may increase levels of norfloxacin.

NYSTATIN

Product names Nyaderm, ratio-Nystatin, and others
Used in the following combined preparations Flagystatin, Viaderm-K.C., and others

GENERAL INFORMATION

Nystatin is an antifungal drug named after the New York State Institute of Health, where it was developed in the early 1950s.

The drug has been used effectively against candidiasis (thrush), an infection caused by the *Candida* yeast. Available in a variety of dosage forms, it is used to treat infections of the skin, mouth, throat, intestinal tract, esophagus, and vagina. As the drug is poorly absorbed into the bloodstream from the digestive tract, it is of little use against *systemic* infections. It is not given by injection.

Nystatin rarely causes *adverse effects* and can be used during pregnancy to treat vaginal candidiasis.

QUICK REFERENCE

Drug group Antifungal drugs (p.124)
Overdose danger rating Low
Dependence rating Low
Prescription needed No
Available as generic Yes

INFORMATION FOR USERS

Follow instructions on the label. Call your physician if symptoms worsen.

How taken

Tablets, pastilles, liquid, vaginal suppositories, cream, ointment.

Frequency and timing of doses
Mouth or throat infections 4 x daily. Liquid should be held in the mouth for several minutes before swallowing.
Intestinal infections 4 x daily.
Skin infections 2–4 x daily.
Vaginal infections Once daily for 2 weeks.

Usual adult dosage range
2–4 million units daily (by mouth); 100,000–200,000 units at night (vaginal suppositories); 1–2 applicatorfuls (vaginal cream); as directed (skin preparations).

Onset of effect
Full beneficial effect may not be felt for 7–14 days.

Duration of action
Up to 6 hours.

Diet advice
None.

Storage
Keep in a closed container in a cool, dry place out of the reach of children. Protect from light.

Missed dose
Take as soon as you remember. Take your next dose as usual.

Stopping the drug
Take the full course. Even if the affected area seems to be cured, the original infection may still be present, and symptoms may recur if treatment is stopped too soon.

Exceeding the dose
An occasional unintentional extra dose is unlikely to be a cause for concern. But if you notice any unusual symptoms, or if a large overdose has been taken, notify your physician.

SPECIAL PRECAUTIONS

Be sure to consult your physician or pharmacist before taking this drug if:
▼ You are taking other medications.

Pregnancy
▼ No evidence of risk to developing fetus. Discuss use with your physician.

Breast-feeding
▼ No evidence of risk.

Infants and children
▼ Reduced dose necessary.

Over 60
▼ No special problems.

Driving and hazardous work
▼ No known problems.

Alcohol
▼ No known problems.

POSSIBLE ADVERSE EFFECTS

Adverse effects are uncommon, and are usually mild and transient. Nausea and vomiting may occur when high doses of the drug are taken by mouth.

Symptom/effect	Frequency		Discuss with physician		Stop taking drug now	Call physician now
	Common	Rare	Only if severe	In all cases		
Diarrhea		●	■			
Nausea/vomiting		●	■			
Rash		●	■		▲	
Difficulty breathing		●		■	▲	▮

INTERACTIONS

None.

PROLONGED USE

No problems expected. Usually given as a course of treatment until the infection is cured.

OLANZAPINE

Product names Zyprexa, Zyprexa Intramuscular, Zyprexa Zydis, and others
Used in the following combined preparations None

GENERAL INFORMATION

Olanzapine is an atypical antipsychotic drug prescribed for the treatment of schizophrenia and mania. It works by blocking several different chemical transmitters, including dopamine, histamine, and serotonin.

In schizophrenia, the drug can be used to treat both "positive" symptoms (delusions, hallucinations, and thought disorders) and "negative" symptoms (blunted mood, emotional and social withdrawal). In mania, olanzapine can be used alone or in combination with other drugs.

The drug stays in the body longer in women, non-smokers, and the elderly. Lower starting and maintenance doses may be used in these groups.

INFORMATION FOR USERS

Your drug prescription is tailored for you. Do not alter dosage without checking with your physician.

How taken

Tablets, oral disintegrating tablets, injection.

Frequency and timing of doses
Once daily.

Usual adult dosage range
Schizophrenia 10mg (starting dose).
Mania 15mg if used alone or 10mg if used in combination with other drugs (starting dose). For both conditions, the dose can be adjusted between 5mg and 20mg daily.

Onset of effect
4–8 hours.

Duration of action
30–38 hours, but longer in women than in men, and longer in the elderly.

Diet advice
None.

Storage
Keep in a closed container in a cool, dry place out of the reach of children. Protect from light.

Missed dose
Take as soon as you remember. If your next dose is due within 8 hours take a single dose now and skip the next.

Stopping the drug
Do not stop the drug without consulting your physician; symptoms may recur.

Exceeding the dose
An occasional unintentional extra dose is unlikely to cause problems. Large overdoses may cause unusual drowsiness, depressed breathing, and low blood pressure. Notify your physician.

POSSIBLE ADVERSE EFFECTS

Unusual drowsiness and weight gain are the most common *adverse effects* of olanzapine.

Symptom/effect	Frequency		Discuss with physician		Stop taking drug now	Call physician now
	Common	Rare	Only if severe	In all cases		
Unusual drowsiness	●		■			
Weight gain	●		■			
Dizziness/fainting	●			■		
Rash	●			■		
Parkinsonism		●		■		
Difficulty urinating		●		■		
Difficulty in regulating body temperature		●		■		

INTERACTIONS

Sedatives All drugs that have a *sedative* effect on the central nervous system may increase the sedative effects of olanzapine.

Anticonvulsant drugs Olanzapine opposes the effect of these drugs.

Carbamazepine, phenytoin, and rifampin These drugs decrease the effect of olanzapine.

Anti-arrhythmics There is an increased risk of arrhythmias when certain of these drugs are used with olanzapine.

Ciprofloxacin, diltiazem, fluvoxamine, paroxetine These drugs may increase the effect of olanzapine.

SPECIAL PRECAUTIONS

Be sure to tell your physician if:
▼ You have an enlarged prostate.
▼ You have kidney or liver problems.
▼ You have diabetes.
▼ You have dementia.
▼ You have glaucoma.
▼ You have epilepsy.
▼ You are taking other medications.

Pregnancy
▼ Discuss risks versus benefits with your physician.

Breast-feeding
▼Safety not established. Discuss with your physician.

Infants and children
▼ Not recommended.

Over 60
▼ Reduced dose necessary. Not indicated in those with dementia. Increased risk of liver, kidney, and heart problems with long-term use.

Driving and hazardous work
▼ Avoid. Olanzapine can cause unusual drowsiness.

Alcohol
▼ Avoid. Alcohol increases the sedative effects of this drug.

PROLONGED USE

Prolonged use of olanzapine may, rarely, cause *tardive dyskinesia*, in which there are involuntary movements of the tongue and face. There is also an increased risk of developing diabetes and raised blood lipid levels. With long-term use in elderly patients, olanzapine also carries a greater risk of stroke than some other antipsychotic drugs.

OMEPRAZOLE

Product names Losec, Nexium, and others
Used in the following combined preparation Vimovo

GENERAL INFORMATION

Omeprazole belongs to a group of drugs called proton pump inhibitors (see p.95), which reduce stomach acid secretion by blocking the stomach's acid-pumping mechanism itself. It is used to treat stomach and duodenal ulcers as well as reflux esophagitis, a condition in which acid from the stomach rises into the esophagus.

Treatment for ulcers is usually given for four to eight weeks, although it may be given for much longer to prevent ulcers in high-risk patients, such as those taking long-term non-steroidal anti-inflammatory drugs (NSAIDs). Omeprazole may also be given with antibiotics to eradicate the *Helicobacter pylori* bacteria that cause many peptic ulcers. Reflux esophagitis may be treated for four to twelve weeks.

Omeprazole causes few serious *side effects*. As with other anti-ulcer drugs, it may mask signs of stomach cancer, so it is prescribed only when the possibility of this disease has been ruled out.

INFORMATION FOR USERS

Your drug prescription is tailored for you. Do not alter dosage without checking with your physician.

How taken

Tablets, capsules, injection, intravenous infusion.

Frequency and timing of doses
Usually once daily.

Usual adult dosage range
10–40mg daily.

Onset of effect
2–5 hours.

Duration of action
Up to 24 hours.

Diet advice
None, although spicy foods and alcohol may exacerbate the underlying condition.

Storage
Keep in a closed container in a cool, dry place out of the reach of children. Omeprazole is very sensitive to moisture. It must not be transferred to another container and must be used within 3 months of opening.

Missed dose
Take as soon as you remember. If your next dose is due within 8 hours, take a single dose now and skip the next.

Stopping the drug
Do not stop the drug without consulting your physician; symptoms may recur.

Exceeding the dose
An occasional unintentional extra dose is unlikely to be a cause for concern. But if you notice any unusual symptoms, or if a large overdose has been taken, notify your physician.

SPECIAL PRECAUTIONS

Be sure to tell your physician if:
▼ You have liver problems.
▼ You have had an allergic reaction to omeprazole.
▼ You are taking other medications.

Pregnancy
▼ Safety in pregnancy not established. Discuss with your physician.

Breast-feeding
▼ The drug may pass into the breast milk. Safety in breast-feeding not established. Discuss with your physician.

Infants and children
▼ Not recommended.

Over 60
▼ No special problems.

Driving and hazardous work
▼ No special problems.

Alcohol
▼ Avoid. Alcohol may aggravate your underlying condition and reduce the beneficial effects of this drug.

POSSIBLE ADVERSE EFFECTS

Adverse effects such as headache and diarrhea are usually mild, and often diminish with continued use of the drug. If you develop a rash, however, you should notify your physician.

Symptom/effect	Frequency		Discuss with physician		Stop taking drug now	Call physician now
	Common	Rare	Only if severe	In all cases		
Headache	●		■			
Diarrhea	●		■			
Constipation/nausea		●	■			
Rash		●		■	▲	

INTERACTIONS

Warfarin The effects of warfarin may be increased by omeprazole.

Phenytoin The effects of phenytoin may be increased by omeprazole.

Clopidogrel The antiplatelet effect of clopidogrel is reduced by omeprazole.

Cyclosporine and tacrolimus Blood levels of these drugs are raised by omeprazole.

Ketoconazole and itraconazole Blood levels of these drugs may be reduced by omeprazole.

PROLONGED USE

Long-term use of omeprazole may increase the risk of certain intestinal infections (such as *Salmonella* and *Clostridium difficile* infections) because of the loss of the natural protection against such infections provided by stomach acid. Prolonged use may also increase the risk of hip fractures in women.

ONDANSETRON

Product names Apo-Ondansetron, Zofran, Zofran ODT, and others
Used in the following combined preparations None

GENERAL INFORMATION

Ondansetron, an anti-emetic, is used especially for treating the nausea and vomiting associated with radiotherapy and anticancer drugs such as cisplatin. It may also be prescribed for the nausea and vomiting that occur after surgery.

The dose given and the frequency will depend on which anti-cancer drug you are having and the dose of that drug. In most instances, you will receive a dose of ondansetron, either by mouth or injection, before infusion of the anti-cancer agent, then tablets for up to five days after the treatment has finished. Ondansetron is less effective against the delayed nausea and vomiting that occur several days after chemotherapy than against symptoms that occur soon after anticancer treatment.

To enhance the effectiveness of ondansetron, it is usually taken with other drugs, such as dexamethasone. Serious adverse effects are unlikely to occur.

INFORMATION FOR USERS

Your drug prescription is tailored for you. Do not alter dosage without checking with your physician.

How taken

Tablets, oral disintegrating tablets, liquid, injection.

Frequency and timing of doses
Normally 2–3 x daily but the frequency will depend on the reason for which it is being used.

Usual adult dosage range
4–32mg daily depending on the reason for which it is being used.

Onset of effect
Within 1 hour.

Duration of action
Approximately 12 hours.

Diet advice
None.

Storage
Keep in a closed container in a cool, dry place out of the reach of children. Protect from light.

Missed dose
Take as soon as you remember. If your next dose is due within 2 hours, take a single dose now and skip the next.

Stopping the drug
Can be safely stopped as soon as you no longer need it.

Exceeding the dose
An occasional unintentional extra dose is unlikely to be a cause for concern. But if you notice any unusual symptoms, or if a large overdose has been taken, notify your physician.

POSSIBLE ADVERSE EFFECTS

Ondansetron is considered to be safe and is generally well tolerated. It does not cause sedation or abnormal muscle movements – adverse effects of some of the other anti-emetics.

Symptom/effect	Frequency		Discuss with physician		Stop taking drug now	Call physician now
	Common	Rare	Only if severe	In all cases		
Constipation	●		■			
Headache	●		■			
Warm feeling in head/stomach	●		■			
Palpitations/chest pain		●		■	▲	■
Dizziness		●		■		
Seizures		●		■	▲	■
Wheezing/itchy rash		●		■	▲	■

INTERACTIONS

Rifampicin This antibiotic may accelerate the breakdown of ondansetron and reduce its effect.

Tramadol The effect of this painkiller may be reduced by ondansetron.

Carbamazepine, phenytoin, and rifampin These antiepileptic drugs may accelerate the breakdown of ondasetron and reduce its effect.

SPECIAL PRECAUTIONS

Be sure to tell your physician if:
▼ You have a long-term liver problem.
▼ You have phenylketonuria.
▼ You have heart rhythm problems.
▼ You are taking other medications.

 Pregnancy
▼ Safety in pregnancy not established. Discuss with your doctor.

 Breast-feeding
▼ The drug passes into the breast milk. Discuss with your doctor.

 Infants and children
▼ Reduced dose necessary.

 Over 60
▼ No special problems.

 Driving and hazardous work
▼ No problems expected.

 Alcohol
▼ No known problems.

PROLONGED USE

Not generally prescribed for long-term treatment.

ORLISTAT

Product name Xenical
Used in the following combined preparations None

GENERAL INFORMATION

Orlistat blocks the action of stomach and pancreatic enzymes (lipases) that digest fats: hence less dietary fat is absorbed and more passes out in the feces. This leads to reduced calorie uptake and helps to produce weight loss as the body burns stored fat to provide energy. The effectiveness of orlistat varies from person to person, and it should only be used to lose weight in conjunction with healthy lifestyle measures.

Because of the way orlistat works, the feces become oily and this can cause flatulence. Part of the drug's effect may be due to people reducing their fat intake in order to avoid these *side effects*.

As fat absorption is greatly reduced, there is a danger that fat soluble vitamins might be lost to the body. Vitamin supplements may be prescribed to compensate for this (see Diet advice, below).

INFORMATION FOR USERS

Follow instructions on the label. Call your physician if symptoms worsen.

How taken

Capsules.

Frequency and timing of doses
Just before, during, or up to 1 hour after each main meal (up to 3 x daily). If a meal is omitted or contains no fat, do not take the dose of orlistat.

Usual adult dosage range
120–360mg daily.

Onset of effect
30 minutes; excretion of excess fecal fat begins about 24–48 hours after the first dose.

Duration of action
Orlistat is not absorbed from the gut, and potentially continues to work as it passes through the intestines. If you stop taking the drug, fecal fat returns to normal in 48–72 hours.

Diet advice
Eat a nutritionally balanced diet that does not contain quite enough calories, and that provides about 30 percent of the calories as fat. Eat lots of fruit and vegetables. The intake of fat, carbohydrate, and protein should be distributed over the three main meals. If a multivitamin supplement is needed, it should be taken at least 2 hours before an orlistat dose or at bedtime.

Storage
Keep in a closed container in a cool dry place. Keep out of the reach of children.

Missed dose
No cause for concern. Take the next dose with the next meal.

Stopping the drug
The drug can be safely stopped as soon as it is no longer needed, but notify your physician.

Exceeding the dose
An occasional unintentional extra dose is unlikely to be a cause for concern. But if you notice any unusual symptoms, or if a large overdose has been taken, notify your physician.

POSSIBLE ADVERSE EFFECTS

Most of the side effects depend on how much fat is eaten, as well as the dose of orlistat.

Symptom/effect	Frequency		Discuss with physician		Stop taking drug now	Call physician now
	Common	Rare	Only if severe	In all cases		
Liquid, oily stools	●		■			
Fecal urgency/flatulence	●		■			
Abdominal/rectal pain	●		■			
Headache		●	■			
Menstrual irregularities		●	■			
Anxiety/fatigue/nausea		●	■			

INTERACTIONS

General note Orlistat reduces absorption of fat-soluble vitamins (A, D, E, and K) so that a multivitamin supplement may be needed. This is particularly important in growing teenagers.

Cyclosporine, oral anticoagulants, amiodarone, and antiepileptics Orlistat may reduce the effects of these drugs.

Acarbose Avoid using orlistat if using acarbose.

SPECIAL PRECAUTIONS

Be sure to tell your physician or pharmacist if:
▼ You have diabetes.
▼ You have chronic malabsorption syndrome.
▼ You have gallbladder or liver problems.
▼ You are taking lipid-lowering drugs.
▼ You are taking other medications.

Pregnancy
▼ Safety not established. Discuss with your physician.

Breast-feeding
▼ Safety not established. Discuss with your physician.

Infants and children
▼ Should not be used in under-18s except on specialist advice.

Over 60
▼ No known problems.

Driving and hazardous work
▼ No special problems.

Alcohol
▼ No special problems.

PROLONGED USE

Orlistat treatment should be stopped after 12 weeks if you have not lost 5 percent of your body weight since the start of treatment. If you have, then the drug may be continued, for up to a maximum of 2 years, until your target weight is approached.

When orlistat treatment is stopped, there may be gradual weight gain.

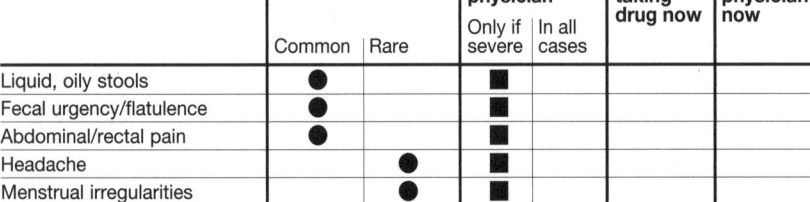

OSELTAMIVIR

Product name Tamiflu
Used in the following combined preparations None

GENERAL INFORMATION

Oseltamivir is an antiviral drug that is used to prevent or treat influenza (flu), a virus that infects and multiplies within the lungs. As well as regular seasonal flu, it is also effective against the avian (bird) flu and swine flu strains of the influenza virus. Oseltamivir works by blocking the entry of the virus into cells where they normally multiply before spreading throughout the body. This prevents or alleviates the typical symptoms of the flu, which include sudden onset of fever, sweating and shivering, cough, runny or stuffy nose, headache, aching muscles, and extreme fatigue. The drug should be taken within 48 hours of the onset of symptoms. It may reduce the duration of symptoms by 1–2 days.

Oseltamivir is not a substitute for seasonal flu vaccination and is not recommended for prevention of seasonal flu. However, because it does not alter the flu vaccine's effectiveness, it can be taken even if you have been vaccinated.

QUICK REFERENCE

Drug group Antiviral drugs (p.119)
Overdose danger rating Low
Dependence rating Low
Prescription needed Yes
Available as generic No

INFORMATION FOR USERS

Your drug prescription is tailored for you. Do not alter dosage without checking with your physician.

How taken

Capsules, suspension.

Frequency and timing of doses
Once or twice daily.

Usual dosage range
Treatment of influenza 13 years of age or older, 75mg twice daily for 5 days.
Prevention 75mg once daily for up to 14 days.
For children 1–12 years of age, dose is based on the weight of the child.

Onset of effect
Within 7 days.

Duration of action
Up to 12 hours.

Diet advice
May be taken with or without food. Taking it with food may make it easier to tolerate the medication.

Storage
Capsules Keep in a closed container in a cool, dry place out of the reach of children.
Suspension Store in refrigerator at 2–8°C. Suspension should be shaken well before use.

Missed dose
If you miss a dose, take it as soon as you remember. If it is near the time of the next dose, skip the missed dose and resume your using dosing schedule. Do not double up to catch up on a missed dose.

Stopping the drug
Do not stop the drug without consulting your physician; symptoms may recur.

Exceeding the dose
An occasional unintentional extra dose is unlikely to cause problems. However, if you notice any unusual symptoms, or if a large overdose has been taken, notify your physician.

SPECIAL PRECAUTIONS

Be sure to tell your physician if:
▼ You have ever had an allergic reaction to oseltamivir.
▼ You have a long-term illness.
▼ You have poor immunity to infections.
▼ You have kidney problems or kidney disease.
▼ You are on any other medications.

Pregnancy
▼ Discuss benefits versus risks with your physician.

Breast-feeding
▼ The drug passes into the breast milk in low amounts. Discuss use with your physician.

Infants and children
▼ Not recommended in children less than one year of age. For all children, discuss follow-up with your physician.

Over 60
▼ No special problems.

Driving and hazardous work
▼ No known problems.

Alcohol
▼ No known problems.

POSSIBLE ADVERSE EFFECTS

Adverse effects are uncommon. Such effects that occur are similar to signs and symptoms of flu and may therefore sometimes be caused by the influenza virus rather than oseltamivir.

Symptom/effect	Frequency		Discuss with physician		Stop taking drug now	Call physician now
	Common	Rare	Only if severe	In all cases		
Nausea/vomiting	●		■			
Dizziness	●		■			
Abdominal pain		●	■			
Headache		●	■			
Rash		●		■		▌
Hallucinations/psychosis		●		■	▲	▌

INTERACTIONS

Probenecid may increase the effect of oseltamivir.

PROLONGED USE

This drug should only be used for 5 days for treatment or for the appropriate recommended duration for prophylaxis. Not prescribed for long-term use.

OXAZEPAM

Product names Apo-Oxazepam, Bio-Oxazepam, Oxpam, and others
Used in the following combined preparations None

GENERAL INFORMATION

Oxazepam belongs to a group of drugs known as the benzodiazepines, which help to relieve anxiety and encourage sleep. The actions and *adverse effects* of this group of drugs are described more fully on page 67.

Oxazepam is used for the short-term treatment of excessive anxiety and may be taken two to four times a day for this condition. When taken 30 minutes to 1 hour before bedtime, it can also help with insomnia. Oxazepam is less likely than some of the other benzodiazepines to accumulate in the body.

Oxazepam, in common with other benzodiazopines, can be habit-forming if taken regularly over a long period of time. Its effects may also diminish with time. For those reasons, treatment should be reviewed regularly.

QUICK REFERENCE

Drug group Benzodiazepine anti-anxiety drugs (p.67)

Overdose danger rating Medium

Dependence rating High

Prescription needed Yes

Available as generic Yes

INFORMATION FOR USERS

Your drug prescription is tailored for you. Do not alter dosage without checking with your physician.

How taken

Tablets.

Frequency and timing of doses
1–4 times daily.

Usual adult dosage range
15–120mg daily.

Onset of effect
Within 30–45 minutes.

Duration of action
Several hours.

Diet advice
None.

Storage
Keep in a closed container in a cool, dry place out of the reach of children.

Missed dose
On a daytime schedule, take the missed dose when you remember. If your next dose is due within 2–3 hours, take a single dose now and skip the next. If taken at bedtime only, a missed dose is no cause for concern.

Stopping the drug
If you have been taking the drug continuously for less than 2 weeks, it can be safely stopped as soon as you feel you no longer need it. If you have been taking the drug for longer, consult your physician, who will supervise a gradual reduction in dosage. Stopping abruptly may lead to withdrawal symptoms (see p.66).

Exceeding the dose
An occasional unintentional extra dose is unlikely to cause problems. Large overdoses may cause unusual drowsiness. Notify your physician immediately and seek medical assistance.

SPECIAL PRECAUTIONS

Be sure to tell your physician if:
▼ You have severe respiratory disease or sleep apnea.
▼ You have or have had any problems with alcohol or drug misuse/abuse.
▼ You have myasthenia gravis.
▼ You have glaucoma.
▼ You have had epileptic seizures.
▼ You have impaired liver or kidney function.
▼ You are taking other medications.

 Pregnancy
▼ Not recommended.

 Breast-feeding
▼ The drug passes into the breast milk. Intermittent and short-term use is generally considered safe. Discuss with your physician.

 Infants and children
▼ Not recommended.

 Over 60
▼ Increased likelihood of adverse effects. Reduced dose may therefore be necessary.

 Driving and hazardous work
▼ Avoid such activities until you have learned how oxazepam affects you because the drug can cause drowsiness, reduced alertness, and slowed reactions.

Alcohol
▼ Avoid. Alcohol increases the sedative effects of the drug.

POSSIBLE ADVERSE EFFECTS

The principal adverse effects of this drug are related to its *sedative* and tranquillizing properties and normally diminish after the first few days of treatment.

Symptom/effect	Frequency		Discuss with physician		Stop taking drug now	Call physician now
	Common	Rare	Only if severe	In all cases		
Daytime drowsiness	●		■			
Dizziness/unsteadiness		●		■		
Headache		●		■		
Nausea/vomiting		●		■		
Amnesia		●		■	▲	
Confusion/disorientation		●		■		▮
Rash		●		■	▲	▮

INTERACTIONS

Sedatives All drugs, including alcohol, that have a sedative effect on the central nervous system are likely to increase the sedative effects of oxazepam. Such drugs include other sleeping and anti-anxiety drugs, antihistamines, antidepressants, *opioid* analgesics, and antipsychotics.

Antacid May decrease the rate of oxazepam absorption; separate administration times.

Cimetidine May decrease breakdown of oxazepam and increase its effect.

PROLONGED USE

Regular use of this drug over several weeks can lead to a reduction in its effect as the body adapts. It may also be habit-forming when taken for extended periods, especially if large doses are taken.

OXYBUTYNIN

Product names Ditropan XL, Oxytrol, Uromax, and others
Used in the following combined preparations None

GENERAL INFORMATION

Oxybutynin is an *anticholinergic* and *antispasmodic* drug used to treat urinary incontinence and frequency in adults and bedwetting in children. It works by reducing bladder contraction, allowing the bladder to hold more urine. The drug stops bladder spasms and delays the desire to empty the bladder. It also has some local *anesthetic* effect.

It is available as tablets and as a *patch* that can be applied to the skin. The patch is usually applied twice weekly.

The drug's usefulness is limited to some extent by its *side effects*, especially in children and the elderly. It can aggravate conditions such as an enlarged prostate or coronary heart disease in the elderly. Children are more susceptible to effects on the central nervous system (CNS), such as restless-ness, disorientation, hallucinations, and convulsions.

INFORMATION FOR USERS

Your drug prescription is tailored for you. Do not alter dosage without checking with your physician.

How taken

Tablets, liquid, patch.

Frequency and timing of doses
2–3 x daily, once daily (XL), twice weekly (patch).

Usual adult dosage range
10–20mg daily.

Onset of effect
1 hour.

Duration of action
Up to 10 hours.

Diet advice
None.

Storage
Keep in a closed container in a cool, dry place out of the reach of children. Protect liquid from light.

Missed dose
Take as soon as you remember. If your next dose is due within 2 hours, take a single dose now and skip the next.

Stopping the drug
Do not stop taking the drug without consulting your physician; symptoms may recur.

OVERDOSE ACTION

 Seek immediate medical advice in all cases. Take emergency action if symptoms such as breathing difficulty, seizures, or loss of consciousness occur.

See Drug poisoning emergency guide (p.526).

POSSIBLE ADVERSE EFFECTS

An adjustment in dosage is necessary in children and the elderly to minimize oxybutynin's *adverse effects*. The drug can also precipitate glaucoma.

Symptom/effect	Frequency		Discuss with physician		Stop taking drug now	Call physician now
	Common	Rare	Only if severe	In all cases		
Dry mouth	●		■			
Blurred vision/eye pain		●	■			
Constipation	●		■			
Nausea	●		■			
Facial flushing	●		■			
Difficulty in passing urine	●			■		
Headache/confusion		●		■		
Dry skin/rash		●		■		

INTERACTIONS

General note Oxybutynin reduces gastric motility (spontaneous stomach movements that move stomach contents into the intestine) and so may affect the absorption of other oral drugs.

Other anticholinergic drugs If oxybutynin is taken with other drugs that have anticholinergic effects, the risk of accumulated side effects is increased.

SPECIAL PRECAUTIONS

Be sure to tell your physician if:
▼ You have liver or kidney problems.
▼ You have hyperthyroidism.
▼ You have heart problems.
▼ You have an enlarged prostate.
▼ You have hiatus hernia.
▼ You have ulcerative colitis.
▼ You have glaucoma.
▼ You have myasthenia gravis.
▼ You are taking other medications.

 Pregnancy
▼ Safety not established. May harm the unborn baby. Discuss with your physician.

 Breast-feeding
▼ The drug passes into the breast milk; safety not established. Discuss with your physician.

 Infants and children
▼ Not recommended under 5 years. Reduced dose necessary in older children.

 Over 60
▼ Reduced dose necessary.

 Driving and hazardous work
▼ Avoid such activities until you have learned how oxybutynin affects you because the drug can cause drowsiness, disorientation, and blurred vision.

 Alcohol
▼ Avoid. Alcohol increases the *sedative* effects of oxybutynin.

PROLONGED USE

No special problems. The need for continued treatment may be reviewed after six months.

PANTOPRAZOLE

Product names Pantoloc, PANTO IV, and others
Used in the following combined preparations None

GENERAL INFORMATION

Pantoprazole is an anti-ulcer drug used to treat stomach and duodenal ulcers as well as reflux esophagitis, a condition in which acid from the stomach rises into the esophagus. It reduces the amount of stomach acid and works in a different way from other anti-ulcer drugs that reduce acid secretion. It may also be used to prevent gastroduodenal ulceration sometimes caused by non-steroidal anti-inflammatory drugs (p.64).

Treatment is usually given for four to eight weeks, depending on where the ulcer is situated. Pantoprazole may also be given with *antibiotics* to eradicate the

Helicobacter pylori bacteria that cause many gastric ulcers. Reflux esophagitis may be treated for four to twelve weeks.

Pantoprazole causes few serious *side effects*. However, because the drug may affect the actions of enzymes in the liver, where many drugs are broken down, it may increase the effects of cyclosporine, warfarin, and phenytoin, and these drugs require more careful monitoring when used with pantoprazole. As with other anti-ulcer drugs, it may mask signs of stomach cancer, so it is used only when the possibility of this disease has been ruled out.

INFORMATION FOR USERS

Your drug prescription is tailored for you. Do not alter dosage without checking with your physician.

How taken

Tablets, injection. Tablets should be swallowed whole and should not be chewed or crushed.

Frequency and timing of doses
Once daily in the morning.

Usual adult dosage range
20–40mg daily.

Onset of effect
1–3 hours

Duration of action
24 hours.

Diet advice
None, although spicy foods and alcohol may exacerbate the underlying condition.

Storage
Keep in a closed container in a cool, dry place out of the reach of children.

Missed dose
If you miss a dose, take it as soon as you remember. If your next dose is within 8 hours, take a single dose now and skip the next.

Stopping the drug
Do not stop the drug without consulting your physician; symptoms may recur.

Exceeding the dose
An occasional unintentional extra dose is unlikely to be a cause for concern. But if you notice any unusual symptoms, or if a large overdose has been taken, notify your physician.

POSSIBLE ADVERSE EFFECTS

Adverse effects such as diarrhea is usually mild, and often diminish with continued use of the drug. If you develop a rash, however, you should notify your physician.

Symptom/effect	Frequency		Discuss with physician		Stop taking drug now	Call physician now
	Common	Rare	Only if severe	In all cases		
Diarrhea	●		■			
Headaches	●		■			
Nausea/vomiting		●	■			
Constipation		●	■			
Dizziness		●	■			
Rash		●		■	▲	∎

INTERACTIONS

Ketoconazole Pantoprazole may decrease the effectiveness of ketoconazole, and ketoconazole may increase the levels of pantoprazole.

Citalopram Pantoprazole may increase the level of citalopram.

Clopidogrel Pantoprazole may decrease the effectiveness of clopidogrel.

Cyclosporine, warfarin, phenytoin Pantoprazole may increase the effects of these drugs and they may require more careful monitoring.

SPECIAL PRECAUTIONS

Be sure to tell your physician if:
▼ You have liver problems.
▼ You have had an allergic reaction to pantoprazole.
▼ You are taking other medications.

Pregnancy
▼ Safety has not been established. Discuss with your physician.

Breast-feeding
▼ Safety in breast-feeding not established. Discuss with your physician.

Infants and children
▼ Not recommended.

Over 60
▼ No special problems.

Driving and hazardous work
▼ No special problems.

Alcohol
▼ Avoid. Alcohol may aggravate your underlying condition and reduce the beneficial effects of this drug.

PROLONGED USE

No problems expected.

PAROXETINE

Product names Paxil, Teva-Paroxetine, and others
Used in the following combined preparations None

GENERAL INFORMATION

Paroxetine is a selective serotonin reuptake inhibitor (SSRI). It is used in the treatment of mild to moderate depression and helps control the anxiety often accompanying it. It is also used to treat generalized anxiety disorder, social phobia, panic disorder, obsessive-compulsive disorders, and post-traumatic stress disorders. Paroxetine is sometimes given to treat severe premenstrual syndrome.

It is less likely than the older tricyclic antidepressants to cause *anticholinergic side effects* such as dry mouth, blurred vision, and difficulty in passing urine, and is much less dangerous if taken in overdose.

The most common *adverse effects* include nausea, diarrhea, drowsiness, sweating, tremor, weakness, insomnia, and sexual problems, such as lack of orgasm.

QUICK REFERENCE

Drug group Antidepressant drug (p.68)

Overdose danger rating Medium

Dependence rating Low

Prescription needed Yes

Available as generic Yes

INFORMATION FOR USERS

Your drug prescription is tailored for you. Do not alter dosage without checking with your physician.

How taken

Tablets.

Frequency and timing of doses
Once daily, in the morning.

Usual adult dosage range
10–40mg daily.

Onset of effect
The onset of therapeutic response usually occurs within 7–14 days of starting treatment, but full antidepressant effect may not be felt for 4 weeks.

Duration of action
Up to 24 hours.

Diet advice
None.

Storage
Keep in a closed container in a cool, dry place out of the reach of children.

Missed dose
Take as soon as you remember.

Stopping the drug
Do not stop the drug without consulting your physician. Stopping abruptly can cause *withdrawal symptoms*.

Exceeding the dose
An occasional unintentional extra dose is unlikely to be a cause for concern. Large doses may cause unusual drowsiness. Notify your physician immediately.

POSSIBLE ADVERSE EFFECTS

Common adverse effects include nausea, diarrhea, drowsiness, sweating, tremor, weakness, insomnia, and sexual dysfunction (lack of orgasm, male ejaculation problems).

Symptom/effect	Frequency		Discuss with physician		Stop taking drug now	Call physician now
	Common	Rare	Only if severe	In all cases		
Nausea	●		■			
Sweating	●		■			
Drowsiness/dizziness	●		■			
Sexual dysfunction (both sexes)	●		■			
Diarrhea	●		■			
Nervousness/anxiety/agitation		●		■		
Rash/itching/hives/joint pain		●		■	▲	▌
Poor appetite/weight loss		●		■		
Convulsions		●		■	▲	▌

INTERACTIONS

General note Any drug that affects the breakdown of others in the liver may alter blood levels of paroxetine or vice versa.

Anticoagulants Paroxetine may increase the effects of these drugs.

Sedatives All *sedatives* are likely to increase the sedative effects of paroxetine.

Antipsychotics and tricyclic antidepressants Paroxetine may increase the *toxicity* of these drugs.

Monoamine oxidase inhibitors (MAOIs) Paroxetine should not be taken during or within 14 days of MAOI treatment because serious reactions may occur.

ASA and non-steroidal anti-inflammatory drugs (NSAIDs) There is an increased risk of gastric bleeding when these drugs are used with paroxetine.

SPECIAL PRECAUTIONS

Be sure to tell your physician if:
▼ You have long-term liver or kidney problems.
▼ You have heart problems or bleeding disorders.
▼ You have glaucoma.
▼ You have a history or a family history of seizures.
▼ You are taking other medications.

Pregnancy
▼ Risks versus benefits need to be assessed. Discuss with your physician.

Breast-feeding
▼ The drug passes into the breast milk. Discuss with your physician.

Infants and children
▼ Not generally recommended under 18 years.

Over 60
▼ Increased likelihood of adverse effects. Reduced dose may be necessary.

Driving and hazardous work
▼Avoid such activities until you have learned how paroxetine affects you because the drug can cause drowsiness.

Alcohol
▼ Avoid. Alcohol may increase the *sedative* effects of this drug.

PROLONGED USE

Withdrawal symptoms may occur if the drug is not stopped gradually. Such symptoms include dizziness, electric shock sensations, anxiety, nausea, and insomnia. These rarely last for more than 1–2 weeks. There is also a small risk of suicidal thoughts and self-harm in children and adolescents, although the drug is rarely used in this age group.

Monitoring Any person experiencing drowsiness confusion, muscle cramps, or seizures should be monitored for low sodium levels in the blood. Under-18s should be monitored for suicidal thoughts and self harm.

PENICILLIN V

Product names Apo-Pen VK, Novo-Pen VK, Nu-Pen VK, and others
Used in the following combined preparations None

GENERAL INFORMATION

Penicillin V, also known as phenoxymethylpenicillin, is a penicillin-type antibiotic that is prescribed for a wide range of infections.

Various commonly occurring respiratory tract infections, such as some types of tonsillitis and pharyngitis, as well as ear infections, often respond well to this drug. It is also effective for the treatment of the gum disease, Vincent's gingivitis.

Penicillin V is also used to treat less common infections caused by the *Streptococcus* bacterium, such as scarlet fever. It is also prescribed long term to prevent the recurrence of rheumatic fever, a rare, although potentially serious condition. It is also used long term to prevent infections following removal of the spleen or in sickle cell disease.

As with other penicillin antibiotics, the most serious *adverse effect* that may rarely occur is an allergic reaction that may cause collapse, wheezing, and a rash in susceptible people.

QUICK REFERENCE

Drug group Penicillin antibiotics (p.114)

Overdose danger rating Low

Dependence rating Low

Prescription needed Yes

Available as generic Yes

INFORMATION FOR USERS

Your drug prescription is tailored for you. Do not alter dosage without checking with your physician.

How taken

Tablets, liquid.

Frequency and timing of doses
2–4 x daily, at least 30 minutes before food.

Usual dosage range
Adults 1.5–2.0 million iu daily (500,000 iu = 300 mg).
Children Reduced dose according to age.

Onset of effect
1–2 days.

Duration of action
Up to 12 hours.

Diet advice
None.

Storage
Keep in a closed container in a cool, dry place out of the reach of children.

Missed dose
Take as soon as you remember. If your next dose is due within 2 hours, take a single dose now and skip the next.

Stopping the drug
Take the full course. Even if you feel better, the original infection may still be present and may recur if the treatment is stopped too soon.

Exceeding the dose
An occasional unintentional extra dose is unlikely to be a cause for concern. But if you notice any unusual symptoms, or if a large overdose has been taken, notify your physician.

SPECIAL PRECAUTIONS

Be sure to tell your physician if:
▼ You have a long-term kidney problem.
▼ You have had a previous allergic reaction to a penicillin or cephalosporin antibiotic.
▼ You have an allergic disorder such as asthma or urticaria.
▼ You are taking other medications.

Pregnancy
▼ No evidence of risk.

Breast-feeding
▼ The drug passes into the breast milk, but at normal doses adverse effects on the baby are unlikely. Discuss with your physician.

Infants and children
▼ Reduced dose necessary.

Over 60
▼ No special problems.

Driving and hazardous work
▼ No known problems.

Alcohol
▼ No known problems.

POSSIBLE ADVERSE EFFECTS

Most people do not experience any serious adverse effects when taking penicillin V.

However, this drug may provoke an allergic reaction in susceptible people.

Symptom/effect	Frequency		Discuss with physician		Stop taking drug now	Call physician now
	Common	Rare	Only if severe	In all cases		
Nausea/vomiting	●		■			
Diarrhea		●	■			
Rash/itching		●		■	▲	▮
Breathing difficulties		●		■	▲	▮

INTERACTIONS

Probenecid increases the level of penicillin V in the blood.

Methotrexate Excretion of this drug may be greatly reduced by penicillin V, leading to toxicity.

PROLONGED USE

Prolonged use may increase the risk of *Candida* infections and diarrhea.

PERINDOPRIL

Product name Coversyl
Used in the following combined preparations Coversyl Plus, Coversyl Plus HD, Coversyl Plus LD

GENERAL INFORMATION

Perindopril is an ACE inhibitor, a group of drugs used to treat high blood pressure and heart failure. The drug relaxes the muscles around the blood vessels, allowing them to dilate and thereby easing blood flow. Perindopril lowers blood pressure promptly but may need to be taken for several weeks to achieve maximum effect. When treating heart failure, perindopril is usually combined with a diuretic. This can give dramatic improvement, relaxing the muscle in blood vessel walls and reducing the workload on the heart.

At the start of treatment ACE inhibitors can cause a very rapid fall in blood pressure. Therefore, the first dose is usually low and taken at bedtime so that the patient can stay lying down.

The most characteristic *adverse effect* of perindopril is a persistent dry cough. This may occur in up to 20 per cent of patients. The throat may become irritated, and the voice husky or hoarse.

INFORMATION FOR USERS

Your drug prescription is tailored for you. Do not alter dosage without checking with your physician.

How taken

Tablets.

Frequency and timing of doses
Once daily, 30 minutes before food. Taken in the morning for the treatment of heart failure.

Usual adult dosage range
2mg initially, then 4–8mg daily.

Onset of effect
30–60 minutes; full beneficial effect may take several weeks.

Duration of action
24 hours.

Diet advice
A low-salt diet may be advised to help control blood pressure.

Storage
Keep in a closed container in a cool, dry place out of the reach of children.

Missed dose
Take as soon as you remember. If your next dose is due within the next 8 hours, take a single dose now, and skip the next.

Stopping the drug
Do not stop the drug without consulting your physician; stopping the drug may lead to worsening of the underlying condition.

Exceeding the dose
An occasional unintentional extra dose is unlikely to cause problems. Large overdoses may cause dizziness or fainting. Notify your physician.

SPECIAL PRECAUTIONS

Be sure to tell your physician if:
▼ You have long-term liver or kidney problems.
▼ You have heart problems.
▼ You have had angioedema or a previous allergic reaction to ACE inhibitors.
▼ You are pregnant or intend to become pregnant.
▼ You are taking other medications.

Pregnancy
▼ Not prescribed. There is evidence of harm to the developing fetus.

Breast-feeding
▼ Safety not established. Discuss with your physician.

Infants and children
▼ Not recommended.

Over 60
▼ Elderly people may be more sensitive to the drug. Reduced dose necessary.

Driving and hazardous work
▼ Avoid such activities until you have learned how perindopril affects you. The drug can cause dizziness and fainting.

Alcohol
▼ Avoid. Alcohol may increase the blood-pressure-lowering and adverse effects of the drug.

Surgery and general anesthetics
▼ Perindopril may need to be stopped before you have a general anesthetic. Discuss with your physician or dentist before any operation.

POSSIBLE ADVERSE EFFECTS

Perindopril may cause a variety of adverse effects but they are usually mild and often disappear soon after treatment has started. It may also cause kidney impairment.

Symptom/effect	Frequency		Discuss with physician		Stop taking drug now	Call physician now
	Common	Rare	Only if severe	In all cases		
Rash	●			■		
Persistent dry cough	●			■		
Mouth ulcers/sore mouth		●		■		
Dizziness		●		■		
Sore throat/fever		●		■		
Swelling of mouth/lips		●		■	▲	▮
Breathing difficulty		●		■	▲	▮

INTERACTIONS

Lithium Blood levels and toxicity of this drug may be raised by perindopril.

Diuretics cause a very rapid fall in blood pressure if taken with perindopril.

Cyclosporine, potassium salts, and potassium-sparing diuretics These drugs increase the risk of high potassium blood levels when taken with perindopril.

Non-steroidal anti-inflammatory drugs (NSAIDs) These drugs may reduce the effects of perindopril. There is also a risk of kidney damage when they are taken together.

Vasodilators (e.g. nitrates) and other antihypertensives may reduce blood pressure even further if taken with perindopril.

PROLONGED USE

No problems expected.

Monitoring Periodic checks on potassium levels, white blood cell count, kidney function, and urine are usually performed.

PERMETHRIN

Product names Kwellada-P, NixCreme Rinse, Nix Dermal Cream
Used in the following combined preparations None

GENERAL INFORMATION

Permethrin is an insecticide used to treat head and pubic lice, and scabies infestations. It works by interfering with the nervous system function of the parasites, causing paralysis and death. Permethrin has the advantage of being less toxic than some of the other types of insecticide, although it is toxic to some animals, such as cats.

Permethrin is applied topically, usually as a shampoo or creme rinse, to treat head lice and as a cream for scabies

infestations. It should not be used on broken skin. Speak to your *pharmacist* and follow the package directions carefully.

For scabies, all family members should be treated at the same time, to prevent recontamination, and the process repeated after a week.

Permethrin is also an ingredient of some insect repellants used to impregnate clothing and mosquito nets in malarial regions.

QUICK REFERENCE

Drug group Drugs to treat skin parasites (p.164)

Overdose danger rating Low

Dependence rating Low

Prescription needed No

Available as generic No

INFORMATION FOR USERS

Follow instructions on the label. Call your physician if symptoms worsen.

How taken

Cream, topical liquid (lotion, shampoo, spray).

Frequency and timing of doses
Once only, repeating after 7 days. Avoid contact with eyes and broken or infected skin.

Usual adult dosage range
As directed.

Onset of effect
Varies depending on formulation; consult product packaging.

Duration of action
Until washed off.

Diet advice
None.

Storage
Keep in a closed container in a cool, dry place out of the reach of children. Protect from light.

Missed dose
Timing of the second application is not rigid; use as soon as you remember.

Stopping the drug
Not applicable

Exceeding the dose
An occasional extra application is unlikely to cause problems. If the drug is accidentally swallowed, take emergency action.

POSSIBLE ADVERSE EFFECTS

In general, permethrin is well tolerated on the skin, although mild skin irritation is common.

Symptom/effect	Frequency		Discuss with physician		Stop taking drug now	Call physician now
	Common	Rare	Only if severe	In all cases		
Itching	●		■			
Reddened skin/stinging	●		■			
Rash		●	■			

INTERACTIONS

None.

SPECIAL PRECAUTIONS

Be sure to consult your physician or pharmacist before taking this drug if:
▼ You have sensitivity to chrysanthemums.
▼ You are taking other medications.

Pregnancy
▼ Safety not established. Discuss risks versus benefits with your physician.

Breast-feeding
▼ Safety not established. Discuss risks versus benefits with your physician.

Infants and children
▼ No special problems.

Over 60
▼ No special problems.

Driving and hazardous work
▼ No special problems.

Alcohol
▼ No special problems.

PROLONGED USE

Permethrin should not be used topically for prolonged periods; it is intended for intermittent use only.

PHENOBARBITAL

Product names Phenobarb, Phenobarb Elixir, Phenobarbital Sodium Injection
Used in the following combined preparations Bellergal Spacetabs

GENERAL INFORMATION

Phenobarbital belongs to the group of drugs known as barbiturates. It is used mainly in the treatment of epilepsy, although this use is declining. It was also used as a sleeping drug and *sedative* before the development of safer drugs. In the treatment of epilepsy, the drug is usually given together with another anticonvulsant drug such as phenytoin. When combined with other drugs, it has been used in anxiety associated with menopausal symptoms. However, there are more effective and safer drugs for this now.

The main disadvantage of the drug is that it often causes unwanted sedation. However, tolerance develops within a week or two. In children and the elderly, it may occasionally cause excessive excitement. Because of their sedative effects, phenobarbital and other barbiturates are sometimes abused.

QUICK REFERENCE

Drug group Barbiturate antiepileptic drugs (p.70)

Overdose danger rating High

Dependence rating High

Prescription needed Yes

Available as generic Yes

INFORMATION FOR USERS

Your drug prescription is tailored for you. Do not alter dosage without checking with your physician.

How taken

Tablets, liquid, injection.

Frequency and timing of doses
Once daily, usually at night.

Usual dosage range
Adults 60–250mg daily (anticonvulsant).

Onset of effect
30–60 minutes (by mouth).

Duration of action
24–48 hours (some effect may persist for up to 6 days).

Diet advice
People taking the drug long-term should eat plenty of fresh green vegetables to prevent possible deficiency of vitamins A, D, K, and folic acid.

Storage
Keep in a closed container in a cool, dry place out of the reach of children.

Missed dose
Take as soon as you remember. If the next dose is due within 10 hours, take a single dose now and skip the next.

Stopping the drug
Do not stop taking the drug without consulting your physician, who may supervise a gradual reduction in dosage. Abrupt cessation may cause fits or lead to restlessness, trembling, and insomnia.

OVERDOSE ACTION

 Seek immediate medical advice in all cases. Take emergency action if unsteadiness, severe weakness, confusion, or loss of consciousness occur.

See Drug poisoning emergency guide (p.526).

SPECIAL PRECAUTIONS

Be sure to tell your physician if:
▼ You have long-term liver or kidney problems.
▼ You have heart problems.
▼ You have poor circulation.
▼ You have porphyria.
▼ You have breathing problems.
▼ You are taking other medications.

 Pregnancy
▼ The drug may affect the fetus and increase the tendency of bleeding in the newborn. Discuss with your physician.

 Breast-feeding
▼ The drug passes into the breast milk and could cause drowsiness in the baby. Discuss with your physician.

 Infants and children
▼ Reduced dose necessary.

 Over 60
▼ Increased likelihood of confusion. Reduced dose may therefore be necessary.

 Driving and hazardous work
▼ Your underlying condition, in addition to the possibility of reduced alertness while taking phenobarbital, may make such activities inadvisable. Discuss with your physician.

 Alcohol
▼ Never drink while under treatment with phenobarbital. Alcohol may interact dangerously with this drug.

POSSIBLE ADVERSE EFFECTS

Most of the adverse effects of phenobarbital are the result of its sedative effect. They can sometimes be minimized by a medically supervised reduction of dosage.

Symptom/effect	Frequency		Discuss with physician		Stop taking drug now	Call physician now
	Common	Rare	Only if severe	In all cases		
Drowsiness	●		■			
Clumsiness/unsteadiness	●		■			
Dizziness/faintness	●			■		
Confusion		●		■		
Rash/localized swellings		●		■	▲	▮
Mouth ulcers		●		■	▲	▮

INTERACTIONS

Antipsychotics, antidepressants, St John's wort, mefloquine, and chloroquine may reduce the anticonvulsant effect of phenobarbital.

Anticoagulants, corticosteroids, oral contraceptives, and protease inhibitors

Phenobarbital may decrease the effect of these drugs.

Sedatives All such drugs are likely to increase the sedative properties of phenobarbital.

PROLONGED USE

With prolonged use, *tolerance* to the drug's sedative effects may develop. *Dependence* may also result, and withdrawal symptoms may occur if the drug is stopped suddenly. Long-term use may also lead to deficiency of vitamins A, D, K, and folic acid.

Monitoring Blood samples may be taken periodically to test blood levels of the drug.

PHENYTOIN/FOSPHENYTOIN

Product names Dilantin, Cerebyx (fosphenytoin), and others
Used in the following combined preparations None

GENERAL INFORMATION

Phenytoin is used to treat epilepsy. It decreases the likelihood of convulsions by reducing abnormal electrical activity within the brain. Fosphenytoin (Cerebryx) is a type of phenytoin given by injection for control of seizures, if oral therapy is not temporarily possible. Some *adverse effects* of phenytoin are more pronounced in children, so it is prescribed for children only when other drugs are unsuitable.

It is recommended that patients remain on the same brand of phenytoin.

QUICK REFERENCE

Drug group Antiepileptic drugs (p.70)

Overdose danger rating High

Dependence rating Low

Prescription needed Yes

Available as generic Yes (phenytoin)

INFORMATION FOR USERS

Your drug prescription is tailored for you. Do not alter dosage without checking with your physician.

How taken

Tablets, chewable tablets, capsules, liquid, injection.

Frequency and timing of doses
1–3 x daily with food or plenty of water. Once daily (extended release capsules).

Usual dosage range
Adults 100–500mg daily.
Children According to age and weight.
Note: A small increase in the dose can cause a disproportionately high drug level in the blood.

Onset of effect
Full anticonvulsant effect may not be felt for 7–10 days.

Duration of action
24 hours.

Diet advice
Folic acid and vitamin D deficiency may occasionally occur while taking this drug. Make sure you eat a balanced diet containing fresh, green vegetables, and dairy products.

Storage
Keep in a tightly closed container in a cool, dry place out of the reach of children.

Missed dose
Take as soon as you remember.

Stopping the drug
Do not stop the drug without consulting your physician; symptoms may recur.

OVERDOSE ACTION

Seek immediate medical advice in all cases. Take emergency action if unsteadiness, severe weakness, confusion, or loss of consciousness occur.

See Drug poisoning emergency guide (p.526).

SPECIAL PRECAUTIONS

Be sure to tell your physician if:
▼ You have long-term liver or kidney problems.
▼ You have diabetes.
▼ You have porphyria.
▼ You are taking other medications.

Pregnancy
▼ The drug may be associated with malformation and a tendency to bleeding in the newborn baby. Folic acid supplements should be taken by the mother. Discuss with your physician and pharmacist.

Breast-feeding
▼ The drug passes into the breast milk, but at normal doses adverse effects on the baby are unlikely. Discuss with your physician.

Infants and children
▼ Reduced dose necessary. Increased likelihood of overgrowth of the gums and excessive growth of body hair.

Over 60
▼ Reduced dose may be necessary.

Driving and hazardous work
▼ Your underlying condition, as well as the effects of phenytoin, may make such activities inadvisable. Discuss with your physician.

Alcohol
▼ Avoid. Alcohol increases the sedative effects of this drug.

POSSIBLE ADVERSE EFFECTS

Phenytoin has a number of adverse effects, many of which appear only after prolonged use. If they become severe, your physician may prescribe a different antiepileptic.

Symptom/effect	Frequency		Discuss with physician		Stop taking drug now	Call physician now
	Common	Rare	Only if severe	In all cases		
Dizziness/headache	●			■		
Nausea/vomiting	●		■			
Insomnia	●		■			
Overgrowth of gums	●		■			
Increased body hair		●	■			
Confusion/unsteadiness		●		■		▮
Rash		●		■		▮
Fever/sore throat/mouth ulcers		●		■		▮

INTERACTIONS

General note Many drugs may interact with phenytoin, causing changes in the phenytoin blood level. The dosage of phenytoin may need to be adjusted.

Cyclosporine Blood levels of cyclosporine may be reduced with phenytoin.

Oral contraceptives Phenytoin may reduce their effectiveness.

Antidepressants, antipsychotics, mefloquine, chloroquine, and St John's wort may reduce the effect of phenytoin.

Warfarin The anticoagulant effect of this drug may be altered. An adjustment in its dosage may be necessary.

PROLONGED USE

There is a slight risk that blood abnormalities may occur. Prolonged use may also lead to adverse effects on skin, gums, and bones. It may also disrupt control of diabetes.

Monitoring Periodic blood tests are performed to monitor levels of the drug in the body and composition of the blood cells and blood chemistry.

PILOCARPINE

Product names Pilopine HS, Salagen Tablets, and others
Used in the following combined preparation None

GENERAL INFORMATION

Pilocarpine is a *miotic* drug used to treat chronic glaucoma and severe glaucoma prior to surgery.

The eye drops are quick-acting but have to be re-applied every four to eight hours. Eye gel is longer acting and needs to be applied only once a day.

Pilocarpine frequently causes blurred vision; and spasm of the eye muscles may cause headaches, particularly at the start of treatment. However, serious *adverse effects* are rare.

Tablets are used to treat dry mouth after radiotherapy to the head and neck.

QUICK REFERENCE

Drug group Drugs for glaucoma (p.156)
Overdose danger rating Medium
Dependence rating Low
Prescription needed Yes
Available as generic Yes

INFORMATION FOR USERS

Your drug prescription is tailored for you. Do not alter dosage without checking with your physician.

How taken

Tablets, eye drops, eye gel.

Frequency and timing of doses
Eye drops 4 x daily (chronic glaucoma). In acute glaucoma, pilocarpine is given at 5-minute intervals until the condition is controlled.
Eye gel Once daily.
Tablets 3 x daily after food with plenty of water.

Usual dosage range
According to formulation and condition. In general, 1–2 eye drops are used per application.
Tablets 15–20mg daily.

Onset of effect
15–30 minutes.

Duration of action
4–8 weeks for maximum effect (tablets); 3–8 hours (eye drops); up to 24 hours (eye gel).

Diet advice
None.

Storage
Keep in a closed container in a cool, dry place out of the reach of children (tablets/eye drops). Discard eye drops 1 month after opening.

Missed dose
Use as soon as you remember. If not remembered until 2 hours before your next dose, skip the missed dose and take the next dose now.

Stopping the drug
Do not stop the drug without consulting your physician; symptoms may recur.

Exceeding the dose
An occasional unintentional extra application is unlikely to cause problems. Excessive use may cause facial flushing, an increase in the flow of saliva, and sweating. If accidentally swallowed, seek medical attention immediately.

POSSIBLE ADVERSE EFFECTS

Alteration in vision is common. Brow ache and eye pain are common at the start of treatment, but usually wear off after a few days.

Symptom/effect	Frequency		Discuss with physician		Stop taking drug now	Call physician now
	Common	Rare	Only if severe	In all cases		
Eye drops/gel						
Blurred vision/poor night vision	●		■			
Headache/brow ache	●		■			
Sweating/chills	●		■			
Eye pain/irritation	●			■		▮
Red, watery eyes		●	■			
Twitching eyelids		●		■		
Tablets						
Nausea/diarrhea	●		■			
Dizziness	●			■		
Urinary frequency	●		■			
Wheezing		●		■	▲	▮

INTERACTIONS

General note A wide range of drugs (including aminoglycoside antibiotics, clindamycin, chloroquine, quinine, quinidine, lithium, and procainamide) may antagonize pilocarpine.

Beta blockers These drugs may reduce the effects of pilocarpine.

Calcium channel blockers These drugs may increase pilocarpine's *systemic* effects.

SPECIAL PRECAUTIONS

Be sure to tell your physician if:
▼ You have asthma.
▼ You have inflamed eyes.
▼ You wear contact lenses.
▼ You have heart, liver, or gastrointestinal problems.
▼ You are taking other medications.

Pregnancy
▼ No evidence of risk at the doses used for chronic glaucoma.

Breast-feeding
▼ The drug passes into the breast milk, but at normal doses adverse effects on the baby are unlikely. Discuss with your physician.

Infants and children
▼ Not usually prescribed.

Over 60
▼ Reduced night vision is particularly noticeable.

Driving and hazardous work
▼ Avoid such activities, especially in poor light, until you have learned how pilocarpine affects you because it may cause short sight and poor night vision.

Alcohol
▼ No known problems.

PROLONGED USE

The effect of the drug may occasionally wear off with prolonged use as the body adapts, but may be restored by changing temporarily to another antiglaucoma drug.

PIOGLITAZONE

Product names Apo-pioglitazone, Co-pioglitazone, Sandoz Pioglitazone, and others
Used in the following combined preparations None

GENERAL INFORMATION

Pioglitazone is used to treat type 2 diabetes mellitus and works by reducing insulin resistance in fatty tissue, skeletal muscle, and in the liver, leading to a decrease in blood glucose levels. It takes 6–12 weeks to reach its full effect. This drug can be used alone or with other antidiabetic drugs such as metformin, but it is not approved for use with insulin. When combined with other antidiabetic drugs, there is a risk of low blood sugar, whose symptoms include shakiness, lightheadedness, sweating, nervousness, sudden change in behaviour, headache, and numbness or tingling around the mouth.

QUICK REFERENCE

Drug group Oral antidiabetics (p.128)

Overdose danger rating High

Dependence rating Low

Prescription needed Yes

Available as generic Yes

INFORMATION FOR USERS

Your drug prescription is tailored for you. Do not alter dosage without checking with your physician.

How taken

Tablets.

Frequency and timing of doses
Usually once daily; may be taken with or without food.

Adult dosage range
Initial dose: 15–30mg once daily; may gradually increase up to a maximum of 45mg daily.

Onset of effect
In 2–4 weeks; full beneficial effects may not be seen until 6–12 weeks.

Duration of action
Up to 24 hours.

Diet advice
An individualized low fat, low carbohydrate diet must be maintained in order for the drug to be fully effective. Follow your physician and dietician's advice.

Storage
Keep in a closed container in a cool, dry place out of the reach of children.

Missed dose
If you remember the same day, take as soon as you remember. If you remember the next day, do not take the missed dose and continue with your regular dosing schedule. Do not double up on your dose.

Stopping the drug
Do not stop the drug without consulting your physician. Stopping the drug may lead to worsening of the underlying condition.

OVERDOSE ACTION

Seek immediate medical advice in all cases. Take emergency action if loss of consciousness occurs.

See Drug poisoning emergency guide (p.526).

SPECIAL PRECAUTIONS

Be sure to tell your physician if:
▼ You have liver problems.
▼ You have heart problems, especially congestive heart failure (CHF).
▼ You have swelling of the ankles.
▼ You have shortness of breath or are easily fatigued.
▼ You have polycystic ovary syndrome.
▼ You are not using birth control, as this drug may increase the chance of conception.
▼ You have osteoporosis or decrease in bone mineral density.
▼ You are taking other medications.

 Pregnancy
▼ Safety in pregnancy not established. Discuss with your physician.

 Breast-feeding
▼ Safety not established. Discuss with your physician.

 Infants and children
▼ Not recommended.

 Over 60
▼ No special problems.

 Driving and hazardous work
▼ No special problems.

 Alcohol
▼ No known problems.

POSSIBLE ADVERSE EFFECTS

If weight gain occurs, especially when used with diabetic drugs, discuss this with your physician.

Symptom/effect	Frequency		Discuss with physician		Stop taking drug now	Call physician now
	Common	Rare	Only if severe	In all cases		
Runny nose	●		■			
Headache	●		■			
Muscle pain	●		■			
Tooth or mouth pain	●		■			
Sore throat	●		■			
Nausea or vomiting		●		■		▮
Loss of appetite		●		■		▮
Dark urine		●		■		
Blurred vision		●		■		▮
Jaundice		●		■		
Edema (swelling)		●		■		▮

INTERACTIONS

Oral contraceptives Pioglitazone may reduce the effectiveness of oral contraceptives by reducing the *hormone* levels in these products.

Ketoconazole This drug may increase the effects of pioglitazone.

PROLONGED USE

Pioglitazone, like other antidiabetic drugs, is used indefinitely.

Monitoring Blood glucose will be measured regularly when on this medication. A liver function test may be done before starting therapy and periodically. Heart performance will be monitored regularly. Weight will be measured periodically.

PIROXICAM

Product names Apo-Piroxicam, Novo-Pirocam, Nu-Pirox, and others
Used in the following combined preparations None

GENERAL INFORMATION

Piroxicam is a non-steroidal anti-inflammatory drug (NSAID) that, like others in this group, reduces pain, stiffness, and inflammation. Blood levels of the drug remain high for many hours after a dose, so it needs to be taken only once daily. Piroxicam is used for osteoarthritis, rheumatoid arthritis, acute attacks of gout, and ankylosing spondylitis. It gives relief of the symptoms of arthritis, although it does not cure the

disease. It is sometimes prescribed in conjunction with slow-acting drugs in rheumatoid arthritis to relieve pain and inflammation while these drugs take effect. The drug may also be given for pain relief after sports injuries, for conditions such as tendinitis and bursitis, and following minor surgery.

Piroxicam carries the highest risk of any of the NSAIDs of causing gastro-intestinal side effects.

QUICK REFERENCE

Drug group Non-steroidal anti-inflammatory drugs (p.102) and drugs for gout (p.105)

Overdose danger rating Medium

Dependence rating Low

Prescription needed Yes

Available as generic Yes

INFORMATION FOR USERS

Your drug prescription is tailored for you. Do not alter dosage without checking with your physician.

How taken

Capsules, suppositories.

Frequency and timing of doses
1–2 x daily with food or plenty of water.

Usual adult dosage range
10–40mg daily.

Onset of effect
Pain relief 3–4 hours; *arthritis* 2–4 weeks for full anti-inflammatory effect; *gout* 4–5 days for full anti-inflammatory effect.

Duration of action
Up to 2 days. Some effect may last for 7–10 days after treatment has been stopped.

Diet advice
None.

Storage
Keep in a closed container in a cool, dry place out of the reach of children. Protect from light.

Missed dose
Take as soon as you remember. If your next dose is due within 4 hours, take a single dose now and skip the next.

Stopping the drug
When taken for short-term pain relief, the drug can be safely stopped as soon as you no longer need it. If prescribed for the long-term treatment of arthritis, however, you should seek medical advice before stopping the drug.

Exceeding the dose
An occasional unintentional extra dose is unlikely to be a cause for concern. Large overdoses may cause nausea and vomiting. Notify your physician.

SPECIAL PRECAUTIONS

Be sure to tell your physician if:
▼ You have liver or kidney problems.
▼ You have heart problems or high blood pressure.
▼ You have had a peptic ulcer, oesophagitis, or acid indigestion.
▼ You have porphyria.
▼ You have asthma.
▼ You are allergic to ASA.
▼ You are taking other medications.

Pregnancy
▼ The drug may increase the risk of adverse effects on the baby's heart and may prolong labour if taken in the third trimester. Discuss with your physician.

Breast-feeding
▼ The drug passes into the breast milk but at normal doses adverse effects are unlikely. Discuss with your physician.

Infants and children
▼ Not recommended under 6 years. Reduced dose necessary.

Over 60
▼ Increased likelihood of adverse effects. Reduced dose may therefore be necessary.

Driving and hazardous work
▼ Avoid such activities until you have learned how piroxicam affects you because the drug can cause dizziness.

Alcohol
▼ Avoid. Alcohol may increase the risk of stomach disorders with piroxicam.

Surgery and general anesthetics
▼ Piroxicam may prolong bleeding. Discuss with your physician or dentist before surgery.

POSSIBLE ADVERSE EFFECTS

Gastrointestinal *side effects*, dizziness, and headache are not generally serious. Black or bloodstained bowel movements should be reported to your physician immediately.

Symptom/effect	Frequency		Discuss with physician		Stop taking drug now	Call physician now
	Common	Rare	Only if severe	In all cases		
Heartburn/indigestion	●		■			
Nausea/vomiting	●		■			
Headache		●	■			
Dizziness/drowsiness		●	■			
Swollen feet or legs		●	■			
Weight gain		●	■			
Rash/itching		●		■	▲	
Wheezing/breathlessness		●		■	▲	▮
Black/bloodstained feces		●		■	▲	▮

INTERACTIONS

General note Piroxicam interacts with many drugs, including other NSAIDs, corticosteroids, and oral anticoagulant drugs, to increase the risk of bleeding and/or peptic ulcers.

Antihypertensive drugs and diuretics The beneficial effects of these drugs may be reduced by piroxicam.

Lithium and methotrexate Piroxicam may raise blood levels of these drugs.

Ciprofloxacin, norfloxacin, and ofloxacin Piroxicam may increase the risk of convulsions when taken with these drugs.

Ritonavir This drug increases blood levels of piroxicam.

PROLONGED USE

There is an increased risk of bleeding from peptic ulcers and in the bowel with prolonged use. There is also a small risk of a heart attack or stroke. To minimize these risks, the lowest effective dose is given for the shortest duration.

PIZOTIFEN

Product names Sandomigran, Sandomigran DS
Used in the following combined preparations None

GENERAL INFORMATION

Pizotifen has a chemical structure similar to that of the tricyclic antidepressants (p.84); it also has similar *anticholinergic* effects. This drug is prescribed for the prevention of migraine headaches in people who suffer frequent, disabling attacks. It is not effective in relieving migraine attacks once they have started. The drug is thought to work by blocking the chemicals (histamine and serotonin) that act on blood vessels in the brain.

The main disadvantage of prolonged use of pizotifen is that it stimulates the appetite and, as a result, often causes weight gain. It is usually prescribed only for people in whom other measures for migraine prevention, such as avoidance of trigger factors, have failed.

INFORMATION FOR USERS

Your drug prescription is tailored for you. Do not alter dosage without checking with your physician.

How taken

Tablets.

Frequency and timing of doses
Start once a day (at night); gradually increase to 3 x daily.

Adult dosage range
1.5–4.5mg daily. Maximum single dose 3mg.

Onset of effect
Full beneficial effects may not be felt for several days.

Duration of action
Effects of this drug may last for several weeks.

Diet advice
Migraine sufferers may be advised to avoid foods that trigger headaches in their case.

Storage
Keep in a closed container in a cool, dry place out of the reach of children. Protect from light.

Missed dose
Take as soon as you remember. If your next dose is due within 4 hours, take a single dose now and skip the next.

Stopping the drug
Do not stop the drug without consulting your physician; symptoms may recur.

Exceeding the dose
An occasional unintentional extra dose is unlikely to cause problems. Large overdoses may cause drowsiness, nausea, palpitations, and seizures. Notify your physician.

SPECIAL PRECAUTIONS

Be sure to tell your physician if:
▼ You have a long-term kidney problem.
▼ You have glaucoma.
▼ You have urinary retention.
▼ You have prostate trouble.
▼ You are taking other medications.

Pregnancy
▼ Safety in pregnancy not established. Discuss with your physician.

Breast-feeding
▼ The drug passes into the breast milk, but at normal doses adverse effects on the baby are unlikely. Discuss with your physician.

Infants and children
▼ Reduced dose usually necessary.

Over 60
▼ No special problems.

Driving and hazardous work
▼ Avoid such activities until you have learned how pizotifen affects you because the drug can cause drowsiness and blurred vision.

Alcohol
▼ Avoid. Alcohol may increase the *sedative* effects of this drug.

POSSIBLE ADVERSE EFFECTS

Drowsiness is a common *adverse effect* that can often be minimized by starting treatment with a low dose that is gradually increased.

Symptom/effect	Frequency		Discuss with physician		Stop taking drug now	Call physician now
	Common	Rare	Only if severe	In all cases		
Weight gain/increased appetite	●		■			
Drowsiness	●		■			
Fatigue	●		■			
Nausea/dizziness		●	■			
Muscle pains		●	■			
Dry mouth		●	■			
Blurred vision		●	■			
Depression		●		■		

INTERACTIONS

Anticholinergic drugs The weak anticholinergic effects of pizotifen may be increased by other anticholinergic drugs, including tricyclic antidepressants.

Sedatives All drugs that have a sedative effect on the central nervous system are likely to increase the sedative properties of pizotifen. These include sleeping drugs, anti-anxiety drugs, *opioid* analgesics, and antihistamines.

PROLONGED USE

Pizotifen often causes weight gain during long-term use. Treatment is usually reviewed every 6 months.

POLYMYXIN B

Product names Only available in combination with other drugs
Used in the following combined preparations Bioderm Ointment, Cortisoporin, Diosporin, Lidomyxin, Maxitrol, Ozonol antibiotic cream, Polysporin antibiotic cream, and others.

GENERAL INFORMATION

Polymyxin B is an *antibiotic* that is effective against certain bacteria. It is used primarily in combination with other antibiotics and corticosteroids to treat skin infections and infections of the eye and ear, such as acute bacterial conjunctivitis, otitis externa, and inflammation of the external auditory canal due to infection. It is also used for bladder irrigation in combination with neomycin, another antibiotic. Many products are available over the counter.

Some products that contain other antibiotics or corticosteroids require a prescription. Do not use the skin product in your eyes or ears.

Follow your physician's or *pharmacist's* instructions for proper application of eye or ear drops. Always wash your hands first. After administering ear drops, remain on your side with the affected ear facing up for 5 to 10 minutes. If applying more than one drop, wait 3 to 5 minutes between drops.

INFORMATION FOR USERS

Check with your pharmacist or physician for an appropriate product and how to use it.

How taken

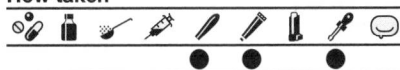

Urethral irrigating solution, topical (ointment and cream for the skin), ophthalmic suspension (for the eye), otic liquid (for the ear).

Frequency and timing of doses
Eye/ear Usually 4–6 x daily.
Skin application Apply 1–4 x daily.

Usual adult dosage range
As instructed by your pharmacist or physician.

Onset of effect
24–48 hours.

Duration of action
4–6 hours.

Diet advice
Not applicable.

Storage
Keep in the original container in a cool, dry place out of the reach of children.

Missed dose
Use as soon as you remember. If it is almost time for the next application, continue with the scheduled time.

Stopping the drug
Complete the recommended treatment schedule. Stopping too soon may cause symptoms to return.

Exceeding the dose
An occasional unintentional extra dose is unlikely to be a cause for concern. If unusual symptoms occur that are of concern, contact your physician.

SPECIAL PRECAUTIONS

Be sure to tell your physician if:
▼ You are allergic to any antibiotics.
▼ You are allergic to foods, dyes, and preservatives.
▼ You have tried self-treatment for this condition before.
▼ You are taking other medications.

Pregnancy
▼ Safety unknown. Discuss with your physician or pharmacist.

Breast-feeding
▼ Safety unknown. Discuss with your physician or pharmacist.

Infants and children
▼ No expected problems. Discuss with physician or pharmacist.

Over 60
▼ No expected problems.

Driving and hazardous work
▼ Eye drops may cause blurred vision; avoid driving or hazardous work.

Alcohol
▼ No problems.

POSSIBLE ADVERSE EFFECTS

The most common *side effect* is local irritation.

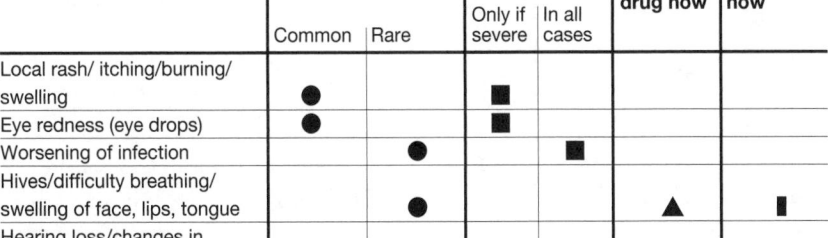

Symptom/effect	Frequency		Discuss with physician		Stop taking drug now	Call physician now
	Common	Rare	Only if severe	In all cases		
Local rash/ itching/burning/ swelling	●		■			
Eye redness (eye drops)	●		■			
Worsening of infection		●		■		
Hives/difficulty breathing/ swelling of face, lips, tongue		●			▲	▮
Hearing loss/changes in hearing (ear drops)		●			▲	▮

PROLONGED USE

Usually used for a short period of treatment.

INTERACTIONS

General note Check with your pharmacist or physician if the eye drops are safe to use with contact lenses. If it is safe, wait at least 15 minutes after using the medication, before putting in your contact lenses. No specific interactions when used on the skin.

PRAMIPEXOLE

Product name Apo-Pramipexole, Ava-Pramipexole, Mirapex, and others
Used in the following combined preparations None

GENERAL INFORMATION

Pramipexole helps relieve signs and symptoms of Parkinson's disease by stimulating dopamine *receptors* in the brain. It can be used alone in the early management of Parkinson's disease, or in combination with levodopa in people who experience wearing off of levodopa's effectiveness.

Pramipexole is quickly absorbed when taken by mouth. Common *side effects* include dizziness, insomnia, and lightheadedness. Rarely, it can cause hallucinations or fidgety movements (dyskinesia), sudden sleep attacks, and problems with impulse control (e.g. compulsive gambling).

QUICK REFERENCE

Drug group Antiparkinsonism drug (p.71)

Overdose danger rating Medium

Dependence rating Low

Prescription needed Yes

Available as generic Yes

INFORMATION FOR USERS

Your drug prescription is tailored for you. Do not alter dosage without checking with your physician.

How taken

Tablets.

Frequency and timing of doses
Up to 3 x daily.

Usual adult dosage range
0.375mg initial dose (0.125mg given 3 x daily); gradually increased. Usual daily dose: 1.5–3mg. Maximum daily dose: 4.5mg.

Onset of effect
Peak effect: 1–3 hours.

Duration of action
8–12 hours.

Diet advice
None.

Storage
Keep in a closed container in a cool, dry place out of the reach of children. Protect from light.

Missed dose
Take as soon as you remember. Do not double a dose.

Stopping the drug
Do not stop taking the drug without consulting your physician; symptoms may recur. Also, suddenly stopping the drug can cause muscular rigidity and altered consciousness. If these occur, you should seek medical help straight away.

Exceeding the dose
An occasional unintentional extra dose is unlikely to cause problems. But if you notice any unusual symptoms, or if a large overdose has been taken, notify your physician right away.

SPECIAL PRECAUTIONS

Be sure to tell your physician if:
▼ You have kidney problems.
▼ You have unusual conditions relating to your eye.
▼ You have experienced an *allergic reaction* to pramipexole.
▼ You are taking other medications.

Pregnancy
▼ Safety not established. Discuss with your physician.

Breast-feeding
▼ Safety not established. Discuss with your physician.

Infants and children
▼ Not recommended.

Over 60
▼ Increased likelihood of adverse effects. Reduced dose necessary.

Driving and hazardous work
▼ Avoid such activities until you have learned how pramipexole affects you because the drug can cause dizziness and sudden sleep attacks. Also, your condition may make it difficult to drive. Check with your physician.

Alcohol
▼ Avoid. Alcohol may increase the sedative effects of this drug.

POSSIBLE ADVERSE EFFECTS

Pramipexole can cause lightheadedness on getting up quickly due to a drop in blood pressure. Getting up slowly can prevent this.

If nausea occurs, taking the drug with food can minimize this.

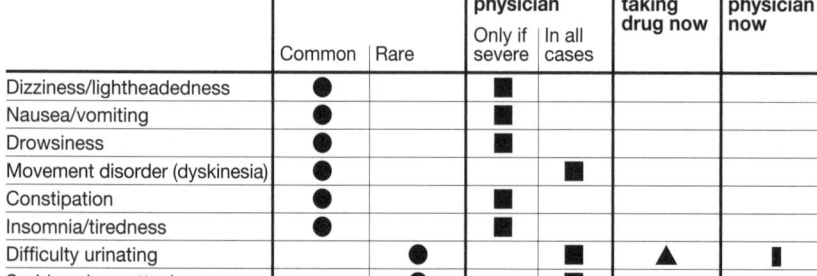

Symptom/effect	Frequency		Discuss with physician		Stop taking drug now	Call physician now
	Common	Rare	Only if severe	In all cases		
Dizziness/lightheadedness	●		■			
Nausea/vomiting	●		■			
Drowsiness	●		■			
Movement disorder (dyskinesia)	●			■		
Constipation	●		■			
Insomnia/tiredness	●		■			
Difficulty urinating		●		■	▲	▮
Sudden sleep attacks		●		■		

INTERACTIONS

Metoclopramide, phenothiazines, theophylline These may decrease the effect of pramipexole. Monitor closely.

Amantadine, cimetidine, diltiazem, quinidine, verapamil, triamterene These may increase the effect of pramipexole. Dose adjustment may be necessary.

Levodopa When pramipexole is initiated, you may have to lower levodopa dose.

Antihypertensives, tricyclic antidepressants, diuretics These drugs can worsen the lightheadedness caused by pramipexole.

PROLONGED USE

No specific problems expected. However, your condition may change with time and the dose of the drug should be regularly re-evaluated.

Monitoring Regular monitoring of your Parkinsonian symptoms are required. You should report any changes to your physician.

PRASUGREL

Product name Effient
Used in the following combined preparations None

GENERAL INFORMATION

Prasugrel is an antiplatelet drug that decreases the risk of clot formation. It is prescribed after a heart attack or unstable angina, along with acetylsalicylic acid (ASA) in patients who will be managed with percutaneous coronary intervention (PCI).

INFORMATION FOR USERS

Your drug prescription is tailored for you. Do not alter dosage without checking with your physician.

How taken

Tablets.

Frequency and timing of doses
Once daily.

Usual adult dosage range
Loading dose of 60mg, then 10mg once daily.

Onset of effect
Within a few hours.

Duration of action
Up to 24 hours.

Diet advice
None.

Storage
Keep in a closed container in a cool, dry place out of the reach of children.

Missed dose
Take a missed dose as soon as you remember. Do not take two doses on the same day.

Stopping the drug
Do not stop taking the drug without consulting your physician; symptoms may recur.

OVERDOSE ACTION

 Seek immediate medical help in all cases. Take emergency action if severe bleeding or loss of consciousness occur.

See Drug poisoning emergency guide (p.526).

SPECIAL PRECAUTIONS

Be sure to tell your physician if:
▼ You have a known history of TIA or stroke.
▼ You have peptic ulcer disease.
▼ You have severe liver problems.
▼ Your body weight is < 60 kg.
▼ You have had recent surgery or an upcoming planned surgery.
▼ You have allergies to medications, including clopidogrel or ticlopidine.
▼ You are taking other medications.

 Pregnancy
▼ No adequate, well-controlled studies. Discuss with your physician.

 Breast-feeding
▼ No adequate, well-controlled studies. Not recommended.

 Infants and children
▼ No data available on safety and efficacy. Not recommended.

 Over 60
▼Not recommended in those ≥ 75 years of age due to increased risk of bleeding.

 Driving and hazardous work
▼ Use caution. Even minor bumps can cause bad bruises and excessive bleeding.

 Alcohol
▼ No special problems.

POSSIBLE ADVERSE EFFECTS

A common *side effect* of prasugrel is bleeding. When on this medication, one may bruise easily and cuts may take longer to heal. Many other medications taken in conjunction with prasugrel can increase the risk of bleeding (see Drug Interactions).

Symptom/effect	Frequency		Discuss with physician		Stop taking drug now	Call physician now
	Common	Rare	Only if severe	In all cases		
Nose bleeds	●		■			
Bleeding gums	●		■			
Blood in your stool or urine/coughing up blood		●		■		▌
Sudden severe headache		●				▌
Dizziness/lightheadedness		●				▌
Fever/yellowish colour of the skin/confusion		●				▌
Allergic reaction (rash, swelling of the face & throat)		●				▌

INTERACTIONS

Anticoagulants Avoid using prasugrel with other anticoagulants such as dabigatran, warfarin, rivaroxaban, and heparin.

Antiplatelet drugs such as clopidogrel and ASA can increase the anticoagulant effect of prasugrel.

Herbs that have an anticoagulant or antiplatelet effect, such as ginseng, licorice and ginkgo, can increase the antiplatelet effect of prasugrel.

NSAIDs can increase the effect of prasugrel.

PROLONGED USE

Monitoring Monitor for bleeding risk.

PRAVASTATIN

Product names Apo-Pravastatin, Pravachol, and others
Used in the following combined preparations None

GENERAL INFORMATION

Pravastatin belongs to the statin group of lipid-lowering drugs. It is prescribed for people with hypercholesterolemia (high levels of cholesterol in the blood) who have not responded to other treatments, such as a special diet, and who are at risk of developing heart disease or stroke. The drug works by blocking the action of an enzyme that is needed for the manufacture of cholesterol, mainly in the liver. As a result, blood levels of cholesterol are lowered, which can help to prevent heart disease and stroke.

Side effects are usually mild and often wear off over time. Pravastatin may raise the levels of liver enzymes but this does not usually indicate serious liver amage. Rarely, it may cause muscle damage, and any unexpected muscle tenderness, pain, or weakness should be reported to your physician.

QUICK REFERENCE

Drug group Lipid-lowering drugs (p.89)

Overdose danger rating Medium

Dependence rating Low

Prescription needed Yes

Available as generic Yes

INFORMATION FOR USERS

Your drug prescription is tailored for you. Do not alter dosage without checking with your physician.

How taken

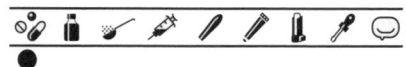

Tablets.

Frequency and timing of doses
Once daily at night.

Usual adult dosage range
10–40mg daily, changed after intervals of at least 4 weeks.

Onset of effect
Within 2 weeks. Full beneficial effect may be felt within 4 weeks.

Duration of action
24 hours.

Diet advice
A low fat diet is usually recommended.

Storage
Keep in a closed container in a cool, dry place out of the reach of children. Protect from light.

Missed dose
Take as soon as you remember. If your next dose is due within 8 hours, do not take the missed dose, but take the next dose as usual.

Stopping the drug
Do not stop taking the drug without consulting your physician; stopping the drug may lead to worsening of the underlying condition.

Exceeding the dose
An occasional unintentional extra dose is unlikely to cause problems. Large overdoses may cause liver problems. Notify your physician.

SPECIAL PRECAUTIONS

Be sure to tell your physician if:
▼ You have had liver or kidney problems.
▼ You have thyroid problems.
▼ You are a heavy drinker.
▼ You have a family history of muscular disorders.
▼ You are diabetic.
▼ You are taking other medications.

Pregnancy
▼ Not recommended. May affect fetal development. Discuss with your physician if you are or plan to become pregnant.

Breast-feeding
▼ The drug passes into the breast milk and may affect the baby. Discuss with your physician.

Infants and children
▼ Not recommended. Reduced dose necessary in older children, under specialist advice.

Over 60
▼ No special problems. Start with a smaller dose.

Driving and hazardous work
▼ No special problems.

Alcohol
▼ Avoid excessive amounts. Alcohol may increatse the risk of developing liver problems with this drug.

PROLONGED USE

Long-term use of pravastatin can affect liver function.

Monitoring Regular blood tests to check liver and muscle function are usually required.

POSSIBLE ADVERSE EFFECTS

Most *adverse effects* are mild and usually disappear with time. You should report any muscle pains, tenderness, or weakness to your physician straight away.

Symptom/effect	Frequency		Discuss with physician		Stop taking drug now	Call physician now
	Common	Rare	Only if severe	In all cases		
Abdominal pain	●		■			
Constipation/diarrhea	●		■			
Nausea/flatulence	●		■			
Sleep disturbance/headache	●		■			
Rash		●		■	▲	
Muscle pain/weakness		●		■	▲	▮
Jaundice		●		■	▲	▮

INTERACTIONS

Anticoagulants Statins can increase the effect of these drugs, although this is less llikely with pravastatin.

Antifungal drugs Taken with statins, itraconazole, ketoconazole, and possibly other antifungal drugs may increase the risk of muscle damage.

Other lipid-lowering drugs (fibrates) Taken with pravastatin, these drugs may increase the risk of muscle damage.

Cyclosporine and other immunosuppressant drugs There is an increased risk of muscle damage if pravastatin is taken with these drugs. They are not usually prescribed together.

PREDNISONE/PREDNISOLONE

Product names Novo-Prednisone, Winpred, and others
Used in the following combined preparations [all with prednisolone] Blephamide, Pred Forte, Pred Mild

GENERAL INFORMATION

Prednisolone, the active form of prednisone, is a powerful corticosteroid, and is used for a wide range of conditions, including some skin diseases, rheumatic disorders, allergic states, and certain blood disorders. It is used in the form of eye drops to reduce inflammation in conjunctivitis or iritis. The drug can also be injected into joints to relieve rheumatoid and other forms of arthritis. Prednisolone is also prescribed with fludrocortisone for pituitary or adrenal gland disorders.

Low doses taken short term (by mouth or topically) rarely cause serious side effects. However, long-term treatment with large doses can cause *systemic* effects, such as osteoporosis, fluid retention, indigestion, diabetes, hypertension, and acne.

QUICK REFERENCE

Drug group Corticosteroids (p.127)
Overdose danger rating Low
Dependence rating Low
Prescription needed Yes
Available as generic Yes

INFORMATION FOR USERS

Your drug prescription is tailored for you. Do not alter dosage without checking with your physician.

How taken

Tablets, liquid, injection, eye drops.

Frequency and timing of doses
1–2 x daily or on alternate days with food (tablets/injection); 2–4 x daily (eye drops).

Usual adult dosage range
Considerable variation. Follow your physician's instructions.

Onset of effect
2–4 days.

Duration of action
12–72 hours.

Diet advice
A low-sodium diet may be recommended when the oral or injected form of the drug is prescribed for extended periods. Follow the advice of your physician.

Storage
Keep in a closed container in a cool, dry place out of the reach of children. Protect from light.

Missed dose
Take as soon as you remember. If your next dose is due within 6 hours, take a single dose now and skip the next.

Stopping the drug
Do not stop the drug without consulting your physician. Abrupt cessation of long-term treatment by mouth or injection may be dangerous.

Exceeding the dose
An occasional unintentional extra dose is unlikely to be a cause for concern. But if you notice any unusual symptoms, or if a large overdose has been taken, notify your physician.

POSSIBLE ADVERSE EFFECTS

The rare but more serious adverse effects occur only when high doses are taken by mouth or injection or for long periods. If taking oral forms, you should avoid close personal contact with chickenpox or herpes zoster, and seek urgent medical attention if exposed.

Symptom/effect	Frequency		Discuss with physician		Stop taking drug now	Call physician now
	Common	Rare	Only if severe	In all cases		
Indigestion	●			■		
Acne	●		■			
Weight gain		●	■			
Muscle weakness		●		■		
Mood changes/depression		●		■		
Black/bloodstained feces		●		■	▲	■

INTERACTIONS

Anticonvulsant drugs Carbamazepine, phenytoin, and phenobarbital can reduce the effects of prednisolone/prednisone.

Vaccines Serious reactions can occur if live vaccines are given with this drug. Discuss with your physician.

Anticoagulant drugs Prednisolone may affect the response to these drugs.

Antihypertensive and antidiabetic drugs and insulin Prednisolone may reduce the effects of these drugs.

Cyclosporine increases the effects of prednisolone.

NSAIDs There is an increased risk of peptic ulcers when these drugs are taken with prednisone.

SPECIAL PRECAUTIONS

Be sure to tell your physician if:
▼ You have had a peptic ulcer.
▼ You have glaucoma.
▼ You have had tuberculosis.
▼ You suffer from depression or psychiatric illness.
▼ You have any infection.
▼ You have diabetes.
▼ You have osteoporosis.
▼ You are taking other medications.

Pregnancy
▼ No evidence of risk with eye drops. Taken as tablets in low doses, harm to the fetus is unlikely. Discuss with your physician.

Breast-feeding
▼ No evidence of risk with drops. Taken by mouth, it passes into the breast milk, but at low doses adverse effects on the baby are unlikely. Discuss with your physician.

Infants and children
▼ Only given when essential. Reduced dose may be necessary.

Over 60
▼ Increased likelihood of adverse effects. Reduced dose may therefore be necessary.

Driving and hazardous work
▼ No known problems.

Alcohol
▼ Keep consumption low. Alcohol may increase the risk of peptic ulcers with prednisolone taken by mouth or injection.

Infection
▼ Avoid exposure to chickenpox, shingles, or measles if you are on systemic treatment.

PROLONGED USE

Prolonged systemic use can lead to such adverse effects as diabetes, glaucoma, cataracts, and fragile bones, and may retard growth in children. Dosages are usually tailored to minimize these effects.

PREGABALIN

Product name Lyrica
Used in the following combined preparations None

GENERAL INFORMATION

Pregabalin is an anti-epileptic drug (see Anticonvulsant drugs, p.70) used to treat pain related to damaged nerves (neuropathic pain) in the hands, fingers, arms, feet, and legs, and other areas as a result of diabetes (diabetic peripheral neuropathy). It is also approved for nerve pain related to rash from shingles (postherpetic neuralgia). Individuals should inform their physician and dentist that they are on this medication.

INFORMATION FOR USERS

Your drug prescription is tailored for you. Do not alter dosage without checking with your physician.

How taken

Capsules.

Frequency and timing of doses
Two or three times daily, with or without food.

Adult dosage range
Initial dose: 150mg daily; maximum of 600mg daily.

Onset of effect
Several weeks for pain relief.

Duration of action
8–12 hours.

Diet advice
None.

Storage
Keep in a closed container in a cool, dry place out of the reach of children.

Missed dose
If you miss a dose, take it as soon as you remember. If it is near the time of the next dose, skip the missed dose and resume your usual dosing schedule. Do not double up to catch up on a missed dose.

Stopping the drug
Do not stop the drug without consulting your physician. Stopping the drug may lead to withdrawal symptoms. If the drug is to be discontinued, gradual decrease in dose over a period of weeks is recommended.

Exceeding the dose
An occasional unintentional extra dose is unlikely to cause problems. Large overdoses may cause serious adverse effects. Notify your physician.

SPECIAL PRECAUTIONS

Be sure to tell your physician if:
▼ You have had problems with alcohol or drug abuse.
▼ You have a low number of platelets.
▼ You or your partner plan on becoming pregnant.
▼ You have heart or kidney disease.
▼ You are on rosiglitazone or thioglitazone for diabetes.
▼ You have congestive heart failure.
▼ You are taking other medications.

Pregnancy
▼ Safety in pregnancy not established. Discuss with your physician.

Breast-feeding
▼ Safety not established. Discuss with your physician.

Infants and children
▼ Not recommended.

Over 60
▼ Dose may be adjusted for changes in kidney function.

Driving and hazardous work
▼ May cause drowsiness. Do not drive a car or operate machinery until the effect of the drug wears off and you feel you are mentally alert.

Alcohol
▼ Avoid alcohol use as it may increase the effect of drowsiness caused by this drug.

POSSIBLE ADVERSE EFFECTS

In general, pregabalin is well tolerated. Common side effects include dizziness, tiredness, blurred vision, weight gain, edema (swelling of arms, feet, etc), dry mouth.

Symptom/effect	Frequency		Discuss with physician		Stop taking drug now	Call physician now
	Common	Rare	Only if severe	In all cases		
Dizziness	●			■		
Tiredness	●			■		
Weight gain	●			■		
Dry mouth	●			■		
Constipation	●			■		
Difficulty concentrating		●		■		
Blurred vision or changes in eyesight		●		■		
Swelling of the eyes, face, or throat		●		■		■

INTERACTIONS

CNS depressants Use of pregabalin with central nervous system depressants (such as benzodiazepines, *opioids*) may result in additional drowsiness and tiredness.

Alcohol May increase drowsiness caused by pregabalin.

PROLONGED USE

No problems expected.

PROBENECID

Product name Benuryl
Used in the following combined preparations None

GENERAL INFORMATION

Probenecid is used in the treatment of high uric acid levels in the blood, associated with gout. As probencid increases the excretion of uric acid through the kidneys, it should not be used in situations where there is an increase in uric acid production, such as in patients receiving chemotherapy. It should also not be used in those with kidney stones or in those with compromised kidney function. Historically, probenecid has also been used in combination with specific beta-lactam antibiotics, such as cefazolin, where it decreases the antibiotic's excretion, thus enhancing its antibacterial effect.

INFORMATION FOR USERS

Your drug prescription is tailored for you. Do not alter dosage without checking with your physician.

How taken

Tablets.

Frequency and timing of doses
Gout: twice daily. With antibiotics, may be taken up to 4 x daily.

Adult dosage range
Gout: 0.5 to 1gm daily. Start with 250mg twice daily for a week, then increase to 500mg twice daily. Maximum daily dose: 2 gm.

Onset of effect
Within 4 hours.

Duration of action
8–12 hours.

Diet advice
Take with food to minimize stomach upset. Ensure adequate fluid intake.

Storage
Keep in a closed container in a cool, dry place out of the reach of children.

Missed dose
If you miss a dose, take it as soon as you remember. If it is near the time of the next dose, skip the missed dose and resume your usual dosing schedule. Do not double-up to catch up on a missed dose.

Stopping the drug
Do not stop the drug without consulting your physician. Stopping the drug may lead to worsening of the underlying condition.

Exceeding the dose
If you notice any unusual symptoms, or if a large overdose has been taken, call your physician and seek medical assistance.

POSSIBLE ADVERSE EFFECTS

Most common side effects include headache, nausea, vomiting, and anorexia. Taking it with food can minimize nausea and vomiting. It can rarely cause a serious blood disorder.

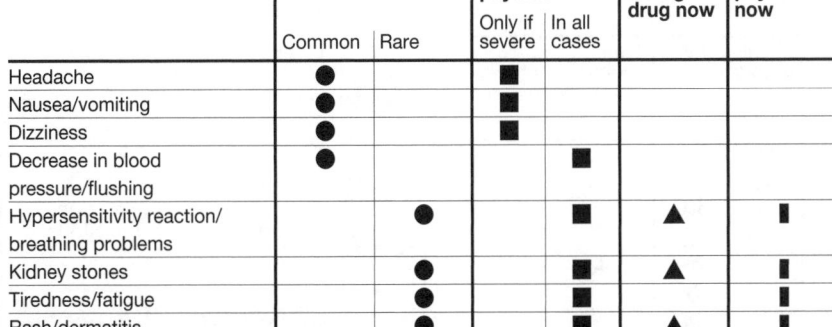

Symptom/effect	Frequency		Discuss with physician		Stop taking drug now	Call physician now
	Common	Rare	Only if severe	In all cases		
Headache	●		■			
Nausea/vomiting	●		■			
Dizziness	●		■			
Decrease in blood pressure/flushing	●			■		
Hypersensitivity reaction/ breathing problems		●		■	▲	▮
Kidney stones		●		■	▲	▮
Tiredness/fatigue		●		■		▮
Rash/dermatitis		●		■	▲	▮

INTERACTIONS

Due to its effect on the kidneys, probenecid can alter excretion of many drugs. Please check with your physician or *pharmacist* before starting any new drug, in particular:

ACE inhibitors, acetaminophen, acyclovir, allopurinol, aminosalicylates, benzodiazepines, cephalosporin antibiotics, dapsone, fexofenedine, furosemide, ganciclovir, ketorolac, morphine, oseltamivir, pramipexole, quinolone antibiotics, sulfinpyrazone, and zidovudine.

SPECIAL PRECAUTIONS

Be sure to tell your physician if:
▼ You are taking ASA or Aspirin.
▼ You have kidney problems.
▼ You have a history of kidney stones.
▼ You have a hypersensitivity to probenecid.
▼ You have or will be receiving chemotherapy.
▼ You are taking other medications.

Pregnancy
▼ Safety in pregnancy not established. Discuss with your physician.

Breast-feeding
▼ Limited safety information. Discuss with your physician.

Infants and children
▼ Not recommended in children < 2 years of age. For use in children 2 years and older, consult their physician.

Over 60
▼ Not recommended with reduced kidney function.

Driving and hazardous work
▼ No special problems.

Alcohol
▼ No special problems.

PROLONGED USE

Serious problems are unlikely, but prolonged use should be followed closely by a physician. Due to many drug interactions, close monitoring required with changes to drug therapy.

Monitoring Kidney function, uric acid level in the blood and urine.

PROCHLORPERAZINE

Product name Apo-Prochlorperazine, PMS-Prochlorperazine, and others
Used in the following combined preparations None

GENERAL INFORMATION

Prochlorperazine was introduced in the late 1950s and belongs to a group of drugs called the phenothiazines, which act on the central nervous system.

In small doses, the drug controls nausea and vomiting, especially when they occur as the *side effects* of medical treatment by drugs or radiation, or of anesthesia. Prochlorperazine may also help the nausea that occurs with inner-ear disorders, for example, vertigo. In large doses, it is used as an antipsychotic to tranquillize, reduce aggressiveness, and suppress abnormal behaviour (see p.69). It thus minimizes and controls the abnormal behaviour of schizophrenia, mania, and other mental disorders. Prochlorperazine does not cure any of these diseases, but it helps to relieve symptoms.

QUICK REFERENCE

Drug group Phenothiazine antipsychotic drug (p.69) and anti-emetic drug (p.74)

Overdose danger rating Medium

Dependence rating Low

Prescription needed Yes

Available as generic Yes

INFORMATION FOR USERS

Your drug prescription is tailored for you. Do not alter the dosage without checking with your physician.

How taken

Tablets, liquid, injection, suppositories.

Frequency and timing of doses
3–4 x daily (tablets); 3–4 x daily (suppositories); 2–3 x daily (injection).

Usual adult dosage range
Nausea and vomiting 20mg initially, then 5–10mg per dose (tablets); 5–25mg per dose (suppositories).
Mental illness 15–40mg daily. Larger doses may be given.

Onset of effect
Within 60 minutes (by mouth or *suppository*); 10–20 minutes (by injection).

Duration of action
3–6 hours.

Diet advice
None.

Storage
Keep in a closed container in a cool, dry place out of the reach of children. Protect from light.

Missed dose
Take as soon as you remember. If your next dose is due within 2 hours, take a single dose now and skip the next.

Stopping the drug
Do not stop the drug without consulting your physician; symptoms may recur.

Exceeding the dose
An occasional unintentional extra dose is unlikely to be a cause for concern. Large overdoses may cause unusual drowsiness and may affect the heart. Notify your physician.

SPECIAL PRECAUTIONS

Be sure to tell your physician if:
▼ You have heart problems.
▼ You have liver or kidney problems.
▼ You have had epileptic seizures.
▼ You have Parkinson's disease.
▼ You have an underactive thyroid gland.
▼ You have prostate problems.
▼ You have glaucoma.
▼ You are taking other medications.

Pregnancy
▼ Safety in pregnancy not established. Discuss with your physician.

Breast-feeding
▼ The drug passes into the breast milk and may affect the baby. Discuss with your physician.

Infants and children
▼ Not recommended in infants weighing less than 10kg and young children. Reduced dose necessary in older children due to increased risk of adverse effects.

Over 60
▼ Increased likelihood of adverse effects. Reduced dose may therefore be necessary.

Driving and hazardous work
▼ Avoid such activities until you have learned how prochlorperazine affects you because it can cause drowsiness and reduced alertness.

Alcohol
▼ Avoid. Alcohol may increase and prolong the sedative effects of this drug.

POSSIBLE ADVERSE EFFECTS

Prochlorperazine has a strong *anticholinergic* effect, which can cause a variety of minor symptoms that often become less marked with time. The most significant adverse effect with high doses is tremor and muscle rigidity of the face and limbs (*parkinsonism*) caused by changes in the balance of brain chemicals.

Symptom/effect	Frequency		Discuss with physician		Stop taking drug now	Call physician now
	Common	Rare	Only if severe	In all cases		
Drowsiness/lethargy	●		■			
Dry mouth	●		■			
Dizziness/fainting	●			■		
Parkinsonism	●			■		
Rash		●		■	▲	
Jaundice/fever		●		■		■
Tensing of muscles		●		■		

INTERACTIONS

Sedatives All drugs with a *sedative* effect are likely to increase the sedative effects of prochlorperazine.

Drugs for parkinsonism Prochlorperazine may block the beneficial effect of these.

Anticholinergic drugs Prochlorperazine may increase the side effects of these drugs.

Antihypertensive drugs Prochlorperazine can increase the effects of these drugs, especially doxazosin.

PROLONGED USE

Use of this drug for more than a few months may lead to the development of involuntary, potentially irreversible, eye mouth, and tongue, movements (*tardive dyskinesia*). Occasionally, *jaundice* may occur.

Monitoring Periodic blood tests may be performed.

PROCYCLIDINE

Product name PMS-Procyclidine
Used in the following combined preparations None

GENERAL INFORMATION

Introduced in the 1950s, procyclidine is an *anticholinergic* drug that is used to treat Parkinson's disease. It is especially helpful in the early stages of the disorder for treating muscle rigidity. It also helps to reduce excess salivation. However, the drug has little effect on the shuffling gait and slow muscular movements that characterize Parkinson's disease.

Procyclidine is also sometimes used to treat *parkinsonism* resulting from treatment with antipsychotic drugs.

The drug may cause various minor *adverse effects* (see below), but these are rarely serious enough to warrant stopping treatment.

INFORMATION FOR USERS

Your drug prescription is tailored for you. Do not alter dosage without checking with your physician.

How taken

Tablets, liquid medication.

Frequency and timing of doses
2–3 x daily.

Usual adult dosage range
5–30mg daily. Dosage is determined individually in order to find the best balance between effective relief of symptoms and the occurrence of adverse effects.

Onset of effect
Within 30 minutes.

Duration of action
8–12 hours.

Diet advice
None.

Storage
Keep in a closed container in a cool, dry place out of the reach of children.

Missed dose
Take as soon as you remember. If your next dose is due within 2 hours, take a single dose now and skip the next.

Stopping the drug
Do not stop the drug without consulting your physician; symptoms may recur.

OVERDOSE ACTION

 Seek immediate medical advice in all cases. Take emergency action if palpitations, seizures, or unconsciousness occur.

See Drug poisoning emergency guide (p.526).

POSSIBLE ADVERSE EFFECTS

The possible adverse effects of procyclidine are mainly the result of its anticholinergic action. Some of the more common symptoms, such as dry mouth, constipation, and blurred vision, may be overcome by adjustment in dosage. Nausea and vomiting, nervousness, and rash have occasionally been reported.

Symptom/effect	Frequency		Discuss with physician		Stop taking drug now	Call physician now
	Common	Rare	Only if severe	In all cases		
Dry mouth	●		■			
Constipation	●		■			
Nervousness/anxiety	●		■			
Drowsiness/dizziness	●			■		
Blurred vision	●			■		
Confusion		●		■		
Difficulty in passing urine		●		■		▮
Palpitations		●		■	▲	▮

INTERACTIONS

Anticholinergic and antihistamine drugs These drugs may increase the adverse effects of procyclidine.

Antidepressant drugs may increase the *side effects* of procyclidine.

Nitroglycerin tablets may be less effective in relief of heart pain, since dry mouth may prevent it from dissolving under the tongue.

SPECIAL PRECAUTIONS

Be sure to tell your physician if:
▼ You have long-term liver or kidney problems.
▼ You suffer from or have a family history of glaucoma.
▼ You have high blood pressure.
▼ You suffer from constipation.
▼ You have prostate trouble.
▼ You are taking other medications.

 Pregnancy
▼ Safety in pregnancy not established. Discuss with your physician.

 Breast-feeding
▼ Safety in breast-feeding not established. Discuss with your physician.

 Infants and children
▼ Not recommended.

 Over 60
▼ Reduced dose may be necessary.

 Driving and hazardous work
▼ Avoid such activities until you have learned how procyclidine affects you because the drug can cause drowsiness, blurred vision, and mild confusion.

 Alcohol
▼ Avoid. Alcohol may increase the sedative effect of this drug.

PROLONGED USE

Prolonged use of this drug may provoke the onset of glaucoma.

Monitoring Periodic eye examinations are usually advised.

PROGUANIL WITH ATOVAQUONE

Product name Malarone
Used in the following combined preparations None

GENERAL INFORMATION

Proguanil is an antimalarial drug given to prevent the development of malaria. Microbial resistance to its effects can occur and this has led to it being used in combination with other drugs.

Atovaquone is an antiprotozoal drug that is also active against the fungus *Pneumocystis carinii* (a cause of pneumonia in people with poor immunity). Atovaquone is less useful on its own for malaria, but when it is combined with proguanil it rapidly treats the infection. The combination is also used for prevention of malaria, especially in areas

where resistance to other drugs is present.

Used for prevention, you should start taking proguanil with atovaquone a day or two before travelling. Continue taking the tablets during your stay, and for 7 days after your return. It is important to take other precautions, such as using an insect repellent at all times and a mosquito net at night. If you develop an illness or fever in the year after your return from a malarial zone, and especially in the first 3 months, go to your physician immediately and tell him or her where you have been.

QUICK REFERENCE

Drug group Antimalarial drugs (p.123)

Overdose danger rating Medium

Dependence rating Low

Prescription needed Yes

Available as generic No

INFORMATION FOR USERS

Your drug prescription is tailored for you. Do not alter dosage without checking with your physician.

How taken

Tablets.

Frequency and timing of doses
Prevention Once daily with food or a milky drink, at the same time each day. Start 1–2 days before travel, and continue for 7 days after return.
Treatment Once daily for 3 days, with food or a milky drink.

Usual adult dosage range
Prevention 1 tablet.
Treatment 4 tablets.

Onset of effect
After 24 hours.

Duration of action
24–48 hours.

Diet advice
Take with food or a milky drink.

Storage
Keep in a closed container in a cool, dry place out of the reach of children.

Missed dose
Take as soon as you remember. If your next dose is due at this time, take both doses together.

Stopping the drug
Do not stop taking the drug for 1 week after leaving a malaria-infected area, otherwise there is a risk that you may develop the disease.

Exceeding the dose
An occasional unintentional extra dose is unlikely to cause problems. Large overdoses may cause abdominal pain and vomiting. Notify your physician.

SPECIAL PRECAUTIONS

Be sure to tell your physician if:
▼ You have a long-term kidney problem.
▼ You have epilepsy.
▼ You have a liver problem.
▼ You are suffering from diarrhea and vomiting.
▼ You have a mental illness.
▼ You are taking other medications.

 Pregnancy
▼ Safety in pregnancy not established, although benefits are generally considered to outweigh risks. Folic acid supplements must be taken. Discuss with your physician.

 Breast-feeding
▼ Safety not established. Discuss with your physician.

 Infants and children
▼ Reduced dose necessary.

 Over 60
▼ No known problems.

 Driving and hazardous work
▼ Avoid until you know how the drug affects you because it may cause dizziness.

 Alcohol
▼ No special problems.

POSSIBLE ADVERSE EFFECTS

Adverse effects are generally fairly mild. The most frequent effects are headache, nausea, vomiting, and abdominal pain.

Symptom/effect	Frequency		Discuss with physician		Stop taking drug now	Call physician now
	Common	Rare	Only if severe	In all cases		
Diarrhoea	●		■			
Nausea/vomiting	●		■			
Abdominal pain/indigestion	●		■			
Mouth ulcers		●	■			
Hair loss		●		■		
Jaundice		●		■		
Swelling of the neck, mouth		●		■		
Rash		●		■		

PROLONGED USE

No known problems.

INTERACTIONS

Rifampin, metoclopramide, and tetracycline antibiotics These drugs reduce the effect of proguanil with atovaquone.

Warfarin The effects of warfarin may be enhanced by proguanil with atovaquone.

PROMETHAZINE

Product names Histanil, PMS-Promethazine, and others
Used in the following combined preparations None

GENERAL INFORMATION

Promethazine is one of a class of drugs known as the phenothiazines, which were developed in the 1950s for their beneficial effect on abnormal behaviour arising from mental illnesses (see Antipsychotics, p.79). Promethazine was found, however, to have effects more like the antihistamines that are used to treat allergies (see p.110) and some types of nausea and vomiting (see Antiemetics, p.74). The drug is widely used to reduce itching in a variety of skin conditions including urticaria (hives),
chickenpox, and eczema. It can also relieve the nausea and vomiting caused by inner ear disturbances such as Ménière's disease and motion sickness. Because of its *sedative* effect, promethazine is sometimes used for short periods as a sleeping medicine, and is also given as *premedication* before surgery.

Promethazine is used in combined preparations together with *opioid* cough suppressants for the relief of coughs and nasal congestion, and it is given at night for its sedative effect.

INFORMATION FOR USERS

Follow instructions on the label. Call your physician if symptoms worsen.

How taken

Tablets, liquid, injection.

Frequency and timing of doses
Allergic symptoms 1–3 x daily or as a single dose at night.
Motion sickness Bedtime on night before travelling, repeating following morning if necessary, then every 6–8 hours as necessary.
Nausea/vomiting Every 4–6 hours as needed.

Usual dosage range (promethazine hydrochloride)
Adults 20–75mg per dose (oral).
Children Reduced dose according to age.

Onset of effect
Within 1 hour. If dose is taken after nausea has started, the onset of effect is delayed.

Duration of action
8–16 hours.

Diet advice
None.

Storage
Keep in a closed container in a cool, dry place out of the reach of children. Protect from light.

Missed dose
No cause for concern, but take as soon as you remember. Adjust the timing of your next dose accordingly.

Stopping the drug
Can be safely stopped as soon as symptoms disappear.

Exceeding the dose
An occasional unintentional extra dose is unlikely to cause problems. Large overdoses may cause drowsiness or agitation, seizures, unsteadiness, and coma. Notify your physician.

SPECIAL PRECAUTIONS

Be sure to consult your physician or pharmacist before taking this drug if:
▼ You have liver or kidney problems.
▼ You have had epileptic seizures.
▼ You have heart disease.
▼ You have glaucoma.
▼ You suffer from asthma or bronchitis.
▼ You have Parkinson's disease.
▼ You have urinary retention or prostate problems.
▼ You are taking other medications.

Pregnancy
▼ Safety in pregnancy not established. Discuss with your physician.

Breast-feeding
▼ The drug passes into the breast milk, but at normal doses adverse effects on the baby are unlikely. Discuss with your physician.

Infants and children
▼ Not recommended for infants under two years. Reduced dose necessary for older children.

Over 60
▼ Adverse effects may be more likely.

Driving and hazardous work
▼ Avoid such activities until you have learned how promethazine affects you because the drug can cause drowsiness.

Alcohol
▼ Avoid. Alcohol may increase the sedative effects of this drug.

Sunlight
▼ Avoid exposure to strong sunlight.

POSSIBLE ADVERSE EFFECTS

Promethazine usually causes only minor *anticholinergic* effects. More serious *adverse effects* generally occur only during long-term use or with abnormally high doses.

Symptom/effect	Frequency		Discuss with physician		Stop taking drug now	Call physician now
	Common	Rare	Only if severe	In all cases		
Drowsiness/lethargy	●		■			
Dry mouth	●		■			
Blurred vision	●		■			
Urinary retention	●			■		
Palpitations		●		■		
Light-sensitive rash		●		■	▲	

INTERACTIONS

Monamine oxidase inhibitors (MAOIs) These drugs may cause a severe reaction if taken with promethazine. Avoid taking promethazine if MAOIs have been taken in the last 14 days.

Skin-prick allergen tests Promethazine should be stopped a week before such a
test as it may produce a false result.

Sedatives All drugs that have a sedative effect are likely to increase the sedative properties of promethazine. Such drugs include other antihistamines, benzodiazepines, and antipsychotics.

PROLONGED USE

Use of this drug for long periods is rarely necessary, but may sometimes cause abnormal movements of the face and limbs (*parkinsonism*). The problem normally disappears when the drug is stopped.

PROPRANOLOL

Product names Apo-Propranolol, Inderal-LA, Nu-Propranolol
Used in the following combined preparations None

GENERAL INFORMATION

Propranolol, a non-cardioselective beta blocker, is mainly used to treat angina, and abnormal heart rhythms but is also helpful in controlling the symptoms of an overactive thyroid gland. Propranolol also helps to reduce the palpitations, sweating, and tremor of severe anxiety and is also used to prevent migraine headaches. The drug is also used to treat hypertension, but this use is declining as more selective beta blockers are now available.

Propranolol is not prescribed to people with asthma, chronic bronchitis, or emphysema because it can cause breathing difficulties. The drug should be used with caution by diabetics, because it affects the body's response to low blood sugar.

QUICK REFERENCE

Drug group Beta blockers (p.83) and anti-anxiety drugs (p.67)

Overdose danger rating High

Dependence rating Low

Prescription needed Yes

Available as generic Yes

INFORMATION FOR USERS

Your drug prescription is tailored for you. Do not alter dosage without checking with your physician.

How taken

Tablets, SR-capsules.

Frequency and timing of doses
2–4 x daily. Once daily (SR-capsules).

Usual adult dosage range
Abnormal heart rhythms 30–160mg daily.
Angina 60–320mg daily.
Hypertension 60–320mg daily.
Migraine prevention; anxiety 40–160mg daily.

Onset of effect
1–2 hours (tablets); after 4 hours (SR-capsules). In hypertension and migraine, it may be several weeks before full benefits are felt.

Duration of action
6–12 hours (tablets); Up to 24 hours (SR-capsules).

Diet advice
None.

Storage
Keep in a closed container in a cool, dry place out of the reach of children. Protect from light.

Missed dose
Take as soon as you remember. If your next dose is due within 2 hours (tablets) or 12 hours (SR-capsules), take a single dose now and skip the next.

Stopping the drug
Do not stop the drug without consulting your physician. Abrupt cessation may lead to worsening of the underlying condition.

OVERDOSE ACTION

 Seek immediate medical advice in all cases. Take emergency action if breathing difficulties, collapse, or loss of consciousness occur.

See Drug poisoning emergency guide (p.526).

SPECIAL PRECAUTIONS

Be sure to tell your physician if:
▼ You have long-term liver or kidney problems.
▼ You have a breathing disorder such as asthma, bronchitis, or emphysema.
▼ You have heart problems.
▼ You have diabetes.
▼ You have psoriasis.
▼ You have poor circulation in the legs.
▼ You are taking other medications.

 Pregnancy
▼ May affect the baby. Discuss with your physician.

 Breast-feeding
▼ The drug passes into the breast milk, but at normal doses adverse effects on the baby are unlikely. Discuss with your physician.

 Infants and children
▼ Reduced dose necessary.

 Over 60
▼ Increased risk of adverse effects.

 Driving and hazardous work
▼ Avoid such activities until you have learned how the drug affects you because it can cause dizziness.

 Alcohol
▼ Avoid excessive intake. Alcohol may increase the blood-pressure-lowering effect of propranolol.

Surgery and general anesthetics
▼ Propranolol may need to be stopped before you have a general anesthetic. Discuss this with your physician or dentist before any surgery.

POSSIBLE ADVERSE EFFECTS

Propranolol's *adverse effects* are common to most beta blockers and tend to diminish with long-term use. Fainting may be a sign that the drug has slowed the heart beat excessively.

Symptom/effect	Frequency		Discuss with physician		Stop taking drug now	Call physician now
	Common	Rare	Only if severe	In all cases		
Lethargy/fatigue	●		■			
Cold hands and feet	●		■			
Nausea/vomiting		●	■			
Nightmares/vivid dreams		●		■	▲	
Rash/dry eyes		●		■	▲	
Fainting/breathlessness		●		■	▲	■
Visual disturbances		●		■	▲	

INTERACTIONS

Antihypertensive drugs Propranolol may enhance the blood-pressure-lowering effect.

Calcium channel blockers may cause low blood pressure, a slow heart beat, and heart failure if used with propranolol.

Cardiac glycosides may increase the heart-slowing effect of propranolol.

Cimetidine may increase the effects of propranolol.

Non-steroidal anti-inflammatory drugs (NSAIDs) e.g., indomethacin may reduce the antihypertensive effect of propranolol.

PROLONGED USE

No problems expected.

PROPYLTHIOURACIL

Product name Propyl-Thyracil
Used in the following combined preparations None

GENERAL INFORMATION

Propylthiouracil is an antithyroid drug that suppresses formation of thyroid *hormones* and is used to manage overactivity of the thyroid gland (hyperthyroidism). In Graves' disease (the most common cause of hyperthyroidism), a course of propylthiouracil alone or combined with thyroxine (so-called "block and replace" therapy) – usually given for 6–18 months – may cure the disorder. In other conditions, propylthiouracil is given until other treatments, such as surgery or radioiodine, take effect. If other treatments are not possible or are declined by the patient, propylthiouracil can be given long-term. It is the treatment of choice for hyperthyroidism in the first trimester of pregnancy. The full effect of the drug may take several weeks, and beta blockers may be given during this period to control symptoms.

The most important *adverse effect* is a reduction in white blood cells (agranulocytosis), increasing the risk of infection. Although this is rare, if you develop a sore throat, mouth ulcers, or a fever, you should see your physician immediately to have your white blood cell count checked.

QUICK REFERENCE

Drug group Drugs for thyroid disorders (p.130)
Overdose danger rating Medium
Dependence rating Low
Prescription needed Yes
Available as generic No

INFORMATION FOR USERS

Your drug prescription is tailored for you. Do not alter dosage without consulting your physician.

How taken

Tablets.

Frequency and timing of doses
1–3 x daily.

Usual dosage range
Initially 150–300mg daily. Usually the dose can be reduced to 50–150mg daily.

Onset of effect
10–20 days. Full beneficial effects may not be felt for 6–10 weeks.

Duration of action
6–8 hours.

Diet advice
Your physician may advise you to avoid foods that are high in iodine (see p.473).

Storage
Keep in a closed container in a cool, dry place out of the reach of children. Protect from light.

Missed dose
Take as soon as you remember. If your next dose is due within 3 hours, take a single dose now and skip the next.

Stopping the drug
Do not stop the drug without consulting your physician; stopping the drug may lead to a recurrence of hyperthyroidism.

Exceeding the dose
An occasional unintentional extra dose is unlikely to cause problems. Large overdoses may cause nausea, vomiting, and headache. Notify your physician.

SPECIAL PRECAUTIONS

Be sure to tell your physician if:
▼ You have long-term liver or kidney problems.
▼ You are pregnant.
▼ You are taking other medications.

 Pregnancy
▼ Prescribed with caution. Risk of goitre and thyroid hormone deficiency (hypothyroidism) in the newborn infant if too high a dose is used. Discuss with your physician.

 Breast-feeding
▼ The drug passes into the breast milk and may affect the baby. Discuss with your physician.

 Infants and children
▼ Reduced dose necessary.

 Over 60
▼ No special problems.

 Driving and hazardous work
▼ No problems expected.

 Alcohol
▼ No known problems.

POSSIBLE ADVERSE EFFECTS

The most important *side effect* is a rare life-threatening reduction in white blood cells (agranulocytosis). This may be indicated by a sore throat or fever and should be reported to your physician immediately.

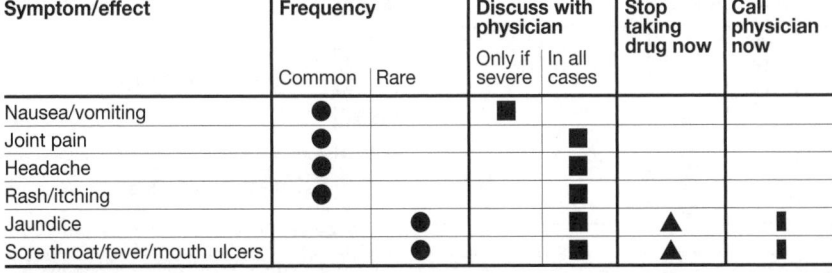

Symptom/effect	Frequency		Discuss with physician		Stop taking drug now	Call physician now
	Common	Rare	Only if severe	In all cases		
Nausea/vomiting	●		■			
Joint pain	●			■		
Headache	●			■		
Rash/itching	●			■		
Jaundice		●		■	▲	▮
Sore throat/fever/mouth ulcers		●		■	▲	▮

INTERACTIONS

None

PROLONGED USE

High doses of propylthiouracil over a prolonged period may rarely reduce the number of white blood cells.

Monitoring Periodic tests of thyroid function are usually required. If you have a sore throat, fever, or mouth ulcers, your white blood cell count must be checked.

PSEUDOEPHEDRINE

Product names Eltor, Sudafed Decongestant 12 Hour, and others
Used in the following combined preparations Actifed Plus, Dimetapp Daytime Cold, Dristan N.D., Sinutab Extra Strength Tablets, and others

GENERAL INFORMATION

Pseudoephedrine, a component of many non-prescription remedies, is a sympathomimetic nasal decongestant. It reduces congestion of the nasal passages and sinuses by narrowing blood vessels in the nose.

Pseudoephedrine should not be given to children under 6 years of age.

INFORMATION FOR USERS

Follow instructions on the label. Call your physician if symptoms worsen.

How taken

Tablets, tablets SR, capsules, oral liquid.

Frequency and timing of doses
Every 3–4 hours (tablets, liquid); every 12 hours (SR tablets).

Usual dosage range
Adults and children 12 years and over Up to 240mg daily.
Children 6–11 years Consult your *pharmacist* or physician.
120mg slow-release preparations are not recommended under 12 years.

Onset of effect
15–30 minutes (tablets and liquid).

Duration of action
4–6 hours (tablets and liquid); 8–12 hours (slow-release preparations).

Diet advice
None.

Storage
Keep in a closed container in a cool, dry place out of the reach of children. Protect from light.

Missed dose
Take as soon as you remember. If your next dose is due within 2 hours, take a single dose now and skip the next.

Stopping the drug
Can be safely stopped as soon as you no longer need it.

OVERDOSE ACTION

Seek immediate medical advice in all cases. Take emergency action if delirium, seizures, or loss of consciousness occur.

See Drug poisoning emergency guide (p.526).

POSSIBLE ADVERSE EFFECTS

High doses may cause anxiety, nausea, dizziness, and, rarely, a marked rise in blood pressure, causing palpitations, headache, and breathlessness.

Symptom/effect	Frequency		Discuss with physician		Stop taking drug now	Call physician now
	Common	Rare	Only if severe	In all cases		
Nervousness/insomnia	●		■			
Nausea/vomiting		●	■			
Dizziness/lightheadedness		●	■			
Hallucinations		●		■		
Rash		●		■	▲	
Palpitations/breathlessness		●		■		▌
Headache		●		■		▌

INTERACTIONS

Antihypertensive drugs Pseudo-ephedrine counteracts the lowered blood pressure from antihypertensive drugs.

Other sympathomimetic drugs increase the risk of adverse effects with this drug.

Monoamine oxidase inhibitors (MAOIs) There is a risk of a dangerous rise in blood pressure if pseudoephedrine is taken with these drugs.

SPECIAL PRECAUTIONS

Be sure to consult your physician or pharmacist before taking this drug if:
▼ You have heart problems.
▼ You have high blood pressure.
▼ You have had glaucoma.
▼ You have diabetes.
▼ You have an overactive thyroid.
▼ You have urinary difficulties.
▼ You have an enlarged prostate.
▼ You are taking other medications.

Pregnancy
▼ Safety in pregnancy not established. Discuss with your physician.

Breast-feeding
▼ The drug passes into the breast milk and may affect the baby. Discuss with your physician.

Infants and children
▼ Not recommended for children under 6 years. Reduced dose necessary in older children. Consult with your physician or pharmacist.

Over 60
▼ Reduced dose may need to be given. Increased likelihood of *adverse effects*.

Driving and hazardous work
▼ Avoid such activities until you have learned how the drug affects you; it can cause dizziness.

Alcohol
▼ No known problems.

PROLONGED USE

Pseudoephedrine is not normally taken for prolonged periods. It should not be taken for longer than 7 days except on the advice of your physician.

PSYLLIUM

Product name Metamucil
Used in the following combined preparation Metamucil Capsules Plus Calcium

GENERAL INFORMATION

This bulk-forming laxative has been extracted from the seeds of Plantago plants since 1934. It is used in the treatment of constipation. Taken by mouth, as powder or granules dissolved in water, psyllium passes through the stomach to the intestines, where it absorbs up to 25 times its volume in water, softening and increasing the volume of bowel movements. It may take several days for improved bowel habits to be established.

Psyllium is also used to reduce the frequency and improve the firmness of bowel movements of people with persistent watery diarrhea or those who have had intestinal surgery such as colostomies and ileostomies. Psyllium may dry up and plug the bowel if the intake of fluids is insufficient.

Serious *side effects* are rare, but the drug may sometimes cause bloating and excess gas, especially at the start of treatment. It should not be taken with-out medical advice for constipation that is accompanied by severe abdominal pain because of the risk of obstructing the bowel. People sensitive to inhaled psyllium may experience allergic reactions while mixing it.

QUICK REFERENCE

Drug group Bulk-forming laxatives (p.97)

Overdose danger rating Low

Dependence rating Low

Prescription needed No

Available as generic Yes

INFORMATION FOR USERS

Follow instructions on label. Call your physician if symptoms worsen.

How taken

Wafers, powder for solution, granules. (Approximately 3g per tsp; check package.)

Frequency and timing of doses
1–3 x daily with at least 240ml of water or fruit juice. Drink liquid immediately after mixing.

Usual adult dosage range
Adults 2.5–30g daily.
Children over 6 years on medical advice only.

Onset of effect
12–24 hours.

Duration of action
Up to 24 hours.

Diet advice
Drink plenty of fluids, at least 240ml, with each dose plus additional liquid during the day.

Storage
Keep in a closed container in a cool, dry place out of the reach of children.

Missed dose
Take as soon as you remember. Resume normal dose thereafter.

Stopping the drug
Can be safely stopped as soon as you no longer need it.

Exceeding the dose
An occasional unintentional extra dose is unlikely to be a cause for concern. But if you notice unusual symptoms, or if a large overdose has been taken, notify your physician.

SPECIAL PRECAUTIONS

Be sure to consult your physician or pharmacist before taking this drug if:
▼ You have severe constipation and/or nausea, vomiting, or abdominal pain.
▼ You have unexplained rectal bleeding.
▼ You have difficulty swallowing.
▼ You are allergic to psyllium products.
▼ You have a known narrowing of the bowel.
▼ You are taking other medications.

Pregnancy
▼ No evidence of risk to the developing baby.

Breast-feeding
▼ No evidence of risk.

Infants and children
▼ Given to children over 6 years only on medical advice.

Over 60
▼ No special problems.

Driving and hazardous work
▼ No known problems.

Alcohol
▼ No known problems.

POSSIBLE ADVERSE EFFECTS

Serious *adverse effects* are rare, but persistent or severe abdominal pain following the use of this (or any) laxative should always receive medical attention.

Symptom/effect	Frequency		Discuss with physician		Stop taking drug now	Call physician now
	Common	Rare	Only if severe	In all cases		
Excess gas		●	■			
Bloating		●	■			
Abdominal pain		●		■		
Wheezing/breathlessness		●		■	▲	▌

INTERACTIONS

General note Psyllium may reduce the absorption of oral anticoagulant drugs, digoxin, salicylates, and other drugs. Spacing of doses may be recommended. Ask your pharmacist.

PROLONGED USE

No problems expected.

x

PYRIDOSTIGMINE

Product names Mestinon, Mestinon-SR
Used in the following combined preparations None

GENERAL INFORMATION

Pyridostigmine is used to treat myasthenia gravis (p.107), an autoimmune condition involving the faulty transmission of nerve impulses to the muscles. Pyridostigmine improves muscle strength by prolonging nerve signals, although it does not cure the disease. In severe cases, it may be prescribed with corticosteroids or other drugs. Pyridostigmine may also be used to reverse temporary paralysis of the bowel and urinary retention following operations.

Cholinergic side effects (e.g. nausea, abdominal cramps, increased salivation and sweating, and diarrhea) usually diappear after reducing the dosage of pyridostigmine, although occasionally an *anticholinergic* drug such as propantheline is needed to counteract these effects.

INFORMATION FOR USERS

Your drug prescription is tailored for you. Do not alter dosage without checking with your physician.

How taken

Tablets, SR-tablets.

Frequency and timing of doses
Every 3–4 hours initially. Thereafter, according to the needs of the individual.
SR-tablets 1–2 x daily.

Usual dosage range
Adults 150mg–1g daily (by mouth) according to response and side effects.
Children Reduced dose necessary according to age and weight.

Onset of effect
30–60 minutes.

Duration of action
3–6 hours.

Diet advice
None.

Storage
Keep in a closed container in a cool, dry place out of the reach of children. Protect from light.

Missed dose
Take as soon as you remember. If your next dose is due within 2 hours, take a single dose now and skip the next.

Stopping the drug
Do not stop the drug without consulting your physician; symptoms may recur.

OVERDOSE ACTION

Seek immediate medical advice in all cases. You may experience severe abdominal cramps, vomiting, weakness, and tremor. Take emergency action if troubled breathing, unusually slow heart beat, seizures, or loss of consciousness occur.

See Drug poisoning emergency guide (p.526).

SPECIAL PRECAUTIONS

Be sure to tell your physician if:
▼ You have a long-term kidney problem.
▼ You have heart problems.
▼ You have had epileptic seizures.
▼ You have asthma.
▼ You have difficulty in passing urine.
▼ You have a peptic ulcer.
▼ You have Parkinson's disease.
▼ You are taking other medications.

Pregnancy
▼ No evidence of risk to the developing fetus in the first 6 months. Large doses near the time of delivery may cause premature labour and temporary muscle weakness in the baby. Discuss with your physician.

Breast-feeding
▼ No evidence of risk, but the baby should be monitored for signs of muscle weakness.

Infants and children
▼ Reduced dose necessary, calculated according to age and weight.

Over 60
▼ Reduced dose may need to be given. Increased likelihood of adverse effects.

Driving and hazardous work
▼ Your underlying condition may make such activities inadvisable. Discuss with your physician.

Alcohol
▼ No special problems.

Surgery and general anesthetics
▼ Pyridostigmine interacts with some anesthetic agents. Make sure your treatment is known to your physician, dentist, and anesthetist before any surgery.

POSSIBLE ADVERSE EFFECTS

Adverse effects of pyridostigmine are usually dose-related and can be avoided by adjusting the dose. Too large a dose can, paradoxically, increase muscle weakness. In rare cases, hypersensitivity may occur leading to an allergic skin rash.

Symptom/effect	Frequency		Discuss with physician		Stop taking drug now	Call physician now
	Common	Rare	Only if severe	In all cases		
Nausea/vomiting	●		■			
Increased salivation	●		■			
Sweating	●		■			
Abdominal cramps/diarrhea	●			■		
Watering eyes/small pupils		●		■		
Muscle twitching/weakness		●		■		■
Rash		●		■		

INTERACTIONS

General note Drugs that suppress the transmission of nerve signals may oppose the effect of pyridostigmine. Such drugs include aminoglycoside *antibiotics*, clindamycin digoxin, procainamide, quinidine, lithium, and chloroquine.

Propranolol may decrease the effectiveness of pyridostigmine.

PROLONGED USE

No problems expected.

PYRIMETHAMINE

Product name Daraprim
Used in the following combined preparations None

GENERAL INFORMATION

Pyrimethamine is a drug used to treat protozoal infections, which include malaria. Because malaria parasites can readily develop resistance to pyrimethamine, the drug is now always given combined with the antibacterial drug sulfadoxine for the treatment of malaria. The activity of the combination greatly exceeds that of either drug alone. Pyrimethamine and sulfadoxine are used with quinine in the treatment of malaria.

Pyrimethamine is not used for the prevention of malaria. Pyrimethamine is sometimes given with another drug, sulfadiazine, to treat toxoplasmosis in people with lowered immunity. Such treatment must be supervised by an expert.

Blood disorders can sometimes arise during prolonged treatment with pyrimethamine, and, because of this, blood counts are monitored regularly and vitamin supplements are given.

INFORMATION FOR USERS

Your drug prescription is tailored for you. Do not alter dosage without checking with your physician.

How taken

Tablets.

Frequency and timing of doses
Taken once only, daily or weekly, depending on the condition being treated.

Usual dosage range
Adults 2–3 tablets.
Children Reduced dose necessary according to age.

Onset of effect
24 hours.

Duration of action
Up to 1 week.

Diet advice
None.

Storage
Keep in a closed container in a cool, dry place out of the reach of children. Protect from light.

Missed dose
If you are being treated for toxoplasmosis, take as soon as you remember. If your next dose is due within 24 hours, take a single dose now and alter the dosing day so that your next dose is one week later.

Stopping the drug
Do not stop taking the drug without discussing it with your physician.

Exceeding the dose
An occasional unintentional extra dose is unlikely to cause problems. Large overdoses may cause trembling, breathing difficulty, seizures, and blood disorders. Notify your physician.

SPECIAL PRECAUTIONS

Be sure to tell your physician if:
▼ You have long-term liver or kidney problems.
▼ You have had epileptic seizures.
▼ You have anemia.
▼ You are allergic to sulfonamides.
▼ You have glucose-6-phosphate dehydrogenase (G6PD) deficiency.
▼ You are taking other medications.

Pregnancy
▼ Pyrimethamine can cause folic acid deficiency in the unborn baby. Discuss with your physician.

Breast-feeding
▼ The drug passes into the breast milk, but at normal doses adverse effects on the baby are unlikely. Discuss with your physician.

Infants and children
▼ Reduced dose necessary.

Over 60
▼ No special problems.

Driving and hazardous work
▼ No special problems.

Alcohol
▼ No known problems.

Sunlight and sunbeds
▼ Avoid excessive exposure to sunlight.

POSSIBLE ADVERSE EFFECTS

Unusual tiredness, weakness, bleeding, bruising, and sore throat may be signs of a blood disorder. Notify your physician promptly if they occur. Breathing difficulties or signs of chest infection should be reported to your physician immediately.

Symptom/effect	Frequency		Discuss with physician		Stop taking drug now	Call physician now
	Common	Rare	Only if severe	In all cases		
Loss of appetite		●	■			
Insomnia		●	■			
Gastric irritation		●		■		
Rash		●		■		▮
Unusual bleeding/bruising		●		■		▮
Sore throat/fever		●		■		▮
Breathing problems		●		■		▮

INTERACTIONS

General note Drugs that suppress the bone marrow or cause folic acid deficiency may increase the risk of serious blood disorders when taken with pyrimethamine.

Such drugs include anticancer and antirheumatic drugs, sulfasalazine, co-trimoxazole, trimethoprim, phenytoin, and phenylbutazone.

PROLONGED USE

Prolonged use of this drug may cause folic acid deficiency, leading to serious blood disorders. Supplements of folic acid may be recommended (in the form of folinic acid).

Monitoring Regular blood cell counts are required during high-dose or long-term treatment.

QUETIAPINE

Product names Seroquel, Teva-Quetiapine, and others
Used in the following combined preparations None

GENERAL INFORMATION

Quetiapine is an atypical antipsychotic drug that is prescribed for the treatment of schizophrenia, as well as for mania and depression in bipolar affective disorder (manic depression). It can be used to treat "positive" symptoms (thought disorders, delusions, and hallucinations) and "negative" symptoms (blunted affect and emotional and social withdrawal in schizophrenia). The drug may be more effective when used for positive symptoms, however.

Elderly people excrete the drug up to 50 per cent more slowly than the usual adult rate. They, therefore, need to be prescribed much lower doses in order to avoid *adverse effects*.

QUICK REFERENCE

Drug group Antipsychotic drugs (p.69)
Overdose danger rating Medium
Dependence rating Low
Prescription needed Yes
Available as generic Yes

INFORMATION FOR USERS

Your drug prescription is tailored for you. Do not alter dosage without checking with your physician.

How taken

Tablets.

Frequency and timing of doses
2 x daily.

Usual adult dosage range
50mg daily (day 1), 100mg daily (day 2), 200mg daily (day 3), 300mg daily (day 4), then changing according to response. Usual dose: 300–600mg daily.

Onset of effect
1–7 days.

Duration of action
Up to 12 hours.

Diet advice
None.

Storage
Keep in a closed container in a cool, dry place out of the reach of children.

Missed dose
Take as soon as you remember. If your next dose is due within 4 hours take a single dose now and skip the next.

Stopping the drug
Do not stop the drug without consulting your physician; symptoms may recur.

Exceeding the dose
An occasional unintentional extra dose is unlikely to cause problems. Large overdoses may cause unusual drowsiness, palpitations, and low blood pressure. Notify your physician.

POSSIBLE ADVERSE EFFECTS

Unusual drowsiness and weight gain are common adverse effects of quetiapine.

Symptom/effect	Frequency		Discuss with physician		Stop taking drug now	Call physician now
	Common	Rare	Only if severe	In all cases		
Unusual drowsiness	●		■			
Weight gain	●		■			
Indigestion/constipation	●		■			
Parkinsonism	●			■		
Dizziness/fainting		●		■		
Stuffy nose/sore throat		●		■		
Palpitations		●		■		

INTERACTIONS

Antiepileptics Quetiapine opposes the effect of these drugs but phenytoin decreases the effect of quetiapine. Other liver *enzyme*-inducing antiepileptic drugs, such as carbamazepine and barbiturates, may have a similar effect.

Sedatives All drugs that have a sedative effect on the central nervous system are likely to increase the sedative properties of quetiapine.

Erythromycin, clarithromycin, ketoconazole, and fluconazole These drugs may increase the effects of quetiapine.

SPECIAL PRECAUTIONS

Be sure to tell your physician if:
▼ You have epilepsy.
▼ You have Parkinson's disease.
▼ You have dementia.
▼ You have liver or kidney problems.
▼ You have heart problems.
▼ You have blood problems.
▼ You are taking other medications.

Pregnancy
▼ Safety not established. Discuss with your physician.

Breast-feeding
▼ Safety not established. Discuss with your physician.

Infants and children
▼ Not recommended.

Over 60
▼ Reduced doses necessary. The elderly eliminate quetiapine much more slowly than younger adults. Not indicated in those with dementia.

Driving and hazardous work
▼ Avoid. Quetiapine can cause drowsiness.

Alcohol
▼ Avoid. Alcohol increases the *sedative* effects of this drug.

PROLONGED USE

Prolonged use of quetiapine may rarely cause *tardive dyskinesia* (in which there are involuntary movements of the tongue and face). There is also a risk of developing diabetes and raised blood lipid levels. With long-term use in elderly patients, quetiapine also carries a greater risk of stroke than some other antipsychotic drugs.

QUINIDINE

Product name Quinidine Sulfate Injection
Used in the following combined preparations None

GENERAL INFORMATION

Although quinidine is one of the oldest of the anti-arrhythmic drugs, it is still used to treat many different abnormal heart rhythms, particularly in cases where a rapid heartbeat causes important symptoms or is life-threatening.

When taken by mouth, the onset of action is slow. It can be given by injection in emergencies when rapid control of an abnormal heart rhythm is required.

Quinidine has several possible *adverse effects*. Diarrhea, nausea, and vomiting, which are common, may be due to its irritant effect. Serious allergic reactions have also occurred. The most serious adverse effect is the possibility of further abnormal heart rhythms that may give rise to palpitations.

INFORMATION FOR USERS

Your drug prescription is tailored for you. Do not alter dosage without checking with your physician.

How taken

Tablets, injection.

Frequency and timing of doses
Every 6 hours (tablets). In some situations, higher doses may be used initially.

Usual adult dosage range
600mg–2.4g daily.

Onset of effect
Within 3 hours.

Duration of action
6–8 hours (tablets).

Diet advice
None.

Storage
Keep in a closed container in a cool, dry place out of the reach of children. Protect from light.

Missed dose
Take as soon as you remember. If your next dose is due within 2 hours, take a single dose now and skip the next.

Stopping the drug
Do not stop taking the drug without consulting your physician; symptoms may recur.

OVERDOSE ACTION

Seek immediate medical advice in all cases. Take emergency action if breathing problems, seizures, or collapse occurs.

See Drug poisoning emergency guide (p.526).

SPECIAL PRECAUTIONS

Be sure to tell your physician if:
▼ You have impaired liver or kidney function.
▼ You have heart failure.
▼ You have myasthenia gravis.
▼ You have had a rash following quinidine on a previous occasion.
▼ You are taking digoxin.
▼ You are taking other medications.

Pregnancy
▼ Safety in pregnancy not established. Discuss with your physician.

Breast-feeding
▼ The drug passes into the breast milk and may affect the baby. Discuss with your physician.

Infants and children
▼ Not usually prescribed.

Over 60
▼ Reduced dose necessary.

Driving and hazardous work
▼ Avoid such activities until you know how quinidine affects you; it can cause dizziness and blurred vision.

Alcohol
▼ No known problems.

POSSIBLE ADVERSE EFFECTS

The most common adverse effects are diarrhea, nausea, and vomiting. If they become severe, a change of drug may be necessary. Vertigo or palpitations may indicate the dose is too high; notify your physician promptly.

Symptom/effect	Frequency		Discuss with physician		Stop taking drug now	Call physician now
	Common	Rare	Only if severe	In all cases		
Diarrhea	●		■			
Nausea/vomiting	●		■			
Dizziness	●		■			
Ringing in the ears		●		■		
Headache/vertigo		●		■		▮
Palpitations		●		■		▮
Lightheadedness		●		■		
Rash		●		■		▮
Blurred vision		●		■		▮

PROLONGED USE

Sudden onset of abnormal heart rhythms or abnormalities of the blood may occur.

Monitoring Periodic checks on blood levels of the drug may be required.

INTERACTIONS

Antihypertensive drugs Quinidine may increase the effects of these drugs.

Anticoagulant drugs Quinidine increases the effects of these drugs.

Phenobarbital and phenytoin reduce the effect of quinidine.

Digoxin Quinidine increases the effects of digoxin; blood levels must be checked.

QUININE

Product names Quinine-Odan, Teva-Quinine, and others
Used in the following combined preparations None

GENERAL INFORMATION

Quinine, obtained from the bark of the cinchona tree, is the earliest antimalarial drug. It often causes *side effects*, but is still given for cases of malaria that are resistant to safer treatments. Owing to the resistance of malaria parasites to chloroquine and other antimalarials, quinine is used, in combination with a second drug, in the treatment of malaria. It is not used for prevention of malaria.

Although not formally approved, quinine has also been used in the treatment of nocturnal leg muscle cramps. At the high doses used to treat malaria, quinine may cause ringing in the ears, headaches, nausea, hearing loss, and blurred vision: a group of symptoms known as cinchonism. In rare cases, it may cause bleeding problems.

INFORMATION FOR USERS

Your drug prescription is tailored for you. Do not alter dosage without checking with your physician.

How taken

Tablets, capsules.

Frequency and timing of doses
Malaria Every 8 hours after meals.

Usual adult dosage range
1.8g daily for 3–7 days (malaria);
200–300mg daily at bedtime (leg cramps).

Onset of effect
1–2 days (malaria); up to 4 weeks (leg cramps).

Duration of action
Up to 24 hours.

Diet advice
None.

Storage
Keep in a closed container in a cool, dry place out of the reach of children. Protect from light.

Missed dose
Take as soon as you remember. If your next dose is due within 4 hours, skip the missed one and return to your normal dosing schedule thereafter.

Stopping the drug
If prescribed for malaria, take the full course. Even if you feel better, the original infection may still be present and may recur if treatment is stopped too soon. If taken for muscle cramps, the drug can safely be stopped as soon as you no longer need it.

OVERDOSE ACTION

Seek immediate medical advice in all cases. Take emergency action if breathing problems, seizures, or loss of consciousness occur.

See Drug poisoning emergency guide (p.526).

SPECIAL PRECAUTIONS

Be sure to consult your physician if:
▼ You have a long-term kidney problem.
▼ You have tinnitus (ringing in the ears).
▼ You have optic neuritis.
▼ You have myasthenia gravis.
▼ You have glucose-6-phosphate dehydrogenase (G6PD) deficiency.
▼ You have heart problems, especially rhythm disturbances.
▼ You are taking other medications.

Pregnancy
▼ Not usually prescribed. May cause defects in the unborn baby. Discuss with your physician.

Breast-feeding
▼ The drug passes into the breast milk, but at normal doses adverse effects on the baby are unlikely. Discuss with your physician.

Infants and children
▼ Reduced dose necessary.

Over 60
▼ No special problems.

Driving and hazardous work
▼ Avoid these activities until you know how quinine affects you because the drug's side effects may distract you.

Alcohol
▼ No known problems.

POSSIBLE ADVERSE EFFECTS

Adverse effects are unlikely with low doses. At antimalarial doses, hearing disturbances, headache, and blurred vision are more common. Nausea and diarrhea may occur.

Symptom/effect	Frequency		Discuss with physician		Stop taking drug now	Call physician now
	Common	Rare	Only if severe	In all cases		
Nausea/vomiting/diarrhea		●		■		
Headache		●		■		
Ringing in ears/giddiness		●		■		
Rash/itching		●		■	▲	▮
Loss of hearing		●		■	▲	▮
Blurred vision		●		■	▲	▮
Bruising/excessive bleeding		●		■	▲	▮

INTERACTIONS

Cimetidine This drug increases the blood levels of quinine.

Mefloquine may cause increased effect on the heart. Do not use with quinine.

Digoxin Quinine increases the blood levels of digoxin, and so the dose of digoxin should be reduced. Discuss with your physician.

PROLONGED USE

Prolonged use of quinine can cause blood disorders.

RALOXIFENE

Product names Evista, PMS-Raloxifene, and others
Used in the following combined preparations None

GENERAL INFORMATION

Raloxifene is a non-steroidal drug that acts on some estrogen receptors (estrogen is a naturally occurring female sex hormone, see p.133). It is a selective estrogen receptor modulator (SERM), which acts like estrogen on bone. It is prescribed to prevent vertebral fractures in postmenopausal women who have osteoporosis or are at increased risk of osteoporosis.

Raloxifene has no beneficial effect on other menopausal problems such as hot flushes. It is not prescribed to women who might become pregnant because it may harm the unborn baby, and it is not prescribed to men.

There is an increased risk of a thrombosis (blood clot) developing in a vein in the leg, but the risk is similar to that due to HRT (see p.133). However, because of this risk, raloxifene is usually stopped if the woman taking it becomes immobile or bedbound, when clots are more likely to form. Treatment is restarted when full activity is resumed.

INFORMATION FOR USERS

Your drug prescription is tailored for you. Do not alter dosage without checking with your physician.

How taken

Tablets.

Frequency and timing of doses
Once daily.

Usual adult dosage range
60mg daily.

Onset of effect
1–4 hours.

Duration of action
24–48 hours.

Diet advice
Calcium supplements are recommended if dietary calcium is low.

Storage
Keep in a closed container in a cool, dry place out of the reach of children. Protect from light.

Missed dose
Take as soon as you remember. If your next dose is due within 8 hours, take a single dose now and skip the next.

Stopping the drug
Do not stop the drug without consulting your physician except under conditions specified in advance, such as immobility, which increases the risk of blood clots forming.

Exceeding the dose
An occasional unintentional extra dose is unlikely to be a cause for concern. But if you notice any unusual symptoms, or if a large overdose has been taken, notify your physician.

SPECIAL PRECAUTIONS

Be sure to tell your physician if:
▼ You have had a blood clot in a vein or a pulmonary embolism.
▼ You have vaginal bleeding.
▼ You have liver or kidney problems.
▼ You are taking other medications.
▼ You have a history of stroke.
▼ You have heart rhythm problems.

Pregnancy
▼ Not prescribed to premenopausal women.

Breast-feeding
▼ Not prescribed to premenopausal women.

Infants and children
▼ Not prescribed.

Over 60
▼ No special problems.

Driving and hazardous work
▼ No special problems.

Alcohol
▼ No special problems.

POSSIBLE ADVERSE EFFECTS

Some *adverse effects* of raloxifene are indications of a thrombosis (blood clot) in a vein in the leg. If a clot occurs somewhere else in the body, there might not be any obvious symptoms.

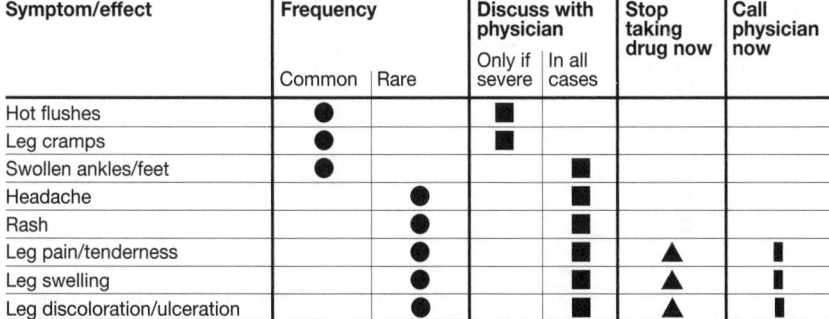

Symptom/effect	Frequency		Discuss with physician		Stop taking drug now	Call physician now
	Common	Rare	Only if severe	In all cases		
Hot flushes	●		■			
Leg cramps	●		■			
Swollen ankles/feet	●			■		
Headache		●		■		
Rash		●		■		
Leg pain/tenderness		●		■	▲	▮
Leg swelling		●		■	▲	▮
Leg discoloration/ulceration		●		■	▲	▮

INTERACTIONS

Cholestyramine This drug reduces the absorption of raloxifene by the body.

PROLONGED USE

Raloxifene is normally used long term. It reduces the risk of some types of breast cancer, but this benefit must be weighed against the increased risk of stroke and venous thrombosis.

Monitoring Liver function tests may be performed periodically.

RAMIPRIL

Product names Altace, CO Ramipril, and others
Used in the following combined preparations Altace HCT

GENERAL INFORMATION

Ramipril belongs to a group of drugs known as ACE (angiotensin converting *enzyme*) inhibitors. It works by dilating the blood vessels, which enables the blood to circulate more easily. The drug is used to treat high blood pressure (p.88), to reduce the strain on the heart in patients with heart failure after a heart attack, and to prevent future strokes and heart attacks. The first dose of an ACE inhibitor can cause the blood pressure to drop very suddenly, so a few hours' bed rest afterwards may be advised.

Side effects such as headache, nausea, and dizziness are usually mild. Like all ACE inhibitors, ramipril can cause the body to retain potassium. In addition, it can cause a persistent dry cough.

INFORMATION FOR USERS

Your drug prescription is tailored for you. Do not alter dosage without checking with your physician.

How taken

Capsules.

Frequency and timing of doses
With water, with or without food.
High blood pressure Usually once daily.
Heart failure after a heart attack 2 x daily.

Usual adult dosage range
High blood pressure 1.25–10mg daily.
Heart failure, or after heart attack 5–10mg daily.

Onset of effect
Within 2 hours; full beneficial effect may take several weeks.

Duration of action
Up to 24 hours.

Diet advice
Your physician may advise you to decrease your salt intake to help control your blood pressure.

Storage
Keep in a closed container in a cool, dry place out of the reach of children.

Missed dose
Take as soon as you remember. If your next dose is due within 6 hours, take a single dose now and skip the next. Subsequently, continue with your usual routine.

Stopping the drug
Do not stop taking the drug without consulting your physician. Treatment of hypertension and heart failure is normally lifelong, it may be necessary to substitute alternative therapy.

Exceeding the dose
If you notice any unusual symptoms or if a large overdose has been taken, notify your physician.

SPECIAL PRECAUTIONS

Be sure to tell your physician if:
▼ You have long-term liver or kidney problems.
▼ You have heart problems.
▼ You have had angioedema or a previous allergic reaction to ACE inhibitors.
▼ You are pregnant or intend to become pregnant.
▼ You are taking other medications.

Pregnancy
▼ Not prescribed. There is evidence of harm to the developing fetus.

Breast-feeding
▼ Safety not established. Discuss with your physician.

Infants and children
▼ Not recommended.

Over 60
▼ Reduced dose may be necessary.

Driving and hazardous work
▼ Avoid such activities until you have learned how ramipril affects you because the drug may cause dizziness and fainting.

Alcohol
▼ Avoid. Alcohol may increase the blood-pressure-lowering and adverse effects of the drug.

Surgery and general anesthetics
▼ Notify your physician or dentist that you are taking ramipril as anesthetics can increase the effects of this drug.

POSSIBLE ADVERSE EFFECTS

Ramipril can cause a variety of side effects, but most are usually mild and transient. An irritating dry cough may persist and necessitate withdrawal of the drug. Rarely, ramipril may cause deterioration of kidney function, digestive tract disturbance, severe rash, or severe swelling of the face accompanied by breathing difficulties.

Symptom/effect	Frequency		Discuss with physician		Stop taking drug now	Call physician now
	Common	Rare	Only if severe	In all cases		
Rash	●			■		
Persistent dry cough	●			■		
Mouth ulcers/sore mouth		●		■		
Dizziness		●		■		
Sore throat/fever		●		■		
Swelling of mouth/lips		●		■	▲	▮
Breathing difficulty		●		■	▲	▮

INTERACTIONS

Non-steroidal anti-inflammatory drugs (NSAIDs) (e.g., ibuprofen) may reduce the antihypertensive effect of ramipril and increase the risk of kidney damage.

Cyclosporine increases the risk of high potassium levels in the blood.

Vasodilators, diuretics, and other antihypertensives These drugs may increase the blood-pressure-lowering effect of ramipril.

Potassium supplements and potassium-sparing diuretics may cause excess levels of potassium in the body.

Lithium Ramipril may cause raised blood lithium levels and toxicity.

PROLONGED USE

No problems expected.

Monitoring Periodic checks on potassium levels, white blood cell count, kidney function, and urine are usually performed.

RANITIDINE

Product names Apo-Ranitidine, CO Ranitidine, Zantac
Used in the following combined preparations None

GENERAL INFORMATION

Ranitidine is an anti-ulcer drug of the antihistamine (H₂) antagonist type (known as H₂ blockers). It reduces acid production by the stomach, allowing ulcers to heal, and is usually given in courses lasting four to eight weeks, with further courses if symptoms recur. It may also be used to protect against ulcers in people taking NSAIDs (p.102), and to reduce the discomfort and ulceration of esophagitis. In clinical practice, ranitidine has been largely replaced by newer proton pump inhibitor anti-ulcer drugs, such as omeprazole. It is available over-the-

counter for the short-term treatment of heartburn and indigestion in those over 16 years old. Unlike the similar drug cimetidine, ranitidine does not increase blood levels of other drugs such as anticoagulants and antiepileptics. Most people experience no serious *side effects* during treatment. As ranitidine promotes healing of the stomach lining, there is a risk that it might mask stomach cancer. It is therefore prescribed only when this possibility has been ruled out.

INFORMATION FOR USERS

Follow instructions on the label. Call your physician if symptoms worsen.

How taken

Tablets, oral liquid, injection.

Frequency and timing of doses
Once daily at bedtime or 2 x daily.

Usual adult dosage range
150–600mg daily, depending on the condition being treated. Usual dose is 150mg twice daily.

Onset of effect
Within 1 hour.

Duration of action
12 hours.

Diet advice
None.

Storage
Keep in a closed container in a cool, dry place out of the reach of children. Protect from light.

Missed dose
Take as soon as you remember. If your next dose is due within 3 hours, take a single dose now and skip the next.

Stopping the drug
Do not stop the drug without consulting your physician; symptoms may recur.

Exceeding the dose
An occasional unintentional extra dose is unlikely to be a cause for concern. But if you notice any unusual symptoms, or if a large overdose has been taken, notify your physician.

POSSIBLE ADVERSE EFFECTS

The *adverse effects* of ranitidine, of which headache is the most common, are usually related to dosage level and almost always disappear when treatment finishes.

Symptom/effect	Frequency		Discuss with physician		Stop taking drug now	Call physician now
	Common	Rare	Only if severe	In all cases		
Headache/dizziness	●		■			
Nausea/vomiting		●	■			
Constipation		●	■			
Diarrhea		●	■			
Jaundice		●		■		
Mental problems/agitation		●		■		
Sore throat/fever		●		■		▮

INTERACTIONS

Ketoconazole Ranitidine may reduce the absorption of ketoconazole. Ranitidine should be taken at least 2 hours after ketoconazole.

Glipizide Ranitidine may increase the absorption of glipizide.

Sucralfate High doses (2g) of sucralfate may reduce the absorption of ranitidine. Sucralfate should be taken at least 2 hours after ranitidine.

SPECIAL PRECAUTIONS

Be sure to tell your physician or pharmacist if:
▼ You have long-term liver or kidney problems.
▼ You have porphyria.
▼ You have had an allergic reaction to ranitidine or to another H₂ blocker.
▼ You are taking other medications.

Pregnancy
▼ Safety in pregnancy not established. Discuss with your physician.

Breast-feeding
▼ The drug passes into the breast milk and may affect the baby. Discuss with your physician.

Infants and children
▼ Reduced dose necessary.

Over 60
▼ No special problems.

Driving and hazardous work
▼ No known problems. Dizziness can occur in a very small proportion of patients.

Alcohol
▼ Avoid. Alcohol may aggravate your underlying condition and reduce the beneficial effects of this drug.

PROLONGED USE

No problems expected.

RASAGILINE

Product name Azilect
Used in the following combined preparations None

GENERAL INFORMATION

Rasagiline is used alone or in combination with another medication to treat Parkinson's disease. It works by inhibiting an *enzyme* called monoamine oxidase type B (MAO-B), which increases dopamine in the brain. It can be used early on in the disease to control symptoms. It can be used with medications such as levodopa as it helps prolong its effect. While on this medication, it is advised that you get up slowly while supporting yourself, to minimize dizziness or lightheadedness. As rasagiline blocks the MAO-B enzyme, it can prevent the breakdown of tyramine, which is a by-product of some foods. When these foods are taken while on this medication, serious *side effects* can occur (see below).

QUICK REFERENCE

Drug group Drugs for Parkinsonism (p. 71)

Overdose danger rating High

Dependence rating Low

Prescription needed Yes

Available as generic No

INFORMATION FOR USERS

Your drug prescription is tailored for you. Do not alter dosage without checking with your physician.

How taken

Tablets.

Frequency and timing of doses
Usually once daily.

Adult dosage range
0.5–1mg daily.

Onset of effect
1 hour.

Duration of action
Up to 24 hours.

Diet advice
Avoid foods rich in tyramine while on, and for 14 days after stopping, rasagiline. These include aged cheeses, salami, fava beans, red wine, soybean products. Consult your dietician.

Storage
Keep in a closed container in a cool, dry place out of the reach of children.

Missed dose
If you miss a dose, take it as soon as you remember. If it is near the time of the next dose, skip the missed dose and resume your usual dosing schedule. Do not double up to catch up on a missed dose.

Stopping the drug
Do not stop the drug without consulting your physician. Stopping the drug may lead to worsening of the underlying condition.

OVERDOSE ACTION

 Seek immediate medical advice in all cases. Take emergency action if chest pain or loss of consciousness occurs.

See Drug poisoning emergency guide (p.526).

SPECIAL PRECAUTIONS

Be sure to tell your physician if:
▼ You have pheochromocytoma.
▼ You have kidney or liver disease.
▼ You have had melanoma.
▼ You are taking herbal remedies such as St John's Wort.
▼ You are taking other medications.

 Pregnancy
▼ Not usually prescribed. Safety in pregnancy not established. Discuss with your physician.

 Breast-feeding
▼ Safety not established. Discuss with your physician.

 Infants and children
▼ Not recommended.

 Over 60
▼ No special problems.

 Driving and hazardous work
▼ May cause drowsiness. Do not drive a car or operate machinery until the effect of the drug wears off and you feel you are mentally alert.

 Alcohol
▼ Avoid alcohol use as it may increase the effect of drowsiness caused by this drug.

PROLONGED USE

No problems expected.

POSSIBLE ADVERSE EFFECTS

Rasigiline may cause some drowsiness and change in bowel pattern.

Symptom/effect	Frequency		Discuss with physician		Stop taking drug now	Call physician now
	Common	Rare	Only if severe	In all cases		
Constipation or diarrhea	●		■			
Drowsiness	●		■			
Mild headache		●	■			
Loss of appetite		●	■			
Unsteadiness		●	■			
Severe headache/ chest pain/blurred vision		●		■	▲	▌
Hallucinations		●		■	▲	▌
Shortness of breath		●		■		▌
Slow or difficult speech		●		■		▌

INTERACTIONS

General note Because of the wide range of possible drug interactions with rasagiline, do not take any medication, whether prescription or nonprescription, without first consulting your physician or *pharmacist*.

Antidepressants, St. John's wort, dextromethorphan, pseudoephedrine, and meperidine The combination of rasagiline with these may cause severe and dangerous reactions. Allow at least 14 days after stopping rasagiline before taking these.

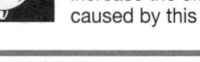

REPAGLINIDE

Product names CO Repaglinide, GlucoNorm, and others
Used in the following combined preparations None

GENERAL INFORMATION

Repaglinide is a drug used to treat Type 2 diabetes that cannot be adequately controlled by diet and exercise alone. It acts in a similar manner to sulfonylurea drugs by stimulating the release of insulin from the pancreas. Therefore, some of the pancreatic cells need to be functioning in order for it to be effective.

Repaglinide is quick acting, but its effects last for only about four hours. The drug is sometimes given with metformin if that drug is not providing adequate diabetic control.

Repaglinide is best taken just before a meal in order for the insulin that is released to cope with the food. If a meal is likely to be missed, the dose of repaglinide should not be taken. If a tablet has been taken and a meal is not forthcoming, some carbohydrate (as specified by your physician or dietician) should be eaten as soon as possible.

INFORMATION FOR USERS

Your drug prescription is tailored for you. Do not alter dosage without checking with your physician.

How taken

Tablets.

Frequency and timing of doses
1–4 x daily (up to 30 minutes before a meal, and up to 4 meals a day). If you are going to miss a meal, do not take the tablet.

Usual adult dosage range
500mcg (starting dose), increased at intervals of 1–2 weeks according to response; 4–16mg daily (maintenance dose).

Onset of effect
30 minutes.

Duration of action
4 hours.

Diet advice
Follow the diet advised by your physician or dietician.

Storage
Keep in a closed container in a cool, dry place out of the reach of children.

Missed dose
Do not take tablets between meals. Discuss with your physician.

Stopping the drug
Do not stop taking the drug without consulting your physician.

Exceeding the dose
An overdose will cause hypoglycaemia with dizziness, sweating, trembling, confusion, and headache. Notify your physician.

SPECIAL PRECAUTIONS

Be sure to tell your physician if:
▼ You have liver or kidney problems.
▼ You are taking other medications.

Pregnancy
▼ Safety not established. Discuss with your physician.

Breast-feeding
▼ Safety not established. Discuss with your physician.

Infants and children
▼ Not recommended.

Over 60
▼ No special problems, but safety not established over 75 years.

Driving and hazardous work
▼ Avoid if low blood sugar without warning signs is likely.

Alcohol
▼ Avoid. Alcohol may upset diabetic control and may increase and prolong the effects of repaglinide.

POSSIBLE ADVERSE EFFECTS

Intestinal problems are common at the start of treatment with repaglinide. However, such adverse effects tend to become less troublesome as treatment continues.

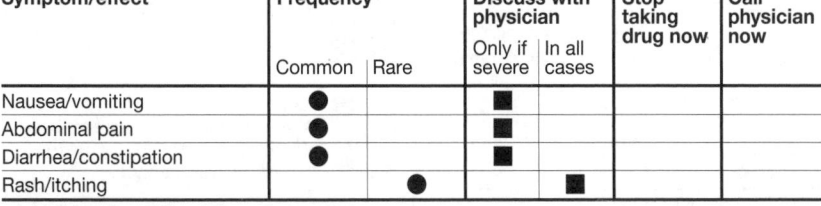

Symptom/effect	Frequency		Discuss with physician		Stop taking drug now	Call physician now
	Common	Rare	Only if severe	In all cases		
Nausea/vomiting	●		■			
Abdominal pain	●		■			
Diarrhea/constipation	●		■			
Rash/itching		●		■		

PROLONGED USE

Repaglinide is usually prescribed indefinitely. No special problems.

Monitoring Periodic monitoring of control of blood glucose levels is necessary.

INTERACTIONS

Monoamine oxidase inhibitors (MAOIs), beta-blockers, ACE inhibitors, and NSAIDs These drugs may increase the effect of repaglinide.

Ketoconazole, erythromycin, and gemfibrozil may increase the effect of repaglinide.

Beta blockers The symptoms of hypoglycemia may be masked by these drugs, especially by non-cardioselective beta blockers (e.g. propranolol).

Oral contraceptives, thiazide diuretics, corticosteroids, danazol, thyroid hormones, and sympathomimetics These drugs may decrease the effect of repaglinide.

Rifampin and carbamazepine may decrease the effect of repaglinide

RIFAMPIN

Product namees Rifadin, Rofact
Used in the following combined preparation Rifater

GENERAL INFORMATION

Rifampin is an antibacterial drug that is highly effective in the treatment of tuberculosis. Taken by mouth, the drug is well absorbed in the intestine and widely distributed throughout the body, including the brain. As a result, it is particularly useful in the treatment of tuberculous meningitis.

Rifampin has also been used to prevent infection in close contacts of those with meningococcal meningitis.

Rifampin is always prescribed with other antibiotics or antituberculous drugs because of the rapid development of resistance in some bacteria.

A harmless red-orange coloration may be imparted to the urine, saliva, and tears, and soft contact lenses may become permanently stained.

QUICK REFERENCE

Drug group Antituberculous drugs (p.118)

Overdose danger rating Medium

Dependence rating Low

Prescription needed Yes

Available as generic Yes

INFORMATION FOR USERS

Your drug prescription is tailored for you. Do not alter dosage without checking with your physician.

How taken

Tablets, capsules, injection (available through Special Access Programme).

Frequency and timing of doses
1 x daily, 30 minutes before breakfast (tuberculosis); 2 x daily (prevention of meningococcal meningitis); 2–4 x daily, 30 minutes before or 2 hours after meals (other serious infections).

Usual adult dosage range
According to weight; usually 450–600mg daily (tuberculosis); 600mg–1.2g daily (other serious infections); 1.2g daily for 2 days (prevention of meningococcal meningitis).

Onset of effect
Over several days.

Duration of action
Up to 24 hours.

Diet advice
None.

Storage
Keep in a closed container in a cool, dry place out of the reach of children. Protect from light.

Missed dose
Take as soon as you remember. If your next dose is due within 6 hours, take a single dose now, then return to normal dosing schedule.

Stopping the drug
Take the full course. Even if you feel better, the original infection may still be present and symptoms may recur if treatment is stopped too soon.

Exceeding the dose
An occasional unintentional extra dose is unlikely to cause problems. Large overdoses may cause liver damage, nausea, vomiting, and lethargy. Notify your physician immediately.

SPECIAL PRECAUTIONS

Be sure to tell your physician if:
▼ You have a long-term liver or kidney problem.
▼ You have porphyria.
▼ You wear contact lenses.
▼ You are taking other medications.

Pregnancy
▼ Safety in pregnancy not established. Discuss with your physician.

Breast-feeding
▼ The drug passes into the breast milk, but at normal doses adverse effects on the baby are unlikely. Discuss with your physician.

Infants and children
▼ Reduced dose necessary.

Over 60
▼ Increased risk of adverse effects. Reduced dose may therefore be necessary.

Driving and hazardous work
▼ No problems expected.

Alcohol
▼ Avoid excessive amounts. Heavy alcohol consumption may increase the risk of liver damage.

POSSIBLE ADVERSE EFFECTS

A harmless red-orange discoloration of body fluids normally occurs. Serious *adverse effects* are rare. *Jaundice* usually improves during treatment but should be reported to your physician. Headache and breathing difficulties may occur after stopping high-dose treatment.

Symptom/effect	Frequency		Discuss with physician		Stop taking drug now	Call physician now
	Common	Rare	Only if severe	In all cases		
Muscle cramps/aches		●		■		
Nausea/vomiting/diarrhea		●	■			
Jaundice		●		■		▮
Flu-like illness		●		■	▲	▮
Rash/itching		●		■		
Easy bruising/bleeding		●		■	▲	▮

PROLONGED USE

Prolonged use of rifampin may cause liver damage.

Monitoring Periodic blood tests may be performed to monitor liver function.

INTERACTIONS

General note Rifampin may reduce the effectiveness of a wide variety of drugs, such as oral contraceptives (in which case alternative contraceptive methods may be necessary), phenytoin, corticosteroids, oral antidiabetics, disopyramide, and oral anticoagulants. Dosage adjustment of these drugs may be necessary at the start or end of treatment with rifampin. Consult your physician or pharmacist for advice.

RISEDRONATE

Product names Actonel, Actonel DR, PMS-Risendronate, and others
Used in the following combined preparations None

GENERAL INFORMATION

Risedronate is given for the prevention and treatment of osteoporosis in post-menopausal women and osteoporosis due to long-term use of corticosteroid drugs in men and women. Risedronate is also beneficial in individuals with Paget's disease.

A calcium supplement and vitamin D may be prescribed with the drug if dietary amounts are not adequate. However, calcium should not be taken at the same time as risedronate because calcium is one of the many substances that reduces its absorption.

Generally, the drug's *side effects* are mild. The most common are diarrhea, nausea and abdominal pain.

INFORMATION FOR USERS

Your drug prescription is tailored for you. Do not alter dosage without checking with your physician.

How taken

Tablets.

Frequency and timing of doses
Once daily or once weekly; take with a full glass of water (not with juice or other drinks) 30 minutes before breakfast or at least 2 hours before or after food. Remain upright for 30 minutes after taking the drug.

Usual adult dosage range
Osteoporosis 5mg daily or 35mg once weekly or 150mg once a month.
Paget's disease 30mg daily for 2 months.

Onset of effect
It may take months to notice an improvement.

Duration of action
Some effects may persist for several weeks or months.

Diet advice
Absorption of risedronate is reduced by foods and drinks, including dairy products such as milk. The drug should be taken on an empty stomach with plain water. The diet must contain adequate calcium and vitamin D; supplements may be given.

Storage
Keep in a closed container in a cool, dry place out of the reach of children.

Missed dose
Daily dose If you missed the dose by a few hours and you can take it on an empty stomach and remain upright for 30 minutes, take the missed dose now. If not, take the next dose at the usual time next morning. *Weekly dose* Take the missed dose at the usual time on the next day. Do not take the weekly dose more than once a week.

Stopping the drug
Do not stop taking the drug without consulting your physician; the underlying condition may worsen.

Exceeding the dose
An occasional unintentional extra dose is unlikely to cause problems. Large overdoses may cause stomach problems including heartburn, irritation, and ulcers. Notify your physician at once, and try to remain upright.

SPECIAL PRECAUTIONS

Be sure to tell your physician if:
▼ You have a history of stomach problems or peptic ulcers.
▼ You have unusual bone pain.
▼ You have impaired kidney function.
▼ You have had a previous allergic reaction to risedronate or other bisphosphonates.
▼ You have problems swallowing or with your esophagus.
▼ You are unable to stay upright for 30 minutes.
▼ You have hypocalcemia.
▼ You are taking other medications.

Pregnancy
▼ Not recommended.

Breast-feeding
▼ Not recommended.

Infants and children
▼ Not recommended.

Over 60
▼ No special problems.

Driving and hazardous work
▼ No special problems.

Alcohol
▼ Avoid. May cause further stomach irritation.

POSSIBLE ADVERSE EFFECTS

The most common side effect caused by risedronate is diarrhea, which is more likely with higher doses.

Symptom/effect	Frequency		Discuss with physician		Stop taking drug now	Call physician now
	Common	Rare	Only if severe	In all cases		
Diarrhea	●		■			
Abdominal pain	●		■			
Bone pain	●		■			
New or worsening heartburn	●			■		
Nausea		●	■			
Rash/itching		●		■		
Eye pain/redness/blurred vision		●		■		
Jaw pain		●		■		
Dull pain in thigh, hip, or groin		●		■		■
Problem swallowing		●		■	▲	

INTERACTIONS

Antacids, calcium, and dairy products can decrease the absorption of risedronate. Take risedronate at least 30 minutes before any calcium tablets, calcium-rich foods or calcium-containing antacids.

PROLONGED USE

In patients with Paget's disease, courses of treatment longer than two months are not usually prescribed but repeat courses may be required. When used to treat or prevent osteoporosis, risedronate may be taken safely long-term.

Monitoring Blood and urine tests may be carried out at intervals. Your doctor may monitor your bone mineral density.

RISPERIDONE

Product names Apo-Risperidone, CO Risperidone, ratio-Risperidone, Risperdal, Risperdal Consta, and others
Used in the following combined preparations None

GENERAL INFORMATION

Risperidone is used to treat patients with acute psychiatric disorders, and long-term psychotic illness such as schizophrenia. It is effective for relieving "positive" symptoms (such as hostility, and hallucinations) and "negative" symptoms (such as emotional and social withdrawal). It may also help with other symptoms often associated with schizophrenia, such as depression and anxiety. Risperidone has less of a *sedative* effect and is less likely to cause movement disorders as a *side effect* than some other antipsychotics.

INFORMATION FOR USERS

Your drug prescription is tailored for you. Do not alter dosage without checking with your physician.

How taken

Tablets, oral disintegrating tablets, liquid.

Frequency and timing of doses
1–2 x daily.

Usual adult dosage range
Schizophrenia and related disorders 2mg daily (starting dose) increasing gradually to 4–6mg daily (usual maintenance dose); maximum 10mg daily.

Onset of effect
Tablets Within 2–3 days, but may take up to 4 weeks before maximum effect is seen.

Duration of action
Approximately 2 days.

Diet advice
None.

Storage
Keep in a closed container in a cool, dry place out of the reach of children. Protect from light.

Missed dose
Take as soon as you remember. If your next dose is due within 3 hours, take a single dose now and skip the next.

Stopping the drug
Do not stop taking the drug without consulting your physician; symptoms may recur.

Exceeding the dose
An occasional unintentional extra dose is unlikely to cause problems. If larger doses have been taken, notify your physician.

SPECIAL PRECAUTIONS

Be sure to tell your physician if:
▼ You have liver or kidney problems.
▼ You have dementia.
▼ You have/had pituitary or breast cancer.
▼ You have heart or circulation problems.
▼ You have had epileptic seizures.
▼ You have Parkinson's disease.
▼ You are taking other medications.

Pregnancy
▼ Short-term nervous system problems may occur in babies when the drug is taken in the third trimester. Discuss with your physician.

Breast-feeding
▼ The drug probably passes into breast milk. Discuss with your physician.

Infants and children
▼ Not recommended under 15 years.

Over 60
▼ Reduced dose necessary. Use with caution in those with dementia.

Driving and hazardous work
▼ Avoid such activities until you have learned how risperidone affects you because the drug may cause difficulty in concentration and slowed reactions.

Alcohol
▼ Avoid. Alcohol may increase the sedative effects of this drug.

Surgery and general anesthetics
▼ Risperidone treatment may need to be stopped before you have a general anesthetic. Discuss this with your physician or dentist before any operation.

POSSIBLE ADVERSE EFFECTS

Risperidone is generally well tolerated with a low incidence of movement disorders. This drug is less sedating than some of the other antipsychotics.

Symptom/effect	Frequency		Discuss with physician		Stop taking drug now	Call physician now
	Common	Rare	Only if severe	In all cases		
Insomnia/anxiety/agitation	●		■			
Headache	●		■			
Difficulty in concentration	●		■			
Weight gain	●		■			
Shakiness/tremor	●			■		
Dizziness/drowsiness		●		■		
Rash		●		■		
Unusual thirst		●		■		
High fever/rigid muscles		●		■	▲	▮

INTERACTIONS

Sedatives All drugs that have a sedative effect on the central nervous system are likely to increase any sedative effect of risperidone.

Fluoxetine This drug increases the blood levels of risperidone and the risk of side effects.

Carbamazepine This drug reduces the effects of risperidone. Other liver-*enzyme* inducing drugs, e.g., phenytoin, may have the same effect.

Drugs for parkinsonism Risperidone may reduce the effect of these drugs.

PROLONGED USE

If used long term, permanent movement disorders (*tardive dyskinesia*) may occur, although they are less likely than with many other antipsychotic drugs.

RITUXIMAB

Product name Rituxan
Used in the following combined preparations None

GENERAL INFORMATION

Rituximab is a monoclonal antibody (p.141) that suppresses the immune system and reduces inflammation. It works by reducing the number of white blood cell that forms part of the immune system. It is used to treat non-Hodgkin's lymphoma (NHL), chronic lymphocytic leukemia (CLL), moderate to severe rheumatoid arthritis (RA) and severely active granulomatosis with polyangiitis (GPA). The drug is given by injection as an intravenous infusion and is administered by a physician or a nurse. Because rituximab supresses the immune system, serious infections can occur or be reactivated. Inform your physician if you have had hepatitis B or tuberculosis.

QUICK REFERENCE

Drug group Anticancer drugs (p.140)

Overdose danger rating Medium

Dependence rating Low

Prescription needed Yes

Available as generic No

INFORMATION FOR USERS

Your drug prescription is tailored for you. Do not alter dosage without checking with your physician.

How taken

Intravenous.

Frequency and timing of doses
NHL: once weekly, initially for four doses; maintenance dose: every 3 months up to 2 years. RA: 2 doses, 2 weeks apart.

Adult dosage range
Dose calculated individually.

Onset of effect
Several days.

Duration of action
Several days.

Diet advice
None.

Storage
Usually stored at 2–8°C. Protect from light.

Missed dose
As this medication is administered by your physician or nurse, it is unlikely to be missed.

Stopping the drug
Do not stop without consulting your physician; the underlying condition may worsen.

Exceeding the dose
Overdosage is unlikely since treatment is carefully monitored and supervised.

SPECIAL PRECAUTIONS

Be sure to tell your physician if:
▼ You have had a cancer of the white blood cells or of the immune system.
▼ You have an irregular heartbeat or any heart conditions.
▼ You have an infection, wound, dental problem or have had recent surgery.
▼ You have hepatitis B, tuberculosis or an infection with other viruses such as chicken pox or West Nile virus.
▼ You have had a previous allergic reaction to infusions.
▼ You have heart or lung disease.
▼ You are taking other medications.
▼ You have an autoimmune disease.

Pregnancy
▼ Not usually prescribed. Safety in pregnancy not established. Discuss with your physician.

Breast-feeding
▼ Safety not established. Discuss with your physician.

Infants and children
▼ Not recommended.

Over 60
▼ No special problems.

Driving and hazardous work
▼ Avoid until you know how rituximab affects you because it can cause dizziness and fatigue.

Alcohol
▼ Avoid excessive amounts. Alcohol may increase the risk of developing liver problems.

POSSIBLE ADVERSE EFFECTS

Infusion reactions such as fever, chills, and headache are common in the first few hours. Tell your physician immediately if you develop any of these symptoms.

Symptom/effect	Frequency		Discuss with physician		Stop taking drug now	Call physician now
	Common	Rare	Only if severe	In all cases		
Nausea/vomiting/heartburn	●		■			
Muscle, back pain/night sweats	●		■			
Burning/tingling of hands/feet	●		■			
Diarrhea	●		■			
Infections	●			■		
Sore throat, fever, chills		●		■		▮
Rash, swollen lips/tongue		●				▮
Difficulty breathing/swallowing		●				▮
Blurred vision, headache		●				▮
Irregular heartbeat		●				▮
Fast breathing/anxiety		●				▮
Chest pain/weakness		●				▮
Skin blisters, sores		●				▮
Abdominal pain		●				▮
Speech or vision changes/confusion/paralysis		●		■	▲	▮

PROLONGED USE

Any infection that develops should be treated promptly. Very rarely, a serious brain infection may develop; you should tell your physician immediately if you develop memory problems, confusion, difficulty walking, or vision problems.

Monitoring Periodic blood tests may be carried out. Body temperature, blood pressure, and heart rate may be monitored when you receive infusions.

INTERACTIONS

Biologic agents and disease modifying drugs (except methotrexate) If used together, monitor for signs of infection.

Cisplatin Caution in using this drug with rituximab as it may affect kidney function.

Antihypertensive drugs may have their blood-pressure-lowering effect enhanced when taken with rituximab.

RIVAROXABAN

Product name Xarelto
Used in the following combined preparations None

GENERAL INFORMATION

Rivaroxaban is used to prevent blood clots in the veins in those undergoing elective hip and knee replacement surgery, for stroke prevention in those with atrial fibrillation (AF), and for treatment of clots in the veins of the legs (deep vein thrombosis).

Rivaroxaban belongs to a group of drugs called anticoagulants and works by inhibiting factor Xa, which is important for clotting. Unlike other oral anticoagulants such as warfarin, routine monitoring is unnecessary.

INFORMATION FOR USERS

Your drug prescription is tailored for you. Do not alter dosage without checking with your physician.

How taken

Tablets.

Frequency and timing of doses
Prevention: Once daily.
Treatment: Usually given twice daily for 3 weeks, then once daily.

Adult dosage range
Clot prevention: 10mg.
Stroke prevention: 20mg taken with food.
Deep vein thrombosis: 20–30mg with food.

Onset of effect
Full beneficial effects may not be felt for 2 weeks.

Duration of action
Up to 12 hours. May take up to 4 weeks to see its full effect.

Diet advice
None.

Storage
Keep in a closed container in a cool, dry place out of the reach of children.

Missed dose
For once daily dosing, take a missed dose as soon as you remember on that day. Do not take two tablets in one day. For twice daily dosing, take the missed dose as soon as you remember. Do not take more than two tablets of the 15mg in one day.

Stopping the drug
Always complete your course of therapy. For long-term therapy, do not stop taking the drug without consulting your physician as it may lead to worsening of the underlying condition.

OVERDOSE ACTION

Seek immediate medical advice in all cases. Take emergency action if severe bleeding or loss of consciousness occur.

See Drug poisoning emergency guide (p.526).

SPECIAL PRECAUTIONS

Be sure to tell your physician if:
▼ You have liver problems.
▼ You have kidney problems.
▼ You have any bleeding disorders.
▼ You have had a bleeding ulcer or have an active ulcer now.
▼ You have had a stroke in the last 6 months.
▼ You are taking other medications.

Pregnancy
▼ Do not use in pregnancy.

Breast-feeding
▼ Safety not established. Not recommended.

Infants and children
▼ Safety and efficacy not established in those less than 18 years of age.

Over 60
▼ Dosage reduction not normally necessary, but dose is adjusted based on kidney function.

Driving and hazardous work
▼ Use caution. Even minor bumps can cause bad bruises and excessive bleeding.

Alcohol
▼ No special problems.

PROLONGED USE

Usually used for a specified time.
Monitoring Adverse effects of bleeding should be monitored.

POSSIBLE ADVERSE EFFECTS

The common *side effect* of rivaroxaban is bleeding, which can be life-threatening. There are many medications and herbs that can increase the risk of bleeding from rivaroxaban (see Drug Interactions).

Symptom/effect	Frequency		Discuss with physician		Stop taking drug now	Call physician now
	Common	Rare	Only if severe	In all cases		
Bleeding from the surgical site		●		■		
Bleeding gums/blood in your stool or urine		●		■		▮
Lightheadedness/dizziness		●		■		▮
Rash/hives/swelling/difficulty breathing (allergic reaction)		●			▲	▮

INTERACTIONS

Ketoconazole, itraconazole, voriconazole, posaconazole, and ritonavir can increase the levels of rivaroxaban and should not be used together.

Azithromycin and clarithromycin may increase the levels of rivaroxaban.

Rifampin, carbamazepine, St John's wort and other drugs may decrease the level of rivaroxaban.

Anticoagulants Avoid using rivaroxaban with other anticoagulants such as dabigatran, warfarin, and heparin.

Antiplatelet drugs and some herbs such as ginseng and ginko can increase the anticoagulant effect of rivaroxaban.

RIVASTIGMINE

Product names Apo-Rivastigmine, Exelon, PMS-Rivastigmine
Used in the following combined preparations None

GENERAL INFORMATION

Rivastigmine is an inhibitor of the *enzyme* anticholinesterase. This enzyme breaks down the naturally occurring *neurotransmitter* acetylcholine to limit its effects. Blocking the enzyme raises the levels of acetylcholine which, in the brain, increases alertness. It has been found that rivastigmine can improve the symptoms of mild to moderate dementia in Alzheimer's disease, or in dementia occurring at least 2 years following the diagnosis of Parkinson's disease, and is used to slow the rate of deterioration in these diseases. The drug is not currently recommended for dementia due to other causes. It is usual to assess anyone being treated with rivastigmine after about three months to decide whether the drug is helping and whether it is worth continuing the treatment. As the disease progresses, the benefit obtained may diminish.

Side effects may include agitation, confusion and depression, which could be thought due to Alzheimer's disease. Weight loss should be monitored.

INFORMATION FOR USERS

Your drug prescription is tailored for you. Do not alter dosage without checking with your physician.

How taken

Capsules, liquid.

Frequency and timing of doses
2 x daily.

Usual adult dosage range
3mg daily (starting dose); 6–12mg daily (maintenance dose).

Onset of effect
30–60 minutes.

Duration of action
8–12 hours.

Diet advice
None.

Storage
Keep in a closed container in a cool, dry place out of the reach of children.

Missed dose
Take as soon as you remember. If your next dose is due within 4 hours, take a single dose now and skip the next. A carer should be overseeing the taking of tablets.

Stopping the drug
Do not stop the drug without consulting your physician; symptoms may recur.

Exceeding the dose
An occasional unintentional extra dose is unlikely to be a problem. Large overdoses may cause nausea, vomiting, and diarrhea. Notify your physician.

SPECIAL PRECAUTIONS

Be sure to tell your physician if:
▼ You have a heart problem.
▼ You have liver or kidney problems.
▼ You have asthma or respiratory problems.
▼ You have a history of peptic ulcers.
▼ You have had an epileptic seizure.
▼ You have a low body weight.
▼ You are taking other medications.

Pregnancy
▼ Safety in pregnancy not established.

Breast-feeding
▼ Not recommended.

Infants and children
▼ Not recommended.

Over 60
▼ No special problems.

Driving and hazardous work
▼ Your underlying condition may make such activities inadvisable. Discuss with your physician.

Alcohol
▼ Avoid. Alcohol increases the sedative effects of rivastigmine.

Surgery and general anesthetics
▼ Treatment with rivastigmine may need to be stopped before you have a general anesthetic. Discuss this with your physician or dentist before any operation.

POSSIBLE ADVERSE EFFECTS

Adverse effects include mental changes and intestinal problems. Although common, these effects are usually quite mild. However, women may be more susceptible to nausea, vomiting, and weight loss.

Symptom/effect	Frequency		Discuss with physician		Stop taking drug now	Call physician now
	Common	Rare	Only if severe	In all cases		
Reduced appetite/weight loss	●			■		
Nausea/abdominal pain	●			■		
Agitation/confusion/depression	●			■		
Drowsiness/dizziness	●			■		
Weakness/trembling	●			■		
Headache/insomnia	●		■			
Sweating/tiredness	●		■			
Convulsions		●		■	▲	■

INTERACTIONS

General note Rivastigmine is a relatively new drug and known interactions with other drugs are not fully established. If you notice changes in the effect of the drug after taking or stopping other medications, discuss this with your physician.

Muscle relaxants used in surgery Rivastigmine may increase the effects of some muscle relaxants, but it may also block the effects of some others.

Anticholinergics may decrease the effectiveness of rivastigmine.

Succinylcholine Rivastigmine may increase the effect of this drug.

PROLONGED USE

May be continued for as long as there is benefit. Stopping the drug leads to a gradual loss of the improvements.

Monitoring Checks at 6-monthly intervals may be performed to test whether the drug is still providing some benefit.

RIZATRIPTAN

Product names CO Rizatriptan ODT, Maxalt, Maxalt RPD
Used in the following combined preparations None

GENERAL INFORMATION

Rizatriptan is a highly effective drug for migraine, usually given when people fail to respond to analgesics (such as ASA and acetaminophen). The drug is effective in the treatment of acute migraine attacks, whether or not they are preceded by an aura, but is not meant to be taken regularly to prevent attacks. Rizatriptan is also used for the acute treatment of cluster headache

(a form of migraine headache). It should be taken as soon as possible after the onset of the attack. Rizatriptan relieves the symptoms of migraine by preventing the dilation of blood vessels in the brain that causes the attack.

The recommended daily maximum is 20mg per day. If you need to use rizatriptan for more than 10 days per month, discuss this with your physician.

QUICK REFERENCE

Drug group Drugs for migraine (p.73)

Overdose danger rating Medium

Dependence rating Low

Prescription needed Yes

Available as generic Yes

INFORMATION FOR USERS

Your drug prescription is tailored for you. Do not alter dosage without checking with your physician.

How taken

Tablets, rapidly disintegrating tablet-wafer (RPD).

Frequency and timing of doses
Should be taken as soon as possible after the onset of an attack. However, it is equally effective at whatever stage it is taken. The dose may be repeated once no sooner than TWO HOURS AFTER; no more than 20mg should be taken in any 24 hour period. RPD to be placed on the tongue (will dissolve).

Usual adult dosage range
Tablets or wafers usual dose: 5mg; some may require 10mg (maximum 24 hour dose: 20mg).

Onset of effect
1–2.5 hours.

Duration of action
3–6 hours.

Diet advice
None unless otherwise advised.

Storage
Keep in a closed container in a cool, dry place out of the reach of children. Protect from light.

Missed dose
Not applicable (taken only to treat a migraine attack).

Stopping the drug
Taken only to treat a migraine attack.

Exceeding the dose
An occasional unintentional extra dose is unlikely to cause concerns. But if you notice any unusual symptoms or if a large overdose has been taken, notify your physician.

SPECIAL PRECAUTIONS

Be sure to tell your physician if:
▼ You have liver or kidney problems.
▼ You have heart problems.
▼ You have high blood pressure.
▼ You have high cholesterol.
▼ You have had a heart attack, stroke or have heart rhythm problems.
▼ You have angina.
▼ You have phenylketonuria.
▼ You are allergic to some medicines or other triptans.
▼ You have ever had temporary paralysis or tingling during a migraine.
▼ You are taking other medications.

 Pregnancy
▼ Safety in pregnancy not established. Discuss with your physician.

 Breast-feeding
▼ Safety in breast-feeding not established. Discuss with your physician.

 Infants and children
▼ Not recommended.

 **Over 60**
▼ Not recommended for patients over 65 years of age.

 Driving and hazardous work
▼ Avoid such activities until you have learned how rizatriptan affects you because the drug can cause drowsiness and fatigue.

 Alcohol
▼ No special problems, but some drinks may provoke migraine in some people (p.69).

Surgery and general anesthetics
▼ Notify your physician or dentist if you have used rizatriptan within 48 hours prior to surgery.

POSSIBLE ADVERSE EFFECTS

Many of the *adverse effects* will disappear after about 1 hour as your body becomes adjusted to the medicine. If the symptoms persist or are severe, contact your physician.

Symptom/effect	Frequency		Discuss with physician		Stop taking drug now	Call physician now
	Common	Rare	Only if severe	In all cases		
Nausea	●		■			
Drowsiness/dizziness	●		■			
Tiredness	●		■			
Headache	●		■			
Dry mouth	●		■			
Chest pain		●		■		▐
Mental/mood changes		●		■		▐
Vision changes		●		■		▐
Cold/tingling/numb hand		●		■		▐

INTERACTIONS

Propranolol, SSRI type of antidepressants These drugs may increase the effect of rizatriptan. A lower dose of rizatriptan is recommended for those on these medications. Discuss with your physician or pharmacist.

Almotriptan, dihydroergotamine, eletriptan, ergotamine, methysergide, naratriptan, sumatriptan, zolmitriptan Rizatriptan should not be taken within 24 hours of having used one of these drugs.

Moclobemide, phenelzine, tranylcypromine Rizatriptan should not be used within 2 weeks of having used these drugs.

PROLONGED USE

Rizatriptan should not be used continuously to prevent migraine but only to treat migraine attacks.

ROSIGLITAZONE

Product name Avandia
Used in the following combined preparation Avandamet

GENERAL INFORMATION

Rosiglitazone is used to treat Type 2 diabetes when all other oral antidiabetic agents have not resulted in adequate control or when other agents are not tolerated. It works by reducing insulin resistance in fatty tissue, skeletal muscle, and in the liver, which leads to a reduction of blood glucose levels. The effects appear gradually and reach their full extent in about 8 weeks.

The drug is usually prescribed with metformin or a sulfonylurea (p.128)

if metformin is contraindicated. The combined treatment can produce a significant improvement in diabetic control. Rosiglitazone works better in obese diabetics, although it often causes weight gain.

Rosiglitazone is not approved for use with insulin. Generally this drug is not used in individuals with heart failure, heart disease, or severe liver disease.

INFORMATION FOR USERS

Your drug prescription is tailored for you. Do not alter dosage without checking with your physician.

How taken

Tablets.

Frequency and timing of doses
1–2 x daily.

Usual adult dosage range
4–8mg daily.

Onset of effect
60 minutes; it can take 8 weeks for full effects to appear.

Duration of action
12–24 hours.

Diet advice
An individualized diabetic diet must be maintained. Follow your physician's advice.

Storage
Keep in a closed container in a cool dry place out of the reach of children.

Missed dose
Take as soon as you remember. If your next dose is due within 2 hours, take a single dose now and skip the next.

Stopping the drug
Do not stop without consulting your physician; the underlying condition may worsen.

OVERDOSE ACTION

 Seek immediate medical advice in all cases. Take emergency action if loss of consciousness occurs.

See Drug poisoning emergency guide (p.526).

SPECIAL PRECAUTIONS

Be sure to tell your physician if:
▼ You have liver problems.
▼ You are anemic.
▼ You have heart failure, angina, or have had heart attack.
▼ You have severe kidney failure.
▼ You are taking other medications.
▼ You are not using birth control.
▼ You have shortness of breath or are easily fatigued.
▼ You have osteoporosis or a decrease in bone mineral density.

 Pregnancy
▼ Safety not established. Discuss with your physician.

 Breast-feeding
▼ Safety not established. Discuss with your physician.

 Infants and children
▼ Not recommended in those younger than 18 years of age.

 Over 60
▼ No special problems.

 Driving and hazardous work
▼ No known problems.

 Alcohol
▼ No known problems.

POSSIBLE ADVERSE EFFECTS

Fatigue and weakness (as a result of anemia) and weight gain (even on a strict diabetic diet) are two of the more common *side effects* of rosiglitazone.

Symptom/effect	Frequency		Discuss with physician		Stop taking drug now	Call physician now
	Common	Rare	Only if severe	In all cases		
Indigestion/flatulence	●		■			
Fatigue/weakness	●			■		
Headache	●			■		
Weight gain	●			■		
Nausea/abdominal pain		●	■			■
Dark urine		●		■		
Dizziness/pins and needles		●		■		
Sleepiness		●		■		
Edema (swelling)		●		■		■
Painful breathing/night cough		●		■		
Blurred vision		●		■		

PROLONGED USE

Rosiglitazone, like other antidiabetic drugs, is used indefinitely.

Monitoring Periodic blood tests of liver function and hemoglobin levels will be performed. Heart performance will be monitored regularly. Weight will be measured at intervals

INTERACTIONS

Gemfibrozil, ritonavir, and ACE inhibitors may increase the effects of rosiglitazone.

Cholestyramine and colestipol can decrease absorption of rosiglitazone.

ROSUVASTATIN

Product names Crestor, Sandoz Rosuvastatin, Teva-Rosuvastatin
Used in the following combined preparations None

GENERAL INFORMATION

Rosuvastatin is a "statin" lipid-lowering drug that blocks the action of an *enzyme* needed for the formation of cholesterol in the liver, resulting in lower blood levels of cholesterol. It is more potent than other statins and can achieve lower cholesterol levels than other statins. The drug is prescribed for people who have not responded to a special diet or less potent statins, and are at risk of developing or have existing coronary heart disease.

Rosuvastatin is usually taken once a day, with or without food, and should be taken at the same time daily. The drug should be continued even when cholesterol levels are normal as the benefits seen with this class of drugs are long-term. *Side effects* are usually mild. Rosuvastatin may raise the levels of various liver enzymes. These enzymes are monitored periodically and do not usually indicate serious liver damage. People of Asian origin are given lower starting doses because the drug behaves more potently in them.

QUICK REFERENCE

Drug group Lipid-lowering drugs (p.89)

Overdose danger rating Medium

Dependence rating Low

Prescription needed Yes

Available as generic Yes

INFORMATION FOR USERS

Your drug prescription is tailored for you. Do not alter dosage without checking with your physician.

How taken

Tablets.

Frequency and timing of doses
Once daily at night.

Adult dosage range
5–40mg daily (5–20mg for patients of Asian origin).

Onset of effect
2–4 weeks to see a change in cholesterol levels.

Duration of action
Up to 24 hours.

Diet advice
A diet low in saturated fat and cholesterol.

Storage
Keep in a closed container in a cool, dry place out of the reach of children.

Missed dose
If you miss a dose, take it as soon as you remember. If it is near the time of the next dose, skip the missed dose and resume your usual dosing schedule.

Stopping the drug
Do not stop the drug without consulting your physician. Stopping the drug may lead to worsening of the underlying condition.

Exeeding the dose
An occasional unintentional extra dose is unlikely to cause problems. Large overdoses may cause liver problems. Notify your physician.

SPECIAL PRECAUTIONS

Be sure to tell your physician if:
▼ You have liver or kidney problems.
▼ You have eye or vision problems.
▼ You have a personal or family history of muscle problems.
▼ You have a thyroid disorder.
▼ You have had problems with alcohol abuse.
▼ You are of Asian origin.
▼ You have porphyria.
▼ You have angina or high blood pressure.
▼ You are taking other medications.

Pregnancy
▼ Contraindicated in pregnancy.

Breast-feeding
▼ Safety not established.
Discuss with your physician.

Infants and children
▼ Not recommended.

Over 60
▼ No special problems.
Dose may need to be adjusted based on kidney function.

Driving and hazardous work
▼ No special problems.

Alcohol
▼ Avoid excessive amounts.
Alcohol may increase the risk of developing liver problems with this drug.

POSSIBLE ADVERSE EFFECTS

Most *adverse effects* are usually mild and transient. However, if you develop muscle tenderness, pain, or weakness, consult your physician at once.

Symptom/effect	Frequency		Discuss with physician		Stop taking drug now	Call physician now
	Common	Rare	Only if severe	In all cases		
Abdominal pain	●		■			
Nausea/flatulence	●		■			
Constipation/diarrhea	●		■			
Headache/sleep disturbance	●		■			
Rash		●		■	▲	
Jaundice		●		■	▲	▌
Muscle pain/weakness		●		■	▲	▌

INTERACTIONS

Antacids These may decrease the amount of rosuvastatin that is absorbed. Take antacid at least 2 hours after taking rosuvastatin.

Cyclosporine and gemfibrozil Both can increase the level of rosuvastatin in the blood and increase the risk for adverse effects; dosage adjustment is recommended.

Estrogens Rosuvastatin increases blood levels of some of these drugs.

Warfarin Rosuvastatin may enhance the effect of warfarin. INR should be monitored before starting rosuvastatin and periodically after.

Lopinavir/ritonavir These drugs can increase the level of rosuvastatin and increase its adverse effects.

Anti-HIV drugs may increase the risk of muscle damage when taken with rosuvastatin.

PROLONGED USE

Prolonged treatment can adversely affect liver function.

Monitoring Regular blood tests to test for muscle toxicity and assess liver function are recommended.

SALBUTAMOL

Product names Airomir, Ventodisks, Ventolin, and others
Used in the following combined preparations Combivent UDV, Mylan-Combo Sterinebs, and others

GENERAL INFORMATION

Salbutamol is a *sympathomimetic bronchodilator* used to treat conditions such as chronic obstructive pulmonary disease (COPD) and asthma, in which the airways become constricted. Although it can be taken by mouth, inhalation is more effective because the drug is delivered directly to the bronchioles, thus giving rapid relief, allowing smaller doses, and causing fewer *side effects*. If you need to use inhaled salbutamol more than 3 times a week, or have to use it at night, you will probably also be prescribed an inhaled corticosteroid to improve control of your asthma.

Compared with some similar drugs, salbutamol has little stimulant effect on the heart rate and blood pressure, making it safer for people with heart problems or high blood pressure. Because it relaxes the muscles of the uterus, it may also be used to prevent premature labour.

QUICK REFERENCE

Drug group Bronchodilators (p.76) and drugs to treat asthma (p.77)

Overdose danger rating Low

Dependence rating Low

Prescription needed Yes

Available as generic Yes

INFORMATION FOR USERS

Your drug prescription is tailored for you. Do not alter dosage without checking with your physician.

How taken

Liquid, injection, inhaler, powder for inhalation, inhalation solution.

Frequency and timing of doses
1–2 inhalations 3–4 x daily when needed (inhaler); 3–4 x daily (liquid).

Usual adult dosage range
Maximum 800mcg daily (inhaler); 6–16mg daily (by mouth).

Onset of effect
Within 5–15 minutes (inhaler); within 30–60 minutes (by mouth).

Duration of action
Up to 6 hours (inhaler); up to 8 hours (by mouth).

Diet advice
None.

Storage
Keep in a closed container in a cool, dry place out of the reach of children. Protect from light. Do not puncture or burn inhalers.

Missed dose
Take as soon as you remember if you need it. If your next dose is due within 2 hours, take a single dose now and skip the next.

Stopping the drug
Do not stop the drug without consulting your physician; symptoms may recur.

Exceeding the dose
An occasional unintentional extra dose is unlikely to be a cause for concern. But if you notice any unusual symptoms, or if a large overdose has been taken, notify your physician.

SPECIAL PRECAUTIONS

Be sure to tell your physician if:
▼ You have heart problems.
▼ You have high blood pressure.
▼ You have an overactive thyroid gland.
▼ You are taking other medications.

Pregnancy
▼ No evidence of risk when used to treat asthma, or to treat or prevent premature labour. Discuss with your physician.

Breast-feeding
▼ The drug passes into the breast milk, but at normal doses adverse effects on the baby are unlikely. Discuss with your physician.

Infants and children
▼ Reduced dose necessary.

Over 60
▼ Use cautiously in those with cardiovascular disease.

Driving and hazardous work
▼ Avoid such activities until you have learned how salbutamol affects you because the drug can cause tremors.

Alcohol
▼ No known problems.

POSSIBLE ADVERSE EFFECTS

Muscle tremor, which particularly affects the hands, anxiety, and restlessness are the most common *adverse effects*. Palpitations and headache are rare.

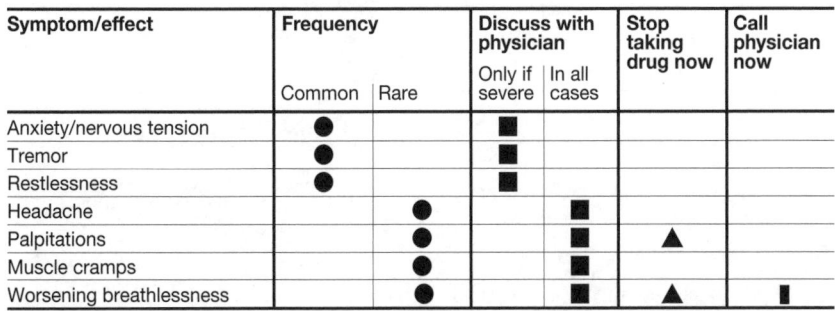

Symptom/effect	Frequency		Discuss with physician		Stop taking drug now	Call physician now
	Common	Rare	Only if severe	In all cases		
Anxiety/nervous tension	●		■			
Tremor	●		■			
Restlessness	●		■			
Headache		●		■		
Palpitations		●		■	▲	
Muscle cramps		●		■		
Worsening breathlessness		●		■	▲	■

INTERACTIONS

Theophylline There is a risk of low potassium levels in the blood occurring if this drug is taken with salbutamol.

Monoamine oxidase inhibitors (MAOIs) can interact with salbutamol to produce a dangerous rise in blood pressure.

Other sympathomimetic drugs may increase the effects of salbutamol, thereby also increasing the risk of adverse effects.

Beta blockers Drugs in this group may reduce the action of salbutamol.

PROLONGED USE

No problems expected. However, you should contact your physician if you find you are needing to use your salbutamol inhaler more than usual. Failure to respond to the drug may be a result of worsening asthma that requires urgent medical attention.

Monitoring Periodic blood tests for potassium may be needed in people on high-dose treatment with salbutamol combined with other asthma drugs and/or diuretics.

SALMETEROL

Product name Serevent
Used in the following combined preparation Advair

GENERAL INFORMATION

Salmeterol is a *sympathomimetic bronchodilator* used to treat conditions, such as asthma, chronic obstructive pulmonary disorder (COPD), and bronchospasm, in which the airways become constricted. Its advantage over salbutamol (p.429) is that it is longer acting. In asthma, it is used as add-on therapy to an inhaled corticosteroid.

Salmeterol relaxes the muscle surrounding the airways in the lungs but, because of its slow onset of effect, it is not used for immediate relief of symptoms of asthma. It is prescribed to prevent attacks, however, and can be helpful in preventing night-time asthma.

Taken by inhalation, salmeterol is delivered directly to the airways. This allows smaller doses to be taken and reduces the risk of *adverse effects*.

INFORMATION FOR USERS

Your drug prescription is tailored for you. Do not alter dosage without checking with your physician.

How taken

Inhaler, powder for inhalation.

Frequency and timing of doses
2 x daily.

Usual adult dosage range
100mcg daily (1 inhalation twice daily).

Onset of effect
10–20 minutes.

Duration of action
12 hours.

Diet advice
None.

Storage
Keep in a cool, dry place out of the reach of children.

Missed dose
Take as soon as you remember. If your next dose is due within 4 hours, take a single dose now and skip the next.

Stopping the drug
Do not stop the drug without consulting your physician; symptoms may recur.

Exceeding the dose
An occasional unintentional extra dose is unlikely to be a cause for concern. But if you notice any unusual symptoms, or if a large overdose has been taken, notify your physician.

SPECIAL PRECAUTIONS

Be sure to tell your physician if:
▼ You have heart problems.
▼ You have high blood pressure.
▼ You have an overactive thyroid.
▼ You are taking other medications.

Pregnancy
▼ No evidence of risk when used to treat asthma. Discuss with your physician.

Breast-feeding
▼ The drug passes into the breast milk, but at normal doses adverse effects on the baby are unlikely. Discuss with your physician.

Infants and children
▼ Reduced dose necessary. Not recommended for children under 4 years.

Over 60
▼ No special problems.

Driving and hazardous work
▼ No special problems.

Alcohol
▼ No known problems.

POSSIBLE ADVERSE EFFECTS

Side effects are usually mild. If wheezing and breathlessness suddenly worsen after using the inhaler (paradoxical bronchospasm), stop taking the drug and notify your physician immediately.

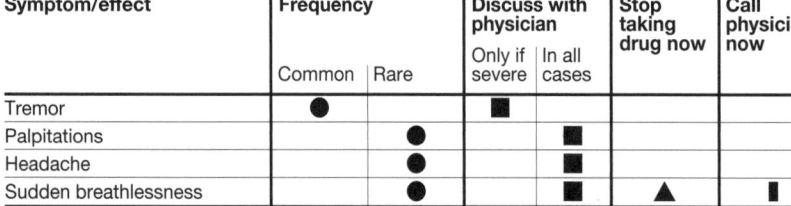

Symptom/effect	Frequency		Discuss with physician		Stop taking drug now	Call physician now
	Common	Rare	Only if severe	In all cases		
Tremor	●		■			
Palpitations		●		■		
Headache		●		■		
Sudden breathlessness		●		■	▲	▮

INTERACTIONS

Oral corticosteroids, theophylline, and diuretics There is an increased risk of low blood potassium levels when high doses of salmeterol are taken with these drugs.

Monoamine oxidase inhibitors (MAOIs) can interact with salmeterol to produce a dangerous rise in blood pressure.

Beta blockers may reduce the action of salmeterol.

Other sympathomimetic drugs may increase the effects of salmeterol, thereby also increasing the risk of adverse effects.

PROLONGED USE

Monitoring Periodic blood tests may be carried out in select individuals to monitor potassium levels.

SELEGILINE

Product names Apo-Selegiline, Mylan-Selegiline, Nu-Selegiline, Teva-Selegiline
Used in the following combined preparations None

GENERAL INFORMATION

Selegiline, also known as deprenyl, is an inhibitor of an *enzyme* in the brain called monoamine oxidase type B (MAO-B). It is used alone or together with levodopa or levodopa-carbidopa combination to treat Parkinson's disease. In patients newly diagnosed with Parkinson's disease, selegiline may delay the need to start levodopa treatment. In combination with levodopa, it works to increase and extend the effects of levodopa.

At usual doses of up to 10mg, there are no dietary restrictions. With doses above 10mg, the risk of dangerous reactions, such as sudden elevation of blood pressure, is increased if selegiline is taken with foods that are high in tyramine content.

INFORMATION FOR USERS

Your drug prescription is tailored for you. Do not alter dosage without checking with your physician.

How taken

Tablets.

Frequency and timing of doses
2 x daily (breakfast and lunch).

Usual adult dosage range
2.5–10mg daily.

Onset of effect
30 minutes to 2 hours.

Duration of action
Variable.

Diet advice
For doses over 10mg/day, avoid foods high in tyramine (mature cheeses, pickled herring, red wine, beer).

Storage
Keep in a cool, dry place out of the reach of children. Protect from light.

Missed dose
Take as soon as you remember. If your next dose is due within 2 hours, take a single dose now and skip the next.

Stopping the drug
Do not stop the drug without consulting your physician; symptoms may recur.

OVERDOSE ACTION

Seek immediate medical advice in all cases. Take emergency action if chest pain or loss of consciousness occurs.

See Drug poisoning emergency guide (p.526).

POSSIBLE ADVERSE EFFECTS

The *adverse effects* associated with selegiline, when taken in combination with levodopa, are usually related to excess levodopa and may require a dosage adjustment. Severe headache, nausea, and/or vomiting or unexplained sweating require immediate medical attention.

Symptom/effect	Frequency		Discuss with physician		Stop taking drug now	Call physician now
	Common	Rare	Only if severe	In all cases		
Nausea/abdominal pain	●		■			
Dizziness/faintness/headache	●		■			
Confusion/hallucinations		●		■		▮
Dry mouth		●	■			
Palpitations/chest pains		●		■	▲	▮
Diarrhea		●		■		
Insomnia/vivid dreams		●		■		

INTERACTIONS

General note Because of the wide range of possible drug interactions, do not take any medication, whether prescription or nonprescription, without first consulting your physician or *pharmacist*.

Oral contraceptives and clopidogrel can increase the effect of selegiline.

Dextromethorphan, SSRIs, and tricyclic antidepressants may cause severe and dangerous reactions when combined with selegiline. Allow at least 14 days after stopping these drugs before taking selegiline.

Fluoxetine Wait 5 weeks after stopping this drug before taking selegiline.

Meperidine should not be used with selegiline.

SPECIAL PRECAUTIONS

Be sure to tell your physician if:
▼ You have impaired liver function.
▼ You have a peptic ulcer.
▼ You have tremors, psychosis, or severe dementia.
▼ You are taking other medications.

Pregnancy
▼ Safety in pregnancy not established. Discuss with your physician.

Breast-feeding
▼ It is not known if the drug passes into the breast milk. Discuss with your physician.

Infants and children
▼ Not recommended.

Over 60
▼ Increased likelihood of adverse effects. Reduced dose may therefore be necessary.

Driving and hazardous work
▼ Avoid such activities until you have learned how the drug affects you; it can cause dizziness.

Alcohol
▼ Avoid. Alcohol may increase the risk of adverse effects.

Surgery and general anesthetics
▼ Selegiline treatment should be withdrawn at least 2 weeks before you have a general anesthetic and some dental treatments. Discuss this with your physician or dentist before any surgery.

PROLONGED USE

No problems expected.

SERTRALINE

Product names Teva-Sertraline, Zoloft, and others
Used in the following combined preparations None

GENERAL INFORMATION

Sertraline is a member of the group of antidepressants called selective serotonin re-uptake inhibitors (SSRIs). These drugs tend to cause less sedation and have different *side effects* from older types of antidepressants. Sertraline elevates mood, increases energy levels, and restores interest in everyday activities. It is used to treat depression, including accompanying anxiety, panic disorder, and obsessive-compulsive disorder. Sertraline is also prescribed for post-traumatic stress disorder.

The drug is usually stopped gradually, because symptoms such as headache, nausea, and dizziness may occur if sertraline is withdrawn suddenly.

INFORMATION FOR USERS

Your drug prescription is tailored for you. Do not alter dosage without checking with your physician.

How taken

Capsules.

Frequency and timing of doses
Once daily, with meal.

Usual adult dosage range
50–200mg daily.

Onset of effect
Some benefits may appear within 14 days, but full effects may take up to 4 weeks.

Duration of action
24 hours.

Diet advice
None.

Storage
Keep in a closed container in a cool, dry place out of the reach of children.

Missed dose
Take as soon as you remember. If your next dose is due within 8 hours, take a single dose now and skip the next.

Stopping the drug
Do not stop the drug without consulting your physician, who may supervise a gradual reduction in dosage.

Exceeding the dose
An occasional unintentional extra dose is unlikely to cause problems. Large overdoses may cause adverse effects. Notify your physician.

SPECIAL PRECAUTIONS

Be sure to tell your physician if:
▼ You have long-term liver or kidney problems.
▼ You have had epileptic seizures.
▼ You have heart problems.
▼ You have a history of bleeding disorders.
▼ You have diabetes.
▼ You have glaucoma.
▼ You have had an allergic reaction to any SSRI.
▼ You have a history of mania.
▼ You are taking other medications.

Pregnancy
▼Discuss benefits versus risks with your physician.

Breast-feeding
▼ Discuss benefits versus risks with your physician.

Infants and children
▼ Not recommended for children under 6 years. For children over 6 years with obsessive-compulsive disorder, reduced dose necessary.

Over 60
▼ No special problems.

Driving and hazardous work
▼ Avoid such activities until you know how sertraline affects you because the drug can cause drowsiness, dizziness, visual disturbances, and hallucinations.

Alcohol
▼ Avoid. SSRIs may increase the *sedative* effects of alcohol.

POSSIBLE ADVERSE EFFECTS

The most common side effects caused by sertraline are restlessness, insomnia, and gastrointestinal problems.

Symptom/effect	Frequency		Discuss with physician		Stop taking drug now	Call physician now
	Common	Rare	Only if severe	In all cases		
Nausea	●		■			
Diarrhea/loose stools	●		■			
Loss of appetite/indigestion	●		■			
Insomnia/sleepiness/anxiety	●		■			
Dizziness/tremor/confusion		●		■		
Palpitations/fainting		●		■		
Sexual dysfunction		●		■		
Rash/itching/skin eruptions		●		■	▲	▮

INTERACTIONS

General note Any drug that affects the breakdown of others in the liver may alter blood levels of sertraline, and vice versa.

St John's wort There is a danger of greatly increasing the effects of both substances.

Monoamine oxidase inhibitors (MAOIs) Sertraline's effects and toxicity are greatly increased by MAOIs.

Clozapine and haloperidol The levels and effects of these drugs are increased by sertraline.

Carbamazepine and phenytoin may decrease the effect of sertraline.

PROLONGED USE

No known problems in adults. There is a small risk of suicidal thoughts and self-harm in children and adolescents, although the drug is rarely used for this age group.

Monitoring Any person experiencing drowsiness, confusion, muscle cramps, or seizures should be monitored for low sodium levels in the blood. Under-18s should be monitored for suicidal thoughts and self-harm.

SILDENAFIL

Product names ratio-Sildenafil R, Revatio, Viagra
Used in the following combined preparations None

GENERAL INFORMATION

Sildenafil is a drug that is used to treat erectile dysfunction. It does not cause an erection directly but allows more blood to flow into the blood vessels of the penis. This drug is also used in the treatment of pulmonary arterial hypertension (PAH).

When used for erectile dysfunction, sildenafil only needs to be taken before sexual activity to produce an erection.

Because it is a vasodilator, sildenafil can cause a small fall in blood pressure while it is active, and it may increase the effect of antihypertensive drugs. The drug is not prescribed with nitrates (see p.84) because it greatly increases their effects.

QUICK REFERENCE

Drug group Drugs for erectile dysfunction (p.152)

Overdose danger rating Medium

Dependence rating Low

Prescription needed Yes

Available as generic Yes

INFORMATION FOR USERS

Your drug prescription is tailored for you. Do not alter dosage without checking with your physician.

How taken

Tablets.

Frequency and timing of doses
Erectile dysfunction (ED): maximum once daily, usually 1 hour before sexual activity; *pulmonary hypertension (PH)*: 3 x daily.

Usual adult dosage range
ED: 25–100mg; PH: 60mg.

Onset of effect
30 minutes.

Duration of action
4 hours.

Diet advice
None, although sildenafil will take longer to work after a meal, especially a high fat meal. It is absorbed faster on an empty stomach.

Storage
Keep in a closed container in a cool, dry place out of the reach of children.

Missed dose
Take the next dose when you need to. Do not use more than one dose in a 24-hour period.

Stopping the drug
For erectile dysfunction, the drug can be safely stopped as soon as it is no longer needed. For pulmonary hypertension, do not stop without consulting your physician; your condition may worsen.

Exceeding the dose
An occasional unintentional extra dose is unlikely to cause problems. Large overdoses may cause headache, dizziness, flushing, and altered vision. Notify your physician.

SPECIAL PRECAUTIONS

Be sure to tell your physician if:
- ▼ You have heart problems.
- ▼ You have had a stroke or heart attack.
- ▼ You have high or low blood pressure.
- ▼ You have sickle cell anemia.
- ▼ You have multiple myeloma.
- ▼ You have leukemia.
- ▼ You have liver or kidney problems.
- ▼ You have an inherited eye problem.
- ▼ You have an abnormality of the penis.
- ▼ You are taking a nitrate drug.
- ▼ You are taking other medications.

Pregnancy
▼ Not prescribed.

Breast-feeding
▼ Not prescribed.

Infants and children
▼ Not prescribed under 18 years, except rarely for pulmonary hypertension on specialist advice.

Over 60
▼ Reduced dose may be necessary.

Driving and hazardous work
▼ Avoid such activities until you have learned how sildenafil affects you because the drug can cause dizziness and altered vision.

Alcohol
▼ No special problems.

POSSIBLE ADVERSE EFFECTS

Most *adverse effects* of sildenafil are common. However, if priapism (a persistent, painful erection) occurs, you should discontinue the drug and consult your physician.

Symptom/effect	Frequency		Discuss with physician		Stop taking drug now	Call physician now
	Common	Rare	Only if severe	In all cases		
Headache	●			■		
Flushing	●			■		
Dizziness	●			■		
Indigestion	●			■		
Nasal congestion	●			■		
Blurred vision	●			■		
Altered colour vision	●			■		
Sudden decrease or loss of vision		●		■		▌
Persistent erection		●		■	▲	▌
Chest pain		●		■	▲	▌

PROLONGED USE

No problems expected.

INTERACTIONS

Nitrates The effects of these drugs are greatly increased by sildenafil, and they should not be used together.

Antihypertensive drugs Sildenafil may enhance the blood-pressure-lowering effect of these drugs.

Cimetidine, erythromycin, nicorandil, ketoconazole (oral), and antivirals (ritonavir) These drugs increase the blood levels and *toxicity* of sildenafil.

Other drugs for erectile dysfunction Safety not established. Not recommended.

SIMVASTATIN

Product names Simvastatin-Odan, Zocor, and others
Used in the following combined preparations None

GENERAL INFORMATION

Simvastatin is a "statin" lipid-lowering drug. It blocks the action of an *enzyme* needed for cholesterol to be manufactured in the liver, resulting in lowered blood levels of cholesterol. The drug is prescribed for people with hyper-cholesterolemia (high levels of cholesterol in the blood) who have not responded to other forms of therapy, such as a special diet, and who are at risk of developing or have existing coronary heart disease,

or stroke. At present it is used only for patients with a high cholesterol level that is not caused by another disease; these high levels are often hereditary.

Side effects are usually mild and often wear off with time. In the body, simvastatin is found mainly in the liver, and it may raise the levels of various liver enzymes. This effect does not usually indicate serious liver damage.

QUICK REFERENCE

Drug group Lipid-lowering drug (p.89)

Overdose danger rating Medium

Dependence rating Low

Prescription needed Yes

Available as generic Yes

INFORMATION FOR USERS

Your drug prescription is tailored for you. Do not alter dosage without checking with your physician.

How taken

Tablets.

Frequency and timing of doses
Once daily in the evening.

Usual adult dosage range
10–80mg daily.

Onset of effect
Within 2 weeks; full beneficial effects may not be felt for 4–6 weeks.

Duration of action
Up to 24 hours.

Diet advice
A low-fat diet is usually recommended.

Storage
Keep in a closed container in a cool, dry place out of the reach of children. Protect from light.

Missed dose
Take as soon as you remember. If your next dose is due within 8 hours, do not take the missed dose, but take the next dose on schedule.

Stopping the drug
Do not stop taking the drug without consulting your physician. Stopping the drug may lead to worsening of the underlying condition.

Exceeding the dose
An occasional unintentional extra dose is unlikely to cause problems. Large overdoses may cause liver problems. Notify your physician.

SPECIAL PRECAUTIONS

Be sure to tell your physician if:
▼ You have liver or kidney problems.
▼ You have eye or vision problems.
▼ You have muscle weakness.
▼ You have a personal or family history of muscular disorders.
▼ You have a thyroid disorder.
▼ You have had problems with alcohol abuse.
▼ You have porphyria.
▼ You have angina.
▼ You have high blood pressure.
▼ You are taking other medications.

Pregnancy
▼ Not recommended. May affect fetal development. Discuss with your physician if you are or intend to become pregnant.

Breast-feeding
▼ Safety not established. Discuss with your physician.

Infants and children
▼ Not recommended.

Over 60
▼ No special problems.

Driving and hazardous work
▼ No special problems.

Alcohol
▼ Avoid excessive amounts. Alcohol may increase the risk of developing liver problems with this drug.

POSSIBLE ADVERSE EFFECTS

Adverse effects are usually mild and do not last long. The most common are those affecting the gastrointestinal system.

Simvastatin may very rarely cause muscle problems, and any muscle pain or weakness should be reported to your physician at once.

Symptom/effect	Frequency		Discuss with physician		Stop taking drug now	Call physician now
	Common	Rare	Only if severe	In all cases		
Abdominal pain	●		■			
Constipation/diarrhea	●		■			
Nausea/flatulence	●		■			
Headache/sleep disturbance	●		■			
Rash		●		■	▲	
Jaundice		●		■	▲	▌
Muscle pain/weakness		●		■	▲	▌
Change in cognition		●		■		▌

INTERACTIONS

Anticoagulants Simvastatin may increase the effect of these. Close monitoring dose adjustment may be required.

Grapefruit juice may increase blood levels of simvastatin.

Carbamazepine and St John's wort reduce blood levels of simvastatin. The dose of simvastatin may need to be increased.

Cyclosporine, immunosuppressants, antivirals and other lipid-lowering drugs These, given with simvastatin, can increase the risk of muscle toxicity; not usually prescribed together.

Itraconazole, ketoconazole erythromycin, protease inhibitors These, given with a statin, may increase the risk of muscle damage.

PROLONGED USE

Prolonged treatment can adversely affect liver function.

Monitoring Regular blood tests to check liver function are recommended. Tests of muscle function may be carried out if problems are suspected.

SITAGLIPTIN PHOSPHATE

Product name Januvia
Used in the following combined preparation Janumet

GENERAL INFORMATION

Sitagliptin is an oral antihyperglycemic agent that works by inhibiting an *enzyme* called dipeptidyl peptidase-4; it is also called a DPP-4 inhibitor. Sitagliptin is used to treat non-insulin-dependent diabetes mellitus (NIDDM, Type 2 diabetes) when metformin alone cannot be used to control blood glucose levels. It can also be used in combination with metformin and other oral anti-diabetic medications, such as a sulfonylurea. The drug helps to increase the insulin level when blood sugar levels are high, such as after a meal, and also decreases the amount of sugar made by the body. This drug is not recommended to be used in those with Type 1 diabetes.

QUICK REFERENCE

Drug group Antihyperglycemic agent (p.128)

Overdose danger rating High

Dependence rating Low

Prescription needed Yes

Available as generic No

INFORMATION FOR USERS

Your drug prescription is tailored for you. Do not alter dosage without checking with your physician.

How taken

Tablets.

Frequency and timing of doses
Take 1 tablet once daily.
The combination product (Janumet) is to be taken twice daily.

Usual adult dosage range
100mg.

Onset of effect
Starts to work within 1–4 hours.

Duration of action
24 hours.

Diet advice
A low-fat, low-sugar diet must be maintained; follow your physician's advice.

Storage
Keep in a closed container in a cool, dry place out of the reach of children.

Missed dose
Once daily regimen: If you remember a missed dose within 12 hours, take it as soon as you remember. If you do not remember until later, do not take the missed dose and do not double up the next one. Instead, go back to your regular schedule.

Stopping the drug
Do not stop taking the drug without consulting with your physician, as it may lead to worsening of the underlying condition.

OVERDOSE ACTION

 Seek immediate medical advice in all cases. Take emergency action if breathing difficulties occur.

See Drug poisoning emergency guide (p.526).

POSSIBLE ADVERSE EFFECTS

Low blood sugar may occur more often when sitagliptin is taken with a sulfonylurea; symptoms should be managed and reported to your physician.

Symptom/effect	Frequency		Discuss with physician		Stop taking drug now	Call physician now
	Common	Rare	Only if severe	In all cases		
Stuffy or runny nose	●		■			
Sore throat/headache	●		■			
Constipation	●		■			
Headache/drowsiness/ weakness/dizziness/ confusion/ a fast heartbeat/sweating		●		■		
Severe abdominal pain/nausea		●			▲	▮
Rash/swelling of the face/difficulty breathing		●			▲	▮

INTERACTIONS

General note May cause hypoglycemia when administered with other drugs that lower blood glucose levels.

ACE inhibitors Sitagliptin may increase the risk of facial swelling when used with ACE inhibitors.

Somatropin may decrease the effectiveness of sitagliptin.

Rifampin can drecrease the level of sitagliptin.

Beta blockers may mask symptoms of low blood sugar when taken with sitagliptin.

SPECIAL PRECAUTIONS

Be sure to tell your physician if:
▼ You have pancreatitis.
▼ You have gall stones.
▼ You have high triglyceride levels.
▼ You have any kidney or liver problems.
▼ You have congestive heart failure.
▼ You have a history of allergic reaction to sitagliptin.
▼ You drink alcohol regularly.
▼ You are taking other medications.

 Pregnancy
▼ Safety not established in pregnancy.

 Breast-feeding
▼ Safety not established in women who are breast-feeding.

 Infants and children
▼ Not recommended for those less than 18 years of age.

 Over 60
▼ Reduced dose usually needed for those over 60 based on kidney function.

 Driving and hazardous work
▼ Avoid driving and hazardous work if you have warning signs of low blood sugar.

 Alcohol
▼ Avoid alcohol as it increases the risk of low blood sugar.

PROLONGED USE

No problems expected.

Monitoring Blood glucose should be monitored.

SODIUM CROMOGLYCATE

Product names Cromolyn, Nalcrom, Nu-Cromolyn, Opticrom, Rhinaris CS Anti-allergic
Used in the following combined preparations None

GENERAL INFORMATION

Sodium cromoglycate is used primarily to prevent allergic conditions. It works by stabilizing cells that release certain substances including histamine, which causes an *allergic reaction*. It reduces redness, itching, and swelling of eyelids and also decreases sneezing and a runny nose.

The capsules are used to treat allergic reactions to certain foods and should be used along with a restriction of causative foods as much as possible.

This drug should not be used when the person has a life-threatening allergy to a specific food. The eye drops are used for allergic conjunctivitis or for conjunctivitis due to hay fever or seasonal allergies. The nasal mist inhaler is also used to prevent allergies.

QUICK REFERENCE

Drug group Anti-allergy drugs (p.109)

Overdose danger rating Low

Dependence rating Low

Prescription needed No (except oral product)

Available as generic Yes

INFORMATION FOR USERS

Follow instructions on the label. Call your physician if symptoms worsen.

How taken

Capsules, nasal mist inhaler, eye drops.

Frequency and timing of doses
Capsules 4 x daily before meals, swallowed whole or dissolved in water.
Nasal inhaler 3–6 x daily.
Eye preparations 4 x daily (drops).

Usual dosage range
800mg daily (capsules); 1 spray/nostril (inhaler); 1–2 drops in each eye per dose (eye drops).

Onset of effect
Varies with dosage, form, and condition treated. Eye conditions and allergic rhinitis may respond after a few days' treatment with drops, while chronic allergic rhinitis may take take 2–6 weeks to show improvement.

Duration of action
4–6 hours. Some effect persists for several days after treatment is stopped.

Diet advice
Capsules: you may be advised to avoid certain foods. Follow your physician's advice.

Storage
Keep in a closed container in a cool, dry place out of the reach of children. Protect from light.

Missed dose
Take as soon as you remember. If your next dose is due within 2 hours, take a single dose now and skip the next.

Stopping the drug
Do not stop the drug without consulting your physician; symptoms may recur.

Exceeding the dose
An occasional unintentional extra dose is unlikely to be a cause for concern. But if you notice any unusual symptoms, or if a large overdose has been taken, notify your physician.

SPECIAL PRECAUTIONS

Be sure to consult your physician or pharmacist before taking this drug if:
▼ You have kidney or liver problems.
▼ You are taking other medications.

Pregnancy
▼ Safety not established with oral capsules. Discuss with your physician.

Breast-feeding
▼ Safety not established with oral capsules. Use other formulations with caution. Discuss with your physician.

Infants and children
▼ Oral capsules not recommended in children under 2 years of age.

Over 60
▼ No special problems.

Driving and hazardous work
▼ No known problems.

Alcohol
▼ No known problems.

POSSIBLE ADVERSE EFFECTS

Side effects are usually mild.

Symptom/effect	Frequency		Discuss with physician		Stop taking drug now	Call physician now
	Common	Rare	Only if severe	In all cases		
Coughing/hoarseness	●		■			
Local irritation	●		■			
Nausea/diarrhea/abdominal discomfort		●	■			
Muscle weakness		●		■	▲	
Wheezing/breathlessness		●		■		
Rash (capsules)/swelling of the face, tongue, throat		●		■	▲	

PROLONGED USE

No problems expected.

INTERACTIONS

None.

SPIRONOLACTONE

Product names Aldactone, Teva-Spironolactone
Used in the following combined preparations Aldactazide, Teva-Spirozine/HCTZ

GENERAL INFORMATION

Spironolactone is a diuretic. It acts by inhibiting a *hormone* called aldosterone, which then results in an increase in the amount of urine that is passed through the kidneys. It is used in the treatment of edema (fluid retention), which can result from heart failure or liver disease (liver cirrhosis) and for hypertension (high blood pressure). It can also be used to counteract overproduction of the hormone aldosterone, which can occur with certain adrenal gland tumors.

Spironolactone causes the kidneys to conserve potassium (potassium-sparing diuretic) and should not be used when there is a high blood level of potassium. The drug is prescribed cautiously in people taking potassium supplements or those with kidney disease. When used for hypertension, it is usually combined with other diuretics.

INFORMATION FOR USERS

Your drug prescription is tailored for you. Do not alter dosage without checking with your physician.

How taken

Tablets.

Frequency and timing of doses
Once daily (with higher doses, the daily dose may be divided into two doses).

Usual adult dosage range
50–100mg (starting dose); may increase up to 200mg.

Onset of effect
Within 2–4 hours.

Duration of action
12–24 hours.

Diet advice
Avoid foods that are high in potassium; for example, dried fruit, bananas, tomatoes, and salt substitutes.

Storage
Keep in a closed container in a cool, dry place out of the reach of children.

Missed dose
If you miss a dose, take it as soon as you remember. However, if it is late in the day, do not take the missed dose. Take the next scheduled dose as usual.

Stopping the drug
Do not stop the drug without consulting your physician; symptoms may recur.

Exceeding the dose
An occasional unintentional extra dose is unlikely to be a cause for concern. But if you notice any unusual symptoms, or if a large overdose has been taken, notify your physician.

POSSIBLE ADVERSE EFFECTS

Generally well tolerated. The main problem is that potassium may be retained by the body, causing muscle weakness and numbness. Rarely, breast enlargement can occur; this is related to the length of therapy and the dose. This is usually resolved by discontinuation of spironolactone.

Symptom/effect	Frequency		Discuss with physician		Stop taking drug now	Call physician now
	Common	Rare	Only if severe	In all cases		
Nausea, vomiting	●		■			
Muscle weakness/cramps		●		■		
Breast enlargement		●		■		
Drowsiness/tiredness		●	■			

INTERACTIONS

Diuretic Spironolactone is commonly used with other diuretics; however, the effect is additive and the dose of other diuretics may need to be decreased.

Lisinopril, ramipril, etc. ACE-inhibitors such as lisinopril, ramipril, etc. can increase blood potassium and this effect will be additive to the effect of spironolactone.

Non-steroidal anti-inflammatory drugs These drugs can counteract the antihypertensive effect of spironolactone, as well as increasing the risk of potassium retention.

SPECIAL PRECAUTIONS

Be sure to tell your physician if:
▼ You have long-term liver or kidney problems.
▼ You are taking potassium supplements.
▼ You have diabetes.
▼ You are taking other medications.

Pregnancy
▼ Safety in pregnancy is not established. Also, diuretics in general may cause a reduction in the blood supply to the developing baby. Discuss with your physician.

Breast-feeding
▼ Not recommended during breast-feeding. Discuss with your physician.

Infants and children
▼ Not recommended.

Over 60
▼ Increased likelihood of adverse effects. Reduced dose necessary.

Driving and hazardous work
▼ No known problems.

Alcohol
▼ No special problems.

PROLONGED USE

Monitoring Blood tests may be carried out to monitor levels of electrolytes in the blood.

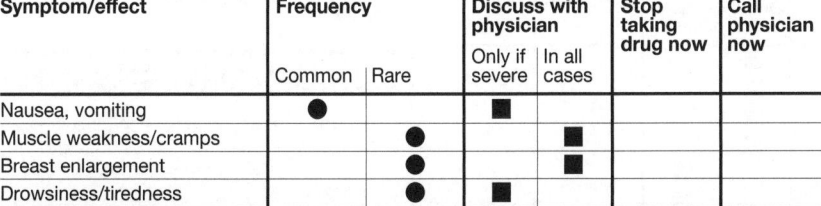

SUCRALFATE

Product names Dom-Sucralfate, Sulcrate, and others
Used in the following combined preparations None

GENERAL INFORMATION

Sucralfate, a drug partly derived from aluminium, is prescribed to treat gastric and duodenal ulcers. It is particularly used to prevent stress-induced ulcers in patients who are seriously ill. The drug does not neutralize stomach acid, but it forms a protective barrier over the ulcer that protects it from attack by digestive juices, giving it time to heal.

If it is necessary during treatment to take antacids to relieve pain, they should be taken at least half an hour before or after taking sucralfate.

There are a few reports of seriously ill patients developing bezoars (balls of indigestible material) in their stomachs while on sucralfate. The safety of the drug for long-term use has not yet been confirmed. Therefore, courses of more than 12 weeks are not recommended.

QUICK REFERENCE

Drug group Ulcer-healing drugs (p.95).

Overdose danger rating Low

Dependence rating Low

Prescription needed Yes

Available as generic Yes

INFORMATION FOR USERS

Your drug prescription is tailored for you. Do not alter dosage without checking with your physician.

How taken

Tablets, liquid.

Frequency and timing of doses
2–4 x daily, 1 hour before each meal and at bedtime, at least 2 hours after food.

Usual dosage range
2–6g daily.

Onset of effect
Some improvement may be noted after one or two doses, but it takes a few weeks for an ulcer to heal.

Duration of action
Up to 5 hours.

Diet advice
Your physician will advise if supplements are needed.

Storage
Keep in a closed container in a cool, dry place out of the reach of children.

Missed dose
Do not make up the dose you missed. Take your next dose on your original schedule.

Stopping the drug
Do not stop the drug without consulting your physician; symptoms may recur.

Exceeding the dose
An occasional unintentional extra dose is unlikely to be a cause for concern. But if you notice any unusual symptoms, or if a large overdose has been taken, notify your physician.

SPECIAL PRECAUTIONS

Be sure to tell your physician if:
▼ You have a long-term kidney problem.
▼ You are taking other medications.

Pregnancy
▼ Safety in pregnancy not established. Discuss with your physician.

Breast-feeding
▼ No evidence of risk.

Infants and children
▼ Not usually prescribed.

Over 60
▼ No special problems.

Driving and hazardous work
▼ Usually no problems, but sucralfate may cause dizziness in some people.

Alcohol
▼ Avoid. Alcohol may counteract the beneficial effect of this drug.

POSSIBLE ADVERSE EFFECTS

Most people do not experience any *adverse effects* while they are taking sucralfate. The most common is constipation, which will diminish as your body adjusts to the drug.

Symptom/effect	Frequency		Discuss with physician		Stop taking drug now	Call physician now
	Common	Rare	Only if severe	In all cases		
Indigestion	●		■			
Constipation	●		■			
Diarrhea		●	■			
Dry mouth		●	■			
Nausea		●		■		
Rash/itching		●		■		
Dizziness/vertigo		●		■		
Insomnia		●		■		

PROLONGED USE

Not usually prescribed for periods longer than 12 weeks at a time. Prolonged use may lead to deficiencies of vitamins A, D, E, and K.

INTERACTIONS

General note Sucralfate may reduce the absorption and effect of a range of drugs, including ranitidine, digoxin, phenytoin, warfarin, levothyroxine, and antibacterials. Take these and other medications at least 2 hours before or after sucralfate.

Antacids and other indigestion remedies These reduce the effectiveness of sucralfate and should be taken more than 30 minutes before or after sucralfate.

SULFAMETHOXAZOLE-TRIMETHOPRIM

Product name Septra
Used in the following combined preparations (Sulfamethoxazole-trimethoprim is a combination of two drugs)

GENERAL INFORMATION

Sulfamethoxazole-trimethoprim is a mixture of two antibacterial drugs. It is prescribed for prevention and treatment of urinary tract infections and treatment of skin, ear, and gastrointestinal infections. Sulfamethoxazole-trimethoprim is also used to treat pneumocystis pneumonia, toxoplasmosis, and the bacterial infection nocardiasis.

Although sulfamethoxazole-trimethoprim was widely prescribed in the past, its use has declined in recent years with the introduction of new, more effective, and safer drugs.

Rare but serious *adverse effects* of sulfamethoxazole-trimethoprim may occur and these include skin rashes, blood disorders, and liver or kidney damage.

QUICK REFERENCE

Drug group Antibacterial drugs (p.117)

Overdose danger rating Medium

Dependence rating Low

Prescription needed Yes

Available as generic Yes

INFORMATION FOR USERS

Your drug prescription is tailored for you. Do not alter dosage without checking with your physician.

How taken

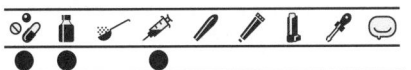

Tablets, tablets double strength (DS), liquid, injection.

Frequency and timing of doses
Normally 2 x daily, preferably with food.

Usual adult dosage range
Usually 4 tablets daily (each standard tablet is 480mg) or 2 DS daily. Higher doses may be used for the treatment of pneumocystis pneumonia, toxoplasmosis, and nocardiasis.

Onset of effect
1–4 hours.

Duration of action
24 hours.

Diet advice
Drink plenty of fluids, particularly in warm weather.

Storage
Keep in a closed container in a cool, dry place out of the reach of children. Protect from light.

Missed dose
Take as soon as you remember. If your normal dose is 480mg, double this; if it is more than 480mg, take one dose only.

Stopping the drug
Take the full course. Even if you feel better, the original infection may still be present and symptoms may recur if treatment is stopped too soon.

Exceeding the dose
An occasional unintentional extra dose is unlikely to be a cause for concern. Large overdoses may cause nausea, vomiting, dizziness, and confusion. Notify your physician.

POSSIBLE ADVERSE EFFECTS

The most common problems are nausea and rash, and itching. Other less common reactions include vomiting, diarrhea, sore tongue, and headache.

Symptom/effect	Frequency		Discuss with physician		Stop taking drug now	Call physician now
	Common	Rare	Only if severe	In all cases		
Rash/itching	●			■	▲	▮
Nausea/vomiting	●			■		
Diarrhea	●		■			
Headache	●			■		
Sore tongue/mouth ulcers		●		■	▲	▮
Jaundice		●		■	▲	▮

INTERACTIONS

Warfarin Sulfamethoxazole-trimethoprim may increase its *anticoagulant* effect; the dose of warfarin may have to be reduced. Blood-clotting status may have to be checked.

Cyclosporine Taking cyclosporine with sulfamethoxazole-trimethoprim can impair kidney function.

Phenytoin Sulfamethoxazole-trimethoprim may cause a build-up of phenytoin in the body; the dose of phenytoin may have to be reduced.

Oral antidiabetic drugs Sulfamethoxazole-trimethoprim may increase the blood sugar lowering effect of these drugs.

Amiodarone Sulfamethoxazole-trimethorpim may increase the risk of irregular heart beats when given with amiodarone.

Methotrexate Sulfamethoxazole-trimethorpim may increase the blood level of methotrexate; regular blood tests may be necessary.

SPECIAL PRECAUTIONS

Be sure to tell your physician if:
▼ You have long-term liver or kidney problems.
▼ You have a blood disorder.
▼ You have glucose-6-phosphate dehydrogenase (G6PD) deficiency.
▼ You are allergic to sulfonamide drugs.
▼ You suffer from porphyria.
▼ You are taking other medications.

Pregnancy
▼ Not usually prescribed. May cause defects in the baby. Discuss with your physician.

Breast-feeding
▼ The drug passes into the breast milk, but at normal levels adverse effects on the baby are unlikely. Discuss with your physician.

Infants and children
▼ Not recommended in infants under 6 weeks old. Reduced dose necessary in older children.

Over 60
▼ Side effects are more likely. Used only when necessary, and often in reduced dosage.

Driving and hazardous work
▼ No known problems.

Alcohol
▼ No known problems.

PROLONGED USE

Long-term use of this drug may lead to folic acid deficiency, which can cause anemia. Folic acid supplements may be needed.

Monitoring Regular blood tests are recommended.

SUMATRIPTAN

Product name Imitrex DF, Teva-Sumatriptan, and others
Used in the following combined preparations None

GENERAL INFORMATION

Sumatriptan is an effective drug for migraine, usually given when people fail to respond to analgesics (such as ASA and acetaminophen). The drug is of considerable value in the treatment of acute migraine attacks, whether or not they are preceded by an aura, but is not meant to be taken regularly to prevent attacks. Sumatriptan is also used for the acute treatment of cluster headache (a form of migraine headache). It should be taken as soon as possible after the onset of the attack, although it will still be of benefit at whatever stage of the attack it is taken.

Sumatriptan relieves the symptoms of migraine by preventing the dilation of blood vessels in the brain, which causes the attack.

INFORMATION FOR USERS

Your drug prescription is tailored for you. Do not alter dosage without checking with your physician.

How taken

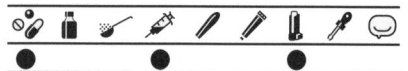

Tablets, injection, nasal spray.

Frequency and timing of doses
Should be taken as soon as possible after the onset of an attack. However, it is equally effective at whatever stage it is taken. If partial response only, the dose may be repeated once after 2 hours. The tablets should be swallowed whole with water.

Usual adult dosage range
Tablets 25–100mg per attack, up to maximum of 200mg in 24 hours if another attack occurs. *Injection* 6mg per attack, up to maximum of 12mg (two injections) in 24 hours if another attack occurs. *Nasal spray* 5–20mg per attack, up to maximum of 40mg (2 puffs) in 24 hours if another attack occurs.

Onset of effect
30 minutes (tablets);10–15 minutes (injection).

Duration of action
Tablets The maximum effect occurs after 2–4 hours.
Injection The maximum effect occurs after 1½–2 hours.

Diet advice
None unless otherwise advised.

Storage
Keep in a closed container in a cool, dry place out of the reach of children. Protect from light.

Missed dose
Not applicable, as it is taken only to treat a migraine attack.

Stopping the drug
Taken only to treat a migraine attack.

Exceeding the dose
An occasional unintentional extra tablet or injection is unlikely to cause problems. But if you notice any unusual symptoms, or if a large overdose has been taken, notify your physician.

SPECIAL PRECAUTIONS

Be sure to tell your physician if:
▼ You have liver or kidney problems.
▼ You have heart problems.
▼ You have high blood pressure.
▼ You have had a heart attack.
▼ You have angina.
▼ You are allergic to some medicines.
▼ You are taking other medications.

Pregnancy
▼ Discuss treatment options with your physician.

Breast-feeding
▼ Discuss treatment options with your physician.

Infants and children
▼ Not recommended.

Over 60
▼ Not recommended for patients over 65 years.

Driving and hazardous work
▼ Avoid such activities until you have learned how sumatriptan affects you because the drug can cause drowsiness.

Alcohol
▼ No special problems, but some drinks may provoke migraine in some people (see p.69).

Surgery and general anesthetics
▼ Notify your physician or dentist if you have used sumatriptan within 48 hours prior to surgery.

POSSIBLE ADVERSE EFFECTS

Many of the *adverse effects* will disappear after about 1 hour as your body becomes adjusted to the medicine. If the symptoms persist or are severe, contact your physician.

Symptom/effect	Frequency		Discuss with physician		Stop taking drug now	Call physician now
	Common	Rare	Only if severe	In all cases		
Pain at injection site	●		■			
Feeling of tingling/heat	●		■			
Flushing	●		■			
Feeling of heaviness/weakness	●		■			
Dizziness		●	■			
Fatigue/drowsiness		●	■			
Palpitations/chest pain		●		■	▲	▮

INTERACTIONS

Antidepressants Monoamine oxidase inhibitors (MAOIs) and some other antidepressants, such as fluvoxamine, fluoxetine, paroxetine, and sertraline, increase the risk of adverse effects with sumatriptan.

Lithium Patients taking lithium should not take sumatriptan due to the high risk of adverse effects.

Other triptans and ergot derivatives (e.g. dihydroergotamine, ergotamine) Do not use these drugs within 24 hours of using sumatriptan.

PROLONGED USE

Sumatriptan should not be used continuously to prevent migraine but only to treat migraine attacks.

TAMOXIFEN

Product names Nolvadex D, Teva-Tamoxifen, and others
Used in the following combined preparations None

GENERAL INFORMATION

Tamoxifen is an anti-estrogen drug (estrogen is a naturally occurring female sex hormone, see p.133). It is used as an anticancer drug for breast cancer because it works against estrogens. Tamoxifen works by blocking the effect of natural estrogens that stimulate the growth of tumours with estrogen receptors (estrogen-receptor-positive tumours). This reduces the risk of tumours recurring after surgical removal of the tumour.

As its effect is specific, tamoxifen has fewer *adverse effects* than most other drugs used for breast cancer. However, it may cause eye damage if high doses are taken for long periods.

INFORMATION FOR USERS

Your drug prescription is tailored for you. Do not alter dosage without checking with your physician.

How taken

Tablets.

Frequency and timing of doses
1–2 x daily.

Usual adult dosage range
20–40mg daily.

Onset of effect
Side effects may be felt within days, but beneficial effects may take 4–10 weeks.

Duration of action
Effects may be felt for several weeks after stopping the drug.

Diet advice
None.

Storage
Keep in a closed container in a cool, dry place out of the reach of children. Protect from light.

Missed dose
Take as soon as you remember. If your next dose is due within 2 hours, take a single dose now and skip the next.

Stopping the drug
Do not stop the drug without consulting your physician; stopping the drug may lead to worsening of your underlying condition.

Exceeding the dose
An occasional unintentional extra dose is unlikely to be a cause for concern. But if you notice any unusual symptoms, or if a large overdose has been taken, notify your physician.

POSSIBLE ADVERSE EFFECTS

These are rarely serious and do not usually require treatment to be stopped. Nausea, vomiting, and hot flushes are the most common reactions. There is a small risk of endometrial cancer (cancer of the uterine lining) developing, so you should notify your physician of any symptoms such as irregular vaginal bleeding as soon as possible.

Symptom/effect	Frequency		Discuss with physician		Stop taking drug now	Call physician now
	Common	Rare	Only if severe	In all cases		
Nausea/vomiting	●		■			
Hot flushes/hair loss	●		■			
Irregular vaginal bleeding	●			■		‖
Irregular vaginal discharge	●			■		‖
Swollen feet/ankles		●	■			
Bone and tumour pain		●		■		
Rash/itching		●		■		
Blurred vision/headache		●		■		

INTERACTIONS

Anticoagulants People treated with anticoagulants such as warfarin usually need a lower dose of the anticoagulant.

SSRI antidepressants may reduce the effectiveness of tamoxifen.

SPECIAL PRECAUTIONS

Be sure to tell your physician if:
▼ You are pregnant or plan to become pregnant.
▼ You have cataracts or poor eyesight.
▼ You suffer from porphyria.
▼ You have a history of venous thrombosis or stroke.
▼ You have or have had low platelets or white blood cells.
▼ You are taking other medications.

Pregnancy
▼ Not usually prescribed. May have effects on the developing baby. Discuss with your physician.

Breast-feeding
▼ Not usually prescribed. Discuss with your physician.

Infants and children
▼ Not prescribed.

Over 60
▼ No special problems.

Driving and hazardous work
▼ Do not drive until you have learned how tamoxifen affects you because the drug can cause dizziness and blurred vision.

Alcohol
▼ No known problems.

PROLONGED USE

There is a risk of damage to the eye with long-term, high-dose treatment.

There is a small increased risk of endometrial cancer and venous thrombosis with long-term treatment but these risks are far outweighed by the benefits of treatment.

Monitoring Eyesight may be tested periodically.

TAMSULOSIN

Product names Flomax CR, Sandoz Tamsulosin, and others
Used in the following combined preparations None

GENERAL INFORMATION

Tamsulosin is a selective alpha-blocker drug used to treat urinary retention due to benign prostatic hyperplasia, or BPH (enlarged prostate gland). The drug relaxes the muscle in the wall of the prostate gland, thereby increasing urine flow.

To exclude other conditions with similar symptoms, your physician will arrange for you to have a physical examination and a special blood test, which may be repeated at intervals during treatment.

Like other alpha-blockers, tamsulosin may lower blood pressure rapidly after the first dose. For this reason, the first dose should be taken at home so that, if dizziness or weakness occur, you can sit or lie down until they have disappeared.

QUICK REFERENCE

Drug group Drugs for urinary disorders (p.154)

Overdose danger rating Medium

Dependence rating Low

Prescription needed Yes

Available as generic Yes

INFORMATION FOR USERS

Your drug prescription is tailored for you. Do not alter dosage without checking with your physician.

How taken

SR capsules, extended release (ER) tablets.

Frequency and timing of doses
Once daily after breakfast.

Usual adult dosage range
400–800mcg.

Onset of effect
1–2 hours.

Duration of action
24 hours.

Diet advice
None.

Storage
Keep in a closed container in a cool, dry place out of the reach of children.

Missed dose
Taken as soon as you remember. If your next dose is due within 4 hours, take a single dose now and skip the next.

Stopping the drug
Do not stop taking the drug without consulting your physician; stopping suddenly may lead to a rise in blood pressure.

Exceeding the dose
An occasional unintentional extra dose is unlikely to cause problems. Large overdoses may produce sedation, dizziness, low blood pressure, and rapid pulse. Notify your physician immediately.

SPECIAL PRECAUTIONS

Be sure to tell your physician if:
▼ You have had low blood pressure.
▼ You have liver or kidney problems.
▼ You have heart failure.
▼ You have a history of depression.
▼ You are taking an MAOI drug.
▼ You are taking drugs for high blood pressure.
▼ You have cataract surgery planned.
▼ You are taking other medications.

Pregnancy
▼ Not prescribed.

Breast-feeding
▼ Not prescribed.

Infants and children
▼ Not prescribed.

Over 60
▼ No special problems.

Driving and hazardous work
▼ Avoid such activities until you have learned how tamsulosin affects you because the drug can cause drowsiness and dizziness.

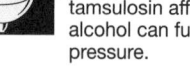

Alcohol
▼ Avoid until you know how tamsulosin affects you because alcohol can further lower blood pressure.

Surgery and general anesthetics
▼ Tamsulosin may need to be stopped. Discuss with your physician or dentist before you have any surgery.

POSSIBLE ADVERSE EFFECTS

Dizziness seems to be the most common *adverse effect*, but this usually improves after the first few doses.

Symptom/effect	Frequency		Discuss with physician		Stop taking drug now	Call physician now
	Common	Rare	Only if severe	In all cases		
Dizziness/weakness/fainting	●			■		
Ejaculatory problems	●		■			
Headache	●		■			
Drowsiness	●		■			
Palpitations	●			■		
Nausea/vomiting		●	■			
Diarrhea/constipation		●	■			
Rash/itching		●		■		

INTERACTIONS

Antidepressants, beta blockers, calcium channel blockers, and diuretics These drugs are likely to increase the blood-pressure-lowering effect of tamsulosin.

PROLONGED USE

No special problems.

TEMAZEPAM

Product names Apo-Temazepam, Novo-Temazepam, Restoril, and others
Used in the following combined preparations None

GENERAL INFORMATION

Temazepam belongs to a group of drugs known as the benzodiazepines. The actions and *adverse effects* of this group of drugs are described more fully under Anti-anxiety drugs (p.67).

Temazepam is used in the short-term treatment of insomnia. Because it is a short-acting drug compared with some other benzodiazepines, it is less likely to cause drowsiness and/or lightheadedness the following day.

For this reason, the drug is not usually effective in preventing early wakening, but hangover is less common than with other benzodiazepines.

Like other benzodiazepine drugs, temazepam can be habit-forming if taken regularly over a long period. Its effects also grow weaker with time. For these reasons, treatment with temazepam is usually only continued for a few days at a time.

QUICK REFERENCE

Drug group Benzodiazepine sleeping drug (p.66)

Overdose danger rating Medium

Dependence rating High

Prescription needed Yes

Available as generic Yes

INFORMATION FOR USERS

Your drug prescription is tailored for you. Do not alter dosage without checking with your physician.

How taken

Capsules.

Frequency and timing of doses
Once daily, 30 minutes before bedtime.

Usual adult dosage range
10–40mg.

Onset of effect
15–40 minutes, or longer.

Duration of action
6–8 hours.

Diet advice
None.

Storage
Keep in a closed container in a cool, dry place out of the reach of children. Protect from light.

Missed dose
If you fall asleep without having taken a dose and wake some hours later, do not take the missed dose. If necessary, return to your normal dose schedule the following night.

Stopping the drug
If you have been taking the drug continuously for less than 2 weeks, it can be safely stopped as soon as you no longer need it. If you have been taking the drug for longer, consult your physician, who may supervise a gradual reduction in dosage. Stopping abruptly may lead to *withdrawal symptoms* (see p.66).

Exceeding the dose
An occasional unintentional extra dose is unlikely to be a cause for concern. Large overdoses may cause severe drowsiness and breathing problems. Notify your physician.

POSSIBLE ADVERSE EFFECTS

The principal adverse effects of this drug are related to its *sedative* and tranquillizing properties. These effects normally diminish after the first few days of treatment.

Symptom/effect	Frequency		Discuss with physician		Stop taking drug now	Call physician now
	Common	Rare	Only if severe	In all cases		
Daytime drowsiness	●		■			
Dizziness/unsteadiness		●		■		
Headache		●		■		
Vivid dreams/nightmares		●		■		
Forgetfulness/confusion		●		■		■

INTERACTIONS

Sedatives All drugs that have a sedative effect on the central nervous system are likely to increase the sedative properties of temazepam. Such drugs include other anti-anxiety and sleeping drugs, *opioid* analgesics, antidepressants, antihistamines, and antipsychotics.

SPECIAL PRECAUTIONS

Be sure to tell your physician if:
▼ You have severe respiratory disease.
▼ You suffer from porphyria.
▼ You suffer from depression.
▼ You have liver or kidney problems.
▼ You have myasthenia gravis.
▼ You have had problems with alcohol or drug abuse.
▼ You are taking other medications.

Pregnancy
▼ Not usually recommended; may cause adverse effects on the newborn baby at the time of delivery. Discuss with your physician.

Breast-feeding
▼ The drug passes into the breast milk, and should be avoided during breast-feeding if possible. Discuss with your physician.

Infants and children
▼ Not recommended.

Over 60
▼ Reduced dose may be necessary. Increased likelihood of adverse effects.

Driving and hazardous work
▼ Avoid such activities until you have learned how temazepam affects you because the drug can cause reduced alertness and slowed reactions.

Alcohol
▼ Avoid. Alcohol may increase the sedative effect of this drug.

PROLONGED USE

Regular use of this drug over several weeks can lead to a reduction in its effect as the body adapts. It may also be habit-forming when taken for extended periods, and withdrawal symptoms may occur when the drug is stopped. Temazepam should not normally be used for longer than 1–2 weeks.

TERAZOSIN

Product names Hytrin, Teva-Terazosin, and others
Used in the following combined preparations None

GENERAL INFORMATION

Terazosin belongs to the group of anti-hypertensive drugs known as alpha blockers and is used to treat high blood pressure (hypertension). The drug works by relaxing the muscles in the blood vessel walls. Terazosin is also used to relieve the obstruction caused by an enlarged prostate (benign prostatic hypertrophy, or BPH), thereby improving the flow of urine.

Dizziness and fainting, especially on standing up, are common at the start of treatment with terazosin because the first dose may cause a marked drop in blood pressure. For this reason, the initial dose that is prescribed is usually low. To avoid experiencing these effects, it is advisable to take the drug just before going to bed.

INFORMATION FOR USERS

Your drug prescription is tailored for you. Do not alter dosage without checking with your physician.

How taken

Tablets.

Frequency and timing of doses
Once daily.

Usual adult dosage range
Hypertension 1mg at bedtime (starting dose) doubled after 7 days if necessary. Usual dosage range 1–5mg.
Benign prostatic hypertrophy 1mg at bedtime (starting dose) doubled after 1–2 weeks if necessary. Usual dosage range 5–10mg.

Onset of effect
Hypertension Within 3 hours.
Benign prostatic hypertrophy Improvements in symptoms can occur as early as 2 weeks after starting treatment. Full beneficial effects may not be felt for 4–6 weeks.

Duration of action
24 hours.

Diet advice
None.

Storage
Keep in a closed container in a cool dry place out of the reach of children.

Missed dose
Do not double up on a dose. Take the next dose at the usual time.

Stopping the drug
Do not stop the drug without consulting your physician. Stopping the drug may lead to an increase in blood pressure.

Exceeding the dose
An occasional unintentional extra dose is unlikely to be a cause for concern. Large overdoses may drop blood pressure and cause dizziness or fainting. Notify your physician.

SPECIAL PRECAUTIONS

Be sure to tell your physician if:
▼ You are taking other medications.

Pregnancy
▼ Safety in pregnancy not established. Discuss with your physician.

Breast-feeding
▼ Safety in breast-feeding not established. Discuss with your physician.

Infants and children
▼ Not recommended.

Over 60
▼ No special problems.

Driving and hazardous work
▼ Avoid such activities until you have learned how terazosin affects you because the drug can cause dizziness, lightheadedness, or drowsiness.

Alcohol
▼ Avoid. Alcohol may increase some of the *adverse effects* of terazosin, such as drowsiness.

Surgery and general anesthetics
▼ Terazosin may need to be stopped. Discuss with your physician or dentist before you have any surgery.

PROLONGED USE

No problems expected.

POSSIBLE ADVERSE EFFECTS

Rarely, headaches occur with terazosin treatment. A common problem with the drug, however, is that it may cause dizziness or fainting when you stand up.

Symptom/effect	Frequency		Discuss with physician		Stop taking drug now	Call physician now
	Common	Rare	Only if severe	In all cases		
Dizziness/faintness	●			■		
Weakness	●		■			
Palpitations	●			■		
Nausea	●		■			
Drowsiness	●		■			
Stuffy nose	●		■			
Ankle swelling	●			■		
Blurred vision	●			■		
Headache		●	■			

INTERACTIONS

Anesthetics, antidepressants, and hypotensive drugs These drugs may enhance the blood-pressure-lowering effect of terazosin.

TERBINAFINE

Product names Lamisil, Nu-Terbinafine, Teva-Terbinafine, and others
Used in the following combined preparations None

GENERAL INFORMATION

Terbinafine is an antifungal drug used to treat fungal infections of the skin and nails, particularly tinea (ringworm). It is also used as a cream for candida (yeast) infections.

Terbinafine has largely replaced older drugs such as griseofulvin because it is more easily absorbed and is therefore more effective.

Tinea infections are treated in two to six weeks, but treatment of nail infections may take up to 6 months.

Rare *adverse effects* of terbinafine include *jaundice* and a severe skin rash, both of which should be reported to your physician without delay.

QUICK REFERENCE

Drug group Antifungal drugs (p.124)

Overdose danger rating Low

Dependence rating Low

Prescription needed Yes

Available as generic Yes

INFORMATION FOR USERS

Your drug prescription is tailored for you. Do not alter dosage without checking with your physician.

How taken

Tablets, cream, skin spray.

Frequency and timing of doses
Once daily (tablets); 1–2 x daily (cream).

Usual adult dosage range
Tinea infections 250mg (tablets).
Candida infections As directed (cream).

Onset of effect
1 hour.

Duration of action
24 hours.

Diet advice
None.

Storage
Keep in a closed container in a cool, dry place out of the reach of children. Protect from light.

Missed dose
Take as soon as you remember. If your next dose is due within 4 hours, take a single dose now and skip the next.

Stopping the drug
Take the full course. Even if you feel better, the original infection may still be present and may recur if treatment is stopped too soon.

Exceeding the dose
An occasional unintentional extra dose is unlikely to be a cause for concern. But if you notice any unusual symptoms, or if a large overdose has been taken, notify your physician.

SPECIAL PRECAUTIONS

Be sure to tell your physician if:
▼ You have liver or kidney problems.
▼ You have psoriasis.
▼ You are taking other medications.

Pregnancy
▼ Safety in pregnancy not established. Discuss with your physician.

Breast-feeding
▼ Safety not established. Discuss with your physician.

Infants and children
▼ Safety not established. Discuss with your physician.

Over 60
▼ No special problems.

Driving and hazardous work
▼ No known problems.

Alcohol
▼ No known problems.

POSSIBLE ADVERSE EFFECTS

Side effects of terbinafine are generally mild and transient.

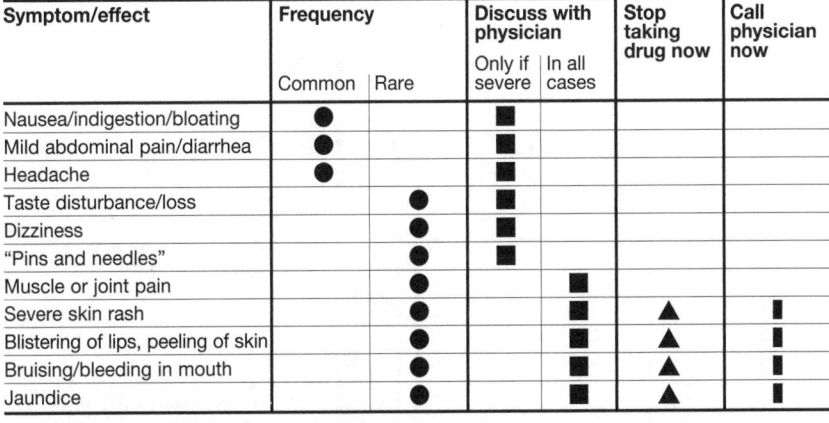

Symptom/effect	Frequency		Discuss with physician		Stop taking drug now	Call physician now
	Common	Rare	Only if severe	In all cases		
Nausea/indigestion/bloating	●		■			
Mild abdominal pain/diarrhea	●		■			
Headache	●		■			
Taste disturbance/loss		●	■			
Dizziness		●	■			
"Pins and needles"		●	■			
Muscle or joint pain		●		■		
Severe skin rash		●		■	▲	❙
Blistering of lips, peeling of skin		●		■	▲	❙
Bruising/bleeding in mouth		●		■	▲	❙
Jaundice		●		■	▲	❙

INTERACTIONS

Oral contraceptives "Breakthrough" bleeding may occur when these are taken with terbinafine.

Rifampin This drug may reduce the blood level and effect of terbinafine.

Cimetidine This drug may increase the blood level of terbinafine.

Cyclosporine Terbinafine may reduce the blood level of cyclosporine.

PROLONGED USE

No special problems.

TERIPARATIDE

Product name Forteo
Used in the following combined preparations None

GENERAL INFORMATION

Teriparatide, a recombinant human analogue of parathyroid hormone, is used in severe osteoporosis in men and in postmenopausal women. It is also used to treat osteoporosis associated with ongoing oral glucocorticoid therapy. It increases the amount of bone formed and increases bone strength and thickness. In studies in severe osteoporosis, it increased bone density and decreased the incidence of new fractures. This drug is not advised for individuals with calcium disorders, Paget's disease, and bone tumors.

Teriparatide is given as an injection into the subcutaneous tissue of the thigh or abdominal wall. It comes as a prefilled delivery device containing 28 doses. The individual should be seated or lying down when receiving this drug as it can cause lightheadedness. It can be self-administered. For those with inadequate dietary intake, supplemental calcium and vitamin D may be recommended. Discuss with your physician.

INFORMATION FOR USERS

Your drug prescription is tailored for you. Do not alter dosage without checking with your physician.

How taken

Injection (subcutaneous).

Frequency and timing of doses
Once daily.

Adult dosage range
20mcg subcutaneously daily for a maximum of 24 months.

Onset of effect
Several weeks to see effect on bone density.

Duration of action
Up to 24 hours.

Diet advice
A diet with calcium (no more than 500mg daily)

and vitamin D (800 IU daily) is recommended. Supplements may be used.

Storage
Store this medication in the refrigerator at all times. Do not freeze it. Protect it from light. Keep out of the reach of children.

Missed dose
If you miss a dose and remember it on that day, take it as soon as you remember. If it is the next day, skip the missed dose and resume your usual dosing schedule. Do not double up to catch up on a missed dose.

Stopping the drug
Do not stop the drug without consulting your physician.

Exeeding the dose
An occasional unintentional extra dose is unlikely to cause problems. Large overdoses may cause changes to calcium levels in the blood and toxicity related to this.

SPECIAL PRECAUTIONS

Be sure to tell your physician if:
▼ You have Paget's disease.
▼ You have other bone disorders including bone tumors.
▼ You have had radiation treatment.
▼ You have had high calcium levels or parathyroid disorder.
▼ You have kidney or liver disorder or heart disease.
▼ You are allergic to mannitol or other medications.
▼ You are taking other medications.

Pregnancy
▼ Safety not established. Discuss with your physician.

Breast-feeding
▼ Safety not established. Not to be used in premenopausal women.

Infants and children
▼ Not recommended in children and adolescents.

Over 60
▼ No special problems.

Driving and hazardous work
▼ No special problems.

Alcohol
▼ No special problems. Individuals with osteoporosis should ensure that strategies are in place to prevent falling, which can result in fractures.

POSSIBLE ADVERSE EFFECTS

This drug is generally well tolerated. Its *side effects* include muscle cramps and, rarely, high calcium levels, nausea, and dizziness.

Symptom/effect	Frequency		Discuss with physician		Stop taking drug now	Call physician now
	Common	Rare	Only if severe	In all cases		
Pain at injection site	●		■			
Weakness	●		■			
Nausea	●		■			
Dizziness	●		■			
Heartburn	●		■			
Fainting		●		■		
Leg cramps		●		■		
Chest pain		●		■	▲	▮
Difficulty breathing		●		■	▲	▮
Fever, chills		●		■		▮

INTERACTIONS

Digoxin Teriparatide should be used cautiously in those on digoxin; increase in calcium levels can result in *adverse effects* from digoxin.

PROLONGED USE

This medication is usually recommended up to 24 months only.

Monitoring Calcium levels will be measured prior to starting therapy and periodically while on the medication. Bone density may be measured yearly.

TESTOSTERONE

Product names Andriol, Androderm, AndroGel, Delatestryl, and others
Used in the following combined preparations None

GENERAL INFORMATION

Testosterone is a male sex *hormone* produced by the testes and, in small quantities, by the ovaries in women. The hormone encourages bone and muscle growth in both men and women and stimulates sexual development in men.

The drug is used to treat testosterone deficiency (hypogonadism) due to pituitary or testicular disorders. It is also used to initiate puberty in male adolescents if it has been delayed because of a deficiency of the natural hormone.

Testosterone can interfere with growth or cause over-rapid sexual development in adolescents. High doses may cause deepening of the voice, excessive hair growth, or hair loss in women.

INFORMATION FOR USERS

Your drug prescription is tailored for you. Do not alter dosage without checking with your physician.

How taken

Capsules, injection, topical gel, patch.

Frequency and timing of doses
2 x daily (capsules); once every 2 weeks to 2 x weekly (injection) depending on condition being treated; once daily (patch); once daily (gel).

Usual dosage range
Varies with method of administration and the condition being treated.

Onset of effect
2–3 days.

Duration of action
1–2 days (capsules and patch); 1–3 weeks (injection); approximately 6 months (implant).

Diet advice
None.

Storage
Keep in a closed container in a cool, dry place out of the reach of children. Protect from light.

Missed dose
No cause for concern, but take as soon as you remember. If your next dose (by mouth) is due within 3 hours, take a single dose now and skip the next.

Stopping the drug
Do not stop taking the drug without consulting your physician.

Exceeding the dose
An occasional unintentional extra dose is unlikely to be a cause for concern. But if you notice unusual symptoms, or if a large overdose was taken, notify your physician.

SPECIAL PRECAUTIONS

Be sure to tell your physician if:
▼ You have long-term liver or kidney problems.
▼ You have heart problems.
▼ You have prostate trouble.
▼ You have high blood pressure.
▼ You have epilepsy or migraine headaches.
▼ You have diabetes.
▼ You are taking other medications.

Pregnancy
▼ Not prescribed. Avoid skin-to-skin transfer of testosterone from other people.

Breast-feeding
▼ Not prescribed. Avoid skin-to-skin transfer of testosterone from other people.

Infants and children
▼ Not prescribed for infants and young children. Reduced dose necessary in adolescents.

Over 60
▼ Rarely required. Increased risk of prostate problems in elderly men. Reduced dose may therefore be necessary.

Driving and hazardous work
▼ No special problems.

Alcohol
▼ No special problems.

POSSIBLE ADVERSE EFFECTS

Most of the more serious *adverse effects* are likely to occur only with long-term treatment with testosterone, and may be helped by a reduction in dosage. Close contact with gel application sites can transfer significant amounts of the hormone to other people; pregnant women and young children are particularly at risk.

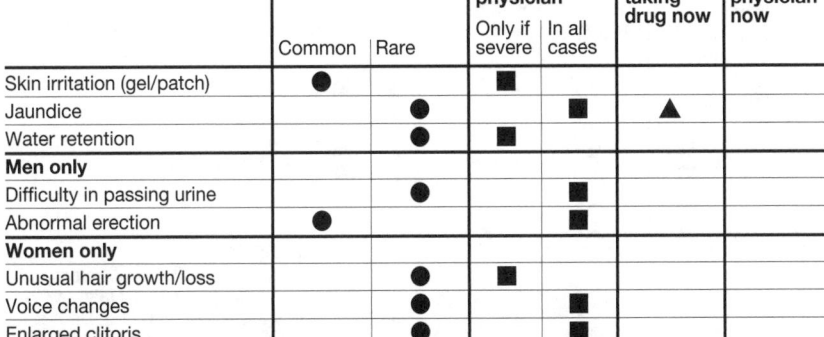

Symptom/effect	Frequency		Discuss with physician		Stop taking drug now	Call physician now
	Common	Rare	Only if severe	In all cases		
Skin irritation (gel/patch)	●		■			
Jaundice		●		■	▲	
Water retention		●	■			
Men only						
Difficulty in passing urine		●		■		
Abnormal erection	●			■		
Women only						
Unusual hair growth/loss		●	■			
Voice changes		●		■		
Enlarged clitoris		●		■		

INTERACTIONS

Anticoagulant drugs Testosterone may increase the effect of these drugs. Dosage of anticoagulant drugs may need to be adjusted accordingly.

Antidiabetic agents As testosterone may lower the blood sugar, dosage of antidiabetic drugs and insulin may need to be reduced.

PROLONGED USE

Prolonged use of this drug may lead to reduced growth in adolescents. In older men, it may accelerate prostate disease.

Monitoring Regular blood tests for the effects of testosterone treatment are necessary, such as red blood cell counts, liver function tests, and PSA (prostate-specific antigen) levels.

TETRACYCLINE

Product names Jaa Tetra, Nu-Tetra, and others
Used in the following combined preparations None

GENERAL INFORMATION

Tetracycline is a very widely used antibiotic. However, the development of drug-resistant bacteria has reduced its effectiveness in many types of infection. Tetracycline is still used for chest infections caused by chlamydia (for example, psittacosis) and myco-plasma microorganisms. Tetracycline is also used in non-specific urethritis and a number of rarer conditions, such as Q fever, Rocky Mountain spotted fever, cholera, and brucellosis. Acne improves with long-term treatment with tetracyline taken by mouth.

Common *side effects* of this drug are nausea, vomiting, and diarrhea. Rashes may also occur. Tetracycline may discolour developing teeth if it is taken by children or by the mother during pregnancy. People with poor kidney function are not prescribed tetracycline because it can cause further deterioration.

INFORMATION FOR USERS

Your drug prescription is tailored for you. Do not alter your dosage without checking with your physician.

How taken

Tablets, capsules.

Frequency and timing of doses
By mouth 4 x daily, at least 1 hour before or 2 hours after meals.
Long-term treatment of acne may require only a single dose daily.

Usual adult dosage range
Infections 1–2g daily.
Acne 250mg–1g daily.

Onset of effect
4–12 hours. Improvement in acne may not be noticed for up to 4 weeks.

Duration of action
Up to 6 hours.

Diet advice
Milk products should be avoided for 1 hour before and 2 hours after taking the drug, since they may impair its absorption.

Storage
Keep in a closed container in a cool, dry place out of the reach of children.

Missed dose
Take as soon as you remember. If your next dose is due within 2 hours, take a single dose now and skip the next.

Stopping the drug
Take the full course. Even if you feel better, the original infection may still be present and may recur if treatment is stopped too soon.

Exceeding the dose
An occasional unintentional extra dose is unlikely to be a cause for concern. But if you notice any unusual symptoms, or if a large overdose has been taken, notify your physician.

POSSIBLE ADVERSE EFFECTS

Adverse effects from skin preparations are rare. When tetracyclines are given by mouth, however, they may cause nausea, vomiting, or diarrhea.

Symptom/effect	Frequency		Discuss with physician		Stop taking drug now	Call physician now
	Common	Rare	Only if severe	In all cases		
Nausea/vomiting	●		■			
Diarrhea	●		■			
Light-sensitive rash		●		■	▲	
Rash/itching		●		■	▲	
Jaundice		●		■	▲	
Headache/visual disturbance		●		■	▲	■

INTERACTIONS

Iron may reduce the effectiveness of tetracycline.

Oral anticoagulants Tetracycline may increase the action of these drugs.

Retinoids may increase the adverse effects of tetracycline.

Methotrexate Tetracycline may increase the risk of methotrexate toxicity.

Oral contraceptives Tetracycline may reduce the effectiveness of oral contraceptives.

Antacids and milk These interfere with the absorption of tetracycline and may reduce their effectiveness. Doses should be separated by 1–2 hours.

SPECIAL PRECAUTIONS

Be sure to tell your physician if:
▼ You have long-term liver or kidney problems.
▼ You have previously suffered an allergic reaction to a tetracycline antibiotic.
▼ You have myasthenia gravis or acute porphyria.
▼ You have systemic lupus erythematosus.
▼ You are taking other medications.

 Pregnancy
▼ Not prescribed. May cause birth defects and may damage teeth and bones of the developing fetus as well as the mother's liver. Discuss with your physician.

 Breast-feeding
▼ Not contraindicated for short term use. Discuss with your physician.

 Infants and children
▼ Not recommended under 12 years. Reduced dose necessary in older children. May discolour developing teeth.

 Over 60
▼ No special problems.

 Driving and hazardous work
▼ No known problems.

 Alcohol
▼ No known problems.

Taking your tablets
▼ To prevent irritation to the esophagus, each dose of the drug should be taken with a full glass of water while standing. Do not lie down immediately afterwards.

PROLONGED USE

No problems expected.

THEOPHYLLINE/AMINOPHYLLINE

Product names [theophylline] Apo-Theo-LA, Theolair, Uniphyl, and others
Used in the following combined preparations None

GENERAL INFORMATION

Theophylline (and aminophylline for injection, which breaks down to theophylline in the body) is used to treat bronchospasm (constriction of the air passages) in patients suffering from asthma, bronchitis, and emphysema.

It is usually taken continuously as a preventative measure, and is added to standard therapy. It can also be used to treat acute attacks in hospital.

Slow-release formulations of the drugs produce beneficial effects lasting for up to 12 hours. These preparations may be prescribed twice daily, but they are also useful as a single dose taken at night to prevent night-time asthma.

Treatment with theophylline must be monitored because the effective dose is very close to the *toxic* dose. Some *adverse effects*, such as indigestion, nausea, headache, and agitation, can be controlled by regulating the dosage and checking blood levels of the drug.

INFORMATION FOR USERS

Your drug prescription is tailored for you. Do not alter dosage without checking with your physician.

How taken

Tablets, SR-tablets, liquid, injection.

Frequency and timing of doses
3–4 x daily (tablets, liquid); every 12 or 24 hours (SR-tablets). The drug should be taken at the same time each day in relation to meals.

Usual dosage range
Adults 400–600mg daily, depending on which product is used.

Onset of effect
Within 30 minutes (by mouth); within 90 minutes (SR-tablets).

Duration of action
Up to 8 hours (by mouth); 12–24 hours (SR-tablets).

Diet advice
None.

Storage
Keep in a closed container in a cool, dry place out of the reach of children.

Missed dose
Take as soon as you remember. If your next dose is due within 2 hours, take half the dose now (short-acting preparations) or forget about the missed dose and take your next dose now (SR-preparations). Return to your normal dose schedule thereafter.

Stopping the drug
Do not stop taking the drug without consulting your physician; stopping the drug may lead to worsening of the underlying condition.

OVERDOSE ACTION

 Seek immediate medical advice in all cases. Take emergency action if chest pains, confusion, or loss of consciousness occur.

See Drug poisoning emergency guide (p.526).

POSSIBLE ADVERSE EFFECTS

Most adverse effects of this drug are related to dosage. These include effects related to the drug's action on the central nervous system, such as agitation and insomnia.

Symptom/effect	Frequency		Discuss with physician		Stop taking drug now	Call physician now
	Common	Rare	Only if severe	In all cases		
Agitation		●		■		
Headache	●			■		
Nausea/vomiting	●		■			
Diarrhea		●	■			
Insomnia		●	■			
Palpitations		●		■	▲	∎

INTERACTIONS

General note Many drugs increase the effect of theophylline (e.g., erythromycin, cimetidine, acyclovir, oral contraceptives, ciprofloxacin, and clarithromycin); others reduce its effect (e.g., carbamazepine, phenytoin, and rifampin). Discuss with your physician.

SPECIAL PRECAUTIONS

Be sure to tell your physician if:
▼ You have a long-term liver problem.
▼ You have angina or irregular heartbeat.
▼ You have high blood pressure.
▼ You have epilepsy.
▼ You have hyperthyroidism.
▼ You have porphyria.
▼ You have peptic ulcers.
▼ You smoke.
▼ You are taking other medications.

 Pregnancy
▼ Safety in pregnancy not established. Discuss with your physician.

 Breast-feeding
▼ The drug passes into the breast milk and may affect the baby. Discuss with your physician.

 Infants and children
▼ Reduced dose necessary according to age and weight.

 Over 60
▼ Reduced dose may be necessary.

 Driving and hazardous work
▼ No known problems.

 Alcohol
▼ Avoid excess as this may alter levels of the drug and may increase gastrointestinal symptoms.

PROLONGED USE

No problems expected.

Monitoring Periodic checks on blood levels of this drug are usually required.

TICAGRELOR

Product name Brilinta
Used in the following combined preparations None

GENERAL INFORMATION

Ticagrelor is an antiplatelet drug used to prevent blood clots in certain conditions; is usually recommended to be administered with low-dose (75 to 150mg) ASA. It is indicated for patients after a heart attack or unstable angina to decrease the risk of stroke, future heart attacks, and complications of cardiovascular disease. Ticagrelor works by preventing platelets in the blood from clumping together. This drug may be held for a few days prior to planned surgery. It is important to take the dose at the same time each day.

INFORMATION FOR USERS

Your drug prescription is tailored for you. Do not alter dosage without checking with your physician.

How taken

Tablets.

Frequency and timing of doses
Twice daily.

Usual adult dosage range
Loading dose of 180mg, then 90mg twice daily.

Onset of effect
Usually within 2–8 hours.

Duration of action
Up to 24 hours

Diet advice
None.

Storage
Keep in a closed container in a cool, dry place out of the reach of children.

Missed dose
Take your next dose at its scheduled time. Do not double up on a dose.

Stopping the drug
Do not stop suddenly without consulting your physician. Stopping the drug may lead to a recurrence of the original condition.

Exceeding the dose
Notify your physician if you have taken an unintentional extra dose even if you don't have symptoms.

SPECIAL PRECAUTIONS

Be sure to tell your physician if:
▼ Be sure to tell your physician if:
▼ You have a known history of TIA or stroke.
▼ You have active peptic ulcer disease.
▼ You have moderate to severe liver problems.
▼ You have a history of gout or increased uric acid levels.
▼ You have had recent surgery or an upcoming planned surgery.
▼ You are taking other medications.

Pregnancy
▼ Limited clinical information available. Discuss with your physician.

Breast-feeding
▼ Use while breast-feeding not recommended. Discuss with your physician.

Infants and children
▼ Safety and efficacy not established in those under 18 years of age; not recommended in this group.

Over 60
▼ No special problems.

Driving and hazardous work
▼ The drug may cause dizziness in some individuals. Use caution. Also, minor bumps can cause bad bruises and excessive bleeding.

Alcohol
▼ No special problems.

POSSIBLE ADVERSE EFFECTS

Bruising may happen easily and cuts may take longer to heal. Many other medications taken with ticagrelor can increase the risk of bleeding (see Drug Interactions).

Symptom/effect	Frequency		Discuss with physician		Stop taking drug now	Call physician now
	Common	Rare	Only if severe	In all cases		
Headache/dizziness	●		■			
Confusion	●			■		
Nausea/vomiting	●		■			
Nose bleeds/bleeding gums	●		■			
Shortness of breath		●		■		
Blood in your stool or urine/coughing up blood		●		■		▮
Sudden severe headache		●			▲	▮
Sudden numbness on one side/difficulty speaking/ walking problems		●			▲	▮
Slowing/ speeding of heart rate		●		■		▮
Increased fatigue/swelling in the legs or feet/shortness of breath		●		■		▮

INTERACTIONS

General note Drugs or herbs that have an antiplatelet or anticoagulant effect can increase these effects in ticagrelor. Avoid using ticagrelor with anticoagulants.

Drugs such as ketconazole, clarithromycin, ritonavir, and atanazavir can increase the level of ticagrelor significantly. Avoid using together.

Drugs such as rifampin, carbamazepine, dexamethasone, and phenytoin can reduce the effectiveness of ticagrelor.

NSAIDs can increase the effect of ticagrelor

Simvastatin and lovastatin Ticagrelor may increase the serum concentration of these drugs.

PROLONGED USE

Monitoring Monitoring required for bleeding risk.

TIMOLOL

Product names PMS-Timolol, Timoptic, Timoptic-XE, and others
Used in the following combined preparations Azarga, Combigan, Cosopt, and others

GENERAL INFORMATION

Timolol is a non-cardioselective beta blocker prescribed to treat angina and hypertension. It may be given after a heart attack to prevent further damage to the heart. Timolol is commonly administered as eye drops to people with certain types of glaucoma and is occasionally given by mouth to prevent migraine.

Timolol can cause breathing difficulties, especially in people with respiratory diseases; this is more likely with tablets although it can also occur in individuals using the eye drops. Timolol may mask the body's response to low blood sugar and, for that reason, is prescribed with caution to those with diabetes on insulin.

QUICK REFERENCE

Drug group Beta blockers (p.83) and drugs for glaucoma (p.156)

Overdose danger rating High

Dependence rating Low

Prescription needed Yes

Available as generic Yes

INFORMATION FOR USERS

Your drug prescription is tailored for you. Do not alter dosage without checking with your physician.

How taken

Tablets, eye drops.

Frequency and timing of doses
1–2 x daily.

Usual adult dosage range
By mouth 10–40mg daily (hypertension); 10–45mg daily (angina); 10–20mg daily (after a heart attack); 10–20mg daily (migraine prevention).

Onset of effect
Within 30 minutes (by mouth).

Duration of action
Up to 24 hours.

Diet advice
None.

Storage
Keep in a closed container in a cool, dry place out of the reach of children.

Missed dose
Take as soon as you remember. If your next dose is due within 3 hours, take a single dose now and skip the next.

Stopping the drug
Do not stop without consulting your physician; the underlying condition may worsen.

OVERDOSE ACTION

 Seek immediate medical advice in all cases of overdose by mouth. Take emergency action if breathing difficulties, palpitations, or loss of consciousness occur.

See Drug poisoning emergency guide (p.526).

SPECIAL PRECAUTIONS

Be sure to tell your physician if:
▼ You have a lung disorder such as asthma, bronchitis, or emphysema.
▼ You have diabetes.
▼ You have myasthenia gravis.
▼ You have poor circulation.
▼ You have psoriasis.
▼ You wear contact lenses (eye drops).
▼ You are taking other medications.

 Pregnancy
▼ Safety in pregnancy not established. Discuss with your physician.

 Breast-feeding
▼ The drug passes into the breast milk, but at normal doses *adverse effects* on the baby are unlikely. Discuss with your physician.

 Infants and children
▼ Not usually prescribed.

 Over 60
▼ Reduced dose may be necessary.

 Driving and hazardous work
▼ Avoid such activities until you have learned how timolol affects you because the tablets may cause drowsiness and the eye drops may cause blurred vision.

 Alcohol
▼ May enhance lowering of blood pressure; avoid excessive amounts.

Surgery and general anesthetics
▼ Timolol may need to be stopped before you have a general anesthetic. Discuss with your physician or dentist before any surgery.

POSSIBLE ADVERSE EFFECTS

Timolol taken by mouth can occasionally provoke or worsen heart problems and asthma. Fainting may be a sign that the drug has slowed the heartbeat excessively.

Symptom/effect	Frequency		Discuss with physician		Stop taking drug now	Call physician now
	Common	Rare	Only if severe	In all cases		
Eye irritation (eye drops)	●		■			
Lethargy/fatigue	●			■		
Cold hands and feet	●			■		
Nausea/vomiting		●		■		
Nightmares/vivid dreams		●		■	▲	
Rash/dry eyes		●		■	▲	
Visual disturbances		●		■	▲	
Faiting/palpitations		●		■	▲	❚
Breathlessness/wheezing		●		■	▲	❚

INTERACTIONS

Decongestants Present in many cough and cold remedies, these drugs can cause a dangerous rise in blood pressure when taken with timolol.

Calcium channel blockers may cause low blood pressure, a slow heartbeat, and heart failure if used with timolol.

Cardiac glycosides (e.g. digoxin) may increase the heart-slowing effect of timolol.

Antihypertensive drugs Timolol may enhance the blood-pressure-lowering effect.

Salbutamol, salmeterol, and other beta agonists The effects of these drugs may be reduced by timolol.

PROLONGED USE

No problems expected.

TIOTROPIUM

Product name Spiriva
Used in the following combined preparations None

GENERAL INFORMATION

Tiotropium is an *anticholinergic* bronchodilator that relaxes the muscles surrounding the bronchioles (airways in the lung). It is used in the maintenance treatment of reversible airway disorders, such as chronic bronchitis. Tiotropium is a long-acting drug, but its effects are felt after only 5 minutes or so. It is not suitable for acute attacks of wheezing or in the emergency treatment of asthma when salbutamol should be used. Tiotropium is taken by inhalation of a powder, and it acts directly and locally on the internal surface of the lungs. The most common *side effect* is a dry mouth.

INFORMATION FOR USERS

Your drug prescription is tailored for you. Do not alter dosage without checking with your physician.

How taken

Powder in capsules for inhaler.

Frequency and timing of doses
Once daily, at the same time each day.

Usual adult dosage range
18mcg daily.

Onset of effect
5 minutes.

Duration of action
24 hours.

Diet advice
None.

Storage
Keep in a closed container in a cool, dry place out of the reach of children.

Missed dose
Take as soon as you remember. If your next dose is due within 8 hours, take a single dose now and skip the next.

Stopping the drug
Do not stop taking the drug without consulting your physician. Symptoms may recur.

Exceeding the dose
An occasional unintentional extra dose is unlikely to be a cause for concern. But if you notice any unusual symptoms, or if a large overdose has been taken, notify your physician.

POSSIBLE ADVERSE EFFECTS

Dry mouth is the most common side effect. If you get the powder in your eyes, it could trigger glaucoma; you should call the physician immediately.

Symptom/effect	Frequency		Discuss with physician		Stop taking drug now	Call physician now
	Common	Rare	Only if severe	In all cases		
Dry mouth/sore throat	●		■			
Constipation	●		■			
Fast heartbeat/palpitations		●		■		
Altered sense of taste		●		■		
Change in voice		●		■		
Difficulty passing urine		●		■		
Rash		●		■		
Wheezing after inhalation		●		■		
Eye pain/blurred vision		●		■		■
Visual halos		●		■		■

INTERACTIONS

Atropine and ipratropium The effects and toxicity of tiotropium are likely to be increased if it is used at the same time as these drugs.

SPECIAL PRECAUTIONS

Be sure to tell your physician if:
▼ You are allergic to atropine or ipratropium.
▼ You have prostate problems.
▼ You have urinary retention.
▼ You have glaucoma.
▼ You have kidney problems.
▼ You are taking other medications.

 Pregnancy
▼ Safety not established. Discuss with your physician.

 Breast-feeding
▼ Safety not established, but the amount present in breast milk is unlikely to harm your baby. Discuss with your physician.

 Infants and children
▼ Not recommended under 18 years of age.

 Over 60
▼ No known problems.

 Driving and hazardous work
▼ No known problems.

 Alcohol
▼ No known problems.

Protecting your eyes
▼ Care must be taken to avoid getting the powder into the eyes as it could trigger glaucoma or make existing glaucoma worse. If you develop eye or vision problems, call your physician immediately.

PROLONGED USE

No known problems.

TIZANIDINE

Product names Apo-Tizanidine, Mylan-Tizanidine, Zanaflex
Used in the following combined preparations None

GENERAL INFORMATION

Tizanidine is a medication used to treat muscle spasms. It can be used in many conditions where spasticity or muscle tone needs to be controlled. The dose should be scheduled such that the peak effect coincides with the time when relief of spasticity is most desirable.

Generally, the drug is well tolerated. The most common *side effects* are constipation, dry mouth, drowsiness, dizziness, and decrease in blood pressure. To minimize side effects, especially the decrease in blood pressure, the dose should be increased gradually.

QUICK REFERENCE

Drug group Muscle relaxants (p.106)

Overdose danger rating Medium

Dependence rating Low

Prescription needed Yes

Available as generic Yes

INFORMATION FOR USERS

Your drug prescription is tailored for you. Do not alter dosage without checking with your physician.

How taken

Tablets.

Frequency and timing of doses
Up to three or four times daily.

Usual adult dosage range
4–8mg (1–2 tablets) two to four times daily; starting dose 4mg once daily.

Onset of effect
Peak effect usually occurs in 1–2 hours.

Duration of action
Effect may last between 3–6 hours.

Diet advice
None.

Storage
Keep in a closed container in a cool, dry place out of the reach of children.

Missed dose
If you miss a dose, take it as soon as you remember. If it is near the time of the next dose, skip the missed dose and resume your using dosing schedule. Do not double up to catch up on a missed dose.

Stopping the drug
Do not stop the drug without consulting your physician. Stopping the drug may lead to worsening of the underlying condition.

Exceeding the dose
An occasional unintentional extra dose is unlikely to cause problems. Large overdoses may cause severe drowsiness, fainting, or trouble breathing. If overdose is suspected, notify your local poison control centre right away.

POSSIBLE ADVERSE EFFECTS

The most common side effects caused by tizanidine are dizziness and dry mouth. Blood pressures can decrease more significantly with higher doses. To minimize dizziness, stand up slowly when arising from a sitting or lying position.

Symptom/effect	Frequency		Discuss with physician		Stop taking drug now	Call physician now
	Common	Rare	Only if severe	In all cases		
Dizziness	●		■			
Drowsiness	●		■			
Nausea	●		■			
Dry mouth	●		■			
Constipation	●		■			
Muscle fatigue/weakness	●		■			
Stomach pain, vomiting		●		■		▮
Yellowing of skin or eyes		●		■		▮
Vision/hearing changes		●		■		▮

INTERACTIONS

All drugs, including alcohol, that cause drowsiness such as anti-anxiety and sleeping drugs, antihistamines, antidepressants, opioid analgesics, and antipsychotics These can increase the sedative properties of tizanidine.

Antihypertensive and diuretic drugs The effect of such drugs may be increased.

Oral contraceptives These may increase the effect of tizanidine; dose of tizanidine may need to be adjusted.

Ciprofloxacin Do not use this drug with tizanidine.

SPECIAL PRECAUTIONS

Be sure to tell your physician if:
▼ You are allergic to tizanidine.
▼ You are taking blood pressure medications.
▼ You have fainted before or have low blood pressure.
▼ You have kidney problems.
▼ You are on any other medications.

Pregnancy
▼ Safety in pregnancy not established. Discuss with your physician.

Breast-feeding
▼ Safety in breast-feeding not established. Discuss with your physician.

Infants and children
▼ Not recommended.

Over 60
▼ Increased likelihood of *adverse effects*. Reduced dose may therefore be necessary. Dose should be adjusted for any changes in kidney function.

Driving and hazardous work
▼ Do not undertake such activities until you have learned how the drug affects you; it can cause reduced alertness and slowed reactions.

Alcohol
▼ Avoid. Can increase side effects of tizanidine. Alcohol increases the *sedative* effects of this drug.

PROLONGED USE

If this medication has been taken for a prolonged time, it should not be stopped suddenly without consulting with your physician.

Monitoring Periodic blood tests may be performed to check for liver function.

TOLTERODINE

Product names Detrol, Detrol LA
Used in the following combined preparations None

GENERAL INFORMATION

Tolterodine is an *anticholinergic* and antispasmodic drug that is similar to oxybutynin. It is used to treat urinary frequency and incontinence in adults. Tolterodine works by reducing contraction of the bladder, allowing it to expand and hold more. It also stops spasms and delays the desire to empty the bladder.

Tolterodine's usefulness is limited to some extent by its *side effects*, and dosage needs to be reduced in the elderly. Children are more susceptible than adults to the drug's anticholinergic effects. Tolterodine can also trigger glaucoma.

QUICK REFERENCE

Drug group Drugs for urinary disorders (p.154)

Overdose danger rating High

Dependence rating Low

Prescription needed Yes

Available as generic No

INFORMATION FOR USERS

Your drug prescription is tailored for you. Do not alter dosage without checking with your physician.

How taken

Tablets, ER capsules.

Frequency and timing of doses
2 x daily, once daily for extended release.

Usual adult dosage range
4mg daily, reduced to 2mg daily, if necessary, to minimize side effects.

Onset of effect
1 hour.

Duration of action
12 hours.

Diet advice
None.

Storage
Keep in a closed container in a cool, dry place out of the reach of children.

Missed dose
Take as soon as you remember. If your next dose is due within 2 hours, take a single dose now and skip the next.

Stopping the drug
Do not stop taking the drug without consulting your physician; symptoms may recur.

OVERDOSE ACTION

Seek immediate medical advice in all cases. Take emergency action if symptoms such as breathing difficulty, seizures, or loss of consciousness occur.

See Drug poisoning emergency guide (p.526).

SPECIAL PRECAUTIONS

Be sure to tell your physician if:
▼ You have liver or kidney problems.
▼ You have thyroid problems.
▼ You have heart problems, especially rhythm disturbances.
▼ You have porphyria.
▼ You have hiatus hernia.
▼ You have prostate problems or urinary retention.
▼ You have ulcerative colitis.
▼ You have glaucoma.
▼ You have myasthenia gravis.
▼ You are taking other medications.

Pregnancy
▼ Safety in pregnancy not established. May harm the unborn baby. Discuss with your physician.

Breast-feeding
▼ Safety not established. Discuss with your physician.

Infants and children
▼ Not recommended. Safety not established.

Over 60
▼ Reduced dose may be necessary.

Driving and hazardous work
▼ Avoid. Tolterodine may cause drowsiness, disorientation, and blurred vision.

Alcohol
▼ Avoid. Alcohol increases the drug's sedative effects.

POSSIBLE ADVERSE EFFECTS

The most common side effects, such as dry mouth, digestive upset, and dry eyes, are the result of the drug's anticholinergic action.

Symptom/effect	Frequency		Discuss with physician		Stop taking drug now	Call physician now
	Common	Rare	Only if severe	In all cases		
Dry mouth/digestive upset	●		■			
Constipation/abdominal pain	●		■			
Headache	●		■			
Dry eyes/blurred vision	●		■			
Drowsiness/nervousness	●		■			
Chest pain		●		■		
Confusion		●		■		
Urinary difficulties		●		■		
Unexplained collapse		●		■	▲	■

INTERACTIONS

General note All drugs that have an anticholinergic effect will have increased side effects when taken with tolterodine.

Domperidone and metoclopramide The effects of these drugs may be decreased by tolterodine.

Erythromycin, clarithromycin, itraconazole, ketoconazole, and miconazole These drugs may increase blood levels of tolterodine.

PROLONGED USE

No special problems. Effectiveness of the drug, and continuing clinical need for it, are usually reviewed after 3–6 months.

Monitoring Periodic eye tests for glaucoma may be performed.

TOPIRAMATE

Product names CO Topiramate, Dom-Topiramate, PMS-Topiramate, Sandoz Topiramate, Topamax, and others
Used in the following combined preparations None

GENERAL INFORMATION

Topiramate is an antiepileptic drug, usually prescribed in combination with other antiepileptics, such as valproic acid, carbamazepine, or phenytoin, for the treatment of epilepsy. It may also be used to prevent migraine headaches and can reduce the frequency of migraines. It is not recommended in children less than 2 years of age. Tablets should be swallowed whole.

Sprinkle capsules can be swallowed whole or sprinkled on a teaspoonful of food and swallowed without chewing.

Topiramate may cause a number of dose-related *side effects*. Some individuals may experience weight loss; if this becomes problematic, an increase in food intake or dietary supplements may be helpful.

INFORMATION FOR USERS

Your drug prescription is tailored for you. Do not alter dosage without checking with your physician.

How taken

Tablets, Sprinkle capsules.

Frequency and timing of doses
Usually twice daily; can sprinkle capsule contents on soft food or swallow whole.

Usual adult dosage range
50mg (starting); 200–400mg daily (maintenance).

Onset of effect
Approximately 4–8 days at a constant dose.

Duration of action
Up to 24 hours.

Diet advice
None.

Storage
Keep in a closed container in a cool, dry place out of the reach of children.

Missed dose
If it is almost time for the next dose, take a single dose now and skip the next. Do not double up on a dose.

Stopping the drug
Do not stop taking the drug without consulting your physician. A gradual reduction is necessary to reduce the risk of rebound seizures.

Exceeding the dose
An occasional unintentional extra dose is unlikely to be a cause for concern. Large overdoses may cause sedation, loss of muscular coordination, nausea, and vomiting. Contact your physician immediately.

POSSIBLE ADVERSE EFFECTS

Generally well tolerated.

Symptom/effect	Frequency		Discuss with physician		Stop taking drug now	Call physician now
	Common	Rare	Only if severe	In all cases		
Headache	●		■			
Dizziness/drowsiness	●		■			
Nervousness	●			■		
Difficulty coordinating muscle movements/speech problems	●			■		
Difficulty concentrating/with memory	●			■		
Tingling in fingers/toes		●		■		
Confusion/mood changes		●		■		
Vision changes		●		■		
Decreased sweating		●		■		

INTERACTIONS

Phenytoin and carbamazepine These drugs can decrease the effectiveness of topiramate and the dose of topiramate may need to be adjusted.

Acetazolamide When taken with topiramate, can increase the risk of kidney stones.

Oral contraceptives Topiramate may decrease the effectiveness of these drugs.

Discuss with your physician.

Metformin When metformin (used in diabetic management) is given with topiramate, blood glucose levels should be closely followed.

CNS depressants Any drugs that affect the CNS can have an additive effect with topiramate.

SPECIAL PRECAUTIONS

Be sure to tell your physician if:
▼ You have long-term liver or kidney problems.
▼ You have a heart condition.
▼ You are taking other medications.

Pregnancy
▼ Discuss treatment options with your physician.

Breast-feeding
▼ Discuss treatment options with your physician.

Infants and children
▼ Not recommended in children younger than 2 years. Reduced dose recommended in children between 2 and 18 years of age.

Over 60
▼ Increased likelihood of adverse effects. Reduced dose may be necessary.

Driving and hazardous work
▼ Avoid such activities until you have learned how topiramate affects you because the drug can cause drowsiness.

Alcohol
▼ Avoid. Alcohol may increase the adverse effects of this drug.

PROLONGED USE

No problems expected.

TRAMADOL

Product names Ralivia, Tridural, Ultram, Zytram XL
Used in the following combined preparations Apo-Tramadol/ACET, Tramacet

GENERAL INFORMATION

Tramadol is a type of opioid analgesic (p.64) used to relieve moderate to severe pain. It is available as regular (RR) and extended release (ER) tablets. The ER tablets should only be used when round-the-clock pain relief is needed in someone who has already been on the regular tablets. There are different forms of ER available. These should be swallowed whole and should not be split, chewed, or crushed.

Tramadol can cause lightheadedness; it is best to get up slowly from a lying or sitting position, while supporting oneself. These drugs are habit-forming. However, most patients prescribed tramadol for pain relief do not become dependent and are able to stop taking them without difficulty.

QUICK REFERENCE

Drug group Opioid analgesics (p.65)
Overdose danger rating High
Dependence rating High
Prescription needed Yes
Available as generic Yes

INFORMATION FOR USERS

Your drug prescription is tailored for you. Do not alter dosage without checking with your physician.

How taken

Tablets, regular (RR) and extended release (ER).

Frequency and timing of doses
RR: every 4–6 hour; ER taken once daily.

Adult dosage range
150–400mg per day.

Onset of effect
Usually within an hour.

Duration of action
RR: 4–6 hours; ER: up to 24 hours, depending on product.

Diet advice
None.

Storage
Keep in a closed container in a cool, dry place out of the reach of children.

Missed dose
If you have been instructed to take the medication regularly, take the missed dose as soon as you remember. However, if it is near the time of the next dose, skip the missed dose and resume your usual dosing schedule. Do not double up to catch up on a missed dose.

Stopping the drug
Do not stop the drug without consulting your physician. Stopping the drug may lead to withdrawal symptoms. Tramadol requires a gradual withdrawal.

OVERDOSE ACTION

 Seek immediate medical advice in all cases. Take emergency action if breathing difficulties, seizures, or loss of consciousness occurs. Notify your physician.

See Drug poisoning emergency guide (p. 526).

SPECIAL PRECAUTIONS

Be sure to tell your physician if:
▼ You have an allergic reaction or sensitivity to the opioid class of drugs.
▼ You have a history of seizures or epileptic seizures.
▼ You have liver or kidney problems.
▼ You have a lung disorder such as asthma or bronchitis.
▼ You have sleep apnea.
▼ You have had problems with alcohol or drug abuse.
▼ You are taking herbal products such as St John's Wort.
▼ You are taking other medications.

 Pregnancy
▼ Safety in pregnancy not established. Discuss with your physician.

 Breast-feeding
▼ Safety not established. Discuss with your physician.

 Infants and children
▼ Safety not established in children at or below 16 years of age. For those 16 and over, see adult dosage and discuss with your physician.

 Over 60
▼ A lower starting dose may be recommended.

 Driving and hazardous work
▼ May cause drowsiness. Do not drive a car or operate machinery until the effect of the drug wears off and you feel you are mentally alert.

 Alcohol
▼ Avoid alcohol use as it may increase the effect of drowsiness caused by this drug.

POSSIBLE ADVERSE EFFECTS

The most common *side effects* are dizziness, nausea, constipation, and headache.

Symptom/effect	Frequency		Discuss with physician		Stop taking drug now	Call physician now
	Common	Rare	Only if severe	In all cases		
Nausea	●		■			
Agitation/anxiety	●			■		
Constipation	●		■			
Dizziness	●		■			
Dry mouth	●		■			
Headache	●		■			
Changes in walking or balance		●		■		
Shortness of breath		●		■		▌
Seizures		●		■		▌
Trouble concentrating/sleeping		●		■		

PROLONGED USE

Dependence may occur if it is taken for extended periods, although this is unusual in patients taking the correct dose for pain relief.

INTERACTIONS

CNS depressants Can have drowsiness and other additive effects.

SSRIs, TCAs, MAOIs, carbamazepine Can increase the potential for seizures.

MAOIs Tramadol must not to be used with, or for 14 days after stopping, MAOIs.

Quinidine, Cimetidine, Ritonavir These drugs can increase the effect of tramadol.

Warfarin Warfarin's effect may change with tramadol; monitor INR.

TRIAMTERENE

Product name Only available as combination product
Used in the following combined preparations Apo-Triazide, Nu-Triazide, Pro-Triazide, and others

GENERAL INFORMATION

Triamterene belongs to the class of drugs known as potassium-sparing diuretics. In combination with thiazide or loop diuretics, this drug is given for the treatment of hypertension and edema (fluid retention). Triamterene, either on its own or, more commonly, with a thiazide diuretic, may be used to treat edema as a complication of heart failure, nephrotic syndrome, or cirrhosis of the liver.

Triamterene has a mild effect on urine flow, which is apparent in 1–2 hours. For this reason, you should avoid taking the drug after about 4 pm. As with other potassium-sparing diuretics, unusually high levels of potassium may build up in the blood if the kidneys are functioning abnormally. Therefore, triamterene is prescribed with caution to people with kidney failure.

QUICK REFERENCE

Drug group Potassium-sparing diuretic (p.85)

Overdose danger rating Low

Dependence rating Low

Prescription needed Yes

Available as generic Yes (in combined products)

INFORMATION FOR USERS

Your drug prescription is tailored for you. Do not alter dosage without checking with your physician.

How taken

Tablets.

Frequency and timing of doses
1–2 x daily after meals or on alternate days.

Usual adult dosage range
50–250mg daily.

Onset of effect
Within 2 hours.

Duration of action
9–12 hours.

Diet advice
Avoid foods that are high in potassium, such as dried fruit and salt substitutes.

Storage
Keep in a closed container in a cool, dry place out of the reach of children.

Missed dose
Take as soon as you remember. However, if it is late in the day, do not take the missed dose, or you may need to get up at night to pass urine. Take the next scheduled dose as usual.

Stopping the drug
Do not stop the drug without consulting your physician; symptoms may recur.

Exceeding the dose
An occasional unintentional extra dose is unlikely to be a cause for concern. But if you notice any unusual symptoms, or if a large overdose has been taken, notify your physician.

SPECIAL PRECAUTIONS

Be sure to tell your physician if:
▼ You have long-term liver or kidney problems.
▼ You have had kidney stones.
▼ You have gout.
▼ You are taking other medications.

Pregnancy
▼ Not usually prescribed. May cause a reduction in the blood supply to the developing fetus. Discuss with your physician.

Breast-feeding
▼ The drug passes into breast milk and may affect the baby. It could also reduce your milk supply. Discuss with your physician.

Infants and children
▼ Not usually prescribed. Reduced dose necessary.

Over 60
▼ Increased likelihood of adverse effects. Reduced dose may therefore be necessary.

Driving and hazardous work
▼ No special problems.

Alcohol
▼ No known problems.

POSSIBLE ADVERSE EFFECTS

Triamterene has few *adverse effects*; the main problem is the possibility of potassium being retained by the body, causing muscle weakness and heart rhythm problems. Triamterene may colour your urine blue but this is not a cause for concern.

Symptom/effect	Frequency		Discuss with physician		Stop taking drug now	Call physician now
	Common	Rare	Only if severe	In all cases		
Digestive disturbance		●	■			
Headache		●	■			
Muscle weakness		●		■		
Rash		●		■		
Dry mouth		●	■			

INTERACTIONS

Lithium Triamterene may increase the blood levels of lithium, leading to an increased risk of lithium *toxicity*.

Non-steroidal anti-inflammatory drugs (NSAIDs) may increase the risk of raised blood levels of potassium.

ACE inhibitors These drugs increase the risk of raised blood levels of potassium with triamterene.

Cyclosporine This drug may increase levels of potassium with triamterene.

PROLONGED USE

Serious problems are unlikely, but levels of salts such as sodium and potassium may occasionally become abnormal during prolonged use.

Monitoring Blood tests may be performed to check on kidney function and levels of body salts.

VALPROIC ACID

Product names Depakene, Epival (divalproex sodium), Nu-Valproic, PHL Dialproex, and others
Used in the following combined preparations None

GENERAL INFORMATION

Valproic acid is an antiepileptict drug that is effective in treating all forms of epilepsy. Divalproex, also an antiepileptic, is chemically related to valproic acid. The action of valproic acid is similar to that of other antiepileptics, reducing electrical discharges in the brain to prevent the excessive build-up of discharges that can lead to epileptic seizures.

Beneficial in long-term treatment, this drug does not have a *sedative* effect. This makes it particularly suitable for children who suffer either from atonic epilepsy (the sudden relaxing of the muscles throughout the body) or from absence seizures (during which the person appears to be daydreaming).

Care should be taken if changing brands.

INFORMATION FOR USERS

Your drug prescription is tailored for you. Do not alter dosage without checking with your physician.

How taken

Capsules, tablets (divalproex), liquid, injection.

Frequency and timing of doses
1–2 x daily, after food.

Usual dosage range
15mg/kg/day (starting dose), gradually increasing until seizures controlled. Maximum dose of 60mg/kg/day.

Onset of effect
Within 60 minutes.

Duration of action
12 hours or more.

Diet advice
None.

Storage
Keep in a tightly closed container in a cool, dry place out of the reach of children. Protect from light.

Missed dose
Take as soon as you remember. If your next dose is due within 2 hours, take a single dose now and skip the next.

Stopping the drug
Do not stop the drug without consulting your physician; symptoms may recur.

Exceeding the dose
An occasional unintentional extra dose is unlikely to cause problems. Large overdoses may lead to coma. Notify your physician.

SPECIAL PRECAUTIONS

Be sure to tell your physician if:
▼ You have long-term liver or kidney problems.
▼ You are taking other medications.
▼ You have porphyria.
▼ You are pregnant or intend to become pregnant.
▼ You have diabetes.

Pregnancy
▼ Not usually prescribed. May cause abnormalities in the unborn baby as well as developmental delay. If prescribed, extra folic acid supplements should also be taken. Discuss seizure control with your physician and *pharmacist* prior to conception if possible.

Breast-feeding
▼ The drug passes into the breast milk, but at normal doses adverse effects on the baby are unlikely. Discuss with your physician.

Infants and children
▼ Reduced dose necessary.

Over 60
▼ Reduced dose may be necessary.

Driving and hazardous work
▼ Your underlying condition, as well as the possibility of reduced alertness while taking valproic acid, may make such activities inadvisable. Discuss with your physician.

Alcohol
▼ Avoid. Alcohol may increase the *sedative* effects of this drug.

POSSIBLE ADVERSE EFFECTS

Most of the *adverse effects* of valproic acid are uncommon and the most serious ones are rare. They include liver failure, and platelet and bleeding abnormalities.

Menstrual periods may become irregular or cease altogether.

Symptom/effect	Frequency		Discuss with physician		Stop taking drug now	Call physician now
	Common	Rare	Only if severe	In all cases		
Temporary loss of hair	●		■			
Weight gain	●		■			
Nausea/indigestion		●		■		
Rash		●		■		■
Drowsiness		●		■		■
Jaundice		●		■		■
Vomiting		●		■		■

INTERACTIONS

Other antiepileptic drugs These drugs may reduce blood levels of valproic acid.

ASA This drug may increase the effects of valproic acid.

Antidepressants, antipsychotics, mefloquine, and chloroquine These drugs may reduce the effectiveness of valproic acid.

Cholestyramine This drug may reduce the absorption of oral valproic acid.

Cimetidine and erythromycin These drugs may increase the effects of valproic acid.

Zidovudine When zidovudine and valproic acid are taken together, the blood levels of zidovudine may increase, leading to increased adverse effects.

PROLONGED USE

Use of this drug may cause liver damage, which is more likely in the first 6 months of use.

Monitoring Periodic blood tests of liver function and blood composition may be carried out.

VALSARTAN

Product names Ava-Valsartan, CO-Valsartan, Diovan, and others
Used in the following combined preparations Ava-Valsartan-HCT, Diovan-HCT, and others

GENERAL INFORMATION

Valsartan is a member of the group of vasodilator drugs called angiotensin-II blockers. Used to treat hypertension, the drug works by blocking the action of angiotensin-II (a naturally occurring substance that constricts blood vessels). This action causes the blood vessel walls to relax, thereby easing blood pressure. It can also be used after a heart attack to improve prognosis in those with heart failure, who cannot take ACE inhibitors. Valsartan is prescribed with caution to people with stenosis (narrowing) of the arteries of the kidneys. A small starting dose may be used initially to minimize the risk of a sudden drop in blood pressure seen early in therapy. This drug is taken once daily when taken for high blood pressure; it is usually taken twice daily in those with heart failure.

QUICK REFERENCE

Drug group Vasodilators (p.84) and Antihypertensive drugs (p.88)

Overdose danger rating Medium

Dependence rating Low

Prescription needed Yes

Available as generic Yes

INFORMATION FOR USERS

Your drug prescription is tailored for you. Do not alter dosage without checking with your physician.

How taken

Tablets and capsules.

Frequency and timing of doses
Once to twice daily.

Adult dosage range
40–320mg daily.

Onset of effect
Within 2 hours; to see changes in blood pressure, it may take 1–2 weeks, with maximum effect in 3–6 weeks.

Duration of action
Up to 24 hours.

Diet advice
None.

Storage
Keep in a closed container in a cool, dry place out of the reach of children.

Missed dose
Take as soon as you remember. If you take the dose daily and your next dose is within 8 hours, take a single dose now and skip the next.

Stopping the drug
Do not stop the drug without consulting your physician. Stopping the drug may lead to worsening of the underlying condition.

Exceeding the dose
An occasional unintentional extra dose is unlikely to cause problems. Large overdoses may cause dizziness and fainting. Notify your physician.

SPECIAL PRECAUTIONS

Be sure to tell your physician if:
▼ You have stenosis of the kidney arteries.
▼ You have kidney or liver problems.
▼ You are at risk for dehydration.
▼ You have experienced angioedema.
▼ You are allergic to valsartan or any other medications.
▼ You are taking other medications.

Pregnancy
▼ Not prescribed. May cause abnormalities in the fetus.

Breast-feeding
▼ Not prescribed. Safety not established.

Infants and children
▼ Not recommended.

Over 60
▼ A reduced dose may be necessary.

Driving and hazardous work
▼ Do not undertake such activities until you have learned how valsartan affects you because the drug can cause dizziness and fatigue.

Alcohol
▼ Avoid. Alcohol may increase the blood-pressure-lowering and *adverse effects* of valsartan.

POSSIBLE ADVERSE EFFECTS

A common *side effect* of this drug is dizziness. When getting out of bed or up from a chair, you should be sure to get up slowly while supporting yourself.

Symptom/effect	Frequency		Discuss with physician		Stop taking drug now	Call physician now
	Common	Rare	Only if severe	In all cases		
Dizziness/fatigue	●		■			
Headache		●	■			
Chills, fever, sore throat		●		■		
Diarrhea	●		■			
Abdominal pain	●		■			
Rash/itching		●		■		
Jaundice		●		■		
Wheezing/facial swelling		●		■	▲	■

INTERACTIONS

Diuretics, vasodilators, and other antihypertensives These drugs may increase the blood-pressure-lowering effects of valsartan.

Potassium supplements, potassium-sparing diuretics, cyclosporine Valsartan increases the effect of these drugs, leading to raised levels of potassium in the blood.

Lithium Valsartan may increase the levels and toxicity of lithium.

Non-steroidal anti-inflammatory drugs (NSAIDs) Certain NSAIDs may interfere with the blood-pressure-lowering effect of valsartan.

PROLONGED USE

No special problems.

Monitoring Periodic checks on blood potassium levels may be performed.

VARENICLINE

Product name Champix
Used in the following combined preparations None

GENERAL INFORMATION

Varenicline is an effective aid to stopping smoking in adults. It works in a similar way to nicotine in the body and helps reduce tobacco cravings. It is often more effective than nicotine replacement therapy or bupropion, and is also more likely to be successful in motivated individuals who are given additional expert advice and support. Discuss how this should be taken with your physician or *pharmacist*. *Adverse effects* are common but not usually serious. Rarely, it may cause suicidal behaviour. You should discontinue treatment and seek immediate medical advice if you become agitated, depressed, or have suicidal thoughts while taking varenicline.

QUICK REFERENCE

Drug group Drugs for treatment of tobacco dependence

Overdose danger rating Medium

Dependence rating Low

Prescription needed Yes

Available as generic No

INFORMATION FOR USERS

Your drug prescription is tailored for you. Do not alter dosage without checking with your physician.

How taken

Tablets.

Frequency and timing of doses
Once to twice daily. Take after a meal, with a full glass of water.

Adult dosage range
0.5–2mg daily.

Onset of effect
3–4 hours.

Duration of action
Up to 24 hours.

Diet advice
None.

Storage
Keep in a closed container in a cool, dry place out of the reach of children.

Missed dose
If you miss a dose, take it as soon as you remember. If it is almost time for the next dose, skip the missed dose and continue your usual dosing schedule. Do not double up to catch up on a missed dose.

Stopping the drug
Do not stop the drug without consulting your physician. Stopping the drug may lead to worsening of the underlying condition.

Exceeding the dose
An occasional unintentional extra dose is unlikely to cause problems. With large overdoses, notify your physician immediately.

SPECIAL PRECAUTIONS

Be sure to tell your physician if:
▼ You are taking nicotine replacement therapy.
▼ You have kidney disease.
▼ You have had heart problems or a stroke.
▼ You have a history of psychiatric problems.
▼ You are pregnant or planning to become pregnant.
▼ You are allergic to varenicline.
▼ You have had problems with alcohol abuse.
▼ You are taking other medications.

Pregnancy
▼ Not recommended in pregnancy. Discuss with your physician.

Breast-feeding
▼ Safety not established. Discuss with your physician.

Infants and children
▼ Not recommended.

Over 60
▼ If there is compromised kidney function, a smaller dose may be recommended.

Driving and hazardous work
▼ May cause drowsiness or dizziness. Do not drive a car or operate machinery until you feel you are mentally alert.

Alcohol
▼ Alcohol may increase the risk of drowsiness and other psychiatric *side effects* caused by this drug.

POSSIBLE ADVERSE EFFECTS

Nausea is the most commonly reported adverse effect and is related to the dose. With continued use, the incidence of nausea can decrease.

Symptom/effect	Frequency		Discuss with physician		Stop taking drug now	Call physician now
	Common	Rare	Only if severe	In all cases		
Nausea/vomiting	●		■			
Abnormal dreams	●			■		
Constipation/flatulence	●		■			
Taste changes	●		■			
Dizziness/drowsiness	●		■			
Sleep disturbance		●		■		
Unusual tiredness/weakness		●		■		
Abdominal pain		●		■		
Allergic reaction (swollen eyelids, lips, throat, shortness of breath)		●	■		▲	▮
Depression/suicidal thoughts		●	■		▲	▮
Confusion, paralysis, change in vision, sudden severe headache		●	■		▲	▮
Chest pain/symptoms of heart attack		●	■		▲	▮

PROLONGED USE

Varenicline is not normally used for prolonged periods.

INTERACTIONS

General note Stopping smoking may alter the effects of many drugs; examples include insulin, theophylline, and warfarin. Consult your physician or pharmacist.

Nicotine When used with nicotine products, *side effects* such as nausea, vomiting, headache, and dizziness may be higher. Combined therapy is not recommended.

VENLAFAXINE

Product names Effexor XR, Pristiq, and others
Used in the following combined preparations None

GENERAL INFORMATION

Venlafaxine is an antidepressant with a chemical structure unlike any other available antidepressant. It combines the therapeutic properties of both the tricyclic antidepressants and selective serotonin reuptake inhibitors (SSRIs), with fewer *anticholinergic adverse effects*.

As with other antidepressants, this drug acts to elevate mood, increase energy levels, and restore interest in everyday pursuits.

Nausea, dizziness, drowsiness or insomnia, and restlessness are common adverse effects. Weight loss may occur initially due to decreased appetite. At high doses, the drug can cause an elevation of blood pressure, which should be monitored during treatment.

INFORMATION FOR USERS

Your drug prescription is tailored for you. Do not alter dosage without checking with your physician.

How taken

Tablets, SR-capsules.

Frequency and timing of doses
Twice daily (tablets); once daily (SR-capsules). The drug should be taken with food.

Usual dosage range
75–150mg daily for outpatients; up to 375mg daily in severely depressed patients.

Onset of effect
Full antidepressant effect may not be felt for 2–4 weeks or more.

Duration of action
About 8–12 hours; up to 24 hours for SR-capsules. Following prolonged treatment, antidepressant effects may persist for up to 6 weeks.

Diet advice
None.

Storage
Keep in the original container in a cool, dry place out of the reach of children.

Missed dose
Do not make up for a missed dose. Just take your next regularly scheduled dose.

Stopping the drug
Do not stop the drug without consulting your physician. Stopping abruptly can cause withdrawal symptoms.

OVERDOSE ACTION

 Seek immediate medical advice in all cases. Take emergency action if fits, slow or irregular pulse, or loss of consciousness occur.

See Drug poisoning emergency guide (p.526).

SPECIAL PRECAUTIONS

Be sure to tell your physician if:
▼ You have had an adverse reaction to any other antidepressants.
▼ You have long-term liver or kidney problems.
▼ You have a heart problem or elevated blood pressure.
▼ You have had epileptic seizures.
▼ You have glaucoma.
▼ You have had problems with alcohol or drug misuse/abuse.
▼ You are taking other medications.

 Pregnancy
▼ Discuss treatment options with your physician.

 Breast-feeding
▼ Not recommended. Discuss with your physician.

 Infants and children
▼ Not recommended under 18 years.

 Over 60
▼ Increased likelihood of adverse effects. Reduced dose may therefore be necessary.

 Driving and hazardous work
▼ Avoid such activities until you have learned how venlafaxine affects you because the drug can cause dizziness, drowsiness, and blurred vision.

  Alcohol
▼ Avoid. Alcohol may increase the sedative effects of this drug.

POSSIBLE ADVERSE EFFECTS

The most common adverse effects are weakness, nausea, restlessness, and drowsiness. Some of these effects may wear off within a few days. Restlessness may include anxiety, nervousness, tremor, abnormal dreams, agitation, and confusion.

Symptom/effect	Frequency		Discuss with physician		Stop taking drug now	Call physician now
	Common	Rare	Only if severe	In all cases		
Nausea	●			■		
Restlessness/insomnia	●			■		
Weakness/blurred vision	●			■		
Drowsiness/dizziness	●			■		
Decreased appetite		●		■		
Sexual dysfunction		●		■	▲	
Rash/itching		●		■	▲	
High blood pressure		●		■		

INTERACTIONS

General note Drugs that affect breakdown of others in the liver may alter blood levels of venlafaxine, and vice versa.

Sedatives All drugs with a *sedative* effect may increase sedative effects of venlafaxine.

Antihypertensive drugs Venlafaxine may reduce the effectiveness of these drugs.

MAOIs Venlafaxine may interact with these drugs to produce a dangerous rise in blood pressure. MAOIs should be stopped at least 14 days before starting venlafaxine.

PROLONGED USE

Withdrawal symptoms may occur if the drug is not stopped gradually. There is also a small risk of suicidal thoughts and self-harm in children and adolescents, although the drug is rarely used for this age group.

Monitoring Blood pressure should be measured periodically if high doses of venlafaxine are prescribed.

VERAPAMIL

Product names Isoptin SR, Mylan-Verapamil, Verelan, and others
Used in the following combined preparation Tarka

GENERAL INFORMATION

Verapamil belongs to a group of drugs known as calcium channel blockers, which interfere with the conduction of signals in the muscles of the heart and blood vessels. It is used in the treatment of hypertension, abnormal heart rhythms, and angina. It reduces the frequency of angina attacks but does not help relieve pain while an attack is in progress. Verapamil increases the ability to tolerate physical exertion and can be used safely by asthmatics.

Verapamil is also prescribed for certain types of abnormal heart rhythm. It can be administered by injection as well as in tablet form for such disorders.

Verapamil is not generally prescribed for people with low blood pressure, slow heart beat, or heart failure because it may worsen these conditions.

QUICK REFERENCE

Drug group Anti-angina drugs (p.87), anti-arrhythmic drugs (p.86), and antihypertensive drugs (p.88)

Overdose danger rating Medium

Dependence rating Low

Prescription needed Yes

Available as generic Yes

INFORMATION FOR USERS

Your drug prescription is tailored for you. Do not alter dosage without checking with your physician.

How taken

Tablets, SR-tablets, injection.

Frequency and timing of doses
2–3x daily (tablets); 1–2x daily (SR-tablets). Injection: as directed by physician.

Usual adult dosage range
120–480mg daily.

Onset of effect
1–2 hours (tablets); 2–3 minutes (injection).

Duration of action
6–8 hours. During prolonged treatment some beneficial effects may last for up to 12 hours. SR-tablets act for 12–24 hours.

Diet advice
Avoid grapefruit juice which may increase blood levels of verapamil.

Storage
Keep in a closed container in a cool, dry place out of the reach of children.

Missed dose
Take as soon as you remember. If your next dose is due within 3 hours (tablets) or 8 hours (SR-tablets), take a single dose now and skip the next.

Stopping the drug
Do not stop the drug without consulting your physician; symptoms may recur.

Exceeding the dose
An occasional unintentional extra dose is unlikely to be a cause for concern. Large overdoses may cause dizziness. Notify your physician.

SPECIAL PRECAUTIONS

Be sure to tell your physician if:
▼ You have a long-term liver problem.
▼ You have heart failure.
▼ You have porphyria.
▼ You are taking other medications.

Pregnancy
▼ Not usually prescribed. May inhibit labour if taken during later stages of pregnancy. Discuss with your physician.

Breast-feeding
▼ The drug passes into the breast milk, but at normal doses adverse effects on the baby are unlikely. Discuss with your physician.

Infants and children
▼ Usually given on specialist advice only. Reduced dose necessary.

Over 60
▼ No special problems.

Driving and hazardous work
▼ Avoid such activities until you have learned how verapamil affects you because the drug can cause dizziness.

Alcohol
▼ Avoid. Alcohol may further reduce blood pressure, causing dizziness or other symptoms.

Surgery and general anesthetics
▼ Verapamil may need to be stopped before surgery. Consult your physician or dentist.

POSSIBLE ADVERSE EFFECTS

The main adverse effect is constipation. Rarely, verapamil may cause gynecomastia (breast enlargement in males) and an increase in gum tissue after long-term use.

Symptom/effect	Frequency		Discuss with physician		Stop taking drug now	Call physician now
	Common	Rare	Only if severe	In all cases		
Constipation	●		■			
Headache	●		■			
Nausea/vomiting	●		■			
Dry mouth	●		■			
Ankle swelling	●			■		
Dizziness/tiredness		●		■		
Breast/gum enlargement		●		■		
Rash		●		■		■

INTERACTIONS

Beta blockers When verapamil is taken with these drugs, there is a slight risk of abnormal heart beat and heart failure.

Carbamazepine The effects of this drug may be enhanced by verapamil.

Cyclosporine The blood levels of this drug may be increased by verapamil and its dose may need to be reduced.

Antihypertensive drugs Blood pressure may be further lowered when these drugs are taken with verapamil.

Digoxin The effects of this drug may be increased if it is taken with verapamil. The dosage of digoxin may need to be reduced.

PROLONGED USE

No problems expected.

WARFARIN

Product names Apo-Warfarin, Coumadin, Taro-Warfarin, and others
Used in the following combined preparations None

GENERAL INFORMATION

Warfarin is an anticoagulant used to prevent blood clots, mainly in areas where blood flow is slowest, particularly in the leg and pelvic veins. Such clots can break off and travel through the bloodstream to the lungs, where they lodge and cause pulmonary embolism. The drug is also used to reduce the risk of clots forming in the heart in people with atrial fibrillation, or after insertion of artificial heart valves. These clots may travel to the brain and cause a stroke.

A widely used oral anticoagulant drug, warfarin requires regular monitoring to ensure proper maintenance dosage. As its full beneficial effects are not felt for two to three days, a faster-acting drug such as heparin is often used to complement the effects of warfarin at the start of treatment.

The most serious *adverse effect*, as with all anticoagulants, is the risk of excessive bleeding, which is usually the result of excessive dosage.

INFORMATION FOR USERS

Your drug prescription is tailored for you. Do not alter dosage without checking with your physician.

How taken

Tablets.

Frequency and timing of doses
Once daily, taken at the same time each day.

Usual dosage range
10mg for 2 days (starting dose); 2–9mg daily at the same time, as determined by blood tests (maintenance dose).

Onset of effect
Within 24–48 hours, with full effect after several days.

Duration of action
2–3 days.

Diet advice
Avoid cranberry juice and major diet changes (especially of salads and vegetables).

Storage
Keep in a closed container in a cool, dry place out of the reach of children. Protect from light.

Missed dose
Take as soon as you remember. Take the following dose on your original schedule.

Stopping the drug
Do not stop taking the drug without consulting your physician; stopping the drug may lead to worsening of the underlying condition.

OVERDOSE ACTION

 Seek immediate medical advice in all cases. Take emergency action if severe bleeding or loss of consciousness occur.

See Drug poisoning emergency guide (p.526).

SPECIAL PRECAUTIONS

Be sure to tell your physician if:
▼ You have long-term liver or kidney problems.
▼ You have high blood pressure.
▼ You have peptic ulcers.
▼ You have a bleeding disorder.
▼ You are taking other medications.

 Pregnancy
▼ Not usually prescribed. If given in early pregnancy, the drug can cause malformations in the unborn child. Taken near the time of delivery, it may cause the mother to bleed excessively. Discuss with your physician.

 Breast-feeding
▼ The drug passes into the breast milk, but at normal doses adverse effects on the baby are unlikely. Discuss with your physician.

 Infants and children
▼ Reduced dose necessary.

 Over 60
▼ No special problems.

 Driving and hazardous work
▼ Use caution. Even minor bumps can cause bad bruises and excessive bleeding.

 Alcohol
▼ Avoid excessive amounts. Alcohol may increase the effects of this drug.

Surgery and general anesthetics
▼ Warfarin may need to be stopped before surgery. Discuss with your physician or dentist.

POSSIBLE ADVERSE EFFECTS

Bleeding is the most common adverse effect with warfarin. Any bruising, dark stools, dark urine, or prolonged bleeding from a minor wound should be reported to your physician at once.

Symptom/effect	Frequency		Discuss with physician		Stop taking drug now	Call physician now
	Common	Rare	Only if severe	In all cases		
Bleeding/bruising	●			■	▲	▮
Fever		●		■	▲	▮
Nausea/vomiting		●		■	▲	▮
Abdominal pain/diarrhea		●		■		
Rash		●		■		
Hair loss		●		■		
Jaundice		●		■		▮

INTERACTIONS

General note A wide variety of drugs, such as ASA, barbiturates, oral contraceptives, cimetidine, diuretics, certain antidepressants, and certain *antibiotics* interact with warfarin, either by increasing or decreasing the anticlotting effect. Consult your *pharmacist* before using over-the-counter medicines.

PROLONGED USE

No special problems.

Monitoring Regular blood tests are performed during treatment. More frequent testing may be needed if there is a significant change in your health.

XYLOMETAZOLINE

Product names Balminil Nasal Decongestant, Otrivin Decongestant Nasal Spray, and others
Used in the following combined preparation None

GENERAL INFORMATION

Xylometazoline is a sympathomimetic nasal decongestant that can be bought over-the-counter to relieve a stuffy nose caused by colds, hayfever, or sinusitis. It works by constricting the small blood vessels in the nose, thereby reducing inflammation and swelling.

   Because the effect of xylometazoline may last for up to 10 hours, it needs to be used only two or three times daily.

Using the drug more often than this will increase the likelihood of adverse effects such as headache, palpitations, and drowsiness. Nor should xylometazoline be used for more than a few days at a time; this may cause "rebound" congestion, making nasal stuffiness worse.

QUICK REFERENCE

Drug group Decongestants (p.79)
Overdose danger rating Medium
Dependence rating Low
Prescription needed No
Available as generic Yes

INFORMATION FOR USERS

Follow instructions on the label. Call your physician if symptoms worsen.

How taken

Nose drops, nasal spray.

Frequency and timing of doses
As needed up to 3 x daily.

Usual dosage range
Adults 2–3 drops or 1–2 sprays in each nostril (0.1 per cent solution).
Children 2-5 years 1 drop or 1 spray in each nostril (0.05 per cent solution).
Children 6 years and over 2–3 drops or 1–2 sprays in each nostril (0.05 per cent solution).

Onset of effect
Within 10 minutes.

Duration of action
Up to 10 hours.

Diet advice
None.

Storage
Keep in a closed container in a cool, dry place out of the reach of children. Protect from light.

Missed dose
No cause for concern. Take only if needed.

Stopping the drug
Can be safely stopped as soon as you no longer need it. Seek medical advice if symptoms persist for more than a few days.

Exceeding the dose
An occasional unintentional extra dose is unlikely to cause problems. Large overdoses or accidental poisoning may cause headaches, insomnia, and drowsiness. Notify your physician.

SPECIAL PRECAUTIONS

Be sure to consult your physician or pharmacist before using this drug if:
▼ You have glaucoma.
▼ You have heart problems.
▼ You have high blood pressure.
▼ You are taking other medications.

Pregnancy
▼ No evidence of risk if used sparingly. However, overuse can cause a rise in blood pressure that could harm the developing baby. Discuss with your physician.

Breast-feeding
▼ The drug passes into the breast milk, but at normal doses adverse effects on the baby are unlikely. Discuss with your physician.

Infants and children
▼ Reduced dose necessary. For children in general, but especially for those under 2 years of age, consult with your health care provider. Reduced dose necessary for all children.

Over 60
▼ Increased likelihood of adverse effects. Reduced dose may therefore be necessary.

Driving and hazardous work
▼ Exercise caution if blurred vision or drowsiness occurs.

Alcohol
▼ No special problems.

POSSIBLE ADVERSE EFFECTS

The adverse effects of xylometazoline are mild and infrequent when the medication is taken for short periods of time. When they do occur it is usually a signal that too much of the drug is being absorbed into the body, and this can be helped by reducing the dose.

Symptom/effect	Frequency		Discuss with physician		Stop taking drug now	Call physician now
	Common	Rare	Only if severe	In all cases		
Headache/lightheadedness		●		■		
Nasal discomfort		●	■			
Insomnia		●		■		
Blurred vision		●	■			
Excessive sneezing		●	■			
Palpitations/tremor		●		■	▲	

INTERACTIONS

Sympathomimetic drugs There is an increased risk of adverse effects when drugs such as ephedrine and pseudoephedrine are taken with xylometazoline.

Monoamine oxidase inhibitors (MAOIs) increase the risk of high blood pressure with xylometazoline, with potentially serious effects. Xylometazoline should not be taken during or within 14 days of MAOI treatment.

PROLONGED USE

Long-term use of this drug may lead to worsening of the condition. Also, it may lead to a rise in blood pressure. The drug increases the risk of lightheadedness, sleeplessness, and palpitations. Courses of longer than a few days are not recommended.

ZANAMIVIR

Product name Relenza
Used in the following combined preparations None

GENERAL INFORMATION

Zanamivir is an antiviral drug used to treat influenza (flu), a virus that infects and multiplies in the lungs. The drug works by attacking the virus and preventing it from multiplying and spreading in the lungs. Zanamivir is not a substitute for flu vaccination, but is used to treat at-risk individuals, for example the elderly and people with long-term illnesses such as chronic heart and lung disease.

Flu causes fever, chills, headache, aches and pains. Other symptoms include sore throat, cough, and nasal symptoms. Taken by inhaler, zanamivir helps to clear these symptoms and may shorten the duration of the illness. Therefore, treatment should begin as soon as possible, and certainly within 48 hours of the onset of symptoms.

Symptoms usually subside in two to seven days, unless complications such as a chest infection occur.

Zanamivir should be used with caution by asthmatic patients because it may provoke wheezing requiring urgent use of a *bronchodilator*.

INFORMATION FOR USERS

Your drug prescription is tailored for you. Do not alter dosage without checking with your physician.

How taken

Inhaled via Diskhaler.

Frequency and timing of doses
2 x daily. Inhale the contents of the blisters one at a time.

Usual dosage range
Adults 20mg (4 x 5mg blisters) daily for 5 days.
Children ≥ 7 years Same dose as in adults.

Onset of effect
Within 7 days.

Duration of action
Up to 12 hours.

Diet advice
None.

Storage
Keep in a cool, dry place out of the reach of children.

Missed dose
Take as soon as you remember. If your next dose is due within 2 hours, take a single dose now and skip the next.

Stopping the drug
Do not stop taking the drug without consulting your physician; symptoms may recur.

Exceeding the dose
An occasional unintentional dose is unlikely to cause problems. However, if you notice any unusual symptoms, or if a large overdose has been taken, notify your physician.

SPECIAL PRECAUTIONS

Be sure to tell your physician if:
▼ You have ever had an allergic reaction to zanamivir or lactose monohydrate.
▼ You have a long-term illness.
▼ You have a lung disease such as asthma.
▼ You have poor immunity to infections.
▼ You are taking other medications.

Pregnancy
▼ Safety in pregnancy not established. Discuss with your physician.

Breast-feeding
▼ Safety in breast-feeding not established. Discuss with your physician.

Infants and children
▼ Not recommended in children < 7 years of age.

Over 60
▼ No special problems.

Driving and hazardous work
▼ No known problems.

Alcohol
▼ No known problems.

POSSIBLE ADVERSE EFFECTS

Adverse effects are uncommon. Such effects that occur are similar to signs and symptoms of flu and may therefore sometimes be caused by the influenza virus rather than zanamivir.

Symptom/effect	Frequency		Discuss with physician		Stop taking drug now	Call physician now
	Common	Rare	Only if severe	In all cases		
Headache		●	■			
Sore throat		●	■			
Cough		●	■			
Nasal symptoms		●	■			
Wheezing/breathlessness		●		■	▲	

PROLONGED USE

This drug should only be used for 5 days and is not prescribed for long-term use.

INTERACTIONS

Inhaled drugs (e.g., salbutamol and beclomethasone) These should be inhaled just before zanamivir is administered.

ZIDOVUDINE/LAMIVUDINE

Product names 3TC, Apo-Zidovudine, Novo-AZT, Retrovir (zidovudine)
Used in the following combined preparations Combivir, Trizivir

GENERAL INFORMATION

Zidovudine and lamivudine are from the same class of drugs – nucleoside analogues – and are used in the treatment of HIV infection. The two drugs are also available combined in one tablet, which is usually prescribed with another class of drug to treat HIV, either a non-nucleoside reverse transcriptase inhibitor or a protease inhibitor. This combination of three drugs is more effective at treating HIV than either a single or double regime of drugs.

Although not a cure for HIV, combination antiretroviral therapy (also known as highly active antiretroviral therapy, or HAART) slows down production of the virus and, therefore, reduces the viral load and consequent damage done to the immune system. The drugs need to be taken regularly and on a long-term basis to remain effective.

QUICK REFERENCE

Drug group Drugs for HIV and immune deficiency (p.144)

Overdose danger rating Medium

Dependence rating Low

Prescription needed Yes

Available as generic No

INFORMATION FOR USERS

Your drug prescription is tailored for you. Do not alter dosage without checking with your physician.

How taken

Tablets.

Frequency and timing of doses
Every 12 hours.

Usual adult dosage range
One tablet.

Onset of effect
1 hour.

Duration of action
12 hours.

Diet advice
None.

Storage
Keep in the original container in a cool, dry place out of the the reach of children.

Missed dose
Take as soon as you remember. If your next dose is due within 2 hours, take a single dose now and skip the next. It is very important not to miss doses on a regular basis as this can lead to the development of drug-resistant HIV.

Stopping the drug
Do not stop taking the drug without consulting your physician.

Exceeding the dose
An occasional unintentional extra dose is unlikely to cause problems. But if you notice any unusual symptoms, or if a large overdose has been taken, notify your physician.

SPECIAL PRECAUTIONS

Be sure to tell your physician if:
▼ You have liver or kidney problems.
▼ You have other infections, such as hepatitis B or C.
▼ You are taking other medications.

Pregnancy
▼ If you are pregnant or planning pregnancy, discuss benefits versus risks with your physician.

Breast-feeding
▼ Safety in breast-feeding not established. Breast-feeding is not recommended by HIV-positive mothers as the virus may be passed to the baby.

Infants and children
▼ Reduced dose necessary.

Over 60
▼ Increased likelihood of adverse effects. Reduced dose may therefore be necessary.

Driving and hazardous work
▼ No special problems.

Alcohol
▼ No known problems.

POSSIBLE ADVERSE EFFECTS

The most common adverse effects of zidovudine/lamivudine are nausea, vomiting, and diarrhea. Sometimes, anemia may develop with prolonged use.

Symptom/effect	Frequency		Discuss with physician		Stop taking drug now	Call physician now
	Common	Rare	Only if severe	In all cases		
Nausea/vomiting	●		■			
Diarrhea	●		■			
Fatigue	●		■			
Skin discoloration		●	■			
Anemia		●		■		
Severe abdominal pain		●		■		■

INTERACTIONS

General note A wide range of drugs may interact with zidovudine and lamivudine causing either an increase in adverse effects or a reduction in the effect of the antiretroviral drugs. Check with your physician or pharmacist before taking any new drugs, including those from the dentist and supermarket, and herbal medicines.

PROLONGED USE

There is an increased risk of serious blood disorders, such as anemia, with long-term use of zidovudine and lamivudine. There may also be redistribution of fat from the limbs to the abdomen, back, and breasts. This may be accompanied by increases in blood levels of lipids and glucose.

Monitoring Regular blood checks will be carried out to monitor the viral load, blood count, and blood lipid and glucose levels.

ZOPICLONE

Product names Apo-Zopiclone, Imovane, Rhovane, and others
Used in the following combined preparations None

GENERAL INFORMATION

Zopiclone is a hypnotic (sleeping drug) used for the short-term treatment of insomnia. Sleep problems can take the form of difficulty in falling asleep, frequent night-time awakenings, and/or early morning awakenings. Hypnotic drugs are given only when non-drug measures – for example, avoidance of caffeine – have proved ineffective. Unlike benzodiazepines, zopiclone possesses no anti-anxiety properties.

Hypnotics are intended for occasional use only. The risk of *dependence* is increased with ongoing, continuous use.

QUICK REFERENCE

Drug group Sleeping drugs (p.66)
Overdose danger rating Medium
Dependence rating Medium
Prescription needed Yes
Available as generic Yes

INFORMATION FOR USERS

Your drug prescription is tailored for you. Do not alter dosage without checking with your physician.

How taken

Tablets.

Frequency and timing of doses
Once daily at bedtime when required. Tablets should be swallowed whole, without sucking or chewing.

Usual dosage range
3.75–7.5mg.

Onset of effect
Within 30 minutes.

Duration of action
4–6 hours.

Diet advice
None.

Storage
Keep in a closed container in a cool, dry place out of the reach of children. Protect from light.

Missed dose
If you fall asleep without having taken a dose and wake some hours later, do not take the missed dose.

Stopping the drug
If you have been taking the drug continuously for less than 1 week, it can be safely stopped as soon as you feel you no longer need it. However, if you have been taking the drug for longer, consult your physician.

Exceeding the dose
An occasional, unintentional extra dose is unlikely to cause problems. Large overdoses may cause prolonged sleep, drowsiness, lethargy, and poor muscle coordination and reflexes. Notify your physician immediately.

POSSIBLE ADVERSE EFFECTS

The most common *adverse effects* of zopiclone are daytime drowsiness, which normally diminishes after the first few days of treatment, and a bitter taste in the mouth. Persistent morning drowsiness or impaired coordination are signs of excessive dose.

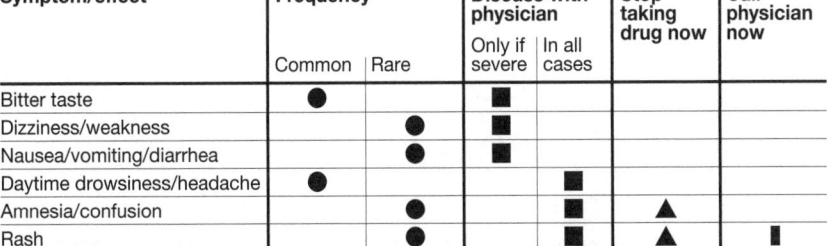

Symptom/effect	Frequency		Discuss with physician		Stop taking drug now	Call physician now
	Common	Rare	Only if severe	In all cases		
Bitter taste	●		■			
Dizziness/weakness		●	■			
Nausea/vomiting/diarrhea		●	■			
Daytime drowsiness/headache	●			■		
Amnesia/confusion		●		■	▲	
Rash		●		■	▲	∎

INTERACTIONS

Sedatives All drugs, including alcohol, that have a *sedative* effect on the central nervous system are likely to increase the sedative effects of zopiclone. Such drugs include other sleeping and anti-anxiety drugs, antihistamines, antidepressants, *opioid* analgesics, and antipsychotics.

Carbamazepine, phenytoin, rifampicin, and St John's wort may reduce the effects of zopiclone.

SPECIAL PRECAUTIONS

Be sure to tell your physician if:
▼ You have or have had any problems with alcohol or drug misuse/abuse.
▼ You have myasthenia gravis.
▼ You have had epileptic seizures.
▼ You have liver or kidney problems.
▼ You are taking other medications.

 Pregnancy
▼ Use in late pregnancy may affect the baby and cause withdrawal symptoms. Discuss with your physician.

 Breast-feeding
▼ The drug passes into the breast milk. Discuss with your physician.

 Infants and children
▼ Not recommended.

 Over 60
▼ Increased likelihood of adverse effects. Reduced dose may therefore be necessary.

 Driving and hazardous work
▼ Avoid such activities until you have learned how zopiclone affects you because the drug can cause drowsiness, reduced alertness, and slowed reactions.

 Alcohol
▼ Avoid. Alcohol increases the sedative effects of this drug.

PROLONGED USE

Intended for occasional use only. The risk of dependence is increased with ongoing, continuous use. Withdrawal symptoms may occur when the drug is stopped. These may include insomnia, anxiety, tremor, confusion, and panic attacks. Withdrawal symptoms are less likely when the drug is used for less than 4 weeks.

A–Z OF VITAMINS, MINERALS, AND SUPPLEMENTS

This section gives detailed information on the major vitamins and minerals that are required by the body for good health – essential chemicals that the body cannot make by itself. These include the main vitamins – A, C, D, E, K, H, and the B vitamins – together with 11 essential minerals. Information on selected supplements is also included. The section on vitamins in Part 3 (p.135) gives in general terms the main sources of the major vitamins and minerals and their roles in the body, while the following profiles discuss each vitamin and mineral in detail.

The following pages may be particularly useful as a guide for those who think their diet lacks sufficient amounts of a certain vitamin or mineral, and for those with disorders of the digestive tract or liver, who may need larger amounts of certain vitamins. The table on p.136 gives the good dietary sources of each one.

The profiles

Vitamins, minerals, and supplements are considered natural health products in Canada and are regulated by the Natural Health Products Directorate. Supplements may not be standardized in how they are manufactured, and the amount of the active substance may vary between products (and from the product used to conduct research).

The profiles here are arranged in alphabetical order and give information under standard headings. Normal daily vitamin and mineral requirements are usually based on the Recommended Dietary Allowance (RDA) or Adequate Intake (AI). This measurement is the amount of the nutrient thought to be enough for about 97–98 per cent of healthy people. The dosages for treating a vitamin or mineral deficiency are usually much higher, but the precise doses need to be determined by your physician.

HOW TO UNDERSTAND THE PROFILES

Each vitamin, mineral, and supplement profile contains information arranged under standard headings to enable you to find the information you need.

Availability
Tells you whether the vitamin, mineral, or supplement is available over the counter or only by prescription.

Other names
Lists the chemical and non-chemical names by which the vitamin or mineral is also known.

Dietary and other natural sources
Tells you how the vitamin or mineral is obtained naturally.

When supplements are helpful
Suggests when your physician may recommend that you take supplements.

Dosage range for treating deficiency
Gives a usual recommended dosage of vitamin or mineral supplements.

Actions on the body
Explains the role played by each vitamin or mineral in maintaining healthy body function.

Normal daily requirement
Gives you a guide to the recommended daily allowance (RDA) of each vitamin or mineral.

Symptoms of deficiency
Describes the common signs of deficiency.

Symptoms and risks of excessive intake
Explains the risks that may accompany excessive intake of each vitamin or mineral and warning signs to look out for.

PANTOTHENIC ACID

Other names Calcium pantothenate, vitamin B₅

Availability
Pantothenic acid, calcium pantothenate, and panthenol are available without prescription in a variety of multivitamin and mineral preparations.

Actions on the body
Pantothenic acid plays a vital role in the activities of many enzymes. It is essential for the production of energy from sugars and fats, for the manufacture of fats, corticosteroids, and sex hormones, for the utilization of other vitamins, for the proper function of the nervous system and the adrenal glands, and for normal growth and development.

Dietary and other natural sources
Pantothenic acid is present in almost all vegetables, cereals, and animal foods. Liver, kidney, heart, fish, and egg yolks are good dietary sources. Brewer's yeast, wheat germ, and royal jelly (the substance on which queen bees feed) are also rich in the vitamin.

Normal daily requirement
No recommended daily allowance (RDA) for pantothenic acid has ever been established, but adult requirements are met by a 4–7mg intake daily.

When supplements are helpful
Most diets provide adequate amounts of pantothenic acid. Any deficiency is likely to occur in malnutrition together with other B vitamin deficiency diseases such as pellagra (see niacin), beriberi (see thiamine), or with alcoholism, and will be treated with B complex supplements. There is no firm evidence that large doses help, as some believe, in the prevention of greying hair, nerve disorders in diabetes, or psychiatric illness.

Symptoms of deficiency
Pantothenic acid deficiency is unlikely to occur unless a person is suffering from malnutrition. However, deficiency produced under experimental conditions can cause malaise, abdominal discomfort, and burning feet.

Dosage range for treating deficiency
Usually 5–10mg per day.

Symptoms and risks of excessive intake
In tests, doses of 1,000mg or more of pantothenic acid have not caused toxic effects. The risk of toxicity is considered to be very low, since pantothenic acid is a water-soluble vitamin that does not accumulate in the tissues. Any excess is eliminated rapidly in the urine. However, very high intakes of 10–20g can cause diarrhea.

POTASSIUM

Other names Potassium chloride, potassium citrate, potassium gluconate

Availability
Salts of potassium in small doses are available in a number of multivitamin and mineral supplements. They are available at higher doses as supplements and in an injectable form, both to be used under medical supervision. Potassium salts are also widely available in sodium-free salt (used as a salt substitute).

Actions on the body
Potassium works together with sodium in the control of the body's water balance, conduction of nerve impulses, contraction of muscle, and maintenance of a normal heart rhythm. Potassium is essential for maintenance of normal blood sugar.

Dietary and other natural sources
The best dietary sources of potassium are leafy green vegetables, tomatoes, oranges, potatoes, and bananas. Lean meat, pulses, chocolate, coffee, and milk are also rich in the mineral. Many methods of food processing may lower the potassium levels found in fresh food.

Normal daily requirement
The recommended daily allowance (RDA) is 2,000mg in adults. There are no extra requirements in pregnancy or breast-feeding.

When supplements are helpful
Most diets contain adequate amounts of potassium, and supplements are rarely required in normal circumstances. However, people who drink large amounts of alcohol or eat lots of salty foods may become marginally deficient. People with a condition called diabetic ketoacidosis or with certain types of kidney disease may be deficient in potassium, but the most common cause is prolonged treatment with diuretics. Long-term use of corticosteroids may also deplete the body's potassium. Prolonged vomiting and diarrhea also cause potassium deficiency, so people who abuse laxatives may be affected. Supplements are usually advised only when symptoms suggest deficiency, or for people at particular risk.

Symptoms of deficiency
Early symptoms of potassium deficiency may include muscle weakness, fatigue, dizziness, and mental confusion. Impairment of nerve and muscle function may progress to cause disturbances of the heart rhythm and paralysis of the skeletal muscles and those of the bowel, which leads to constipation.

Dosage range for treating deficiency
Depends on the preparation, the individual, and the cause and severity of deficiency. In general, daily doses equivalent to 20-40mmol/day of potassium chloride are given to prevent deficiency (for example, in people treated with diuretics that deplete potassium). Doses equivalent to 40–60mmol of potassium chloride daily are used to treat deficiency. Potassium supplements should be taken with a full glass of water, and may be taken after a meal to avoid gastric irritation.

Symptoms and risks of excessive intake
Blood potassium levels are normally regulated by the kidneys, and any excess is rapidly eliminated in the urine. Massive doses cause serious disturbances of the heart rhythm and muscular paralysis. In people with impaired kidney function, excess potassium may build up and the risk of potassium poisoning is increased. People on hemodialysis treatment need to take a carefully controlled low-potassium diet.

476

BIOTIN

Other names Coenzyme R, vitamin B$_7$

Availability
Biotin is available without a prescription, alone and in a wide variety of multivitamin and mineral preparations.

Actions on the body
Biotin plays a vital role in the activities of several *enzymes*. It is essential for the breakdown of carbohydrates and fatty acids in the diet for conversion into energy, for the manufacture of fats, and for excretion of the products of protein breakdown.

Dietary and other natural sources
Traces of biotin are present in a wide variety of foods. Dietary sources rich in this vitamin include liver, nuts, yeast, peas, beans, egg yolks, cauliflower, and mushrooms. A large proportion of the biotin we require is manufactured by bacteria in the intestine.

Normal daily requirement
Daily adequate intake (AI) amounts of biotin are: 5mcg (0–6 months); 6mcg (7–12 months); 8mcg (1–3 years); 12mcg (4–8 years); 20mcg (9–13 years); 25mcg (14–18 years); 30mcg (19 years and over); 35mcg (while breast-feeding).

When supplements are helpful
Adequate amounts of biotin are provided in most diets and by the bacteria living in the intestine, so supplements are rarely needed. However, deficiency can occur with prolonged, excessive consumption of raw egg whites (as in eggnogs), because these contain a protein – avidin – that prevents absorption of the vitamin in the intestine. The risk of deficiency is also increased during long-term treatment with antibiotics or sulfonamide antibacterial drugs, which may destroy the biotin-producing bacteria in the intestine. However, additional biotin is not usually necessary with a balanced diet.

Symptoms of deficiency
Deficiency symptoms include weakness, tiredness, poor appetite, hair loss, muscle pain, and depression. Severe deficiency is rare but may cause eczema of the face and body, and inflammation of the tongue.

Dosage range for treating deficiency
Depends on the individual and on the nature and severity of the disorder. Dietary deficiency can be treated with doses of 150–300mcg of biotin daily. Deficiency of biotin resulting from a genetic defect that limits use of the vitamin by body cells can be treated with very large doses of 5mg given once or twice daily.

Symptoms and risks of excessive intake
None known.

CALCIUM

Other names Calcium acetate, calcium carbonate, calcium chloride, calcium citrate, calcium gluconeptonate, calcium gluconate, calcium lactate, calcium phosphate

Availability
Oral forms are available without a prescription. Injectable forms of calcium are available only under medical supervision.

Actions on the body
The most abundant mineral in the body, calcium makes up more than 90 per cent of the hard matter in bones and teeth. It is essential for the formation and maintenance of strong bones and healthy teeth, as well as blood clotting, transmission of nerve impulses, and muscle contraction.

Dietary and other natural sources
The main dietary sources of calcium are milk and dairy products, sardines, dark green leafy vegetables, beans, peas, and nuts. Calcium may also be obtained by drinking water in hard water areas.

Normal daily requirement
The recommended dietary requirements for elemental calcium are: 200mg (birth–6 months); 260mg (7–12 months); 700mg (1–3 years); 1,000mg (4–8 years); 1,300mg (9–18 years); 1,000mg (19–50 years); 1,000mg (males aged 51–70 years); 1,200mg (females aged 51–70 years); 1,200 (over 70 years). The daily requirement of calcium in pregnancy and during breast-feeding is 1,000mg.

When supplements are helpful
Unless a sufficient amount of dairy products is consumed (a glass of milk contains approximately 300mg) the diet may not contain enough calcium, and supplements may be needed. Breast-feeding women are especially vulnerable to calcium deficiency because breast-feeding demands large amounts of calcium, which may be extracted from the skeleton if intake is not adequate. Osteoporosis (fragile bones) has been linked to dietary calcium deficiency, but supplements alone may not be enough to treat this condition. Other treatment is usually necessary (see Drugs for bone disorders, p.108). Avoid single doses of over 500mg of elemental calcium.

Symptoms of deficiency
When dietary intake is inadequate, the body obtains the calcium it needs from the skeleton. Long-term deficiency of calcium may lead to increased fragility of the bones. Osteoporosis results in increased risk of fractures, particularly of the vertebrae, hip, and wrist. Severe deficiency, resulting in low levels of calcium in the blood, causes abnormal stimulation of the nervous system, resulting in cramp-like spasms in the hands, feet, and face. Vitamin D deficiency is the main cause of the bone-softening diseases rickets and osteomalacia.

Dosage range for treating deficiency
Vitamin D helps with calcium absorption and is needed for treatment of all cases of calcium deficiency, such as rickets and osteomalacia (p.108). Oral supplements of up to 800IU vitamin D daily may be advised for children with rickets, and 800IU to 1,000IU daily may be given for osteoporosis and osteomalacia. Severe calcium deficiency is treated in hospital by intravenous injection of calcium.

Symptoms and risks of excessive intake
Excessive intake of calcium may reduce the amount of iron and zinc absorbed and may also cause constipation and nausea. There are concerns related to increase in cardiac problems if excess supplementation is used; it is preferable to obtain the required calcium from foods and only use supplements if this is inadequate. There is an increased risk of palpitations and, for susceptible people, of calcium deposits in the kidneys leading to kidney stones and kidney damage. These symptoms do not usually develop unless excessive calcium is consumed.

CHROMIUM

Other name Chromium picolinate

Availability
Chromium supplements are available without prescription. However, only a very small proportion of chromium in the supplements is absorbed by the body (possibly 1–2 per cent).

Actions on the body
Chromium plays a vital role in the activities of several *enzymes*. It is involved in the breakdown of sugar for conversion into energy and in the manufacture of certain fats. The mineral works together with insulin and is thus essential to the body's ability to use sugar. Chromium may also be involved in the manufacture of proteins in the body.

Dietary and other natural sources
Traces of chromium are present in a wide variety of foods. Meat, dairy products, and wholemeal cereals are good sources of this mineral.

Normal daily requirement
Chromium is a trace element and only minute quantities are required. Daily adequate intake (AI) amounts are: 0.2mcg (0–6 months); 5.5mcg (7–12 months); 11mcg (1–3 years); 15mcg (4–8 years); 25mcg (males aged 9–13 years; females aged 19–50 years); 21mcg (females aged 9–13 years); 35mcg (males aged 14–50 years); 24mcg (females aged 14–18 years); 30mcg (males aged 51 and over); 20mcg (females aged 51 and over); 30mcg (during pregnancy); 45mcg (while breast-feeding).

When supplements are helpful
Most people who eat a healthy diet containing plenty of fresh or unprocessed foods receive adequate amounts of chromium. The use of chromium in diabetes is under investigation, but diabetics and those with diabetes-like symptoms may benefit from additional chromium. Supplements may also be helpful if symptoms suggest chromium deficiency.

Symptoms of deficiency
Chromium deficiency is very rare in Canada and typically occurs mainly in patients given long-term intravenous feeding. A diet of too many processed foods may contribute to chromium deficiency. Inadequate intake of chromium over a prolonged period may impair the body's ability to use sugar, leading to high blood sugar levels. However, in most cases, there are no symptoms. In some people, there may be diabetes-like symptoms such as tiredness, mental confusion, and numbness or tingling of the hands and feet. Deficiency may worsen pre-existing diabetes and may depress growth in children. It has also been suggested that chromium deficiency may contribute to the development of atherosclerosis (narrowing of the arteries).

Dosage range for treating deficiency
Since chromium deficiency is very rare, there are no recommendations to treat deficiency to-date. Discuss with your physician.

Symptoms and risks of excessive intake
Chromium is poisonous in excess. Levels that produce symptoms are usually obtained from occupational exposure or industrial waste in drinking water or the atmosphere, not from excessive dietary intake. Symptoms include inflammation of the skin and, if inhaled, damage to the nasal passages. People who are repeatedly exposed to chromium fumes have a higher-than-average risk of developing lung cancer. High levels may reduce kidney function.

CO-ENZYME Q$_{10}$

Other names Ubiquinone-10, ubidecarenone, CoQ$_{10}$

Availability
Co-enzyme Q$_{10}$, also known as CoQ$_{10}$, is available without a prescription.

Actions on the body
Co-enzyme Q$_{10}$ is a natural substance in the body and is used to produce energy for cell growth. It is also an antioxidant, protecting cells from damage caused by harmful molecules. CoQ$_{10}$ is naturally present in foods.

Dietary and other natural sources
Peanuts, soy oil, fish such as sardines and mackerel, and organ meats (heart, liver) are particularly high in CoQ$_{10}$.

Normal daily requirement
There is no specific recommended daily allowance for Co-enzyme Q$_{10}$.

When supplements are helpful
CoQ$_{10}$ has been studied in patients with heart failure and is thought to protect the heart muscle from damage caused by some prescription drugs. However, not all scientists agree that it has beneficial effects. In general, it may have potential benefits for heart health and as an antioxidant.

Symptoms of deficiency
No specific deficiency noted.

Dosage range for treating deficiency
There is no specific deficiency range. When used for heart health, CoQ$_{10}$ has been used in doses ranging from 30–100 mg, taken one to three times daily. Rarely, CoQ$_{10}$ may increase liver enzymes or affect thyroid *hormone* levels. CoQ$_{10}$ may decrease the effect of some drugs when taken concurrently, such as warfarin. Other drugs, such as those used for high cholesterol (statins) or for diabetes, may decrease the level of CoQ$_{10}$. Liver function tests and blood glucose levels may need to be periodically monitored. Individuals on co-enzyme Q$_{10}$ should be monitored by their physician and *pharmacist*. Women who are breast-feeding should consult their physician as safety in this situation has not been established.

Symptoms and risks of excessive intake
No specific *adverse effects* related to high doses have been reported. May adversely affect liver function.

COPPER

Other names Copper chloride, copper chloride dihydrate, copper gluconate, copper sulfate

Availability
Copper supplements are available in oral combined products without a prescription.

Actions on the body
Copper is an essential constituent of several proteins and *enzymes*. It plays an important role in the development of red blood cells, helps to form the dark pigment that colours hair and skin, and helps the body to use vitamin C. It is essential for the formation of collagen and elastin – proteins found in ligaments, blood vessel walls, and the lungs – and for the proper formation and maintenance of strong bones. It is also required for central nervous system activity.

Dietary and other natural sources
Most unprocessed foods contain copper. Liver, shellfish, nuts, mushrooms, wholemeal cereals, and dried pulses are particularly rich sources. Soft water may dissolve copper from pipes.

Normal daily requirement
The recommended dietary allowances (RDA) for copper are: 0.2mg (birth–6 months); 0.22mg (7 months–1 year); 0.34mg (1–3 years); 0.44mg (4–8 years); 0.7mg (9–13 years); 0.89mg (14–18 years); and 0.9mg (19 years and over). Daily requirement during pregnancy is 1mg, and rises to 1.3mg when breast-feeding.

When supplements are helpful
A diet that regularly includes a selection of the foods mentioned above provides sufficient copper. Supplements are rarely necessary. However, physicians may advise additional copper for malnourished infants and children.

Symptoms of deficiency
Copper deficiency is very rare. The major change is *anemia* due to failure of production of red blood cells, the main symptoms of which are pallor, fatigue, shortness of breath, and palpitations. In severe cases, abnormal bone changes may occur. An inherited copper deficiency disorder called Menke's syndrome (kinky hair disease) results in brain degeneration, retarded growth, sparse and brittle hair, and weak bones.

Dosage range for treating deficiency
This depends on the individual and on the nature and severity of the disorder.

Symptoms and risks of excessive intake
The tolerable upper intake level for copper is 10mg/day. Amounts larger than this can produce toxic effects. Symptoms of poisoning include nausea, vomiting, abdominal pain, diarrhea, and general aches and pains. Large overdoses of copper may cause destruction of red blood cells (hemolytic anemia), and liver and kidney damage. In Wilson's disease, an inherited disorder, the patient cannot excrete copper and suffers from long-term copper poisoning and gradually develops liver and brain damage. The disease is treated with *chelating agents* such as penicillamine. Acute copper poisoning may occur in people who regularly drink homemade alcohol distilled through copper tubing.

FLUORIDE

Other name Sodium fluoride

Availability
Sodium fluoride may be added to drinking water and is available over-the-counter in single- or multiple-ingredient preparations. It is also available in mouth rinses, toothpastes, tablets, gels, and oral drops.

Actions on the body
Fluoride helps to prevent tooth decay and contributes to the strength of bones. It is thought to work on the teeth by strengthening the mineral composition of the tooth enamel, making it more resistant to attack by acid in the mouth. Fluoride is most effective when taken during the formation of teeth in childhood, since it is then incorporated into the tooth itself. It may also strengthen developing bones.

Dietary and other natural sources
Fluoride has been added to drinking water in many areas, and water is therefore a prime source of this mineral (fluoride levels in water vary from area to area, and untreated water also contains a small amount of fluoride). Foods and beverages grown or prepared in areas with fluoride-treated water may also contribute fluoride. Tea and sea fish are also rich in fluoride.

Normal daily requirement
Daily adequate intake (AI) amounts for fluoride are: 0.01mg (0–6 months); 0.5mg (7–12 months); 0.7mg (1–3 years); 1mg (4–8 years); 2mg (9–13 years); 3mg (males aged 14–18 years; females aged 14 and over); 4mg (males aged 19 years and over).

When supplements are helpful
Fluoride supplements are not usually necessary for adults, particularly those who use a fluoride toothpaste, although a dentist may recommend supplements for people who are especially prone to tooth decay. For children, supplements are not generally advised unless the drinking water contains a very low level of fluoride; infants less than 6 months old should not be given supplements even if the drinking water is low in fluoride. In all cases, supplements should only be used on the advice of a dentist. See below for more information about dosage ranges for supplements.

Symptoms of deficiency
Fluoride deficiency increases the risk of tooth decay, especially in children.

Dosage range for treating deficiency
Dietary supplements are not usually advised unless the drinking water contains less than 0.7 parts per million (ppm) of fluoride. In such cases, the recommended dosage depends on the level of fluoride in the water and the age of the child; supplements are not recommended for infants under 6 months old. When the drinking water contains less than 0.3ppm, the recommended daily dose is: 0.25mg (6 months–3 years); 0.5mg (4–8 years); and 1mg (9–13 years). When the drinking water contains 0.3–0.7ppm, supplements are not recommended for children under 3 years old; the recommended daily dose for older children is 0.25mg (3–6 years) and 0.5mg (over 6 years).

Symptoms and risks of excessive intake
Prolonged intake of water containing high concentrations of fluoride may lead to mottled or brown discoloration of the enamel in developing teeth, a condition known as fluorosis. Suggestions of a link between fluoridation of the water supply and cancer are without foundation. A child or adult who has taken a number of fluoride tablets may become seriously unwell and eventually lose consciousness. Give milk if the person is conscious, and seek immediate medical help (see p.526).

FOLIC ACID

Other names Folacin, vitamin B$_9$, folate, pteroylglutamic acid

Availability
Folic acid is available without prescription, alone and in a variety of multivitamin and mineral preparations. Strengths of over 1,000mcg (1mg) are available only on prescription.

Actions on the body
Folic acid is essential for the activities of several *enzymes*. It is required for the manufacture of nucleic acids – the genetic material of cells – and thus for the processes of growth and reproduction. It is vital for the formation of red blood cells by the bone marrow and the development and function of the central nervous system.

Dietary and other natural sources
The best sources are leafy green vegetables, yeast extract, and liver. Root vegetables, oranges, nuts, dried pulses, and egg yolks are also rich sources.

Normal daily requirement
Recommended dietary allowances as folate are: 0.065mg (birth–6 months); 0.08mg (7 months–1 year); 0.15mg (1–3 years); 0.20mg (4–8 years); 0.30mg (9–13 years); 0.40mg (14 years and over). For women considering pregnancy, the following are recommended to decrease incidence of fetal congenital problems; women with no personal health risks, on a healthy folate-rich diet, should take a daily supplement of a multivitamin with folic acid (0.4–1mg) for at least 2-3 months before conception; 0.60mg throughout pregnancy; after childbirth, 0.5mg for 4–6 weeks while breast-feeding. Women with health risks (epilepsy, Type 1 Diabetes mellitus, obesity, family history of neural tube defect) should consume a folate-rich diet and a daily multivitamin with 4mg folic acid to be started 3 months before conception and for the first 10–12 weeks of pregnancy.

When supplements are helpful
A varied diet containing fresh fruit and vegetables usually provides adequate amounts. However, minor deficiency is fairly common, and can be corrected by the addition of one uncooked fruit or vegetable or a glass of fruit juice daily. Supplements are recommended for women before and during pregnancy for the prevention of neural tube defects such as spina bifida. Supplements may also be needed in premature or low-birth-weight infants and those fed on goat's milk (breast and cow's milk contain adequate amounts of the vitamin). Physicians may recommend additional folic acid for people on hemodialysis, those who have certain blood disorders, psoriasis, certain conditions in which absorption of nutrients from the intestine is impaired, severe alcoholism, or liver disease. Supplements may be helpful if you are a heavy drinker or if you are taking certain drugs that deplete folic acid. Such drugs include antiepileptics, antimalarial drugs, estrogen-containing contraceptives, certain analgesics, corticosteroids, and sulfonamide antibacterial drugs.

Symptoms of deficiency
Folic acid deficiency leads to abnormally low numbers of red blood cells (*anemia*). The main symptoms include fatigue, loss of appetite, nausea, diarrhea, and hair loss. Mouth sores are common and the tongue is often sore. Deficiency may also cause poor growth in infants and children.

Dosage range for treating deficiency
Symptoms of anemia are usually treated with 0.25–1mg of folic acid daily (some may need higher doses), together with vitamin B$_{12}$. A lower maintenance dose may be substituted once the anemia has responded.

Symptoms and risks of excessive intake
Folic acid may worsen the neurological symptoms of a coexisting vitamin B$_{12}$ deficiency and should never be taken to treat anemia without a full medical investigation of the cause of the anemia.

GLUCOSAMINE

Other names Glucosamine sulfate, Glucosamine hydrochloride

Availability
Glucosamine is available without a prescription. It is available mainly as tablets or *capsules*, and as a sulfate salt (glucosamine sulfate) or hydrochloride or hydroiodide. Most of the studies have been conducted with glucosamine sulfate. It is also available in combination with another natural product, chondroitin.

Actions on the body
Glucosamine is a natural component of cartilage found in human joints and is thought to be able to provide some protection from damage to the cartilage.

Dietary and other natural sources
There are no food sources of glucosamine. Supplements are generally derived from the outer shells of crabs, shrimp, and lobsters.

Normal daily requirement
There are no specific recommended dietary allowances for glucosamine.

When supplements are helpful
Glucosamine has been studied in the treatment of osteoarthritis, especially of the knee. It is thought to provide benefit by strengthening the cartilage in the joints. Although some smaller studies with glucosamine have shown improvement in pain and joint movement associated with osteoarthritis, others have not shown a benefit. In the studies where benefit was observed, there was some indication that glucosamine may allow for reduced doses of pain medications such as non-steroidal anti-inflammatory drugs.

Symptoms of deficiency
No specific deficiency noted.

Dosage range for treating deficiency
In studies with glucosamine sulfate in osteoarthritis, doses of 1500mg daily have been used; this is usually recommended to be taken as 500mg three times daily with food. There is some indication that a higher dose, up to 2000mg a day, may be needed with glucosamine hydrochloride. Glucosamine may need to be tried for at least 4 weeks in order to evaluate its beneficial effects. Blood glucose may need to be monitored in those with diabetes or on medications that can affect blood glucose. Individuals on glucosamine may require ongoing monitoring by their physician and *pharmacist*. Pregnant women or women who are breast-feeding should consult their physician, as safety in these situations has not been established.

Symptoms and risks of excessive intake
Upset stomach, heart burn, and diarrhea are some of its *side effects*. It is unclear whether there are any serious effects of excessive intake.

IODINE

Other names Potassium iodide, potassium iodate, sodium iodide

Availability
Iodine supplements are available without prescription as kelp tablets and in several multivitamin and mineral preparations. Iodine skin preparations are also available without a prescription for antiseptic use. A small amount of iodine is routinely added to most table salts in order to prevent iodine deficiency from occurring. Treatments for thyroid suppression are available only on prescription.

Actions on the body
Iodine is essential for the formation of thyroid *hormone*, which regulates the body's energy production, promotes growth and development, and helps burn excess fat.

Dietary and other natural sources
Seafood is the best source of iodine, but bread and dairy products such as milk are the main sources of this mineral in most diets. Iodized table salt is also a good source. Iodine may also be inhaled from the atmosphere in coastal regions.

Normal daily requirement
The recommended dietary allowances (RDA) for iodine in micrograms (mcg) are: 110mcg (birth–6 months); 130mcg (7–12 months); 90mcg (1–3 years); 90mcg (4–8 years); 120mcg (9–13 years); and 150mcg (14 years and over). Daily requirement during pregnancy is 220mcg, and rises to 290mcg when breast-feeding; one vitamin tablet with calcium and iodine daily is recommended for nursing mothers.

When supplements are helpful
Most diets contain adequate amounts of iodine and use of iodized table salt can usually make up for any deficiency. Supplements are rarely necessary except on medical advice. However, excessive intake of raw cabbage or nuts reduces uptake of iodine into the thyroid gland and it may lead to deficiency if iodine intake is otherwise low. Kelp supplements may be helpful.

Adults exposed to radiation from radioactive iodine released into the environment may be given 100mg of iodine as a single dose (as potassium iodate 170mg) to prevent their thyroid gland absorbing the radioactive material; a lower dose is given to children according to age.

Iodine is used to treat people with thyrotoxicosis before surgery on the thyroid gland.

Symptoms of deficiency
Deficiency may result in a goitre (enlargement of the thyroid gland) and hypothyroidism (deficiency of thyroid hormone). Symptoms of hypothyroidism include tiredness, physical and mental slowness, weight gain, facial puffiness, and constipation. Babies born to iodine-deficient mothers are lethargic and difficult to feed. Left untreated, many show poor growth and mental retardation.

Dosage range for treating deficiency
Iodine deficiency may be treated with doses of 150mcg of iodine daily, and then followed up by ensuring that iodized table salt is used.

Symptoms and risks of excessive intake
The amount of iodine that occurs naturally in food is non-toxic, but prolonged use of large amounts (6mg or more daily) may suppress the activity of the thyroid gland. Large overdoses of iodine compounds may cause abdominal pain, vomiting, bloody diarrhea, and swelling of the thyroid and salivary glands.

IRON

Other names Ferrous fumarate, ferrous gluconate, ferrous sulfate, iron dextran, iron-polysaccharide complex, sodium ferric gluconate complex

Availability
Ferrous sulfate, ferrous fumarate, ferrous gluconate, and iron-polysaccharide complex are all available without prescription, alone and in multivitamin and mineral preparations. Iron dextran, an injectable form, is available only on prescription.

Actions on the body
Iron has an important role in the formation of red blood cells (which contain two-thirds of the body's iron) and is a vital component of the oxygen-carrying pigment hemoglobin. It is involved in the formation of myoglobin, a pigment that stores oxygen in muscles for use during exercise. It is also an essential component of several *enzymes*, and is involved in the uptake of oxygen by the cells and the conversion of blood sugar to energy.

Dietary and other natural sources
Liver is the best dietary source of iron. Meat (especially organ offal), eggs, chicken, fish, leafy green vegetables, dried fruit, enriched or wholemeal cereals, breads and pastas, nuts, and dried legumes are also rich sources. Iron is better absorbed from meat, eggs, chicken, and fish than from vegetables. Foods containing vitamin C enhance iron absorption from non-heme food sources such as vegetables.

Normal daily requirement
The recommended dietary allowances (RDA) for elemental iron are: 0.27mg (birth–6 months); 11mg (7–12 months); 7mg (1–3 years); 10mg (4–8 years); 8mg (9–13 years); 11mg (males aged 14–18 years); 15mg (females aged 14–18 years); 8mg (males aged 19 years and over); 18mg (females 19–50 years); and 8mg (females 51 years and over). Requirements may be increased during pregnancy (27mg) and while breast-feeding (10mg for 18 years and under; 9mg for 19–50 years).

When supplements are helpful
Most diets supply adequate amounts of iron. However, larger amounts are necessary during pregnancy. Supplements may be given throughout pregnancy and for 2 to 3 months after childbirth to maintain and replenish adequate iron stores in the mother. Premature babies may be prescribed supplements from a few weeks after birth to prevent deficiency. Supplements may be helpful in young vegetarians, women with heavy menstrual periods, and people with chronic blood loss due to disease (for example, peptic ulcer). Iron is available as iron salts (e.g., ferrous sulfate or ferrous gluconate). Always clarify whether a dosage refers to elemental iron or a specific salt of iron.

Symptoms of deficiency
Iron deficiency causes *anemia*; symptoms include pallor, fatigue, shortness of breath, and palpitations. Apathy, irritability, and lowered resistance to infection may also occur. Iron deficiency may also affect intellectual performance and behaviour.

Dosage range for treating deficiency
Depends on the individual and the nature and severity of the condition. In adults, iron-deficiency anemia is usually treated with 100mg of elemental iron (usually as ferrous sulphate or gluconate) daily. In children, the dose is reduced according to age and weight. Iron supplements of 30–60mg daily may be given during pregnancy.

Symptoms and risks of excessive intake
An overdose of iron tablets is extremely dangerous. Pain in the abdomen, nausea, and vomiting may be followed by abdominal bloating, dehydration, and dangerously lowered blood pressure. Immediate medical attention must be sought (see p.526). Keep out of the reach of children.

Excessive long-term intake, especially when it is taken with large amounts of vitamin C, may in susceptible individuals cause iron to accumulate in organs, causing congestive heart failure, cirrhosis of the liver, and diabetes mellitus. This condition is known as hemochromatosis.

LUTEIN

Other names Luteol, xanthophyll; also as a combined product with zeaxanthin (Visionex and Vitalux)

Availability
Lutein is considered to be a natural health product in Canada and is regulated by the Natural Health Products Directorate. Supplements may not be standardized in how they are manufactured, and the amount of the active substance may vary between products (and from the product used to conduct research on which health claims are based). Lutein is available without a prescription. It may also be included as an additive in some food products.

Actions on the body
Lutein is a component of the lens and retina of the eye. Along with fatty acids, which are components of these tissues, lutein is thought to act as an antioxidant and absorb certain types of harmful light.

Dietary and other natural sources
Lutein is naturally found in dark green, leafy vegetables such as spinach, kale, turnip greens, collard greens, broccoli, and also in highly coloured foods such as corn and egg yolks.

Normal dietary requirement
There is no specific recommended dietary allowance for lutein.

When supplements are helpful
Some tissues in the eyes are susceptible to damage. Research has been conducted to see if lutein, and zeaxanthin, can prevent macular degeneration and cataract formation. Studies to-date indicate that there may be some benefit. However, better controlled studies are needed to demonstrate conclusively such a benefit.

Symptoms of deficiency
No specific deficiency noted.

Dosage range for treating deficiency
There is no specific deficiency range. Studies that examined the use of lutein in people with age-related macular degeneration used doses ranging from 5mg to 20mg per day. Individuals on lutein may need ongoing monitoring by their physician and *pharmacist*. Pregnant women and women who are breast-feeding should consult their physician as the safety in these situations has not been established.

Symptoms and risks of excessive intake
No specific *adverse effects* have been reported.

MAGNESIUM

Other names Magnesium carbonate, magnesium citrate, magnesium hydroxide, magnesium sulfate

Availability
Magnesium is available without prescription in a variety of multivitamin and mineral preparations. Magnesium is also an ingredient of numerous over-the-counter antacid and laxative preparations, but it is not absorbed well from these sources.

Actions on the body
About 60 per cent of the body's magnesium is found in bones and teeth. Magnesium is essential for the formation of healthy bones and teeth, the transmission of nerve impulses, and the contraction of muscles. It activates several *enzymes*, and is important in the conversion of carbohydrates, fats, and proteins into energy.

Dietary and other natural sources
The best dietary sources of magnesium are leafy green vegetables. Nuts, wholemeal cereals, soya beans, cheese, and seafood are also rich in magnesium. Drinking water in hard water areas is also a source of this mineral.

Normal daily requirement
The recommended dietary allowances (RDA) for magnesium are: 30mg (birth–6 months); 75mg (7–12 months); 80mg (1–3 years); 130mg (4–8 years); 240mg (9–13 years); 410mg (males aged 14–18 years); 360mg (females aged 14–18 years); 400mg (males aged 19–30); 310mg (females aged 19–30); 420mg (males aged 31 years and over); and 320mg (females aged 31 years and over). Daily requirements do not increase much during pregnancy (350–360mg) and drop back to 310–320mg while breast-feeding.

When supplements are helpful
A varied diet provides adequate amounts of magnesium, particularly in hard water areas. Supplements are usually necessary only on medical advice for deficiency of magnesium associated with certain conditions in which absorption from the intestine is impaired, which occurs in repeated vomiting or diarrhea, advanced kidney disease, severe alcoholism, or prolonged treatment with certain diuretic drugs. Some anti-ulcer drugs (proton pump inhibitors) may also cause magnesium deficiency. Intravenous magnesium is used to treat eclampsia, cardiac arrhythmias, and myocardial infarction.

Estrogens and estrogen-containing oral contraceptives may reduce blood magnesium levels, but women who are on adequate diets do not need supplements.

Symptoms of deficiency
The symptoms of magnesium deficiency include anxiety, restlessness, tremors, confusion, palpitations, irritability, depression, and disorientation. Severe magnesium deficiency causes marked overstimulation of the nervous system, and results in seizures and cramp-like spasms of the hands and feet. Inadequate intake may be a factor in the development of coronary heart disease, and may also lead to calcium deposits in the kidneys, resulting in kidney stones.

Dosage range for treating deficiency
This depends on the individual and on the nature and severity of the disorder. Severe deficiency is usually treated in hospital by injection of magnesium sulfate.

Symptoms and risks of excessive intake
Magnesium toxicity (hypermagnesemia) is rare, but can occur in people with impaired kidney function after prolonged intake of the large amounts that are found in antacid or laxative preparations. Symptoms include nausea, vomiting, dizziness (due to a drop in blood pressure), and muscle weakness. Very large increases in magnesium in the blood may cause fatal respiratory failure or heart arrest.

NIACIN

Other names Niacinamide, nicotinamide, nicotinic acid, vitamin B$_3$

Availability
Niacin is available without prescription in a wide variety of single-ingredient and multivitamin and mineral preparations. It is also available as an extended-release, prescription-only product (Niaspan®) and as slow-release formulations. However, high doses of nicotinic acid are available only on prescription.

Actions on the body
Niacin plays a vital role in the activities of many *enzymes* and is important in producing energy from blood sugar, and in the manufacture of fats. Niacin is essential for the proper working of the nervous system, for a healthy skin and digestive system, and for the manufacture of steroid *hormones*.

Dietary and other natural sources
Liver, lean meat, poultry, fish, wholemeal cereals, nuts, and dried pulses are the best dietary sources of niacin.

Normal daily requirement
The recommended dietary allowances (RDA) for niacin are: 2mg (birth–6 months); 4mg (7–12 months); 6mg (1–3 years); 8mg (4–8 years); 12mg (9–13 years); 16mg (males aged 14 years and over); and 14mg (females aged 14 years and over). Daily requirements increase during pregnancy (18mg) and during breast-feeding (17mg).

When supplements are helpful
Most Canadian diets provide adequate amounts of niacin, and dietary deficiency is rare. Supplements are required for niacin deficiency associated with bowel disorders in which absorption from the intestine is impaired, and for people with liver disease or severe alcoholism. They may also be required for elderly people on poor diets. Large doses of niacin (up to 6g daily) are sometimes prescribed in the treatment of hyperlipidemia, especially for high levels of low-density lipoprotein (LDL) and triglycerides (over-the-counter products should not be used to treat hyperlipidemia). There is no convincing medical evidence that niacin helps psychiatric disorders (except those associated with pellagra).

Symptoms of deficiency
Severe niacin deficiency causes pellagra (literally, rough skin). Symptoms include sore, red, cracked skin in areas exposed to sun, friction, or pressure, inflammation of the mouth and tongue, abdominal pain and distension, nausea, diarrhea, and mental disturbances such as depression, anxiety, and dementia.

Dosage range for treating deficiency
For severe pellagra, adults are usually treated with 300–500mg daily by mouth, and children are usually given 100–300mg daily. For less severe deficiency, doses of 25–50mg are given.

Symptoms and risks of excessive intake
At doses of over 50mg used to treat hyperlipidemia, niacin may cause transient itching, flushing, tingling, or headache. These symptoms diminish after a few weeks with repeated administration. Niacin in the form that occurs naturally in the body (nicotinamide), is free of these effects. Large doses of niacin may cause nausea and may aggravate a peptic ulcer. *Side effects* may be reduced by taking the drug on a full stomach. At doses of over 2g daily (which have been used to treat hyperlipidemia), there is a risk of gout, liver damage, and high blood sugar levels, leading to extreme thirst. High doses of niacin should be used cautiously if the individual is also on statins for high cholesterol, due to a higher risk of liver and muscle problems when both are taken together.

OMEGA-3 FATTY ACIDS

Other names Omega-3 acid ethyl esters, Omega-3 oils

Availability
Omega-3 Fatty Acids (OFAs) are available without a prescription. Preparations include *capsules*, oil, and liquid.

Actions on the body
There are many types of OFAs; some are found in plants and some in fish. Plant OFAs (such as flaxseed and soy bean oil) are broken down and used differently in the body from the longer-chain OFAs found in fish. Fish oil fatty acids contain a combination of omega-3 ethyl esters called eicosapentaenoic acid (EPA) and docosahexaenoic acid (DHA). Omega-3-acids are polyunsaturated and are considered an essential fatty acid, as these cannot be made by the body. They may have many potential benefits and continue to be researched (see When supplements are helpful, below).

Dietary and other natural sources
Eicosapentaenoic acid (EPA) and docosahexaenoic acid (DHA): are found in salmon, trout, mackerel, sardines, and herring. Plant OFAs are found in flax seeds, walnuts, and canola oil.

Normal daily requirement
There is no specific recommended dietary allowance for OFAs.

When supplements are helpful
It appears that omega-3 fatty acids can reduce the risk of some types of heart disease. However, studies indicate that the fish oils may have a more positive benefit in those with heart problems than the plant fatty acids, especially after a heart attack. A small percent of the plant oils is converted to the longer chain fatty acids in the body. Fish oils can decrease the amount of triglycerides (TG) (a type of cholesterol) in the blood. These may be used along with lifestyle changes, an appropriate diet, and exercise to decrease high triglycerides. There are several studies that are currently ongoing in evaluating the specific benefit of these in decreasing the risk of heart disease. Omega-3 oils are also being evaluated in decreasing the risk of eye problems such as macular degeneration and in inflammatory conditions such as arthritis. Although this product is available without a prescription, its use should be considered in conjunction with the individual's other medical conditions and medications in consultation with a physician.

Symptoms of deficiency
No specific deficiency noted.

Dosage range for treating deficiency
As there is no specific deficiency range, there are no recommendations to treat deficiency to-date. One study evaluating the potential benefits of omega-3 oils had participants eat 2 servings of fatty fish per week; in another study, participants took 850mg of omega-3 fatty acids daily. The Heart and Stroke Foundation recommends that eating fish twice weekly in those with heart disease may be beneficial. Higher doses may be needed to decrease high triglycerides and for use in other conditions. Individuals on omega-3 oils may require monitoring by their health care provider. There is also potential for interaction with medicines such as warfarin. Pregnant or breast-feeding women should consult their physician, as safety in these situations has not been established.

Symptoms and risks of excessive intake
High doses may cause excessive bleeding in some. There is concern about contaminants like mercury in some types of fish.

PANTOTHENIC ACID

Other names Calcium pantothenate, vitamin B$_5$

Availability
Pantothenic acid, calcium pantothenate, and panthenol are available without prescription in a variety of multivitamin and mineral preparations.

Actions on the body
Pantothenic acid plays a vital role in the activities of many *enzymes*. It is essential for the production of energy from sugars and fats, for the manufacture of fats, corticosteroids, and sex *hormones*, for the utilization of other vitamins, for the proper function of the nervous system and the adrenal glands, and for normal growth and development.

Dietary and other natural sources
Pantothenic acid is present in almost all vegetables, cereals, and animal foods. Liver, kidney, heart, fish, and egg yolks are good dietary sources. Brewer's yeast, wheat germ, and royal jelly (the substance on which queen bees feed) are also rich in the vitamin.

Normal daily requirement
Daily adequate intake (AI) amounts for pantothenic acid are: 1.7mg (0–6 months); 1.8mg (7–12 months); 2mg (1–3 years); 3mg (4–8 years); 4mg (9–13 years); 5mg (19 years and over); 6mg (during pregnancy); 7mg (while breast-feeding).

When supplements are helpful
Most diets provide adequate amounts of pantothenic acid. Any deficiency is likely to occur in malnutrition together with other B vitamin deficiency diseases such as pellagra (see niacin), beriberi (see thiamine), or with alcoholism, and will be treated with B complex supplements. There is no firm evidence that large doses help, as some believe, in the prevention of greying hair, nerve disorders in diabetes, or psychiatric illness.

Symptoms of deficiency
Pantothenic acid deficiency is unlikely to occur unless a person is suffering from malnutrition. However, deficiency produced under experimental conditions can cause malaise, abdominal discomfort, and burning feet.

Dosage range for treating deficiency
Usually 5–10mg per day.

Symptoms and risks of excessive intake
In tests, doses of 1,000mg or more of pantothenic acid have not caused toxic effects. The risk of toxicity is considered to be very low, since pantothenic acid is a water-soluble vitamin that does not accumulate in the tissues. Any excess is eliminated rapidly in the urine. However, very high intakes of 10–20g can cause diarrhea.

POTASSIUM

Other names Potassium chloride, potassium citrate, potassium gluconate

Availability
Salts of potassium in small doses are available in a number of multivitamin and mineral supplements. They are available at higher doses as supplements and in an injectable form, both to be used under medical supervision. Potassium salts are also widely available in sodium-free or low-sodium salt (used as a salt substitute). However, these salt substitutes should be avoided by people with impaired kidney function and those taking drugs that cause potassium retention, such as potassium-sparing diuretics.

Actions on the body
Potassium works together with sodium in the control of the body's water balance, conduction of nerve impulses, contraction of muscle, and maintenance of a normal heart rhythm. Potassium is essential for maintenance of normal blood sugar.

Dietary and other natural sources
The best dietary sources of potassium are leafy green vegetables, tomatoes, oranges, potatoes, and bananas. Lean meat, pulses, chocolate, coffee, and milk are also rich in the mineral. Many methods of food processing may lower the potassium levels found in fresh food.

Normal daily requirement
No recommended dietary allowance (RDA) for potassium has been established, but adult requirements are met by a 40–80mmol intake daily.

When supplements are helpful
Most diets contain adequate amounts of potassium, and supplements are rarely required in normal circumstances. However, people who drink large amounts of alcohol or eat lots of salty foods may become marginally deficient. People with a condition called diabetic ketoacidosis or with certain types of kidney disease may be deficient in potassium, but the most common cause is prolonged treatment with diuretics. Long-term use of corticosteroids may also deplete the body's potassium. Prolonged vomiting and diarrhea also cause potassium deficiency, so people who abuse laxatives may be affected. Supplements are advised only when laboratory tests have confirmed a deficiency.

Symptoms of deficiency
Early symptoms of potassium deficiency may include muscle weakness, fatigue, dizziness, and mental confusion. Impairment of nerve and muscle function may progress to cause disturbances of the heart rhythm and paralysis of the skeletal muscles and those of the bowel, which leads to constipation.

Dosage range for treating deficiency
Depends on the preparation, the individual, and the cause and severity of deficiency. In general, daily doses equivalent to 20-40mmol/day of potassium chloride are given to prevent deficiency (for example, in people treated with diuretics that deplete potassium). Doses equivalent to 40–60mmol of potassium chloride daily are used to treat deficiency. Potassium supplements should be taken with a full glass of water, and may be taken after a meal to avoid gastric irritation.

Symptoms and risks of excessive intake
Blood potassium levels are normally regulated by the kidneys, and any excess is rapidly eliminated in the urine. Massive doses cause serious disturbances of the heart rhythm and muscular paralysis. In people with impaired kidney function, excess potassium may build up and the risk of potassium poisoning is increased.

PYRIDOXINE

Other names Pyridoxine hydrochloride, vitamin B_6

Availability
Pyridoxine and pyridoxine hydrochloride are available without prescription in a variety of single-ingredient and multivitamin and mineral preparations. Pyroxidine is also available as an injection to be used under medical supervision.

Actions on the body
Pyridoxine plays a vital role in the activities of many *enzymes*. This B vitamin is essential for the release of carbohydrates stored in the liver and muscles for energy; for the breakdown and use of proteins, carbohydrates, and fats from food; and for the manufacture of niacin (vitamin B_3). It is needed for the production of red blood cells and antibodies, for healthy skin. It is also important for normal function of the central nervous system.

Dietary and other natural sources
Liver, chicken, fish, wholemeal cereals, wheat germ, and eggs are rich in this vitamin. Bananas, avocados, and potatoes are also good sources.

Normal daily requirement
The recommended dietary allowances (RDA) for pyridoxine are: 0.1mg (birth–6 months); 0.3mg (7–12 months); 0.5mg (1–3 years); 0.6mg (4–8 years); 1.0mg (9–13 years); 1.3mg (males aged 14–50 years); 1.2mg (females aged 14–18 years); 1.3mg (females aged 19–50 years); 1.7mg (males aged 51 and over); and 1.5mg (females aged 51 and over); 1.6mg (during pregnancy); 2mg (while breast-feeding).

When supplements are helpful
Most balanced diets contain adequate amounts of pyridoxine, and it is also manufactured in small amounts by bacteria that live in the intestine. However, breast-fed infants and elderly people may require additional pyridoxine. Supplements may be given on medical advice together with other B vitamins to people with certain conditions in which absorption from the intestine is impaired. They may also be used to treat a form of *anemia* (sideroblastic) and certain rare genetic disorders termed pyridoxine dependency conditions. Supplements may also be recommended to prevent or treat deficiency caused by alcoholism, oral contraceptives, and treatment with drugs such as isoniazid, penicillamine, and hydralazine.

Symptoms of deficiency
Pyridoxine deficiency is rare unless it is due to drug treatment Deficiency may cause weakness, nervousness, irritability, depression, skin disorders, inflammation of the mouth and tongue, and cracked lips. in adults, it may cause *anemia* (abnormally low levels of red blood cells). Convulsions may occur in infants.

Dosage range for treating deficiency
Depends on the individual and the nature and severity of the disorder. In general, deficiency is treated with 2.5–10mg daily in adults. Once signs of deficiency are corrected, a lower dose of 2.5mg daily can be used. Deficiency resulting from genetic defects that prevent use of the vitamin is treated with doses of 10–100mg daily in infants and 10–250mg daily in adults and children. More studies are needed to determine whether pyroxidine has a clear benefit in the treatment of premenstrual syndrome.

Symptoms and risks of excessive intake
The tolerable upper limit for pyridoxine is 100mg/day. Larger doses taken over a prolonged period may severely damage the nervous system, resulting in unsteadiness, numbness, and clumsiness of the hands.

RIBOFLAVIN

Other names Vitamin B_2, vitamin G

Availability
Riboflavin is available without a prescription, alone and in a wide variety of multivitamin and mineral preparations.

Actions on the body
Riboflavin plays a vital role in the activities of several *enzymes*. It is involved in the breakdown and utilization of carbohydrates, fats, and proteins and in the production of energy in cells using oxygen. It is needed for utilization of other B vitamins and for production of steroid *hormones* (by the adrenal glands).

Dietary and other natural sources
Riboflavin is found in most foods. Good dietary sources are liver, milk, cheese, eggs, leafy green vegetables, wholemeal cereals, and pulses. Brewer's yeast is also a rich source of the vitamin.

Normal daily requirement
The recommended dietary allowances (RDA) for riboflavin are: 0.3mg (birth–6 months); 0.4mg (7–12 months); 0.5mg (1–3 years); 0.6mg (4–8 years); 0.9mg (9–13 years); 1.3mg (males aged 14 and over); 1mg (females 14–18 years); and 1.1mg (females aged over 18 years). Daily requirements rise by 0.3mg in pregnancy and by 0.5mg when breast-feeding.

When supplements are helpful
A balanced diet generally provides adequate amounts of riboflavin. Supplements may be beneficial in people on very low-calorie diets and elderly people on poor diets. Riboflavin requirements may also be increased by prolonged use of phenothiazine antipsychotics, tricyclic antidepressants, and estrogen-containing oral contraceptives. Supplements are required for riboflavin deficiency associated with chronic diarrheal illnesses in which absorption of nutrients from the intestine is impaired. Riboflavin deficiency is also common among alcoholics. As with other B vitamins, the need for riboflavin is increased by injury, surgery, severe illness, and psychological stress. In all cases, treatment with supplements works best in a complete B-complex formulation.

Symptoms of deficiency
Prolonged deficiency may lead to chapped lips, cracks, and sores in the corners of the mouth, a red, sore tongue, and skin problems in the genital area. The eyes may itch, burn, and become unusually sensitive to light.

Dosage range for treating deficiency
Usually treated with 5–30mg daily in combination with other B vitamins.

Symptoms and risks of excessive intake
Excessive intake may cause diarrhea, polyuria (the production of excessive amounts of urine), and a yellow-orange discoloration of the urine.

SELENIUM

Other name Selenium sulfide

Availability
Selenium is available without a prescription alone and in a multivitamin and mineral preparation. Selenium sulfide is the active ingredient of several antidandruff shampoos.

Actions on the body
Selenium is a trace element that is an essential part of an *enzyme* system that protects cells against damage by oxygen radicals (it is an *antioxidant* like vitamins A, C, and E).

Dietary and other natural sources
Meat, fish, wholemeal cereals, and dairy products are good dietary sources. The amount of selenium found in vegetables depends on the content of the mineral in the soil where they were grown. Selenium is found in foodstuffs combined in amino acids.

Normal daily requirement
The recommended dietary allowances (RDA) for selenium are: 15mcg (birth–6 months); 20mcg (7–12 months); 20mcg (1–3 years); 30mcg (4–8 years); 40mcg (9–13 years); and 55mcg (14 years and over). There is a slight extra requirement of 5mcg daily during pregnancy, and 15mcg extra daily are required when breast-feeding.

When supplements are helpful
Most normal diets provide adequate amounts of selenium, and supplements are, therefore, rarely necessary. At present, there is no conclusive medical evidence to support some claims that selenium may provide protection against cancer or that it prolongs life. A daily intake of more than 150mcg is not recommended, except on the advice of a physician.

Symptoms of deficiency
Long-term lack of selenium may result in loss of stamina and degeneration of tissues, leading to premature ageing. Severe deficiency may cause muscle pain and tenderness, and can eventually lead to a fatal form of heart disease in children in areas where selenium levels in the diet are very low – for example in one remote part of China.

Dosage range for treating deficiency
Depends on the individual and on the nature and severity of the disorder. Severe selenium deficiency may be treated under medical supervision with doses of up to 200mcg daily.

Symptoms and risks of excessive intake
Excessive intake may cause hair and nail loss, tooth decay and loss, fatigue, nausea, vomiting, and garlic breath. Total daily intake should not exceed 400mcg; large overdoses may be fatal.

SODIUM

Other names Sodium bicarbonate (baking soda), sodium chloride (table salt), sodium phosphate

Availability
Sodium is widely available in the form of common table salt (sodium chloride). Sodium bicarbonate is used in many over-the-counter antacids and is available as an injection. Sodium phosphate is a laxative to be used under medical supervision. Sodium chloride is also available as an injection and an inhalation solution.

Actions on the body
Sodium works with potassium in control of the water balance in the body, conduction of nerve impulses, contraction of muscles, and maintenance of a normal heart rhythm.

Dietary and other natural sources
Sodium is present in almost all foods as a natural ingredient, or as an extra ingredient added during processing. The main sources are table salt, processed foods, cheese, breads and cereals, and smoked, pickled, or cured meats and fish. High concentrations are found in pickles and snack foods, including potato crisps and olives. Sodium is also present in water that has been treated with water softeners. Manufactured foods may also contain sodium compounds such as monosodium glutamate.

Normal daily requirement
There is no clearly defined recommended dietary allowance (RDA) for sodium, but Health Canada recommends an intake of 1.5g per day for adults to promote good health. Most diets contain far more sodium than what is needed: the average consumption of sodium in Canada is 3g daily. One teaspoon of table salt contains about 2g of sodium.

When supplements are helpful
The need for supplementation is rare in temperate climates, even with "low-salt" diets. In tropical climates, however, sodium supplements may help to prevent cramps and possibly heatstroke occurring as a result of sodium lost through excessive perspiration during heavy work. Sodium supplements may be given on medical advice to replace salt loss due to prolonged diarrhea and vomiting, particularly in infants. They may also be given to prevent or treat deficiency due to certain kidney disorders, cystic fibrosis, adrenal gland insufficiency, use of diuretics, or severe bleeding (as intravenous infusion).

Symptoms of deficiency
Sodium deficiency caused by dietary insufficiency is rare. It is usually a result of conditions that increase loss of sodium from the body, such as diarrhea, vomiting, and excessive perspiration. Early symptoms include lethargy, muscle cramps, and dizziness. In severe cases, there may be a marked drop in blood pressure leading to confusion, fainting, and palpitations.

Dosage range for treating deficiency
Depends on the individual and on the nature and severity of symptoms. In extreme cases, intravenous sodium chloride may be required.

Symptoms and risks of excessive intake
Excessive sodium intake is thought to contribute to the development of high blood pressure, which may increase the risk of heart disease, stroke, and kidney damage. Other *adverse effects* include abnormal fluid retention, which leads to swelling of the legs and face. Large overdoses, even of table salt, may cause seizures or *coma* and could be fatal. Table salt should never be used as an *emetic*.

THIAMINE

Other names Thiamine hydrochloride, vitamin B_1

Availability
Thiamine is available without prescription in single-ingredient and a variety of multivitamin and mineral preparations.It is also available on prescription only as an injection.

Actions on the body
Thiamine plays a vital role in the activities of many *enzymes*. It is essential for the breakdown and utilization of fats, alcohol, and carbohydrates. It is important for a healthy nervous system, healthy muscles, and normal heart function.

Dietary and other natural sources
Thiamine is present in all unrefined food. Good dietary sources include wholemeal or enriched cereals and breads, brown rice, pasta, liver, kidneys, meat, fish, beans, nuts, eggs, and most vegetables. Wheat germ and bran are excellent sources.

Normal daily requirement
The recommended dietary allowances (RDA) for thiamine are: 0.2mg (birth–6 months); 0.3mg (7–12 months); 0.5mg (1–3 years); 0.6mg (4–8 years); 0.9mg (9–13 years); 1.2mg (males aged over 14 years); 1mg (females aged 14–18 years); and 1.1mg (females aged over 18 years). Daily requirements rise by 0.3mg in pregnancy and when breast-feeding.

When supplements are helpful
A balanced diet generally provides adequate amounts of thiamine. However, supplements may be helpful in elderly people on poor diets or those with high energy requirements caused, for example, by overactivity of the thyroid or heavy manual work. As with other B vitamins, requirements of thiamine are increased during severe illness, surgery, serious injury, and prolonged psychological stress. Additional thiamine is usually necessary on medical advice for deficiency associated with conditions in which absorption of nutrients from the intestine is impaired, and for prolonged liver disease or severe alcoholism.

Symptoms of deficiency
Deficiency may cause fatigue, irritability, loss of appetite, and disturbed sleep, confusion, loss of memory, depression, abdominal pain, constipation, and beriberi, a disorder that affects the nervous systems (so-called "dry" beriberi) and heart ("wet" beriberi). Symptoms of beriberi include tingling or burning sensations in the legs, cramps and tenderness in the calf muscles, incoordination, palpitations, seizures, and heart failure. In chronic alcoholics and in malnutrition, thiamine deficiency may lead to a characteristic deterioration of central nervous system function known as Wernicke-Korsakoff's syndrome. The syndrome results in paralysis of the eye muscles, severe memory loss, and dementia, for which urgent treatment is needed.

Dosage range for treating deficiency
Depends on the nature and severity of the disorder but, in general, for mild chronic deficiency 5–30mg by mouth should be taken daily. Injections of the vitamin are sometimes given when deficiency is very severe or when symptoms have appeared suddenly.

Symptoms and risks of excessive intake
The risk of *adverse effects* is very low because any excess is rapidly eliminated in the urine. However, prolonged use of large doses of thiamine may deplete other B vitamins and should therefore be taken in a vitamin B complex formulation. There is a risk of *allergic reactions* with thiamine injections.

VITAMIN A

Other names Beta-carotene, retinol

Availability
Retinol and beta-carotene are available without prescription in various single-ingredient and multivitamin and mineral preparations. Derivatives of vitamin A (isotretinoin and tretinoin) are used in prescription-only treatments for acne and psoriasis.

Actions on the body
Vitamin A is essential for normal growth and strong bones and teeth in children. It is necessary for normal vision and healthy cell structure. It helps to keep skin healthy and protect the linings of the mouth, nose, throat, lungs, and digestive and urinary tracts against infection. Vitamin A is also necessary for fertility in both sexes. Beta-carotene is an important antioxidant (i.e., it protects the body from cell damage).

Dietary and other natural sources
Liver (the richest source), fish liver oils, eggs, dairy products, orange and yellow vegetables and fruits (carrots, tomatoes, apricots, and peaches), and leafy green vegetables are good dietary sources. Vitamin A is also added to margarine.

Normal daily requirement
The recommended dietary allowances (RDA) for vitamin A are: 400mcg (birth–6 months); 500mcg (7–12 months); 300mcg (1–3 years); 400mcg (4–8 years); 600mcg (9–13 years); 900mcg (males aged 14 and over); 700mcg (females aged 14 and over); 770mcg (pregnancy); and 1,300mcg (breast-feeding).

When supplements are helpful
Most diets provide adequate amounts of vitamin A. Diets very low in fat or protein can lead to deficiency. Supplements are often given to young children in developing countries. They may also be needed by people with cystic fibrosis, obstruction of the bile ducts, overactivity of the thyroid gland, and certain intestinal disorders, and by people on long-term treatment with certain lipid-lowering drugs (e.g., cholestyramine and orlistat), which reduce absorption of the vitamin from the intestine. They are recommended with other vitamins for pregnant women, children under 5 years, and nursing mothers. High dose supplementation is not recommended due to risk of toxicity.

Symptoms of deficiency
Night blindness (difficulty in seeing in dim light) is the earliest symptom of deficiency; others include dry, rough skin, loss of appetite, and diarrhea. Resistance to infection is decreased. Eyes may become dry and inflamed. Severe deficiency may lead to corneal ulcers.

Dosage range for treating deficiency
Deficiency is treated by oral doses of up to 30,000 mcg daily in adults.

Symptoms and risks of excessive intake
Prolonged excessive intake (7.5–15mg daily) in adults can cause loss of appetite, diarrhea, dry or itchy skin, and hair loss. Fatigue and irregular menstruation are common. Headache, weakness, and vomiting may result from increased pressure of the fluid surrounding the brain. In extreme cases, bone pain and enlargement of the liver and spleen may occur. High doses of beta-carotene may turn the skin orange but are not dangerous. Large doses can increase the effect of warfarin. Excessive intake in pregnancy may lead to birth defects (see box, below).

VITAMIN A AND PREGNANCY

Very large doses of vitamin A in the early weeks of pregnancy can, rarely, cause defects in the baby, leading to damage of the central nervous system, face, eyes, ears, or palate. Pregnant women and those considering pregnancy should keep to the prescribed dose and not take extra vitamin A or eat liver products such as pâté (one serving of liver may contain 4–12 times the dose recommended for pregnancy). No other dietary restrictions are considered necessary.

VITAMIN B12

Other names Cyanocobalamin, hydroxocobalamin, methylcobalamin

Availability
Vitamin B_{12} is available without prescription in a wide variety of preparations. Cyanocobalamin is given by injection only under medical supervision.

Actions on the body
Vitamin B_{12} plays a vital role in the activities of several *enzymes*. It is essential for the manufacture of the genetic material of cells and thus for growth and development. The formation of red blood cells by the bone marrow is particularly dependent on this vitamin. It is also involved in the utilization of folic acid and carbohydrates in the diet, and is necessary for maintaining a healthy nervous system.

Dietary and other natural sources
Liver is the best dietary source of vitamin B_{12}. Almost all animal products, as well as seaweed, are also rich in the vitamin, but vegetables are not.

Normal daily requirement
Only minute quantities of vitamins B_{12} are required. Recommended dietary allowances (RDA) are: 0.4mcg (birth–6 months); 0.5mcg (7–12 months); 0.9mcg (1–3 years); 1.2mcg (4–8 years); 1.8mcg (9–13 years); 2.4mcg (14 years and over); 2.6mcg (pregnancy); and 2.8mcg (breast-feeding).

When supplements are helpful
A balanced diet usually provides more than adequate amounts of this vitamin, and deficiency is generally due to impaired absorption from the intestine rather than low dietary intake. However, a strict vegetarian or vegan diet lacking in eggs or dairy products is likely to be deficient in vitamins B_{12}, and supplements are usually needed. Another cause of deficiency is pernicious *anemia*, in which absorption of the vitamin is impaired due to inability of the stomach to secrete a special substance – known as intrinsic factor – that normally combines with the vitamin so that it can be taken up in the intestine. Supplements are also prescribed on medical advice in certain bowel disorders, such as celiac disease and various other causes of malabsorption, after surgery to the stomach or intestine, and in fish tapeworm infestation.

Symptoms of deficiency
Vitamins B_{12} deficiency usually develops over months or years – the liver can store up to 6 years' supply. Deficiency leads to anemia. The mouth and tongue often become sore. The brain and spinal cord may also be affected, leading to numbness and tingling of the limbs, memory loss, and depression.

Dosage range for treating deficiency
Depends on the individual and on the type and severity of deficiency. Pernicious anemia (due to impaired absorption of vitamins B_{12}) is treated in adults with injections of 0.1mg–1mg (100–1,000mcg) on alternate days for 1–2 weeks, then 0.1–0.2mg per week until blood counts are normal, then 1mg every 2–3 months. Higher monthly doses of up to 1,000mcg of B_{12}, together with folic acid, may be given if the deficiency is severe. Children are treated with a total of 30–50mcg daily. Dietary deficiency is usually treated with oral supplements of 50–150mcg or more daily (35–50mcg twice daily in infants). Deficiency that results from a genetic defect preventing use of the vitamin is treated with 250mcg every three weeks throughout life.

Symptoms and risks of excessive intake
Harmful effects from high doses of vitamins B_{12} are rare. *Allergic reactions* may in rare cases occur with preparations given by injection.

VITAMIN C

Other name Ascorbic acid

Availability
Vitamin C is available without prescription in a wide variety of single-ingredient and multivitamin and mineral preparations. Ascorbic acid can also be given by injection under specialized medical supervision.

Actions on the body
Vitamin C plays an essential role in the activities of several *enzymes*. It is vital for the growth and maintenance of healthy bones, teeth, gums, ligaments, and blood vessels, and is an important component of all body organs. Vitamin C is also recognized as an important antioxidant (i.e., it protects the body against cell damage and may prevent fat deposits from building up in the blood vessels) and is important for the manufacture of certain *neurotransmitters* and adrenal hormones. It is required for the utilization of folic acid and absorption of iron. This vitamin is also necessary for normal immune responses to infection and for wound healing.

Dietary and other natural sources
Vitamin C is found in most fresh fruits and vegetables. Citrus fruits, tomatoes, potatoes, and leafy green vegetables are good dietary sources. This vitamin is easily destroyed by cooking; some fresh, uncooked fruit and vegetables should be eaten daily. Adding a daily source of vitamin C, such as a glass of orange juice, is also recommended.

Normal daily requirement
The recommended dietary allowances (RDA) for vitamin C are: 40mg (birth–6 months); 50mg (7–12 months); 15mg (1–3 years); 25mg (4–8 years); 45mg (9–13 years); 75mg (males aged 14–18 years); 65mg (females aged 14–18 years); 90mg (males aged over 19 years); 75mg (females aged over 19 years); 85mg (pregnancy); and 120mg (breast-feeding).

When supplements are helpful
A healthy diet generally contains sufficient quantities of vitamin C. However, it is used up more rapidly after a serious injury, major surgery, burns, and in extremes of temperature. Supplements may be necessary to prevent or treat deficiency in the elderly and chronically sick, for smokers, and in severe alcoholism. They are recommended with other vitamins for pregnant women, children under 5 years, and nursing mothers. Women taking estrogen-containing contraceptives may also require supplements. Although many people take larger doses (1g daily) for the prevention or treatment of colds, there is no convincing evidence that vitamin C in large doses prevents them.

Symptoms of deficiency
Mild deficiency may cause weakness and aches and pains. Severe deficiency results in scurvy, the symptoms of which include inflamed, bleeding gums, nosebleeds, excessive bruising, and internal bleeding. In adults, teeth become loose. In children, there is abnormal bone and tooth development. Wounds fail to heal and become infected. Deficiency of vitamin C often leads to *anemia* (abnormally low levels of red blood cells), the symptoms of which are pallor, fatigue, shortness of breath, and palpitations. Untreated scurvy may cause seizures, *coma*, and death.

Dosage range for treating deficiency
For scurvy, 100–250mg of vitamin C is given daily for several weeks.

Symptoms and risks of excessive intake
The risk of harmful effects is low, since excess vitamin C is excreted in the urine. However, doses of over 3g daily may cause diarrhea, nausea, and stomach cramps. Kidney stones may occasionally develop.

VITAMIN D

Other names Alfacalcidol, calcifediol, calciferol, calcitriol, cholecalciferol, ergocalciferol, vitamin D_2, vitamin D_3

Availability
Vitamin D and its analogs are available without prescription in a variety of single-ingredient, multivitamin and mineral preparations. Injections are given only under medical supervision.

Actions on the body
Vitamin D (together with parathyroid *hormone*) helps regulate the balance of calcium and phosphate in the body. It aids in the absorption of calcium from the intestinal tract, and is essential for strong bones and teeth.

Dietary and other natural sources
Margarine (to which vitamin D is added by law), oily fish (sardines, herring, salmon, and tuna), liver, dairy products, and egg yolks are usually good sources of this vitamin. It is also formed by the action of ultraviolet rays in sunlight on chemicals naturally present in the skin. Sunlight is a major source of vitamin D for most people.

Normal daily requirement
The recommended dietary allowances (RDA) for vitamin D are: 10mcg (birth–12 months); 15mcg (1–70 years); 20mcg (over 70 years); and 15mcg (women who are pregnant or breast-feeding). 1mcg of cholecalciferol equals 40 international units (IU) of vitamin D.

When supplements are helpful
Vitamin D requirements are small and are usually met by dietary sources and normal exposure to sunlight. However, a poor diet and inadequate sunlight may lead to deficiency; dark-skinned people, night-shift workers, and those who live north of 40 degrees latitude in winter are more at risk. In areas of moderate sunshine, supplements may be given to infants. Premature infants, strict vegetarians, vegans, and the elderly may benefit from supplements of this vitamin. Supplements are usually necessary on medical advice to prevent and treat vitamin D deficiency-related bone disorders, and for conditions in which absorption from the intestine is impaired, deficiency due to liver disease, certain kidney disorders, prolonged use of certain drugs, genetic defects, and hypoparathyroidism. Supplements are recommended with other vitamins for pregnant women, breast-fed full-term infants, children under 5 years, and nursing mothers. They are also recommended with calcium to prevent or treat osteoporosis in young children and bone loss in older adults.

Symptoms of deficiency
Long-term deficiency leads to low blood levels of calcium and phosphate, which results in softening of the bones. In children, this causes abnormal bone development (rickets), and in adults, osteomalacia, causing backache, muscle weakness, bone pain, and fractures.

Dosage range for treating deficiency
In general, rickets caused by dietary deficiency is treated initially with 1,000–4,000 IU of vitamin D daily, depending on the age of the child, followed by a maintenance dose of 400 IU. Osteomalacia caused by deficiency of vitamin D is treated initially with 3,000 daily–40,000 IU weekly, followed by a daily maintenance dose of 400 IU. Deficiency caused by impaired intestinal absorption is treated with doses of up to 10,000 IU daily.Osteoporosis is treated with 400–1,000 IU daily for adults less than 50 years, and 800–2,000 IU for older adults and those at high risk.

Symptoms and risks of excessive intake
Always discuss doses greater than 2,000 IU with your physician. Prolonged excessive use disrupts the balance of calcium and phosphate in the body and may lead to abnormal calcium deposits in the soft tissues, blood vessel walls, and kidneys and retarded growth in children. Excess calcium may lead to symptoms such as weakness, unusual thirst, increased urination, gastrointestinal disturbances, and depression.

VITAMIN E

Other names Alpha tocopherol, alpha tocopheryl acetate, tocofersolan

Availability
Vitamin E is available without prescription in many single-ingredient and multivitamin and mineral preparations. It is also available as a component of a multivitamin injection, and is included in skin creams. Alpha tocopherol is the most powerful form of vitamin E.

Actions on the body
Vitamin E, a potent anti-oxidant, is vital for healthy cell structure, for slowing the effects of the ageing process on cells, and for maintaining the activities of certain *enzymes*. Vitamin E protects the lungs and other tissues from damage caused by pollutants, and protects red blood cells against destruction by poisons in the bloodstream. It also helps to maintain healthy red blood cells, and is involved in the production of energy in the heart and muscles. Current evidence does not support its use to prevent heart disease, cancer, or dementia.

Dietary and other natural sources
Some vegetable oils are good sources. Other sources rich in this vitamin include leafy green vegetables, wholemeal cereals, and wheat germ.

Normal daily requirement
Vitamin E is measured in milligrams of alpha-tocopherol equivalents (mg alpha-TE). Approximately 3–15mg daily are recommended.The recommended dietary allowances (RDA) are: 4mg alpha-TE as alpha tocopherol (birth–6months); 5mg alpha-TE (7–12 months); 6mg alpha-TE (1–3 years); 7mg alpha-TE (4–8 years); 11mg alpha-TE (9–13 years); 15mg alpha-TE (over 14 years); 15mg alpha-TE (pregnancy); and 19mg alpha-TE (breast-feeding).

When supplements are helpful
A normal diet supplies adequate amounts of vitamin E, and supplements are rarely necessary. However, people who consume large amounts of polyunsaturated fats in vegetable oils, especially if used in cooking at high temperatures, may need supplements. Supplements of vitamin E are also recommended for premature infants and people with impaired intestinal absorption, liver disease in children, or cystic fibrosis. They may also be needed for people on long-term treatment with certain lipid-lowering drugs (e.g., cholestyramine and orlistat).

Symptoms of deficiency
Vitamin E deficiency leads to destruction of red blood cells (hemolysis) and eventually *anemia* (abnormally low levels of red blood cells), symptoms of which may include pallor, fatigue, shortness of breath, and palpitations. In infants, deficiency may cause irritability and fluid retention.

Dosage range for treating deficiency
Doses are generally four to five times the RDA in adults and children, for the relevant sex and age group.

Symptoms and risks of excessive intake
Harmful effects are rare, but there is a risk of diarrhea and abdominal pain with doses of more than 1g per day. Prolonged use of over 250mg daily may lead to nausea, abdominal pain, vomiting, and diarrhea. Long-term use of over 400mg daily has been linked to an increased risk of certain types of cancer.

VITAMIN K

Other names Phytonadione, vitamin K$_1$

Availability
Vitamin K is available without prescription in several multivitamin and mineral preparations. Injectable and oral preparations of vitamin K alone are used to treat bleeding disorders, and are to be used only under close medical supervision. Oral vitamin K tablets are available through a Special Access Programme.

Actions on the body
Vitamin K is necessary for the formation in the liver of several substances that promote the formation of blood clots (blood clotting factors), including prothrombin (clotting factor II).

Dietary and other natural sources
The best dietary sources of vitamin K are leafy green vegetables and root vegetables, fruits, seeds, cow's milk, and yoghurt. Alfalfa is also an excellent source. In adults and children, the intestinal bacteria manufacture a large part of the vitamin K that is required.

Normal daily requirement
The recommended dietary allowances (RDA) are: 2mcg (birth–6 months); 2.5mcg (7–12 months); 30mcg (1–3 years); 55mcg (4–8 years); 60mcg (9–13 years); 75mcg (14–18 years); 120mcg (males aged over 19 years); and 90mcg (females aged over 19 years). There are no extra requirements in pregnancy or breast-feeding. It is also recommended that newborns be given a vitamin K injection of 1mg shortly after birth.

When supplements are helpful
Vitamin K requirements are generally met adequately by dietary intake and by manufacture of the vitamin by bacteria that live in the intestine. Supplements are given routinely to newborn babies, since they lack intestinal bacteria capable of producing the vitamin and are therefore more at risk of deficiency than adults are. In adults and children, additional vitamin K is usually necessary only on medical advice for deficiency associated with prolonged use of *antibiotics* or sulfonamide antibacterials that destroy bacteria in the intestine, or when absorption of nutrients from the intestine is impaired. These conditions include liver disease, obstruction of the bile duct, and intestinal disorders causing chronic diarrhea. Vitamin K may also be given to reduce blood loss during labour or after surgery in people who have been taking oral anticoagulants. Vitamin K also reverses the effect of an overdose of warfarin, an oral anticoagulant.

Symptoms of deficiency
Vitamin K deficiency leads to low levels of prothrombin (hypoprothrombinemia) and other clotting factors, resulting in delayed blood clotting and a tendency to bleed. This may cause easy bruising, oozing from wounds, nosebleeds, and bleeding from the gums, intestine, urinary tract, and, rarely, in the brain. (These effects are the same as those due to an overdose of warfarin, which counteracts vitamin K.)

Dosage range for treating deficiency
Depends on the individual and on the nature and severity of the disorder.

Symptoms and risks of excessive intake
Excess dietary intake of vitamin K has no known harmful effects. *Adverse effects* are extremely rare with vitamin K preparations taken by mouth.

ZINC

Other names Zinc gluconate, zinc hydroxide, zinc oxide, zinc sulfate, zinc pyrithione

Availability
Zinc supplements are available without prescription in single-ingredient and multivitamin and mineral preparations. Zinc sulfate is used in ocular solutions. Zinc is also one ingredient included in a variety of topical formulations used for the treatment of minor skin irritations, dandruff, acne, hemorrhoids, and fungal infections.

Actions on the body
Zinc plays a vital role in the activities of over 100 *enzymes*. It is essential for the manufacture of proteins and nucleic acids (the genetic material of cells), and is involved in the function of the *hormone* insulin in the utilization of carbohydrates. It is necessary for normal functioning of the immune system, a normal rate of growth, development of the reproductive organs, normal function of sperm, and healing of wounds and burns.

Dietary and other natural sources
Zinc is present in small amounts in a wide variety of foods. The mineral is better absorbed from animal sources than from plant sources. Protein-rich foods such as lean meat and seafood are the best sources of the mineral. Wholemeal breads and cereals, as well as dried pulses, are also good dietary sources.

Normal daily requirement
The recommended dietary allowances (RDA) for zinc are: 2mg (birth–6 months); 3mg (7 months–3 years); 5mg (4–8 years); 8mg (9–13 years); 11mg (males aged over 14 years); 9mg (females 14–18 years); 8mg (females aged 19 and over); 11mg (pregnancy); and 12mg (breast-feeding).

When supplements are helpful
A balanced diet containing natural, unprocessed foods usually provides adequate amounts of zinc. Dietary deficiency is rare, and is likely only in people who are generally malnourished, such as debilitated elderly people on poor diets. Supplements are usually recommended on medical advice for those with reduced absorption of the mineral due to certain intestinal disorders, such as cystic fibrosis; for those with increased zinc requirements due to sickle cell disease or major burns; and for those with liver damage occurring, for example, as a result of excessive alcohol intake. It has been suggested that zinc supplements may shorten the duration of the common cold, but scientific studies provide limited evidence. Studies do suggest that zinc may be beneficial when taken at the onset of symptoms.

Symptoms of deficiency
Deficiency may cause loss of appetite and impair the sense of taste. In children, it may also lead to poor growth and, in severe cases, to delayed sexual development and short stature. Severe, prolonged lack of zinc may result in a rare skin disorder involving hair loss, rash, inflamed areas of skin with pustules, and inflammation around the mouth, tongue, eyelids, and around the fingernails.

Dosage range for treating deficiency
Depends on the individual and on the cause and severity of the deficiency.

Symptoms and risks of excessive intake
Large overdoses of zinc salts in powder form are corrosive to tissues and may cause burns in the mouth and throat. Prolonged use of high doses may interfere with the absorption of copper, leading to deficiency, and may cause nausea, vomiting, headache, fever, malaise, and abdominal pain.

DRUGS OF ABUSE

The purpose of these pages is to clarify the medical facts concerning certain drugs (or classes of drugs) that are commonly known to be abused. Their physical and mental effects, sometimes combined with a dangerous habit-forming potential, have led to their use outside a medical context. Some of the drugs listed in this section are illegal, while others have legitimate medical uses – such as anti-anxiety and sleeping drugs – and are also discussed in other parts of the book. Alcohol, nicotine, and solvents, although not medical drugs, are nevertheless drugs in a pharmacological sense and carry a substantial risk of abuse. These substances are not illegal, but the sale of alcohol and tobacco products to young people is regulated by law, and the sale of solvents by voluntary agreement.

The individual profiles are designed to instruct and inform the reader, enabling him or her to understand how these drugs affect the body, to become more aware of the hazards of drug abuse, and to be able to recognize signs of drug abuse in other people.

Since a large proportion of drug abusers are young people, the following pages may serve as a useful source of reference for parents and teachers who are concerned that young people under their care may be taking drugs.

The drugs of abuse profiles

The profiles are arranged in alphabetical order under their medical names, with street names, drug categories, and cross-references to other parts of the book where appropriate. Each profile contains information on that drug under standard headings. Topics covered include the various ways it is taken, its habit-forming potential, its legitimate medical uses, its legal status, its effects and risks, the signs of abuse, and *interactions* with other drugs.

HOW TO UNDERSTAND THE PROFILES

Each drug of abuse profile contains standard headings under which you will find information covering important aspects of the drug.

Drug category
Categorizes the drug according to its principal effects on the body, with cross-references to other parts of the book where relevant.

Other common names
Lists the usual, alternative, and street names of each drug.

How taken
Tells you the various forms in which each substance is taken.

Short-term effects
Explains the immediate mental and physical effects of the drug.

Signs of abuse
Describes the outward effects of taking the drug, both short- and long-term, that concerned observers may notice.

Practical points
Gives tips on how to avoid abuse of the drug and suggests ways to stop or reduce intake.

BENZODIAZEPINES

Other common names Tranquilizers, temmies
Drug category Central nervous system depressants (see Sleeping drugs, p.66, and Anti-anxiety drugs, p.67)

Habit-forming potential
The addictive potential of benzodiazepines is much lower than that of some other central nervous system depressants such as barbiturates. However, use of these drugs can lead to physical and psychological dependence on their sedative effects, especially when taken regularly long-term and in higher than normal doses.

How taken
By mouth as tablets or capsules, or by injection.

Legitimate uses
Benzodiazepines are commonly prescribed mainly for short-term treatment of anxiety and stress, as well as for relief of sleeplessness. They are also used in *anesthesia*, both as *premedication* and for induction of general anesthesia. Other medical uses include the management of alcohol withdrawal, control of epileptic fits, and relief of muscle spasms. Benzodiazepines are listed under the Benzodiazepines and Other Targeted Substances schedule (Controlled Drugs and Substances Act, Part IV) of the Food and Drugs Act.

Short-term effects
Benzodiazepines can reduce mental activity. In moderate doses, they may also cause unsteadiness, reduce alertness, and slow the body's reactions, thus impairing driving ability as well as increasing the risk of accidents. Benzodiazepines may also cause amnesia (loss of memory regarding events that occurred while the person was under the influence of the drug). Any benzodiazepine in a high-enough dose induces sleep. Very large overdoses may cause depression of the breathing mechanism and death can occur.

Long-term effects and risks
Benzodiazepines tend to lose their sedative effect with longterm use. This may lead the user to increase the dose progressively, a manifestation of tolerance and physical dependence. Older people may become apathetic or confused when taking these drugs. On stopping the drug, the chronic user may develop *withdrawal symptoms* that may include anxiety, panic attacks, palpitations, shaking, insomnia, headaches, dizziness, aches and pains, nausea, loss of appetite, and clumsiness. Symptoms can last for days or weeks. This can be minimized by stopping the drug gradually. Babies born to women who use benzodiazepines regularly may suffer withdrawal symptoms during the first week of life.

Signs of abuse
Abuse can occur by injection in young people. Another type of abuser is a middle-aged or elderly person who may have been taking these drugs by prescription for months or years. He or she is usually unaware of the problem, and may freely admit to taking "nerve" or sleeping pills in normal or large quantities. Problems usually occur only if people attempt to cut down or stop taking the drugs without medical advice.

Interactions
Benzodiazepines increase the sedation with any drug that has a sedative effect on the central nervous system. These include other anti-anxiety and sleeping drugs, alcohol, *opioid* analgesics, antipsychotics, tricyclic antidepressants, and antihistamines.

Practical points
Benzodiazepines should normally be used for courses of two weeks' duration or less. If these drugs have been taken for longer than two weeks, it is usually best to reduce the dose gradually to minimize the risk of withdrawal symptoms. If you have been taking benzodiazepines for many months or years, it is best to consult your physician to work out a dose reduction programme. If possible, it will help to tell your family and friends and enlist their support.

CANNABIS

Other common names Marijuana, marihuana, grass, pot, dope, reefers, weed, hash, ganja, skunk, skunkweed
Drug category Central nervous system depressant, hallucinogen, anti-emetic.
Cannabis sativa extract; brand name Sativex

Habit-forming potential
There is evidence that regular users of cannabis can become physically and psychologically dependent on its effects.

How taken
Usually smoked, either like tobacco or through a "bong" pipe. May be eaten, often in cakes or biscuits, or brewed like tea and drunk.
Sativex (cannabidiol): a spray formulation to be used under the tongue or inside of the cheek. Approved for neuropathic pain management in patients with multiple sclerosis (MS).

Legitimate uses
Preparations of the leaves and resin of the cannabis plant have been in use for over 2,000 years. Introduced into Western medicine in the mid-19th century, cannabis was formerly taken for many complaints, including anxiety, insomnia, rheumatic disorders, migraine, painful menstruation, strychnine poisoning, and opioid withdrawal. Today, cannabis derivatives – for example, nabilone – can be prescribed with certain restrictions for the relief of nausea and vomiting caused by treatment with anticancer drugs. Cannabis is listed under the Food and Drugs Act, Restricted Drugs, Part I (Controlled Drugs and Substances Act). An exception to this is under the Marihuana Medical Access Regulations, where an application can be placed to receive an authorization to possess cannabis for medical illness, such as terminal illness.

Short-term effects
In small doses, the drug promotes a feeling of relaxation and well-being, enhances auditory and visual perception, and increases talkativeness. Appetite is usually increased. However, in some individuals the drug may have little or no effect.
Under the influence of the drug, short-term memory may be impaired and driving ability and coordination are disrupted. Confusion, emotional distress, and loss of the sense of time can result. Hallucinations may occur in rare cases. The effects last for one to three hours after smoking cannabis and for up to 12 hours or longer after it is eaten, but reaction times remain slowed for 24 hours after a single use of the drug so that driving ability may remain impaired without the person being aware of it.

Long-term effects and risks
Cannabis smoking increases the risk of bronchitis and lung cancer. Regular users may become apathetic and lethargic, and neglect their work or studies, and personal appearance. In susceptible people, heavy use may trigger depression or psychotic illness such as schizophrenia. Cannabis is thought by some physicians to increase the likelihood of experimentation with other drugs.
Since cannabis may increase the heart rate and lower blood pressure, people with heart disorders may be at risk from adverse effects of this drug. Regular use of cannabis may reduce fertility in both men and women and, if used during pregnancy, may contribute to premature birth.

Signs of abuse
The cannabis user may appear unusually talkative or drunk under the influence of the drug. Appetite is increased. The user may become defensive or aggressive when challenged about the drug.
Cannabis smoke has a distinct herbal smell that may linger in the hair and clothes. Burns may occur on clothing as a result of pieces of lighted cannabis falling from the cigarette.

Interactions
Cannabis may increase the risk of sedation with any drugs that have a *sedative* effect on the central nervous system. These include anti-anxiety drugs, sleeping drugs, *general anaesthetics*, opioid analgesics, antipsychotics, tricyclic antidepressants, antihistamines, and alcohol.

487

Habit-forming potential
Explains to what extent the drug is likely to produce physical or psychological *dependence*.

Legitimate uses
Describes the accepted medical uses of the substance, if any.

Long-term effects and risks
Explains the serious long-term effects on health and the risks involved with regular use of the drug.

Interactions
Describes interactions that may occur with other drugs.

ALCOHOL

Other common names Booze, drink (includes beer, wine, alcopops, hard liquor, and spirits); also known as ethyl alcohol or ethanol
Drug category Central nervous system depressant; sedative

Habit-forming potential

It is difficult to measure the habit-forming potential of alcohol because individual responses vary so widely. There is certainly a behaviour called alcoholism that is characterized by a person's inability to control intake. Regular drinking and heavy drinking do not cause alcoholism but, like alcoholism itself, carry significant health risks. Alcoholism involves psychological and physical *dependence*, evidenced by large daily consumption, heavy weekend drinking, or periodic binges.

How taken

Orally, in the form of wines, beers and cider, and a wide range of spirits and liqueurs. Alcopops, the lemonade or fruit juice-based drinks, actually contain as much alcohol (5%) as beer or cider.

The alcohol content of drinks

Glasses vary in the amount they hold, so approximate volumes are quoted to help comparisons:

1 UNIT of alcohol = 1 glass of wine (125ml)

½ pint of alcopops (250ml)

½ pint of beer or cider (250ml)

¼ pint of super strong lager (125ml)

1 pub glass of port or sherry

1 single shot of whisky, gin, vodka, or brandy

Pub measures of sherry, port, and spirits are usually less generous than drinks at home.

Legitimate uses

The legal age to possess, consume, or purchase alcohol varies with each province, with many, such as Ontario, having the legal age for all of these three categories as 19 years. The manufacture and sale of alcoholic drinks is closely regulated by both provincial and federal laws.

Absorption of alcohol

Alcohol is rapidly absorbed from the stomach and particularly from the small intestine. Very strong drinks such as neat spirits are actually absorbed more slowly than weaker ones (as the alcohol reduces stomach movements that would push it into the intestine). Very dilute drinks are absorbed relatively slowly due to the large amount of water. In between these extremes, the stronger drinks will give higher blood levels; sherry and port are at about the "optimum" concentration. The presence of bubbles of carbon dioxide (in champagne, lemonade, and lager) may help to speed up absorption. So will mixing drinks; for example, drinking a glass of spirits as a "chaser" after drinking beer will produce a higher concentration that is absorbed more quickly.

Food in the stomach slows the rate of absorption of alcohol. Full cream milk, in which the fat is present in small droplets with a large surface area, seems particularly efficient for this purpose. Even the amount of carbohydrate in beer slows alcohol absorption a little, compared to a solution of alcohol in water at the same strength. Slowing the rate of absorption means that some of the alcohol can be broken down (metabolized, detoxified) before the rest is absorbed. This reduces the blood level and hence the effects of alcohol.

One unit of alcohol is the equivalent of about 15ml of pure alcohol, which is the amount that the average human adult male can break down in 1 hour. If you drink at a faster rate, your blood alcohol level will continue to rise. It will then take as many hours for your body to rid itself of all the alcohol as the number of units you have drunk. For example, if you had five pints of beer (10 units) in a few hours, it will, on average, take around 10 hours to be removed from your blood. However, there is considerable variation in these figures. Women achieve higher blood levels than men after drinking the same amount (because women's bodies contain a lower percentage of water, into which the alcohol is distributed, and they break down alcohol significantly slower than men of the same weight). A large-framed adult will have a lower blood level of alcohol than a smaller person after they have had the same amount to drink.

Short-term effects

Alcohol acts as a central nervous system depressant, reducing anxiety, tension, and inhibitions. In moderate quantities, it creates a feeling of relaxation and confidence, and increases sociability and talkativeness, but does not improve mental performance. Moderate amounts also dilate small blood vessels, especially in the skin, leading to flushing and a feeling of warmth. Increasing amounts progressively impair concentration and judgement and reactions are increasingly slowed. Accidents, particularly driving accidents, are more likely. As blood alcohol levels rise, violent or aggressive behaviour is possible. Speech is slurred, and the person becomes unsteady, staggers, and may experience double vision and loss of balance. Nausea and vomiting are frequent; incontinence may also occur. Loss of consciousness may follow if blood alcohol levels continue to rise, and there is a risk of death from choking on vomit or cessation of breathing. Blood alcohol levels of only 3–4 times the legal driving limit are thus potentially fatal.

In addition to alcohol's effects on the central nervous system, it has a number of other effects. The most noticeable to the drinker is its diuretic action. Beer drinkers will be particularly aware of this, but dehydration after drinking any kind of alcohol is responsible for much of the headache and other symptoms described as a "hangover" because the water removed comes from organs such as the brain. The best means of prevention is to drink less, or at least to drink a glass of water for each unit of alcohol, during the same time period.

Alcoholic drinks are not the same as "alcohol." They contain other chemical ingredients that might have *side effects*; for example, the juniper oil in gin acts as a diuretic. It is thought that many of the ingredients in drinks can add to the hangover experience, perhaps by delaying alcohol metabolism. Congeners – complex organic molecules such as polyphenols, higher alcohols, and histamine, which occur in varying amounts in different alcoholic drinks – may also have toxic effects.

Long-term effects and risks

Heavy drinkers risk developing liver diseases, such as alcoholic hepatitis, liver cancer, cirrhosis, or fatty liver (excess fat deposits that may lead to cirrhosis). High blood pressure, strokes, and heart failure may also result from heavy drinking. Inflammation of the stomach (gastritis) and peptic ulcers are more common in alcoholics, who also have a higher than average risk of developing a dementia-like illness.

Long-term heavy drinking is generally associated with physical dependence. An alcoholic may appear to be sober, even after heavy drinking, because of built-up tolerance. But a reverse tolerance effect is frequently seen in alcoholics, where relatively little alcohol can rapidly produce a state of intoxication. As well as health problems, alcohol dependence is associated with a range of personal and social problems. Alcoholics may suffer from anxiety and depression, and because they often eat poorly, they are at risk of various nutritional deficiency diseases, particularly deficiency of thiamine (see p.479).

Drinking during pregnancy can cause fetal abnormalities and poor physical and mental development in infants; drinking moderate to large amounts of alcohol (6 or more units per day or binges of over 5 units several times a week) is associated with miscarriage, low birth weight, and mental retardation. Drinking during the first trimester is the most harmful for the baby and should be avoided, and it is safest to avoid drinking alcohol entirely for the duration of your pregnancy.

About 4 per cent of breast cancers in women may be related to alcohol intake. In developed countries, the risk of breast cancer rises with increased alcohol consumption.

Signs of abuse

Alcohol consumption may be getting out of control if any or all of the following signs are noted:

- changes in drinking pattern (for example, early morning drinking or a switch from beer to spirits);
- changes in drinking habits (such as drinking alone or having a drink before an appointment or interview);
- neglect of personal appearance;
- personality changes or furtive behaviour;
- poor eating habits;
- increasingly frequent or prolonged bouts of intoxication with memory lapses (blackouts) about events that occurred during drinking episodes.

Physical symptoms of heavy drinking may include nausea, vomiting, or shaking in the morning, abdominal pain, and cramps. The face may look red due to enlarged blood vessels. There may also be weakness in the legs and hands, general unsteadiness, poor memory, and incontinence.

Attempts to stop heavy drinking should always be made under medical supervision. The sudden stopping of heavy drinking, if not treated, can lead to delirium tremens (severe shaking, confusion, hallucinations, and occasionally fatal convulsions). These symptoms begin after one to four days of abstinence and last for up to three days. Drugs such as atenolol and benzodiazepines given short term under medical supervision, can control *withdrawal symptoms*.

Practical points

If you drink alcohol, know what your limits are. They vary from person to person, and your capacity depends a good deal on your body weight, age, experience, and mental and emotional state. However, you can use a "rule of thumb" guide to judge the body's ability to break down alcohol. Generally, the body can break down only about one unit of alcohol per hour, which means that alcoholic drinks should be spaced about one hour apart. If you drink faster than this, your blood alcohol is likely to rise above the "legal" limit for driving. But lower levels than this can affect judgement and reaction times, so the safest advice is not to drink at all if you plan to drive.

Drinking guidelines suggest that men should have no more than a total of 14 drinks a week, and women should have no more than nine each week. The weekly allowance of units should not be "saved up" in order to have a binge at the weekend. The usual recommendation is for no more than two standard drinks at each occasion. If you are a woman and are pregnant, or you are trying to conceive, the safest course is abstinence.

If you find that you are having trouble controlling your drinking, seek help and advice from your physician or from an organization, such as Alcoholics Anonymous, which is dedicated to helping people with this particular problem.

Even if you do not have a control problem with alcohol, you should still avoid drinking heavily because alcohol can have harmful effects on many parts of your body.

INTERACTIONS WITH OTHER DRUGS

Alcohol interacts with a wide variety of drugs and it is important to be aware of the *interactions* if you are on medication and want to have a drink. The main drug categories and their effects when taken with alcohol are shown below.

Type of drug	For example	Effects
Anti-anxiety drugs	Diazepam, lorazepam	Increased risk of sedation
Sleeping drugs	Temazepam, zopiclone	Increased risk of sedation
General anesthetics	Thiopental	Increased risk of sedation
Antipsychotics	Chlorpromazine, haloperidol	Increased risk of sedation
Tricyclic antidepressants	Amitriptyline, desipramine, trimipramine	Increased risk of sedation
Antihistamines	Chlorpheniramine, promethazine	Increased risk of sedation
Antimuscarinics	Hyoscine	Increased risk of sedation
Muscle relaxants	Baclofen, tizanidine	Increased risk of sedation
Cannabis derivatives	Nabilone	Increased risk of sedation
Opioid analgesics	Morphine, dihydrocodeine, meperidine	Increased risk of sedation, fall in blood pressure, coma, death
Antidepressants, SSRIs	Citalopram, paroxetine	Possibly increased alcohol effects
Antihypertensives	Nifedipine, atenolol, losartan, captopril	Fall in blood pressure
	Clonidine,	Increased risk of sedation
Drugs of abuse	Barbiturates, heroin, solvents	Coma, death
Salicylates	ASA	Risk of stomach bleeding
Antibacterials	Metronidazole	Unpleasant reactions, including nausea, vomiting, headache, palpitations, flushing
Cytotoxics	Procarbazine	Unpleasant reactions, including nausea, vomiting, headache, palpitations, flushing
Antidiabetics	Insulin	Increased hypoglycemia
	Sulfonylureas	Possibly increased effects
MAOIs	Phenelzine, tranylcypromine	Dangerous rise in blood pressure with tyramine in red wine; fall in blood pressure with other alcoholic drinks
Anticoagulants	Warfarin	Increased risk of bleeding
Antiepileptics	Carbamazepine	CNS side effects increased
Dopamine-boosters	Bromocriptine	Reduced tolerance to drug

AMPHETAMINE

Other common names Speed, uppers, bennies, whizz, blues
(see also Ecstasy, p.488)
Drug category Central nervous system stimulant (see p.72)

Habit-forming potential
Regular use of amphetamine or methamphetamine rapidly
leads to the development of *tolerance*, so that larger and larger
doses are required to achieve the same effect. Users become
psychologically dependent on the drug's effects. Toxic effects
can occur at relatively low doses.

How taken
Usually swallowed as tablets or powder. Sometimes sniffed
or mixed with water and injected.

Legitimate uses
During the 1950s and 1960s, amphetamine was widely given
as an appetite suppressant. This use of the drug to suppress
appetite has been stopped because of the risk of *dependence*
and abuse. Amphetamine was used to maintain wakefulness by
drivers and pilots. It is still prescribed as dexamphetamine for
attention deficit disorder (hyperactivity) and narcolepsy (see
also Nervous system stimulants, p.72). Amphetamine is
classified under the Food and Drugs Act, Part 3 (controlled
Drugs and Substances Act). Possession without a prescription
is illegal.

Short-term effects
In small doses, amphetamine increases mental alertness and
physical energy. Breathing and heart rate speed up, the pupils
dilate, appetite decreases, and dryness of the mouth is common.
As these effects wear off, depression and fatigue may follow. At
high doses, amphetamine may cause tremor, sweating, anxiety,
headache, palpitations, and chest pain. Large doses may cause
delusions, confusion, hallucinations, delirium, collapse, aggressive
behaviour, convulsions, coma, and death.

Long-term effects and risks
Regular use frequently leads to muscle damage, weight loss,
and constipation. People who use amphetamine regularly may
also become emotionally unstable; psychosis may develop.
Severe depression and suicide are associated with withdrawal.
Heavy long-term use reduces resistance to infection and also
carries a risk of damage to the heart and blood vessels, leading
to strokes and heart failure.

Use of amphetamine in early pregnancy may increase the
risk of birth defects, especially in the heart. Taken throughout
pregnancy, amphetamine leads to premature birth and low
birth weight.

Signs of abuse
The amphetamine user may appear unusually energetic, cheerful,
and excessively talkative while under the influence of the drug.
Restlessness, agitation, and a lack of interest in food are typical
symptoms; personality changes, psychotic reactions, and
paranoid delusions may also occur. Regular users may exhibit
unusual sleeping patterns, staying awake for two or three nights
at a stretch, then sleeping for up to 48 hours afterwards. Mood
swings are common.

Interactions
Amphetamine interacts with a variety of drugs. It causes an
increase in blood pressure, thus opposing the effect of
antihypertensive drug treatments. Taken with monoamine
oxidase inhibitors (MAOIs), it may lead to a dangerous rise
in blood pressure. It also increases the risk of abnormal
heart rhythms with digitalis drugs, levodopa, and certain
anesthetics that are given by inhalation. Amphetamine
counteracts the *sedative* effects of drugs that depress the
central nervous system.

BARBITURATES

Other common names Barbs, downers
Drug category Central nervous system depressant (see also
Sleeping drugs, p.66), sedative

Habit-forming potential
Long-term, regular use of barbiturates can be habit-forming.
Both physical and psychological *dependence* may occur.

How taken
By mouth in the form of *capsules* or tablets. Occasionally
mixed with water and injected.

Legitimate uses
In the past, barbiturates were widely prescribed as sleeping
drugs. Since the 1960s, however, they have been almost
completely replaced by benzodiazepines, which may also be
addictive but are less likely to cause death from overdose.

The widest uses of barbiturates today are in *anesthesia*
(thiopental) and for epilepsy (phenobarbital).

Most barbiturates are listed under Schedule G of the Food
and Drugs Act (Controlled Drugs and Substances Act, Part IV).

Short-term effects
The short-term effects are similar to those of alcohol. A low
dose produces relaxation, while larger amounts make the
user more intoxicated and drowsy. Coordination is impaired
and slurred speech, clumsiness, and confusion may occur.
Increasingly large doses may produce loss of consciousness,
coma, and death caused by depression of the person's
breathing mechanism.

Long-term effects and risks
The greatest risk of long-term barbiturate use is physical
dependence. In an addicted person, sudden withdrawal of
the drug precipitates a withdrawal syndrome that varies in
severity, depending partly on the type of barbiturate, its dose,
and the duration of use, but primarily on the availability and
administration of supportive treatment, including appropriate
medication. Symptoms may include irritability, disturbed sleep,
nightmares, nausea, vomiting, weakness, tremors, and extreme
anxiety. Abrupt withdrawal after several months of use may
cause convulsions, delirium, fever, and coma lasting for up to
one week. Long-term, heavy use of barbiturates increases the
risk of accidental overdose. The risk of chest infections is also
increased because the cough reflex is suppressed by long-term,
heavy use of these drugs.

Use of barbiturates during pregnancy may cause fetal
abnormalities and, used regularly in the last three months,
may lead to *withdrawal symptoms* in the newborn baby.

Signs of abuse
Long-term heavy use of barbiturates may cause prolonged
bouts of intoxication with memory lapses ("blackouts"), neglect
of personal appearance and responsibilities, personality changes,
and episodes of severe depression.

Interactions
Barbiturates interact with a wide variety of drugs and increase
the risk of sedation with any drug that has a *sedative* effect on
the central nervous system. These include anti-anxiety drugs,
opioid analgesics, antipsychotics, antihistamines, and tricyclic
antidepressants. High doses taken with alcohol can lead to a
fatal coma.

Barbiturates also increase the activity of certain *enzymes*
in the liver, leading to an increase in the breakdown of certain
drugs, thus reducing their effects. Tricyclic antidepressants,
phenytoin, griseofulvin, and corticosteroids are affected in this
way. However, the toxicity of an acetaminophen overdose is
likely to be greater in people taking barbiturates.

BENZODIAZEPINES

Other common names Tranquillizers, temmies
Drug category Central nervous system depressants (see Sleeping drugs, p.66, and Anti-anxiety drugs, p.67)

Habit-forming potential
The addictive potential of benzodiazepines is much lower than that of some other central nervous system depressants such as barbiturates. However, use of these drugs can lead to physical and psychological *dependence*, especially when taken regularly long-term and in higher than normal doses.

How taken
By mouth as tablets or *capsules*, or by injection.

Legitimate uses
Benzodiazepines are commonly prescribed mainly for short-term treatment of anxiety and stress, as well as for relief of sleeplessness. They are also used in *anesthesia,* both as *premedication* and for induction of general anesthesia. Other medical uses include the management of alcohol withdrawal, control of epileptic seizures, and relief of muscle spasms. Benzodiazepines are listed under the Benzodiazepines and Other Targeted Substances schedule (Controlled Drugs and Substances Act, Part IV) of the Food and Drugs Act.

Short-term effects
Benzodiazepines can reduce mental activity. In moderate doses, they may also cause unsteadiness, reduce alertness, and slow the body's reactions, thus impairing driving ability as well as increasing the risk of accidents. Benzodiazepines may also cause anterograde amnesia (loss of memory regarding events that occurred while the person was under the influence of the drug). Any benzodiazepine in a high-enough dose induces sleep. Large overdoses (especially by intravenous injection) may cause depression of the breathing mechanism and death can occur, especially when the drug is mixed with alcohol or other CNS drugs.

Long-term effects and risks
Benzodiazepines tend to lose their *sedative* effect with long-term use (more than a few weeks). This may lead the user to increase the dose progressively, a manifestation of *tolerance* and physical dependence. Older people may become apathetic or confused when taking these drugs. On stopping the drug, the chronic user may develop *withdrawal symptoms* that may include anxiety, panic attacks, palpitations, shaking, insomnia, headaches, dizziness, aches and pains, nausea, loss of appetite, and clumsiness. Symptoms can last for days or weeks. This can be minimized by stopping the drug gradually. Babies born to women who use benzodiazepines regularly may suffer withdrawal symptoms during the first week of life.

Signs of abuse
Abuse can occur by injection in young people. Another type of abuser is a middle-aged or elderly person who may have been taking these drugs by prescription for months or years. He or she is usually unaware of the problem, and may freely admit to taking "nerve" or sleeping pills in normal or large quantities. Problems usually occur only if people attempt to cut down or stop taking the drugs without medical advice.

Interactions
Benzodiazepines increase the risk of sedation with any drug that has a sedative effect on the central nervous system. These include other anti-anxiety and sleeping drugs, alcohol, *opioid* analgesics, antipsychotics, tricyclic antidepressants, and antihistamines.

Practical points
Benzodiazepines should normally be used for courses of two weeks' duration or less. If these drugs have been taken for longer than two weeks, it is usually best to reduce the dose gradually to minimize the risk of withdrawal symptoms. If you have been taking benzodiazepines for many months or years, it is best to consult your physician to work out a dose reduction program. If possible, it will help to tell your family and friends and enlist their support.

CANNABIS

Other common names Marijuana, marihuana, grass, pot, dope, reefers, weed, hash, ganja, skunk, skunkweed
Drug category Central nervous system depressant, hallucinogen, anti-emetic.
Cannabis sativa extract; brand name Sativex

Habit-forming potential
There is evidence that regular users of cannabis can become physically and psychologically *dependent* on its effects. Those who smoke cannabis mixed with tobacco may also become addicted to nicotine.

How taken
Usually smoked, either like tobacco or through a "bong" pipe. May be eaten, often in cakes or biscuits, or brewed like tea and drunk.
Sativex (cannabidiol): a spray formulation to be used under the tongue or inside of the cheek. Approved for neuropathic pain management in patients with multiple sclerosis (MS).

Legitimate uses
The leaves and resin of the plants *Cannabis sativa* and *C. indica* have been in use for over 2,000 years. Introduced into Western medicine in the mid-19th century, cannabis was formerly taken for many complaints, including anxiety, insomnia, rheumatic disorders, migraine, painful menstruation, strychnine poisoning, and *opioid* withdrawal. Today, cannabis derivatives – for example, nabilone – can be prescribed with certain restrictions for the relief of nausea and vomiting caused by treatment with anticancer drugs. Cannabis is listed under the Food and Drugs Act, Restricted Drugs, Part 4 (Controlled Drugs and Substances Act). An exception to this is under the Marihuana Medical Access Regulations, where an application can be placed to receive an authorization to possess cannabis for medical illness, such as terminal illness.

Short-term effects
In small doses, the drug promotes a feeling of relaxation and well-being, enhances auditory and visual perception, and increases talkativeness. Appetite is usually increased. However, in some individuals the drug may have little or no effect.
Under the influence of the drug, short-term memory may be impaired and driving ability and coordination are disrupted. Confusion, emotional distress, and loss of the sense of time can result. Hallucinations may occur in rare cases. The effects last for one to three hours after smoking cannabis and for up to 12 hours or longer after it is eaten, but reaction times remain slowed for 24 hours after a single use of the drug so that driving ability may remain impaired without the person being aware of it.

Long-term effects and risks
Cannabis smoking increases the risk of bronchitis and lung cancer. Regular users may become apathetic and lethargic, and neglect their work or studies and personal appearance. In susceptible people, heavy use may trigger depression or psychotic illness such as schizophrenia. Cannabis is thought by some physicians to increase the likelihood of experimentation with other drugs.
Since cannabis may increase the heart rate and lower blood pressure, people with heart disorders may be at risk from *adverse effects* of this drug. Regular use of cannabis may reduce fertility in both men and women and, if used during pregnancy, may contribute to premature birth.

Signs of abuse
The cannabis user may appear unusually talkative or drunk under the influence of the drug. Appetite is increased. The user may become defensive or aggressive when challenged about use of the drug. Cannabis smoke has a distinct herbal smell that may linger in the hair and clothes.

Interactions
Cannabis may increase the risk of sedation with any drugs that have a *sedative* effect on the central nervous system. These include anti-anxiety drugs, sleeping drugs, *general anaesthetics*, opioid analgesics, antipsychotics, tricyclic antidepressants, antihistamines, and alcohol.

COCAINE

Other common names Coke, crack, nose candy, snow
Drug category Central nervous system stimulant and local anesthetic (p.64)

Habit-forming potential
Taken regularly, cocaine is habit-forming. Users may become psychologically dependent on its physical and psychological effects, and may step up their intake to maintain or increase these effects or to prevent the feelings of severe fatigue and depression that may occur after the drug is stopped. The risk of *dependence* is especially pronounced with the form of cocaine known as "freebase" or "crack" (see below).

How taken
Smoked, sniffed through a tube ("snorted"), or injected.

Legitimate uses
Cocaine was formerly widely used as a *local anesthetic*. It is still sometimes given for *topical* anesthesia in the eye, mouth, and throat prior to minor surgery or other procedures. However, because of its *side effects* and potential for abuse, cocaine has now been replaced in most cases by safer *local anesthetic* drugs. Cocaine is classified under the Narcotic Control Act.

Short-term effects
Cocaine is a central nervous system stimulant. In moderate doses it overcomes fatigue and produces feelings of wellbeing. Appetite is reduced. Physical effects include an increase in heart rate and blood pressure, dilation of the pupils, tremor, and increased sweating. Large doses can lead to agitation, anxiety, paranoia, and hallucinations. Paranoia may cause violent behaviour. Very large doses cause seizures, heart failure, and rapid death. In some people, seizures and heart attack may occur after only moderate doses.

Long-term effects and risks
Heavy, regular use of cocaine can cause restlessness, anxiety, hyperexcitability, nausea, insomnia, and weight loss. Continued use may cause increasing paranoia and psychosis. Repeated sniffing also damages the membranes lining the nose and may eventually lead to the destruction of the septum (the structure separating the nostrils). Regular cocaine use leads to increased atheroma (fatty deposits in the arteries) and consequent risk of heart attacks.

Signs of abuse
The cocaine user may appear unusually energetic and exuberant under the influence of the drug and show little interest in food. Heavy, regular use may lead to disturbed eating and sleeping patterns. Agitation, mood swings, aggressive behaviour, and suspiciousness of other people may also be signs of a heavy user.

Interactions
Cocaine can increase blood pressure, thus opposing the effect of antihypertensive drugs. Taken with monoamine oxidase inhibitors (MAOIs), it can cause a dangerous rise in blood pressure. It also increases the risk of *adverse effects* on the heart when taken with certain general anesthetics.

CRACK

This potent form of cocaine is taken in the form of crystals that are smoked by vaporizing with a flame and inhaling the fumes. Highly addictive, crack appears to have more intense effects than other forms of cocaine and it is associated with an increased risk of abnormal heart rhythms, high blood pressure, heart attacks, stroke, and death. Other consequences of crack abuse include coughing of black phlegm, wheezing, irreversible lung damage, hoarseness, and parched lips, tongue, and throat from inhaling the hot fumes. Mental deterioration, personality changes, social withdrawal, paranoia or violent behaviour, and suicide attempts may occur.

ECSTASY

Other common names E, MDMA, XTC, methylenedioxy-methamphetamine. Other slang names vary from place to place
Drug category Central nervous system stimulant

Habit-forming potential
As with other amphetamines, regular use leads to *tolerance*, so that higher doses are required to achieve the same effect. Users may become psychologically dependent on the effects of the drug and the lifestyle that surrounds its use.

How taken
By mouth in tablet or *capsule* form.

Legitimate uses
Although there have been claims that ecstasy may have a place in psychotherapy, it currently has no legitimate medical use. The drug is classified under the Food and Drugs Act, Restricted Drugs (Part 4).

Short-term effects
Ecstasy is most commonly used as a dance drug at "raves" or parties to increase the emotional effects of dancing to fast music and to enable users to dance for many hours. *Adverse effects* are more commonly due to "recreational" doses rather than to an overdose. Ecstasy stimulates the central nervous system, leading to increased wakefulness and energy and suppression of thirst, tiredness, and sleep. It can produce tight clenching of the jaw muscles (sometimes leading to involuntary tooth grinding) and stiffness in other muscles. The drug also increases the heart rate and raises the blood pressure. Various complications may occur, in particular, heatstroke due to prolonged dancing without replacing fluids lost by sweating. Heatstroke can lead to muscle breakdown, kidney failure, problems with the blood clotting mechanism, convulsions, and death. In some cases there may be low sodium levels and brain swelling due to excessive intake of fluid in the absence of sufficient exertion to sweat it off. These patients may experience vomiting, headaches, and drowsiness. Liver damage and stroke have also occurred.

Long-term effects and risks
There is increasing evidence that ecstasy can impair both short- and long-term memory. In addition, some cases of psychiatric illness have been reported, such as schizophrenia and depression. Sleep disturbances and a craving for chocolate have also been reported. There may be an increased likelihood of developing depression even years after stopping the drug.

Signs of abuse
Ecstasy causes dilated pupils. Behaviour may be excitable or agitated. The ecstasy user may experience weight loss, tooth damage as a result of jaw-clenching, and anxiety.

Interactions
Ecstasy interacts with a variety of drugs. If it is taken with monoamine oxidase inhibitors (MAOIs), ecstasy may lead to a dangerous rise in blood pressure. It also increases the risk of abnormal heart rhythms with digoxin, levodopa, and certain anesthetics given by inhalation. Ecstasy tends to counteract the *sedative* effects of drugs that depress the central nervous system, and its effect on the mind is reduced by these drugs. SSRI antidepressants (such as fluoxetine) appear to block the psychoactive effects of ecstasy, which often prompts users to take higher doses of ectasy to overcome this blocking effect.

GHB

Other common names Liquid X, GBH, Liquid E, gamma hydroxybutyrate, sodium oxybate
Drug category Central nervous system depressant

Habit-forming potential
GHB is addictive if taken regularly in large doses.

How taken
By mouth. Often sold as a liquid in bottles, but it may be presented in a *capsule* or as a powder that is commonly dissolved in water to produce a clear, colourless liquid that often has a salty taste. It may also be injested as a number of other drugs that break down in the body to form GHB; for example, GBL (gamma-butyrolacone) and the industrial solvent 1,4BD (1,4 butanediol).

Legitimate uses
GHB is a naturally occurring chemical produced in the body in small amounts. Originally developed as an anesthetic, it has been used in the treatment of narcolepsy, insomnia, and alcohol and *opioid* withdrawal, but currently has no recognized medical use. Possession of GHB is illegal.

Short-term effects
GHB is a central nervous system depressant. Its effects are somewhat similar to alcohol, with talkativeness, cheerfulness, and euphoria occurring soon after taking an average dose. Most people become drowsy but recover within 4–8 hours of ingestion. Some users may experience confusion, headache, or gastrointestinal symptoms such as vomiting or stomach pain. Excessive doses may cause unconsciousness, and seizures, slowed heart rate, low blood pressure, and respiratory arrest have been reported. Recovery may take 96 hours, and hospital treatment may be necessary. Deaths have occurred after taking excessive doses of GHB, either from cardiorespiratory depression or from accidents while intoxicated by the drug.

Long-term effects and risks
Users may suffer a "hung-over" state for 2–3 days, and insomnia and dizziness may linger for up to 2 weeks. Longer-term effects of the drug have not been well studied. Stopping after prolonged use may cause a withdrawal syndrome.

Signs of abuse
As the drug is taken in liquid form it is difficult to estimate the correct dose, and the response to a low dose varies widely. Many abusers simply "guzzle" it until they reach an adequate high. This is often achieved only shortly before becoming unconscious, so sudden unconsciousness on the dance floor, for example, may be caused by GHB intoxication. In such cases, the person may later wake up suddenly, after apparently having been in a deep coma. Abnormally long-lasting hangovers and dizziness may be signs of abuse.

Interactions
The effects will be increased by other central nervous system depressants – for example, alcohol, benzodiazepines, and antipsychotics. GHB may also add to the effects of *opioid* analgesic drugs and muscle relaxants. It is sometimes mixed with amphetamines to prolong the "high" for several hours.

KETAMINE

Other common names Kit-Kat, Special K, Super K, vitamin K
Drug category General anesthetic with analgesic properties (see p.64)

Habit-forming potential
Likely to lead to psychological addiction if taken regularly.

How taken
Usually swallowed as the liquid pharmaceutical preparation or as tablets/capsules, produced mainly by heating the liquid anesthetic to evaporate the water, leaving ketamine crystals. Sometimes smoked or sniffed as a powder. The smoke has a characteristic bitter taste and produces a high rapidly. Ketamine may also be injected into a muscle, and this is the preferred route of administration for heavy users. The drug is usually taken alone in a quiet place because the effects can be disturbing if the drug is taken in a noisy or crowded environment.

Legitimate uses
A *general anesthetic* with analgesic properties, used both in human and veterinary medicine (it is on the WHO list of essential drugs for any health care system). It is related to phencyclidine.

Short-term effects
The effects may depend on mood and environment, but have a rapid onset. Ketamine stimulates the cardiovascular system, producing a racing heart. There are a number of psychological effects that may occur, including hallucinations and a feeling of paralysis in which the user cannot move or speak but is still fully conscious and can see and hear. Actions or words may be repeated persistently, or the user may have an "out of body" experience. Users may be unconcerned whether they live or die. Due to the analgesic effects, the user is unlikely to feel pain. Severe reactions, usually due to overdose, may include convulsions, depression of the breathing mechanism, or heart failure.

Long-term effects and risks
The long-term use of ketamine may interfere with memory, learning, and attention span. Users may also experience flashbacks. Psychosis may occur. There have also been reports that regular use of ketamine causes inflammation of the bladder and ureters, which can cause cystitis-like spasms ("K-cramps"), bladder pain, and blood in the urine. In some cases, it has necessitated surgical removal of the bladder.

Signs of abuse
Strange behaviour may suggest the psychological effects of ketamine. Painful injuries (such as cigarette burns) appear to go unnoticed.

Interactions
Barbiturates lengthen the duration of action that results from ketamine use, and in combination there is a risk of respiratory depression. Use of ketamine together with theophylline or aminophylline may increase the likelihood of convulsions. Alcoholics tend to be resistant to ketamine, although the psychological effects may be exaggerated during the recovery period.

KHAT

Other common names Cat, chaat, mriaa, quat
Drug category Central nervous system stimulant

Habit-forming potential
Dependence on khat is exclusively psychological. The main active constituent of khat is cathinone, an amphetamine-like substance that is responsible for khat's potential for causing psychological dependence.

How taken
Khat is composed of the leaves and small twigs of a plant (*Catha edulis*) that grows on high ground in many tropical countries. A large amount of the leaves or stems are chewed, and the plant material is kept in the cheek while the juice is swallowed. Occasionally it is dried and drunk as a tea because cathinone is unstable in the fresh leaves.

Legitimate uses
Khat has no legitimate medical uses. The drug is widely used as a social stimulant in many Middle East and African countries, and is often taken at celebrations and gatherings. It has also been used as a traditional remedy to treat depression, fatigue, obesity, and gastric ulcers. However, the authorities in these countries are increasingly concerned about its *adverse effects* on health.

Short-term effects
Khat produces appetite suppression, dry mouth, euphoria, increased alertness, talkativeness, and hyperactivity. Gastrointestinal *side effects* are common, as well as a mild rise in the blood pressure, pulse, respiratory rate, and temperature. Insomnia, poor concentration, and malaise are also common side effects. Aggressive verbal outbursts and hallucinations may occur as a result of khat use, and psychosis has occurred. Mental depression and sedation may follow withdrawal after heavy or regular use.

Long-term effects and risks
Constipation is a very common side effect and stomach ulcers are quite common in regular users of khat. Men may experience erectile dysfunction and reduced sex drive. Khat use may contribute to the risk of high blood pressure in young adults. Chronic use during pregnancy may lead to low birth weight, and the drug is excreted in breast milk.

Signs of abuse
The drug causes a brownish-green staining of the teeth. Weight loss may occur as a result of appetite suppression.

Interactions
It causes additive effects with other phenylalkylamines, including amphetamine, to cause mental stimulation, a fast heart rate and high blood pressure.

LSD

Other common names Lysergide, diethylamide, lysergic acid, lysergic acid diethylamide, acid, haze, microdots
Drug category Hallucinogen

Habit-forming potential
Although it is not physically addictive, LSD may cause psychological *dependence*. After several days of regular use, a person develops a *tolerance* to its actions. A waiting period must pass before resumption of the drug will produce the original effects.

How taken
By mouth, as tiny coloured tablets (known as "microdots"), or absorbed onto small squares of paper, gelatin sheets, or sugar cubes.

Legitimate uses
None. Early interest of the medical profession in LSD focused on its possible use in psychotherapy, but additional studies suggested that it could lead to psychosis in susceptible people. LSD is listed under the Food and Drugs Act, Restricted Drugs, Part 4 (Schedule III, Controlled Drugs and Substances Act).

Short-term effects
The effects of usual doses of LSD last for about 4–12 hours, beginning almost immediately after taking the drug. Initial effects include restlessness, dizziness, a feeling of coldness with shivering, and an uncontrollable desire to laugh. The subsequent effects include distortions in vision and, in some cases, in the perception of sound. Introspection is often increased and mystical, pseudoreligious experiences may occur. Loss of emotional control, unpleasant or terrifying hallucinations, and overwhelming feelings of anxiety, despair, or panic may occur (a "bad trip"), particularly if the user is suffering from underlying anxiety or depression. Suicide may be attempted. Driving and other hazardous tasks are extremely dangerous. Some people under the influence of this drug have fallen off high buildings, mistakenly believing they could fly.

Long-term effects and risks
The effects of long-term LSD use include an increase in the risk of mental disturbances, including severe depression. In those with existing psychological difficulties, it may lead to lasting mental problems (e.g., permanent psychosis). In addition, for months or even years after last taking the drug, some frequent users experience brief but vivid recurrences of LSD's effects ("flashbacks"), which cause anxiety and disorientation. There is no evidence of lasting physical ill-effects from LSD use.

Signs of abuse
A person under the influence of LSD may be behaving strangely but rarely shows any other outward signs of intoxication. Occasionally, a user who is drugged with LSD may seem overexcited, or appear withdrawn or confused.

Interactions
Chlorpromazine reduces the effects of LSD, so it can be used to treat a person who is acutely disturbed. Interactions with other drugs acting on the brain, such as alcohol, may increase the likelihood of unpredictable or violent behaviour. Lysergide abusers who are given SSRI antidepressants (e.g., fluoxetine, paroxetine, or sertraline) may experience onset or worsening of flashbacks. When LSD is given to those taking lithium or tricyclic antidepressants, it may sometimes cause dissociative fugue states during which the users are unaware of their surroundings and may injure themselves.

MESCALINE

Other common names Peyote, cactus buttons, big chief
Drug category Hallucinogen

Habit-forming potential
Mescaline has a low habit-forming potential; it does not cause physical *dependence* and does not usually lead to psychological dependence. After several days of taking mescaline, the user develops a tolerance for further doses of the drug, thus discouraging regular daily use.

How taken
By mouth as *capsules*, or in the form of peyote cactus buttons, eaten fresh or dried, drunk as tea, or ground up and smoked with cannabis.

Legitimate uses
The peyote cactus has been used by Native Mexicans for over 2,000 years, both in religious rituals and as a herbal remedy for various ailments ranging from wounds and bronchitis to failing vision. Mescaline is listed under the Food and Drugs Act, Restricted Drugs, Part 4 (Schedule III, Controlled Drugs and Substances Act).

Short-term effects
Mescaline alters visual and auditory perception, although true hallucinations are rare. Appetite is reduced under the influence of this drug. There is also a risk of unpleasant mental effects, particularly in people who are anxious or depressed.

Peyote may have additional effects caused by several other active substances (in addition to mescaline) in the plant. Strychnine-like chemicals may cause nausea, vomiting, and, occasionally, tremors and sweating, which usually precede the perceptual effects of mescaline by up to 2 hours.

Long-term effects and risks
The long-term effects of mescaline have not been well studied. It may increase the risk of mental disturbances, particularly in people with existing psychological problems. Studies have shown that, after taking mescaline, most of the drug concentrates in the liver rather than in the brain, and it may therefore have special risks for people with impaired liver function.

Signs of abuse
Mescaline or peyote abuse may not have obvious signs. Users might sometimes appear withdrawn, disoriented, or confused.

Interactions
The combination of alcohol and peyote, although common, is recognized to be dangerous. There is a risk of temporary derangement, leading to disorientation, panic, and violent behaviour. Vomiting is likely to occur.

NICOTINE

Other common names Found in tobacco products
Drug category Central nervous system stimulant (see also p.371)

Habit-forming potential
The nicotine in tobacco is largely responsible for tobacco *addiction* in over one-third of the population who are cigarette smokers. Most are also probably psychologically *dependent* on the process of smoking. Most people who start go on to smoke regularly, and most become physically dependent on nicotine. Stopping can produce temporary *withdrawal symptoms* that include nausea, headache, diarrhea, hunger, drowsiness, fatigue, insomnia, irritability, depression, inability to concentrate, and craving for cigarettes.

How taken
Usually smoked in the form of cigarettes, cigars, and pipe tobacco. Sometimes sniffed (tobacco snuff) or chewed (chewing tobacco).

Legitimate uses
There are no legal restrictions on tobacco use. Its sale, however, is restricted to those over the age of 18. Nicotine chewing gum, lozenges, inhalers, or slow-release patches may be prescribed on a temporary basis, along with behaviour modification therapy to help people who want to give up smoking.

Short-term effects
Nicotine stimulates the sympathetic nervous system (see p.63). In regular tobacco users, it increases concentration, relieves tension and fatigue, and counters boredom and monotony. These effects are short-lived, thus encouraging frequent use. Physical effects include narrowing of blood vessels, increase in heart rate and blood pressure, and reduction in urine output. First-time users often feel dizzy and nauseated, and may vomit.

Long-term effects and risks
Nicotine taken regularly may cause a rise in fatty acids in the bloodstream. This effect, combined with the effects of the drug on heart rhythm and blood vessel size, may increase the risk of diseases of the heart and circulation, including angina, high blood pressure, peripheral vascular disease, stroke, and coronary thrombosis. In addition, its stimulatory effects may lead to excess production of stomach acid, and thereby increase the risk of peptic ulcers.

Other well-known risks of tobacco smoking, such as chronic lung diseases, *adverse effects* on pregnancy, and cancers of the lung, mouth, and throat, may be due to other harmful ingredients in tobacco smoke. It is now believed that the main cancer-causing chemical in tobacco smoke is benzo (a) pyrene diol epoxide (a tarry substance).

Signs of abuse
Regular smokers often have yellow, tobacco-stained fingers and teeth and bad breath. The smell of tobacco may linger on hair and clothes. A smoker's cough or shortness of breath are usually early signs of established lung damage or heart disease.

Interactions
Cigarette smoking reduces the blood levels of a variety of drugs and reduces their effects. Such drugs include the benzodiazepines, tricyclic antidepressants, theophylline, propranolol, heparin, and caffeine. Diabetics may require larger doses of insulin. The health risks involved in taking oral contraceptives are increased by smoking.

Practical points
▼ Don't start smoking; nicotine is highly addictive.
▼ If you smoke already, give up now even if you have not yet suffered adverse effects. There are various strategies to help you with this.
▼ Ask your physician or *pharmacist* for advice and support.
▼ Inquire about self-help groups in your neighbourhood for people trying to give up smoking.

NITRITES

Other common names Amyl nitrite, butyl nitrite, poppers, snappers
Drug category Vasodilators (see also p.84)

Habit-forming potential
Nitrites do not cause physical *dependence*; major *withdrawal symptoms* have never been reported. However, users may become psychologically dependent on the stimulant effect of these drugs.

How taken
By inhalation, usually from small bottles with screw or plug tops or from small glass ampules that are broken.

Legitimate uses
Amyl nitrite was originally introduced as a treatment for angina but has now largely been replaced by safer, longer-acting drugs. It is still available as an *antidote* for cyanide poisoning. Butyl and isobutyl nitrites are not used medically.

Short-term effects
Nitrites increase the flow of blood by relaxing blood vessel walls. They give the user a rapid "high", felt as a strong rush of energy. Less pleasant effects include an increase in heart rate, intense flushing, dizziness, fainting, pounding headache, nausea, and coughing. High doses may cause fainting, and regular use may produce a blue discoloration of the skin due to alteration of hemoglobin in the red blood cells.

Long-term effects and risks
Nitrites are very quick-acting drugs. Their effects start within 30 seconds of inhalation and last for about 5 minutes. Regular users may become *tolerant* to these drugs, thus requiring higher doses to achieve the desired effects. Lasting physical damage, including cardiac problems, can result from chronic use of these drugs, and deaths have occurred.

The risk of *toxic* effects is increased in those with low blood pressure. Nitrites may also precipitate the onset of glaucoma in susceptible people, by increasing pressure inside the eye.

Signs of abuse
Nitrites have a pungent, fruity odour. They evaporate quickly; the contents of a small bottle left uncapped in a room usually disappear within 2 hours. Unless someone is actually taking the drug or is suffering from an overdose, the only sign of abuse may be a bluish skin discoloration, although this is rare. Overdose is usually through swallowing rather than inhaling, and can result in collapse, convulsions, and coma.

Interactions
The blood-pressure-lowering effect of these drugs is greatly increased by sildenafil, tadalafil, and vardenafil (drugs for erectile dysfunction) and their concomitant use should be avoided. In susceptible individuals, the effect may be to precipitate a stroke or heart attack. Alcohol, beta blockers, calcium channel blockers, and tricyclic antidepressants also increase the blood-pressure-lowering effects of nitrites, thus increasing the risk of dizziness and fainting.

OPIOIDS (HEROIN)

Other common names Horse, junk, smack, scag, H, diamorphine, morphine, opium
Drug category Central nervous system depressant

Habit-forming potential
Opioid analgesics include not only those drugs derived from the opium poppy (opium and morphine) but also synthetic drugs whose medical actions are similar to those of morphine (meperidine, methadone, and dextropropoxyphene). Frequent use of these drugs leads to *tolerance*, and all have a potential for *dependence*. Among them, heroin is the most potent, widely abused, and dangerous. It is also associated with criminal behaviour.

After only a few weeks of use, *withdrawal symptoms* may occur when the drug is stopped; fear of such withdrawal effects may be a strong inducement to go on using the drug. In heavy users, the drug habit is often coupled with a lifestyle that revolves around its use.

How taken
A white or speckled brown powder, heroin is smoked, sniffed, or injected. Other opioids may be taken by mouth.

Legitimate uses
Heroin is widely used in countries such as Britain and Belgium for the treatment of acute severe pain. Although Canadian drug regulations were changed in the 1980s to allow heroin to be prescribed in hospital, it is rarely used. Heroin and morphine are powerful cough suppressants. Other opioids, such as morphine and methadone, are used as analgesics. Most opioids are listed under Schedule I of the Controlled Drugs and Substances Act of the Food and Drugs Act. Mild opioids such as codeine are also sometimes included in cough suppressant and antidiarrheal medications.

Short-term effects
Strong opioids induce a feeling of contentment and well-being. Pain is dulled and the activity of the nervous system is depressed; breathing and heart rate are slowed and the cough reflex is inhibited. First-time users often feel nauseated and vomit. With higher doses, there is increasing drowsiness, sometimes leading to coma and, in rare cases, death from respiratory arrest.

Long-term effects and risks
The long-term regular use of opioids leads to constipation, reduced sexual drive, disruption of menstrual periods, and poor eating habits. Poor nutrition and personal neglect may lead to general ill health.

Street drugs are often mixed ("cut") with other substances, such as caffeine, quinine, talcum powder, and flour, that can damage blood vessels, affect the lungs, or lead to the formation of blood clots. There is also a risk of abscesses at the injection site. Dangerous infections, such as hepatitis, syphilis, and human immunodeficiency virus (HIV), may be transmitted via unclean or shared needles.

After several weeks of regular use, sudden withdrawal of opioids produces a flu-like withdrawal syndrome beginning 6–24 hours after the last dose. Symptoms may include runny nose and eyes, hot and cold sweats, sleeplessness, aches, tremor, anxiety, nausea, vomiting, diarrhea, muscle spasms, and abdominal cramps. These effects are at their worst 48–72 hours after withdrawal and fade after 7–10 days.

Signs of abuse
An opioid abuser may exhibit such signs as apathy, neglect of personal appearance and hygiene, loss of appetite and weight, loss of interest in former hobbies and social activities, personality changes, and furtive behaviour. Users resort to crime to continue financing their habit. Signs of intoxication include pinpoint pupils and a drowsy or drunken appearance.

Interactions
Opioids dangerously increase the risk of sedation with any drug that has a *sedative* effect on the central nervous system, including benzodiazepines and alcohol.

PHENCYCLIDINE

Other common names PCP, angel dust, crystal, ozone
Drug category General anesthetic (see p.64), hallucinogen

Habit-forming potential
There is little evidence that phencyclidine causes physical *dependence*. Some users become psychologically dependent on this drug and *tolerant* to its effects.

How taken
May be sniffed, used in smoking mixtures (in the form of angel dust), eaten (as tablets), or, in rare cases, injected.

Legitimate uses
Although it was once used as an anesthetic (and was a forerunner of ketamine), it no longer has any medical use. Its use in veterinary medicine has also been discontinued. Phencyclidine's effects on behaviour (see below) make it one of the most dangerous of all drugs of abuse.

Short-term effects
Phencyclidine taken in small amounts generally produces a "high", but sometimes leads to anxiety or depression. Coordination of speech and movement deteriorates, and thinking and concentration are impaired. Hallucinations and violent behaviour may occur. Other possible effects include increases in blood pressure and heart rate, dilation of the pupils, dryness of the mouth, tremor, numbness, and greatly reduced sensitivity to pain, which may make it difficult to restrain a person who has become violent under the influence of the drug. Shivering, vomiting, muscle weakness, and rigidity may also occur. Higher doses lead to coma or stupor and seizures. The recovery period is often prolonged, with alternate periods of sleep and waking, usually followed by memory blackout of the whole episode.

Long-term effects and risks
Repeated phencyclidine use may lead to paranoia, auditory hallucinations, violent behaviour, anxiety, severe depression, and schizophrenia. While depressed, the user may attempt suicide by overdosing on the drug. Heavy users may also develop brain damage, which may cause memory blackouts, disorientation, visual disturbances, and speech difficulties.

Deaths due to prolonged convulsions, cardiac or respiratory arrest, and ruptured blood vessels in the brain have been reported. After high doses or prolonged coma, there is also a risk of mental derangement, which may be permanent.

Signs of abuse
The phencyclidine user may appear drunk while under the influence of the drug. Hostile or violent behaviour and mood swings with bouts of depression may be more common with heavy use.

Interactions
Using phencyclidine may inhibit the effects of *anticholinergic* drugs, as well as beta blockers and antihypertensive drugs.

SOLVENTS

Other common names Inhalants, glue
Drug category Central nervous system depressant

Habit-forming potential
There is a low risk of physical *dependence* with solvent abuse, but regular users may become psychologically dependent. Young people with family and personality problems are at particular risk of becoming habitual users of solvents.

How taken
By breathing in the fumes, usually from a plastic bag placed over the nose and/or mouth or from a cloth or handkerchief soaked in the solvent.

Legitimate uses
Solvents are used in a wide variety of industrial, domestic, and cosmetic products. They function as aerosol propellants for spray paints, hair lacquer, lighter fuel, and deodorants. They are used in adhesives, paints, paint stripper, lacquers, gasoline, and cleaning fluids.

Short-term effects
The short-term effects of solvents include lightheadedness, dizziness, confusion, and progressive drowsiness; loss of coordination occurs with increasing doses. Accidents of all types are more likely. Heart rhythm might be disturbed, sometimes fatally. Large doses can lead to disorientation, hallucinations, and loss of consciousness. Nausea, vomiting, and headaches may also occur.

Long-term effects and risks
One of the greatest risks of solvent abuse is accidental death or injury while intoxicated. Some products, especially aerosol gases, butane gas, and cleaning fluids, may seriously disrupt heart rhythm or cause heart failure and sometimes death. Aerosols and butane gas can also cause suffocation by sudden cooling of the airways and these are particularly dangerous if squirted into the mouth. Butane gas has been known to ignite in the mouth. Aerosol products, such as deodorant and paint, may suffocate the user by coating the lungs. People have suffocated while sniffing solvents from plastic bags placed over their heads. There is also a risk of death from inhalation of vomit and depression of the breathing mechanism.

Long-term misuse of solvent-based cleaning fluids can cause permanent liver or kidney damage, while long-term exposure to benzene (found in plastic cements, lacquers, paint remover, gasoline, and cleaning fluid) may lead to blood and liver disorders. Hexane-based adhesives may cause nerve damage leading to numbness and tremor. Repeated sniffing of leaded gasoline may cause lead poisoning.

Regular daily use of solvents can lead to pallor, fatigue, and forgetfulness. Heavy use may affect the student's school performance and lead to weight loss, depression, and general deterioration of health.

Signs of abuse
Most abusers are adolescents between the ages of 10 and 17, although the average age, 14–15, for this type of drug abuse is thought to be falling.

Obvious signs of solvent abuse include a chemical smell on the breath and traces of glue or solvents on the body or clothes. Other signs include furtive behaviour, uncharacteristic moodiness, unusual soreness or redness around the mouth, nose, or eyes, and a persistent cough.

Interactions
Sniffing solvents increases the risk of sedation with any drug that has a *sedative* effect on the central nervous system. Such drugs include anti-anxiety and sleeping drugs, *opioids*, tricyclic antidepressants, antipsychotics, and alcohol.

ALTERNATIVE MEDICINE

Alternative, or complementary, medicine has become increasingly popular in recent years. Agrowing number of people consult alternative practitioners as well as, or instead of, their own physicians, and the use of alternative remedies has become considerably more widespread. Physicians are also more likely to refer some patients to alternative practitioners or to recommend the use of alternative treatments. However, there is little evidence of how alternative medicines work or of the safety and effectiveness of many of these remedies.

All natural health products (NHPs) sold in Canada are controlled by the Natural Health Products Regulations.

Although many medicines are derived from plant matter, the use of plants and other natural substances to aid healing can be found in different cultures all around the world. Many modern alternative remedies are based on these traditional therapies. Most alternative practitioners believe that an illness is caused by an imbalance in the body, which must be restored to treat the illness. Many aim to treat the whole body rather than just certain symptoms. Before using a Natural Health Product, discuss its safety and efficacy with your health care practitioner.

Natural Health Products Regulations
Health Canada defines Natural Health Products as including vitamins, minerals, herbal remedies, homeopathic medicines, traditional Chinese and Ayurvedic medicines, probiotics and other products like amino acids and essential fatty acids. Natural Health Products Regulations came into effect as of January 1, 2004. All natural products require a product licence and are legally authorized for sale in Canada by the Natural Health Products Directorate. All products must display a product identification number preceded by NPN or, in the case of a homeopathic medicine, preceded by DIN-HM on their labels. Standard labelling requirements for natural products should include information on product name, quantity of product in the bottle, recommended conditions of use, and any special storage conditions. Recommended conditions of use include its recommended use or purpose, dose, dosage form, route of administration, warnings, cautions, contraindications, and possible *adverse effects*. Health Canada also requires that these products be monitored for adverse reactions and that these be reported to Health Canada.

Buying alternative medicines
Most alternative medicines are available over the counter from *pharmacies* and health shops. Only buy products from a reputable manufacturer, who will usually provide information leaflets and instructions for use. Other medicines can only be dispensed by suitably trained and registered practitioners. Some alternative practitioners are also medically trained and qualified.

Using alternative medicines
You may be able to treat yourself for minor, short-lived conditions, such as a cold, but professional advice should always be sought for more serious or persistent complaints. Always follow the instructions given when taking alternative medicines, and never exceed the recommended dose. Certain herbs and preparations contain ingredients that can be harmful if not used with care.

Some alternative medicines can interact with other drugs or affect pre-existing disorders in an adverse way. You should therefore tell your practitioner about any drugs you are taking as well as any pre-existing illnesses. You should also inform your physician or *pharmacist* about any alternative remedies you are taking before you start taking conventional drugs. Do not stop or reduce conventional treatment without asking your physician's advice.

HOMEOPATHY

The aim of homeopathy is to stimulate the body's powers of self-healing. Treatment is based on the concept of "like cures like" and uses the principle that the body can be stimulated to overcome illness if a patient is given extremely dilute doses of a substance that, at full strength, would produce symptoms of the illness. For example, minute doses of pollen are used to treat hayfever and allergic asthma.

Creating homeopathic remedies
There are at least 2000 homeopathic remedies. They are made from extracts of plants, animals, or minerals. These extracts are then infused in alcohol and water to make a tincture. This is then diluted repeatedly, in a process that is known as potentiation.

Homeopathic practitioners believe that the more dilute the remedy, the stronger the effect it will have. A few drops of the tincture are usually added to sugar tablets, creams, or other substances for administration.

How homeopathy works
One theory of how homeopathy works is that an electromagnetic imprint of the homeopathic substance remains after dilution, even though no molecules of the original substance are present. This imprint is believed to stimulate a response in the body. Some homeopathic practitioners believe that the imprint acts on the flow of energy in the body rather than on physical processes.

However, these findings are not reproducible and the basic principles underlying homeopathy are still generally regarded with scepticism.

Using homeopathic remedies
Homeopathic remedies are available as sugar tablets, powders, tinctures, oils, creams, and ointments. Tablets should be sucked or chewed. Tinctures are usually diluted in water and taken internally or applied externally. Ointments, oils, and creams are applied externally to the skin. Your homeopathic practitioner can

COMMON HOMEOPATHIC REMEDIES

Coughs, colds, and 'flu	**Bruises, sprains, and minor injuries**
Aconite	Arnica
Bryonia	Hypericum
Gelsemium	Ruta.grav.
Hayfever	**Menopause**
Allium	Calcarea
Arsen. alb.	Graphites
Euphrasia	Sepia
Nat. mur.	Sulfur
Indigestion	**Insomnia and exhaustion**
Acid. phos.	Arnica
Bryonia	Arsen. alb.
Carbo veg.	Coffea
Nux vom.	Nux vom.
Irritable bowel syndrome	
Argent. nit.	**Stress**
Arsen. alb.	Ignatia
Cantharis	Nux vom.
Nux vom.	Sepia
Headaches and migraine	**Depression**
Aconite	Lycopodium
Belladonna	Nat. mur.
Hypericum	Pulsatilla
Nat. mur.	Sulfur
Eczema and dermatitis	**Anxiety**
Graphites	Argent. nit.
Nat. mur.	Arsen. alb.
	Gelsemium
	Phos.

provide specific recommendations on how to take the remedy; usually they are taken at least 30 minutes before or after eating or drinking.

As homeopathic remedies are highly diluted, they are very unlikely to cause *side effects*. However, in some cases, symptoms being treated may worsen briefly at the start of treatment before getting better.

WESTERN HERBAL MEDICINE

Western herbal medicines are extracted from the leaves, flowers, roots, seeds, berries, fruits, or bark of whole plants. They differ from modern drugs derived from herbs in that they use parts of the whole plant instead of isolating a single active ingredient. Many herbalists believe that the therapeutic effect of the whole plant is greater and safer than that of its isolated constituents. Several herbs may be combined in one remedy, and products should indicate which part of the plant has been used. The World Health Organization acknowledges that Western herbal medicine plays an important role in healthcare.

How Western herbal medicine works

The use of specific herbs is based on their recognized actions on the body. Although research into the use of herbal medicines is limited, evidence supports the claims made for the effectiveness of several herbal medicines. These include echinacea, which appears to stimulate the immune system, and St John's wort (*hypericum perforatum*), which seems to be effective in treating mild depression.

Using Western herbal remedies

Herbal remedies are available in a range of forms including infusions or teas, decoctions, tinctures, tablets, creams, lotions, ointments, and oils. *Side effects* are not common, although allergic reactions may occur. In general, herbal remedies should be avoided during pregnancy or breast-feeding, and they should not be taken by young children or by elderly people without professional advice.

Some interactions between herbal medicines and conventional drugs have been reported, with some causing serious problems; some combinations are dangerous. Their potential interactions can be predicted from the known effects of a plant. Plant remedies that could interfere with conventional drugs include liquorice, blue cohosh, broom, ginger, and St John's wort. It is important that you discuss potential interactions between herbal medicines and conventional drugs with your pharmacist or physician before use.

COMMON WESTERN HERBAL REMEDIES

Minor injuries and bruises
Comfrey
Marigold
St John's wort

Coughs and colds
Echinacea
Garlic
Ginger

Nausea and vomiting
Chamomile
Fennel
Ginger
Peppermint

Headaches and migraine
Chamomile
Feverfew
Lavender

Acne
Echinacea
Dandelion root
Nettle

Premenstrual syndrome
Agnus castus
Cramp bark
Dandelion
Gamolenic acid
Marigold

Chronic fatigue
Astragalus
Echinacea
Ginseng
Goldenseal
Yellow dock root

Stress
Chamomile
Ginseng
Hops
Motherwort
Passion flower
Valerian
Vervain

CHINESE HERBAL MEDICINE

Chinese herbal medicine is part of the ancient system of healing known as Traditional Chinese Medicine (TCM). Medicines are derived from hundreds of different plant species. Parts used may include the flowers, leaves, fruits, stalks, seeds, or bark. Chinese herbal medicine is different from Western medicine in that it regards symptoms as being due to disharmony in the body and tries to treat the underlying cause in order to restore balance. Western medicine tends to concentrate on specific symptoms. In China, TCM is taught at university level and practised in all hospitals.

How Chinese herbal medicine works

TCM is based around the concepts of *yin* and *yang*, two complementary but opposing forces. If these forces are disturbed, disease occurs. Different symptoms indicate excess *yin* or *yang*. Another belief is that each internal organ is associated with one of the five elements – fire, earth, metal, water, and wood.

Herbal remedies are used to restore balance between all these forces within the body. Herbs are classified under one of the five elements and according to their *yin* and *yang* qualities.

Although some studies have shown an improvement in symptoms following the use of Chinese herbal medicines, the concepts underlying traditional Chinese medicine cannot be explained by Western

science and many Western physicians are still sceptical.

Using Chinese herbal remedies

Herbs are generally prescribed by the practitioner as a formula containing several different ingredients, usually up to 15 in combination. Each herb performs a particular function and is used for a specific purpose. The herbs are usually boiled in water to make a decoction or tea but may also be available as tablets, pills, powders, pastes, ointments, creams, and lotions. Medicine is usually taken daily at the start of treatment.

A large range of Chinese herbal medicines for minor conditions can be bought over-the-counter from health shops, pharmacies, Chinese herbalists, or Chinese medicine centres. More complex remedies and formulas are prescribed by a practitioner.

Although side effects are uncommon, some Chinese medicinal plants can have toxic effects. In particular, some remedies have been associated with liver damage. Additionally, recent analysis of a small sample of Chinese herbal cream showed that a significant proportion contained potent corticosteroids, which can be harmful if used inappropriately.

COMMON CHINESE HERBAL REMEDIES

Coughs and colds
Astragalus root
Balloon flower
Fritillary
Plantain

Eczema
Chinese gentian
Chinese wormwood
Peony root
Rehmannia

Irritable bowel syndrome
Chinese angelica
Chinese rhubarb
Dandelion
Magnolia bark
Poria

Arthritis
Aconite
Chinese angelica
Cinnamon
Ginger
Liquorice

Headaches and migraine
Cassia
Chrysanthemum

Menopause
Chinese angelica
Ginseng
Peony
Rehmannia
Thorowax root

Insomnia
Fleeceflower
Poria
Wild jujube

AIDS
Chinese bitter melon
Ginseng
Lentinan
Red sage
White peony

DRUGS IN SPORT

The use of drugs to improve athletic performance ("doping") has been universally condemned by sporting authorities. Certain drugs give the athlete an unfair advantage and may also endanger health. The World Anti-Doping Agency (WADA) currently oversees the drug code that is used in most competitive sports worldwide. If traces of a prohibited substance are found by means of a urine test, the athlete is banned from the competition and risks lifelong exclusion from the sport. It is not only prescribed medications that affect athletic performance; everyday items such as cigarettes, alcohol, tea, and coffee can also have an effect. Drugs of any kind should be taken by athletes only under strict medical supervision and must be declared in writing to the relevant medical authority before the competition.

Many drugs affect the performance of athletes who are taking them. Some have been prescribed by physicians to treat specific medical conditions but are abused by athletes who want to benefit from the body-building and general performance-improving effects of these drugs. Others are everyday non-prescribed substances, such as caffeine and nicotine, which have a relatively minor effect on performance. However, even these substances can cause drug levels in the athlete's body to rise to unacceptable levels if taken in excess. Further information on prohibited substances is available from www.wada-ama.org.

Detecting drugs
Drugs can be detected in the urine and other body fluids. Increasingly sensitive tests are constantly being devised to check for prohibited substances. These tests are performed frequently in most sports, during competitions and in training.

Prohibited substances
WADA publishes a list of substances that are banned at all times, both in and out of competition. There are five classes of these banned substances: anabolic androgenic agents (e.g. anabolic steroids); peptide hormones, growth factors, and related substances (e.g. erythropoietin and growth hormone); beta 2 agonists (except when taken for therapeutic reasons, e.g. salbutamol), except specific drugs in certain circumstances; hormone antagonists and modulators (e.g. anti-estrogens such as clomifene); and diuretics and other masking agents. Many other drugs, such as stimulants, narcotics, cannabinoids, glucocorticsteroids, and alcohol (above a level of 0.1g per litre) are banned in most sports.

Legitimate medications
Certain prescribed drugs are allowed to be taken legitimately by athletes for certain medical disorders, such as asthma or epilepsy – known as therapeutic use exemption. Prescribed medicines must be declared in writing to the appropriate medical authority before any competition. Other prescribed drugs may not make any noticeable difference to athletic performance, but the underlying disorder for which the drugs are being taken may make strenuous exercise inadvisable. The athlete should also be careful when using certain over-the-counter preparations, as many contain low doses of prohibited substances.

TYPES OF DRUGS AND PRACTICES

Antibiotics
These drugs may occasionally impair ability by causing nausea or diarrhea.

Antihistamines
Preparations containing chlorpheniramine or diphenhydramine may cause drowsiness, dizziness, or blurred vision.

Anti-inflammatory drugs
Using anti-inflammatory drugs to relieve pain in muscles, tendons, or ligaments can be dangerous; masking pain may result in aggravation of an injury.

Asthma drugs
An asthma drug should not contain isoprenaline, ephedrine, or phenylephrine, which are prohibited stimulants. However, inhalers containing salbutamol and specific required medicines may be used.

Blood doping
This illegal practice involves removing blood from an athlete during training and replacing it shortly before a competition. After the blood is removed, the volume and number of red blood cells in the remaining blood is naturally replenished. When stored blood is reinfused, the hemoglobin content of the blood is increased, enhancing the blood's ability to deliver oxygen to muscles. A similar effect is achieved by erythropoietin (epoietin).

Caffeine
Although caffeine is listed as a prohibited stimulant, disqualification results only if large quantities (more than 12mg/litre) are detected in the urine sample.

Cocaine
This illegal and highly addictive stimulant is prohibited in sport. Dangerous *side effects* include heart arrhythmias, negative personality changes, and damage to the nasal lining after regular inhalation. A high dose can trigger convulsions or psychosis and may cause death.

Cough and cold remedies
Avoid preparations that contain codeine, ephedrine, pseudoephedrine, or phenylephrine for 12 hours before a competition. Drugs that can be used legally include antibiotics and antihistamines, steam inhalations, dextromethorphan, guaifenesin, and acetaminophen.

Diarrhea remedies
Any preparation containing opioids, such as morphine, must be avoided. However, diphenoxylate, loperamide, or electrolytes may be used.

Dieting drugs
Most diet drugs contain a prohibited stimulant or diuretic.

Hay fever remedies
Many remedies contain the prohibited stimulants ephedrine, pseudoephedrine, or phenylephrine, and should be stopped 24 hours before competition. However, nasal sprays that contain steroids or xylometazoline and sodium cromoglycate eye drops can be used legally. See also Antihistamines, p.110.

Liniment
Used as a counter irritant on the pain *receptors* in the skin, it is important that application of liniment does not mask pain to the point where further damage to an injury may result after exertion.

Nicotine
Available from tobacco products as well as from nicotine transdermal patches, nicotine reduces the flow of blood through the muscles. Carbon monoxide from smoking decreases the available oxygen carried round the body, thereby reducing the capacity for exercise.

Painkillers
Strong painkillers such as meperidine and morphine, known as opioid analgesics, are prohibited in sport. Weaker painkillers – for example, acetaminophen, ibuprofen, ASA, and *local anesthetics* in spray, ointment, or cream form – are permitted, but their use can mask pain, resulting in the aggravation of an injury.

Sleeping drugs
Many sports authorities ban sedatives, so a sleeping drug should not be taken less than 24 hours before a competition.

MEDICINES AND TRAVEL

Low cost air transport has resulted in enormous growth in international travel for both business and pleasure in recent years. This expansion has been paralleled by a more adventurous approach to leisure destinations. Few areas of the world are not on someone's itinerary and travellers are more likely than ever before to visit destinations with health hazards they have not encountered before and with poorly developed health services. Although few travellers run into serious medical problems, it is worth paying a little attention to the health aspects of travel when planning a trip. This should help to prevent problems later on and to ensure that any that do arise will not be serious. Risks can be minimized by seeking information about the country you are visiting, checking out facilities before you travel, and being prepared for both minor and major medical emergencies.

BEFORE YOU GO

If you take medicines regularly
Pack sufficient supplies to last for the entire trip. Some drugs may not be available at your destination or may require a local prescription. If any of your medicines are opioid or controlled drugs (see p.13), check with your physician or *pharmacist* as these may be stopped by Customs in some countries. Take your prescription record with you or ask your physician to give you a letter with details of the drugs you have been prescribed to show to Customs abroad and to Canadian Customs on your return. If you are worried about taking a prescription medicine into another country, you could ask the relevant embassy whether there might be a problem.

... and even if you don't
Take a few everyday medicines with you, including:
- a motion sickness remedy
- simple painkillers (e.g. acetaminophen or ibuprofen)
- an antidiarrheal and rehydration salts for traveller's diarrhea
- a laxative for constipation caused by changes in diet or routine
- an antiseptic cream for small injuries
- a bite/sting relief spray or cream for insect bites
- a high-protection factor (SPF 25+) sunscreen lotion
- an insect repellent

If you are going to a high risk area for malaria, start taking antimalarial drugs (p.123) a week or two before going to ensure that any intolerable *side effects* become apparent before departure.

If you are going outside the usual tourist routes, backpacking, or living among the local people, you might need to carry an emergency sterile syringe and needle kit. If you are intending to stay away for a long time, see your dentist for a check-up before you leave.

Vaccinations
Vaccinations are not normally necessary when travelling to Western Europe, the U.S., Australia, or New Zealand (although you should make sure that your tetanus and poliomyelitis boosters are up to date). However, consult your physician if you are visiting other destinations. If you are taking children with you, check that they have had the full set of routine childhood vaccinations as well as any vaccinations that are necessary for the areas you will be travelling in.

If you are visiting an area where there is yellow fever, an International Certificate of Vaccination will be needed. You may also need this certificate in the future. Many countries that you might want to visit require an International Certificate of Vaccination if you have already been to a country where yellow fever is present.

You are at risk of other infectious diseases in many parts of the world and appropriate vaccinations are a wise precaution. For example, there is a zone across northern India, Nepal, Bhutan, Pakistan, continuing in a wide band across Africa from the Sahara down to Kenya, that is called the "Meningitis Belt." Anyone intending to visit this zone should have the combined A, C, W135, and Y meningococcal vaccine. Visitors to Saudi Arabia, especially for the Hajj or Umrah pilgrimages, may also be required to have had this combined vaccine.

You may need extra vaccinations if you are planning to stay for a long time or backpacking. For example, hepatitis A vaccine would be sensible for anyone travelling to a developing country, but a long-stay traveller should consider having hepatitis B vaccine and BCG (tuberculosis) as well. Anyone travelling into remote areas is recommended to have rabies vaccination.

All immunization should be completed well before departure as the vaccinations do not give instant protection (BCG needs 3 months), and some need more than one dose to be effective.

Health Canada (see Further Information p.501) provides information and Travel Health Advisories to Canadians. Their Travel Medicine Program (TMP) lists travel clinics across Canada, specific diseases prevalent in parts of the world, and other relevant information.

Outbreaks of disease
Some infectious diseases are endemic (constantly or generally present). For example, dengue fever is found throughout the tropics; only the severity of the illness varies. Other diseases appear as definite outbreaks or epidemics; influenza is an example. While we are accustomed to think of influenza as a winter illness, it may occur at any time, especially in the tropics. If you or family members are likely to be at special risk and did not get the latest influenza booster, it would be worth checking whether there is an outbreak of influenza (or any other serious infectious disease) in the area you are planning to visit.

You could ask your physician or travel insurance company about the risk of disease in the country you are visiting. If you have access to the Internet, the best source of information on serious outbreaks of disease is the website of the Centers for Disease Control and Prevention (www.cdc.gov).

Insurance
Being taken ill when you are abroad can be expensive. Even if you are only travelling to the U.S., in the event of serious illness or accident you will need to show your insurance coverage in order to receive medical treatment. You should always take out travel health insurance, which can be inexpensive, before you leave. If you have a regular annual policy, check that it is kept up to date and is valid for the entire travel period and for any activities that you may be planning (such as skiing or watersports).

WHILE YOU ARE TRAVELLING

Travel sickness
If you are prone to travel sickness, take a travel sickness medicine about half an hour before you start your journey. Ask your physician or pharmacist for advice on which drug to choose. Do not drink alcohol if taking travel sickness drugs as alcohol can interact with the drugs and may make you excessively sleepy.

Dehydration and other cabin problems
The dry atmosphere inside the cabin of a passenger plane makes it very easy to become dehydrated, especially if you over-indulge in alcoholic drinks. Drink plenty of non-alcoholic fluids and limit alcoholic drinks, and you will feel fresher when you reach your destination.

Sitting still during a long-haul flight may lead to thrombosis (a blood clot) in the leg veins. A single tablet of soluble ASA taken with food before a long-haul flight may give protection. Discuss this with your physician before taking it and ensure that this is an appropriate medication for you. Once on the flight, get up and walk around the cabin now and again; also practise ankle- and knee-flexing exercises to try to help your circulation. Flight socks can help, too.

Taking medicines

International travel, in which time zones are crossed and airline meals are served at apparently random intervals, may make it difficult to decide when to take your regular medicines. Fortunately, precise timing is not critical with most medicines; take them at the correct intervals (e.g. every 8 hours for a drug normally taken 3 times a day) regardless of the clock time, then adjust to the original schedule upon arrival at your destination.

However, the timing of some drugs is much more crucial. For example, progestin-only oral contraceptives (p.149), must be taken at intervals of almost exactly 24 hours in order to remain effective; a delay of more than 3 hours will interfere with contraceptive protection. Timing is less critical with the combined (estrogen and progestin) oral contraceptive drugs.

People with insulin-dependent diabetes also face problems when travelling as their insulin dosage regimen is governed by the clock and by the timing of their meals (p.128). Such individuals should always consult their physician or diabetic educator before travelling long distances.

Jet lag

Rapid travel across time zones can cause physical and psychological stress. Business travellers should try to avoid major decisions on the first day after arrival, and all travellers should have a quiet adjustment period of at least a day to settle into the new day/night timing. Those on regular medication should seek advice from their physician about dosage adjustment before travelling.

Melatonin can shift the body clock when taken 15–30 minutes before bedtime in the new time zone, and repeated for the following 2–4 days. Melatonin is now available as a Natural Health Product in Canada.

TRAVEL IMMUNIZATION

The immunizations that you will need before travelling depend on the area of the world you intend to visit, although some diseases can be contracted almost anywhere. Wherever you are planning to go, make sure that you have been immunized against tetanus and polio and have had booster doses if necessary. Advice on other necessary immunizations may change from time to time. Before you travel, it is advisable to ask your physician, *pharmacist*, or travel clinic about vaccination for specific areas of the world as they should have the most up-to-date information.

Disease	Number of doses	When effective	Period of protection	Who should be immunized
Diphtheria	1 injection	Immediately	10 years	People travelling to countries where it is endemic and expatriates living in developing countries.
Hepatitis A	2 injections, 6–12 months apart	2–4 weeks after 1st dose	10 years	Frequent travellers to the Mediterranean or developing countries.
Hepatitis B	3 injections, 1 month between 1st and 2nd doses, 5 months between 2nd and 3rd doses	Immediately after 2nd dose	3–5 years	People travelling to countries in which hepatitis B is prevalent; those who might need medical or dental treatment while travelling in a developing country; and people likely to have unprotected sex.
Japanese B encephalitis	2–3 injections 1–2 weeks apart	10–14 days after last dose	About 2 years	People staying for an extended period in rural areas of the Indian subcontinent, China, Southeast Asia, and the Far East.
Meningitis A, C, W135, and Y	1 injection	After 15 days	3–5 years	People travelling to sub-Saharan Africa, Nepal, Bhutan, Pakistan, and Brazil; quadrivalent vaccine and immunization certificate needed if travelling to Saudi Arabia for the Hajj at Mecca.
Rabies	3 injections, 1 week between 1st and 2nd doses, 3 weeks between 2nd and 3rd doses	Immediately after 3rd dose	2–3 years	People travelling to areas where rabies is endemic and who are at high risk (veterinary surgeons, people working with animals, and those travelling into remote country).
Typhoid	1 injection or 3 oral doses	10 days after last dose or injection	3 years	People travelling to areas with poor sanitation.
Yellow fever	1 injection	After 10 days	10 years	People travelling to parts of South America and Africa.
Cholera	2 oral doses, 1–6 weeks apart	1 week	2 years	People at high risk (relief and aid workers or health professionals working in endemic countries).

ON ARRIVAL

Insect bites
Many microbial and viral diseases are spread by insect bites; taking steps to prevent these bites can help minimize risks. Ticks, sand flies, simulium flies, tsetse flies, and mosquitoes are among the insect carriers of disease. Although usually thought of as tropical problems, ticks, sand flies, and mosquitoes may spread some of the diseases mentioned here as far from the tropics as Europe, North America and the Mediterranean.

Viral diseases borne by insects include dengue fever, yellow fever, Japanese encephalitis, phlebotomus fever (sand fly fever), Colorado tick fever, West Nile virus, and many others. Insects also transmit protozoal parasitical diseases, for example: malaria, filariasis, leishmaniasis, Lyme disease, river blindness, and trypanosomiasis (African sleeping sickness).

To reduce the chance of being bitten wear long sleeved shirts and trousers, apply insect repellent regularly, and sleep under an insecticide-impregnated mosquito bed net or in screened accommodation sprayed with an insecticide just before bedtime and protected by an insecticide vaporizer.

Malaria prevention
Travellers to malaria-affected areas should protect themselves by taking antimalarial tablets regularly (p.123) and taking steps to prevent mosquito bites (see above).

Traveller's diarrhea
This unpleasant, although usually short-lived, condition affects up to 50 per cent of all travellers to the developing world and is usually the result of different local bacteria. The condition is largely avoidable by drinking only mineral water and other bottled beverages or sterilized water and avoiding ice in drinks, uncooked and unpeeled fruit and vegetables, salads, and meat that is not freshly and thoroughly cooked. Be cautious about shellfish, even if it seems to have been cooked. Avoid buying cooked food from street vendors. When brushing teeth, rinse with bottled water, not tap water. People who are careful about water often overlook this.

If you do get traveller's diarrhea, it normally disappears quickly without medicines, and so your primary concern should be on preventing the dehydration that may accompany it, especially in young children, by using rehydration salts. Commercial packs of oral rehydration salts are available from pharmacies in Canada.

Although antidiarrheal drugs are of no value in reducing the overall duration of traveller's diarrhea, they might be useful for people who wish to reduce the frequency of bowel movements.

Loperamide (p.338) and diphenoxylate are often used for this purpose. Remember that severe diarrhea can reduce both the absorption and the effectiveness of medicines that are taken by mouth. Discuss with your physician and *pharmacist* when it may be appropriate to take antidiarrheal drugs.

Typhoid and cholera are two serious diseases spread by contaminated food and drink that may start like traveller's diarrhea. If you are going to a country where typhoid or cholera is endemic, you should be vaccinated against it before you travel, but you must still observe all precautions. Do not hesitate to call local medical help if diarrhea seems to be getting worse.

Eating raw, salted, dried, or pickled fish may lead to liver fluke or tapeworm infestations, particularly in the Far East.

Sun
In North America, thousands of people develop skin cancer each year, and these numbers are increasing by 8 per cent annually. Sun-induced skin damage can be avoided by following a few simple precautions. Travellers, especially those with fair skins, should avoid exposure to the hottest sun (from 11 am to 3 pm), apply a high-protection factor (25+) sunscreen protecting against both UVA and UVB to exposed skin, and use a wide-brimmed hat and clothing for additional sun protection. There is no such thing as a healthy tan.

A traveller who is unaccustomed to hot climates may experience heat exhaustion and even sunstroke, causing weakness, dizziness, nausea, muscle cramps, and eventually unconsciousness. Rarely, severe sunstroke may be fatal. Drinking plenty of non-alcoholic fluids, limiting exposure to the sun, especially during the hottest part of the day, and avoiding physical exertion until you are acclimatized can usually prevent this developing.

Bites and stings
Seek expert advice if stung or bitten by any unfamiliar wildlife or by any mammal, and try to avoid such incidents by following local advice on where it is safe to walk or swim. Tropical and subtropical rivers and lakes may contain parasitic flukes such as bilharzia that will infest visitors who drink, bathe, or swim in them. Walking outdoors with bare feet is a bad idea in many areas; hookworms and threadworms in the soil are able to penetrate the skin and enter the body, passing through tissues, the bloodstream, and the lungs before parasitizing the intestines to suck blood. If hiking, always wear good walking shoes or boots and long trousers with the bottoms tucked into your socks. Keep to paths and avoid walking in long grass.

ON RETURN

If you have any unusual symptoms such as persistent diarrhea or unexplained fever after you have travelled, see your physician right away and inform him or her of which country or countries you have visited. If you were taking anti-malarial drugs while you were travelling, you may need to continue to take them for 4 weeks after your return, depending on the type of tablets taken.

INTERACTIONS OF TRAVEL DRUGS

Two or more drugs taken at the same time may interact and therefore, if you are taking regular medication, it is advisable to consider what the potential interaction might be when it is combined with some common drugs that may be taken while you are travelling. For more details on the interactions of particular drugs consult your physician or pharmacist.

Travel (motion) sickness drugs
• **Dimenhydrinate** Nitrates (taken sublingually) may have a reduced effect because of dry mouth, which is a *side effect* of dimenhydrinate. Alcohol and sedative drugs increase the *sedative* effect of dimenhydrinate.
• **Antihistamines** These drugs may negate the effect of anti-arrhythmics and increase the effect of sedatives.

Painkillers
• **Acetaminophen** The effect of anti-coagulant drugs may be increased if taken with acetaminophen.
• **ASA and other NSAIDs** When taken with other NSAIDs, the effect is increased; there is an increased risk of bleeding if these drugs are taken with anticoagulants. ASA and NSAIDs increase the toxicity of methotrexate. When taken with ACE inhibitors, these drugs may reduce their antihypertensive effects. The effects of lithium may be increased when combined with ASA and other NSAIDs.

Antidiarrheal drugs
Alcohol increases the sedative effects of opioid analgesics when they are taken as antidiarrheals. Antidiarrheal drugs may increase the adverse effects of MAOIs and the overall effects of anti-epileptic drugs. There is a greater risk of toxicity when antiviral (HIV) drugs are taken with antidiarrheal drugs.

Drugs for malaria prevention
• **Chloroquine and mefloquine** The effect of amiodarone and quinidine may be decreased with chloroquine, and mefloquine may antagonize antiepileptic drugs. Chloroquine and mefloquine may increase digoxin levels and toxicity.
• **Proguanil** This may increase the effects of warfarin.

PART

5

GLOSSARY AND INDEX

FURTHER INFORMATION
GLOSSARY
GENERAL INDEX
DRUG POISONING EMERGENCY GUIDE

FURTHER INFORMATION

It is important to have as much information as possible about any *medications* that you, or someone that you are caring for, are taking. All medications, whether prescribed or bought over-the-counter should come with a patient information leaflet. Always read these leaflets. If you are still in doubt about anything to do with a medication, you should ask your physician or *pharmacist*.

Organizations should be able to provide general information on medications. Some of these societies are listed below. Further information is usually also available from your local hospital, as well as social services and local libraries. If you have access to the Internet you will also be able to find hundreds of websites that offer information.

Although much of the available advice on medications and drugs is useful and reliable, some information may sometimes be misleading, oversimplified, or even wrong. Always be careful of following advice that does not appear to be from a qualified source, and discuss the matter with your physician or pharmacist if you are unsure.

GENERAL INFORMATION

Canadian Medical Association
1867 Alta Vista Drive
Ottawa, ON   K1G 5W8
Tel: (888) 855-2555
www.cma.ca

Canadian Pharmacists Association
1785 Alta Vista Drive
Ottawa, ON   K1G 3Y6
Tel: (800) 917-9489
www.pharmacists.ca

Canadian Public Health Association
1565 Carling Avenue
Suite 300
Ottawa, ON   K1Z 8R1
Tel: (613) 725-3769
www.cpha.ca

Canadian Red Cross
170 Metcalfe Street
Suite 300
Ottawa, ON   K2P 2P2
Tel: (613) 740-1900
www.redcross.ca

College of Family Physicians of Canada
2630 Skymark Avenue
Mississauga, ON   L4W 5A4
Tel: (905) 629-0900
www.cfpc.ca

Food and Drug Administration (U.S.)
10903 New Hampshire Avenue
Silver Spring, MD   20993-0002
USA
Tel: (888) 463-6332
www.fda.gov

Health Canada
A.L. 0900C2
Ottawa, ON   K1A 0K9
Tel: (613) 957-2991
www.hc-sc.gc.ca

Health Canada Therapeutic Products Directorate
www.hc-sc.gc.ca/dhp-mps/prodpharma/index-eng.php

Kid's Health (U.S.)
www.kidshealth.org

World Health Organization
Avenue Appia 20
1211 Geneva 27
Switzerland
Tel: 0041 22 791 2111
www.who.int

DRUG DEPENDENCE

Alcoholics Anonymous
www.aacanada.com

Canadian Assembly of Narcotics Anonymous
www.canaacna.org

Canadian Centre on Substance Abuse
75 Albert Street
Suite 500
Ottawa, ON   K1P 5E7
Tel: (613) 235-4048
www.ccsa.ca

Centre for Addiction and Mental Health
24 Hour Information Line: (800) 463-6273
www.camh.net

DRUG REACTIONS

Asthma Society of Canada
124 Merton Street
Suite 401
Toronto, Ontario   M4S 2Z2
Tel: (866) 787-4050
www.asthma.ca

Canadian MedicAlert Foundation
2005 Sheppard Avenue East
Suite 800
Toronto, ON   M2J 5B4
Tel: (416) 696-0267
or 1-800-668-1507
www.medicalert.ca

MedEffect Canada
www.hc-sc.gc.ca/dhp-mps/medeff/index-eng.php

Motherisk
The Hospital for Sick Children
555 University Avenue
Toronto, ON   M5G 1X8
Tel: (416) 813-6780
www.motherisk.org

SPECIFIC CONDITIONS

Alzheimer Society of Canada
20 Eglinton Avenue West
Suite 1600
Toronto, ON   M4R 1K8
Tel: (416) 488-8772
www.alzheimer.ca

Arthritis Society
393 University Avenue
Suite 1700
Toronto, ON   M5G 1E6
Tel: (416) 979-7228
www.arthritis.ca

Canadian AIDS Society
190 O'Connor Street
Suite 800
Ottawa, ON   K2P 2R3
Tel: (613) 230-3580
www.cdnaids.ca

Canadian Association of the Deaf
251 Bank Street
Suite 203
Ottawa, ON   K2P 1X3
Tel: (613) 565-2882
www.cad.ca

Canadian Cancer Society
55 St. Clair Avenue West
Suite 300
Toronto, ON   M4V 2Y7
Tel: (416) 961-7223
www.cancer.ca

The Canadian Continence Foundation
P.O. Box 417
Peterborough, ON   K9J 6Z3
Tel: (705) 750-4600
www.canadiancontinence.ca

Canadian Diabetes Association
1400-522 University Avenue
Toronto, ON   M5G 2R5
Tel: (800) 226-8464
www.diabetes.ca

Canadian Lung Association
1750 Courtwood Crescent
Suite 300
Ottawa, ON   K2C 2B5
Tel: (613) 569-6411
or 1-888-566-5864
www.lung.ca

Canadian Mental Health Association
Phenix Professional Building
595 Montreal Road
Suite 303
Ottawa, ON   K1K 4L2
www.cmha.ca

Canadian National Institute for the Blind
1929 Bayview Avenue
Toronto, ON   M4G 3E8
Tel: (416) 486-2500
www.cnib.ca

Canadian Pain Society
1143 Wentworth Street West
Suite 202
Oshawa, ON   L1J 8P7
Tel: (905) 404-9545
www.canadianpainsociety.ca

Heart & Stroke Foundation of Canada
222 Queen Street
Suite 1402
Ottawa, ON   K1P 5V9
Tel: (613) 569-4361
www.heartandstroke.ca

Menopause—Society of Obstetricians and Gynaecologists of Canada
780 Echo Drive
Ottawa, ON   K1S 5R7
Tel: (800) 561-2416
www.menopauseandu.ca

Osteoporosis Canada
1090 Don Mills Road
Suite 301
Toronto, ON   M3C 3R6
Tel: (800) 463-6842
www.osteoporosis.ca

ALTERNATIVE MEDICINE
Canadian Association of Naturopathic Doctors
20 Holly Street
Suite 200
Toronto, ON   M4S 3B1
Tel: (800) 551-4381
www.cand.ca

Chinese Medicine & Acupuncture Association of Canada
www.cmaac.ca

Homeopathic Medical Council of Canada
31 Adelaide Street East
Box 605
Toronto, ON   M5C 2J8
Tel: (416) 788-4622
www.hmcc.ca

DRUGS IN SPORT
Canadian Olympic Committee
21 St. Clair Avenue East
Suite 900
Toronto, ON   M4T 1L9
Tel: (416) 962-0262
www.olympic.ca

Sport Canada
15 Eddy Street
16th Floor
Gatineau, QC   K1A 0M5
Tel: (819) 997-0055
www.pch.gc.ca/sportcanada

MEDICINES AND TRAVEL
Canadian Society for International Health
1 Nicholas Street
Suite 1105
Ottawa, ON   K1N 7B7
Tel: (613) 241-5785
www.csih.org

Centers for Disease Control and Prevention (U.S.)
1600 Clifton Road
Atlanta GA   30333
USA
Tel: (800) 232-4636
www.cdc.gov/travel

Centre for Travel and Tropical Medicine
Travel Clinic
123 Edward Street
Toronto, ON   M5G 1E2
Pre Travel Tel: (416) 730-5700
Post Travel Tel: (416) 340-3675
www.uhn.ca/Clinics_&_Services/clinics/travel_tropical_medicine.asp

Department of Foreign Affairs and International Trade
125 Sussex Drive
Ottawa, ON   K1A 0G2
Tel: (800) 267-6788
www.voyage.gc.ca

McGill Centre For Tropical Diseases
Montreal General Hospital
1650 Cedar Avenue
Room L10-509
Montreal, QC   H3G 1A4
Tel: (514) 934-8049
www.medicine.mcgill.ca/tropmed

Travel Health
Public Health Agency of Canada
www.travelhealth.gc.ca

GLOSSARY

The following pages contain definitions of drug-related terms whose technical meanings are not explained in detail elsewhere in the book, or for which an easily located precise explanation may be helpful. These are words that may not be familiar to the general reader, or that have a slightly different meaning in a medical context from that in ordinary use. Some of the terms included refer to particular drug actions or effects; others describe methods of drug administration. A few medical conditions that may occur as a result of drug use are also defined. All words printed in *italics* in the main text are included as entries in this glossary.

The glossary is arranged in alphabetical order. To avoid repetition, where relevant, entries include cross-references to further information on that topic located in other sections of the book, or to another glossary term.

A

Activator
See *Agonist*.

Addiction
Addiction or psychological dependence refers to the use of substances, including *opioid* medications, to alter mood. It is usually associated with compulsive use, continued use, and craving.

Adjuvant
A drug or chemical that enhances the therapeutic effect of another drug. One example of an adjuvant is aluminium, which is added to certain vaccines in order to enhance the immune response, thereby increasing the protection that is given by the vaccine.

Adrenergic
See *Sympathomimetic*.

Adverse effect
Like side effect and adverse reaction, this is a term that refers to any unwanted effects of a drug. When drugs are taken they are distributed throughout the body and their actions are unlikely to be restricted to just the intended organ or tissue. Other parts of the body contain *receptors* like those at which the drug is aimed. The drug molecule may fit other, different receptors well enough to affect them as well. Most of these unwanted effects are dose-related, increasing as the dose is increased, and are commonly referred to as "side effects." Other unwanted adverse effects appear not to be dose-related, such as an *idiosyncrasy* or an *allergic reaction*. See also Adverse effects (p.15).

Adverse reaction
See *Adverse effect*.

Agonist
A term meaning to have a stimulating effect. An agonist drug (often called an activator) is one that binds to a *receptor* and activates it. This may trigger an increase or decrease in a particular activity in that cell, depending on the physiological effects of activating that particular receptor.

Allergic reaction
An allergic reaction or allergy is one that appears not on first exposure to a drug but on a subsequent occasion. Causes and symptoms are similar to a reaction caused by other allergens. See Allergy (p.109) and *Anaphylaxis*.

Amoebicide
A drug that kills amoebae (single-celled microorganisms). See also Antiprotozoal drugs (p.122).

Anemia
A condition in which the concentration of the oxygen-carrying pigment of the blood, hemoglobin, is below normal. Many different disorders may cause anemia, and it may sometimes occur as a result of drug treatment. Severe anemia may cause fatigue, pallor, and occasionally, breathing difficulty.

Anesthetic, general
A drug or drug combination given to produce unconsciousness before and during surgery or potentially painful investigative procedures. General anesthesia is usually induced by injection of a drug such as thiopental, and maintained by inhalation of the fumes of a volatile liquid such as halothane or a gas such as nitrous oxide mixed with oxygen. Intravenous maintenance anesthesia is also possible depending on the type and duration of operation. See also *Premedication*.

Anesthetic, local
A drug applied topically or injected to numb sensation in a small area. See also Local anesthetics (p.64).

Analeptic
A drug given in hospital that stimulates breathing. See also Respiratory stimulants (p.72).

Analgesia
Relief of pain, usually by drugs. See also Analgesics (p.64).

Anaphylaxis
A severe reaction to an allergen such as a bee sting or a drug (see Allergy, p.109). Symptoms may include rash, swelling, breathing difficulty, and collapse. See also Anaphylactic shock (p.528).

Antagonist
A term meaning to have an opposing effect. An antagonist drug (often called a blocker) binds to a *receptor* without activating it and prevents any other substance from occupying that receptor.

Antibiotic
A substance that kills or arrests the growth of bacteria. Originally, antibiotics were produced by microorganisms such as moulds, but most are now produced synthetically. See also Antibiotics (p.114), Antifungal drugs (p.124), and Antibacterial drugs (p.117).

Antibody
A protein manufactured by lymphocytes (a type of white blood cell) to neutralize an antigen (foreign protein) in the body. The formation of antibodies against an invading microorganism is part of the body's defence against infection. *Immunization* carried out to increase the body's resistance to a specific disease involves either injection of specific antibodies or administration of a *vaccine* that stimulates antibody production. See also Vaccines and immunization (p.120).

Anticholinergic
A drug that blocks the action of acetylcholine. Acetylcholine, a *neurotransmitter* secreted by the endings of nerve cells, allows certain nerve impulses to be transmitted, including those that relax some involuntary muscles, tighten others, and affect the release of saliva. Anticholinergic drugs are used to treat urinary incontinence because they relax the bladder's squeezing muscles while tightening those of the sphincter. Anticholinergic drugs also relax the muscles of the intestinal wall, helping to relieve irritable bowel syndrome (p.98). See also Autonomic nervous system (p.63).

Antidote
A substance used to neutralize or counteract the effects of a poison. A few poisons have a specific antidote.

Antineoplastic
An anticancer drug (p.140).

Antioxidant
A substance that delays deterioration due to free radicals (unstable oxygen atoms). free radicals are generated by the body's normal processes and are thought to play a role in aging and disease. Vitamins A, C, and E are antioxidants. See also Vitamins (p.135).

Antiperspirant
A substance that is applied to the skin to reduce excess sweating. Antiperspirants reduce the activity of the sweat glands or block the ducts carrying sweat to the skin surface.

Antipyretic
A type of drug that reduces fever. The most commonly used antipyretic drugs are ASA and acetaminophen.

Antiseptic
A chemical that destroys bacteria and sometimes other microorganisms. Antiseptics may be applied to the skin or other areas to prevent infection. See also Anti-infective skin preparations (p.163).

Antispasmodic
A drug that reduces spasm (abnormally strong or inappropriate contraction) of the digestive-tract muscles. The pain caused by intestinal spasm is known as colic. These drugs may be used to relieve irritable bowel syndrome (p.98).

Antitussive
A drug that prevents or relieves a cough. See also Drugs to treat coughs (p.80).

Aperient
A mild laxative. See Laxatives (p.97).

Astringent
A substance that causes tissue to dry and shrink by reducing its ability to absorb water. Astringents are used in a number of *antperspirants* and skin tonics to remove excessive moisture from the skin surface. They are also used in ear drops for inflammation of the outer ear because they promote healing of inflamed tissue.

B

Bactericidal
A term used to describe a drug that kills bacteria. See also Antibiotics (p.114) and Antibacterials (p.117).

Bacteriostatic
A term used to describe a drug that stops the growth or multiplication of bacteria. See also Antibiotics (p.114) and Antibacterials (p.117).

Balm
A soothing or healing preparation applied to the skin.

Bioavailability
The proportion of a dose of a drug that enters the bloodstream and so reaches the body tissues, usually expressed as a percentage of the dose given. Injection of a drug directly into a vein produces 100 per cent bioavailability. Drugs given by mouth generally have a lower bio-availability because some of the drug may

not pass through the gut wall, and some may be broken down in the liver before reaching the rest of the body.

Blocker
See *Antagonist*.

Body mass index (BMI)
An indicator of healthy body weight. BMI is calculated by dividing a person's weight in kilograms by the square of his or her height in metres. The normal range is 18.5–24.9.

Body salts
Also known as electrolytes, these are minerals that are present in body fluids such as blood, urine, and sweat, and within cells. These salts play an important role in regulating water balance, the acidity of the blood, conduction of nerve impulses, and muscle contraction. The balance between the various body salts can be upset by such conditions as diarrhea and vomiting. The balance may also be altered by the action of drugs such as diuretics (p.85).

Bronchoconstrictor
A substance that causes the airways in the lungs to narrow. An attack of asthma may be caused by the release of bronchoconstrictor substances such as histamine or certain prostaglandins.

Bronchodilator
A drug that widens the airways. See Bronchodilators (p.76).

C

Capsule
See p.19.

Cathartic
A drug that stimulates bowel action to produce a soft or liquid0 bowel movement. See also Laxatives (p.97).

Chelating agent
A chemical used in the treatment of poisoning by metals such as iron, lead, arsenic, and mercury. The chelating agent combines with the metal to form a less poisonous substance and, in some cases, increases excretion of the poison in the urine. Penicillamine is a commonly used chelating agent.

Chemotherapy
The drug treatment of cancer or infections. *Cytotoxic* drugs (see also p.140) and *antibiotics* (see also p.114) are examples of drugs used in chemotherapy.

Cholinergic
A drug, also called *parasympathomimetic*, that acts by stimulating the parasympathetic nervous system. See also Autonomic nervous system (p.63).

Coma
A state of unconsciousness and unresponsiveness to external stimuli such as noise and pain. Coma results from damage to or disturbance of part of the brain, which may occur, for example, through trauma or drug overdose.

Contraindication
A factor in a person's current condition, medical history, or genetic make-up that may increase the risks of an *adverse effect* from a drug, to the extent that the drug should not be prescribed (called an absolute contraindication), or should only be prescribed with caution (called a relative contraindication).

Counter-irritant
Another term for *rubefacient*.

Cycloplegic
The action of paralysing the ciliary muscle in the eye. This muscle alters the shape of the lens when it contracts, enabling the eye to focus on objects. A cycloplegic drug prevents this action, thereby making both examination of, and surgery on, the eye easier. See also Drugs affecting the pupil (p.158).

Cytotoxic
A drug that kills or damages cells. Drugs with this action are most commonly used to treat cancer. Although these drugs are primarily intended to affect abnormal cells, they may also kill or damage healthy ones. See also Anticancer drugs (p.140).

D

Dependence
A term that relates to the psychological or physical dependence on a substance, or both, and implies a loss of control over drug use and/or compulsive use. Psychological dependence involves intense mental cravings if a drug is unavailable or withdrawn. Physical dependence causes physical withdrawal symptoms (sweating, shaking, abdominal pain, and convulsions) if the substance is not taken. Dependence also implies loss of control over intake. See also Drug dependence (p.23).

Depot injection
Injection into a muscle of a drug that has been specially formulated to provide for a slow, steady absorption of its active ingredients by the surrounding blood vessels.The drug may be mixed with oil or wax. Alternatively, some drugs may be injected under the skin using an applicator. This is known as an implant injection. The release period can be made to last up to several weeks. See also Methods of administration (p.17).

Designer drugs
A group of unlicensed substances whose only purpose is to duplicate the effects of certain illegal drugs of abuse or to provide even stronger ones. Designer drugs differ

chemically in some minor degree from the original drug, enabling the user and supplier to evade prosecution for dealing in, or possession of, an illegal drug. They are very dangerous because their effects are unpredictable, they are often highly potent, and they may contain impurities.

Double-blind
A test used to determine the effectiveness of a new drug compared to an existing medicine or a *placebo*. Neither patients nor the physicians administering the drug know who is receiving which substance. Only after the test is completed and the patients' responses are recorded is the identity of those who received the new drug revealed. Double-blind trials are performed for almost all new drugs. See also Testing and approving new drugs (p.12).

Drip
A non-medical term for *intravenous infusion*.

E

Electrolyte
See *Body salts*.

Elixir
A clear, sweetened liquid, often containing alcohol, that forms the base for many liquid medicines such as those used to treat coughs.

Embrocation
An ointment or liniment rubbed on to the skin to relieve joint pain, muscle cramp, or muscle injury. An embrocation usually contains a *rubefacient*.

Emetic
Any substance that causes a person to vomit. An emetic may work by irritating the lining of the stomach and/or by stimulating the part of the brain that controls vomiting. Emetics such as ipecac (ipecacuanha) may be used in the treatment of drug overdose but are not generally very effective. See also Drug poisoning emergency guide (p.526).

Emollient
A substance having a soothing, softening effect when applied to the skin. An emollient also has a moisturizing effect, preventing loss of water from the skin surface by forming an oily film. See also Bases for skin preparations (p.163).

Emulsion
A combination of two liquids that do not normally mix together but, on addition of a third substance (known as an emulsifying agent), can be mixed to give a complex liquid consisting of droplets of one liquid suspended in the other. An example of an emulsion is liquid paraffin. The medicine bottle may have to be shaken well before use to ensure that the two liquids are thoroughly mixed.

Endorphins
A group of substances occurring naturally in the brain. Released in response to pain, they bind to specialized receptors and reduce the perception of pain. *Opioid* analgesics such as morphine work by mimicking the action of endorphins. See also Analgesics (p.64).

Enteric coated
Treatment of a drug to give it a coating so that, after being taken orally by the individual, it passes safely and unaltered through the stomach and is released in the intestine. This can minimize stomach upsets caused by the drugs.

Enzyme
A protein that controls the rate of one or more chemical reactions in the body. There are thousands of enzymes active in the body. Each type of cell produces a specific range of enzymes. Cells in the liver contain enzymes that stimulate the breakdown of nutrients and drugs; cells in the digestive tract release enzymes that help digest food. Some drugs work by altering the activity of enzymes – for example, certain anticancer drugs halt tumour growth by altering enzyme function in cancer cells.

Epidural injection
An injection that resembles an *intrathecal injection* but delivers the drug into a more superficial space around the spine. Usually a local anesthetic and analgesic are injected or infused together to provide regional anesthesia for operations such as cesarean section or for post-operative pain relief.

Excitatory
A term meaning having a stimulating or enhancing effect. A chemical released from a nerve ending that causes muscle contraction is having an excitatory effect. See also *Inhibitory*.

Expectorant
A type of cough remedy that enhances the production of sputum (phlegm) and is used in the treatment of a productive (sputum-producing) cough. See also Drugs to treat coughs (p.80).

F

Formula, chemical
A way of expressing the constituents of a chemical in symbols and numbers. Every known chemical substance has a formula. Water has the formula H_2O, indicating that it is composed of two hydrogen atoms (H_2) and one oxygen atom (O). All drugs have much more complicated formulae than that of water.

Formulary
A list of drugs produced as a guide to prescribers and other health professionals with the aim of aiding choice. Local formularies are frequently found in hospitals and are sometimes used by groups of physicians.

G

Gel
A viscous, usually translucent, jelly-like formulation of a drug for application to the skin.

Generic name
The official name for a substance that is therapeutically active. The term generic is distinct from a *product name*, which is a term chosen by a manufacturer for its version of a product containing a generic drug. For example: nitrazepam is a generic name; Mogadon is a brand name for a product that contains nitrazepam. See also How drugs are classified (p.13).

H

Half-life
A term used in *pharmacology* for the time taken to reduce the concentration of the drug in the blood by half. Knowledge of the half-life of a drug helps to determine frequency of dosage.

Hallucinogen
A drug that causes hallucinations (unreal perceptions of surroundings and objects). Common hallucinogens include the drugs of abuse LSD (p.490) and cannabis (p.487). Alcohol taken in large amounts may have an hallucinogenic effect; hallucinations may also occur during withdrawal from alcohol (p.484). Certain prescribed drugs can cause hallucinations (e.g. SSRI and other anti-depressants, *opioids* and dopamine agents).

Hormone
A chemical released directly into the bloodstream by a gland or tissue. The body produces numerous hormones, each of which has a specific range of functions – for example, controlling the *metabolism* of cells, growth, sexual development, and the body's response to stress or illness. Hormone-producing glands make up the endocrine system; the kidneys, intestine, and brain also release hormones. See also Hormones and endocrine system (p.126).

I

Idiosyncrasy
Some *adverse effects* appear not to be dose related. Where such an effect happens on the first use of a drug and is *pharmacologically* unexpected, the phenomenon is called idiosyncrasy, or an idiosyncratic reaction. This happens because people are different genetically; they may lack a particular *enzyme* or an enzyme may be less active than usual. In normal life this may not cause any problems. Because of this difference, they may react differently to a drug.

Immunization

The process of inducing immunity (resistance to infection) as a preventive measure against the spread of infectious diseases. See Vaccines and immunization (p.120).

Indication

The term used to describe a disorder, symptom, or condition for which a drug or treatment may be prescribed. For example, indications for the use of beta blockers include angina and high blood pressure (hypertension).

Infusion pump

A machine for administering a continuous, controlled amount of a drug or other fluid through a needle inserted into a vein or under the skin. It consists of a small battery-powered pump that controls the flow of fluid from a syringe into the needle. The pump may be strapped to the patient and pre-programmed to deliver the fluid at a constant rate. See also Methods of administration (p.17).

Inhaler

A device used for administering a drug in powder or vapour form, used principally in the treatment of respiratory disorders such as asthma and chronic bronchitis. The kinds of drugs that are often administered by this method include corticosteroids and *broncho-dilators*. See also Methods of administration (p.17) and Inhalers (p.77).

Inhibitory

A term meaning to have a blocking effect on cell activity, e.g., a chemical that prevents muscle contraction has an inhibitory effect. See also *Antagonist* and *Excitatory*.

Inoculation

A method of administering biological substances, such as microorganisms, to produce immunity to disease by scratching the *vaccine* into the skin. See also Vaccines and immunization (p.120).

Interaction

See p.16.

Intramuscular injection

Injection of a drug into a muscle, usually located in the upper arm or buttock. The drug is absorbed into the bloodstream from the muscle. See also Methods of administration (p.17).

Intrathecal injection

An injection of a drug into the space around the brain or spinal cord. This route is used to minimize *systemic* effects of a drug while allowing high drug levels to be achieved within the enclosed nervous tissue. It is used for some anticancer drugs, antispasticity drugs (e.g. baclofen), and analgesic drugs (e.g. morphine) to provide pain relief. Local anesthetic drugs are injected by this route to provide spinal anesthesia. See also *Epidural injection*.

Intravenous infusion

Prolonged, slow injection of fluid (often a solution of a drug) into a vein. The fluid flows at a controlled rate from a bag or bottle through a fine tube inserted into an opening in a vein. An intravenous infusion may also be administered via an *infusion pump*.

Intravenous injection

Direct injection of a drug into a vein, putting the drug immediately into the circulation. Because it has a rapid effect, intravenous injection is useful in an emergency. See also Methods of administration (p.17).

JL

Jaundice

A condition in which the skin and whites of the eyes take on a yellow coloration, caused by an accumulation in the blood of the yellow-brown bile pigment bilirubin. Jaundice is a sign of many disorders of the liver. A drug may cause jaundice as an *adverse effect* either by damaging the liver or by causing an increase in the breakdown of red blood cells in the circulation. See also Liver and kidney disease, p.22.

Liniment

A liquid medicine for application to the skin with friction, that is, to be rubbed in. See also *Embrocation*.

Lotion

A liquid preparation that may be applied to large areas of skin. See also Bases for skin preparations (p.163).

M

Medication

Any substance prescribed to treat illness. See *Medicine*.

Medicine

A medication or drug that is taken in order to maintain, improve, or restore health.

Metabolism

The term used to describe all chemical processes in the body that involve either the formation of new substances or the breakdown of substances to release energy or detoxify foreign substances. The metabolism provides the energy that is required to keep the body functioning at rest – that is, to maintain breathing, heart beat, and body temperature and to replace worn tissues. It also provides the energy needed during exertion. This energy is produced by the metabolism from the breakdown of foods.

Miotic

A drug that constricts the pupil. *Opioid* drugs such as morphine have a miotic effect, and someone who is taking one of these drugs has very small, pinpoint pupils. The pupil is sometimes deliberately narrowed by other miotic drugs, such as pilocarpine, in the treatment of glaucoma. See also Drugs for glaucoma (p.156) and Drugs affecting the pupil (p.158).

Mucolytic

A drug that liquefies mucus secretions in the airways. See also Drugs to treat coughs (p.80).

Mydriatic

A drug that dilates (widens) the pupil. *Anti-cholinergic* drugs, such as atropine, have this effect and they may cause *photophobia* as a consequence. Mydriatic drugs may occasionally provoke the onset of glaucoma. These drugs are also used to facilitate examination of the retina at the back of the eye. See also Drugs affecting the pupil (p.158).

N

Narcotic

Originating from the Greek word for numbness or stupor and once applied to drugs derived from the opium poppy, the word narcotic no longer has a precise medical meaning; some American sources use the term to mean any potent abused drug. Narcotic analgesic, a term largely replaced by *opioid* analgesic, is used to refer to opium-derived and synthetic drugs that have pain-relieving properties and other effects similar to those of morphine (see Analgesics, p.64). See also Opioids (p.492)

Nebulizer

A method of administering a drug to the airways and lungs in aerosol form through a facemask. The apparatus includes an electric or hand-operated pump that sends a stream of air or oxygen through a length of tubing into a small canister containing the drug in liquid form. This inflow of gas causes the drug to be dispersed into a fine mist, which is then carried through another tube into the facemask. Inhalation of this drug mist is much easier than inhaling from a pressurized aerosol. See also *Inhaler*.

Neuroleptic

A drug used to treat psychotic illness. See Antipsychotic drugs (p.69).

Neurotransmitter

A chemical released from a nerve ending after receiving an electrical impulse. A neuro-transmitter may carry a message from the nerve to another nerve so that the electrical impulse passes on, or to a muscle to stimulate contraction, or to a gland to stimulate secretion of a particular hormone. Acetylcholine and noradrenaline are examples of neurotransmitters. Many drugs either mimic or block the action of neurotransmitters. See also Brain and nervous system (p.62).

O

Opioid
A group of drugs (also called *narcotic analgesics*) that are given to relieve pain, treat diarrhea, and suppress coughs. See Opioids (p.492).

Orphan drug
A drug that is effective for a rare medical condition, but that may not be marketed by a drug manufacturer because of the small profit potential compared with the high costs of development and production. These drugs can usually be obtained by special request.

OTC
The abbreviation for over-the-counter. Over-the-counter drugs can be bought from a *pharmacy* without a prescription. See also Managing your drug treatment (p.25).

P

Parasympathomimetic
A drug that is prescribed to stimulate the parasympathetic nervous system (see Autonomic nervous system, p.63). These drugs (also called *cholinergic* drugs) are used as *miotics* and to stimulate bladder contraction in urinary retention (see Drugs used in urinary disorders, p.154).

Parkinsonism
Neurological symptoms including tremor of the hands, muscle rigidity, and slowness of movement that resemble Parkinson's disease. Parkinsonism may be caused by prolonged treatment with an antipsychotic drug. See Drugs for parkinsonism (p.71).

Patch
See *Transdermal patch.*

Pharmacist
A registered health professional (often called a "chemist") concerned with the preparation, manufacture, and dispensing of drugs. Pharmacists can advise on the correct use of drugs and can help detect potential interactions between your medications.

Pharmacodynamics
A word used to describe the effects or actions that a drug produces in the body. For example, pain relief is a pharmacodynamic effect that may stem from a drug.

Pharmacokinetics
The term used to describe how the body deals with a drug from the point it enters the body to the point at which it acts (usually a *receptor*). This includes how it is absorbed into the bloodstream, distributed to different tissues, broken down, and excreted from the body.

Pharmacologist
A scientist concerned with the study of the *pharmacodynamics* and *pharmacokinetics* of drugs. Pharmacologists form one of the groups responsible for scientific research into new drugs and new uses for existing drugs. Clinical pharmacologists are usually qualified physicians.

Pharmacology
The science of the origin, appearance, chemistry, and action of drugs.

Pharmacopoeia
A publication (in book or electronic form) that describes the drugs used in medicine. The term pharmacopoeia usually refers to an official national publication (such as the U.S. Pharmacopoeia) that sets standards and describes the methods used to identify drugs and determine their purity. These publications are used for reference by the medical profession.

Pharmacy
A term that is used to describe the science and technology involved in the study of drugs. The term is also used to refer to the place where the practise of preparing drugs, making up prescriptions, and dispensing the drugs is carried out.

Photophobia
Dislike of bright light. Certain drugs (notably *mydriatics*) and diseases may induce photophobia.

Photosensitivity
An abnormal reaction of the skin to light, often causing reddening. Photosensitivity may be caused by certain drugs.

Placebo
A "medicine", often in tablet or capsule form, that contains no medically active ingredient. Placebos are frequently used in clinical trials of new drugs (see *Double-blind*). See also Placebo response (p.15).

Poison
A substance that, in relatively small amounts, disrupts the structure and/or function of cells, causing harmful and sometimes fatal effects. Many drugs are poisonous if taken in overdose.

Premedication
The term applied to drugs given to patients between one and two hours before an operation. The premedication usually contains an *opioid* analgesic to help relieve pain and anxiety and to reduce the dose of anesthetic needed to produce unconsciousness (see also *Anesthetic, general*). In some cases, an *anticholinergic* drug is also included to reduce secretions in the airways.

Prescription
A written instruction from the physician to the *pharmacist*, detailing the name of the drug to be dispensed, the dosage, how often it has to be taken, and other instructions as necessary. A prescription is written and signed by a physician and carries the name and address of the patient for whom the drug is prescribed. The pharmacist keeps a record, often computerized, of all prescriptions dispensed to each patient. See also Managing your drug treatment (p.25).

Product name
The name chosen by a manufacturer for its particular version of a product containing a generic drug, e.g., Viagra is a product name for the generic drug sildenafil. See also *Generic name* and How drugs are classified (p.13).

Prophylactic
A drug, procedure, or piece of equipment used to prevent disease. The process of prevention is called prophylaxis. For example, a course of drugs given to a traveller to prevent malarial infection is known as malaria prophylaxis.

Proprietary
A term now applied to a drug that is sold over-the-counter and having its name registered to a private manufacturer, i.e., a proprietor.

Prostaglandin
A fatty (organic) acid that acts in a similar way to a hormone. Prostaglandins occur in many different tissues and have various effects. These include causing inflammation in damaged tissue, lowering blood pressure, and stimulating contractions in labour.

Psychedelic
Derived from the Greek word for "soul" and "to manifest," the term refers to a drug that changes cognition and perception by the brain. This often includes intense visual hallucinations. Most psychedelics are drugs of abuse, although some have legitimate therapeutic uses (e.g. ketamine). An alternative term is an entheogen, although this is often restricted to psychedelics used in religious or spiritual rituals (e.g. peyote).

Purgative
A drug that helps eliminate feces from the body, to relieve constipation or to empty the bowel/intestine before surgery. See also *Cathartic* and Laxatives (p.97).

Pyrogen
A substance that causes a rise in temperature.

R

Receptor
A specific site with a characteristic chemical and physical structure that binds a drug. Receptors are usually located on the surface of a cell, although some are located inside the cell (e.g. the receptors that bind steroid *hormones*). Natural body chemicals such as neurotransmitters and hormones bind to their specific receptors to initiate a response in the cell. Most drugs have their effects by binding to receptors and either activating or blocking them. Hence the drug may mimic or inhibit the normal cell response to activation of that receptor. See also *Agonist* and *Antagonist*.

Replication
The duplication of genetic material (DNA or RNA) in a cell as part of the process of cell division that enables a tissue to grow or a virus to multiply.

Rubefacient
A preparation, also known as a counter-irritant, that, when applied to an area of skin, causes it to redden by increasing blood flow in vessels in that area. A rubefacient such as methyl salicylate may be included in an *embrocation* or a *liniment*.

S

Sedative
A drug that dampens the activity of the central nervous system. Sleeping drugs (p.66) and anti-anxiety drugs (p.67) have a sedative effect, and many other drugs, including antihistamines (p.110) and antidepressants (p.68), can produce sedation as a *side effect*.

Side effect
See *Adverse effect*.

Sterile
A term meaning free from living micro-organisms. Drugs that are administered by certain methods, such as by injection and *bladder irrigation/instillation*, must be sterile to avoid causing infection. See also *Pyrogen*.

Subcutaneous injection
A method of giving a drug by which the drug is injected under the skin. It is then slowly absorbed over a few hours into surrounding blood vessels. Insulin is given in this way. See also Methods of administration (p.17).

Sublingual
A term meaning under the tongue. Some drugs are administered sublingually in tablet or spray form. The drug is rapidly absorbed through the lining of the mouth. Nitrate drugs may be given this way to provide rapid relief of an angina attack. See also Methods of administration (p.17).

Suppository
A bullet-shaped pellet usually containing a drug for insertion into the rectum or vagina. See also Methods of administration (p.17).

Sympatholytic
A term that means blocking the effect of the sympathetic nervous system. Sympatholytic drugs work either by reducing the release of the stimulatory *neurotransmitter* norepinephrine (noradrenaline) from nerve endings, or by occupying the receptors to which the neurotransmitters epinephrine (adrenaline) and noradrenaline normally bind, thereby preventing their normal actions. Beta blockers are examples of sympatholytic drugs. See also Autonomic nervous system (p.63).

Sympathomimetic
Having the same effect as stimulation of the sympathetic nervous system to cause, for example, an increase in the heart rate and widening of the airways. A drug having a sympathomimetic action may work either by causing the release of the stimulatory *neurotransmitter* norepinephrine (noradrenaline) from the nerve endings or by mimicking neurotransmitter action (see Autonomic nervous system, p.63). The sympathomimetic drugs include certain bronchodilators (p.76) and decongestants (p.79).

Syrup
A solution of sucrose (sugar) in water. Syrup is used as a basis for some liquid medicines because it acts as an *antioxidant*; bacteria, fungi, and moulds do not grow in it; and its sweetness hides the taste of some drugs. Syrups are not suitable for diabetics.

Systemic
Having a generalized effect, causing physical or chemical changes in tissues throughout the body. For a drug to have a systemic effect it must be absorbed into the bloodstream, usually via the digestive tract, by injection or by rectal *suppository*.

T

Tablet
See p.19.

Tardive dyskinesia
Abnormal, uncontrolled movements, mainly of the face, tongue, mouth, and neck, that may be caused by prolonged treatment with anti-psychotic drugs. This condition is distinct from *parkinsonism,* which may also be caused by such drugs. See also Antipsychotic drugs (p.69).

Tolerance
The need to take a higher dosage of a specific drug to maintain the same physical or mental effect. Tolerance occurs during prolonged treatment with *opioid* analgesics and benzodiazepines. See also Drug dependence (p.23).

Tonics
A diverse group of remedies prescribed or bought over-the-counter for relieving vague symptoms such as malaise, lethargy, and loss of appetite, for which no obvious cause can be found. Tonics sometimes contain vitamins and minerals, but there is no scientific evidence that such ingredients have anything other than a *placebo* effect. Nevertheless, many individuals feel better after taking a tonic for a few weeks.

Topical
The term used to describe the application of a drug to the site where it is intended that it should have its effect. Disorders of the skin, eye, outer ear, nasal passages, anus, and vagina are often treated with drugs applied topically.

Toxic reaction
Unpleasant and possibly dangerous symptoms caused by a drug, the result of an overdose. See also The effects of drugs (p.15).

Toxin
A poisonous substance such as a harmful chemical released by bacteria.

Tranquillizer, major
A drug used to treat psychotic illness such as schizophrenia. See Antipsychotic drugs (p.69).

Tranquillizer, minor
This is an older term for a sedative drug used to treat anxiety and emotional tension. See Anti-anxiety drugs (p.67).

Transdermal patch
An adhesive patch that is impregnated with the drug and placed on the skin. The drug is slowly absorbed through the skin into the underlying blood vessels. Drugs administered in this way include nicotine, nitrates, travel sickness remedies, and estrogens. See also Methods of administration (p.17).

V

Vaccine
A substance administered to induce active immunity against a specific infectious disease (see Vaccines and immunization, p.120).

Vasoconstrictor
A drug that narrows blood vessels, often prescribed to reduce nasal congestion (see Decongestants, p.79). These drugs are also frequently given with injected local anesthetics (p.64) (see also *Anesthetic, local*). Ephedrine is a commonly prescribed vasoconstrictor.

Vasodilator
A drug that widens blood vessels. See Vasodilators (p.84).

W

Wafer
A thin wafer that is impregnated with a drug and placed on the tongue. The wafer slowly dissolves and the drug is absorbed through the lining of the mouth into the surrounding blood vessels.

Withdrawal symptom
Any symptom caused by abrupt stopping of a drug. These symptoms occur as a result of physical *dependence* on a drug. Drugs that may cause withdrawal symptoms after prolonged use include *opioids*, benzo-diazepines, and nicotine. Withdrawal symptoms vary according to each drug, but common examples include sweating, shaking, anxiety, nausea, and abdominal pain. See also Drug dependence (p.23).

THE GENERAL INDEX

This General Index contains references to the information in all sections of the book. It can be used to look up topics such as groups of drugs, individual drug names, diseases, and conditions. References for generic and brand-name drugs are

also listed, with references to the listing in the Drug Finder (pp.33–59).

Entries that contain a page reference followed by the letter "g" indicate that the entry is defined in the Glossary on the page specified (pp.503–508).

N

O

P

DRUG POISONING EMERGENCY GUIDE

The information on the following pages is intended to give practical advice for dealing with a known or suspected drug poisoning emergency. Although many of the first-aid techniques described can be used in a number of different types of emergency, these instructions apply specifically to drug overdose or poisoning.

Emergency action is necessary in any of the following circumstances:
● If a person has taken an overdose of any of the high-danger drugs listed in the box on p.528.
● If a person has taken an overdose of a less dangerous drug, but has one or more of the danger symptoms listed (right).
● If a person has taken, or is suspected of having taken, an overdose of an unknown drug.
● If an infant or child has swallowed, or is suspected of having swallowed any medications or any drug of abuse.

What to do
If you are faced with a drug poisoning emergency, it is important to carry out first aid and arrange immediate medical help in the correct order. The Priority Action Decision Chart (below left) will help you to assess the situation and to determine your priorities. The following information should help you to remain calm in an emergency if you ever need to deal with a case of drug poisoning.

DANGER SYMPTOMS

Take emergency action if the person has one or more of the following symptoms:
● Drowsiness or unconsciousness
● Shallow, irregular, or stopped breathing
● Vomiting
● Seizures

PRIORITY ACTION DECISION CHART

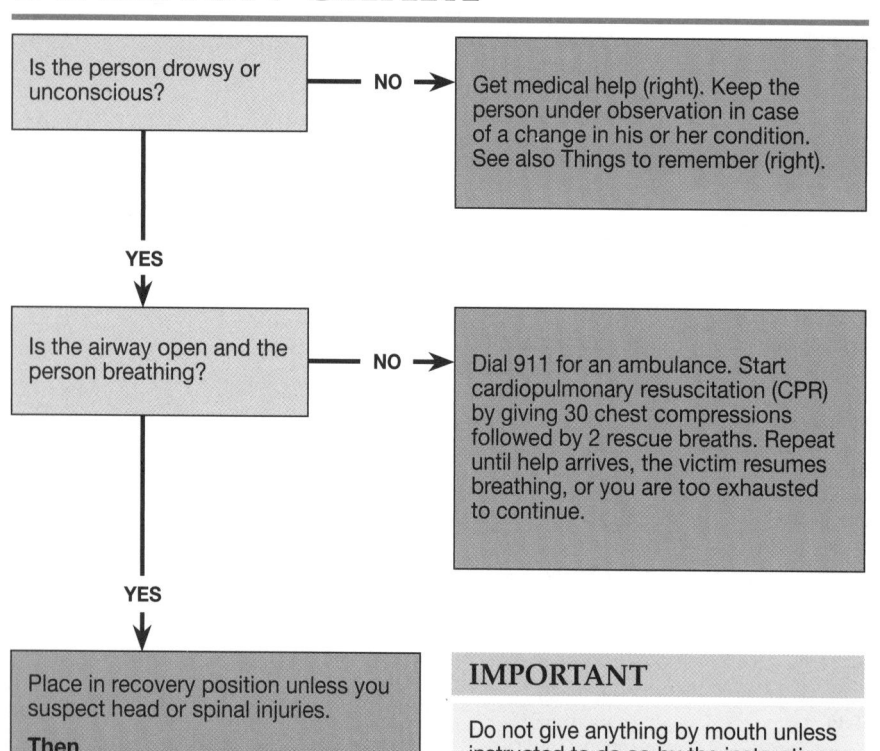

Is the person drowsy or unconscious? — **NO** → Get medical help (right). Keep the person under observation in case of a change in his or her condition. See also Things to remember (right).

YES

Is the airway open and the person breathing? — **NO** → Dial 911 for an ambulance. Start cardiopulmonary resuscitation (CPR) by giving 30 chest compressions followed by 2 rescue breaths. Repeat until help arrives, the victim resumes breathing, or you are too exhausted to continue.

YES

Place in recovery position unless you suspect head or spinal injuries.
Then
Get medical help (right). Keep the person under observation in case of a change in his or her condition.

IMPORTANT

Do not give anything by mouth unless instructed to do so by the instructions on the label of the substance or by a doctor. Fluids may hasten absorption of the drug, increasing the danger.

GETTING MEDICAL HELP

In an emergency, a calm person who is competent in first aid should stay with the victim, while others summon help. However, if you have to deal with a drug poisoning emergency on your own, use first aid (see the Priority Action Decision Chart, left) before getting help.

Calling 911 for an ambulance may be the quickest method of transport to hospital. Then call your physician or your local Poison Control Center for advice. If possible, tell them what drug has been taken and how much, and the age of the victim. Follow the physician's or hospital's instructions precisely.

THINGS TO REMEMBER

Effective treatment of drug poisoning depends on the physician making a rapid assessment of the type and amount of drug taken. Collecting evidence that will assist the diagnosis will help. After you have carried out first aid, look for empty or opened medicine (or other) containers. Keep any of the drug that is left, together with its container (or syringe), and give these to the nurse or physician. Save any vomit for analysis by the hospital.

ESSENTIAL FIRST AID

CARDIOPULMONARY RESUSCITATION (CPR)

OPENING THE AIRWAY

Open the airway (steps 1 and 2). If the victim is breathing, place him or her in the recovery position (right). If there is no rise and fall of the chest and you can feel no movement of exhaled air, immediately start CPR by giving 30 chest compressions (below), then 2 rescue breaths (see Rescue breathing, below right).

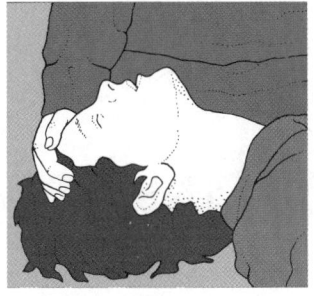

1 Lay the victim on his or her back on a firm surface. Place one hand on the victim's forehead and gently tilt the head back. Wipe any vomit from around the mouth.

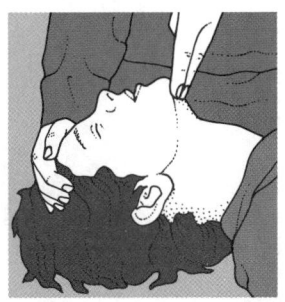

2 Place two fingers under the point of the victim's chin, and lift his or her jaw. Then look, listen, and feel for breathing.

CHEST COMPRESSIONS

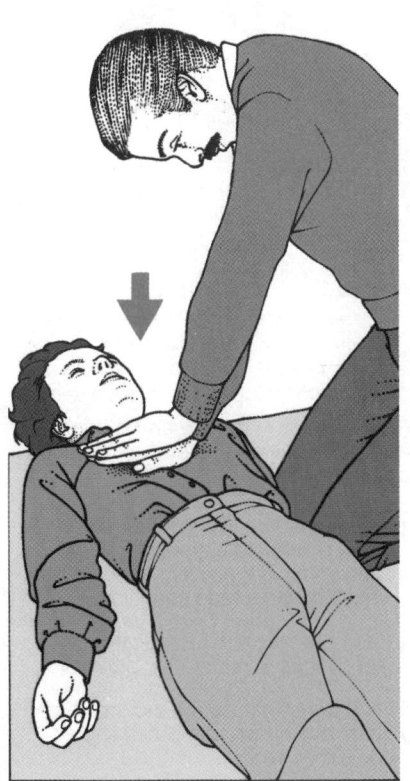

This technique is used to continue output of blood from a stopped heart. It does not usually restart a heart that has stopped.

Chest compression involves putting repeated pressure on the centre of the chest with the heels of both hands, at a rate of 100 compressions per minute (see Priority action decision chart, left). After each set of 30 compressions, give two rescue breaths (see Rescue breathing, right).

RECOVERY POSITION

The recovery position is the safest position for an unconscious or drowsy person. It allows the person to breathe easily and will help to prevent choking if vomiting occurs. A drug poisoning victim should be placed in the recovery position if more urgent first aid, such as CPR, is not necessary. Place the victim on his or her side with one leg bent. Tilt the head back to keep the airway open, and support it in this position by placing the victim's hand under the cheek. Cover him or her with a blanket for warmth.

RESCUE BREATHING

If the victim is not breathing, start CPR by giving 30 chest compressions (see Chest compressions, left). Follow this with 2 rescue breaths (steps 3 and 4). Continue the sequence of 30 chest compressions and 2 rescue breaths until help arrives, the victim recovers, or you are too exhausted to continue.

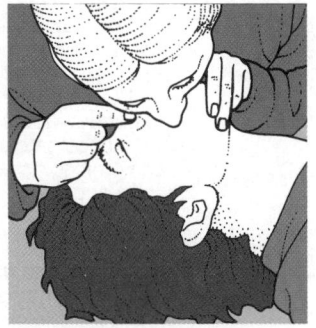

3 Pinch the victim's nostrils closed with the hand that is on the forehead. Take a deep breath, seal your mouth over the victim's, and give 2 breaths in succession.

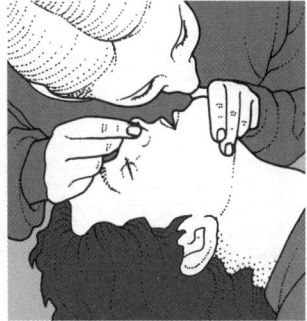

4 After each breath, turn to watch the chest falling while you listen for the sound of air leaving the victim's mouth.

DEALING WITH A SEIZURE

Certain types of drug poisoning may provoke seizures. These may occur whether the person is conscious or not. The victim usually falls to the ground twitching or making uncontrolled movements of the limbs and body. If you witness a seizure, remember the following points:

● Do not try to hold the person down.

● Loosen clothing around neck if possible.

● Do not attempt to put anything into the person's mouth.

● Try to ensure that the person does not suffer injury by keeping him or her away from dangerous objects or furniture.

● Once the seizure is over, place the person in the recovery position (p.527).

HIGH-DANGER DRUGS

The following is a list of drugs given a high overdose rating in the drug profiles or included in the drugs of abuse. If you suspect that someone has taken an overdose of any of these drugs, seek immediate medical attention.

Acetaminophen
Amitriptyline
ASA
Atropine

Betahistine
Bupropion

Chloroquine
Clomipramine
Codeine
Colchicine

Digoxin

Epinephrine
   (adrenaline)

Fentanyl

Gliclazide
Glyburide

Heparin
Hydrocodone
Hydromorphone

Imipramine
Insulin
Isoniazid

Lithium

Mefloquine
Metformin
Methadone
Methylphenidate
Metoprolol
Morphine

Phenobarbital
Procyclidine
Propranolol
Pseudoephedrine
Pyridostigmine

Quinidine
Quinine

Rosiglitazone

Selegiline

Theophylline/
   aminophylline
Timolol

Venlafaxine

Warfarin

Drugs of abuse
Alcohol
Amphetamines
Barbiturates
Benzodiazepines
Cannabis
   (marijuana)
Cocaine
   (including crack)
Ecstasy
GHB
Ketamine
Khat
LSD
Mescaline
Nicotine
Nitrites
Opioids
   (including heroin)
Phencyclidine
Solvents

DEALING WITH ANAPHYLACTIC SHOCK

Anaphylactic shock can occur as the result of a severe *allergic reaction* to a drug (such as penicillin). Blood pressure drops dramatically and the airways may become narrowed. The reaction usually occurs within minutes of taking the drug. The main symptoms are:

● Breathing difficulty

● Pallor

● Blotchy red rash

● Anxiety

● Swelling of tongue or throat

1 If the person is consious but having breathing difficulties, he or she is usually more comfortable sitting up. If the breathing is normal, lay him or her down, face up, with legs raised above the level of the heart to ensure adequate circulation of the blood.

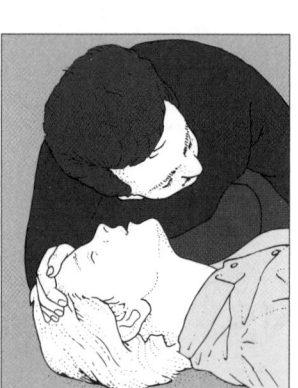

2 If the person becomes unconsious, ensure that he or she is breathing. If breathing has stopped, immediate mouth-to-mouth resuscitation should be carried out as described on p.527.

3 Phone for medical help. While waiting, cover the person with a blanket or other article of clothing. If you have to leave the person, place him or her in the recovery position. Do not attempt to administer anything by mouth.

DEALING WITH VOMITING

Vomiting is the body's response to many things, including contaminated food, viral infections, and severe pain. It also occurs as an *adverse effect* of some drugs and as a result of drug overdose.

Do not attempt to provoke vomiting by pushing fingers down the victim's throat. When vomiting does occur, remember the following:

● Vomiting can be a sign of poisoning.

● Vomiting due to drugs is usually a result of an overdose rather than a *side effect*. Check in the relevant drug profile whether vomiting is a possible adverse effect of the suspected drug. If vomiting appears to be due to an overdose, get medical help urgently.

● Even if vomiting has stopped, keep the person under observation in case he or she loses consciousness or has a seizure.

● If the person is drowsy and is vomiting, place him or her in the recovery position (p.527).

1 Ensure that the victim leans well forward to avoid either choking or inhaling vomit. If the victim appears to be choking, encourage coughing.

2 Keep the vomit for later analysis (see Things to remember, p.526).

3 Give water to rinse the mouth. This water should be spat out; it should not be swallowed.